I[illegible] TO E[illegible]BEDDED SYSTEMS

ABOUT THE AUTHOR

Shibu has over nine years of hands-on experience in the Embedded & Real Time System domain with solid background on all phases of Embedded Product Development Life Cycle. He holds a B-Tech Degree (Hons) in Instrumentation & Control Engineering from the University of Calicut. He started his professional career as Research Associate in the VLSI and Embedded Systems Group of India's prime Electronics Research & Development Centre (ER&DCI—under the ministry of Information & Communication Technology, Govt. of India) Thiruvananthapuram Unit. He has conducted research activities in the embedded domain for Contactless Smart Card Technology and Radio Frequency Identification (RFID). He has developed a variety of products in the Contactless Smart Card & RFID Technology platform using industry's most popular 8-bit microcontroller—*8051*.

Shibu has sound working knowledge in Embedded Hardware development using EDA Tools and firmware development in Assembly Language and Embedded C using a variety of IDEs and cross-compilers for various 8/16/32 bit microprocessors/microcontrollers and System on Chips. He is also an expert in RTOS based Embedded System design for various RTOSs including Windows CE, VxWorks, MicroC/OS-II and RTX-51. He is well versed in various industry standard protocols and bus interfaces. Presently, he is engaged with the Embedded Systems & Product Engineering practice unit of Infosys Technologies Ltd (www.infosys.com), Thiruvananthapuram Unit.

INTRODUCTION TO EMBEDDED SYSTEMS

Shibu K V

Technical Architect
Mobility & Embedded Systems Practice
Infosys Technologies Ltd.,
Trivandrum Unit, Kerala

McGraw Hill Education (India) Private Limited
NEW DELHI

McGraw Hill Education Offices

New Delhi New York St Louis San Francisco Auckland Bogotá Caracas
Kuala Lumpur Lisbon London Madrid Mexico City Milan Montreal
San Juan Santiago Singapore Sydney Tokyo Toronto

McGraw Hill Education (India) Private Limited

Published by McGraw Hill Education (India) Private Limited
P-24, Green Park Extension, New Delhi 110 016

Eleventh reprint 2014
RYCDRRDURBYYX

ISBN (13 digit): 978-0-07-014589-4
ISBN (10 digit): 0-07-014589-X

Vice President and Managing Director: *Ajay Shukla*
General Manager: Publishing—SEM & Tech Ed: *Vibha Mahajan*
Manager—Sponsoring: *Shalini Jha*
Associate Sponsoring Editor: *Nilanjan Chakravarty*
Development Editor: *Surbhi Suman*
Jr Manager—Production: *Anjali Razdan*

General Manager—Production: *Rajender P Ghansela*

Typeset at The Composers, 260, C.A. Apt., Paschim Vihar, New Delhi 110063 and printed at Sanat Printers, 312 EPIP, HSIDC, Kundli, Sonepat, Haryana

I dedicate this book to all Infoscions, my wife, my unborn kid, my parents, my friends and my loved ones

Contents

Part 2
Design and Development of Embedded Product

Preface

There exists a common misconception amongst students and young practising engineers that embedded system design is 'writing 'C' code'. This belief is absolutely wrong and I strongly emphasise that embedded system design refers to the design of embedded hardware, embedded firmware in 'C' or other supporting languages, integrating the hardware and firmware, and testing the functionalities of both.

Embedded system design is a highly specialised branch of Electronics Engineering where the technological advances of electronics and the design expertise of mechanical engineering work hand-in-hand to deliver cutting edge technologies and high-end products to a variety of diverse domains including consumer electronics, telecommunications, automobile, retail and banking applications. Embedded systems represent an integration of computer hardware, software along with programming concepts for developing special-purpose computer systems, designed to perform one or a few dedicated functions.

The embedded domain offers tremendous job opportunities worldwide. Design of embedded system is an art, and it demands talented people to take up the design challenges keeping the time frames in mind. The biggest challenge faced by the embedded industry today is the lack of skilled manpower in the domain. Though most of our fresh electronics and computer science engineering graduates are highly talented, they lack proper training and knowledge in the embedded domain. Lack of suitable books on the subject is one of the major reasons for this crisis. Although various books on embedded technology are available, almost none of them are capable of delivering the basic lessons in a simple and structured way. They are written from a high-end perspective, which are appropriate only for the practising engineers.

This book 'Introduction to Embedded Systems' is the first-of-its-kind, which will appeal as a comprehensive introduction to students, and as a guide to practising engineers and project managers. It has been specially designed for undergraduate courses in Computer Science & Engineering, Information Technology, Electrical Engineering, Electronics & Communication Engineering and Instrumentation & Control Engineering. Also, it will be a valuable reference for the students of BSc / MSc / MTech (CS/IT/Electronics), MCA and DOEACC 'B' level courses.

The book has been organised in such a way to provide the fundamentals of embedded systems; the steps involved in the design and development of embedded hardware and firmware, and their integration; and the life cycle management of embedded system development. Chapters 1 to 4 have been structured to give the readers a basic idea of an embedded system. Chapters 5 to 13 have been organised to give an in-depth knowledge on designing the embedded hardware and firmware. They would be very helpful to practising embedded system engineers. Chapter 15 dealing with the design life cycle of an embedded system would be beneficial to both practising engineers as well as project managers. Each chapter begins with learning objectives, presenting the concepts in simple language supplemented with ample tables, figures and solved examples. An important part of this book comes at the end of each chapter where you will find a brief summary, list of keywords, objective questions (in multiple-choice format) and review questions. To aid students commence experimentation in the laboratory, lab assignments have been provided in relevant chapters. An extremely beneficial segment at the end of the book is the overview of PIC & AVR Family of Microcontrollers & ARM Processors as well as innovative design case studies presenting real-world situations.

The major highlights of this book are as follows.

- Brings an entirely different approach in the learning of embedded system. It looks at embedded systems as a whole, specifies what it is, what it comprises of, what is to be done with it and how to go about the whole process of designing an embedded system.
- Follows a design- and development-oriented approach through detailed explanations for Keil Micro Vision (i.e., embedded system/integrated development environment), ORCAD (PCB design software tool) and PCB Fabrication techniques.
- Practical implementation such as washing machines, automotives, and stepper motor and other I/O device interfacing circuits.
- Programming concepts: deals in embedded C, delving into basics to unravelling advance level concepts.
- Complete coverage of the *8051* microcontroller architecture and assembly language programming.
- Detailed coverage of RTOS internals, multitasking, task management, task scheduling, task communication and synchronisation. Ample examples on the various task scheduling policies.
- Comprehensive coverage on the internals of MicroC/OS-II and VxWorks RTOS kernels.
- Written in lucid, easy-to-understand language with strong emphasis on examples, tables and figures.
- Useful reference for practicing engineers not well conversant with embedded systems and their applications.
- Rich Pedagogy includes objective questions, lab assignments, solved examples and review questions.

The comprehensive online learning centre—http://www.mhhe.com/shibu/es1e—accompanying this book offers valuable resources for students, instructors and professionals.

For Instructors

- PowerPoint slides (chapter-wise)
- A brief chapter on Embedded Programming Language C++/ Java
- Case studies that are given in the book and one new case study on heart beat monitoring system
- Solution manual (chapter-wise)
- Short questions, quizzes in the category of fill in the blanks, true/false and multiple choice questions (25); programming questions with solution (5). (Level of difficulty: hard)
- Chapter-wise links to important websites and important text materials

For Students

- Chapter-wise tutorials
- A brief chapter on Embedded Programming Language C++/ Java
- Case studies that are given in the book and one new case study on heart beat monitoring system
- Answers for objective questions/selected review questions and hints for lab assignments provided in the book.
- Short questions, self-test quizzes in the category of fill in the blanks, true/false and multiple choice questions (25); programming questions with solutions (5). (Level of difficulty: easy/medium)
- List of project ideas
- Chapter-wise links to important websites and important text materials.

This book is written purely on the basis of my working knowledge in the field of embedded hardware and firmware design, and expertise in dealing with the life cycle management of embedded systems. A few descriptions and images used in this book are taken from websites with prior written copyright permissions from the owner of the site/author of the articles.

The design references and data sheets of devices including the parametric reference used in the illustrative part of this book are taken from the following websites. Readers are requested to visit these sites for getting updates and more information on design articles. Also, you can order some free samples from some of the sites for your design.

www.intel.com	Intel Corporation
www.maxim-ic.com	Maxim/Dallas Semiconductor
www.atmel.com	Atmel Corporation
www.analog.com	Analog Devices
www.microchip.com	Microchip Technology
www.ti.com	Texas Instruments
www.nxp.com	NXP Semiconductors
www.national.com	National Semiconductor
www.fairchildsemi.com	Fairchild Semiconductor
www.intersil.com	Intersil Corporation
www.freescale.com	Freescale Semiconductor
www.xilinx.com	Xilinx (Programmable Devices)
www.orcad.com	Cadence Systems (Orcad Tool)
www.keil.com	Keil (MicroVision 3 IDE)
www.embedded.com	Online Embedded Magazine
www.elecdesign.com	Electronic Design Magazine

I would be looking forward to suggestions for further improvement of the book. You may contact me at the following email id—tmh.csefeedback@gmail.com. Kindly mention the title and author name in the subject line. Wish you luck as you embark on an exhilarating career path!

Shibu K V

Acknowledgements

I take this opportunity to thank ***Mr Mohammed Rijas*** (Group Project Manager, Mobility and Embedded Systems Practice, Infosys Technologies Ltd Thiruvananthapuram) and ***Mr Shafeer Badharudeen*** (Senior Project Manager, Mobility and Embedded Systems Practice, Infosys Technologies Ltd Thiruvananthapuram) for their valuable suggestions and guidance in writing this book. I am also grateful to my team and all other members of the Embedded Systems Group, Infosys Technologies for inspiring me to write this book. I acknowledge my senior management team at the Embedded Systems and Mobility practice, Infosys Technologies—***Rohit P, Srinivasa Rao M, Tadimeti Srinivasan, Darshan Shankavaram and Ramesh Adiga***—for their constant encouragement and appreciation of my efforts. I am immensely grateful to ***Mr R Ravindra Kumar*** (Senior Director, CDAC Thiruvananthapuram) for giving me an opportunity to work with the Hardware Design Group of CDAC (Erstwhile ER&DCI), ***Mrs K G Sulochana*** (Joint Director CDAC Thiruvananthapuram) for giving me the first embedded project to kick start my professional career and also for all the support provided to me during my tenure with CDAC. I convey my appreciation to ***Mr Biju C Oommen*** (Addl. Director, Hardware Design Group, CDAC Thiruvananthapuram), who is my great source of inspiration, for giving me the basic lessons of embedded technology, ***Mr S Krishna Kumar Rao, Mr Sanju Gopal, Ms Deepa R S, Mr Shaji N M*** and ***Mr Suresh R Pillai*** for their helping hand during my research activities at CDAC, and ***Mr Praveen V L*** whose contribution in designing the graphics of this book is noteworthy. I extend my heartfelt gratitude to all my friends and ex-colleagues of Hardware Design Group CDAC Thiruvananthapuram—without their prayers and support, this book would not have been a reality. Last but not the least, I acknowledge my beloved friend ***Dr Sreeja*** for all the moral support provided to me during this endeavor, and my family members for their understanding and support during the writing of this book.

A token of special appreciation to ***Mr S Krishnakumar Rao*** (Deputy Director, Hardware Design Group, CDAC Thiruvananthapuram) for helping me in compiling the section on VLSI Design and ***Mr Shameerudheen P T*** for his help in compiling the section on PCB Layout Design using Orcad Layout Tool.

I would like to extend my special thanks to the following persons for coordinating and providing timely feedback on all requests to the concerned product development/service companies, semiconductor manufacturers and informative web pages.

Angela Williams of Keil Software
Natasha Wan, ***Jessen Wehrwein*** and ***Scott Wayne*** of Analog Devices
Derek Chan of Atmel Asia
Moe Rubenzahl of Maxim Dallas Semiconductor
Mark Aaldering and ***Theresa Warren*** of Xilinx
Anders Edholm of Electrolux
Vijayeta Karol of Honda Siel Cars India Ltd
Mark David of Electronic Design Magazine
Vidur Naik of Adidas India Division
Steven Kamin of Cadence Design Systems
Deepak Pingle and ***Pralhad Joshi*** of Advanced Micronic Devices Limited (AMDL)
Regina Kim of WIZnet Inc.
Taranbir Singh Kochar of Siemens Audiology India Division
Crystal Whitcomb of Linksys—A Division of Cisco Systems
Kulbhushan Seth of Casio India Co. Pvt. Ltd
Jitesh Mathur and ***Meggy Chan*** of Philips Medical Systems
John Symonds of Burn Technology Limited
Citron Chang of Advantech Equipment Corp
Michael Barr of Netrino Consultants Networks
Peggy Vezina of GM Media Archive
David Mindell of MIT
Frank Miller of pulsar.gs
Gautam Awasthi of Agilent Technologies India Pvt. Ltd

A note of acknowledgement is due to the following reviewers for their valuable suggestions for the book.

Bimal Raj Dutta
Shri Ram Murti Smarak College of Engineering & Technology, Bareilly

Nilima Fulmare
Hindustan College of Science & Technology, Agra

P K Mukherjee
Institute of Technology, Banaras Hindu University, Varanasi

Kalyan Mahato
Government College of Engineering & Leather Technology, Kolkata

P Kabisatpathy
College of Engineering & Technology, Bhubaneswar

P K Dutta
North Eastern Regional Institute of Science and Technology College, Itanagar

Prabhat Ranjan
Dhirubhai Ambani Institute of Information and Communication Technology (DAIICT), Gandhinagar
Lyla B Das
National Institute of Technology Calicut (NITC), Calicut

Finally, I thank the publishing team at McGraw-Hill Education India, more specifically Vibha Mahajan, Shalini Jha, Nilanjan Chakravarty, Surbhi Suman, Dipika Dey, Anjali Razdan and Baldev Raj for their praiseworthy initiatives and efficient management of the book.

SHIBU K V

Visual Preview

Learning Objectives

LEARNING OBJECTIVES

- ✓ *Learn what an Embedded System is*
- ✓ *Learn the difference between Embedded Systems and General Computing Systems*
- ✓ *Know the history of Embedded Systems*
- ✓ *Learn the classification of Embedded Systems based on performance, complexity and the era in which they evolved*
- ✓ *Know the domains and areas of applications of Embedded Systems*
- ✓ *Understand the different purposes of Embedded Systems*
- ✓ *Analysis of a real life example on the bonding of embedded technology with human life*

Each chapter begins with ***Learning Objectives*** *which provides readers with specific outcomes they should be able to achieve after mastering the chapter content.*

Sections and Sub-sections

6.2 THE *8051* INSTRUCTION SET

As mentioned earlier, the *8051 Instruction Set* is broadly classified into five categories namely; *Data transfer instructions*, *Arithmetic instructions*, *Logical instructions*, *Boolean instructions* and *Program control transfer instructions*. The following sections describe each of them in detail.

6.2.1 Data Transfer Instructions

Data transfer instructions transfer data between a source and destination. The source can be an internal data memory, a register, external data memory, code memory or immediate data. Destination may be an internal data memory, external data memory or a register.

6.2.1.1 Internal Data Transfer Operations Internal data transfer instructions perform the movement of data between, register, memory location, accumulator and stack. MOV instruction is used for data transfer between register, memory location and accumulator. PUSH and POP instructions transfer data between memory location/register and stack. The following table summarises the various internal data transfer instructions.

Each chapter has been neatly divided into ***Sections and Sub-sections*** *so that the subject matter is studied in a logical progression of ideas and concepts.*

Solved Examples

Example 1

The accumulator register contains 80H and B register contains 8FH. Add accumulator content with B register. Explain the output of the summation and the status of the carry flag after the addition operation.

Adding 80H with 8FH results in 10FH. Since 10FH requires more than 8 bits to represent, the accumulator holds the least significant 8 bits of the result (Here 0FH). The carry bit CY present in the Program Status Word (PSW) reg is set to indicate that the output of the addition operation resulted in a number greater than FFH. Figure 6.11 illustr the addition operation and the involvement of Carry bit (CY).

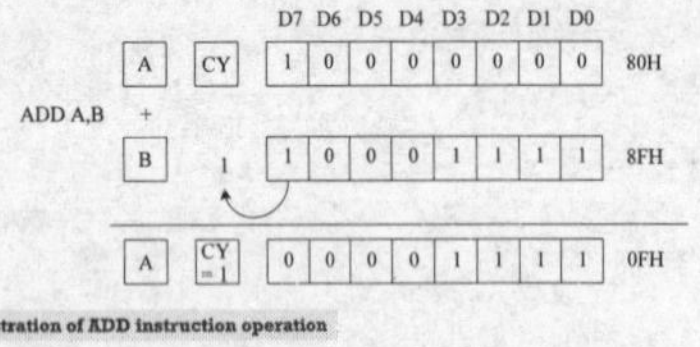

Fig. 6.11 **Illustration of ADD instruction operation**

Example 2

Register R0 contains 0BH. Add the contents of register R0 with the sum obtained in the previous example using *ADDC* instruction. Explain the output of the summation and the status of the carry flag after the addition operation.

Provided at appropriate locations, ***Solved Examples*** *aid in understanding of the fundamentals of embedded hardware and firmware design.*

Photographs

Photographs of important concepts, designs and architectural descriptions bring the subject to life.

Some embedded systems store the collected data for processing and analysis. Such systems incorporate a built-in/plug-in storage memory for storing the captured data. Some of them give the user a meaningful representation of the collected data by visual (graphical/quantitative) or audible means using display units [Liquid Crystal Display (LCD), Light Emitting Diode (LED), etc.] buzzers, alarms, etc. Examples are: measuring instruments with storage memory and monitoring instruments with storage memory used in medical applications. Certain embedded systems store the data and will not give a representation of the same to the user, whereas the data is used for internal processing.

A digital camera is a typical example of an embedded system with data collection/storage/representation of data. Images are captured and the captured image may be stored within the memory of the camera. The captured image can also be presented to the user through a graphic LCD unit.

Fig. 1.1 A digital camera for image capturing/storage/display
(Photo courtesy of Casio-Model EXILIM ex-Z850 (www.casio.com))

1.6.2 Data Communication

Embedded data communication systems are deployed in applications ranging from complex satellite communication systems to simple home networking systems. As mentioned earlier in this chapter, the data collected by an embedded terminal may require transferring of the same to some other system located remotely. The transmission is achieved either by a wire-line medium or by a wireless medium. Wire-line medium was the most common choice in all olden days embedded systems. As technology is changing, wireless medium is becoming the de-facto standard for data communication in embedded systems. A wireless medium offers cheaper connectivity solutions and make the communication link free from the hassle of wire bundles. Data can either be transmitted by analog means or by digital means. Modern industry trends are settling towards digital communication.

The data collecting embedded terminal itself can incorporate data communication units like wireless

Fig. 1.2 A wireless network router for data communication
(Photo courtesy of Linksys (www.linksys.com). A division of CISCO system)

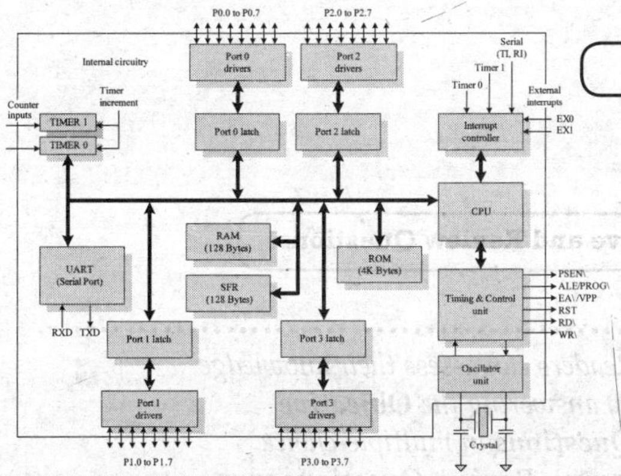

Fig. 5.1 *8051* Architecture—Block diagram representation

5.3.2 The Memory Organisation

8051 is built around the *Harvard* processor architecture. The program and data memory of *8051* is logically separated and they physically reside separately. Separate address spaces are assigned for data memory and program memory. *8051*'s address bus is 16bit wide and it can address up to 64KB (2^{16}) memory.

5.3.2.1 The Program (Code) Memory The basic *8051* architecture provides lowest 4K bytes of program memory as on-chip memory (built-in chip memory). In *8031*, the ROMless counterpart of *8051*, all program memory is external to the chip. Switching between the internal program memory and external program memory is accomplished by changing the logic level of the pin External Access (EA\). Tying EA\ pin to logic 1 (V_{CC}), configures the chip to execute instructions from program memory up to 4K (program memory location up to 0FFFH) from internal memory and 4K (program memory location from 1000H) onwards from external memory, while connecting EA\ pin to logic 0 (GND) configures the chip to external program execution mode, where the entire code memory is executed from the external memory. Remember External Access pin is an active low pin (Normally referred as EA\). The control signal for external program memory execution is PSEN\ (Program Strobe Enable). For internal program

Illustrations

Effective and accurate ***Illustrations*** *demonstrate the concepts, design problems and steps involved in the design of embedded systems.*

Chapter Summary and Keywords

Summary

- ✓ An embedded system is an Electronic/Electro-mechanical system designed to perform a specific function and is a combination of both hardware and firmware (Software).
- ✓ A general purpose computing system is a combination of generic hardware and general purpose operating system for executing a variety of applications, whereas an embedded system is a combination of special purpose hardware and embedded OS/firmware for executing a specific set of applications.
- ✓ Apollo Guidance Computer (AGC) is the first recognised modern embedded system and 'Autonetics D-17', the guidance computer for the Minuteman-I missile, was the first mass-produced embedded system.
- ✓ Based on the complexity and performance requirements, embedded systems are classified into small-scale, medium-scale and large-scale/complex.
- ✓ The presence of embedded systems vary from simple electronic toys to complex flight and missile control systems.
- ✓ Embedded systems are designed to serve the purpose of any one or a combination of data collection/storage/representation, data communication, data (signal) processing, monitoring, control or application specific user interface.

*Bulleted **Summary** gives a recap of the various topics illustrated in the chapter and **Keywords** highlight the important chapter terminology.*

Keywords

Embedded system	: An electronic/electro-mechanical system which is designed to perform a specific function and is a combination of both hardware and firmware
Microprocessor	: A silicon chip representing a Central Processing Unit (CPU)
Microcontroller	: A highly integrated chip that contains a CPU, scratchpad RAM, special and general purpose register arrays and integrated peripherals
DSP	: Digital Signal Processor is a powerful special purpose 8/16/32 bit microprocessor designed specifically to meet the computational demands and power constraints
ASIC	: Application Specific Integrated Circuit is a microchip designed to perform a specific or unique application
Sensor	: A transducer device that converts energy from one form to another for any measurement or control purpose
Actuator	: A form of transducer device (mechanical or electrical) which converts signals to corresponding physical action (motion)
LED	: Light Emitting Diode. An output device producing visual indication in the form of light in accordance with current flow
Buzzer	: A piezo-electric device for generating audio indication. It contains a piezo-electric diaphragm which produces audible sound in response to the voltage applied to it
Operating system	: A piece of software designed to manage and allocate system resources and execute other pieces of software
Electro Cardiogram (ECG)	: An embedded device for heartbeat monitoring
SCADA	: Supervisory Control and Data Acquisition System. A data acquisition system used in industrial control applications
RAM	: Random Access memory. Volatile memory
ADC	: Analog to Digital Converter. An integrated circuit which converts analog signals to digital

Objective and Review Questions

*Readers can assess their knowledge by answering the **Objective Questions** in multiple-choice format. **Review Questions** spur students to apply and integrate chapter content.*

Objective Questions

1. Embedded systems are
   (a) General purpose (b) Special purpose
2. Embedded system is
   (a) An electronic system (b) A pure mechanical system
   (c) An electro-mechanical system (d) (a) or (c)
3. Which of the following is not true about embedded systems?
   (a) Built around specialised hardware (b) Always contain an operating system
   (c) Execution behaviour may be deterministic (d) All of these
   (e) None of these
4. Which of the following is not an example of a 'Small-scale Embedded System'?
   (a) Electronic Barbie doll (b) Simple calculator
   (c) Cell phone (d) Electronic toy car
5. The first recognised modern embedded system is
   (a) Apple Computer (b) Apollo Guidance Computer (AGC)
   (c) Calculator (d) Radio Navigation System
6. The first mass produced embedded system is
   (a) Minuteman-I (b) Minuteman-II
   (c) Autonetics D-17 (d) Apollo Guidance Computer (AGC)
7. Which of the following is (are) an intended purpose(s) of embedded systems?
   (a) Data collection (b) Data processing (c) Data communication
   (d) All of these (e) None of these
8. Which of the following is an (are) example(s) of embedded system for data communication?
   (a) USB Mass storage device (b) Network router
   (c) Digital camera (d) Music player
   (e) All of these (f) None of these
9. A digital multi meter is an example of an embedded system for
   (a) Data communication (b) Monitoring (c) Control (d) All of these
   (e) None of these
10. Which of the following is an (are) example(s) of an embedded system for signal processing?
    (a) Apple iPOD (media player device) (b) SanDisk USB mass storage device
    (c) Both (a) and (b) (d) None of these

Review Questions

1. What is an embedded system? Explain the different applications of embedded systems.
2. Explain the various purposes of embedded systems in detail with illustrative examples.
3. Explain the different classifications of embedded systems. Give an example for each.

Lab Assignments

Lab Assignments

1. Write a 'C' program to find the *endianness* of the processor in which the program is running. If the processor is big endian, print "The processor architecture is Big endian", else print "The processor architecture is Little endian" on the console window. Execute the program separately on a PC with Windows, Linux and MAC operating systems.
2. Draw the interfacing diagram for connecting an LED to the port pin of a microcontroller. The LED is turned ON when the microcontroller port pin is at Logic '0'. Calculate the resistance required to connect in series with the LED for the following design parameters.
   (a) LED voltage drop on conducting = 1.7V
   (b) LED current rating = 20 mA
   (c) Power Supply Voltage = 5V
3. Design an RC (Resistor-Capacitor) based reset circuit for producing an active low Power-On reset pulse of width 0.1 milli seconds.
4. Design a zener diode and transistor based brown-out protection circuit with active low reset pulse for the following design parameters.

To aid students conduct experiments in the laboratory, ***Lab Assignments*** *have been provided at the end of relevant chapters.*

Appendix

II

Design Case Studies

Case Studies

1. DIGITAL CLOCK

Design and Implement a Digital Clock as per the requirements given below.

1. Use a 16 character 2-line display for displaying the current Time. Display the time in DAY HH:MM:SS format on the first line. Display the message 'Have A Nice Day!' on the second line. DAY represents the day of the Week (SUN, MON, TUE, WED, THU, FRI and SAT). HH represents the hour in 2 digit format. Depending on the format settings it may vary from 00 to 12 (12 Hour Format) or from 00 to 23 (24 Hour format). MM represents the minute in 2 digit format. It varies from 00 to 59. SS represents the seconds in 2 digit format. It varies from 00 to 59. The alignment of display character should be centre justified (Meaning if the characters to display are 12, pack it with 2 blank space each at right and left and then display).
2. Interface a Hitachi HD44780 compatible LCD with 8051 microcontroller as per the following interface details
   Data Bus: Port P2
   Register Select Control line (RS): Port Pin P1.4
   Read/Write Control Signal (RW): Port Pin P1.5
   LCD Enable (E): P1.6
3. The Backlight of the LCD should be always ON
4. Use AT89C51/52 or AT89S8252 microcontroller. Use a crystal Oscillator with frequency 12.00 MHz. This will provide accurate timing of 1 microsecond/machine cycle.
5. A 2 × 2 matrix key board (4 keys) is interfaced to Port P1 of the microcontroller. The key details are MENU key connected to Row 0, and Column 0 of the matrix; ESC key connected to Row 0, and Column 1 of the matrix; UP key connected to Row 1, and Column 0 of the matrix; DOWN key connected to Row 1, and Column 1 of the matrix. The Rows 0, 1 and columns 0, 1 of matrix keyboard are interfaced to Port pins P1.0, P1.1, P1.2 and P1.3 respectively.
6. The hour (HH) and minutes (MM) should be adjustable through a Menu Screen. The Menu screen is invoked by

A comprehensive set of five ***Case Studies,*** *at the end of the book demonstrate the applications of theoretical concepts.*

Appendix

I

Overview of PIC and AVR Family of Microcontrollers and ARM Processors

Appendix on different family of Microprocessors and Controllers

INTRODUCTION TO PIC® FAMILY OF MICROCONTROLLERS

PIC® is a popular 8/16/32 bit RISC microcontroller family from Microchip Technology (www.microchip.com). The 8bit PIC family comprises the products PIC10F, PIC12F, PIC16F and PIC18F. They differ in the amount of program memory supported, performance, instruction length and pin count. Based on the architecture, the 8bit PIC family is grouped into three namely;

Baseline Products based on the original PIC architecture. They support 12bit instruction set with very limited features. They are available in 6 to 40 pin packages. The 6 pin 10F series, some 12F series (8 pin 12F629) and some 16F series (The 20-pin 16F690 and 40-pin 16F887) falls under this category.

Mid-Range This is an extension to the baseline architecture with added features like support for interrupts, on-chip peripherals (Like A/D converter, Serial Interfaces, LCD interface, etc.), increased memory, etc. The instruction set for this architecture is 14bit wide. They are available in 8 to 64 pin packages with operating voltage in the range 1.8V to 5.5V. Some products of the 12F (The 8 pin 12F629) and the 16F (20-pin 16F690 and 40-pin 16F887) series comes under this category.

High Performance The PIC 18F J and K series comes under this category. The memory density for these devices is very high (Up to 128KB program memory and 4KB data memory). They provide built-in support for advanced peripherals and communication interfaces like USB, CAN, etc. The instruction set for this architecture is 16bit wide. They are capable of delivering a speed of 16MIPS.

As mentioned earlier we have a bunch of devices to select for our design, from the PIC 8bit family. Some of them have limited set of I/O capabilities, on-chip Peripherals, data memory (SRAM) and program memory (FLASH) targeting low end applications. The 12F508 controller is a typical example for this. It contains 512 × 12 bits of program memory, 25 bytes of RAM, 6 I/O lines and comes in an 8-pin package. On the other hand some of the PIC family devices are feature rich with a bunch of on-chip peripherals (Like ADC, UART, I2C, SPI, etc.), higher data and program storage memory, targeting high end applications. The 16F877 controller is a typical example for this. It contains 8192 × 14 bits of FLASH program memory, 368 bytes of RAM, 256 bytes of EEPROM, 33 I/O lines, On-chip peripherals like 10-bit A/D converter, 3-Timer units, USART, Interrupt Controller, etc. It comes in a 40-pin package.

Here, the 16F877 device is selected as the candidate for illustrating the generic PIC architecture. Figure A1.1 illus-

The ***Appendix*** *section is intended to give an overview of PIC & AVR family of microcontrollers & ARM processor.*

PART 1

EMBEDDED SYSTEM: UNDERSTANDING THE BASIC CONCEPTS

Understanding the basic concepts is essential in the learning of any subject. Designing an *Embedded System* is not a herculean task if you know the fundamentals. Like any general computing systems, Embedded Systems also possess a set of characteristics which are unique to the embedded system under consideration. In contrast to the general computing systems, Embedded Systems are highly domain and application specific in nature, meaning; they are specifically designed for certain set of applications in certain domains like consumer electronics, telecom, automotive, industrial control, measurement systems etc. Unlike general computing systems it is not possible to replace an embedded system which is specifically designed for an application catering to a specific domain with another embedded system catering to another domain. The designer of the embedded system should be aware of its characteristics, and its domain and application specific nature.

An embedded system is an electrical/electro mechanical system which is specifically designed for an application catering to a specific domain. It is a combination of specialised hardware and firmware (software), which is tailored to meet the requirements of the application under consideration. An embedded system contains a processing unit which can be a microprocessor or a microcontroller or a System on Chip (SoC) or an Application Specific Integrated Circuit (ASIC)/Application Specific Standard Product (ASSP) or a Programmable Logic Device (PLD) like FPGA or CPLD, an I/O subsystem which facilitates the interfacing of sensors and actuators which acts as the messengers from and to the '*Real world*' to which the embedded system is interacting, on-board and external communication interfaces for communicating between the various on-board subsystems and chips which builds the embedded system and external systems to which the embedded system interacts, and other supervisory systems and support units like watchdog timers, reset circuits, brown-out protection circuits, regulated power supply unit, clock generation circuit etc. which empower and monitor the functioning of the embedded system. The design of embedded system has two aspects: The hardware design which takes care of the selection of the processing unit, the various I/O sub systems and communication interface and the inter connection among them, and the design of the embedded firmware which deals with configuring the various sub systems, implementing data communication and processing/controlling algorithm requirements. Depending on the response requirements and the type of applications for which the embedded system is designed, the embedded system can be a *Real-time* or a Non-real time system. The response requirements for a real-time system like *Flight Control System, Airbag Deployment System* for Automotive etc, are time critical and the hardware and firmware design aspects for such systems should take these into account, whereas the response requirements for non-real time systems like *Automatic Teller Machines* (*ATM*), *Media Playback Systems* etc, need not be time critical and missing deadlines may be acceptable in such systems.

Like any other systems, embedded systems also possess a set of quality attributes, which are the non-functional requirements like security, scalability, availability, maintainability, safety, portability etc. The non-functional requirements for the embedded system should be identified and should be addressed properly in the system design. The designer of the embedded system should be aware of the different non-functional requirement for the embedded system and should handle this properly to ensure high quality.

This section of the book is dedicated for describing the basic concepts of Embedded Systems. The chapters in this section are organised in a way to give the readers a comprehensive introduction to '*Embedded Systems, their application areas and their role in real life*', '*The different elements of a typical Embedded System*', the basic lessons on '*The characteristics and quality attributes of Embedded Systems*', '*Domain and Application specific usage examples for Embedded Systems*' and the '*Hardware and Software Co-design approach for Embedded System Design*', and a detailed introduction to '*The architecture and programming concepts for 8051 Microcontroller – The 8bit Microcontroller selected for our design examples*'. We will start the section with the chapter on '*Introduction to Embedded Systems*'

1 Introduction to Embedded Systems

LEARNING OBJECTIVES

- ✓ *Learn what an Embedded System is*
- ✓ *Learn the difference between Embedded Systems and General Computing Systems*
- ✓ *Know the history of Embedded Systems*
- ✓ *Learn the classification of Embedded Systems based on performance, complexity and the era in which they evolved*
- ✓ *Know the domains and areas of applications of Embedded Systems*
- ✓ *Understand the different purposes of Embedded Systems*
- ✓ *Analysis of a real life example on the bonding of embedded technology with human life*

Our day-to-day life is becoming more and more dependent on "embedded systems" and digital techniques. Embedded technologies are bonding into our daily activities even without our knowledge. Do you know the fact that the refrigerator, washing machine, microwave oven, air conditioner, television, DVD players, and music systems that we use in our home are built around an embedded system? You may be traveling by a 'Honda' or a 'Toyota' or a 'Ford' vehicle, but have you ever thought of the genius players working behind the special features and security systems offered by the vehicle to you? It is nothing but an intelligent embedded system. In your vehicle itself the presence of specialised embedded systems vary from intelligent head lamp controllers, engine controllers and ignition control systems to complex air bag control systems to protect you in case of a severe accident. People experience the power of embedded systems and enjoy the features and comfort provided by them. Most of us are totally unaware or ignorant of the intelligent embedded systems giving us so much comfort and security. Embedded systems are like reliable servants–they don't like to reveal their identity and neither they complain about their workloads to their owners or bosses. They are always sitting in a hidden place and are dedicated to their assigned task till their last breath. This book gives you an overview of embedded systems, the various steps involved in their design and development and the major domains where they are deployed.

1.1 WHAT IS AN EMBEDDED SYSTEM?

An embedded system is an electronic/electro-mechanical system designed to perform a specific function and is a combination of both hardware and firmware (software).

Every embedded system is unique, and the hardware as well as the firmware is highly specialised to the application domain. Embedded systems are becoming an inevitable part of any product or equipment in all fields including household appliances, telecommunications, medical equipment, industrial control, consumer products, etc.

1.2 EMBEDDED SYSTEMS vs. GENERAL COMPUTING SYSTEMS

The computing revolution began with the general purpose computing requirements. Later it was realised that the general computing requirements are not sufficient for the embedded computing requirements. The embedded computing requirements demand 'something special' in terms of response to stimuli, meeting the computational deadlines, power efficiency, limited memory availability, etc. Let's take the case of your personal computer, which may be either a desktop PC or a laptop PC or a palmtop PC. It is built around a general purpose processor like an Intel® Centrino or a Duo/Quad† core or an AMD Turion™ processor and is designed to support a set of multiple peripherals like multiple USB 2.0 ports, Wi-Fi, ethernet, video port, IEEE1394, SD/CF/MMC external interfaces, Bluetooth, etc and with additional interfaces like a CD read/writer, on-board Hard Disk Drive (HDD), gigabytes of RAM, etc. You can load any supported operating system (like Windows® XP/Vista/7, or Red Hat Linux/Ubuntu Linux, UNIX etc) into the hard disk of your PC. You can write or purchase a multitude of applications for your PC and can use your PC for running a large number of applications (like printing your dear's photo using a printer device connected to the PC and printer software, creating a document using Microsoft® Office Word tool, etc.) Now let us think about the DVD player you use for playing DVD movies. Is it possible for you to change the operating system of your DVD? Is it possible for you to write an application and download it to your DVD player for executing? Is it possible for you to add a printer software to your DVD player and connect a printer to your DVD player to take a printout? Is it possible for you to change the functioning of your DVD player to a television by changing the embedded software? The answers to all these questions are 'NO'. Can you see any general purpose interface like Bluetooth or Wi-Fi on your DVD player? Of course 'NO'. The only interface you can find out on the DVD player is the interface for connecting the DVD player with the display screen and one for controlling the DVD player through a remote (May be an IR or any other specific wireless interface). Indeed your DVD player is an embedded system designed specifically for decoding digital video and generating a video signal as output to your TV or any other display screen which supports the display interface supported by the DVD Player. Let us summarise our findings from the comparison of embedded system and general purpose computing system with the help of a table:

General Purpose Computing System	Embedded System
A system which is a combination of a generic hardware and a General Purpose Operating System for executing a variety of applications	A system which is a combination of special purpose hardware and embedded OS for executing a specific set of applications
Contains a General Purpose Operating System (GPOS)	May or may not contain an operating system for functioning

†The illustration given here is based on the processor details available till Dec 2008. Since processor technology is undergoing rapid changes, the processor names mentioned here may not be relevant in future.

Applications are alterable (programmable) by the user (It is possible for the end user to re-install the operating system, and also add or remove user applications)	The firmware of the embedded system is pre-programmed and it is non-alterable by the end-user (There may be exceptions for systems supporting OS kernel image flashing through special hardware settings)
Performance is the key deciding factor in the selection of the system. Always, 'Faster is Better'	Application-specific requirements (like performance, power requirements, memory usage, etc.) are the key deciding factors
Less/not at all tailored towards reduced operating power requirements, options for different levels of power management.	Highly tailored to take advantage of the power saving modes supported by the hardware and the operating system
Response requirements are not time-critical	For certain category of embedded systems like mission critical systems, the response time requirement is highly critical
Need not be deterministic in execution behaviour	Execution behaviour is deterministic for certain types of embedded systems like 'Hard Real Time' systems

However, the demarcation between desktop systems and embedded systems in certain areas of embedded applications are shrinking in certain contexts. Smart phones are typical examples of this. Nowadays smart phones are available with RAM up to 256 MB and users can extend most of their desktop applications to the smart phones and it waives the clause "Embedded systems are designed for a specific application" from the characteristics of the embedded system for the mobile embedded device category. However, smart phones come with a built-in operating system and it is not modifiable by the end user. It makes the clause: "The firmware of the embedded system is unalterable by the end user", still a valid clause in the mobile embedded device category.

1.3 HISTORY OF EMBEDDED SYSTEMS

Embedded systems were in existence even before the IT revolution. In the olden days embedded systems were built around the old vacuum tube and transistor technologies and the embedded algorithm was developed in low level languages. Advances in semiconductor and nano-technology and IT revolution gave way to the development of miniature embedded systems. The first recognised modern embedded system is the Apollo Guidance Computer (AGC) developed by the MIT Instrumentation Laboratory for the lunar expedition. They ran the inertial guidance systems of both the Command Module (CM) and the Lunar Excursion Module (LEM). The Command Module was designed to encircle the moon while the Lunar Module and its crew were designed to go down to the moon surface and land there safely. The Lunar Module featured in total 18 engines. There were 16 reaction control thrusters, a descent engine and an ascent engine. The descent engine was 'designed to' provide thrust to the lunar module out of the lunar orbit and land it safely on the moon. MIT's original design was based on 4K words of fixed memory (Read Only Memory) and 256 words of erasable memory (Random Access Memory). By June 1963, the figures reached 10K of fixed and 1K of erasable memory. The final configuration was 36K words of fixed memory and 2K words of erasable memory. The clock frequency of the first microchip proto model used in AGC was 1.024 MHz and it was derived from a 2.048 MHz crystal clock. The computing unit of AGC consisted of approximately 11 instructions and 16 bit word logic. Around 5000 ICs (3-input NOR gates, RTL logic) supplied by Fairchild Semiconductor were used in this design. The user interface unit of AGC is known as DSKY (display/keyboard). DSKY looked like a calculator type keypad with an array of numerals. It was used for inputting the commands to the module numerically.

The first mass-produced embedded system was the guidance computer for the Minuteman-I missile in 1961. It was the '*Autonetics **D-17***' guidance computer, built using discrete transistor logic and a hard-disk for main memory. The first integrated circuit was produced in September 1958 but computers using them didn't begin to appear until 1963. Some of their early uses were in embedded systems, notably used by NASA for the Apollo Guidance Computer and by the US military in the Minuteman-II intercontinental ballistic missile.

1.4 CLASSIFICATION OF EMBEDDED SYSTEMS

It is possible to have a multitude of classifications for embedded systems, based on different criteria. Some of the criteria used in the classification of embedded systems are:

1. Based on generation
2. Complexity and performance requirements
3. Based on deterministic behaviour
4. Based on triggering.

The classification based on deterministic system behaviour is applicable for 'Real Time' systems. The application/task execution behaviour for an embedded system can be either deterministic or non-deterministic. Based on the execution behaviour, Real Time embedded systems are classified into *Hard* and *Soft*. We will discuss about hard and soft real time systems in a later chapter. Embedded Systems which are 'Reactive' in nature (Like process control systems in industrial control applications) can be classified based on the trigger. Reactive systems can be either *event triggered* or *time triggered.*

1.4.1 Classification Based on Generation

This classification is based on the order in which the embedded processing systems evolved from the first version to where they are today. As per this criterion, embedded systems can be classified into:

1.4.1.1 First Generation The early embedded systems were built around 8bit microprocessors like 8085 and Z80, and 4bit microcontrollers. Simple in hardware circuits with firmware developed in Assembly code. Digital telephone keypads, stepper motor control units etc. are examples of this.

1.4.1.2 Second Generation These are embedded systems built around 16bit microprocessors and 8 or 16 bit microcontrollers, following the first generation embedded systems. The instruction set for the second generation processors/controllers were much more complex and powerful than the first generation processors/controllers. Some of the second generation embedded systems contained embedded operating systems for their operation. Data Acquisition Systems, SCADA systems, etc. are examples of second generation embedded systems.

1.4.1.3 Third Generation With advances in processor technology, embedded system developers started making use of powerful 32bit processors and 16bit microcontrollers for their design. A new concept of application and domain specific processors/controllers like Digital Signal Processors (DSP) and Application Specific Integrated Circuits (ASICs) came into the picture. The instruction set of processors became more complex and powerful and the concept of instruction pipelining also evolved. The processor market was flooded with different types of processors from different vendors. Processors like Intel Pentium, Motorola 68K, etc. gained attention in high performance embedded requirements. Dedicated embedded real time and general purpose operating systems entered into the embedded market. Embedded systems spread its ground to areas like robotics, media, industrial process control, networking, etc.

1.4.1.4 Fourth Generation The advent of System on Chips (SoC), reconfigurable processors and multicore processors are bringing high performance, tight integration and miniaturisation into the embedded device market. The SoC technique implements a total system on a chip by integrating different functionalities with a processor core on an integrated circuit. We will discuss about SoCs in a later chapter. The fourth generation embedded systems are making use of high performance real time embedded operating systems for their functioning. Smart phone devices, mobile internet devices (MIDs), etc. are examples of fourth generation embedded systems.

1.4.1.5 What Next? The processor and embedded market is highly dynamic and demanding. So 'what will be the next smart move in the next embedded generation?' Let's wait and see.

1.4.2 Classification Based on Complexity and Performance

This classification is based on the complexity and system performance requirements. According to this classification, embedded systems can be grouped into:

1.4.2.1 Small-Scale Embedded Systems Embedded systems which are simple in application needs and where the performance requirements are not time critical fall under this category. An electronic toy is a typical example of a small-scale embedded system. Small-scale embedded systems are usually built around low performance and low cost 8 or 16 bit microprocessors/microcontrollers. A small-scale embedded system may or may not contain an operating system for its functioning.

1.4.2.2 Medium-Scale Embedded Systems Embedded systems which are slightly complex in hardware and firmware (software) requirements fall under this category. Medium-scale embedded systems are usually built around medium performance, low cost 16 or 32 bit microprocessors/microcontrollers or digital signal processors. They usually contain an embedded operating system (either general purpose or real time operating system) for functioning.

1.4.2.3 Large-Scale Embedded Systems/Complex Systems Embedded systems which involve highly complex hardware and firmware requirements fall under this category. They are employed in mission critical applications demanding high performance. Such systems are commonly built around high performance 32 or 64 bit RISC processors/controllers or Reconfigurable System on Chip (RSoC) or multi-core processors and programmable logic devices. They may contain multiple processors/controllers and co-units/hardware accelerators for offloading the processing requirements from the main processor of the system. Decoding/encoding of media, cryptographic function implementation, etc. are examples for processing requirements which can be implemented using a co-processor/hardware accelerator. Complex embedded systems usually contain a high performance Real Time Operating System (RTOS) for task scheduling, prioritization and management.

1.5 MAJOR APPLICATION AREAS OF EMBEDDED SYSTEMS

We are living in a world where embedded systems play a vital role in our day-to-day life, starting from home to the computer industry, where most of the people find their job for a livelihood. Embedded technology has acquired a new dimension from its first generation model, the Apollo guidance computer, to the latest radio navigation system combined with in-car entertainment technology and the microprocessor based "Smart" running shoes launched by Adidas in April 2005. The application areas and the products in the embedded domain are countless. A few of the important domains and products are listed below:

1. *Consumer electronics:* Camcorders, cameras, etc.
2. *Household appliances:* Television, DVD players, washing machine, fridge, microwave oven, etc.
3. *Home automation and security systems:* Air conditioners, sprinklers, intruder detection alarms, closed circuit television cameras, fire alarms, etc.
4. *Automotive industry:* Anti-lock breaking systems (ABS), engine control, ignition systems, automatic navigation systems, etc.
5. *Telecom:* Cellular telephones, telephone switches, handset multimedia applications, etc.
6. *Computer peripherals:* Printers, scanners, fax machines, etc.
7. *Computer networking systems:* Network routers, switches, hubs, firewalls, etc.
8. *Healthcare:* Different kinds of scanners, EEG, ECG machines etc.
9. *Measurement & Instrumentation:* Digital multi meters, digital CROs, logic analyzers PLC systems, etc.
10. *Banking & Retail:* Automatic teller machines (ATM) and currency counters, point of sales (POS)
11. *Card Readers:* Barcode, smart card readers, hand held devices, etc.

1.6 PURPOSE OF EMBEDDED SYSTEMS

As mentioned in the previous section, embedded systems are used in various domains like consumer electronics, home automation, telecommunications, automotive industry, healthcare, control & instrumentation, retail and banking applications, etc. Within the domain itself, according to the application usage context, they may have different functionalities. Each embedded system is designed to serve the purpose of any one or a combination of the following tasks:

1. Data collection/Storage/Representation
2. Data communication
3. Data (signal) processing
4. Monitoring
5. Control
6. Application specific user interface

1.6.1 Data Collection/Storage/Representation

Embedded systems designed for the purpose of data collection performs acquisition of data from the external world. Data collection is usually done for storage, analysis, manipulation and transmission. The term "data" refers all kinds of information, viz. text, voice, image, video, electrical signals and any other measurable quantities. Data can be either analog (continuous) or digital (discrete). Embedded systems with analog data capturing techniques collect data directly in the form of analog signals whereas embedded systems with digital data collection mechanism converts the analog signal to corresponding digital signal using analog to digital (A/D) converters and then collects the binary equivalent of the analog data. If the data is digital, it can be directly captured without any additional interface by digital embedded systems.

The collected data may be stored directly in the system or may be transmitted to some other systems or it may be processed by the system or it may be deleted instantly after giving a meaningful representation. These actions are purely dependent on the purpose for which the embedded system is designed. Embedded systems designed for pure measurement applications without storage, used in control and instrumentation domain, collects data and gives a meaningful representation of the collected data by means of graphical representation or quantity value and deletes the collected data when new data arrives at the data collection terminal. Analog and digital CROs without storage memory are typical examples of this. Any measuring equipment used in the medical domain for monitoring without storage functionality also comes under this category.

Some embedded systems store the collected data for processing and analysis. Such systems incorporate a built-in/plug-in storage memory for storing the captured data. Some of them give the user a meaningful representation of the collected data by visual (graphical/quantitative) or audible means using display units [Liquid Crystal Display (LCD), Light Emitting Diode (LED), etc.] buzzers, alarms, etc. Examples are: measuring instruments with storage memory and monitoring instruments with storage memory used in medical applications. Certain embedded systems store the data and will not give a representation of the same to the user, whereas the data is used for internal processing.

Fig. 1.1 **A digital camera for image capturing/storage/display**
(Photo courtesy of Casio-Model EXILIM ex-Z850 (www.casio.com))

A digital camera is a typical example of an embedded system with data collection/storage/representation of data. Images are captured and the captured image may be stored within the memory of the camera. The captured image can also be presented to the user through a graphic LCD unit.

1.6.2 Data Communication

Embedded data communication systems are deployed in applications ranging from complex satellite communication systems to simple home networking systems. As mentioned earlier in this chapter, the data collected by an embedded terminal may require transferring of the same to some other system located remotely. The transmission is achieved either by a wire-line medium or by a wireless medium. Wire-line medium was the most common choice in all olden days embedded systems. As technology is changing, wireless medium is becoming the de-facto standard for data communication in embedded systems. A wireless medium offers cheaper connectivity solutions and make the communication link free from the hassle of wire bundles. Data can either be transmitted by analog means or by digital means. Modern industry trends are settling towards digital communication.

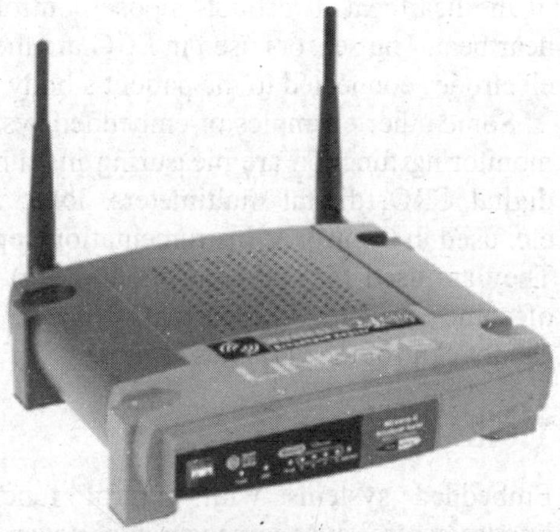

Fig. 1.2 **A wireless network router for data communication**
(Photo courtesy of Linksys (www.linksys.com). A division of CISCO system)

The data collecting embedded terminal itself can incorporate data communication units like wireless modules (Bluetooth, ZigBee, Wi-Fi, EDGE, GPRS, etc.) or wire-line modules (RS-232C, USB, TCP/IP, PS2, etc.). Certain embedded systems act as a dedicated transmission unit between the sending and receiving terminals, offering sophisticated functionalities like data packetizing, encrypting and decrypting. Network hubs, routers, switches, etc. are typical examples of dedicated data transmission embedded systems. They act as mediators in data communication and provide various features like data security, monitoring etc.

1.6.3 Data (Signal) Processing

As mentioned earlier, the data (voice, image, video, electrical signals and other measurable quantities) collected by embedded systems may be used for various kinds of data processing. Embedded systems with signal processing functionalities are employed in applications demanding signal processing like speech coding, synthesis, audio video codec, transmission applications, etc.

A digital hearing aid is a typical example of an embedded system employing data processing. Digital hearing aid improves the hearing capacity of hearing impaired persons.

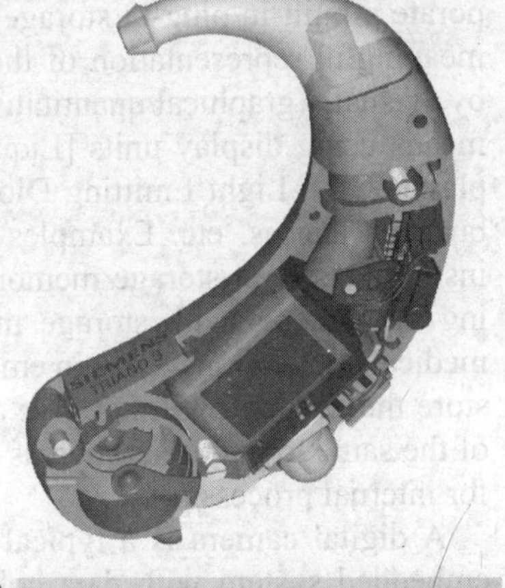

Fig. 1.3 **A digital hearing aid employing signal processing technique**
(Siemens TRIANO 3 Digital hearing aid; Siemens Audiology Copyright© 2005)

1.6.4 Monitoring

Embedded systems falling under this category are specifically designed for monitoring purpose. Almost all embedded products coming under the medical domain are with monitoring functions only. They are used for determining the state of some variables using input sensors. They cannot impose control over variables. A very good example is the electro cardiogram (ECG) machine for monitoring the heartbeat of a patient. The machine is intended to do the monitoring of the heartbeat. It cannot impose control over the heartbeat. The sensors used in ECG are the different electrodes connected to the patient's body.

Some other examples of embedded systems with monitoring function are measuring instruments like digital CRO, digital multimeters, logic analyzers, etc. used in Control & Instrumentation applications. They are used for knowing (monitoring) the status of some variables like current, voltage, etc. They cannot control the variables in turn.

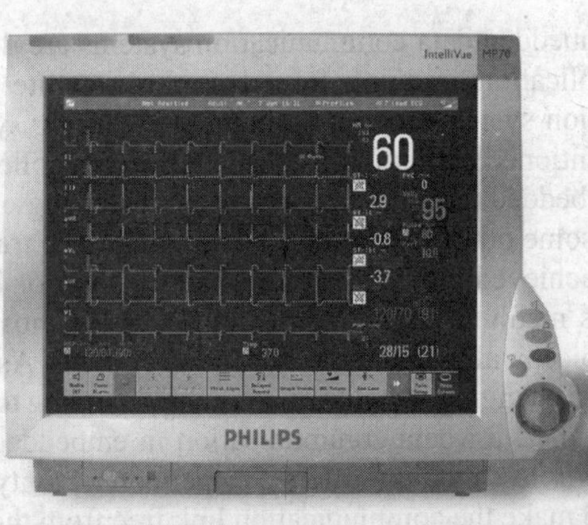

Fig. 1.4 **A patient monitoring system for monitoring heartbeat**
(Photo courtesy of Philips Medical Systems (www.medical.philips.com/))

1.6.5 Control

Embedded systems with control functionalities impose control over some variables according to the changes in input variables. A system with control functionality contains both sensors and actuators. Sensors are connected to the input port for capturing the changes in environmental variable or measuring variable. The actuators connected to the output port are controlled according to the changes in input variable to put an impact on the controlling variable to bring the controlled variable to the specified range.

Air conditioner system used in our home to control the room temperature to a specified limit is a typical example for embedded system for control purpose. An airconditioner contains a room temperature-sensing element (sensor) which may be a thermistor and a handheld unit for setting up (feeding) the desired temperature. The handheld unit may be connected to the central embedded unit residing inside the airconditioner through a wireless link or through a wired link. The air compressor unit acts as the actuator. The compressor is controlled according to the current room temperature and the desired temperature set by the end user.

Fig. 1.5 **"An Airconditioner for controlling room temperature. Embedded System with Control functionality"**
(Photo courtesy of Electrolux Corporation (www.electrolux.com/au))

Here the input variable is the current room temperature and the controlled variable is also the room temperature. The controlling variable is cool air flow by the compressor unit. If the controlled variable and input variable are not at the same value, the controlling variable tries to equalise them through taking actions on the cool air flow.

1.6.6 Application Specific User Interface

These are embedded systems with application-specific user interfaces like buttons, switches, keypad, lights, bells, display units, etc. Mobile phone is an example for this. In mobile phone the user interface is provided through the keypad, graphic LCD module, system speaker, vibration alert, etc.

1.7 'SMART' RUNNING SHOES FROM ADIDAS—THE INNOVATIVE BONDING OF LIFESTYLE WITH EMBEDDED TECHNOLOGY

After three years of extensive research work, Adidas launched the "Smart" running shoes in the market in April 2005. The term "Smart Shoe" may sound gimmicky. But adaptive cushioning provided by the shoe makes sense, and the design engineering behind the shoes is very impressive. The shoe constantly adapts its shock-absorbing characteristics to customize its value to the individual runner, depending on the running style, pace, body weight, and running surface. The shoe uses a magnetic sensing system to measure cushioning level, which is adjusted via a digital signal processing unit that controls a motor-driven cable system.

Fig. 1.6 **An embedded system with an application-specific user interface**
(Photo courtesy of Nokia Mobile Handsets (www.nokia.com))

A hall effect sensor is positioned at the top of the "cushioning element", and the magnet is placed at the bottom of the element. As the cushioning compresses on each impact, the sensor measures the distance from top to bottom of mid-sole (accurate to 0.1 mm). About 1000 readings per second are taken and relayed to the shoe's microprocessor. The Microprocessor (MPU) is positioned under the arch of the shoe. It runs an algorithm that compares the compression messages received from the sensor to a preset range of proper cushioning levels, so it understands if the shoe is too soft or too firm. Then the MPU sends a command to a micro motor, housed in the mid-foot. The micro motor turns a lead screw to lengthen or shorten a cable secured to the walls of a plastic-cushioning element. When the cable is shortened, the cushioning element is pulled taut and compresses very little. A longer cable allows for a more cushioned feel. A replaceable 3-V battery powers the motor and lasts for about 100 hours of running.

The Portland, Ore-based Adidas Innovation Team that developed the shoe was led by Christian DiBenedetto. It also included electromechanical engineer Mark Oleson, as well as a footwear developer and two industrial designers. Oleson explains that the team chose a magnetic sensor because it could measure the amount of compression in addition to the time it took to reach full compression. Gathering sensor data, he says, meant little without building a comparative "running context". So one of the first steps in developing the MPU algorithms was building this database. Runners wore test shoes that gathered information about various compression levels during a run. Then the runners were interviewed to learn their thoughts about the different cushion levels. "When the two matched up, that helped validate our sensor," says Oleson.

Adaptations in the cushioning element account for the change of running surface and pace of the runner, and they're made gradually over an average of four running steps. The goal is for the runner not to feel any sudden changes. Adaptations are made during the "swing" phase rather than the "stance" phase of the stride (i.e. when the foot is off the ground). If the shoe's owner prefers a more cushioned or a firmer "ride," adjustments can be made via "+" and "–" buttons that also activate the intelligent functions of the shoe.

LED indicators confirm when the electronics are turned on (The lights do not remain on when the shoes are in use). If the shoes aren't turned on, they operate like old-fashioned "manual" running shoes. The shoes turn off if their owner is either inactive or at a walking pace for 10 minutes.

Source Electronic Design
www.electronicdesign.com/Articles/Index.cfm?AD=1&ArticleID=10113
Re-printed with permission

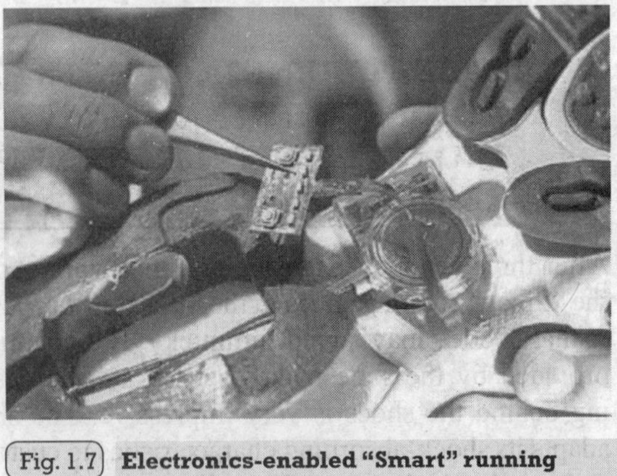

Fig. 1.7 **Electronics-enabled "Smart" running shoes from Adidas**
(Photo courtesy of Adidas – Salomon AG (www.adidas.com))

Summary

- ✓ An embedded system is an Electronic/Electro-mechanical system designed to perform a specific function and is a combination of both hardware and firmware (Software).
- ✓ A general purpose computing system is a combination of generic hardware and general purpose operating system for executing a variety of applications, whereas an embedded system is a combination of special purpose hardware and embedded OS/firmware for executing a specific set of applications.
- ✓ Apollo Guidance Computer (AGC) is the first recognised modern embedded system and 'Autonetics D-17', the guidance computer for the Minuteman-I missile, was the first mass-produced embedded system.
- ✓ Based on the complexity and performance requirements, embedded systems are classified into small-scale, medium-scale and large-scale/complex.
- ✓ The presence of embedded systems vary from simple electronic toys to complex flight and missile control systems.
- ✓ Embedded systems are designed to serve the purpose of any one or a combination of data collection/storage/representation, data communication, data (signal) processing, monitoring, control or application specific user interface.

Keywords

Embedded system : An electronic/electro-mechanical system which is designed to perform a specific function and is a combination of both hardware and firmware

Microprocessor : A silicon chip representing a Central Processing Unit (CPU)

Microcontroller : A highly integrated chip that contains a CPU, scratchpad RAM, special and general purpose register arrays and integrated peripherals

DSP : Digital Signal Processor is a powerful special purpose 8/16/32 bit microprocessor designed specifically to meet the computational demands and power constraints

ASIC : Application Specific Integrated Circuit is a microchip designed to perform a specific or unique application

Sensor : A transducer device that converts energy from one form to another for any measurement or control purpose

Actuator : A form of transducer device (mechanical or electrical) which converts signals to corresponding physical action (motion)

LED : Light Emitting Diode. An output device producing visual indication in the form of light in accordance with current flow

Buzzer : A piezo-electric device for generating audio indication. It contains a piezo-electric diaphragm which produces audible sound in response to the voltage applied to it

Operating system : A piece of software designed to manage and allocate system resources and execute other pieces of software

Electro Cardiogram (ECG) : An embedded device for heartbeat monitoring

SCADA : Supervisory Control and Data Acquisition System. A data acquisition system used in industrial control applications

RAM : Random Access memory. Volatile memory

ADC : Analog to Digital Converter. An integrated circuit which converts analog signals to digital form

Bluetooth	:	A low cost, low power, short range wireless technology for data and voice communication
Wi-Fi	:	Wireless Fidelity is the popular wireless communication technique for networked communication of devices

Objective Questions

1. Embedded systems are
   (a) General purpose (b) Special purpose
2. Embedded system is
   (a) An electronic system (b) A pure mechanical system
   (c) An electro-mechanical system (d) (a) or (c)
3. Which of the following is not true about embedded systems?
   (a) Built around specialised hardware (b) Always contain an operating system
   (c) Execution behaviour may be deterministic (d) All of these
   (e) None of these
4. Which of the following is not an example of a 'Small-scale Embedded System'?
   (a) Electronic Barbie doll (b) Simple calculator
   (c) Cell phone (d) Electronic toy car
5. The first recognised modern embedded system is
   (a) Apple Computer (b) Apollo Guidance Computer (AGC)
   (c) Calculator (d) Radio Navigation System
6. The first mass produced embedded system is
   (a) Minuteman-I (b) Minuteman-II
   (c) Autonetics D-17 (d) Apollo Guidance Computer (AGC)
7. Which of the following is (are) an intended purpose(s) of embedded systems?
   (a) Data collection (b) Data processing (c) Data communication
   (d) All of these (e) None of these
8. Which of the following is an (are) example(s) of embedded system for data communication?
   (a) USB Mass storage device (b) Network router
   (c) Digital camera (d) Music player
   (e) All of these (f) None of these
9. A digital multi meter is an example of an embedded system for
   (a) Data communication (b) Monitoring (c) Control (d) All of these
   (e) None of these
10. Which of the following is an (are) example(s) of an embedded system for signal processing?
    (a) Apple iPOD (media player device) (b) SanDisk USB mass storage device
    (c) Both (a) and (b) (d) None of these

Review Questions

1. What is an embedded system? Explain the different applications of embedded systems.
2. Explain the various purposes of embedded systems in detail with illustrative examples.
3. Explain the different classifications of embedded systems. Give an example for each.

2 The Typical Embedded System

LEARNING OBJECTIVES

- ✓ *Learn the building blocks of a typical Embedded System*
- ✓ *Learn about General Purpose Processors (GPPs), Application Specific Instruction Set Processors (ASIPs), Microprocessors, Microcontrollers, Digital Signal Processors, RISC & CISC processors, Harvard and Von-Neumann Processor Architecture, Big-endian v/s Little endian processors, Load Store operation and Instruction pipelining*
- ✓ *Learn about different PLDs like Complex Programmable Logic Devices (CPLDs), Field Programmable Gate Arrays (FPGAs), etc.*
- ✓ *Learn about the different memory technologies and memory types used in embedded system development*
- ✓ *Learn about Masked ROM (MROM), PROM, OTP, EPROM, EEPROM and FLASH memory for embedded firmware storage*
- ✓ *Learn about Serial Access Memory (SAM), Static Random Access Memory (SRAM), Dynamic Random Access Memory (DRAM) and Nonvolatile SRAM (NVRAM)*
- ✓ *Understand the different factors to be considered in the selection of memory for embedded systems*
- ✓ *Understand the role of sensors, actuators and their interfacing with the I/O subsystems of an embedded system*
- ✓ *Learn about the interfacing of LEDs, 7-segment LED Displays, Piezo Buzzer, Stepper Motor, Relays, Optocouplers, Matrix keyboard, Push button switches, Programmable Peripheral Interface Device (e.g. 8255 PPI), etc. with the I/O subsystem of the embedded system*
- ✓ *Learn about the different communication interfaces of an embedded system*
- ✓ *Understand the various chip level communication interfaces like I2C, SPI, UART, 1-wire, parallel bus, etc.*
- ✓ *Understand the different wired and wireless external communication interfaces like RS-232C, RS-485, Parallel Port, USB, IEEE1394, Infrared (IrDA), Bluetooth, Wi-Fi, ZigBee, GPRS, etc.*
- ✓ *Know what embedded firmware is and its role in embedded systems*
- ✓ *Understand the different system components like Reset Circuit, Brown-out protection circuit, Oscillator Unit, Real-Time Clock (RTC) and Watchdog Timer unit*
- ✓ *Understand the role of PCB in embedded systems*

A typical embedded system (Fig. 2.1) contains a single chip controller, which acts as the master brain of the system. The controller can be a Microprocessor (e.g. *Intel 8085*) or a microcontroller (e.g. Atmel AT89C51) or a Field Programmable Gate Array (FPGA) device (e.g. *Xilinx Spartan*) or a Digital Signal Processor (DSP) (e.g. *Blackfin® Processors* from Analog Devices) or an Application Specific Integrated

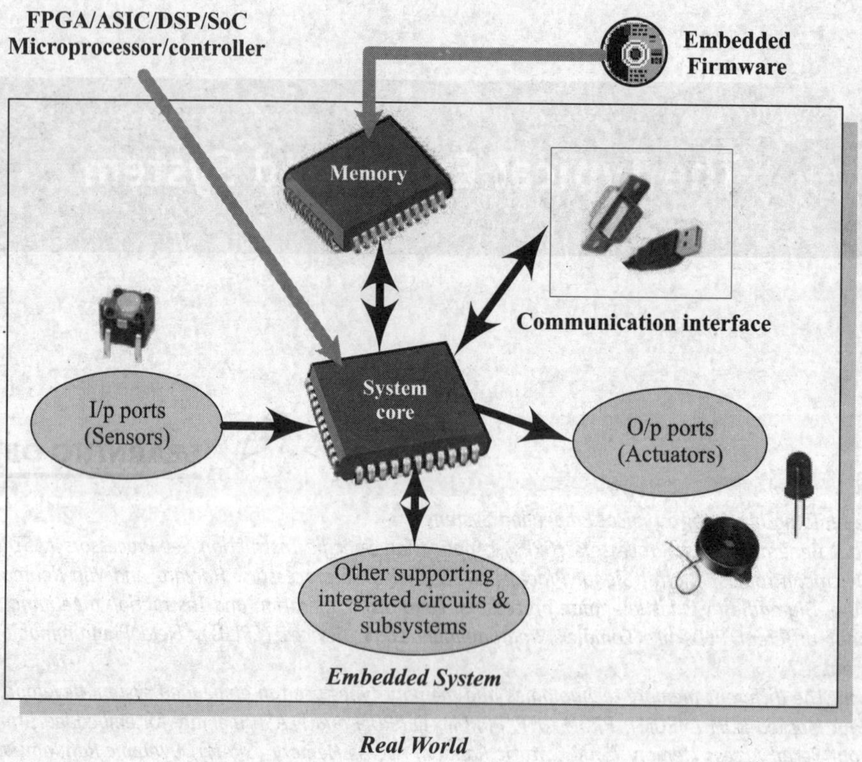

Fig. 2.1 **Elements of an embedded system**

Circuit (ASIC)/Application Specific Standard Product (ASSP) (e.g. ADE7760 Single Phase Energy Metreing IC from) Analog Devices for energy metering applications).

Embedded hardware/software systems are basically designed to regulate a physical variable or to manipulate the state of some devices by sending some control signals to the Actuators or devices connected to the O/p ports of the system, in response to the input signals provided by the end users or Sensors which are connected to the input ports. Hence an embedded system can be viewed as a reactive system. The control is achieved by processing the information coming from the sensors and user interfaces, and controlling some actuators that regulate the physical variable.

Key boards, push button switches, etc. are examples for common user interface input devices whereas LEDs, liquid crystal displays, piezoelectric buzzers, etc. are examples for common user interface output devices for a typical embedded system. It should be noted that it is not necessary that all embedded systems should incorporate these I/O user interfaces. It solely depends on the type of the application for which the embedded system is designed. For example, if the embedded system is designed for any handheld application, such as a mobile handset application, then the system should contain user interfaces like a keyboard for performing input operations and display unit for providing users the status of various activities in progress.

Some embedded systems do not require any manual intervention for their operation. They automatically sense the variations in the input parameters in accordance with the changes in the real world, to which they are interacting through the sensors which are connected to the input port of the system. The sensor information is passed to the processor after signal conditioning and digitisation. Upon receiving the sensor data the processor or brain of the embedded system performs some pre-defined operations with the help of the firmware embedded in the system and sends some actuating signals to the actuator connected to the output port of the embedded system, which in turn acts on the controlling variable to bring the controlled variable to the desired level to make the embedded system work in the desired manner.

The Memory of the system is responsible for holding the control algorithm and other important configuration details. For most of embedded systems, the memory for storing the algorithm or configuration data is of fixed type, which is a kind of Read Only Memory (ROM) and it is not available for the end user for modifications, which means the memory is protected from unwanted user interaction by implementing some kind of memory protection mechanism. The most common types of memories used in embedded systems for control algorithm storage are OTP, PROM, UVEPROM, EEPROM and FLASH. Depending on the control application, the memory size may vary from a few bytes to megabytes. We will discuss them in detail in the coming sections. Sometimes the system requires temporary memory for performing arithmetic operations or control algorithm execution and this type of memory is known as "working memory". Random Access Memory (RAM) is used in most of the systems as the working memory. Various types of RAM like SRAM, DRAM and NVRAM are used for this purpose. The size of the RAM also varies from a few bytes to kilobytes or megabytes depending on the application. The details given under the section "Memory" will give you a more detailed description of the working memory.

An embedded system without a control algorithm implemented memory is just like a new born baby. It is having all the peripherals but is not capable of making any decision depending on the situational as well as real world changes. The only difference is that the memory of a new born baby is self-adaptive, meaning that the baby will try to learn from the surroundings and from the mistakes committed. For embedded systems it is the responsibility of the designer to impart intelligence to the system.

In a controller-based embedded system, the controller may contain internal memory for storing the control algorithm and it may be an EEPROM or FLASH memory varying from a few kilobytes to megabytes. Such controllers are called controllers with on-chip ROM, e.g. Atmel AT89C51. Some controllers may not contain on-chip memory and they require an external (off-chip) memory for holding the control algorithm, e.g. Intel 8031AH.

2.1 CORE OF THE EMBEDDED SYSTEM

Embedded systems are domain and application specific and are built around a central core. The core of the embedded system falls into any one of the following categories:

1. General Purpose and Domain Specific Processors
   - 1.1 Microprocessors
   - 1.2 Microcontrollers
   - 1.3 Digital Signal Processors
2. Application Specific Integrated Circuits (ASICs)
3. Programmable Logic Devices (PLDs)
4. Commercial off-the-shelf Components (COTS)

If you examine any embedded system you will find that it is built around any of the core units mentioned above.

2.1.1 General Purpose and Domain Specific Processors

Almost 80% of the embedded systems are processor/controller based. The processor may be a microprocessor or a microcontroller or a digital signal processor, depending on the domain and application. Most of the embedded systems in the industrial control and monitoring applications make use of the commonly available microprocessors or microcontrollers whereas domains which require signal processing such as speech coding, speech recognition, etc. make use of special kind of digital signal processors supplied by manufacturers like, Analog Devices, Texas Instruments, etc.

2.1.1.1 Microprocessors A Microprocessor is a silicon chip representing a central processing unit (CPU), which is capable of performing arithmetic as well as logical operations according to a pre-defined set of instructions, which is specific to the manufacturer. In general the CPU contains the Arithmetic and Logic Unit (ALU), control unit and working registers. A microprocessor is a dependent unit and it requires the combination of other hardware like memory, timer unit, and interrupt controller, etc. for proper functioning. Intel claims the credit for developing the first microprocessor unit *Intel 4004*, a 4bit processor which was released in November 1971. It featured 1K data memory, a 12bit program counter and 4K program memory, sixteen 4bit general purpose registers and 46 instructions. It ran at a clock speed of 740 kHz. It was designed for olden day's calculators. In 1972, 14 more instructions were added to the 4004 instruction set and the program space is upgraded to 8K. Also interrupt capabilities were added to it and it is renamed as *Intel 4040*. It was quickly replaced in April 1972 by *Intel 8008* which was similar to *Intel 4040*, the only difference was that its program counter was 14 bits wide and the *8008* served as a terminal controller. In April 1974 Intel launched the first 8 bit processor, the *Intel 8080*, with 16bit address bus and program counter and seven 8bit registers (A-E,H,L: BC, DE, and HL pairs formed the 16bit register for this processor). *Intel 8080* was the most commonly used processors for industrial control and other embedded applications in the 1975s. Since the processor required other hardware components as mentioned earlier for its proper functioning, the systems made out of it were bulky and were lacking compactness.

Immediately after the release of *Intel 8080*, Motorola also entered the market with their processor, *Motorola 6800* with a different architecture and instruction set compared to *8080*.

In 1976 Intel came up with the upgraded version of *8080 – Intel 8085*, with two newly added instructions, three interrupt pins and serial I/O. Clock generator and bus controller circuits were built-in and the power supply part was modified to a single +5 V supply.

In July 1976 Zilog entered the microprocessor market with its *Z80 processor* as competitor to *Intel*. Actually it was designed by an ex-Intel designer, *Frederico Faggin* and it was an improved version of Intel's *8080* processor, maintaining the original *8080* architecture and instruction set with an 8bit data bus and a 16bit address bus and was capable of executing all instructions of *8080*. It included 80 more new instructions and it brought out the concept of register banking by doubling the register set. *Z80* also included two sets of index registers for flexible design.

Technical advances in the field of semiconductor industry brought a new dimension to the microprocessor market and twentieth century witnessed a fast growth in processor technology. 16, 32 and 64 bit processors came into the place of conventional 8bit processors. The initial 2 MHz clock is now an old story. Today processors with clock speeds up to 2.4 GHz are available in the market. More and more competitors entered into the processor market offering high speed, high performance and low cost processors for customer design needs.

Intel, AMD, Freescale, IBM, TI, Cyrix, Hitachi, NEC, LSI Logic, etc. are the key players in the processor market. Intel still leads the market with cutting edge technologies in the processor industry.

Different instruction set and system architecture are available for the design of a microprocessor. Harvard and Von-Neumann are the two common system architectures for processor design. Processors based on Harvard architecture contains separate buses for program memory and data memory, whereas processors based on Von-Neumann architecture shares a single system bus for program and data memory. We will discuss more about these architectures later, under a separate topic. Reduced Instruction Set Computing (RISC) and Complex Instruction Set Computing (CISC) are the two common Instruction Set Architectures (ISA) available for processor design. We will discuss the same under a separate topic in this section.

2.1.1.2 General Purpose Processor (GPP) vs. Application-Specific Instruction Set Processor (ASIP) A General Purpose Processor or GPP is a processor designed for general computational tasks. The processor running inside your laptop or desktop (Pentium 4/AMD Athlon, etc.) is a typical example for general purpose processor. They are produced in large volumes and targeting the general market. Due to the high volume production, the per unit cost for a chip is low compared to ASIC or other specific ICs. A typical general purpose processor contains an Arithmetic and Logic Unit (ALU) and Control Unit (CU). On the other hand, Application Specific Instruction Set Processors (ASIPs) are processors with architecture and instruction set optimised to specific-domain/application requirements like network processing, automotive, telecom, media applications, digital signal processing, control applications, etc. ASIPs fill the architectural spectrum between general purpose processors and Application Specific Integrated Circuits (ASICs). The need for an ASIP arises when the traditional general purpose processor are unable to meet the increasing application needs. Most of the embedded systems are built around application specific instruction set processors. Some microcontrollers (like automotive AVR, USB AVR from Atmel), system on chips, digital signal processors, etc. are examples for application specific instruction set processors (ASIPs). ASIPs incorporate a processor and on-chip peripherals, demanded by the application requirement, program and data memory.

2.1.1.3 Microcontrollers A Microcontroller is a highly integrated chip that contains a CPU, scratch pad RAM, special and general purpose register arrays, on chip ROM/FLASH memory for program storage, timer and interrupt control units and dedicated I/O ports. Microcontrollers can be considered as a super set of microprocessors. Since a microcontroller contains all the necessary functional blocks for independent working, they found greater place in the embedded domain in place of microprocessors. Apart from this, they are cheap, cost effective and are readily available in the market.

Texas Instrument's *TMS 1000* is considered as the world's first microcontroller. We cannot say it as a fully functional microcontroller when we compare it with modern microcontrollers. TI followed Intel's *4004/4040*, 4 bit processor design and added some amount of RAM, program storage memory (ROM) and I/O support on a single chip, there by eliminated the requirement of multiple hardware chips for self-functioning. Provision to add custom instructions to the CPU was another innovative feature of TMS 1000. TMS 1000 was released in 1974.

In 1977 Intel entered the microcontroller market with a family of controllers coming under one umbrella named *MCS-48*™ family. The processors came under this family were *8038HL*, *8039HL*, *8040AHL*, *8048H*, *8049H* and *8050AH*. *Intel 8048* is recognised as Intel's first microcontroller and it was the most prominent member in the MCS-48™† family. It was used in the original IBM PC keyboard. The inspiration behind *8048* was Fairchild's *F8* microprocessor and Intel's goal of developing a low cost and small size processor. The design of *8048* adopted a true Harvard architecture where program and data memory shared the same address bus and is differentiated by the related control signals.

†MCS-48™ is a trade mark owned by Intel

Eventually Intel came out with its most fruitful design in the 8bit microcontroller domain–the *8051 family* and its derivatives. It is the most popular and powerful 8bit microcontroller ever built. It was developed in the 1980s and was put under the family MCS-51. Almost 75% of the microcontrollers used in the embedded domain were *8051 family* based controllers during the 1980–90s. *8051* processor cores are used in more than 100 devices by more than 20 independent manufacturers like Maxim, Philips, Atmel, etc. under the license from Intel. Due to the low cost, wide availability, memory efficient instruction set, mature development tools and Boolean processing (bit manipulation operation) capability, *8051 family* derivative microcontrollers are much used in high-volume consumer electronic devices, entertainment industry and other gadgets where cost-cutting is essential.

Another important family of microcontrollers used in industrial control and embedded applications is the **PIC** family micro controllers from Microchip Technologies (It will be discussed in detail in a later section of this book). It is a high performance RISC microcontroller complementing the CISC (complex instruction set computing) features of *8051*. The terms RISC and CISC will be explained in detail in a separate heading.

Some embedded system applications require only 8bit controllers whereas some embedded applications requiring superior performance and computational needs demand 16/32bit microcontrollers. Infineon, Freescale, Philips, Atmel, Maxim, Microchip etc. are the key suppliers of 16bit microcontrollers. Philips tried to extend the *8051* family microcontrollers to use for 16bit applications by developing the Philips XA (eXtended Architecture) microcontroller series.

8bit microcontrollers are commonly used in embedded systems where the processing power is not a big constraint. As mentioned earlier, more than 20 companies are producing different flavours of the *8051* family microcontroller. They try to add more and more functionalities like built in SPI, I2C serial buses, USB controller, ADC, Networking capability, etc. So the competitive market is driving towards a one-stop solution chip in microcontroller domain. High processing speed microcontroller families like ARM11 series are also available in the market, which provides solution to applications requiring hardware acceleration and high processing capability.

Freescale, NEC, Zilog, Hitachi, Mitsubishi, Infineon, ST Micro Electronics, National, Texas Instruments, Toshiba, Philips, Microchip, Analog Devices, Daewoo, Intel, Maxim, Sharp, Silicon Laboratories, TDK, Triscend, Winbond, Atmel, etc. are the key players in the microcontroller market. Of these Atmel has got special significance. They are the manufacturers of a variety of Flash memory based microcontrollers. They also provide In-System Programmability (which will be discussed in detail in a later section of this book) for the controller. The Flash memory technique helps in fast reprogramming of the chip and thereby reduces the product development time. Atmel also provides another special family of microcontroller called AVR (it will be discussed in detail in a later chapter), an 8bit RISC Flash microcontroller, fast enough to execute powerful instructions in a single clock cycle and provide the latitude you need to optimise power consumption.

The instruction set architecture of a microcontroller can be either RISC or CISC. Microcontrollers are designed for either general purpose application requirement (general purpose controller) or domain-specific application requirement (application specific instruction set processor). The *Intel 8051* microcontroller is a typical example for a general purpose microcontroller, whereas the automotive AVR microcontroller family from Atmel Corporation is a typical example for ASIP specifically designed for the automotive domain.

2.1.1.4 Microprocessor vs Microcontroller The following table summarises the differences between a microcontroller and microprocessor.

Microprocessor	Microcontroller
A silicon chip representing a central processing unit (CPU), which is capable of performing arithmetic as well as logical operations according to a pre-defined set of instructions	A microcontroller is a highly integrated chip that contains a CPU, scratchpad RAM, special and general purpose register arrays, on chip ROM/FLASH memory for program storage, timer and interrupt control units and dedicated I/O ports
It is a dependent unit. It requires the combination of other chips like timers, program and data memory chips, interrupt controllers, etc. for functioning	It is a self-contained unit and it doesn't require external interrupt controller, timer, UART, etc. for its functioning
Most of the time general purpose in design and operation	Mostly application-oriented or domain-specific
Doesn't contain a built in I/O port. The I/O port functionality needs to be implemented with the help of external programmable peripheral interface chips like 8255	Most of the processors contain multiple built-in I/O ports which can be operated as a single 8 or 16 or 32 bit port or as individual port pins
Targeted for high end market where performance is important	Targeted for embedded market where performance is not so critical (At present this demarcation is invalid)
Limited power saving options compared to microcontrollers	Includes lot of power saving features

2.1.1.5 Digital Signal Processors Digital Signal Processors (DSPs) are powerful special purpose 8/16/32 bit microprocessors designed specifically to meet the computational demands and power constraints of today's embedded audio, video, and communications applications. Digital signal processors are 2 to 3 times faster than the general purpose microprocessors in signal processing applications. This is because of the architectural difference between the two. DSPs implement algorithms in hardware which speeds up the execution whereas general purpose processors implement the algorithm in firmware and the speed of execution depends primarily on the clock for the processors. In general, DSP can be viewed as a microchip designed for performing high speed computational operations for 'addition', 'subtraction', 'multiplication' and 'division'. A typical digital signal processor incorporates the following key units:

Program Memory Memory for storing the program required by DSP to process the data

Data Memory Working memory for storing temporary variables and data/signal to be processed.

Computational Engine Performs the signal processing in accordance with the stored program memory. Computational Engine incorporates many specialised arithmetic units and each of them operates simultaneously to increase the execution speed. It also incorporates multiple hardware shifters for shifting operands and thereby saves execution time.

I/O Unit Acts as an interface between the outside world and DSP. It is responsible for capturing signals to be processed and delivering the processed signals.

Audio video signal processing, telecommunication and multimedia applications are typical examples where DSP is employed. Digital signal processing employs a large amount of real-time calculations. Sum of products (SOP) calculation, convolution, fast fourier transform (FFT), discrete fourier transform (DFT), etc, are some of the operations performed by digital signal processors.

Blackfin®† processors from Analog Devices is an example of DSP which delivers breakthrough signal-processing performance and power efficiency while also offering a full 32-bit RISC MCU programming model. Blackfin processors present high-performance, homogeneous software targets, which allows flexible resource allocation between hard real-time signal processing tasks and non real-time control tasks. System control tasks can often run in the shadow of demanding signal processing and multimedia tasks.

2.1.1.6 RISC vs. CISC Processors/Controllers The term RISC stands for Reduced Instruction Set Computing. As the name implies, all RISC processors/controllers possess lesser number of instructions, typically in the range of 30 to 40. CISC stands for Complex Instruction Set Computing. From the definition itself it is clear that the instruction set is complex and instructions are high in number. From a programmers point of view RISC processors are comfortable since s/he needs to learn only a few instructions, whereas for a CISC processor s/he needs to learn more number of instructions and should understand the context of usage of each instruction (This scenario is explained on the basis of a programmer following Assembly Language coding. For a programmer following C coding it doesn't matter since the cross-compiler is responsible for the conversion of the high level language instructions to machine dependent code). Atmel AVR microcontroller is an example for a RISC processor and its instruction set contains only 32 instructions. The original version of *8051* microcontroller (e.g. *AT89C51*) is a CISC controller and its instruction set contains 255 instructions. Remember it is not the number of instructions that determines whether a processor/controller is CISC or RISC. There are some other factors like pipelining features, instruction set type, etc. for determining the RISC/CISC criteria. Some of the important criteria are listed below:

RISC	CISC
Lesser number of instructions	Greater number of Instructions
Instruction pipelining and increased execution speed	Generally no instruction pipelining feature
Orthogonal instruction set (Allows each instruction to operate on any register and use any addressing mode)	Non-orthogonal instruction set (All instructions are not allowed to operate on any register and use any addressing mode. It is instruction-specific)
Operations are performed on registers only, the only memory operations are load and store	Operations are performed on registers or memory depending on the instruction
A large number of registers are available	Limited number of general purpose registers
Programmer needs to write more code to execute a task since the instructions are simpler ones	Instructions are like macros in C language. A programmer can achieve the desired functionality with a single instruction which in turn provides the effect of using more simpler single instructions in RISC
Single, fixed length instructions	Variable length instructions
Less silicon usage and pin count	More silicon usage since more additional decoder logic is required to implement the complex instruction decoding.
With Harvard Architecture	Can be Harvard or Von-Neumann Architecture

I hope now you are clear about the terms RISC and CISC in the processor technology. Isn't it?

†Blackfin® is a Registered trademark of Analog Devices Inc.

2.1.1.7 Harvard vs. Von-Neumann Processor/Controller Architecture The terms Harvard and Von-Neumann refers to the processor architecture design.

Microprocessors/controllers based on the **Von-Neumann** architecture shares a single common bus for fetching both instructions and data. Program instructions and data are stored in a common main memory. Von-Neumann architecture based processors/controllers first fetch an instruction and then fetch the data to support the instruction from code memory. The two separate fetches slows down the controller's operation. Von-Neumann architecture is also referred as **Princeton** architecture, since it was developed by the Princeton University.

Microprocessors/controllers based on the **Harvard** architecture will have separate data bus and instruction bus. This allows the data transfer and program fetching to occur simultaneously on both buses. With Harvard architecture, the data memory can be read and written while the program memory is being accessed. These separated data memory and code memory buses allow one instruction to execute while the next instruction is fetched ("pre-fetching"). The pre-fetch theoretically allows much faster execution than Von-Neumann architecture. Since some additional hardware logic is required for the generation of control signals for this type of operation it adds silicon complexity to the system. Figure 2.2 explains the Harvard and Von-Neumann architecture concept.

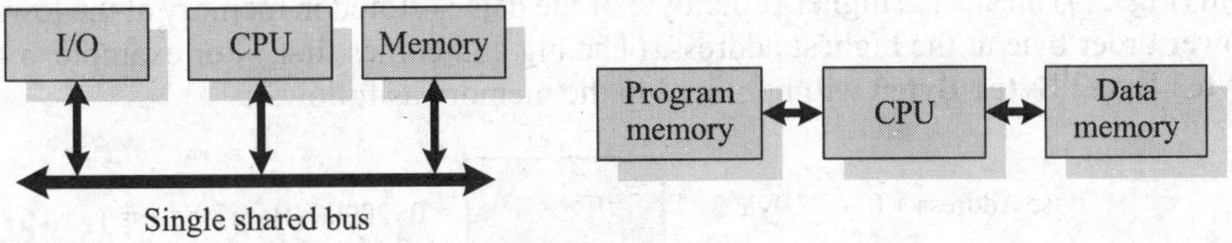

Fig. 2.2 **Harvard vs Von-Neumann architecture**

The following table highlights the differences between Harvard and Von-Neumann architecture.

Harvard Architecture	Von-Neumann Architecture
Separate buses for instruction and data fetching	Single shared bus for instruction and data fetching
Easier to pipeline, so high performance can be achieved	Low performance compared to Harvard architecture
Comparatively high cost	Cheaper
No memory alignment problems	Allows self modifying codes†
Since data memory and program memory are stored physically in different locations, no chances for accidental corruption of program memory	Since data memory and program memory are stored physically in the same chip, chances for accidental corruption of program memory

2.1.1.8 Big-Endian vs. Little-Endian Processors/Controllers Endianness specifies the order in which the data is stored in the memory by processor operations in a multi byte system (Processors whose word size is greater than one byte). Suppose the word length is two byte then data can be stored in memory in two different ways:

1. Higher order of data byte at the higher memory and lower order of data byte at location just below the higher memory.
2. Lower order of data byte at the higher memory and higher order of data byte at location just below the higher memory.

†Self-modifying code is a code/instruction which modifies itself while execution.

Little-endian (Fig. 2.3) means the lower-order byte of the data is stored in memory at the lowest address, and the higher-order byte at the highest address. (The little end comes first.) For example, a 4 byte long integer **Byte3 Byte2 Byte1 Byte0** will be stored in the memory as shown below:

Base Address + 0	Byte 0	Byte 0	0×20000 (Base Address)
Base Address + 1	Byte 1	Byte 1	0×20001 (Base Address + 1)
Base Address + 2	Byte 2	Byte 2	0×20002 (Base Address + 2)
Base Address + 3	Byte 3	Byte 3	0×20003 (Base Address + 3)

Fig. 2.3 Little-Endian operation

Big-endian (Fig. 2.4) means the higher-order byte of the data is stored in memory at the lowest address, and the lower-order byte at the highest address. (The big end comes first.) For example, a 4 byte long integer **Byte3 Byte2 Byte1 Byte0** will be stored in the memory as follows‡:

Base Address + 0	Byte 3	Byte 3	0×20000 (Base Address)
Base Address + 1	Byte 2	Byte 2	0×20001 (Base Address + 1)
Base Address + 2	Byte 1	Byte 1	0×20002 (Base Address + 2)
Base Address + 3	Byte 0	Byte 0	0×20003 (Base Address + 3)

Fig. 2.4 Big-Endian operation

2.1.1.9 Load Store Operation and Instruction Pipelining As mentioned earlier, the RISC processor instruction set is orthogonal, meaning it operates on registers. The memory access related operations are performed by the special instructions *load* and *store*. If the operand is specified as memory location, the content of it is loaded to a register using the *load* instruction. The instruction *store* stores data from a specified register to a specified memory location. The concept of **Load Store Architecture** is illustrated with the following example:

Suppose x, y and z are memory locations and we want to add the contents of x and y and store the result in location z. Under the load store architecture the same is achieved with 4 instructions as shown in Fig. 2.5.

The first instruction *load R1, x* loads the register R1 with the content of memory location x, the second instruction *load R2,y* loads the register R2 with the content of memory location y. The instruction

‡ Note that the base address is chosen arbitrarily as 0×20000

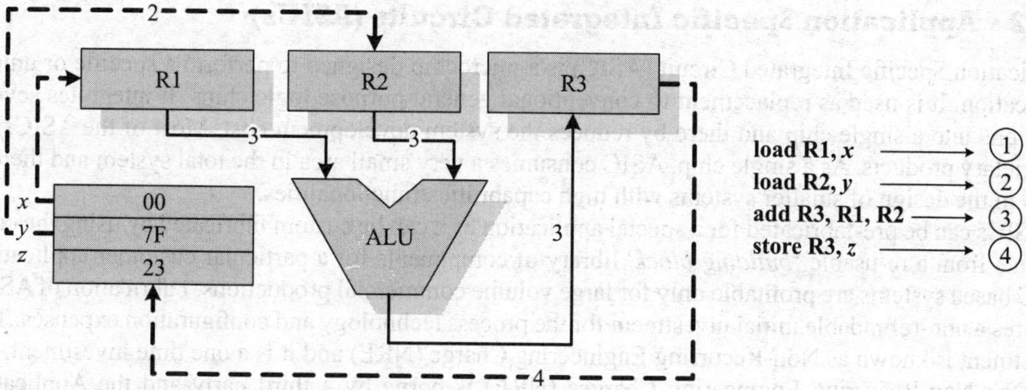

Fig. 2.5 The concept of load store architecture

add R3, R1, R2 adds the content of registers R1 and R2 and stores the result in register R3. The next instruction *store R3,z* stores the content of register R3 in memory location *z*.

The conventional instruction execution by the processor follows the fetch-decode-execute sequence. Where the 'fetch' part fetches the instruction from program memory or code memory and the decode part decodes the instruction to generate the necessary control signals. The execute stage reads the operands, perform ALU operations and stores the result. In conventional program execution, the fetch and decode operations are performed in sequence. For simplicity let's consider decode and execution together. During the decode operation the memory address bus is available and if it is possible to effectively utilise it for an instruction fetch, the processing speed can be increased. In its simplest form instruction pipelining refers to the overlapped execution of instructions. Under normal program execution flow it is meaningful to fetch the next instruction to execute, while the decoding and execution of the current instruction is in progress. If the current instruction in progress is a program control flow transfer instruction like jump or call instruction, there is no meaning in fetching the instruction following the current instruction. In such cases the instruction fetched is flushed and a new instruction fetch is performed to fetch the instruction. Whenever the current instruction is executing the program counter will be loaded with the address of the next instruction. In case of jump or branch instruction, the new location is known only after completion of the jump or branch instruction. Depending on the stages involved in an instruction (fetch, read register and decode, execute instruction, access an operand in data memory, write back the result to register, etc.), there can be multiple levels of instruction pipelining. Figure 2.6 illustrates the concept of Instruction pipelining for single stage pipelining.

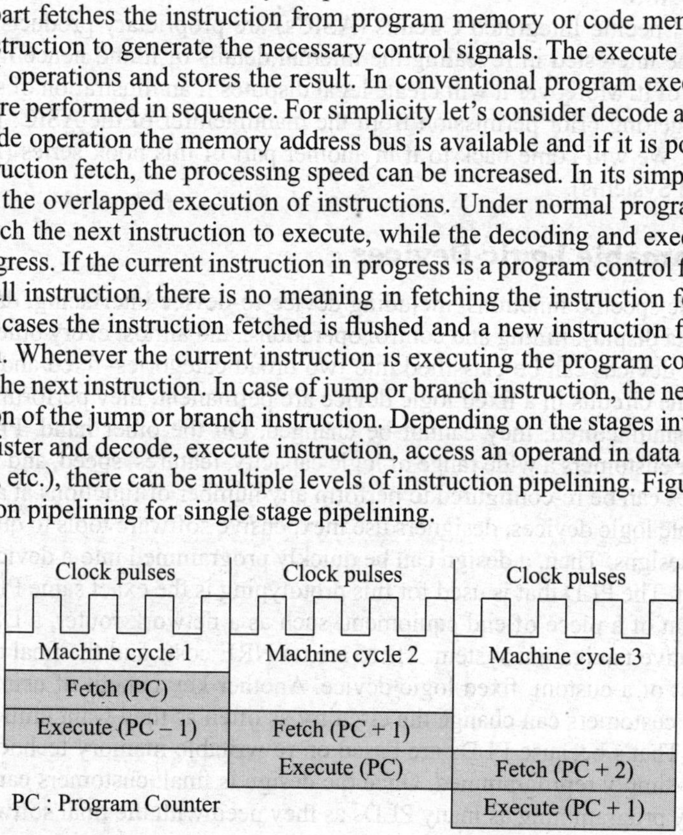

Fig. 2.6 The single-stage pipelining concept

2.1.2 Application Specific Integrated Circuits (ASICs)

Application Specific Integrated Circuit (ASIC) is a microchip designed to perform a specific or unique application. It is used as replacement to conventional general purpose logic chips. It integrates several functions into a single chip and there by reduces the system development cost. Most of the ASICs are proprietary products. As a single chip, ASIC consumes a very small area in the total system and thereby helps in the design of smaller systems with high capabilities/functionalities.

ASICs can be pre-fabricated for a special application or it can be custom fabricated by using the components from a re-usable '*building block*' library of components for a particular customer application. ASIC based systems are profitable only for large volume commercial productions. Fabrication of ASICs requires a non-refundable initial investment for the process technology and configuration expenses. This investment is known as Non-Recurring Engineering Charge (NRE) and it is a one time investment.

If the Non-Recurring Engineering Charges (NRE) is borne by a third party and the Application Specific Integrated Circuit (ASIC) is made openly available in the market, the ASIC is referred as Application Specific Standard Product (ASSP). The ASSP is marketed to multiple customers just as a general-purpose product is, but to a smaller number of customers since it is for a specific application. "The ADE7760 Energy Metre ASIC developed by Analog Devices for Energy metreing applications is a typical example for ASSP".

Since Application Specific Integrated Circuits (ASICs) are proprietary products, the developers of such chips may not be interested in revealing the internal details of it and hence it is very difficult to point out an example of it. Moreover it will create legal disputes if an illustration of such an ASIC product is given without getting prior permission from the manufacturer of the ASIC. For the time being, let us forget about it. We will come back to it in another part of this book series (Namely, Designing Advanced Embedded Systems).

2.1.3 Programmable Logic Devices

Logic devices provide specific functions, including device-to-device interfacing, data communication, signal processing, data display, timing and control operations, and almost every other function a system must perform. Logic devices can be classified into two broad categories–fixed and programmable. As the name indicates, the circuits in a fixed logic device are permanent, they perform one function or set of functions–once manufactured, they cannot be changed. On the other hand, Programmable Logic Devices (PLDs) offer customers a wide range of logic capacity, features, speed, and voltage characteristics–and these devices can be re-configured to perform any number of functions at any time.

With programmable logic devices, designers use inexpensive software tools to quickly develop, simulate, and test their designs. Then, a design can be quickly programmed into a device, and immediately tested in a live circuit. The PLD that is used for this prototyping is the exact same PLD that will be used in the final production of a piece of end equipment, such as a network router, a DSL modem, a DVD player, or an automotive navigation system. There are no NRE costs and the final design is completed much faster than that of a custom, fixed logic device. Another key benefit of using PLDs is that during the design phase customers can change the circuitry as often as they want until the design operates to their satisfaction. That's because PLDs are based on re-writable memory technology–to change the design, the device is simply reprogrammed. Once the design is final, customers can go into immediate production by simply programming as many PLDs as they need with the final software design file.

2.1.3.1 CPLDs and FPGAs The two major types of programmable logic devices are Field Programmable Gate Arrays (FPGAs) and Complex Programmable Logic Devices (CPLDs). Of the two, FPGAs offer the highest amount of logic density, the most features, and the highest performance. The largest FPGA now shipping, part of the Xilinx **Virtex™**† line of devices, provides eight million "system gates" (the relative density of logic). These advanced devices also offer features such as built-in hardwired processors (such as the IBM power PC), substantial amounts of memory, clock management systems, and support for many of the latest, very fast device-to-device signaling technologies. FPGAs are used in a wide variety of applications ranging from data processing and storage, to instrumentation, telecommunications, and digital signal processing.

CPLDs, by contrast, offer much smaller amounts of logic–up to about 10,000 gates. But CPLDs offer very predictable timing characteristics and are therefore ideal for critical control applications. CPLDs such as the Xilinx **CoolRunner™**† series also require extremely low amounts of power and are very inexpensive, making them ideal for cost-sensitive, battery-operated, portable applications such as mobile phones and digital handheld assistants.

Advantages of PLD Programmable logic devices offer a number of important advantages over fixed logic devices, including:

- PLDs offer customers much more flexibility during the design cycle because design iterations are simply a matter of changing the programming file, and the results of design changes can be seen immediately in working parts.
- PLDs do not require long lead times for prototypes or production parts–the PLDs are already on a distributor's shelf and ready for shipment.
- PLDs do not require customers to pay for large NRE costs and purchase expensive mask sets–PLD suppliers incur those costs when they design their programmable devices and are able to amortize those costs over the multi-year lifespan of a given line of PLDs.
- PLDs allow customers to order just the number of parts they need, when they need them, allowing them to control inventory. Customers who use fixed logic devices often end up with excess inventory which must be scrapped, or if demand for their product surges, they may be caught short of parts and face production delays.
- PLDs can be reprogrammed even after a piece of equipment is shipped to a customer. In fact, thanks to programmable logic devices, a number of equipment manufacturers now tout the ability to add new features or upgrade products that already are in the field. To do this, they simply upload a new programming file to the PLD, via the Internet, creating new hardware logic in the system.

Over the last few years programmable logic suppliers have made such phenomenal technical advances that PLDs are now seen as the logic solution of choice from many designers. One reason for this is that PLD suppliers such as Xilinx are "fabless" companies; instead of owning chip manufacturing foundries, Xilinx outsource that job to partners like Toshiba and UMC, whose chief occupation is making chips. This strategy allows Xilinx to focus on designing new product architectures, software tools, and intellectual property cores while having access to the most advanced semiconductor process technologies. Advanced process technologies help PLDs in a number of key areas: faster performance, integration of more features, reduced power consumption, and lower cost.

FPGAs are especially popular for prototyping ASIC designs where the designer can test his design by downloading the design file into an FPGA device. Once the design is set, hardwired chips are produced for faster performance.

Just a few years ago, for example, the largest FPGA was measured in tens of thousands of system gates and operated at 40 MHz. Older FPGAs also were relatively expensive, costing often more than $150 for the most advanced parts at the time. Today, however, FPGAs with advanced features offer

† **Virtex™** and **CoolRunner™** are the registered trademarks of Xilinx Inc.

millions of gates of logic capacity, operate at 300 MHz, can cost less than $10, and offer a new level of integrated functions such as processors and memory.

2.1.4 Commercial Off-the-Shelf Components (COTS)

A Commercial Off-the-Shelf (**COTS**) product is one which is used '*as-is*'. COTS products are designed in such a way to provide easy integration and interoperability with existing system components. The COTS component itself may be developed around a general purpose or domain specific processor or an Application Specific Integrated circuit or a programmable logic device. Typical examples of COTS hardware unit are remote controlled toy car control units including the RF circuitry part, high performance, high frequency microwave electronics (2–200 GHz), high bandwidth analog-to-digital converters, devices and components for operation at very high temperatures, electro-optic IR imaging arrays, UV/IR detectors, etc. The major advantage of using COTS is that they are readily available in the market, are cheap and a developer can cut down his/her development time to a great extent. This in turn reduces the time to market your embedded systems.

The TCP/IP plug-in module available from various manufactures like 'WIZnet', 'Freescale', 'Dynalog', etc. are very good examples of COTS product (Fig. 2.7). This network plug-in module gives the TCP/IP connectivity to the system you are developing. There is no need to design this module yourself and write the firmware for the TCP/IP protocol and data transfer. Everything will be readily supplied by the COTS manufacturer. What you need to do is identify the COTS for your system and give the plug-in option on your board according to the hardware plug-in connections given in the specifications of the COTS. Though multiple vendors supply COTS for the same application, the major problem faced by the end-user is that there are no operational and manufacturing standards. A Commercial off-the-shelf (COTS) component manufactured by a vendor need not have hardware plug-in and firmware interface compatibility with one manufactured by a second vendor for the same application. This restricts the end-user to stick to a particular vendor for a particular COTS. This greatly affects the product design.

Fig. 2.7 An example of a COTS product for TCP/IP plug-in from WIZnet
(WIZnet NM7010A Plug in Module-Courtesy of WIZnet http://www.wiznet.co.kr/en/)

The major drawback of using COTS components in embedded design is that the manufacturer of the COTS component may withdraw the product or discontinue the production of the COTS at any time if a rapid change in technology occurs, and this will adversely affect a commercial manufacturer of the embedded system which makes use of the specific COTS product.

2.2 MEMORY

Memory is an important part of a processor/controller based embedded systems. Some of the processors/controllers contain built in memory and this memory is referred as **on-chip memory**. Others do not contain any memory inside the chip and requires external memory to be connected with the controller/processor to store the control algorithm. It is called **off-chip memory**. Also some working memory is required for holding data temporarily during certain operations. This section deals with the different types of memory used in embedded system applications.

2.2.1 Program Storage Memory (ROM)

The program memory or code storage memory of an embedded system stores the program instructions and it can be classified into different types as per the block diagram representation given in Fig. 2.8.

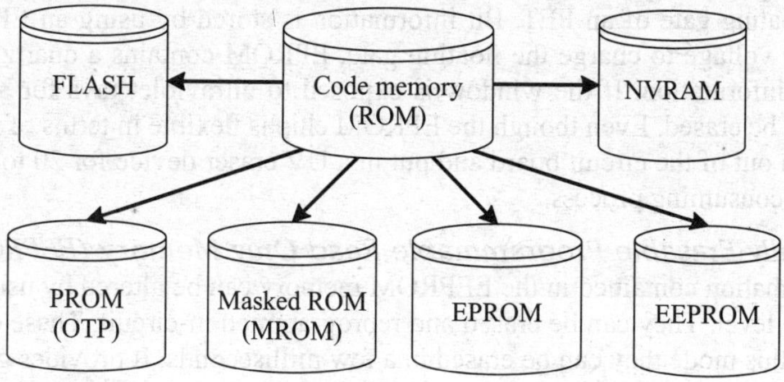

Fig. 2.8 **Classification of Program Memory (ROM)**

The code memory retains its contents even after the power to it is turned off. It is generally known as non-volatile storage memory. Depending on the fabrication, erasing and programming techniques they are classified into the following types.

2.2.1.1 Masked ROM (MROM) Masked ROM is a one-time programmable device. Masked ROM makes use of the hardwired technology for storing data. The device is factory programmed by masking and metallisation process at the time of production itself, according to the data provided by the end user. The primary advantage of this is low cost for high volume production. They are the least expensive type of solid state memory. Different mechanisms are used for the masking process of the ROM, like

1. Creation of an enhancement or depletion mode transistor through channel implant.
2. By creating the memory cell either using a standard transistor or a high threshold transistor. In the high threshold mode, the supply voltage required to turn ON the transistor is above the normal ROM IC operating voltage. This ensures that the transistor is always off and the memory cell stores always logic 0.

Masked ROM is a good candidate for storing the embedded firmware for low cost embedded devices. Once the design is proven and the firmware requirements are tested and frozen, the binary data (The firmware cross compiled/assembled to target processor specific machine code) corresponding to it can be given to the MROM fabricator. The limitation with MROM based firmware storage is the inability to modify the device firmware against firmware upgrades. Since the MROM is permanent in bit storage, it is not possible to alter the bit information.

2.2.1.2 Programmable Read Only Memory (PROM) / (OTP) Unlike Masked ROM Memory, One Time Programmable Memory (OTP) or PROM is not pre-programmed by the manufacturer. The end user is responsible for programming these devices. This memory has *nichrome* or *polysilicon* wires arranged in a matrix. These wires can be functionally viewed as fuses. It is programmed by a PROM programmer which selectively burns the fuses according to the bit pattern to be stored. Fuses which are not blown/burned represents a logic "1" whereas fuses which are blown/burned represents a logic "0". The default state is logic "1". OTP is widely used for commercial production of embedded systems whose proto-typed versions are proven and the code is finalised. It is a low cost solution for commercial production. OTPs cannot be reprogrammed.

2.2.1.3 Erasable Programmable Read Only Memory (EPROM) OTPs are not useful and worth for development purpose. During the development phase the code is subject to continuous changes and using an OTP each time to load the code is not economical. Erasable Programmable Read Only Memory (EPROM) gives the flexibility to re-program the same chip. EPROM stores the bit information by charging the floating gate of an FET. Bit information is stored by using an EPROM programmer, which applies high voltage to charge the floating gate. EPROM contains a quartz crystal window for erasing the stored information. If the window is exposed to ultraviolet rays for a fixed duration, the entire memory will be erased. Even though the EPROM chip is flexible in terms of re-programmability, it needs to be taken out of the circuit board and put in a UV eraser device for 20 to 30 minutes. So it is a tedious and time-consuming process.

2.2.1.4 Electrically Erasable Programmable Read Only Memory (EEPROM) As the name indicates, the information contained in the EEPROM memory can be altered by using electrical signals at the register/Byte level. They can be erased and reprogrammed in-circuit. These chips include a chip erase mode and in this mode they can be erased in a few milliseconds. It provides greater flexibility for system design. The only limitation is their capacity is limited when compared with the standard ROM (A few kilobytes).

2.2.1.5 FLASH FLASH is the latest ROM technology and is the most popular ROM technology used in today's embedded designs. FLASH memory is a variation of EEPROM technology. It combines the re-programmability of EEPROM and the high capacity of standard ROMs. FLASH memory is organised as sectors (blocks) or pages. FLASH memory stores information in an array of floating gate MOSFET transistors. The erasing of memory can be done at sector level or page level without affecting the other sectors or pages. Each sector/page should be erased before re-programming. The typical erasable capacity of FLASH is 1000 cycles. W27C512 from WINBOND (www.winbond.com) is an example of 64KB FLASH memory.

2.2.1.6 NVRAM Non-volatile RAM is a random access memory with battery backup. It contains static RAM based memory and a minute battery for providing supply to the memory in the absence of external power supply. The memory and battery are packed together in a single package. The life span of NVRAM is expected to be around 10 years. *DS1644* from Maxim/Dallas is an example of 32KB NVRAM.

2.2.2 Read-Write Memory/Random Access Memory (RAM)

RAM is the data memory or working memory of the controller/processor. Controller/processor can read from it and write to it. RAM is volatile, meaning when the power is turned off, all the contents are destroyed. RAM is a direct access memory, meaning we can access the desired memory location directly without the need for traversing through the entire memory locations to reach the desired memory position (i.e. random access of memory location). This is in contrast to the Sequential Access Memory (SAM), where the desired memory location is accessed by either traversing through the entire memory or through a 'seek' method. Magnetic tapes, CD ROMs, etc. are examples of sequential access memories. RAM generally falls into three categories: Static RAM (SRAM), dynamic RAM (DRAM) and non-volatile RAM (NVRAM) (Fig. 2.9).

2.2.2.1 Static RAM (SRAM) Static RAM stores data in the form of voltage. They are made up of flip-flops. Static RAM is the fastest form of RAM available. In typical implementation, an SRAM cell (bit) is realised using six transistors (or 6 MOSFETs). Four of the transistors are used for building the

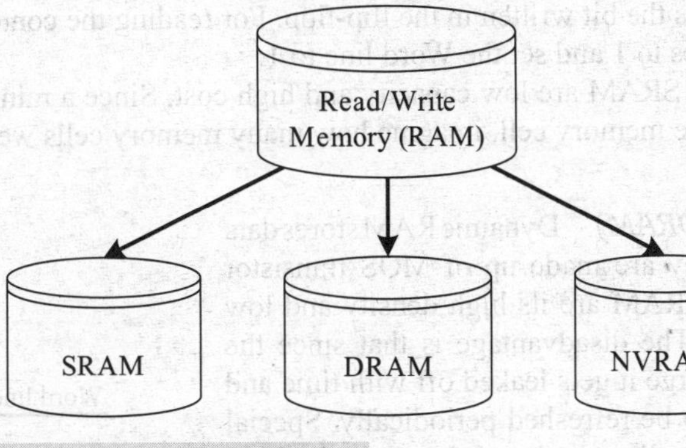

Fig. 2.9 **Classification of Working Memory (RAM)**

latch (flip-flop) part of the memory cell and two for controlling the access. SRAM is fast in operation due to its resistive networking and switching capabilities. In its simplest representation an SRAM cell can be visualised as shown in Fig. 2.10:

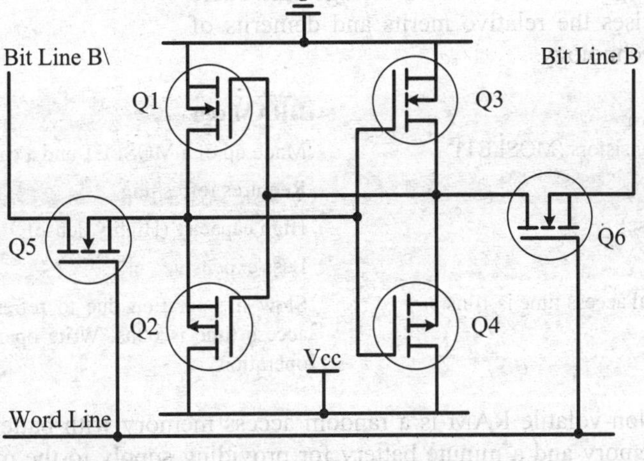

Fig. 2.10 **SRAM cell implementation**

This implementation in its simpler form can be visualised as two-cross coupled inverters with read/write control through transistors. The four transistors in the middle form the cross-coupled inverters. This can be visualised as shown in Fig. 2.11.

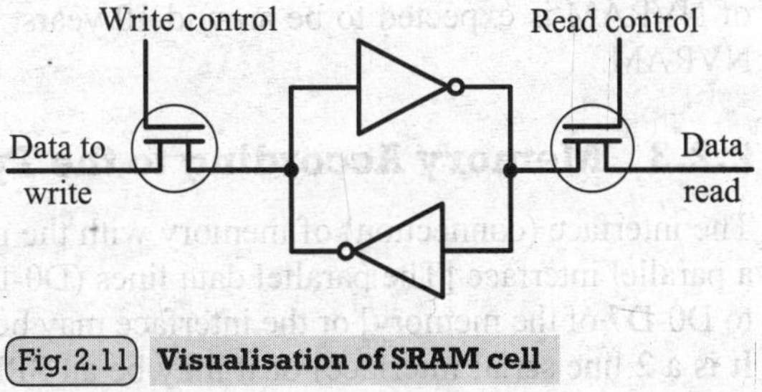

Fig. 2.11 **Visualisation of SRAM cell**

From the SRAM implementation diagram, it is clear that access to the memory cell is controlled by the line Word Line, which controls the access transistors (MOSFETs) Q5 and Q6. The access transistors control the connection to bit lines B & B\. In order to write a value to the memory cell, apply the desired value to the bit control lines (For writing 1, make B = 1 and B\ =0; For writing 0, make B = 0 and B\ =1) and assert the Word Line (Make Word line high). This operation latches the bit written in the flip-flop. For reading the content of the memory cell, assert both B and B\ bit lines to 1 and set the Word line to 1.

The major limitations of SRAM are low capacity and high cost. Since a minimum of six transistors are required to build a single memory cell, imagine how many memory cells we can fabricate on a silicon wafer.

2.2.2.2 Dynamic RAM (DRAM) Dynamic RAM stores data in the form of charge. They are made up of MOS transistor gates. The advantages of DRAM are its high density and low cost compared to SRAM. The disadvantage is that since the information is stored as charge it gets leaked off with time and to prevent this they need to be refreshed periodically. Special circuits called DRAM controllers are used for the refreshing operation. The refresh operation is done periodically in milli-seconds interval. Figure 2.12 illustrates the typical implementation of a DRAM cell.

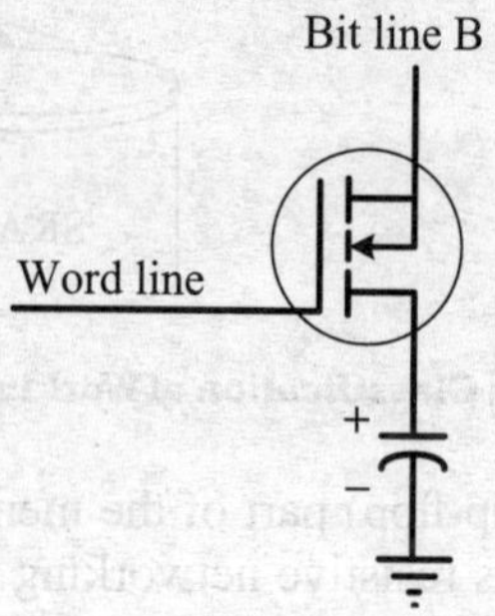

Fig. 2.12 **DRAM cell implementation**

The MOSFET acts as the gate for the incoming and outgoing data whereas the capacitor acts as the bit storage unit. Table given below summarises the relative merits and demerits of SRAM and DRAM technology.

SRAM cell	DRAM cell
Made up of 6 CMOS transistors (MOSFET)	Made up of a MOSFET and a capacitor
Doesn't require refreshing	Requires refreshing
Low capacity (Less dense)	High capacity (Highly dense)
More expensive	Less expensive
Fast in operation. Typical access time is 10ns	Slow in operation due to refresh requirements. Typical access time is 60ns. Write operation is faster than read operation.

2.2.2.3 NVRAM Non-volatile RAM is a random access memory with battery backup. It contains static RAM based memory and a minute battery for providing supply to the memory in the absence of external power supply. The memory and battery are packed together in a single package. NVRAM is used for the non-volatile storage of results of operations or for setting up of flags, etc. The life span of NVRAM is expected to be around 10 years. DS1744 from Maxim/Dallas is an example for 32KB NVRAM.

2.2.3 Memory According to the Type of Interface

The interface (connection) of memory with the processor/controller can be of various types. It may be a parallel interface [The parallel data lines (D0-D7) for an 8 bit processor/controller will be connected to D0-D7 of the memory] or the interface may be a serial interface like I2C (Pronounced as I Square C. It is a 2 line serial interface) or it may be an SPI (Serial peripheral interface, 2+*n* line interface where *n* stands for the total number of SPI bus devices in the system). It can also be of a single wire interconnection (like Dallas 1-Wire interface). Serial interface is commonly used for data storage memory like EEPROM. The memory density of a serial memory is usually expressed in terms of kilobits, whereas that of a parallel interface memory is expressed in terms of kilobytes. Atmel Corporations AT24C512 is an example for serial memory with capacity 512 kilobits and 2-wire interface. Please refer to the section 'Communication Interface' for more details on I2C, SPI and 1-Wire Bus.

2.2.4 Memory Shadowing

Generally the execution of a program or a configuration from a Read Only Memory (ROM) is very slow (120 to 200 ns) compared to the execution from a random access memory (40 to 70 ns). From the timing parameters it is obvious that RAM access is about three times as fast as ROM access. Shadowing of memory is a technique adopted to solve the execution speed problem in processor-based systems. In computer systems and video systems there will be a configuration holding ROM called Basic Input Output Configuration ROM or simply BIOS. In personal computer systems BIOS stores the hardware configuration information like the address assigned for various serial ports and other non-plug '*n*' play devices, etc. Usually it is read and the system is configured according to it during system boot up and it is time consuming. Now the manufactures included a RAM behind the logical layer of BIOS at its same address as a shadow to the BIOS and the first step that happens during the boot up is copying the BIOS to the shadowed RAM and write protecting the RAM then disabling the BIOS reading. You may be thinking that what a stupid idea it is and why both RAM and ROM are needed for holding the same data. The answer is: RAM is volatile and it cannot hold the configuration data which is copied from the BIOS when the power supply is switched off. Only a ROM can hold it permanently. But for high system performance it should be accessed from a RAM instead of accessing from a ROM.

2.2.5 Memory Selection for Embedded Systems

Embedded systems require a program memory for holding the control algorithm (For a super-loop based design) or embedded OS and the applications designed to run on top of it (for OS based designs), data memory for holding variables and temporary data during task execution, and memory for holding non-volatile data (like configuration data, look up table etc) which are modifiable by the application (Unlike program memory, which is non-volatile as well unalterable by the end user). The memory requirement for an embedded system in terms of RAM and ROM (EEPROM/FLASH/NVRAM) is solely dependent on the type of the embedded system and the applications for which it is designed. There is no hard and fast rule for calculating the memory requirements. Lot of factors need to be considered when selecting the type and size of memory for embedded system. For example, if the embedded system is designed using SoC or a microcontroller with on-chip RAM and ROM (FLASH/EEPROM), depending on the application need the on-chip memory may be sufficient for designing the total system. As a rule of thumb, identify your system requirement and based on the type of processor (SoC or microcontroller with on-chip memory) used for the design, take a decision on whether the on-chip memory is sufficient or external memory is required. Let's consider a simple electronic toy design as an example. As the complexity of requirements are less and data memory requirement are minimal, we can think of a microcontroller with a few bytes of internal RAM, a few bytes or kilobytes (depending on the number of tasks and the complexity of tasks) of FLASH memory and a few bytes of EEPROM (if required) for designing the system. Hence there is no need for external memory at all. A PIC microcontroller device which satisfies the I/O and memory requirements can be used in this case. If the embedded design is based on an RTOS, the RTOS requires certain amount of RAM for its execution and ROM for storing the RTOS image (Image is the common name given for the binary data generated by the compilation of all RTOS source files). Normally the binary code for RTOS kernel containing all the services is stored in a non-volatile memory (Like FLASH) as either compressed or non-compressed data. During boot-up of the device, the RTOS files are copied from the program storage memory, decompressed if required and then loaded to the RAM for execution. The supplier of the RTOS usually gives a rough estimate on the run time RAM requirements and program memory requirements for the RTOS. On top of this add the RAM requirements for executing user tasks and ROM for storing user applications. On a safer side, always add a buffer value to the total estimated RAM and ROM size requirements. A smart phone device with Windows mobile operating system is a typical example for embedded device with OS. Say 64MB RAM and 128MB ROM are the minimum requirements for running the Windows mobile device, indeed you need extra RAM and ROM for running user applications. So while building the system, count the memory for that also and arrive at a value which is always at the safer side, so that you won't end up in a situation where you don't have sufficient memory to install and run user applications. There are two parameters for representing a memory. The first one is the size of the memory chip (Memory density expressed in terms of number of memory bytes per chip). There is no option to get a memory chip with the exact required number of bytes. Memory chips come in standard sizes like 512bytes, 1024bytes (1 kilobyte), 2048bytes (2 kilobytes), 4Kb,† 8Kb, 16Kb, 32Kb, 64Kb, 128Kb, 256Kb, 512Kb, 1024Kb (1 megabytes), etc. Suppose your embedded application requires only 750 bytes of RAM, you don't have the option of getting a memory chip with size 750 bytes, the only option left with is to choose the memory chip with a size closer to the size needed. Here 1024 bytes is the least possible option. We cannot go for 512 bytes, because the minimum requirement is 750 bytes. While you select a memory size, always keep in mind the address range supported by your processor. For example, for a processor/controller with 16 bit address bus, the maximum number of memory locations that can be addressed is 2^{16} = 65536 bytes = 64Kb. Hence it is meaningless to select a 128Kb memory chip for a processor with 16bit wide address bus. Also, the entire memory range supported by the processor/controller may not be available to the memory chip alone. It may be shared between I/O, other ICs and memory. Suppose the address bus is 16bit wide and only the lower 32Kb address range is assigned to the memory chip, the memory size maximum required is 32Kb only. It is not worth to use a memory chip with size 64Kb in such a situation. The second parameter that needs to be considered in selecting a memory is the word size of the memory. The word size refers to the number of memory bits that can be read/write together at a time. 4, 8, 12, 16, 24, 32, etc. are the word sizes supported by memory chips. Ensure that the word size supported by the memory chip matches with the data bus width of the processor/controller.

FLASH memory is the popular choice for ROM (program storage memory) in embedded applications. It is a powerful and cost-effective solid-state storage technology for mobile electronics devices and other consumer applications. FLASH memory comes in two major variants, namely, NAND and NOR FLASH. NAND FLASH is a high-density low cost non-volatile storage memory. On the other hand, NOR FLASH is less dense and slightly expensive. But it supports the Execute in Place (XIP) technique for program execution. The XIP technology allows the execution of code memory from ROM itself without the need for copying it to the RAM as in the case of conventional execution method. It is a good practice to use a combination of NOR and NAND memory for storage memory requirements, where NAND can be used for storing the program code and or data like the data captured in a camera device. NAND FLASH doesn't support XIP and if NAND FLASH is used for storing program code, a DRAM can be used for copying and executing the program code. NOR FLASH supports XIP and it can be used as the memory for bootloader or for even storing the complete program code.

The EEPROM data storage memory is available as either serial interface or parallel interface chip. If the processor/controller of the device supports serial interface and the amount of data to write and read to and from the device is less, it is better to have a serial EEPROM chip. The serial EEPROM saves the address space of the total system. The memory capacity of the serial EEPROM is usually expressed in

†Kb—Kilobytes

bits or kilobits. 512 bits, 1Kbits, 2Kbits, 4Kbits, etc. are examples for serial EEPROM memory representation. For embedded systems with low power requirements like portable devices, choose low power memory devices. Certain embedded devices may be targeted for operating at extreme environmental conditions like high temperature, high humid area, etc. Select an industrial grade memory chip in place of the commercial grade chip for such devices.

2.3 SENSORS AND ACTUATORS

At the very beginning of this chapter it is already mentioned that an embedded system is in constant interaction with the Real world and the controlling/monitoring functions executed by the embedded system is achieved in accordance with the changes happening to the Real world. The changes in system environment or variables are detected by the sensors connected to the input port of the embedded system. If the embedded system is designed for any controlling purpose, the system will produce some changes in the controlling variable to bring the controlled variable to the desired value. It is achieved through an actuator connected to the output port of the embedded system. If the embedded system is designed for monitoring purpose only, then there is no need for including an actuator in the system. For example, take the case of an ECG machine. It is designed to monitor the heart beat status of a patient and it cannot impose a control over the patient's heart beat and its order. The sensors used here are the different electrode sets connected to the body of the patient. The variations are captured and presented to the user (may be a doctor) through a visual display or some printed chart.

2.3.1 Sensors

A sensor is a transducer device that converts energy from one form to another for any measurement or control purpose. This is what I "by-hearted" during my engineering degree from the transducers paper.

If we look back to the "Smart" running shoe example given at the end of Chapter 1, we can identify that the sensor which measures the distance between the cushion and magnet in the smart running shoe is a magnetic hall effect sensor (Please refer back).

2.3.2 Actuators

Actuator is a form of transducer device (mechanical or electrical) which converts signals to corresponding physical action (motion). Actuator acts as an output device.

Looking back to the "Smart" running shoe example given at the end of Chapter 1, we can see that the actuator used for adjusting the position of the cushioning element is a micro stepper motor (Please refer back).

2.3.3 The I/O Subsystem

The I/O subsystem of the embedded system facilitates the interaction of the embedded system with the external world. As mentioned earlier the interaction happens through the sensors and actuators connected to the input and output ports respectively of the embedded system. The sensors may not be directly interfaced to the input ports, instead they may be interfaced through signal conditioning and translating systems like ADC, optocouplers, etc. This section illustrates some of the sensors and actuators used in embedded systems and the I/O systems to facilitate the interaction of embedded systems with external world.

2.3.3.1 Light Emitting Diode (LED) Light Emitting Diode (LED) is an important output device for visual indication in any embedded system. LED can be used as an indicator for the status of various signals or situations. Typical examples are indicating the presence of power conditions like 'Device ON', 'Battery low' or 'Charging of battery' for a battery operated handheld embedded devices.

Light Emitting Diode is a *p-n* junction diode (Refer Analog Electronics fundamentals to refresh your memory for *p-n* junction diode ☺) and it contains an anode and a cathode. For proper functioning of the LED, the anode of it should be connected to +ve terminal of the supply voltage and cathode to the –ve terminal of supply voltage. The current flowing through the LED must be limited to a value below the maximum current that it can conduct. A resister is used in series between the power supply and the LED to limit the current through the LED. The ideal LED interfacing circuit is shown in Fig. 2.13.

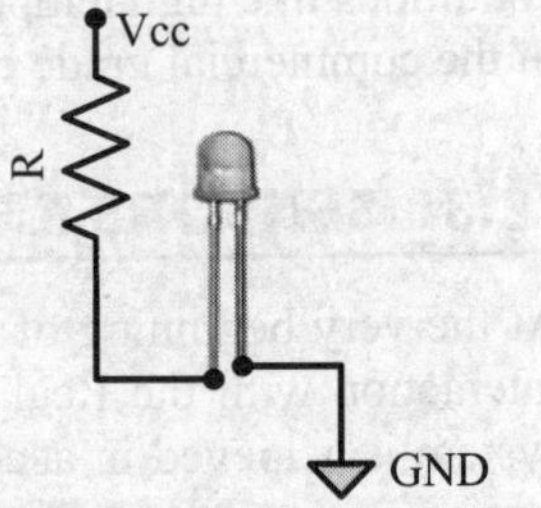

Fig. 2.13 **LED interfacing**

LEDs can be interfaced to the port pin of a processor/controller in two ways. In the first method, the anode is directly connected to the port pin and the port pin drives the LED. In this approach the port pin 'sources' current to the LED when the port pin is at logic High (Logic '1'). In the second method, the cathode of the LED is connected to the port pin of the processor/controller and the anode to the supply voltage through a current limiting resistor. The LED is turned on when the port pin is at logic Low (Logic '0'). Here the port pin 'sinks' current. If the LED is directly connected to the port pin, depending on the maximum current that a port pin can source, the brightness of LED may not be to the required level. In the second approach, the current is directly sourced by the power supply and the port pin acts as the sink for current. Here we will get the required brightness for the LED.

2.3.3.2 7-Segment LED Display The 7-segment LED display is an output device for displaying alpha numeric characters. It contains 8 light-emitting diode (LED) segments arranged in a special form. Out of the 8 LED segments, 7 are used for displaying alpha numeric characters and 1 is used for representing 'decimal point' in decimal number display. Figure 2.14 explains the arrangement of LED segments in a 7-segment LED display.

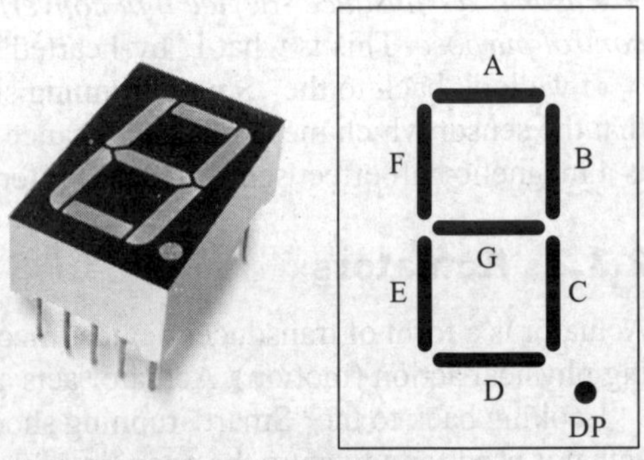

Fig. 2.14 **7-Segment LED Display**

The LED segments are named A to G and the decimal point LED segment is named as DP. The LED segments A to G and DP should be lit accordingly to display numbers and characters. For example, for displaying the number 4, the segments F, G, B and C are lit. For displaying 3, the segments A, B, C, D, G and DP are lit. For displaying the character 'd', the segments B, C, D, E and G are lit. All these 8 LED segments need to be connected to one port of the processor/controller for displaying alpha numeric digits. The 7-segment LED displays are available in two different configurations, namely; Common Anode and Common Cathode. In the common anode configuration, the anodes of the 8 segments are connected commonly whereas in the common cathode configuration, the 8 LED segments share a common cathode line. Figure 2.15 illustrates the Common Anode and Cathode configurations.

Based on the configuration of the 7-segment LED unit, the LED segment's anode or cathode is connected to the port of the processor/controller in the order 'A' segment to the least significant port pin and DP segment to the most significant port pin.

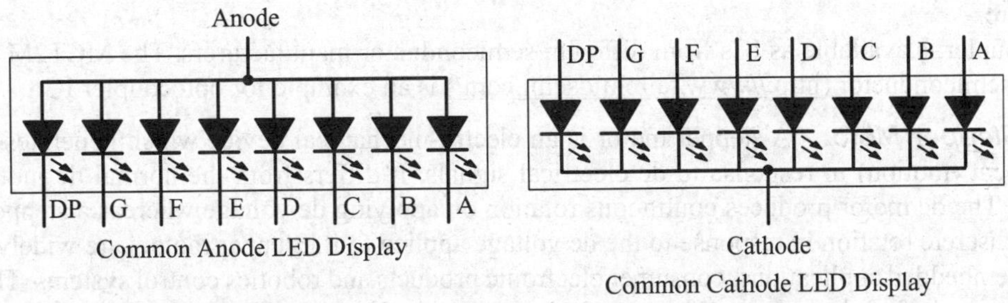

Fig. 2.15 Common anode and cathode configurations of a 7-segment LED Display

The current flow through each of the LED segments should be limited to the maximum value supported by the LED display unit. The typical value for the current falls within the range of 20mA. The current through each segment can be limited by connecting a current limiting resistor to the anode or cathode of each segment. The value for the current limiting resistors can be calculated using the current value from the electrical parameter listing of the LED display.

For common cathode configurations, the anode of each LED segment is connected to the port pins of the port to which the display is interfaced. The anode of the common anode LED display is connected to the 5V supply voltage through a current limiting resistor and the cathode of each LED segment is connected to the respective port pin lines. For an LED segment to lit in the Common anode LED configuration, the port pin to which the cathode of the LED segment is connected should be set at logic 0.

7-segment LED display is a popular choice for low cost embedded applications like, Public telephone call monitoring devices, point of sale terminals, etc.

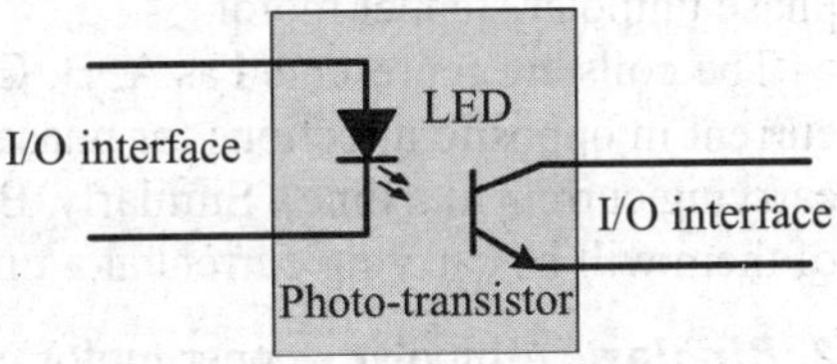

Fig. 2.16 An optocoupler device

2.3.3.3 Optocoupler Optocoupler is a solid state device to isolate two parts of a circuit. Optocoupler combines an LED and a photo-transistor in a single housing (package). Figure 2.16 illustrates the functioning of an optocoupler device.

In electronic circuits, an optocoupler is used for suppressing interference in data communication, circuit isolation, high voltage separation, simultaneous separation and signal intensification, etc. Optocouplers can be used in either input circuits or in output circuits. Figure 2.17 illustrates the usage

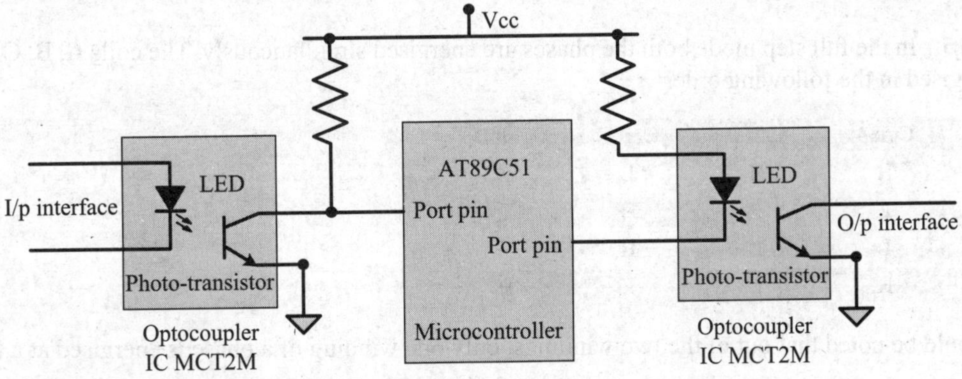

Fig. 2.17 Optocoupler in Input and Output circuit

of optocoupler in input circuit and output circuit of an embedded system with a microcontroller as the system core.

Optocoupler is available as ICs from different semiconductor manufacturers. The MCT2M IC from Fairchild semiconductor (http://www.fairchildsemi.com/) is an example for optocoupler IC.

2.3.3.4 Stepper Motor A stepper motor is an electro-mechanical device which generates discrete displacement (motion) in response to dc electrical signals. It differs from the normal dc motor in its operation. The dc motor produces continuous rotation on applying dc voltage whereas a stepper motor produces discrete rotation in response to the dc voltage applied to it. Stepper motors are widely used in industrial embedded applications, consumer electronic products and robotics control systems. The paper feed mechanism of a printer/fax makes use of stepper motors for its functioning.

Based on the coil winding arrangements, a two-phase stepper motor is classified into two. They are:

1. Unipolar
2. Bipolar

1. Unipolar A unipolar stepper motor contains two windings per phase. The direction of rotation (clockwise or anticlockwise) of a stepper motor is controlled by changing the direction of current flow. Current in one direction flows through one coil and in the opposite direction flows through the other coil. It is easy to shift the direction of rotation by just switching the terminals to which the coils are connected. Figure 2.18 illustrates the working of a two-phase unipolar stepper motor.

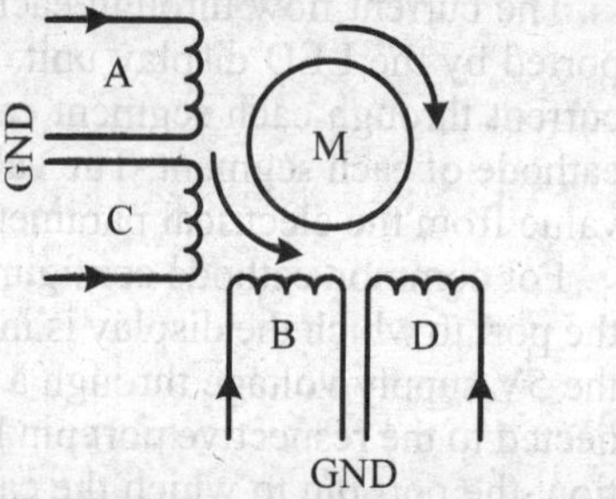

Fig. 2.18 **2-Phase unipolar stepper motor**

The coils are represented as A, B, C and D. Coils A and C carry current in opposite directions for phase 1 (only one of them will be carrying current at a time). Similarly, B and D carry current in opposite directions for phase 2 (only one of them will be carrying current at a time).

2. Bipolar A bipolar stepper motor contains single winding per phase. For reversing the motor rotation the current flow through the windings is reversed dynamically. It requires complex circuitry for current flow reversal. The stator winding details for a two phase unipolar stepper motor is shown in Fig. 2.19.

The stepping of stepper motor can be implemented in different ways by changing the sequence of activation of the stator windings. The different stepping modes supported by stepper motor are explained below.

Full Step In the full step mode both the phases are energised simultaneously. The coils A, B, C and D are energised in the following order:

Step	Coil A	Coil B	Coil C	Coil D
1	H	H	L	L
2	L	H	H	L
3	L	L	H	H
4	H	L	L	H

It should be noted that out of the two windings, only one winding of a phase is energised at a time.

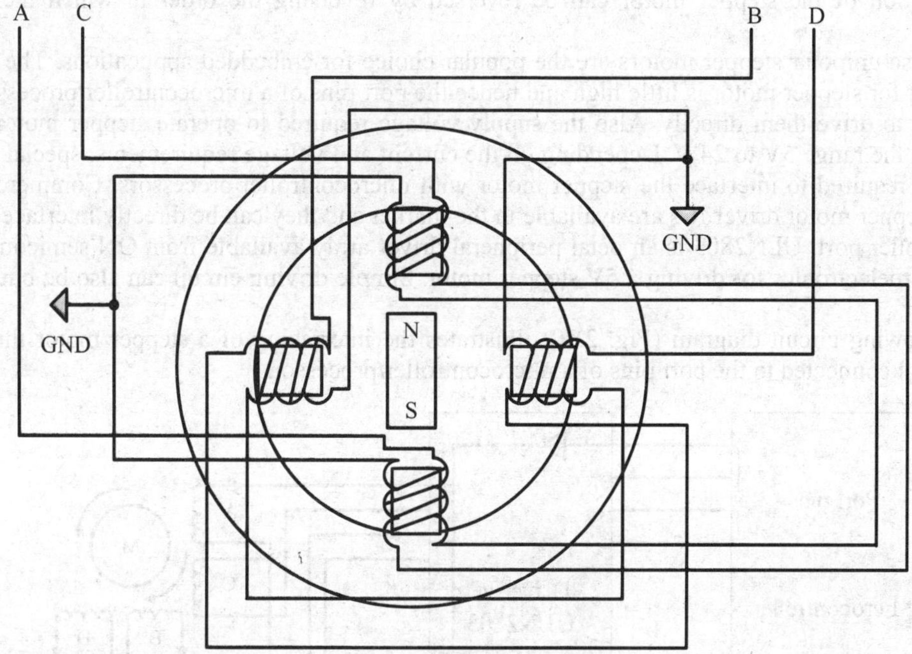

Fig. 2.19 **Stator Winding details for a 2 Phase unipolar stepper motor**

Wave Step In the wave step mode only one phase is energised at a time and each coils of the phase is energised alternatively. The coils A, B, C and D are energised in the following order:

Step	Coil A	Coil B	Coil C	Coil D
1	H	L	L	L
2	L	H	L	L
3	L	L	H	L
4	L	L	L	H

Half Step It uses the combination of wave and full step. It has the highest torque and stability. The coil energising sequence for half step is given below.

Step	Coil A	Coil B	Coil C	Coil D
1	H	L	L	L
2	H	H	L	L
3	L	H	L	L
4	L	H	H	L
5	L	L	H	L
6	L	L	H	H
7	L	L	L	H
8	H	L	L	H

The rotation of the stepper motor can be reversed by reversing the order in which the coil is energised.

Two-phase unipolar stepper motors are the popular choice for embedded applications. The current requirement for stepper motor is little high and hence the port pins of a microcontroller/processor may not be able to drive them directly. Also the supply voltage required to operate stepper motor varies normally in the range 5V to 24 V. Depending on the current and voltage requirements, special driving circuits are required to interface the stepper motor with microcontroller/processors. Commercial off-the-shelf stepper motor driver ICs are available in the market and they can be directly interfaced to the microcontroller port. ULN2803 is an octal peripheral driver array available from ON semiconductors and ST microelectronics for driving a 5V stepper motor. Simple driving circuit can also be built using transistors.

The following circuit diagram (Fig. 2.20) illustrates the interfacing of a stepper motor through a driver circuit connected to the port pins of a microcontroller/processor.

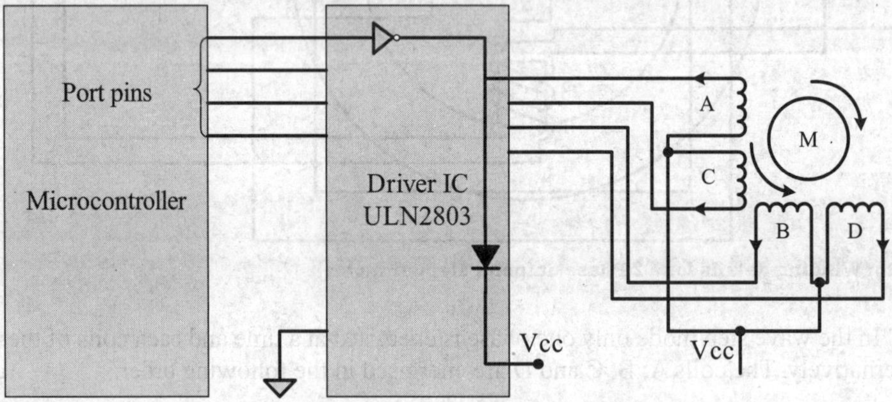

Fig. 2.20 **Interfacing of stepper motor through driver circuit**

2.3.3.5 Relay Relay is an electro-mechanical device. In embedded application, the 'Relay' unit acts as dynamic path selectors for signals and power. The 'Relay' unit contains a relay coil made up of insulated wire on a metal core and a metal armature with one or more contacts.

'Relay' works on electromagnetic principle. When a voltage is applied to the relay coil, current flows through the coil, which in turn generates a magnetic field. The magnetic field attracts the armature core and moves the contact point. The movement of the contact point changes the power/signal flow path. 'Relays' are available in different configurations. Figure 2.21 given below illustrates the widely used relay configurations for embedded applications.

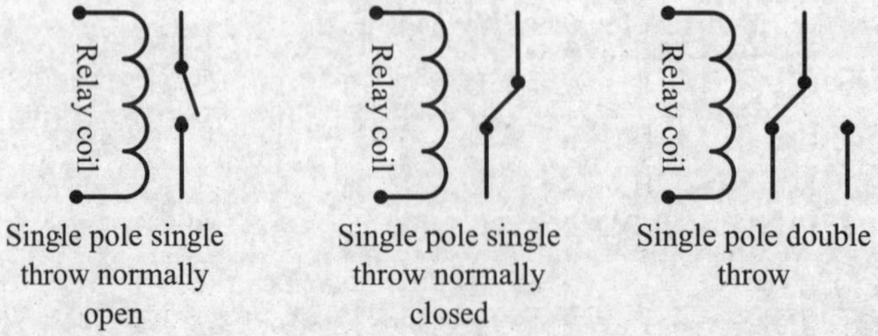

Fig. 2.21 **Relay configurations**

The **Single Pole Single Throw** configuration has only one path for information flow. The path is either open or closed in normal condition. For normally Open Single Pole Single Throw relay, the circuit is normally open and it becomes closed when the relay is energised. For normally closed Single Pole Single Throw configuration, the circuit is normally closed and it becomes open when the relay is energised. For Single Pole Double Throw Relay, there are two paths for information flow and they are selected by energising or de-energising the relay.

The Relay is normally controlled using a relay driver circuit connected to the port pin of the processor/controller. A transistor is used for building the relay driver circuit. Figure 2.22 illustrates the same.

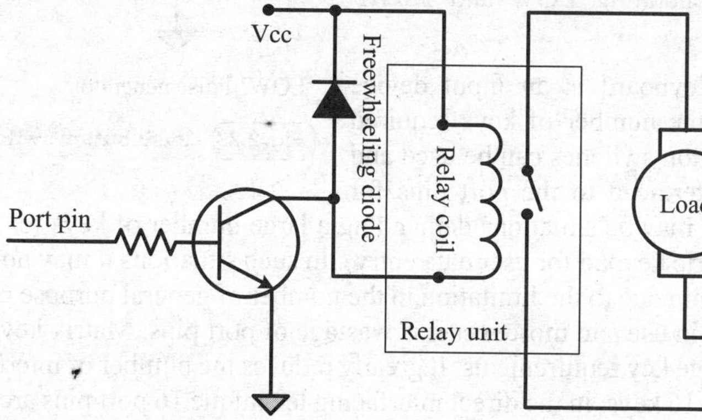

Fig. 2.22 **Transistor based Relay driving circuit**

A free-wheeling diode is used for free-wheeling the voltage produced in the opposite direction when the relay coil is de-energised. The freewheeling diode is essential for protecting the relay and the transistor.

Most of the industrial relays are bulky and requires high voltage to operate. Special relays called 'Reed' relays are available for embedded application requiring switching of low voltage DC signals.

2.3.3.6 Piezo Buzzer Piezo buzzer is a piezoelectric device for generating audio indications in embedded application. A piezoelectric buzzer contains a piezoelectric diaphragm which produces audible sound in response to the voltage applied to it. Piezoelectric buzzers are available in two types. 'Self-driving' and 'External driving'. The 'Self-driving' circuit contains all the necessary components to generate sound at a predefined tone. It will generate a tone on applying the voltage. External driving piezo buzzers supports the generation of different tones. The tone can be varied by applying a variable pulse train to the piezoelectric buzzer. A piezo buzzer can be directly interfaced to the port pin of the processor/control. Depending on the driving current requirements, the piezo buzzer can also be interfaced using a transistor based driver circuit as in the case of a 'Relay'.

2.3.3.7 Push Button Switch It is an input device. Push button switch comes in two configurations, namely 'Push to Make' and 'Push to Break'. In the 'Push to Make' configuration, the switch is normally in the open state and it makes a circuit contact when it is pushed or pressed. In the 'Push to Break' configuration, the switch is normally in the closed state and it breaks the circuit contact when it is pushed or pressed. The push button stays in the 'closed' (For Push to Make type) or 'open' (For Push to Break type) state as long as it is kept in the pushed state and it breaks/makes the circuit connection when it is released. Push button is used for generating a momentary pulse. In embedded application push button is generally used as reset and start switch and pulse generator. The Push button is normally connected to the port pin of the host processor/controller. Depending on the way in which the push button interfaced to the controller, it can generate either a 'HIGH' pulse or a 'LOW' pulse. Figure 2.23 illustrates how the push button can be used for generating 'LOW' and 'HIGH' pulses.

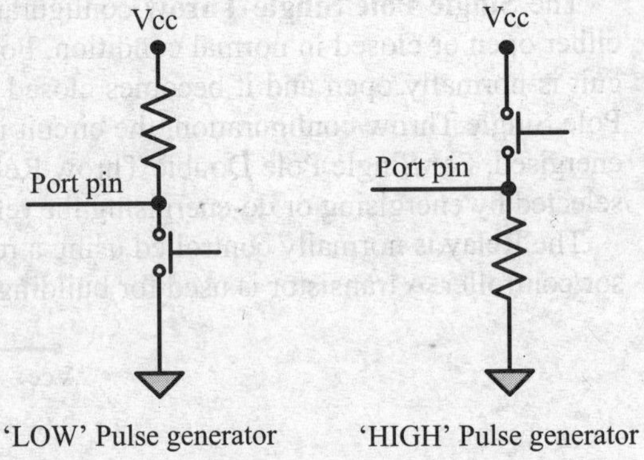

Fig. 2.23 **Push button switch configurations**

2.3.3.8 Keyboard Keyboard is an input device for user interfacing. If the number of keys required is very limited, push button switches can be used and they can be directly interfaced to the port pins for reading. However, there may be situations demanding a large number of keys for user input (e.g. PDA device with alpha-numeric keypad for user data entry). In such situations it may not be possible to interface each keys to a port pin due to the limitation in the number of general purpose port pins available for the processor/controller in use and moreover it is wastage of port pins. Matrix keyboard is an optimum solution for handling large key requirements. It greatly reduces the number of interface connections. For example, for interfacing 16 keys, in the direct interfacing technique 16 port pins are required, whereas in the matrix keyboard only 8 lines are required. The 16 keys are arranged in a 4 column × 4 Row matrix. Figure 2.24 illustrates the connection of keys in a matrix keyboard.

In a matrix keyboard, the keys are arranged in matrix fashion (i.e. they are connected in a row and column style). For detecting a key press, the keyboard uses the scanning technique, where each row of the matrix is pulled low and the columns are read. After reading the status of each columns corresponding to a row, the row is pulled high and the next row is pulled low and the status of the columns are read. This process is repeated until the scanning for all rows are completed. When a row is pulled low and if a key connected to the row is pressed, reading the column to which the key is connected will give logic 0. Since keys are mechanical devices, there is a possibility for de-bounce issues, which may give multiple key press effect for a single key press. To prevent this, a proper key de-bouncing technique should be applied. Hardware key de-bouncer circuits and software key de-bounce techniques are the key debouncing techniques available. The software key de-bouncing technique doesn't require any additional hardware and is easy to implement. In the software de-bouncing technique, on detecting a key-press, the key is read again after a de-bounce delay. If the key press is a genuine one, the state of the key will remain as 'pressed' on the second read also. Pull-up resistors are connected to the column lines to limit the current that flows to the Row line on a key press.

2.3.3.9 Programmable Peripheral Interface (PPI) Programmable Peripheral Interface (PPI) devices are used for extending the I/O capabilities of processors/controllers. Most of the processors/controllers provide very limited number of I/O and data ports and at times it may require more number of I/O ports than the one supported by the controller/processor. A programmable peripheral interface device expands the I/O capabilities of the processor/controller. *8255A* is a popular PPI device for 8bit processors/controllers. *8255A* supports 24 I/O pins and these I/O pins can be grouped as either three 8-bit parallel ports (Port A, Port B and Port C) or two 8bit parallel ports (Port A and Port B) with Port C in any one of the following configurations:

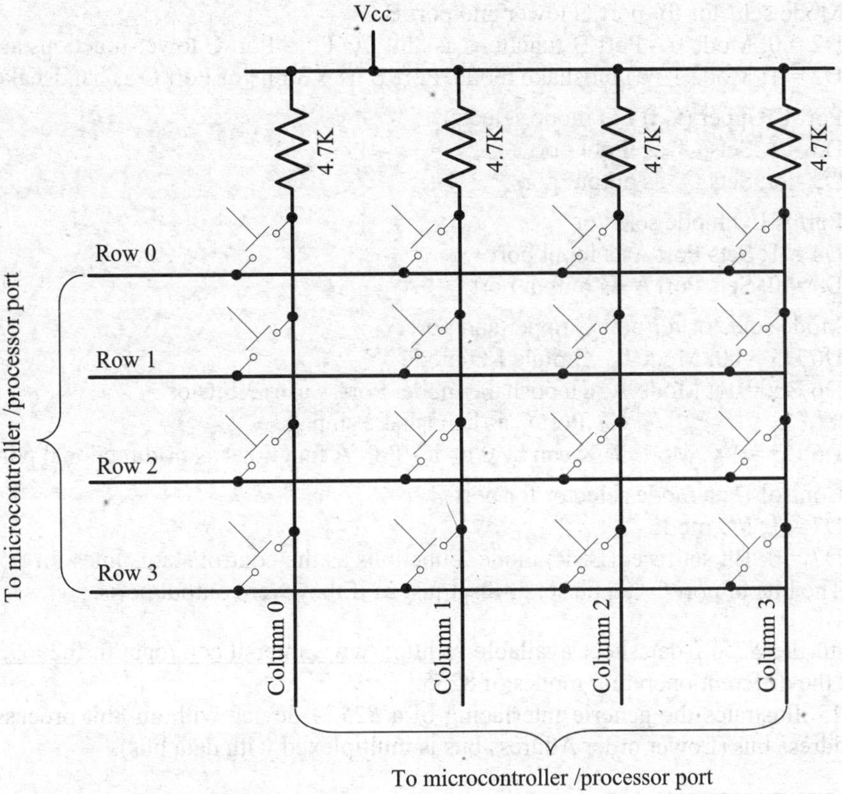

Fig. 2.24 **Matrix keyboard Interfacing**

1. As 8 individual I/O pins
2. Two 4bit ports namely Port C_{UPPER} (C_U) and Port C_{LOWER} (C_L)

This is configured by manipulating the control register of *8255A*. The control register holds the configuration for Port A, Port B and Port C. The bit details of control register is given below:

D7	D6	D5	D4	D3	D2	D1	D0

The table given below explains the meaning and use of each bit.

Bit	Description
D0	Port C Lower (C_L) I/O mode selector D0 = 1; Sets C_L as input port D0 = 0; Sets C_L as output port
D1	Port B I/O mode selector D1 = 1; Sets port B as input port D1 = 0; Sets port B as output port

D2	Mode selector for port C lower and port B D2 = 0; Mode 0 – Port B functions as 8bit I/O Port. Port C lower functions as 4bit port. D2 = 1; Mode 1 – Handshake mode. Port B uses 3 bits of Port C as handshake signals
D3	Port C Upper (C_U) I/O mode selector D3 = 1; Sets C_U as input port D3 = 0; Sets C_U as output port
D4	Port A I/O mode selector D4 = 1; Sets Port A as input port D4 = 0; Sets Port A as output port
D5, D6	Mode selector for port C upper and port A D6 D5 = 00; Mode 0 – Simple I/O mode D6 D5 = 01; Mode 1 – Handshake mode. Port A uses 3 bits of Port C as handshake signals D6 D5 = 1X; Mode 2. X can be 0 or 1 – Port A functions as bi-directional port
D7	Control/Data mode selector for port C D7 = 1; I/O mode. D7 = 0; Bit set/reset (BSR) mode. Functions as the control/status lines for ports A and B. The bits of port C can be set or reset just as if they were output ports.

Please refer to the *8255A* datasheet available at http://www.intersil.com/data/fn/fn2969.pdf for more details about the different operating modes of 8255.

Figure 2.25 illustrates the generic interfacing of a *8255A* device with an 8bit processor/controller with 16bit address bus (Lower order Address bus is multiplexed with data bus).

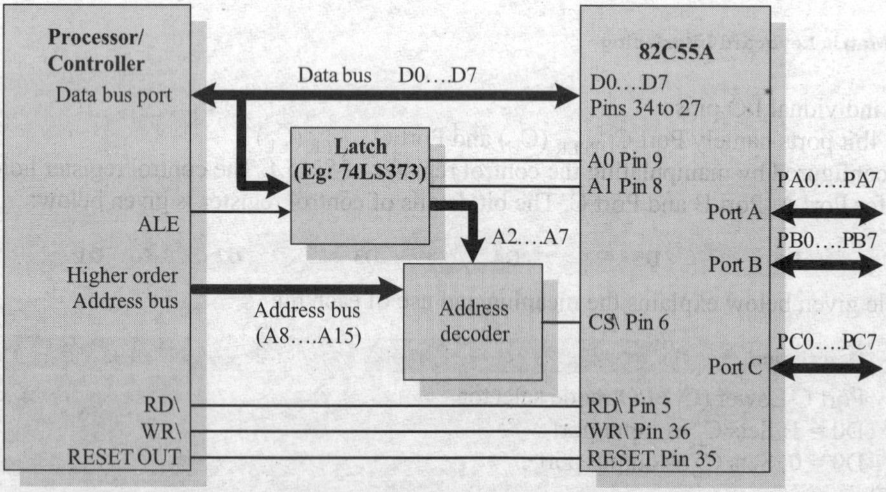

Fig. 2.25 **Interfacing of *8255* with an 8 bit microcontroller**

The ports of *8255* can be configured for different modes of operation by the processor/controller.

2.4 COMMUNICATION INTERFACE

Communication interface is essential for communicating with various subsystems of the embedded system and with the external world. For an embedded product, the communication interface can be viewed in two different perspectives; namely; Device/board level communication interface (Onboard Communication Interface) and Product level communication interface (External Communication Interface). Embedded product is a combination of different types of components (chips/devices) arranged on a printed circuit board (PCB). The communication channel which interconnects the various components within an embedded product is referred as device/board level communication interface (onboard communication interface). Serial interfaces like I2C, SPI, UART, 1-Wire, etc and parallel bus interface are examples of 'Onboard Communication Interface'.

Some embedded systems are self-contained units and they don't require any interaction and data transfer with other sub-systems or external world. On the other hand, certain embedded systems may be a part of a large distributed system and they require interaction and data transfer between various devices and sub-modules. The 'Product level communication interface' (External Communication Interface) is responsible for data transfer between the embedded system and other devices or modules. The external communication interface can be either a wired media or a wireless media and it can be a serial or a parallel interface. Infrared (IR), Bluetooth (BT), Wireless LAN (Wi-Fi), Radio Frequency waves (RF), GPRS, etc. are examples for wireless communication interface. RS-232C/RS-422/RS-485, USB, Ethernet IEEE 1394 port, Parallel port, CF-II interface, SDIO, PCMCIA, etc. are examples for wired interfaces. It is not mandatory that an embedded system should contain an external communication interface. Mobile communication equipment is an example for embedded system with external communication interface.

The following section gives you an overview of the various 'Onboard' and 'External' communication interfaces for an embedded product. We will discuss about the various physical interface, firmware requirements and initialisation and communication sequence for these interfaces in a dedicated book titled '*Device Interfacing*', which is planned under this series.

2.4.1 Onboard Communication Interfaces

Onboard Communication Interface refers to the different communication channels/buses for interconnecting the various integrated circuits and other peripherals within the embedded system. The following section gives an overview of the various interfaces for onboard communication.

2.4.1.1 Inter Integrated Circuit (I2C) Bus The Inter Integrated Circuit Bus (I2C–Pronounced 'I square C') is a synchronous bi-directional half duplex (one-directional communication at a given point of time) two wire serial interface bus. The concept of I2C bus was developed by 'Philips semiconductors' in the early 1980s. The original intention of I2C was to provide an easy way of connection between a microprocessor/microcontroller system and the peripheral chips in television sets. The I2C bus comprise of two bus lines, namely; Serial Clock–SCL and Serial Data–SDA. SCL line is responsible for generating synchronisation clock pulses and SDA is responsible for transmitting the serial data across devices. I2C bus is a shared bus system to which many number of I2C devices can be connected. Devices connected to the I2C bus can act as either 'Master' device or 'Slave' device. The 'Master' device is responsible for controlling the communication by initiating/terminating data transfer, sending data and generating necessary synchronisation clock pulses. 'Slave' devices wait for the commands from the master and respond upon receiving the commands. 'Master' and 'Slave' devices can act as either transmitter or receiver. Regardless whether a master is acting as transmitter or receiver, the synchronisation clock signal is generated by the 'Master' device only. I2C supports multi masters on the same bus. The following bus interface diagram shown in Fig. 2.26 illustrates the connection of master and slave devices on the I2C bus.

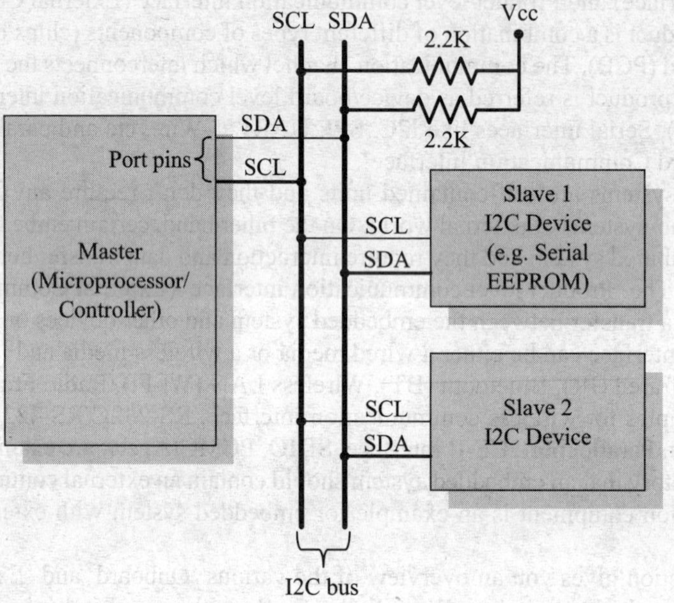

Fig. 2.26 **I2C Bus Interfacing**

The I2C bus interface is built around an input buffer and an open drain or collector transistor. When the bus is in the idle state, the open drain/collector transistor will be in the floating state and the output lines (SDA and SCL) switch to the 'High Impedance' state. For proper operation of the bus, both the bus lines should be pulled to the supply voltage (+5V for TTL family and +3.3V for CMOS family devices) using pull-up resistors. The typical value of resistors used in pull-up is 2.2K. With pull-up resistors, the output lines of the bus in the idle state will be 'HIGH'.

The address of a I2C device is assigned by hardwiring the address lines of the device to the desired logic level. The address to various I2C devices in an embedded device is assigned and hardwired at the time of designing the embedded hardware. The sequence of operations for communicating with an I2C slave device is listed below:

1. The master device pulls the clock line (SCL) of the bus to 'HIGH'
2. The master device pulls the data line (SDA) 'LOW', when the SCL line is at logic 'HIGH' (This is the 'Start' condition for data transfer)
3. The master device sends the address (7 bit or 10 bit wide) of the 'slave' device to which it wants to communicate, over the SDA line. Clock pulses are generated at the SCL line for synchronising the bit reception by the slave device. The MSB of the data is always transmitted first. The data in the bus is valid during the 'HIGH' period of the clock signal

4. The master device sends the Read or Write bit (Bit value = 1 Read operation; Bit value = 0 Write operation) according to the requirement
5. The master device waits for the acknowledgement bit from the slave device whose address is sent on the bus along with the Read/Write operation command. Slave devices connected to the bus compares the address received with the address assigned to them
6. The slave device with the address requested by the master device responds by sending an acknowledge bit (Bit value = 1) over the SDA line
7. Upon receiving the acknowledge bit, the Master device sends the 8bit data to the slave device over SDA line, if the requested operation is 'Write to device'. If the requested operation is 'Read from device', the slave device sends data to the master over the SDA line
8. The master device waits for the acknowledgement bit from the device upon byte transfer complete for a write operation and sends an acknowledge bit to the Slave device for a read operation
9. The master device terminates the transfer by pulling the SDA line 'HIGH' when the clock line SCL is at logic 'HIGH' (Indicating the 'STOP' condition)

I2C bus supports three different data rates. They are: Standard mode (Data rate up to 100kbits/sec (100 kbps)), Fast mode (Data rate up to 400kbits/sec (400 kbps)) and High speed mode (Data rate up to 3.4Mbits/sec (3.4 Mbps)). The first generation I2C devices were designed to support data rates only up to 100kbps. The new generation I2C devices are designed to operate at data rates up to 3.4Mbits/sec.

2.4.1.2 Serial Peripheral Interface (SPI) Bus The Serial Peripheral Interface Bus (SPI) is a synchronous bi-directional full duplex four-wire serial interface bus. The concept of SPI was introduced by Motorola. SPI is a single master multi-slave system. It is possible to have a system where more than one SPI device can be master, provided the condition only one master device is active at any given point of time, is satisfied. SPI requires four signal lines for communication. They are:

Master Out Slave In (MOSI): Signal line carrying the data from master to slave device. It is also known as Slave Input/Slave Data In (SI/SDI)

Master In Slave Out (MISO): Signal line carrying the data from slave to master device. It is also known as Slave Output (SO/SDO)

Serial Clock (SCLK): Signal line carrying the clock signals

Slave Select (SS): Signal line for slave device select. It is an active low signal

The bus interface diagram shown in Fig. 2.27 illustrates the connection of master and slave devices on the SPI bus.

The master device is responsible for generating the clock signal. It selects the required slave device by asserting the corresponding slave device's slave select signal 'LOW'. The data out line (MISO) of all the slave devices when not selected floats at high impedance state.

The serial data transmission through SPI bus is fully configurable. SPI devices contain a certain set of registers for holding these configurations. The serial peripheral control register holds the various configuration parameters like master/slave selection for the device, baudrate selection for communication, clock signal control, etc. The status register holds the status of various conditions for transmission and reception.

SPI works on the principle of 'Shift Register'. The master and slave devices contain a special shift register for the data to transmit or receive. The size of the shift register is device dependent. Normally it is a multiple of 8. During transmission from the master to slave, the data in the master's shift register is shifted out to the MOSI pin and it enters the shift register of the slave device through the MOSI pin of the slave device. At the same time the shifted out data bit from the slave device's shift register enters

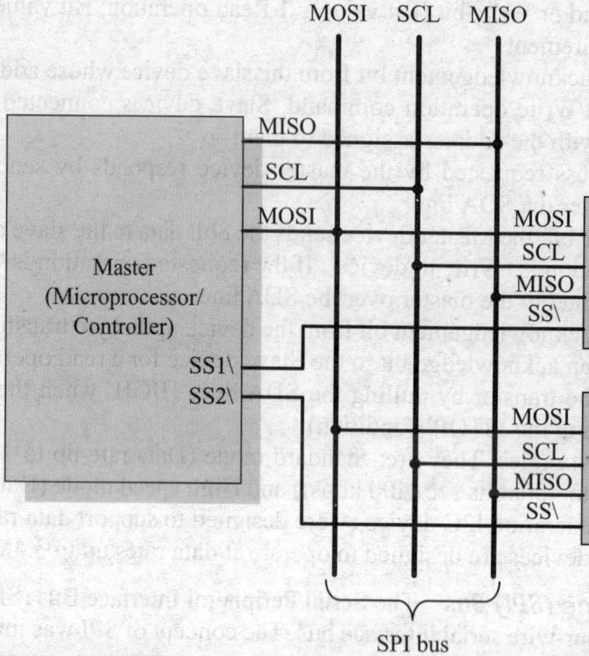

Fig. 2.27 **SPI bus interfacing**

the shift register of the master device through MISO pin. In summary, the shift registers of 'master' and 'slave' devices form a circular buffer. For some devices, the decision on whether the LS/MS bit of data needs to be sent out first is configurable through configuration register (e.g. LSBF bit of the SPI control register for Motorola's 68HC12 controller).

When compared to I2C, SPI bus is most suitable for applications requiring transfer of data in 'streams'. The only limitation is SPI doesn't support an acknowledgement mechanism.

2.4.1.3 Universal Asynchronous Receiver Transmitter (UART) Universal Asynchronous Receiver Transmitter (UART) based data transmission is an asynchronous form of serial data transmission. UART based serial data transmission doesn't require a clock signal to synchronise the transmitting end and receiving end for transmission. Instead it relies upon the pre-defined agreement between the transmitting device and receiving device. The serial communication settings (Baudrate, number of bits per byte, parity, number of start bits and stop bit and flow control) for both transmitter and receiver should be set as identical. The start and stop of communication is indicated through inserting special bits in the data stream. While sending a byte of data, a start bit is added first and a stop bit is added at the end of the bit stream. The least significant bit of the data byte follows the 'start' bit.

The 'start' bit informs the receiver that a data byte is about to arrive. The receiver device starts polling its 'receive line' as per the baudrate settings. If the baudrate is 'x' bits per second, the time slot available for one bit is $1/x$ seconds. The receiver unit polls the receiver line at exactly half of the time slot available for the bit. If parity is enabled for communication, the UART of the transmitting device adds a parity bit (bit value is 1 for odd number of 1s in the transmitted bit stream and 0 for even number of 1s). The UART of the receiving device calculates the parity of the bits received and compares it with the received parity bit for error checking. The UART of the receiving device discards the 'Start', 'Stop' and 'Parity' bit from the received bit stream and converts the received serial bit data to a word (In the case of 8 bits/byte, the byte is formed with the received 8 bits with the first received bit as the LSB and last received data bit as MSB).

For proper communication, the 'Transmit line' of the sending device should be connected to the 'Receive line' of the receiving device. Figure 2.28 illustrates the same.

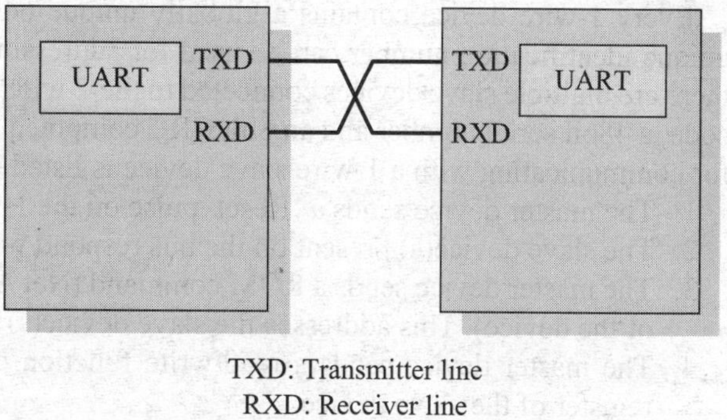

Fig. 2.28 **UART Interfacing**

In addition to the serial data transmission function, UART provides hardware handshaking signal support for controlling the serial data flow. UART chips are available from different semiconductor manufacturers. National Semiconductor's 8250 UART chip is considered as the standard setting UART. It was used in the original IBM PC.

Nowadays most of the microprocessors/controllers are available with integrated UART functionality and they provide built-in instruction support for serial data transmission and reception.

2.4.1.4 1-Wire Interface 1-wire interface is an asynchronous half-duplex communication protocol developed by Maxim Dallas Semiconductor (http://www.maxim-ic.com). It is also known as **Dallas 1-Wire® protocol**. It makes use of only a single signal line (wire) called DQ for communication and follows the master-slave communication model. One of the key feature of 1-wire bus is that it allows power to be sent along the signal wire as well. The 12C slave devices incorporate internal capacitor (typically of the order of 800 pF) to power the device from the signal line. The 1-wire interface supports a single master and one or more slave devices on the bus. The bus interface diagram shown in Fig. 2.29 illustrates the connection of master and slave devices on the 1-wire bus.

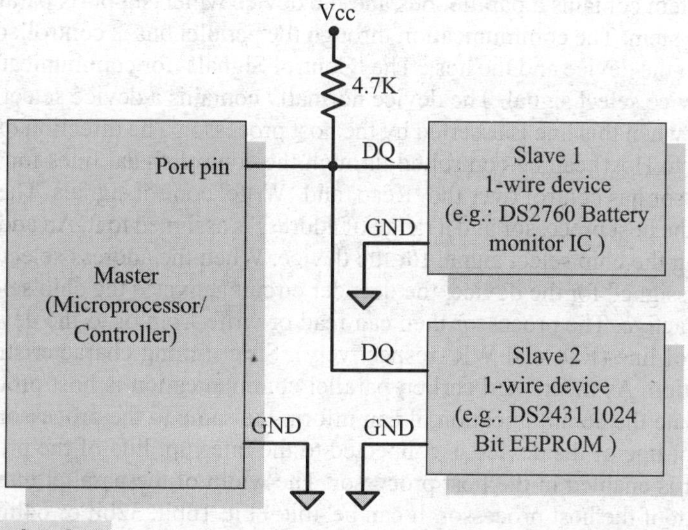

Fig. 2.29 **1-Wire Interface bus**

Every 1-wire device contains a globally unique 64bit identification number stored within it. This unique identification number can be used for addressing individual devices present on the bus in case there are multiple slave devices connected to the 1-wire bus. The identifier has three parts: an 8bit family code, a 48bit serial number and an 8bit CRC computed from the first 56 bits. The sequence of operation for communicating with a 1-wire slave device is listed below.

1. The master device sends a 'Reset' pulse on the 1-wire bus.
2. The slave device(s) present on the bus respond with a 'Presence' pulse.
3. The master device sends a ROM command (Net Address Command followed by the 64bit address of the device). This addresses the slave device(s) to which it wants to initiate a communication.
4. The master device sends a read/write function command to read/write the internal memory or register of the slave device.
5. The master initiates a Read data/Write data from the device or to the device

All communication over the 1-wire bus is master initiated. The communication over the 1-wire bus is divided into timeslots of 60 microseconds. The 'Reset' pulse occupies 8 time slots. For starting a communication, the master asserts the reset pulse by pulling the 1-wire bus 'LOW' for at least 8 time slots (480µs). If a 'slave' device is present on the bus and is ready for communication it should respond to the master with a 'Presence' pulse, within 60µs of the release of the 'Reset' pulse by the master. The slave device(s) responds with a 'Presence' pulse by pulling the 1-wire bus 'LOW' for a minimum of 1 time slot (60µs). For writing a bit value of 1 on the 1-wire bus, the bus master pulls the bus for 1 to 15µs and then releases the bus for the rest of the time slot. A bit value of '0' is written on the bus by master pulling the bus for a minimum of 1 time slot (60µs) and a maximum of 2 time slots (120µs). To Read a bit from the slave device, the master pulls the bus 'LOW' for 1 to 15µs. If the slave wants to send a bit value '1' in response to the read request from the master, it simply releases the bus for the rest of the time slot. If the slave wants to send a bit value '0', it pulls the bus 'LOW' for the rest of the time slot.

2.4.1.5 Parallel Interface The on-board parallel interface is normally used for communicating with peripheral devices which are memory mapped to the host of the system. The host processor/controller of the embedded system contains a parallel bus and the device which supports parallel bus can directly connect to this bus system. The communication through the parallel bus is controlled by the control signal interface between the device and the host. The 'Control Signals' for communication includes 'Read/Write' signal and device select signal. The device normally contains a device select line and the device becomes active only when this line is asserted by the host processor. The direction of data transfer (Host to Device or Device to Host) can be controlled through the control signal lines for 'Read' and 'Write'. Only the host processor has control over the 'Read' and 'Write' control signals. The device is normally memory mapped to the host processor and a range of address is assigned to it. An address decoder circuit is used for generating the chip select signal for the device. When the address selected by the processor is within the range assigned for the device, the decoder circuit activates the chip select line and thereby the device becomes active. The processor then can read or write from or to the device by asserting the corresponding control line (RD\ and WR\ respectively). Strict timing characteristics are followed for parallel communication. As mentioned earlier, parallel communication is host processor initiated. If a device wants to initiate the communication, it can inform the same to the processor through interrupts. For this, the interrupt line of the device is connected to the interrupt line of the processor and the corresponding interrupt is enabled in the host processor. The width of the parallel interface is determined by the data bus width of the host processor. It can be 4bit, 8bit, 16bit, 32bit or 64bit etc. The bus width supported by the device should be same as that of the host processor. The bus interface diagram shown in Fig. 2.30 illustrates the interfacing of devices through parallel interface.

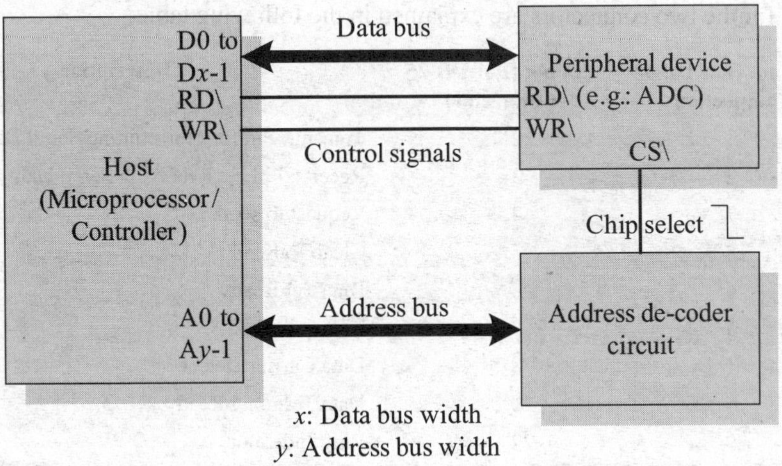

Fig. 2.30 **Parallel Interface Bus**

Parallel data communication offers the highest speed for data transfer.

2.4.2 External Communication Interfaces

The External Communication Interface refers to the different communication channels/buses used by the embedded system to communicate with the external world. The following section gives an overview of the various interfaces for external communication.

2.4.2.1 RS-232 C & RS-485 RS-232 C (Recommended Standard number 232, revision C from the Electronic Industry Association) is a legacy, full duplex, wired, asynchronous serial communication interface. The RS-232 interface is developed by the Electronics Industries Association (EIA) during the early 1960s. RS-232 extends the UART communication signals for external data communication.

UART uses the standard TTL/CMOS logic (Logic 'High' corresponds to bit value 1 and Logic 'Low' corresponds to bit value 0) for bit transmission whereas RS-232 follows the EIA standard for bit transmission. As per the EIA standard, a logic '0' is represented with voltage between +3 and +25V and a logic '1' is represented with voltage between -3 and -25V. In EIA standard, logic '0' is known as 'Space' and logic '1' as 'Mark'. The RS-232 interface defines various handshaking and control signals for communication apart from the 'Transmit' and 'Receive' signal lines for data communication. RS-232 supports two different types of connectors, namely; DB-9: 9-Pin connector and DB-25: 25-Pin connector. Figure 2.31 illustrates the connector details for DB-9 and DB-25.

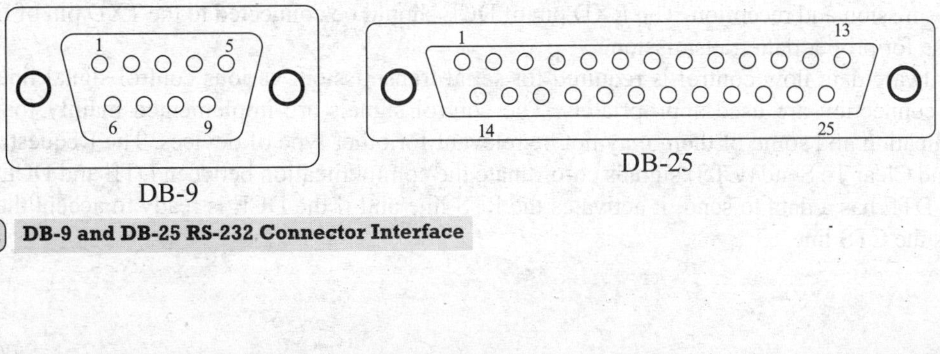

Fig. 2.31 **DB-9 and DB-25 RS-232 Connector Interface**

The pin details for the two connectors are explained in the following table:

Pin Name	Pin no: (For DB-9 Connector)	Pin no: (For DB-25 Connector)	Description
TXD	3	2	Transmit Pin for Transmitting Serial Data
RXD	2	3	Receive Pin for Receiving Serial Data
RTS	7	4	Request to send.
CTS	8	5	Clear To Send
DSR	6	6	Data Set Ready
GND	5	7	Signal Ground
DCD	1	8	Data Carrier Detect
DTR	4	20	Data Terminal Ready
RI	9	22	Ring Indicator
FG		1	Frame Ground
SDCD		12	Secondary DCD
SCTS		13	Secondary CTS
STXD		14	Secondary TXD
TC		15	Transmission Signal Element Timing
SRXD		16	Secondary RXD
RC		17	Receiver Signal Element Timing
SRTS		19	Secondary RTS
SQ		21	Signal Quality detector
NC		9	No Connection
NC		10	No Connection
NC		11	No Connection
NC		18	No Connection
NC		23	No Connection
NC		24	No Connection
NC		25	No Connection

RS-232 is a point-to-point communication interface and the devices involved in RS-232 communication are called 'Data Terminal Equipment (DTE)' and 'Data Communication Equipment (DCE)'. If no data flow control is required, only TXD and RXD signal lines and ground line (GND) are required for data transmission and reception. The RXD pin of DCE should be connected to the TXD pin of DTE and vice versa for proper data transmission.

If hardware data flow control is required for serial transmission, various control signal lines of the RS-232 connection are used appropriately. The control signals are implemented mainly for modem communication and some of them may not be relevant for other type of devices. The Request To Send (RTS) and Clear To Send (CTS) signals co-ordinate the communication between DTE and DCE. Whenever the DTE has a data to send, it activates the RTS line and if the DCE is ready to accept the data, it activates the CTS line.

The Data Terminal Ready (DTR) signal is activated by DTE when it is ready to accept data. The Data Set Ready (DSR) is activated by DCE when it is ready for establishing a communication link. DTR should be in the activated state before the activation of DSR.

The Data Carrier Detect (DCD) control signal is used by the DCE to indicate the DTE that a good signal is being received.

Ring Indicator (RI) is a modem specific signal line for indicating an incoming call on the telephone line.

The 25 pin DB connector contains two sets of signal lines for transmit, receive and control lines. Nowadays DB-25 connector is obsolete and most of the desktop systems are available with DB-9 connectors only.

As per the EIA standard RS-232 C supports baudrates up to 20Kbps (Upper limit 19.2 Kbps) The commonly used baudrates by devices are 300bps, 1200bps, 2400bps, 9600bps, 11.52Kbps and 19.2Kbps. 9600 is the popular baudrate setting used for PC communication. The maximum operating distance supported by RS-232 is 50 feet at the highest supported baudrate.

Embedded devices contain a UART for serial communication and they generate signal levels conforming to TTL/CMOS logic. A level translator IC like MAX 232 from Maxim Dallas semiconductor is used for converting the signal lines from the UART to RS-232 signal lines for communication. On the receiving side the received data is converted back to digital logic level by a converter IC. Converter chips contain converters for both transmitter and receiver.

Though RS-232 was the most popular communication interface during the olden days, the advent of other communication techniques like Bluetooth, USB, Firewire, etc are pushing down RS-232 from the scenes. Still RS-232 is popular in certain legacy industrial applications.

RS-232 supports only point-to-point communication and not suitable for multi-drop communication. It uses single ended data transfer technique for signal transmission and thereby more susceptible to noise and it greatly reduces the operating distance.

RS-422 is another serial interface standard from EIA for differential data communication. It supports data rates up to 100Kbps and distance up to 400 ft. The same RS-232 connector is used at the device end and an RS-232 to RS-422 converter is plugged in the transmission line. At the receiver end the conversion from RS-422 to RS-232 is performed. RS-422 supports multi-drop communication with one transmitter device and receiver devices up to 10.

RS-485 is the enhanced version of RS-422 and it supports multi-drop communication with up to 32 transmitting devices (drivers) and 32 receiving devices on the bus. The communication between devices in the bus uses the 'addressing' mechanism to identify slave devices.

2.4.2.2 Universal Serial Bus (USB) Universal Serial Bus (USB) is a wired high speed serial bus for data communication. The first version of USB (USB1.0) was released in 1995 and was created by the USB core group members consisting of Intel, Microsoft, IBM, Compaq, Digital and Northern Telecom. The USB communication system follows a star topology with a USB host at the centre and one or more USB peripheral devices/USB hosts connected to it. A USB host can support connections up to 127, including slave peripheral devices and other USB hosts. Figure 2.32 illustrates the star topology for USB device connection.

USB transmits data in packet format. Each data packet has a standard format. The USB communication is a host initiated one. The USB host contains a host controller which is responsible for controlling the data communication, including establishing connectivity with USB slave devices, packetizing and formatting the data. There are different standards for implementing the USB Host Control interface; namely Open Host Control Interface (OHCI) and Universal Host Control Interface (UHCI).

The physical connection between a USB peripheral device and master device is established with a USB cable. The USB cable supports communication distance of up to 5 metres. The USB standard uses two different types of connector at the ends of the USB cable for connecting the USB peripheral device and host device. 'Type A' connector is used for upstream connection (connection with host) and Type B connector is used for downstream connection (connection with slave device). The USB connector present in desktop PCs or laptops are examples for 'Type A' USB connector. Both Type A and Type B connectors contain 4 pins for communication. The Pin details for the connectors are listed in the table given below.

Pin no:	Pin name	Description
1	V_{BUS}	Carries power (5V)
2	D–	Differential data carrier line
3	D+	Differential data carrier line
4	GND	Ground signal line

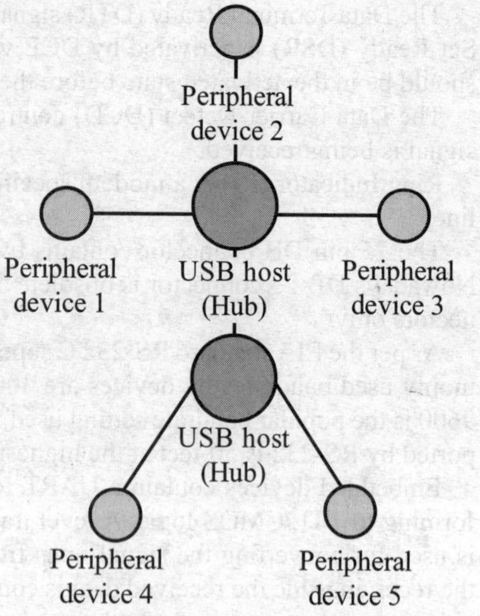

Fig. 2.32 **USB Device Connection topology**

USB uses differential signals for data transmission. It improves the noise immunity. USB interface has the ability to supply power to the connecting devices. Two connection lines (Ground and Power) of the USB interface are dedicated for carrying power. It can supply power up to 500 mA at 5 V. It is sufficient to operate low power devices. Mini and Micro USB connectors are available for small form factor devices like portable media players.

Each USB device contains a Product ID (PID) and a Vendor ID (VID). The PID and VID are embedded into the USB chip by the USB device manufacturer. The VID for a device is supplied by the USB standards forum. PID and VID are essential for loading the drivers corresponding to a USB device for communication.

USB supports four different types of data transfers, namely; Control, Bulk, Isochronous and Interrupt. **Control transfer** is used by USB system software to query, configure and issue commands to the USB device. **Bulk transfer** is used for sending a block of data to a device. Bulk transfer supports error checking and correction. Transferring data to a printer is an example for bulk transfer. **Isochronous data** transfer is used for real-time data communication. In Isochronous transfer, data is transmitted as streams in real-time. Isochronous transfer doesn't support error checking and re-transmission of data in case of any transmission loss. All streaming devices like audio devices and medical equipment for data collection make use of the isochronous transfer. **Interrupt transfer** is used for transferring small amount of data. Interrupt transfer mechanism makes use of polling technique to see whether the USB device has any data to send. The frequency of polling is determined by the USB device and it varies from 1 to 255 milliseconds. Devices like Mouse and Keyboard, which transmits fewer amounts of data, uses Interrupt transfer.

USB.ORG (www.usb.org) is the standards body for defining and controlling the standards for USB communication. Presently USB supports four different data rates namely; Low Speed (1.5Mbps), Full Speed (12Mbps), High Speed (480Mbps) and Super Speed (4.8Gbps). The Low Speed and Full Speed specifications are defined by USB 1.0 and the High Speed specification is defined by USB 2.0. USB 3.0

defines the specifications for Super Speed. USB 3.0 is expected to be in action by year 2009. There is a move happening towards wireless USB for data transmission using Ultra Wide Band (UWB) technology. Some laptops are already available in the market with wireless USB support.

2.4.2.3 IEEE 1394 (Firewire) *IEEE 1394* is a wired, isochronous high speed serial communication bus. It is also known as High Performance Serial Bus (HPSB). The research on 1394 was started by Apple Inc. in 1985 and the standard for this was coined by IEEE. The implementation of it is available from various players with different names. Apple Inc's (www.apple.com) implementation of 1394 protocol is popularly known as ***Firewire***. ***i.LINK*** is the *1394* implementation from Sony Corporation (www.sony.net) and ***Lynx*** is the implementation from Texas Instruments (www.ti.com). *1394* supports peer-to-peer connection and point-to-multipoint communication allowing 63 devices to be connected on the bus in a tree topology. *1394* is a wired serial interface and it can support a cable length of up to 15 feet for interconnection.

The *1394* standard has evolved a lot from the first version *IEEE 1394–1995* released in 1995 to the recent version *IEEE 1394–2008* released in June 2008. The *1394* standard supports a data rate of 400 to 3200Mbits/second. The *IEEE 1394* uses differential data transfer (The information is sent using differential signals through a pair of twisted cables. It increases the noise immunity) and the interface cable supports 3 types of connectors, namely; 4-pin connector, 6-pin connector (alpha connector) and 9 pin connector (beta connector). The 6 and 9 pin connectors carry power also to support external devices (In case an embedded device is connected to a PC through an *IEEE 1394* cable with 6 or 9 pin connector interface, it can operate from the power available through the connector.) It can supply unregulated power in the range of 24 to 30V. (The Apple implementation is for battery operated devices and it can supply a voltage in the range 9 to 12V.) The table given below illustrates the pin details for 4, 6 and 9 pin connectors.

Pin name	Pin no: (4 Pin Connector)	Pin no: (6 Pin Connector)	Pin no: (9 Pin Connector)	Description
Power		1	8	Unregulated DC supply. 24 to 30V
Signal Ground		2	6	Ground connection
TPB–	1	3	1	Differential Signal line for Signal line B
TPB+	2	4	2	Differential Signal line for Signal line B
TPA–	3	5	3	Differential Signal line for Signal line A
TPA+	4	6	4	Differential Signal line for Signal line A
TPA(S)			5	Shield for the differential signal line A. Normally grounded
TPB(S)			9	Shield for the differential signal line B. Normally grounded
NC			7	No connection

There are two differential data transfer lines A and B per connector. In a *1394* cable, normally the differential lines of A are connected to B (TPA+ to TPB+ and TPA–to TPB–) and vice versa.

1394 is a popular communication interface for connecting embedded devices like Digital Camera, Camcorder, Scanners to desktop computers for data transfer and storage.

Unlike USB interface (Except USB OTG), *IEEE 1394* doesn't require a host for communicating between devices. For example, you can directly connect a scanner with a printer for printing. The data-rate supported by *1394* is far higher than the one supported by *USB2.0 interface*. The *1394* hardware implementation is much costlier than USB implementation.

2.4.2.4 Infrared (IrDA) Infrared (IrDA) is a serial, half duplex, line of sight based wireless technology for data communication between devices. It is in use from the olden days of communication and you may be very familiar with it. The remote control of your TV, VCD player, etc. works on Infrared data communication principle. Infrared communication technique uses infrared waves of the electromagnetic spectrum for transmitting the data. IrDA supports point-point and point-to-multipoint communication, provided all devices involved in the communication are within the line of sight. The typical communication range for IrDA lies in the range 10 cm to 1 m. The range can be increased by increasing the transmitting power of the IR device. IR supports data rates ranging from 9600bits/second to 16Mbps. Depending on the speed of data transmission IR is classified into Serial IR (SIR), Medium IR (MIR), Fast IR (FIR), Very Fast IR (VFIR) and Ultra Fast IR (UFIR). SIR supports transmission rates ranging from 9600bps to 115.2kbps. MIR supports data rates of 0.576Mbps and 1.152Mbps. FIR supports data rates up to 4Mbps. VFIR is designed to support high data rates up to 16Mbps. The UFIR specs are under development and it is targeting a data rate up to 100Mbps.

IrDA communication involves a transmitter unit for transmitting the data over IR and a receiver for receiving the data. Infrared Light Emitting Diode (LED) is the IR source for transmitter and at the receiving end a photodiode acts as the receiver. Both transmitter and receiver unit will be present in each device supporting IrDA communication for bidirectional data transfer. Such IR units are known as 'Transceiver'. Certain devices like a TV remote control always require unidirectional communication and so they contain either the transmitter or receiver unit (The remote control unit contains the transmitter unit and TV contains the receiver unit).

'Infra-red Data Association' (IrDA - http://www.irda.org/) is the regulatory body responsible for defining and licensing the specifications for IR data communication. IrDA communication has two essential parts; a physical link part and a protocol part. The physical link is responsible for the physical transmission of data between devices supporting IR communication and protocol part is responsible for defining the rules of communication. The physical link works on the wireless principle making use of Infrared for communication. The IrDA specifications include the standard for both physical link and protocol layer.

The IrDA control protocol contains implementations for Physical Layer (PHY), Media Access Control (MAC) and Logical Link Control (LLC). The Physical Layer defines the physical characteristics of communication like range, data rates, power, etc.

IrDA is a popular interface for file exchange and data transfer in low cost devices. IrDA was the prominent communication channel in mobile phones before Bluetooth's existence. Even now most of the mobile phone devices support IrDA.

2.4.2.5 Bluetooth (BT) Bluetooth is a low cost, low power, short range wireless technology for data and voice communication. Bluetooth was first proposed by 'Ericsson' in 1994. Bluetooth operates at 2.4GHz of the Radio Frequency spectrum and uses the Frequency Hopping Spread Spectrum (FHSS) technique for communication. Literally it supports a data rate of up to 1Mbps and a range of approximately 30 feet for data communication. Like IrDA, Bluetooth communication also has two essential parts; a physical link part and a protocol part. The physical link is responsible for the physical transmission of data between devices supporting Bluetooth communication and protocol part is responsible for defining the rules of communication. The physical link works on the wireless principle making use of RF waves for communication. Bluetooth enabled devices essentially contain a Bluetooth wireless radio for the transmission and reception of data. The rules governing the Bluetooth communication is implemented in the 'Bluetooth protocol stack'. The Bluetooth communication IC holds the stack. Each Bluetooth device will have a 48 bit unique identification number. Bluetooth communication follows packet based data transfer.

Bluetooth supports point-to-point (device to device) and point-to-multipoint (device to multiple device broadcasting) wireless communication. The point-to-point communication follows the master-slave relationship. A Bluetooth device can function as either master or slave. When a network is formed with one Bluetooth device as master and more than one device as slaves, it is called a Piconet. A Piconet supports a maximum of seven slave devices.

Bluetooth is the favourite choice for short range data communication in handheld embedded devices. Bluetooth technology is very popular among cell phone users as they are the easiest communication channel for transferring ringtones, music files, pictures, media files, etc. between neighbouring Bluetooth enabled phones.

The Bluetooth standard specifies the minimum requirements that a Bluetooth device must support for a specific usage scenario. The Generic Access Profile (GAP) defines the requirements for detecting a Bluetooth device and establishing a connection with it. All other specific usage profiles are based on GAP. Serial Port Profile (SPP) for serial data communication, File Transfer Profile (FTP) for file transfer between devices, Human Interface Device (HID) for supporting human interface devices like keyboard and mouse are examples for Bluetooth profiles.

The specifications for Bluetooth communication is defined and licensed by the standards body 'Bluetooth Special Interest Group (SIG)'. For more information, please visit the website www.bluetooth.org.

2.4.2.6 Wi-Fi Wi-Fi or Wireless Fidelity is the popular wireless communication technique for networked communication of devices. Wi-Fi follows the IEEE 802.11 standard. Wi-Fi is intended for network communication and it supports Internet Protocol (IP) based communication. It is essential to have device identities in a multipoint communication to address specific devices for data communication. In an IP based communication each device is identified by an IP address, which is unique to each device on the network. Wi-Fi based communications require an intermediate agent called Wi-Fi router/Wireless Access point to manage the communications. The Wi-Fi router is responsible for restricting the access to a network, assigning IP address to devices on the network, routing data packets to the intended devices on the network. Wi-Fi enabled devices contain a wireless adaptor for transmitting and receiving data in the form of radio signals through an antenna. The hardware part of it is known as Wi-Fi Radio.

Wi-Fi operates at 2.4GHz or 5GHz of radio spectrum and they co-exist with other ISM band devices like Bluetooth. Figure 2.33 illustrates the typical interfacing of devices in a Wi-Fi network.

For communicating with devices over a Wi-Fi network, the device when its Wi-Fi radio is turned ON, searches the available Wi-Fi network in its vicinity and lists out the Service Set Identifier (SSID) of the available networks. If the network is security enabled, a password may be required to connect to a particular SSID. Wi-Fi employs different security mechanisms like Wired Equivalency Privacy (WEP) Wireless Protected Access (WPA), etc. for securing the data communication.

Wi-Fi supports data rates ranging from 1Mbps to 150Mbps (Growing towards higher rates as technology progresses) depending on the standards (802.11a/b/g/n) and access/modulation method. Depending on the type of antenna and usage location (indoor/outdoor), Wi-Fi offers a range of 100 to 300 feet.

2.4.2.7 ZigBee ZigBee is a low power, low cost, wireless network communication protocol based on the IEEE 802.15.4-2006 standard. ZigBee is targeted for low power, low data rate and secure applications for Wireless Personal Area Networking (WPAN). The ZigBee specifications support a robust mesh network containing multiple nodes. This networking strategy makes the network reliable by permitting messages to travel through a number of different paths to get from one node to another.

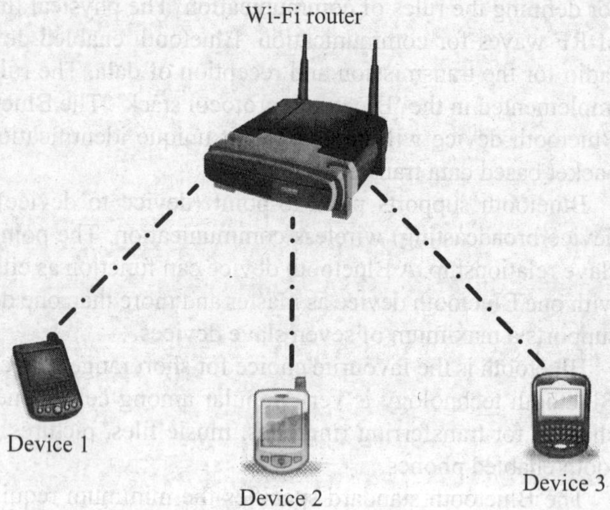

Fig. 2.33 **Wi-Fi network**

ZigBee operates worldwide at the unlicensed bands of Radio spectrum, mainly at 2.400 to 2.484 GHz, 902 to 928 MHz and 868.0 to 868.6 MHz. ZigBee Supports an operating distance of up to 100 metres and a data rate of 20 to 250Kbps.

In the ZigBee terminology, each ZigBee device falls under any one of the following ZigBee device category.

ZigBee Coordinator (ZC)/Network Coordinator: The ZigBee coordinator acts as the root of the ZigBee network. The ZC is responsible for initiating the ZigBee network and it has the capability to store information about the network.

ZigBee Router (ZR)/Full function Device (FFD): Responsible for passing information from device to another device or to another ZR.

ZigBee End Device (ZED)/Reduced Function Device (RFD): End device containing ZigBee functionality for data communication. It can talk only with a ZR or ZC and doesn't have the capability to act as a mediator for transferring data from one device to another.

The diagram shown in Fig. 2.34 gives an overview of ZC, ZED and ZR in a ZigBee network.

ZigBee is primarily targeting application areas like home & industrial automation, energy management, home control/security, medical/patient tracking, logistics & asset tracking and sensor networks & active RFID. Automatic Meter Reading (AMR), smoke detectors, wireless telemetry, HVAC control, heating control, lighting controls, environmental controls, etc. are examples for applications which can make use of the ZigBee technology.

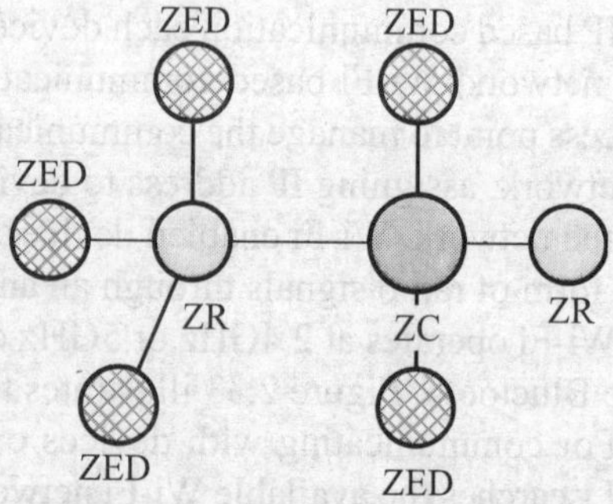

Fig. 2.34 **A ZigBee network model**

The specifications for ZigBee is developed and managed by the ZigBee alliance (www.zigbee.org), a non-profit consortium of leading semiconductor manufacturers, technology providers, OEMs and end-users worldwide.

2.4.2.8 General Packet Radio Service (GPRS) General Packet Radio Service (GPRS) is a communication technique for transferring data over a mobile communication network like GSM. Data is sent as packets in GPRS communication. The transmitting device splits the data into several related packets. At the receiving end the data is re-constructed by combining the received data packets. GPRS supports a theoretical maximum transfer rate of 171.2kbps. In GPRS communication, the radio channel is concurrently shared between several users instead of dedicating a radio channel to a cell phone user. The GPRS communication divides the channel into 8 timeslots and transmits data over the available channel. GPRS supports Internet Protocol (IP), Point to Point Protocol (PPP) and X.25 protocols for communication.

GPRS is mainly used by mobile enabled embedded devices for data communication. The device should support the necessary GPRS hardware like GPRS modem and GPRS radio. To accomplish GPRS based communication, the carrier network also should have support for GPRS communication. GPRS is an old technology and it is being replaced by new generation data communication techniques like EDGE, High Speed Downlink Packet Access (HSDPA), etc. which offers higher bandwidths for communication.

2.5 EMBEDDED FIRMWARE

Embedded firmware refers to the control algorithm (Program instructions) and or the configuration settings that an embedded system developer dumps into the code (Program) memory of the embedded system. It is an un-avoidable part of an embedded system. There are various methods available for developing the embedded firmware. They are listed below.

1. Write the program in high level languages like Embedded C/C++ using an Integrated Development Environment (The IDE will contain an editor, compiler, linker, debugger, simulator, etc. IDEs are different for different family of processors/controllers. For example, Keil micro vision3 IDE is used for all family members of *8051* microcontroller, since it contains the generic *8051* compiler C51).
2. Write the program in Assembly language using the instructions supported by your application's target processor/controller.

The instruction set for each family of processor/controller is different and the program written in either of the methods given above should be converted into a processor understandable machine code before loading it into the program memory.

The process of converting the program written in either a high level language or processor/controller specific Assembly code to machine readable binary code is called '*HEX File Creation*'. The methods used for '*HEX File Creation*' is different depending on the programming techniques used. If the program is written in Embedded C/C++ using an IDE, the cross compiler included in the IDE converts it into corresponding processor/controller understandable '*HEX File*'. If you are following the Assembly language based programming technique (method 2), you can use the utilities supplied by the processor/controller vendors to convert the source code into '*HEX File*'. Also third party tools are available, which may be of free of cost, for this conversion.

For a beginner in the embedded software field, it is strongly recommended to use the high level language based development technique. The reasons for this being: writing codes in a high level language is easy, the code written in high level language is highly portable which means you can use the same code to run on different processor/controller with little or less modification. The only thing you need to do is re-compile the program with the required processor's IDE, after replacing the include files for that particular processor. Also the programs written in high level languages are not developer dependent. Any skilled programmer can trace out the functionalities of the program by just having a look at the program. It will be much easier if the source code contains necessary comments and documentation lines. It is very easy to debug and the overall system development time will be reduced to a greater extent.

The embedded software development process in assembly language is tedious and time consuming. The developer needs to know about all the instruction sets of the processor/controller or at least s/he should carry an instruction set reference manual with her/him. A programmer using assembly language technique writes the program according to his/her view and taste. Often he/she may be writing a method or functionality which can be achieved through a single instruction as an experienced person's point of view, by two or three instructions in his/her own style. So the program will be highly dependent on the developer. It is very difficult for a second person to understand the code written in Assembly even if it is well documented.

We will discuss both approaches of embedded software development in a later chapter dealing with design of embedded firmware, in detail. Two types of control algorithm design exist in embedded firmware development. The first type of control algorithm development is known as the infinite loop or '*super loop*' based approach, where the control flow runs from top to bottom and then jumps back to the top of the program in a conventional procedure. It is similar to the *while (1) { };* based technique in C. The second method deals with splitting the functions to be executed into tasks and running these tasks using a scheduler which is part of a General Purpose or Real Time Embedded Operating System (GPOS/RTOS). We will discuss both of these approaches in separate chapters of this book.

2.6 OTHER SYSTEM COMPONENTS

The other system components refer to the components/circuits/ICs which are necessary for the proper functioning of the embedded system. Some of these circuits may be essential for the proper functioning of the processor/controller and firmware execution. Watchdog timer, Reset IC (or passive circuit), brown-out protection IC (or passive circuit), etc. are examples of circuits/ICs which are essential for the proper functioning of the processor/controllers. Some of the controllers or SoCs integrate these components within a single IC and doesn't require such components externally connected to the chip for proper functioning. Depending on the system requirement, the embedded system may include other integrated circuits for performing specific functions, level translator ICs for interfacing circuits with different logic levels, etc. The following section explains the essential circuits for the proper functioning of the processor/controller of the embedded system.

2.6.1 Reset Circuit

The reset circuit is essential to ensure that the device is not operating at a voltage level where the device is not guaranteed to operate, during system power ON. The reset signal brings the internal registers and the different hardware systems of the processor/controller to a known state and starts the firmware execution from the reset vector (Normally from vector address 0x0000 for conventional processors/controllers. The reset vector can be relocated to an address for processors/controllers supporting bootloader). The reset signal can be either active high (The processor undergoes reset when the reset pin of the processor is at logic high) or active low (The processor undergoes reset when the reset pin of the processor is at logic low). Since the processor operation is synchronised to a clock signal, the reset pulse should be wide enough to give time for the clock oscillator to stabilise before the internal reset state starts. The reset signal to the processor can be applied at power ON through an external passive reset circuit comprising a Capacitor and Resistor or through a standard Reset IC like MAX810 from Maxim Dallas (www.maxim-ic.com). Select the reset IC based on the type of reset signal and logic level (CMOS/TTL) supported by the processor/controller in use. Some microprocessors/controllers contain built-in internal reset circuitry and they don't require external reset circuitry. Figure 2.35 illustrates a resistor capacitor based passive reset circuit for active high and low configurations. The reset pulse width can be adjusted by changing the resistance value *R* and capacitance value *C*.

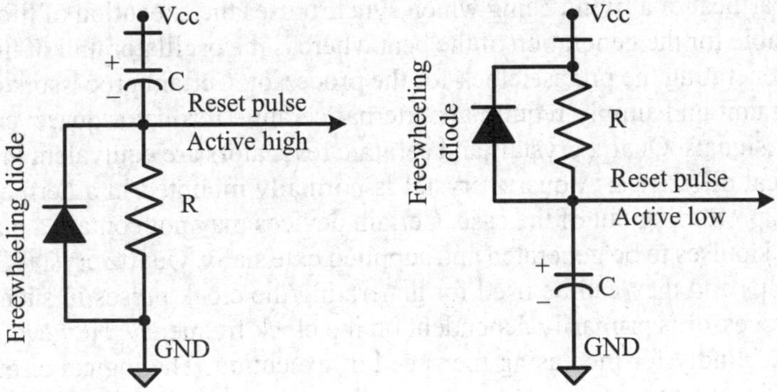

Fig. 2.35 **RC based reset circuit**

2.6.2 Brown-out Protection Circuit

Brown-out protection circuit prevents the processor/controller from unexpected program execution behaviour when the supply voltage to the processor/controller falls below a specified voltage. It is essential for battery powered devices since there are greater chances for the battery voltage to drop below the required threshold. The processor behaviour may not be predictable if the supply voltage falls below the recommended operating voltage. It may lead to situations like data corruption. A brown-out protection circuit holds the processor/controller in reset state, when the operating voltage falls below the threshold, until it rises above the threshold voltage. Certain processors/controllers support built in brown-out protection circuit which monitors the supply voltage internally. If the processor/controller doesn't integrate a built-in brown-out protection circuit, the same can be implemented using external passive circuits or supervisor ICs. Figure 2.36 illustrates a brown-out circuit implementation using Zener diode and transistor for processor/controller with active low Reset logic.

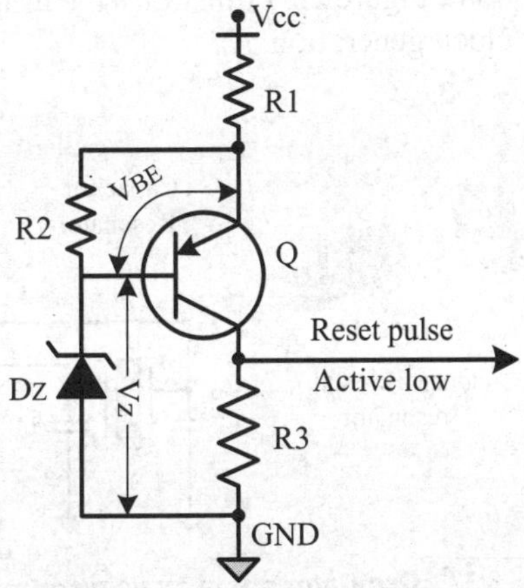

Fig. 2.36 **Brown-out protection circuit with Active low output**

The Zener diode Dz and transistor Q forms the heart of this circuit. The transistor conducts always when the supply voltage V_{cc} is greater than that of the sum of V_{BE} and V_z (Zener voltage). The transistor stops conducting when the supply voltage falls below the sum of V_{BE} and V_Z. Select the Zener diode with required voltage for setting the low threshold value for *Vcc*. The values of R1, R2, and R3 can be selected based on the electrical characteristics (Absolute maximum current and voltage ratings) of the transistor in use. Microprocessor Supervisor ICs like DS1232 from Maxim Dallas (www.maxim-ic.com) also provides Brown-out protection.

2.6.3 Oscillator Unit

A microprocessor/microcontroller is a digital device made up of digital combinational and sequential circuits. The instruction execution of a microprocessor/controller occurs in sync with a clock signal. It is analogous to the heartbeat of a living being which synchronises the execution of life. For a living being, the heart is responsible for the generation of the beat whereas the oscillator unit of the embedded system is responsible for generating the precise clock for the processor. Certain processors/controllers integrate a built-in oscillator unit and simply require an external ceramic resonator/quartz crystal for producing the necessary clock signals. Quartz crystals and ceramic resonators are equivalent in operation, however they possess physical difference. A quartz crystal is normally mounted in a hermetically sealed metal case with two leads protruding out of the case. Certain devices may not contain a built-in oscillator unit and require the clock pulses to be generated and supplied externally. Quartz crystal Oscillators are available in the form chips and they can be used for generating the clock pulses in such a cases. The speed of operation of a processor is primarily dependent on the clock frequency. However we cannot increase the clock frequency blindly for increasing the speed of execution. The logical circuits lying inside the processor always have an upper threshold value for the maximum clock at which the system can run, beyond which the system becomes unstable and non functional. The total system power consumption is directly proportional to the clock frequency. The power consumption increases with increase in clock frequency. The accuracy of program execution depends on the accuracy of the clock signal. The accuracy of the crystal oscillator or ceramic resonator is normally expressed in terms of +/-ppm (Parts per million). Figure 2.37 illustrates the usage of quartz crystal/ceramic resonator and external oscillator chip for clock generation.

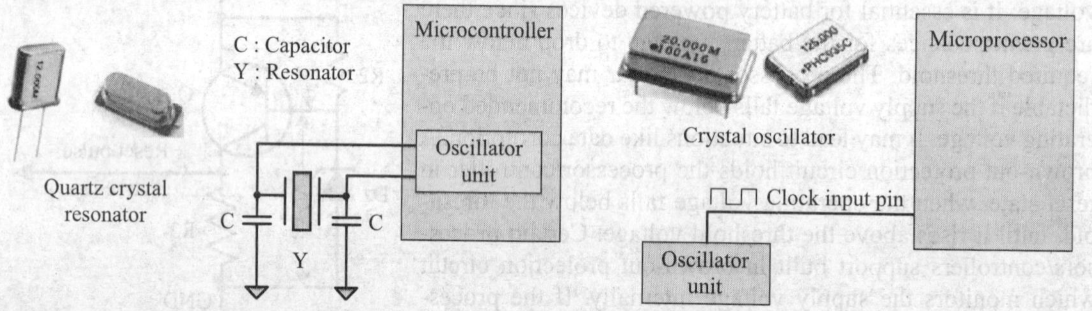

Fig. 2.37 **Oscillator circuitry using quartz crystal and quartz crystal oscillator**

2.6.4 Real-Time Clock (RTC)

Real-Time Clock (RTC) is a system component responsible for keeping track of time. RTC holds information like current time (In hours, minutes and seconds) in 12 hour/24 hour format, date, month, year, day of the week, etc. and supplies timing reference to the system. RTC is intended to function even in the absence of power. RTCs are available in the form of Integrated Circuits from different semiconductor manufacturers like Maxim/Dallas, ST Microelectronics etc. The RTC chip contains a microchip for holding the time and date related information and backup battery cell for functioning in the absence of power, in a single IC package. The RTC chip is interfaced to the processor or controller of the embedded system. For Operating System based embedded devices, a timing reference is essential for synchronising the operations of the OS kernel. The RTC can interrupt the OS kernel by asserting the interrupt line of the processor/controller to which the RTC interrupt line is connected. The OS kernel identifies the interrupt in terms of the Interrupt Request (IRQ) number generated by an interrupt controller. One IRQ can be assigned to the RTC interrupt and the kernel can perform necessary operations like system date time updation, managing software timers etc when an RTC timer tick interrupt occurs. The RTC can be configured to interrupt the processor at predefined intervals or to interrupt the processor when the RTC register reaches a specified value (used as alarm interrupt).

2.6.5 Watchdog Timer

In desktop Windows systems, if we feel our application is behaving in an abnormal way or if the system hangs up, we have the 'Ctrl + Alt + Del' to come out of the situation. What if it happens to our embedded system? Do we really have a 'Ctrl + Alt + Del' to take control of the situation? Of course not ☹, but we have a watchdog to monitor the firmware execution and reset the system processor/microcontroller when the program execution hangs up. A watchdog timer, or simply a watchdog, is a hardware timer for monitoring the firmware execution. Depending on the internal implementation, the watchdog timer increments or decrements a free running counter with each clock pulse and generates a reset signal to reset the processor if the count reaches zero for a down counting watchdog, or the highest count value for an upcounting watchdog. If the watchdog counter is in the enabled state, the firmware can write a zero (for upcounting watchdog implementation) to it before starting the execution of a piece of code (subroutine or portion of code which is susceptible to execution hang up) and the watchdog will start counting. If the firmware execution doesn't complete due to malfunctioning, within the time required by the watchdog to reach the maximum count, the counter will generate a reset pulse and this will reset the processor (if it is connected to the reset line of the processor). If the firmware execution completes before the expiration of the watchdog timer you can reset the count by writing a 0 (for an upcounting watchdog timer) to the watchdog timer register. Most of the processors implement watchdog as a built-in component and provides status register to control the watchdog timer (like enabling and disabling watchdog functioning) and watchdog timer register for writing the count value. If the processor/controller doesn't contain a built in watchdog timer, the same can be implemented using an external watchdog timer IC circuit. The external watchdog timer uses hardware logic for enabling/disabling, resetting the watchdog count, etc instead of the firmware based 'writing' to the status and watchdog timer register. The Microprocessor supervisor IC DS1232 integrates a hardware watchdog timer in it. In modern systems running on embedded operating systems, the watchdog can be implemented in such a way that when a watchdog timeout occurs, an interrupt is generated instead of resetting the processor. The interrupt handler for this handles the situation in an appropriate fashion. Figure 2.38 illustrates the implementa-

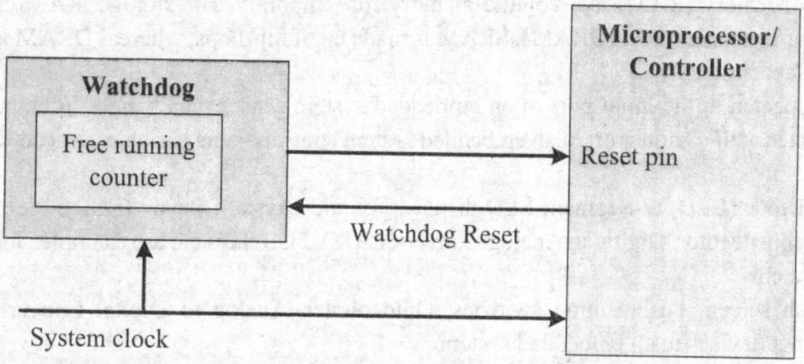

Fig. 2.38 **Watchdog timer for firmware execution supervision**

tion of an external watchdog timer based microprocessor supervisor circuit for a small scale embedded system.

2.7 PCB AND PASSIVE COMPONENTS

Printed Circuit Board (PCB) is the backbone of every embedded system. After finalising the components and the inter-connection among them, a schematic design is created and according to the schematic the PCB is fabricated. This will be described in detail in a chapter dedicated for "Embedded Hardware Design and Development". PCB acts as a platform for mounting all the necessary components as per the design requirement. Also it acts as a platform for testing your embedded firmware. Apart from the above-mentioned important subsystems of an embedded system, you can find some passive electronic components like resistor, capacitor, diodes, etc. on your board. They are the co-workers of various chips contained in your embedded hardware. They are very essential for the proper functioning of your embedded system. For example for providing a regulated ripple-free supply voltage to the system, a regulator IC and spike suppressor filter capacitors are very essential.

Summary

- ✓ The core of an embedded system is usually built around a commercial off-the-shelf component or an application specific integrated circuit (ASIC) or a general purpose processor like a microprocessor or microcontroller or application specific instruction set processors (ASIP like DSP, Microcontroller, etc.) or a Programmable Logic Device (PLD) or a System on Chip (SoC)
- ✓ Processors/controllers support either Reduced Instruction Set Computing (RISC) or Complex Instruction Set Computing (CISC)
- ✓ Microprocessors/controllers based on the Harvard architecture will have separate data bus and instruction bus, whereas Microprocessors/controllers based on the Von-Neumann architecture shares a single common bus for fetching both instructions and data
- ✓ The Big-endian processors store the higher-order byte of the data in memory at the lowest address, whereas Little-endian processors store the lower-order byte of data in memory at the lowest address
- ✓ Field Programmable Gate Arrays (FPGAs) and Complex Programmable Logic Devices (CPLDs) are the two major types of programmable logic devices
- ✓ The Read Only Memory (ROM) is a non-volatile memory for storing the firmware and embedded OS files. MROM, PROM (OTP), EPROM, EEPROM and FLASH are the commonly used firmware storage memory
- ✓ Random Access Memory (RAM) is a volatile memory for temporary data storage. RAM can be either Static RAM (SRAM) or Dynamic RAM (DRAM). SRAM is made up of flip-flops, whereas DRAM is made up of MOS Transistor and Capacitor
- ✓ The sensors connected to the input port of an embedded system senses the changes in input variables and the actuators connected at the output port of an embedded system controls some variables in accordance with changes in input
- ✓ Light Emitting Diode (LED), 7-Segment LED displays, Liquid Crystal Display (LCD), Piezo Buzzer, Speaker, Optocoupler, Stepper Motor, Digital to Analog Converters (DAC), Relays etc are examples for output devices of an embedded system
- ✓ Keyboard, Touch screen, Push Button switches, Optocoupler, Analog to Digital Converter (ADC) etc are examples for Input devices in an embedded system

- ✓ The Programmable Peripheral Interface (PPI) device extends the I/O capabilities of the processor used in embedded system
- ✓ I2C, SPI, UART, 1-Wire, Parallel bus etc are examples for onboard communication interface and RS-232C, RS-485, USB, IEEE1394 (FireWire), Wi-Fi, ZigBee, Infrared (IrDA), Bluetooth, GPRS, etc. are examples for external communication interface
- ✓ The control algorithm for the embedded device is known as Embedded Firmware. Embedded firmware can be developed on top of an embedded operating system or without an operating system
- ✓ The reset circuit ensures that the device is not operating at a voltage level where the device is not guaranteed to operate, during system power ON. The reset signal brings the internal registers and the different hardware systems of the processor/controller to a known state and starts the firmware execution from the reset vector
- ✓ The brown-out protection circuit prevents the processor/controller from unexpected program execution behaviour when the supply voltage to the processor/controller falls below a specified voltage
- ✓ The oscillator unit generates clock signals for synchronising the operations of the processor
- ✓ The time keeping activity for the embedded system is performed by the Real Time Clock (RTC) of the system. RTC holds current time, date, month, year, day of the week, etc.
- ✓ The watchdog timer monitors the firmware execution and resets the processor or generates an Interrupt in case the execution time for a task is exceeding the maximum allowed limit
- ✓ Printed circuit board or PCB acts as a platform for mounting all the necessary hardware components as per the design requirement

Keywords

COTS : Commercial-off-the-Shelf. Commercially available ready to use component

ASIC : Application Specific Integrated Circuit is a microchip designed to perform a specific or unique application

ASSP : Application Specific Standard Product—An ASIC marketed to multiple customers just as a general-purpose product is, but to a smaller number of customers

Microprocessor : A silicon chip representing a Central Processing Unit (CPU)

GPP : General Purpose Processor or GPP is a processor designed for general computational tasks

ASIP : Application Specific Instruction Set processors are processors with architecture and instruction set optimized to specific domain/application requirements

Microcontroller : A highly integrated chip that contains a CPU, scratchpad RAM, Special and General purpose Register Arrays and Integrated peripherals

DSP : Digital Signal Processor is a powerful special purpose 8/16/32 bit microprocessors designed specifically to meet the computational demands and power constraints

RISC : Reduced Instruction Set Computing. Refers to processors with Reduced and Orthogonal Instruction Set

CISC : Refers to processors with Complex Instruction Set Computing

Harvard Architecture : A type of processor architecture with separate buses for program instruction and data fetch

Von-Neumann Architecture : A type of processor architecture with a shared single common bus for fetching both instructions and data

Big-Endian : Refers to processors which store the higher-order byte of the data in memory at the lowest address

Little-Endian : Refers to processors which store the lower-order byte of the data in memory at the lowest address

FPGA	: Field Programmable Gate Array Device. A programmable logic device with reconfigurable function. Popular for prototyping ASIC designs
MROM	: Masked ROM is a one-time programmable memory, which uses the hardwired technology for storing data
OTP	: One Time Programmable Read Only Memory made up of nichrome or polysilicon wires arranged in a matrix
EPROM	: Erasable Programmable Read Only Memory. Reprogrammable ROM. Erased by exposing to UV light
EEPROM	: Electrically Erasable Programmable Read Only Memory. Reprogrammable ROM. Erased by applying electrical signals
FLASH	: Electrically Erasable Programmable Read Only Memory. Same as EEPROM but with high capacity and support for block level memory erasing
RAM	: Random Access memory. Volatile memory
SRAM	: Static RAM. A type of RAM, made up of flip-flops
DRAM	: Dynamic RAM. A type of RAM, made up of MOS Transistor and Capacitor
NVRAM	: Non-volatile SRAM. Battery-backed SRAM
ADC	: Analog to Digital Converter. An integrated circuit which converts analog signals to digital form
LED	: Light Emitting Diode. An output device which produces visual indication in the form of light in accordance with current flow
7-Segment LED Display	: The 7-segment LED display is an output device for displaying alpha numeric characters. It contains 8 light-emitting diode (LED) segments arranged in a special form
Optocoupler	: A solid state device to isolate two parts of a circuit. Optocoupler combines an LED and a photo-transistor in a single housing (package)
Stepper motor	: An electro-mechanical device which generates discrete displacement (motion) in response to dc electrical signals
Relay	: An electro-mechanical device which acts as dynamic path selector for signals and power
Piezo Buzzer	: A piezo-electric device for generating audio indication. It contains a piezo-electric diaphragm which produces audible sound in response to the voltage applied to it
Push Button switch	: A mechanical device for electric circuit 'make' and 'break' operation
PPI	: Programmable Peripheral Interface is a device for extending the I/O capabilities of processors/controllers
I2C	: The Inter Integrated Circuit Bus (I2C–Pronounced 'I square C') is a synchronous bi-directional half duplex two wire serial interface bus.
SPI	: The Serial Peripheral Interface Bus (SPI) is a synchronous bi-directional full duplex four wire serial interface bus
UART	: The Universal Asynchronous Receiver Transmitter is an asynchronous communication implementation standard
1-Wire interface	: An asynchronous half-duplex communication protocol developed by Maxim Dallas Semiconductor. It is also known as Dallas 1-Wire® protocol.
RS-232 C	: Recommended Standard number 232, revision C from the Electronic Industry Association, is a legacy, full duplex, wired, asynchronous serial communication interface
RS-485	: The enhanced version of RS-232, which supports multi-drop communication with up to 32 transmitting devices (drivers) and 32 receiving devices on the bus
USB	: Universal Serial Bus is a wired high speed serial bus for data communication
IEEE 1394	: A wired, isochronous high speed serial communication bus
Firewire	: The Apple Inc.'s implementation of the 1394 protocol

Infrared (IrDA)	:	A serial, half duplex, line of sight based wireless technology for data communication between devices
Bluetooth	:	A low cost, low power, short range wireless technology for data and voice communication
Wi-Fi	:	Wireless Fidelity is the popular wireless communication technique for networked communication of devices
ZigBee	:	A low power, low cost, wireless network communication protocol based on the IEEE 802.15.4-2006 standard. ZigBee is targeted for low power, low data-rate and secure applications for Wireless Personal Area Networking (WPAN)
GPRS	:	General Packet Radio Service is a communication technique for transferring data over a mobile communication network like GSM
Reset Circuit	:	A passive circuit or IC device to supply a reset signal to the processor/controller of the embedded system
Brown-out Protection Circuit	:	A passive circuit or IC device to protect the processor from unexpected program execution flow due to the drop in power supply voltage
RTC	:	Real Time Clock is a system component keeping track of time
Watchdog Timer (WDT)	:	Timer for monitoring the firmware execution
PCB	:	Printed Circuit Board is the place holder for arranging the different hardware components required to build the embedded product

Objective Questions

1. Embedded hardware/software systems are basically designed to
   (a) Regulate a physical variable (b) Change the state of some devices
   (c) Measure/Read the state of a variable/device (d) Any/All of these
2. Little Endian processors
   (a) Store the lower-order byte of the data at the lowest address and the higher-order byte of the data at the highest address of memory
   (b) Store the higher-order byte of the data at the lowest address and the lower-order byte of the data at the highest address of memory
   (c) Store both higher order and lower order byte of the data at the same address of memory
   (d) None of these
3. An integer variable with value 255 is stored in memory location at 0x8000. The processor word length is 8 bits and the processor is a big endian processor. The size of integer is considered as 4 bytes in the system. What is the value held by the memory location 0x8000?
   (a) 0xFF (b) 0x00 (c) 0x01 (d) None of these
4. The instruction set of RISC processor is
   (a) Simple and lesser in number (b) Complex and lesser in number
   (c) Simple and larger in number (d) Complex and larger in number
5. Which of the following is true about CISC processors?
   (a) The instruction set is non-orthogonal
   (b) The number of general purpose registers is limited
   (c) Instructions are like macros in C language
   (d) Variable length Instructions
   (e) All of these
   (f) None of these

6. Which of the following processor architecture supports easier instruction pipelining?
   (a) Harvard (b) Von Neumann (c) Both of them (d) None of these
7. Microprocessors/controllers based on the Harvard architecture will have separate data bus and instruction bus. This allows the data transfer and program fetching to occur simultaneously on both buses. State True or False
   (a) True (b) False
8. Which of the following is one-time programmable memory?
   (a) SRAM (b) PROM (c) FLASH (d) NVRAM
9. Which of the following memory type is best suited for development purpose?
   (a) EEPROM (b) FLASH (c) UVEPROM
   (d) OTP (e) (a) or (b)
10. EEPROM memory is alterable at byte level. State True or False
    (a) True (b) False
11. Non-volatile RAM is a Random Access Memory with battery backup. State True or False
    (a) True (b) False
12. Execution of program from ROM is faster than the execution from RAM. State True or False
    (a) True (b) False
13. Dynamic RAM stores data in the form of voltage. State True or False
    (a) True (b) False
14. The control algorithm (Program instructions) and or the configuration settings that are kept in the code (Program) memory of the embedded system are known as Embedded Software. State True or False
    (a) True (b) False
15. Which of the following is an example for Wireless Communication interface?
    (a) RS-232C (b) Wi-Fi (c) Bluetooth
    (d) EEE1394 (e) both (b) and (c)
16. Which of the following is (are) examples for Application Specific Instruction set Processor(s)
    (a) Intel Centrino (b) Atmel Automotive AVR
    (c) AMD Turion (d) Microchip CAN PIC (e) All of these (f) both (b) and (d)
17. How many memory cells are present in 1Kb RAM
    (a) 1024 (b) 8192 (c) 512 (d) 4096
    (e) None of these
18. Which of the following memory supports Execute in Place (XIP)?
    (a) EEPROM (b) NOR FLASH (c) NAND FLASH
    (d) both (b) and (c) (e) None of these
19. How many memory cells are present in 1Kb Serial EEPROM
    (a) 1024 (b) 8192 (c) 512 (d) 4096
    (e) None of these
20. Which of the following is (are) example(s) for the input subsystem of an embedded system dealing with digital data?
    (a) ADC (b) Optocoupler (c) DAC (d) All of them
    (e) only (a) and (b)
21. Which of the following is (are) example(s) for the output subsystem of an embedded system dealing with digital data?
    (a) LED (b) Optocoupler (c) Stepper Motor (d) All of these
    (e) only (a) and (c)
22. Which of the following is true about optocouplers
    (a) Optocoupler acts as an input device only
    (b) Optocoupler acts as an output device only
    (c) Optocoupler can be used in both input and output circuitry
    (d) None of these

23. Which of the following is true about a unipolar stepper motor
    (a) Contains only a single winding per stator phase (b) Contains two windings per stator phase
    (c) Contains four windings per stator phase (d) None of these
24. Which of the following is (are) true about normally open single pole relays?
    (a) The circuit remains open when the relay is not energised
    (b) The circuit remains closed when the relay is energised
    (c) There are two output paths
    (d) Both (a) and (b) (e) None of these
25. What is the minimum number I/O line required to interface a 16-Key matrix keyboard?
    (a) 16 (b) 8 (c) 4 (d) 9
26. Which is the optimal row-column configuration for a 24 key matrix keyboard?
    (a) 6×4 (b) 8×3 (c) 12×2 (d) 5×5
27 Which of the following is an example for on-board interface in the embedded system context?
    (a) I2C (b) Bluetooth (c) SPI (d) All of them
    (e) Only (a) and (c)
28. What is the minimum number of interface lines required for implementing I2C interface?
    (a) 1 (b) 2 (c) 3 (d) 4
29. What is the minimum number of interface lines required for implementing SPI interface?
    (a) 2 (b) 3 (c) 4 (d) 5
30. Which of the following are synchronous serial interface?
    (a) I2C (b) SPI (c) UART (d) All of these
    (e) Only (a) and (b)
31. RS-232 is a synchronous serial interface. State True or False
    (a) True (b) False
32. What is the maximum number of USB devices that can be connected to a USB host?
    (a) Unlimited (b) 128 (c) 127 (d) None of these
33. In the ZigBee network, which of the following ZigBee entity stores the information about the network?
    (a) ZigBee Coordinator (b) ZigBee Router
    (c) ZigBee Reduced Function Device (d) All of them
34. What is the theoretical maximum data rate supported by GPRS
    (a) 8Mbps (b) 12Mbps (c) 100Kbps (d) 171.2Kbps
35. GPRS communication divides the radio channel into __________ timeslots
    (a) 2 (b) 3 (c) 5 (d) 8

Review Questions

1. Explain the components of a typical embedded system in detail
2. Which are the components used as the core of an embedded system? Explain the merits, drawbacks, if any, and the applications/domains where they are commonly used
3. What is Application Specific Integrated Circuit (ASIC)? Explain the role of ASIC in Embedded System design?
4. What is the difference between Application Specific Integrated Circuit (ASIC) Application Specific Standard Product (ASSP)?
5. What is the difference between microprocessor and microcontroller? Explain the role of microprocessors and controllers in embedded system design?
6. What is Digital Signal Processor (DSP)? Explain the role of DSP in embedded system design?
7. What is the difference between RISC and CISC processors? Give an example for each.

8. What is processor architecture? What are the different processor architectures available for processor/controller design? Give an example for each.
9. What is the difference between big-endian and little-endian processors? Give an example of each.
10. What is Programmable Logic Device (PLD)? What are the different types of PLDs? Explain the role of PLDs in Embedded System design.
11. What is the difference between PLD and ASIC?
12. What are the advantages of PLD over fixed logic device?
13. What are the different types of memories used in Embedded System design? Explain the role of each.
14. What are the different types of memories used for Program storage in Embedded System Design?
15. What is the difference between Masked ROM and OTP?
16. What is the difference between PROM and EPROM?
17. What are the advantages of FLASH over other program storage memory in Embedded System design?
18. What is the difference between RAM and ROM?
19. What are the different types of RAM used for Embedded System design?
20. What is memory shadowing? What is its advantage?
21. What is Sensor? Explain its role in Embedded System Design? Illustrate with an example.
22. What is Actuator? Explain its role in Embedded System Design? Illustrate with an example.
23. What is Embedded Firmware? What are the different approaches available for Embedded Firmware development?
24. What is the difference between General Purpose Processor (GPP) and Application Specific Instruction Set Processor (ASIP). Give an example for both.
25. Explain the concept of Load Store architecture and instruction pipelining.
26. Explain the operation of Static RAM (SRAM) cell.
27. Explain the merits and limitations of SRAM and DRAM as Random Access Memory.
28. Explain the difference between Serial Access Memory (SAM) and Random Access Memory (RAM). Give an example for both.
29. Explain the different factors that needs to be considered in the selection of memory for Embedded Systems.
30. Explain the different types of FLASH memory and their relative merits and de-merits.
31. Explain the different Input and output subsystems of Embedded Systems.
32. What is stepper motor? How is it different from ordinary dc motor?
33. Explain the role of Stepper motor in embedded applications with examples.
34. Explain the different step modes for stepper motor.
35. What is Relay? What are the different types of relays available? Explain the role of relay in embedded applications.
36. Explain the operation of the transistor based Relay driver circuit.
37. Explain the operation of a Matrix Keyboard.
38. What is Programmable Peripheral Interface (PPI) Device? Explain the interfacing of 8255 PPI with an 8bit microprocessor/controller.
39. Explain the different on-board communication interfaces in brief.
40. Explain the different external communication interfaces in brief.
41. Explain the sequence of operation for communicating with an I2C slave device.
42. Explain the difference between I2C and SPI communication interface.
43. Explain the sequence of operation for communicating with a 1-Wire slave device.
44. Explain the RS-232 C serial interface in detail.
45. Explain the merits and limitations of Parallel port over Serial RS-232 interface.
46. Explain the merits and limitations of IEEE1394 interface over USB.
47. Compare the operation of ZigBee and Wi-Fi network.
48. Explain the role of Reset circuit in Embedded System.
49. Explain the role of Real Time Clock (RTC) in Embedded System.
50. Explain the role of Watchdog Timer in Embedded System.

Lab Assignments

1. Write a 'C' program to find the *endianness* of the processor in which the program is running. If the processor is big endian, print "The processor architecture is Big endian", else print "The processor architecture is Little endian" on the console window. Execute the program separately on a PC with Windows, Linux and MAC operating systems.
2. Draw the interfacing diagram for connecting an LED to the port pin of a microcontroller. The LED is turned ON when the microcontroller port pin is at Logic '0'. Calculate the resistance required to connect in series with the LED for the following design parameters.
   (a) LED voltage drop on conducting = 1.7V
   (b) LED current rating = 20 mA
   (c) Power Supply Voltage = 5V
3. Design an RC (Resistor-Capacitor) based reset circuit for producing an active low Power-On reset pulse of width 0.1 milli seconds.
4. Design a zener diode and transistor based brown-out protection circuit with active low reset pulse for the following design parameters.
   (a) Use BC327 PNP transistor for the design
   (b) The supply voltage to the system is 5V
   (c) The reset pulse is asserted when the supply voltage falls below 4.7V

3 Characteristics and Quality Attributes of Embedded Systems

LEARNING OBJECTIVES

- ✓ *Learn the characteristics describing an embedded system*
- ✓ *Learn the non-functional requirements that needs to be addressed in the design of an embedded system*
- ✓ *Learn the important quality attributes of the embedded system that needs to be addressed for the operational mode (online mode) of the system. This includes Response, Throughput, Reliability, Maintainability, Security, Safety, etc.*
- ✓ *Learn the important quality attributes of the embedded system that needs to be addressed for the non-operational mode (offline mode) of the system. This includes Testability, Debug-ability, Evolvability, Portability, Time to prototype and market, Per unit cost and revenue, etc.*
- ✓ *Understand the Product Life Cycle (PLC)*

No matter whether it is an embedded or a non-embedded system, there will be a set of characteristics describing the system. The non-functional aspects that need to be addressed in embedded system design are commonly referred as quality attributes. Whenever you design an embedded system, the design should take into consideration of both the functional and non-functional aspects. The following topics give an overview of the characteristics and quality attributes of an embedded system.

3.1 CHARACTERISTICS OF AN EMBEDDED SYSTEM

Unlike general purpose computing systems, embedded systems possess certain specific characteristics and these characteristics are unique to each embedded system. Some of the important characteristics of an embedded system are:

1. Application and domain specific
2. Reactive and Real Time
3. Operates in harsh environments
4. Distributed
5. Small size and weight
6. Power concerns

3.1.1 Application and Domain Specific

If you closely observe any embedded system, you will find that each embedded system is having certain functions to perform and they are developed in such a manner to do the intended functions only. They cannot be used for any other purpose. It is the major criterion which distinguishes an embedded system from a general purpose system. For example, you cannot replace the embedded control unit of your microwave oven with your air conditioner's embedded control unit, because the embedded control units of microwave oven and airconditioner are specifically designed to perform certain specific tasks. Also you cannot replace an embedded control unit developed for a particular domain say telecom with another control unit designed to serve another domain like consumer electronics.

3.1.2 Reactive and Real Time

As mentioned earlier, embedded systems are in constant interaction with the Real world through sensors and user-defined input devices which are connected to the input port of the system. Any changes happening in the Real world (which is called an Event) are captured by the sensors or input devices in Real Time and the control algorithm running inside the unit reacts in a designed manner to bring the controlled output variables to the desired level. The event may be a periodic one or an unpredicted one. If the event is an unpredicted one then such systems should be designed in such a way that it should be scheduled to capture the events without missing them. Embedded systems produce changes in output in response to the changes in the input. So they are generally referred as Reactive Systems.

Real Time System operation means the timing behaviour of the system should be deterministic; meaning the system should respond to requests or tasks in a known amount of time. A Real Time system should not miss any deadlines for tasks or operations. It is not necessary that all embedded systems should be Real Time in operations. Embedded applications or systems which are mission critical, like flight control systems, Antilock Brake Systems (ABS), etc. are examples of Real Time systems. The design of an embedded Real time system should take the worst case scenario into consideration.

3.1.3 Operates in Harsh Environment

It is not necessary that all embedded systems should be deployed in controlled environments. The environment in which the embedded system deployed may be a dusty one or a high temperature zone or an area subject to vibrations and shock. Systems placed in such areas should be capable to withstand all these adverse operating conditions. The design should take care of the operating conditions of the area where the system is going to implement. For example, if the system needs to be deployed in a high temperature zone, then all the components used in the system should be of high temperature grade. Here we cannot go for a compromise in cost. Also proper shock absorption techniques should be provided to systems which are going to be commissioned in places subject to high shock. Power supply fluctuations, corrosion and component aging, etc. are the other factors that need to be taken into consideration for embedded systems to work in harsh environments.

3.1.4 Distributed

The term distributed means that embedded systems may be a part of larger systems. Many numbers of such distributed embedded systems form a single large embedded control unit. An automatic vending machine is a typical example for this. The vending machine contains a card reader (for pre-paid vending systems), a vending unit, etc. Each of them are independent embedded units but they work together to perform the overall vending function. Another example is the Automatic Teller Machine (ATM). An ATM contains a card reader embedded unit, responsible for reading and validating the user's ATM card, transaction unit for performing transactions, a currency counter for dispatching/vending currency to the authorised person and a printer unit for printing the transaction details. We can visualise these as independent embedded systems. But they work together to achieve a common goal.

Another typical example of a distributed embedded system is the Supervisory Control And Data Acquisition (SCADA) system used in Control & Instrumentation applications, which contains physically distributed individual embedded control units connected to a supervisory module.

3.1.5 Small Size and Weight

Product aesthetics is an important factor in choosing a product. For example, when you plan to buy a new mobile phone, you may make a comparative study on the pros and corns of the products available in the market. Definitely the product aesthetics (size, weight, shape, style, etc.) will be one of the deciding factors to choose a product. People believe in the phrase "Small is beautiful". Moreover it is convenient to handle a compact device than a bulky product. In embedded domain also compactness is a significant deciding factor. Most of the application demands small sized and low weight products.

3.1.6 Power Concerns

Power management is another important factor that needs to be considered in designing embedded systems. Embedded systems should be designed in such a way as to minimise the heat dissipation by the system. The production of high amount of heat demands cooling requirements like cooling fans which in turn occupies additional space and make the system bulky. Nowadays ultra low power components are available in the market. Select the design according to the low power components like low dropout regulators, and controllers/processors with power saving modes. Also power management is a critical constraint in battery operated application. The more the power consumption the less is the battery life.

3.2 QUALITY ATTRIBUTES OF EMBEDDED SYSTEMS

Quality attributes are the non-functional requirements that need to be documented properly in any system design. If the quality attributes are more concrete and measurable it will give a positive impact on the system development process and the end product. The various quality attributes that needs to be addressed in any embedded system development are broadly classified into two, namely 'Operational Quality Attributes' and 'Non-Operational Quality Attributes'.

3.2.1 Operational Quality Attributes

The operational quality attributes represent the relevant quality attributes related to the embedded system when it is in the operational mode or 'online' mode. The important quality attributes coming under this category are listed below:

1. Response
2. Throughput
3. Reliability
4. Maintainability
5. Security
6. Safety

3.2.1.1 Response Response is a measure of quickness of the system. It gives you an idea about how fast your system is tracking the changes in input variables. Most of the embedded systems demand fast response which should be almost Real Time. For example, an embedded system deployed in flight control application should respond in a Real Time manner. Any response delay in the system will create potential damages to the safety of the flight as well as the passengers. It is not necessary that all embedded systems should be Real Time in response. For example, the response time requirement for an electronic toy is not at all time-critical. There is no specific deadline that this system should respond within this particular timeline.

3.2.1.2 Throughput Throughput deals with the efficiency of a system. In general it can be defined as the rate of production or operation of a defined process over a stated period of time. The rates can be expressed in terms of units of products, batches produced, or any other meaningful measurements. In the case of a Card Reader, throughput means how many transactions the Reader can perform in a minute or in an hour or in a day. Throughput is generally measured in terms of 'Benchmark'. A 'Benchmark' is a reference point by which something can be measured. Benchmark can be a set of performance criteria that a product is expected to meet or a standard product that can be used for comparing other products of the same product line.

3.2.1.3 Reliability Reliability is a measure of how much % you can rely upon the proper functioning of the system or what is the % susceptibility of the system to failures.

Mean Time Between Failures (MTBF) and Mean Time To Repair (MTTR) are the terms used in defining system reliability. MTBF gives the frequency of failures in hours/weeks/months. MTTR specifies how long the system is allowed to be out of order following a failure. For an embedded system with critical application need, it should be of the order of minutes.

3.2.1.4 Maintainability Maintainability deals with support and maintenance to the end user or client in case of technical issues and product failures or on the basis of a routine system checkup. Reliability and maintainability are considered as two complementary disciplines. A more reliable system means a system with less corrective maintainability requirements and vice versa. As the reliability of the system increases, the chances of failure and non-functioning also reduces, thereby the need for maintainability is also reduced. Maintainability is closely related to the system availability. Maintainability can be broadly classified into two categories, namely, 'Scheduled or Periodic Maintenance (preventive maintenance)' and 'Maintenance to unexpected failures (corrective maintenance)'. Some embedded products may use consumable components or may contain components which are subject to wear and tear and they should be replaced on a periodic basis. The period may be based on the total hours of the system usage or the total output the system delivered. A printer is a typical example for illustrating the two types of maintainability. An inkjet printer uses ink cartridges, which are consumable components and as per the printer manufacturer the end user should replace the cartridge after each '*n*' number of printouts to get quality prints. This is an example for '**Scheduled or Periodic maintenance**'. If the paper feeding part of the printer fails the printer fails to print and it requires immediate repairs to rectify this problem. This is an example of '**Maintenance to unexpected failure**'. In both of the maintenances (scheduled and repair), the printer needs to be brought offline and during this time it will not be available for the user. Hence it is obvious that maintainability is simply an indication of the availability of the product for use. In any embedded system design, the ideal value for availability is expressed as

$$A_i = \text{MTBF}/(\text{MTBF} + \text{MTTR})$$

where A_i = Availability in the ideal condition, MTBF = Mean Time Between Failures, and MTTR = Mean Time To Repair

3.2.1.5 Security Confidentiality, 'Integrity', and 'Availability' (The term 'Availability' mentioned here is not related to the term 'Availability' mentioned under the 'Maintainability' section) are the three major measures of information security. Confidentiality deals with the protection of data and application from unauthorised disclosure. Integrity deals with the protection of data and application from unauthorised modification. Availability deals with protection of data and application from unauthorized users. A very good example of the 'Security' aspect in an embedded product is a Personal Digital Assistant (PDA). The PDA can be either a shared resource (e.g. PDAs used in LAB setups) or an individual one. If it is a shared one there should be some mechanism in the form of a user name and password to access into a particular person's profile–This is an example of 'Availability'. Also all data and applications present in the PDA need not be accessible to all users. Some of them are specifically accessible to administrators only. For achieving this, Administrator and user levels of security should be implemented –An example of Confidentiality. Some data present in the PDA may be visible to all users but there may not be necessary permissions to alter the data by the users. That is Read Only access is allocated to all users–An example of Integrity.

3.2.1.6 Safety 'Safety' and 'Security' are two confusing terms. Sometimes you may feel both of them as a single attribute. But they represent two unique aspects in quality attributes. Safety deals with the possible damages that can happen to the operators, public and the environment due to the breakdown of an embedded system or due to the emission of radioactive or hazardous materials from the embedded products. The breakdown of an embedded system may occur due to a hardware failure or a firmware failure. Safety analysis is a must in product engineering to evaluate the anticipated damages and determine the best course of action to bring down the consequences of the damages to an acceptable level. As stated before, some of the safety threats are sudden (like product breakdown) and some of them are gradual (like hazardous emissions from the product).

3.2.2 Non-Operational Quality Attributes

The quality attributes that needs to be addressed for the product 'not' on the basis of operational aspects are grouped under this category. The important quality attributes coming under this category are listed below.

1. Testability & Debug-ability
2. Evolvability
3. Portability
4. Time to prototype and market
5. Per unit and total cost.

3.2.2.1 Testability & Debug-ability Testability deals with how easily one can test his/her design, application and by which means he/she can test it. For an embedded product, testability is applicable to both the embedded hardware and firmware. Embedded hardware testing ensures that the peripherals and the total hardware functions in the desired manner, whereas firmware testing ensures that the firmware is functioning in the expected way. Debug-ability is a means of debugging the product as such for figuring out the probable sources that create unexpected behaviour in the total system. Debug-ability has two aspects in the embedded system development context, namely, hardware level debugging and firmware level debugging. Hardware debugging is used for figuring out the issues created by hardware problems whereas firmware debugging is employed to figure out the probable errors that appear as a result of flaws in the firmware.

3.2.2.2 Evolvability Evolvability is a term which is closely related to Biology. Evolvability is referred as the non-heritable variation. For an embedded system, the quality attribute 'Evolvability' refers to the ease with which the embedded product (including firmware and hardware) can be modified to take advantage of new firmware or hardware technologies.

3.2.2.3 Portability Portability is a measure of 'system independence'. An embedded product is said to be portable if the product is capable of functioning 'as such' in various environments, target processors/controllers and embedded operating systems. The ease with which an embedded product can be ported on to a new platform is a direct measure of the re-work required. A standard embedded product should always be flexible and portable. In embedded products, the term 'porting' represents the migration of the embedded firmware written for one target processor (e.g. Intel x86) to a different target processor (say Hitachi SH3 processor). If the firmware is written in a high level language like 'C' with little target processor-specific functions (operating system extensions or compiler specific utilities), it is very easy to port the firmware for the new processor by replacing those 'target processor-specific functions' with the ones for the new target processor and re-compiling the program for the new target processor-specific settings. Re-compiling the program for the new target processor generates the new target processor-specific machine codes. If the firmware is written in Assembly Language for a particular family of processor (say x86 family), it will be very difficult to translate the assembly language instructions to the new target processor specific language and so the portability is poor.

If you look into various programming languages for application development for desktop applications, you will see that certain applications developed on certain languages run only on specific operating systems and some of them run independent of the desktop operating systems. For example, applications developed using Microsoft technologies (e.g. Microsoft Visual C++ using Visual studio) is capable of running only on Microsoft platforms and will not function on other operating systems; whereas applications developed using 'Java' from Sun Microsystems works on any operating system that supports Java standards.

3.2.2.4 Time-to-Prototype and Market Time-to-market is the time elapsed between the conceptualisation of a product and the time at which the product is ready for selling (for commercial product) or use (for non-commercial products). The commercial embedded product market is highly competitive and time to market the product is a critical factor in the success of a commercial embedded product. There may be multiple players in the embedded industry who develop products of the same category (like mobile phone, portable media players, etc.). If you come up with a new design and if it takes long time to develop and market it, the competitor product may take advantage of it with their product. Also, embedded technology is one where rapid technology change is happening. If you start your design by making use of a new technology and if it takes long time to develop and market the product, by the time you market the product, the technology might have superseded with a new technology. Product prototyping helps a lot in reducing time-to-market. Whenever you have a product idea, you may not be certain about the feasibility of the idea. Prototyping is an informal kind of rapid product development in which the important features of the product under consideration are developed. The time to prototype is also another critical factor. If the prototype is developed faster, the actual estimated development time can be brought down significantly. In order to shorten the time to prototype, make use of all possible options like the use of off-the-shelf components, re-usable assets, etc.

3.2.2.5 Per Unit Cost and Revenue Cost is a factor which is closely monitored by both end user (those who buy the product) and product manufacturer (those who build the product). Cost is a highly sensitive factor for commercial products. Any failure to position the cost of a commercial product at a nominal rate, may lead to the failure of the product in the market. Proper market study and cost benefit analysis should be carried out before taking a decision on the per-unit cost of the embedded product. From a designer/product development company perspective the ultimate aim of a product is to generate marginal profit. So the budget and total system cost should be properly balanced to provide a marginal profit. Every embedded product has a product life cycle which starts with the design and development phase. The product idea generation, prototyping, Roadmap definition, actual product design and development are the activities carried out during this phase. During the design and development phase there is only investment and no returns. Once the product is ready to sell, it is introduced to the market. This stage is known as the Product Introduction stage. During the initial period the sales and revenue will be low. There won't be much competition and the product sales and revenue increases with time. In the growth phase, the product grabs high market share. During the maturity phase, the growth and sales will be steady and the revenue reaches at its peak. The Product Retirement/Decline phase starts with the drop in sales volume, market share and revenue. The decline happens due to various reasons like competition from similar product with enhanced features or technology changes, etc. At some point of the decline stage, the manufacturer announces discontinuing of the product. The different stages of the embedded products life cycle–revenue, unit cost and profit in each stage–are represented in the following Product Life-cycle graph.

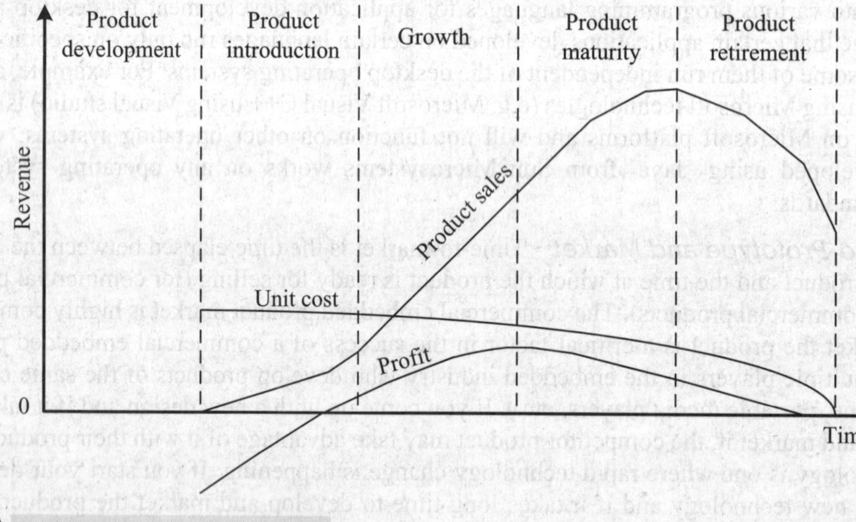

Fig. 3.1 **Product life cycle (PLC) curve**

From the graph, it is clear that the total revenue increases from the product introduction stage to the product maturity stage. The revenue peaks at the maturity stage and starts falling in the decline/retirement stage. The unit cost is very high during the introductory stage (a typical example is cell phone; if you buy a new model of cell phone during its launch time, the price will be high and you will get the same model with a very reduced price after three or four months of its launching). The profit increases with increase in sales and attains a steady value and then falls with a dip in sales. You can see a negative value for profit during the initial period. It is because during the product development phase there is only investment and no returns. Profit occurs only when the total returns exceed the investment and operating cost.

Summary

- ✓ There exists a set of characteristics which are unique to each embedded system.
- ✓ Embedded systems are application and domain specific.
- ✓ Quality attributes of a system represents the non-functional requirements that need to be documented properly in any system design.
- ✓ The operational quality attributes of an embedded system refers to the non-functional requirements that needs to be considered for the operational mode of the system. Response, Throughput, Reliability, Maintainability, Security, Safety, etc. are examples of operational quality attributes.
- ✓ The non-operational quality attributes of an embedded system refers to the non-functional requirements that needs to be considered for the non-operational mode of the system. Testability, debug-ability, evolvability, portability, time-to-prototype and market, per unit cost and revenue, etc. are examples of non-operational quality attributes.
- ✓ The product life cycle curve (PLC) is the graphical representation of the unit cost, product sales and profit with respect to the various life cycle stages of the product starting from conception to disposal.
- ✓ For a commercial embedded product, the unit cost is peak at the introductory stage and it falls in the maturity stage.
- ✓ The revenue of a commercial embedded product is at the peak during the maturity stage.

Keywords

Quality attributes : The non-functional requirements that need to be addressed in any system design

Reactive system : An embedded system which produces changes in output in response to the changes in input

Real-Time system : A system which adheres to strict timing behaviour and responds to requests in a known amount of time

Response : It is a measure of quickness of the system

Throughput : The rate of production or operation of a defined process over a stated period of time

Reliability : It is a measure of how much % one can rely upon the proper functioning of a system

MTBF : Mean Time Between Failures–The frequency of failures in hours/weeks/months

MTTR : Mean Time To Repair–Specifies how long the system is allowed to be out of order following a failure

Time-to-prototype : A measure of the time required to prototype a design

Product life-cycle (PLC) : The representation of the different stages of a product from its conception to disposal

Product life cycle curve : The graphical representation of the unit cost, product sales and profit with respect to the various life cycle stages of the product starting from conception to disposal

Objective Questions

1. Embedded systems are application and domain specific. State True or False
   (a) True (b) False
2. Which of the following is true about Embedded Systems?
   (a) Reactive and Real Time (b) Distributed (c) Operates in harsh environment
   (d) All of these (e) None of these
3. Which of the following is a distributed embedded system?
   (a) Cell phone (b) Notebook Computer (c) SCADA system (d) All of these
   (e) None of these
4. Quality attributes of an embedded system are
   (a) Functional requirements (b) Non-functional requirements
   (c) Both (d) None of these
5. Response is a measure of
   (a) Quickness of the system (b) How fast the system tracks changes in Input
   (c) Both (d) None of these
6. Throughput of an embedded system is a measure of
   (a) The efficiency of the system (b) The output over a stated period of time
   (c) Both (d) None of these
7. Benchmark is
   (a) A reference point (b) A set of performance criteria
   (c) (a) or (b) (d) None of these
8. Mean Time Between Failures (MTBF) and Mean Time To Repair (MTTR) defines the reliability of an embedded system. State True or False
   (a) True (b) False
9. MTBF gives the frequency of failures of an embedded system. State True or False
   (a) True (b) False
10. Which of the following is true about the quality attribute 'maintainability'?
    (a) The corrective maintainability requirement for a highly reliable embedded system is very less
    (b) Availability of an embedded system is directly related to the maintainability of the system
    (c) Both of these
    (d) None of these
11. The Mean Time Between Failure (MTBF) for an embedded product is very high. This means:
    (a) The product is highly reliable
    (b) The availability of the product is very high
    (c) The preventive maintenance requirement for the product is very less
    (d) All of these
    (e) None of these
12. The Mean Time Between Failure (MTBF) of an embedded product is 4 months and the Mean Time To Repair (MTTR) of the product is 2 weeks. What is the availability of the product?
    (a) 100% (b) 50% (c) 89% (d) 10%
13. Which of the following are the three measures of information security in embedded systems?
    (a) Confidentiality, secrecy, integrity (b) Confidentiality, integrity, availability
    (c) Confidentiality, transparency, availability (d) Integrity, transparency, availability

14. You are working on a mission critical embedded system development project for a client and the client and your company has signed a Non Disclosure Agreement (NDA) on the disclosure of the project-related information. You share the details of the project you are working with your friend. Which aspect of Information security you are violating here?
    (a) Integrity (b) Confidentiality (c) Availability (d) None of these
15. Which of the following is an example of 'gradual' safety threat from an embedded system?
    (a) Product blast due to overheating of the battery (b) UV emission from the embedded product
    (c) Both of these (d) None of these
16. Non operational quality attributes are
    (a) Non-functional requirements (b) Functional requirements
    (c) Quality attributes for an offline product (d) (a) and (c)
    (e) None of these
17. Which of the following is (are) an operational quality attribute?
    (a) Testability (b) Safety (c) Debug-ability (d) Portability
    (e) All of these
18. Which of the following is (are) non-operational quality attribute?
    (a) Reliability (b) Safety (c) Maintainability (d) Portability
    (e) All of these (f) None of these
19. In the Information security context, Confidentiality deals with the protection of data and application from unauthorised disclosure. State True or False
    (a) True (b) False
20. What are the two different aspects of debug-ability in the embedded system development context?
    (a) Hardware & Firmware debug-ability (b) Firmware & Software debug-ability
    (c) None of these
21. For an embedded system, the quality attribute 'Evolvability' refers to
    (a) The upgradability of the product (b) The modifiability of the product
    (c) Both of these (d) None of these
22. Portability is a measure of 'system independence'. State True or False
    (a) True (b) False
23. For a commercial embedded product the *unit cost* is high during
    (a) Product launching (b) Product maturity
    (c) Product growth (d) Product discontinuing
24. For a commercial embedded product the sales volume is high during
    (a) Product launching (b) Product maturity
    (c) Product growth (d) Product discontinuing

Review Questions

1. Explain the different characteristics of embedded systems in detail.
2. Explain quality attribute in the embedded system development context? What are the different Quality attributes to be considered in an embedded system design.
3. What is operational quality attribute? Explain the important operational quality attributes to be considered in any embedded system design.
4. What is non-operational quality attribute? Explain the important non-operational quality attributes to be considered in any embedded system design.
5. Explain the quality attribute *Response* in the embedded system design context.
6. Explain the quality attribute *Throughput* in the embedded system design context.

7. Explain the quality attribute *Reliability* in the embedded system design context.
8. Explain the quality attribute *Maintainability* in the embedded system design context.
9. The availability of an embedded product is 90%. The Mean Time Between Failure (MTBF) of the product is 30 days. What is the Mean Time To Repair (MTTR) in days/hours for the product?
10. Explain the quality attribute *Information Security* in the embedded system design context.
11. Explain the quality attribute *Safety* in the embedded system design context.
12. Explain the significance of the quality attributes *Testability and Debug-ability* in the embedded system design context.
13. Explain the quality attribute *Portability* in the embedded system design context.
14. Explain *Time-to-market*? What is its significance in product development?
15. Explain *Time-to-prototype*? What is its significance in product development?
16. Explain the *Product Life-cycle* curve of an embedded product development.

4 Embedded Systems—Application- and Domain-Specific

LEARNING OBJECTIVES

- ✓ *Illustrate the domain and application specific aspect of embedded systems with examples*
- ✓ *Know the presence of embedded systems in automotive industry*
- ✓ *Learn about High Speed Electronic Control Units (HECUs) and Low Speed Electronic Control Units (LECUs) employed in automotive applications*
- ✓ *Learn about the Controller Area Network (CAN), Local Interconnect Network (LIN) and Media Oriented System Transport (MOST) communication buses used in automotive applications*
- ✓ *Know the semiconductor chip providers, tools and platform providers and solution providers for automotive embedded applications*

As mentioned in the previous chapter on the characteristics of embedded systems, embedded systems are application and domain specific, meaning; they are specifically built for certain applications in certain domains like consumer electronics, telecom, automotive, industrial control, etc. In general purpose computing, it is possible to replace a system with another system which is closely matching with the existing system, whereas it is not the case with embedded systems. Embedded systems are highly specialised in functioning and are dedicated for a specific application. Hence it is not possible to replace an embedded system developed for a specific application in a specific domain with another embedded system designed for some other application in some other domain. The following sections are intended to give the readers some idea on the application and domain specific characteristics of embedded systems.

4.1 WASHING MACHINE—APPLICATION-SPECIFIC EMBEDDED SYSTEM

People experience the power of embedded systems and enjoy the features and comfort provided by them, but they are totally unaware or ignorant of the intelligent embedded players working behind the products providing enhanced features and comfort. Washing machine is a typical example of an embedded system providing extensive support in home automation applications (Fig. 4.1).

As mentioned in an earlier chapter, an embedded system contains sensors, actuators, control unit and application-specific user interfaces like keyboards, display units, etc. You can see all these components in a washing machine if you have a closer look at it. Some of them are visible and some of them may be invisible to you.

The actuator part of the washing machine consists of a motorised agitator, tumble tub, water drawing pump and inlet valve to control the flow of water into the unit. The sensor part consists of the water temperature sensor, level sensor, etc. The control part contains a microprocessor/controller based board with interfaces to the sensors and actuators. The sensor data is fed back to the control unit and the control unit generates the necessary actuator outputs. The control unit also provides connectivity to user interfaces like keypad for setting the washing time, selecting the type of material to be washed like light, medium, heavy duty, etc. User feedback is reflected through the display unit and LEDs connected to the control board. The functional block diagram of a washing machine is shown in Fig. 4.2.

EWF 1495

Fig. 4.1 **Washing Machine – Typical example of an embedded system**
(Photo courtesy of Electrolux Corporation (www.electrolux.com/au))

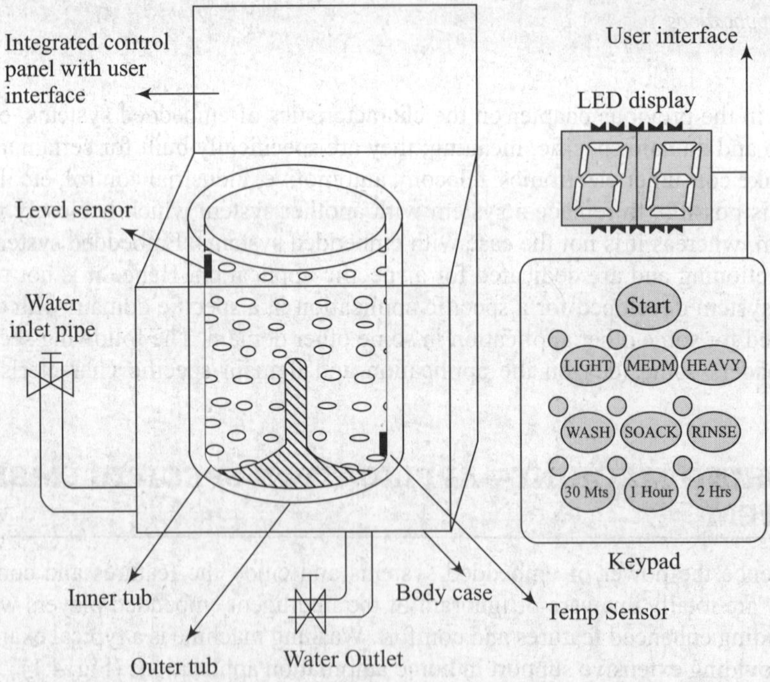

Fig. 4.2 **Washing machine – Functional block diagram**

Washing machine comes in two models, namely, top loading and front loading machines. In top loading models the agitator of the machine twists back and forth and pulls the cloth down to the bottom of the tub. On reaching the bottom of the tub the clothes work their way back up to the top of the tub where the agitator grabs them again and repeats the mechanism. In the front loading machines, the clothes are tumbled and plunged into the water over and over again. This is the first phase of washing.

In the second phase of washing, water is pumped out from the tub and the inner tub uses centrifugal force to wring out more water from the clothes by spinning at several hundred Rotations Per Minute (RPM). This is called a '*Spin Phase*'. If you look into the keyboard panel of your washing machine you can see three buttons namely* *Wash*, *Spin* and *Rinse*. You can use these buttons to configure the washing stages. As you can see from the picture, the inner tub of the machine contains a number of holes and during the spin cycle the inner tub spins, and forces the water out through these holes to the stationary outer tub from which it is drained off through the outlet pipe.

It is to be noted that the design of washing machines may vary from manufacturer to manufacturer, but the general principle underlying in the working of the washing machine remains the same. The basic controls consist of a timer, cycle selector mechanism, water temperature selector, load size selector and start button. The mechanism includes the motor, transmission, clutch, pump, agitator, inner tub, outer tub and water inlet valve. Water inlet valve connects to the water supply line using at home and regulates the flow of water into the tub.

The integrated control panel consists of a microprocessor/controller based board with I/O interfaces and a control algorithm running in it. Input interface includes the keyboard which consists of wash type selector namely* *Wash*, *Spin* and *Rinse*, cloth type selector namely* *Light*, *Medium*, *Heavy duty* and washing time setting, etc. The output interface consists of LED/LCD displays, status indication LEDs, etc. connected to the I/O bus of the controller. It is to be noted that this interface may vary from manufacturer to manufacturer and model to model. The other types of I/O interfaces which are invisible to the end user are different kinds of sensor interfaces, namely, water temperature sensor, water level sensor, etc. and actuator interface including motor control for agitator and tub movement control, inlet water flow control, etc.

4.2 AUTOMOTIVE – DOMAIN-SPECIFIC EXAMPLES OF EMBEDDED SYSTEM

The major application domains of embedded systems are consumer, industrial, automotive, telecom, etc., of which telecom and automotive industry holds a big market share.

Figure 4.3 gives an overview of the various types of electronic control units employed in automotive applications.

4.2.1 Inner Workings of Automotive Embedded Systems

Automotive embedded systems are the one where electronics take control over the mechanical systems. The presence of automotive embedded system in a vehicle varies from simple mirror and wiper controls to complex air bag controller and antilock brake systems (ABS). Automotive embedded systems are normally built around microcontrollers or DSPs or a hybrid of the two and are generally known as Electronic Control Units (ECUs). The number of embedded controllers in an ordinary vehicle varies

*Name may vary depending on the manufacturer.

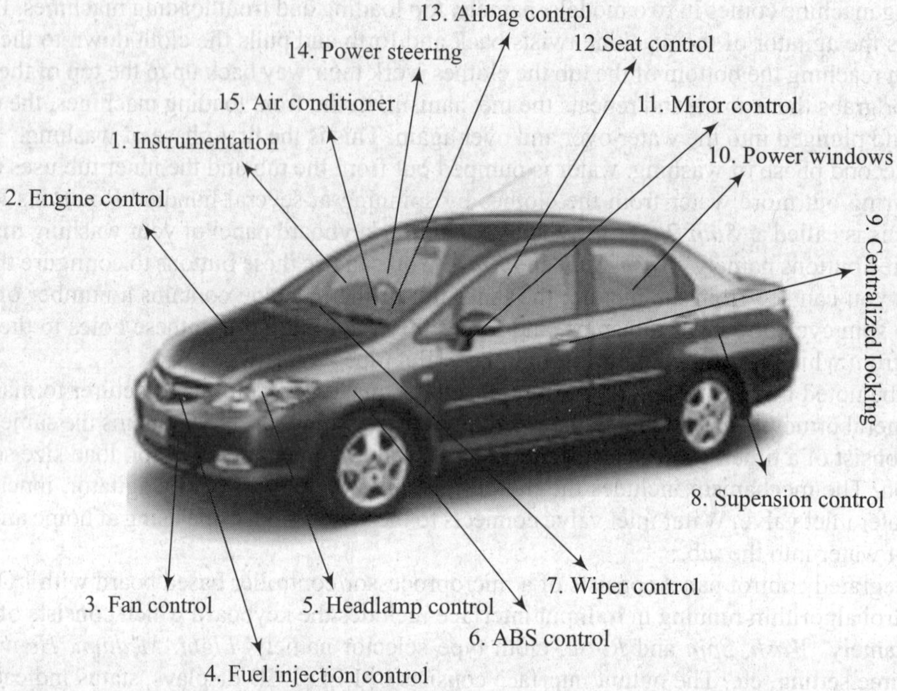

Fig. 4.3 Embedded system in the automotive domain
(Photo courtesy of Honda Siel Car India (www.hondacarindia.com))

from 20 to 40 whereas a luxury vehicle like Mercedes S and BMW 7 may contain 75 to 100 numbers of embedded controllers. Government regulations on fuel economy, environmental factors and emission standards and increasing customer demands on safety, comfort and infotainment forces the automotive manufactures to opt for sophisticated embedded control units within the vehicle. The first embedded system used in automotive application was the microprocessor based fuel injection system introduced by Volkswagen 1600 in 1968.

The various types of electronic control units (ECUs) used in the automotive embedded industry can be broadly classified into two–High-speed embedded control units and Low-speed embedded control units.

4.2.1.1 High-speed Electronic Control Units (HECUs) High-speed electronic control units (HECUs) are deployed in critical control units requiring fast response. They include fuel injection systems, antilock brake systems, engine control, electronic throttle, steering controls, transmission control unit and central control unit.

4.2.1.2 Low-speed Electronic Control Units (LECUs) Low-Speed Electronic Control Units (LECUs) are deployed in applications where response time is not so critical. They generally are built around low cost microprocessors/microcontrollers and digital signal processors. Audio controllers, passenger and driver door locks, door glass controls (power windows), wiper control, mirror control, seat control systems, head lamp and tail lamp controls, sun roof control unit etc. are examples of LECUs.

4.2.2 Automotive Communication Buses

Automotive applications make use of serial buses for communication, which greatly reduces the amount of wiring required inside a vehicle. The following section will give you an overview of the different types of serial interface buses deployed in automotive embedded applications.

4.2.2.1 Controller Area Network (CAN) The CAN bus was originally proposed by Robert Bosch, pioneer in the Automotive embedded solution providers. It supports medium speed (ISO11519-class B with data rates up to 125 Kbps) and high speed (ISO11898 class C with data rates up to 1Mbps) data transfer. CAN is an event-driven protocol interface with support for error handling in data transmission. It is generally employed in safety system like airbag control; power train systems like engine control and Antilock Brake System (ABS); and navigation systems like GPS. The protocol format and interface application development for CAN bus will be explained in detail in another volume of this book series.

4.2.2.2 Local Interconnect Network (LIN) LIN bus is a single master multiple slave (up to 16 independent slave nodes) communication interface. LIN is a low speed, single wire communication interface with support for data rates up to 20 Kbps and is used for sensor/actuator interfacing. LIN bus follows the master communication triggering technique to eliminate the possible bus arbitration problem that can occur by the simultaneous talking of different slave nodes connected to a single interface bus. LIN bus is employed in applications like mirror controls, fan controls, seat positioning controls, window controls, and position controls where response time is not a critical issue.

4.2.2.3 Media-Oriented System Transport (MOST) Bus The Media-oriented system transport (MOST) is targeted for automotive audio/video equipment interfacing, used primarily in European cars. A MOST bus is a multimedia fibre-optic point-to-point network implemented in a star, ring or daisy-chained topology over optical fibre cables. The MOST bus specifications define the physical (electrical and optical parameters) layer as well as the application layer, network layer, and media access control. MOST bus is an optical fibre cable connected between the Electrical Optical Converter (EOC) and Optical Electrical Converter (OEC), which would translate into the optical cable MOST bus.

4.2.3 Key Players of the Automotive Embedded Market

The key players of the automotive embedded market can be visualised in three verticals namely, silicon providers, solution providers and tools and platform providers.

4.2.3.1 Silicon Providers Silicon providers are responsible for providing the necessary chips which are used in the control application development. The chip may be a standard product like microcontroller or DSP or ADC/DAC chips. Some applications may require specific chips and they are manufactured as Application Specific Integrated Chip (ASIC). The leading silicon providers in the automotive industry are:

Analog Devices (www.analog.com): Provider of world class digital signal processing chips, precision analog microcontrollers, programmable inclinometer/accelerometer, LED drivers, etc. for automotive signal processing applications, driver assistance systems, audio system, GPS/Navigation system, etc.

Xilinx (www.xilinx.com): Supplier of high performance FPGAs, CPLDs and automotive specific IP cores for GPS navigation systems, driver information systems, distance control, collision avoidance, rear seat entertainment, adaptive cruise control, voice recognition, etc.

Atmel (www.atmel.com): Supplier of cost-effective high-density Flash controllers and memories. Atmel provides a series of high performance microcontrollers, namely, ARM®[1], AVR®[2], and 80C51. A wide range of Application Specific Standard Products (ASSPs) for chassis, body electronics, security, safety and car infotainment and automotive networking products for CAN, LIN and FlexRay are also supplied by Atmel.

Maxim/Dallas (www.maxim-ic.com): Supplier of world class analog, digital and mixed signal products (Microcontrollers, ADC/DAC, amplifiers, comparators, regulators, etc), RF components, etc. for all kinds of automotive solutions.

NXP semiconductor (www.nxp.com): Supplier of 8/16/32 Flash microcontrollers.

Renesas (www.renesas.com): Provider of high speed microcontrollers and Large Scale Integration (LSI) technology for car navigation systems accommodating three transfer speeds: high, medium and low.

Texas Instruments (www.ti.com): Supplier of microcontrollers, digital signal processors and automotive communication control chips for Local Inter Connect (LIN) bus products.

Fujitsu (www.fmal.fujitsu.com): Supplier of fingerprint sensors for security applications, graphic display controller for instrumentation application, AGPS/GPS for vehicle navigation system and different types of microcontrollers for automotive control applications.

Infineon (www.infineon.com): Supplier of high performance microcontrollers and customised application specific chips.

NEC (www.nec.co.jp): Provider of high performance microcontrollers.

There are lots of other silicon manufactures which provides various automotive support systems like power supply, sensors/actuators, optoelectronics, etc. Describing all of them is out of the scope of this book. Readers are requested to use the Internet for finding more information on them.

4.2.3.2 Tools and Platform Providers Tools and platform providers are manufacturers and suppliers of various kinds of development tools and Real Time Embedded Operating Systems for developing and debugging different control unit related applications. Tools fall into two categories, namely embedded software application development tools and embedded hardware development tools. Sometimes the silicon suppliers provide the development suite for application development using their chip. Some third party suppliers may also provide development kits and libraries. Some of the leading suppliers of tools and platforms in automotive embedded applications are listed below.

ENEA (www.enea.com): Enea Embedded Technology is the developer of the OSE Real-Time operating system. The OSE RTOS supports both CPU and DSP and has also been specially developed to support multi-core and fault-tolerant system development.

The MathWorks (www.mathworks.com): It is the world's leading developer and supplier of technical software. It offers a wide range of tools, consultancy and training for numeric computation, visualisation, modelling and simulation across many different industries. MathWork's breakthrough product is MATLAB–a high-level programming language and environment for technical computation and numerical analysis. Together MATLAB, SIMULINK, Stateflow and Real-Time Workshop provide top quality tools for data analysis, test & measurement, application development and deployment, image processing and development of dynamic and reactive systems for DSP and control applications.

[1] ARM® is the registered trademark of ARM Holdings.
[2] AVR® is the registered trademark of Atmel Corporation.

Keil Software (www.keil.com**):** The Integrated Development Environment Keil Microvision from Keil software is a powerful embedded software design tool for 8051 & C166 family of microcontrollers.

Lauterbach (http://www.lauterbach.com/)**:** It is the world's number one supplier of debug tools, providing support for processors from multiple silicon vendors in the automotive market.

ARTiSAN (www.artisansw.com)**:** Is the leading supplier of collaborative modelling tools for requirement analysis, specification, design and development of complex applications.

Microsoft (www.microsoft.com)**:** It is a platform provider for automotive embedded applications. Microsoft's WindowsCE is a powerful RTOS platform for automotive applications. Automotive features are included in the new WinCE Version for providing support for automotive application developers.

4.2.3.3 Solution Providers Solution providers supply OEM and complete solution for automotive applications making use of the chips, platforms and different development tools. The major players of this domain are listed below.

Bosch Automotive (www.boschindia.com)**:** Bosch is providing complete automotive solution ranging from body electronics, diesel engine control, gasoline engine control, powertrain systems, safety systems, in-car navigation systems and infotainment systems.

DENSO Automotive (www.globaldensoproducts.com)**:** Denso is an Original Equipment Manufacturer (OEM) and solution provider for engine management, climate control, body electronics, driving control & safety, hybrid vehicles, embedded infotainment and communications.

Infosys Technologies (www.infosys.com)**:** Infosys is a solution provider for automotive embedded hardware and software. Infosys provides the competitive edge in integrating technology change through cost-effective solutions.

Delphi (www.delphi.com)**:** Delphi is the complete solution provider for engine control, safety, infotainment, etc., and OEM for spark plugs, bearings, etc.

……and many more. The list is incomplete. Describing all providers is out of the scope of this book.

Summary

- ✓ Embedded systems designed for a particular application for a specific domain cannot be replaced with another embedded system designed for another application for a different domain
- ✓ Consumer, industrial, automotive, telecom, etc. are the major application domains of embedded systems. Telecom and automotive industry are the two segments holding a big market share of embedded systems
- ✓ Automotive embedded systems are normally built around microcontrollers or DSPs or a hybrid of the two and are generally known as Electronic Control Units (ECUs)
- ✓ High speed Electronic Control Units (HECUs) are deployed in critical control units requiring fast response, like fuel injection systems, antilock brake system, etc.
- ✓ Low speed Electronic Control Units (LECUs) are deployed in applications where response time is not so critical. They are generally built around low cost microprocessors/microcontrollers and digital signal processors. Audio controllers, passenger and driver door locks, door glass controls, etc., are examples for LECUs.
- ✓ Automotive applications use serial buses for communication. Controller Area Network (CAN), Local Interconnect Network (LIN), Media Oriented System Transport (MOST) bus, etc. are the important automotive communication buses.

- ✓ CAN is an event driven serial protocol interface with support for error handling in data transmission. It is generally employed in safety system like airbag control, powertrain systems like engine control and Antilock Brake Systems (ABS).
- ✓ LIN bus is a single master multiple slave (up to 16 independent slave nodes) communication interface. LIN is a low speed, single wire communication interface with support for data rates up to 20Kbps and is used for sensor/actuator interfacing.
- ✓ The Media Oriented System Transport (MOST) bus is targeted for automotive audio video equipment interfacing. MOST bus is a multimedia fibre-optic point-to-point network implemented in a star, ring or daisy-chained topology over optical fibres cables
- ✓ The key players of the automotive embedded market can be classified into 'Silicon Providers', 'Tools and Platform Providers' and 'Solution Providers'

Keywords

ECU : Electronic Control Unit. The generic term for the embedded control units in automotive application

HECU : High-speed Electronic Control Unit. The high-speed embedded control unit deployed in automotive applications

LECU : Low-speed Electronic Control Unit. The low-speed embedded control unit deployed in automotive applications

CAN : Controller Area Network. An event driven serial protocol interface used primarily for automotive applications

LIN : Local Interconnect Network. A single master multiple slave, low speed serial bus used in automotive application

MOST : Media Oriented System Transport Bus. A multimedia fibre-optic point-to-point network implemented in a star, ring or daisy-chained topology over optical fibres cables

Objective Questions

1. In Automotive systems, High-speed Electronic Control Units (HECUs) are deployed in
   (a) Fuel injection systems (b) Antilock brake systems
   (c) Power windows (d) Wiper control (e) Only (a) and (b)
2. In Automotive systems, Low speed electronic control units (LECUs) are deployed in
   (a) Electronic throttle (b) Steering controls (c) Transmission control (d) Mirror control
3. The first embedded system used in automotive application is the microprocessor based fuel injection system introduced by ______ in 1968
   (a) BMW (b) Volkswagen 1600 (c) Benz E Class (d) KIA
4. CAN bus is an event driven protocol for communication. State True or False
   (a) True (b) False
5. Which of the following serial bus is (are) used for communication in Automotive Embedded Applications?
   (a) Controller Area Network (CAN) (b) Local Interconnect Network (LIN)
   (c) Media Oriented System Transport (MOST) bus (d) All of these (e) None of these
6. Which of the following is true about LIN bus?
   (a) Single master multiple slave interface (b) Low speed serial bus
   (c) Used for sensor/actuator interfacing (d) All of these (e) None of these

7. Which of the following is true about MOST bus?
   (a) Used for automotive audio video system interfacing
   (b) It is a fibre optic point-to-point network
   (c) It is implemented in star, ring or daisy-chained topology
   (d) All of these (e) None of these
8. Which of the following is (are) example(s) of Silicon providers for automotive applications?
   (a) Maxim/Dallas (b) Analog Devices (c) Xilinx (d) Atmel
   (e) All of these (f) None of these

Review Questions

1. Explain the role of embedded systems in automotive domain.
2. Explain the different electronic control units (ECUs) used in automotive systems.
3. Explain the different communication buses used in automotive application.
4. Give an overview of the different market players of the automotive embedded application domain.

5 Designing Embedded Systems with 8bit Microcontrollers—*8051*

LEARNING OBJECTIVES

- ✓ *Understand the different factors that need to be considered while selecting a microcontroller for an embedded design*
- ✓ *Know why 8051 is the popular choice for low cost low performance embedded system design*
- ✓ *Learn the A to Z of 8051 microcontroller architecture*
- ✓ *Learn the Internals of the 8051 microcontroller*
- ✓ *Learn the program memory and internal data memory organisation of 8051*
- ✓ *Learn the Paged Data memory access and Von-Neumann memory model implementation for 8051*
- ✓ *Learn about the organisation of lower 128 bytes RAM for data memory, upper 128 bytes RAM for SFR and upper 128bytes RAM for Internal Data memory (IRAM)*
- ✓ *Learn about the CPU registers and general purpose registers of 8051*
- ✓ *Learn about the Oscillator unit and speed of execution of 8051*
- ✓ *Learn about the different I/O ports, organisation of the ports, the internal implementation of the port pins, the different registers associated with the ports and the operation of ports*
- ✓ *Learn about interrupts and its significance in embedded applications*
- ✓ *Learn about the Interrupt System of 8051, the interrupts supported by 8051, interrupt priorities, different registers associated with configuring the interrupts, Interrupt Service Routine and their vector address*
- ✓ *Learn about the Timer/Counter units supported by 8051 and configuring the Timer unit for Timer/Counter operation. Learn the different registers associated with timer units and the different modes of operations supported by Timer/Counter units*
- ✓ *Learn about the Serial Port of the 8051, the different control, status and data registers associated with it*
- ✓ *Learn the different modes of operations supported by the Serial port and setting the baudrate for each mode*
- ✓ *Learn about the Power-On Reset circuit implementation for 8051*
- ✓ *Learn about the different power saving modes supported by 8051*
- ✓ *Learn the difference between 8051 and 8052*

A recent survey on the microcontroller industry reveals that 8bit microcontrollers account for more than 40% of the total sales in the microcontroller industry. Among the 8bit microcontrollers, the *8051* family is the most popular, cost effective and versatile device offering extensive support in the embedded application domain. Looking back to the history of microcontrollers you can find that the 8bit microcontroller industry has travelled a lot from its first popular model *8031AH* built by Intel in 1977 to the advanced 8bit microcontroller built by Maxim/Dallas recently, which offers high performance 4 Clock, 75MHz operation *8051* microcontroller core (Remember the original 8031 core was 12 Clock with support for a maximum system clock of 6MHz, so a performance improvement of 3 times on the original version in execution) with extensive support for networking by integrating 10/100 Ethernet MAC with IEEE 802.3 MMI, CAN bus for automotive application support, RS-232 C interface for legacy serial applications, SPI serial interface for board level device inter connect, 1-wire interface for connecting to low cost multi-drop sensors and actuators, and 16MB addressing space for code and data memory.

5.1 FACTORS TO BE CONSIDERED IN SELECTING A CONTROLLER

Selection of a microcontroller for any application depends on some design factors. A good designer finalises his selection based on a comparative study of the design factors. The important factors to be considered in the selection process of a microcontroller are listed below.

5.1.1 Feature Set

The important queries related to the feature set are: Does the microcontroller support all the peripherals required by the application, say serial interface, parallel interface, etc.? Does it satisfy the general I/O port requirements by the application? Does the controller support sufficient number of timers and counters? Does the controller support built-in ADC/DAC hardware in case of signal processing applications? Does the controller provide the required performance?

5.1.2 Speed of Operation

Speed of operation or performance of the controller is another important design factor. The number of clocks required per instruction cycle and the maximum operating clock frequency supported by the processor greatly affects the speed of operation of the controller. The speed of operation of the controller is usually expressed in terms of million instructions per second (MIPS).

5.1.3 Code Memory Space

If the target processor/controller application is written in C or any other high level language, does the controller support sufficient code memory space to hold the compiled hex code (In case of controllers with internal code memory)?

5.1.4 Data Memory Space

Does the controller support sufficient internal data memory (on chip RAM) to hold run time variables and data structures?

5.1.5 Development Support

Development support is another important factor for consideration. It deals with–Does the controller manufacture provide cost-effective development tools? Does the manufacture provide product samples for prototyping and sample development stuffs to alleviate the development pains? Does the controller support third party development tools? Does the manufacture provide technical support if necessary?

5.1.6 Availability

Availability is another important factor that should be taken into account for the selection process. Since the product is entirely dependent on the controller, the product development time and time to market the product solely depends on its availability. By technical terms it is referred to as *Lead time*. Lead time is the time elapsed between the purchase order approval and the supply of the product.

5.1.7 Power Consumption

The power consumption of the controller should be minimal. It is a crucial factor since high power requirement leads to bulky power supply designs. The high power dissipation also demands for cooling fans and it will make the overall system messy and expensive. Controllers should support idle and power down modes of operation to reduce power consumption.

5.1.8 Cost

Last but not least, cost is a big deciding factor in selecting a controller. The cost should be within the reachable limit of the end user and the targeted user should not be *high tech*. Remember the ultimate aim of a product is to *gain marginal benefit*.

5.2 WHY *8051* MICROCONTROLLER

8051 is a very versatile microcontroller featuring powerful Boolean processor which supports bit manipulation instructions for real time industrial control applications. The standard *8051* architecture supports 6 interrupts (2 external interrupts, 2 timer interrupts and 2 serial interrupts), two 16bit timers/counters, 32 I/O lines and a programmable full duplex serial interface. Another fascinating feature of *8051* is the way it handles interrupts. The interrupts have two priority levels and each interrupt is allocated fixed 8 bytes of code memory. This approach is very efficient in real time application. Though *8051* is invented by Intel, today it is available in the market from more than 20 vendors and with more than 100 variants of the original *8051* flavour, supporting CAN, USB, SPI and TCP/IP interfaces, integrated ADC/DAC, LCD Controller and extended number of I/O ports. Another remarkable feature of *8051* is its low cost. The *8051* flash microcontroller (*AT89C51*) from Atmel is available in the market for less than 1US$ per piece. So imagine its cost for high volume purchases.

5.3 DESIGNING WITH *8051*

5.3.1 The *8051* Architecture

The basic *8051* architecture consist of an 8bit CPU with Boolean processing capability, oscillator driver unit, 4K bytes of on-chip program memory, 128 bytes of internal data memory, 128 bytes of special function register memory area, 32 general purpose I/O lines organised into four 8bit bi-directional ports, two 16bit timer units and a full duplex programmable UART for serial data transmission with configurable baudrates. Figure 5.1 illustrates the basic 8051 architecture.

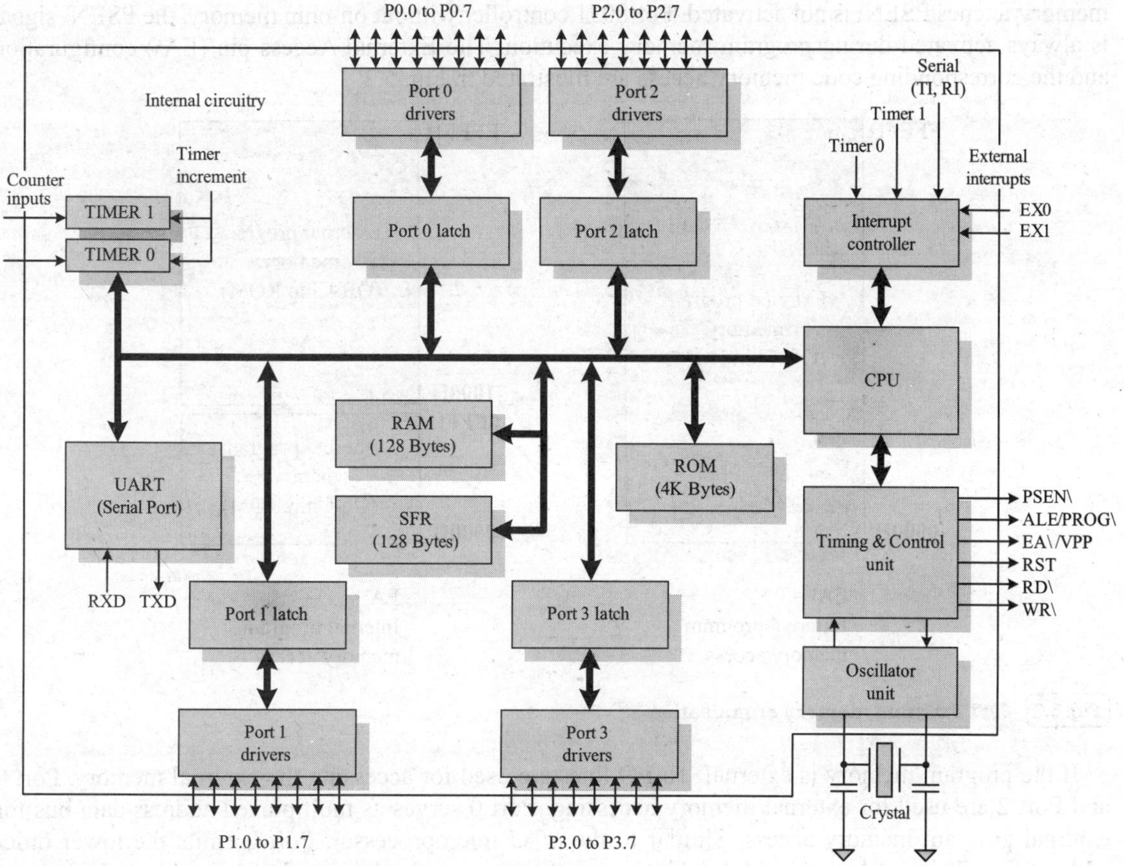

Fig. 5.1 **8051 Architecture—Block diagram representation**

5.3.2 The Memory Organisation

8051 is built around the *Harvard* processor architecture. The program and data memory of *8051* is logically separated and they physically reside separately. Separate address spaces are assigned for data memory and program memory. *8051*'s address bus is 16bit wide and it can address up to 64KB (2^{16}) memory.

5.3.2.1 The Program (Code) Memory The basic *8051* architecture provides lowest 4K bytes of program memory as on-chip memory (built-in chip memory). In *8031*, the ROMless counterpart of *8051*, all program memory is external to the chip. Switching between the internal program memory and external program memory is accomplished by changing the logic level of the pin External Access (EA\). Tying EA\ pin to logic 1 (V_{CC}), configures the chip to execute instructions from program memory up to 4K (program memory location up to 0FFFH) from internal memory and 4K (program memory location from 1000H) onwards from external memory, while connecting EA\ pin to logic 0 (GND) configures the chip to external program execution mode, where the entire code memory is executed from the external memory. Remember External Access pin is an active low pin (Normally referred as EA\). The control signal for external program memory execution is PSEN\ (Program Strobe Enable). For internal program memory fetches PSEN\ is not activated. For 8031 controller without on-chip memory, the PSEN\ signal is always activated during program memory execution. The External Access pin (EA\) configuration and the corresponding code memory access are illustrated in Fig. 5.2.

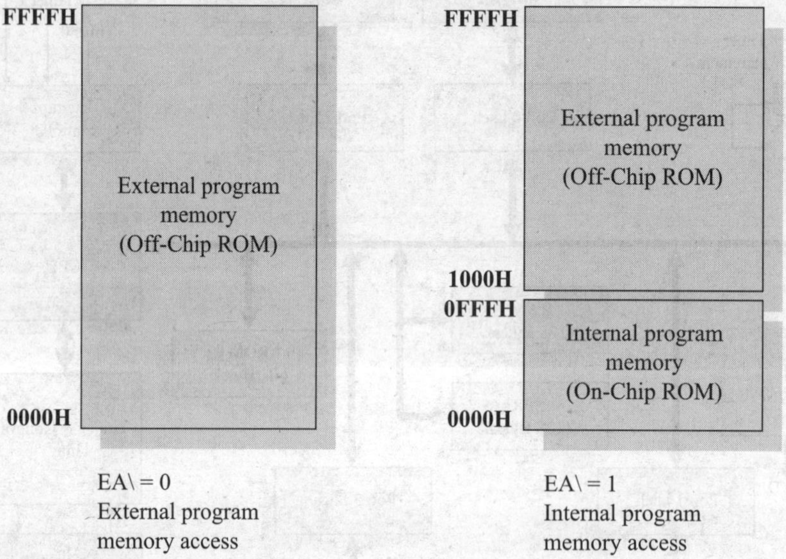

Fig. 5.2 ***8051* Program memory organisation**

If the program memory is external, 16 I/O lines are used for accessing the external memory. Port 0 and Port 2 are used for external memory accessing. Port 0 serves as multiplexed address/data bus for external program memory access. Similar to the *8085* microprocessor, Port 0 emits the lower order address first. This can be latched to an 8bit external latch with the Address Latch Enable (ALE) signal emitted by *8051*. Once the address outing is over, Port 0 functions as input port for data transfer from the corresponding memory location. The address from which the program instruction to be fetched is supplied by the 16bit register, Program Counter (PC), which is part of the CPU. The Program Counter is a 16bit register made up of two 8bit registers. The lower order byte of program counter register is held by the PCL register and higher order by the PCH register. PCL and PCH in combination serve as a 16bit register. During external program memory fetching, Port 0 emits the contents of PCL and Port 2 emits the contents of PCH register. Port 0 emits the contents of PCL only for a fixed duration allowing the external latch to hold the content on arrival of the ALE signal. Afterwards Port 0 goes into high impedance state, waiting for the arrival of data from the corresponding memory location of external memory. Whereas Port 2 continues emitting the contents of PCH register throughout the external memory fetch. Once the PSEN\ signal is active, data from the program memory is clocked into Port 0. Remember, during external program memory access Port 0 and Port 2 are dedicated for it and cannot be used as general purpose I/O ports. The interfacing of an external program memory chip is illustrated in Fig. 5.3.

5.3.2.2 The Data Memory The basic 8051 architecture supports 128 bytes of internal data memory and 128 bytes of *Special Function Register* memory. Special Function Register memory is not available for the user for general data memory applications. The address range for internal user data memory is 00H to 7FH. Special Function Registers are residing at memory area 80H to FFH. *8051* supports interface for 64 Kbytes of external data memory. The control signals used for external data memory

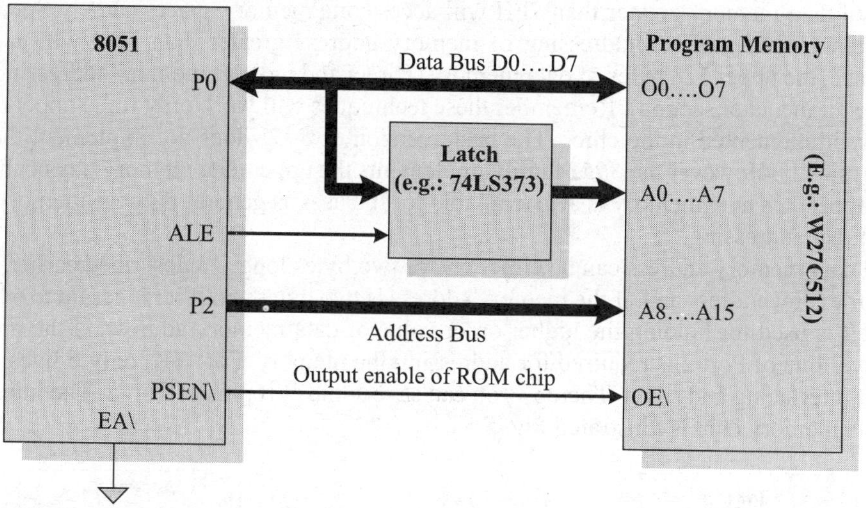

Fig. 5.3 **8051 External Program Memory chip (ROM) interfacing**

access are RD\ and WR\ and the 16bit register holding the address of external data memory address to be accessed is *Data Pointer* (*DPTR*). Similar to the Program Counter, the Data Pointer is also made up of two 8bit registers, namely, DPL (holding the lower order 8bit) and DPH (holding the higher order 8bit). The program counter is not accessible to the user whereas DPTR is accessible to the user and the contents of DPTR register can be modified. In external data memory operations, Port 0 emits the content of DPL and Port 2 emits the content of DPH. Port 0 is address/data multiplexed in external data memory operations also. The internal and external data memory model of *8051* is diagrammatically represented in Fig. 5.4.

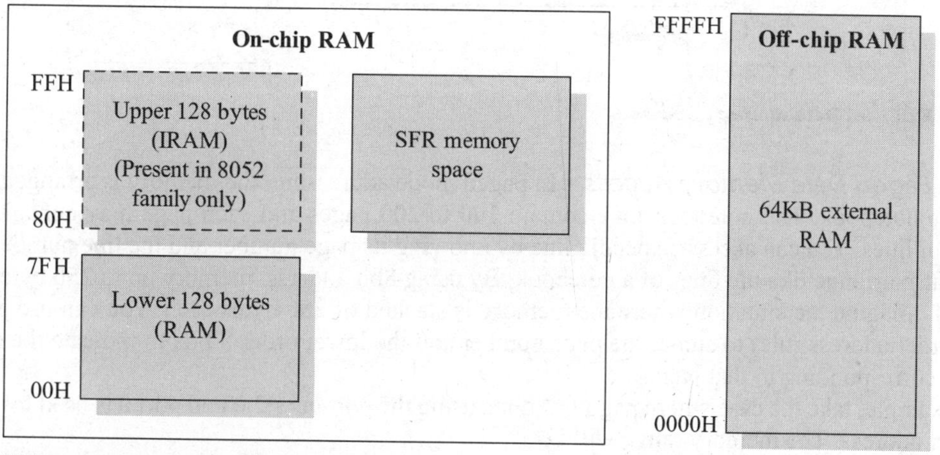

Fig. 5.4 **Data memory map for *8051***

Internal data memory addresses are always one byte long. So it can accommodate up to 256 bytes of internal data memory (Ranging from 0 to 255). However the addressing techniques used in *8051* can accommodate 384 bytes using a simple memory addressing technique. The technique is: Direct addressing of data memory greater than 7FH will access one memory space, namely Special Function Register memory and indirect addressing of memory address greater than 7FH will access another memory space, the upper 128 bytes of data memory (Direct and indirect memory addressing will be discussed in detail in a later section). Remember these techniques will work only if the upper data memory is physically implemented in the chip. The basic version of *8051* does not implement the upper data memory physically. However the *8052* family implements the upper data memory physically in the chip and so the upper 128 byte memory is also available for the user as general purpose memory, if accessed through indirect addressing.

External data memory address can be either one or two bytes long. As described earlier, Port 0 emits the lower order 8bit address and, if the memory address is two bytes and if it ranges up to 64K, the entire bits of Port 2 is used for holding the higher order value of data memory address. If the memory range is 32K, only 7 bits of Port 2 is required for addressing the memory. For 16K, only 6 lines of Port 2 are required for interfacing and so on. Thereby you can save some port pins of Port 2. The interfacing of an external data memory chip is illustrated Fig. 5.5.

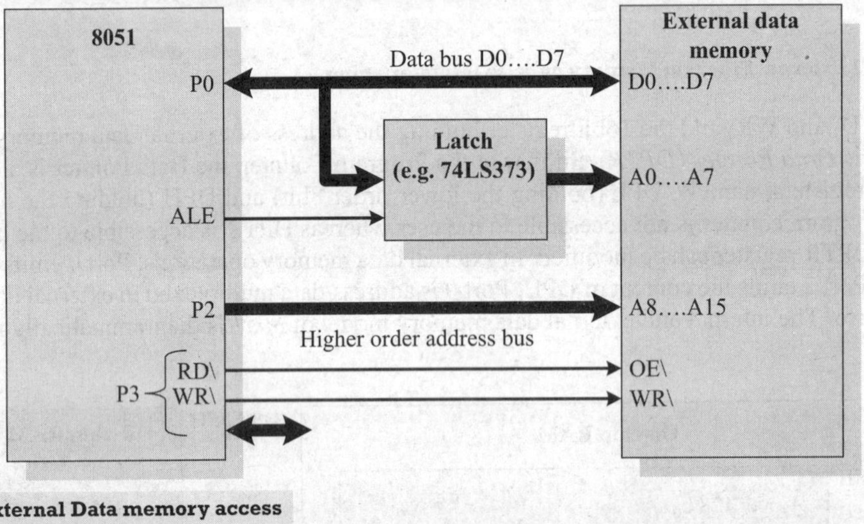

Fig. 5.5 External Data memory access

5.3.2.3 Paged Data Memory Access In paged mode addressing, the memory is arranged like the lines of a notebook. The notebook may contain 100 to 200 pages and each page may contain a fixed number of lines. You can access a specific line by knowing its page number and the line number. Memory can also arrange like the lines of a notebook. By using 8bit address, memory up to 256 bytes can be accessed. Imagine the situation where the memory is stacked of 256 bytes each. You can use port pins (High order address rule) to signal the page number and the lower order 8 bits to indicate the memory location corresponding to that page.

For example, take the case where paging is done using the port pin P2.0 and port 0 is used for holding the lower address. The memory range will be

Page selector (P2.0)	Lower order address	Address range
0	00H to FFH	000H to 0FFH
1	00H to FFH	100H to 1FFH

5.3.2.4 The Von-Neumann Memory Model for 8051 The code memory and data memory of *8051* can be combined together to give the Von-Neumann architectural benefit for *8051*. A single memory chip with read/write option can be used for this. The program memory can be allocated to the lower memory space starting from 0000H and data memory can be assigned to some other specific area after the code memory. For program memory fetching and data memory read operations combine the PSEN\ and RD\ signals using an AND gate and connect it to the Output Enable (OE\) signal of the memory chip as shown in Fig. 5.6.

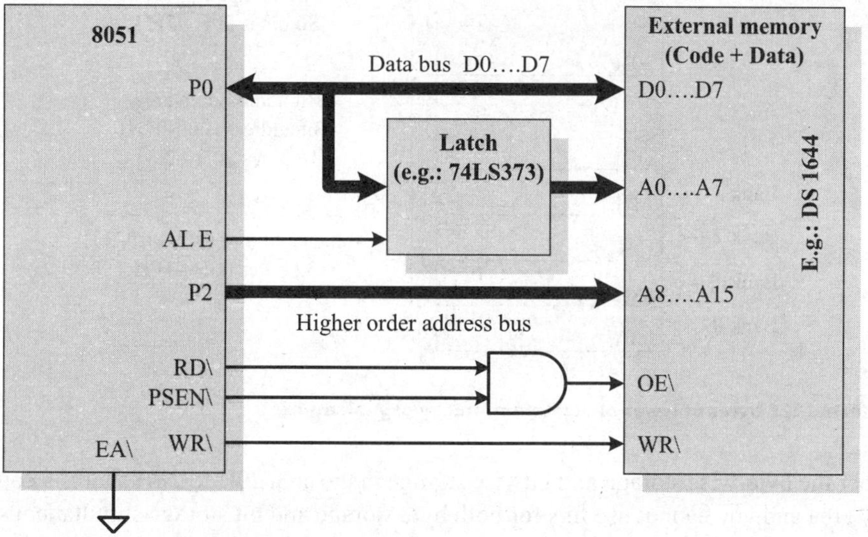

Fig. 5.6 **Combining Code memory and Data memory**

The Von-Neumann memory model is very helpful in evaluation boards for the controller, which allows modification of code memory on the fly. The major drawbacks of using a single chip for program and data memory are

- Accidental corruption of program memory
- Reduction in total memory space. In separate program and data memory model the total available memory is 128KB (64KB program memory + 64KB Data memory) whereas in the combined model the total available memory is only 64KB

5.3.2.5 Lower 128 Byte Internal Data Memory (RAM) Organisation This memory area is volatile; meaning the contents of these locations are not retained on power lose. On power up these memory locations contain random data. The lowest 32 bytes of RAM (00H to 1FH) are grouped into 4 banks of 8 registers each. These registers are known as R0 to R7 registers which are used as temporary data storage registers during program execution. The effective usage of these registers reduces the code memory requirement since register instructions are shorter than direct memory addressing instructions. The next 16 bytes of RAM with address 20H to 2FH is a bit addressable memory area. It accommodates 128 bits (16 bytes x 8), which can be accessed by direct bit addressing. The address of bits ranges from 00H to 7FH. This is very useful since 8051 is providing extensive support for Boolean operations (Bit Manipulation Operations). Also it saves memory since flag variables can be set up with these bits and there is no need to waste one full byte of memory for setting up a flag variable. These 16 bytes can also be used as byte variables. The context in which these bytes are used as either byte variable or bit variable is determined by the type of instruction. If the instruction is a bit manipulation instruction and the operand is given as a direct address in the range 00H to 7FH, it is treated as a bit variable. The lower 128 bytes of internal RAM for *8051* family members is organised as shown in Fig. 5.7.

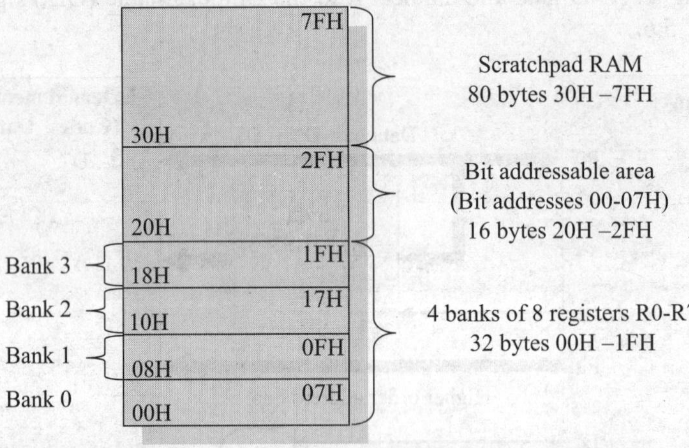

Fig. 5.7 **Internal 128 bytes of lower order data memory organisation**

Remember the byte-wise storage and bitwise storage in the area 20H to 2FH shares a common physical memory area and you cannot use this for both byte storage and bit storage simultaneously. If you do so, depending on the usage, the byte variables and bit variables may get corrupted and it may produce unpredicted results in your application. This is explained more precisely using the following table.

B7	B6	B5	B4	B3	B2	B1	B0	Byte Address
7FH	7EH	7DH	7CH	7BH	7AH	79H	78H	2FH
77H	76H	75H	74H	73H	72H	71H	70H	2EH
6FH	6EH	6DH	6CH	6BH	6AH	69H	68H	2DH
67H	66H	65H	64H	63H	62H	61H	60H	2CH
5FH	5EH	5DH	5CH	5BH	5AH	59H	58H	2BH
57H	56H	55H	54H	53H	52H	51H	50H	2AH
4FH	4EH	4DH	4CH	4BH	4AH	49H	48H	29H
47H	46H	45H	44H	43H	42H	41H	40H	28H
3FH	3EH	3DH	3CH	3BH	3AH	39H	38H	27H
37H	36H	35H	34H	33H	32H	31H	30H	26H
2FH	2EH	2DH	2CH	2BH	2AH	29H	28H	25H
27H	26H	25H	24H	23H	22H	21H	20H	24H
1FH	1EH	1DH	1CH	1BH	1AH	19H	18H	23H

17H	16H	15H	14H	13H	12H	11H	10H	22H
0FH	0EH	0DH	0CH	0BH	0AH	09H	08H	21H
07H	06H	05H	04H	03H	02H	01H	00H	20H

B0, B1, B3 ...B7 represents the bit addresses. Now let's have a look at the following piece of Assembly code:

```
ORG 0000H          ; Reset Vector. Assembler directive
LJMP 0050H         ; Jump to location 0050H. Avoid conflicts in ISR Code
ORG 0050H          ; Location 0050H. Assembler directive
MOV 20H, #00H      ; Clear memory location 20H
SETB 01H           ; Store logic 1 in bit address 01H.
MOV 20H, #0F0H     ; Load memory location 20H with F0H
END                ; End of program. Assembler directive
```

This piece of assembly code sets the bit with bit address 01H and loads the memory location 20H with value F0H. Don't worry about the different instructions used here. We will discuss about the 8051 instruction set in a later chapter. The *MOV 20H, #00H* instruction clears the memory location 20H. The *SETB 01H* instruction stores logic 1 in the bit address 01H. In reality the bit address 01H is the bit 1 of the memory location pointed by address 20H. Executing the instruction *SETB 01H* changes the contents of memory location 20H to 02H (00000010b. Only bit 1 is in logic 1 state). The instruction *MOV 20H, #F0H* alters the content of memory location 20H with F0H (11110000b). This overwrites the information held by bit address 01H and leads to data corruption. So be careful while using bitwise storage and byte-wise storage simultaneously.

The next 80 bytes of RAM with address space 30H to 7FH is used as general purpose scratchpad RAM. Though memory spaces 00H to 2FH have specific usage, they can also be used as general purpose scratchpad (Read/Write) RAM. The lower 128 byte RAM can be accessed by either direct addressing or indirect addressing.

5.3.2.6 The Upper 128 bytes RAM (Special Function Registers) The upper 128 bytes of RAM when accessed by direct addressing, accesses the Special Function Registers (SFRs). SFRs include port latches, status and control bits, timer control and value registers, CPU registers, stack pointer, accumulator, etc. Some of the SFR registers are only byte level accessible and some of them are both byte-wise and bit-wise accessible. SFRs with address ends in 0H and 8H are both bit level and byte level accessible. In the standard 8051 architecture, among the 128 bytes, only a few bytes are occupied by the SFR and the rest are left unused and are reserved for future implementations. The table given below explains the SFR implementation for standard *8051* architecture.

Memory Address	SFR Name	Memory Address	SFR Name	Memory Address	SFR Name
80H	Port 0	8AH	TL0	A0H	Port 2
81H	SP	8BH	TL1	A8H	IE
82H	DPL	8CH	TH0	B0H	Port 3
83H	DPH	8DH	TH1	B8H	IP
87H	PCON	90H	Port 1	D0H	PSW
88H	TCON	98H	SCON	E0H	A
89H	TMOD	99H	SBUF	F0H	B

SFR memory is not available to the user for general purpose scratchpad RAM usage. However the user can modify the contents of some of the SFR according to the program requirements. Some of the SFRs are Read Only. Some of the SFR memory spaces are not implemented in the basic 8051 version. They are reserved for future use and users are instructed not to do anything with this reserved SFR space. Reading from the unimplemented SFR memory address returns random data and writing to this memory location will not produce any effect. Each of the SFRs will be discussed in detail in the sections covering their usage.

5.3.2.7 Upper 128 Bytes of Scratchpad RAM (IRAM) Variants of *8051* and the *8052* architecture where the upper 128 bytes of RAM are physically implemented in the chip can be used as general purpose scratchpad RAM by indirect addressing. They are generally known as IRAM. The address of IRAM ranges from 80H to FFH and the access is indirect. Registers R0 and R1 are used for indirect addressing. For example, for accessing the IRAM located at address 80H, load R0 or R1 with 80H and use the indirect memory access instruction. The following piece of assembly code illustrates the same.

```
MOV    R0,#80H  ; Load IRAM address 80H in indirect register
MOV    A,@R0    ; Load Accumulator with IRAM content at address 80H
```

5.3.3 Registers

Registers of *8051* can be broadly classified into CPU Registers and Scratchpad Registers.

5.3.3.1 CPU Registers Accumulator, B register, Program Status Word (PSW), Stack Pointer (SP), Data Pointer (DPTR, Combination of DPL and DPH), and Program Counter (PC) constitute the CPU registers. They are described in detail below.

Accumulator (ACC) (SFR-E0H) It is the most important CPU register which acts as the heart of all CPU related Arithmetic operations. Accumulator is an implicit operand in most of the arithmetic operations. Accumulator is a bit addressable register.

ACC.7	ACC.6	ACC.5	ACC.4	ACC.3	ACC.2	ACC.1	ACC.0

B Register (SFR-F0H) It is a CPU register that acts as an operand in multiply and division operations. It also stores the remainder in division and MSB in multiplication Instruction. B can also be used as a general purpose register for programming.

Program Status Word (PSW) (SFR-D0H) It is an 8-bit, bit addressable Special Function register signalling the status of accumulator related operations and register bank selector for the scratch pad registers R0 to R7. The bit details of PSW register is given below.

PSW.7	PSW.6	PSW.5	PSW.4	PSW.3	PSW.2	PSW.1	PSW.0
CY	AC	F0	RS1	RS0	OV		P

The table given below explains the meaning and use of each bit.

Bit	Name	Explanation
CY	Carry flag	Sets when a carry occurs on the addition of two 8-bit numbers or when a borrow occurs on the subtraction of two 8-bit numbers.
AC	Auxiliary carry flag	Sets when a carry generated out of bit 3 (bit index starts from 0) on addition

F0	Flag 0	General purpose user programmable flag (PSW.5)
OV	Over flow	Sets when overflow occurs. OV is set if there is a carry-out of bit 6 but not out of bit 7, or a carry-out of bit 7 but not bit 6; otherwise OV is cleared. When adding signed integers, OV indicates a negative number produced as the sum of two positive operands, or a positive sum from two negative operands.
P	Parity flag	Set or cleared by hardware each instruction cycle to indicate an odd or even number of 1s in the accumulator. 'P' is set to 1 if the number of 1s in the accumulator content is odd else reset to 0.
PSW.1	General flag	User programmable general purpose bit
RS0 RS1	Register bank selector	The bit status and bank selected is given in the following table

The following table illustrates the possible combinations for the register bank select bits, the corresponding register bank number and the address for the scratchpad registers R0-R7 in the specified register bank.

RS1	RS0	Register Bank	Register Address
0	0	0	00H-07H
0	1	1	08H-0FH
1	0	2	10H-17H
1	1	3	18H-1FH

The power-on reset value for the bits RS1 and RS2 are 0 and the default register bank for scratchpad registers R0 to R7 is 0 and the address range for R0 to R7 is 00H to 07H. A programmer can change the register bank by changing the values of RS1 and RS0. The following piece of assembly code illustrates the selection of bank 2 for the scratchpad registers R0 to R7.

```
CLR RS0      ; Clear bit RS1
SETB RS1     ; Set bit RS1. Bank 2 is selected
```

Data Pointer (DPTR) (DPL: SFR-82H, DPH: SFR-83H) It is a combination of two 8-bit register namely DPL (Lower 8-bit holder of DPTR) and DPH (Higher order 8-bit holder of DPTR). DPTR holds the 16-bit address of the external memory to be read or written in external data memory operations. DPH and DPL can be used as two independent 8-bit general purpose registers for application programming.

Program Counter (PC) It is a 16-bit register holding the address of the code memory to be fetched. It is an integral part of the CPU and it is hidden from the programmer (It is not accessible to the programmer).

Stack Pointer (SP) (SFR-81H) It is an 8-bit register holding the current address of stack memory. Stack memory stores the program counter address, other memory and register values during a sub routine/function call. On power on reset the stack pointer register value is set as 07H. The stack pointer address and bank 0, address of R7 is same when the controller is at reset, so care should be taken for selecting SP address. It is the responsibility of the programmer to assign sufficient stack memory by entering the starting address of stack into the Stack Pointer register. Care should be taken to avoid the overflow of stacks and merging of stack memory with data memory. This will result in un-predicted program flow. The stack grows up in memory.

5.3.3.2 Scratchpad Registers (R0 to R7) The scratchpad registers R0 to R7 is located in the lower 32 bytes of internal RAM. It can be on one of the four banks, which is selected by the register selector bits RS0 and RS1 of the PSW register. On power on reset, by default, RS0 and RS1 are 0 and the default bank selected is bank 0. There are eight scratchpad registers and they are named as R0, R1…R7. The register names and their memory address corresponding to bank 0 are given below.

R7	R6	R5	R4	R3	R2	R1	R0
07H	06H	05H	04H	03H	02H	01H	00H

As the bank number changes the register address also offsets by the memory address bank number multiplied by 8. Though you can select between the register banks 0 and 3, there will be only one active register bank at a time and it depends on the RS0 and RS1 bits of Program Status Word (PSW). Registers R0 to R7 are used as general purpose working registers. R0 and R1 also handle the role of index addressing or indirect addressing register (@R0 and @R1 instructions). R0 and R1 can also be used for external memory access in place of DPTR, if the memory address is 8-bit wide ((MOVX A, @R0) – will be discussed later).

5.3.4 Oscillator Unit

The program execution is dependent on the clock and the oscillator unit is responsible for generating the clock signals. All *8051* family microcontrollers contain an on-chip oscillator. This contains all necessary oscillator driving circuits. The only external component required is a ceramic crystal resonator. The *8051* on chip oscillator circuit provides external interface option through two pins of the microcontroller, namely, XTAL1 and XTAL2.

If you are using a ceramic resonator, you can connect it across the XTAL1 and XTAL2 pins of the chip with two external capacitors. Capacitors with values 15pF, 22pF, 33pF, etc. are used with the crystal resonator. This is the cheapest solution since the total cost for a ceramic resonator and two capacitors is always less than a standalone oscillator module.

If an external stand alone oscillator unit is used, the output signal of the oscillator unit should be connected to the pin XTAL1 of the chip and the pin XTAL2 should be left unconnected for a CMOS* type microcontroller (80C51). For an NMOS** type microcontroller, the oscillator output signal should be connected to the Pin XTAL2 and the pin XTAL1 should be grounded (Fig. 5.8).

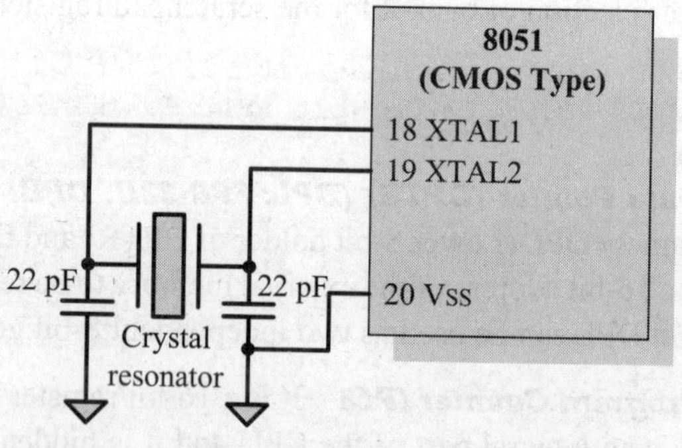

Fig. 5.8 **Circuit configuration for using on-chip oscillator**

* CMOS—Complementary metal–oxide–semiconductor field effect transistor technology for digital circuit design. CMOS features less power consumption and high logic density on an integrated circuit.

** NMOS—*n*-type metal-oxide-semiconductor field effect transistor technology for digital circuit design. It is an old technology and possesses the drawback of noise susceptibility and slow logic transition. In modern designs it is supplanted by CMOS technology.

You may be thinking why an oscillator circuit is required? The answer is–The microcontroller chip is made up of digital combinational and sequential circuits and they require a clock to drive the digital circuitry. The clock is supplied by this oscillator circuit and the operational speed of the chip is dependent on the clock speed.

5.3.4.1 Execution Speed The execution speed of the processor is directly proportional to the oscillator clock frequency. Increasing the clock speed will have direct impact on the speed of program execution. But the internal processor core design will always have certain limitations on the maximum clock frequency on which it can be operated. During program execution the instructions stored in the code memory is fetched, decoded and corresponding action is initiated. Each instruction fetching consists of the number of *machine cycles*. The instruction set of 8051 contains single cycle to four machine cycle instructions.

Each machine cycle is made up of a sequence of states called *T states*. The original 8051 processor's machine cycle consists of 6 T states and is named S1, S2, S3…S6. Each T states in turn consist of two oscillator periods (Clock cycles) and so one machine cycle contains 12 clock cycles. For a one machine cycle instruction to execute, it takes 12 clock cycles. If the system clock frequency is 12MHz, it takes 1microsecond (1μs) time to execute one machine cycle. The machine cycle, T state and clock cycle relationship is illustrated in the following Fig. 5.9.

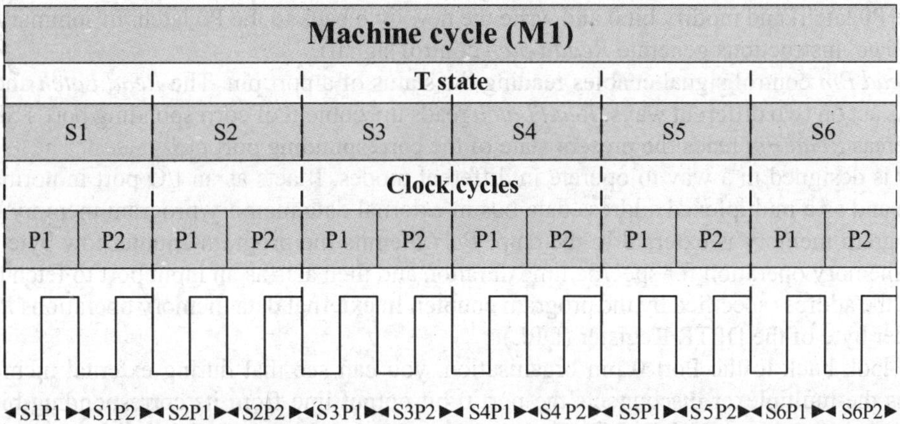

Fig. 5.9 Machine Cycles, T state & clock periods

5.3.5 Port

Port is a group of Input/Output (I/O) lines. Each port has its own port control unit, port driver and buffers. The original version of *8051* supports 32 I/O lines grouped into 4 I/O ports, consisting of 8 I/O lines per port. The ports are named as *Port 0*, *Port 1*, *Port 2* and *Port 3*. One output driver and one input buffer is associated with each I/O line. All four ports are bi-directional and an 8bit latch (Special Function Register) is associated with each port.

5.3.5.1 Port 0 PORT 0 is a bi-directional port, which is used as a multiplexed address/data bus in external data memory/program memory operations. Port 0 pin organisation is illustrated in Fig. 5.10.

Each pin of Port 0 possesses a bit latch which is part of the Special Function Register (SFR) for Port 0, P0. The latch is a D flip flop and it clocks in a logic value (either logic 1 or logic 0) from the internal

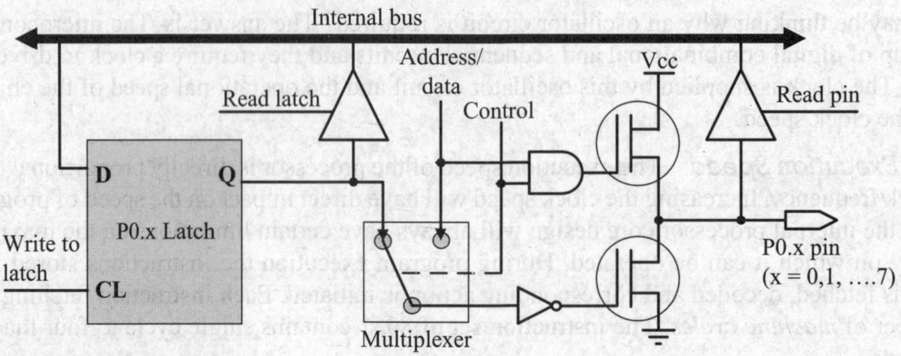

Fig. 5.10 Port 0 pin organisation

bus when a write to the corresponding latch signal is issued by the internal control unit. Apart from the write to latch operation you can read the contents of the corresponding Port 0 Pin latch by activating a *Read Latch* signal. The *Read Latch* signal is asserted on executing an instruction with a read from the corresponding 'port latch' instruction (e.g. *ANL P0*, A reads the P0 latch, logical AND it with accumulator and loads the latch with the result. Similarly, the instruction *MOV P0.0,C* reads the Port 0 byte (8 bits of the P0 latch) and modify bit 0 and write the new byte back to the P0 latch. In summary all '*Read-Modify-Write*' instructions generate *Read Latch* control signal).

The *Read Pin* control signal enables reading the status of a port pin. The *Read Latch* and *Read Pin* operations act on two different ways. *Read Latch* reads the content of corresponding port's SFR/SFR bit latch whereas *Read Pin* reads the present state of the corresponding port pin.

Port 0 is designed in a way to operate in different modes. It acts as an I/O port in normal mode of operation and as a multiplexed address data bus in external data memory/program memory operations. If the program memory is external to the chip, *Port 0* emits the program counter low byte in external program memory operation for specific time duration and then acts as an input port to fetch the instruction from the address specified by the program counter. In external data memory operations P0 emits the lower order byte of the DPTR Register (DPL).

If you look back to the Port 0 pin organisation, you can see that during external memory related operations the multiplexer disconnects the port 0 bit output line from its corresponding bit latch and directly connect it to the ADDRESS/DATA line and the output driver circuitry is driven according to the ADDRESS/DATA line and the control.

The output drivers of Port 0 are formed by two FETs, out of which the top FET functions as the internal port pull-up. The pull-up FET driver for Port 0 is active only when the address line is emitting 1s during external memory operations. The pull-up FET will be off on all other conditions and the Port 0 pins which are used as output pins will become open drain (Open Collector for TTL logic). On writing a 1 to the corresponding port bit SFR latch, the bottom FET is turned off and the pin floats and it enters in a high impedance state.

In order to make any Port 0 pin an input pin, a logic 1 should be written to the corresponding Port 0 SFR latch bit and an external pull-up resistor (in the range of Kilo ohms, typically 4.7K) should be connected across the corresponding Port 0 pin and power supply V_{CC}, which will act as a bypass to the internal pull-up FET.

If Port 0 is used for external memory or device interfacing, it should be equipped with external pull-up resistors to provide noise immunity to Port 0 data lines.

When configured as O/p port by writing 1s to the Port 0 SFR, all Port 0 pins floats and it is said to be in a high impedance state. Port 0 is a true bi-directional port.

Port 0 SFR (P0) (SFR-80H) Port 0 SFR is a bit addressable Special Function Register that acts as the bit latch for each Port 0 pins.

BIT 7	BIT 6	BIT 5	BIT 4	BIT 3	BIT 2	BIT 1	BIT 0
P0.7	P0.6	P0.5	P0.4	P0.3	P0.2	P0.1	P0.0

During external memory operations P0 SFR gets 1s written into it. The reset value of Port 0 SFR is FFH (All latch bits set to 1)

5.3.5.2 Port 1 PORT 1 is a bi-directional port which is used as a general purpose I/O port. The Port 1 pin organisation is given in Fig. 5.11.

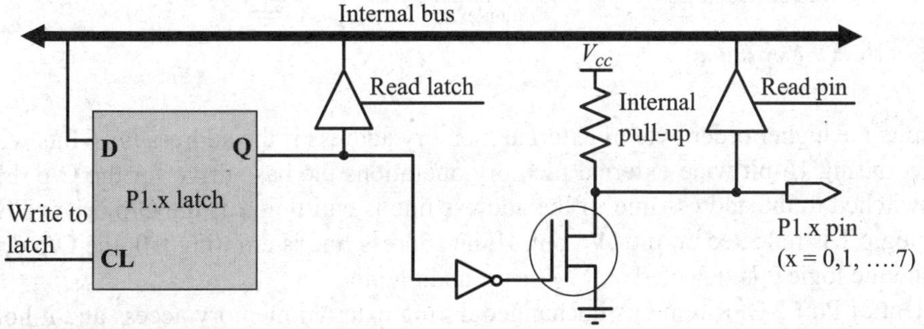

Fig. 5.11 **Port 1 pin organisation**

As seen in the pin organisation, Port 1 pin contains an internal pull-up resistor. In order to make the Port 1 pins as input line, the corresponding SFR latch bit for Port 1 should be kept as 1. Writing a 1 into any of the P1 SFR bit latch turns off the output driver FET and produces logic high at the corresponding port pin. The internal pull up for Port 1 is fixed and weak. When Port 1 pins are configured as inputs (by writing a 1 to the corresponding Port 1 SFR bit latch) the pins are pulled high and they can source current when an externally connected device pulls the port pin to low, signaling a logic 0 at the corresponding input line and places logic 0 to the internal bus in response to a *Read Pin* command. If the externally connected device forces logic high, the *Read Pin* control signal generated by a *Read Pin* related command (e.g. *MOV A,P1*, *MOV C,P1.0,* etc.) places logic high into the internal bus.

Since Port 1 holds fixed internal pull ups and are capable of sourcing current, it is known as *Quasi Bi-directional*.

Port 1 SFR (P1) (SFR- 90H) It is also a bit addressable Special Function Register that acts as the bit latch for each pin of Port 1. The bit details of Port1 SFR is given below.

BIT 7	BIT 6	BIT 5	BIT 4	BIT 3	BIT 2	BIT 1	BIT 0
P1.7	P1.6	P1.5	P1.4	P1.3	P1.2	P1.1	P1.0

The reset value of Port 1 SFR is FFH (All bit latches set to 1).

5.3.5.3 Port 2 Port 2 is designed to operate in two different modes. It acts as general purpose I/O port in normal operational mode and acts as higher order address bus in external data memory/program memory operations. Figure 5.12 illustrates the Port 2 pin organisation.

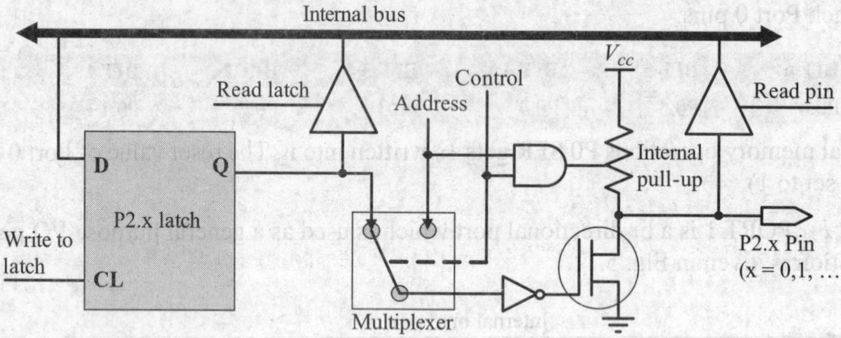

Fig. 5.12 **Port 2 pin organisation**

Port 2 emits the higher order byte of external memory address if the address is 16 bits wide. As seen in the figure, during 16-bit wide external memory operations the base drive for the O/p driver FET is internally switched to the address line. If the address line is emitting a 1, the O/p driver FET is turned off and the logic 1 is reflected on the O/p pin. If the address line is emitting a 0, the O/p driver FET is turned on and the logic 0 is reflected at the corresponding pin.

The content of Port 2 SFR remains unchanged during external memory access and it holds the previous content as such. It is to be noted that if Port 2 is in external memory operation it cannot be used as general purpose I/O line. When not used for external memory access, Port 2 can be used as general purpose I/O port. During normal operation mode, the internal multiplexer switches the base line (GATE) of O/p FET to the D latch O/p of corresponding SFR bit latch. In normal operation mode when a 1 is written into any of the P2 bit latch, the O/p driver FET is turned off and as in the case of Port 1 this line acts as an I/p line. P2 is a *Quasi bi-directional* port.

Port 2 SFR (P2) (SFR- A0H) It is a bit addressable Special Function Register that acts as the bit latch for each pins of Port 2. The reset value of Port 2 SFR is FFH (All bit latches set to 1).

BIT 7	BIT 6	BIT 5	BIT 4	BIT 3	BIT 2	BIT 1	BIT 0
P2.7	P2.6	P2.5	P2.4	P2.3	P2.2	P2.1	P2.0

5.3.5.4 Port 3 Port 3 is a general purpose I/O port which is also configurable for implementing alternative functions. Port 3 Pin configuration is shown in Fig. 5.13.

Port 3 is identical to Port 1 in operation. All the settings that need to be done for configuring Port 1 as I/O port is applicable to Port 3 also. The only difference is that the SFR latch for Port 3 is P3. Port 3 supports alternate I/O functions. The alternate I/O functions supported by Port 3 and the pins used for these alternate functions are tabulated below.

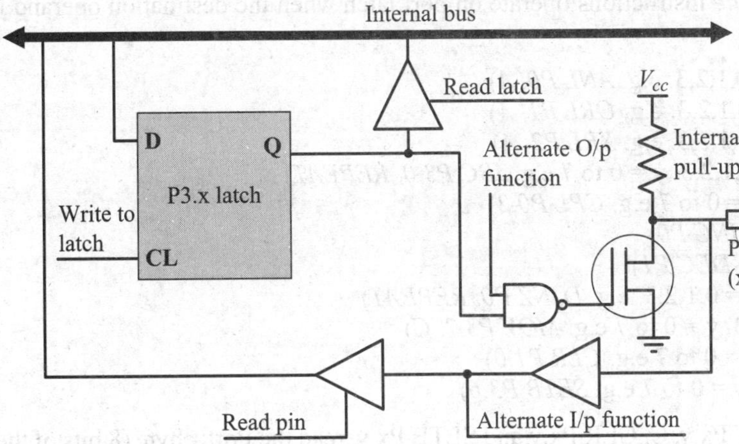

Fig. 5.13 **Port 3 pin organisation**

Port Pin	Alternate I/O Function
P3.0	RXD (Receive Pin – Serial Input Port Pin) – Input line
P3.1	TXD (Transmit Pin – Serial O/p Pin) – Output line
P3.2	INT0\ (External Interrupt 0 line) – Input line
P3.3	INT1\ (External Interrupt 1 line) – Input line
P3.4	T0 (Counter 0 External Input line) – Input line
P3.5	T1 (Counter 1 External Input line) – Input line
P3.6	WR\ (Write signal for External data memory access) – O/p line
P3.7	RD\ (Read signal for External data memory access) – O/p line

It is obvious from the table that all 8 pins of Port 3 are having some alternate I/O function associated with them. From the Port 3 pin configuration it is clear that the alternate I/O functions will come into action only if the corresponding SFR bit latch is set to logic 1. Otherwise the port pin remains at logic 0.

Port 3 SFR (P3) (SFR-B0H) It is a bit addressable Special Function Register that acts as the bit latch for each pin of Port 3. Reset value of Port 3 SFR is FFH (All bit latches set to 1).

BIT 7	BIT 6	BIT 5	BIT 4	BIT 3	BIT 2	BIT 1	BIT 0
P3.7	P3.6	P3.5	P3.4	P3.3	P3.2	P3.1	P3.0

5.3.5.5 'Read Port Latch' and 'Read Port Pin' Operations As we discussed earlier, the 'Port Read' operations fall into two categories namely, *Read Latch* and *Read Pin*. The *Read Latch* operation reads the content of the corresponding port latch. The port architecture for all 4 ports contains necessary circuit for reading the *Port Latch* for all port pins. The read *Port Latch* operation is triggered by the control signal *Read Latch*. The *Read Latch* control signal is generated internally on executing an instruction implementing the *Read Latch* operation. The *Read-Modify-Write* instructions which reads the port, modifies it and re-writes it to the port, operates on the port latch instead of port pins. The following *Read-Modify-Write* instructions operate on port latch when the destination operand is a Port or a Port bit.

ANL Px, <source> (x= 0,1,2,3. e.g. *ANL P0, A*)
ORL Px, <source> (x= 0,1,2,3. e.g. *ORL P1, A*)
XRL Px, <source> (x= 0,1,2,3. e.g. *XRL P2, A*)
JBC Px.y, LABEL (x= 0,1,2,3. y = 0 to 7 e.g. *JBC P3.0, REPEAT*)
CPL Px.y (x= 0,1,2,3. y = 0 to 7 e.g. *CPL P0.2*)
INC Px (x= 0,1,2,3. e.g. *INC P0*)
DEC Px (x= 0,1,2,3. e.g. *DEC P1*)
DJNZ Px, LABEL Px (x= 0,1,2,3. e.g. *DJNZ P0, REPEAT*)
MOV Px.y, C (x= 0,1,2,3. y = 0 to 7 e.g. *MOV P3.7, C*)
CLR Px.y (x= 0,1,2,3. y = 0 to 7 e.g. *CLR P1.0*)
SETB Px.y (x= 0,1,2,3. y = 0 to 7 e.g. *SETB P3.6*)

The instructions MOV Px.y, C, CLR Px.y and SETB Px.y, read the Port *x* byte (8 bits of the P*x* latch) and modify bit *y* and write the new byte back to the P*x* latch.

The following assembly code snippet illustrates the *Read Latch* operation.

```
MOV P0, #0FH        ; Configure P0.0 to P0.3 pins as input pins
MOV A, #0FH         ; Load Accumulator with 0FH
ANL P0, A           ; Read P0 latch, logical AND with Accumulator-
                    ; content and load P0 latch with the result
```

Executing the instruction *MOV P0, #0FH* loads the Port 0 latch with 0FH (The latches for port pins P0.0 to P0.3 are set). Now Port pins P0.0 to P0.3 acts as input pins. Executing the instruction *MOV A, #0FH* loads the accumulator with 0FH. The *ANL P0, A* instruction reads the P0 latch and logical AND it with accumulator and rewrites the P0 latch with the ANDed result. The status of port pins configured as input port has no effect on the instruction ANL P0, A. Suppose P0.0 pin (Not P0.0 latch bit) is at logic 0 and pins P0.1 to P0.3 are at logic 1 at the time of executing the instruction *ANL P0, A*, still Port 0 latch is loaded with 0FH and not 0EH.

The *Read Pin* operation reads the status of a port pin when the corresponding port pin is configured as input pin (When the corresponding port latch bit is loaded with logic 1). The port architecture for all 4 ports contains necessary circuit for reading the *Port Pin* for all ports. The read *Port Pin* operation is triggered by the control signal *Read Pin*. The *Read Pin* control signal is generated internally on executing an instruction implementing the *Read Pin* operation. *MOV A, Px, MOV C, Px.y* are examples for *Read Pin* instructions. The following code snippet illustrates the '*Read Pin*' operation.

```
MOV P0, #0FH        ; Configure P0.0 to P0.3 pins as input pins
MOV A, P0           ; Load Accumulator with P0 Port pin status
```

Executing the instruction *MOV P0, #0FH* loads the Port 0 latch with 0FH (The latches for port pins P0.0 to P0.3 are set). Now Port pins P0.0 to P0.3 act as input pins. Executing the instruction *MOV A, P0* loads accumulator with the Pin status of pins P0.0 P0.3. Suppose P0.0 pin is at logic 0 and pins P0.1 to P0.3 are at logic 1 at the time of executing the instruction *MOV A, P0*, the accumulator is loaded with 0EH.

5.3.5.6 Source and Sink Currents for 8051 Ports

Source Current The term *source current* refers to how much current the *8051* port pin can supply to drive an externally connected device. The device can be an LED, a buzzer or a TTL logic device. For TTL family of *8051* devices the source current is defined in terms of TTL logic. TTL logic has two logic levels namely logic 1 (High) and logic 0 (Low). The typical voltage levels for logic *Low* and *High* is given in the following table.

Logic Level	Input signal level		Output signal level		V_{cc}
	Min	Max	Min	Max	
Low	0V	0.8V	0V	0.5V	5V
High	2V	5V	2.7V	5V	5V

The logic levels are defined for a TTL gate acting as input and output. For logic 0 the input voltage level is defined as any voltage below 0.8V and the current is 1.6mA sinking current to ground through a TTL input. According to the *8051* design reference, the maximum current that a port pin (For an LS TTL logic based 8051 devices) can source is 60 µA.

Sink Current It refers to the maximum current that the *8051* port pin can absorb through a device which is connected to an external supply. The device can be an LED, a buzzer or a TTL logic device (For TTL logic based 8051 devices). Pins of Ports P1, P2 and P3 can sink a maximum current of 1.6 mA. Port 0 pins can sink currents up to 3.2 mA. Under steady state the maximum sink current is limited by the criteria: Maximum Sink Current per port pin = 10 mA, Maximum Sink current per 8-bit port for port 0 = 26 mA, Maximum Sink Current per 8-bit port for port 1, 2, & 3 = 15 mA, Maximum total Sink current for all output pin = 71 mA (As per the AT89C51 Datasheet). Figure 5.14 illustrates the circuits for source, sink and ideal port interfacing for *8051* port pins.

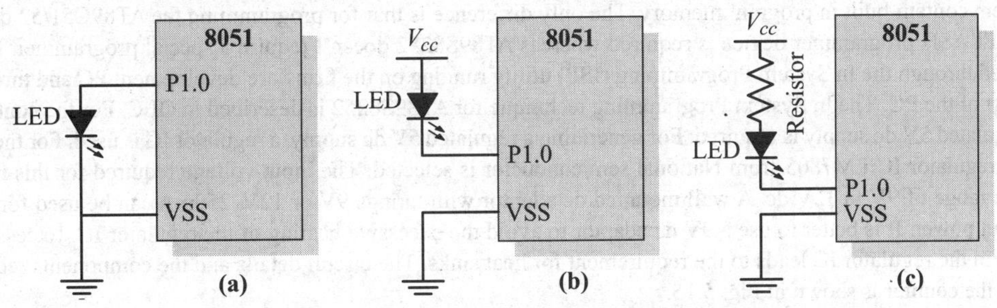

Fig. 5.14 **(a) Current Sourcing, (b) Current Sinking (c) Ideal Port pin interface for *8051***

Figure 5.14(a) illustrates the current sourcing for port pins. Since *8051* port pins are only capable of sourcing less than 1 mA current, the brightness of LED will be very poor. Figure 5.14(b) illustrates the current sinking for port pins. In this configuration, the forward voltage of LED while conducting is approximately 2V and the supply voltage 5V (V_{cc}) is distributed across the LED and the internal TTL circuitry. The extra 3V has to be dropped across the internal TTL circuitry and this will lead to high power dissipation, which in turn will result in the damage of the LED or the port pin. This type of design is not recommended in embedded design. Instead the current through the LED is limited by connecting the LED to the power supply through a resistor as shown in Fig. 5.14(c). In this configuration, the port pin should be at Logic 0 for the LED to conduct. For a 2.2V LED, the drop across Resistor is calculated as Supply voltage – (LED Forward Voltage + TTL Low Voltage) = 5 – (2.2 + 0.8) = 2.0V. The Resistance value is calculated as 2V / (Required LED Current). Refer LED data sheet for LED current. If the resistance value is not properly selected, it may lead to the flow of high current through the LED and may damage the LED.

Example 1

Design an 8051 microcontroller based system for displaying the binary numbers from 0 to 255 using 8 LEDs as per the specifications given below:

1. Use Atmel's AT89C51/52 or AT89S8252 (Flash microcontroller with In System Programming (ISP) support) for designing the system.
2. Use a 12MHz crystal resonator for generating the necessary clock signal for the controller.
3. Use on-chip program memory for storing the program instructions.
4. The 8 LEDs are connected to the port pins P2.0 to P2.7 of the microcontroller and are arranged in a single row with the LED connected to P2.0 at the rightmost position (LSB) and the LED connected to P2.7 at the leftmost position (MSB).
5. The LEDs are connected to the port pins through pull-up resistors of 470 ohms and will conduct only when the corresponding port pin is at logic 0.
6. Each LED represents the corresponding binary bit of a byte and it reflects the logic levels of the bit through turning ON and OFF the LED (The LED is turned on when the bit is at logic 1 and off when the LED is at logic 0).
7. The counting starts from 0 (All LEDs at turned OFF state) and increments by one. The counter is incremented at the rate of 5 seconds.
8. When the counter is at 255 (0FFH, all LEDs are in the turn ON state), the next increment resets the counter to 00H and the counting process is repeated.

The design of this system has two parts. The first part is the design of the microcontroller based hardware circuit. The hardware circuit part can be wired on a breadboard for simplifying the development. The controller for this can be chosen as either AT89C51/52 or AT89S8252. Both of these controllers are from the *8051* family and are pin compatible. Both of them contain built in program memory. The only difference is that for programming the AT89C51/52 device an EEPROM/FLASH programmer device is required whereas AT89S8252 doesn't require a special programmer. It can be programmed through the In System Programming (ISP) utility running on the firmware development PC and through the parallel port of the PC. The In System Programming technique for AT89S8252 is described in OLC. For the controller to work, a regulated 5V dc supply is required. For generating a regulated 5V dc supply, a regulator IC is used. For the current design the regulator IC LM7805 from National semiconductor is selected. The input voltage required for this regulator IC is in the range of 9V to 12V dc. A wall mounted dc adaptor with ratings 9V or 12V, 250mA can be used for supplying the input power. It is better to use a 9V dc adaptor to avoid the excessive heating of the regulator IC. Excessive heat production in the regulator IC leads to the requirement for heat sinks. The circuit details and the components required to implement the counter is shown in Fig. 5.15.

The circuit shows the minimal components and the interconnection among them to make the controller operational. As mentioned earlier, it requires a regulated 5V dc supply for powering the controller. The 12 MHZ crystal resonator in combination with the external 22 picofarad (pF) capacitors drives the on-chip oscillator unit and generates the required clock signal for the controller. The RC circuit connected to the RST pin of the controller provides Power-On reset for the controller. The capacitor and resistor values are selected in such a way that the reset pulse is active (high) for at least 2 machine cycle duration. The diode in the reset circuitry is used as freewheeling diode and it is not mandatory. The 0.1 Microfarad (0.1 MFD) capacitor connected to the power supply line filters the spurious (noise) signals from the power supply line. For proper driving, the LEDs should be connected to the respective port pins through pull-up resistors. The pull-up resistor values are determined by the forward voltage of LEDs and the current rating of the LEDs. The current design uses 470 ohms as the pull up resistor. If you are not sure about the forward voltage and current ratings of the LED, it is better to start with a high value (say 8.2K) for the resistor and replace it with successive low value resistors (4.2 K, 2.7K, 1 K, 870 E, 470 E etc.) till you feel that the brightness of the LED while it is conducting is reasonably good. The controller contains on-chip program memory and it can be used for storing the firmware. In order to use the on-chip program memory, the EA\ pin should be tied to V_{CC}. Pulling the EA\ pin to V_{CC} through a high value resistor ensures that the pin draws very minimal amount of current.

The second part is the design and development of program code (firmware) for implementing the binary counter and displaying the counter content using the LEDs interfaced to Port 2. The firmware requirement can be modelled in the form of a flow chart as given in Fig. 5.16.

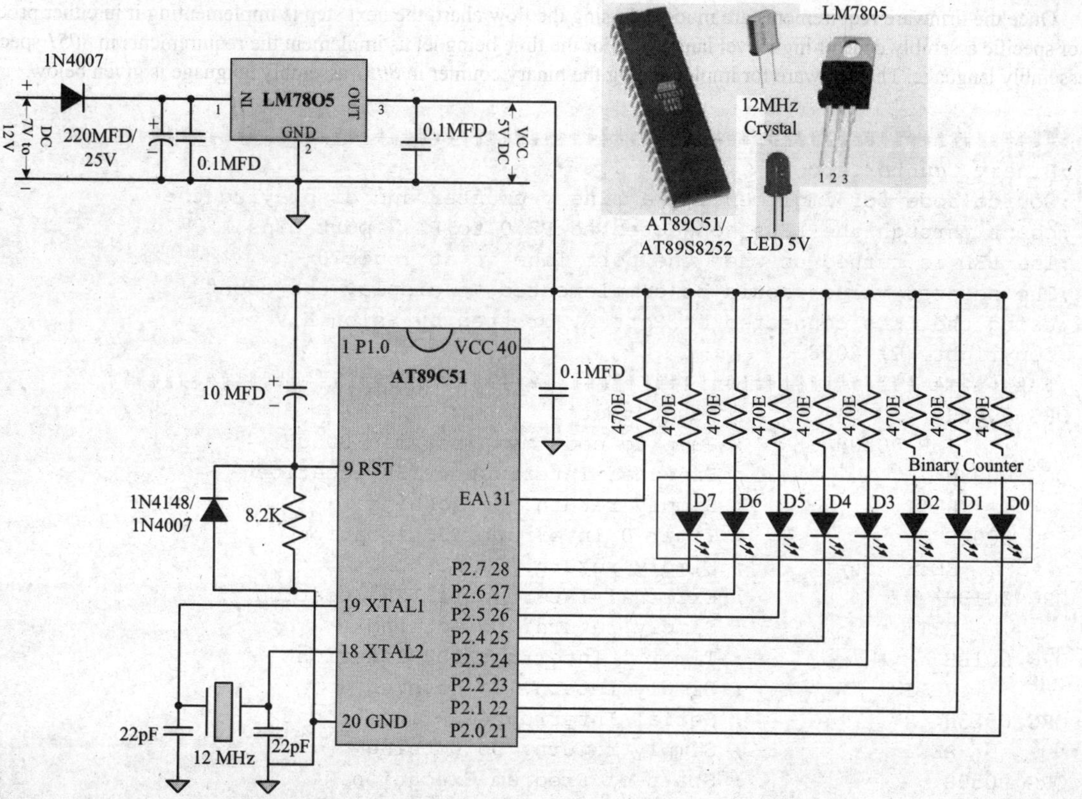

Fig. 5.15 **Binary number display circuit using *8051* and LEDs**

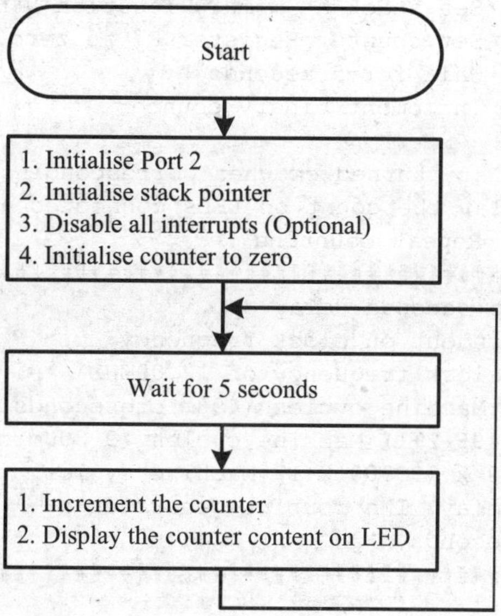

Fig. 5.16 **Flow chart for Binary Number Display using LEDs**

Once the firmware requirements are modelled using the flow chart, the next step is implementing it in either processor specific assembly code or high level language. For the time being let us implement the requirements in *8051* specific assembly language. The firmware for implementing the binary counter in *8051* assembly language is given below.

```
;####################################################################
;Binary_Counter.src
;Source code for implementing a binary counter and displaying the
;count through the LEDs connected to P2.0 to P2.7 port pins
;The LED is turned on when the port line is at logic 0
;The counter value should be complemented to display the count
;using the LEDs connected at Port 2. Written by Shibu K V
;Copyright (C) 2008
;####################################################################
ORG 0000H              ; Reset vector
        JMP 0050H      ; Jump to code mem location 0050H
ORG 0003H              ; External Interrupt 0 ISR location
        RETI           ; Simply return. Do nothing
ORG 000BH              ; Timer 0 Interrupt ISR location
        RETI           ; Simply return. Do nothing
ORG 0013H              ; External Interrupt 1 ISR location
        RETI           ; Simply return. Do nothing
ORG 001BH              ; Timer 1 Interrupt ISR location
        RETI           ; Simply return. Do nothing
ORG 0023H              ; Serial Interrupt ISR location
        RETI           ; Simply return. Do nothing
ORG 0050H              ; Start of Program Execution
        MOV P2, #0FFH  ; Turn off all LEDs
        CLR EA         ; Disable All interrupts
        MOV SP, #08H   ; Set stack at memory location 08H
        MOV R7,#00H    ; Set counter Register R7 to zero.
REPEAT: CALL DELAY     ; Wait for 5 seconds
        INC R7         ; Increment binary counter
        MOV A, R7      ;
        CPL A; The LED's are turned on when corresponding bit is 0
        MOV P2, A ; Display the count on LEDs connected at Port 2
        JMP REPEAT     ; Repeat counting
;####################################################################
;Routine for generating 5 seconds delay
;Delay generation is dependent on clock frequency
;This routine assumes a clock frequency of 12.00MHZ
;LOOP1 generates 248 x 2 Machine cycles (496microseconds) delay
;LOOP2 generates 200 x (496+2+1) Machine cycles (99800microseconds)
;delay. LOOP3 generate 50 x (99800+2+1) Machine cycles
;(4990150microseconds) delay. The routine generates a-
;precise delay of 4.99 seconds
;####################################################################
```

```
DELAY:   MOV R2, #50
LOOP1:   MOV R1, #200
LOOP2:   MOV R0, #248
LOOP3:   DJNZ R0, LOOP3
         DJNZ R1, LOOP2
         DJNZ R2, LOOP1
         RET
END ; END of Assembly Program
```

Once the assembly code is written and checked for syntax errors, it is converted into a controller specific machine code (hex file) using an assembler program. The conversion can be done using a freely/commercially available assembler program for *8051* or an IDE based tool (like Keil microvison 3). The final stage is embedding the hex code in the program memory of the controller. If the controller used is AT89C51, the program can be embedded using a FLASH programmer device. For controllers supporting In System Programming (ISP), like AT89S8252, the hex file can be directly loaded into the program memory of the controller using an ISP application running on the development PC.

Example 2

Design an *8051* microcontroller based control system for controlling a 5V, 2-phase 6-wire stepper motor. The system should satisfy the following:

1. Use Atmel's AT89C51/52 or AT89S8252 (Flash microcontroller with In System Programming (ISP) support) for designing the system.
2. Use a 12 MHz crystal resonator for generating the necessary clock signal for the controller.
3. Use on-chip program memory for storing the program instructions.
4. The wires of the stepper motor are marked corresponding to the coils (A, B, C & D) and Ground (2 wires)
5. Use the octal peripheral driver IC ULN2803 from National semiconductors for driving the stepper motor.
6. Step the motor in 'Full step' mode with a delay of 1 sec between the steps.
7. Connect the coil drives to Port 1 in the order Coil A to P1.0, Coil B to P1.1, Coil C to P1.2, and Coil D to P1.3

Refer to the description on stepper motors given in Chapter 2 to get an understanding of unipolar stepper motors and the coil energising sequence for 'Full step' mode.

Figure 5.17 illustrates the interfacing of stepper motor through the driver circuit connected to Port 1 of 8051. The flow chart given in Fig. 5.18 models the firmware requirements for interfacing the stepper motor.

From the pulse sequence for running the stepper motor in 'Full step' it is clear that the pulse sequence for next step is obtained by right shifting the current pulse sequence. The initial pulse sequence required is H, H, L, L at coils A, B, C & D respectively (Please refer to the stepper motor section in Chapter 2). In our case we have only 4 bits to shift and our controller is an 8bit controller. Performing a right shift operation of the accumulator moves the LS bit of accumulator to the MS bit position (Bit position 7 in 0–7 numbering). We want the LS bit to be available at 3rd bit position after each rotation. This can be achieved by some bit manipulation operation. We can also achieve it by loading the MS nibble of accumulator with the same initial sequence HHLL. In this example we are not using Port P1 for any other operation. Hence the values of port pins P1.4 to P1.7 are irrelevant in our case. But in real life scenario it may not be the case always. The firmware implementation for this is given below:

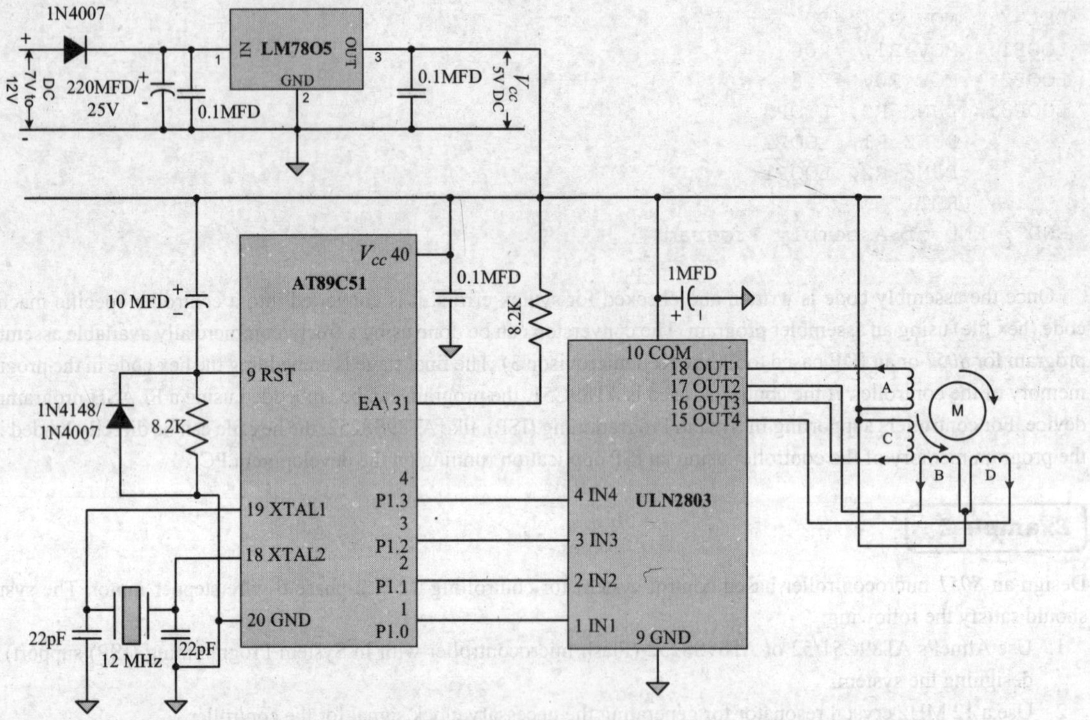

Fig. 5.17 **Stepper Motor Interfacing circuit for 8051**

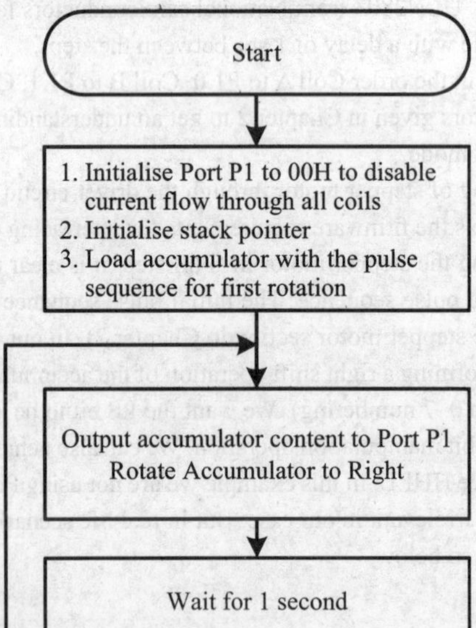

Fig. 5.18 **Flow chart for Implementing Stepper Motor Interfacing**

```
;####################################################################
;Stepper_motor.src. Firmware for Interfacing stepper motor
;The stator coils A, B, C and Dare controlled through Port pins P1.0,
;P1.1, P1.2 and P1.3 respectively.
;Accumulator is used for generating the pulse sequence for 'Fullstep'
;The initial pulse sequence is represented by 0CH
;Written & Compiled for A51 Assembler. Written by Shibu K V
;Copyright (C) 2008
;####################################################################
ORG 0000H               ; Reset vector
        JMP 0100H       ; Jump to code mem location 0100H to start-
                        ; execution
ORG 0003H               ; External Interrupt 0 ISR location
        RETI            ; Simply return. Do nothing
ORG 000BH               ; Timer 0 Interrupt ISR location
        RETI            ; Simply return. Do nothing
ORG 0013H               ; External Interrupt 1 ISR location
        RETI            ; Simply return. Do nothing
ORG 001BH               ; Timer 1 Interrupt ISR location
        RETI            ; Simply return. Do nothing
ORG 0023H               ; Serial Interrupt ISR location
        RETI            ; Simply return. Do nothing
;####################################################################
; Start of main Program
ORG 0100H
        MOV P1, #00H    ; Turn off the drives to all stator coils
        MOV SP, #08H    ; Set stack at memory location 08H
        MOV A, #0CCH    ; Load the initial pulse sequence
REPEAT: MOV P1, A       ; Load Port P1 with pulse sequence
        RR A            ; Rotate Accumulator to right
        CALL DELAY      ; Wait for 1 second
        JMP REPEAT      ; Load Port P1 with new pulse sequence
;####################################################################
;Routine for generating 1 second delay
;Delay generation is dependent on clock frequency
;This routine assumes a clock frequency of 12.00MHz
;LOOP1 generates 248 x 2 Machine cycles (496microseconds) delay
;LOOP2 generates 200 x (496+2+1) Machine cycles (99800microseconds)
;delay. LOOP3 generate 10 x (99800+2+1) Machine cycles
;(998030microseconds) delay. ;The routine generates a-
; precise delay of 0.99 seconds
;####################################################################
DELAY:  MOV R2, #10
LOOP1:  MOV R1, #200
LOOP2:  MOV R0, #248
LOOP3:  DJNZ R0, LOOP3
        DJNZ R1, LOOP2
        DJNZ R2, LOOP1
        RET
END     ;END of Assembly Program
```

Example 3

Design an *8051* microcontroller based system for interfacing the Programmable Peripheral Interface (PPI) device 8255. The system should satisfy the following:

1. Use Atmel's AT89C51/52 or AT89S8252 (Flash microcontroller with In System Programming (ISP) support) for designing the system
2. Use a 12 MHz crystal resonator for generating the necessary clock signal for the controller. Use on-chip program memory for storing the program instructions
3. Use Intersil Corporation's (wwww.intersil.com) 82C55A PPI device
4. Allocate the address space 8000H to FFFFH to 8255. Initialise the Port A, Port B and Port C of *8255* as Output ports in Mode0

Here we are allocating the address space 8000H to FFFFH to 8255. Hence the 8255 is activated when the 15th bit of address line becomes 1. Here we have to use a single *NOT* gate to invert the A15 line before applying it to the Chip Select (CS\) line of *8255*. In this configuration *8255* requires only four address space namely 8000H for Port A, 8001H for Port B, 8002H for Port C and 8003H for the Control Register. Rest of the address space 8004H to FFFFH is left unused. Here we have the luxury of using the entire address range since we don't have any other devices to connect. In real life applications it may not be the case. We may have multiple devices sharing the entire address space 0000H to FFFFH and we need to select each device in their own address space. In such scenarios the address lines A2 to A15 needs to be decoded using a combination of logic gates (NAND, AND, NOT, OR, NOR) and decoders. Figure 5.19 illustrates the interfacing of *8255* with *8051*.

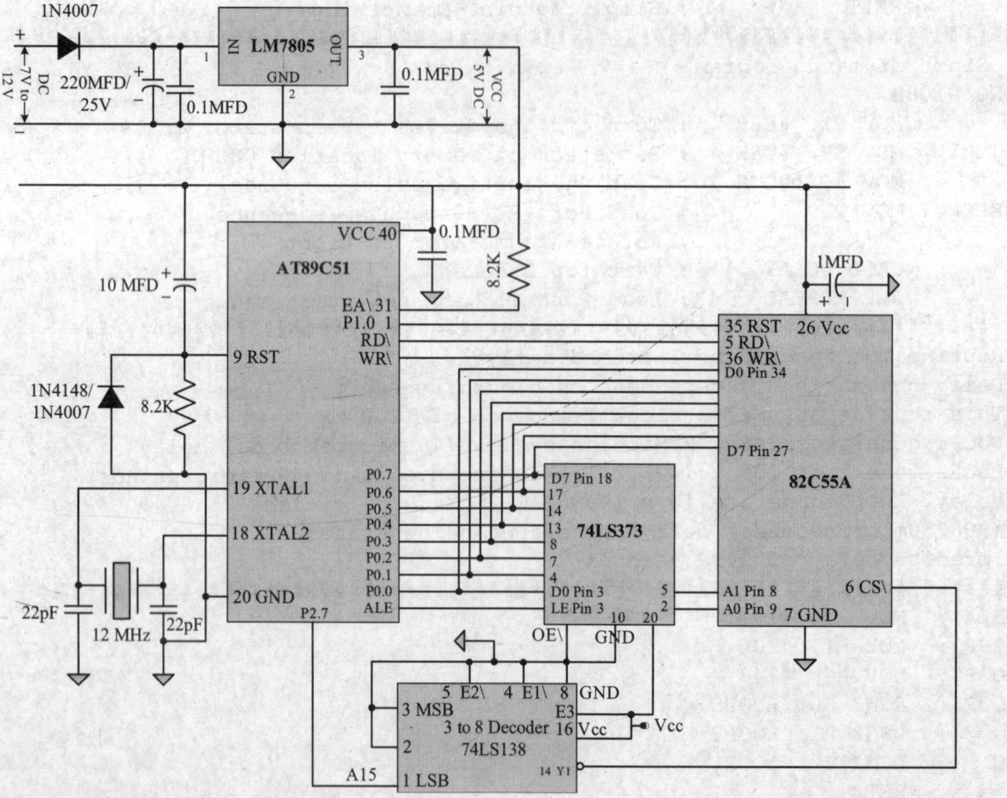

Fig. 5.19 **Interfacing *8255* PPI with *8051***

The Octal latch 74LS373 latches the lower order address bus (A0-A7) which is multiplexed with the data bus (D0-D7). A 3 to 8 decoder chip, 74LS138, decodes the address bus to generate the Chip Select (CS\) signal for *8255*. Here we have only one address line (A15) to decode. The rest of the 2 input lines to the decoder (Pins 2 & 3) are grounded. Our intention is to assert the CS\ signal of *8255* when A15 line is 1. The I/p condition corresponds to this is 001. The decoded output for this is Output 1 (Y1). You can replace the decoder with a NOT Logic IC. The reset line of 8255 is controlled through port pin P1.0. The Reset of *8255* is active high and when *8051* is initialised, the port pin P1.0 automatically generates a reset high signal for *8255*.

The flow chart given in Fig. 5.20 models the firmware requirements for interfacing *8255* with *8051* controller.

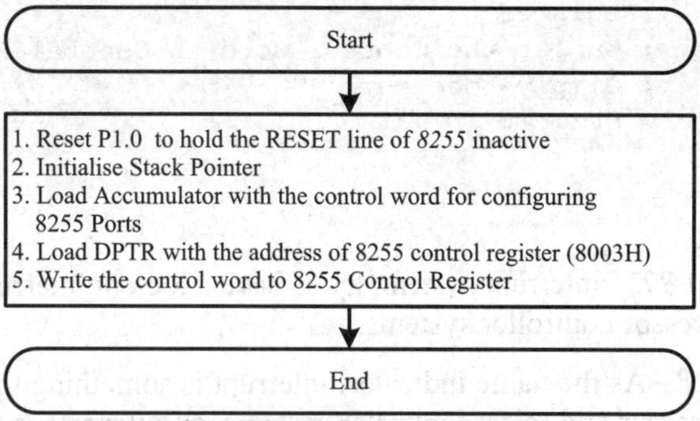

Fig. 5.20 **Flow chart for Interfacing 8255 with *8051***

The control word for configuring all the *8255* ports as output ports in mode 0 is shown below. Please refer to the section on Programmable Peripheral Interface (PPI) given in Chapter 2 for more details on *8255*'s control register.

D7	D6	D5	D4	D3	D2	D1	D0
1	0	0	0	0	0	0	0

The firmware implementation for this is given below.

```
;####################################################################
;8255.src. Firmware for Interfacing 8255A PPI
;8255 is memory mapped at 8000H to FFFFH. The address assignment for
;various port and control register are: Port A : 8000H,
;Port B : 8001H, Port C : 8002H, Control Register : 8003H
;Reset of 8255 is controlled through P1.0 of 8051
;Written & Compiled for A51 Assembler. Written by Shibu K V
;Copyright (C) 2008
;####################################################################
ORG 0000H           ; Reset vector
      JMP MAIN      ; Jump to the address location pointed by
                    ; the Label 'MAIN' to start execution
ORG 0003H           ; External Interrupt 0 ISR location
      RETI          ; Simply return. Do nothing
ORG 000BH           ; Timer 0 Interrupt ISR location
      RETI          ; Simply return. Do nothing
ORG 0013H           ; External Interrupt 1 ISR location
      RETI          ; Simply return. Do nothing
ORG 001BH           ; Timer 1 Interrupt ISR location
      RETI          ; Simply return. Do nothing
```

```
ORG 0023H               ; Serial Interrupt ISR location
        RETI            ; Simply return. Do nothing
;####################################################################
; Start of main Program
MAIN:   CLR P1.0        ; De-activate 8255 Reset line
        MOV SP, #08H    ; Set stack at memory location 08H
        MOV A, #80H     ; Load the initial Control Word
        MOV DPTR,#8003H; Load DPTR with the address of Control
                        ;Register
        MOVX @DPTR, A   ; Output the Control word to Control Register
        JMP $           ; Simply Loop here
END     ;END of Assembly Program
```

5.3.6 Interrupts

Before going to the details of *8051* interrupt system, let us have a look at interrupts in general and how interrupts work in microprocessor/controller systems.

5.3.6.1 What is Interrupt? As the name indicates, interrupt is something that produces some kind of interruption. In microprocessor and microcontroller systems, an interrupt is defined as a signal that initiates changes in normal program execution flow. The signal that generates changes in normal program execution flow may come from an external device connected to the microprocessor/controller, requesting the system that it needs immediate attention or the interrupt signal may come from some of the internal units of the processor/controller such as timer overflow indication signal. The first type of interrupt signals are referred as external interrupts.

5.3.6.2 Why Interrupts? From a programmer point of view interrupt is a boon. Interrupts are very useful in situations where you need to read or write some data from or to an externally connected device. Without interrupts, the normal procedure adopted is polling the device to get the status. You can write your program in two ways to poll the device. In the first method your program polls the device continuously till the device is ready to send data to the controller or ready to accept data from the controller. This technique achieves the desired objective effectively by sacrificing the processor time for that single task. Also there is a chance for the program hang up and the total system to crash in certain situations where the external device fails or stops functioning. Another approach for implementing the polling technique is to schedule the polling operation on a time slice basis and allocate the total time on a shared basis to rest of the tasks also. This leads to much more effective utilisation of the processor time. The biggest drawback of this approach is that there is a chance for missing some information coming from the device if the total tasks are high in number. Your device polling will get another chance to poll the device only after the other tasks are done at least once.

Here comes the role of interrupts. If the external device supports interrupt, you can connect the interrupt pin of the device to the interrupt line of the controller. Enable the corresponding interrupt in firmware. Write the code to handle the interrupt request service in a separate function and put the other tasks in the main program code. Here the main program is executed normally and when the external device asserts an interrupt, the main program is interrupted and the processor switches the program execution to the interrupt request service. On finishing the execution of the interrupt request service, the program flow is automatically diverted back to the main stream and the main program resumes its execution exactly from the point where it got interrupted.

5.3.6.3 Use of Interrupts In any interrupt based systems, interrupts are mainly used for accomplishing the following tasks:

1. I/O data transfer between peripheral devices and processor/controller
2. Timing applications
3. Handling emergency situations (e.g. switch off the system when the battery status falls below the critical limit in battery operated systems)
4. Context switching/Multitasking/Real-Time application programming
5. Event driven programming

5.3.7 The *8051* Interrupt System

I hope by now you got reasonably good information on interrupts and interrupt handling. Now let us move on to the interrupt system of *8051* microcontroller. The basic *8051* and its ROMless counterpart 8031AH supports five interrupt sources; namely two external interrupts, two timer interrupts and the serial interrupt. The serial interrupt is an ORed combination of the two serial interrupts; Receive Interrupt (RI) and Transmit Interrupt (TI).

5.3.7.1 Enabling Interrupts The interrupt system of *8051* can be enabled or disabled totally under software control. This is achieved by setting or clearing the global interrupt enable bit of the Special Function Register Interrupt Enable (IE). Also, each interrupt can be enabled or disabled individually by setting or clearing the corresponding interrupt enable bit in the SFR Interrupt Enable.

Interrupt Enable (IE) (SFR- A8H) The bit details of the Interrupt Enable Register is given below:

IE.7	IE.6	IE.5	IE.4	IE.3	IE.2	IE.1	IE.0
EA	RSD	RSD	ES	ET1	EX1	ET0	EX0

The table given below explains the meaning and use of each bit.

Bit	Name	Description
EA	Enable All	EA = 0 disable all interrupts. EA = 1 enable all interrupts, which are individually enabled by setting their corresponding enable bit in Interrupt Enable SFR.
RSD	Reserved	Unimplemented. Reserved for future use
ES	Enable Serial	ES = 1 enables Serial Interrupt. ES = 0 disables it
ET1	Enable Timer 1	ET1 = 1 enable Timer1 Interrupt. ET1 = 0 disables it
EX1	Enable External 1	EX1 = 1 enable External Interrupt 1. EX1 = 0 disables it
ET0	Enable Timer 0	ET0=1 enable Timer0 Interrupt. ET0=0 disables it
EX0	Enable External 0	EX0=1 enable External Interrupt 0. EX0 = 0 disables it

The following code snippet illustrates the enabling of Timer 0 interrupt and disabling of all other interrupts.

```
ORL IE, #10000010B    ; Set bits EA & ET0. Preserve other
                      ; bits as such
ANL IE, #11100010B    ; Reset bits ES, ET1, EX1 and EX0.
                      ; Preserve other bits as such
```

The instruction *ORL IE, #10000010B* sets the global interrupt enabler bit *EA(IE.7)* and the Timer 0 Interrupt enabler bit *ET0 (IE.1)*. The status of all other bits in the IE register is preserved. The instruction *ANL IE, #11100010B* preserves the status of the global interrupt enabler bit *EA(IE.7)*, the *RSD (IE.6 & IE.5)* bits and the Timer 0 Interrupt enabler bit *ET0 (IE.1)* and resets the Serial interrupt enabler bit *ES(IE.4)*, Timer 1 Interrupt enabler bit *ET1 (IE.3)*, External Interrupt 1 enabler bit *EX1 (IE.2)* and External Interrupt 0 enabler bit *EX0 (IE.0)*. This ensures that the reserved bits *RSD (IE.6 & IE.5)* are left untouched. The same can also be achieved by individually setting or clearing the corresponding bits of IE register using *SETB* and *CLR* instructions. This requires more number of instructions to achieve the result.

Note: Though the corresponding interrupt bits are 'set' in the IE register, the Interrupts will not be enabled and serviced if the global interrupt enabler, EA bit of the Interrupt Enable Register (IE) is 0.

5.3.7.2 Setting Interrupt Priorities In a Real World application, interrupts can occur at any time (asynchronous behaviour) and different interrupts may occur simultaneously. This may confuse the processor on deciding which interrupt is to be serviced first. This arbitration problem is resolved by setting interrupt priorities. Interrupt priority is configured under software control. The Special Function Register Interrupt Priority (IP) Register is the one holding the interrupt priority settings for each interrupt.

Interrupt Priority Register (IP) (SFR-B8H) The bit details of the Interrupt Priority Register is explained in the table below.

IP.7	IP.6	IP.5	IP.4	IP.3	IP.2	IP.1	IP.0
RSD	RSD	RSD	PS	PT1	PX1	PT0	PX0

The table given below explains the meaning and use of each bit in the IP register.

Bit	Name	Description
RSD	Reserved	Unimplemented. Reserved for future use
PS	Serial interrupt priority	PS = 1 sets priority to Serial Interrupt
PT1	Timer 1 interrupt priority	PT1 = 1 sets priority to Timer1 Interrupt
PX1	External 1 interrupt priority	PX1 = 1 sets priority to External Interrupt 1
PT0	Timer 0 interrupt priority	PT0 = 1 sets priority to Timer 0 interrupt
PX0	External 0 interrupt priority	EX0 = 1 sets priority to External interrupt 0

The interrupt control system of *8051* contains latches to hold the status of each interrupt. The status of each interrupt flags are latched and updated during S5P2 of every machine cycle (Refer to machine cycles for information on S5P2). The latched samples are polled during the following machine cycle. If the flag for an enabled interrupt is found to be set in S5P2 of the previous cycle, the interrupt system transfers the program flow to the corresponding interrupt's service routine in the code memory (Provided none of the conditions described in section "Different conditions blocking an interrupt" blocks the vectoring of the interrupt). The Interrupt Service Routine address for each interrupt in the code memory is listed below.

Interrupt number	Interrupt source	ISR Location in code memory
0	External interrupt 0	0003H
1	Timer 0 interrupt	000BH

2	External interrupt 1	0013H
3	Timer 1 interrupt	001BH
4	Serial interrupt	0023H

It is to be noted that each Interrupt Service Routine (ISR) is allocated 8 bytes of code memory in the code memory space.

From the IP Register architecture it is obvious that each interrupt can be individually programmed to one of two priority levels by setting or clearing the corresponding priority bit in the Interrupt Priority Register. Some general info on *8051* interrupts is given below:

1. If two interrupt requests of different priority levels are received simultaneously, the request of higher priority interrupt is serviced.
2. If interrupt requests of the same priority level are received simultaneously, the order in which the interrupt flags are polled internally is served first. First polled first served. (Also known as internal polling sequence.)
3. A low-priority interrupt can always be interrupted by a high priority interrupt.
4. A low-priority interrupt in progress can never be interrupted by another low priority interrupt.
5. A high priority interrupt in progress cannot be interrupted by a low priority interrupt or an interrupt of equal priority.

5.3.7.3 Different conditions blocking an Interrupt It is not necessary that an interrupt should be serviced immediately on request. The following situations can block an interrupt request or delay the servicing of an interrupt request in *8051* architecture.

1. All interrupts are globally disabled by clearing the Enable All (EA) bit of Interrupt Enable register.
2. The interrupt is individually disabled by clearing its corresponding enable bit in the Interrupt Enable Register (IE).
3. An interrupt of higher priority or equal priority is already in progress.
4. The current polling machine cycle is not the final cycle in the execution of the instruction in progress (To ensure that the instruction in progress will be completed before vectoring to the interrupt service routine. In this state the LCALL generation to the ISR location is postponed till the completion of the current instruction).
5. The instruction in execution is RETI or a write to the IE/IP Register. (Ensures the interrupt related instructions will not make any conflicts).

In the first three conditions the interrupt is not serviced at all whereas conditions 4 and 5 services the interrupt request with a delay.

5.3.7.4 Returning from an Interrupt Service Routine An Interrupt Service Routine should end with an RETI instruction as the last executable instruction for the corresponding ISR. Executing the RETI instruction informs the interrupt system that the service routine for the corresponding interrupt is finished and it clears the corresponding priority-X (X=1 High priority) interrupt in progress flag by clearing the corresponding flip flop. This enables the system to accept any interrupts with low priority or equal priority of the interrupt which was just serviced. Remember an interrupt of higher priority can always interrupt a lower priority even if the corresponding priority's interrupt in progress flag is set. Executing the RETI instruction POPs (retrieves) the Program Counter (PC) content from stack and the program flow is brought back to the point where the interruption occurred.

In operation, RETI is similar to RET where RETI indicates return from an Interrupt Service Routine and RET indicates return from a normal routine. RETI clears the interrupt in progress flag as well as POPs (retrieves) the content of the Program Counter register to bring the program flow back to the point where it got interrupted. RET instruction only POPs the content of the Program Counter register and brings the program flow back to the point where the interruption occurred.

Will a non serviced Interrupt be serviced later? This is a genuine doubt raised by beginners in the *8051* based system design. The answer is '*No*'. Each interrupt polling sequence is a new one and it happens at S5P2 of each machine cycle. If an interrupt is not serviced in a machine cycle for the reason that it occurred simultaneously with another high priority interrupt, will be lost. There is no mechanism in place for holding the non serviced interrupts in queue and marking them as pending interrupts and servicing them later.

5.3.7.5 Priority Levels for 8051 Interrupts By default the *8051* architecture supports two levels of priority which is already explained in the previous sections. The first priority level is determined by the settings of the Interrupt Priority (IP) register. The second level is determined by the internal hardware polling sequence. The internal polling sequence based priority determination comes into action if two or more interrupt requests of equal priority occurs simultaneously. The internal polling based priority within the same level of priority is listed below in the descending order of priority.

Interrupt	Priority
External interrupt 0	HIGHEST
Timer 0 overflow interrupt	↓
External interrupt 1	
Timer 1 overflow interrupt	
Serial interrupt	LOWEST

5.3.7.6 What Happens when an Interrupt Occurs? On identifying the interrupt request number, the following actions are generated by the processor:

1. Complete the execution of instruction in progress.
2. The Program Counter (PC) content which is the address of the next instruction in code memory which will be executed in normal program flow is pushed automatically to the stack. Program Counter Low byte (PCL) is pushed first and Program Counter High (PCH) byte is pushed next.
3. Clear the corresponding interrupt flags if the interrupt is a timer or external interrupt (only for transition activated (edge triggered) configuration).
4. Set interrupt in progress flip flop.
5. Generate a long call (LCALL) to the corresponding Interrupt Service Routine address in the code memory (Known as vectoring of interrupt).

5.3.7.7 Interrupt Latency In the 8051 architecture, the interrupt flags are sampled and latched at S5P2 of each machine cycle. The latched samples are polled during S5P2 of the following machine cycle to find out their state. If the polling process identifies a priority interrupt flag's flip flop as set, an LCALL to its ISR location is generated (If and only if none of the conditions listed under the topic ***"Different conditions blocking an interrupt"*** blocks it). Interrupt latency is the time elapsed between the assertion of the interrupt and the start of the ISR for the same.

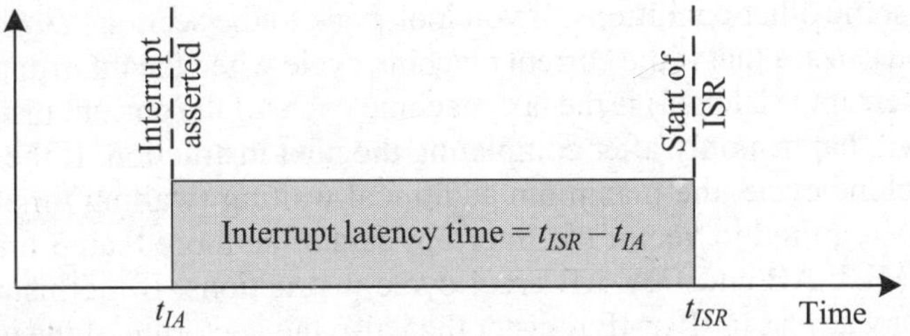

Fig. 5.21 Interrupt Latency

Interrupt latency is highly significant in real-time applications and is very crucial in time-critical applications. Interrupt latency can happen due to various reasons. For external interrupts there is no synchronisation with the system (asynchronous in behaviour) and so it can occur at any point of time. But the processor latches each interrupt flag only at S5P2 of each machine cycle. So there is no point even if the interrupt occurs at S1P1 of the machine cycle. It is latched only at S5P2 of the current machine cycle and the latched interrupts flags are polled at S5P2 of the following machine cycle and an LCALL is generated to the corresponding ISR, if no other conditions block the call. So this delay itself contributes a significant part in interrupt latency. Even if the ISR is entered some delay can be happened by the number of register contents to be stored (PUSH instructions) and other actions to be taken before executing the ISR task. The interrupt latency part which contributes the delay in servicing the ISR is the sum of the following time delays.

Time between the interrupt assertion to the start of state S5 of current machine cycle (polling cycle) + (Time for S5 & S6) + Remaining machine cycles for the current instruction in execution (The current execution should not be RETI or instructions accessing registers IE or IP, if so there will be an additional delay of the execution time for the next instruction) + LCALL generation time. The LCALL generation time is 12 T States (2 Machine cycles).

If the current machine cycle (the polling cycle) is the last cycle of the current instruction in execution and the current instruction in execution is other than RETI or instruction accessing IE or IP register, the interrupt vectoring happens at the shortest possible time and it is given as

Time between the interrupt asserted to start of state S5 of current machine cycle (polling cycle) + (S5+S6 T state + 12 clock)
= Time between the Interrupt Asserted to the start of state S5 + $(((1+1+12) \times 2)/f_{osc})$ seconds. (1 T state = 2 clock cycles and 1 clock cycle = $1/f_{osc}$)

The minimum time required to identify an interrupt by the system is one machine cycle, i.e. if an interrupt occurs at S5 of a machine cycle, it is latched and it is identified as an interrupt at state S5 of next machine cycle (Polling cycle). Hence the minimum time from interrupt assertion to S5 of the polling machine cycle is 1 machine cycle (12 clock periods). The maximum time required to identify an interrupt by the system is approximately 2 machine cycles. Assume the interrupt is asserted at state S6 of a machine cycle, it is latched at S5 of next machine cycle and the latched value is polled at S5 of next machine cycle. Hence the minimum time between the 'Interrupt Asserted' to state S5 of the current machine cycle (polling cycle) is 6 T States (1 machine cycle). That means State S6 of previous machine cycle to state S5 of current machine cycle. Hence the minimum acknowledgement time will be 20 T States (Since 1 machine cycle = 6 T states. The approximate response delay will be 3 machine cycles).

3 machine cycles is the minimum response delay for acknowledging an interrupt in a single interrupt system. There may have additional wait times which come as an addition to the minimum response

delay, depending on some other conditions. If you look back to the section "***Different conditions blocking an Interrupt***" you can see that if the current machine cycle when the interrupt asserted (The machine cycle at which the interrupt is latched) is the last machine cycle of the current instruction in progress, the interrupt vectoring will happen only after completing the next instruction. If the instruction in progress is not in its final machine cycle, the maximum additional waiting (waiting time excluding the LCALL generation time) time required to vector the Interrupt cannot be more than 3 machine cycles since the longest instructions MUL AB and DIV AB are 4 cycle instructions. If the instruction in progress is a RETI instruction or any access to IP or IE register then also the vectoring of the interrupt service routine will be delayed till the execution of next instruction. If the next instruction following the RETI or IP/IE register related instruction is MUL AB or DIV AB, the additional wait time will be 5 machine cycles (RETI and IP/IE related instructions are 2 machine cycle instructions).

In brief, the response time for interrupt in 8051 system is always more than 3 machine cycles and less than 9 machine cycles.

5.3.7.8 Configuring External Interrupts 8051 supports two external interrupts, namely, *External interrupt 0* and *External interrupt 1*. These are hardware interrupts. Two port pins of Port 3 serve the purpose of external interrupt input line. External interrupts are usually used for connecting peripheral devices. The external interrupt assertion can be either level triggered or edge triggered depending on the external device connected to the interrupt line. From the *8051* side it is configurable and the configuration is done at the SFR Timer/Counter Control Register (TCON). Bits TCON.0 and TCON.2 of TCON register configures the same for External Interrupt 0 and 1 respectively. TCON.0 is also known as Interrupt 0 type control bit (IT0). Setting this bit to 1 configures the external interrupt 0 as falling edge triggered. Clearing the bit configures the external interrupt 0 as low level triggered. Similarly, TCON.2 is known as Interrupt 1 type control bit (IT1). Setting this bit to 1 configures the external interrupt 1 as falling edge triggered. Clearing this bit configures the external interrupt 1 as low level triggered.

For external interrupts, the interrupt line should be asserted by the externally connected device to a minimum time period of the interval between two consecutive latching, i.e. S6P1 of previous machine cycle to S5P2 of current machine cycle (1 Machine cycle). Otherwise it may not be identified by the processor (Only interrupts which are found asserted during the latching time (S5P2) will be identified).

5.3.7.9 Single Stepping Program with the Help of External Interrupts Single stepping is the process of executing the program instruction by instruction. This can be achieved with the help of the external interrupt 0 or 1 and a small firmware modification. This works on the basic principle that an interrupt request will not be acknowledged if an interrupt of equal priority is in progress and if the instruction in progress when the interrupt is asserted is a RETI instruction, the vectoring will happen only after executing an instruction from the main program, which is interrupted by the interrupt. If the external interrupt is in the asserted state, the interrupt vectoring happens after executing one instruction from the main program. This execution switching between the main program and ISR can be achieved by a simple ISR firmware modification. Connecting a push button switch to the external interrupt line 0 through a resistor is the only hardware change needed for a *single step* operation (Fig. 5.22). Configure INT0 as level triggered in firmware. Activating the push button asserts the INT0 interrupt and the processor starts executing the ISR for interrupt 0. At the end, the ISR waits for a 1 to 0 transition at the INT0 line that asserts the external interrupt 0 again. The next instruction that is going to be executed on asserting the INT0 is *RETI* and according to the general interrupt vectoring principle the processor will go back to the point in the main code where it got interrupted and after completing one instruction it will again come back to the INT0 ISR. This process is repeated.

Single stepping can also be done with external interrupt 1. Make external interrupt 1 as level triggered and connect the hardware set up to pin P3.3 (external interrupt 1 line) and modify the ISR for external interrupt 1 as explained for external interrupt 0 ISR. It will work fine. Single stepping is a very useful method in debugging the application. It gives an insight into the various effects produced by the execution of an instruction, like registers and memory locations modified as a result of the execution of an instruction.

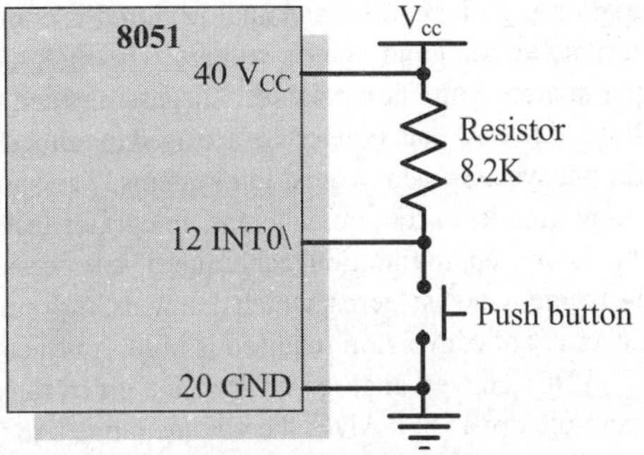

Fig. 5.22 **Hardware setup for single stepping program with external interrupt**

Example 1

Design an *8051* microcontroller based data acquisition system for interfacing the Analog to Digital Converter ADC, ADC0801 from National semiconductors. The system should satisfy the following:

1. Use Atmel's AT89C51/52 or AT89S8252 (Flash microcontroller with In System Programming (ISP) support) for designing the system. Use a 12MHZ crystal resonator for generating the necessary clock signal for the controller. Use on-chip program memory for storing the program instructions.
2. The data lines of the ADC is interfaced to Port 2 of the microcontroller. The control signals (RD\, WR\, CS\) to the ADC is supplied through Port 3 pins of microcontroller.
3. The Analog voltage range for conversion is from 0V to 5. The varying analog input voltage is generated from the 5V supply voltage (Vcc) using a variable resistor (Potentiometer). The ADC asserts its interrupt line to interrupt the microcontroller when the AD conversion is over and data is available at the ADC data port.
4. The microcontroller reads the data on receiving the interrupt and stores it in the memory. The successive data conversion is initiated after reading the converted data for a sample. Only the most recent 16 samples are stored in the microcontroller memory.

This example is a good starting point for a discussion on data converters and their use in embedded applications. The processing/controlling unit (The core of the embedded system) of every embedded system is made up of digital systems and they work only on digital data. The processor/controller is capable of dealing with binary (digital) data only. As mentioned in the beginning, embedded systems are in constant interaction with the real world through sensors and actuators. In most of the situations, the signals which are handled by embedded systems fall into the category 'analog'. Analog signals are continuous in nature. Most of the embedded systems used in control and instrumentation applications include the monitoring or control of at least one analog signal. The thermocouple-based temperature sensing system used in industrial control is a typical example for this. The thermocouple generates millivoltage (mV) in response to the changes in temperature. This voltage signals are filtered and signal conditioned and then applied to the monitoring system for monitoring and control purpose. Digital systems are not capable of handling analog signals as such for processing. The analog input signal from sensors needs to be digitized (quantized) before inputting to the digital systems. In a similar fashion, the output from digital systems are digital (discrete) in nature and they cannot be applied directly to analog systems which require continuous signals for their operation. The problem of handling the analog and digital data in embedded systems is handled by data converters. Data converters fall into two categories, namely; Analog to Digital Converters (ADC) and Digital to Analog Converters (DAC). Analog to Digital Converter (ADC) converts analog signals to corresponding digital representation, whereas Digital to Analog Converter (DAC) converts digital signals to the corresponding analog representation.

ADCs are used at the input stage of the processor/controller and DACs are used at the output stage of the processor/controller. ADCs and DACs are available in the form of Integrated Circuits (ICs) from different manufacturers. These chips are used for interfacing the processor/controller with sensors/actuators which produces/requires analog signals.

Analog to digital conversion can be accomplished through different conversion techniques. **Successive approximation** and **integrator** are the two commonly adopted analog to digital conversion techniques. In the successive approximation technique, the input analog signal is compared against a reference voltage. The reference voltage is adjusted till it matches the input analog voltage. The integrator technique changes the input voltage to time and compares the new parameters with known values. Discussing each technique in detail is out of the scope of this book (The current scope is limited to how data converters are used in embedded system designs) and readers are advised to refer books dedicated on digital systems/data acquisition systems. The successive approximation technique is faster in data conversion and at the same time less accurate, whereas, integrator technique is highly accurate but the conversion speed is slow compared to successive approximation technique. The successive approximation ADCs are used in embedded systems like control and instrumentation systems, which demands high conversion speed. The Integrator type ADCs are used in systems where the accuracy of conversion required is high. A typical example is a digital multimeter.

ADCs convert analog voltages in a given range to a binary data within the range supported by the ADC register. For example, for an 8bit ADC, the voltage range 0 to 5 V is represented with binary data 00H to FFH. The voltage range (5-0) is split across the 256 (0 to 255) steps. Hence the resolution of the ADC is represented as 1/256, meaning the binary data is incremented by one for a rise in 1/256 V in the input voltage. The resolution offered by the ADC depends on the input voltage range and the register width of the ADC. ADC can be used for the conversion of +ve as well as –ve voltage and range of I/p with offset from 0. It is the responsibility of the firmware developer to interpret all these conditions based on the system design. For example, if the input voltage is in the range 1 to 5V, the ADC represents 1 as 00H and 5 as FFH. The firmware developer should handle this appropriately.

The IC ADC0801ADC from National Semiconductor is an example for successive approximation ADC. The ADC0801 is designed in such a way that its tri-stated output latches can directly drive the processor/controller data bus/port. ADC0801 appears as a memory location or I/O port to the processor/controller and it doesn't require any additional bus interface logic. The logic inputs and outputs of ADC0801 meets both TTL and CMOS voltage level specifications and it can be used with processors/controllers from the CMOS/TTL logic family without using any interface conversion logic. ADC0801 supports input voltage range from 0 to 5V and two inputs, $V_{IN}(+)$ and $V_{IN}(-)$ for differential analog voltages. The input signal is applied to $V_{IN}(+)$ and $V_{IN}(-)$ is grounded for converting single ended positive voltages. For single ended negative voltage conversion, the input voltage is applied to $V_{IN}(-)$ and $V_{IN}(+)$ is grounded. ADC0801 provides an option for adjusting the span (range) of input voltage for conversion. The span adjustment is achieved by applying a voltage, which is half of the required span, at the $V_{REF}/2$ (Pin N0. 9) of ADC0801. For example, if the required span is 3V, apply a voltage 1.5V at pin $V_{REF}/2$. This converts the input voltage range 0V to 3V to digital data 00H to FFH. Keeping the $V_{REF}/2$ pin unconnected sets the span to 5V (The input varies from 0V to 5V). If the span is less than 5 and the range of input signal starts with an offset from 0V, the same can be achieved by applying corresponding voltages at pins $V_{REF}/2$ and $V_{IN}(-)$. As an example consider the requirement where, the span is 3V and range is from 0.5V to 3.5V, a voltage of 1.5V is applied to Pin $V_{REF}/2$ and 0.5V to pin $V_{IN}(-)$.The AD converter requires a clock signal for its operation. The minimal hardware connection required to build the AD converter system is shown in Fig. 5.23.

The AD converter contains an internal clock generator circuit. For putting the chip into operation, either an external clock or the built in clock generator can be used. ADC0801 provides a pin, CLK IN (Pin No. 4), for connecting external clock signal. The external clock signals can be generated using an oscillator circuit or the clock signal available from the CLK OUT pin of the microcontroller can be applied to the CLK IN. The internal clock generator circuit of the ADC can be used for generating the necessary clock signal to the system by connecting an external resistor and capacitor across the pins CLK IN and CLK R as shown in the schematic. The CLK IN pin is internally connected to the input pin of a Schmitt trigger and CLK R is connected to the o/p pin of the Schmitt triggers as shown in Fig. 5.24.

The frequency of the circuit is represented as $f_{CLK} = 1/1.1\ RC$. The frequency range for ADC0801 is in the range 100 kHz to 800 kHz

ADC0801 requires three necessary control signals namely; RD\, WR\, CS\ for its operation. The CS\ signal is used for activating the ADC chip. For starting a conversion, the CS\ and WR\ signals should be asserted low. The internal Successive Approximation Register (SAR) of the chip is reset and the output data lines of the ADC enter high impedance state on asserting the WR\ signal. The data conversion begins when the WR\ signal makes a transition from asserted state to high. The ADC asserts the line INTR\ on completion of the conversion. This signal generates an interrupt at the processor. The converted digital data is available on the data bus of the ADC from the moment when the INTR\ line is asserted low. The INTR\ signal is reset when the RD\ signal is asserted low by the processor.

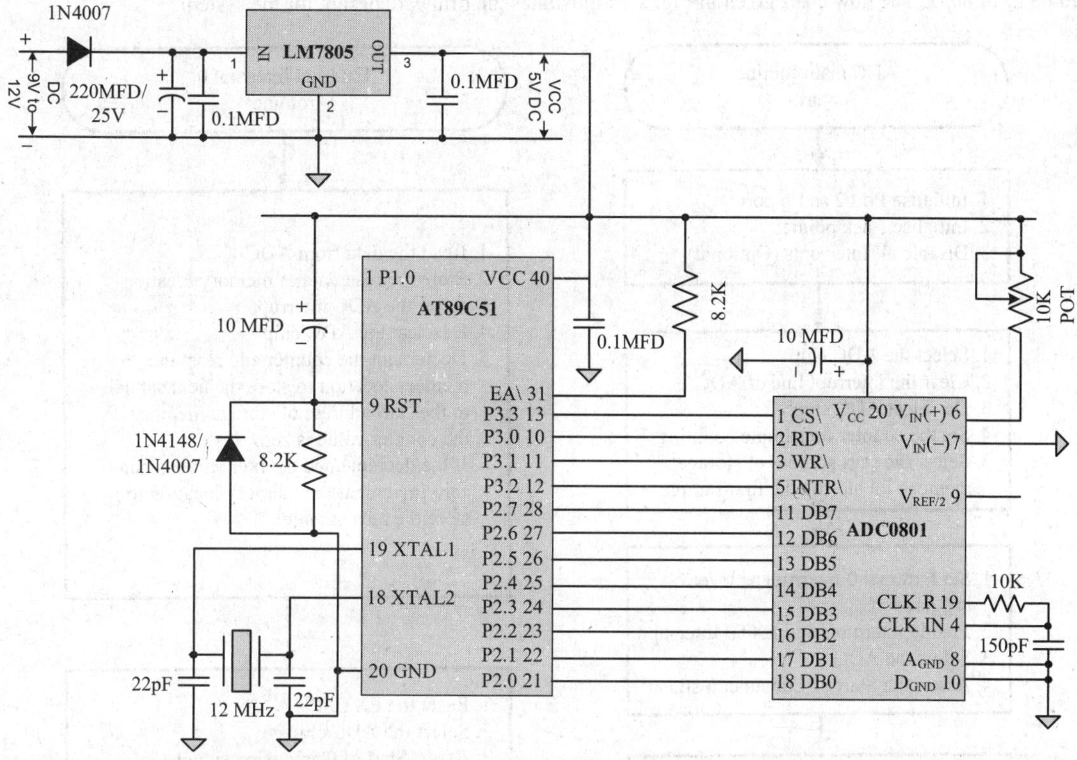

Fig. 5.23 **Interfacing *ADC0801* with *8051***

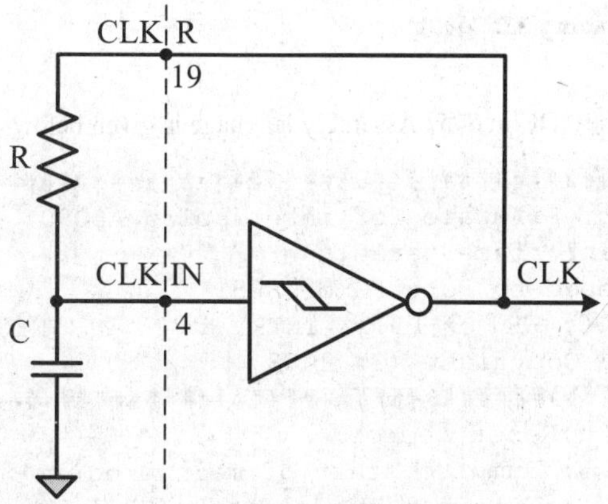

Fig. 5.24 **Schmitt Trigger Circuit**

In the current design, a potentiometer is used for varying the voltage from 0V to 5V. The data lines of the ADC are interfaced to Port 2 of the controller. The control signals to the ADC are supplied through the pins of Port 3. Port Pin P3.3 supplies the Chip Select (CS\) signal and Port Pin P3.0 supplies the RD\ Signal to the ADC. The WR\ signal to ADC is supplied through Port Pin P3.1. The INTR\ signal line of ADC is interfaced to the External Interrupt 0 (INT0\) line (Port Pin P3.2) of *8051*. The flow chart given in Fig. 5.25 illustrates the firmware design for the system.

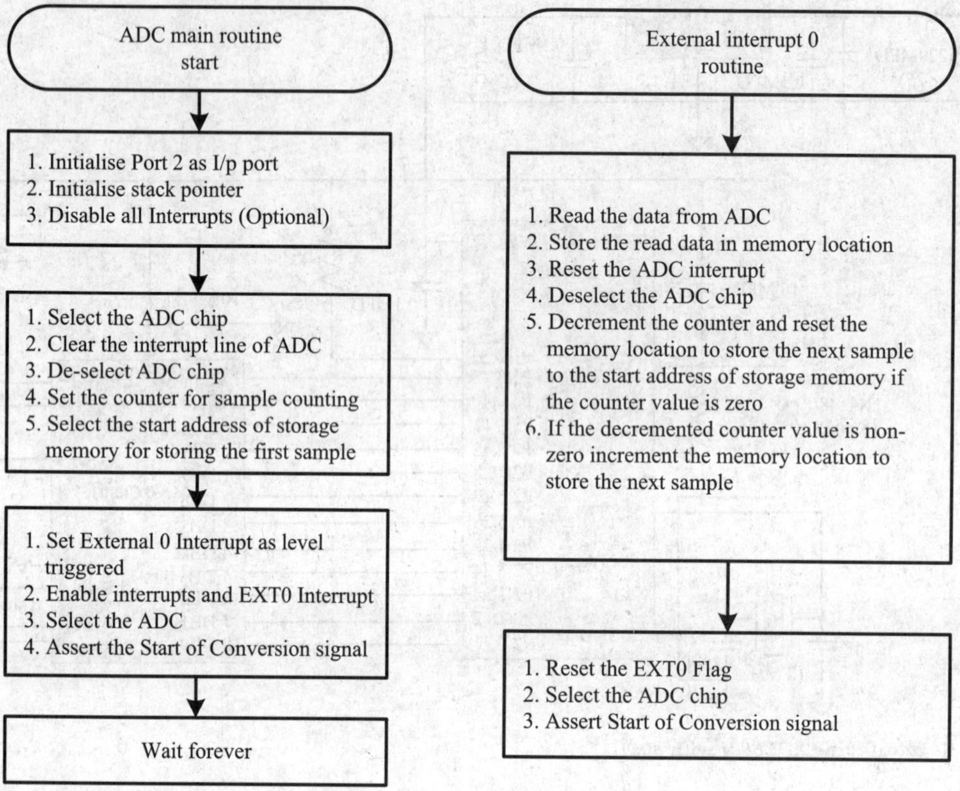

Fig. 5.25 **Flow chart for interfacing ADC0801**

The firmware for interfacing the ADC in *8051* Assembly language is given below.

```
;#####################################################################
;adc0801_interrupt.src. Firmware for interfacing ADC801 with 8051
;ADC - 8051 Physical Interface details
;ADC Data lines connected to Port P2 of 8051
;CS\ →P3.3; RD\ → P3.0; WR\ → P3.1; INTR\ → P3.2 (INT0\)
;Written by Shibu K V. Copyright (C) 2008
;#####################################################################
ORG 0000H              ;Reset vector
        JMP 0050H      ; Jump to start of main program
ORG 0003H              ; External Interrupt 0 ISR location
        ; The ISR will not fit in 8 bytes size.
        ; Hence it is implemented as separate routine
        CALL EXTERNAL_INTR0 ; Function implementing Extnl 0 routine
        RETI           ; Return
```

```
ORG 000BH                ; Timer 0 Interrupt ISR location
      RETI               ; Simply return. Do nothing
ORG 0013H                ; External Interrupt 1 ISR location
      RETI               ; Simply return. Do nothing
ORG 001BH                ; Timer 1 Interrupt ISR location
      RETI               ; Simply return. Do nothing
ORG 0023H                ; Serial Interrupt ISR location
      RETI               ; Simply return. Do nothing
;#####################################################################
ORG 0050H                ; Start of main Program
      MOV P2, #0FFH      ; Configure Port2 as input Port
      MOV SP, #08H       ; Set stack at memory location 08H
      CLR P3.3           ; Select ADC
      CLR P3.0           ; Clear ADC interrupt line by asserting ADC
                         ; RD\
      SETB P3.3          ; De-select ADC
      MOV R0, #16        ; Set the counter for 16 samples
      MOV R1, #20H       ; Set start of sample storage memloc as 20H
      CLR IT0            ; Set External Interrupt 0 as low-level
                         ; triggered
      MOV IE, #10000001b ; Enable only External 0 interrupt
      CLR P3.3           ; Select ADC
      CLR P3.1           ; Trigger ADC Conversion; Reset ADC SAR
      NOP                ; Hold the WR\Signal low for 2 machine cycles
      NOP
      SETB P3.1          ; Toggle WR\ line from 0 to 1 to initiate-
                         ; conversion
      JMP $              ; Loop for ever
;#####################################################################
; Routine for handling External 0 Interrupt
; External 0 Interrupt is asserted when ADC finishes data conversion
;#####################################################################
EXTERNAL_INTR0:
      MOV @R1, P2
      CLR P3.0           ; Assert RD\ Signal to clear INTR\ ADC Signal
                         ; line
      NOP
      NOP
      SETB P3.0
      SETB P3.3          ; De-select ADC
      DJNZ R0, RETURN
      ; The 16 samples are taken
      ; overwrite the previous samples with new
      MOV R1, #1FH ; 20H is the mem loc holding the start of sample
      MOV R0, #16        ; Reload Sample counter with 16
RETURN: INC R1           ; Increment mem loc to hold next sample
      CLR IE0            ; Clear the interrupt 0 edge detect flag
      CLR P3.3           ; Select ADC
```

```
        CLR P3.1        ; Trigger ADC Conversion; Reset ADC SAR
        NOP             ; Hold the WR\Signal low for 2 machine cycles
        NOP
        SETB P3.1       ; Toggle WR\ line to initiate conversion
        RET
END     ; END of Assembly Program
```

5.3.8 Timer Units

Timers are very essential for generating precise time reference in any system. Timers can be implemented in either software or hardware. Hardware timers are dedicated hardware units and are highly precise in operation. The Standard 8051architecture supports two 16bit hardware timers that can be configured to operate in either timer mode or external event counting mode. The timers are named as *Timer 0* and *Timer 1*. If the timers are configured in timer function mode, the corresponding timer register is incremented once in each machine cycle. Since one machine cycle consists of six T-States (12 clock cycles), the timer increment rate is 1/12th of the oscillator frequency ($f_{osc}/12$).

If the timer unit is configured for counter mode, the timer register is incremented in response to a one to zero transition at the corresponding external port pin for counter mode. The external input pins are sampled during S5P2 of each machine cycle. If the sample shows a high in S5P2 of one machine cycle and a low in any of the next sampling time, the counter register is incremented by one. The count is updated only at S3P1 of the machine cycle following the machine cycle in which the transition is detected. It is obvious that it takes a minimum of two machine cycles to identify a 1 to 0 transition (2 machine cycle corresponds to 24 clock periods). So the maximum count rate for external events is $f_{osc}/24$, where f_{osc} is the oscillator frequency (Clock frequency). Timer 0 and Timer 1 can be configured as timer unit or counter unit by using timer/counter mode select bit of the special function register Timer/counter Mode Control (TMOD). Timer 0 and Timer 1 can be operated in four different modes. The mode selection is done by the timer mode select bits of TMOD register.

Timer/Counter Mode Control Register (TMOD) (SFR-89H)

BIT 7	BIT 6	BIT 5	BIT 4	BIT 3	BIT 2	BIT 1	BIT 0
GATE	C/T	M1	M0	GATE	C/T	M1	M0
Timer 1 Configuration				Timer 0 Configuration			

The following table explains the meaning and use of each bit in the TMOD register.

Bit	Name	Description
GATE	Gating control	If this bit is set to 1 in the corresponding timer configuration nibble of TMOD, the corresponding timer/counter will be enabled only when the INT0 /INT1 (INT0 corresponds Timer 0 /Counter 0 & INT1 corresponds Timer 1/Counter 1) line is high and the corresponding timer/counter's run bit TR is enabled in the TCON register. If GATE bit is 0, the timer/counter will run when the corresponding timer/counter's run bit TR is enabled in the TCON register.

C/T	Counter/Timer selector	Counter or timer mode select bit. If this bit is set to 1 in the corresponding timer configuration nibble of TMOD register, the corresponding timer will act as a counter. If the bit is cleared in the corresponding timer configuration nibble of TMOD register, the corresponding timer will function as timer unit.
M1	Mode select bits	The Timer/Counter operation 'mode select' bits. It can be one among the 4 modes.
M0		

The values for bits M0 and M1 and the corresponding mode of operation for the timer/counter is explained in the table given below.

Mode Select Bits		Description
M1	M0	
0	0	Mode 0. 8bit timer with divided by 32 prescaler.
0	1	Mode 1. 16bit timer.
1	0	Mode 2. Autoreload mode. Configures timer register as 8bit timer/counter with auto reload. The lower byte of timer register only gets incremented and when a roll over from FFH to 00H occurs, the lower byte of register is re-loaded with the higher byte of the corresponding timer register. The higher byte always holds the reload value. Timer *x* can be viewed as two 8bit registers namely (TLx) & (THx) where *x* = timer number (0 or 1)
1	1	Mode 3. Timer 1 in this mode simply holds its count. It is similar to disabling the Timer 1 run control bit TR1. Timer 0 in this mode configures as two 8bit registers TL0 and TH0. TL0 is configured by the Timer 0 configuration nibble and TH0 is configured by the Timer 1 configuration nibble.

Timer/Counter Control Register (TCON) (SFR-88H) It is a bit addressable special function register that holds the timer/counter interrupt flags and run control bits.

BIT 7	BIT 6	BIT 5	BIT 4	BIT 3	BIT 2	BIT 1	BIT 0
TF1	TR1	TF0	TR 0	IE1	IT1	IE0	IT 0

The following table explains the meaning and use of each bit in the TCON register.

Bit	Name	Description
TF1	Timer/Counter 1 overflow flag	Set by hardware when timer/counter 1 overflows. The flag is automatically cleared when timer 1 interrupt is vectored.
TR1	Timer/Counter 1 Run control	TR1=1 Start timer/counter1 TR1=0 Stops timer/counter 1
TF0	Timer/Counter 0 overflow flag	Set by hardware when timer/counter 0 overflows. The flag is automatically cleared when timer 0 interrupt is vectored.
TR0	Timer/Counter 0 Run control	TR0 = 1 Start Timer/Counter 0 TR0 = 0 Stops Timer/Counter 0
IE1	External Interrupt 1 edge detect flag	Set by hardware when external interrupt 1 edge is detected. Cleared by hardware when interrupt is vectored

IT1	External Interrupt 1 type control	IT1 = 1 Configures the external interrupt 1 to edge triggered (Falling Edge) IT1= 0 Configures the external interrupt 1 to level triggered (Low level)
IE0	External interrupt 0 edge detect flag	Set by hardware when external interrupt 0 edge is detected. Cleared by hardware when interrupt is vectored
IT0	External interrupt 0 type control	IT0 = 1 Configures the external interrupt 0 to edge triggered (Falling edge) IT0 = 0 Configures the external interrupt 0 to level triggered (Low level)

5.3.8.1 Timer/Counter in Mode 0 Timer/Counter-0 and Timer/Counter-1 in mode 0 acts as a 13bit timer/counter (Fig. 5.26). The 13bit register is formed by all 8 bits of TH0 and the lower 5 bits of TL0 for Timer/Counter-0 (All 8 bits of TH1 and the lower 5 bits of TL1 for Timer/Counter-1). The timer/counter mode selection is done by the bit C/T of the register TMOD. Timer/Counter-0 & Timer/Counter-1 has separate selection bits as described earlier. If Timer/Counter-0 is configured as timer and if the corresponding run control bit for Timer/Counter-0 (TR0 in Timer Control Register (TCON)) is set, registers TL0 & TH0 functions as a 13bit register and starts incrementing from its current value. The timer register is incremented by one on each machine cycle. When the 13bit Timer register rolls over from all 1s to all 0s (FF1FH to 0000H), the corresponding timer overflow flag TF0, present in TCON register is set. If the Timer 0 interrupt is in the enabled state and no other conditions block the Timer 0 interrupt, Timer 0 interrupt is generated and is vectored to its corresponding vector address 000BH. On vectoring the interrupt, the TF0 flag is automatically cleared. Operation of Timer 1 in mode 0 is same as that of Timer 0 except that for Timer 1, the 13bit timer register is formed by the registers TL1 and TH1 and the corresponding Timer run control bit is TR1. The Timer 1 overflow flag is TF1 and the corresponding interrupt vector location for Timer 1 is 001BH. It is advised to set the GATE control bit to 0 for timer operations. If the GATE control is set to 1, the timer register is incremented in accordance with each machine cycle only if the corresponding Interrupt line INTRx is high (INT0 for Timer 0 and INT1 for Timer 1).

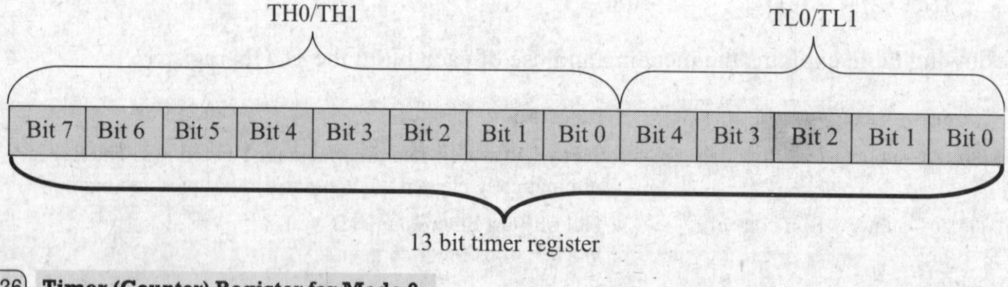

Fig. 5.26 Timer (Counter) Register for Mode 0

Figure 5.27 illustrates the operation of Timer/Counter in Mode 0

It is to be noted that for mode 0 operation, the lower 5 bits of TL0/TL1 (Bit 0 to Bit 4) and all 8 bits of TH0/TH1 forms the 13bit register. When the 5 bits of TL0 rolls over from all 1s (IFH) to all 0s (00H), TH0 is incremented by one. The upper 3 bits of TL0/TL1 is indeterminate (Don't care bits). TH0/TH1

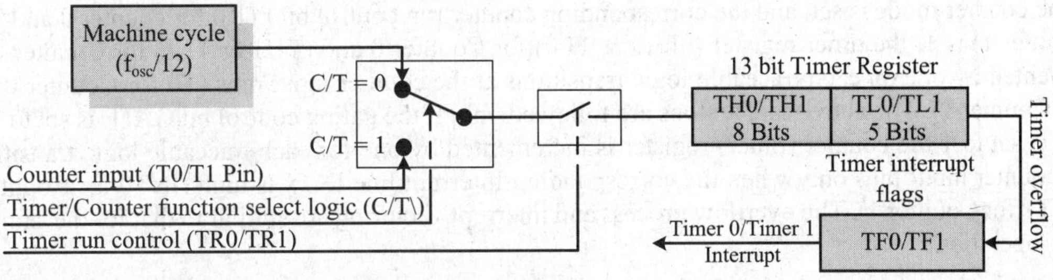

Fig. 5.27 **Timer (Counter) 0/ Timer (Counter) 1 in Mode 0**

runs in its full 8bit mode and act as the 8bit counter whereas, only the 5 least significant bits of TL0/TL1 undergoes changes in accordance with machine cycle and so TL0/TL1 is said to be acting as a prescaler 32 for the 8bit counter TH0/TH1. The timer interrupt is generated when the 13bit timer register rolls over from all 1s to all 0s, i.e. when TH0 count is FFH and TL0 count rolls from 1FH to 00H. The count range for mode 0 is 0000H to 1FFFH.

5.3.8.2 Timer/Counter in Mode 1 Mode 1 operation of Timer (Counter) 0/ Timer (Counter) 1 is similar to that of mode 0 except the timer register size (Fig. 5.28). The timer register is 16bit wide in mode 1. The timer/counter mode selection is done by the bit C/T of the register TMOD. Timer (Counter) 0 and Timer (Counter) 1 has separate selection bits as described earlier. If Timer 0 is configured as a timer and if the corresponding run control bit for Timer 0 (TR0 in Timer Control Unit (TCON)) is set, registers TL0 and TH0 functions as 16bit register and starts incrementing from its current value. The timer register is incremented by one on each machine cycle. When the timer register rolls over from all 1s to all 0s (FFFFH to 0000H), the corresponding timer overflow flag TF0, present in TCON register is set. If Timer 0 interrupt is in the enabled state and no other conditions block the Timer 0 interrupt, Timer 0 interrupt is generated and is vectored to its corresponding vector address 000BH. On vectoring the interrupt, the TF0 flag is automatically cleared. Operation of Timer 1 in mode 1 is same as that of Timer 0 except that for Timer 1 the 16bit timer register is formed by the registers TL1 and TH1 and the corresponding Timer run control bit is TR1. The Timer 1 overflow flag is TF1 and the corresponding interrupt vector location for Timer 1 is 001BH.

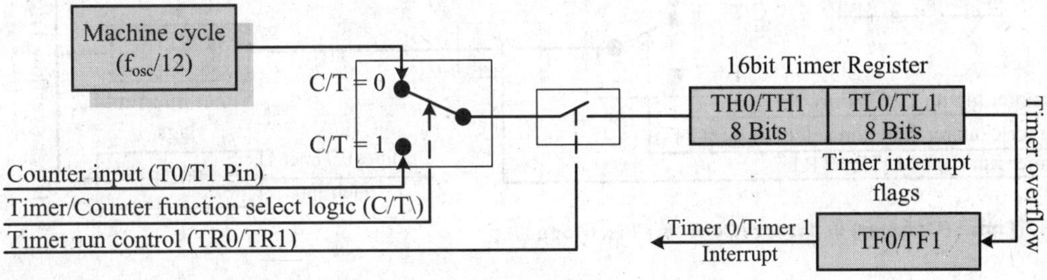

Fig. 5.28 **Timer (Counter) 0/ Timer (Counter) 1 in Mode 1**

It is advised to set the GATE control bit to 0 for timer operations. If the GATE control is set to 1, the timer register is incremented in accordance with each machine cycle only if the corresponding Interrupt line INTx is high (INT0 for Timer 0 and INT1 for Timer 1).

If the counter mode is set, and the corresponding counter run control bit (TR0 for counter 0 and TR1 for counter 1) is 1, the timer register ((TH0 & TL0) for Counter 0 and (TH1 & TL1) for Counter 1) is incremented by one on each traceable logic transitions at the counter input pins (T0 for Counter 0 and T1 for Counter 1). The above said actions are followed only if the gating control bit GATE is set to 0. If GATE is set to 1 the counter (timer) register is incremented by one for each traceable logic transitions at the counter input pins only when the corresponding Interrupt line INTx is high (INT0 for Counter 0 and INT1 for Counter 1). The overflow process and interrupt vectoring are similar to that for the Timer0/ Timer1 operation.

5.3.8.3 Timer/Counter in Mode 2 (Auto Reload Mode) Timer (Counter) 0/ Timer (Counter) 1 in mode 2 acts as 8bit timer/counter (TL0 for Timer (Counter) 0 and TL1 for Timer (Counter) 1) with auto reload on the timer/counter register overflow (TL0 or TL1) (Fig. 5.29). The timer/counter mode selection is done by the bit C/T of the register TMOD. Timer (Counter) 0 & Timer (Counter) 1 has separate selection bits as described earlier. If Timer 0 is configured as timer and if the corresponding run control bit for Timer 0 (TR0) in Timer Control Unit (TCON)) is set, register TL0 functions as 8bit register and starts incrementing from its current value. The timer register is incremented by one on each machine cycle. When the Timer register rolls over from all 1s to all 0s (FFH to 00H), the corresponding timer overflow flag TF0, present in TCON register is set and TL0 is reloaded with the value from TH0. TH0 remains unchanged. If Timer 0 interrupt is in the enabled state and no other conditions block the Timer 0 interrupt, it is vectored to the corresponding vector address 000BH. On vectoring the interrupt, the TF0 flag is automatically cleared. Operation of Timer 1 in mode 2 is same as that of Timer 0 except that for Timer 1 the 8bit timer register is formed by the register TL1 and the corresponding Timer run control bit is TR1. The Timer 1 overflow flag is TF1 and the corresponding interrupt vector location is 001BH. It is advised to set the GATE control bit to 0 for timer operations. If the GATE control is set to 1, the timer register is incremented in accordance with each machine cycle only if the corresponding Interrupt line INTx is high (INT0 for Timer 0 and INT1 for Timer 1).

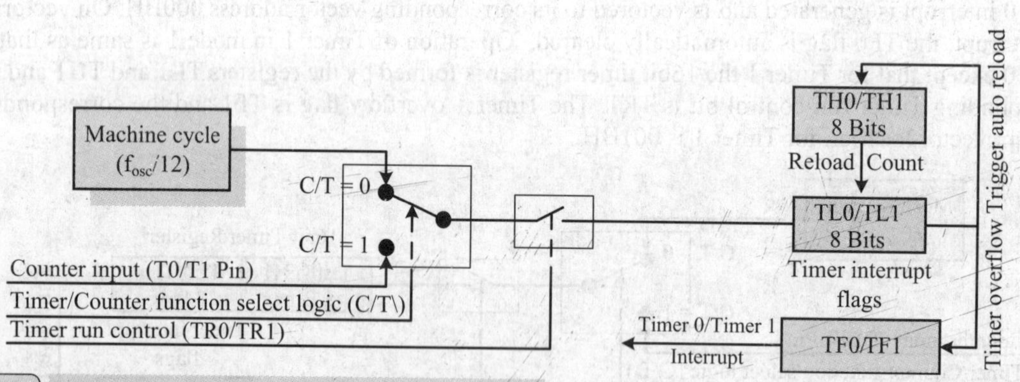

Fig. 5.29 **Timer (Counter) 0/ Timer (Counter) 1 in Mode 2**

If the counter mode is set, and the corresponding counter run control bit (TR0 for counter 0 and TR1 for counter 1) is 1, the timer register (TL0 for Counter 0 and TL1 for Counter 1) is incremented by one on each traceable logic transitions at the counter input pins (T0 for Counter 0 and T1 for Counter1). The above said actions are followed only when the gating control bit GATE is set to 0. If GATE is set to 1, the timer register is incremented by one for each traceable logic transitions at the counter input pins only if the corresponding Interrupt line INTx (INT0 for Counter 0 and INT1 for Counter 1) is high. The overflow process and interrupt vectoring are similar to that of Timer0/Timer1 operation. Timer 1 in Mode 2 is generally used for baudrate generation in serial data transmission.

5.3.8.4 Timer/Counter in Mode 3 Timer/Counter 0 in mode 3 functions as two separate 8bit Timers/Counters (Fig. 5.30). TL0 acts as the timer/counter register for Timer/Counter 0 and TH0 acts as the timer/counter register for Timer/Counter 1. TL0 uses the Timer 0 control bits namely TR0, GATE, C/T, INT0 and TF0. TL0 can run in either counter/timer mode by setting or clearing the C/T bit. Counter operation is controlled by GATE, INT0 pin, T0 pin and TR0 bit as explained earlier. But the operation is similar to that of Timer 0 in mode 3. In mode 3, TH0 supports only timer function and does not support counter function. TH0 counts only the machine cycles, not external events.

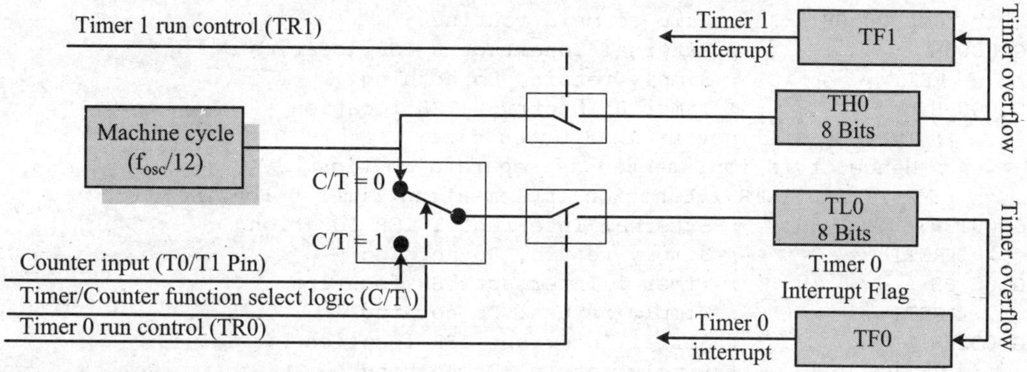

Fig. 5.30 **Timer (Counter) 0 in Mode 3**

The actual Timer 1 (TH1 TL1), when configured to run in mode 3, by using the Timer 1 configuration bits, stops its functioning and simply holds its count.

Thus mode 3 provides an extra 8bit timer. The original Timer 1 (TH1 TL1) can be turned on and off by switching it out and into mode 3 and it can run in either mode 0, mode 1 or mode 2 apart from mode 3 since the acting Timer 1, TH0 in mode 3 is forced to run as an 8bit timer by default, by putting Timer 0 configuration bits to mode 3 (M0, M1 of Timer 0 Control Register = 1). The only shortcoming is that since TH0 is responsible generating Timer 1 interrupt when Timer 0 is configured in mode 3, no interrupt is generated by the actual Timer 1 (TH1 TL1) when it runs in mode 0, 1 or 2 with Timer 0 in mode 3. But still Timer 1 can use for applications that doesn't require Timer interrupts like baudrate generation.

Example 1

Implement the example 1 given under '*Ports*' section (Binary Counter implementation) using timer interrupts.

In the example given under the '*Ports*' section, the display delay is implemented using a delay generator loop. The delay generation can be easily implemented using a timer and the required operations following the delay can be implemented in the timer interrupt handling routine.

8051 provides two timer units and they can be operated in four different modes. The timer units in mode 1 acts as a 16bit timer unit which counts machine cycles from 0 (0000H) to 65535 (FFFFH) and generates timer interrupt when rolls over from 65535 (FFFFH) to 0 (0000H). If the system clock is 12MHz, the timer interrupt is asserted after every 65536 microseconds (0.0655 seconds), if the counter is started with an initial count 00H. For generating a delay of 1 second, the timer interrupt should be generated multiple times. If one timer interrupt generates 50000 microseconds, 100 such interrupts are required to generate a delay of 5 seconds. For generating a delay of 50000 microseconds, the timer should be loaded with a count 65536 – 50000 = 15536 (3CB0H). The following assembly code illustrates the use of timer and timer interrupts for implementing the binary counter requirement. Timer 0 is used for this.

```
;#######################################################################
;binary_counter_timer.src
;Application for implementing binary counter using Timer Interrupt
;The LED is turned on when the port line is at logic 0
;Written by Shibu K V. Copyright (C) 2008
;#######################################################################
ORG 0000H              ; Reset vector
      JMP 0050H        ; Jump to main routine
ORG 0003H              ; External Interrupt 0 ISR location
      RETI             ; Simply return. Do nothing
ORG 000BH              ; Timer 0 Interrupt ISR location
      ; The ISR will not fit in 8 bytes size.
      ; Hence it is implemented as separate routine
      JMP TIMER0_INTR ; Function implementing Timer 0 routine
ORG 0013H              ; External Interrupt 1 ISR location
      RETI             ; Simply return. Do nothing
ORG 001BH              ; Timer 1 Interrupt ISR location
      RETI             ; Simply return. Do nothing
ORG 0023H              ; Serial Interrupt ISR location
      RETI             ; Simply return. Do nothing
ORG 0050H              ; Start of Program Execution
      MOV P2, #0FFH  ; Turn off all LEDs
      ORL IE, #10000010B ; Enable Timer 0 Interrupt
      ANL IE, #11100010B ; Disable all interrupts Except Timer 0
      MOV SP, #08H     ; Set stack at memory location 08H
      MOV R7,#00H      ; Set counter Register R7 to zero.
      CLR TR0
      ;Load Timer 0 with count corresponding to 50000 microseconds
      MOV TL0, #0B8H
      MOV TH0, #3CH
      MOV R0, #100     ; Load The multiplier for the time delay
      ; Configure Timer 0 as Timer in mode 1 (16 bit Timer)
      MOV TMOD, #00000001b
      SETB TR0         ; Start Timer 0
      JMP $            ; Loop for ever
;#######################################################################
; Routine for handling Timer 0 Interrupt
; Checks whether the timer runs for generating the desired delay
; If so display increment the binary counter and display the count
; Load Timer 0 Register and the multiplier for generating next-
; 5 seconds delay
; If the delay generation is not complete (R0>0) simply return
;#######################################################################
```

```
TIMER0_INTR:
        DJNZ R0, RETURN
        INC R7              ; Increment binary counter
        MOV A, R7           ;
        CPL A; The LED's are turned on when corresponding bit is 0
        MOV P2, A ; Display the count on LEDs connected at Port 2
        MOV R0, #100        ; Load the multiplier for the time delay
RETURN: MOV TH0, #3CH
        MOV TL0, #0B8H
        RETI
END     ;END of Assembly Program
```

It should be noted that the Timer 0 ISR involves lot of activities including binary counter increment and display and hence the delay between the successive count display may not be exactly 5 seconds. The timer count can be adjusted to take these operations into account or the displaying of the count can be moved to the main routine and synchronization between main routine and ISR can be implemented through a flag. It is left to the readers as an exercise.

5.3.9 Serial Port

The standard *8051* supports a full duplex (simultaneous data transmission and reception), receive buffered (supports the pipelining system of the reception of second byte before the previously received byte is read from the receive buffer) standard serial interface for serial data transmission. The Special Function Register SBUF provides a common interface to both serial reception and transmission registers. The serial reception and transmission register exist physically as two separate registers but they are accessed by a read/write to the SBUF register. The Serial communication module contains a Transmit control unit and a Receive control unit. The transmit control unit is responsible for handling the serial data transmission and receive control unit is responsible for handling all serial data reception related operations. The Serial Port can be operated in four different modes. The mode selection is configured by setting or clearing the SM0 and SM1 bits of the Special Function Register Serial Port Control SCON.

Serial Port Control Register (SCON) (SFR-98H) SCON is a bit addressable Special Function Register holding the Serial Port Control related bits. The details of SCON bits are given below.

SCON. 7	SCON. 6	SCON. 5	SCON. 4	SCON. 3	SCON. 2	SCON. 1	SCON. 0
SM0	SM1	SM2	REN	TB8	RB8	TI	RI

The following table explains the meaning and use of each bit in the SCON register.

Bit	Name	Description
SM0	Serial port mode selector	Sets the serial port operation mode
SM1		
SM2	Multiprocessor communication flag	SM2 = 1 Enable Multiprocessor communication SM2 = 0 Disable Multiprocessor communication
REN	Serial data reception enable	REN = 1 Enables reception REN = 0 Disables serial data reception
TB8		9th Data bit that will be transmitted in Modes 2 & 3. Setting/Clearing under software control

RB8		9th Data bit received in Modes 2 & 3. Counterpart for TB8. In Mode 1, if multiprocessor mode is disabled, RB8 will be the stop bit received in serial transmission. RB8 is not used in Mode 0. RB8 is Software controllable
TI	Transmit interrupt	Set by internal circuitry at the end of transmission of the 8th bit in Mode 0. For other modes it is set at the beginning of the stop bit (9th bit). TI should be cleared by firmware
RI	Receive interrupt	Set by internal circuitry at the end of reception of the 8th bit in Mode 0. For other modes it is set on half way of reception of the stop bit (9th bit). RI should be cleared by firmware.

5.3.9.1 Serial Communication Modes As mentioned earlier, *8051* supports four different modes of operation for Serial data communication. The mode is selected by the SM0 and SM1 bits of SCON register. The table given below gives the different combinations of SM0 and SM1 and the serial communication modes corresponding to it.

SM0	SM1	Mode	Type
0	0	0	Shift Register
0	1	1	8 bit UART
1	0	2	9 bit UART
1	1	3	9 bit UART

Mode 0 The Mode 0 operation of serial port is same as that of the operation of a clocked shift register. In Mode 0 operation Pin RXD (Port Pin P3.0) is used for transmitting and receiving serial data and Pin TXD (Port Pin P3.1) outputs the shift clock. 8 data bits are transmitted in this mode with LSB first. The baudrate* is fixed for this mode and it is 1/12 of the oscillator frequency. Mode 0 is half duplex, meaning it supports only unidirectional communication at a time. It can be either transmission or reception. Serial data transmission is initiated by a write access to the SBUF register (Any Instruction that uses SBUF as the destination register. E.g. MOV SBUF, A; ANL SBUF, A; MOV SBUF, #data etc). The write to SBUF loads a 1 to the MSB of the transmit shift register which acts as the stop bit in the serial transmission. The contents of SBUF register is shifted out to the RXD Pin in the order LSB first. The bit shifting occurs in each machine cycle until all bits including the stop bit is shifted out. The bit shift rate is same as the machine cycle rate and hence the transmission rate in mode 0 is $1/12^{th}$ of the oscillator frequency. The Transmit Interrupt TI is set by the Transmit Control unit when all the 8 bits are shifted out. The TXD pin outputs the transmit shift clock during data transmission. Serial data reception is enabled only when the reception enable bit, REN is set 1 and the Receive Interrupt bit, RI is in the cleared state. A 'write to SCON' (Clear RI/Set REN) initiates the data reception. The receive control unit samples the receive pin, RXD during each machine cycle and places the sample at the LSB of the receive shift register and left shifts the receive shift register. The Receive Interrupt (RI) is set when all the 8 data bits are received. Pin TXD outputs the receive shift clock throughout the reception process.

Mode 1 In Mode 1, serial data pin TXD transmits the serial data and pin RXD receives the serial data. Mode 1 is a full duplex mode, meaning it supports simultaneous reception and transmission of

* Baudrate is defined as the number of bits per second.

serial data. 10 bits are transmitted or received in Mode 1. The 10 bits are formed by the start bit, 8 data bits and one stop bit. The stop bit on reception is moved to RB8 bit of SCON. The baudrate is variable and it can be configured for different bauds. Similar to Mode 0, transmission is triggered by a write access to the SBUF register in Mode 1. A 'write to SBUF' signal loads a 1, which acts as the stop bit, to the 9th bit position of the transmit shift register and informs the transmit control unit that a serial data transmission is requested. Unlike Mode 0 where transmission is synchronized to 'write to SBUF' signal, in Mode 1, the transmission is synchronized to a divide-by-16 counter. The divide-by-16 counter count rate is dependent on the timer 1 overflow rate. The transmission starts with sending the start bit (logic 0), when the divide-by-16 counter rolls over after the 'write to SBUF' signal. The transmit register contents are shifted out to the TXD pin (P3.1 Port pin) at the successive rollover of the divide-by-16 counter. The Transmit Interrupt TI is set by the transmit control unit when all the 8 bits are shifted out. Figure 5.31 illustrates the bit transmission with respect to time in Mode 1.

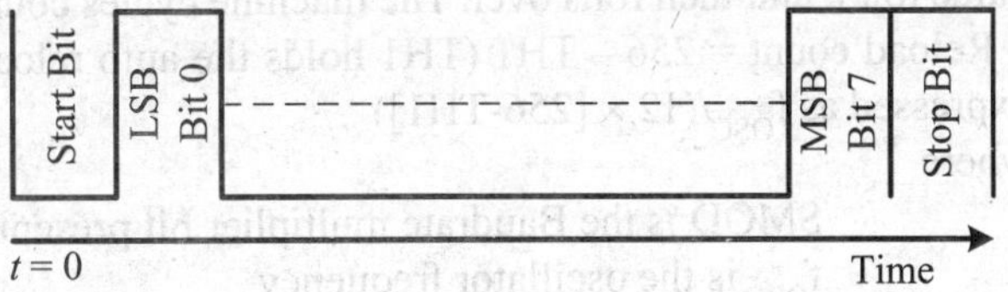

Fig. 5.31 **Bit Transmission with respect to time in Mode 1**

Serial data reception is triggered by a 1 to 0 transition detected at the Receive pin RXD. The RXD pin is sampled at a rate of 16 times the baudrate. On detecting a 1 to 0 transition at the RXD pin, the divided-by-16 counter is reset and 1FFH is loaded into the receive shift register. The divide-by-16 counter divides the bit time of a bit (1/baudrate) into 16 time frames. In order to reduce noise in input data, the RXD pin is sampled at 7th, 8th and 9th frames of the bit time. If the value remains the same for at least two of the samples, it is taken as the data bit. If the value obtained for the first bit time (start bit) is not 0, the receiver circuitry resets and it will look for another 1 to 0 transition as a valid start bit condition. On receiving a valid start bit it is placed in the receive shift register at the rightmost position after shifting the present contents of the receive shift register to the left by one. As data bits enter into the rightmost position, the initially loaded 1s in the receive shift register is shifted out through the left most position. As the reception goes on, when the start bit (the first received 0 bit) reaches at the left most position of the receive shift register, the Receiver unit is informed that only one more bit reception is required and to load the SBUF with the contents of receive shift register after the reception of next bit, move the next receiving bit (stop bit) into RB8 and set the Receive Interrupt RI. The signal to load SBUF and RB8 and set RI is generated only when Receive Interrupt RI = 0 and Bit SM2 in SCON is 0 or received stop bit = 1 at the time of generation of the final shift pulse. If both of these conditions are not met, the received byte is not moved into SBUF else the received byte is moved into SBUF, the received stop bit is placed in the RB8 bit, present in the SCON register and the Receive Interrupt (RI) is activated. After the reception of the stop bit, irrespective of the above-mentioned meeting criteria, the receiver unit looks for the next 1 to 0 transition at the RXD pin for catching the next byte.

Baudrates for Mode 1 As mentioned earlier, the baudrate for Mode 1 is variable. Mode 1 baudrate is dependent on the operating frequency and Timer 1 overflow rate. The bit transmission rate in mode 1 is dependent on the divide-by-16 counter overflow rate. The count rate of divide-by-16 counter is dependent on the timer 1 overflow rate. Depending on the value of the SMOD bit, the divide-by-16 counter is incremented directly on the overflow of Timer 1 or after the two consecutive overflow of the timer 1. If SMOD is 0, the divide-by-16 counter is incremented only after two consecutive overflow of timer 1. If SMOD is 1, the divide-by-16 counter is incremented with the overflow of timer 1. The baudrate in Mode 1 expressed as:

$$\text{Baudrate} = ((2^{SMOD}) \times \text{Timer 1 Overflow rate})/(16 \times 2)$$

For baudrate generation operations, Timer 1 interrupt should be disabled. It is advised to run Timer 1 in the timer mode for baudrate generation operation. Normally Timer 1 is configured in Mode 2 (Auto reload mode) for baudrate generation. In this case the equation will become

$$\text{Baudrate} = 2^{SMOD} \times f_{OSC}/((12 \times [256\text{-TH1}]) \times 16 \times 2)$$

(Timer 1 in mode 2 is incremented at each machine cycle. One machine cycle contains 12 clock periods and so the timer 1 increment rate is f_{OSC} / 12. In Auto reload mode the timer counts from Auto reload value to FF and then rolls over. The machine cycles counted in mode 2 for overflow is expressed as 256 – Reload count = 256 – TH1 (TH1 holds the auto reload count). Hence, Timer 1 overflow rate can be expressed as $f_{OSC}/(12 \times [256\text{-TH1}])$

where

SMOD is the Baudrate multiplier bit present in PCON SFR

f_{OSC} is the oscillator frequency

TH1 is the Timer 1 Auto re-load value.

For achieving low baudrates, Timer 1 can be configured in Mode 1 to run as 16bit timer with interrupt enabled. In Timer 1 interrupt handler write the code to re-load Timer 1 with the count required to get the desired baudrate.

Theoretically the maximum baudrate that can be achieved with Timer 1 running in Mode 1 is given as

$$\text{Max baudrate} = 2^{SMOD} \times f_{OSC}/(12 \times 16 \times 2)$$

Re-load Timer 1 with FFFFH in Timer 1 interrupt handler.

Minimum baudrate that can be achieved with Timer 1 running in Mode 1 is given as Min Baudrate = $2^{SMOD} \times f_{OSC}/(12 \times 16 \times 2 \times 65536)$.

There is no need of re-loading Timer 1

The commonly used baudrates for Mode 1 of serial communication, required oscillator frequency, timer mode and Timer 1 reload value for auto reload mode of Timer 1 are tabulated below. Timer 1 is assumed to be run in the timer mode (Not in counter mode) for all these calculations.

Baudrate	f_{OSC}(MHz)	SMOD	Timer 1	
			Timer Mode	Reload Value
9600	11.0592	0	2	FDH
4800	11.0592	0	2	FAH
2400	11.0592	0	2	F4H
1200	11.0592	0	2	E8H
137.5	11.0592	0	2	1DH
2400	11.0592	1	2	E8H
4800	11.0592	1	2	F4H
9600	11.0592	1	2	FAH
19200	11.0592	1	2	FDH
110	6.00	0	2	72H

Mode 1 baudrate 9600 is the most compatible to communicate with PC's COM port.

Modes 2 & 3 11 bits are transmitted in Modes 2 & 3. The 11 bits are formed by the 8 data bits, 1 start bit (0), 1 stop bit (1) and a programmable bit that acts as the 9th data bit. Mode 2 & 3 are also full duplex and serial data is transmitted through the pin TXD and reception is carried out through the pin RXD. TB8 bit of SCON register is transmitted as the 9th bit. TB8 is programmable; it can be set to either 1 or 0. TB8 bit can be used as a parity bit for transmission. The parity bit of PSW reflects the parity of Accumulator content. If the data byte to be sent is the Accumulator content, the parity bit of PSW can be directly moved to TB8 bit of SCON for transmitting it as the 9th data bit, which will give the functionality of a parity enabled serial data transmission. On reception of serial data, the 9th data bit is moved to the RB8 bit of SCON register. If the serial reception is also parity enabled, RB8 can be used for checking the parity of the received byte. The bits of the received byte can be XORed and the resulting bit can be compared to the received 9th bit (which is present in the RB8 bit of SCON) in firmware to check whether the parity bit matches with the parity of the received byte. This ensures error free reception of data. The received stop bit is ignored in Modes 2 & 3. Mode 2 and Mode 3 of Serial communication is similar in all respect except that the Mode 2 and Mode 3 baudrates are different.

Mode 2 baudrate is fixed and is given as $2^{SMOD} \times f_{OSC}/64$

Depending on the SMOD bit, it can be either $f_{OSC}/64$ or $f_{OSC}/32$

Mode 3 baudrate is same as that of Mode 1. Refer back to Mode 1 baudrate for details.

5.3.9.2 Multiprocessor/Controller Communication Support Multiprocessor/controller communication implements communication between multiple processors/controllers connected to the same serial interface bus. Each processor is assigned an address which is set in the firmware.

One of the processor/controller acts as the master controller and the other controllers act as slave controllers (Fig. 5.32).

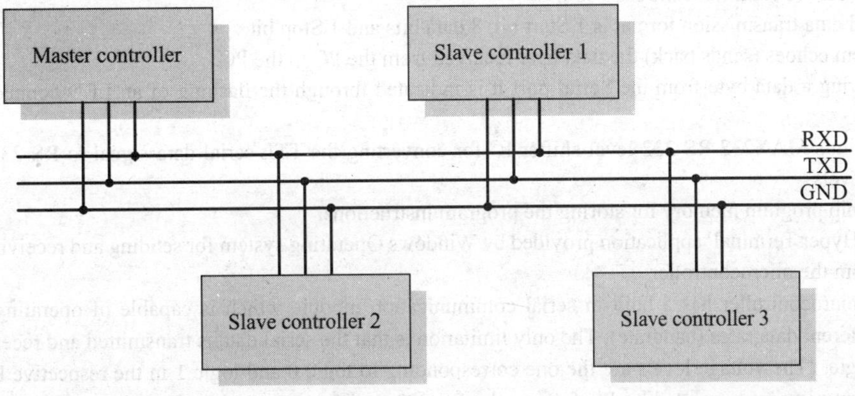

Fig. 5.32 Multiprocessor communication setup

Modes 2 & 3 of *8051* serial transmission supports multiprocessor communication if the SM2 bit present in the SCON register is set for each controller. In Modes 2 & 3 operation, 9 data bits and a stop bit are received. The received 9th data bit goes to the RB8 bit of SCON register. With SM2 set, the serial port interrupt is activated on reception of the stop bit only if the received RB8 bit is 1. When the master processor/controller wants to transmit a block of data to any one of the slave controllers, it sends out the address byte of the slave controller, to which it wants to communicate. The 9th data bit that will be sending along with the address byte will be 1. If the multiprocessor mode is enabled in slaves, on receiving the address byte the receive interrupt is activated and each slave controller can use the interrupt handler to examine whether the received address byte is matching to its assigned address (which is stored in the firmware). If a slave finds that the received address byte is matching with its address, it clears its SM2 bit and waits to receive the data byte block from the master. The data bytes are sent along with a 9th data bit which is 0. If the 9th data bit is 1 it implies that the incoming byte is an address byte and if it is 0, it informs the controller that the incoming bytes are data bytes. Once a slave is selected, it clears its SM2 bit and generates interrupt for all incoming data bytes while all other slaves ignore the received bytes since their SM2 bit is still in the set condition. To enable the multiprocessor communication again in the selected slave which is presently involved in the transmission it should be informed the end of reception of data bytes through some mechanism. On receiving the end of data byte reception information, the slave sets the SM2 bit and brings back the slave controller into multiprocessor communication enabled mode.

Setting SM2 bit in Mode 0 will not produce any effect in transmission/reception. If SM2 is set in Mode 1 the validity of the received stop bit is checked. If SM2 = 1 and Mode = 1, receive interrupt RI is generated only if the received stop bit is 1.

Example 1

Design an *8051* microcontroller based system for serial data communication with a PC as per the requirements given below.

1. Use Atmel's AT89C51/52 or AT89S8252 (Flash microcontroller with In System Programming (ISP) support) for designing the system.
2. The baudrate for communication is 9600.
3. The serial data transmission format is 1 Start bit, 8 data bits and 1 Stop bit.
4. The system echoes (sends back) the data byte received from the PC to the PC.
5. On receiving a data byte from the Serial port it is indicated through the flashing of an LED connected to a port pin.
6. Use Maxim's MAX232 RS-232 level shifter IC for converting the TTL serial data signal to RS-232 compatible voltage levels.
7. Use on-chip program memory for storing the program instructions.
8. Use the 'Hyper Terminal' application provided by Windows Operating system for sending and receiving serial data to and from the microcontroller.

The *8051* microcontroller has a built-in serial communication module which is capable of operating in different modes with different data rates (baudrate). The only limitation is that the serial data is transmitted and received in either TTL/CMOS logic. (The voltage levels are the one corresponding to logic 0 and logic 1 in the respective logic family.) The serial communication supported by PC follows the RS-232 Serial communication standard and the voltage levels are entirely different from the TTL/CMOS logic. The voltage levels for RS-232 is +/–12 V (We will discuss about the RS-232 Protocol, voltage level and electrical characteristics in a dedicated book, which is planned under this book series.) For translating the RS-232 voltage levels to the TTL/CMOS compatible voltage level, an RS-232 translator chip is required between the PC interface and the microcontroller interface. The RS-232 translator chip is available from different chip manufacturers and the MAX232 IC from Maxim Dallas Semiconductors is a very popular level translator IC. The Serial data is usually routed to an RS-232 connector (DB Connector). The RS-232 connector comes in two different pin counts namely; DB9 – 9 Pin connector and DB25 – 25-Pin connector. For proper data communication, the Transmit Pin of one device (Here either PC or microcontroller) should be connected to the receive pin of the other device and vice versa. This can be done at the microcontroller board side by connecting the TXDOUT pin of MAX232 to the RX (Receive) pin of DB connector and the RXDIN Pin of MAX232 to the TX (Transmit) pin of DB9 connector. An RS-232 cable is used for connecting the PC COM Port with DB Connector of the microcontroller board. For the above configuration, the RS-232 cable should be 1-1 wired meaning, the RXD and TXD lines of the connectors present at both ends are 1-1 connected. If the Serial lines are not used in the cross over mode in the microcontroller board, a twisted cable (cable with RXD pin connected to TXD pin of the other end connector and TXD pin connected to RXD pin) can be used for establishing the proper communication. The hardware connection for implementing the serial communication is given in Fig. 5.33.

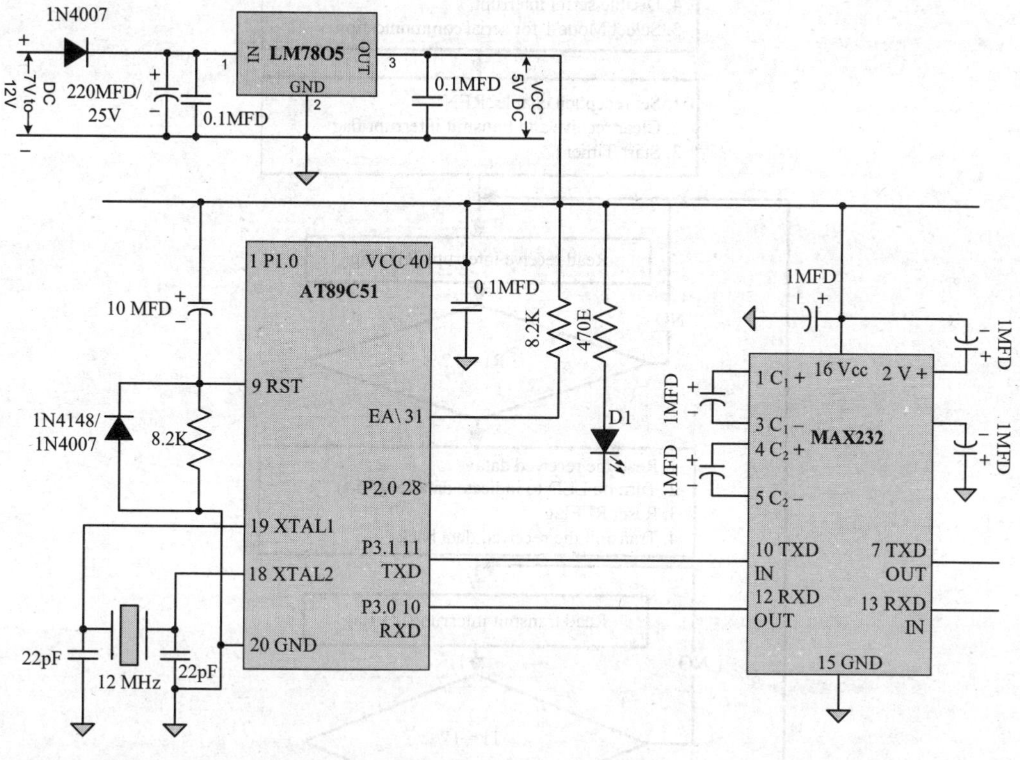

Fig. 5.33 **Serial communication circuit implementation using *8051***

For implementing the serial data communication as 1 Start bit + 8 Data bits + 1 Stop bit with a data rate (baudrate) of 9600, the serial port should be configured in mode 1. Timer 1 should be configured to run in auto reload mode (Mode 2) to generate the required baudrate. With an operating clock frequency of 11.0592 MHz, Timer 1 in mode 2 should be reloaded with a count 0FDH for generating a baudrate of 9600 (Refer section **Baudrates for Mode 1:** for more details on baudrate generation for serial communication in mode 1).

The flow chart given in Fig. 5.34 illustrates the firmware design for implementing serial data communication.

The firmware for Implementing Serial communication in 8051 Assembly language is given below.

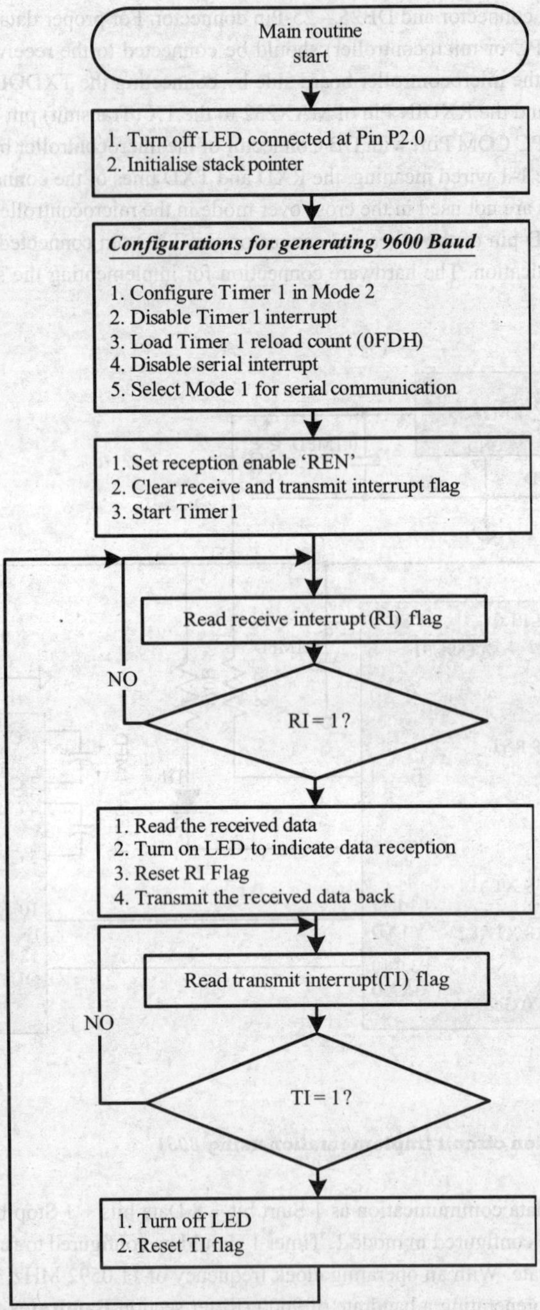

Fig. 5.34 Flow chart for implementing polling based serial communication

```
;#####################################################################
;serial_polling.src
;Firmware for Implementing Serial Communication with PC
;Written by Shibu K V. Copyright (C) 2008
;#####################################################################
ORG 0000H               ; Reset vector
      JMP 0050H         ; Jump to start of main program
ORG 0003H               ; External Interrupt 0 ISR location
      RETI              ; Simply return. Do nothing
ORG 000BH               ; Timer 0 Interrupt ISR location
      RETI              ; Simply return. Do nothing
ORG 0013H               ; External Interrupt 1 ISR location
      RETI              ; Simply return. Do nothing
ORG 001BH               ; Timer 1 Interrupt ISR location
      RETI              ; Simply return. Do nothing
ORG 0023H               ; Serial Interrupt ISR location
      RETI              ; Simply return. Do nothing
;#####################################################################
ORG 0050H               ; Start of main program
      SETB P2.0         ; Turn off data reception indicator LED
      MOV SP, #08H      ; Set stack at memory location 08H
      CLR TR1           ; Stop Timer 1
      MOV TMOD, #00100000B ; Set Timer 1 in Mode 2 (Autoreload)
      CLR EA            ; Disable all interrupts
      MOV TH1, #0FDH    ; Reload count for Timer 2
      MOV TL1, #0FDH
      ; Select Mode 1 for serial Communication
      ; SM0 = 0, SM1 = 1, SM2 = 0
      ; Set REN
      ; TB8 = 0, RB8 = 0, TI =0, RI =0
      MOV SCON, #01010000B
      ANL PCON, #01111111B ; Reset baudrate doubler bit
      SETB TR1          ; Start Timer 1
      ; Read Receive Interrupt (RI) flag
      ; Check whether data reception occurred
      ; If not, loop till RI=1
RECEIVE:JNB RI, RECEIVE
      ; Data received
      CLR P2.0          ; Turn ON LED to indicate data reception
      ; Read the received data
      MOV A, SBUF
      CLR RI            ; Reset RI flag
      MOV SBUF, A       ; Transmit back the received data
      ; Read Transmit Interrupt (TI) flag
      ; Check whether data transmission completed
      ; If not, wait till completion (loop till TI=1)
      JNB TI, $
      ; Data Transmitted
      SETB P2.0         ; Turn off Indicator LED
      CLR TI            ; Reset Transmit Interrupt flag
      JMP RECEIVE       ; Wait for next data to arrive
END     ; END of Assembly Program
```

The firmware polls the serial interrupt flags and takes the corresponding actions when either the receive interrupt or transmit interrupt flag is set. This approach is CPU-intensive and the CPU is dedicated for serial data communication. Another approach in which the serial communication is handled is the interrupt based communication approach. The flow chart given in Fig. 5.35 models the interrupt based serial communication.

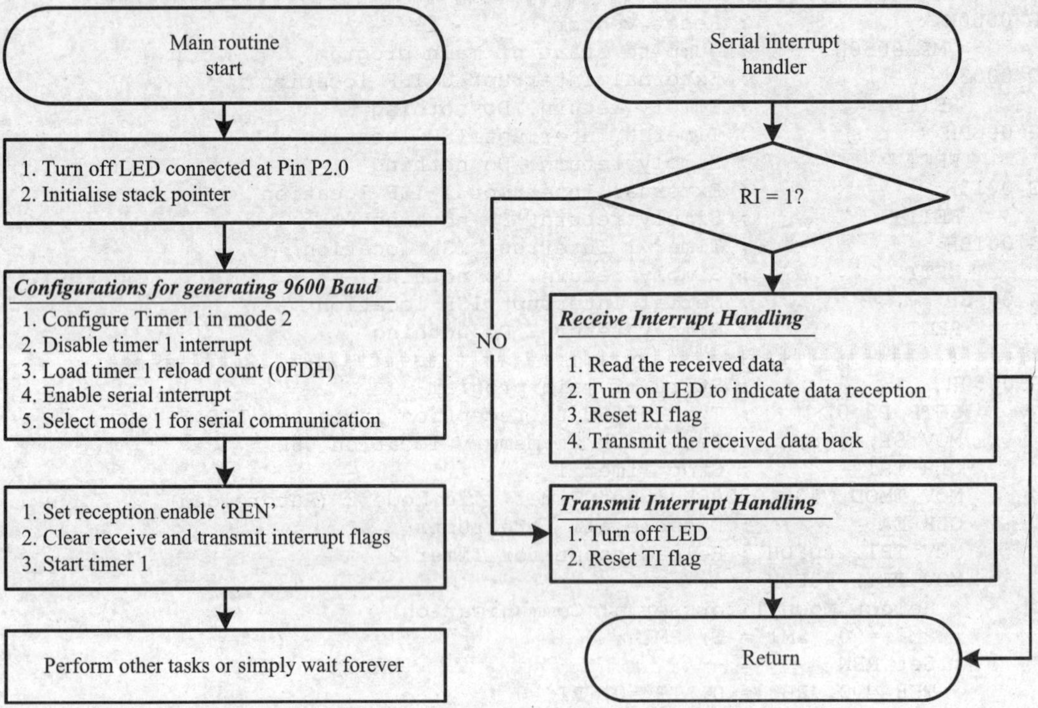

Fig. 5.35 **Flow chart for implementing interrupt based serial communication**

The firmware implementation for the interrupt based serial data communication is given below.

```
;#####################################################################
;serial_interrupt.src
;Firmware for Implementing Serial Communication with PC
;Serial Data reception and transmission handled through Interrupts
;Written by Shibu K V. Copyright (C) 2008
;#####################################################################
ORG 0000H               ; Reset vector
      JMP 0050H         ; Jump to start of main routine
ORG 0003H               ; External Interrupt 0 ISR location
      RETI              ; Simply return. Do nothing
ORG 000BH               ; Timer 0 Interrupt ISR location
      RETI              ; Simply return. Do nothing
ORG 0013H               ; External Interrupt 1 ISR location
      RETI              ; Simply return. Do nothing
ORG 001BH               ; Timer 1 Interrupt ISR location
      RETI              ; Simply return. Do nothing
ORG 0023H               ; Serial Interrupt ISR location
    ; Interrupt handling will not fit in 8 bytes
```

```
        ; Call the routine where interrupt is handled
        CALL SERIAL_INTERRUPT
        RETI            ; Return
;######################################################################
ORG 0050H               ; Start of main Program
        SETB P2.0       ; Turn off data reception indicator LED
        MOV SP, #08H    ; Set stack at memory location 08H
        CLR TR1         ; Stop Timer 1
        MOV TMOD, #00100000B ; Set Timer 1 in Mode 2 (Autoreload)
        MOV IE, #10010000B ; Enable only serial interrupt
        MOV TH1, #0FDH ; Reload count for Timer 2
        MOV TL1, #0FDH
        ; Select Mode 1 for serial Communication
        ; SM0 = 0, SM1 = 1, SM2 = 0.
        ; REN = 1, TB8 = 0, RB8 = 0, TI = 0, RI = 0
        MOV SCON, #01010000B
        ANL PCON, #01111111B ; Reset baudrate doubler bit
        SETB TR1        ; Start Timer 1
        JMP $           ; Simply Loop here
 #####################################################################
;Routine for handling Serial Interrupt (Both RI & TI)
;Only one Interrupt available for Transmission and Reception
;Check whether the interrupt is TI or RI
;Perform the actions corresponding to the Interrupt and then Return
;######################################################################
SERIAL_INTERRUPT:
        ; Check whether the interrupt is Receive Interrupt (RI)
        JNB RI, CHECK_TI
        ; Receive Interrupt occurred
        ; Data received
        CLR P2.0        ; Turn ON LED to indicate data reception
        MOV A, SBUF     ; Read the received data
        CLR RI          ; Reset RI flag
        MOV SBUF, A     ; Transmit back the received data
        ; Receive Interrupt processing completed
        ; Return
        RET
CHECK_TI:
        ; Transmit Interrupt occurred
        ; Data Transmitted
        SETB P2.0       ; Turn off Indicator LED
        CLR TI          ; Reset Transmit Interrupt flag
        ; Transmit Interrupt processing completed
        ; Return
        RET
END     ;END of Assembly Program
```

This design will not be complete without explaining the PC side application responsible for sending and receiving serial data to and from the *8051* based system connected to the serial port (Communication Port 1, COM 1) of the PC. The *8051* based system should be connected to the serial port using one of the cables (twisted/ one-to-one), as per the design requirement, as explained earlier. Figure 5.36 illustrates the interfacing of the microcontroller board to the COM port of the PC.

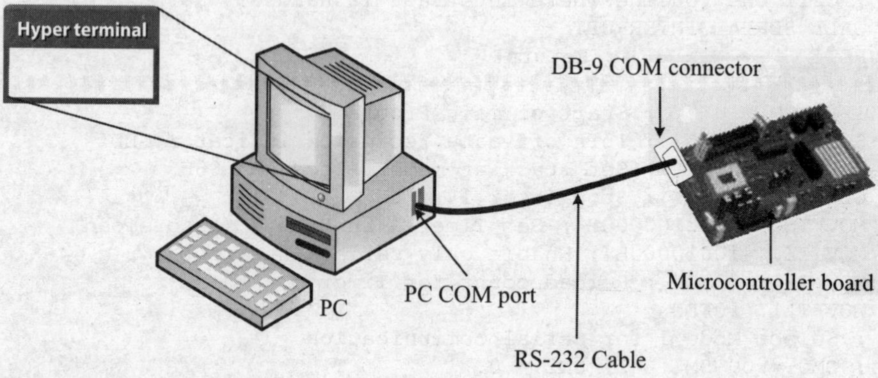

Fig. 5.36 **Serial Port Interfacing with PC**

The Microsoft ® Windows Operating System (Windows 9x/XP is used in our example) provides a built-in serial communication terminal program called '*Hyper terminal*'. The '*Hyper terminal*' application can be launched through *Start* → *All Programs* → *Accessories* → *Communications* → *Hyper terminal*

The *Hyper terminal* application will request for a *Connection Description* while launching a new instance of the application. Provide a connection description name (say *8051*) in the *Connection Description* wizard. Discard the *Connect To* wizard by *Cancel*. Select *Properties* tab from the *File* menu of the *Hyper terminal* application. A new window describing the *Properties* of the *Hyper terminal* connection is displayed. From the *Connect To* tab of the new Window, select the com number to which the 8051 system is connected, say COM1, against the *Connect using:* option. Now select the *Configure..* button. A new configuration window is displayed for configuring the *Port Settings* for the selected COM port. Configure the *Bit per second:* to 9600, *Data bits:* to 8, *Parity:* to *None*, *Stop bits:* to 1 and *Flow control:* to *None*. Save the *Port Settings* through the *Apply* button. Exit the *Port Settings* window by invoking the *OK* button. Start the communication by invoking the *Call* option from the *Call* menu (This can also be achieved by pressing the *Telephone* icon on the hyper terminal window). Now you are ready to communicate with the 8051 system connected to the communication port configured as per the requirement. Start sending data by typing on the hyper terminal application. You can see the data echoed by the 8051 system on the hyper terminal application. The hyper terminal application can be stopped by invoking the *Disconnect* option from the *Call* menu. (This can also be achieved by pressing the *Telephone Hang-up* icon on the hyper terminal window.)

5.3.10 Reset Circuitry

Reset is necessary to bring the different internal register values and associated internal hardware circuitry to a known state. Before putting the 8051 controller into operation a reset should be applied to the controller. As mentioned earlier, applying a reset loads the registers with default known values and loads the Program Counter (PC) with 0000H. This ensures that the program execution starts from the start of the code memory (0000H) and stack will reset to the memory location 07H. Reset can be of two types: hardware and software reset. Hardware reset brings all associated hardware units to a well-defined initial state. *8051* provides a pin named RST for applying the hardware reset.

The reset signal must be kept active until all the three of the following conditions are met

1. The power supply must be in the specified range.
2. The oscillator must reach a minimum oscillation level to ensure a good noise to signal ratio and a correct internal duty cycle generation.
3. The reset pulse width duration must be at least two machine cycles (24 Clock periods) when conditions 1 and 2 are met.

If one of the conditions is not satisfied, the microcontroller may not startup properly. To ensure a good startup, the reset pulse width has to be wide enough to cover the period of time, where the electrical conditions are not met. Please refer to the note given on the 'On line Learning Centre', on the important parameters that should be taken into account for determining the reset pulse width.

The C51 family of microcontrollers support two kinds of reset input. The first one is a pure input which allows an external device or circuitry to reset the microcontroller. The second one is bidirectional, in which the microcontroller is capable of resetting an external device. In actual practice a power on reset (unidirectional input) is given to the *8051* controller by connecting an external resistor and capacitor as shown in Fig. 5.37.

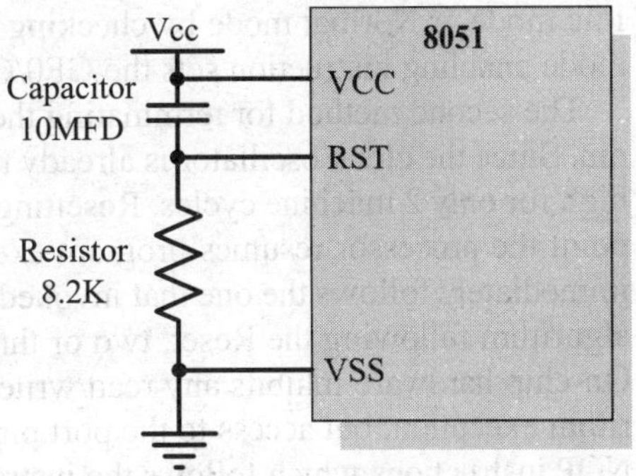

Fig. 5.37 **Power on reset circuitry for *8051***

When the power supply is turned on, initially the capacitor acts as short circuit and the full applied voltage appears across the resistor (RST pin becomes at logic 1). The capacitor starts charging gradually and the applied voltage is build across the capacitor (RST pin becomes at logic 0). The time taken by the capacitor to get charged to a voltage V_c, which brings the RST pin to logic LOW, is calculated as

$$V_c = V_f - (V_f - V_i) \times e^{-t/RC}$$

V_c = voltage at which RST pin logic high changes to LOW

V_f = final voltage (VDD =5 V)

V_i = initial voltage (=0 V)

RC = time constant of resistor capacitor circuit $(8.2 \times 10^3 \times 10 \times 10^{-6})$

The reset pulse width '*t*' can be calculated from the above equation with V_c = The voltage across RST pin which makes the RST pin at logic 0 and V_f = 5V. The pulse width will be of the order of milliseconds to seconds. This ensures that the RST pin remains HIGH for enough time to allow the oscillator to start up (A few milliseconds), the power supply to stabilise plus two machine cycles. It is to be noted that the port pins will be in a random state until the oscillator is started and the internal reset algorithm writes 1 to the corresponding port SFRs.

5.3.11 Power Saving Modes

For applications like battery operated systems where power consumption is critical, the CMOS version of *8051* provides power reduced modes of operation namely *IDLE* and *POWER DOWN* modes.

5.3.11.1 IDLE Mode The *IDLE* mode is activated by setting the bit PCON.0 of the SFR power control register (PCON). The instruction setting the PCON.0 bit pushes the processor into an idle state where the internal clock to the processor is temporarily suspended. Before putting the CPU into idle state, the various CPU statuses like Stack Pointer (SP), Program Counter (PC), Program Status Word (PSW) and Accumulator and all other register values are preserved as such. All port pins will hold the logical states they had at the moment at which the idle mode is activated by setting the PCON.0 bit. ALE and PSEN remains at logic high during Idle Mode. The interrupt, Timer and Serial port sections continue functioning since the clock signal is not withdrawn for the same. The Idle mode is terminated by asserting any enabled interrupt. The interrupt can be any one of the external interrupt (INT0 or INT1) or Serial Interrupt. On asserting the interrupt, the IDL bit (PCON.0) is cleared and the interrupt routine is serviced. After executing the RETI instruction, the next instruction executing will be the instruction which follows immediately the instruction that put the processor in Idle Mode. Two general purpose flag bits GF0 & GF1 present in the PCON register can be used for giving an indication for whether an interrupt occurred in normal mode or Idle Mode. Since PCON register is not a bit addressable register, the instruction which sets the IDLE Mode control bit PCON.0 can also set the flags either GF0 or GF1 or both. When an interrupt occurs its service routine can examine whether the interrupt occurred in the Idle mode or Normal mode by checking the status of GF0 or GF1 bits of PCON (valid only if the Idle mode enabling instruction sets the GF0/GF1 bit along with PCON.0).

The second method for terminating the idle mode is the application of a reset input signal at the RST pin. Since the clock oscillator is already running and it is in the stable state, the RST pin need to be held high for only 2 machine cycles. Resetting the processor clears the IDL bit (PCON.0) directly and at this point the processor resumes program execution from where it left off, that is, at the instruction which immediately follows the one that invoked the idle mode. When the internal circuitry undergoes the reset algorithm following the Reset, two or three machine cycles of program execution may take place. The On-chip hardware inhibits any read/write access to the scratchpad RAM during the internal reset algorithm execution, but access to the port pins are not inhibited. Hence it is advised to put a minimum of 3 NOP instructions which follows the instruction that triggers the idle mode.

Power Control Register (PCON) (SFR-87H) It is the Special Function Register holding the power control bits and baudrate multiplier bit. PCON is not a bit addressable register. The details of PCON bits are given below.

BIT 7	BIT 6	BIT 5	BIT 4	BIT 3	BIT 2	BIT 1	BIT 0
SMOD	RSD	RSD	RSD	GF1	GF0	PD	IDL

The following table explains the meaning and use of each bit in the PCON register.

Bit	Name	Description
SMOD	Baudrate multiplier	If Serial port is operating in Modes 1, 2 or 3 and timer 1 is used for baudrate generation, setting SMOD to 1 doubles the baudrate
RSD	Reserved	Unimplemented. Reserved for future use. Users are advised not to modify it
GF1	General purpose flag bit 1	User programmable bit. Can be set or reset under firmware control
GF0	General purpose flag bit 0	User programmable bit. Can be set or reset under firmware control
PD	Power down control bit	PD = 1 Invokes power down mode.
IDL	Idle mode control bit	IDL = Invoke Idle mode

The NMOS version of 8051 devices implement only SMOD bit in PCON register. The other 4 bits are available only in CMOS versions. Reset value of PCON is 0XXX0000 (X denotes don't care. It may be either 0 or 1). PD bit always take precedence over IDL bit and if an instruction sets both IDL and PD bits to 1, action corresponding to PD = 1 is performed and it masks the IDL bits activity.

5.3.11.2 Power Down Mode When the PD bit (PCON.1) is set by an instruction, the Power Down mode is activated. The CPU stops executing instructions; clock signal to all internal hardware including timer unit, interrupt system and CPU is terminated. The contents of internal RAM and SFR are maintained. All ports continue emitting their respective SFR contents. ALE and PSEN signals are held at low. Power Down mode can only be terminated through hardware reset. All SFRs are brought into their reset

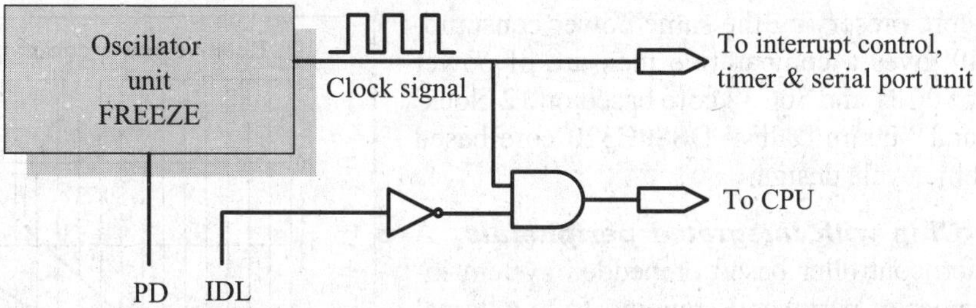

Fig. 5.38 **Power down and IDLE mode operation**

values. However the on-chip RAM retains their contents to that of the values when the Power Down mode is entered. The supply voltage V_{cc} to the controller can be brought down to as low as 2V when the controller is in Power Down mode. However before terminating the Power Down mode with a hardware reset, the supply voltage V_{cc} should be brought into the normal operating level. If the hardware reset is applied to the controller to terminate the processor before bringing the operating voltage to the nominal level, the controller may behave in an unexpected way. Hence reset should not be activated before V_{cc} is brought to its normal operating level, and the reset signal should be held active till the oscillator is re-started and becomes stabilised.

5.3.11.3 Power Consumption V/s Oscillator Frequency Average Power consumption is directly proportional to the operating frequency (Clock frequency). Increasing the clock frequency (subject to the condition that it will not exceed the maximum supported frequency by the system core) increases the execution speed of the controller. But it also has a direct impact on the total power consumption. Figure 5.39 illustrates the typical power curve for a generic *8051* microcontroller.

Generally, the current consumption v/s operating frequency characteristics is linear with a dc offset. The dc quiescent current is generated by static on-chip circuitry such as op amps, comparators, etc. This current is a constant drain current typically in the range of 1mA. From the power curve it is obvious that as the operating speed demand is high, the power consumption also goes high. So there is always a trade-off between processing power and power consumption with the generic *8051* design. Some techniques used to achieve high processing speeds by maintaining the power consumption to the least possible are explained below.

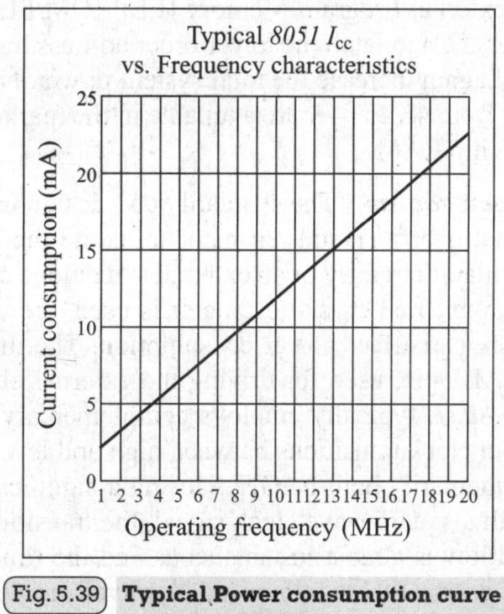

Fig. 5.39 **Typical Power consumption curve for generic *8051***
Copyright Maxim Integrated Products (http://www.maxim-ic.com) used by permission

High-speed core The original *8051* design was based on a 12 clock/machine cycle and two fetches per machine cycle architecture. The high speed core uses 4 clocks or 1 clock per machine cycle design. Comparing this with the original 12 clock/machine cycle for the same operating frequency, the performance will be approximately 3 times for the 4 clock core and 12 times for the 1 clock core preserving the same power consumption. Figure 5.40 gives a comparative measure of power consumption for 80C31 and 80C32 core based on 12 clock/machine cycle and Maxim/Dallas' DS80C320 core based on 4 clock/machine cycle design.

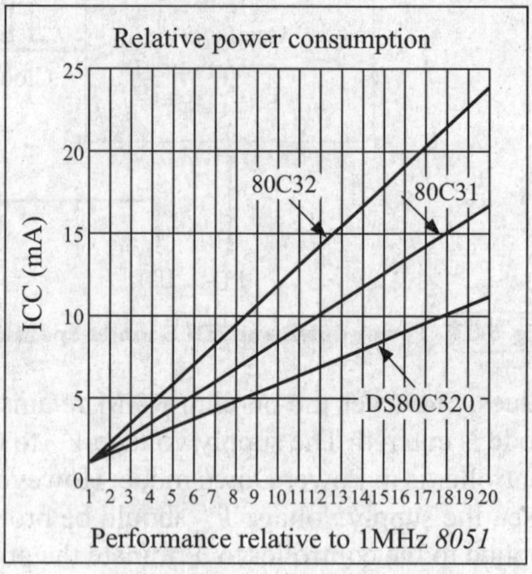

Fig. 5.40 **Power Consumption curve for normal core v/s Reduced Clock cycle**
Copyright Maxim Integrated Products (http://www.maxim-ic.com) used by permission

Use of Single Chip with integrated peripherals A typical *8051* microcontroller based embedded system incorporates a number of peripherals ranging from external UART to reset ICs (e.g. DS1232 from Maxim Integrated Products/Dallas Semiconductor), brown-out circuits and watch dog timers. Using these chips as separate ICs will definitely increase the total system power consumption. An effective way of reducing this kind of power consumption is the use of a single chip that integrates the *8051* controller and the related necessary chips in a single chip. Apart from significant reduction in power consumption, this approach also reduces the space required for placing the components on the PCB and thereby makes the embedded product much more compact one.

Use of On-chip program memory and RAM Use of external Program Memory (EEPROM/FLASH) and RAM requires an additional latch circuit (e.g. 74LS373) to latch the lower order address bus from the multiplexed address/data bus. Adding this chip will again increase the total system power. Nowadays controllers with internal program memory ranging from 4K to 64K are available in the market. Some manufacturers provide extra RAM up to 1 KB as on-chip RAM.

Clock source The standard *8051* design uses either an external quartz crystal resonator to excite the internal on-chip oscillator circuitry or an external standalone crystal oscillator. If an external crystal oscillator is used, the waveform of the clock can affect power consumption. The input stage of the XTAL1 pin, used for driving the external clock signals into the *8051*, typically employs complementary drivers. As the input clock transitions between high and low, the drivers will momentarily both be ON, causing a significant current rush. With a square wave clock signal, the transition between high and low is almost instantaneous and the time in which both drivers are ON is minimised. A waveform with a slower rise and fall time, such as a sine or triangle wave, will take long time to complete the transition and both drivers will be on for a long time. This will increase the current and power consumption. A comparison diagram for power consumption for different clock waves is given in Fig. 5.41.

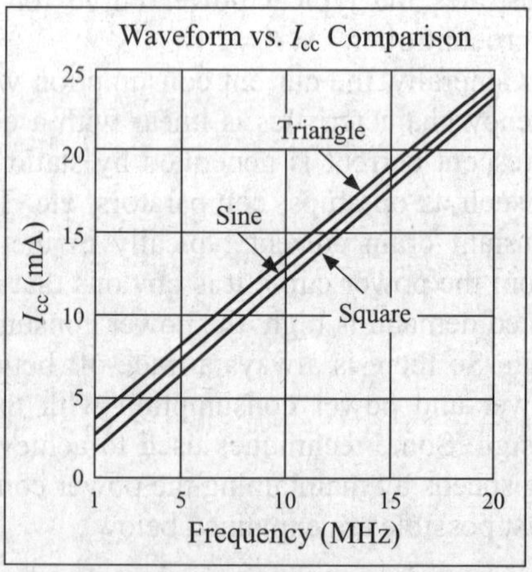

Fig. 5.41 **Power consumption curve for different clock waves**
Copyright Maxim Integrated Products (http://www.maxim-ic.com). used by permission.

5.3.11.4 On Circuit Emulation (ONCE) Mode The On Circuit Emulation (ONCE) Mode helps in testing and debugging the system without removing the microcontroller from the circuit. The ONCE mode is invoked through the following steps:

1. Pulling the ALE pin while the controller is in reset and PSEN is high
2. Holding the ALE pin low as Reset is de-activated

In ONCE mode, Port 0 pins stay in the floating state and other Port pins, ALE and PSEN are pulled high weakly internally. The oscillator circuit remains active. With these conditions an emulator or another controller can be used for driving the circuit. Normal operation of the target controller can be restored by applying a normal reset.

5.4 THE *8052* MICROCONTROLLER

The *8052* microcontroller is a member of the *8051* family and it can be considered as the 'big' brother of *8051*. *8052* is pin to pin compatible with the standard *8051* microcontroller. The only difference between the *8051* and *8052* is that *8052* contains certain additional functionalities. The *8052* architecture implements the upper 128 bytes of user data RAM physically on the chip and application programmers can access this memory through indirect addressing, whereas the standard *8051* architecture doesn't implement the upper 128 bytes of data RAM physically on the chip. *8052* also implements an additional 16bit timer (Timer 2) and thus the total number of timers available in *8052* is three, whereas the standard *8051* architecture implements only two timers. T2CON is the SFR register implemented in *8052* for controlling the timer 2 operations. The 16bit timer register is formed by the register pair TH2 and TL2. Timer 2 supports interrupt and the interrupt vector location for Timer 2 is 002BH. Timer 2 supports a special mode of operation called 'Capture Mode' and when the timer is in capture mode the contents of TH2 and TL2 is captured to the capture SFR RCAP2H and RCAP2L respectively when a 1 to 0 transition is detected at the P1.1 pin of the microcontroller. The timer 2 interrupt is also generated if the timer 2 interrupt is in the enabled state.

5.5 *8051/52* VARIANTS

Lot of variants are available for the basic *8051* architecture from different microcontroller manufactures including Atmel, Maxim/Dallas, etc. We will have a glance through on some of them.

5.5.1 Atmel's AT89C51RD2/ED2

The AT89C51RD2 from Atmel Corporation is a high speed *8052* core compatible microcontroller. It contains six 8bit I/O ports, three 16bit Timers/Counters, 256 bytes of user data RAM, 9 interrupt sources with 4 levels of priority and 64 Kbytes of on-chip In System Programmable FLASH memory for program storage. It also contains 1792 bytes of on-chip expanded RAM (XRAM), SPI port, pulse width modulation (PWM) unit, integrated watch dog timer (WDT), integrated power monitor for Power On reset and power supply fail detect, dual full duplex serial port and dual Data Pointer Register (DPTR). The 89C51RD2 controller can be operated in standard mode and high-speed mode. The standard mode of operation requires 12 clocks per machine cycle, whereas the high-speed mode (Also known as X2 mode) requires only 6 clock periods per machine cycle for instruction fetch and execution. Standard mode supports clock speed of up to 60 MHz and high speed mode supports clock speed up to 30 MHz. It also supports variable length MOVX instruction for synchronising the data communication with slow RAM/peripheral devices. It also contains 2Kbytes of FLASH bootloader containing the low level FLASH memory programming routines and default serial loader. The 89C51ED2 version is similar to the RD2 version in all respect and it supports 2Kbytes of On-Chip EEPROM memory for non-volatile data storage.

5.5.2 Maxim/Dallas' *DS80C320/ DS80C323*

The *DS80C320/DS80C323* microcontrollers from Maxim/Dallas are high speed low power microcontrollers compatible with the standard *80C31/80C32* architecture. It contains four 8bit I/O ports, three 16bit timers/counters, 256 bytes of user data RAM, 13 total interrupt sources with six external, with 3 levels of priority, programmable watch dog timer (WDT), integrated power monitor for Power On reset and power supply fail detect and dual Data Pointer Register (DPTR). The high speed core of *DS80C320/ DS80C323* uses 4 clocks or 1 clock per machine cycle design. Comparing this with the original 12 clock/machine cycle for the same operating frequency, the performance will be approximately 3 times for the 4 clock core and 12 times for the 1 clock core preserving the same power consumption.

Summary

- ✓ Feature set, speed of operation, code memory space, data memory space, development support, availability, power consumption, cost, etc. are the important factors that need to be considered in the selection of a microcontroller for an embedded design
- ✓ The basic *8051* architecture consist of an 8bit CPU with Boolean processing capability, oscillator driver unit, 4K bytes of on-chip program memory, 128 bytes of internal data memory, 128 bytes of special function register memory area, 32 general purpose I/O lines organised into four 8bit bi-directional ports, two 16bit timer units and a full duplex programmable UART for serial data transmission with configurable baudrates
- ✓ *8051* is built around the 'Harvard' processor architecture. The program and data memory of *8051* is logically separated and they physically reside separately. Separate address spaces are assigned for data memory and program memory. *8051*'s address bus is 16bit wide and it can address up to 64KB memory
- ✓ The Program Strobe Enable (PSEN) signal is activated during the external program memory fetching operation, whereas it is not activated if the program memory is internal to the microcontroller. The Program Counter (PC) Register supplies the address from which the program instruction to be fetched.
- ✓ The *8051* architecture implements 8 general purpose registers with names R0 to R7 and they are available in 4 different banks
- ✓ The lower 128 byte RAM of *8051* is organised into register banks, Bit addressable memory and Scratchpad RAM
- ✓ Accumulator, B register, Program Status Word (PSW), Stack pointer (SP), Data pointer (DPTR, combination of DPL and DPH), and Program Counter (PC) constitute the CPU registers of *8051*
- ✓ The instruction fetch operation consists of a number of machine cycles and one machine cycle consists of 12 clock periods for the standard *8051* architecture
- ✓ *8051* supports 4 bi-directional ports. The ports are named as Port 0, 1, 2 and 3. Each port contains 8 bidirectional port pins
- ✓ The 'Read Latch' operation for all port pins return the content of the corresponding pin's latch, whereas the 'Read Pin' operation returns the status of the port pin
- ✓ The basic *8051* and its ROMless counterpart *8031*AH supports five interrupt sources; namely two external interrupts, two timer interrupts and the serial interrupt. The serial interrupt is an ORed combination of the two serial interrupts; Receive Interrupt (RI) and Transmit Interrupt (TI). An interrupt vector is assigned to each interrupts in the program memory and 8 bytes of code memory location is allocated for writing the ISR corresponding to each interrupt

- ✓ The interrupt system of *8051* can be enabled or disabled totally under software control by setting or clearing the global interrupt enable bit of the Special Function Register Interrupt Enable (IE).
- ✓ The *8051* architecture supports two levels of interrupt priority. The first priority level is determined by the settings of the Interrupt Priority (IP) register. The second level is determined by the internal hardware polling sequence
- ✓ An interrupt service routine always ends with the instruction RETI. The RETI instruction informs the interrupt system that the service routine for the corresponding interrupt is finished and it clears the corresponding priority-X interrupt in progress flag by clearing the corresponding flip flop
- ✓ The basic *8051* architecture supports two timer units namely Timer 0 and Timer 1. The timer units can be configured to operate as either timer or counter. The timers support four modes of operation namely Mode 0, 1, 2 and 3
- ✓ The standard *8051* supports a full duplex, receive buffered serial interface for serial data transmission
- ✓ The CMOS version of *8051* supports two power down modes, namely, IDLE and POWERDOWN. They are activated by setting the corresponding bit in Special Function Register PCON
- ✓ The on circuit emulation (ONCE) mode of *8051* helps in testing and debugging the *8051* microcontroller based system without removing the microcontroller from the circuit
- ✓ The *8052* microcontroller architecture supports an additional 16bit timer and it supports capture mode for timer operation in addition to the four modes supported by *8051*. It also implements the upper 128bytes of user data RAM physically on the chip

Keywords

MIPS : Million instructions per second–A measure of processor speed

Microcontroller : A highly integrated chip that contains a CPU, scratchpad RAM, Special and General purpose register Arrays and Integrated peripherals

Code Memory : Memory for storing program instructions

Data Memory : Memory for holding temporary data during program execution

Register : Data holding unit made up of flip-flops

On-Chip Memory : Memory internal to the microcontroller

Port : An I/O unit which groups a number of I/O pins together and provides a control/status register for controlling the I/O pins and monitoring the pin status

ALE : Address latch enable. A control signal generated by the processor/controller for indicating the arrival of valid address signal on the address/data multiplexed bus

Program Counter : CPU register which holds the address of the program memory location from which the next instruction is to be fetched (Its width depends on the processor architecture)

Data Pointer Register (DPTR) : 16bit register which holds the address of external data memory address to be accessed, in 8051 architecture

Special Function Register : Register holding the status and control information and data associated with the various configurations, status and data for on-chip peripheral units like Timer, Interrupt Controller, etc.

Accumulator : CPU register which holds the results of all CPU related arithmetic operations

B Register : CPU register that acts as an operand in multiply and division operations, in *8051* architecture

Program Status Word (PSW) : 8bit, bit addressable special function register signalling the status of accumulator related operations and register bank selector for the scratchpad registers R0 to R7, in *8051* architecture

Stack Pointer (SP) : 8bit register holding the current address of stack memory in *8051* architecture

Machine Cycle	: The fundamental unit of instruction execution. One instruction execution may require one or more machine cycles. Under standard *8051* architecture, one machine cycle corresponds to 12 clock periods
Source Current	: The maximum current a port pin can supply to drive an externally connected device
Sink Current	: The maximum current a port pin can absorb through a device which is connected to an external supply
Interrupt	: Signal that initiates changes in normal program execution flow
Interrupt Service Routine (ISR)	: Piece of code representing the actions to be done when an interrupt occurs
Interrupt Vector	: The start address of the program memory where the ISR corresponding to an interrupt is to be located
Interrupt Latency	: The time elapsed between the assertion of the interrupt and the start of the ISR for the same
Timer	: A hardware or software unit which generates time delays. Hardware timers generate more precise time delays
Serial Port	: The I/O unit which transmits and receives data in serial format
Multiprocessor Communication	: A serial communication implementation for communicating between multiple processors on the same serial bus. Only one device acts as the master and rest act as slave at any given point of time
High-Speed Core	: A processor core which requires lesser number of clock periods for instruction fetch, decode and execution

Objective Questions

1. What is the size of internal data memory supported by the standard *8051* architecture
   (a) 64 bytes (b) 128 bytes (c) 256 bytes (d) 1024 bytes
   (e) No internal data memory
2. What is the size of a 'Special Function Register' memory supported by the standard *8051* architecture
   (a) 64 bytes (b) 128 bytes (c) 256 bytes (d) 1024 bytes
   (e) No internal SFR memory
3. What is the size of an internal program memory supported by the standard *8051* architecture
   (a) 128 bytes (b) 1024 bytes (c) 2 Kbytes (d) 4 Kbytes
   (e) No internal program memory
4. What is the number of general purpose I/O lines supported by the standard *8051* architecture
   (a) 8 (b) 16 (c) 32 (d) 64
5. The general purpose I/O lines of a standard *8051* is grouped into
   (a) Two 8-bit bi-directional ports (b) Four 8-bit bi-directional ports
   (c) Two 16-bit bi-directional ports (d) Four 16-bit bi-directional ports
6. What is the number of timer units supported by a standard *8051* architecture
   (a) Two 16-bit timers (b) Three 16-bit timers (c) Two 8-bit timers (d) One 16-bit timer
7. The UART of the standard *8051* controller is
   (a) Half duplex with configurable baudrate (b) Half duplex with fixed baudrate
   (c) Full duplex with configurable baudrate (d) Full duplex with fixed baudrate
8. The standard 8051 controller is built around
   (a) Harvard Architecture (b) Von Neumann Architecture (c) None of these
9. Which of the following is *True* for a *8051* controller?
   (a) The program and data memory of *8051* is logically separated

(b) The program and data memory of *8051* physically resides separately.
(c) Separate address spaces are assigned for data memory and program memory
(d) All of these (e) None of these

10. The address bus of *8051* is
(a) 8-bit wide (b) 16-bit wide (c) 32-bit wide (d) 20-bit wide
11. Which of the following is *True* about external program memory access?
(a) Port 0 acts as the data bus and Port 2 acts as the higher order address bus
(b) Port 2 acts as the data bus and Port 0 acts as the higher order address bus
(c) Port 0 acts as the multiplexed address/data bus and Port 2 acts as the higher order address bus
(d) Port 2 acts as the multiplexed address/data bus and Port 0 acts as the higher order address bus
12. Name the register holding the address of the memory location holding the next instruction to fetch
(a) DPTR (b) PC (c) SP (d) None of these
13. Name the register holding the address of the external data memory to be accessed in 16bit external data memory operation
(a) DPTR (b) PC (c) SP (d) None of these
14. For standard *8051* architecture, the internal data memory address is
(a) 8bit wide (b) 4bit wide (c) 16bit wide (d) None of these
15. The external data memory is 4 Kbytes in size and it is arranged in paged addressing mode where 1 page consists of 256 bytes. Port 2 is used as the page selector. How many port bits are required for implementing the paging?
(a) 1 (b) 2 (c) 3 (d) 4
16. Which of the following conditions should be satisfied to implement the Von-Neumann memory model for *8051*?
(a) The data memory and code memory should be stored in a single memory chip (RAM/NVRAM)
(b) The external access pin should be tied to logic 0
(c) The external access pin should be tied to logic 1
(d) The PSEN\ and RD\ signals of 8051 should be ANDed to generate the output enable (OE\) of the memory chip
(e) (a) (b) and (d) (f) (a) (c) and (d)
17. What is the number of general purpose registers supported by the standard *8051* architecture
(a) 1 (b) 8 (c) 16 (d) 32
18. What is the number of bit variables supported by *8051* in the internal data memory area?
(a) 8 (b) 16 (c) 32 (d) 64
(e) 128
19. Bit address 07H contains logic 1, what is the value of bit 07H after executing the instruction MOV 20H, #01H
(a) 0 (b) 1
20. Memory location 81H contains F0H. What will be the value of Accumulator after executing the instruction *MOV A, 81H*
(a) 81H (b) 00H (c) F0H (d) Random data
21. The target controller is a standard *8051*. Memory location 81H contains F0H. What will be the value of accumulator after executing the instructions
MOV R0, #81H
MOV A, @R0
(a) 81H (b) 00H (c) F0H (e) Random data
22. Name the register signalling the status of accumulator related operations
(a) A (b) B (c) PSW (d) SP
(e) None of these
23. How many user programmable general purpose bits are available in the status register of *8051*?
(a) 0 (b) 1 (c) 2 (d) 3
(e) 4
24. The accumulator content is 02H. What will be the status of the 'parity bit P' of the Status Register?
(a) 1 (b) 0

25. The accumulator contains 0FH. The overflow (OV) carry (C) flag and Auxiliary carry flag (AC) are in the set state. What will be status of these flags after executing the instruction *ADD A, #1*
(a) OV = 0; C = 0; AC = 0 (b) OV = 0; C = 0; AC = 1
(c) OV = 1; C = 1; AC = 1 (d) OV = 1; C = 1; AC = 0
26. The register bank selector bits RS0, RS1 are 0 and 1. What is the physical address of register R0?
(a) 00H (b) 08H (c) 0FH (d) 10H
(e) 18H
27. The machine cycle for a standard *8051* controller consists of
(a) 2T States (b) 4T States (c) 6T States (d) 8T States
28. Which port of *8051* is 'true-bidirectional'?
(a) Port 0 (b) Port 1 (c) Port 2 (d) Port 3
29. For configuring a port pin as input port, the corresponding port pins bit latch should be at
(a) Logic 0 (b) Logic 1
30. Port 2 latch contains A5H. What will be the value of Port 2 latch after executing the following instructions?
MOV DPTR, #0F00H
MOV A, #0FFH
MOVX @DPTR, A
(a) 00H (b) 0FH (c) A5H (d) FFH
31. The alternate I/O function for the pins of Port 3 will come into action only when the corresponding bit latch is
(a) 1 (b) 0
32. The interrupts Timer 0 and serial interrupt are enabled individually in the interrupt enable register and high priority is given to Timer 0 interrupt by setting the Timer 0 priority selector in the interrupt priority register. It is observed that the serial interrupt is not at all occurring. What could be the reasons for this?
(a) The global interrupt enable bit (EA) is not in the set state
(b) The Serial interrupt always occurs with Timer 0 interrupt
(c) There is no Serial data transmission or reception activity happening in the system
(d) None of these (e) (a) or (b) or (c)
33. Timer 0 and External 0 interrupts are enabled in the system and are given a priority of 1. Incidentally, the Timer 0 interrupt and External 0 interrupt occurred simultaneously. Which interrupt will be serviced by the *8051* CPU?
(a) Timer 0 (b) External 0
(c) External 0 interrupt is serviced first and after completing it Timer 0 interrupt is serviced
(d) None of them are serviced
34. What is the maximum ISR size allocated for each interrupt in the standard 8051 Architecture
(a) 1 Byte (b) 4 Byte (c) 8 Byte (d) 16 Byte
35. What is the minimum interrupt acknowledgement latency in a single interrupt system for standard *8051* architecture
(a) 1 Machine cycle (b) 2 Machine cycle (c) 3 Machine cycle (d) 8 Machine cycle
36. External 0 interrupt is asserted and latched at S5P2 of the first machine cycle of the instruction *MUL AB*. What will be the minimum interrupt acknowledgement latency time?
(a) 6 Machine cycles (b) 5 Machine cycles (c) 3 Machine cycles (d) 2 Machine cycles
37. What is the minimum duration in which the external interrupt line should be asserted to identify it as a valid interrupt for level triggered configuration?
(a) 1 Machine cycle (b) 3 T States (c) 2 Machine cycles (d) 3 Machine cycles
38. What is the timer increment rate for timer operation for standard *8051* architecture
(a) Oscillator Frequency/6 (b) Oscillator Frequency/12
(c) Same as Oscillator Frequency (d) Oscillator Frequency/24
39. What is the maximum count rate for counting external events for standard *8051* architecture
(a) Oscillator Frequency/6 (b) Oscillator Frequency/12
(c) Same as Oscillator Frequency (d) Oscillator Frequency/24
40. Which is the 'Timer' used for baudrate generation for serial communication?
(a) Timer 0 (b) Timer 1

41. The 'Timer' used for baudrate generation should run in
    (a) Mode 0 (b) Mode 1 (c) Mode 2 (d) Mode 3
42. For 'Mode 0' operation, the 13 bit register is formed by
    (a) 8 bits of TH0/TH1 and least significant 5 bits of TL0/TL1
    (b) 8 bits of TH0/TH1 and most significant 5 bits of TL0/TL1
    (c) 8 bits of TL0/TL1 and least significant 5 bits of TH0/TH1
    (d) 8 bits of TL0/TL1 and most significant 5 bits of TH0/TH1
43. The serial port of the standard *8051* architecture is
    (a) Full duplex (b) Half duplex (c) 'Receive' buffered (d) (a) and (c)
    (e) (b) and (c)
44. Name the 'Register' which acts as the 'Receive' and 'Transmit' buffer in serial communication operation?
    (a) SCON (b) PCON (c) SBUF (d) Accumulator
45. Which of the following is (are) true about 'Mode 0' operation of serial communication
    (a) The baudrate is variable (b) The baudrate is given as oscillator frequency/12
    (c) The baudrate is same as oscillator frequency (d) The baudrate is given as oscillator frequency/2
46. The 'Auto Reload' count for 'Timer 1' is FDH and the operating frequency is 11.0592 MHz and baudrate doubler bit SMOD is 0. What is the baudrate for communication?
    (a) 2400 (b) 4800 (c) 9600 (d) 19200
47. What will be the value of 'Program Counter (PC)' after a proper power on reset?
    (a) FFFFH (b) 0000H (c) Random value (d) 0001H
48. What will be the value of internal RAM after a reset?
    (a) 00H (b) FFH
    (c) The value before reset if the system is resetted during operation
    (d) Random if the system is resetted immediately after Power ON
    (e) (c) or (d)
49. Which of the following is (are) 'True' about 'IDLE' mode?
    (a) The internal clock to the processor is temporarily suspended
    (b) The various CPU status like SP, PC, PSW, Accumulator and all other register values are preserved
    (c) All port pins will retain their logical state
    (d) ALE and PSEN are pulled high
    (e) All of these (f) (a), (b) and (c) only
50. A reset signal is applied to the *8051* processor when it is in the 'Idle' mode. How will the system behave?
    (a) The idle mode setting bit IDL is cleared
    (b) The processor resumes program execution from where it left off
    (c) The processor resumes program execution from 0000H
    (d) (a) and (b) only (e) (a) and (c) only

Review Questions

1. Explain the various factors to be considered while selecting a microcontroller for an embedded system design.
2. Explain the architecture of the *8051* microcontroller with a block diagram.
3. Explain the different operating modes of *8051* (Hint: normal operation mode, power saving mode and ONCE mode)
4. Explain the code memory organisation for *8051* for internal and external program memory access.
5. Explain the data memory organisation for standard *8051* controller.
6. Explain the *Von-Neumann* memory model implementation for *8051* based system. What are the merits and demerits of using a *Von-Neumann* memory model?
7. Explain the memory organisation for lower 128 bytes of internal RAM for standard *8051* architecture.

8. Explain how Port 0 acts as a normal I/O port and multiplexed address data bus for external data/program memory access?
9. What is the difference between *Read Latch* and *Read Pin* operation for port lines?
10. Why is Port 0 known as *true-bidirectional*?
11. Why is Port 1 known as *quasi-bidirectional*?
12. Explain how Port 2 acts as a normal I/O port and higher order address bus for external data/program memory access?
13. Explain how Port 3 acts as a normal I/O port and an alternate I/O function port?
14. What is the difference between RET and RETI instructions for indicating the end of a subroutine call?
15. Explain how a third priority level can be achieved in *8051* interrupt system?
16. What is *interrupt latency*? What is the minimum and maximum interrupt latency time for a single interrupt system in standard *8051* architecture? Explain in detail.
17. Explain the different conditions that block or delay the vectoring of an interrupt.
18. Explain the different actions generated by the processor on identifying an interrupt request number.
19. The external interrupt INT0 is enabled, and set to be level triggered. The Port pin P3.2 is set at logic 0. Explain the behaviour of the system.
20. Explain the operation of Timer 0 in *Mode 0*. Why is *Mode 0* operation known as 8-bit Timer with a divide by 32 prescaler?
21. Explain the *auto reload* mode of operation of a timer. Give an example for the usage of Timer 1 in *auto reload* mode.
22. Explain the *Mode 1* operation of *serial communication*. How is *configurable baudrate* achieved for serial communication in *Mode 1*? What is the *Timer 1* auto reload count for a baudrate of 9600 bits/second for a system working at 11.0592MHz?
23. What is *multiprocessor communication*? Explain the multiprocessor communication for *8051* for serial communication *Mode 2*.
24. How a 'power on reset' can be implemented for an *8051*-based system? Explain the changes that happen to various registers and internal RAM on a proper reset.
25. Explain the two power saving modes *Idle* and *Power Down* modes for *8051*. What is the difference between the two? Explain the methods of terminating each of the power saving modes.
26. Explain the *Power consumption* v/s *Operating Frequency* characteristics for an *8051* based system. Why do the characteristics curve contain an offset from the origin?
27. What are the different techniques that can be adopted for reducing the power consumption of an *8051* based system?
28. What is *On Circuit Emulation (ONCE)* mode? How is *ONCE* mode enabled? What is the use *ONCE* mode in system design?
29. Explain the difference between *8051* and *8052* microcontroller.
30. Only Timer 0 interrupt is enabled in the system and it is assigned a priority of 1. It is observed that the timer interrupt occurred only once and it is not occurring even though the timer roll over happens. The program does not contain any instruction for disabling the global interrupt enable flag IE and Timer 0 interrupt. What could be the reason?

Lab Assignments

1. Write an *8051* assembly language program for transmitting 1 byte data through the serial port with a ninth bit which is used as an even parity bit. The program should configure the serial communication settings as: Baudrate = 9600, 1 start bit, 1 stop bit and also depending on the parity of the data byte to be sent, the parity bit should be set properly.

2. Write an *8051* assembly language program for receiving an even parity enabled 8-bit data through the serial port. The program should configure the serial communication settings as: Baudrate = 9600, 1 start bit, 1 stop bit. Upon receiving the data byte, the parity of it is calculated and it is verified with the parity bit received. Use interrupts for implementing the serial data reception
3. Develop a hardware system to single step the program written for *8051*. The firmware running in the controller sends the register contents A, B, PSW and R0 to R7 on executing each instruction to a program running on PC. Develop a PC application to capture the register details and display it. Use RS-232 UART communication for sending the debug info to PC. Use the following configuration settings for the RS-232 link: Baudrate = 9600, 1 start bit, 1 stop bit, No parity.
4. Develop an *8051*-based system for detecting the keypress of a pushbutton switch connected to the port pin P1.0 of the microcontroller. Implement the key de-bouncing for the push button in firmware (Upon detecting a keypress, the firmware waits for 20 milliseconds and then checks the push button switch again, if the switch remains in the depressed state, the key press is identified as a valid key depression). For a valid keypress, a buzzer connected to port pin P1.1 is activated for a period of 1 second. Use a BC547 transistor-based driver circuit for driving the buzzer.
5. Implement the above requirement using a hardware key de-bounce circuit and connecting the push button switch to the external interrupt 0 pin of the controller. Implement the buzzer control logic in the Interrupt Service Routine for External Interrupt 0.
6. Develop an *8051*-based system for detecting the keypress of an array of 8 pushbutton switches connected to the port pins P1.0 to P1.7 of the microcontroller. Using an AND gate generate an external interrupt signal when any one of the push button switch is depressed. Identify which push button is depressed by scanning the status of the push button connected port pins, in the interrupt service routine for the external interrupt. The port pins are scanned in the order P1.0 to P1.7. Even if multiple push buttons are depressed, the first identified push button switch is recognised as the valid keypress. Use a hardware key de-bounce circuit/IC for implementing the key de-bouncing for all push buttons. An 8 ohm speaker is connected to port pin P2.0. Generate different tones (by varying the frequency (say 100Hz, 200Hz, 300Hz, 500Hz, etc) of the pulse generated at the port pin in which the speaker is connected, corresponding to each push button press. Use BC547 transistor based driver circuit for driving the speaker.
7. Design an *8051* based system for interfacing an RF transceiver ***(e.g. RF Modem from SUNROM Technologies http://www.sunrom.com/index.php?main_page=product_info&cPath=89&products_id=560)*** and a relay driver circuit using an NPN transistor for driving a normally open relay with coil voltage 12V for switching Alternating Current with ratings 5Amps and 50Hz. Connect a 100W/240V bulb through the relay. Turn ON and OFF the bulb in response to the command received by the RF transceiver. The commands are sent by an application running on PC through an RF transceiver.
8. Implement the above system using infrared (IR) remote control and receiver, supporting the RC5 protocol (e.g. TV remote and SFH 506-36 IR receiver unit (Use the reference design http://www.atmel.com/dyn/resources/prod_documents/doc1473.pdf from Atmel for SFH 506 interfacing)), in place of the RF based control implementation.
9. Develop a miniature 'Traffic Light Control' system based on *8051* and LEDs for controlling the 'Red' 'Green' and 'Yellow' signal lights present at a junction where four roads meet. The 'Green' and 'Red' signal will be on for a duration of 30 seconds and 'Yellow' for 5 seconds.
10. Develop a simple electronic calculator using 8051 microcontroller with 16 push button keys arranged in a 4×4 matrix for representing digits 0 to 9, operators +, –, ×, %, = and 'Clear' button. Use two 7-segment LEDs for displaying the result. Only single digit operations are allowed. The system requirements are listed below.
    (a) Upon power on both the 7-Segment LEDs display 0
    (b) When a numeric key is pressed, it is displayed on the rightmost 7-segment LED
    (c) Enter the first operand (digit) by pressing the corresponding push button
    (d) To perform an operation (+, –, ×, %) press the corresponding push button
    (e) Now press the second operand (digit)
    (f) Press the '=' operator for displaying the result of the operation
    (g) Pressing the 'Clear' key at any point clears the display and displays '0' on both LED displays. For division operation, display the quotient as result.

6 Programming the *8051* Microcontroller

LEARNING OBJECTIVES

- ✓ *Learn how to program the 8051 microcontroller using Assembly Language*
- ✓ *Understand what an instruction and instruction set is*
- ✓ *Learn the direct, indirect, register, immediate and indexed addressing modes supported by 8051. Learn about register instructions and register specific instructions supported by 8051*
- ✓ *Learn the different instructions supported by 8051 instruction set architecture*
- ✓ *Learn the internal and external data transfer instructions, data exchange instructions, Stack memory related data transfer instructions and code memory read instructions supported by 8051*
- ✓ *Learn the addition and subtraction, multiplication and division, increment and decrement, and decimal adjust instructions supported by 8051*
- ✓ *Learn the different logical instructions (Rotate, Shift, Complement, etc.) supported by 8051*
- ✓ *Learn the bit manipulation instructions supported by 8051*
- ✓ *Learn the different program execution control transfer instructions supported by 8051*
- ✓ *Learn the unconditional program control transfer instructions (Jump, Subroutine Call, return from ISR and function call, etc.) supported by 8051*
- ✓ *Learn the conditional program control transfer instructions (Decrement and Jump if non zero, Compare and jump if not equal, Jump if carry flag is set or not set, Jump if a specified bit is set or not, etc.) supported by 8051*

As you learned in the basic *8085/8088* microprocessor class, an *Instruction* consists of two parts namely; *Opcode* and *Operand* (s). The opcode tells the processor what to do on executing an instruction. The operand(s) is the parameter(s) required by opcode to complete the action. The term *Instruction Set* refers to the set of instructions supported by a processor/controller architecture. The instruction set of *8051* family microcontroller is broadly classified into five categories namely; *Data transfer instructions*, *Arithmetic instructions*, *Logical instructions*, *Boolean instructions* and *program control transfer instructions*. Before going to the details of each type of instructions, it is essential to understand the different addressing modes supported by the *8051* microcontroller.

6.1 DIFFERENT ADDRESSING MODES SUPPORTED BY *8051*

The term '*addressing mode*' refers to "How the operand is specified in an instruction" along with opcode. The operand may be one or a combination of the following–memory location(s), contents of memory location(s), register(s), or constant. Depending on the type of operands, the addressing modes are classified as follows.

6.1.1 Direct Addressing

The operand is specified as an 8 bit memory address. For *8051* processor, only the lower 128 byte internal data memory and the SFRs are directly accessible.

For example, *MOV A, 07H* (Moves the content of memory location 07H to the accumulator. 07H refers to the address of data memory at location 7. If memory location 07H contains the value 255, executing this instruction will modify the content of *A* to 255) uses MOV as opcode and *A*, 07H as operands (Fig. 6.1).

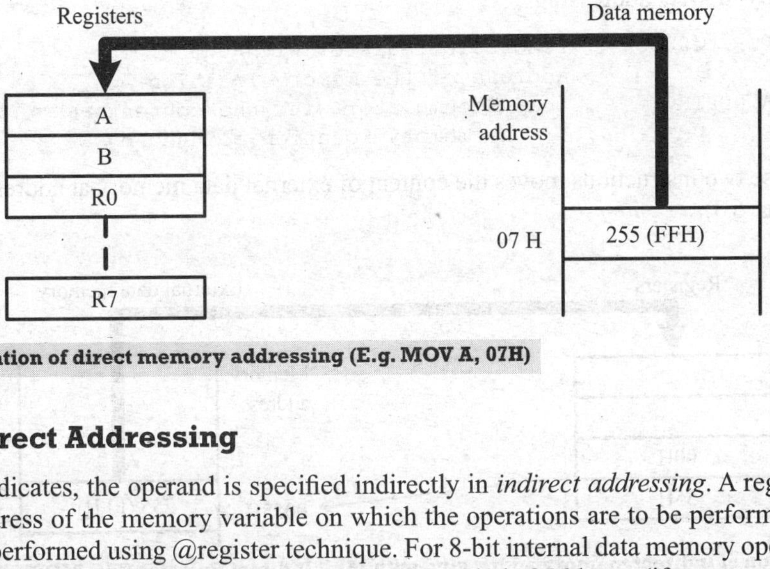

Fig. 6.1 **Illustration of direct memory addressing (E.g. MOV A, 07H)**

6.1.2 Indirect Addressing

As the name indicates, the operand is specified indirectly in *indirect addressing*. A register is used for holding the address of the memory variable on which the operations are to be performed. The indirect operations are performed using @register technique. For 8-bit internal data memory operations, register R0 or R1 is used as the indirect addressing register. The whole 256 bytes (if present physically on the chip) can be accessed by indirect addressing.

```
E.g.   MOV R0, #55H   ; Load R0 with 55H, The address of mem loc
       MOV A,@R0      ; Load Accumulator with the contents of the-
                      ; memory location pointed by R0
```

Register R0 is loaded with 55H (85 in decimal) on executing the first instruction. Here R0 is used as the indirect addressing register and data memory 55H is the memory variable on which the operations are performed. Executing the second instruction moves the contents of memory address 55H to the accumulator. This can be interpreted as MOV A, content @Memory Address 55H. Suppose 55H contains 255, executing the second instruction will load the accumulator with 255 (Fig. 6.2).

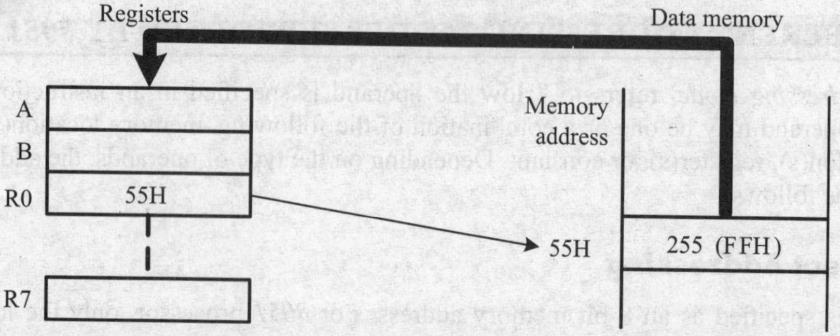

Fig. 6.2 **Illustration of indirect memory addressing with 8bit indirect register (E.g. MOV A, @R0)**

Among the scratchpad registers R0 to R7, only R0 and R1 can be used for indirect addressing. For 16bit external data memory/memory mapped register operations, 16bit register DPTR is used as the indirect addressing register. The whole 64K bytes of the external memory (if present physically on chip) can be accessed by indirect addressing.

```
E.g.   MOV DPTR, #0055H  ; Load DPTR register with 0055H, The-
                         ; address of the memory location
       MOVX A,@DPTR      ; Load Accumulator with the contents-
                         ; of the memory location pointed by DPTR
```

Executing these two instructions moves the content of external data memory at address 0055H to the Accumulator (Fig. 6.3).

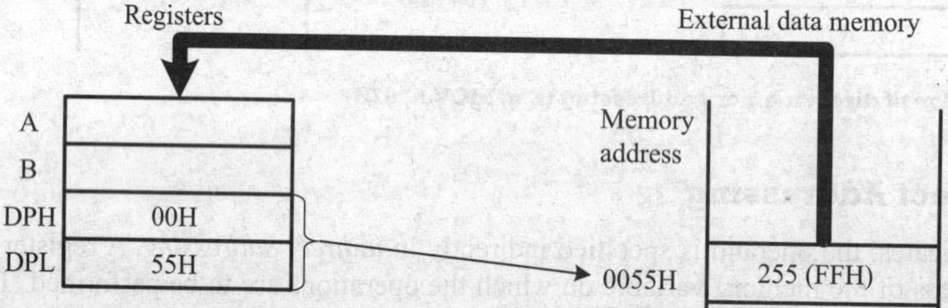

Fig. 6.3 **Illustration of Indirect memory addressing with 16bit Indirect Register (E.g. MOVX A, @DPTR)**

Indirect addressing is same as the pointer concept in C Programming. Indirect addressing is commonly used for operations similar to pointer based operations in C Programming like array, external memory access, etc.

6.1.3 Register Addressing

Register addressing is of two types. In some instructions, the register operand is implicitly specified by some bits of the opcode. These types of instructions are referred as *Register Instructions*. Some instructions implicitly work on certain specific registers. They are known as *Register Specific Instructions*.

6.1.3.1 Register Instructions In register instructions, the register operand is specified by some bits of the opcode itself. If scratchpad registers R0 to R7 are used as operands, they can be specified along with the opcode by using the last 3 bits of the opcode. Such instructions are code efficient since the opcode itself specifies one operand; it eliminates the need for storing the operand as a byte in code memory and also saves the time in fetching the operand. Generally register variable access is faster than general memory access.

```
E.g.    MOV R0, 01H
```

This is a two byte instruction where the first operand R0 is indicated by the last 3 bits of the opcode byte.

Register to register data transfer is not allowed and hence instructions like *MOV R1, R2* are invalid.

6.1.3.2 Register Specific Instructions Some of the *8051* instructions are specific to certain registers. Examples are accumulator and data pointer specific instructions.

```
E.g.    ADD A, #50
```

During the assembly process, this instruction is converted to a two byte instruction in which *A* is implicitly specified by the opcode corresponding to ADD.

6.1.4 Immediate Constants

Constants can be an operand for some instructions. If an instruction makes use of a constant data as the operand, the type of addressing is called *immediate addressing*. In immediate addressing, a constant follows the opcode as operand in code memory. An immediate constant is represented with a leading '#' symbol in the assembly code. A leading '#' tells the assembler that the operand is a constant. For example, if you want to load accumulator with the constant 9, the following instruction will do it.

```
        MOV A, #09
```

6.1.5 Indexed Addressing

Indexed addressing is used for program memory access. This addressing mode is used for reading look up table from code memory and is Read Only. A 16bit register is used for holding the base address of the lookup table. The offset of the table entry from which the data to be retrieved is loaded in Accumulator. The instruction *MOVC* is used for indexed addressing.

```
E.g.    MOV DPTR, #2008H
        MOV A, #00
        MOVC A, @A+DPTR
```

The above example assumes that the lookup table is at memory location 2008H and so the base address of the lookup table is 2008H. The first instruction loads the base pointer address 2008H to the base pointer register DPTR. The table index is provided by the accumulator register. To access the corresponding entry of the table, load accumulator with the offset from the base address. For accessing the base element the offset should be 0. The second instruction loads the offset to accumulator. For example, if you want to access the entry which is just above the base entry, the accumulator should be loaded with 1. Executing the third instruction moves the content of the table entry at memory location 0+2008H to the accumulator. Since the offset address register, accumulator, is an 8bit register, the maximum size of the look up table is 256 bytes (Base address + 0 to Base address + 255).

Another register, which is 16bit wide, used for indexed addressing is Program Counter (PC). The only difference in using PC for indexed addressing when compared to DPTR is that the PC is not available to user for direct manipulation and user cannot directly load the desired base address to the PC register by a *MOV* instruction as in the case of DPTR. Instead the desired address is loaded to the PC by diverting the program flow to the location where the Lookup table is held in the code memory by using a CALL instruction.

First the desired table index is loaded to the accumulator register and a call is made to the location where the lookup table is stored. For this type of tables, the index should be within 1 to 255 (including both). 0 cannot be used as an index since the execution of *MOVC A,@A+DPTR* increments the PC to the address of the RET instruction's memory location. If you use a 0 index along with the PC, the contents retrieved will be the binary data corresponding to the RET instruction. Code memory lookup tables are usually used for storing string constants and other configuration data. Another use of indexed addressing is the 'case jump' instruction in *8051*. Here the jump instruction's destination address is calculated as the sum of the base pointer (PC) and the Accumulator data.

Example 1

Write an assembly program to display the numbers from 0 to 9 on a 7-segment common-anode LED display which is connected to Port 2 of the *8051*. The seven segment codes for displaying the numerals 0 to 9 on the common anode LED is stored as lookup table in the code memory starting at 0050H. Use DPTR register for holding the base address of the table.

Please refer to the section on 7-segment LED Display given in Chapter 2 for more details on 7-segment LED Display. Figure 6.4 illustrates the interfacing of common anode LED Display with Port 2 of *8051*.

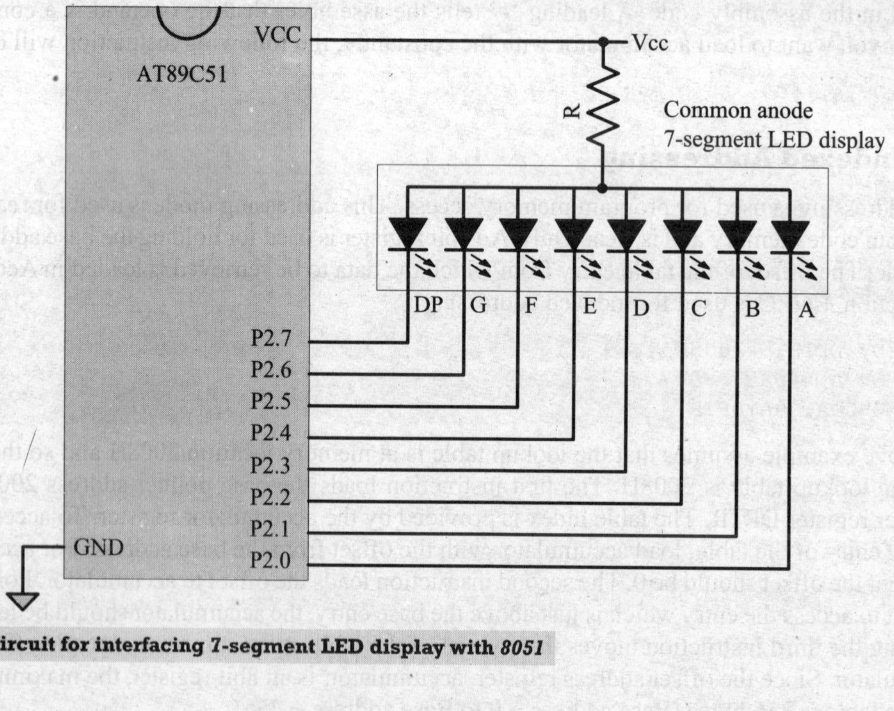

Fig. 6.4 **Circuit for interfacing 7-segment LED display with *8051***

Now we need to design the different bit patterns (code) to be outputted to the Port 2 pins to display the numbers from 0 to 9 on the LED Display. The following table explains the same. Refer to the LED segment arrangement diagram given earlier for clarification.

Digit	DP P2.7	G P2.6	F P2.5	E P2.4	D P2.3	C P2.2	B P2.1	A P2.0	Code (Hex)
0	1	1	0	0	0	0	0	0	C0
1	1	1	1	1	1	0	0	1	F9
2	1	0	1	0	0	1	0	0	A4
3	1	0	1	1	0	0	0	0	B0
4	1	0	0	1	1	0	0	1	99
5	0	0	0	1	0	0	1	0	12
6	0	0	0	0	0	0	1	0	02
7	1	1	1	1	1	0	0	0	F8
8	1	0	0	0	0	0	0	0	80
9	1	0	0	1	0	0	0	0	90

Now the codes for displaying the digits and the port interfacing for the LED display is complete. The next step required for setting up the decimal counter for counting from 0 to 9 is the development of firmware. The flow chart given in Fig. 6.5 illustrates the firmware requirements for building the decimal counter.

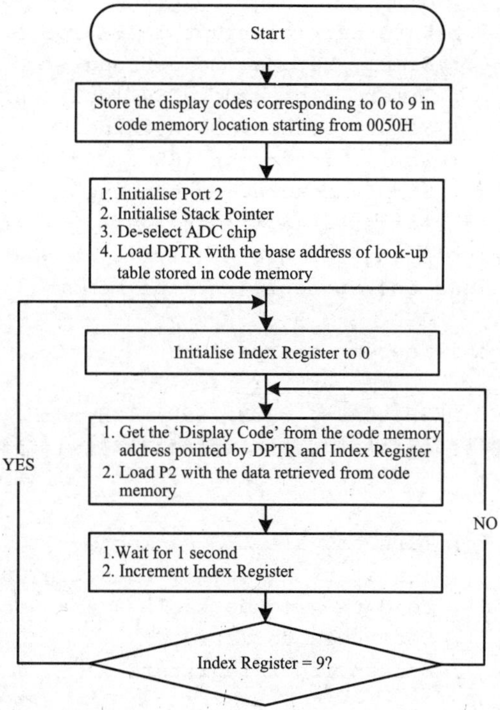

Fig. 6.5 **Flowchart for displaying digits using 7-Segment LED Display**

The firmware for implementing the decimal counter is given below.

```
;####################################################################
;7_Segment_LED_DPTR.src
;Firmware for Implementing Decimal Counter and displaying count in
;7 Segment LED Display
;The display code for displaying digits 0 to 9 are stored in code-
;memory starting from code memory address 0050H.
;The DPTR register holds the base address of the lookup table-
;holding the display codes. Accumulator is used as the index-
;register for retrieving the codes corresponding to 0 to 9
;from code memory. Written & Compiled for A51 Assembler
;Written by Shibu K V. Copyright (C) 2008
;####################################################################
ORG 0023H
ORG 0000H                ; Reset vector
       JMP 0100H         ; Jump to code mem location 0100H to start-
                         ; execution
ORG 0003H                ; External Interrupt 0 ISR location
       RETI              ; Simply return. Do nothing
ORG 000BH                ; Timer 0 Interrupt ISR location
       RETI              ; Simply return. Do nothing
ORG 0013H                ; External Interrupt 1 ISR location
       RETI              ; Simply return. Do nothing
ORG 001BH                ; Timer 1 Interrupt ISR location
       RETI              ; Simply return. Do nothing
                         ; Serial Interrupt ISR location
       RETI              ; Simply return. Do nothing
;####################################################################
;Define the codes for displaying the digits from 0 to 9
;The codes are stored in a lookup table in code memory-
;starting from 0050h
;The DB definition usage is assembler specific
ORG 0050H
DECIMAL_CODES: DB 0C0H, 0F9H, 0A4H, 0B0H, 99H, 12H, 02H, 0F8H, 80H,90H
;####################################################################
; Start of main Program
ORG 0100H
       MOV P2, #0FFH     ; Turn off all LED segments
       MOV SP, #08H      ; Set stack at memory location 08H
       MOV DPTR,#0050H   ; Load the lookup table start address
RESET: CLR A             ; Set index to zero.
       MOV R7,A          ; Backup index register
```

```
REPEAT: MOVC A,@A+DPTR   ; Get the display code
        MOV P2, A        ; Load P2 with Display code
        CALL DELAY       ; Wait for 1 second
        INC R7           ; Increment index
        MOV A, R7
        CJNE A, #10, REPEAT   ; Are all 9 digits displayed?
        ; All 9 digits displayed. Reset counter to 0
        JMP RESET
;###################################################################
;Routine for generating 1 second delay
;Delay generation is dependent on clock frequency
;This routine assumes a clock frequency of 12.00MHZ
;LOOP1 generates 248 x 2 Machine cycles (496microseconds) delay
;LOOP2 generates 200 x (496+2+1) Machine cycles (99800microseconds)
;delay. LOOP3 generate 10 x (99800+2+1) Machine cycles
;(998030microseconds) delay
;The routine generates a precise delay of 0.99 seconds
;###################################################################
DELAY:  MOV R2, #10
LOOP1:  MOV R1, #200
LOOP2:  MOV R0, #248
LOOP3:  DJNZ R0, LOOP3
        DJNZ R1, LOOP2
        DJNZ R2, LOOP1
        RET
END     ;END of Assembly Program
```

6.2 THE *8051* INSTRUCTION SET

As mentioned earlier, the *8051 Instruction Set* is broadly classified into five categories namely; *Data transfer instructions*, *Arithmetic instructions*, *Logical instructions*, *Boolean instructions* and *Program control transfer instructions*. The following sections describe each of them in detail.

6.2.1 Data Transfer Instructions

Data transfer instructions transfer data between a source and destination. The source can be an internal data memory, a register, external data memory, code memory or immediate data. Destination may be an internal data memory, external data memory or a register.

6.2.1.1 Internal Data Transfer Operations Internal data transfer instructions perform the movement of data between, register, memory location, accumulator and stack. MOV instruction is used for data transfer between register, memory location and accumulator. PUSH and POP instructions transfer data between memory location/register and stack. The following table summarises the various internal data transfer instructions.

Instruction Mnemonic	Action	Comments	Machine Cycles	Exec. Time (μs)
MOV <dest>, <src>	<dest> = <src>	Copies the content of <src> to <dest>. <dest> can be one of the registers B, R0, R1, … R7, any SFR, a direct internal data memory or an internal data memory pointed indirectly by the indirect addressing register R0 or R1 and @. <src> can be any of the above said locations or an immediate constant. (General register to register based direct and indirect data transfer (e.g. MOV R0, R1; MOV @R0, @R1; MOV @R0, R1; MOV R0, @R1; etc) is not allowed in the case of registers R0 to R7)	2†	$2^*(f_{OSC}/12)$
MOV A,< src >	A= <src>	Copies the content of <src> to Accumulator. <src> can be registers B, R0, R1, … R7, any SFR, a direct internal data memory, or an internal data memory pointed indirectly by indirect addressing register R0 or R1 and @ or an immediate constant	1	$f_{OSC}/12$
MOV < dest >, A	<dest> =A	Copies the content of A to destination. <dest> can be registers B, R0, R1, …R7, any SFR, or a direct internal data memory or an internal data memory pointed indirectly by indirect addressing register R0 or R1 and @	1	$f_{OSC}/12$
MOV DPTR,#const	DPTR=16bit data (const)	Loads DPTR register with a 16bit data (immediate addressing)	2	$2^*(f_{OSC}/12)$
PUSH <src>	SP=SP+1 (@ SP)=<src>	Increment Stack Pointer register by one and stores the content of <src> at the location pointed by SP register.	2	$2^*(f_{OSC}/12)$
POP <dest>	<dest> = @ SP SP = SP-1	Retrieve the content from the location pointed by stack pointer to <dest> and decrement SP register by one	2	$2^*(f_{OSC}/12)$
XCH A,<byte>	temp = A A = byte byte = temp	Exchange data between accumulator and a memory location/ register/a memory location pointed indirectly by indirect addressing register.	1	$f_{OSC}/12$
XCHD A,@Ri (i=0 or 1)		Exchanges the low nibble (lower 4 bits) of 'A' with the low nibble of data pointed by indirect addressing Register R0 or R1	1	$f_{OSC}/12$

MOV instruction copies the content of source to destination. Only the destination is modified. The source data remains unchanged.

6.2.1.2 Stack Memory Related Data Transfer '*Stack*' is an internal memory for storing variables temporarily. Stack memory is normally used for storing the data during subroutine calls. In *8051*, by default the stack memory is allocated from the memory location 07H onwards by loading the stack pointer (SP) register with 07H on power on reset. PUSH instruction stores data on stack memory. The PUSH instruction first increments the SP by one and copies the data to the memory location pointed by the SP register. POP instruction retrieves the data, which is stored on the stack memory using PUSH instruction. POP instruction copies the data stored in memory location pointed by SP register to the variable

† For all data transfer instruction involving an immediate constant as the source, and scratchpad register R0 to R7 as the destination (e.g. MOV R0,#00; MOV @R0, #00) the execution cycle is 1 machine cycle.

given along with POP instruction and decrements the SP by one. In *8051* architecture the stack memory grows upward in memory and follows Last In First Out (LIFO) method. PUSH and POP instructions use only direct addressing mode and hence the instructions PUSH R0, PUSH R1, PUSH A, etc. are not valid. They are valid only if the arguments are used with absolute addressing. Hence the valid instructions corresponding to them are PUSH AR0, PUSH AR1, and PUSH ACC, etc. The operation of PUSH and POP instructions are illustrated in Fig. 6.6 and Fig. 6.7.

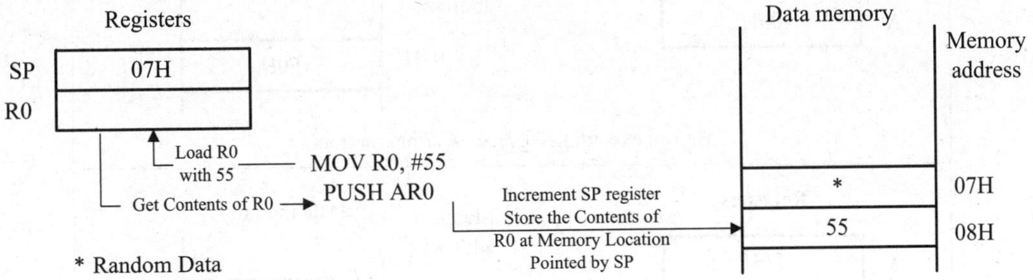

Fig. 6.6 **Illustration of *PUSH* instruction**

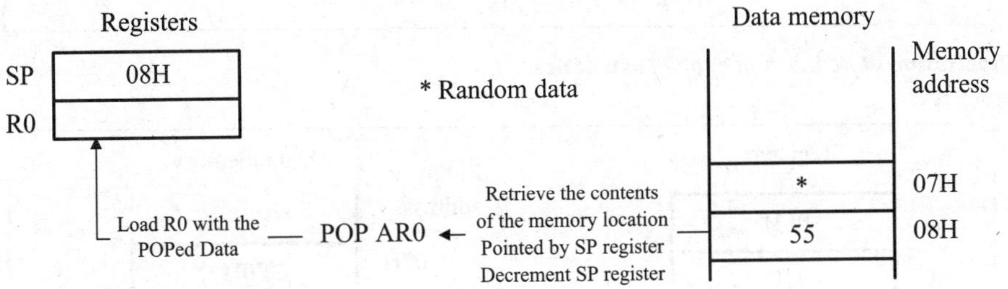

Fig. 6.7 **Illustration of *POP* instruction**

The upper 128 bytes of RAM are not implemented physically in the basic *8051* architecture and its ROMless counterpart 8031. With these devices, if the SP is set to a location in the upper 128 byte area, the PUSHed bytes will be lost and POPed bytes will be indeterminate.

6.2.1.3 Data Exchange Instructions The data exchange instructions exchange data between a memory location and the accumulator register. Data exchange instructions modify both memory location and accumulator register. *8051* supports two data exchange instructions, namely, *XCH A, <memloc>* and *XCHD A, @Ri*.

The *XCH A,<memloc>* instruction performs the exchange of the data at memory location '*memloc*' with the accumulator. By using MOV instructions the *XCH* instruction can be implemented as

```
MOV     R0, A
MOV     A, memloc        ; 'memloc' is a memory in the range
                         ; 00H to 7FH
MOV     memloc, R0
```

It requires three instructions and 4 machine cycles and a temporary variable R0 to achieve this. Whereas the *XCH A, <memloc>* accomplishes this task with a single instruction and one machine cycle.

The *XCHD A,@Ri* (where $i = 0$ or 1) instruction exchanges the low nibbles between the accumulator and the data memory pointed by the indirect memory register R0 or R1. Both *XCH* and *XCHD* are accumulator specific instructions. The operation of *XCH A, <memloc>* and *XCHD A,@Ri* instructions are illustrated in Figs 6.8 and 6.9.

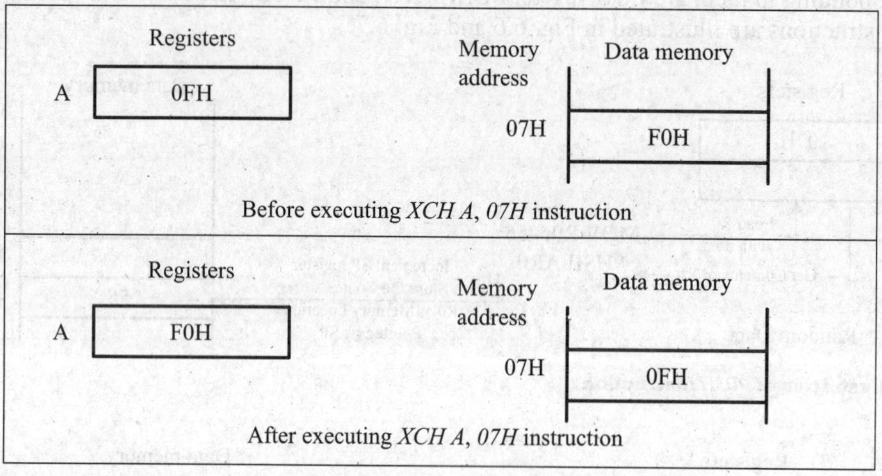

Fig. 6.8 **Illustration of *XCH A, <memloc>* Instruction**

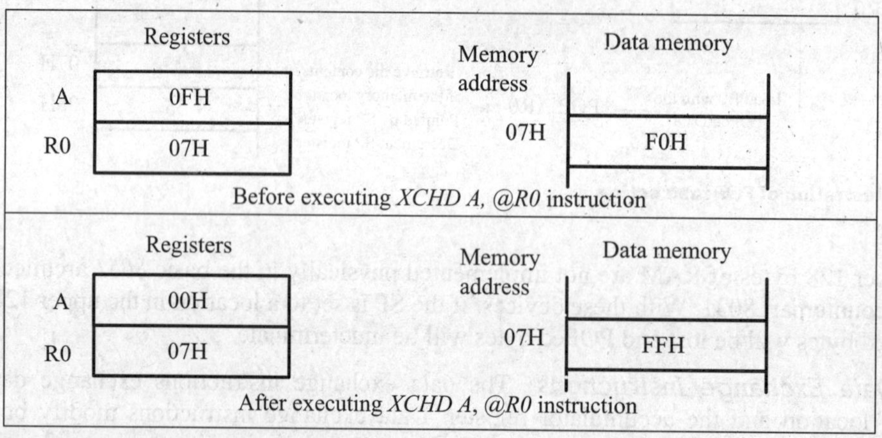

Fig. 6.9 **Illustration of *XCHD A,@Ri* Instruction**

6.2.1.4 External Data Memory Instructions External data memory instructions are used for transferring data between external memory and processor. The registers involved in external data memory instructions are the Data Pointer (DPTR) or the indirect addressing register R0/R1 and the accumulator. Only indirect addressing works on external data memory operations. If the external data memory is 16bit wide, a 16bit register DPTR is used for holding the 16 bit address to function as the external memory pointer. During 16bit external data memory operations Port 0 emits the content of DPL register (Lower order 8bit address) and Port 2 emits the content of DPH register (Higher order 8 bit address).

If the external data memory is only 8bit wide, either the DPTR or the indirect address register R0 or R1 can be used for holding the 8bit address to function as the external memory pointer. If DPTR is used as the memory pointer register, Port 0 emits the content of DPL register (Lower order 8bit address) and Port 2 emits the content of DPH register. If R0 or R1 is used as the memory pointer register, Port 0 emits the contents of R0 or R1 register (Lower order 8bit address) and Port 2 emits the contents of its SFR register (P2 SFR). The instruction mnemonic used for external data transfer operation is *MOVX* and depending on the memory pointer register the operand will be R0, R1 or DPTR. The accumulator is the implicit operand in *MOVX* instruction. The direction of external data memory operation (Read or write operation) is determined by the use of the accumulator register. If the accumulator register is used as the source register, the external data memory operation is a Write operation and the WR\ signal is also asserted. The external data memory operation is a Read operation if the accumulator is used as destination register. This also generates the RD\ signal.

External data memory related instructions are listed in the table given below.

Instruction Mnemonic	Comments	Machine Cycles	Exec. Time (µs)
MOVX A,@Ri	Read the content of external data memory (8bit address) pointed by R0 or R1 to accumulator	2	2* (f_{OSC}/12)
MOVX @Ri,A	Write accumulator content to external data memory (8bit address) pointed by R0 or R1	2	2* (f_{OSC}/12)
MOVX A,@DPTR	Read the content of external data memory (16 bit address) pointed by DPTR register to accumulator	2	2* (f_{OSC}/12)
MOVX @DPTR,A	Write accumulator content to external data memory (16bit address) pointed by DPTR register	2	2* (f_{OSC}/12)

The following sample code illustrates how to read and write from and to an 8bit external memory.

```
; Method-1
; Using Indirect register R0

        MOV R0, #055H      ; Let 55H be the external data memory
                           ; address
        MOVX A,@R0         ; Reads the content of 55H to accumulator
        MOV A, #00H        ; Clear Accumulator
        MOVX @R0, A        ; Writes 0 to external memory 55H
; Method-2
; Using Data Pointer (DPTR) Register
        MOV DPTR, #55H     ; Let 55H be the external data memory
                           ; address
        MOVX A,@DPTR       ; Reads the content of 55H to accumulator
        MOV A, #00H        ; Clear Accumulator
        MOVX @DPTR, A      ; Writes 0 to external memory 55H
```

The following sample code illustrates how to read and write data from and to a 16bit external memory.

```
MOV DPTR, #2055H  ; Let 2055H be the external data memory
                  ; address
MOVX A,@DPTR      ; Reads the content of 2055H to Accumulator
MOV A, #01H       ; Load Accumulator with 1
MOVX @DPTR, A     ; Writes 1 to external memory 2055H
```

Below is given the Instruction fetch and execute sequence for the *MOVX* instruction.

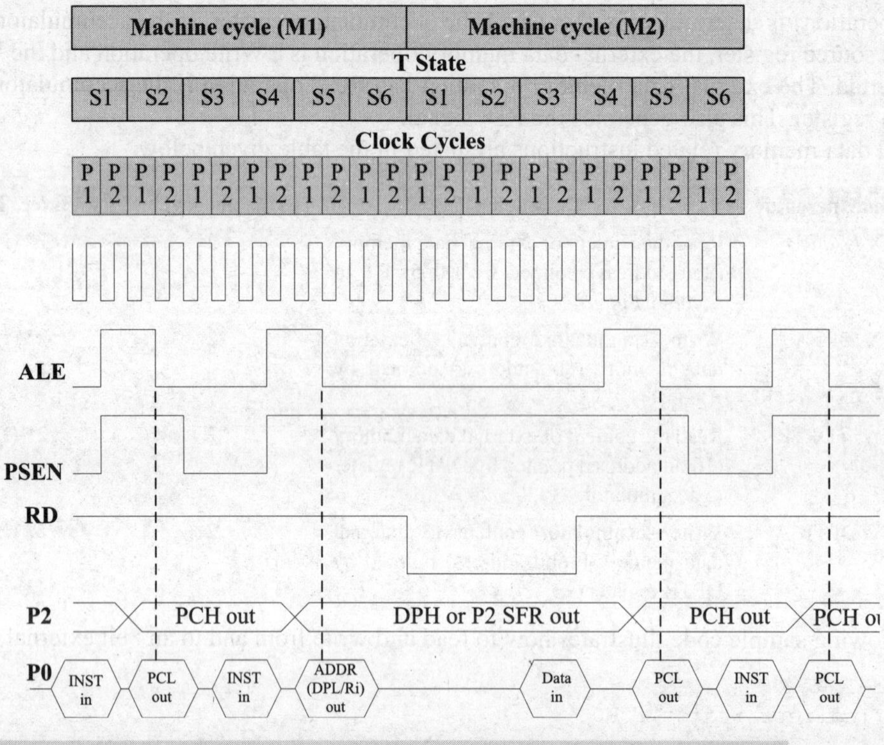

Fig. 6.10 **Timing diagram for MOVX instruction when the program memory is external**

MOVX is a two machine cycle instruction. The opcode fetching starts at state-1 (S1) of the first machine cycle and it is latched to the instruction register. A second program memory fetch occurs at State 4 (S4) of the same machine cycle. Program memory fetches are skipped during the second machine cycle. This is the only time program memory fetches are skipped. The instruction-fetch and execute sequence and timing remains the same regardless the physical location of program memory (it can be either internal or external). If the program memory is external, the Program Strobe Enable (PSEN) is asserted low on each program memory fetch and it is activated twice per machine cycle (Fig. 6.10). Since there is no program fetch associated with the second machine cycle of *MOVX* instruction, PSEN is not asserted during this (two PSEN signals are skipped). During the second machine cycle of *MOVX* instruction, the address and data bus are used for data memory access.

The lower order address bus is multiplexed with the data bus in *8051* and Port 0 outputs the lower order address bus during external memory operations and it is available at S5-S6 states of the first machine cycle. Since it is available only for a short duration of 1 to 1.5 states, it should be latched. The trigger for latch is provided by the signal Address Latch Enable (ALE). ALE is asserted twice in each machine cycle (during S1 Phase 2 (S1P2) and S4 Phase 2 (S4P2)). Since data is outputted to or read from the external memory at State 1 (S1) to State 3 (S3) of the second machine cycle, during a MOVX instruction, ALE is not emitted at S1P2 of the second machine cycle. Without a MOVX instruction ALE is emitted twice per each machine cycle and it can be used as a clock signal to any device.

The control signal PSEN is not asserted if the program memory is internal to the chip. However, ALE signal is asserted even if the program memory is internal.

The external data memory timing for external data memory write is similar to the Read operation except that the control signal used is WR\ instead of RD\ and the data for writing is available in the place of '*Data in*' in the above timing diagram . The timing for all signals remains the same.

6.2.1.5 Code Memory Read Instructions Code memory read instruction is used for reading from the code memory. There is only one instruction for code memory read operation and it is *MOVC*. Detailed description of *MOVC* instruction is given in an earlier section with subtitle "***Indexed Addressing***". Please refer back.

6.2.2 Arithmetic Instructions

Arithmetic instructions perform basic arithmetic operations including addition, subtraction, multiplication, division, increment and decrement. The various arithmetic instructions supported by *8051* are listed below.

Instruction Mnemonic	Action	Comments	Machine Cycles	Exec. Time (μs)
ADD A,<loc>	A = A+<loc>	Add the content of <loc> with accumulator and stores the result in accumulator. <loc> can be registers B, R0, R1, …R7 or any SFR or an immediate constant or an internal data memory or an internal data memory pointed indirectly by indirect addressing register R0 or R1 and @	1	$f_{osc}/12$
ADDC A,<loc>	A= A+<loc> + Carry bit (PSW.7)	Add the content of <loc> with accumulator and carry bit and stores the result in accumulator. <loc> can be registers B, R0,R1, …R7 or any SFR or an immediate constant or an internal data memory or an internal data memory pointed indirectly by indirect addressing register R0 or R1 and @	1	$f_{osc}/12$
SUBB A,<loc>	A=A-<loc>- Carry bit (PSW.7)	Subtract the content of <loc> from accumulator and borrow bit and stores the result in accumulator. <loc> can be registers B, R0,R1, …R7 or any SFR or an internal data memory or an immediate constant or an internal data memory pointed indirectly by indirect addressing register R0 or R1 and @	1	$f_{osc}/12$

INC A	A=A+1	Increments accumulator content by one. (Accumulator Specific Instruction)	1	$f_{OSC}/12$
INC <loc>	<loc > = <loc> + 1	Increments the content of <loc> by 1. <loc> can be registers B, R0,R1, ...R7, or any SFR or an internal data memory or an internal data memory pointed indirectly by indirect addressing register R0 or R1 and @	1	$f_{OSC}/12$
INC DPTR	DPTR = DPTR + 1	Increments the content of 16bit register DPTR by one. (DPTR Specific Instruction)	2	$2*(f_{OSC}/12)$
DEC A	A = A – 1	Decrements accumulator content by one. (Accumulator Specific Instruction)	1	$f_{OSC}/12$
DEC <loc>	<loc > = <loc> – 1	Decrements the content of <loc> by 1. <loc> can be registers B, R0, R1, ...R7 or any SFR or an internal data memory or an internal data memory pointed indirectly by indirect addressing register R0 or R1 and @	1	$f_{OSC}/12$
MUL AB	A=AxB	Multiplies accumulator with B register and stores the result in accumulator & B (Lower order byte of result in accumulator and higher order byte in B register)	4	$4*(f_{OSC}/12)$
DIV AB	A = integer part of [A/B] B=Remainder of [A/B]	Divides accumulator with B register and stores the result in accumulator and remainder in B register	4	$4*(f_{OSC}/12)$
DA A		Decimal adjust Accumulator. Used in BCD arithmetic	1	$f_{OSC}/12$

6.2.2.1 Addition and Subtraction The *8051* supports the addition of 8bit binary numbers and stores the sum in the accumulator register. The instructions *ADD A,<loc>* and *ADDC A,<loc>* are used for performing addition operations. Both of these instructions are accumulator specific, meaning the accumulator is an implicit operand in these instructions. The *ADD A,<loc>* is used for performing a normal addition and the carry flag gets modified accordingly on executing this instruction. If the addition results in an output greater than FFH, the carry flag is set and the accumulator content will be the final result–FFH + carry. The carry flag is reset when the result of an addition is less than or equal to FFH. The *ADDC A,<loc>* instruction operates in the same way as that of *ADD A,<loc>* instruction except that it adds the *carry flag* with *A* and *<loc>*. The changes to the carry flag on executing this instruction remains the same as that of executing the *ADD A, <loc>* instruction. Executing these instructions modify the content of accumulator only and *<loc>* remains unchanged.

The instruction *SUBB A, <loc>* performs the subtraction operation. The carry flag acts as the borrow indicator in the subtraction operation. The *SUBB A, <loc>* instruction subtracts the borrow flag and the contents pointed by *<loc>* from accumulator and modifies the accumulator with the result. The content of *<loc>* remains unchanged. For performing a normal subtraction operation, first clear the carry flag and then call the *SUBB A, <loc>* instruction. The carry (borrow) flag gets modified accordingly on executing this instruction. If the subtraction results in a –ve number ('A' less than (*<loc>* + Carry)), the borrow (carry) flag is set and the accumulator content will be the 2's complement* representation of the result (e.g. Accumulator contains 0FEH and borrow (carry) flag is 0, executing the instruction SUBB A, #0FFH results in –1 which is represented in the accumulator by the 2's complement form of 1. Hence the content of accumulator becomes FFH (2's complement form of 1) and the borrow (carry) flag is also set). The carry flag is reset when the result of a subtraction is +ve ('A' is greater than (*<loc>* + Carry)). The *SUBB A, <loc>* instruction is accumulator specific, meaning accumulator is an implicit operand for this instruction.

Example 1

The accumulator register contains 80H and B register contains 8FH. Add accumulator content with B register. Explain the output of the summation and the status of the carry flag after the addition operation.

Adding 80H with 8FH results in 10FH. Since 10FH requires more than 8 bits to represent, the accumulator holds only the least significant 8 bits of the result (Here 0FH). The carry bit CY present in the Program Status Word (PSW) register is set to indicate that the output of the addition operation resulted in a number greater than FFH. Figure 6.11 illustrates the addition operation and the involvement of Carry bit (CY).

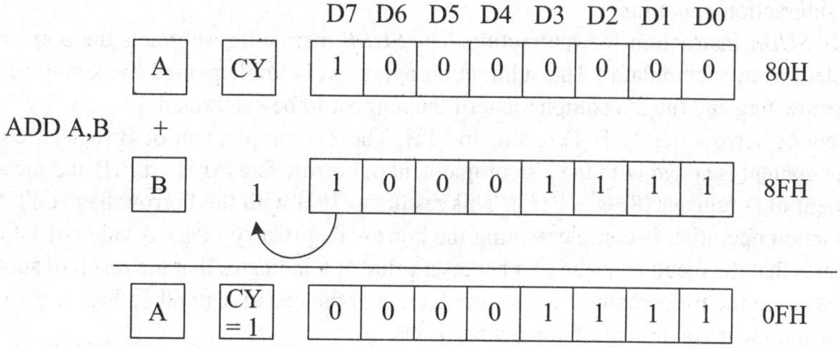

Fig. 6.11 **Illustration of ADD instruction operation**

Example 2

Register R0 contains 0BH. Add the contents of register R0 with the sum obtained in the previous example using *ADDC* instruction. Explain the output of the summation and the status of the carry flag after the addition operation.

The instruction *ADDC A, R0* adds accumulator content with contents of register R0 and the carry flag (*CY*). Before executing this instruction, the accumulator contains the sum of previous addition operation, which is 0FH and the carry flag (*CY*) is in the set state. Register R0 contains 0BH. Executing the instruction *ADDC A, R0* adds 0FH with 0BH and 1. The resulting output is 1BH which is less than FFH. This resets the carry flag. Accumulator register holds the sum. It should be noted that each addition operation sets or resets the carry flag based on the result of addition, regardless of the previous condition of the carry flag. Figure 6.12 explains the *ADDC* operation.

* 2's complement of a number = 1's complement of the number +1

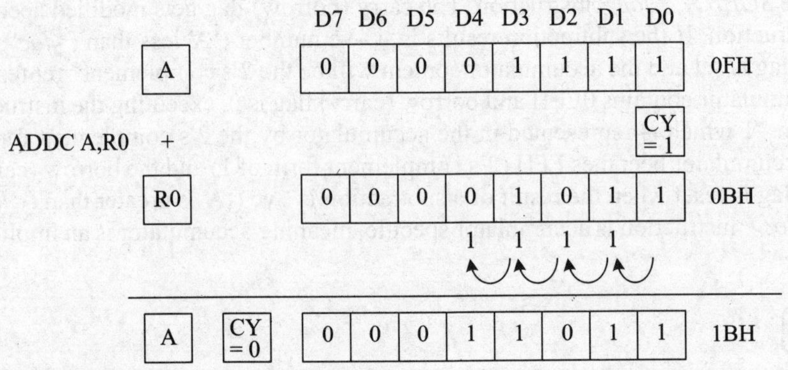

Fig. 6.12 **Illustration of ADDC instruction operation**

Example 3

The accumulator register contains 8FH and B register contains 0FH. The borrow Flag (*CY*) is in the set state. Subtract the contents of accumulator with borrow and B register. Explain what is the output of the subtraction and the status of the borrow flag after the subtraction operation.

8051 supports only *SUBB* instruction for subtraction. The *SUBB* instruction subtracts the borrow flag (*CY*) and the number to be subtracted, from accumulator. The subtraction operation is implemented by adding accumulator with the 2's complement of borrow flag and the 2's complement of the number to be subtracted.

The 2's complement of borrow flag (*CY*=1) results in FFH. The 2's complement of B register content (0FH) yields F1H. The accumulator content is added with the 2's complement of borrow flag (8FH + FFH) and the result (8E) is added with the 2's complement of B register (8EH + F1H). This results in 7FH with the borrow flag (*CY*) in the set state. The final step in the subtraction operation is complementing the borrow flag (Carry Flag). A value of 1 for borrow flag after complementing indicates that the result is negative whereas a value of 0 indicates that the result of subtraction is positive. If the result is negative, accumulator contains the 2's complement of the negative number. Figure 6.13 illustrates subtract with borrow operation and the involvement of borrow bit (*CY*).

6.2.2.2 Multiplication and Division The instruction *MUL AB* multiplies two 8bit unsigned numbers and stores the 16bit result in the register pair *A, B*. The accumulator stores the lower order 8 bits of the result and B register stores the higher order 8 bits of the result. The overflow flag (OV) is set when the product is greater than 0FFH and cleared otherwise. The carry flag becomes cleared state irrespective of the product.

The *DIV AB* instruction divides the content of accumulator register with the content of B register and stores the integer part of the quotient (A/B) in accumulator and the modulus (A%B) in B register (e.g. If A contains 03H and B contains 02H, executing the instruction *DIV AB* loads accumulator with 01H (3/2) and B register with 01H (3%2). *8051* does not have a divide by zero interrupt mechanism to indicate a divide by zero error. However *8051* indicates the divide by zero condition by setting the overflow flag (*OV*) in the Program Status Word (*PSW*) register. The values returned in A and B are undefined for a divide-by-zero operation.

The overflow flag (OV) and carry flag (CY) are cleared for normal division operation.

MUL and *DIV* instructions are accumulator and register *B* specific instructions. They work only with these two registers. If register *B* is not used for multiplication and division, it can be used for temporary storage.

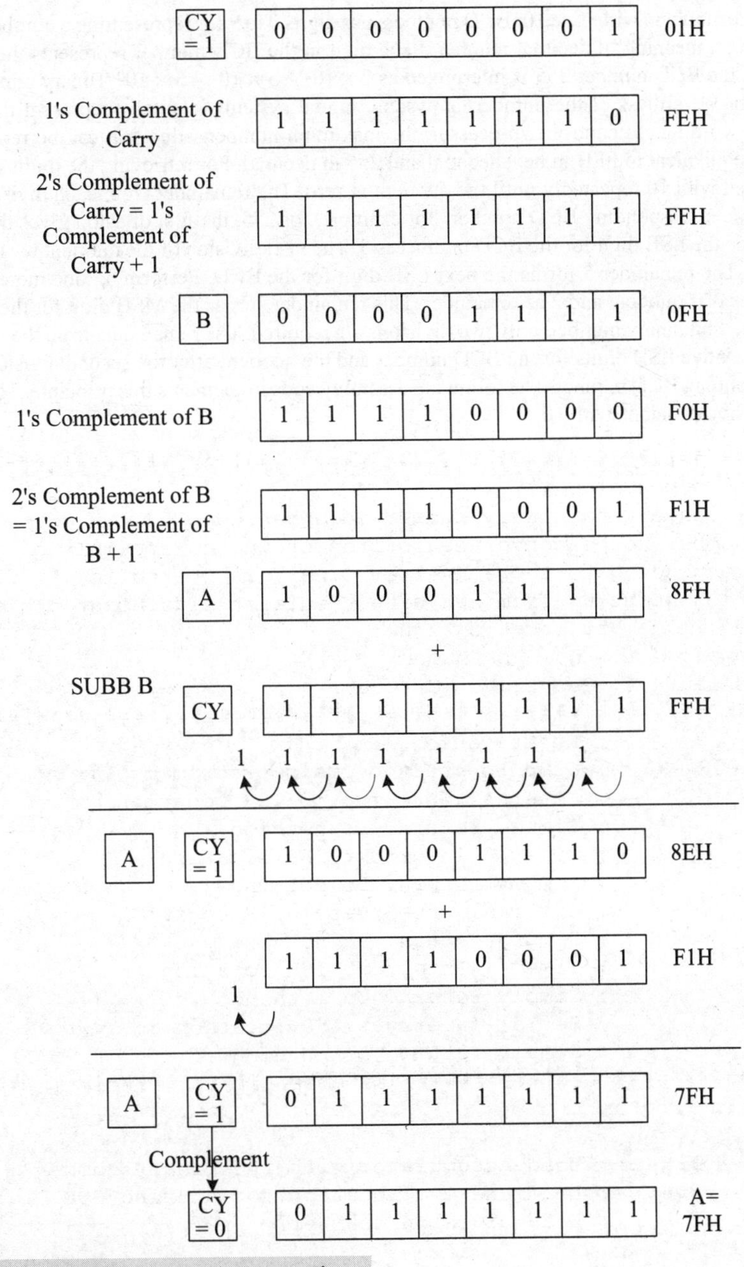

Fig. 6.13 **Illustration of SUBB instruction operation**

Example 1

Convert the binary number FFH present in the accumulator to unpacked BCD and store the resultant 3 digit BCD number in consecutive memory locations starting from 20H

BCD numbers are numbers with base 10. BCD numbers use digits 0 to 9 for representing a number. They are normally used for representing a meaningful decimal number. Each digit in the BCD number represents the consecutive powers of 10. For example, the BCD number 255 is interpreted as $2 \times 10^2 + 5 \times 10^1 + 5 \times 10^0$. Binary numbers follow the base 2 numbering system. Regardless of the numbering system, digital systems internally represent the numbers in binary format. For an 8bit word length controller/processor, the maximum number value that can be represented in binary is 11111111, which is equivalent to FFH in hexadecimal and 255 in decimal. For retrieving the digits of a decimal number, the number is divided with 10 repeatedly until the quotient is zero. The remainder from each division gives the successive LSB digits of the corresponding BCD number. For example, for 255, the first division gives the quotient as 25 and remainder as 5, hence the LSB digit for the BCD number is 5. The next division of the quotient by 10 gives 2 as quotient and 5 as remainder. The remainder 5 forms the next LSB digit for the BCD. Performing one more division with 10 on the quotient (2) gives 0 as quotient and 2 as remainder. This remainder acts as the MSB digit for the corresponding BCD number. In fact for an 8bit binary number, only two divisions are required. The remainders from the two consecutive divisions form the consecutive LSB digits for the BCD number and the quotient after the second division becomes the MSB digit for the corresponding BCD number. The following assembly code implements this principle. The *DIVAB* instruction performs the successive divisions with 10.

```
;######################################################################
;binary_unpacked_bcd.src
;Firmware for converting binary number to unpacked BCD
;The binary number to be converted is present in the accumulator
;The BCD corresponding to the converted binary is stored in-
;memory location starting from 20H with the least significant digit
;of BCD stored in memory location 20H
;Written & Compiled for A51 Assembler
;Written by Shibu K V. Copyright (C) 2008
;######################################################################
ORG 0000H               ; Reset vector
      JMP 0100H         ; Jump to start of main program
ORG 0003H               ; External Interrupt 0 ISR location
      RETI              ; Simply return. Do nothing
ORG 000BH               ; Timer 0 Interrupt ISR location
      RETI              ; Simply return. Do nothing
ORG 0013H               ; External Interrupt 1 ISR location
      RETI              ; Simply return. Do nothing
ORG 001BH               ; Timer 1 Interrupt ISR location
      RETI              ; Simply return. Do nothing
ORG 0023H               ; Serial Interrupt ISR location
      RETI              ; Simply return. Do nothing
;######################################################################
; Start of main Program
ORG 0100H
      MOV A, #0FFH      ; Load Accumulator with the binary number
      MOV R0, #20H      ; Load the mem location for storing BCD Digit
      MOV R1, #2        ; Load division counter
CONTINUE:MOV B, #10
      DIV AB
      MOV @R0,B         ; B holds the remainder, which is the BCD
      INC R0            ; Increment mem loc to store next BCD Digit
      DJNZ R1,CONTINUE
      MOV @R0,A         ; The last BCD digit is the quotient
      JMP $             ; Loop forever
END   ;END of Assembly Program
```

Example 2

Convert the packed BCD number '98' stored in the accumulator to corresponding binary number and store the result in accumulator.

The packed BCD number is stored using a single byte. The higher 4 bits of the byte store the most significant digit of the packed BCD number and the lower 4 bits store the least significant digit of the BCD number. Hence the accumulator representation of packed BCD is 10001000b (98H). The binary value corresponding to this packed BCD is the binary representation of $9 \times 10^1 + 8 \times 10^0 = 9 \times 10 + 8 \times 1 = 90 + 8$.

```
;####################################################################
;packedbcd_to_binary.src
;Firmware for converting packed BCD to binary
;The BCD number to be converted is present in accumulator
;The resultant binary number is held in Accumulator register
;Written & assembled for A51 Assembler
;Written by Shibu K V. Copyright (C) 2008
;####################################################################
ORG 0000H              ; Reset vector
      JMP 0100H        ; Jump to start of main program
ORG 0003H              ; External Interrupt 0 ISR location
      RETI             ; Simply return. Do nothing
ORG 000BH              ; Timer 0 Interrupt ISR location
      RETI             ; Simply return. Do nothing
ORG 0013H              ; External Interrupt 1 ISR location
      RETI             ; Simply return. Do nothing
ORG 001BH              ; Timer 1 Interrupt ISR location
      RETI             ; Simply return. Do nothing
ORG 0023H              ; Serial Interrupt ISR location
      RETI             ; Simply return. Do nothing
;####################################################################
; Start of main Program
ORG 0100H
      MOV A, #98H      ; Packed BCD representing 98
      MOV R0, A        ; Backup BCD number
      SWAP A           ; Extract the MSB of packed BCD
      ANL A, #0FH      ; Extract the MSB of packed BCD
      MOV B, #10       ;
      MUL AB           ; Get the positional weight for MSB digit
      MOV R1, A        ; Store the temporary result
      MOV A, R0        ; Retrieve the original BCD number
      ANL A, #0FH      ; Extract the LSB of packed BCD
      ADD A,R1         ; Final result
      JMP $            ; Loop forever
END   ;END of Assembly Program
```

6.2.2.3 Increment and Decrement The increment instruction (*INC*) increments the content of the location pointed by the operand. The *INC A* instruction is an accumulator specific instruction which increments the content of accumulator. Executing the instruction *INC A* will not modify the carry flag. The *INC* <*loc*> instruction increments the content pointed by <*loc*>. If the content pointed by the operand of *INC* instruction is FFH, on executing the *INC* instruction, the content simply rolls over to 00H. None of the status bits are modified to indicate this rollover. *INC DPTR* instruction is DPTR register specific instruction and it increments the content of 16bit DPTR register by one. The following piece of assembly code illustrates the usage of *INC* instruction.

```
MOV 00H,#80H     ; Load Data memory location 00H (R0) with 80H
MOV A,#0FFH      ; Load Accumulator with FFH
MOV DPTR,#00FFH ; Load DPTR with 00FFH
INC 00H          ; Increment the contents of Data memory-
                 ; location 00H. It becomes 81H
INC A            ; Increment the content of Accumulator. It-
                 ; becomes 00H
INC DPTR         ; Increment the content of DPTR Register. It-
                 ; becomes 0100H
```

The decrement instruction (*DEC*) decrements the content of the location pointed by the operand. The *DEC A* instruction is an accumulator specific instruction which decrements the content of accumulator. Executing the instruction *DEC A* will not modify the carry flag. The *DEC <loc>* instruction decrements the content pointed by *<loc>*. If the content pointed by the operand of *DEC* instruction is 00H, executing the *DEC* instruction simply rolls over it to FFH. None of the status bits are modified to indicate this. The following code snippet illustrates the usage of *DEC* instruction.

```
MOV 00H,#80H     ; Load Data memory location 00H (R0) with 80H
MOV A,#0FFH      ; Load Accumulator with FFH
DEC 00H          ; Decrement the contents of Data memory-
                 ; location 00H. It becomes 7FH
DEC A            ; Decrement the content of Accumulator. It-
                 ; becomes FEH
```

There is no specific instruction to decrement the DPTR register content by one in *8051* instruction set. However decrementing the DPTR can be achieved by using other instructions in the optimal way.

6.2.2.4 Decimal Adjust The *DA A* instruction adjusts the accumulator content to give a meaningful BCD result in BCD arithmetic. Binary Coded Decimal (BCD) is a number representation in numeric systems. In the BCD number system, numerals from 0 to 9 are used for representing a number. Based on the number of BCD digits represented in a single byte, the BCD numbers are known as packed and unpacked BCDs. In the unpacked BCD representation, a single BCD digit (0 to 9) is represented by a single byte whereas in the packed BCD representation two BCD digits (00 to 99) are represented using a single byte. *ADD* and *ADDC* instructions used for BCD addition should follow a *DA A* instruction to bring the Accumulator content to a meaningful BCD result. It should be noted that the *DA A* instruction will not convert a binary number to a BCD. The *DA A* instruction always follow the *ADD* instruction.

Example 1

Write an assembly program to add two packed BCD numbers '28' and '12' stored in consecutive memory locations starting from data memory address 50H. The result of the addition should be adjusted for BCD.

The Assembly code snippet shown below illustrates the implementation.

```
;######################################################################
;BCD_addition.src
;Firmware for adding two packed BCD numbers
;The BCD numbers to be added are present in the memlocation 50H & 51H
;The resultant BCD number is held in Accumulator register
;After addition the result is adjusted for BCD
;Written & assembled for A51 Assembler
;Written by Shibu K V. Copyright (C) 2008
;######################################################################
ORG 0000H               ; Reset vector
      JMP 0100H         ; Jump start of main program
ORG 0003H               ; External Interrupt 0 ISR location
      RETI              ; Simply return. Do nothing
ORG 000BH               ; Timer 0 Interrupt ISR location
      RETI              ; Simply return. Do nothing
ORG 0013H               ; External Interrupt 1 ISR location
      RETI              ; Simply return. Do nothing
ORG 001BH               ; Timer 1 Interrupt ISR location
      RETI              ; Simply return. Do nothing
ORG 0023H               ; Serial Interrupt ISR location
      RETI              ; Simply return. Do nothing
;######################################################################
; Start of main Program
ORG 0100H
      MOV 050H, #28H    ; Packed BCD representing 28
      MOV 051H, #12H    ; Packed BCD representing 12
      MOV A, 050H       ; Move the first BCD number to Accumulator
      ADD A, 051H       ; Add with second BCD number
      DA A              ; Decimal adjust the result
      JMP $             ; Loop forever
END     ;END of Assembly Program
```

If the accumulator is not adjusted for decimal, after the addition, the accumulator content will be 3AH. Adjusting the accumulator for decimal, after the addition operation, produces a meaningful result, 40H (Which is the sum of the BCDs 28 and 12).

6.2.3 Logical Instructions

Logical instructions perform logical operations such as 'ORing', 'ANDing', 'XORing', complementing, clearing, bit rotation and swapping nibbles of a byte, etc. The list of logical instructions supported by 8051 is tabulated below.

<table>
<tr><th>Instruction Mnemonic</th><th>Action</th><th>Comments</th><th>Machine Cycle</th><th>Exec. Time (µs)</th></tr>
<tr><td>ORL A,<loc></td><td>A = A|<loc></td><td>Perform bitwise logical OR the content of Accumulator with the content of <loc> and stores the result in Accumulator. <loc> can be registers B, R0, R1, …R7, or any SFR, an immediate constant, an internal data memory or an internal data memory pointed indirectly by indirect addressing register R0 or R1 and @</td><td>1</td><td>$f_{OSC}/12$</td></tr>
<tr><td>ORL <loc>,A</td><td><loc> = A|<loc></td><td>Bitwise logical OR the content of the accumulator with the content of <loc> and stores the result in memory location <loc>. <loc> can be any SFR or an internal data memory</td><td>1</td><td>$f_{OSC}/12$</td></tr>
<tr><td>ORL <loc>,#const</td><td><loc> = <loc>|const</td><td>Bitwise logical OR the content of <loc> with an immediate constant and stores the result in memory location <loc>. <loc> can be any SFR or an internal data memory</td><td>2</td><td>$2*(f_{OSC}/12)$</td></tr>
<tr><td>ANL A,<loc></td><td>A=A&<loc></td><td>Bitwise logical AND the content of the accumulator with the content of <loc> and stores the result in Accumulator. <loc> can be B, R0, R1, …R7, or any SFR, an internal data memory or an immediate constant or an internal data memory pointed indirectly by indirect addressing register R0 or R1 and @</td><td>1</td><td>$f_{OSC}/12$</td></tr>
<tr><td>ANL <loc>,A</td><td><loc> = A&<loc></td><td>Bitwise logical AND the content of the accumulator with the content of <loc> and stores the result in memory location <loc>. <loc> can be any SFR or an internal data memory</td><td>1</td><td>$f_{OSC}/12$</td></tr>
<tr><td>ANL <loc>,#const</td><td><loc> = <loc>&const</td><td>Bitwise logical AND the content of <loc> with an immediate constant and stores the result in memory location <loc>. <loc> can be any SFR or an internal data memory</td><td>2</td><td>$2*(f_{OSC}/12)$</td></tr>
<tr><td>XRL A,<loc></td><td>A = A^<loc></td><td>Bitwise logical XOR the content of the accumulator with the content of <loc> and stores the result in Accumulator. <loc> can be B, R0, R1, …R7, or any SFR, an internal data memory or an immediate constant or an internal data memory pointed indirectly by indirect addressing register R0 or R1 and @</td><td>1</td><td>$f_{OSC}/12$</td></tr>
</table>

XRL <loc>,A	<loc> = A^<loc>	Logical XOR the content of the accumulator with the content of <loc> and stores the result in memory location <loc>. <loc> can be any SFR or an internal data memory	1	$f_{osc}/12$
XRL <loc>,#const	<loc> = <loc> ^ const	Logical XOR the content of <loc> with an immediate constant and stores the result in memory location <loc>. <loc> can be any SFR or an internal data memory	2	$2*(f_{osc}/12)$
CLR A	A = 00H	Clear the content of accumulator (Loads 0 to Accumulator)	1	$f_{osc}/12$
CPL A	A = ~A	Complement the content of the accumulator. 1s are replaced by 0s and 0s by 1s.	1	$f_{osc}/12$
RL A	A = A<1	Rotate the Accumulator content 1 bit to the left. The MSB of the accumulator is shifted out to the LSB position of the accumulator	1	$f_{osc}/12$
RLC A	A = A<1	Rotate the accumulator content 1 bit to the left through carry bit. The MSB of the accumulator is shifted out to carry bit and content of carry bit enters at the LSB position of the Accumulator	1	$f_{osc}/12$
RR A	A = A>1	Rotate the accumulator content 1 bit to the right. The LSB of the Accumulator is shifted out to the MSB position of the Accumulator	1	$f_{osc}/12$
RRC A	A = A>1	Rotate the accumulator content 1 bit to the right through carry bit. The LSB of the accumulator is shifted out to carry bit and content of carry bit enters at the MSB position of the accumulator	1	$f_{osc}/12$
SWAP A	Before swap A = Nib2 Nib1 After swap A = Nib1 Nib2	Exchanges between the low nibble and high nibble of the accumulator.	1	$f_{osc}/12$

The *ANL* instruction performs bitwise *AND*ing operation. The operation of *ANL* instruction is illustrated below. Suppose the Accumulator contains 80H and if it is *AND*ed with an immediate constant 80H, the following actions shown in Fig. 6.14 take place.

Accumulator	1	0	0	0	0	0	0	0	80H
AND operation	&	&	&	&	&	&	&	&	
Constant	1	0	0	0	0	0	0	0	80H
Result in accumulator	1	0	0	0	0	0	0	0	80H

Fig. 6.14 Illustration of ANL instruction operation

Similarly the *ORL* instruction performs the bitwise *OR*ing operation. For example, let us assume that the accumulator contains 01H and it is *OR*ed with an immediate data 80H. The result will be 81H and it is stored in the accumulator. It is explained in Fig. 6.15.

Accumulator	0	0	0	0	0	0	0	1	01H
'OR' operation	|	|	|	|	|	|	|	|	
Constant	1	0	0	0	0	0	0	0	80H
Result in accumulator	1	0	0	0	0	0	0	1	81H

Fig. 6.15 **Illustration of ORL instruction operation**

The *XRL* instruction performs the bitwise *XOR*ing operation. The principle of *XOR* is that if both the *XOR*ing bits are same (both are either 0 or 1) the output bit is 0 and if the *XOR*ing bits are complement to each other the output bit is 1. For example, if the accumulator content is 81H and an *XOR* operation of the accumulator with an immediate constant 80H yields 01H as output. The *XRL* instruction operation is explained in Fig. 6.16.

Accumulator	1	0	0	0	0	0	0	1	81H
'XOR' operation	^	^	^	^	^	^	^	^	
Constant	1	0	0	0	0	0	0	0	80H
Result in accumulator	0	0	0	0	0	0	0	1	01H

Fig. 6.16 **Illustration of XRL instruction operation**

The *CLR A* and *CPL A* instructions are accumulator specific instructions. The *CLR A* instruction clears the content of accumulator (loads accumulator with 00H), whereas the *CPL A* instruction complements the accumulator content (negates the accumulator content). Both *CLR A* and *CPL A* instructions are single machine cycle instructions.

Assuming accumulator contains F0H, Fig. 6.17 illustrates the operation of *CLR A* and *CPL A* instructions.

Rotate instructions rotates the bits of the Accumulator. All Rotate instructions are Accumulator specific instructions and Accumulator is the implicit register for rotate operations. Accumulator bits can be either rotated to left or right.

The *RL A* instruction rotates the accumulator bits to the left by one position and the MSB of the accumulator comes in place of the LSB. For example, the accumulator contains 80H, after executing an *RL A* instruction, the contents of the accumulator will become 01H. It is illustrated in Fig. 6.18.

The *RLC A* instruction is similar in operation to *RL A* instruction except that in *RLC A* instruction the MSB of the Accumulator is shifted to the Carry bit (CY) and the content of carry flag at the moment

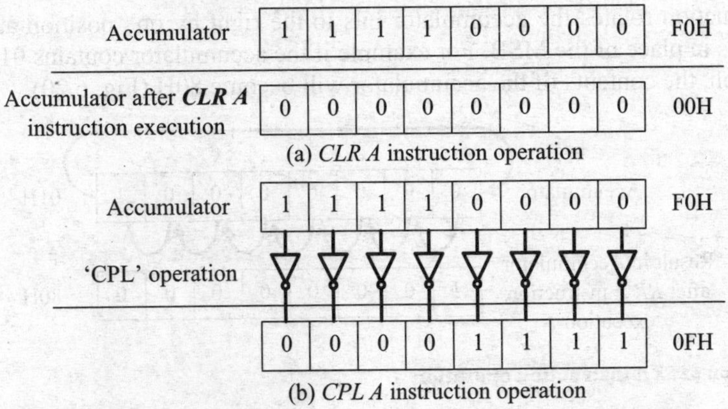

Fig. 6.17 **Illustration of (a) *CLR A* instruction operation (b) *CPL A* instruction operation**

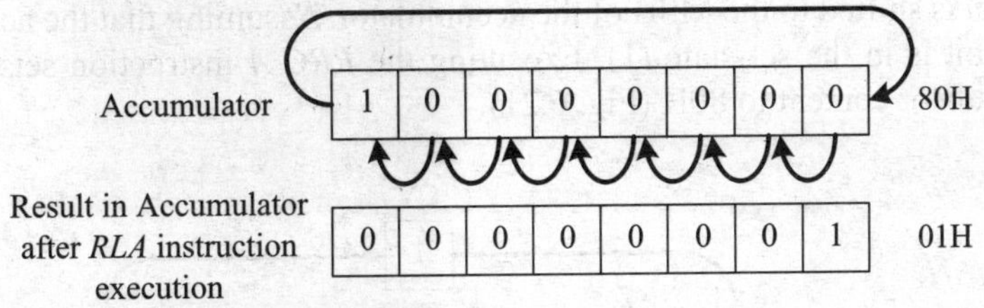

Fig. 6.18 **Illustration of *RL A* instruction operation**

of execution of the *RLC A* instruction is shifted to the LSB of Accumulator. The operation of *RLC A* instruction is illustrated in Fig. 6.19. Assuming the Accumulator contains 80H and the carry bit is in the cleared state (0). Executing the *RLC A* instruction sets the carry flag and modifies the Accumulator content to 00H.

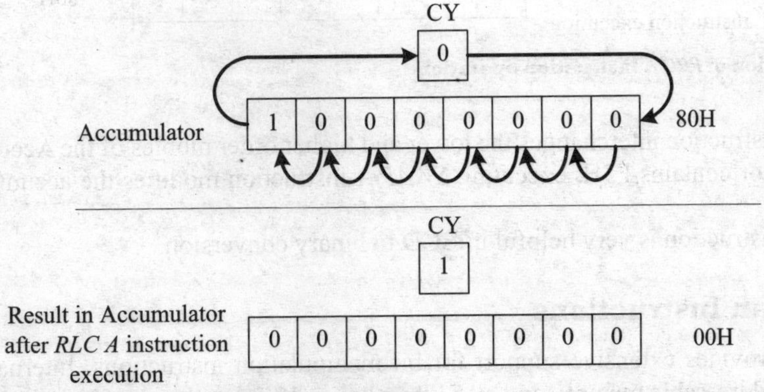

Fig. 6.19 **Illustration of *RLC A* instruction operation**

One more execution of the ***RLC A*** instruction will change the accumulator content to 01H and resets the carry flag.

The *RR A* instruction rotates the accumulator bits to the right by one position and the LSB of the accumulator comes in place of the MSB. For example if the accumulator contains 01H, after executing the *RR A* instruction, the contents of the accumulator will become 80H (Fig. 6.20).

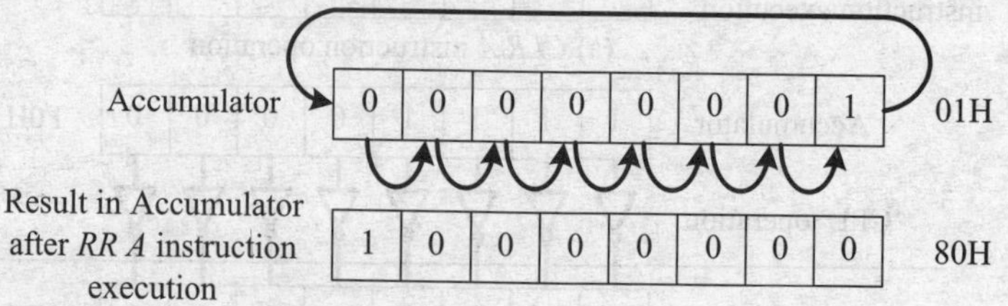

Fig. 6.20 **Illustration of *RR A* instruction operation**

The *RRC A* instruction is similar to *RLC A* instruction except that in *RRC A* instruction the LSB of the accumulator is shifted to the carry bit (CY) and the content of carry flag at the moment of execution of *RRC A* instruction is shifted to the MSB of the accumulator. Assuming that the accumulator contains 01H and the carry bit is in the set state (1). Executing the *RRC A* instruction sets the carry flag and modifies the accumulator content to 80H (Fig. 6.21).

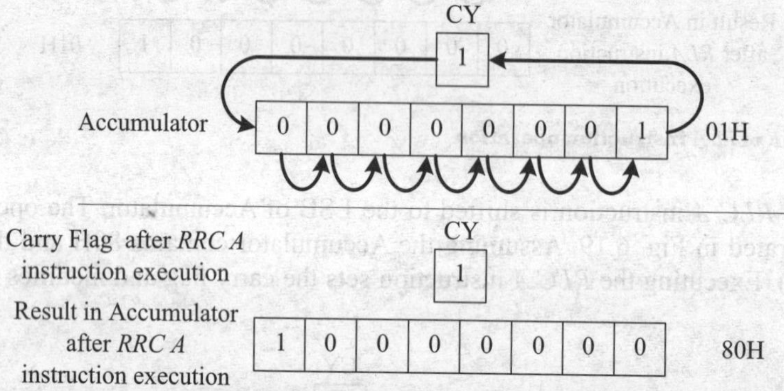

Fig. 6.21 **Illustration of *RRC A* instruction operation**

The *SWAP A* instruction interchanges the lower and higher order nibbles of the Accumulator. Assuming the accumulator contains F5H, executing *SWAP A* instruction modifies the accumulator content to 5FH.

The *SWAP A* instruction is very helpful in BCD to binary conversion.

6.2.4 Boolean Instructions

The *8051* CPU provides extensive support for bit manipulation instructions. Internal RAM of *8051* contains 128 bit-addressable memory and all SFRs whose address ends with 0H and 8H are bit addressable. Boolean instructions are used for performing various operations like bit transfer, bit manipulation, logical operations on bits, program control transfer based on bit state, etc.

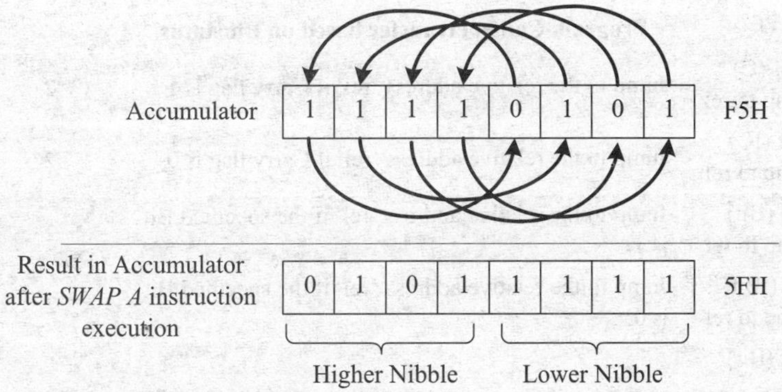

Fig. 6.22 **Illustration of *SWAP A* instruction operation**

The carry bit '*C*', present in the Special Function Register *PSW*, takes the role of accumulator in all bit related operations. The various Boolean instructions supported by the *8051* CPU are listed below. It is to be noted that all bit access is through direct addressing only.

Instruction Mnemonic	Action	Comments	Machine Cycles	Exec. Time (μs)
		Bit manipulation & transfer Instructions		
MOV C, Bit	C = Bit	Moves Bit to carry flag	1	$f_{OSC}/12$
MOV Bit, C	Bit = C	Moves carry flag to Bit	2	$2*(f_{OSC}/12)$
CLR C	C = 0	Clears carry flag	1	$f_{OSC}/12$
CLR Bit	Bit = 0	Clears specified Bit	1	$f_{OSC}/12$
SETB C	C = 1	Sets carry flag	1	$f_{OSC}/12$
SETB Bit	Bit = 1	Sets specified Bit	1	$f_{OSC}/12$
		Logical Operations on Bits		
ANL C, Bit	C = C & Bit	Logical AND Carry flag with Bit and store the result in Carry flag	2	$2*(f_{OSC}/12)$
ANL C, /Bit	C = C & (.NOT. Bit†)	Logical AND the complemented value of Bit with Carry flag and store the result in Carry flag	2	$2*(f_{OSC}/12)$
ORL C, Bit	C = C | Bit	Logical OR Carry flag with Bit and store the result in Carry flag	2	$2*(f_{OSC}/12)$
ORL C, /Bit	C= C | (.NOT. Bit††)	Logical OR the complemented value of Bit with Carry flag. Result in Carry flag	2	$2*(f_{OSC}/12)$
CPL C	C=.NOT.C	Complements the Carry flag	1	$f_{OSC}/12$
CPL Bit	C=.NOT. Bit	Complements Bit	1	$f_{OSC}/12$

† The actual state of the bit remains unchanged. If bit 0H is in the cleared state, executing the instruction ANL C, /0H will not change the state of bit 0H to set.

†† The actual state of the Bit remains unchanged. If bit 0H is in the cleared state, executing the instruction ORL C, /0H will not change the state of bit 0H to set.

Program Control transfer based on Bit status				
JC rel	If (C) Jump to rel	Jump to the relative address 'rel' if Carry flag is 1	2	2*(f_{osc}/12)
JNC rel	If (!C) Jump to rel	Jump to the relative address 'rel' if Carry flag is 0	2	2*(f_{osc}/12)
JB Bit, rel	If (Bit) Jump to rel	Jump to the relative address 'rel' if the specified Bit is 1	2	2*(f_{osc}/12)
JNB Bit, rel	If (!Bit) Jump to rel	Jump to the relative address 'rel' if the specified Bit is 0	2	2*(f_{osc}/12)
JBC Bit, rel	If (Bit) { Clear Bit; Jump to rel; }	If the specified Bit is 1, clear the bit and jump to the relative address 'rel'	2	2*(f_{osc}/12)

The Boolean instructions are very useful in bit manipulation operation for bit-addressable SFRs. Manipulation of port status registers (P0 to P3) is a typical example. The usage of Boolean instructions is illustrated below.

```
MOV C, P2.0      ; Load carry flag with Port pin 2.0's status.
MOV P2.0, C      ; Load Port 2.0 latch with content of carry flag
SETB C           ; Set the carry flag
CLR C            ; Clear carry flag
ANL C, P2.0      ; Logical AND P2.0 Latch bit with Carry flag and
                 ; load Carry  bit with the result
```

The *JC rel* and *JNC rel* instructions has got special significance in comparison operation. The *8051* supports only one compare instruction, *CJNE*, which checks only for the equality of the register/data pair compared. There is no built in instruction for checking above or below condition (*Compare and jump if above* and *Compare and jump if below*). These conditions can be checked by using the *JC* and *JNC* instructions in combination with the *CJNE* instruction. The *CJNE* instruction followed by the *JNC* instruction implements the *Compare and jump if above* condition and the *CJNE* instruction followed by the *JC* instruction implements the *Compare and jump if below* condition. The following code snippet illustrates the same. Assume that the accumulator content is 50H and it is compared against 51H.

```
//Implementation of Compare and Jump if above
          CJNE A, #51H,above?
          ; Check whether accumulator content is greater than 51H
          ; The Carry flag is cleared if Accumulator >= const
above?:   JNC acc_high
          ; Accumulator < 51H. Do the rest of processing here
acc_high: ; Accumulator >= 51H. Do the rest of processing here

//Implementation of Compare and Jump if below
          CJNE A, #51H, below?
          ; Check whether accumulator content is less than 51H
          ; The Carry flag is set if Accumulator < const
```

```
below?:   JC acc_low
          Accumulator >= 51H. Do the rest of processing here
acc_low: ; Accumulator < 51H. Do the rest of processing here
```

6.2.5 Program Control Transfer Instructions

The Program control transfer instructions change the program execution flow. The *8051* instruction set supports two types of program control transfer instructions namely; Unconditional program control instructions and Conditional program control instructions. They are explained below.

6.2.5.1 Unconditional Program Control Transfer Instructions The unconditional program control instructions transfer the program flow to any desired location in the code memory. The unconditional program control instructions supported by *8051* are listed below.

Instruction Mnemonic	Action	Comments	Machine Cycles	Exec. Time (µs)
JMP address		Jump to the specified address	2	$2^*(f_{OSC}/12)$
JMP @A+DPTR		Jump to the address (A+DPTR)	2	$2^*(f_{OSC}/12)$
CALL address		Call subroutine located at the code memory 'address'	2	$2^*(f_{OSC}/12)$
RET		Return from a subroutine	2	$2^*(f_{OSC}/12)$
RETI		Return from an Interrupt routine	2	$2^*(f_{OSC}/12)$
NOP		No operation (Do nothing)	1	$f_{OSC}/12$

Jump Instructions The instruction *JMP* represents three type of jumps. They are *SJMP*, *LJMP* and *AJMP* and they are used in appropriate contexts. If the programmer is not interested in analysing the contexts, he/she can simply use the *JMP* instruction.

SJMP instruction stands for Short Jump. The destination address is given as an offset to the current address held by the Program Counter (PC). The *SJMP* instruction is a two byte instruction consisting of the opcode for *SJMP* and the relative offset address which is one byte. The jump distance for the SJMP instruction is limited to the range of –128 to +127 bytes relative to the instruction following the jump.

LJMP instruction stands for Long Jump. The destination address for *LJMP* is given as the real physical address of the code memory location to which the jump is intended. The *LJMP* instruction is a three byte instruction consisting of the opcode for *LJMP* and the two byte physical address of the location to which the program flow is to be diverted. The jump location can be anywhere within the 64K program memory.

The third type of jump instruction *AJMP* stands for Absolute Jump. The *AJMP* instruction encodes the destination address as 11-bit constant. The instruction is two byte long consisting of the opcode, which itself contains higher 3 bits of the 11-bit constant. Rest 8 bits of the destination address is held by the second byte of the instruction. When an *AJMP* instruction is executed, these 11 bits are substituted for the lower 11 bits in the Program Counter (PC). The higher 5 bits of the Program Counter remains the same. Hence the destination will be within the same 2K block of the current instruction. In general *AJMP* is used for jumping within a memory block.

The programmer need not bother about handling these three jumps, what he/she can do is simply provide the destination address as label or a 16 bit constant. The assembler converts the *JMP* instruction to any of the three jump instruction depending on the context.

Case jumps for diverting program execution flow dynamically can be implemented using *JMP @A+DPTR* instruction. The destination address is computed during run time as the sum of the DPTR register content and accumulator. Normally DPTR is loaded with the address of a jump table which holds jump instructions to the memory location corresponding to a 'case'. For an *n*-way branching requirement, the accumulator is loaded with 0 through *n*–1. The following code snippet illustrates the implementation of a switch case statement using *JMP @ A+DPTR*.

```
//switch case in 'Embedded C'
switch (var)
{
Case0:
// Action…
Case1:
// Action…
Case2:
// Action…
}
```

Corresponding switch case implementation in *8051* Assembly using *JMP @ A+DPTR*

```
var EQU 50H ;Assume memory location 50H is holding variable 'var'
        MOV DPTR, #CASE_TABLE ;Load the base address of jump table
        MOV A,var; Load Accumulator with the case index
        RL A ; Convert the case table index to corresponding offset
        JMP @A+DPTR ; Jump to the case condition
;#####################################################################
CASE_TABLE:
        AJMP CASE0  ; Jump to location implementing code for CASE0
        AJMP CASE1  ; Jump to location implementing code for CASE1
        AJMP CASE2  ; Jump to location implementing code for CASE2
CASE0:              ; Action corresponding to case0
CASE1:              ; Action corresponding to case1
CASE2:              ; Action corresponding to case2
```

Locations CASE0, CASE1 and CASE2 should contain the action item to be implemented for each case statement.

The subroutine calling instruction *CALL* is of two types; namely *LCALL* and *ACALL*. *LCALL* is a three byte instruction of which the first byte represents the opcode and the second and third bytes hold the physical address of the program memory where the subroutine, which is to be executed, is located. For *LCALL* the subroutine can be anywhere within the 64K byte of program memory. *ACALL* is similar to *AJMP*. *ACALL* is a two byte instruction of which the first byte holds the opcode as well as the higher 3 bits of the 11-bit address of the location where the subroutine is located. The second byte holds the remaining 8 bits of the address location. *ACALL* is used for calling a subroutine which is within the 2K block of the instruction, calling the subroutine.

RET instruction performs return from a subroutine call. Executing the *RET* instruction brings the program flow back to the instruction following the *CALL* to the subroutine. *RETI* performs the return from an interrupt routine. *RETI* instruction is similar to the *RET* instruction in all respect except that the *RETI* informs the interrupt system that the interrupt in progress is serviced.

The *NOP* instruction does not perform anything specific. It simply forces the CPU to wait for one machine cycle. It is very useful for generating short waits. It simply eats up the processor time. For example, if you need a short delay between the toggling of a control line/device select line or port pin, simply add some *NOP* instructions. The following code snippet illustrates the usage of NOP instruction in programming.

```
SETB P2.0        ; Pull P2.0 line HIGH
NOP              ; Hold P2.0 line HIGH for 2 machine cycles
NOP
CLR P2.0         ; Release P2.0 line
```

6.2.5.2 Conditional Program Control Transfer Instructions The conditional program control transfer instructions transfer the program flow depending on certain conditions. The program flow is diverted from the normal line only if a specified condition is met. The conditional program control transfer instructions supported by *8051* are listed below.

Instruction Mnemonic	Action	Comments	Machine Cycles	Exec. Time (μs)
JZ rel	If (A == 0) Jump to 'rel'	Jump to the relative address 'rel' if Accumulator content is zero.	2	$2*(f_{osc}/12)$
JNZ rel	If (A != 0) Jump to 'rel'	Jump to the relative address 'rel' if Accumulator content is non zero.	2	$2*(f_{osc}/12)$
DJNZ <loc>, rel	<loc>=<loc>–1 If(<loc>!=0) Jump to 'rel'	Decrement the contents of <loc> and jumps to the relative address 'rel' if content of <loc> is non zero <loc> can be a direct memory or scratchpad registers R0 through R7 or any SFR.	2	$2*(f_{osc}/12)$
CJNE A, <loc>, rel	If (A!=<loc>) Jump to 'rel'	Compares the content of Accumulator with the content of <loc> and jumps to the relative address 'rel' if both are not equal. <loc> can be a direct memory or an immediate constant.	2	$2*(f_{osc}/12)$
CJNE <loc>, #data, rel	If (<loc>!= #data) Jump to 'rel'	Compares the content of <loc> with an immediate constant and jumps to the relative address 'rel' if both are not equal. <loc> can be a memory pointed indirectly or register R0 through R7 or Accumulator.	2	$2*(f_{osc}/12)$

All the conditional branching instructions specify the destination address by relative offset method and so the jump locations are limited to –128 to +127 bytes from the instruction following the conditional jump instruction. Even if the user specifies the actual address, the assembler converts it to an offset at the time of assembling the code.

Unlike the *8085* and *8086* CPU architecture, there is no zero flag for *8051*. The instructions JZ and JNZ instructions implement the zero flag check functionality by checking the accumulator content for zero. DJNZ instruction is used for setting up loop control and generating delays. CJNE instruction compares two variables and check whether they are equal. CJNE instruction in combination with the carry flag can be used for testing the conditions 'greater than', 'greater than or equal' and 'less than'. The two bytes in the operand field of CJNE are taken as unsigned integers. If the first is less than the second, the Carry bit is set (1). If the first is greater than or equal to the second, the carry bit is cleared. Boolean instructions are also used for conditional program control transfer. Please refer to the "Program Control Transfer based on bit status" under the Boolean Instructions section for more details.

Please refer to the Online Learning Centre for the Complete 8051 Instruction Set reference

Summary

- ✓ An Instruction consists of two parts namely; Opcode and Operand(s). The Opcode tells the processor what to do on executing an instruction. Operand(s) is the parameter(s) required by opcode to complete the action
- ✓ Addressing Mode refers to the way in which an operand is specified in an instruction along with the opcode
- ✓ Direct Addressing, Indirect Addressing, Register Addressing, Immediate Addressing and Indexed Addressing are the addressing modes supported by *8051*
- ✓ Instructions in which the register operand is implicitly specified by some bits of the opcode referred as register Instructions, whereas instructions which implicitly work on certain specific registers are known as Register Specific Instructions
- ✓ The instruction set of *8051* family microcontroller is broadly classified into five categories, namely; Data transfer instructions, Arithmetic instructions, Logical instructions, Boolean instructions and Program Control Transfer instructions
- ✓ 'Stack' is an internal memory for storing variables temporarily. The instruction PUSH saves data to the stack and the instruction POP retrieves the pushed data from the stack memory
- ✓ Data transfer instructions transfer data between a source and destination. The data transfer can be between register or memory (internal or external). Arithmetic instructions perform arithmetical operations like addition, subtraction, multiplication, division, increment and decrement
- ✓ Logical instructions perform logical operations such as 'ORing', 'ANDing', 'XORing', complementing, clearing, bit rotation and swapping nibbles of a byte, etc
- ✓ Boolean instructions perform various operations like bit transfer, bit manipulation, logical operations on bits, program control transfer based on bit state, etc. The carry bit 'C', present in the Special Function Register PSW, takes the role of Accumulator in all bit related operations
- ✓ Program Control transfer instructions change the program execution flow. The *8051* instruction set supports two types of program control transfer instructions namely; Unconditional program control instructions and Conditional program control instructions
- ✓ The unconditional program control instructions transfer the program flow to any desired location in the code memory. JMP, CALL, RET, RETI and NOP are the unconditional program control transfer instructions in *8051* instruction set
- ✓ The conditional program control transfer instructions transfer the program flow depending on certain conditions. The program flow is diverted from the normal line only if a specified condition is met. Jump on Zero (JZ), Jump on Non Zero (JNZ), Decrement and Jump if Non Zero (DJNZ), Compare and Jump if not equal (CJNE), Jump if specified bit is set (JB), Jump if specified bit is not set (JNB), Jump if the bit is set and clear the bit (JBC), Jump if Carry flag is set (JC) and Jump if Carry flag is not set (JNC) are the conditional program control transfer instructions in *8051*
- ✓ The DJNZ instruction is used for setting up loop control and generating delays. CJNE instruction compares two variables and check whether they are equal. CJNE instruction in combination with the Carry flag can be used for testing the conditions 'greater than', 'greater than or equal' and 'less than'

Keywords

Opcode : The command that tells the processor what to do on executing an instruction

Operand(s) : The parameter(s) required by an opcode to complete the action

Addressing Mode : The way in which an operand is specified in an instruction along with opcode

Direct Addressing : The addressing mode in which the operand is specified as direct memory address

Indirect Addressing : The addressing mode in which the operand is specified as memory address indirectly, using indirect addressing registers

Register Addressing : Addressing mode in which the operand is specified as Registers

Register Instructions : Instructions in which the register operand is implicitly specified by some bits of the opcode

Register Specific Instructions : Instructions which implicitly work on certain specific registers only

Immediate Addressing : Addressing mode in which the operand is specified as immediate constants

Indexed Addressing : Addressing mode in which the operand is specified through an index register

Data Transfer Instructions : Instructions for transferring data between a source and destination

Stack : Internal memory for storing variables temporarily

PUSH : Instruction for pushing data to the stack memory

POP : Instruction for retrieving the pushed data bytes from stack memory

Data Exchange Instructions : Instructions for exchanging data between a memory location and the accumulator register in *8051* architecture

External Data Memory Instruction : Instruction for transferring data between external memory and processor

Arithmetic Instructions : Instructions for performing basic arithmetic operations including addition, subtraction, multiplication, division, increment and decrement

2's Complement : A binary data representation used in subtraction operation

Binary Coded Decimal (BCD): Numbers with base 10. Represented using digits 0 to 9

Unpacked BCD : A single BCD digit (0 to 9) represented in a single byte

Packed BCD : Two BCD digits (00 to 99) represented using a single byte

Decimal Adjust Accumulator (DAA) : An instruction for adjusting the accumulator content to give a meaningful BCD, after BCD arithmetic

Logical Instructions : Instructions for performing logical operations such as 'ORing', 'ANDing', 'XORing', complementing, clearing, bit rotation and swapping nibbles of a byte, etc

Boolean Instructions : Instructions for performing various operations like bit transfer, bit manipulation, logical operations on bits, program control transfer based on bit state, etc

Objective Questions

1. What are the different addressing modes supported by *8051*?
   (a) Direct Addressing (b) Indirect Addressing (c) Register Addressing (d) Indexed Addressing
   (e) Immediate Addressing (f) All of these
2. Which is the addressing mode for the instruction MOV A, #50H
   (a) Direct (b) Indirect (c) Immediate (d) None of these
3. Which is the addressing mode for the instruction MOV A, 50H
   (a) Direct (b) Indirect (c) Immediate (d) None of these
4. Which is the addressing mode for the instruction MOV A, @R0
   (a) Direct (b) Indirect (c) Immediate (d) None of these

5. Which is the addressing mode for the instruction MOVC A, @A+DPTR
(a) Direct (b) Indirect (c) Immediate (d) None of these
6. Code memory starting from 0050H holds a lookup table of 10 bytes. The first element of the lookup table is 00H. What is the content of accumulator after executing the following piece of code?

```
        MOV A, #00H
        LCALL TABLE
        NOP
ORG 004EH
TABLE:  MOVC A, @A+PC
        RET
```

(a) 00H (b) 22 (c) 22H (d) Undefined
(e) None of these
7. Register R0 contains 50H and Accumulator contains 01H. What will be the contents of R0 and A after executing the instruction MOV A,R0
(a) R0 = 01H; A = 01H (b) R0 = 50H; A = 01H (c) R0 = 01H; A = 50H (d) R0 = 50H; A = 50H
(e) None of these
8. Data memory location 00H contains F0H and Stack Pointer (SP) contains 07H. What will be the contents of memory location 00H and SP after executing the instruction *PUSH 00H*
(a) Data memory location 00H = 07H; SP = 07H (b) Data memory location 00H = F0H; SP = 07H
(c) Data memory location 00H = F0H; SP = 08H (d) Data memory location 00H = F0H; SP = 06H
(e) None of these
9. Data memory location 00H contains F0H and Stack Pointer (SP) contains 08H. The memory location 08H contains 0FH. What will be the contents of memory location 00H, 08H and SP after executing the instruction *POP 00H*
(a) Memory location 00H = 0FH; Memory location 08H = F0H; SP = 08H
(b) Memory location 00H = F0H; Memory location 08H = F0H; SP = 07H
(c) Memory location 00H = 0FH; Memory location 08H = 0FH; SP = 07H
(d) Memory location 00H = 0FH; Memory location 08H = 0FH; SP = 09H
(e) None of these
10. Data memory location 0FH contains 00H and the accumulator contains FFH. What will be the contents of data memory location 0FH and the accumulator after executing the instruction *XCH A, 0FH*
(a) Memory location 0FH = 00H; Accumulator = FFH
(b) Memory location 0FH = 00H; Accumulator = 00H
(c) Memory location 0FH = FFH; Accumulator = 00H
(d) Memory location 0FH = FFH; Accumulator = FFH
(e) None of these
11. Data memory location 0FH contains A5H, Accumulator contains 5AH and register R0 contains 0FH. What will be the contents of data memory location 0FH, Register R0 and accumulator after executing the instruction *XCHD A, @R0*
(a) Memory location 0FH = A5H; Accumulator = 5AH; R0 = 0FH
(b) Memory location 0FH = 55H; Accumulator = AAH; R0 = 0FH
(c) Memory location 0FH = AAH; Accumulator = 55H; R0 = 0FH
(d) Memory location 0FH = A5H; Accumulator = 55H; R0 = AAH
(e) None of these
12. Register DPTR holds 2050H. Explain the result of executing the instruction *MOVX @DPTR, A*
(a) P2 SFR = 20H; P1 SFR = 50H during the first machine cycle; RD\ signal is asserted once
(b) P2 SFR = 50H; P1 SFR = 20H during the first machine cycle; RD\ signal is asserted once
(c) P2 SFR = 20H; P1 SFR = 50H during the first machine cycle; WR\ signal is asserted once
(d) P2 SFR = 50H; P1 SFR = 20H during the first machine cycle; WR\ signal is asserted once
(e) None of these

13. The Program Strobe Enable (PSEN) signal is asserted during program fetching if
    (a) The program memory is external to the controller
    (b) The Program memory is internal to the controller
    (c) The Program memory is either internal or external to the controller
14. How many program fetches occur per machine cycle?
    (a) 1 (b) 2 (c) 3 (d) 4
15. How many 'program memory fetches' are skipped during the execution of *MOVX* instruction?
    (a) 1 (b) 2 (c) 3 (d) 4
16. The Address Latch Enable (ALE) signal is asserted how many times in a machine cycle?
    (a) 1 (b) 2 (c) 3 (d) 4
17. How many times the ALE signal is skipped during the execution of a *MOVX* instruction?
    (a) 1 (b) 2 (c) 3 (d) 4
18. Which of the following is true about *MOVC* instruction
    (a) Used for reading from Program memory (b) Uses Indexed Addressing technique
    (c) Both a & b (d) None of these
19. The content of Accumulator is FFH and the Carry Flag is in the cleared state. What will be the contents of Accumulator and carry flag after executing the instruction *ADD A,#1*
    (a) Accumulator = 01H; Carry flag = 1 (b) Accumulator = 01H; Carry flag = 0
    (c) Accumulator = 00H; Carry flag = 0 (d) Accumulator = 00H; Carry flag = 1
20. Accumulator register contains 0FH and the Carry flag CY is in the set state. What will be the state of Carry flag after executing the instruction *ADD A,#0F0H*
    (a) 1 (b) 0 (c) Indeterminate
21. The content of the accumulator is FFH and the Carry flag is in the cleared state. What will be the contents of the accumulator and carry flag after executing the instruction *ADDC A,#1*
    (a) Accumulator = 01H; Carry flag = 1 (b) Accumulator = 01H; Carry flag = 0
    (c) Accumulator = 00H; Carry flag = 0 (d) Accumulator = 00H; Carry flag = 1
22. Accumulator register contains 0FH and the Carry flag CY is in the cleared state. What will be the contents of Carry flag and Accumulator after executing the instruction *SUBB A,#0F0H*
    (a) Accumulator = E1H; Carry flag = 1 (b) Accumulator = E1H; Carry flag = 0
    (c) Accumulator = 1FH; Carry flag = 0 (d) Accumulator = 1FH; Carry flag = 1
23. Accumulator register contains F0H and the Carry flag CY is in the cleared state. What will be the contents of the Carry flag and the accumulator after executing the instruction *SUBB A,#0FH*
    (a) Accumulator = E1H; Carry flag = 1 (b) Accumulator = E1H; Carry flag = 0
    (c) Accumulator = 1FH; Carry flag = 0 (d) Accumulator = 1FH; Carry flag = 1
24. Accumulator register contains 0FFH and the B register contains 02H. What will be the contents of the Accumulator and B register after executing the instruction *MUL AB*
    (a) Accumulator = 0FEH; B = 01H (b) Accumulator = 00H; B = 0FEH
    (c) Accumulator = 0FEH; B = 00H (d) Accumulator = 01H; B = 0FEH
25. Accumulator register contains 0FFH, B register contains 02H and the Carry flag is in the cleared state. What will be the contents of the Carry flag and Overflow flag after executing the instruction *MUL AB*
    (a) Carry flag = 1; Overflow flag = 0
    (b) Carry flag = 0; Overflow flag = Remains same as the previous value
    (c) Carry flag = 1; Overflow flag = 1
    (d) Carry flag = 0; Overflow flag = 1
26. Accumulator register contains 0FFH, B register contains 02H and the Overflow flag is in the cleared state. What will be the contents of the Carry flag and Overflow flag after executing the instruction *MUL AB*
    (a) Carry flag = remains same as the previous value; Overflow flag = 0
    (b) Carry flag = remains same as the previous value; Overflow flag = 1
    (c) Carry flag = 1; Overflow flag = 1
    (d) Carry flag = 0; Overflow flag = 1

27. Accumulator contains 0FFH and the B Register contains 02H. What will be the contents of the accumulator and B register after executing the instruction *DIV AB*
 (a) Accumulator = 01H; B = 7FH
 (b) Accumulator = 7FH; B = 01H
 (c) Accumulator = 7FH; B = 00H
 (d) Accumulator = 00H; B = 7FH
28. Accumulator register contains 0FFH and the B register contains 0H. What will be the contents of the accumulator, B register and Overflow flag after executing the instruction *DIV AB*
 (a) Accumulator = 00H; B = 00H; Overflow flag = 1
 (b) Accumulator = 0FFH; B = 00H; Overflow flag = 0
 (c) Accumulator = Undefined; B = Undefined; Overflow flag = 1
 (d) Accumulator = Undefined; B = Undefined; Overflow flag = 0
29. Accumulator register contains 0FFH and the Carry flag CY is in the cleared state. What will be the contents of Carry flag and the accumulator after executing the instruction *INC A*
 (a) Accumulator = 00H; Carry flag = 1
 (b) Accumulator = 00H; Carry flag = 0
 (c) Accumulator = 01H; Carry flag = 0
 (d) Accumulator = 01H; Carry flag = 1
30. Accumulator register contains 00H and the Carry flag CY is in the cleared state. What will be the contents of Carry flag and Accumulator after executing the instruction *DEC A*
 (a) Accumulator = 00H; Carry flag = 1
 (b) Accumulator = 00H; Carry flag = 0
 (c) Accumulator = FFH; Carry flag = 0
 (d) Accumulator = FFH; Carry flag = 1
31. DPTR contains 2050H. What will be the content of DPTR after executing the following instructions

```
        XCH   A, DPL
        DEC   A
        CJNE  A, #0FFH, skip_dec
        DEC   DPH
skip_dec:
        XCH   A, DPL
```

 (a) 2050H (b) 2049H (c) 2051H (d) 204FH
32. Accumulator register contains 0FH. What will be the content of the accumulator after executing the instruction *DA A*
 (a) 0FH (b) 15 H (c) 15 (d) 00H
33. Accumulator register contains the BCD number 28. What will be the content of the accumulator after executing the instruction *ADD A,#12H*
 (a) 40H (b) 3AH (c) 40 (d) None of these
34. Accumulator register contains the BCD number 28. What will be the content of the accumulator after executing the following instructions

```
ADD A,#12H
DAA
```

 (a) 40H (b) 3AH (c) 40 (d) None of these
35. Accumulator register contains 0FH. What will be the content of the accumulator after executing the instruction *ORL A, #0F0H*
 (a) 0FH (b) F0H (c) FFH (d) 00H
36. Accumulator register contains 0FH. What will be the content of the accumulator after executing the instruction *ANL A, #0F0H*
 (a) 0FH (b) F0H (c) FFH (d) 00H
37. Accumulator register contains 0AAH. What will be the content of the accumulator after executing the instruction *XRL A, #0D5H*
 (a) AAH (b) 7FH (c) D5H (d) FFH
38. Accumulator register contains 7FH and carry flag is in the set state. What will be the contents of Accumulator and carry flag after executing the instruction *CLR A*
 (a) Accumulator = 7FH; Carry flag = 0
 (b) Accumulator = 7FH; Carry flag = 1
 (c) Accumulator = 00H; Carry flag = 0
 (d) Accumulator = 00H; Carry flag = 1

39. What changes will happen on executing the instruction *CLR 00H*
   (a) The code memory location 00H becomes 00H
   (b) The data memory location 00H becomes 00H
   (c) The external data memory location 00H becomes 00H
   (d) The LS Bit of the data held by data memory location 20H becomes 0
40. Accumulator register contains 0FH and carry flag is in the set state. What will be the contents of the Accumulator and carry flag after executing the instruction *CPL A*
   (a) Accumulator = 0FH; Carry flag = 0 (b) Accumulator = 0FH; Carry flag = 1
   (c) Accumulator = F0H; Carry flag = 0 (d) Accumulator = F0H; Carry flag = 1
41. Accumulator register contains 01H and carry flag is in the set state. What will be the contents of Accumulator and carry flag after executing the instruction *RL A*
   (a) Accumulator = 02H; Carry flag = 0 (b) Accumulator = 02H; Carry flag = 1
   (c) Accumulator = 80H; Carry flag = 0 (d) Accumulator = 80H; Carry flag = 1
42. Accumulator register contains 01H and carry flag is in the set state. What will be the contents of Accumulator and carry flag after executing the instruction *RLC A*
   (a) Accumulator = 02H; Carry flag = 0 (b) Accumulator = 02H; Carry flag = 1
   (c) Accumulator = 03H; Carry flag = 0 (d) Accumulator = 03H; Carry flag = 1
43. Accumulator register contains 01H and carry flag is in the set state. What will be the contents of the accumulator and carry flag after executing the instruction *RR A*
   (a) Accumulator = 02H; Carry flag = 0 (b) Accumulator = 02H; Carry flag = 1
   (c) Accumulator = 80H; Carry flag = 0 (d) Accumulator = 80H; Carry flag = 1
44. Accumulator register contains 01H and carry flag is in the set state. What will be the contents of the accumulator and carry flag after executing the instruction *RRC A*
   (a) Accumulator = 80H; Carry flag = 0 (b) Accumulator = 80H; Carry flag = 1
   (c) Accumulator = 03H; Carry flag = 0 (d) Accumulator = 03H; Carry flag = 1
45. Accumulator register contains 5FH. What will be the content of the accumulator after executing the instruction *SWAP A*
   (a) 00H (b) F5H (c) 5FH (d) 00H
46. What changes will happen on executing the instruction *CPL 00H*
   (a) The code memory location 00H becomes 00H
   (b) The data memory location 00H becomes 00H
   (c) The external data memory location 00H becomes 00H
   (d) The LS Bit of the data held by data memory location 20H is complemented
47. The carry bit is in the set state and the port status bit P1.0 is in the cleared state. What will be the values of Carry bit and P1.0 after executing the instruction *ANL C, /P1.0*
   (a) Carry flag = 0; P1.0 = 0 (b) Carry flag = 0; P1.0 = 1
   (c) Carry flag = 1; P1.0 = 0 (d) Carry flag = 1; P1.0 = 1
48. The Carry bit is in the cleared state and the Port status bit P1.0 is in the cleared state. What will be the values of Carry bit and P1.0 after executing the instruction *ORL C, /P1.0*
   (a) Carry flag = 0; P1.0 = 0 (b) Carry flag = 0; P1.0 = 1
   (c) Carry Flag = 1; P1.0 = 0 (d) Carry flag = 1; P1.0 = 1
49. Which of the following Jump instruction is the optimal instruction if the offset (relative displacement of jump location from the current instruction location) of the jump location is greater than 127 and less than –128 and is within the same 2K block of the current instruction
   (a) AJMP (b) SJMP (c) LJMP (d) All of these
50. The program execution needs to be diverted to a location within the 2K memory block of the current instruction and the 11 least significant bits of the code memory address to which the jump is intended is 050FH. The *AJMP* instruction is used for implementing the jump. What is the machine code for implementing the AJMP instruction for jumping to the specified location?
   (a) 01H, 0FH, 05H (b) 01H, 05H, 0FH (c) A1H, 0FH (d) None of these

51. Which of the following Jump instruction encodes the jump location as absolute memory address
    (a) SJMP (b) AJMP (c) LJMP (d) All of these
    (e) only (b) and (c)
52. All the conditional branching instructions specify the destination address by
    (a) Relative offset method (b) Absolute address method
    (c) Either relative or absolute address method (d) None of these

Review Questions

1. Explain with examples the different addressing modes supported by *8051* CPU
2. What is the difference between Register Instructions and Register Specific Instructions? Give an example for each
3. What is the difference between Immediate addressing and Indexed addressing? State where these addressing techniques are used. Give an example for each.
4. What is Data transfer instruction? Explain the different data transfer instructions supported by *8051* CPU
5. Explain the arithmetic operations/instructions supported by *8051* CPU
6. Accumulator register contains 01H and Carry flag is in the state. What will be the contents of accumulator and Carry flag on executing the instruction

   RR A

   RR C A
7. Examine the following piece of code and explain whether the program will work in the expected way. Justify your statement

   MOV P1.0, P1.2
8. In the following code snippet, the jump location is intended to a memory address with offset beyond +127. Suggest a workaround to solve this issue

   CJNE A,#01H, JUMP_HERE

   ....

   ....

   ;The relative address of label ' JUMP_HERE ' is greater than 127 JUMP_HERE: XCH A,B
9. Explain the stack memory related data transfer instructions in detail
10. Explain the data exchange instructions in detail with examples
11. Explain the timing diagram for the *MOVX* instruction execution when the program memory is internal to the processor
12. Explain the difference between *ADD*, *ADDC* and *DAA* instructions. Explain the significance of *DAA* instruction?
13. Explain the instruction for division operation. How is a divide by zero condition handled in the *8051* architecture?
14. Explain the different logical operations supported by *8051* and the corresponding instruction in detail
15. Explain the different Boolean instructions supported by *8051*
16. Explain the different unconditional program control transfer instructions supported by *8051*
17. Explain the different conditional program control transfer instructions supported by *8051*
18. Explain the implementation of *switch() case* statement using jump tables
19. The *8051* status register doesn't contain a zero flag. Explain how the *8051* architecture implements the Jump on zero and Jump on non-zero conditions
20. Explain the difference between *LCALL* and *ACALL* for subroutine invocation? Which one is faster in execution and why?
21. Explain the difference between *RET* and *RETI* instructions
22. Explain the different types of jumps supported by *8051* architecture. Which one is faster in execution and why?

Lab Assignments

1. A lookup table with 6 bytes is stored in code memory location starting from 8000H. Write a small *8051* assembly program to read the lookup table
2. Implement a BCD counter to count from 00 to 99 with a delay of 1 second between the successive counts. Display the count using two 7-Segment LED displays in multiplexed configuration
3. Optimise the following piece of code (Rewrite the code with instructions/operations giving the same functionality) for memory size and performance

```
ORG 0000H
          JB  P1.0, PORT_SET
          MOV A, #50H
          LJMP SKIP
PORT_SET: CLR P1.0
SKIP:     LCALL DELAY
ORG 0050H
DELAY: NOP
                     NOP
                     RET
```

4. Write a *8051* assembly language program using timer interrupt for generating a 50 Hz square wave at the port pin P1.0. The oscillator frequency applied to the microcontroller is 12.00MHz
5. Write a *8051* assembly language program for generating a 5 kHz square wave at the port pin P1.0. The oscillator frequency applied to the microcontroller is 12.00 MHz.
6. Write a *8051* Assembly language program to generate the Fibonacci series of a given number. Assume the number whose Fibonacci number is to be calculated is received from the hyper terminal application running on a PC to which the microcontroller is interfaced. Upon receiving the number from the hyper terminal application, the Fibonacci series for the number is generated and it is sent to the hyper terminal application running on the PC. The program also inserts the character ',' to separate the two consecutive numbers in the series while sending it. The numbers are sent with their corresponding ASCII value (e.g. 0 is sent as 30H). The serial communication parameter settings for both hyper terminal application and microcontroller program are: baudrate = 9600, 1 start bit, 8 data bits, 1 stop bit, No parity. Use a crystal resonator with frequency 11.0592MHz for designing the microcontroller hardware.
7. Write a *8051* assembly language program to find the largest number from an array of 10 numbers. The array is located in the data memory and the start address of the array is 20H.
8. Write a *8051* assembly language program to generate a PWM signal of ON time 100 microseconds and duty cycle of 39.06%, at port pin P1.0
9. Explain with code snippet how the *8051* timer can be used for the measurement of the width of an unknown pulse
10. It is required by an experimental setup to count the number of pulses arrived during a time period of 50 milliseconds. Explain with code snippets how it can be implemented using the *8051* timers.

7 Hardware Software Co-Design and Program Modelling

LEARNING OBJECTIVES

- ✓ *Learn about the co-design approach for embedded hardware and firmware development*
- ✓ *Know the fundamental issues in model, architecture and language selection for hardware software co-design and partitioning the system requirements into hardware and software (firmware)*
- ✓ *Learn about the different computational models used in Embedded System design*
- ✓ *Learn about Data Flow Graphs (DFG) Model, Control Data Flow Graph (CDFG), State Machine Model, Sequential Program Model, Concurrent/Communicating Model and Object Oriented Model for embedded design*
- ✓ *Learn about Unified Modelling Language (UML) for system modelling, the building blocks of UML, different types of diagrams supported by UML for requirements modelling and design*
- ✓ *Learn about the different tools for UML modelling*
- ✓ *Learn about the trade-offs like performance, cost, etc. to be considered in the partitioning of a system requirement into either hardware or software*

In the traditional embedded system development approach, the hardware software partitioning is done at an early stage and engineers from the software group take care of the software architecture development and implementation, whereas engineers from the hardware group are responsible for building the hardware required for the product. There is less interaction between the two teams and the development happens either serially or in parallel. Once the hardware and software are ready, the integration is performed. The increasing competition in the commercial market and need for reduced 'time-to-market' the product calls for a novel approach for embedded system design in which the hardware and software are co-developed instead of independently developing both.

During the co-design process, the product requirements captured from the customer are converted into system level needs or processing requirements. At this point of time it is not segregated as either hardware requirement or software requirement, instead it is specified as functional requirement. The system level processing requirements are then transferred into functions which can be simulated and verified against performance and functionality. The Architecture design follows the system design. The partition of system level processing requirements into hardware and software takes place during the architecture design phase. Each system level processing requirement is mapped as either hardware and/or software requirement. The partitioning is performed based on the hardware-software trade-offs. We will discuss the various hardware software tradeoffs in hardware software co-design in a separate topic. The architectural design results in the detailed behavioural description of the hardware requirement and the definition of the software required for the hardware. The processing requirement behaviour is usually captured using computational models and ultimately the models representing the software processing requirements are translated into firmware implementation using programming languages.

7.1 FUNDAMENTAL ISSUES IN HARDWARE SOFTWARE CO-DESIGN

The hardware software co-design is a problem statement and when we try to solve this problem statement in real life we may come across multiple issues in the design. The following section illustrates some of the fundamental issues in hardware software co-design.

Selecting the model In hardware software co-design, models are used for capturing and describing the system characteristics. A model is a formal system consisting of objects and composition rules. It is hard to make a decision on which model should be followed in a particular system design. Most often designers switch between a variety of models from the requirements specification to the implementation aspect of the system design. The reason being, the objective varies with each phase; for example at the specification stage, only the functionality of the system is in focus and not the implementation information. When the design moves to the implementation aspect, the information about the system components is revealed and the designer has to switch to a model capable of capturing the system's structure. We will discuss about the different models in a later section of this chapter.

Selecting the Architecture A model only captures the system characteristics and does not provide information on 'how the system can be manufactured?'. The *architecture* specifies how a system is going to implement in terms of the number and types of different components and the interconnection among them. Controller architecture, Datapath Architecture, Complex Instruction Set Computing (CISC), Reduced Instruction Set Computing (RISC), Very Long Instruction Word Computing (VLIW), Single Instruction Multiple Data (SIMD), Multiple Instruction Multiple Data (MIMD), etc. are the commonly used architectures in system design. Some of them fall into Application Specific Architecture Class (like controller architecture), while others fall into either general purpose architecture class (CISC, RISC, etc.) or Parallel processing class (like VLIW, SIMD, MIMD, etc.).

The **controller architecture** implements the finite state machine model (which we will discuss in a later section) using a state register and two combinational circuits (we will discuss about combinational circuits in a later chapter). The state register holds the present state and the combinational circuits implement the logic for next state and output.

The **datapath architecture** is best suited for implementing the data flow graph model where the output is generated as a result of a set of predefined computations on the input data. A datapath represents a channel between the input and output and in datapath architecture the datapath may contain registers, counters, register files, memories and ports along with high speed arithmetic units. Ports connect the datapath to multiple buses. Most of the time the arithmetic units are connected in parallel with pipelining support for bringing high performance.

The **Finite State Machine Datapath** (FSMD) architecture combines the controller architecture with datapath architecture. It implements a controller with datapath. The controller generates the control input whereas the datapath processes the data. The datapath contains two types of I/O ports, out of which one acts as the control port for receiving/sending the control signals from/to the controller unit and the second I/O port interfaces the datapath with` external world for data input and data output. Normally the datapath is implemented in a chip and the I/O pins of the chip acts as the data input output ports for the chip resident data path.

The **Complex Instruction Set Computing** (CISC) architecture uses an instruction set representing complex operations. It is possible for a CISC instruction set to perform a large complex operation (e.g. Reading a register value and comparing it with a given value and then transfer the program execution to a new address location (The CJNE instruction for 8051 ISA)) with a single instruction. The use of a single complex instruction in place of multiple simple instructions greatly reduces the program memory access and program memory size requirement. However it requires additional silicon for implementing microcode decoder for decoding the CISC instruction. The datapath for the CISC processor is complex. On the other hand, Reduced Instruction Set Computing (RISC) architecture uses instruction set representing simple operations and it requires the execution of multiple RISC instructions to perform a complex operation. The data path of RISC architecture contains a large register file for storing the operands and output. RISC instruction set is designed to operate on registers. RISC architecture supports extensive pipelining.

The **Very Long Instruction Word** (VLIW) architecture implements multiple functional units (ALUs, multipliers, etc.) in the datapath. The VLIW instruction packages one standard instruction per functional unit of the datapath.

Parallel processing architecture implements multiple concurrent Processing Elements (PEs) and each processing element may associate a datapath containing register and local memory. Single Instruction Multiple Data (SIMD) and Multiple Instruction Multiple Data (MIMD) architectures are examples for parallel processing architecture. In SIMD architecture, a single instruction is executed in parallel with the help of the Processing Elements. The scheduling of the instruction execution and controlling of each PE is performed through a single controller. The SIMD architecture forms the basis of re-configurable processor (We will discuss about re-configurable processors in a later chapter). On the other hand, the processing elements of the MIMD architecture execute different instructions at a given point of time. The MIMD architecture forms the basis of multiprocessor systems. The PEs in a multiprocessor system communicates through mechanisms like shared memory and message passing.

Selecting the language A programming language captures a 'Computational Model' and maps it into architecture. There is no hard and fast rule to specify this language should be used for capturing this model. A model can be captured using multiple programming languages like C, C++, C#, Java, etc. for software implementations and languages like VHDL, System C, Verilog, etc. for hardware implementations. On the other hand, a single language can be used for capturing a variety of models. Certain languages are good in capturing certain computational model. For example, C++ is a good candidate for capturing an object oriented model. The only pre-requisite in selecting a programming language for capturing a model is that the language should capture the model easily.

Partitioning System Requirements into hardware and software So far we discussed about the models for capturing the system requirements and the architecture for implementing the system. From an implementation perspective, it may be possible to implement the system requirements in either hardware or software (firmware). It is a tough decision making task to figure out which one to opt. Various hardware software trade-offs are used for making a decision on the hardware-software partitioning. We will discuss them in detail in a later section of this chapter.

7.2 COMPUTATIONAL MODELS IN EMBEDDED DESIGN

Data Flow Graph (DFG) model, State Machine model, Concurrent Process model, Sequential Program model, Object Oriented model, etc. are the commonly used computational models in embedded system design. The following sections give an overview of these models.

7.2.1 Data Flow Graph/Diagram (DFG) Model

The Data Flow Graph (DFG) model translates the data processing requirements into a data flow graph. The Data Flow Graph (DFG) model is a data driven model in which the program execution is determined by data. This model emphasises on the data and operations on the data which transforms the input data to output data. Indeed Data Flow Graph (DFG) is a visual model in which the operation on the data (process) is represented using a block (circle) and data flow is represented using arrows. An inward arrow to the process (circle) represents input data and an outward arrow from the process (circle) represents output data in DFG notation.

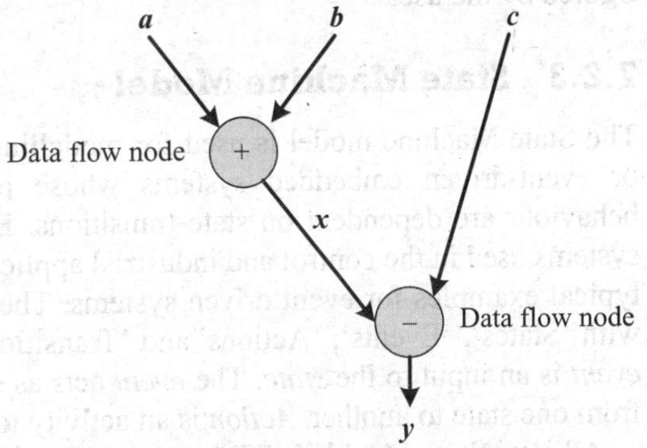

Fig. 7.1 Data flow graph (DFG) model

Embedded applications which are computational intensive and data driven are modeled using the DFG model. DSP applications are typical examples for it. Now let's have a look at the implementation of a DFG. Suppose one of the functions in our application contains the computational requirement $x = a + b$; and $y = x - c$. Figure 7.1 illustrates the implementation of a DFG model for implementing these requirements.

In a DFG model, a data path is the data flow path from input to output. A DFG model is said to be acyclic DFG (ADFG) if it doesn't contain multiple values for the input variable and multiple output values for a given set of input(s). Feedback inputs (Output is fed back to Input), events, etc. are examples for non-acyclic inputs. A DFG model translates the program as a single sequential process execution.

7.2.2 Control Data Flow Graph/Diagram (CDFG)

We have seen that the DFG model is a data driven model in which the execution is controlled by data and it doesn't involve any control operations (conditionals). The Control DFG (CDFG) model is used for modelling applications involving conditional program execution. CDFG models contains both data operations and control operations. The CDFG uses Data Flow Graph (DFG) as element and conditional (constructs) as decision makers. CDFG contains both data flow nodes and decision nodes, whereas DFG contains only data flow nodes. Let us have a look at the implementation of the CDFG for the following requirement.

If flag = 1, $x = a + b$; else $y = a - b$;

This requirement contains a decision making process. The CDFG model for the same is given in Fig. 7.2.

The control node is represented by a 'Diamond' block which is the decision making element in a normal flow chart based design. CDFG translates the requirement, which is modeled to a concurrent process model. The decision on which process is to be executed is determined by the control node.

A real world example for modelling the embedded application using CDFG is the capturing and saving of the image to a format set by the user in a digital still camera where everything is data driven starting from the Analog Front End which converts the CCD sensor generated analog signal to Digital Signal and the task which stores the data from ADC to a frame buffer for the use of a media processor which performs various operations like, auto correction, white balance adjusting, etc. The decision on, in which format the image is stored (formats like JPEG, TIFF, BMP, etc.) is controlled by the camera settings, configured by the user.

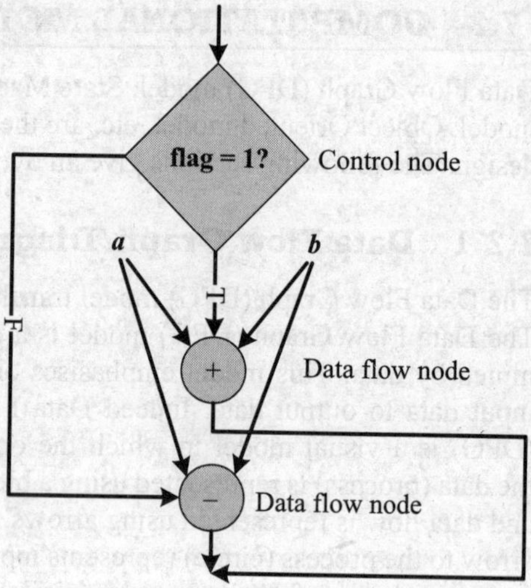

Fig. 7.2 **Control Data Flow Graph (CDFG) Model**

7.2.3 State Machine Model

The State Machine model is used for modelling reactive or event-driven embedded systems whose processing behaviour are dependent on state transitions. Embedded systems used in the control and industrial applications are typical examples for event driven systems. The State Machine model describes the system behaviour with 'States', 'Events', 'Actions' and 'Transitions'. *State* is a representation of a current situation. An *event* is an input to the *state*. The *event* acts as stimuli for state transition. *Transition* is the movement from one state to another. *Action* is an activity to be performed by the state machine.

A Finite State Machine (FSM) model is one in which the number of states are finite. In other words the system is described using a finite number of possible states. As an example let us consider the design of an embedded system for driver/passenger 'Seat Belt Warning' in an automotive using the FSM model. The system requirements are captured as.

1. When the vehicle ignition is turned on and the seat belt is not fastened within 10 seconds of ignition ON, the system generates an alarm signal for 5 seconds.
2. The Alarm is turned off when the alarm time (5 seconds) expires or if the driver/passenger fastens the belt or if the ignition switch is turned off, whichever happens first.

Here the states are 'Alarm Off', 'Waiting' and 'Alarm On' and the events are 'Ignition Key ON', 'Ignition Key OFF', 'Timer Expire', 'Alarm Time Expire' and 'Seat Belt ON'. Using the FSM, the system requirements can be modeled as given in Fig. 7.3.

The 'Ignition Key ON' event triggers the 10 second timer and transitions the state to 'Waiting'. If a 'Seat Belt ON' or 'Ignition Key OFF' event occurs during the wait state, the state transitions into 'Alarm Off'. When the wait timer expires in the waiting state, the event 'Timer Expire' is generated and it transitions the state to 'Alarm On' from the 'Waiting' state. The 'Alarm On' state continues until a 'Seat Belt ON' or 'Ignition Key OFF' event or 'Alarm Time Expire' event, whichever occurs first. The occurrence of any of these events transitions the state to 'Alarm Off'. The wait state is implemented using a timer. The timer also has certain set of states and events for state transitions. Using the FSM model, the timer can be modeled as shown in Fig. 7.4.

As seen from the FSM, the timer state can be either 'IDLE' or 'READY' or 'RUNNING'. During the normal condition when the timer is not running, it is said to be in the 'IDLE' state. The timer is said to be in the 'READY' state when the timer is loaded with the count corresponding to the required time

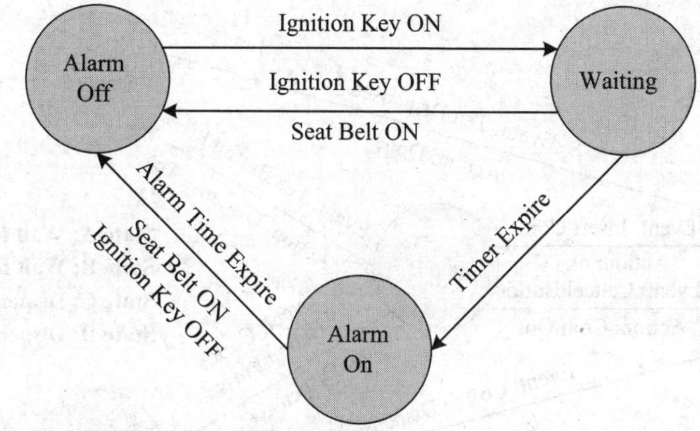

Fig. 7.3 **FSM Model for Automatic seat belt warning system**

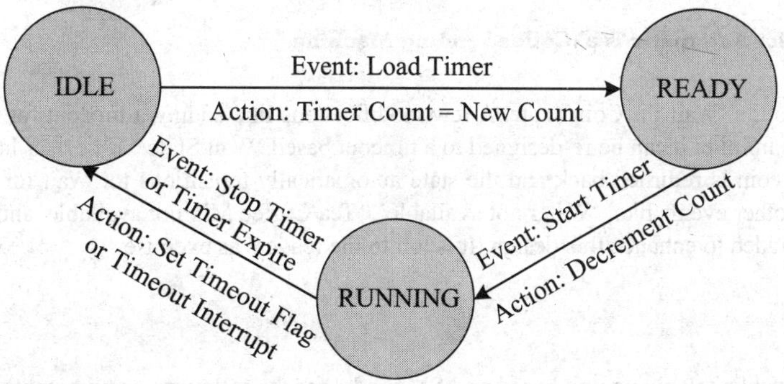

Fig. 7.4 **FSM Model for timer**

delay. The timer remains in the 'READY' state until a 'Start Timer' event occurs. The timer changes its state to 'RUNNING' from the 'READY' state on receiving a 'Start Timer' event and remains in the 'RUNNING' state until the timer count expires or a 'Stop Timer' even occurs. The timer state changes to 'IDLE' from 'RUNNING' on receiving a 'Stop Timer' or 'Timer Expire' event.

Example 1

Design an automatic tea/coffee vending machine based on FSM model for the following requirement.

The tea/coffee vending is initiated by user inserting a 5 rupee coin. After inserting the coin, the user can either select 'Coffee' or 'Tea' or press 'Cancel' to cancel the order and take back the coin.

The FSM representation for the above requirement is given in Fig. 7.5.

In its simplest representation, it contains four states namely; 'Wait for coin' 'Wait for User Input', 'Dispense Tea' and 'Dispense Coffee'. The event 'Insert Coin' (5 rupee coin insertion), transitions the state to 'Wait for User Input'. The system stays in this state until a user input is received from the buttons 'Cancel', 'Tea' or 'Coffee' (Tea and Coffee are the drink select button). If the event triggered in 'Wait State' is 'Cancel' button press, the coin is pushed out and the state transitions to 'Wait for Coin'. If the event received in the 'Wait State' is either 'Tea' button press, or 'Coffee' button press, the state changes to 'Dispense Tea' and 'Dispense Coffee' respectively. Once the coffee/tea vending is over, the respective

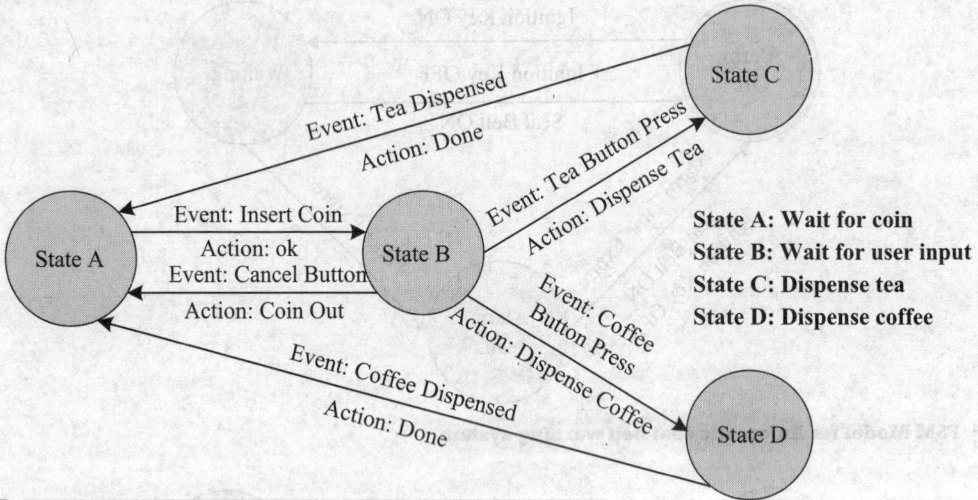

Fig. 7.5 **FSM Model for Automatic Tea\Coffee Vending Machine**

states transitions back to the 'Wait for Coin' state. A few modifications like adding a timeout for the 'Wait State' (Currently the 'Wait State' is infinite; it can be re-designed to a timeout based 'Wait State'. If no user input is received within the timeout period, the coin is returned back and the state automatically transitions to 'Wait for Coin' on the timeout event) and capturing another events like, 'Water not available', 'Tea/Coffee Mix not available' and changing the state to an 'Error State' can be added to enhance this design. It is left to the readers as exercise.

Example 2

Design a coin operated public telephone unit based on FSM model for the following requirements.

1. The calling process is initiated by lifting the receiver (off-hook) of the telephone unit
2. After lifting the phone the user needs to insert a 1 rupee coin to make the call.
3. If the line is busy, the coin is returned on placing the receiver back on the hook (on-hook)
4. If the line is through, the user is allowed to talk till 60 seconds and at the end of 45th second, prompt for inserting another 1 rupee coin for continuing the call is initiated
5. If the user doesn't insert another 1 rupee coin, the call is terminated on completing the 60 seconds time slot.
6. The system is ready to accept new call request when the receiver is placed back on the hook (on-hook)
7. The system goes to the 'Out of Order' state when there is a line fault.

The FSM model shown in Fig. 7.6, is a simple representation and it doesn't take care of scenarios like, user doesn't insert a coin within the specified time after lifting the receiver, user inserts coins other than a one rupee etc. Handling these scenarios is left to the readers as exercise.

Most of the time state machine model translates the requirements into sequence driven program and it is difficult to implement concurrent processing with FSM. This limitation is addressed by the Hierarchical/Concurrent Finite State Machine model (HCFSM). The HCFSM is an extension of the FSM for supporting concurrency and hierarchy. HCFSM extends the conventional state diagrams by the AND, OR decomposition of States together with inter level transitions and a broadcast mechanism for communicating between concurrent processes. HCFSM uses statecharts for capturing the states, transitions, events and actions. The Harel Statechart, UML State diagram, etc. are examples for popular statecharts used for the HCFSM modelling of embedded systems. In statecharts, the state is usually represented using geometric shapes like rounded rectangle, rectangle, ellipse, circle, etc. The Harel Statechart uses a rounded rectangle for representing state. Arrows are used for representing the state transition and they are marked with the event associated with the state transition. Sometimes an optional parenthesized condition is also labeled with the arrow. The condition specifies on what

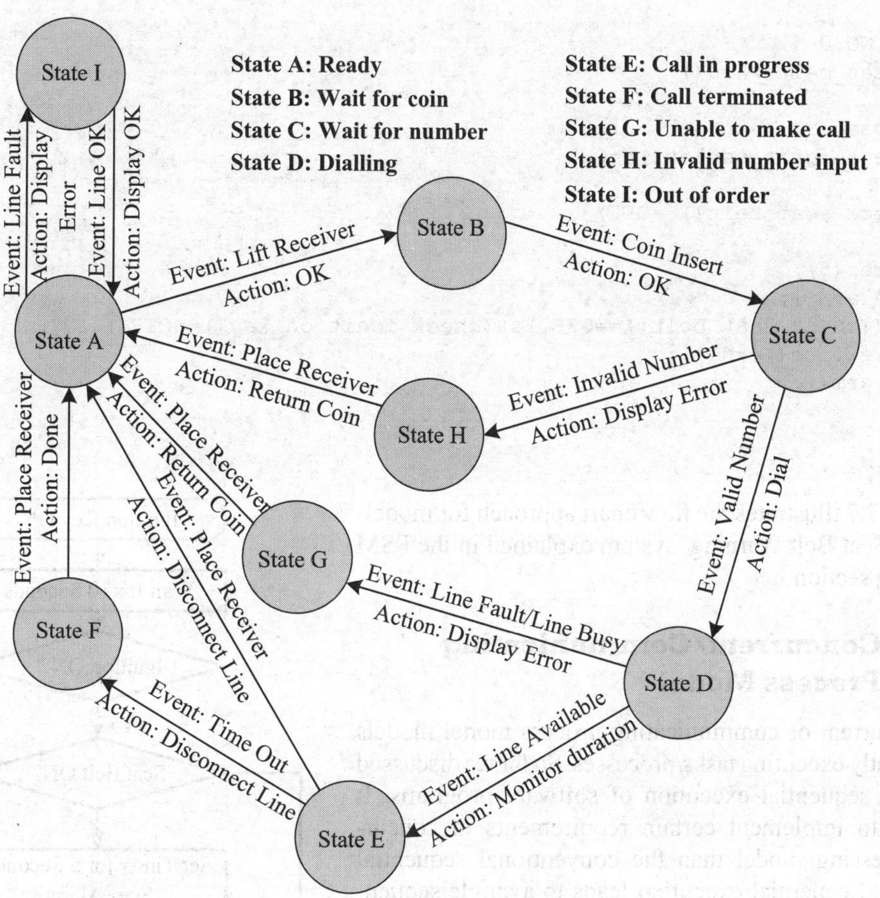

Fig. 7.6 **FSM Model for Coin Operated Telephone System**

basis the state transition happens at the occurrence of the specified event. Lots of design tools are available for state machine and statechart based system modelling. The IAR *visualSTATE* (http://www.iar.com/website1/1.0.1.0/371/1/index.php) from IAR systems is a popular visual modelling tool for embedded applications.

7.2.4 Sequential Program Model

In the sequential programming Model, the functions or processing requirements are executed in sequence. It is same as the conventional procedural programming. Here the program instructions are iterated and executed conditionally and the data gets transformed through a series of operations. FSMs are good choice for sequential program modelling. Another important tool used for modelling sequential program is Flow Charts. The FSM approach represents the states, events, transitions and actions, whereas the Flow Chart models the execution flow. The execution of functions in a sequential program model for the 'Seat Belt Warning' system is illustrated below.

```
#define ON 1
#define OFF 0
#define YES 1
```

```
#define NO 0
void seat_belt_warn()
{
wait_10sec();
if (check_ignition_key()==ON)
{
if (check_seat_belt()==OFF)
{
set_timer(5);
start_alarm();
while ((check_seat_belt()==OFF )&&(check_ignition_key()==OFF )&&
(timer_expire()==NO));
stop_alarm();
}
}
}
```

Figure 7.7 illustrates the flow chart approach for modelling the 'Seat Belt Warning' system explained in the FSM modelling section.

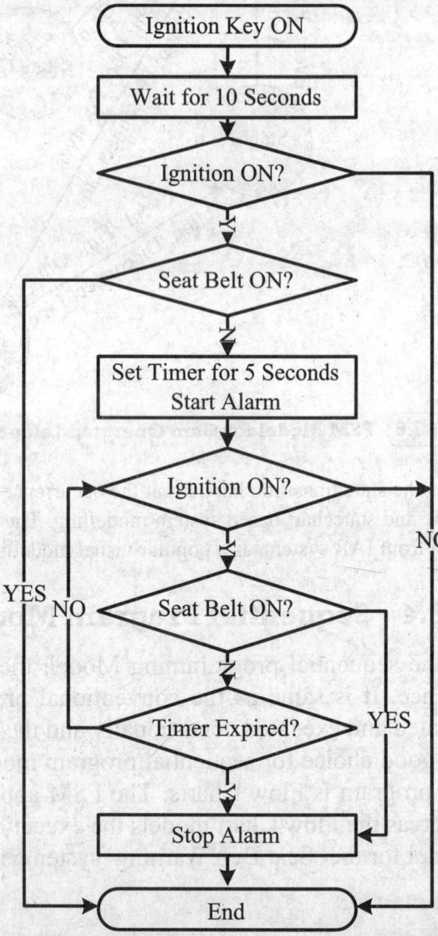

Fig. 7.7 **Sequential Program Model for seat belt warning system**

7.2.5 Concurrent/Communicating Process Model

The concurrent or communicating process model models concurrently executing tasks/processes. So far we discussed about the sequential execution of software programs. It is easier to implement certain requirements in concurrent processing model than the conventional sequential execution. Sequential execution leads to a single sequential execution of task and thereby leads to poor processor utilisation, when the task involves I/O waiting, sleeping for specified duration etc. If the task is split into multiple subtasks, it is possible to tackle the CPU usage effectively, when the subtask under execution goes to a wait or sleep mode, by switching the task execution. However, concurrent processing model requires additional overheads in task scheduling, task synchronisation and communication. As an example for the concurrent processing model let us examine how we can implement the 'Seat Belt Warning' system in concurrent processing model. We can split the tasks into:

1. Timer task for waiting 10 seconds (wait timer task)
2. Task for checking the ignition key status (ignition key status monitoring task)
3. Task for checking the seat belt status (seat belt status monitoring task)

4. Task for starting and stopping the alarm (alarm control task)
5. Alarm timer task for waiting 5 seconds (alarm timer task)

We have five tasks here and we cannot execute them randomly or sequentially. We need to synchronise their execution through some mechanism. We need to start the alarm only after the expiration of the 10 seconds wait timer and that too only if the seat belt is OFF and the ignition key is ON. Hence the alarm control task is executed only when the wait timer is expired and if the ignition key is in the ON state and seat belt is in the OFF state. Here we will use events to indicate these scenarios. The *wait_timer_expire* event is associated with the timer task event and it will be in the reset state initially and it is set when the timer expires. Similarly, events *ignition_on* and *ignition_off* are associated with the task ignition key status monitoring and the events *seat_belt_on* and *seat_belt_off* are associated with the task seat belt status morning. The events *ignition_off* and *ignition_on* are set and reset respectively when the ignition key status is OFF and reset and set respectively when the ignition key status is ON, by the ignition key status monitoring task. Similarly the events *seat_belt_off* and *seat_belt_on* are set and reset respectively when the seat belt status is OFF and reset and set respectively when the seat belt status is ON, by the seat belt status monitoring task. The events *alarm_timer_start* and *alarm_timer_expire* are associated with the alarm timer task. The *alarm_timer_start* event will be in the reset state initially and it is set by the alarm control task when the alarm is started. The *alarm_timer_expire* event will be in the reset state initially and it is set when the alarm timer expires. The alarm control task waits for the signaling of the event *wait_timer_expire* and starts the alarm timer and alarm if both the events *ignition_on* and *seat_belt_off* are in the set state when the event *wait_timer_expire* signals. If not the alarm control task simply completes its execution and returns. In case the alarm is started, the alarm control task waits for the signalling of any one of the events *alarm_timer_expire* or *ignition_off* or *seat_belt_on*. Upon signalling any one of these events, the alarm is stopped and the alarm control task simply completes its execution and returns. Figure 7.8 illustrates the same.

It should be noted that the method explained here is just one way of implementing a concurrent model for the 'Seat Belt Warning' system. The intention is just to make the readers familiar with the concept of multi tasking and task communication/synchronisation. There may be other ways to model the same requirements. It is left to the readers as exercise. The concurrent processing model is commonly used for the modelling of 'Real Time' systems. Various techniques like 'Shared memory', 'Message Passing', 'Events', etc. are used for communication and synchronising between concurrently executing processes. We will discuss these techniques in a later chapter.

7.2.6 Object-Oriented Model

The object-oriented model is an object based model for modelling system requirements. It disseminates a complex software requirement into simple well defined pieces called objects. Object-oriented model brings re-usability, maintainability and productivity in system design. In the object-oriented modelling, object is an entity used for representing or modelling a particular piece of the system. Each object is characterised by a set of unique behaviour and state. A class is an abstract description of a set of objects and it can be considered as a 'blueprint' of an object. A class represents the state of an object through member variables and object behaviour through member functions. The member variables and member functions of a class can be private, public or protected. Private member variables and functions are accessible only within the class, whereas public variables and functions are accessible within the class as well as outside the class. The protected variables and functions are protected from external access. However classes derived from a parent class can also access the protected member functions and variables. The concept of object and class brings abstraction, hiding and protection.

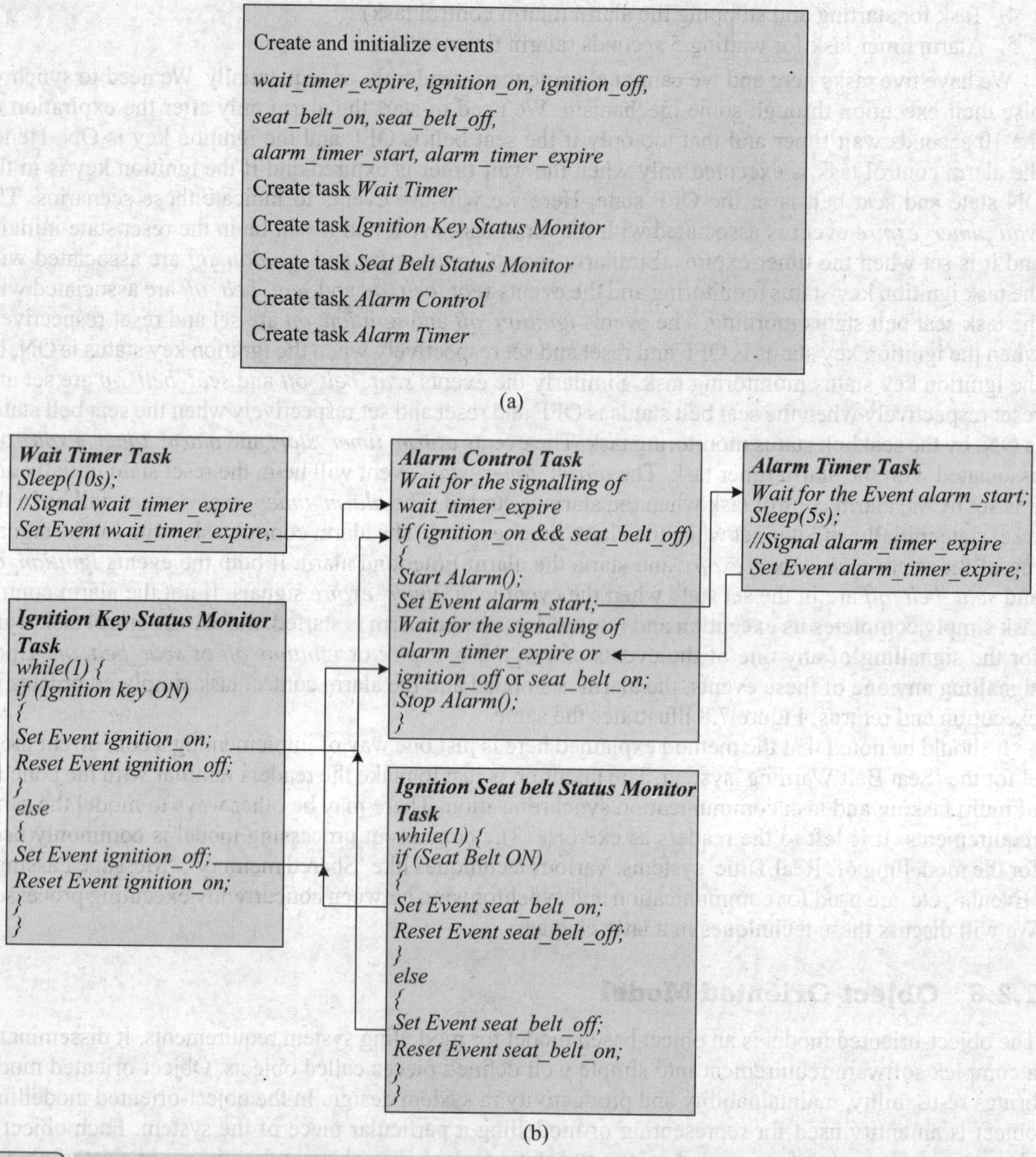

Fig. 7.8 **(a) Tasks for 'Seat Belt Warning System' (b) Concurrent processing Program model for 'Seat Belt Warning System'**

7.3 INTRODUCTION TO UNIFIED MODELLING LANGUAGE (UML)

Unified Modelling Language (UML) is a visual modelling language for Object Oriented Design (OOD). UML helps in all phases of system design through a set of unique diagrams for requirements capturing, designing and deployment.

7.3.1 UML Building Blocks

'Things', 'Relationships' and 'Diagrams' are the fundamental building blocks of UML.

7.3.1.1 Things A 'Thing' is an abstraction of the UML model. The 'Things' in UML are classified into:

Structural things: Represents mostly the static parts of a UML model. They are also known as 'classifiers'. Class, interface, use case, use case realisation (collaboration), active class, component and node are the structural things in UML.

Behavioural things: Represents mostly the dynamic parts of a UML model. Interaction, state machine and activity are the behavioural things in UML.

Grouping things: Are the organisational parts of a UML model. Package and sub-system are the grouping things in UML.

Annotational things: Are the explanatory parts of a UML model. *Note* is the Annotational thing in UML.

The table given below gives a snapshot of various structural, behavioural, grouping and Annotational things in UML.

Thing	Element	Description	Representation
	Class	A template describing a set of objects which share the same attributes, relationships, operations and semantics. It can be considered as a blueprint of object.	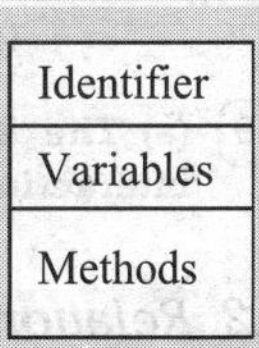 Identifier / Variables / Methods
Structural	Active Class	Class presenting a thread of control in the system. It can initiate control activity. Active class is represented in the same way as that of a class but with thick border lines.	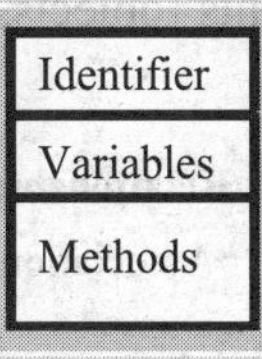 Identifier / Variables / Methods
	Interface	A collection of externally visible operations which specify a service of a class. It is represented as a circle attached to the class	
	Use case	Defines a set of sequence of actions. It is normally represented with an ellipse indicating the name.	 Name
	Collaboration (Use case Realisation)	Interaction diagram specifying the collaboration of different use cases. It is normally represented with a dotted ellipse indicating the name.	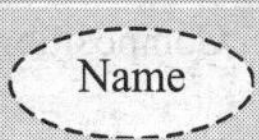 Name
	Component	Physical packaging of classes and interfaces.	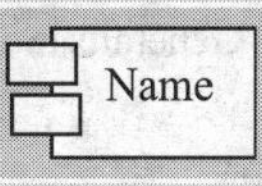 Name
	Node	A computational resource existing at run time. Represented using a cube with name.	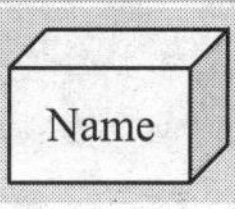 Name

Behavioural	Interaction	Behaviour comprising a set of objects exchanging messages to accomplish a specific purpose. Represented by arrow with name of operation	Name →
	State Machine	Behaviour specifying the sequence of states in response to events, through which an object traverses during its lifetime.	Name
Grouping	Package	Organises elements into packages. It is only a conceptual thing. Represented as a tabbed folder with name.	Name
Annotational	Note	Explanatory element in UML models. Contains formal informal explanatory text. May also contain embedded image.	Text

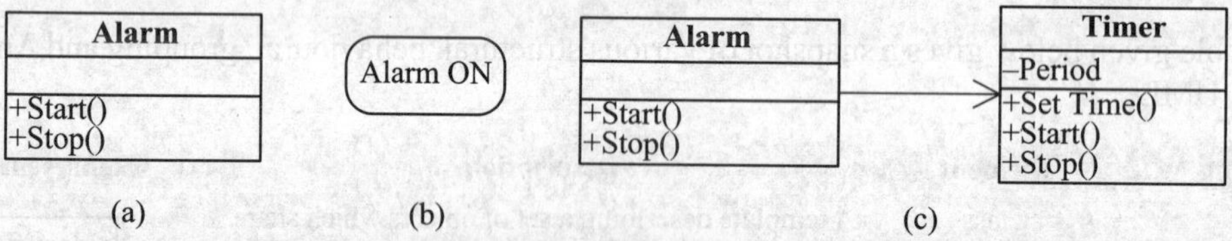

Fig. 7.9 **(a) The Alarm Class. (b) State Representation for 'Alarm ON' state. (c) Alarm – Timer Class interaction for the Seat belt Warning System**

7.3.1.2 Relationships As the name indicates, they express the type of relationship between UML elements (objects, classes, etc). The table given below gives a snapshot of the various relationships in UML.

Relationship	Description	Representation
Association	It is a structural relationship describing the link between objects. The association can be one-to-one or one-to-many. Aggregation and Composition are the two variants of Association.	relationship →
Aggregation	It represents is "a part of" relationship. Represented by a line with a hollow diamond at the end.	a part of ——◇
Composition	Aggregation with strong ownership relation to represent the component of a complex object. Represented by a line with a solid diamond at the end.	——◆
Generalisation	Represents a parent-child relationship. The parent may be more generalised and child being specialised version of the parent object.	Child → Parent

Dependency	Represents a relationship in which one element (object, class) uses or depends on another element (object, class). Represented by a dotted arrow with head pointing to the dependent element.	- - - - - - - - - ->
Realisation	The relationship between two elements in which one element realises the behaviour specified by the other element.	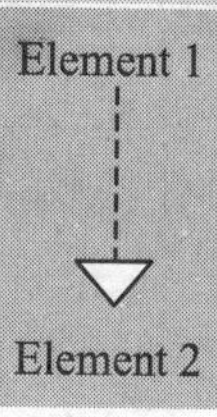

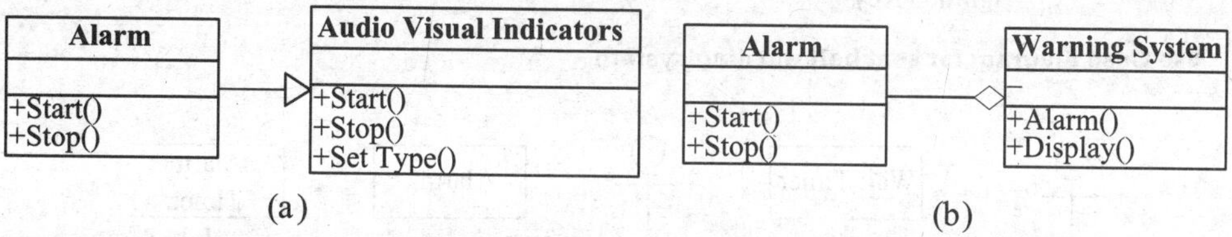

Fig. 7.10 (a) Alarm is a special type of Audio Visual Indicator (Generalisation), (b) Alarm is a part of Warning System (Aggregation)

7.3.1.3 UML Diagrams UML Diagrams give a pictorial representation of the static aspects, behavioural aspects and organisation and management of different modules (classes, packages, etc.) of the system. UML diagrams are grouped into Static Diagrams and Behavioural Diagrams.

Static Diagrams Diagram representing the static (structural) aspects of the system. Class Diagram, Object Diagram, Component Diagram, Package Diagram, Composite Structure Diagram and Deployment Diagram falls under this category. The table given below gives a snapshot of various static diagrams.

Diagram	Description
Object diagram	Gives a pictorial representation of a set of objects and their relationships. It represents the structural organisation between objects.
Class diagram	Gives a pictorial representation of the different classes in a UML model, their interfaces, the collaborations, interactions and relationship between the classes, etc. It captures the static design of the system.
Component diagram	It is a pictorial representation of the implementation view of a system. It comprises components (physical packaging of classes and interfaces), relationships and associations among the components.
Package diagram	It is a representation of the organisation of packages and their elements. Package diagrams are mostly used for organising use case diagrams and class diagrams.
Deployment diagram	It is a pictorial representation of the configuration of run time processing nodes and the components associated with them.

Behavioural Diagrams These are diagrams representing the dynamic (behavioural) aspects of the system. Use Case Diagram (Fig. 7.11), Sequence Diagram (Fig. 7.12), State Diagram, Communication

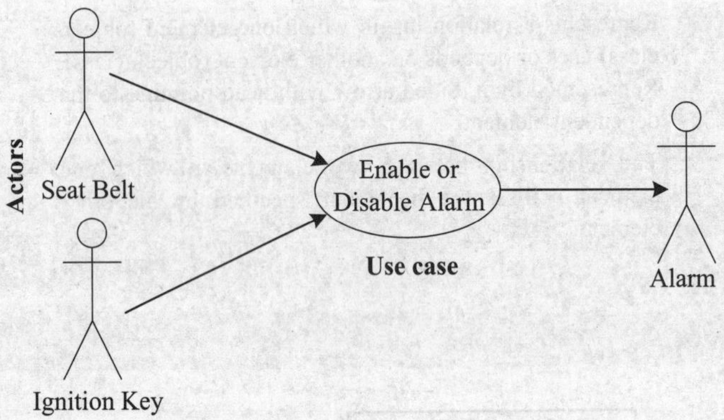

Fig. 7.11 **Use Case diagram for seat belt warning system**

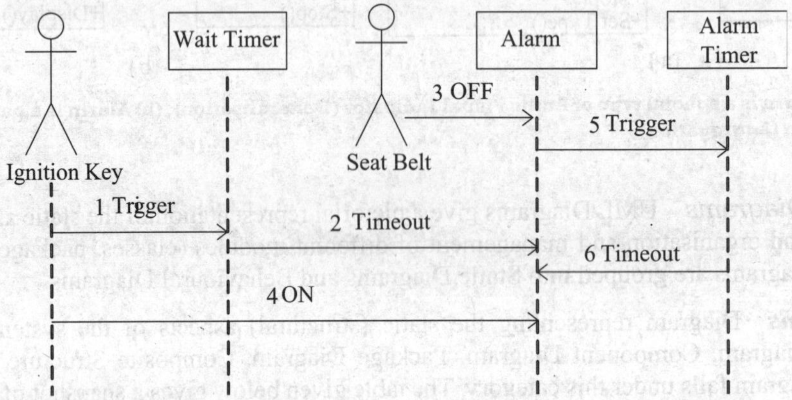

Fig. 7.12 **Sequence diagram for one possible sequence for the seat belt warning system**

Diagram, Activity Diagram, Timing Diagram and Interaction Overview Diagram are the behavioural diagrams in UML model. The table given below gives a snapshot of the important behavioural diagrams.

Diagram	Description
Use Case diagram	Use Case diagrams are used for capturing system functionality as seen by users. It is very useful in system requirements capturing. Use case diagram comprise use cases, *actors* (users) and the relationship between them. In use case diagram, an *actor* is one (or something) who (or which) interacts with the system and use case is the sequence of interaction between the actor and system.
Sequence diagram	Sequence diagram is a type of interaction diagram representing object interactions with respect to time. It emphasises on the time ordering of messages. Best suited for the interaction modelling of real-time systems.
Collaboration (Communication) diagram	Collaboration or Communication diagram is a type of interaction diagram representing the object interaction and 'how they are linked together'. It gives emphasis to the structural organisation of objects that send and receive messages. In short, it represents the collaboration of objects using messages.

State Chart diagram	A diagram showing the states, transitions, events and activities similar to a state machine representation. Best suited for modelling reactive systems.
Activity diagram	It is a special type of state chart diagram showing activity to activity transition in place of state transition. It emphasises on the flow control among objects.

7.3.2 The UML Tools

The tools for building UML based models and diagrams are available from different vendors. Some of them are commercial and some of them are either free or open source. The table given below gives a summary of the popular UML modelling tools.

Tool	Provider/Comments
Rational Rose Enterprise	IBM Software (http://www-01.ibm.com/software/awdtools/developer/rose/enterprise/index.html)
Rational System Developer	Eclipse† based tool from IBM Software (http://www-01.ibm.com/software/awdtools/developer/systemsdeveloper/index.html)
Telelogic Rhapsody	UML/SysML-based model-driven development tool for real-time or embedded systems from IBM Software (http://www-01.ibm.com/software/awdtools/rhapsody/)
Borland® Together®	Borland (www.borland.com)
Enterprise Architect	Sparx Systems (http://www.sparxsystems.com)
ARTiSAN Studio	Artisan Software Tools Inc (http://www.artisansoftwaretools.com/)
Microsoft® Visio	Microsoft Corporation. The Microsoft Visio (Part of Microsoft® Office product) supports UML model Diagram generation. www.microsoft.com/office/visio

Some of the tools generate the skeletal code (stub) for the classes and application in programming languages like C++, C#, Java, etc.

7.4 HARDWARE SOFTWARE TRADE-OFFS

Certain system level processing requirements may be possible to develop in either hardware or software. The decision on which one to opt is based on the trade-offs and actual system requirement. For example, if the embedded system under consideration involves some multimedia codec‡ requirement. The media codec can be developed in either software or using dedicated hardware chip (like ASIC or ASSP). Here the trade-off is performance and re-configurability. A codec developed in hardware may be much more efficient, optimised with low processing and power requirements. It is possible to develop the same codec in software using algorithm. But the software implementation need not be optimised for performance, speed and power efficiency. On the other hand, a codec developed in software is re-usable and re-configurable. With certain modification it can be configured for other codec implementations, whereas a codec developed in a fixed hardware (like ASIC/ASSP) is fixed and it cannot be changed.

Memory size is another important hardware software trade-off. Evaluate how much memory is required if the system requirement under consideration is implemented in software (firmware). Embedded systems are highly memory constrained and embedded designers don't have the luxury of using lavish

† Eclipse is an open source Integrated Development Environment (IDE). Visit www.eclipse.org for more details.

‡ Multimedia codec is a compression and de-compression algorithm for compressing and de-compression of raw data media files (audio and video data)

memory for implementing requirements. On the other hand, evaluate the gate count required (Normally hardware chips are implemented using logic gates and the density of the chip is expressed in terms of the number of gates used in the design (millions of gates ☺)), if the required feature is going to implement in hardware.

Effort required in terms of man hours, if the required feature is going to build in either software or custom hardware implementation using VHDL or any other hardware description languages and the cost for each are another important hardware-software trade-off in any embedded system development.

To summarise, the important hardware-software trade-offs in embedded system design are

1. Processing speed and performance
2. Frequency of change (Re-configurability)
3. Memory size and gate count
4. Reliability
5. Man hours (Effort) and cost

Summary

- ✓ Model selection, Architecture selection, Language selection, Hardware Software partitioning, etc. are some of the main points in the hardware-software co-design
- ✓ A model captures and describes the system characteristics. The architecture specifies how a system is going to implement in terms of the number and types of different components and the interconnection among them
- ✓ Controller architecture, Datapath architecture, Complex Instruction Set Computing (CISC), Reduced Instruction Set Computing (RISC), Very long Instruction Word Computing (VLIW), Single Instruction Multiple Data (SIMD), Multiple Instruction Multiple Data (MIMD), etc. are the commonly used architectures in system design
- ✓ Data Flow Graph (DFG) Model, State Machine Model, Concurrent Process Model, Sequential Program model, Object Oriented model, etc. are the commonly used computational models in embedded system design
- ✓ A programming language captures a 'Computational Model' and maps it into architecture. A model can be captured using multiple programming languages like C, C++, C#, Java, etc. for software implementations and languages like VHDL, System C, Verilog, etc. for hardware implementations
- ✓ The Hierarchical/Concurrent Finite State Machine Model (HCFSM) is an extension of the FSM for supporting concurrency and hierarchy. HCFSM extends the conventional state diagrams by the AND, OR decomposition of States together with inter level transitions and a broadcast mechanism for communicating between concurrent processes
- ✓ HCFSM uses statecharts for capturing the states, transitions, events and actions. The Harel Statechart, UML State diagram, etc. are examples for popular statecharts for the HCFSM modelling of embedded systems
- ✓ In the sequential model, the functions or processing requirements are executed in sequence. It is same as the conventional procedural programming
- ✓ The concurrent or communicating process model models concurrently executing tasks/processes
- ✓ The object oriented model is an object based model for modelling system requirements
- ✓ Unified Modelling Language (UML) is a visual modelling language for Object Oriented Design (OOD). Things, Relationships and Diagrams are the fundamental building blocks of UML
- ✓ UML diagrams give a pictorial representation of the static aspects, behavioural aspects and organisation and management of different modules. Static Diagrams, Object diagram, Usecase diagram, Sequence diagram, Statechart diagram etc. are the different UML diagrams
- ✓ Hardware-Software trade-offs are the parameters used in the decision making of partitioning a system requirement into either hardware or software. Processing speed, performance, frequency of changes, memory size and gate count requirements, reliability, effort, cost, etc. are examples for hardware-software trade-offs

Keywords

Hardware-Software Co-design	: The modern approach for the interactive 'together' design of hardware and firmware for embedded systems
Controller Architecture	: Architecture implementing the Finite State Machine model using a state register and two combinational circuits
Datapath Architecture Datapath	: Architecture implementing the Data Flow Graph model
	: A channel between the input and output. The datapath may contain registers, counters, register files, memories and ports along with high speed arithmetic units
Finite State Machine Datapath (FSMD) Architecture	: Architecture combining the controller architecture with datapath architecture
Complex Instruction Set Computing (CISC) Architecture	: Architecture which uses instruction set representing complex operations
Reduced Instruction Set Computing (RISC) Architecture	: Architecture which uses instruction set representing simple operations
Very Long Instruction Word (VLIW) Architecture	: Architecture implementing multiple functional units (ALUs, multipliers, etc.) in the datapath
Parallel Processing Architecture	: Architecture implementing multiple concurrent Processing Elements (PEs)
Single Instruction Multiple Data (SIMD) Architecture	: Architecture in which a single instruction is executed in parallel with the help of the processing elements
MIMD Architecture	: Architecture in which the processing elements execute different instructions at a given point of time
Programming Language	: An entity for capturing a 'Computational Model' and maps it into architecture
Data Flow Graph (DFG) Model	: A data driven model in which the program execution is determined by data
Control DFG (CDFG) Model	: A model containing both data operations and control operations. The CDFG uses Data Flow Graph (DFG) as element and conditional (constructs) as decision makers
State Machine Model	: A model describing the system behaviour with 'States', 'Events', 'Actions' and 'Transitions'
Statechart	: An entity for capturing the states, transitions, events and actions
Harel Statechart	: A type of statechart
Finite State Machine (FSM) Model	: A state machine model with finite number of states
Hierarchical/Concurrent Finite State Machine Model (HCFSM)	: An extension of the FSM for supporting concurrency and hierarchy
Sequential Model	: Model for capturing sequential processing requirements
Concurrent or Communicating Process Model	: Model for capturing concurrently executing tasks/process requirements
Object Oriented Model	: Object based model for modelling system requirements
Unified Modelling Language (UML)	: A visual modelling language for Object Oriented Design
UML Diagram	: Diagram giving a pictorial representation of the static aspects, behavioural aspects and organisation and management of different modules

Static Diagram	: UML diagram representing the static (structural) aspects of the system
Behavioural Diagram	: UML diagram representing the dynamic (behavioural) aspects of the system
Object Diagram	: Static UML diagram giving the pictorial representation of objects and their relationships
Class Diagram	: Static UML diagram showing the pictorial representation of the different classes in a UML model, their interfaces, the collaborations, interactions and relationship between classes, etc.
Usecase Diagram	: Behavioural UML diagram for capturing system functionality as seen by users
Sequence Diagram	: Behavioural UML diagram representing object interactions with respect to time
Statechart Diagram	: Behavioural UML diagram showing the states, transitions, events and activities similar to a state machine representation
Hardware-Software trade-offs	: The parameters used in the decision making of partitioning a system requirement into either hardware or software

Objective Questions

1. Which of the following programming model is best suited for modelling a data driven embedded system
   (a) State Machine (b) Data Flow Graph (c) Harel Statechart Model
   (d) None of these
2. Which of the following programming model is best suited for modelling a Digital Signal Processing (DSP) embedded system
   (a) Finite State Machine (b) Data Flow Graph (c) Object Oriented Model
   (d) UML
3. Which of the following architecture is best suited for implementing a Digital Signal Processing (DSP) embedded system
   (a) Controller Architecture (b) CISC (c) Datapath Architecture (d) None of these
4. Which of the following is a multiprocessor architecture?
   (a) SIMD (b) MIMD (c) VLIW (d) All
   (e) (a) and (b) (f) (b) and (c)
5. Which of the following model is best suited for modelling a reactive embedded system?
   (a) Finite State Machine (FSM) (b) DFG (c) Control DFG
   (d) Object Oriented Model
6. Which of the following models is best suited for modelling a reactive real time embedded system?
   (a) Finite State Machine (b) DFG (c) Control DFG
   (d) Hierarchical/Concurrent Finite State Machine Model
7. Which of the following model is best suited for modelling an embedded system demanding multitasking capabilities with data sharing?
   (a) Finite State Machine (b) DFG (c) Control DFG
   (d) Communicating Process Model
8. Which of the following is a hardware description language?
   (a) C (b) System C (c) VHDL (d) C++
   (e) (b) and (c)

9. Which of the following is a structural thing in UML?
   (a) Class (b) Interaction (c) State Machine (d) Activity
   (e) None of these
10. Which of the following is a behavioural thing in UML?
   (a) Class (b) Interface (c) State Machine (d) Component
   (e) None of these
11. Which of the following is not a static diagram in UML?
   (a) Class Diagram (b) Object Diagram (c) Use case Diagram (d) Component Diagram
   (e) None of these
12. Which of the following is not a behavioural diagram in UML?
   (a) State Diagram (b) Object Diagram (c) Use case Diagram (d) Sequence Diagram
   (e) None of these
13. Which of the following UML diagrams is best suited for Requirements Capturing?
   (a) State Diagram (b) Use case Diagram (c) Object Diagram (d) Sequence Diagram
   (e) None of these
14. Which of the following UML diagram represents object interactions with respect to time?
   (a) State Diagram (b) Sequence Diagram (c) Object Diagram (d) Use case Diagram
   (e) None of these
15. Which of the following UML interaction diagram(s) emphasises on structural organisation of objects?
   (a) Collaboration Diagram (b) Sequence Diagram (c) State Diagram (d) Use case Diagram
   (e) None of these
16. Which of the following is (are) trade-offs in hardware software partitioning?
   (a) Processing speed (b) Memory requirement (c) Cost (d) All of these
   (e) None of these

Review Questions

1. What is hardware software co-design? Explain the fundamental issues in hardware software co-design
2. Explain the difference between SIMD, MIMD and VLIW architecture
3. What is Computational model? Explain its role in hardware software co-design
4. Explain the different computational models in embedded system design
5. What is the difference between Data Flow Graph (DFG) and Control Data Flow Graph (CDFG) model? Explain their significance in embedded system design
6. What is State and State Machine? Explain the role of State Machine in embedded system design
7. What is the difference between Finite State Machine Model (FSM) and Hierarchical/Concurrent Finite State Machine Model (HCFSM)?
8. What is 'Statechart'? Explain its role in embedded system design
9. Explain the 'Sequential' Program model with an example
10. Explain the 'Concurrent/Communicating' program model. Explain its role in 'Real Time' system design
11. Explain the 'Object-Oriented' program model for embedded system design. Under which circumstances an Object-Oriented model is considered as the best suited model for embedded system design?
12. Explain the role of programming languages in system design
13. What are the building blocks of UML? Explain in detail.
14. Explain the different types of UML diagrams and their significance in each stage of the system development life cycle
15. Explain the important hardware software 'trade-offs' in hardware software partitioning?

Lab Assignments

1. Draw the Data Flow Graph (DFG) model for the FIR filter implementation $y[n] = a0 \times [n] + a1 \times [n-1] + a2 \times [n-2] + a3 \times [n-3] + \ldots + a(n-1) \times [1]$
2. Draw the sequence diagram for the automatic coffee vending machine using UML
3. Model the following automatic teller machine (ATM) requirement using UML statecharts.
   (a) The transaction is started by user inserting a valid ATM card
   (b) Upon detecting the card, the system prompts for a Personal Identification Number (PIN).
   (c) The card is validated against the PIN and on successful validation, the system displays the following options: 'Balance Enquiry', 'Cash Withdrawal' and 'Cancel'
   (d) If the user selects 'Cash Withdrawal', the system prompts for entering the amount to withdraw and upon entering the amount it asks whether a printed receipt is required for the transaction. Upon receiving an input for this, the system verifies the available balance, deduct the amount to withdraw, dispense the cash, prints the transaction receipt (if the user answer to the system query 'whether a printed receipt is required for the transaction' is 'YES') and returns back to the original state to accept a new transaction request.
   (e) If the user selects the option 'Balance Enquiry' in step 'c', the system prompts the message whether a printed receipt is required for the transaction. If user response is 'YES', the balance is printed and the system returns to the original state to accept new transaction request. If the user input is 'NO' to the query 'whether a printed receipt is required for the transaction', the balance amount is displayed on the screen for 30 seconds and the system returns back to the original state to accept a new transaction request.
   (f) If the user selects the option 'Cancel' in step 'c', the system returns back to the original state to accept a new transaction request.
   (g) If there is no response from the user for a period of 30 seconds in steps 'b', 'c', 'd' and 'e' and if the time interval between the two consecutive digit entering for the PIN exceeds 30 seconds, the system displays the message 'User Failed to Respond within the specified Time' for 10 seconds and returns back to the original state to accept a new transaction request.

PART 2

DESIGN AND DEVELOPMENT OF EMBEDDED PRODUCT

I hope by now you got a reasonably good knowledge on embedded systems, the different elements of an embedded system, their application areas and domains, their characteristics and quality attributes. Now it is time to move on to the various steps involved in the design of embedded systems. As mentioned in Chapter 2 of the previous section, embedded systems are built around a central core which can be a Commercial-off-the-Shelf Component (COTS) or an Application Specific Integrated Circuit/Application Specific Standard Product (ASIC/ASSP) or a Programmable Logic Device (PLD) or a General Purpose Processor (Microprocessor/General Purpose Microcontrollers) or Application Specific Instruction Set Processors (Special Purpose Microcontrollers/Digital Signal Processors). Describing all of them in detail is outside the scope of this book and for the time being we will be dealing with the design of embedded systems using Application Specific Instruction Set Processor and the scope of this design is again limited to designing with Microcontroller. The target microcontroller selected for the design approach is *8051* - Industry's most popular 8bit microcontroller. The architecture details of the basic *8051* controller and the instructions supported by it are already explained in some of the previous chapters. In the next sections we will explore the possibilities of how the *8051* controller can be embedded into different applications and how the *8051* can be programmed for various embedded applications.

The embedded product design starts with product requirements specification and analysis. When a requirement arises for an embedded product, the requirements are listed out including the hardware features required, the functionalities to be supported, the product aesthetics (look '*n*' feel) etc. On finalising the requirements, the various hardware components and peripherals required to implement the hardware features are identified and the interconnection among them are defined, the control algorithm for controlling the various hardware and peripherals are developed, product aesthetics like look and feel, enclosure unit, etc. are defined and the control algorithm is transformed to controller specific instructions using the firmware development tools and finally the hardware and firmware are integrated together and the resulting product is tested for the required functionalities as per the requirement specifications. The mechanical design of the product takes care of the product aesthetics and develops a suitable enclosure for the product. Various standards like International Organisation for Standards (ISO) and models like Capability Maturity Model (CMM), Process Capability Maturity Model (PCMM) etc. are used in the entire design life cycle management. There will be well-defined documentation structure (Templates) for the entire design life cycle. The Requirement Specification Document records the entire requirement for the product. Formal verifications of this document will be carried out before the system design starts and it is termed as "Document Reviews". Once the requirement specifications are finalised the preliminary design and detailed designs are carried out. The preliminary design and detailed design deals with the different modules of the total system and what all hardware/firmware components are required to build these modules, how these modules are interconnected and how they are controlled..

The chapters in this section are organised in a way to give the readers the basic lessons on "Embedded Hardware Design and Development", "Embedded Firmware Design and Development", "Integration and testing of the Embedded Hardware and Firmware", "Product Enclosure Development" and Embedded Product Development Life Cycle Management". We will start the section with Embedded Hardware Design and Development.

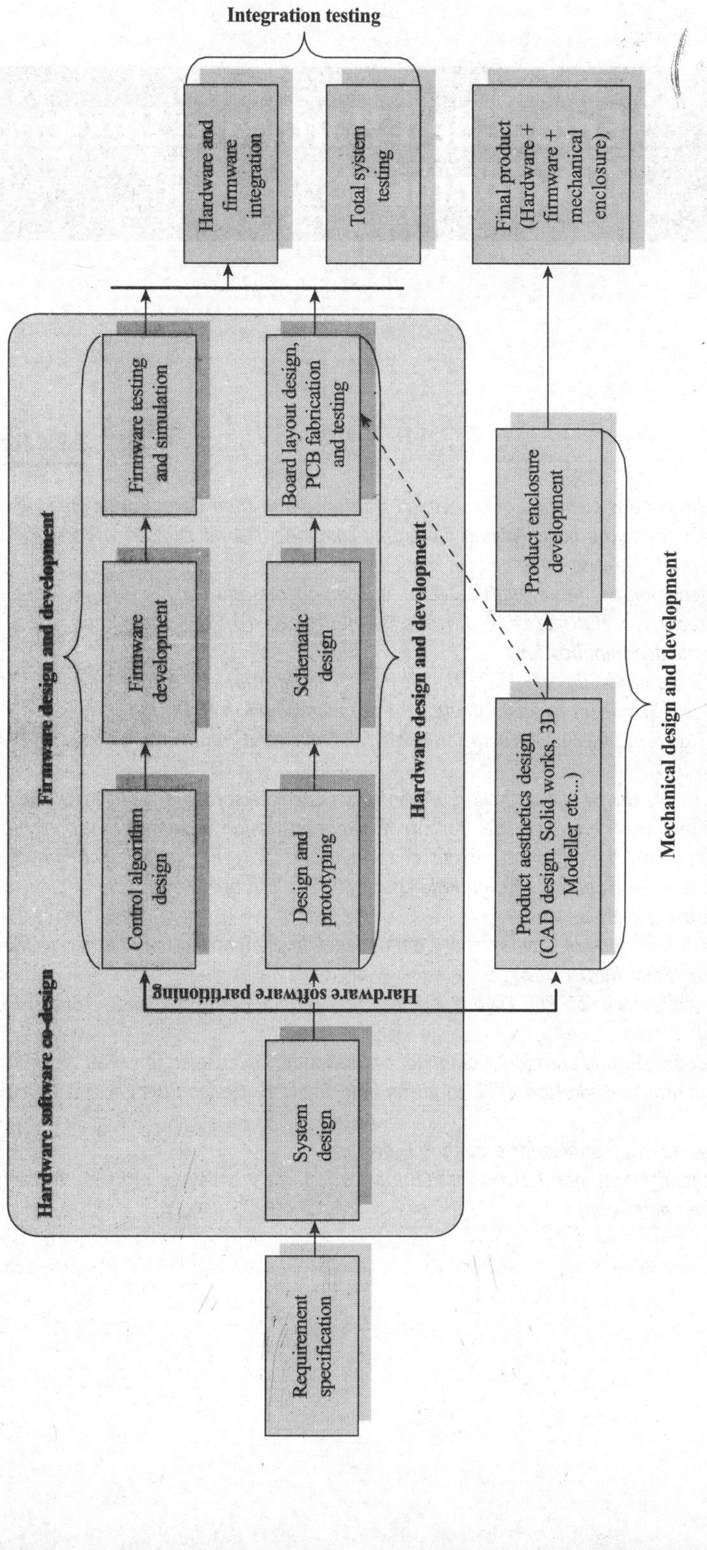

Typical Embedded product design and development approach

8 Embedded Hardware Design and Development

LEARNING OBJECTIVES

- ✓ Learn about the various elements of Embedded Hardware and their design principles
- ✓ Refresh knowledge on the basic Analog Electronic components and circuits – Resistor, Capacitor, Diode, Inductor, Transistor etc. and their use in embedded applications
- ✓ Refresh knowledge on the basic Digital Electronic components and circuits – Logic Gates, Buffer ICs, Latch ICs, Decoder and Encoder ICs, Multiplexer (MUX) and De-multiplexer (D-MUX), Combinational and Sequential Circuits and their use in embedded applications
- ✓ Learn about Integrated Circuits (ICs), the degree of integration in various types of Integrated Circuits, Analog, Digital and Mixed Signal Integrated Circuits, the steps involved in IC Design
- ✓ Learn about Electronic Design Automation tools for Embedded Hardware Design and EDA tools for Printed Circuit Board Design
- ✓ Familiarise with the usage of the Orcad EDA tool from Cadence software for Printed Circuit Board Design
- ✓ Familiarise with the different entities for circuit diagram design (schematic design) using the Orcad CaptureCIS tool. Familiarise with the different entities of the Capture CIS tool like 'Drawing Canvas', 'Drawing Tool', 'Drawing Details', 'Part Number creation', 'Design Rule Check (DRC)', 'Bill of Material (BoM)' creation, 'Netlist file creation for PCB blueprint design, etc.
- ✓ Familiarise with the usage of 'Layout' tool from Cadence for generating the PCB design files from the circuit diagram description file (From Netlist file)
- ✓ Learn the building blocks of 'PCB Layout' – Footprints (Component Packages), Routes/Traces, Layers, Via, Marking text and graphics, etc.
- ✓ Learn about Board Outline creation, Component placement, Layer selection, PCB Track Routing, Assembly note creation, Text and graphics addition, PCB Mounting hole creation, Design Rule Checking, Gerber file creation, etc. using Layout tool
- ✓ Learn the important guidelines for a good PCB design
- ✓ Learn about the different mechanisms for PCB fabrication, different types of PCBs, How a finished PCB looks like and how it is made operational

As mentioned at the beginning of this book, an embedded system is a combination of special purpose hardware and software (firmware). The hardware of embedded system is built around analog electronic components and circuits, digital electronic components and circuits, and integrated circuits (ICs). A printed circuit board (PCB) provides a platform for placing all the necessary hardware components for building an embedded product, like a chess board where you can move the pawns, rookies and bishop. If you are building a simple hardware or a test product, you can use a bread-board to interconnect the various components. For a commercial product you cannot go for a bread-board as an interconnection platform since they make your product bulky and the breadboard connections are highly unstable and your product may require thousands of inter connections. Printed circuit boards (PCB) act as the backbone of embedded hardware. This chapter is organised in such a way to refresh the reader's knowledge on various analog and digital electronic components and circuits, familiarise them with Integrated Circuit designing and provide them the fundamentals of printed circuit boards, its design and development using electronic design automation (EDA) tools.

8.1 ANALOG ELECTRONIC COMPONENTS

Resistors, capacitors, diodes, inductors, operational amplifiers (OpAmps), transistors, etc. are the commonly used analog electronic components in embedded hardware design. A *resistor* limits the current flowing through a circuit. Interfacing of LEDs, buzzer, etc. with the port pins of microcontroller through current limiting resistors is a typical example for the usage of resistors in embedded application. *Capacitors* and *inductors* are used in signal filtering and resonating circuits. Reset circuit implementation, matching circuits for RF designs, power supply decoupling, etc. are examples for the usage of capacitors in embedded hardware circuit. Electrolytic capacitors, ceramic capacitors, tantalum capacitors, etc. are the commonly used capacitors in embedded hardware design. Inductors are widely used for filtering the power supply from ripples and noise signals. Inductors with inductance value in the *microhenry* (μH) range are commonly used in embedded applications for filter and matching circuit implementation.

P-N Junction diode, Schottky diode, Zener diode, etc. are the commonly used diodes in embedded hardware circuits. A schottky diode is same as a P-N junction diode except that its forward voltage drop (voltage drop across diode when conducting) is very low (of the order of 0.15V to 0.45) when compared to ordinary P-N junction diode (of the order of 0.7V to 1.7V). Also the current switching time of schottky diode is very small compared to the ordinary P-N junction diode. A zener diode acts as normal P-N junction diode when forward biased. It also permits current flow in the reverse direction, if the voltage is greater than the junction breakdown voltage. It is normally used for voltage clamping applications. Reverse polarity protection, voltage rectification (AC-DC converters), freewheeling of current produced in inductive circuits, clamping of voltages to a desired level (e.g., Brown-out protection circuit implementation using zener diode), etc. are examples for the usage of diodes in embedded applications.

Transistors in embedded applications are used for either switching or amplification purpose. In switching application, the transistor is in either ON or OFF state. In amplification operation, the transistor is always in the ON state (partially ON). The current is below saturation current value and the current through the transistor is variable. The common emitter configuration of NPN transistor is widely used in switching and driving circuits in embedded applications. Relay, buzzer and stepper motor driving circuits are examples for common emitter configuration based driver circuit implementation using transistor (Please refer to Chapter 2).

8.2 DIGITAL ELECTRONIC COMPONENTS

Digital electronics deal with digital or discrete signals. Microprocessors, microcontrollers and system on chips (SoCs) work on digital principles. They interact with the rest of the world through digital I/O interfaces and process digital data. Embedded systems employ various digital electronic circuits for 'Glue logic' implementation. 'Glue logic' is the custom digital electronic circuitry required to achieve compatible interface between two different integrated circuit chips. Address decoders, latches, encoders/decoders, etc. are examples for glue logic circuits. Transistor Transistor Logic (TTL), Complementary Metal Oxide Semiconductor (CMOS) logic etc are some of the standards describing the electrical characteristics of digital signals in a digital system. The following sections give an overview of the various digital I/O interface standards and the digital circuits/components used in embedded system development.

8.2.1 Open Collector and Tri-State Output

Open collector is an I/O interface standard in digital system design. The term 'open collector' is commonly used in conjunction with the output of an Integrated Circuit (IC) chip. It facilitates the interfacing of IC output to other systems which operate at different voltage levels. In the open collector configuration, the output line from an IC circuit is connected to the base of an NPN transistor. The collector of the transistor is left unconnected (floating) and the emitter is internally connected to the ground signal of IC. Figure 8.1 illustrates an open collector output configuration.

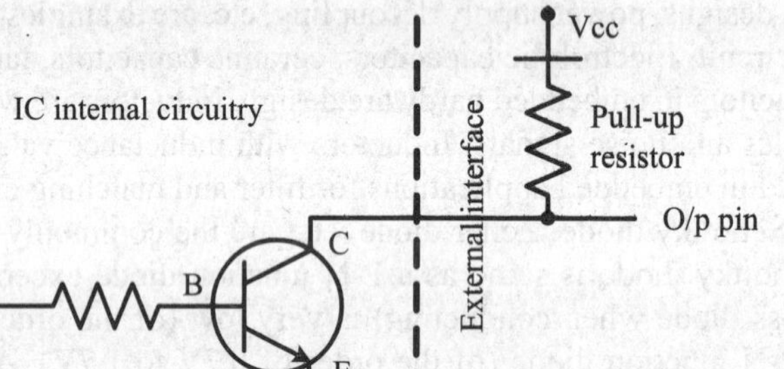

Fig. 8.1 **Open collector output configuration**

For the output pin to function properly, the output pin should be pulled, to the desired voltage for the o/p device, through a pull-up resistor. The output signal of the IC is fed to the base of an open collector transistor. When the base drive to the transistor is ON and the collector is in open state, the o/p pin floats. This state is also known as 'high impedance' state. Here the output is neither driven to logic 'high' nor logic 'low'. If a pull-up resistor is connected to the o/p pin, when the base drive is ON, the o/p pin becomes at logic 0 (0V). With a pull-up resistor, if the base driver is 0, the o/p will be at logic high (Voltage = V_{cc}). The advantage of open collector output in embedded system design is listed below.

1. It facilitates the interfacing of devices, operating at a voltage different from the IC, with the IC. Thereby, it eliminates the need for additional interface circuits for connecting devices at different voltage levels.

2. An open collector configuration supports multi-drop connection, i.e., connecting more than one open collector output to a single line. It is a common requirement in modern embedded systems supporting communication interfaces like I2C, 1-Wire, etc. Please refer to the various interfaces described in Chapter 2 under the section 'Onboard Communication Interfaces'.
3. It is easy to build 'Wired AND' and 'Wired OR' configuration using open collector output lines.

The output of a standard logic device has two states, namely 'Logic 0 (LOW)' and 'Logic 1 (HIGH), and the output will be at any one of these states at a given point of time, whereas tri-state devices have three states for the output, namely, 'Logic 0 (LOW)', 'Logic 1 (HIGH) and 'High Impedance (FLOAT)'. A tri-state logic device contains a device activation line called 'Device Enable'. When the 'Device Enable' line is activated (set at 'Logic 1' for an active 'HIGH' enable input and at 'Logic 0' for an active 'LOW' enable input), the device acts like a normal logic device and the output will be in any one of the logic conditions, 'Logic 0 (LOW)' or 'Logic 1 (HIGH)'. When the 'Device Enable' line is de-activated (set at 'Logic 0' for an active 'HIGH' enable input and at 'Logic 1' for an active 'LOW' enable input), the output of the logic device enters in a high impedance state and the device is said to be in the floating state. The tri-stated output condition produces the effect of 'removing' the device from a circuit and allows more than one devices to share a common bus. With multiple 'tri-stated' devices share a common bus, only one 'device' is allowed to drive the bus (drive the bus to either 'Logic 0' or 'Logic 1') at any given point of time and rest of the devices should be in the 'tri-stated' condition.

8.2.2 Logic Gates

Logic gates are the building blocks of digital circuits. Logic gates control the flow of digital information by performing a logical operation of the input signals. Depending on the logical operation, the logic gates used in digital design are classified into–AND, OR, XOR, NOT, NAND, NOR and XNOR. The logical relationship between the output signal and the input signals for a logic gate is represented using a *truth table*. Figure 8.2 illustrates the *truth table* and symbolic representation of each logic gate.

8.2.3 Buffer

A buffer circuit is a logic circuit for amplifying the current or power. It increases the driving capability of a logic circuit. A tri-state buffer is a buffer with *Output Enable* control. When the Output Enable control is active (Low for Active low enable and High for Active high enable), the tri-state buffer functions as a buffer. If the *Output Enable* is not active, the output of the buffer remains at high impedance state (Tri-stated). Tri-state buffers are commonly used as drivers for address bus and to select the required device among multiple devices connected to a shared data bus. Tri-state buffers are available as either unidirectional or bi-directional buffers. 74LS244/74HC244 is an example of unidirectional octal buffer. It contains 8 individual buffers which are grouped into two. Each buffer group has its own output enable line. Figure 8.3 illustrates the 74LS244 buffer device.

IC 74LS245 is an example of bi-directional tri-state buffer. It allows data flow in both directions, one at a time. The data flow direction can be set by the direction control line. One buffer is allocated for the data line associated with each direction. Figure 8.4 illustrates the 74LS245 octal bi-directional buffer.

8.2.4 Latch

A latch is used for storing binary data. It contains an input data line, clock or gating control line for triggering the latching operation and an output line. The gating signal can be either a positive edge (raising

AND Gate –Truth Table

I_1	I_2	O
0	0	0
0	1	0
1	0	0
1	1	1

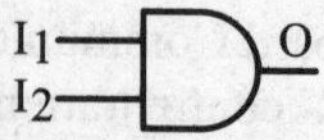

NAND Gate –Truth Table

I_1	I_2	O
0	0	1
0	1	1
1	0	1
1	1	0

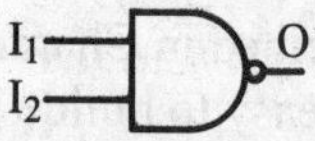

OR Gate –Truth Table

I_1	I_2	O
0	0	0
0	1	1
1	0	1
1	1	1

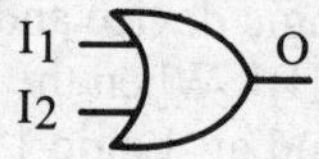

NOR Gate –Truth Table

I_1	I_2	O
0	0	1
0	1	0
1	0	0
1	1	0

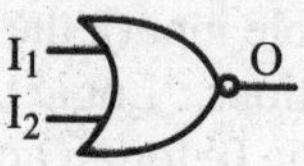

NOT Gate –Truth Table

I	O
0	1
1	0

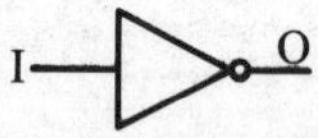

XOR Gate –Truth Table

I_1	I_2	O
0	0	0
0	1	1
1	0	1
1	1	0

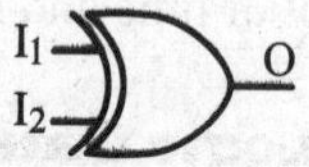

XNOR Gate –Truth Table

I_1	I_2	O
0	0	1
0	1	0
1	0	0
1	1	1

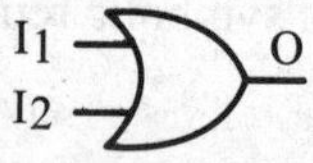

Fig. 8.2 **Logic Gates Truth Table and Symbolic representation**

edge) or a negative edge (falling edge). Whenever a latch trigger happens, the data present on the input line is latched. The latched data is available on the output line of the latch until the next trigger. D flip flop is a typical example of a latch (refer to your Digital Electronics course material—there exist different types of latches namely S-R, J-K, D, T, etc.). In electronic circuits, latches are commonly used for latching data, which is available only for a short duration. A typical example is the lower order address information in a multiplexed address-data bus system. Latches are available as integrated circuits, IC 74LS373 being a typical example. It contains 8 individual D latches.

The 74LS373 latch IC is commonly used for latching the lower order address byte in a multiplexed address data bus system. The address latch enable (ALE) pulse generated by the processor, when the address bits are available on the multiplexed bus, is used as the latch trigger. Figure 8.6 illustrates the usage of latches in address latching.

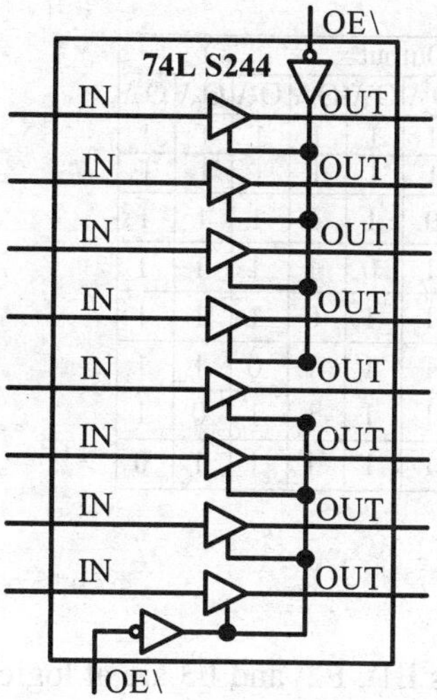

Fig. 8.3 **74LS244 Octal Buffer IC**

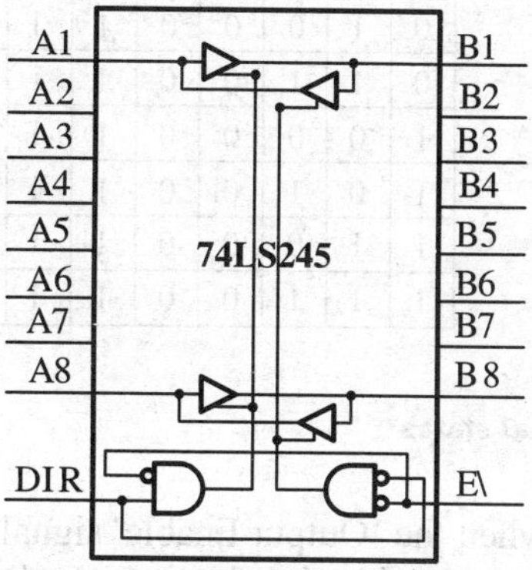

Fig. 8.4 **74LS245 Octal bidirectional Buffer IC**

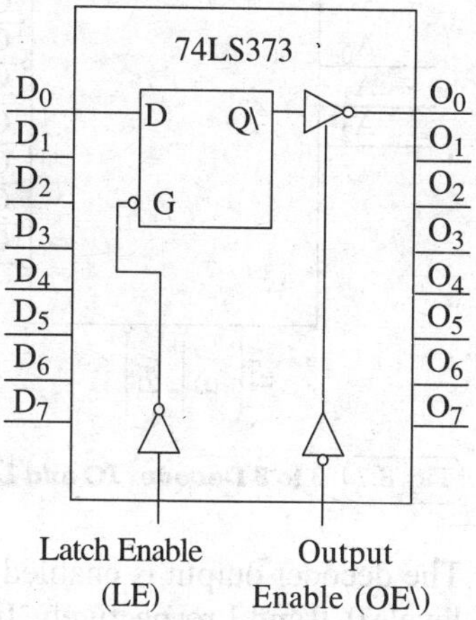

Fig. 8.5 **74LS373 Octal Latch IC**

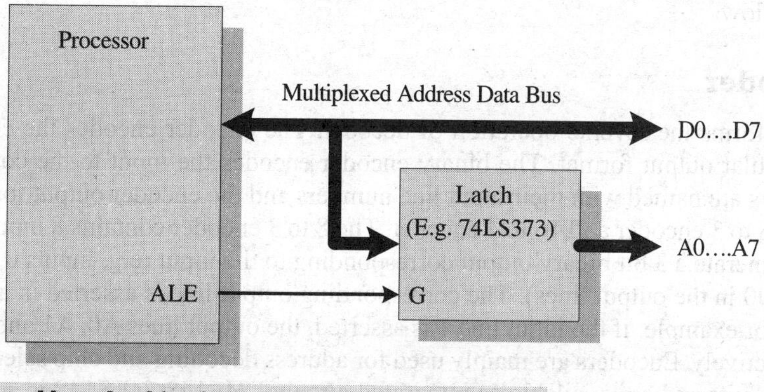

Fig. 8.6 **Latch IC for address latching in multiplexed address data-bus**

8.2.5 Decoder

A decoder is a logic circuit which generates all the possible combinations of the input signals. Decoders are named with their input line numbers and the possible combinations of the input as output. Examples are 2 to 4 decoder, 3 to 8 decoder and 4 to 16 decoder. The 3 to 8 decoder contains 3 input signal lines and it is possible to have 8 different configurations with the 3 lines (000 to 111 in the input line corresponds to 0 to 7 in the output line). Depending on the input signal, the corresponding output line is asserted. For example, for the input state 001, the output line 2 is asserted. Decoders are mainly used for address decoding and chip select signal generation in electronic circuits and are available as integrated circuits. 74LS138/74AHC138 is an example for 3 to 8 decoder IC. Figure 8.7 illustrates the 74AHC138 decoder and the function table for it.

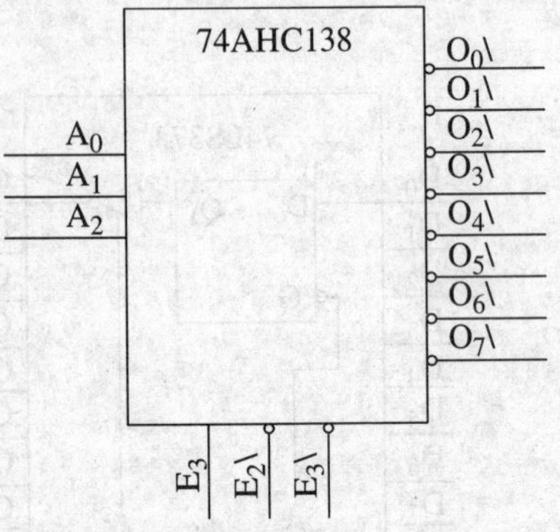

Input						Output							
A_2	A_1	A_0	E_1\	E_2\	E_3\	O_0\	O_1\	O_2\	O_3\	O_4\	O_5\	O_6\	O_7\
0	0	0	0	0	1	0	1	1	1	1	1	1	1
0	0	1	0	0	1	1	0	1	1	1	1	1	1
0	1	0	0	0	1	1	1	0	1	1	1	1	1
0	1	1	0	0	1	1	1	1	0	1	1	1	1
1	0	0	0	0	1	1	1	1	1	0	1	1	1
1	0	1	0	0	1	1	1	1	1	1	0	1	1
1	1	0	0	0	1	1	1	1	1	1	1	0	1
1	1	1	0	0	1	1	1	1	1	1	1	1	0

Fig. 8.7 **3 to 8 Decoder IC and I/O signal states**

The decoder output is enabled only when the 'Output Enable' signal lines E1\, E2\ and E3 are at logic levels 0, 0 and 1 respectively. If the output-enable signals are not at the required logic state, all the output lines are forced to the inactive (High) state. The output line corresponding to the input state is asserted 'Low' when the 'Output Enable' signal lines are at the required logic state (Here E1\=E2\=0 and E3 =1). The output line can be directly connected to the chip select pin of a device, if the chip select logic of the device is active low.

8.2.6 Encoder

An encoder performs the reverse operation of decoder. The encoder encodes the corresponding input state to a particular output format. The binary encoder encodes the input to the corresponding binary format. Encoders are named with their input line numbers and the encoder output format. Examples are 4 to 2 encoder, 8 to 3 encoder and 16 to 4 encoder. The 8 to 3 encoder contains 8 input signal lines and it is possible to generate a 3 bit binary output corresponding to the input (e.g. inputs 0 to 7 are encoded to binary 111 to 000 in the output lines). The corresponding output line is asserted in accordance with the input signals. For example, if the input line 1 is asserted, the output lines A0, A1 and A2 are asserted as 0, 1 and 1 respectively. Encoders are mainly used for address decoding and chip select signal generation in electronic circuits and are available as integrated circuits. 74F148/74LS148 is an example of 8 to 3 encoder IC. Figure 8.8 illustrates the 74F148/74LS148 encoder and the function table for it.

The encoder output is enabled only when the 'Enable Input (EI)' signal line is at logic 0. A 'High' on the Enable Input (EI) forces all outputs to the inactive (High) state and allows new data to settle without producing erroneous information at the outputs. The group signal (GS) is active-Low when any input is Low: this indicates when any input is active. The Enable Output (EO) is active-Low when all inputs are at logic 'High'. 74LS148/74F148 is a priority encoder and it provides priority encoding of the inputs to ensure that only the highest order data line is encoded when multiple data lines are asserted (e.g., when both input lines 1 and 6 are asserted, only 6 is encoded and the output will be 001. It should be noted that the encoded output is an inverted value of the corresponding binary data. (e.g., the output lines A2, A1 and A0 will be at logic levels 000 when the input 7 is asserted). Encoding of keypress in a keyboard is a typical example for an application requiring encoder. The encoder converts each keypress to a binary code.

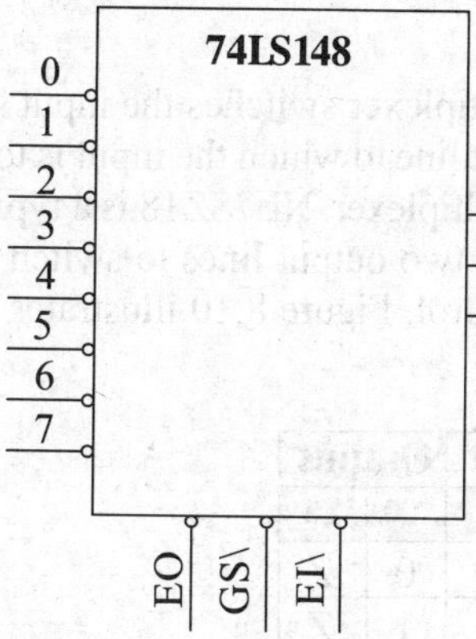

Input									Output				
7	6	5	4	3	2	1	0	E1	GS	E0	A2	A1	A0
1	1	1	1	1	1	1	0	0	0	1	1	1	1
1	1	1	1	1	1	0	1	0	0	1	1	1	0
1	1	1	1	1	0	1	1	0	0	1	1	0	1
1	1	1	1	0	1	1	1	0	0	1	1	0	0
1	1	1	0	1	1	1	1	0	0	1	0	1	1
1	1	0	1	1	1	1	1	0	0	1	0	1	0
1	0	1	1	1	1	1	1	0	0	1	0	0	1
0	1	1	1	1	1	1	1	0	0	1	0	0	0

Fig. 8.8 **8 to 3 Encoder IC and I/O signal states**

8.2.7 Multiplexer (MUX)

A multiplexer (MUX) can be considered as a digital switch which connects one input line from a set of input lines, to an output line at a given point of time. It contains multiple input lines and a single output line. The inputs of a MUX are said to be multiplexed. It is possible to connect one input with the output line at a time. The input line is selected through the MUX control lines. 74S151 is an example for 8 to 1 multiplexer IC. Figure 8.9 illustrates the 74S151 multiplexer and the function table for it.

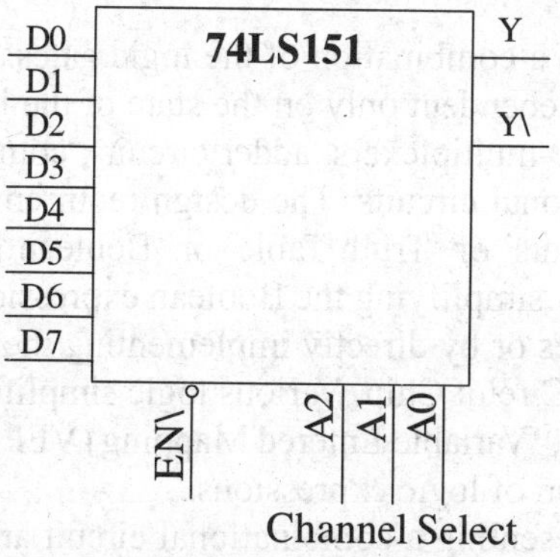

Input				Output	
A2	A1	A0	EN\	Y	Y\
0	0	0	0	D0	D0\
0	0	1	0	D1	D1\
0	1	0	0	D2	D2\
0	1	1	0	D3	D3\
1	0	0	0	D4	D4\
1	0	1	0	D5	D5\
1	1	0	0	D6	D6\
1	1	1	0	D7	D7\
x	x	x	1	0	1

x: Don't care

Fig. 8.9 **8 to 1 multiplexer IC and I/O signal states**

The multiplexer is enabled only when the 'Enable signal (EN)' line is at logic 0. A 'High' on the EN line forces the output to the inactive (Low) state. The input signal is switched to the output line through the channel select control lines A2, A1 and A0. In order to select a particular input line, apply its binary equivalent to the channel select lines A0, A1 and A2 (e.g. set A2A1A0 as 000 for selecting Input D0, and as 001 for selecting channel D1, etc.).

8.2.8 De-multiplexer (D-MUX)

A de-multiplexer performs the reverse operation of multiplexer. De-multiplexer switches the input signal to the selected output line among a number of output lines. The output line to which the input is to be switched is selected by the output selector control lines. The 1 to 2 de-multiplexer, NL7SZ18 is a typical example for 1 to 2 de-multiplexer IC. It contains a single input line and two output lines to switch the input line. The output switching is controlled by the output selector control. Figure 8.10 illustrates the NL7SZ18 de-multiplexer and the function table for it.

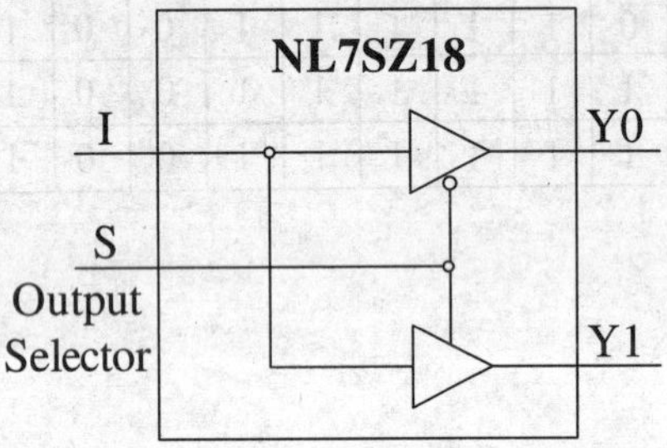

Input		Output	
S	I	Y0	Y1
0	0	0	Z
0	1	1	Z
1	0	Z	0
1	1	Z	1

Z : High Impedance

Fig. 8.10 **1 to 2 De-multiplexer IC and I/O signal states**

When one output line is selected by the output selector control (S), the other output line remains in the High impedance state.

8.2.9 Combinational Circuits

In digital system design, a combinational circuit is a combination of the logic gates. The output of the combinational circuit, at a given point of time, is dependent only on the state of the inputs at the given point of time. Encoders, decoders, multiplexers, de-multiplexers, adder circuits, comparators, multiple input gates, etc. are examples of digital combinational circuits. The design requirements for a combinational circuit are expressed as 'A set of statements' or 'Truth Table' or 'Boolean Expressions'. The combinational circuit can be implemented either by simplifying the Boolean expression/Truth table and realising the simplified expression using logic gates or by directly implementing the logic expressions using an 'Off-the-shelf' Medium Scale Integrated Circuit Chip. Various logic simplification techniques like 'Karnaugh Map (K Map)', 'Algebraic method', 'Variable Entered Mapping (VEP)' and 'Quine-McCluskey method,' etc. are used for the simplification of logic expressions.

In digital system design, logical functions representing a combinational circuit are expressed as either 'Sum of Products (SOP)' or 'Product of Sums (POS)' form. The SOP form represents the logic as the sum of the products of the logical variables whereas the POS form represents the logic as the product of sums of the logical variable.

The expression $Y = AB + \overline{B}C + AC$ is an example for SOP form representation of the logical function. Here Y is the output signal and A, B and C are the input signals.

The expression $Y = (A+B)\ (B+C)\ (A+C)$ is an example for POS form representation of the logical function. Here Y is the output signal and A, B and C are the input signals.

'Karnaugh map' or K-map is the easiest logic simplification technique for arriving at the logic expression when the 'Truth Table' of the combinational circuit is given. Depending on the number of input signal variables, K-maps are named as 2-variable, 3-variable, 4-variable, etc. K-map is the most suitable candidate for handling input variables up to 6. Now let us try to implement a 2 input half adder combinational circuit, for adding two one-bit numbers, using the K-map technique. The 'Truth Table' and the corresponding K-map drawing† for the 2 input 'half adder' circuit is given below.

Input		Output	
B	A	O	C
0	0	0	0
0	1	1	0
1	0	1	0
1	1	0	1

C : Carry

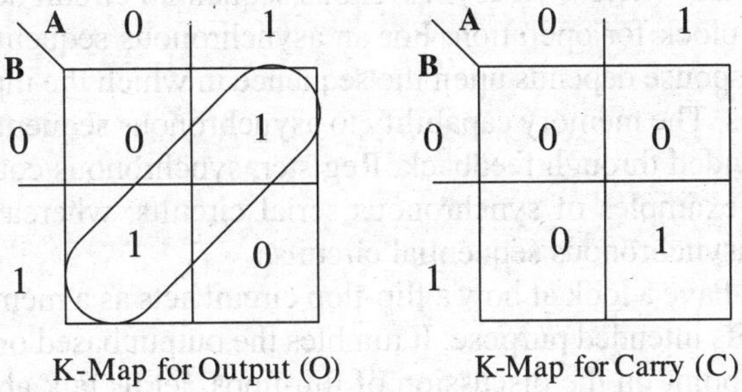

Fig. 8.11 Truth Table and K-map representation for Half Adder

The simplified logical expression for the output (Y) and carry (C) of half adder is given below.

$$Y = \overline{A}B + A\overline{B}$$
$$C = AB$$

The logical expression $\overline{A}B + A\overline{B}$ represents an *XOR* gate. Please refer to the 'truth table' of *XOR* gate given under the '*Logic Gates*' section. Using K-map it can be represented as:

XOR Gate - T ruth Table

I_1	I_2	O
0	0	0
0	1	1
1	0	1
1	1	0

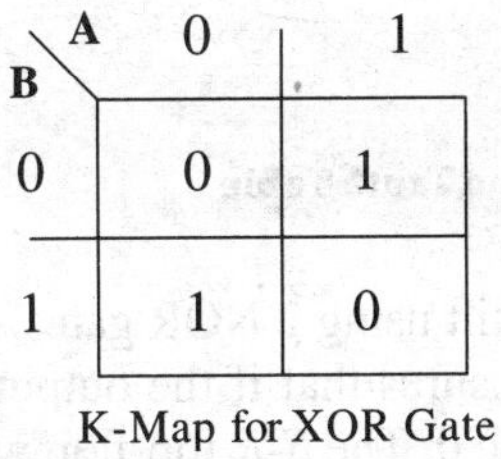

Fig. 8.12 Truth Table and K-map representation for XOR Gate

Hence, the half adder circuit can be realised using an *XOR* and an *AND* gate. The circuit implementation is shown in Fig. 8.13.

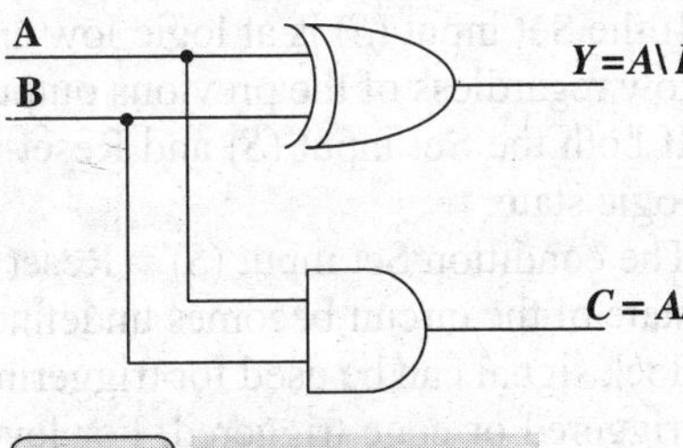

Fig. 8.13 Half Adder Circuit Implementation

8.2.10 Sequential Circuits

Digital logic circuit, whose output at any given point of time depends on both the present and past inputs, is known as sequential circuits. Hence, sequential circuits contain a memory element for holding the previous input states. In general, a sequential circuit can be visualised as a combinational circuit with memory elements.

† Please refer the book '*Modern Digital Electronics* by *R P Jain*' for more details on the K-map drawing and simplification methods.

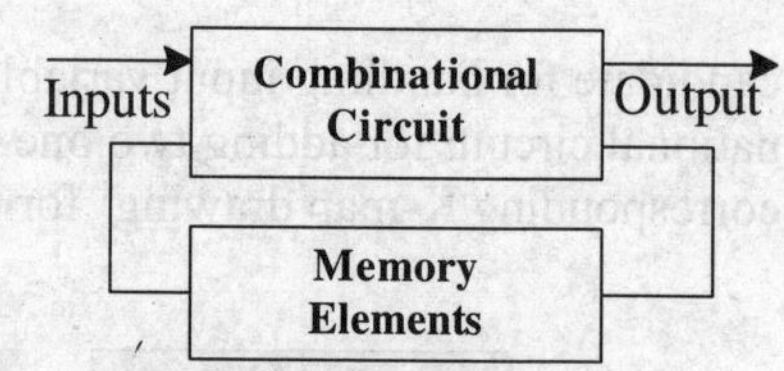

Fig. 8.14 **Visualisation of Sequential Circuit**

Flip-flops act as the basic building blocks of sequential circuits. Sequential circuits are of two types, namely–synchronous (clocked) sequential circuits and asynchronous sequential circuits. The operation of a synchronous sequential circuit is synchronised to a clock signal, whereas an asynchronous sequential circuit does not require a clock for operation. For an asynchronous sequential circuit, the response depends upon the sequence in which the input signal changes. The memory capability to asynchronous sequential circuit is provided through feedback. Register, synchronous counters, etc. are examples of synchronous serial circuits, whereas ripple or asynchronous counter is an example for asynchronous sequential circuits.

Now let us have a look at how a flip-flop circuit acts as a memory storage element. The name *flip-flop* is conveying its intended purpose. It tumbles the output based on the input and other controlling signals. As a starting point on the discussion of flip-flops, let us talk about Set Reset (*S-R*) flip-flop. The logic circuit and the I/O states for an *S-R* flip-flop are given in Fig. 8.15.

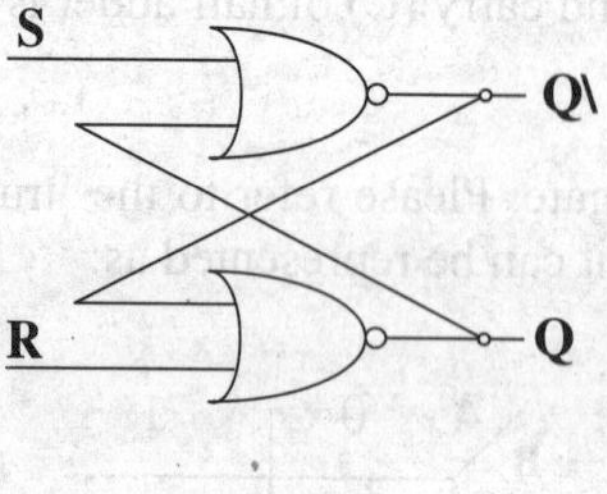

Input		Output	
S	R	Previous State	Present State
0	0	0	0
0	0	1	1
0	1	0	0
0	1	1	0
1	0	0	1
1	0	1	1
1	1	0	x
1	1	1	x

Fig. 8.15 **S-R Flip-Flop and Truth Table**

The *S-R* flip-flop is built using 2 NOR gates. The output of each NOR gate is fed back as input to the other NOR gate. This ensures that if the output of one NOR gate is at logic 1, the output of the other NOR gate will be at logic 0. The *S-R* flip-flop works in the following way.

1. If the Set input (*S*) is at logic high and Reset input (*R*) is at logic low, the output remains at logic high regardless of the previous output state.
2. If the Set input (*S*) is at logic low and Reset input (*R*) is at logic high, the output remains at logic low regardless of the previous output state.
3. If both the Set input (*S*) and Reset input (*R*) are at logic low, the output remains at the previous logic state.
4. The condition Set input (*S*) = Reset input (*R*) = Logic high (1) will lead to race condition and the state of the circuit becomes undefined or indeterminate (*x*).

A clock signal can be used for triggering the state change of flip-flops. The clock signal can be either level triggered or edge triggered. For level triggered flip-flops, the output responds to any changes in input signal, if the clock signal is active (i.e., if the clock signal is at logic 1 for 'HIGH' level triggered and at logic 0 for 'LOW' level triggered clock signal). For edge triggered flip-flops, the output state changes only when a clock trigger happens regardless of the changes in the input signal state. The clock trigger signal can be either a positive edge (A 0 to 1 transition) or a negative edge (A 1 to 0 transition). Figure 8.16 illustrates the implementation of an edge triggered *S-R* flip-flop.

The clocked *S-R* flip-flop functions in the same way as that of *S-R* flip-flop. The only difference is that the output state changes only with a clock trigger. Even though there is a change in the input state, the output remains unchanged until the next clock trigger. When a clock trigger occurs, the output state changes in accordance with the values of *S* and *R* at the time of the clock trigger.

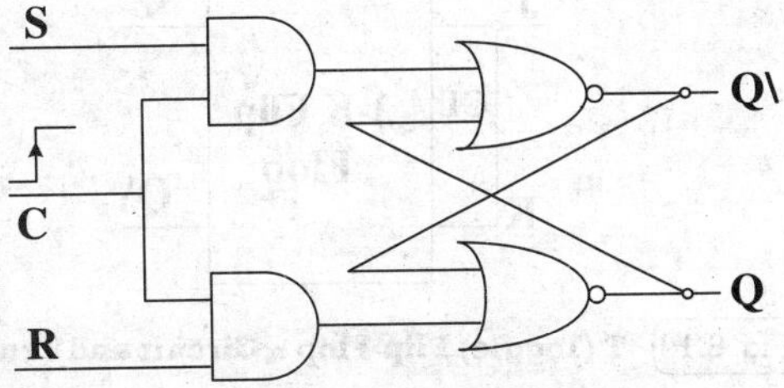

Fig. 8.16 **Clocked S-R Flip-Flop**

We have seen that the input condition *S*=*R*= 1 is undefined in an *S-R* flip-flop. The *J-K* flip-flop augments the behavior of *S-R* flip by interpreting the input state *S*=*R*=1 as a toggle command. The logic circuit and the I/O states for a *J-K* flip-flop are given in Fig. 8.17.

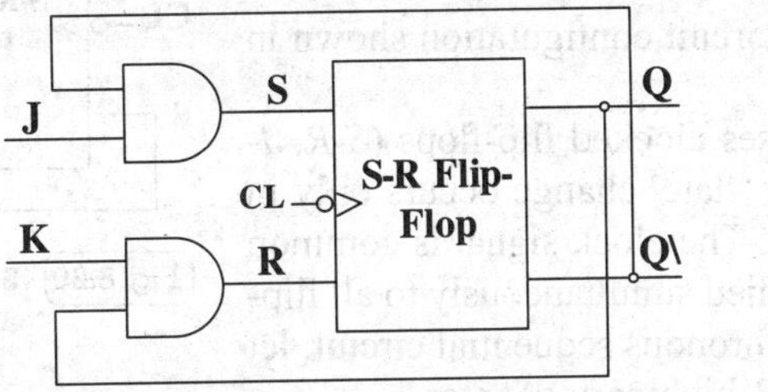

Input		Output	
J	K	Previous State	Present State
0	0	0	0
0	0	1	1
0	1	0	0
0	1	1	0
1	0	0	1
1	0	1	1
1	1	0	1
1	1	1	0

Fig. 8.17 **J-K Flip-Flop Implementation and Truth Table**

From the circuit implementation, it is clear that for a *J-K* flip-flop, *S* = *JQ*\ and *R* = *KQ*. The *J-K* flip-flop operates in the following way:

1. When *J* = 1 and *K* = 0, the output remains in the set state.
2. When *J* = 0 and *K* = 1, the output remains in the reset state.
3. When *J* = *K* = 0, the output remains at the previous logic state.
4. When *J* = 1 and *K* = 1, the output toggles its state.

A D-type (Delay) flip-flop is formed by connecting a *NOT* gate in between the *S* and *R* inputs of an *S-R* flip-flop or by connecting a *NOT* gate between the *J* and *K* inputs of a *J-K* flip-flop. Figure 8.18 illustrates a D-type flip-flop and its I/O states.

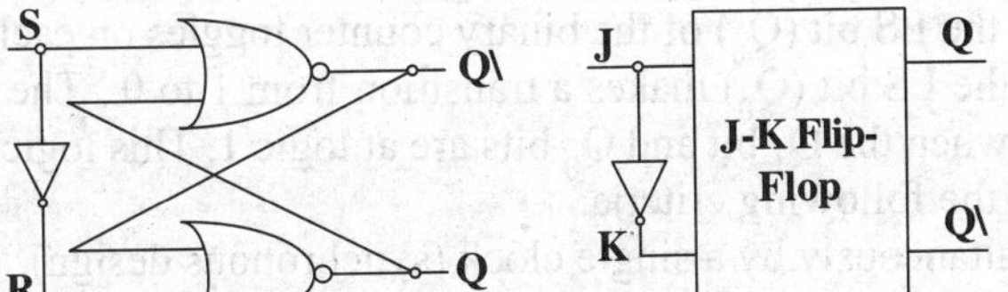

Input	Output
D	Q
0	0
1	1

Fig. 8.18 **D-Type Flip-Flop – Circuit and Truth Table**

This flip-flop is known with the so-called name 'Delay' flip-flop for the following reason–the input to the flip-flop appears at the output at the end of the clock pulse (for falling edge triggering).

A Toggle flip-flop or T flip-flop is formed by combining the *J* and *K* inputs of a *J-K* flip-flop. Figure 8.19 illustrates a T flip-flop and its I/O states.

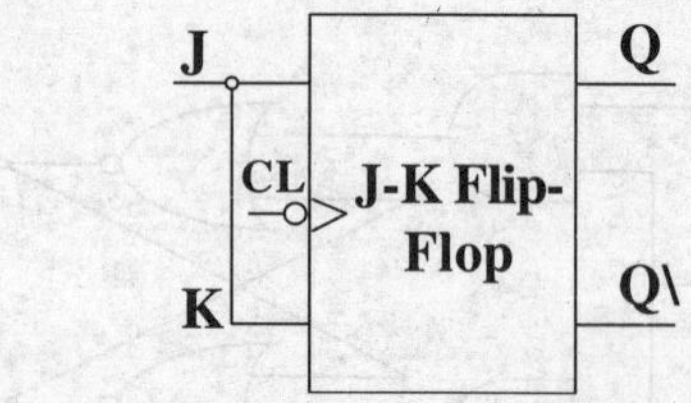

Input	Output
T	Q_{n+1}
0	Q_n
1	Q_n\

Q_{n+1} : Present Output
Q_n : Previous Output

Fig. 8.19 **T (Toggle) Flip-Flop – Circuit and Truth Table**

When the '*T*' input is held at logic 1, the T flip-flop toggles the output with each clock signal. An S-R flip-flop cannot be converted to a 'T' flip-flop by combining the inputs S and R. The logic state S=R=1 is not defined in the *S-R* flip-flop. However, an *S-R* flip-flop can be configured for toggling the output with the circuit configuration shown in Fig. 8.20.

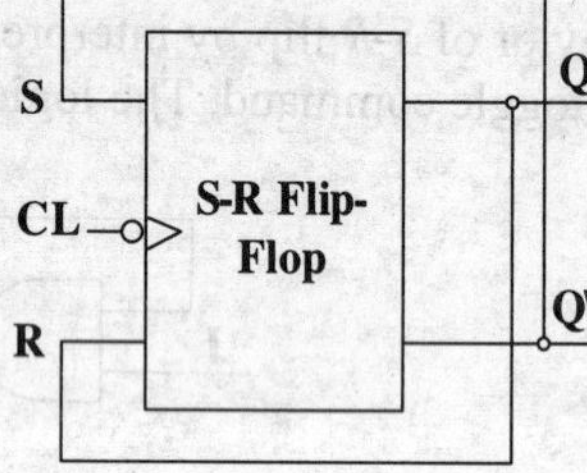

Fig. 8.20 **S-R Flip-Flop acting as Toggle switch**

The synchronous sequential circuit uses clocked flip-flops (*S-R*, *J-K*, *D*, *T* etc.) as memory elements and a 'state' change occurs only in response to a synchronising clock signal. The clock signal is common to all flip-flops and the clock pulse is applied simultaneously to all flip-flops. As an illustrative example for synchronous sequential circuit, let us consider the design of a synchronous 3-bit binary counter.

The counting sequence for a 3-bit binary counter is given below.

Count	Q_2	Q_1	Q_0
0	0	0	0
1	0	0	1
2	0	1	0
3	0	1	1
4	1	0	0
5	1	0	1
6	1	1	0
7	1	1	1

From the count sequence, it is clear that the LS bit (Q_0) of the binary counter toggles on each count and the next LS bit (Q_1) toggles only when the LS bit (Q_0) makes a transition from 1 to 0. The Bit (Q_2) of the binary counter toggles its state only when the Q_1 bit and Q_0 bits are at logic 1. This logic circuit can be realised with 3 T flip-flops satisfying the following criteria:

1. All the T flip-flops are driven simultaneously by a single clock (synchronous design).
2. The output of the T flip-flop representing the Q_0 bit is initially set at 0. The input line of Q_0 flip-flop is connected to logic 1 to ensure toggling of the output with input clock signal.
3. Since Q_1 bit changes only when Q_0 makes a transition from 1 to 0, the output of the T flip-flop representing Q_0 is fed as input to the T flip-flop representing the Q_1 bit.
4. The output bit Q_2 changes only when $Q_0 = Q_1 = 1$. Hence the input to the flip-flop representing bit Q_2 is fed by logically ANDing Q_0 and Q_1.

The circuit realisation of 3-bit binary counter using 3 T flip-flops is given in Fig. 8.21.

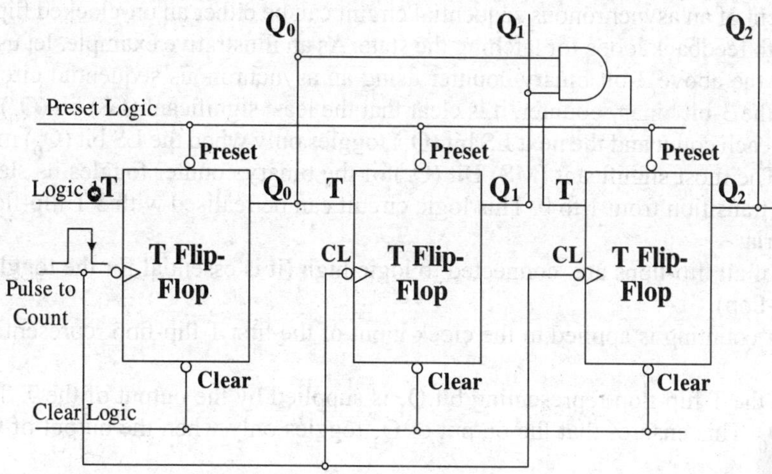

Fig. 8.21 **Binary Counter Implementation using T Flip-Flops**

The Preset line is used for setting the output of flip-flop, whereas the Clear line is used for resetting the output of flip-flops. The counter changes in accordance with the count pulses.

Another example for synchronous sequential circuit is 'register'. A register can be considered as a group of bits holding information. A D flip-flop can be used for holding a 'bit' information. An 8 bit wide register can be visualised as the combination of 8 D flip-flops. The bit storing operation is controlled by the signal associated with a latch write (like a write to latch pulse). The figure given below illustrates the implementation of a 4 bit register using D flip-flops.

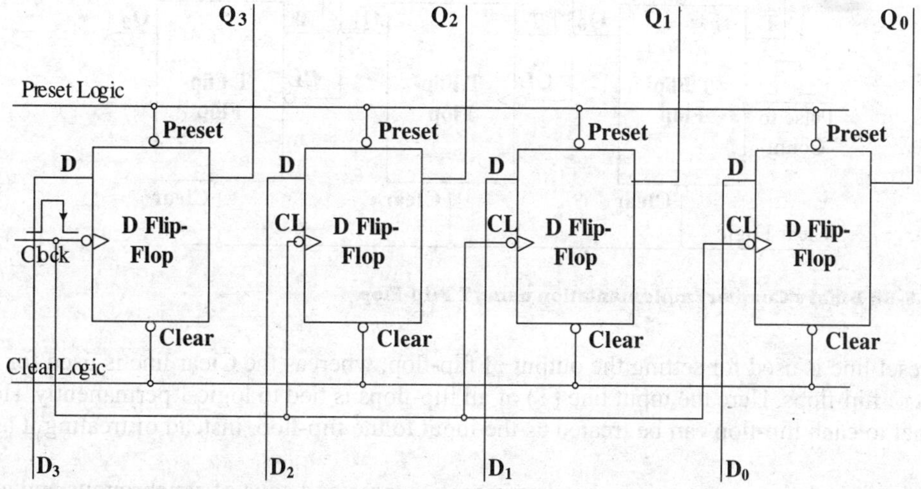

Fig. 8.22 **4 bit Register Implementation using D Flip-Flops**

The state of an asynchronous sequential circuit changes instantaneously with changes in input signal state. The asynchronous sequential circuit doesnot require a synchronising clock signal for its operation. The memory element of an asynchronous sequential circuit can be either an un-clocked flip-flop or logical gate circuits with feedback loops for latching the state. As an illustrative example, let us explore how we can implement the above 3-bit binary counter using an asynchronous sequential circuit. From the count sequence of the 3-bit binary counter, it is clear that the least significant (LS) bit (Q_0) of the binary counter toggles on each count and the next LS bit (Q_1) toggles only when the LS bit (Q_0) makes a transition from 1 to 0. The most significant (MS) Bit (Q_2) of the binary counter toggles its state only when the Q_1 bit makes a transition from 1 to 0. This logic circuit can be realised with 3 T flip-flops satisfying the following criteria:

1. The T input of all flip-flops are connected to logic high (it is essential for the toggling condition of the T Flip-flop).
2. The pulse for counting is applied to the clock input of the first T flip-flop representing the LS bit Q_0.
3. The clock to the T flip-flop representing bit Q_1 is supplied by the output of the T flip-flop representing bit Q_0. This ensures that the output of Q_1 toggles only when the output of Q_0 transitions from 1 to 0.
4. The clock to the T flip-flop representing bit Q_2 is supplied by the output of the T flip-flop representing bit Q_1. This ensures that the output of Q_2 toggles only when the output of Q_1 transitions from 1 to 0.

The circuit realisation of the 3-bit binary counter using 3 T flip-flops in an asynchronous sequential circuit is given below.

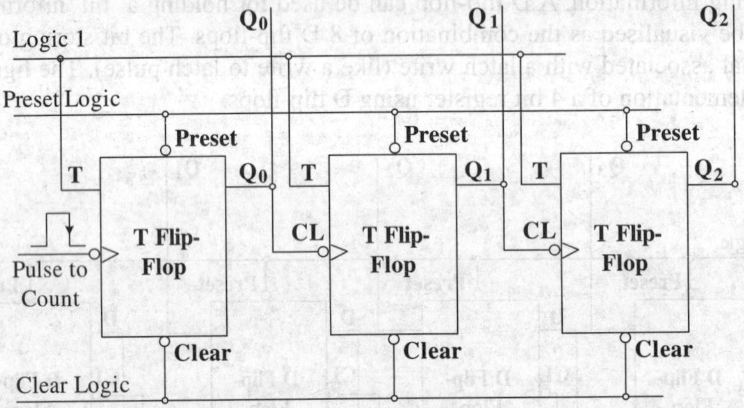

Fig. 8.23 **3-Bit Binary Counter Implementation using T Flip-Flop**

The Preset line is used for setting the output of flip-flop, whereas the Clear line is used for resetting the output of flip-flops. Here the input line (T) of all flip-flops is tied to logic 1 permanently. Hence, the clock signal to each flip-flop can be treated as the input to the flip-flop, instead of treating it as a clock pulse.

The table given below summarises the characteristics, pros and cons of synchronous and asynchronous sequential circuits.

Synchronous Sequential Circuit	Asynchronous Sequential Circuit
Clocked flip-flops act as the memory element in the circuit. All flip-flops are clocked to the same clock signal.	Un-clocked flip-flops or logic gate circuits with feedback loops act as the memory element in the circuit.
The output state of the circuit changes only with clock trigger.	The output state change happens instantaneously with changes in input state.
The speed of operation depends on the maximum supported clock frequency.	Faster than synchronous sequential circuits.

The output state of asynchronous circuit changes instantaneously with input signals; hence the speed of operation of asynchronous sequential circuits is high compared to that of synchronous sequential circuits. Asynchronous sequential circuits are preferred over synchronous sequential circuits for applications requiring high speeds and applications in which the input state change can happen asynchronously. Asynchronous sequential circuits are cheaper to develop, compared to synchronous sequential circuits.

8.3 VLSI AND INTEGRATED CIRCUIT DESIGN

In the beginning of the electronics revolution we started building electronic circuits around the early vacuum tube technologies. As technology progressed, transistors came into the picture and we shifted our circuit designs to transistor based technology. In the ancient times thousands of individual transistors were required to build a digital or analog functionality. The transistors were interconnected using conductive wires for building the required functionality. As technology gained new dimensions, the concept of miniaturisation evolved and researchers and designers were able to build the required functionality within a single silicon wafer, in places of thousands of interconnected transistors. An integrated circuit (IC) is a miniaturised form of an electronic circuit containing transistors and other passive electronic components. In an IC, the circuits, required for building the functionality (say Processing logic: CPU), are built on the surface of a thin silicon wafer. The first integrated circuit was designed in the 1950s. Depending on the number of integrated components, the degree of integration within an integrated circuit (IC) is known as:

Small-Scale Integration (SSI): Integrates one or two logic gate(s) per IC, e.g. LS7400

Medium-Scale Integration (MSI): Integrates up to 100 logic gates in an IC. The decade Counter 7490 is an example for MSI device

Large-Scale Integration (LSI): Integrates more than 1000 logic gates in an IC

Very Large-Scale Integration (VLSI): Integrates millions of logic gates in an IC. Pentium processor is an example of a VLSI Device.

The IC design methodology has evolved over the years from the first generation design, SSI to designs with millions of logic gates. The gate count is a measure of the complexity of the IC. In today's world almost all IC designs fall under the category VLSI and it is a common practice to term IC design as VLSI design. Depending on the type of circuits integrated in the IC, the IC design is categorised as:

Digital Design: Deals with the design of integrated circuits handling digital signals and data. The I/O requirement for such an IC is always digital. Microprocessor/microcontroller, memory, etc. are examples of digital design.

Analog Design: Deals with the design of integrated circuits handling analog signals and data. Analog design gives more emphasis to the physics aspects of semiconductor devices such as gain, power dissipation, resistance, etc. RF IC design, Op-Amp design, voltage regulator IC design, etc. are examples for Analog IC Design.

Mixed Signal Design: In today's world, most of the applications require the co-existence of digital signals and analog signals for functioning. Mixed signal design involves design of ICs, which handle both digital and analog signals as well as data. Design of an analog-to-digital converter is an example for mixed signal IC design.

Integrated circuit design or VLSI design involves a number of steps namely, system specification, functional or architectural design, functional simulation, logic synthesis, physical layout (placement and routing) and timing simulation. As in the case of any other system design, VLSI design also starts with the system specification in which the requirements of the chip under development are listed out. The system specification captures information on 'what the chip does?', the input and output to the chip, timing constraints, power dissipation requirements, etc. (e.g. For an IC for AND gate implementation, the intended function is logical ANDing of input signals and input per gate is 2 and output is 1). The functional design or architectural design involves identifying the various functional modules in the design and their interconnections. It represents an abstraction of the chip under development. computer aided design (CAD) tools are available for architectural design. The functional aspects of a chip can be captured using CAD tools with various methods like block diagrams, truth tables, flow charts, state diagrams, schematic diagrams and Hardware Description Language (HDL). This process of entering the system description into the CAD tool is known as Design Entry. The truth table based design entry uses the truth table of a logic function. This method is suitable for the realisation of logic function implementation involving lesser number of logic variables. The schematic capture based design entry uses the schematic diagram created with an EDA tool (Please refer to the section on Schematic Capture using Capture CIS of this chapter for more details on Schematic Capture). Flow charts can also be used for design entry because of their inherent flow structure to describe any sequential flow. State diagrams are employed to display state machines graphically. State diagrams are used for modelling sequential circuits, characterised by a finite number of states and state-transitions. A Hardware Description Language (HDL) based design flow involves describing the design (circuit) to be realised in a Hardware Description Language like Very High Speed Integrated Circuit HDL (VHDL) or Verilog HDL. HDL is similar to software application programming languages but is used for describing hardware.

The functional simulation process simulates the functioning of the circuit captured using one of the above-mentioned design entry techniques, using a functional simulation tool. During simulation, input stimuli are applied to the circuit and the output is verified for the required functionality. The logic synthesis phase involving optimisation and mapping transforms the design into a gate level netlist corresponding to the logic resource available in the target chip. The chip design may be for the development of a custom ASIC or for implementation of the required functionalities of the IC in a standard Programmable Integrated Circuit like CPLD or FPGA. In case of CPLD, the logic gates are realised in terms of the gates available in the *macrocells* of the CPLD, whereas for FPGAs the logic gates are realised in terms of the Look Up Tables (LUTs). The optimisation and mapping process optimises the logic expressions for speed, area and power and maps the design to the target technology (FPGA, CPLD, etc.) keeping their functionality unaltered. The physical design or layout design is the process of implementing the circuit using the logic resources present in the final device (CPLD, FPGA) or creating the logic partitioning, floor planning, placement, routing, pin assignment, etc for a custom IC (ASIC), using a supported CAD tool. The Timing Simulation is performed using CAD tools for analysing the propagation delay of the circuit, for a particular technology like FPGA, CPLD, etc. For custom ICs (ASICs), the physical design converts the circuit description into geometric description in the form of a GDSII file. The GDSII file is sent to a semiconductor fab for fabricating the IC. The IC is fabricated in silicon wafer and finally it is packaged with the necessary pin layouts. The following section gives you an overview of the VHDL based VLSI design.

8.3.1 VHDL for VLSI Design

Very High Speed Integrated Circuit HDL or VHDL is a hardware description language used in VLSI design. VHDL is a technology independent description, which enables creation of designs targeted for a chosen technology (like CPLD, FPGA, etc.) using synthesis tools. This enables one keep up with the fast development of semiconductor technology. VHDL can be used for describing the functionality and behaviour of the system (Behavioural representation), or describing the actual gate and register levels of the system [Register Transfer Level (RTL) representation]. VHDL supports concurrent, sequential, hierarchical and timing modelling. The concurrent modelling describes the activities happening in parallel, whereas sequential modelling describes the activities in a serial fashion one after another. Hierarchical model describes the structural aspects, and timing model models the timing requirements of the design. Like any other programming language, VHDL also possess certain set of rules and characteristics. The following table gives a snapshot of the important rules and characteristics specific to VHDL

Type	Representation/Remark
Comment	-- (Start with two adjacent hyphens)
Identifier	Reserved words and programmer chosen names for entity and signal description. Supports any length and characters A-Z, a-z, numbers 0-9 and special character underscore (_). Non-case sensitive. Must start with a character
character	ASCII character in single quote. e.g. 'A', 'a', etc
string	Characters grouped in double quotes, e.g. "VHDL"
Bit strings	Arrays of bits with base Binary (B), Octal (O) or Hexadecimal (X). e.g. B"100" Only 1 and 0 allowed in string O"127" numerals only 0 to 7 are allowed X"1F9" Numerals 0 to 9 and letters A to F, and a to f are allowed in string
Numerals	*universal_integer* does not include points, e.g. 100 *universal_real* include a point, e.g. 100.1 The special character '_' can be used for increasing the readability e.g. 1000 can be represented as 1_000 Character E or e can be used for including exponent, e.g. 1E3 '#' can be used for describing the base of the numbering system, e.g. 2#011# Number base 2 and representing number 3. Base can be between 2 and 16

if statement	**if** condition **then**
	--Corresponding actions
	else
	--Corresponding actions
	end if;

case statement	**case** expression **when** case 0 --statements or case ; **when** case 1 --statements or case 1; --………….. **when others** --statements or default case; **end case**;
Loop statement	**loop** --Body of loop; **end loop;**
while loop	**while** expression **loop** --Body of loop; **end loop;**
for loop	**for** item **in** start item to end item **loop** --Body of loop; **end loop;**
Important Syntax Rules	1. Reserved words are written in bold letters 2. All statements end with a semicolon (;) 3. | is used for separating mutually exclusive alternatives 4. ( ) is used for clarifying the order in which a rule is evaluated 5. {} used for representing optional things that may occur once or many times or never 6. [ ] used for representing optional things that may occur once or never

The basic structure of a VHDL design consists of an entity, architecture and signals. The entity declaration defines the name of the function being modelled and its interface ports to the outside world, their direction and type. The basic syntax for an entity declaration is given below.

```
Entity name-of-entity is
Port (list of interface ports and their types);
Entity item declarations;
Begin
Statements;
End entity name-of-entity
```

The architecture describes the internal structure and behaviour of the model. Architecture can define a circuit structure using individually connected modules or model its behaviour using suitable statements. The basic syntax of architecture body is given below

```
Architecture name-of-architecture of name-of-entity is
Begin
Statements;
End architecture name-of-architecture;
```

Signals in VHDL carry data. A signal connects an output and an input of two components (e.g. Gates, flip-flops, etc.) of a circuit. A signal must be defined prior to its use.

e.g. **Signal** a: **bit**; This is an example of a signal 'a' which can take values of type bit.
Once a signal has been defined, values can be assigned to the signal.
e.g. a <= '1'; In this example a value '1' is assigned to the signal 'a'.

Similar to software languages like 'C', where functions are stored in a library which can be re-used, in VHDL also all compiled modules are stored in library. Packages are also stored in a library. A package may contain functions, types, components, etc. For using components from a particular library, first the library and packages must be specified in the VHDL code as

```
Library name-of-library;
Use name-of-library.name-of-package.ALL;
```

When a VHDL module is compiled, it is saved in the work library by default. As per the VHDL standard the work library is always visible and need not be specified in the VHDL code. If other packages or libraries are to be used, they must be defined before the entity declaration.
e.g.

```
Library ieee;
Use ieee.std_logic_1164.ALL;
```

The above library definition defines that all data types, functions, etc available in the package std_logic_1164 in the library *ieee* can be used in the underlying entity. As an example for VHDL based design, let us consider the design of a D flip-flop. The VHDL description of the D Flip-flop is given below.

```
Library ieee;
Use ieee.std_logic_1164.all;
Entity DFF is
Port (D, CLK: in bit; Q: out bit);
End DFF;
Architecture DFF-ARCH of DFF is
Begin
Process (D, CLK)
Begin
        If CLK='1' and CLK'event then
Q <= D;
End if;
End Process;
End DFF_ARCH;
```

In the above example "DFF" is the name of the model and D, CLK, Q are the interface ports. The architecture describes the internal structure and behaviour of the model. In the above example, the architecture "DFF-ARCH" describes the D flip-flop function.

The HDL model of the circuit is then complied and loaded in an HDL simulator. The simulator enables the designer to apply the input stimuli to the design and observe whether the output response is as expected. If there are any functional errors, the HDL code is corrected and the design re-simulated, till the design meets the functional specifications. In the above example on simulation, by applying a clock and data inputs the model functions like a D-flip-flop. The design is now ready for synthesis. A synthesiser tool compiles the source code to an optimised technology dependent circuit at the gate level. The inputs to a synthesiser are the HDL code, a technology library, and constraints. The constraints are in terms of the area and speed requirements of the circuit to be realised in the target technology. This process is done in two phases:

Compilation: The HDL is translated to a generic netlist

Optimisation: The generic netlist is mapped to a target technology (ASIC/FPGA) satisfying the requirements of area and speed.

On synthesis, the VHDL model described above results in a D flip-flop to be realised as shown in Fig. 8.24.

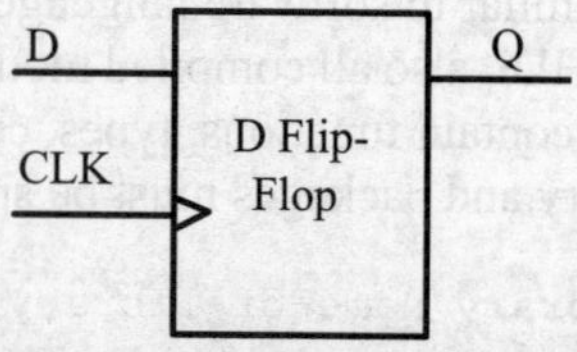

Fig. 8.24 **Realisation of a D Flip-Flop using VHDL**

The next phase of implementation is physical layout (Place and Route). In the case of an FPGA implementation, during the placement stage the various instances in the netlist are mapped and their relative position inside the target FPGA resources is fixed. During the routing phase, the interconnection between the various placed instances is done as per the netlist to realise the circuit. Once the layout is complete, the final step is timing simulation. The design is now re-simulated with the actual component and interconnect delays to verify the functionality. Figure 8.25 illustrates the various steps involved in a HDL based design.

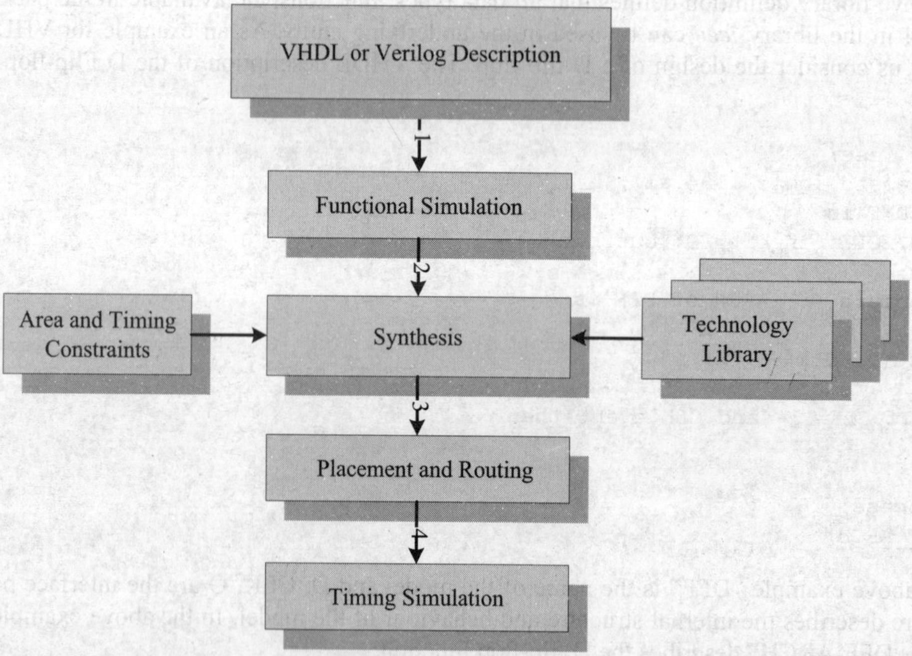

Fig. 8.25 **The HDL based VLSI Design Process**

8.4 ELECTRONIC DESIGN AUTOMATION (EDA) TOOLS

Early embedded products were built around the old transistor and vacuum tube technologies, where the designers built the PCB with their hands, oil paper, pencil, pen, ruler and copper plates. The process of building a PCB was highly cumbersome in ancient times where the designers sketch the required connections using pen, pencil and ruler on papers and the finished sketch was used for etching the connections on a copper plate and it took weeks and months time to finish a PCB. The more the inter connections involved in the hardware, the more difficult was the process. The accuracy and finishing of the PCB was highly dependent on the artistic skills of the designer. Today the scenario is totally changed. Advances in computer technology and IT brought out highly sophisticated and automated tools for PCB design and fabrication. The process of manual sketching the PCB has given way to software packages that gives an automatic routing and layout for your product in a few seconds. These software packages are widely known as Electronic Design Automation (EDA) tools and various manufactures offer these tools for different operating systems (Windows, UNIX, Linux etc). EDA tool is a set of Computer Aided Design/Manufacturing (CAD/CAM) software packages which helps in designing and manufacturing the electronic hardware like integrated circuits, printed circuit board, etc. The key players of the EDA tool industry are Cadence, Protel, Altium, Cadsoft, Redac, Merco, etc. OrCAD, Cadstar, Protel, Eagle, etc. are the popular EDA tool packages available in the market for PCB design. Of these, I feel Cadence OrCAD as the most flexible and user friendly tool. The reference tool used for hardware design throughout this book is OrCAD. An evaluation copy with limited features (for Windows OS) is available for free download from the Cadence website www.cadence.com. Readers can use this tool for their hardware design. Remember this tool is a demo version and you cannot use this for any commercial design and it does not provide you the full features of the licensed version.

8.5 HOW TO USE THE OrCAD EDA TOOL?

Install the demo version of the OrCAD Software for a PC with Microsoft® Operating System (Windows XP/Vista or any other version supported by the tool). If the installation is successful you can see the installed software under the group name ***OrCAD xx.x*†** ***Demo*** under the ***All programs*‡** tab which can be selected through the '***Start***' menu of your desktop. The '***OrCAD xx.x*† *Demo***' contains three main tools namely '*Capture CIS Demo*'–The schematic creation tool, '*Layout Demo*'–PCB Layouting Tool, and 'PSpice AD Demo'–The circuit simulation tool along with a set of documentation. Let us have a look at these tools to get an idea on how they are used in PCB Designing.

8.6 SCHEMATIC DESIGN USING OrCAD CAPTURE CIS

Schematic is a way of representing the different components (can be an electronic component like resistor, integrated circuit, capacitor, etc. or a mechanical/electromechanical component like push button switch, relay, etc.) involved in a hardware product and how each components are interconnected together. You can create a schematic design either by hand sketch on a paper or by electronic sketch using CAD tool. The OrCAD capture CIS tool is an electronic schematic design tool. To create a schematic using this, execute the 'Capture CIS Demo' application. The following window will appear on your desktop (Fig. 8.26).

Create a new project by choosing the 'New Project' tab from the File menu of Capture CIS (File→New→Project…)*. The following dialog box appears on the screen (Fig. 8.27).

Type a name for the project (say, for example, 8051_project1). Choose the 'Schematic' option for 'Create New Project Using' and select a location for the new project by filling the 'Location' box and

† *xx.x* Represents the version number of the tool. If the version is 10.0, xx.x becomes 10.0

‡ The explanation given here is for Microsoft® Windows XP operating system

* The 'Menu' option may vary with change in version of the application. If you find it different from the one explained here, please refer to the user's manual of the application provided by Cadence.

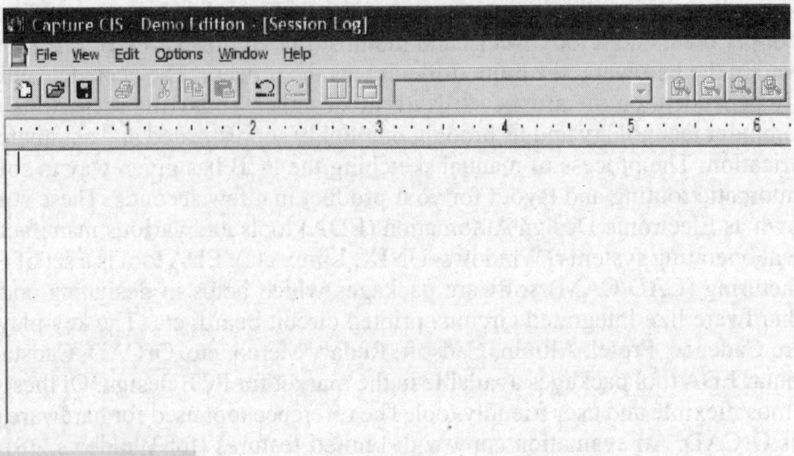

Fig. 8.26 **OrCAD Capture CIS Tool**

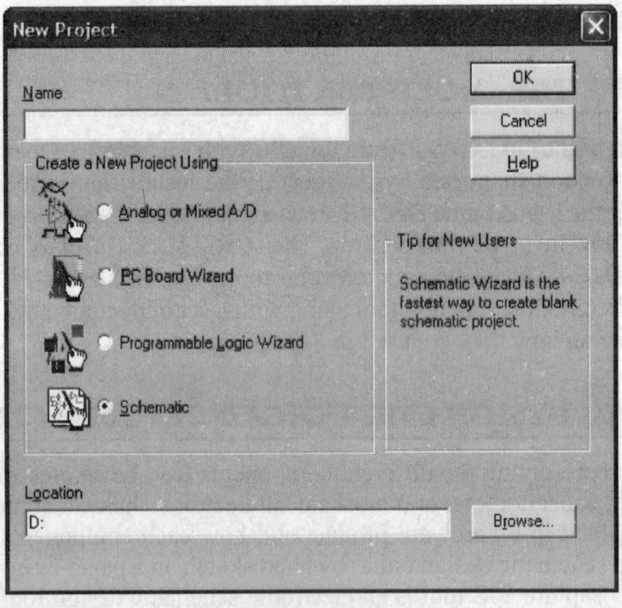

Fig. 8.27 **New Project Creation using OrCAD Capture CIS Tool**

finally click the OK button. Now a schematic capture project is created at the specified location with the specified name and the schematic tool opens default page (PAGE1) with various schematic drawing tools on the right side for creating the schematic (Fig. 8.28). Close the default page by clicking the page close button 'X'. Now you will be taken to the project window where you can view the following categories.

On creating a new project, two files are created at the location for the new project with extensions *.opj* and *.dsn*. The file names will be the same as that of the project name. The *.opj* file stands for OrCAD

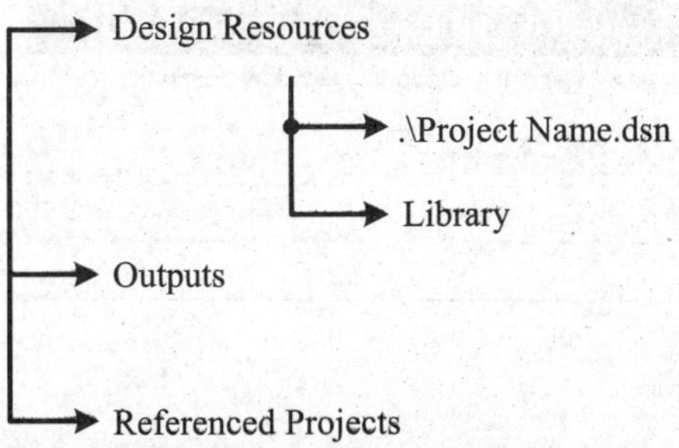

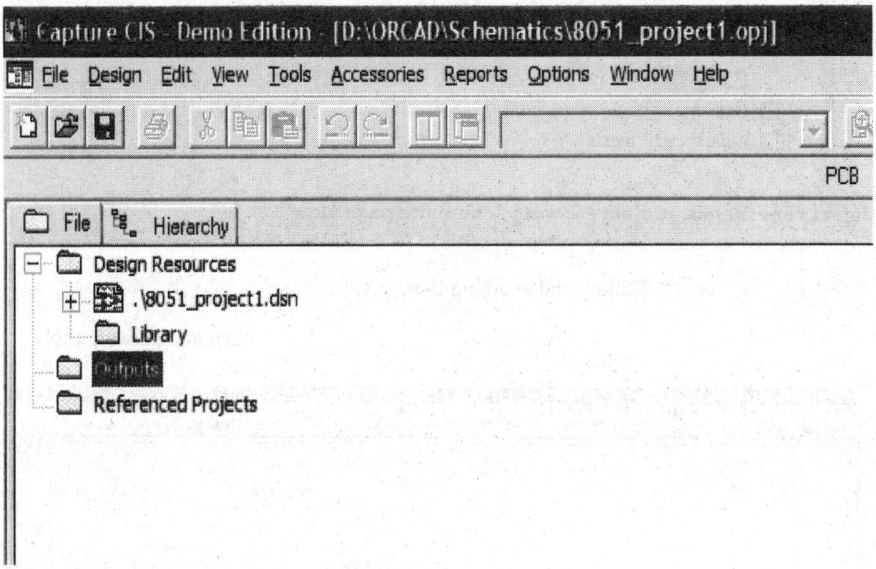

Fig. 8.28 **Project view for New project created on Capture CIS**

project file and it holds all project related settings for the project. The *.dsn* file represents the data source name file holding the schematic drawing settings and data.

The *.dsn* tab in the project window is an expandable tab and it contains the 'SCHEMATIC' and 'Design Cache' details as shown in Fig. 8.29.

To start with the schematic design, double click on the 'PAGE1' tab under the 'SCHEMATIC1' node. It will take you to the schematic drawing canvas along with the drawing tools on the right side of the canvas. 'PAGE1' is created by default on creating a new project. You can change the name of it by right clicking 'PAGE1' and choosing the 'Rename option'. The schematic drawing canvas details are given in Fig. 8.30.

8.6.1 The Drawing Canvas

The drawing canvas is the area on which the different schematic components are placed and interconnected according to the requirements.

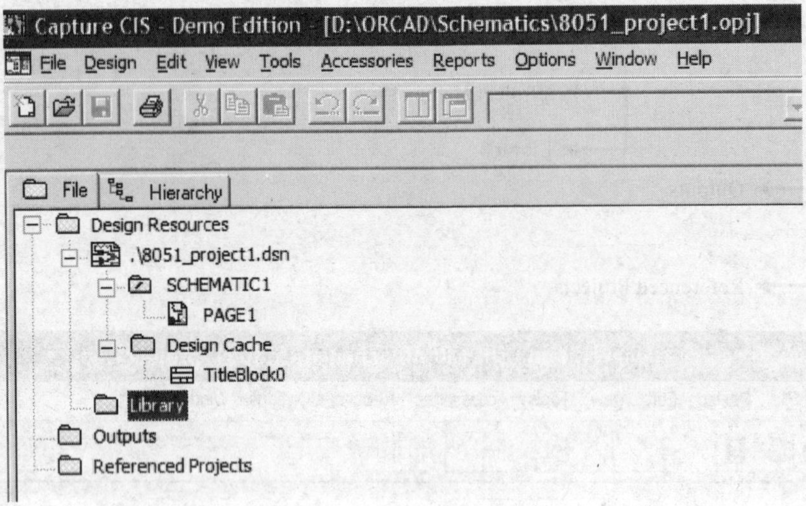

Fig. 8.29 **Project view for new project showing Schematic page view**

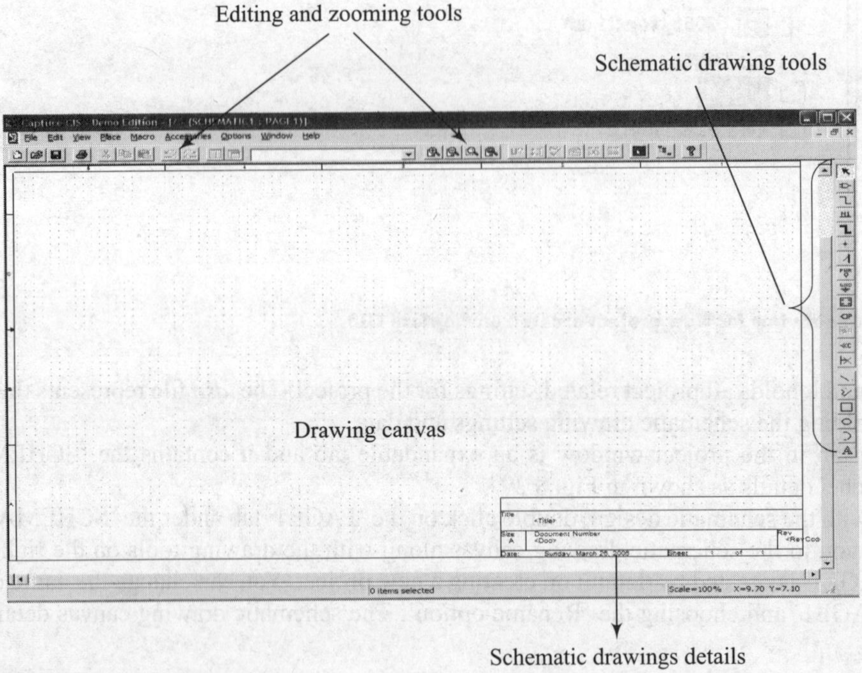

Fig. 8.30 **Schematic drawing canvas**

8.6.2 Schematic Drawing Tools

Schematic drawing tools are the various tools available in the canvas editor to place a component

(Resistor, capacitor, IC, etc), to interconnect different components (a connection between two points), to add a text description, etc. The available schematic drawing tools and their usage are described in the following sections.

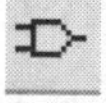
Place Part: Component placing tool. Place various components like resistor, capacitor, different ICs, etc on the drawing canvas. Invoking this button pops up a place part dialog box as shown in Fig. 8.31.

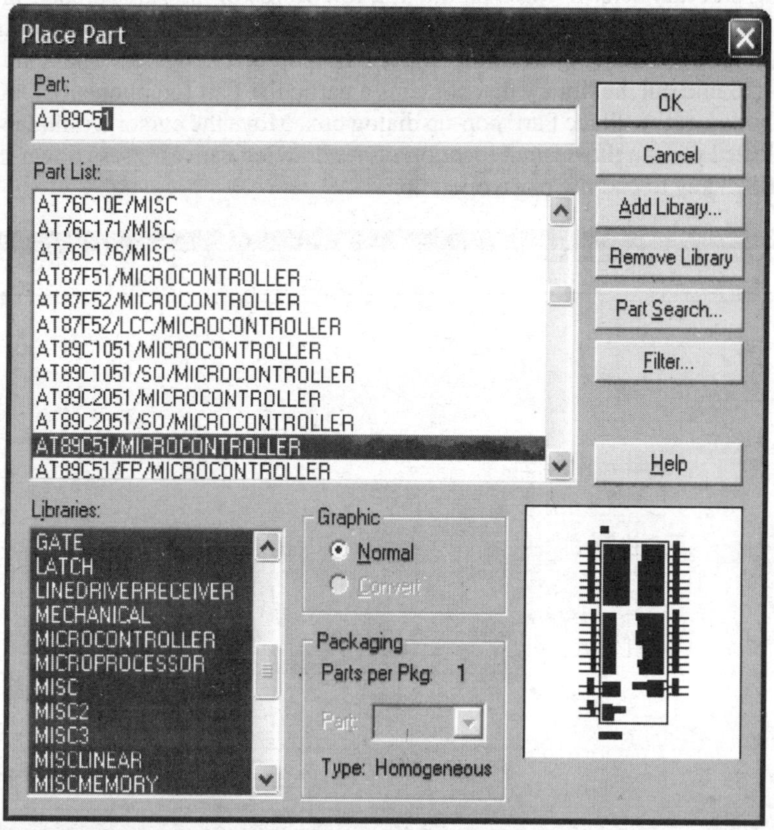

Fig. 8.31 **Selecting a component to place in the schematic canvas**

The manufacturer of different ICs and other components give them a Part Number/Part Name and the component is identified by this name/number. OrCAD incorporates a number of libraries to incorporate the skeletal drawing of these components. The library is located at the path /OrCAD Root Directory/tools/capture/library, where /OrCAD Root Directory is the installation directory of OrCAD tool. You can add these libraries using the '***Add Library…***' button. Add the library you want by using this button. Each library contains specific skeletal drawings. For example, the Library 'GATE' contains the skeletal diagram (Pin Diagram) of almost all available Logic Gate ICs from different manufacturers. Similarly, the Library 'MICROCONTROLLER' contains the skeletal sketch (Pin Diagram) for almost all commercially available microcontrollers. If you are not sure about the component you are going to use belongs to which library, select all libraries by pressing 'Ctrl + A' key in the 'Libraries' box (remember the libraries will only be seen in the Libraries section if you add the libraries explicitly to your project using the 'Add Library' option). If you are certain, on which library the component you are going to add belongs, you can select that particular library by clicking it on the libraries section. For example, if you want to add AT89C51 microcontroller, you can go for two options either use the 'MICROCONTROLLER' library or use the entire libraries.

To select a component, type its name under the 'Part:' section. The part selector supports auto complete for selecting part numbers. If you type the first few words of the part number, the auto complete will display the list of components starting with the typed part number. A preview of the selected component is also shown on the right corner of the 'Place Part' pop-up dialog box. The 'Part Search…' function will help you to find out the library that contains a particular Part (component). Once you select the part, click 'OK' button of the 'Place Part' pop-up dialog box. Move the cursor within the drawing canvas and place the selected part on the desired location of the drawing canvas. Press down the mouse cursor and then press 'ESC' key to end the place operation.

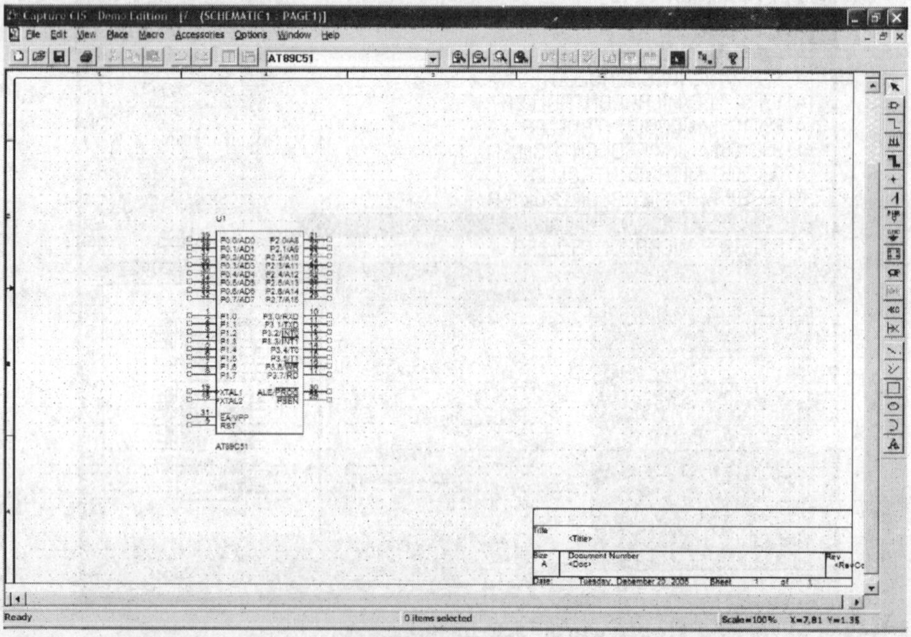

Fig. 8.32 **Placing component in the schematic canvas**

Place Wire: Component interconnection tool. It interconnects various components like resistor, capacitor, different ICs etc within the drawing canvas. Choose this tool and click at the starting point where the connection needs to be started and move the mouse till the end point of the connection. The wire follows the mouse movement. Press 'Esc' when you are done with the connecting action.

Place Net Alias: Tool for interconnecting various components like resistor, capacitor, different ICs, etc within the drawing canvas without using a direct interconnection using 'Place Wire' Techniques. This is used if the number of interconnections within a drawing is large and complex. Clicking this tool pops-up a dialog box to input the Net Alias name. Input the Alias name and Press OK button.

Now your mouse pointer carries the Net Alias. Move the mouse pointer to the start point where the connection starts and place it there. Take the tool again, select the same Net Alias and place it at the other end, where the connection needs to be terminated. If you add the same Net Alias each to different interconnection points, each of them gets connected together. The schematic diagram given in Fig. 8.33 illustrates the use of '*Place Net Alias*' tool.

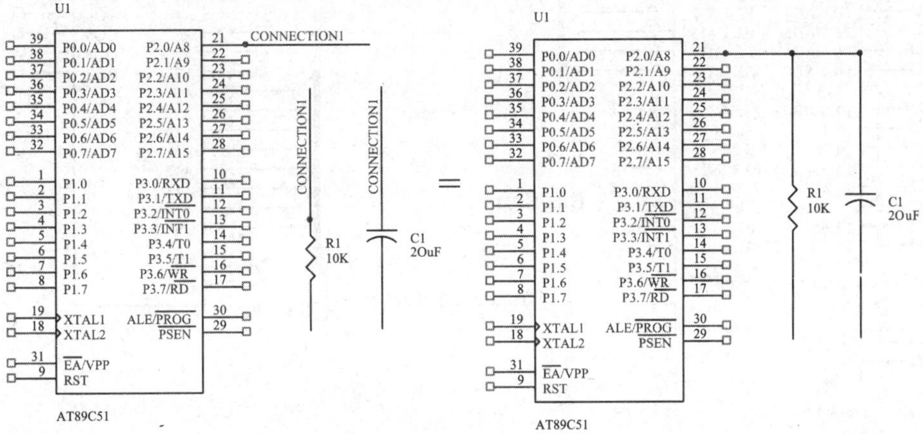

Fig. 8.33 **Illustration of using 'Place Net Alias' Tool**

Place Bus: Places an address or data bus in the schematic. You can avoid connecting individual wires of the bus one-to-one between the source and destination if this is used in combination with the 'Place bus entry' Tool. For *8051*, the address bus A0–A7 and A8–A15 and the data bus D0–D7 can be represented using this.

Place Bus Entry: Used in combination with the Place Bus Tool. It connects each individual lines of the bus into the common bus.

Place Port: This tool associates a group of connections together and it is referred as port. Port connection is of three types; namely bidirectional connector, incoming port connector and outgoing connector. The bidirectional port connector connects a bidirectional port, e.g. D0–D7 of Data bus (P0) for 8051. The outgoing connector implies that the corresponding port is originating from the device (output line) and is intended to feed as an input line to other devices. For example, the address lines of 8051, A8–A15 originates from the chip and it should be connected to the I/p line of any other device requiring these lines. The address lines (A8, A9, A10 to A15) are grouped using the 'Place Bus' tool and each address pins (A8, A9, …, A15) are connected to the address bus using the 'Place Bus Entry' tool. Finally the bus is made available to the rest of the devices by connecting an outgoing Port to the bus. The port holds a name and if the same name is used by a bus with an incoming Port, it will give the same result as they are interconnected together directly. The same is illustrated in Fig. 8.34.

Place Junction: This tool places a junction implicitly on any part of the wiring. This tool can be used in the same way as other tools, click on the tool, move it to the desired point on the wiring already done and press the mouse. Press 'Esc' Key to end the process.

Place Power: Used for placing a power connection to the power line or to the power supply pin of different components.

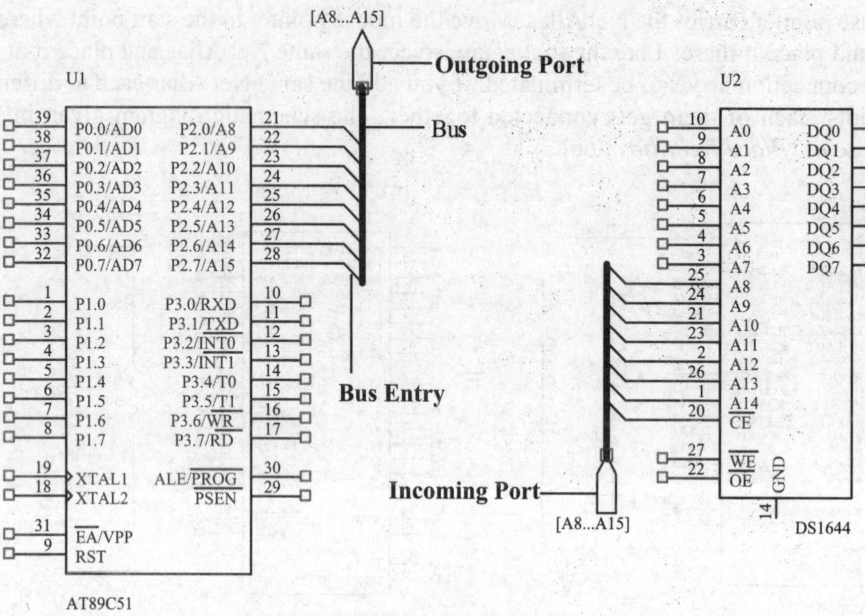

Fig. 8.34 **Illustration of Bus, Bus Entry and Port tool usage**

Place Ground: Used for placing a ground connection to the ground line or to the ground pin of different components.

Place No Connect: Some components may have some pins left unconnected. The No connect tool is used for representing non-connected pins.

Place off Page Connector: For modularity, the schematic can be drawn in different pages with each page representing the associated hardware for that particular module. For example, the schematic can be drawn on different pages for power supply module, processor module, PC interface module etc. If a connection is required from one page to another page it is achieved by using the 'Off Page Connector' tool. If a connection is going out from a page to other pages, it is represented using an outgoing 'off Page Connector' (Fig. 8.36) in that page and if a connection is coming into a page from any other pages it is represented using an incoming 'off Page Connector' in that page.

8.6.2.1 Schematic Part Creation, Formatting and Labelling Tools Certain parts may not be available as readymade part in the Part library of the tool. In such situations, if you know the Pin number for the part you want to create, you can create it using the following part creation tools. Labeling tools are used for putting text labels and others in the canvas to give more readability and understanding of the schematic drawing.

Place Rectangle: Creates a rectangle within the drawing canvas. This rectangle can either be used as an outline to a New Part to be created or as an outline to a labelling text or to isolate some part of the schematic from other area to give visibility.

Place Line: Used for creating Pins on the Rectangular Part for part creation. When used as a formatting tool it is used for drawing lines to separate different areas of the schematic diagram.

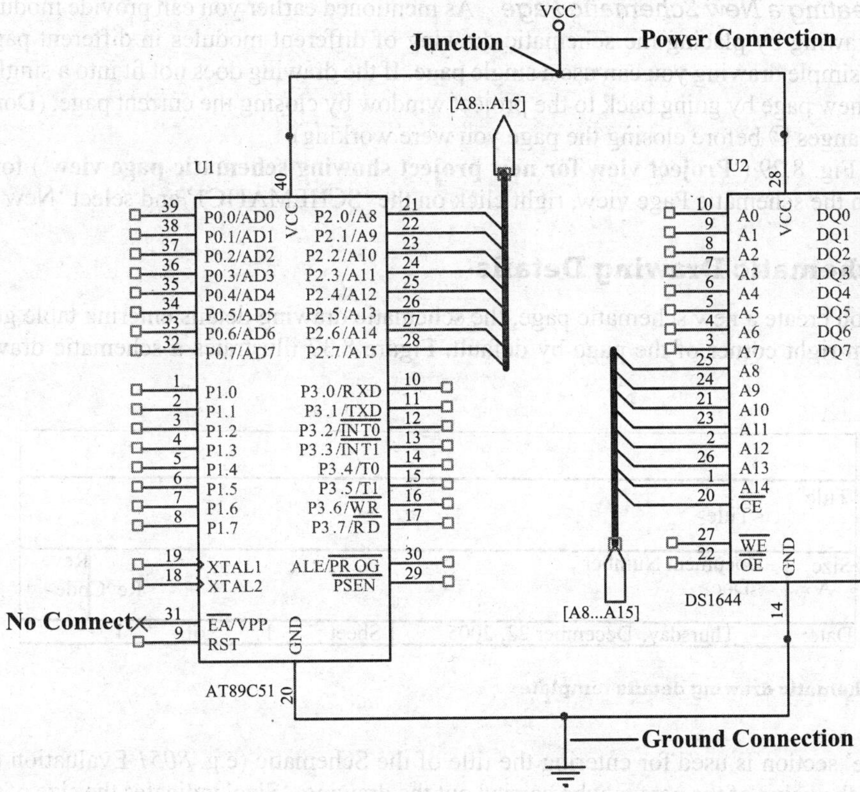

Fig. 8.35 **Illustration of Junction, Power, Ground and No Connect tool usage**

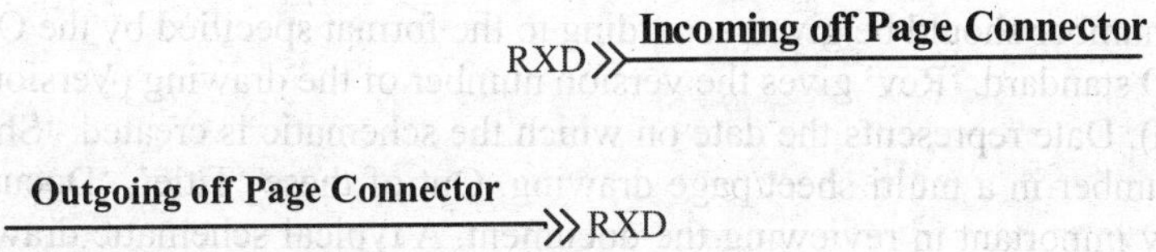

Fig. 8.36 **Illustration of off Page Connector**

Place Poly line: Tool used for creating poly lines on the drawing page.

Place Ellipse: Place an elliptical shape within the drawing canvas.

Place Arc: Tool used for placing different forms of arcs and circle in the drawing area.

Place text: Tool used for creating text labels for documenting the drawing and to add Pin names, description, Part Number etc in the new part creation.

8.6.2.2 Creating a New Schematic Page As mentioned earlier you can provide modularity to the schematic drawing by placing the schematic drawing of different modules in different pages. If your drawing is a simple drawing you can use a single page. If the drawing does not fit into a single page, you can create a new page by going back to the project window by closing the current page. (Don't forget to save your changes ☺ before closing the page you were working).

Refer the Fig. 8.29 ('**Project view for new project showing schematic page view**') for schematic page view. In the schematic Page view, right click on the 'SCHEMATIC1' and select 'New Page'

8.6.3 Schematic Drawing Details

Whenever you create a new schematic page, the schematic drawing details entering table gets attached to the bottom right corner of the page by default. Figure 8.37 illustrates a schematic drawing details template.

Title	<Title>		
Size A	Document Number <Doc>		Rev <RevCode>
Date:	Thursday, December 22, 2005	Sheet 1 of 1	

Fig. 8.37 **Schematic drawing details template**

The 'Title' section is used for entering the title of the Schematic (e.g. *8051* Evaluation board). You can also add the name of the person who carried out the drawing. 'Size' indicates the size of the drawing page. To get the details of the 'Size' take the 'Schematic Page Properties…' tab from the 'Options' menu when the page is in the opened state. (Options → Schematic Page Properties). Whatever values you set there is taken as the default value for a page.

The document number should be given according to the format specified by the QA standard you are following, e.g. ISO standard. 'Rev' gives the version number of the drawing (Version number increases with each revision). Date represents the date on which the schematic is created. 'Sheet No.' represents the Sheet/Page Number in a multi sheet/page drawing. Out of these 'Title', 'Document Number' and 'Rev Code' is very important in reviewing the document. A typical schematic drawing details table is illustrated in Fig. 8.38.

Title	8051 Evaluation Board		
Size A	Document Number PROJ_CODE : 001		Rev 2
Date:	Thursday, December 22, 2005	Sheet 1 of 2	

Fig. 8.38 **Schematic drawing details table**

I hope the basic lessons of schematic design creation and how different tools are used for creating a schematic diagram has been covered in this section. Now let's create a complete schematic diagram using the Capture CIS tool (Fig. 8.39). Part of this schematić (Power Supply Part) is available for download from the Online Learning Centre web page of this book.

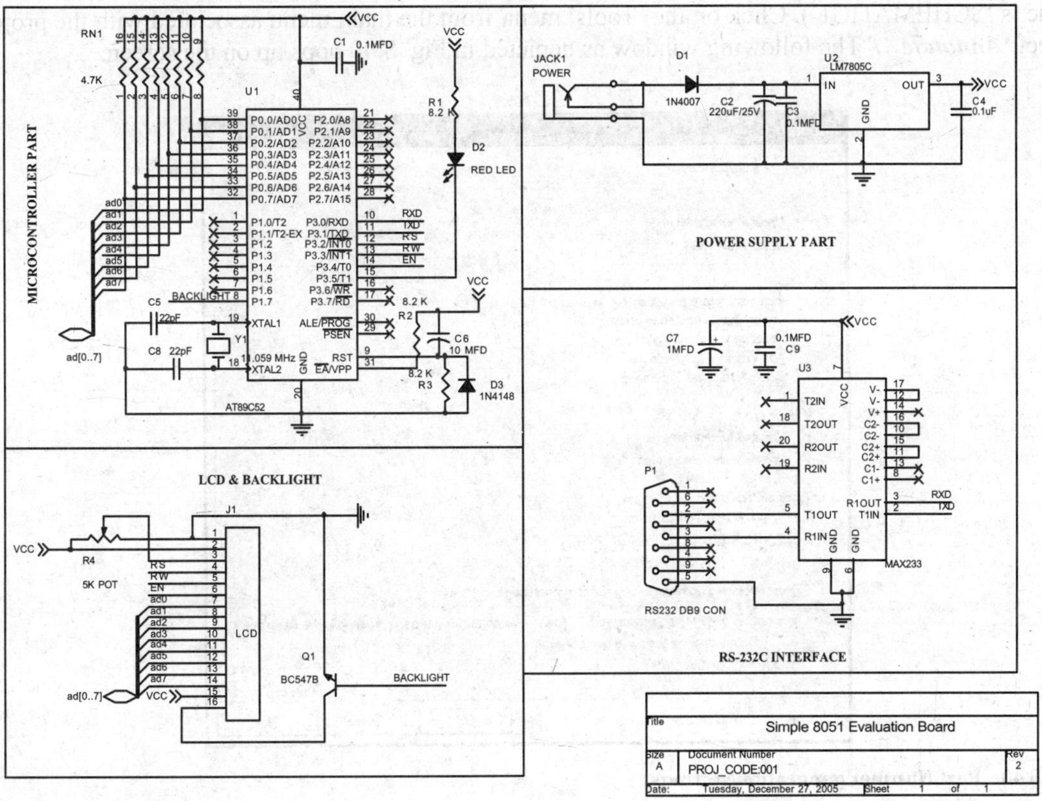

Fig. 8.39 **Finished schematic**

Once the schematic is finished, part numbers should be assigned to the various components present in the schematic and error checking should be performed. If there are no errors, you can proceed to the next step, the netlist creation. The following sections illustrate each of these steps, namely 'Part Number Creation', 'Design Rule Check' and 'Net List Creation'.

8.6.4 Creating Part Numbers

Part Number is the name assigned to each component in the schematic diagram. It is required to identify and distinguish the components in the schematic diagram. Normally part number is given in the order in which they are present in the schematic page. Certain naming convention rules are followed for this. For example, capacitors are named with the letter *C* with suffix *x* (C_x where x = 1, 2, 3….); resistors are named as *Rx* (x = 1, 2, 3….) and ICs with *Ux*, etc. This is automatically validated by the design tool itself, if you follow the steps listed below. The suffix 1, 2, 3, etc. are allocated by the tool depending on the relative positioning of the component within the schematic Page (*x* and *y* co-ordinates of the component). The topmost component is given the reference number 1 and reference number 2 to the next component, and so on.

To generate automatic Part numbers, close all schematic pages and come back to the project view and highlight the *dsn* name or schematic name (In our example the *dsn* is '*8051*_project1.dsn' and schematic name is 'SCHEMATIC1'). Click on the 'Tools' menu from the main menu associated with the project. Select '***Annotate…***' The following window as depicted in Fig. 8.40 pops up on the screen.

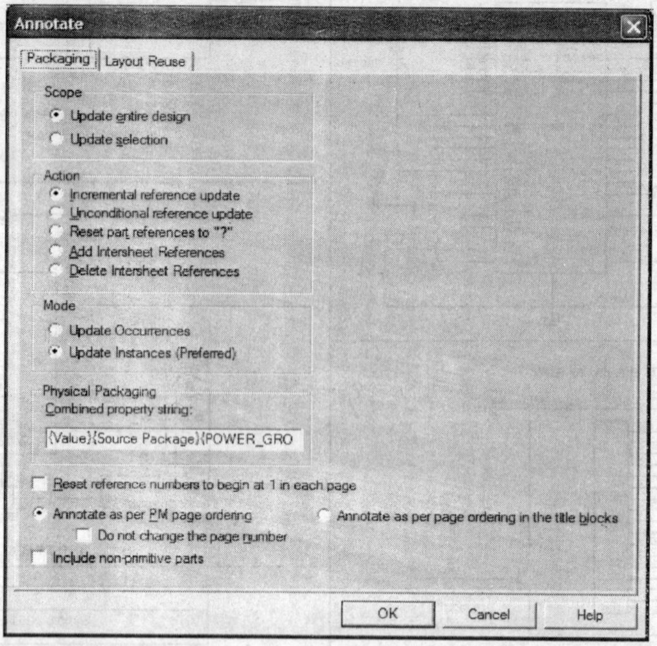

Fig. 8.40 **Part Number generation settings**

From the pop-up window, select the option '***Update entire design***' for '***Scope***', '***Reset part references to "?"***' for '***Action***' and '***Update Instances***' for '***Mode***' and then press the OK button. This prompts for a confirmation. If you respond yes to the confirmation, every part number is re-set with "?" ('C?', 'R?', etc.). If you open the schematic page you can see this. The action performed is to reset all references to a default value. To assign the part numbers, go to the 'Tools' menu again and take 'Annotate…' option. The same window pops up. Choose the option '***Incremental reference update***' for '***Action***' item and keep the rest same as the above settings. Pressing 'OK' button prompts again for user confirmation and if you confirm it, the design part number is updated automatically. It is to be noted that no two components will have the same Part Number. Eventhough there are two or more capacitors or ICs or resistors present in the schematic diagram with the same values (e.g. 0.1MFD (Microfarad) for capacitor or 8.2K (kilo ohms) for resistors, etc.) different part numbers should be used for them. Part numbers are very helpful in PCB routing, soldering of components in the finished PCB and in the creation of Bill of Materials (BoM).

8.6.5 Design Rules Check

Design Rules Check (DRC) is performed for checking any possible errors in the schematic diagram, like duplicate part references, missing off-page connector connections, unconnected nets, unconnected power and ground pins, etc. For performing the DRC check, highlight the *dsn* name or schematic name from the project window and select '***Design Rules Check...***' option from the '***Tools***' menu. The following window as shown in Fig. 8.41 pops up.

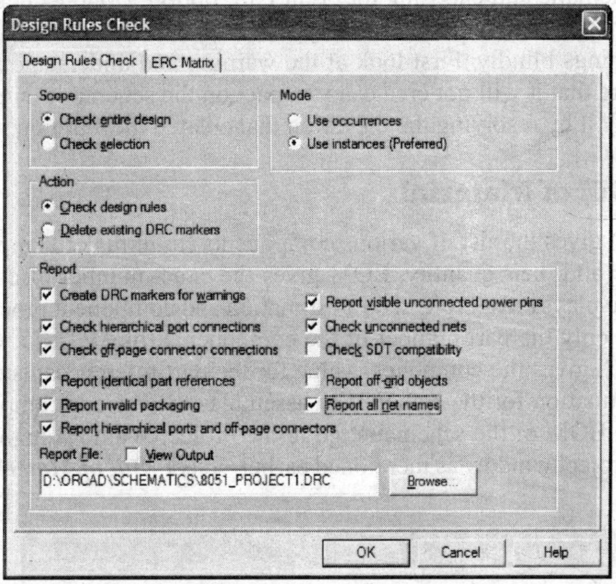

Fig. 8.41 **DRC settings window**

Select the option '***Check entire design***' from '***Scope***', '***Check design rules***' from '***Action***'. Check the following options among the '***Report***' category by selecting the corresponding check box.

Report

- Create DRC markers for warnings
- Check hierarchical port connections
- Check off-page connector connections
- Report identical part references
- Report invalid packaging
- Report hierarchical ports and off-page connectors
- Report visible unconnected power pins
- Check unconnected nets
- Report all net names

You can select the location for the DRC report file to be created. By default it is generated with name '***project name.drc***' (e.g. *8051*_project1.drc) and it is created at the project location directory.

The ***.drc*** file gives you the details of any errors present in the schematic along with the point (x & y co-ordinates) in schematic diagram where the error is occurred. Sometimes the ***.drc*** may report warnings. You can ignore some of the warnings. But you must look into the warnings and should confirm that the warnings will not create any issue in the total circuit. Examples of warnings that may be ignored are "Bi-directional pin connected to input pin", "Output pin connected to Power line". The second example is a very common one where the o/p pin of regulator gives the regulated supply and it usually gets connected to the power pins of other ICs in the circuit. Here, though the o/p Pin of the regulator IC is giving the o/p power, the 'Pin Type' will be output and you are connecting that pin to a 'Pin Type' power of other ICs. This is a possible Pin type conflict. You can either discard this warning or can avoid this warning by changing the 'Pin Type' of the regulator o/p Pin to 'power' by right clicking the Regulator IC component in the schematic and choosing the 'Edit Part' option. Double click on the pin, for which you want to change the 'Type', choose the desired type.

Don't ignore all warnings blindly. First look at the warning and understand its consequence in the schematic. If you are sure that it will not create any impact on the schematic, simply ignore it or if you have enough time, rectify it by resolving the condition that created the warning.

8.6.6 Creating Bill of Materials

Bill of Materials (BOM) gives the list of various components (in terms of component type and value) present in the schematic and their quantity. BOM gives the exact number of components required to fabricate a board and so it plays a vital role in cost estimation and component procurement. When a PCB is fabricated, it contains only the part number of the components (like R1, C1, C2, U1, etc.). BOM is the cross-link chart which gives the component value for the part references listed on the PCB. Bill of Material is a useful information for the person who assembles the various components on the finished PCB. For generating the BOM of the schematic, go to the Project Window, highlight the *.dsn* name or schematic name in the Project window as mentioned earlier, select '***Bill of Materials...***' option from the '***Tools***' menu (Fig. 8.42).

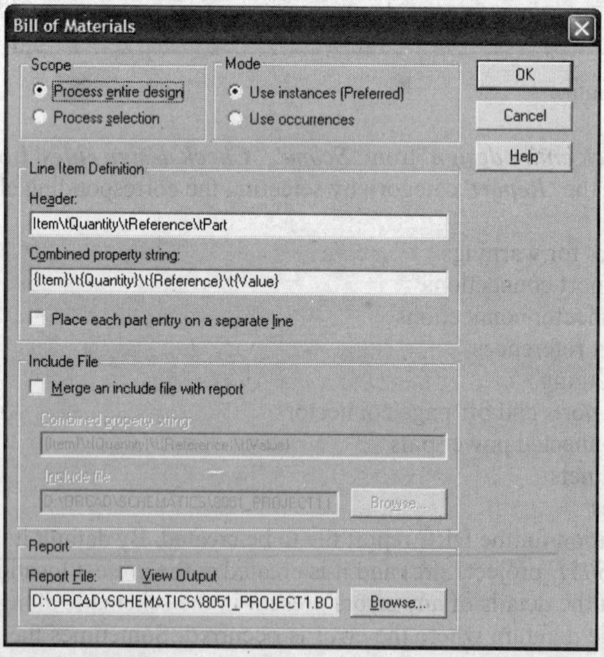

Fig. 8.42 **Bill of Material (BOM) creation**

Select '***Process entire design***' from '***Scope***' and '***Use instances (Preferred)***' from '***Mode***'. The default location for the report file is the Project directory and the BOM name is the project name with extension ***.bom***. You can change the report file location by giving the desired path name in the edit box present in the '***Report***' section. Press 'OK' to proceed. The BOM is generated automatically and it is visible under the '***Outputs***' section of the Project Window. The BOM can be opened for viewing by double clicking on the ***.bom*** file. A sample BOM file is shown in Fig. 8.43.

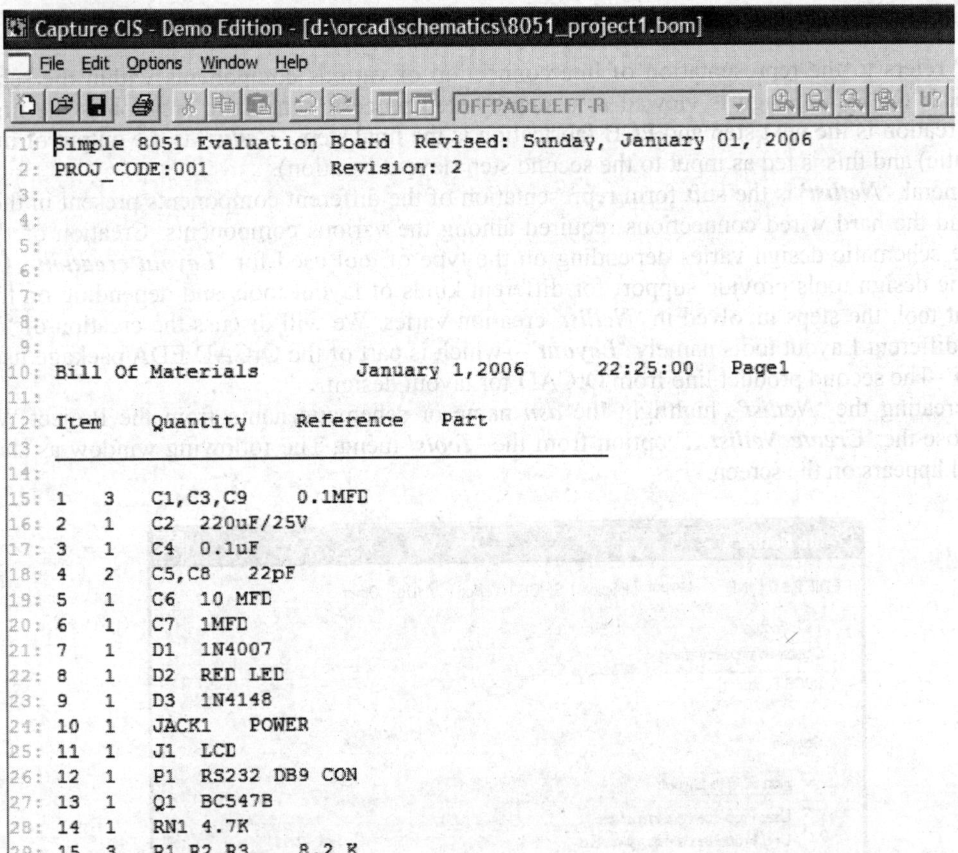


```
Simple 8051 Evaluation Board  Revised: Sunday, January 01, 2006
PROJ_CODE:001                 Revision: 2







Bill Of Materials         January 1,2006       22:25:00    Page1

Item     Quantity    Reference    Part
________________________________________________________

1    3    C1,C3,C9     0.1MFD
2    1    C2   220uF/25V
3    1    C4   0.1uF
4    2    C5,C8    22pF
5    1    C6   10 MFD
6    1    C7   1MFD
7    1    D1   1N4007
8    1    D2   RED LED
9    1    D3   1N4148
10   1    JACK1    POWER
11   1    J1   LCD
12   1    P1   RS232 DB9 CON
13   1    Q1   BC547B
14   1    RN1 4.7K
15   3    R1,R2,R3     8.2 K
16   1    R4   5K POT
17   1    U1   AT89C52
18   1    U2   LM7805C
19   1    U3   MAX233
20   1    Y1   11.059 MHz
```

Fig. 8.43 **Sample BOM**

If you observe the BOM closely, you can find that the BOM gives different types of information to the different type of users. Take the first item in the BOM list. For a person who is interested in procuring the components, the first line of BOM gives the information on the quantity required for capacitor with value 0.1MFD per board is 3. For a person who is involved in the assembling of components on the board, the first line gives the information, the part numbers with reference values C1, C3, C9 should be soldered with capacitors with value 0.1MFD.

8.6.7 Netlist Creation

'*Netlist*' refers to the representation of interconnection of various components within the schematic diagram. If the PCB design is viewed as a step-by-step process, schematic creation is the first step, layout creation is the next step and PCB fabrication is the final step. '*Netlist*' is the output of first step (schematic) and this is fed as input to the second step (layout creation).

In general, '*Netlist*' is the soft form representation of the different components present in the schematic and the hard wired connections required among the various components. Creation of '*Netlist*' from the schematic design varies depending on the type of tool used for '***Layout creation***'. OrCAD schematic design tools provide support for different kinds of layout tools and depending on the type of layout tool, the steps involved in '*Netlist*' creation varies. We will discuss the creation of '*Netlist*' for two different Layout tools namely '***Layout***'—which is part of the OrCAD EDA package itself and '***Allegro***'–The second product line from OrCAD for layout design.

For creating the '*Netlist*', highlight the *dsn* name or schematic name from the Project Window and choose the '***Create Netlist...***' option from the '***Tools***' menu. The following window as shown in Fig. 8.44 appears on the screen.

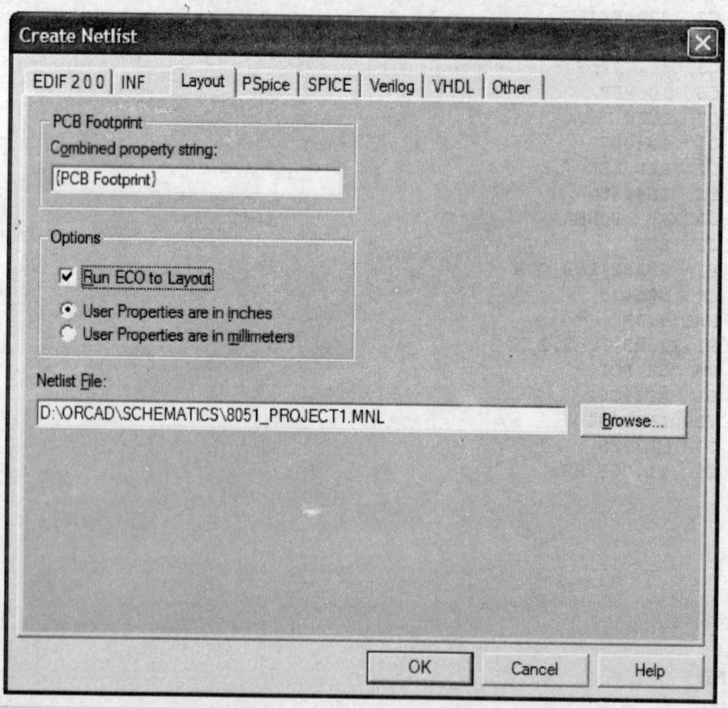

Fig. 8.44 **Netlist creation for 'Layout' tool**

If you plan to use OrCAD '***Layout***' as the layout tool, select the tab '***Layout***' from the pop-up window and select the options as given in Fig. 8.44 and proceed. The '***Netlist***' is generated automatically with extension ***.mnl*** and it will be shown in the '***Output***' section of your project window.

If Cadence '***Allegro***' is your layout tool, select the tab '***Other***' instead of '***Layout***' from the 'Create Netlist' pop-up window as shown in Fig. 8.45.

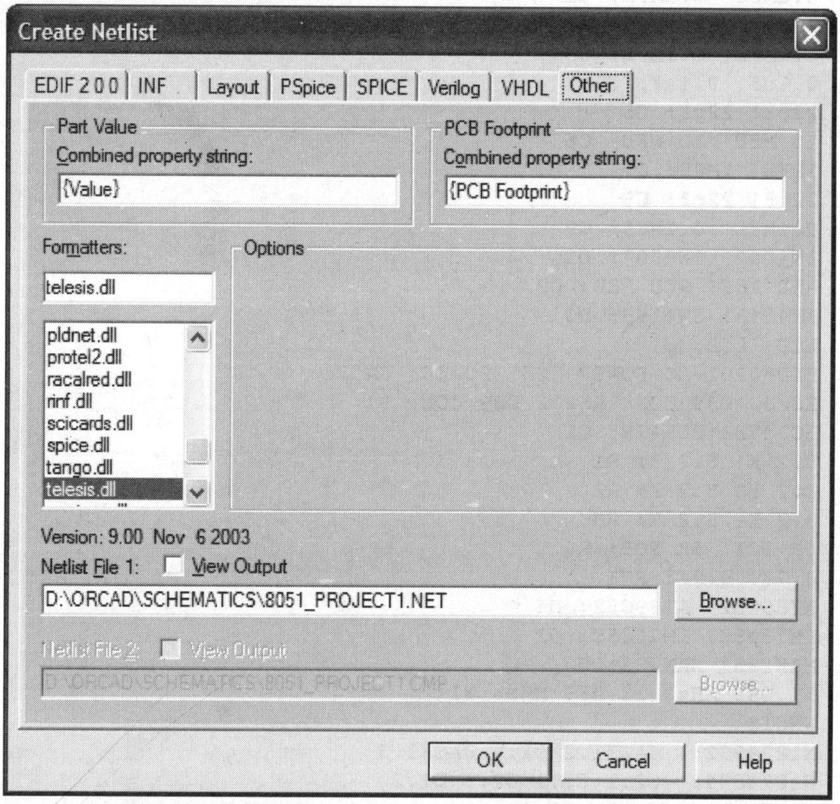

Fig. 8.45 **Netlist Creation for 'Allegro' Tool**

Select '***telesis.dll***' from the '***Formatters***' option and change the '***Netlist***' file creation directory if you want (By default the '***Netlist***' file is generated at the project directory with same name as the project name and extension *.net*) and press 'OK' to proceed.

The '***Netlist***' file is generated automatically and it is visible in the 'Outputs' section of the project window. If you open the '***Netlist***' by double clicking the ***.net*** file from the 'Outputs' section, a file describing the various nets is displayed. A sample '***Netlist***' file generated in '***telesis***' format for "***Allegro***" layout tool is shown in Fig. 8.46.

On a closer look at this file, you can find that it is a representation of the packages (will be described in a later section of this chapter) for various components of the schematic and a 'soft form' representation of the interconnections among the components present in the schematic. The ***.net*** list file contains two sections namely–PACKAGES section and NETS section. The packages section defines the packages of different components in the schematic and the NETS section lists out the various connections in

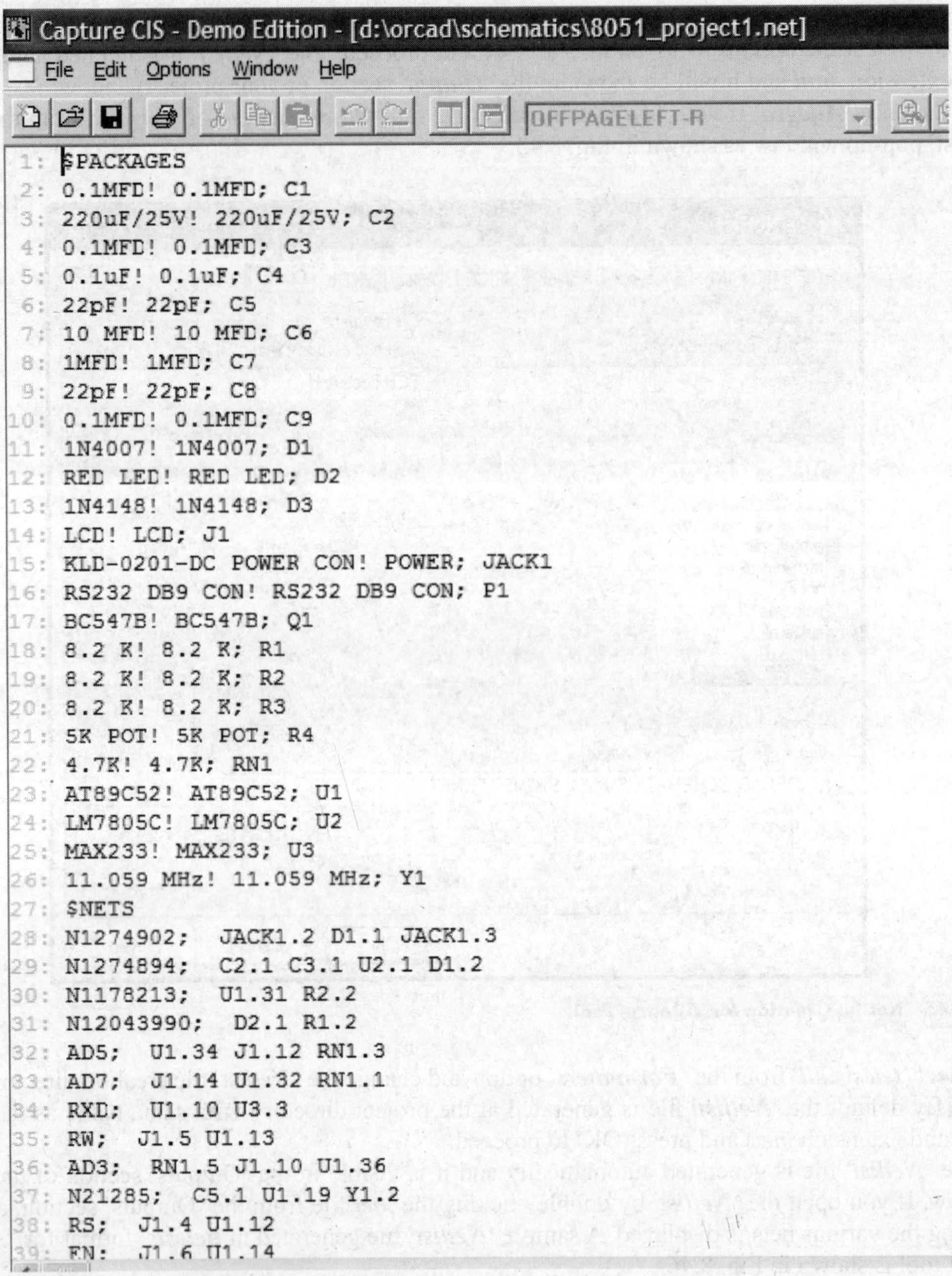


```
$PACKAGES
0.1MFD! 0.1MFD; C1
220uF/25V! 220uF/25V; C2
0.1MFD! 0.1MFD; C3
0.1uF! 0.1uF; C4
22pF! 22pF; C5
10 MFD! 10 MFD; C6
1MFD! 1MFD; C7
22pF! 22pF; C8
0.1MFD! 0.1MFD; C9
1N4007! 1N4007; D1
RED LED! RED LED; D2
1N4148! 1N4148; D3
LCD! LCD; J1
KLD-0201-DC POWER CON! POWER; JACK1
RS232 DB9 CON! RS232 DB9 CON; P1
BC547B! BC547B; Q1
8.2 K! 8.2 K; R1
8.2 K! 8.2 K; R2
8.2 K! 8.2 K; R3
5K POT! 5K POT; R4
4.7K! 4.7K; RN1
AT89C52! AT89C52; U1
LM7805C! LM7805C; U2
MAX233! MAX233; U3
11.059 MHz! 11.059 MHz; Y1
$NETS
N1274902;  JACK1.2 D1.1 JACK1.3
N1274894;  C2.1 C3.1 U2.1 D1.2
N1178213;  U1.31 R2.2
N12043990;  D2.1 R1.2
AD5;  U1.34 J1.12 RN1.3
AD7;  J1.14 U1.32 RN1.1
RXD;  U1.10 U3.3
RW;  J1.5 U1.13
AD3;  RN1.5 J1.10 U1.36
N21285;  C5.1 U1.19 Y1.2
RS;  J1.4 U1.12
EN;  J1.6 U1.14
```

Fig. 8.46 **Netlist file generated for 'Allegro' Tool**

the schematic. A group of connections is given a net name and the component parts which are getting interconnected at that net are listed against the net name. In the net list file given above, the first net is named as N1274902 and it represent the interconnection of Pin 2 & 3 of Jack JACK1 and Pin 1 of Diode D1. You can verify this interconnection by referring back to the schematic diagram in which Pins 2 & 3 of JACK1 is connected to Pin 1 of Diode D1. The '*.net*' file is fed as input to the layout tool for generating the PCB layout.

8.7 THE PCB LAYOUT DESIGN

Layout design is the process of creating the blueprint of the actual PCB from the '*Netlist*' file. The layout file generated for a '*Netlist*' file is given for the final PCB fabrication. Whenever we plan to build a new house, we usually approach a designer to build the 'plan' for the house. The 'plan' contains all information regarding the house, like number of rooms, area of each room, window and door positions for each room, number of floors (single or multistoried house), etc. A '***Layout***' file is similar to the 'plan' for a house in the sense, the '***Layout***' file contains the information on different components present, their physical appearance (footprint), the component placement, interconnection among the components, number of layers for inter connection etc for the PCB.

8.7.1 The Building blocks of Layout

Before going to the details of the usage of the '*Layout Tool*' let's have a brief discussion on 'What is meant by Layout file creation and what all are there in the layout file'. 'Footprints', 'Routes/Traces', 'Layers' 'Vias', 'Marking text and graphics' are the basic building blocks of Layout.

8.7.1.1 Footprint (Package) Footprint is a pictorial representation of a component when it is looked from the top (top view of a component). It is a 1:1 representation of the bottom portion of a component. Imagine you have a chip and a sand-filled box in your hand and if you place the chip on top of the sand-filled box and press it gently, you will get the exact impression of the chip including the body and pin shape of the chip when the chip is removed from the sand. This is what is exactly meant by a footprint.

Package and footprints are two identical terms used interchangeably in PCB layout design. In layout, both the terms represent the same identity. But technically they are two different entities. Footprint can be viewed as a subset of package. Package is a three-dimensional drawing showing all measurements of the component, viz. length, width, thickness for the body as well as pins of the component. Package drawing contains 'Top View', 'Side View' and 'End View' of the component. Out of this, 'Top View' is important in PCB layout design. It gives the space requirement for the component within the board, the orientation of pins, width of pin holes (for through hole components) and the size of pin pads (for surface mount components). The 'Side View' and 'End View' of the component have nothing to do with the board space requirement except in cases where a plug-in board is supposed to put on top of the current board. 'Side view' gives an idea about the component height. In layout, the 'Top view' of the component is known as '***Footprint***'.

Different manufactures produce same chip/component with different names and a large number of chips/components are available in the market. If each manufacturer starts developing chips/components with their own package, it will be very difficult for a layout designer to create a footprint for all. Hence there is a standard for packages and each chip manufacturer should develop chips according to any one of the standard packages supported. The standard package's footprint is available as library in the Layouting Tool and the layout designer can choose that '***Footprint***' for a component. Some of the commonly available packages are explained below.

Single In-line Package Single In-line Package is a single line package where the pins are arranged in a single row with specific pitch spacing. The pins can be either 'Through hole' pins or 'Surface mount leads'. For 'Through hole' pins, the footprint represents the number of pins by drills or vias and

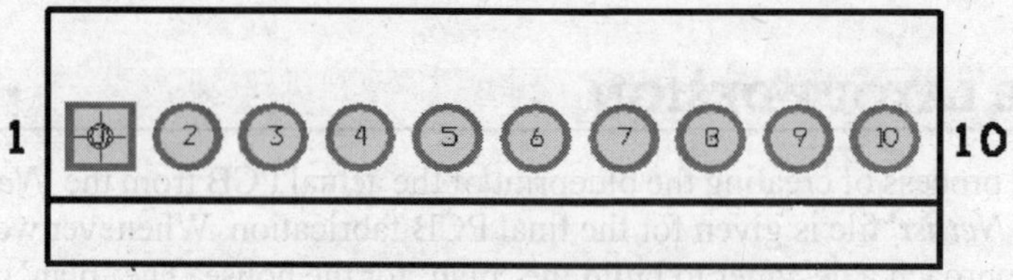

10 Pin Single In-line Packages (SIP) Through Hole

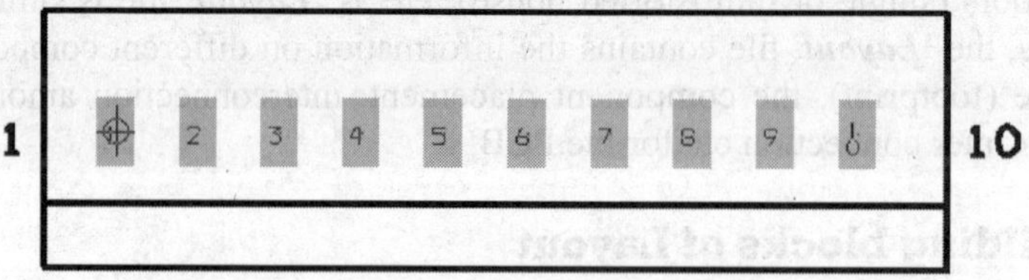

10 Pin Single In-line Package (SIP) Surface Mount

Fig. 8.47 **Single In-line Package (SIP) Footprint**

the dimensional details of the drill are same as that of the pin dimensions. If the pins are surface mount pins, they are represented in the footprint as pads. For 'Through hole' pins, the first pin is indicated by a square pad with a drill/via. The footprint of a 10 pin SIP package is given in Fig. 8.47. SIP package is commonly used for connector parts.

Dual In-line Package Dual In-line Package (DIP) is a commonly used 'through hole' package for Integrated Circuits from the early days of IC technology. DIP contains chip body and through hole pins on both sides of the body of the chip. DIP package itself is varying, depending on the body width of the IC, the pin spacing (lead pitch), etc. The commonly used DIP is with inch pin spacing and 0.3 inch to 0.6 inch body width. The number of pins for DIP varies from 8 to 64 in an even number multiple. An example of the package drawings and footprint of DIP is shown in Fig. 8.48.

The body of the chip is encapsulated in plastic, ceramic or some other material. Depending on this, the Dual In-Line Package is named as PDIP (Plastic DIP), CDIP (Ceramic DIP), etc. (see Fig. 8.49).

Dimensions in Inches and (Millimetres)

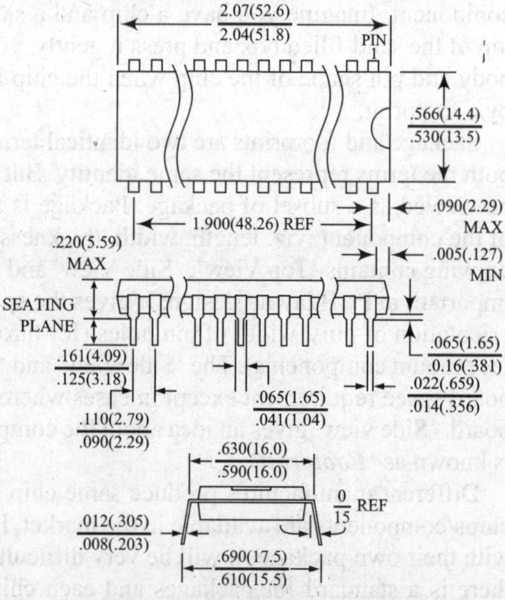

Fig. 8.48 **Package Drawing for 40 Pin Plastic Dual In-line Package (PDIP)**
Courtesy of Atmel (www.atmel.com)

Zigzag Inline Package (ZIP) ZIP package is a modified form of DIP. DIP contains leads (pins) symmetric to both sides of the body of the package, whereas ZIP holds pins in a zigzag manner as shown in Fig. 8.50.

If you observe this package, you can identify that the pin numbering for this is entirely different from that of the DIP. In DIP, the pins are numbered in incremental order in one direction starting from the topmost pin (Left topmost pin) and on the second row the pin numbering continues from the bottom pin (Right bottommost pin) whereas in the case of ZIP, the pins are arranged in zigzag form and the numbering of pins also is zigzag starting from the first pin as shown in Fig. 8.50.

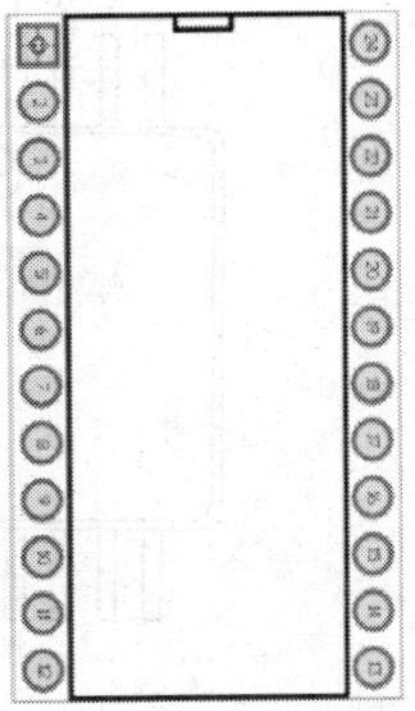

Fig. 8.49 **PCB Footprint for 24 Pin Dual In-line Package (DIP)**

Small Outline Integrated Circuit (SOIC) Package SOIC is a rectangular surface mount package with eight or more gull wing leads. The leads protrude from the longer edge of the package. SOIC packages come in a variety of body widths, namely narrow body (150 mils (1 millimetre = 39.37 mils)) and wide body (300 mils). The standard SOIC lead pitch is nominally 50 mils (1.27 mm). The pin count for SOIC package varies from 8 to 28 Fig. 8.51.

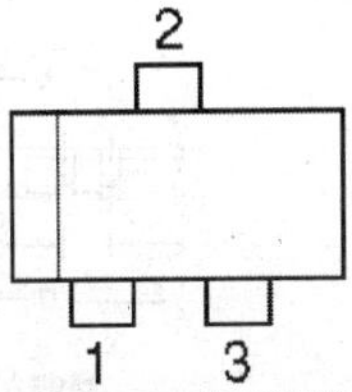

Fig. 8.50 **Zigzag In-line Package (ZIP)**

Thin Shrink Small Outline Package (TSSOP) Thin shrink small outline package is a surface mount package with very small body size and smaller lead pitch. TSSOP comes in the following sizes 3.0 mm × 0.85 mm (Width × Height), 4.4 mm × 0.9 mm (Width × Height) and 6.1 mm × 0.9 mm (Width × Height). Lead count for TSSOP ranges from 8 to 56. Its standard lead pitch is 0.65mm. The package drawing details of TSSOP is shown in Fig. 8.52.

Quad Flat Pack (QFP) So far we discussed about packages with leads (pins) only on the two sides of the body of the chip. There are chips with leads/pins on all four sides of the chip. These chip packages are called Quad Flat Pack (QFP). QFP itself is available in different packages namely Plastic Quad Flat Pack (PQFP), Thin Quad Flat Pack (TQFP), (VQFP), etc. A footprint of 84 pin PQFP is shown in Fig. 8.53.

With this we are concluding the discussion on footprints/packages. There are lots of other packages/footprints remaining. Describing all of them in detail is beyond the scope of this book. The aim of this session was to give the readers a basic understanding of packages and the commonly used

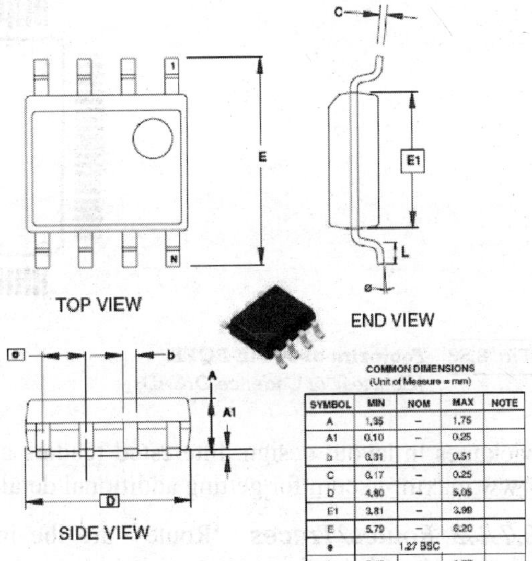

COMMON DIMENSIONS
(Unit of Measure = mm)

SYMBOL	MIN	NOM	MAX	NOTE
A	1.35	–	1.75	
A1	0.10	–	0.25	
b	0.31	–	0.51	
C	0.17	–	0.25	
D	4.80	–	5.05	
E1	3.81	–	3.99	
E	5.79	–	6.20	
e	1.27 BSC			
L	0.40	–	1.27	
θ	0°	–	8°	

Fig. 8.51 **Package drawing for 8 Pin SOIC**
Courtesy of Atmel (www.atmel.com)

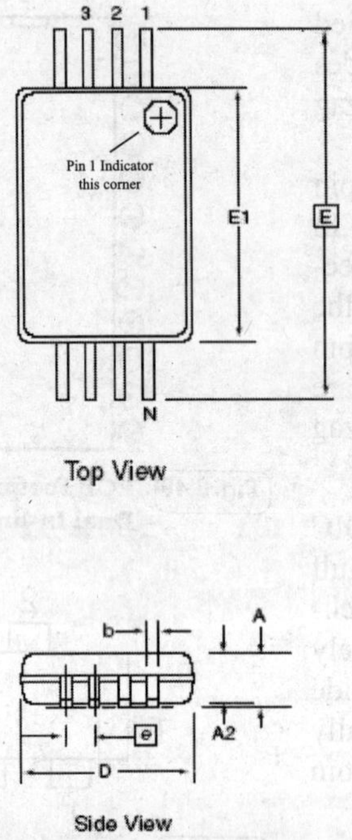

COMMON DIMENSIONS
(Unit of Measure = mm)

SYMBOL	MIN	NOM	MAX	NOTE
D	2.90	3.00	3.10	2, 5
E		6.40 BSC		
E1	4.30	4.40	4.50	3, 5
A	–	–	1.20	
A2	0.80	1.00	1.05	
b	0.19	–	0.30	4
e		0.65 BSC		
L	0.45	0.60	0.75	
L1		1.00 REF		

Fig. 8.52 **8 Pin TSSOP Package**
Courtesy of Atmel (www.atmel.com)

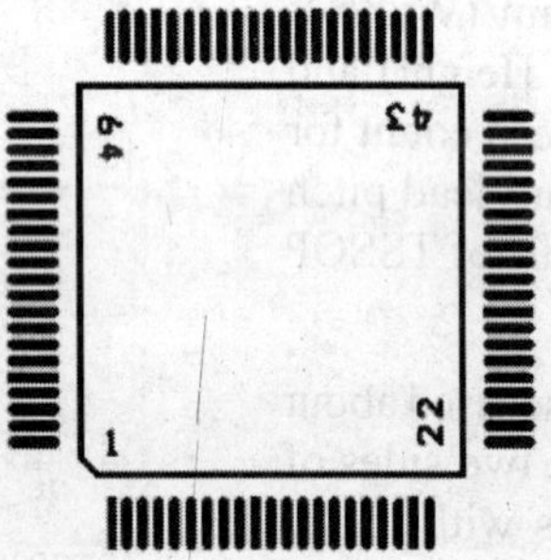

Fig. 8.53 **Footprint of 84 Pin PQFP**
(Courtesy of Cadence OrCAD)

packages in layout design. Interested readers are requested to visit the websites www.atmel.com and www.maxim-ic.com for getting additional details on packages.

8.7.1.2 Routes/Traces 'Routes' are the interconnection among the pins/leads of various components. In schematic capture, it is represented as an electrical connection line. Whereas in layout, the interconnection is represented as copper track interconnection among the leads/pins of different footprints. This copper interconnection is known as 'PCB Track'. The width of the copper track can be set to various values during layout to represent tracks with different widths. Commonly used track widths are 5 mils, 7 mils, 12 mils (1 mm= 39.37 mils), etc. Proper track width should be allocated to tracks connecting to power supply line and ground line. Some reference chart is available for determining the minimum track width required for carrying a particular current (e.g. For carrying a current of 500 mA, the track width should be minimum 12 mils, etc). The routes and footprint of a PCB layout are shown in Fig. 8.54.

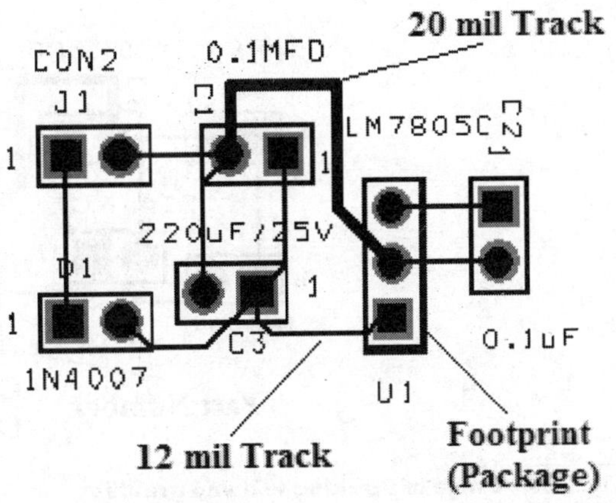

Fig. 8.54 **Routes (Track) and footprint of a PCB layout**

8.7.1.3 Layers 'Layers' act as the 'Multiple planes' for performing the routing operation, if the number of interconnections in a design is high. Normally the routing is done on the top and bottom layers of the PCB. If the complexity of the circuit increases, additional layers are added in between the top and bottom layers and the track routing is done on this layers. It is also advised to allocate separate layers with copper spreading for power supply and ground connections. This avoids noise and electromagnetic interference issues in printed circuit board.

8.7.1.4 Via In a 'Multilayer' board, the interconnection among various layers is provided through conductive drill holes. These drill holes are known as 'via'. Drilling is done on the physical PCB using Computer Numeric Control (CNC) drill machines or laser drills. The drilled holes should be copper plated or riveted (Inserting a rivet into the drill hole) to establish the necessary inter-electrical connection among the various layers. 'Vias' are also known as through holes. If the through hole is plated or riveted for establishing electrical connection, it is called 'Plated Through Hole (PTH). If non-plated, it is referred as none-PTH. Figure 8.55 illustrates 'via' and 'PTH' in PCB layout.

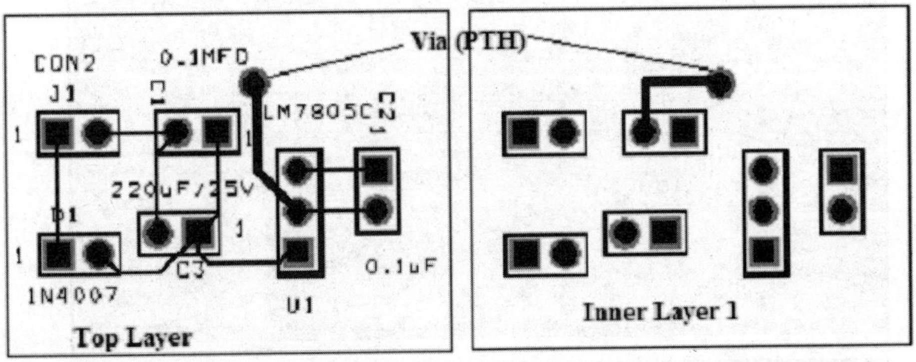

Fig. 8.55 **Illustration of Multiple layers and PTH**

8.7.1.5 Marking Text and Graphics Marking text and graphics provide information like part number, part name, polarities of polar components (like capacitors, diodes, etc.), pin number, product name, company name, board name, graphic outline of components, etc. These text and graphics are printed on PCB after fabrication (Fig. 8.56). Refer to section **Silk Screen** for more details.

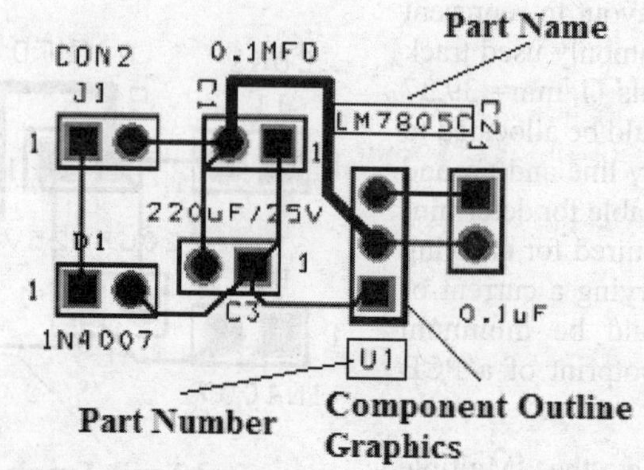

Fig. 8.56 **Usage of marking text and graphics**

8.7.2 Layout Design with OrCAD Layout Tool

To create a PCB layout using OrCAD Layout tool, execute "*Layout Demo*†" from the '*Start Menu*'. You can see the following tool window on your PC screen (Fig. 8.57).

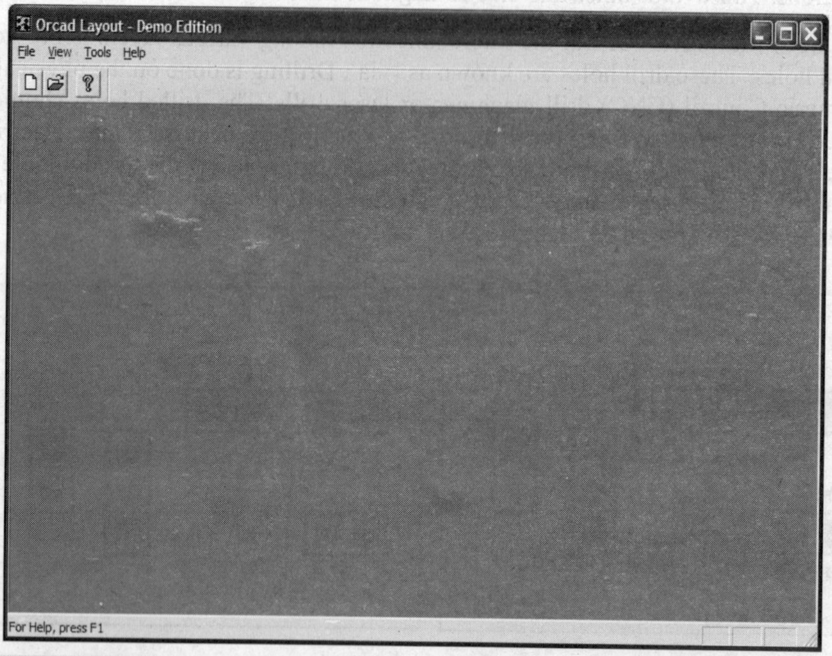

Fig. 8.57 **OrCAD Layout Tool**

† The name given here indicates the name of the demo version tool. It may be different for the commercial version of the tool. Please refer to the OrCAD documentation for more details.

Select '*New*' from the '*File*' menu. A pop up window (AutoECO) describing the inputs to be fed to the tool appears on the screen (Fig. 8.58).

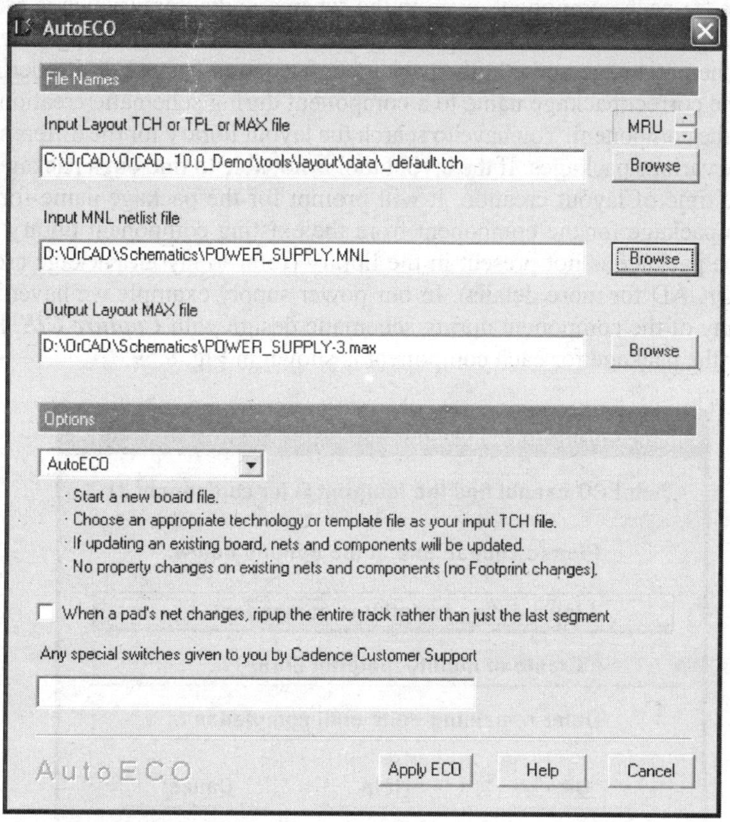

Fig. 8.58 **Creating a New PCB Layout using Layout Tool**

The AutoECO pop up window contains the following sections.

Layout TCH or TPL or Max file This is the reference template and you can select the _default.tch file for this. Clicking on the 'Browse' button by the side of the edit box for this section guides you to the directory containing the tch/tpl/max file. Select '_default.tch' from it.

Input MNL netlist File This is the section for inputting the '*Netlist*' file created using OrCAD '*Capture CIS*' schematic design tool. The file extension of the '*Netlist*' file specifically created for '*Layout*' in the Capture CIS tool is '*.MNL*'. This '*Netlist*' file, containing the component information and component interconnection is going to be transferred to a PCB layout format. In our case the netlist file for the design for power supply part of the 8051_Project is POWER_SUPPLY.MNL.

Output File Section This is the O/p file generated in layout corresponding to the *.MNL* '*Netlist*' file input. By default its name appears same as netlist name and the file extension is '*.MAX*'

Select the default values for all other options and press 'Apply ECO' button to create the new layout file. The '*Netlist*' is processed and if it is error free, the layout tool associates each component's package (footprint) as per the '*Netlist*' file. The '*Netlist*' file associates a package to each component as per the package value given for each component given in the schematic diagram (which is created using Capture CIS). To assign a package value to a component at the time of schematic design itself, right click the component in the schematic page and edit the package information from 'Edit Properties…' section. If you do not assign the correct package name to a component during schematic creation, a default package is associated to the component. You have to search the layout library for the different package names corresponding to the various packages. If the layout tool is not able to find out a package associated with a component, at the time of layout creation, it will prompt for the package name for the component. You should select a package for the component from the existing component library or should create a new package if the package is not present in the library (refer to layout package creation and usage documentation by OrCAD for more details). In our power supply example we haven't associated any package name for any of the component during schematic design with ***Capture CIS***. Hence the layout tool will prompt for the package for each component is shown in Fig. 8.59.

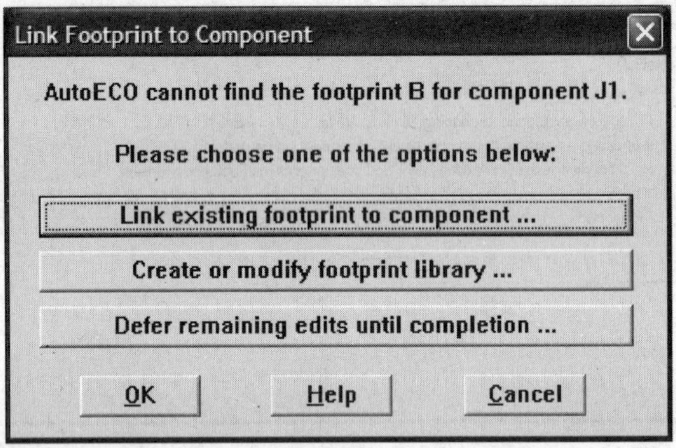

Fig. 8.59 Package (footprint) selection for component

Select the option "Link existing footprint to component…" and link a footprint to the component (Fig. 8.60)

The set of available footprint libraries and the footprints available in the selected library is listed on the footprint selection dialog box. As you move between different footprints, its preview also is shown on the selection dialog box. Since we are using the demo version, the number of footprint libraries and footprints within each library are limited. Select the footprint fitting to the package of your component in terms of size. Repeat the selection for all components.

On completion of the footprint assignment and '*Netlist*' verification, Layout generates an 'AutoECO' report describing the errors, if any. Accept the report if it is error free. Now you can see the package of various components placed on a layouting canvas (Separate Window along with the drill chart). The interconnections among various components are represented in the form of lines as shown in Fig. 8.61.

8.7.2.1 Board Outline Creation To start with the physical layout process, the first step is assigning the physical board size (PCB size in length × width) to the layout area where the components are

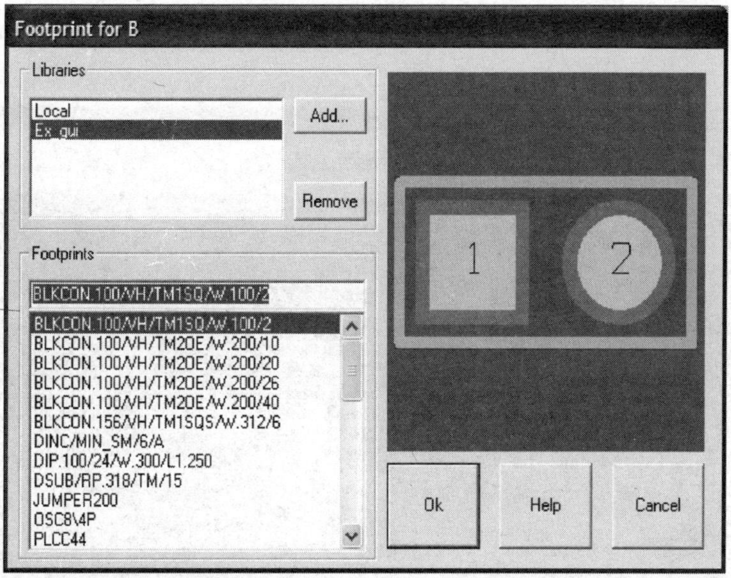

Fig. 8.60 **Package (footprint) selection for component**

going to be placed. For this, the datum (reference point) needs to be fixed first. Move the datum to a convenient location using the command '***Move Datum***' from '***Tool***' menu (Tool→Dimension→Move Datum). Place the datum at the desired position by clicking on the desired point on the layout window after executing the '***Move Datum***' command. Press 'ESC' key to exit the command. Move the drill chart to a convenient location by executing the command '***Move Drill Chart***' from the '***Tool***' menu (Tool→ Drill Chart→ Move Drill Chart). After selecting this command, click on the desired portion where you want to place the drill chart. The drill chart will be moved to that location. Press 'ESC' to exit the drill chart movement operation.

Datum acts as the reference point (0,0) for the design. All measurements are taken with respect to the datum. The co-ordinate left to the datum is taken as –ve and right to datum is taken as +ve. Also co-ordinate on top of datum is +ve and bottom one is –ve. The co-ordinates are displayed as per the co-ordinate system selected during the '*Netlist*' file creation. If the selected system is in inches, the co-ordinate positions are shown in inches. If it is in metric, the co-ordinate system is represented in millimetres in the layout tool (Fig. 8.62).

After fixing the datum, provide an outline to the layout by using the obstacle tool from the tool window. Select the '***Obstacle***' tool from the Tool window (Tool→Obstacle→Select Tool) and click at the datum to start the layout boundary. Move the cursor up till the y co-ordinate reaches the desired width of your layout (PCB width) and then move the cursor towards the right till the x co-ordinate reaches the desired length of your layout (PCB length). Now move the cursor down from this position. Once the cursor reaches a point which is in line with the datum, a rectangle with width and length set for your layout is formed. Press 'ESC' key to stop the execution of '***Obstacle***' creation command. The boundary for your layout (Blueprint of original PCB) is ready and you need to move all the components inside this boundary and arrange them within that boundary and interconnect the various components as per the connections coming from various components. For this, various '*layout tools*' are required. Before

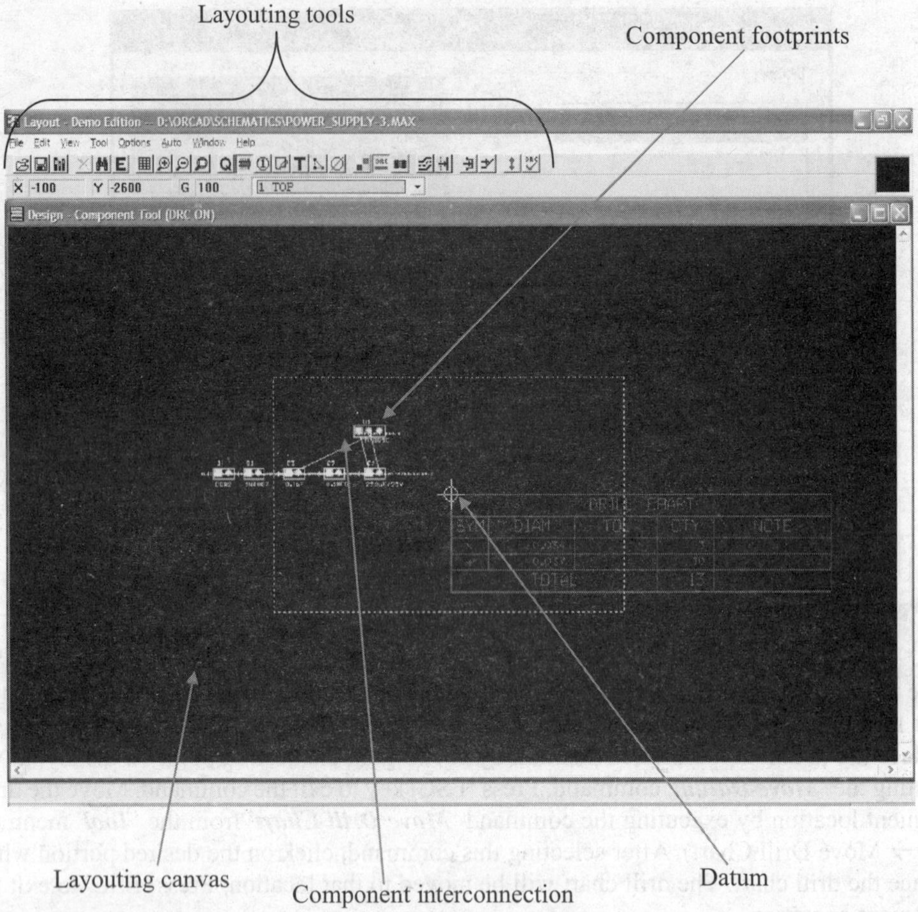

Fig. 8.61 **Component Packages (footprint) placed at the layout tool**

proceeding to the next steps let's have a quick glance at the important tools used from the tool window for this. Figure 8.63 illustrates the different layout tools.

Component Tool: Selects a component. Mainly used for positioning the selected component within the selected boundary of the layout.

Zooming Tools: Zooms in and out the selected portion of the Layout.

Obstacle Tool: Allows the drawing and editing of obstacles such as board outline, outline of components (parts) etc.

Text Tool: Inserts texts in the selected area. It is used for placing and editing Part Number, value, notes etc on the layout area. After selecting this tool right click on the layout window and input the required parameters.

Online DRC: Error checking option. If the online DRC option is selected (ON) during the component layout and inter-connection, any errors occurred (Package to package distance error, track to track distance less than the set value, connection error, etc.) at the layout operation is indicated in real time.

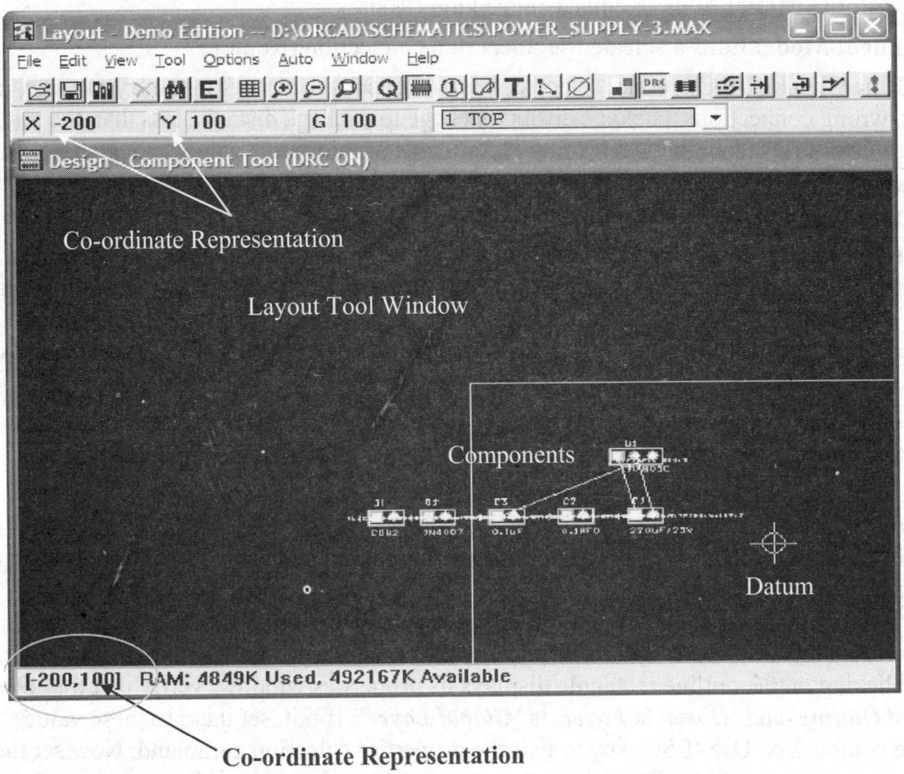

Fig. 8.62 **Co-ordinate representation in layout tool**

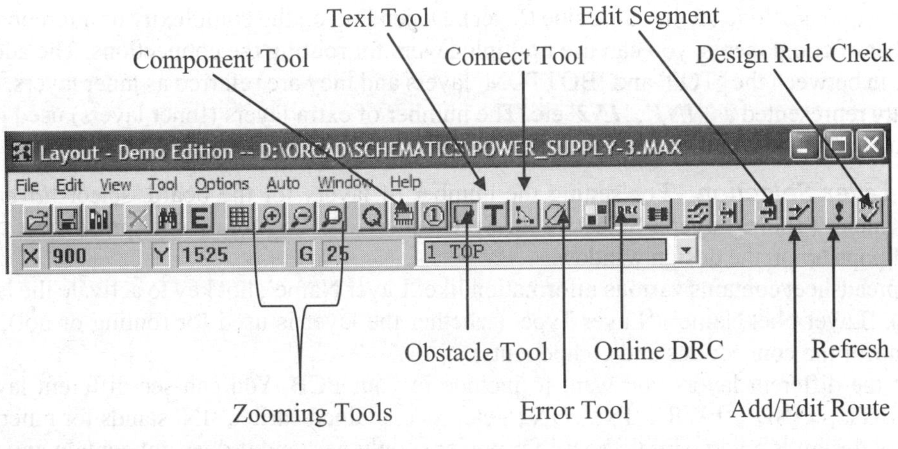

Fig. 8.63 **Different layouting tools (Tool Window)**

Add/Edit Route Mode: Adds or edits a connection (Route)

Edit Segment Mode: Edits a selected segment of a connection (Route)

Design Rule Check (DRC): When selected, this tool checks the errors in the layout, like, missing connections, wrong connections, package errors (package to package distance less than the minimum value set), trace errors (Distance between routes less than the minimum value set), etc. Normally DRC is performed at the end of layouting. If the online DRC was not kept 'ON' during layouting, at the end of layouting, you should run DRC command to verify that there are no errors in layouting the board.

Connect Tool: Inserts a new connection between any components which is not present in the original schematic/netlist. It is useful in situations where you need to add an extra connection apart from the original schematic/netlist. Adding an extra connection without modifying the original netlist file will generate DRC errors. DRC will assume it as a connection made by mistake. If you added it deliberately, you can ignore the error.

Error Tool: Error tool gives the complete description of an error in the layout. Select the error tool and click at the error mark on the layout window to get the corresponding error's description.

Refresh Tool: Refreshes the layout window.

There are lots of other tools also available for layout process. Describing all of them is out of the scope of this book. Readers are requested to get the details of the rest of the tools using the '***Help***' provided by Layout Demo tool.

We have already fixed the board outline for the design using the obstacle tool. Ensure that the obstacle tool created the obstacle as 'board outline', by checking the properties of the board outline rectangle. Double clicking on the outline rectangle displays its properties window. Verify that the '***Obstacle Type***' is '***Board Outline***' and '***Obstacle Layer***' is '***Global Layer***'. If not, set them to these values from the appropriate combo box. Use 'ESC' key to exit the properties selection command. Now set the number of layers required for your PCB. For a through hole component based board we require at least two layers namely; '***TOP***' and '***BOT***' (bottom) layers. The component is placed usually at '***TOP***' layer and inter connections (routes) are created at the '***BOTTOM***' layer. For Surface Mount Device (SMD) components based boards, the minimum number of layers required is one, where both component placement and interconnection are done on the same side (layer). Depending on the complexity of interconnections and the number of components, you can use multiple layers for routing the connections. The additional layers come in between the 'TOP' and 'BOTTOM' layers and they are referred as inner layers. Inner layers are usually represented as '***IN1***', '***IN2***' etc. The number of extra layers (Inner layers) used in the layout (PCB) solely depends on the complexity and number of inter-connections.

8.7.2.2 Layer Selection For setting the number of layers for the board, select '*layer tool*' from the Tool menu (Tool→Layer→Select From Spreadsheet…). The following spreadsheet as shown in Fig. 8.64 pops up on the design window.

The spreadsheet contains various information like 'Layer Name', hot key to activate the layer ('Layer Hotkey'), 'Layer NickName', 'Layer Type' (whether the layer is used for routing or not), and Mirror Layer (mirror the connections and components).

Select the different layers you want to include in your PCB. You can see different layers namely 'TOP', 'BOT', 'GND', 'PWR', 'IN1', 'IN2', etc. As explained earlier, 'IN' stands for inner layers. Our illustrative design is a very simple board for power supply part and it does not contain any inner layers and separate Ground and Power layers. Disable whatever layers we are not using in the design by double clicking on the corresponding cell of '***Layer type***' and set it to 'Unused'. For a double sided through hole

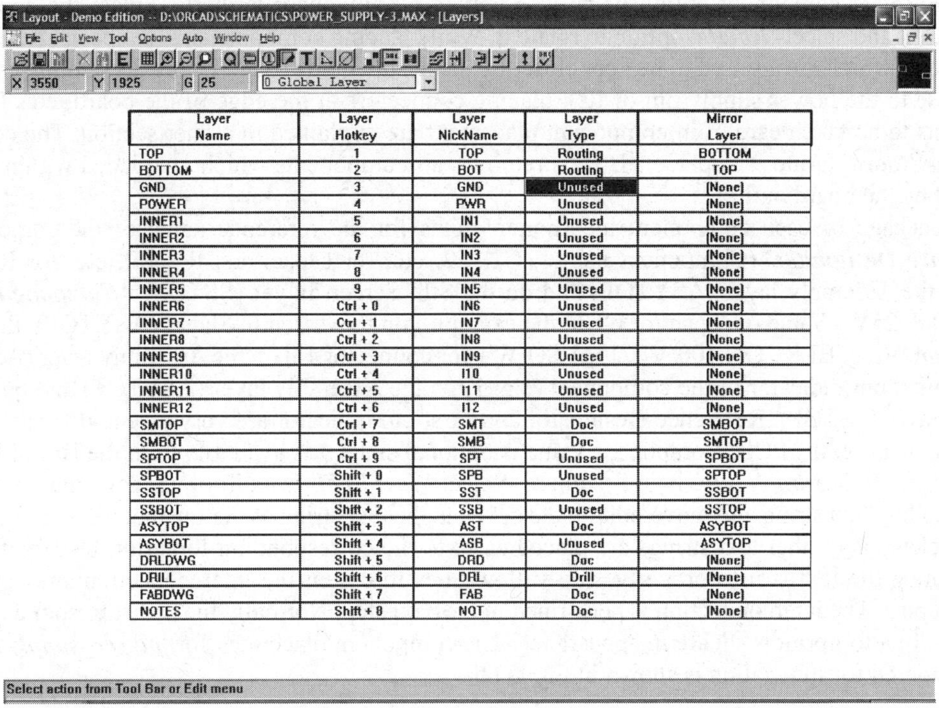

Layer Name	Layer Hotkey	Layer NickName	Layer Type	Mirror Layer
TOP	1	TOP	Routing	BOTTOM
BOTTOM	2	BOT	Routing	TOP
GND	3	GND	Unused	[None]
POWER	4	PWR	Unused	[None]
INNER1	5	IN1	Unused	[None]
INNER2	6	IN2	Unused	[None]
INNER3	7	IN3	Unused	[None]
INNER4	8	IN4	Unused	[None]
INNER5	9	IN5	Unused	[None]
INNER6	Ctrl + 0	IN6	Unused	[None]
INNER7	Ctrl + 1	IN7	Unused	[None]
INNER8	Ctrl + 2	IN8	Unused	[None]
INNER9	Ctrl + 3	IN9	Unused	[None]
INNER10	Ctrl + 4	I10	Unused	[None]
INNER11	Ctrl + 5	I11	Unused	[None]
INNER12	Ctrl + 6	I12	Unused	[None]
SMTOP	Ctrl + 7	SMT	Doc	SMBOT
SMBOT	Ctrl + 8	SMB	Doc	SMTOP
SPTOP	Ctrl + 9	SPT	Unused	SPBOT
SPBOT	Shift + 0	SPB	Unused	SPTOP
SSTOP	Shift + 1	SST	Doc	SSBOT
SSBOT	Shift + 2	SSB	Unused	SSTOP
ASYTOP	Shift + 3	AST	Doc	ASYBOT
ASYBOT	Shift + 4	ASB	Unused	ASYTOP
DRLDWG	Shift + 5	DRD	Doc	[None]
DRILL	Shift + 6	DRL	Drill	[None]
FABDWG	Shift + 7	FAB	Doc	[None]
NOTES	Shift + 8	NOT	Doc	[None]

Fig. 8.64 **PCB Layer Selection**

PCB with components placed at TOP layer and routing at Bottom layer, the minimum layers required are Top Layer ('TOP'), Bottom Layer ('BOT'), Solder Mask Bottom ('SMBOT'), Silk Screen Top (SSTOP) for legend printing, Assembly Top ('ASYTOP') for giving component assembly notes, Drill drawing ('DRLDWG') and 'DRILL'. Keep the '***Layer Type***' of all other layers to 'Unused' and close the spreadsheet. The layers Solder mask, Silk screen, etc. are explained in a separate section of PCB fabrication. Please refer it for more details.

8.7.2.3 Component Placement Component placement is the process of moving components into the layout area within the board outline and arranging them properly within the area. Components can be placed either automatically or manually. If the automatic placement option is selected, '*Layout*' automatically arranges the components within the area covered by the board outline. Select the Automatic component placement option from menu (Auto→Place→Board) to enable automatic placement. Auto place option is normally used with boards with lesser number of components and interconnections. For boards with large number of components and interconnections, the auto place option need not be an optimised one, especially when the board size requirement, component placement, routing, etc. are critical. Manual placing is the advised method in such situations. Manual placement involves moving of the component manually to the desired location on the layout area and placing it appropriately. To activate manual placement, select the '***Component***' icon from the tool window or '***Select Tool***' from the '***Tool***' menu (Tool→Component→Select Tool). Click on the component and move it to the desired position within the area defined by the board outline. Move all components like this. Place the components in a way facilitating their easy interconnection. For easy interconnection, components should be oriented properly. Rotate component option helps in orienting a component properly. Select the component, right click it and select '***Rotate***' option to rotate it. While placing components, give special care to place components which are advised to be kept closer by the design guide (e.g. Placing decoupling capacitors very close to the power supply pin of IC), placing connectors at the edge of the board, etc. The various points to be taken care of in component placement are explained in a later section. The command '***Unplace Board***' (Auto→Unplace→Board) removes all components which are placed within the area bounded by the board outline.

The package of each component incorporates texts for the reference name of the component—'***Reference Designator***' (Component names, C1, C2, etc. for capacitors, R1, R2, etc. for Resistors, etc.) on the Assembly layer (ASYTOP) and on the Silk Screen Layer (SSTOP), '***Component Value***' (e.g. 220uF/25V - Value of capacitor C1 in the example) on the Assembly layer (ASYTOP), the '***Footprint Name***' (e.g. BLKCON.100/VH/TM1 SQ/W.1 for connector J1) on the Assembly layer (ASYTOP) and the First pin indicator of the component (e.g. 1) on the Assembly layer (ASYTOP) and on the Silk Screen Layer (SSTOP). Reference Designator and First pin indicator are very essential for assembling the component on the PCB. Component Value is optional since it is available from the Bill of Material (BOM) file. '***Footprint Name***' is not required. Select '***Text Tool***' from Tool window and click on the corresponding text string and move/edit/delete or rotate the text string as per the requirement. Unwanted text is deleted and other text strings are placed close to the corresponding footprint. Use rotate option for orienting the text strings properly. The yellow lines represent the interconnection among various footprint pins. The interconnection is performed in the next step. Normally the pad corresponding to pin number 1 of a footprint is square in appearance. The component placement for '***power_supply.mnl***' net file considered for illustration is shown in Fig. 8.65.

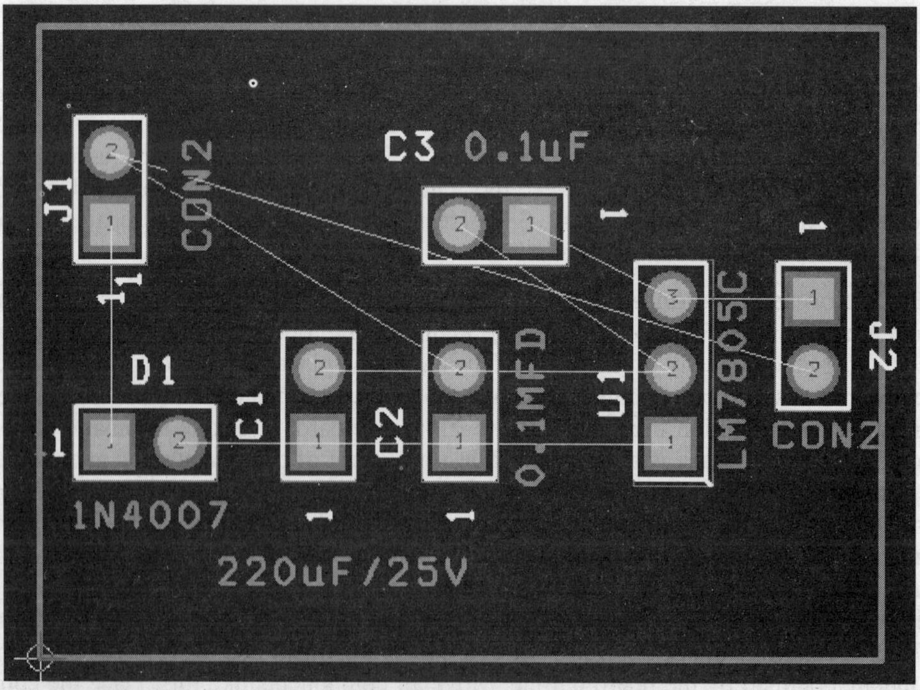

Fig. 8.65 **Component Placement, Datum and Board outline**

8.7.2.4 PCB Track Routing Routing deals with interconnecting the various components as per the capture schematic diagram. The routing information is passed to the layout tool from schematic capture through the '*Netlist*' file. Routing is performed after component placement. First the components are arranged in the desired manner. The interconnection among various components is shown in the layout as 'Yellow lines'. The interconnection lines of a net are referred as 'rats' in PCB terminology. 'Route/track' represents the actual copper path present on the PCB. The track properties of the physical board are determined by the 'Route' in the layout.

Similar to component placement, routing can also be performed either automatically or manually. If automatic routing command is executed, the sweeps are executed automatically and the complete board is routed automatically. Execute the '***Autoroute***' command (Auto→Autoroute→Board) from the menu for routing the board automatically. Auto routing is suitable for boards with lesser number of routes (Interconnections). For complex routing, auto routing is comparatively inefficient and requires multiple layers, more layout area and route connecting holes across different layer (PTH). Manual routing is the best choice for routing complex boards. Though it takes lots of time (of the order weeks) to route a complex board, manual routing provides highly optimised layout with minimal number of layers and plated through holes. Complex boards can be autorouted if the time required to complete the board is critical and the number of layers involved as well as number of plated through holes (PTH) in the board is not a constraint. For a double sided, 'Through hole' board, normally the components are placed at the 'TOP' layer and track routing is done at the bottom ('BOT') layer. If the board is a multilayer board and the number of interconnection are very high, layout contains multiple layers (Inner layers; IN1, IN2 etc). In multilayer boards, apart from inner layers, there may be separate layers for ground 'GND' and power 'PWR'. These layers are usually spread with copper. For multilayer boards the connections are routed through different layers and the continuation of a connection from one layer to the other layer is achieved through a special mechanism called 'via'. Via is a drill hole connecting a route from one layer to another route present in a different layer. Vias are copper plated or riveted to maintain electrical connectivity between the two connecting routes.

While working with multilayered layouts, as routing progresses, the layout area becomes congested with the different tracks routed on various layers. To avoid this you can selectively turn ON and OFF different layers. Say, for example, if you are placing tracks on the second inner layer (IN2) and you feel the routes which are already placed on the first inner layer (IN1) is creating difficulties in placing the routes on the second inner layer, you can turn off the first inner layer. Any layer can be turned off while routing by selecting the corresponding layer from the layer selection combo box and pressing the minus key† '-' on the keyboard. This removes the selected layer from view. To activate the layer, press '-' key again (Toggling with '-' key). Layers like Assembly Layers (AST, ASB), Silk Screen Layers (SST, SSB) can always be switched OFF till the layout process is complete. Other layers are switched ON and OFF conveniently according to the routing process. Layer selection enabling and disabling is depicted in Fig. 8.66.

By default the different layers of the layout are colour coded with different colours to distinguish them. The default colours† for different layers are given below:

Global layer = Yellow
Top = Green
Bottom (BOT) = Red
Inner Layer 1 (IN1) = Aqua

† May change with change in tool version.

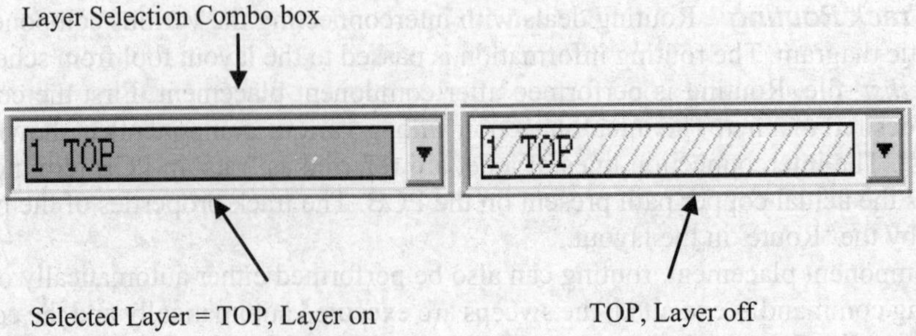

Fig. 8.66 **Layer selection, enabling and disabling**

Inner Layer 2 (IN2) = Blue
Silk screen Top (SST) = White
Assembly Top (AST) = Green
Drill Details (DRD) = Red

The colour code for different layers can be edited with the '***Colour Settings***' Tool from the '*Layout Tool*' window or by executing the '***Colours…***' command (Options→Colours…) from the '***Options***' menu. Invoking the 'Colour Settings' pops up a colour selection spreadsheet. Double click on the present colour for the layer in the spreadsheet and select the desired colour from the color selection window (Note: Always perform the layout operation with the default colours provided by a layout tool for different colours. Changing the colour of the layer is for user convenience only).

Defining Global spacing The following spacing parameters should be set before starting the routing (component interconnection) of the board.

Track-to-Track: Track-to-track spacing specifies the minimum space required between two adjacent tracks, and between tracks and adjacent obstacles. Normally the track to track spacing is set as 12 mil (1 mm= 39.37 mils). The track to track spacing is a critical criterion in PCB fabrication. Always set a track to track space value supported by the PCB fabricator. Nowadays PCBs with 6mil track to track separation is possible with latest PCB fabrication techniques.

Track-to-Via Spacing: Track-to-via spacing specifies the minimum space required between via and an adjacent track. Normal value is 12 mils

Track-to-Pad Spacing: Specifies the minimum space required between pads (Pin pads of components) and tracks of different nets. Normally used value is 12 mils

Via-to-Via Spacing: Specifies the minimum space required between two adjacent vias. Normally used value is 12 mil

Via-to-Pad Spacing: Specifies the minimum space required between pads and adjacent vias.

Pad-to-Pad Spacing: Specifies the minimum space required between two adjacent pads.

Select the '**Global Spacing**' command (Options→Global Spacing…) from the '**Options**' menu and set the desired values for all spacing in the 'Route Spacing' spreadsheet pop-up window.

Manual routing of Board Now all pre-requisite for routing is through. To start with the routing process, select the layer on which the routing operation is carrying out, from the layers selection combo box. Follow the steps given below:

1. Select the '***Edit Segment Mode***' tool from the tools window (or execute the command Tool→Track→Select Tool from the Tool menu)
2. From the View menu, choose Zoom In, click on the screen to magnify the routing area you are working on, and then press ESC to end the zoom command
3. Select a ratsnest (A point from which the yellow line indicating an interconnection starts). The cursor changes to a small-size cross† and the ratsnest is attached to the pointer
4. Drag the pointer to draw a track on your layout area. Right clicking the left mouse button, anchors the track at the nearest pad on the net
5. Continue to move the cursor to draw additional segments of the track, clicking the left mouse button to create vertices (corners) in the track as you route. You can delete a routed segment by placing the cursor over the segment and pressing DELETE key
6. Click the left mouse button to complete the route. The cursor changes to a regular-size cross and the ratsnest disappears from the cursor
7. Select the completed route and choose Lock from the pop-up menu. This locks the route you created so that it cannot be moved if the board is later autorouted
8. Repeat the process for all rats of the layout. On completing a track drawing, the rat representing it is replaced with the route
9. For adding a via (through hole) to connect the route (track) to a track placed on other layers, right click the mouse on the desired location, while you are dragging the mouse to draw a track. Select the '***Add Via***' option
10. To draw the tracks on a different layer select the layer from the layer selection combo and proceed
11. To change the width of the track, right click on the track and select the '***Change Width***' option. Type the desired track width and execute. The normal value for track width is 12 mil. The minimum width of track depends on the value supported by PCB fabricators and the comments from the component manufacturer like the track width of the signal lines should be this much, etc. Nowadays fabrication of PCBs with track width 6 mil is possible. Ensure that proper track width is provided to tracks representing power supply lines and ground. There is a standard guideline for track width selection for power supply lines. Follow these guidelines strictly
12. If possible reduce the track length from a component to ground and always connect the ground tracks coming from different components in a '***star***' model. This eliminates ground elevation problems in PCB

8.7.2.5 Placement & Routing Statistics Placement and routing statistics ensures that all components are placed in the layout and all nets are routed perfectly. It is mandatory to verify the same to ensure that nothing is missed from the components and routes section. For verifying the placing and routing statistics follow the steps given below.

1. Select the '***View Spreadsheet***' toolbar button and choose '***Statistics***'. The Statistics spreadsheet window is displayed
2. Scroll until you find the '***Placed***' and '***Routed***' rows, showing the placing and routing statistics. The statistics should be 100% for both. A statistics value less than 100 for 'Placed' indicates some components are missed from placing. Similarly if the statistics for 'Routed' is less than 100, the routing is incomplete, meaning some tracks are yet to be routed
3. Close the spreadsheet when you have finished viewing the statistics

† Depends on the tool version in use.

8.7.2.6 Adding/Editing Texts in Layout Design

Text strings in '*Layout*' is used for creating Assembly notes and labels. To create/edit/delete a text string, select the '***Text Tool***' from the Tools Menu (Tool→Text→Select Tool from Tool menu). Right click on the layout window for inserting a new text string and select the '***new***' option (or Press '***Insert***' key of keyboard). The following text properties window appears on the screen depicted in Fig. 8.67.

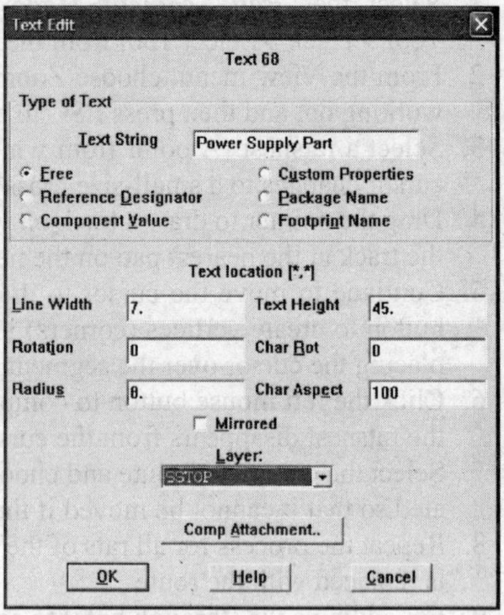

Fig. 8.67 **Text Edit Dialog Box**

Adding a Text String

1. From the 'Type of Text' group box, select the type of text that you want to create
2. Select the '***Free***' option or the '***Custom Properties***' option for adding assembly note and labels. Type a text string into the '***Text String***' text box
3. Edit the 'Line Width', 'Rotation', 'Radius', 'Text Height', 'Char Rot' (character rotation) and Char Aspect (character aspect) text boxes as desired
4. Select the Mirrored option if you want the text to appear mirrored on the layer (useful for placing text on the bottom of the board)
5. Select the target layer from the 'Layer drop-down list' (If the text is to be printed on the silkscreen layer, select the corresponding silkscreen layer (e.g. SST–Silkscreen Top). For assembly texts choose the corresponding assembly layer (e.g. AST–Assembly Top)
6. If you want the text to be attached to a component, choose the '***Comp Attachment***' button, select the '***Attach to Component***' option, input the component's reference designator (e.g. C1, U1, etc), then press OK button
7. Press OK button to close the Text Edit dialog box
8. Position the text on the screen and click the left mouse button to place it

Moving a Text String For moving a text string in the layout area, follow the steps given below.

1. Select the '***Text Tool***' from the Tools menu
2. Click on the text, which is to be moved, with the left mouse button. Text gets attached to the cursor
3. Move the mouse to position the text in the new location
4. Click the left mouse button to place the text

Editing a Text String Execute the following steps to edit an existing text in layout

1. Select the '***Text Tool***' from the the Tools menu
2. Double click on the text which is to be edited, with the left mouse button. The 'Text Edit' window pops-up
3. Perform the required changes on the Text Edit Dialog box and press OK
4. Press 'ESC' key to exit the text edit mode

Deleting a Text String Follow the steps given below to delete a text string.

1. Select the '***Text Tool***' from Tools menu
2. Select the text by clicking on it with the left mouse button
3. Press the DELETE key

8.7.2.7 Assembly Notes Assembly notes are useful information for those who are assembling components on the PCB. To provide useful information, layout should contain component information like name of the component (C1, R1, D1, L1, U1, etc.), pin number of component, polarity of the component, if any, point indicating the placement of an IC, etc. Some information (Like component name, pin number, etc.) embeds with the '*Netlist*' file by default and they appear on the layout at the time of placing the component. The assembly note information is kept on the Assembly layer (e.g. Assembly Top Layer (AST)). If the same information is present on assembly and silk screen (SST or SSB) layers, you can remove it from one of the layers. Use the 'Text Tool' from Tools menu (or Tool→Text→Select Tool from Tools menu) to add, delete, modify or rotate Assembly note Texts.

Apart from the text information, graphic information can also be added to the Assembly layer. Symbols of diode, capacitor, etc. showing the polarity are typical examples. Use the obstacle tool to create symbols on the assembly layer. For performing any operation with the assembly layer, select the assembly layer (e.g. AST) from the layer selection combo box. Now select the obstacle tool and draw whatever symbol you want (e.g. A diode symbol is created as the combination of a triangle obstacle and three line obstacles). You can group the obstacles together by right clicking on the layout area where the obstacles are present and moving the mouse icon in a rectangle area which contains all the obstacles that needs to be moved together. After all obstacles of the group are selected, hold down the right button of mouse and move the group of obstacles to the area in layout where you want to place them. Set the '***Obstacle Type***' of the obstacle/obstacle group to '***Free track***' by editing the obstacle/obstacle group properties. An obstacle/obstacle group can be linked to a component by editing the properties of the obstacle/obstacle group (obstacles selected together). Enable Obstacle tool, right click on the obstacle/ obstacle group and select the option '***Comp Attachment…***' from the '***Edit Obstacle***' pop-up window. Give the Reference name of the component to which the obstacle is to be linked (say C1, U1, etc.) on the '***Reference designator***' edit box. Linking the assembly not obstacles to the component moves it along with the component whenever the component is re-arranged in the layout window.

8.7.2.8 Drill Details To set the pad stack and drill dimensions of the vias used in the layout, execute the steps given below.

1. Select the pin tool from the '***Tool***' menu (Tool→Pin→Select Tool)
2. Click on the via with left mouse button
3. Select '***View Spreadsheet***' from Tools menu
4. Set the pad stack size and drill diameter

8.7.2.9 PCB Mounting Hole Creation Mounting holes are required for mounting the PCB on the enclosure. PCB is fixed to the enclosure using screws and washers. PCB should contain mounting holes and the size of the mounting hole is determined by the mounting screws. The size of the screw is expressed as M2, M3, etc. The '***Capture CIS***' schematic tool does not contain a part for mounting holes and we cannot add mounting hole information to schematic diagram. Mounting holes are directly added to the layout. Follow the steps given below to add a mounting hole to the PCB layout.

1. Select the '***Component Tool***' button from the toolbar
2. Right click on the layout window and select New (or Tool→Component→New… from the 'Tool' menu). The 'Add Component' dialog box appears on the screen
3. Select the 'Footprint' button. The 'Select Footprint dialog' box is displayed
4. In the Libraries group box, select the library '***LAYOUT***'. Use the Add button, if necessary, to add this library to the list of available libraries
5. In the footprints group box, select a mounting hole (OrCAD provides three types of mounting holes: MTHOLE1, MTHOLE2, and MTHOLE3)

6. Press OK to close the 'Select Footprint' dialog box
7. Tick the 'Non-Electric' option, and then press 'OK' to close the 'Add Component' dialog box. The mounting hole gets attached to the cursor
8. Place the mounting hole on the desired area of your board layout by clicking the left mouse button
9. Select '***Padstack***' command from the Tool menu (Tool→Padstack→Select from Spreadsheet). Scroll down to the "100R110" section of the spreadsheet, double click on the name and select '***Non-Plated***' option

Note: This feature is not available with the demo version of the software. Only the full featured version supports it.

8.7.2.10 Design Rule Check (DRC) Design Rule Check (DRC) is performed to verify the layout is meeting all design criteria and there are no errors in the layout. If online DRC is enabled, any error in layout is automatically reported at the design time itself. If online DRC is ON, a white rectangle box (DRC Box) appears on the layout window. Keep the layout area within this rectangle so that any errors at the time of placing or routing are notified by online DRC. If the layout is not fitting in the current DRC box, execute the following steps to incorporate the entire layout area within the board outline to the DRC Box.

1. Select '***Zoom DRC/Route Box***' from the View menu. The cursor shape changes to the zoom cursor 'Z'
2. Move the cursor to the target location and click the left mouse button. Layout zooms in at the new location, centering it on the screen
3. Adjust the click till the layout area fits into the DRC Box

The final DRC check is performed by executing the '***Design Rule Check***'. Executing DRC checks the layout for all kinds of design rule errors, missing connections and components, etc. DRC reports all errors. The description of each error can be obtained using the error tool (Tool→Error→Select Tool). If there is any error in the layout process, rectify it before proceeding to the next stage (creation of gerber files)

8.7.2.11 Cleanup Design Cleanup design command enhances the manufacturability of the board. Executing it automatically smoothens and checks for both aesthetic and manufacturing problems that might have been created in the process of manual or automatic routing. The design should be cleaned up at least once, at the end of the layout process. For cleaning up the design, execute the command '***Cleanup Design***' from the '***Auto***' menu (Auto→Cleanup Design…). Cleanup command corrects the problems listed below.

- Acute angles
- Bad copper share
- Pad exits
- Overlapping vias.

8.7.2.12 Gerber File Creation Gerber file creation is the final stage in the '***Layout***' process (PCB design process). Gerber file transforms the '***Layout***' into PCB fabricating tool understandable format. All the component info, layer info, routing info, drill info etc are included in the gerber file. Gerber is a universally accepted file exchange protocol between the PCB manufacturer and PCB designer.

Follow the sequence of operations listed below for generating gerber file corresponding to the design.

1. Save the layout file (The file is saved with extension '***.max***' and with the name given at the time of creating a new design)

2. Execute '***Post Process Settings***' command from '***Options***' menu (Options→Post Process Settings…). The '***Post Process***' window appears
3. In the '***Post Process***' window ensure that the '***Batch Enabled***' option is set '***Yes***' only to the layers which are selected during the layout design process
4. Ensure that the 'Device' option for all entry is '***EXTENTED GERBER***'
5. Right click on the '***Post Process***' window and select '***Run Batch***' (or execute '***Run Post Processor***' from '***Auto***' menu after closing the '***Post Processor***' window)
6. The gerber file is generated automatically and the confirmation and path of the created file is provided in the form of message boxes

Corresponding to each layer of the '***Layout***', a file is created with the layer name as extension (e.g. '***power_supply.top***' for TOP layer). This file contains all information related to that layer. The '***.tap***' file gives the drill detail information for CNC drilling. All these files (files corresponding to each layer and '.tap' file) are sent to the PCB manufacturer for fabricating the PCB.

8.7.2.13 Finished Layout An example of a finished layout is given in Fig. 8.68. This layout is created for our '***power_supply.mnl***' netlist example.

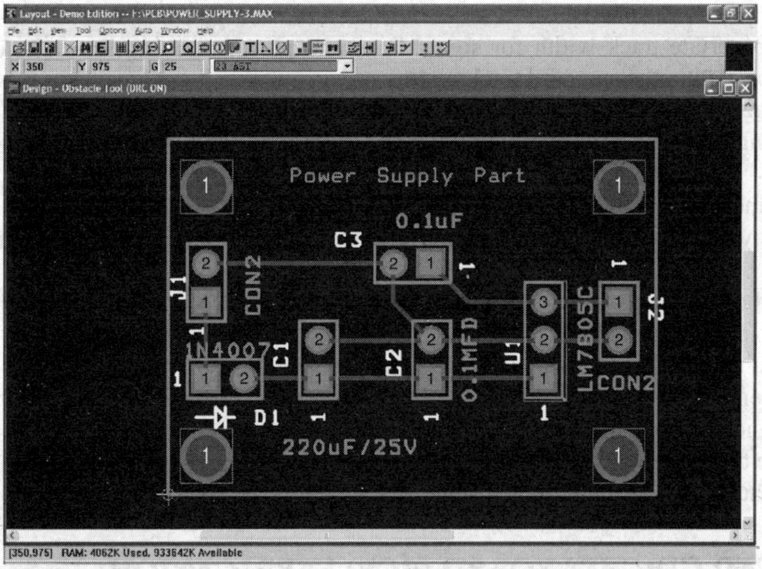

Fig. 8.68 **Finished Layout**

The layout contains component footprints, tracks, mounting holes, top and bottom layer, silkscreen top layer and assembly top layer. The tracks are routed at the bottom layer and they are shown in red colour. The white coloured text and diode symbol is assembly note and they are drawn on the assembly top layer. Green coloured texts are labels and they are drawn on the silkscreen top layer. Save the layout file. The file extension for layout file is '***.max***'. The '***.max***' file can be opened with the '*Layout Demo*' Tool at any time for viewing the routing/placing and modifying.

8.7.3 Guidelines for PCB Layout

The proper functioning of the PCB as well as its dimensions depends on the positioning of the various components and the interconnection among them within the '***Layout***' design. PCB manufacturer fabricates the PCB as per the layout files. An inefficient layout leads to an inefficient PCB. As a rule of thumb, follow the basic guidelines given below, while laying the components and interconnecting them in the '***Layout***'.

1. Place the components inside the layout area within the board outline, keeping the physical size of the PCB in mind
2. Always keep the minimum component to component distance while placing components
3. Place connectors towards the edge of the PCB and consider the enclosure thickness while placing connectors
4. Keep the number of layers minimal. As the number of layers increases, the complexity of the board and fabrication cost also increases and it is very difficult to debug the connections against any non-functioning
5. Use lesser number of vias in the board. Board strength reduces with increase in number of vias.
6. Provide sufficient fixing holes on the board. Arrange fixing holes in a way providing maximum strength/support to the board
7. Provide appropriate track width for signal lines and power carrying lines (Refer to the design guideline for getting the standard track width)
8. Keep the track to track spacing at least the minimum value supported by the PCB fabricator
9. Avoid routing of signal lines over power lines. (If not it may create Electromagnetic Interference issues)
10. Always connect ground point of different components in star model to avoid ground elevation. If possible provide a separate ground plane (layer) and directly connect all ground connections to this plane
11. Take care of components which need to be kept closer (Like decoupling capacitors for ICs)
12. Avoid sharp edges for tracks
13. Provide neat and easily understandable Assembly notes
14. Avoid the congestion of routes on a layer
15. For double side component mounting, before placing a component on the bottom side of the PCB, consider the components height and the clearance between the bottom side of PCB and the enclosure when the PCB is in the mounted state

8.8 PRINTED CIRCUIT BOARD (PCB) FABRICATION

A Printed Circuit Board (PCB) is a platform for placing electronic and electro mechanical components and interconnecting them without discrete wires. Printed Circuit Board (PCB) consists of printed conductive wires (called PCB Tracks) and component layouts attached to an insulator sheet. The insulator sheet is referred as substrate and it is usually made up of 'Glass Epoxy—A fibre glass reinforced epoxy material' or 'Pertinax—A phenol formaldehyde resin'. The normal thickness of this substrate sheet is 1.6 mm. PCB is also known as Printed Wiring Board (PWB). The finished PCB layout looks exactly the same as the Physical PCB with all its layers representing the layers physically present in the PCB and routes of the layout represent the tracks of the PCB. The final step in the hardware design is the fabrication of the PCB. For executing this, all information contained in the layout should be transferred to the

PCB fabrication tool understandable format. The Gerber file created from the layout along with drill details serve the purpose of transferring this information from layout to PCB fabrication tool. Gerber is a universally accepted standard for transferring relative co-ordinates and track information and component details of a layout for PCB fabrication. Gerber files are a collection of art works. In a multilayer PCB, each layer has its own art file representing the component co-ordinates, component info and track info for that layer. The drill details file provides the drilling information (drill hole diameter, plating, etc.) of different vias (PTH) present in the layout. The actual drilling is performed on the PCB using Computer Numeric Control (CNC) drills or laser and the drilling is controlled in accordance with the drill details file.

8.8.1 Different Types of PCB

Depending on the complexity of connections involved and component density, the PCB tracks may be routed through a single layer or multiple layers and the component placement may be either on one side (top or bottom of PCB) and or on both sides (top and bottom of PCB). According to this, PCBs are generally classified into the following categories.

8.8.1.1 Single Sided PCB For simple and small circuits, only one layer (either the top layer or bottom layer) is used for routing the connections. Such PCBs are known as single sided PCBs, where all the connections and tracks are present on one side. If the components used in the design are all surface mount devices (SMD), the component placement as well as the track creation is done on one side. If some components are 'Through hole' components and the track routing is done only on one layer, the 'Through hole' components should be placed on the opposite side of the PCB layer holding the tracks.

8.8.1.2 Double Sided PCB If track routing is done on both sides of the PCB and component placement is also done on both sides, the PCB is called as 'Double side Mounting PCB'. In 'Double side Mounting PCB', the connection required from one side to the other side for circuit connectivity is achieved through 'Plated Through Holes (PTH)'. The PTH/via is a drilled hole which is either copper electroplated or riveted with small rivets. The via may be a visible via with a cylindrical hole and plating on both PCB sides or a completely buried via in which the drill hole is totally filled with conductive material like copper. It is advised to use less via as possible in a board and use buried via, in case of any via required. The major issue in using buried via is fabrication cost. In ancient times the circuit connection between two end points of a drill hole was achieved through inserting a conductive wire and soldering the ends of the wire to the circuit on the pads present on both sides of the board.

8.8.1.3 Multilayer PCB If the complexity of connections in the circuit to be fabricated is high, routing of connections is performed using multiple layers. Multiple layered PCBs, contain additional routing layers called 'inner layers' apart from the top and bottom layers. The number of layers required and the connections on each layer is fixed at the routing time itself and each layer in the layout represents a physical layer in the PCB. The number of inner layers may vary from 1 to 16 depending on the circuit complexity. It is a common practice to allocate separate layers for 'Ground' and 'Power Supply' in multilayer PCBs. The separate ground layer and power layer reduces the effect of any accidental antenna loop formation in the circuit. All layers of the PCB are fabricated separately and finally they are stacked and glued together. Alignment marks are provided on each layer for aligning the layers properly for stacking them. The final PCB looks like a single PCB, though it contains PCB layers inside. The required interconnections between the tracks of different internal layers are established through drill holes called 'via'. The 'via' may be a copper electroplated drill hole or a riveted 'Plated Through Hole'.

8.8.1.4 Piggy-Back/Plug-in/Daughter PCB Piggy-back/plug-in/daughter PCBs are designed to plug into some other PCBs. The Piggy-back PCB may itself be a single sided/double side mounting or multilayer PCB. Most of the COTS component comes as piggy-back/plug-in PCBs.

8.8.1.5 Flexible PCB Flexible PCBs are highly flexible compared to normal PCBs. Normal PCBs use rigid substrate for copper etching platform and they are 'rigid' in nature, whereas flexible PCBs use flexible substrates like plastic as the substrate sheet and the copper film are deposited on top of it. Flexible PCBs are widely used in fabricating 'Antennas' for RF systems and applications requiring connectors as a flexible PCB, like membrane keypad connectors LCD connectors, etc.

8.8.2 PCB Fabrication Methods

PCB fabrication is the process of creating physical PCB from the layout files supplied in the form of gerber files and drill detail files. Three common techniques are adopted for this. They are described in detail in the following sections.

8.8.2.1 Photo Engraving (PCB Etching) Photo engraving is the oldest technology used in PCB fabrication. It is the most popular technology and even today also it plays a vital role in PCB fabrication. Photo engraving is based on the photographic technique (Technique similar to the one used in developing photographs from a negative film) and it makes use of photo masks and chemical etching. To adopt photo engraving technique, the different layers of the layout should be converted into a film very similar to the negatives of photograph. The gerber photo plotter files are inputted to a photo plotting machine and it produces the photo-plot (PCB film) of each layer. The process of creation of PCB film from art files is termed as 'Photo plotting'. The tracks and copper using areas in the layer are opaque (black) and other portions are transparent in the films. These PCB films are used as 'Photo mask' for photo engraving.

Copper coated on a substrate sheet is used as the metal for photo engraving. A photo sensitive material called 'photo resist', which is resistant to acids and other etching materials is applied to the copper sheet. The 'photo mask (PCB film for the corresponding layer)' is kept on top of the photo resist material coated copper sheet and it is aligned properly. This sheet is then exposed to strong ultraviolet rays. The places on the target copper clad board where the PCB film is transparent gets hardened and the opaque regions remain as such. The photo resist is then developed by washing in a solvent that removes the unhardened parts. Finally, the copper area to be engraved (removed) is exposed to an acid or other etching compound which dissolves the exposed parts of the copper sheet. Ferric chloride or ammonium per sulphate chemical bath is used for removing the unwanted copper from the substrate. Each layer of the PCB is fabricated like this and then the required vias are drilled on each layer. Finally all layers are stacked together exactly as present in the layout design to form the finished PCB. Vias used for interconnecting various layers are copper plated or a conductive rivet is inserted into them to establish circuit connections.

8.8.2.2 PCB Milling PCB milling is a straightforward and more precise technique for fabricating PCBs. It uses 2 or 3 axial milling machine to mill away the unwanted copper from a copper cladded substrate which is used for each layer. The milling is done on the basis of gerber file for each layer. Here no PCB films are created and it is a chemical free process. PCB milling machine operates in a way similar to a photo plotter and receives the commands from the host software that controls the position of the milling head in the x and y axes (for 2 axial milling) and x, y and z axes (for 3 axial milling). Compared to photo engraving, the accuracy of PCB milling is very high. PCB milling accuracy is dependent only on milling system accuracy and the milling bits. With milling technique it is very easy to create sharp track edges, pads, etc. on the PCB. Both milling process and engraving process are 'subtractive' process since copper is removed from the substrate board to create electrical isolation.

8.8.2.3 PCB Printing PCB printing is the latest technology adopted in PCB fabrication. As the name indicates PCB printing is similar to the ordinary printing. The only difference is that instead of ink and toner, conductive ink is used and papers are replaced by substrates. Also special types of printers are used for the same.

8.8.3 How a finished PCB looks like and how it is made operational

As mentioned earlier, all the layers of the ***'Layout file'*** are transformed into corresponding physical layer using any of the above-mentioned fabrication techniques and after fabrication of all layers, they are stacked and glued together in the same order as they present in the ***'Layout file'***. The conductive drill holes are plated with copper, or riveted using appropriate rivets. Now the top layer and bottom layer are the only visible layers and they contain the top layer and bottom layer tracks (if any) and component placement copper spread pads (for Surface Mount Devices) and through hole pads (for through hole components). If you examine this PCB you can see the tracks and component layouts but you may not be able to identify which component layout is corresponding to a component given in the 'schematic diagram', since there is no visual indication marks provided on the PCB at this stage, describing the component name, its value (if needed) and the component polarity if any (for polar components like capacitors). Next step is the printing of component 'Part reference Number' details on the top/bottom layer where component layout is done.

8.8.3.1 Solder Mask One more step is involved in the PCB fabrication process before printing the part reference text and layout outlines. In the etched/milled or printed PCB the copper tracks are exposed and there is a chance for corrosion and abrasion. To avoid this, a plastic layer is deposited on top of the PCB. This plastic layer is known as 'Solder Mask'. Solder mask protects all the copper track and spreading from exposure to the surrounding atmosphere. Solder mask also resists the "bead-up" of solder (wetting by solder; where solder is a conductive lead material for fixing components to the pad and track) and prevents the solder used for fixing components from flowing in the PCB. Solder mask is exposed in points which are intended for soldering components. The commonly used solder mask is green coloured and that's why PCBs are green coloured in appearance. Solder mask is applied to top and bottom layers of PCB depending on the presence of copper components. Solder masks are also available in other colours like red, black, blue, etc.

8.8.3.2 Silk Screen The process of printing the part reference information for various components on top of the solder mask layer is called ***'Silk Screen printing or Legend printing'*** and the printings are referred to ***'Silk Screen legend'***. This legend provides readable information on component part numbers and placement of components like where the first pin should come, or the polarity information like + and – of components and also the layout boundaries of the components. This information is necessary for placing the components while assembling the components on the PCB and also for repairing. The printing is performed using ***'Silk screens'***. It can also be done using Inkjet printers. Silk screen printing is done on top and/or bottom layer of the PCB depending on the placement of components on these layers. The silk screen layout file corresponding to the top layer is 'Silk Screen Top (SST)' and for bottom layer it is 'Silk Screen Bottom (SSB)'.

8.8.3.3 Testing PCB The PCB manufacturer itself conducts a preliminary test, after fabricating the PCB to ensure that all the nets (connections) in the gerber file supplied by the end user got interconnected according to the gerber files. This test is known as "Bare Board Test (BBT)". BBT is conducted at the manufacturing setup and the PCB is delivered to the end user only after ensuring the BBT is correct.

Checking the internal connections within a multilayered board is very difficult. However the end user can conduct tests like "Visual Inspection", on receiving the PCB. "Visual Inspection" is performed to ensure there are no 'shorts' within the visible part of the PCB. A magnifying glass is used for examining the board. It is advised to perform a Visual Inspection test always, before soldering the components. Nowadays tests like JTAG Boundary scanning is available for testing the interconnection among various ICs present in the board using the boundary scan cells of the ICs and JTAG interface.

8.8.3.4 Component Assembly Component assembly is the process of soldering the circuit components like capacitors, resistors, ICs, connectors, etc. on the PCB. The components are connected to the PCB through soldering. The soldering technique may be either manual or automated. In manual soldering process, components are soldered on the board by soldering experts using soldering iron and soldering lead. The Bill of Materials generated for the schematic diagram is used as the reference part number and value selector for the components and the legend printed on the PCB helps in finding out which component is to be placed on which part of the PCB. In automated soldering process, machines are used for executing the soldering operation. Here also human intervention is required. Various soldering techniques like re-flow soldering, etc. are used. Techniques like X-ray are used for inspecting the correctness of machine soldering in lead free component assemblies.

It is not recommended to assemble all components in a single stretch for the first time in a proto model development. Split the circuit into different modules like power supply module, processor module, etc. and assemble the components for one module at a time preferably starting with the power supply part of the board and ensure that each module is working properly. Examine the expected output of each module and ensure you are getting the correct output. Move on to the next modules only after getting the correct output from the last assembled module. If you are not getting the expected output, ensure that all components necessary for the functioning of that module is assembled properly, examine the input and output signals of the modules using hardware debugging tools like Multimeter, CRO, Logic Analyser, etc. Make necessary changes in the PCB circuits if required. Most of the times adding of additional components, cutting of tracks, etc. may be required in the first board since we are using it for the first time and we are not familiar with the component and system behaviour in it. Hence this board will be an experimenting board–More precisely "Prototype Board" in embedded technical term. The drawbacks of the circuits in the proto board and the circuit and component modifications, required if any, are included in the next versions of the proto board and it goes into commercial production once it functions in the expected way. It is strongly advised to fabricate lesser number of PCBs in the first run.

Run small test applications on the processor part to ensure that the processor part is working properly. For example, if the board contains some LEDs or buzzers connected to the output ports of the processor, you can write small firmware program to manipulate their status (like blinking LED, turning buzzer ON and OFF, etc.). This helps in ensuring the processor part is functioning properly. You may find it very difficult to do a modulewise assembling and testing, but remember it is a one-time process and once you identify the problems with a board you can apply the remedial measures to all boards and go for a mass assembly. The proverb "A stitch in time saves nine" is really meaningful in the case of embedded hardware design. If you spend some effort for this it will definitely help you in saving the additional time, effort and money in debugging.

If you assemble all the components together in a single stretch for the first time and power it ON, you can see your product functioning properly only if you are a very lucky person ☺. Otherwise it may end up in a board blast or damage. Moreover you won't learn anything on the hardware and the mystery behind how it functions, if it starts functioning in the first run itself. Debugging the hardware only gives you sufficient knowledge on it (from a developer perspective). From a product development company perspective, the product should function fully in the first run itself. The design is always well checked, simulated and debugged before fabrication to avoid all possible problems. Still there may be chances for problems, since hardware functioning is unpredictable.

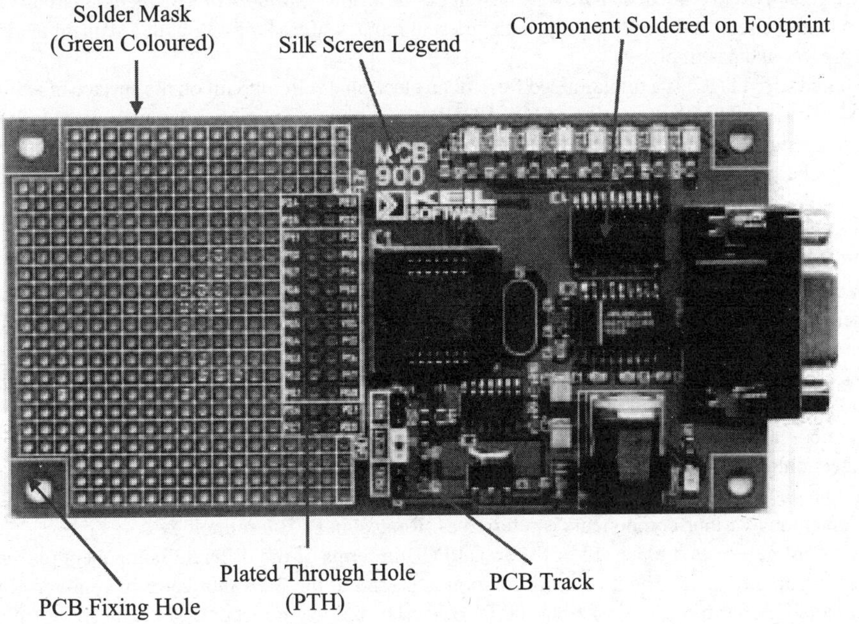

Fig. 8.69 **Finished PCB with components Assembled (Top view)**
Courtesy of Keil (www.keil.com)

8.8.3.5 Conformal Coating The embedded product need not be deployed in a controlled environment always. Hence the PCB along with the components assembled on it should withstand all the extreme operating conditions. The environment where the PCB is going to deploy may be a dusty one, highly humid one, etc. Presence of metal dust particles and conducting corroding particles may create electrical short-circuiting or corroding of the PCB. A special coating called '***Conformal coating***' is applied over the PCB to prevent this. Conformal coating should only be applied after assembling all the components. Dilute solution of silicon rubber or epoxy is used as the conformal coating material. The assembled PCB is either dipped in the conformal solution or the conformal solution is sprayed on the assembled PCB. Another technique used for conformal coating is sputtering of plastic on to the PCB in a vacuum chamber. The major disadvantage of using a conformal coating is, servicing of the board and replacement of the components, in case of any damage, is extremely difficult, since the coating is a permanent one.

Summary

- ✓ The hardware of embedded system contains analog electronic components like resistors, capacitors, inductors, OpAmps, diodes, transistors, MOSFETs, etc., Digital electronic components like logic gates, buffers, encoders and decoders, multiplexers and de-multiplexers, latches, etc. and digital sequential and combinational circuits, Analog, digital and mixed Integrated Circuits (ICs) and Printed Circuit Board
- ✓ Open collector is a special transistor configuration for interfacing the output signals from Integrated Circuits with other systems which operate at the same or different voltage level as that of the IC
- ✓ A digital circuit used in embedded hardware design can be a *Combinational* or a *Sequential* circuit. The output of a combinational circuit is dependent only on the present input, whereas the output of a sequential circuit depends on both present and past inputs
- ✓ An Integrated Circuit (IC) is a miniaturised form of an electronics circuit built on the surface of a thin silicon wafer. VLSI design deals with the design of ICs. VHDL is a hardware description language used in VLSI design
- ✓ Electronic Design Automation (EDA) tool is a set of Computer Aided Design / Manufacturing (CAD/CAM) software packages which help in designing and manufacturing the electronic hardware like integrated circuits, printed circuit board, etc.
- ✓ OrCAD is a popular EDA tool for PCB design from Cadence Design Systems (www.cadence.com). CaptureCIS is the OrCAD tool for circuit creation (schematic capturing), Layout is the PCB layout tool and pSPICE is the circuit simulation tool
- ✓ The schematic capturing tool converts the component details and the interconnection among them in an electronic circuit to a soft form representation called *netlist*
- ✓ Packages are standard entities for describing a component in PCB design. PDIP, ZIP, SOIC, TSSOP, VQFP, PQFP are examples for standard packages.
- ✓ Netlist file contains information about the packages for different components of the circuit diagram, and the interconnection among the different components represented in the form of 'NET's
- ✓ The multiple planes used for interconnecting different components in a PCB is known as 'Layers' and the interconnection among various components is referred as 'Routes' in PCB terminology
- ✓ The layout tool generates a blueprint of the actual PCB in terms of the different component placement, the interconnection among them. The layout information is passed to the PCB fabricator in a universally acceptable standard called gerber file for fabricating the PCB. Gerber file is a collection of art files corresponding to the different layers of the PCB and drill details for the vias and holes present on the PCB
- ✓ PCB is a platform for placing electronic and electromechanical components and interconnecting them without discrete wires. PCB contains printed conductive wires (called PCB tracks) and component layouts attached to an insulator sheet. The insulator sheet is referred as substrate and it is usually made up of 'Glass Epoxy—A fibre glass reinforced epoxy material' or 'Pertinax—A phenol formaldehyde resin'. The normal thickness of this substrate sheet is 1.6 mm
- ✓ PCB etching (Photo engraving), PCB milling and PCB printing are the commonly used PCB fabrication techniques to develop a PCB from the gerber file information
- ✓ PCBs can be classified into Single Sided PCB, Double Sided PCB, Multilayer PCB, etc., based on the number of layers and component placement

Keywords

Open Collector : An NPN transistor configuration with emitter connected to ground and collector left unconnected. It is an I/O interface standard in electronic circuits

Logic Gate	:	Analog/Digital Circuit which produces the output as the output corresponding to the logical operation performed on the input signals
Buffer	:	Logic circuit for increasing the driving capability of a logic circuit in digital electronic circuits
Latch	:	Logic circuit for latching data in digital circuits
Decoder	:	Logic circuit for generating all the possible combinations of the input signals in digital circuit
Encoder	:	Logic circuit for encoding the input signals to a particular output format
Multiplexer	:	Logic circuit which acts as a switch which connects one input line from a set of input lines, to an output line at a given point of time
De-Multiplexer	:	Logic circuit which performs the reverse operation of multiplexer
Combinational Circuit	:	A digital circuit which is a combination of logic gates. The output of the combinational circuit at a given point of time is dependent only on the state of the inputs at the given point of time
Sequential Circuit	:	A digital logic circuit whose output at any given point of time depends on both the present and past inputs
Integrated Circuit (IC)	:	A miniaturised implementation of an electronics circuit containing transistors and other passive electronic components in a silicon wafer
VLSI Design	:	IC design
VHDL	:	A Hardware Description Language for VLSI design
Electronic Design Automation (EDA) tool	:	A set of Computer Aided Design / Manufacturing (CAD/CAM) software packages which helps in designing and manufacturing the electronic hardware
OrCAD	:	A popular EDA tool for PCB design from Cadence Design Systems
Package	:	An entity representing the physical characteristics (length, width, number of pins, type of pins (surface mount or through hole), pin size, etc.) of a hardware component (like IC, capacitor, etc.) in electronic circuit
Netlist file	:	A soft form representation of the package of components and the interconnection among the components in an electronic circuit
Footprint	:	A pictorial representation of a component when it is looked from the top (top view of a component)
Routes	:	The interconnection among the pins/leads of various components in a PCB
Layers	:	The 'Multiple planes' for performing the routing operation, if the number of interconnections in a design is high in a PCB
Vias	:	The conductive drill holes for providing electrical connectivity among various layers in a 'Multilayer' PCB
Gerber File	:	A universally acceptable standard for representing layout information for PCB fabrication
Printed Circuit Board (PCB)	:	A platform for placing electronic and electromechanical components and interconnecting them without discrete wires.
PCB Etching (Photo engraving)	:	A subtractive method for fabricating the PCB
PCB Milling	:	A subtractive method for fabricating the PCB
PCB Printing	:	An additive method for fabricating the PCB
Single Sided PCB	:	PCB with a single layer for routing and connections
Double Sided PCB	:	PCB with track routing and component placement done on both sides of the PCB

Multilayer PCB	:	PCB with multiple layers for track routing
Piggy-back/plug-in/daughter PCB	:	PCB designed to plug into some other PCBs
Flexible PCB	:	PCB with flexible substrate for copper depositing for tracks and footprint
Solder Mask	:	A plastic layer deposited on the copper tracks of the PCB to protect it from corrosion and abrasion
Silk Screen	:	The legend for printing readable information on the PCB
Conformal Coating	:	A protective coating made up of dilute solution of silicon rubber or epoxy for protecting the PCB from extreme environmental conditions

Objective Questions

1. Which of the following analog electronic component is used for clamping of voltage in electronic circuits
   (a) Schottky diode (b) Transistor (c) TRIAC (d) Zener diode
2. Which of the following analog electronic component(s) is (are) used for noise signal filtering in electronic circuits
   (a) Capacitor (b) Transistor (c) Inductor (d) All of these
   (e) Only (a) and (c)
3. Which of the following is (are) true about Open Collector configuration?
   (a) The emitter of the transistor is grounded (b) The emitter of the transistor is open
   (c) The collector of the transistor is open (d) The collector of the transistor is grounded
   (e) (a) and (c) (f) (b) and (d)
4. The logic expression $Y = \bar{A}B + A\bar{B}$ represents the logic gate
   (a) AND (b) NAND (c) OR (d) XOR
   (e) NOR
5. Which of the following is an example for Buffer IC?
   (a) 74LS00 (b) 74LS244 (c) 74LS08 (d) 74LS373
   (e) None of these
6. Which of the following digital circuits is used for selecting one input from a set of inputs and connecting it to an output line
   (a) Buffer (b) Latch (c) Multiplexer (d) De-Multiplexer
   (e) None of these
7. Combinational circuits contain a memory element. State True or False
   (a) True (b) False
8. Half Adder is an example of Sequential circuit. State True or False
   (a) True (b) False
9. Which of the following flip-flop is known as Delay Flip-Flop
   (a) S-R (b) J-K (c) D (d) T
10. For an S-R flip-flop, the previous output state is 0 and the current input state is $S = R = 1$, what is the current output state?
    (a) 1 (b) 0 (c) Undefined
11. Which of the following flip-flop is known as Toggle Flip-Flop
    (a) S-R (b) J-K (c) D (d) T
12. For a J-K Flip-Flop, the previous output state is 1 and the current input state is $J = K = 0$, what is the current output state?
    (a) 1 (b) 0 (c) Undefined

13. For a J-K Flip-Flop, the previous output state is 0 and the current input state is J=K=1, what is the current output state?
(a) 1 (b) 0 (c) Undefined
14. For a T Flip-Flop, the previous output state is 1 and the current input state is 1, what will be the current output state on applying a clock pulse?
(a) 1 (b) 0 (c) Undefined
15. The number of logic gates present in an IC is 500. The integration type of the IC is?
(a) MSI (b) SSI (c) LSI (d) VLSI
16. The type of integration for a microprocessor chip is
(a) MSI (b) SSI (c) LSI (d) VLSI
17. The design of an integrated circuit with built-in ADC is an example for
(a) Analog (b) Digital (c) Mixed signal (d) None of these
18. In embedded hardware design context, schematic represents
(a) The physical arrangement of various components present in the hardware product
(b) The different components involved in a hardware product and the interconnection among them
(c) Both of these (d) None of these
19. In embedded hardware design context, Bill of Materials (BoM) represents
(a) The type and value of each components present in the hardware
(b) The quantity of different components present in the hardware
(c) Both of these (d) None of these
20. In embedded hardware design context, 'Netlist' is
(a) The soft form representation of the different components of a hardware and the interconnection among them
(b) The output file generated from schematic design (c) The input file for the PCB layout design
(d) All of these (e) None of these
21. In embedded hardware design context, 'Layout' is
(a) A soft form representation of the PCB
(b) Software 'Blueprint' representing the physical placement of components in a hardware
(c) All of these (d) None of these
22. Which of the following are the building blocks of a 'layout'?
(a) Footprints (b) Routes (c) Layers (d) Vias
(e) All of these (f) (a) and (b)
23. What is 'Footprint' in the 'Layout' context?
(a) The 'Top view' of a component
(b) The three-dimensional representation of a component
(c) Both of these (d) None of these
24. Which of the following package(s) contain pins/pads on only one side of the component?
(a) Zigzag In-line Package (ZIP) (b) Single In-line Package (SIP)
(c) Dual In-line Package (DIP) (d) All of these (e) None of these
25. Which of the following is a Surface Mount Package?
(a) PDIP (b) TSSOP (c) SOIC (d) All of these
(e) only (b) and (c)
26. Which of the following package(s) contain(s) pins/pads on the four sides of the component?
(a) VQFP (b) SOICS (c) TSSOP (d) PQFP
(e) (a) and (d)
27. The representation of interconnection among various components of a hardware in 'Layout' is known as
(a) Footprint (b) Route/Trace (c) Layer (d) None of these
28. In embedded hardware design context, a 'via' is a
(a) conductive drill hole (b) interconnection among two components (c) Ground line
(d) Power line (e) None of these

29. Which is (are) the layers of 'Layout' used for printing 'Assembly Notes'?
    (a) AST (b) ASB (c) TOP (d) BOT
    (e) (a) and (b)
30. What is gerber file in the PCB Design context?
    (a) File containing the component PCB layout info, routing info, drill details, etc. in a universally accepted file exchange protocol format
    (b) File containing the component PCB layout info, routing info, drill details, etc. in a proprietary file exchange protocol format
    (c) A collection of art works in a gerber format for each layer of the PCB
    (d) (a) and (c) (e) None of these
31. Which of the following is(are) true about a single sided PCB?
    (a) Only a single layer is used for routing the connections between components
    (b) Components are placed on only one side of the PCB
    (c) All of these (d) None of these
32. Which of the following is(are) true about flexible PCB?
    (a) Highly flexible compared to normal PCB (b) Uses flexible substrate for etching
    (c) Commonly used for the fabrication of Antennas, membrane keyboards, etc.
    (d) All of these (e) None of these
33. Which of the following technique(s) is(are) used for PCB fabrication
    (a) Photo Engraving (b) PCB Milling (c) PCB printing (d) All of these
34. Which of the following is(are) subtractive process for PCB fabrication?
    (a) Photo Engraving (b) PCB printing (c) PCB Milling (d) All of these
    (e) None of these (f) only (a) and (c)
35. Which of the following is(are) true about 'Solder Mask'?
    (a) It is a conductive layer (b) It is a non-conductive layer
    (c) It protects the copper tracks from corrosion (d) It prevents the 'wetting' of solder
    (e) (b), (c) and (d)
36. Which of the following is(are) true about 'Conformal Coating'?
    (a) It is a conductive layer (b) It is a non-conductive layer
    (c) It is a coating over the PCB to protect PCB
    (d) Dilute solution of silicon rubber or epoxy, or plastic is used as the conformal coating material
    (e) (b), (c) and (d)

Review Questions

1. Explain the role of the analog electronic components resistor, transistor, capacitor and diode in embedded hardware design. Draw a circuit used in embedded application using these components
2. Explain the role of logic gates in embedded hardware design. Draw a circuit using the 'AND' and 'OR' gate ICs in embedded application
3. What is open collector? State its significance in embedded hardware development
4. Explain the role of de-coders in embedded hardware development. Draw the circuit diagram for interfacing a 3-bit binary decoder with 8051. Explain the functioning of the circuit
5. What is a combinational circuit? Draw a combinational circuit for embedded application development
6. What is a sequential circuit? Draw a sequential circuit and explain its functioning
7. Explain the difference between digital combinational and sequential circuits
8. Explain the difference between synchronous and asynchronous sequential circuits. Give an example for both
9. What is an Integrated Circuit (IC)? Explain the different types of integrations for ICs. Give an example for each

10. Explain the different types of IC design. Give an example for each
11. Explain the different steps involved in VHDL based IC design
12. What is Electronic Design Automation (EDA) tool. Explain the role of EDA tools in embedded system design
13. What is schematic? Explain the role of schematic in embedded hardware design
14. Explain 'Bill of Material' (BoM) in embedded hardware design context. What is the use of BoM in Embedded Hardware design and development?
15. What is '*Netlist*' in the Embedded Hardware design context? Explain its role in hardware design
16. Explain the terms 'Layout' and 'Layout Design' in the hardware design context
17. What are the building blocks of a 'Layout'? Explain them in detail
18. What is the difference between 'Package' and 'Footprint'? Explain the significance of both in embedded hardware design
19. What is 'Package' in the embedded hardware design context? What is 'Through hole' package and 'Surface Mount' package?
20. What is the difference between 'Single In-line Package' (SIP) and 'Dual In-line Package' (DIP)?
21. What are the commonly available DIP packages?
22. What is 'Zigzag In-line Package' (ZIP)?
23. Explain the commonly used '*Surface Mount Packages*' in detail
24. What is '*layer*' in the embedded hardware design context?
25. What is '*via*'? What is the difference between '*via*' and '*Through hole*'?
26. What is '*Through hole*'? What are the different types of '*Through holes*' used in PCB design?
27. What is '*Assembly Note*'? What is the role of '*Assembly Notes*' in embedded hardware design?
28. What is '*gerber*'? What is '*gerber file*' in PCB design context?
29. Explain the general guidelines for an efficient PCB layout
30. Explain PCB in the Hardware Design context? Explain the different types of PCBs
31. What is '*Flexible PCB*'? What is its role in Embedded Systems?
32. Explain the different PCB fabrication techniques. State the merits and drawbacks of each
33. Explain the '*PCB etching*' process in detail
34. What is '*Solder Mask*'? Explain its significance in PCB fabrication
35. What is '*Silk Screen*' and '*Silk Screen Printing*'? Explain their significance in PCB fabrication
36. What is '*Conformal Coating*' in the PCB context? Explain its significance in hardware maintenance.

Lab Assignments

1. Draw the schematic diagram using CaptureCIS for encoding the keys connected to the input lines of the 8 to 3 encoder 74LS148 and reading the encoded output using the AT89C51 microcontroller as per the requirements given below
   (a) The Enable Input (EI) line of the encoder is permanently grounded
   (b) The output lines A0 to A2 of the encoder are interfaced to P1.0 to P1.2 of the microcontroller
   (c) Assume that a regulated supply of 5V is fed to the board from an external ac-dc adaptor. Use a power jack on the board for connecting the external supply. Use filter capacitor 0.1MFD/12V along with the jack
   (d) Use a crystal frequency of 12MHz for the microcontroller
2. Develop the PCB layout for the above requirement using 'Layout' tool. The package details for the components are given below
   Microcontroller : PDIP 40, 74LS148 : PDIP 16, Capacitor : Use a 2 Pin Package from the design Library, Crystal : Use the through hole package (or 2 Pin package) for crystal from the Layout design library, Power Jack : Use the power jack package from the library

3. Draw the schematic diagram using CaptureCIS to interface the 3 to 8 decoder 74LS138 with the AT89C51 microcontroller as per the requirements given below
   (a) LEDs are connected to the 8 output lines of the decoder in such a way that anode is connected to 5V supply and cathode to the output pin of the decoder
   (b) The enable lines E1\ and E2\ are grounded permanently and E3 is connected to the supply voltage VCC through a high value current limiting resistor
   (c) The input lines A0, A1 and A2 of the microcontroller are connected to the Port pins P1.0 to P1.2 of the microcontroller
   (d) Assume that a regulated supply of 5V is fed to the board from an external ac-dc adaptor. Use a power jack on the board for connecting the external supply. Use filter capacitor 0.1MFD/12V along with the jack
   (e) Use a crystal frequency of 12MHz for the microcontroller
4. Develop the PCB layout for the above requirement using 'Layout' tool. The package details for the components are given below
   Microcontroller : PDIP 40, 74LS138 : PDIP 16, Capacitor : Use a 2 Pin Package from the design library, Crystal : Use the through hole package (or 2 Pin package) for crystal from the Layout design library, Power Jack : Use the power jack package from the library
5. Draw the schematic diagram using CaptureCIS for interfacing the Tri-State Buffer 74LS244 in memory mapped configuration with AT89C51 microcontroller as per the requirements given below
   (a) DIP switches are connected to the 8 input lines of the tri-state buffer through resistors 4.7K. The input line is at logic high when the switch is at open state and at logic low when the switch is at closed state
   (b) The output lines of the buffer are connected to the data bus port P0 of the microcontroller
   (c) The Port 0 pins are pulled to the supply voltage through 4.7K resistor
   (d) The address for the tri-state buffer is assigned as 00F8H. Use logic gates AND, NAND and 3 to 8 decoder IC to decode the address line and generate the address selection pulse for the buffer
   (e) The address selection pulse along with the RD\ signal of the microcontroller is used for enabling the buffer
   (f) Assume that a regulated supply of 5V is fed to the board from an external ac-dc adaptor. Use a power jack on the board for connecting the external supply. Use filter capacitor 0.1MFD/12V along with the jack
   (g) Use a crystal frequency of 12MHz for the microcontroller
6. Develop the PCB layout for the above requirement using 'Layout' tool. The package details for the components are given below
   Microcontroller : PDIP 40, 74LS244 : PDIP 20, Capacitor : Use a 2 Pin Package from the design library, AND and NAND Gates : Use respective DIP package for the IC in use, 74LS138 3-8 decoder: PDIP 16, Crystal : Use the through hole package (or 2 Pin package) for crystal from the Layout design library, Power Jack : Use the power jack package from the library
7. Draw the schematic diagram using CaptureCIS to de-multiplex the lower order address of 8051 with the latch 74LS373 as per the requirements given below
   (a) The output control line of the latch is permanently grounded
   (b) The ALE signal of the microcontroller is connected to the Enable line (G) of the latch
   (c) The Port 0 pins are pulled to the supply voltage through 4.7K resistor
   (d) The de-multiplexed address bus is connected to an 8-pin jumper (connector)
   (e) Use a crystal frequency of 12MHz for the microcontroller
   (f) Assume that a regulated supply of 5V is fed to the board from an external ac-dc adaptor. Use a power jack on the board for connecting the external supply. Use filter capacitor 0.1MFD/12V along with the jack
8. Draw the schematic diagram using CaptureCIS to interface a common cathode 7-Segmnet LED display through a 74LS373 latch in memory mapped configuration with AT89C51 microcontroller as per the requirements given below
   (a) The output control line of the latch is permanently grounded

(b) The address for the latch is assigned as FF00H. Use logic gates AND, NAND and 3 to 8 decoder IC to decode the address line and generate the address selection pulse for the buffer
(c) The address selection pulse along with the write signal WR\ of the microcontroller is used for enabling the latch
(d) Use a crystal frequency of 12MHz for the microcontroller
(e) Assume that a regulated supply of 5V is fed to the board from an external ac-dc adaptor. Use a power jack on the board for connecting the external supply. Use filter capacitor 0.1MFD/12V along with the jack

9. Develop the PCB layout for the above requirement using 'Layout' tool. The package details for the components are given below
   Microcontroller : PDIP 40, 74LS373 : PDIP 20, Capacitor : Use a 2 pin package from the design library, AND and NAND Gates : Use respective DIP package for the IC in use, 74LS138 3-8 decoder: PDIP 16, 7-segment LED: Use the available package from the layout design library, Crystal : Use the through hole package (or 2 pin package) for crystal from the Layout design library, power jack : Use the power jack package from the library.
10. Draw the schematic diagram for interfacing the AD570 AD converter from analog device, to the AT89C51 microcontroller as per the requirements given below
    (a) Assume that the supply voltages +5V and –15V are available externally and they are connected to the circuit using a power jack.
    (b) The data line of the ADC is interfaced to Port P0
    (c) The start pulse for conversion is applied through port pin P1.0
    (d) The ADC uses interrupt of microcontroller for indicating the data conversion completion
    (e) The analog input signal for conversion is supplied to the AD Converter from external source through a jumper (connector)
11. Draw the schematic diagram for interfacing the DM9370 7-segment decoder driver, from Fairchild semiconductor, for driving a common anode 7-segment LED display with the AT89C51 microcontroller as per the requirements given below
    (a) Use 330E external current limiting resistor for connecting the 7-segment LED display with the DM9370 IC
    (b) The DM9370 is memory mapped with the microcontroller and it is activated by a write to memory location 8000H
    (c) Assume that a regulated supply of 5V is fed to the board from an external ac-dc adaptor. Use a power jack on the board for connecting the external supply. Use filter capacitor 0.1MFD/12V along with the jack
    (d) Use a crystal frequency of 12MHz for the microcontroller

9 Embedded Firmware Design and Development

LEARNING OBJECTIVES

- ✓ *Learn the different steps involved in the design and development of firmware for embedded systems*
- ✓ *Learn about the different approaches for embedded firmware design and development, the merits and limitations of each*
- ✓ *Learn about the different languages for embedded firmware development and the merits and limitations of each*
- ✓ *Learn about assembly language and instruction mnemonics*
- ✓ *Learn the steps involved in converting an Assembly Language program to machine executable code*
- ✓ *Learn about the assembler, linker, locater and object to hex file converter*
- ✓ *Learn the advantages and drawbacks of Assembly language based firmware development*
- ✓ *Learn the various steps involved in the conversion of a program written in high level language to machine executable code*
- ✓ *Learn about the advantages and limitations of high level language based embedded firmware development*
- ✓ *Learn the different ways of mixing assembly language with high level language for embedded application development*
- ✓ *Learn about the fundamentals of embedded firmware design using Embedded 'C'*
- ✓ *Learn the similarities and differences between conventional 'C' programming and 'C' programming for Embedded application development*
- ✓ *Learn the difference between native and cross-platform development*
- ✓ *Learn about Keywords and Identifiers, Data types, Storage Classes, Arithmetic and Logic Operations, Relational Operations, Branching Instructions, Looping Instructions, Arrays and Pointers, Characters and Strings, Functions, Function Pointers, Structures and Unions, Preprocessors and Macros, Constant Declarations, Volatile Variables, Delay generation and Infinite loops, Bit manipulation operations, Coding Interrupt Service Routines, Recursive and Reentrant functions, and Dynamic memory allocation in Embedded C*

The embedded firmware is responsible for controlling the various peripherals of the embedded hardware and generating response in accordance with the functional requirements mentioned in the requirements for the particular embedded product. Firmware is considered as the master brain of the embedded system. Imparting intelligence to an Embedded system is a one time process and it can happen at any stage, it can be immediately after the fabrication of the embedded hardware or at a later stage. Once intelligence is imparted to the embedded product, by embedding the firmware in the hardware, the product starts functioning properly and will continue serving the assigned task till hardware breakdown occurs or a corruption in embedded firmware occurs. In case of hardware breakdown, the damaged component may need to be replaced by a new component and for firmware corruptions the firmware should be re-loaded, to bring back the embedded product to the normal functioning. Coming back to the newborn baby example, the newborn baby is very adaptive in terms of intelligence, meaning it learns from mistakes and updates its memory each time a mistake or a deviation in expected behaviour occurs, whereas most of the embedded systems are less adaptive or non-adaptive. For most of the embedded products the embedded firmware is stored at a permanent memory (ROM) and they are nonalterable by end users. Some of the embedded products used in the Control and Instrumentation domain are adaptive. This adaptability is achieved by making use configurable parameters which are stored in the alterable permanent memory area (like NVRAM/FLASH). The parameters get updated in accordance with the deviations from expected behaviour and the firmware makes use of these parameters for creating the response next time for similar variations.

Designing embedded firmware requires understanding of the particular embedded product hardware, like various component interfacing, memory map details, I/O port details, configuration and register details of various hardware chips used and some programming language (either target processor/controller specific low level assembly language or a high level language like C/C++/JAVA).

Embedded firmware development process starts with the conversion of the firmware requirements into a program model using modelling tools like UML or flow chart based representation. The UML diagrams or flow chart gives a diagrammatic representation of the decision items to be taken and the tasks to be performed (Fig. 9.1). Once the program model is created, the next step is the implementation of the tasks and actions by capturing the model using a language which is understandable by the target processor/controller. The following sections are designed to give an overview of the various steps involved in the embedded firmware design and development.

9.1 EMBEDDED FIRMWARE DESIGN APPROACHES

The firmware design approaches for embedded product is purely dependent on the complexity of the functions to be performed, the speed of operation required, etc. Two basic approaches are used for Embedded firmware design. They are '*Conventional Procedural Based Firmware Design*' and '*Embedded Operating System (OS) Based Design*'. The conventional procedural based design is also known as '*Super Loop Model*'. We will discuss each of them in detail in the following sections.

9.1.1 The Super Loop Based Approach

The Super Loop based firmware development approach is adopted for applications that are not time critical and where the response time is not so important (embedded systems where missing deadlines are acceptable). It is very similar to a conventional procedural programming where the code is executed task by task. The task listed at the top of the program code is executed first and the tasks just below the top are executed after completing the first task. This is a true procedural one. In a multiple task based system, each task is executed in serial in this approach. The firmware execution flow for this will be

1. Configure the common parameters and perform initialisation for various hardware components memory, registers, etc.
2. Start the first task and execute it
3. Execute the second task
4. Execute the next task
5. :
6. :
7. Execute the last defined task
8. Jump back to the first task and follow the same flow

From the firmware execution sequence, it is obvious that the order in which the tasks to be executed are fixed and they are hard coded in the code itself. Also the operation is an infinite loop based approach. We can visualise the operational sequence listed above in terms of a 'C' program code as

```
void main ()
{
Configurations ();
Initializations ();
while (1)
{
Task 1 ();
Task 2 ();
:
:
Task n ();
}
}
```

Almost all tasks in embedded applications are non-ending and are repeated infinitely throughout the operation. From the above 'C' code you can see that the tasks 1 to n are performed one after another and when the last task (n^{th} task) is executed, the firmware execution is again re-directed to *Task 1* and it is repeated forever in the loop. This repetition is achieved by using an infinite loop. Here the while (1) { } loop. This approach is also referred as ***'Super loop based Approach'***.

Since the tasks are running inside an infinite loop, the only way to come out of the loop is either a hardware reset or an interrupt assertion. A hardware reset brings the program execution back to the main loop. Whereas an interrupt request suspends the task execution temporarily and performs the corresponding interrupt routine and on completion of the interrupt routine it restarts the task execution from the point where it got interrupted.

The ***'Super loop based design'*** doesn't require an operating system, since there is no need for scheduling which task is to be executed and assigning priority to each task. In a super loop based design, the priorities are fixed and the order in which the tasks to be executed are also fixed. Hence the code for performing these tasks will be residing in the code memory without an operating system image.

This type of design is deployed in low-cost embedded products and products where response time is not time critical. Some embedded products demands this type of approach if some tasks itself are sequential. For example, reading/writing data to and from a card using a card reader requires a sequence of operations like checking the presence of card, authenticating the operation, reading/writing, etc. it should strictly follow a specified sequence and the combination of these series of tasks constitutes a single task-namely data read/write. There is no use in putting the sub-tasks into independent tasks and running them parallel. It won't work at all.

A typical example of a '***Super loop based***' product is an electronic video game toy containing keypad and display unit. The program running inside the product may be designed in such a way that it reads the keys to detect whether the user has given any input and if any key press is detected the graphic display is updated. The keyboard scanning and display updating happens at a reasonably high rate. Even if the application misses a key press, it won't create any critical issues; rather it will be treated as a bug in the firmware ☺. It is not economical to embed an OS into low cost products and it is an utter waste to do so if the response requirements are not crucial.

The '***Super loop based design***' is simple and straight forward without any OS related overheads. The major drawback of this approach is that any failure in any part of a single task will affect the total system. If the program hangs up at some point while executing a task, it will remain there forever and ultimately the product stops functioning. There are remedial measures for overcoming this. Use of Hardware and software Watch Dog Timers (WDTs) helps in coming out from the loop when an unexpected failure occurs or when the processor hangs up. This, in turn, may cause additional hardware cost and firmware overheads.

Another major drawback of the '***Super loop***' design approach is the lack of real timeliness. If the number of tasks to be executed within an application increases, the time at which each task is repeated also increases. This brings the probability of missing out some events. For example in a system with Keypads, according to the '***Super loop design***', there will be a task for monitoring the keypad connected I/O lines and this need not be the task running while you press the keys (That is key pressing event may not be in sync with the keypad press monitoring task within the firmware). In order to identify the key press, you may have to press the keys for a sufficiently long time till the keypad status monitoring task is executed internally by the firmware. This will really lead to the lack of real timeliness. There are corrective measures for this also. The best advised option in use interrupts for external events requiring real time attention. Advances in processor technology brings out low cost high speed processors/controllers, use of such processors in super loop design greatly reduces the time required to service different tasks and thereby are capable of providing a nearly real time attention to external events.

Throughout this book under the title '***Embedded Firmware Design and Development***', we will be discussing only the '***Super loop based design***'. Again the discussion is narrowed to super loop based firmware development for 8051 controller.

9.1.2 The Embedded Operating System (OS) Based Approach

The Operating System (OS) based approach contains operating systems, which can be either a General Purpose Operating System (GPOS) or a Real Time Operating System (RTOS) to host the user written application firmware. The General Purpose OS (GPOS) based design is very similar to a conventional PC based application development where the device contains an operating system (Windows/Unix/Linux, etc. for Desktop PCs) and you will be creating and running user applications on top of it. Example of a GPOS used in embedded product development is Microsoft® Windows XP Embedded. Examples of Embedded products using Microsoft® Windows XP OS are Personal Digital Assistants (PDAs), Hand held devices/Portable devices and Point of Sale (PoS) terminals. Use of GPOS in embedded products merges the demarcation of Embedded Systems and general computing systems in terms of OS. For Developing applications on top of the OS, the OS supported APIs are used. Similar to the different hardware specific drivers, OS based applications also require '***Driver software***' for different hardware present on the board to communicate with them.

Real Time Operating System (RTOS) based design approach is employed in embedded products demanding Real-time response. RTOS respond in a timely and predictable manner to events. Real Time operating system contains a Real Time kernel responsible for performing pre-emptive multitasking, scheduler for scheduling tasks, multiple threads, etc. A Real Time Operating System (RTOS) allows flexible scheduling of system resources like the CPU and memory and offers some way to communicate between tasks. We will discuss the basics of RTOS based system design in a later chapter titled '*Designing with Real Time Operating Systems (RTOS)*'.

'*Windows CE*', '*pSOS*', '*VxWorks*', '*ThreadX*', '*MicroC/OS-II*', '*Embedded Linux*', '*Symbian*' etc are examples of RTOS employed in embedded product development. Mobile phones, PDAs (Based on Windows CE/Windows Mobile Platforms), handheld devices, etc. are examples of 'Embedded Products' based on RTOS. Most of the mobile phones are built around the popular RTOS 'Symbian'.

9.2 EMBEDDED FIRMWARE DEVELOPMENT LANGUAGES

As mentioned in Chapter 2, you can use either a target processor/controller specific language (Generally known as Assembly language or low level language) or a target processor/controller independent language (Like C, C++, JAVA, etc. commonly known as High Level Language) or a combination of Assembly and High level Language. We will discuss where each of the approach is used and the relative merits and de-merits of each, in the following sections.

9.2.1 Assembly Language based Development

'*Assembly language*' is the human readable notation of '*machine language*', whereas '*machine language*' is a processor understandable language. Processors deal only with binaries (1s and 0s). Machine language is a binary representation and it consists of 1s and 0s. Machine language is made readable by using specific symbols called '*mnemonics*'. Hence machine language can be considered as an interface between processor and programmer. Assembly language and machine languages are processor/controller dependent and an assembly program written for one processor/controller family will not work with others.

Assembly language programming is the task of writing processor specific machine code in mnemonic form, converting the mnemonics into actual processor instructions (machine language) and associated data using an assembler.

Assembly Language program was the most common type of programming adopted in the beginning of software revolution. If we look back to the history of programming, we can see that a large number of programs were written entirely in assembly language. Even in the 1990s, the majority of console video games were written in assembly language, including most popular games written for the Sega Genesis and the Super Nintendo Entertainment System. The popular arcade game NBA Jam released in 1993 was also coded entirely using the assembly language.

Even today also almost all low level, system related, programming is carried out using assembly language. Some Operating System dependent tasks require low-level languages. In particular, assembly language is often used in writing the low level interaction between the operating system and the hardware, for instance in device drivers.

The general format of an assembly language instruction is an Opcode followed by Operands. The Opcode tells the processor/controller what to do and the Operands provide the data and information required to perform the action specified by the opcode. It is not necessary that all opcode should have Operands following them. Some of the Opcode implicitly contains the operand and in such situation no operand is required. The operand may be a single operand, dual operand or more. We will analyse each of them with the *8051* ASM instructions as an example.

```
MOV A, #30
```

This instruction mnemonic moves decimal value 30 to the 8051 Accumulator register. Here *MOV A* is the Opcode and 30 is the operand (single operand). The same instruction when written in machine language will look like

01110100 00011110

where the first 8 bit binary value 01110100 represents the opcode *MOV A* and the second 8 bit binary value 00011110 represents the operand 30.

The mnemonic *INC A* is an example for instruction holding operand implicitly in the Opcode. The machine language representation of the same is 00000100. This instruction increments the *8051* Accumulator register content by 1.

The mnemonic *MOV A, #30* explained above is an example for single operand instruction.

LJMP 16bit address is an example for dual operand instruction. The machine language for the same is

```
00000010      addr_bit15 to addr_bit 8      addr_bit7 to addr_bit 0
```

The first binary data is the representation of the LJMP machine code. The first operand that immediately follows the opcode represents the bits 8 to 15 of the 16bit address to which the jump is required and the second operand represents the bits 0 to 7 of the address to which the jump is targeted.

Assembly language instructions are written one per line. A machine code program thus consists of a sequence of assembly language instructions, where each statement contains a mnemonic (Opcode + Operand). Each line of an assembly language program is split into four fields as given below

LABEL OPCODE OPERAND COMMENTS

LABEL is an optional field. A 'LABEL' is an identifier used extensively in programs to reduce the reliance on programmers for remembering where data or code is located. LABEL is commonly used for representing

- A memory location, address of a program, sub-routine, code portion, etc.
- The maximum length of a label differs between assemblers. Assemblers insist strict formats for labelling. Labels are always suffixed by a colon and begin with a valid character. Labels can contain number from 0 to 9 and special character _ (underscore).

Labels are used for representing subroutine names and jump locations in Assembly language programming. It is to be noted that 'LABEL' is not a mandatory field; it is optional only.

The sample code given below using *8051* Assembly language illustrates the structured assembly language programming.

```
;####################################################################
;       SUBROUTINE FOR GENERATING DELAY
;       DELAY PARAMETR PASSED THROUGH REGISTER R1
;       RETURN VALUE NONE
;       REGISTERS USED: R0, R1
;####################################################################
```

```
DELAY:   MOV     R0, #255       ; Load Register R0 with 255
         DJNZ    R1, DELAY      ; Decrement R1 and loop till
                                ; R1= 0
         RET                    ; Return to calling program
```

The Assembly program contains a main routine which starts at address 0000H and it may or may not contain subroutines. The example given above is a subroutine, where in the main program the subroutine is invoked by the Assembly instruction

LCALL DELAY

Executing this instruction transfers the program flow to the memory address referenced by the 'LABEL' DELAY.

It is a good practice to provide comments to your subroutines before the beginning of it by indicating the purpose of that subroutine, what the input parameters are and how they are passed to the subroutines, which are the return values, how they are returned to the calling function, etc. While assembling the code a ';' informs the assembler that the rest of the part coming in a line after the ';' symbol is comments and simply ignore it. Each Assembly instruction should be written in a separate line. Unlike C and other high level languages, more than one ASM code lines are not allowed in a single line.

In the above example the *LABEL* DELAY represents the reference to the start of the subroutine DELAY. You can directly replace this LABEL by putting the desired address first and then writing the Assembly code for the routine as given below.

```
ORG 0100H
        MOV R0, #255        ; Load Register R0 with 50H
        DJNZ R1, 0100H      ; Decrement R1 and loop till R1= 0
        RET                 ; Return to calling program
```

The advantage of using a label is that the required address is calculated by the assembler at the time of assembling the program and it replaces the Label. Hence even if you add some code above the LABEL 'DELAY' at a later stage, it won't create any issues like code overlapping, whereas in the second method where you are implicitly telling the assembler that this subroutine should start at the specified address (in the above example 0100H). If the code written above this subroutine itself is crossing the 0100H mark of the program memory, it will be over written by the subroutine code and it will generate unexpected results☺. Hence for safety don't assign any address by yourself, let us refer the required address by using labels and let the assembler handle the responsibility for finding out the address where the code can be placed. In the above example you can find out that the label DELAY is used for calling the subroutine as well as looping (using jumping instruction based on decision-DJNZ). You can also use the normal jump instruction to jump to the label by calling *LJMP DELAY*

The statement *ORG 0100H* in the above example is not an assembly language instruction; it is an assembler directive instruction. It tells the assembler that the Instructions from here onward should be placed at location starting from 0100H. The Assembler directive instructions are known as 'pseudo-ops'. They are used for

1. Determining the start address of the program (e.g. ORG 0000H)
2. Determining the entry address of the program (e.g. ORG 0100H)
3. Reserving memory for data variables, arrays and structures (e.g. var EQU 70H
4. Initialising variable values (e.g. val DATA 12H)

The *EQU* directive is used for allocating memory to a variable and *DATA* directive is used for initialising a variable with data. No machine codes are generated for the 'pseudo-ops'.

Till now we discussed about Assembly language and how it is used for writing programs. Now let us have a look at how assembly programs are organised and how they are translated into machine readable codes.

The Assembly language program written in assembly code is saved as *.asm* (Assembly file) file or an *.src* (source) file. Any text editor like 'notepad' or 'WordPad' from Microsoft® or the text editor provided by an Integrated Development (IDE) tool can be used for writing the assembly instructions.

Similar to 'C' and other high level language programming, you can have multiple source files called modules in assembly language programming. Each module is represented by an '*.asm*' or '*.src*' file similar to the '*.c*' files in C programming. This approach is known as 'Modular Programming'. Modular programming is employed when the program is too complex or too big. In 'Modular Programming', the entire code is divided into submodules and each module is made re-usable. Modular Programs are usually easy to code, debug and alter. Conversion of the assembly language to machine language is carried out by a sequence of operations, as illustrated below.

9.2.1.1 Source File to Object File Translation Translation of assembly code to machine code is performed by assembler. The assemblers for different target machines are different and it is common that assemblers from multiple vendors are available in the market for the same target machines. Some target processor's/controller's assembler may be proprietary and is supplied by a single vendor only. Some assemblers are freely available in the internet for downloading. Some assemblers are commercial and requires licence from the vendor. A51 Macro Assembler from Keil software is a popular assembler for the 8051 family microcontroller. The various steps involved in the conversion of a program written in assembly language to corresponding binary file/machine language is illustrated in Fig. 9.1.

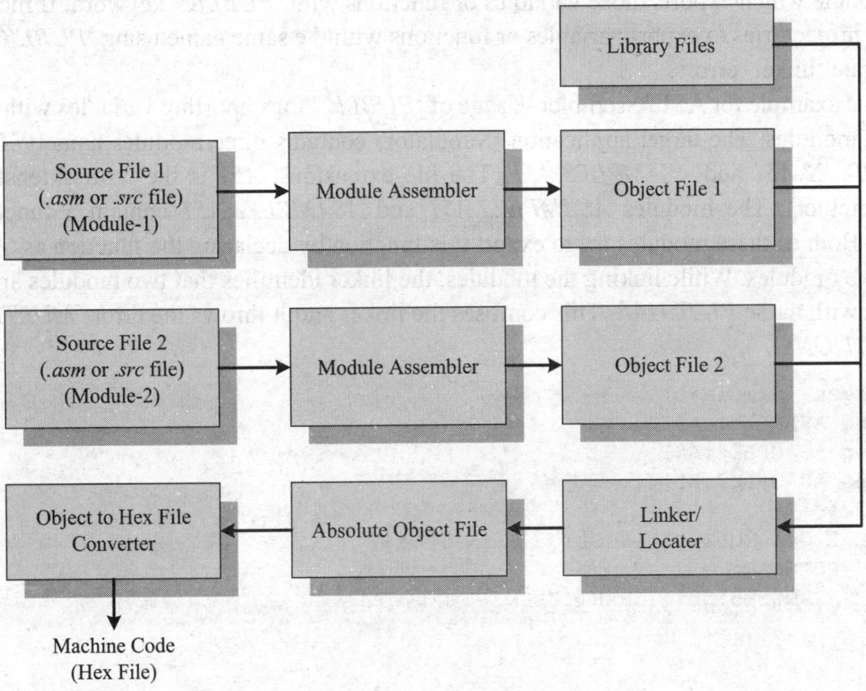

Fig. 9.1 **Assembly language to machine language conversion process**

Each source module is written in Assembly and is stored as *.src* file or *.asm* file. Each file can be assembled separately to examine the syntax errors and incorrect assembly instructions. On successful assembling of each *.src*/*.asm* file a corresponding object file is created with extension '*.obj*'. The object file does not contain the absolute address of where the generated code needs to be placed on the program memory and hence it is called a re-locatable segment. It can be placed at any code memory location and it is the responsibility of the linker/locater to assign absolute address for this module. Absolute address allocation is done at the absolute object file creation stage. Each module can share variables and subroutines (functions) among them. Exporting a variable/function from a module (making a variable/function from a module available to all other modules) is done by declaring that variable/function as *PUBLIC* in the source module.

Importing a variable or function from a module (taking a variable or function from any one of other modules) is done by declaring that variable or function as *EXTRN* (EXTERN) in the module where it is going to be accessed. The '*PUBLIC*' Keyword informs the assembler that the variables or functions declared as '*PUBLIC*' needs to be exported. Similarly the '*EXTRN*' Keyword tells the assembler that the variables or functions declared as '*EXTRN*' needs to be imported from some other modules. While assembling a module, on seeing variables/functions with keyword '*EXTRN*', the assembler understands that these variables or functions come from an external module and it proceeds assembling the entire module without throwing any errors, though the assembler cannot find the definition of the variables and implementation of the functions. Corresponding to a variable or function declared as '*PUBLIC*' in a module, there can be one or more modules using these variables or functions using '*EXTRN*' keyword. For all those modules using variables or functions with '*EXTRN*' keyword, there should be one and only one module which exports those variables or functions with '*PUBLIC*' keyword. If more than one module in a project tries to export variables or functions with the same name using '*PUBLIC*' keyword, it will generate 'linker' errors.

Illustrative example for A51 Assembler–Usage of '*PUBLIC*' for importing variables with same name on different modules. The target application (Simulator) contains three modules namely *ASAMPLE1.A51*, *ASAMPLE2.A51* and *ASAMPLE3.A51* (The file extension . *A51* is the .asm extension specific to A51 assembler). The modules *ASAMPLE2.A51* and *ASAMPLE3.A51* contain a function named *PUTCHAR*. Both of these modules try to export this function by declaring the function as '*PUBLIC*' in the respective modules. While linking the modules, the linker identifies that two modules are exporting the function with name *PUTCHAR*. This confuses the linker and it throws the error '*MULTIPLE PUBLIC DEFINITIONS*'.

```
Build target 'Simulator'
assembling ASAMPLE1.A51...
assembling ASAMPLE2.A51...
assembling ASAMPLE3.A51...
linking...
*** ERROR L104: MULTIPLE PUBLIC DEFINITIONS
 SYMBOL:   PUTCHAR
 MODULE:   ASAMPLE3.obj (CHAR_IO)
```

If a variable or function declared as '*EXTRN*' in one or two modules, there should be one module defining these variables or functions and exporting them using '*PUBLIC*' keyword. If no modules in a project export the variables or functions which are declared as '*EXTRN*' in other modules, it will generate 'linker' warnings or errors depending on the error level/warning level settings of the linker.

Illustrative example for A51 Assembler–Usage of *EXTRN* without variables exported. The target application (Simulator) contains three modules, namely, *ASAMPLE1.A51*, *ASAMPLE2.A51* and *ASAMPLE3.A51* (The file extension .A51 is the .asm extension specific to A51 assembler). The modules *ASAMPLE1.A51* imports a function named *PUT_CRLF* which is declared as '*EXTRN*' in the current module and it expects any of the other two modules to export it using the keyword '*PUBLIC*'. But none of the other modules export this function by declaring the function as '*PUBLIC*' in the respective modules. While linking the modules, the linker identifies that there is no function exporting for this function. The linker generates a warning or error message '*UNRESOLVED EXTERNAL SYMBOL*' depending on the linker 'level' settings.

```
*** WARNING L1: UNRESOLVED EXTERNAL SYMBOL
 SYMBOL:   PUT_CRLF
 MODULE:   ASAMPLE1.obj  (SAMPLE)
```

9.2.1.2 Library File Creation and Usage Libraries are specially formatted, ordered program collections of object modules that may be used by the linker at a later time. When the linker processes a library, only those object modules in the library that are necessary to create the program are used. Library files are generated with extension '*.lib*'. Library file is some kind of source code hiding technique. If you don't want to reveal the source code behind the various functions you have written in your program and at the same time you want them to be distributed to application developers for making use of them in their applications, you can supply them as library files and give them the details of the public functions available from the library (function name, function input/output, etc). For using a library file in a project, add the library to the project.

If you are using a commercial version of the assembler/compiler suite for your development, the vendor of the utility may provide you pre-written library files for performing multiplication, floating point arithmetic, etc. as an add-on utility or as a bonus☺.

'*LIB51*' from Keil Software is an example for a library creator and it is used for creating library files for A51 Assembler/C51 Compiler for *8051* specific controller.

9.2.1.3 Linker and Locater Linker and Locater is another software utility responsible for "linking the various object modules in a multi-module project and assigning absolute address to each module". Linker generates an absolute object module by extracting the object modules from the library, if any and those *obj* files created by the assembler, which is generated by assembling the individual modules of a project. It is the responsibility of the linker to link any external dependent variables or functions declared on various modules and resolve the external dependencies among the modules. An absolute object file or module does not contain any re-locatable code or data. All code and data reside at fixed memory locations. The absolute object file is used for creating hex files for dumping into the code memory of the processor/controller.

'*BL51*' from Keil Software is an example for a Linker & Locater for A51 Assembler/C51 Compiler for 8051 specific controller.

9.2.1.4 Object to Hex File Converter This is the final stage in the conversion of Assembly language (mnemonics) to machine understandable language (machine code). Hex File is the representation of the machine code and the hex file is dumped into the code memory of the processor/controller. The hex file representation varies depending on the target processor/controller make. For Intel processors/controllers the target hex file format will be 'Intel HEX' and for Motorola, the hex file should be in 'Motorola HEX' format. HEX files are ASCII files that contain a hexadecimal representation of target application. Hex file is created from the final 'Absolute Object File' using the Object to Hex File Converter utility.

'*OH51*' from Keil software is an example for Object to Hex File Converter utility for A51 Assembler/C51 Compiler for *8051* specific controller.

9.2.1.5 Advantages of Assembly Language Based Development Assembly Language based development was (is☺) the most common technique adopted from the beginning of embedded technology development. Thorough understanding of the processor architecture, memory organisation, register sets and mnemonics is very essential for Assembly Language based development. If you master one processor architecture and its assembly instructions, you can make the processor as flexible as a gymnast. The major advantages of Assembly Language based development is listed below.

Efficient Code Memory and Data Memory Usage (Memory Optimisation) Since the developer is well versed with the target processor architecture and memory organisation, optimised code can be written for performing operations. This leads to less utilisation of code memory and efficient utilisation of data memory. Remember memory is a primary concern in any embedded product (Though silicon is cheaper and new memory techniques make memory less costly, external memory operations impact directly on system performance).

High Performance Optimised code not only improves the code memory usage but also improves the total system performance. Through effective assembly coding, optimum performance can be achieved for a target application.

Low Level Hardware Access Most of the code for low level programming like accessing external device specific registers from the operating system kernel, device drivers, and low level interrupt routines, etc. are making use of direct assembly coding since low level device specific operation support is not commonly available with most of the high-level language cross compilers.

Code Reverse Engineering Reverse engineering is the process of understanding the technology behind a product by extracting the information from a finished product. Reverse engineering is performed by 'hawkers' to reveal the technology behind 'Proprietary Products'. Though most of the products employ code memory protection, if it may be possible to break the memory protection and read the code memory, it can easily be converted into assembly code using a dis-assembler program for the target machine.

9.2.1.6 Drawbacks of Assembly Language Based Development Every technology has its own pros and cons. From certain technology aspects assembly language development is the most efficient technique. But it is having the following technical limitations also.

High Development Time Assembly language is much harder to program than high level languages. The developer must pay attention to more details and must have thorough knowledge of the architecture, memory organisation and register details of the target processor in use. Learning the inner details of the processor and its assembly instructions is highly time consuming and it creates a delay impact in product development. One probable solution for this is use a readily available developer who is well versed in the target processor architecture assembly instructions. Also more lines of assembly code are required for performing an action which can be done with a single instruction in a high-level language like 'C'.

Developer Dependency There is no common written rule for developing assembly language based applications whereas all high level languages instruct certain set of rules for application development. In assembly language programming, the developers will have the freedom to choose the different memory location and registers. Also the programming approach varies from developer to developer depending on his/her taste. For example moving data from a memory location to accumulator can be achieved through different approaches. If the approach done by a developer is not documented properly at the development stage, he/she may not be able to recollect why this approach is followed at a later stage or when a new developer is instructed to analyse this code, he/she also may not be able to understand what is done and why it is done. Hence upgrading an assembly program or modifying it on a later stage is very difficult. Well documenting the assembly code is a solution for reducing the developer dependency in assembly language programming. If the code is too large and complex, documenting all lines of code may not be productive.

Non-Portable Target applications written in assembly instructions are valid only for that particular family of processors (e.g. Application written for Intel x86 family of processors) and cannot be re-used for another target processors/controllers (Say ARM11 family of processors). If the target processor/controller changes, a complete re-writing of the application using the assembly instructions for the new target processor/controller is required. This is the major drawback of assembly language programming and it makes the assembly language applications non-portable.

"Though Assembly Language programming possesses lots of drawback, as a developer, from my personal experience I prefer assembly language based development. Once you master the internals of a processor/controller, you can really perform magic with the processor/controller and can extract the maximum out of it."

9.2.2 High Level Language Based Development

As we have seen in the earlier section, Assembly language based programming is highly time consuming, tedious and requires skilled programmers with sound knowledge of the target processor architecture. Also applications developed in Assembly language are non-portable. Here comes the role of high level languages. Any high level language (like C, C++ or Java) with a supported cross compiler (for converting the application developed in high level language to target processor specific assembly code – We will discuss cross-compilers in detail in a later section) for the target processor can be used for embedded firmware development. The most commonly used high level language for embedded firmware application development is '*C*'. You may be thinking why '*C*' is used as the popular embedded firmware development language. The answer is "*C* is the well defined, easy to use high level language with extensive cross platform development tool support". Nowadays Cross-compilers for *C++* is also emerging out and embedded developers are making use of *C++* for embedded application development.

The various steps involved in high level language based embedded firmware development is same as that of assembly language based development except that the conversion of source file written in high level language to object file is done by a cross-compiler, whereas in Assembly language based development it is carried out by an assembler. The various steps involved in the conversion of a program written in high level language to corresponding binary file/machine language is illustrated in Fig. 9.2.

The program written in any of the high level language is saved with the corresponding language extension (.c for C, .cpp for C++ etc). Any text editor like 'notepad' or 'WordPad' from Microsoft® or the

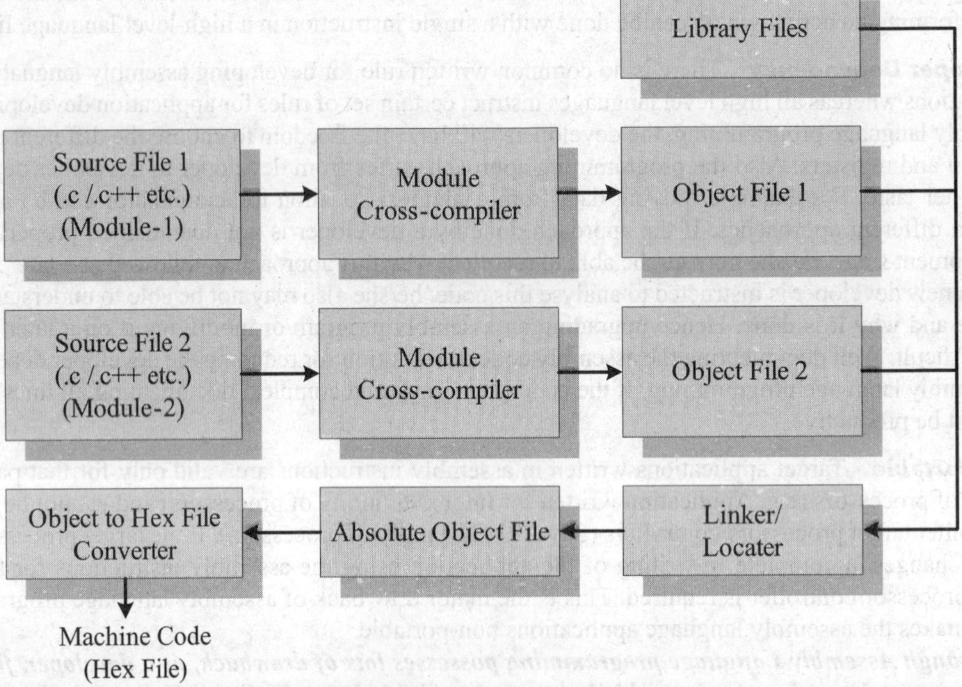

Fig. 9.2 **High level language to machine language conversion process**

text editor provided by an Integrated Development (IDE) tool supporting the high level language in use can be used for writing the program. Most of the high level languages support modular programming approach and hence you can have multiple source files called modules written in corresponding high level language. The source files corresponding to each module is represented by a file with corresponding language extension. Translation of high level source code to executable object code is done by a cross-compiler. The cross-compilers for different high level languages for the same target processor are different. It should be noted that each high level language should have a cross-compiler for converting the high level source code into the target processor machine code. Without cross-compiler support a high level language cannot be used for embedded firmware development. C51 Cross-compiler from Keil software is an example for Cross-compiler. C51 is a popular cross-compiler available for 'C' language for the *8051* family of micro controller. Conversion of each module's source code to corresponding object file is performed by the cross compiler. Rest of the steps involved in the conversion of high level language to target processor's machine code are same as that of the steps involved in assembly language based development.

As an example of high level language based embedded firmware development, we will discuss how 'Embedded C' is used for embedded firmware development, in a later section of this chapter.

9.2.2.1 Advantages of High Level Language Based Development

Reduced Development Time Developer requires less or little knowledge on the internal hardware details and architecture of the target processor/controller. Bare minimal knowledge of the memory organisation and register details of the target processor in use and syntax of the high level language are the only pre-requisites for high level language based firmware development. Rest of the things will be taken care of by the cross-compiler used for the high level language. Thus the ramp up time required by the developer in understanding the target hardware and target machine's assembly instructions is waived off by the cross compiler and it reduces the development time by significant reduction in developer effort. High level language based development also refines the scope of embedded firmware development from a team of specialised architects to anyone knowing the syntax of the language and willing to put little effort on understanding the minimal hardware details. With high level language, each task can be accomplished by lesser number of lines of code compared to the target processor/controller specific Assembly language based development.

Developer Independency The syntax used by most of the high level languages are universal and a program written in the high level language can easily be understood by a second person knowing the syntax of the language. Certain instructions may require little knowledge of the target hardware details like register set, memory map etc. Apart from these, the high level language based firmware development makes the firmware, developer independent. High level languages always instruct certain set of rules for writing the code and commenting the piece of code. If the developer strictly adheres to the rules, the firmware will be 100% developer independent.

Portability Target applications written in high level languages are converted to target processor/controller understandable format (machine codes) by a cross-compiler. An application written in high level language for a particular target processor can easily be converted to another target processor/controller specific application, with little or less effort by simply re-compiling/little code modification followed by re-compiling the application for the required target processor/controller, provided, the cross-compiler has support for the processor/controller selected. This makes applications written in high level language highly portable. Little effort may be required in the existing code to replace the target processor specific header files with new header files, register definitions with new ones, etc. This is the major flexibility offered by high level language based design.

9.2.2.2 Limitations of High Level Language Based Development The merits offered by high level language based design take advantage over its limitations. Some cross-compilers available for high level languages may not be so efficient in generating optimised target processor specific instructions. Target images created by such compilers may be messy and non-optimised in terms of performance as well as code size. For example, the task achieved by cross-compiler generated machine instructions from a high level language may be achieved through a lesser number of instructions if the same task is hand coded using target processor specific machine codes. The time required to execute a task also increases with the number of instructions. However modern cross-compilers are tending to adopt designs incorporating optimisation techniques for both code size and performance. High level language based code snippets may not be efficient in accessing low level hardware where hardware access timing is critical (of the order of nano or micro seconds).

The investment required for high level language based development tools (Integrated Development Environment incorporating cross-compiler) is high compared to Assembly Language based firmware development tools.

9.2.3 Mixing Assembly and High Level Language

Certain embedded firmware development situations may demand the mixing of high level language with Assembly and vice versa. High level language and assembly languages are usually mixed in three ways; namely, mixing Assembly Language with High Level Language, mixing High Level Language with Assembly and In-line Assembly programming.

9.2.3.1 Mixing Assembly with High level language (e.g. Assembly Language with 'C') Assembly routines are mixed with 'C' in situations where the entire program is written in 'C' and the cross compiler in use do not have a built in support for implementing certain features like Interrupt Service Routine functions (ISR) or if the programmer wants to take advantage of the speed and optimised code offered by machine code generated by hand written assembly rather than cross compiler generated machine code. When accessing certain low level hardware, the timing specifications may be very critical and a cross compiler generated binary may not be able to offer the required time specifications accurately. Writing the hardware/peripheral access routine in processor/controller specific Assembly language and invoking it from 'C' is the most advised method to handle such situations.

Mixing 'C' and Assembly is little complicated in the sense—the programmer must be aware of how parameters are passed from the 'C' routine to Assembly and values are returned from assembly routine to 'C' and how 'Assembly routine' is invoked from the 'C' code.

Passing parameter to the assembly routine and returning values from the assembly routine to the caller 'C' function and the method of invoking the assembly routine from 'C' code is cross compiler dependent. There is no universal written rule for this. You must get these informations from the documentation of the cross compiler you are using. Different cross compilers implement these features in different ways depending on the general purpose registers and the memory supported by the target processor/controller. Let's examine this by taking Keil C51 cross compiler for 8051 controller. The objective of this example is to give an idea on how C51 cross compiler performs the mixing of Assembly code with 'C'.

1. Write a simple function in C that passes parameters and returns values the way you want your assembly routine to.
2. Use the *SRC* directive (*#PRAGMA SRC* at the top of the file) so that the *C* compiler generates an *.SRC* file instead of an *.OBJ* file.
3. Compile the *C* file. Since the *SRC* directive is specified, the *.SRC* file is generated. The *.SRC* file contains the assembly code generated for the C code you wrote.
4. Rename the *.SRC* file to *.A51* file.
5. Edit the *.A51* file and insert the assembly code you want to execute in the body of the assembly function shell included in the .A51 file.

As an example consider the following sample code (Extracted from Keil C51 documentation)

```
#pragma SRC
unsigned char my_assembly_func (unsigned int argument)
{
return (argument + 1);  // Insert dummy lines to access all args and
                        // retvals
}
```

This C function on cross compilation generates the following assembly *SRC* file.

```
NAME     TESTCODE
?PR?_my_assembly_func?TESTCODE            SEGMENT CODE
         PUBLIC   _my_assembly_func
; #pragma SRC
; unsigned char my_assembly_func (
```

```
        RSEG  ?PR?_my_assembly_func?TESTCODE
        USING   0
_my_assembly_func:
;---- Variable 'argument?040' assigned to Register 'R6/R7' ----
; SOURCE LINE # 2
;   unsigned int argument)
; {
; SOURCE LINE # 4
; return (argument + 1);    // Insert dummy lines to access all args
; and retvals
; SOURCE LINE # 5
        MOV     A,R7
        INC     A
        MOV     R7,A
; }
; SOURCE LINE # 6
?C0001:
        RET
; END OF _my_assembly_func
        END
```

The special compiler directive *SRC* generates the Assembly code corresponding to the 'C' function and each lines of the source code is converted to the corresponding Assembly instruction. You can easily identify the Assembly code generated for each line of the source code since it is implicitly mentioned in the generated *.SRC* file. By inspecting this code segments you can find out which registers are used for holding the variables of the 'C' function and you can modify the source code by adding the assembly routine you want.

9.2.3.2 Mixing High level language with Assembly (e.g. 'C' with Assembly Language)

Mixing the code written in a high level language like '*C*' and Assembly language is useful in the following scenarios:

1. The source code is already available in Assembly language and a routine written in a high level language like 'C' needs to be included to the existing code.
2. The entire source code is planned in Assembly code for various reasons like optimised code, optimal performance, efficient code memory utilisation and proven expertise in handling the Assembly, etc. But some portions of the code may be very difficult and tedious to code in Assembly. For example 16bit multiplication and division in *8051* Assembly Language.
3. To include built in library functions written in 'C' language provided by the cross compiler. For example Built in Graphics library functions and String operations supported by 'C'.

Most often the functions written in 'C' use parameter passing to the function and returns value/s to the calling functions. The major question that needs to be addressed in mixing a 'C' function with Assembly is that how the parameters are passed to the function and how values are returned from the function and how the function is invoked from the assembly language environment. Parameters are passed to the function and values are returned from the function using CPU registers, stack memory and fixed memory. Its implementation is cross compiler dependent and it varies across cross compilers. A typical example is given below for the Keil C51 cross compiler

C51 allows passing of a maximum of three arguments through general purpose registers R2 to R7. If the three arguments are *char* variables, they are passed to the function using registers R7, R6 and R5 respectively. If the parameters are *int* values, they are passed using register pairs (R7, R6), (R5, R4) and (R3, R2). If the number of arguments is greater than three, the first three arguments are passed through registers and rest is passed through fixed memory locations. Refer to C51 documentation for more details. Return values are usually passed through general purpose registers. R7 is used for returning *char* value and register pair (R7, R6) is used for returning *int* value. The 'C' subroutine can be invoked from the assembly program using the subroutine call Assembly instruction (Again cross compiler dependent).

```
E.g.  LCALL    _Cfunction
```

Where *Cfunction* is a function written in 'C'. The prefix _ informs the cross compiler that the parameters to the function are passed through registers. If the function is invoked without the _ prefix, it is understood that the parameters are passed through fixed memory locations.

9.2.3.3 Inline Assembly Inline assembly is another technique for inserting target processor/controller specific Assembly instructions at any location of a source code written in high level language 'C'. This avoids the delay in calling an assembly routine from a 'C' code (If the Assembly instructions to be inserted are put in a subroutine as mentioned in the section mixing assembly with 'C'). Special keywords are used to indicate that the start and end of Assembly instructions. The keywords are cross-compiler specific. C51 uses the keywords *#pragma asm* and *#pragma endasm* to indicate a block of code written in assembly.

```
E.g.    #pragma asm
        MOV A, #13H
        #pragma endasm
```

Important Note:

*The examples used for illustration throughout the section **Mixing Assembly & High Level Language** is Keil C51 cross compiler specific. The operation is cross compiler dependent and it varies from cross compiler to cross compiler. The intention of the author is just to give an overall idea about the mixing of Assembly code and High level language 'C' in writing embedded programs. Readers are advised to go through the documentation of the cross compiler they are using for understanding the procedure adopted for the cross compiler in use.*

9.3 PROGRAMMING IN EMBEDDED C

Whenever the conventional 'C' Language and its extensions are used for programming embedded systems, it is referred as ***'Embedded C'*** programming. Programming in 'Embedded C' is quite different from conventional Desktop application development using 'C' language for a particular OS platform. Desktop computers contain working memory in the range of Megabytes (Nowadays Giga bytes) and storage memory in the range of Giga bytes. For a desktop application developer, the resources available are surplus in quantity and s/he can be very lavish in the usage of RAM and ROM and no restrictions are imposed at all. This is not the case for embedded application developers. Almost all embedded systems are limited in both storage and working memory resources. Embedded application developers should be aware of this fact and should develop applications in the best possible way which optimises the code memory and working memory usage as well as performance. In other words, the hands of an embedded application developer are always tied up in the memory usage context☺.

9.3.1 'C' v/s. 'Embedded C'

'C' is a well structured, well defined and standardised general purpose programming language with extensive bit manipulation support. 'C' offers a combination of the features of high level language and assembly and helps in hardware access programming (system level programming) as well as business package developments (Application developments like pay roll systems, banking applications, etc). The conventional 'C' language follows ANSI standard and it incorporates various library files for different operating systems. A platform (operating system) specific application, known as, compiler is used for the conversion of programs written in 'C' to the target processor (on which the OS is running) specific binary files. Hence it is a platform specific development.

Embedded 'C' can be considered as a subset of conventional 'C' language. Embedded 'C' supports all 'C' instructions and incorporates a few target processor specific functions/instructions. It should be noted that the standard ANSI 'C' library implementation is always tailored to the target processor/controller library files in Embedded 'C'. The implementation of target processor/controller specific functions/instructions depends upon the processor/controller as well as the supported cross-compiler for the particular Embedded 'C' language. A software program called 'Cross-compiler' is used for the conversion of programs written in Embedded 'C' to target processor/controller specific instructions (machine language).

9.3.2 Compiler vs. Cross-Compiler

Compiler is a software tool that converts a source code written in a high level language on top of a particular operating system running on a specific target processor architecture (e.g. Intel x86/Pentium). Here the operating system, the compiler program and the application making use of the source code run on the same target processor. The source code is converted to the target processor specific machine instructions. The development is platform specific (OS as well as target processor on which the OS is running). Compilers are generally termed as '*Native Compilers*'. A native compiler generates machine code for the same machine (processor) on which it is running.

Cross-compilers are the software tools used in cross-platform development applications. In cross-platform development, the compiler running on a particular target processor/OS converts the source code to machine code for a target processor whose architecture and instruction set is different from the processor on which the compiler is running or for an operating system which is different from the current development environment OS. Embedded system development is a typical example for cross-platform development where embedded firmware is developed on a machine with Intel/AMD or any other target processors and the same is converted into machine code for any other target processor architecture (e.g. 8051, PIC, ARM etc). Keil C51 is an example for cross-compiler. The term 'Compiler' is used interchangeably with 'Cross-compiler' in embedded firmware applications. Whenever you see the term 'Compiler' related to any embedded firmware application, please understand that it is referring the cross-compiler.

9.3.3 Using 'C' in 'Embedded C'

The author takes the privilege of assuming the readers are familiar with 'C' programming. Teaching 'C' is not in the scope of this book. If you are not familiar with 'C' language syntax and 'C' programming technique, please get a handle on the same before you proceed. Readers are advised to go through books by 'Brian W. Kernighan and Dennis M. Ritchie (K&R)' or 'E. Balagurusamy' on 'C' programming.

This section is intended only for giving readers a basic idea on how 'C' Language is used in embedded firmware development.

Let us brush up whatever we learned in conventional 'C' programming. Remember we will only go through the peripheral aspects and will not go in deep.

9.3.3.1 Keywords and Identifiers *Keywords* are the reserved names used by the 'C' language. All *keywords* have a fixed meaning in the 'C' language context and they are not allowed for programmers for naming their own variables or functions. ANSI 'C' supports 32 keywords and they are listed below. All 'C' supported keywords should be written in '*lowercase*' letters.

auto	Double	int	struct
break	else	long	switch
case	enum	register	typedef
char	extern	return	union
const	float	short	unsigned
continue	for	signed	void
default	goto	sizeof	volatile
do	if	static	while

Identifiers are user defined names and labels. Identifiers can contain letters of English alphabet (both upper and lower case) and numbers. The starting character of an identifier should be a letter. The only special character allowed in identifier is underscore (_).

9.3.3.2 Data Types Data type represents the type of data held by a variable. The various data types supported, their storage space (bits) and storage capacity for 'C' language are tabulated below.

Data Type	Size (Bits)	Range	Comments
char	8	–128 to +127	Signed character
signed char	8	–128 to +127	Signed character
unsigned char	8	0 to +255	Unsigned character
short int	8	–128 to +127	Signed short integer
signed short int	8	–128 to +127	Signed short integer
unsigned short int	8	0 to +255	Unsigned short integer
int	16	–32,768 to +32,767	Signed integer
signed int	16	–32,768 to +32,767	Signed integer
unsigned int	16	0 to +65,535	Unsigned integer
long int	32	–2147,483,648 to +2,147,483,647	Signed long integer
signed long int	32	–2147,483,648 to +2,147,483,647	Signed long integer
unsigned long int	32	0 to +4,294,967,295	Unsigned long integer
float	32	3.4E-38 to 3.4E+38	Signed floating point
double	64	1.7E-308 to 1.7E+308	Signed floating point (Double precision)
long double	80	3.4E-4932 to 3.4E+4932	Signed floating point (Long Double precision)

The data type size and range given above is for an ordinary 'C' compiler for 32 bit platform. It should be noted that the storage size may vary for data type depending on the cross-compiler in use for embedded applications.

Since memory is a big constraint in embedded applications, select the optimum data type for a variable. For example if the variable is expected to be within the range 0 to 255, declare the same as an '*unsigned char*' or '*unsigned short int*' data type instead of declaring it as '*int*' or '*unsigned int*'. This will definitely save considerable amount of memory.

9.3.3.3 Storage Class Keywords related to storage class provide information on the scope (visibility or accessibility) and life time (existence) of a variable. 'C' supports four types of storage classes and they are listed below.

Storage class	Meaning	Comments
auto	Variables declared inside a function. Default storage class is auto	Scope and accessibility is restricted within the function where the variable is declared. No initialization. Contains random values at the time of creation
register	Variables stored in the CPU register of processor. Reduces access time of variable	Same as auto in scope and access. The decision on whether a variable needs to be kept in CPU register of the processor depends on the compiler
static	Local variable with life time same as that of the program	Retains the value throughout the program. By default initialises to zero on variable creation. Accessibility depends on where the variable is declared
extern	Variables accessible to all functions in a file and all files in a multiple file program	Can be modified by any function within a file or across multiple files (variable needs to be exported by one file and imported by other files using the same)

Apart from these four storage classes, 'C' literally supports storage class '*global*'. An '*auto or static*' variable declared in the public space of a file (declared before the implementation of all functions including main in a file) is accessible to all functions within that file. There is no explicit storage class for '*global*'. The way of declaration of a variable determines whether it is global or not.

9.3.3.4 Arithmetic Operations The list of arithmetic operators supported by 'C' are listed below

Operator	Operation	Comments
+	Addition	Adds variables or numbers
–	Subtraction	Subtracts variables or numbers
*	multiplication	multiplies variables or numbers
/	Division	Divides variables or numbers
%	Remainder	Finds the remainder of a division

9.3.3.5 Logical Operations Logical operations are usually performed for decision making and program control transfer. The list of logical operations supported by 'C' are listed below

Operator	Operation	Comments
&&	Logical AND	Performs logical AND operation. Output is true (logic 1) if both operands (left to and right to of && operator) are true
||	Logical OR	Performs logical OR operation. Output is true (logic 1) if either operand (operands to left or right of || operator) is true
!	Logical NOT	Performs logical Negation. Operand is complemented (logic 0 becomes 1 and vice versa)

9.3.3.6 Relational Operations Relational operations are normally performed for decision making and program control transfer on the basis of comparison. Relational operations supported by 'C' are listed below.

Operator	Operation	Comments
<	less than	Checks whether the operand on the left side of '<' operator is less than the operand on the right side. If yes return logic one, else return logic zero
>	greater than	Checks whether the operand on the left side of '>' operator is greater than the operand on the right side. If yes return logic one, else return logic zero
<=	less than or equal to	Checks whether the operand on the left side of '<=' operator is less than or equal to the operand on the right side. If yes return logic one, else return logic zero
>=	greater than	Checks whether the operand on the left side of '>=' operator is greater than or equal to the operand on the right side. If yes return logic one, else return logic zero
==	Checks equality	Checks whether the operand on the left side of '==' operator is equal to the operand on the right side. If yes return logic one, else return logic zero
!=	Checks non-equality	Checks whether the operand on the left side of '!=' operator is not equal to the operand on the right side. If yes return logic one, else return logic zero

9.3.3.7 Branching Instructions Branching instructions change the program execution flow conditionally or unconditionally. Conditional branching depends on certain conditions and if the conditions are met, the program execution is diverted accordingly. Unconditional branching instructions divert program execution unconditionally.

Commonly used conditional branching instructions are listed below

Conditional branching instruction	Explanation

//if statement
if (expression)
{
statement1;
statement2;
…………;
}
statement 3;
…………..;
	Evaluates the expression first and if it is true executes the statements given within the { } braces and continue execution of statements following the closing curly brace (}). Skips the execution of the statements within the curly brace { } if the expression is false and continue execution of the statements following the closing curly brace (}).
	
	One way branching

//if else statement
if (expression)
{
if_statement1;
if_statement2;
……………;
}
else
{
else_statement1;
	Evaluates the expression first and if it is true executes the statements given within the { } braces following if (expression) and continue execution of the statements following the closing curly brace (}) of else block. Executes the statements within the curly brace { } following the else, if the expression is false and continue execution of statements following the closing curly brace (}) of else.

else_statement2; ………………; } statement 3;	Two way branching

//switch case statement
switch (expression)
{
    case value1:
        break;
    case value2:
        break;
    default:
        break;
}
	Tests the value of a given expression against a list of case values for a matching condition. The expression and case values should be integers. value1, value2, etc. are integers. If a match found, executes the statement following the case and breaks from the switch. If no match found, executes the default case.
	
	Used for multiple branching.

//Conditional operator
// ?exp1 : exp2
 	
(expression) ?exp1: exp2
 	
E.g.
  if (x>y)
  a=1;
  else
  a=0;
can be written using conditional operator as
a=(x>y)? 1:0
	Used for assigning a value depending on the (expression). (expression) is calculated first and if it is greater than 0, evaluates exp1 and returns it as a result of operation else evaluate exp2 and returns it as result. The return value is assigned to some variable.
	
	It is a combination of if else with assignment statement.
	
	Used for two way branching

//unconditional branching goto label	goto is used as unconditional branching instruction. goto transfers the program control indicated by a label following the goto statement. The label indicated by goto statement can be anywhere in the program either before or after the goto label instruction. goto is generally used to come out of deeply nested loops in abnormal conditions or errors.

9.3.3.8 Looping Instructions Looping instructions are used for executing a particular block of code repeatedly till a condition is met or wait till an event is fired. Embedded programming often uses the looping instructions for checking the status of certain I/o ports, registers, etc. and also for producing delays. Certain devices allow write/read operations to and from some registers of the device only when the device is ready and the device ready is normally indicated by a status register or by setting/clearing certain bits of status registers. Hence the program should keep on reading the status register till the device ready indication comes. The reading operation forms a loop. The looping instructions supported by 'C' are listed below.

Looping instruction	Explanation

//while statement
while (expression)
{
body of while loop
}
	Entry controlled loop statement.
	The expression is evaluated first and if it is true the body of the loop is entered and executed. Execution of 'body of while loop' is repeated till the expression becomes false.

// do while loop
do
{
body of do loop
}
while (expression);
	The 'body of the loop' is executed at least once. At the end of each execution of the 'body of the loop', the while condition (expression) is evaluated and if it is true the loop is repeated, else loop is terminated.

//for loop
for (initialisation; test for condition; update variable)
{
body of for loop
}
	Entry controlled loop. Enters and executes the 'body of loop' only if the test for condition is true. *for* loop contains a loop control variable which may be initialised within the initialisation part of the loop. Multiple variables can be initialised with ',' operator.

//exiting from loop break; goto label	Loops can be exited in two ways. First one is normal exit where loop is exited when the expression/test for condition becomes false. Second one is forced exit. break and goto statements are used for forced exit. break exits from the innermost loop in a deeply nested loop, whereas goto transfers the program flow to a defined label.

//skipping portion of a loop
while (expression)
{
…………..;
if (condition);
continue;
…………..;
}
	Certain situation demands the skipping of a portion of a loop for some conditions. The 'continue' statement used inside a loop will skip the rest of the portion following it and will transfer the program control to the beginning of the loop.
	//for loop with skipping

//do while with skipping
do
{
…………….;
if (condition)
continue;
…………….;
}
while (expression);
	for (initialisation; test for condition; update variable)
	{
	…………….;
	if (condition)
	continue;
	…………….;
	}

Every 'for' loop can be replaced by a 'while' loop with a counter.

Let's consider a typical example for a looping instruction in embedded C application. I have a device which is memory mapped to the processor and I'm supposed to read the various registers of it (except status register) only after the contents of its status register, which is memory mapped at 0x3000 shows device is ready (say value 0x01 means device is ready). I can achieve this by different ways as given below.

```
//#################################################################
//using while loop
//#################################################################

char *status_reg = (char *) 0x3000; //Declares memory mapped register

while (*status_reg!=0x01);       //Wait till status_reg = 0x01

//#################################################################
//using do while loop
//#################################################################

char *status_reg = (char*) 0x3000;

do
{

} while (*status_reg!=0x01); Loop till status_reg = 0x01

//#################################################################
//using for loop
//#################################################################

char *status_reg = (char*) 0x3000;

for (;(*status_reg!=0x01););
```

The instruction *char *status_reg = (char*) 0x3000;* declares *status_reg* as a character pointer pointing to location 0x3000. The character pointer is used since the external device's register is only 8bit wide. We will discuss the pointer based memory mapping technique in a later section. In order to avoid compiler optimisation, the pointer should be declared as volatile pointer. We will discuss the same also in another section.

9.3.3.9 Arrays and Pointers Array is a collection of related elements (data types). Arrays are usually declared with data type of array, name of the array and the number of related elements to be placed in the array. For example the following array declaration

```
char arr [5];
```

declares a character array with name 'arr' and reserves space for 5 character elements in the memory as in Fig. 9.3[†].

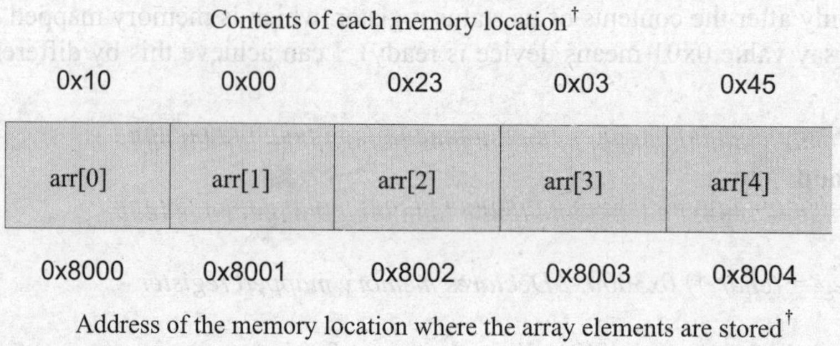

Fig. 9.3 Array representation in memory

The elements of an array are accessed by using the array index or subscript. The index of the first element is '0'. For the above example the first element is accessed by arr[0], second element by arr[1], and so on. In the above example, the array starts at memory location 0x8000 (arbitrary value taken for illustration) and the address of the first element is 0x8000. The '*address of*' operator (&) returns the address of the memory location where the variable is stored. Hence &arr[0] will return 0x8000 and &arr[1] will return 0x8001, etc. The name of the array itself with no index (subscript) always returns the address of the first element. If we examine the first element arr[0] of the above array, we can see that the variable arr[0] is allocated a memory location 0x8000 and the contents of that memory location holds the value for arr[0] (Fig. 9.4).

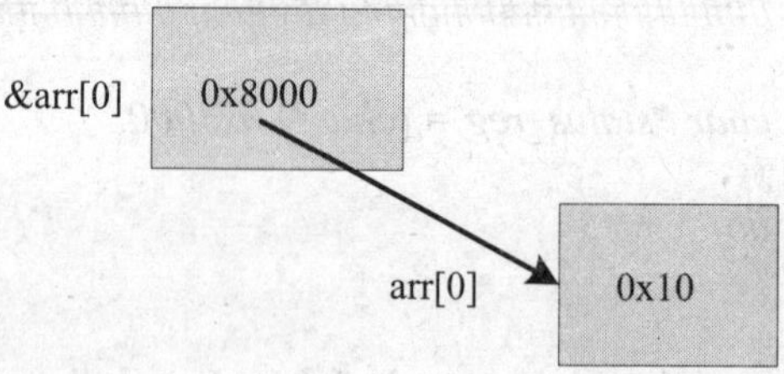

Fig. 9.4 Array element address and content relationship

Arrays can be initialised by two methods. The first method is initialising the entire array at the time of array declaration itself. Second method is selective initialisation where any member can be initialised or altered with a value.

```
//Initialization of array at the time of declaration

unsigned char arr[5] = {5, 10, 20, 3, 2};
unsigned char arr[ ] = {5, 10, 20, 3, 2};

//Selective initialization

unsigned char arr[5];

arr[0] = 5;
arr[1] = 10;
arr[2] = 20;
arr[3] = 3;
arr[4] = 2;
```

† Arbitrary value taken for illustration.

A few important points on Arrays

1. The '*sizeof()*' operator returns the size of an array as the number of bytes. E.g. '*sizeof (arr)*' in the above example returns 5. If arr[ ] is declared as an integer array and if the byte size for integer is 4, executing the '*sizeof (arr)*' instruction for the above example returns 20 (5 × 4).
2. The '*sizeof()*' operator when used for retrieving the size of an array which is passed as parameter to a function will only give the size of the data type of the array.

```
E.g.
    void test (char *p);              //Function declaration
    char arr [5] = {5, 10, 20, 3, 2};       //Array data type char

    void main ( )
    {
    test (arr);
    }

    void test (char *p)
    {
    printf ("%d", sizeof (*p));
    }
```

This code snippet will print '1' as the output, though the user expects 5 (size of arr) as output. The output is equivalent to sizeof (char), size of the data type of the array.

3. Use the syntax '*extern array type array name [ ]*' to access an array which is declared outside the current file. For example '*extern char arr[ ]*' for accessing the array '*arr[ ]*' declared in another file
4. Arrays are not equivalent to pointers. But the expression '*array name*' is equivalent to a pointer, of type specified by the array, to the first element of an array, e.g. '*arr*' illustrated for sizeof () operator is equivalent to a character pointer pointing to the first element of array '*arr*'.
5. Array subscripting is commutative in 'C' language and '*arr[k]*' is same as '**((arr)+(k))*' where '*arr[k]*' is the content of kth element of array '*arr*' and '*(arr)*' is the starting address of the array arr and *k* is the index of the array or offset address for the 'k^{th}' element from the base address of array. '**((arr) + (k))*' is the content of array for the index *k*.

Pointers *Pointer* is a flexible at the same time most dangerous feature, capable of creating potential damages leading to firmware crash, if not used properly. Pointer is a memory pointing based technique for variable access and modification. Pointers are very helpful in

1. Accessing and modifying variables
2. Increasing speed of execution
3. Accessing contents within a block of memory
4. Passing variables to functions by eliminating the use of a local copy of variables
5. Dynamic memory allocation (Will be discussed later)

To understand the pointer concept, let us have a look at the data memory organisation of a processor. For a processor/controller with 128 bytes user programmable internal RAM (e.g. AT89C51), the memory is organised as

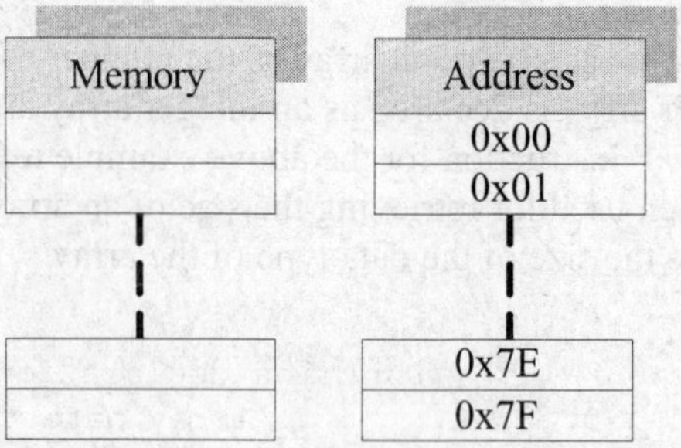

Fig. 9.5 **Data memory organisation for *8051***

If we declare a character variable, say *char input*, the compiler assigns a memory location to the variable anywhere within the internal memory 0x00 to 0x7F. The allocation is left to compiler's choice unless specified explicitly (Let it be 0x45 for our example). If we assign a value (say 10) to the variable ***input*** (input=10), the memory cell representing the variable input is loaded with 10.

Variable Name	Memory Address	Content
input	*0x45*	*10*

Fig. 9.6 **Relationship between variable name, address and data held by variable**

The contents of memory location 0x45 (representing the variable *input*) can be accessed and modified by using a pointer of type same as the variable (*char* for the variable *input* in the example). It is accomplished by the following method.

```
char input;     //Declaring input as character variable
char *p; //Declaring a character pointer p (* denotes p is a pointer)
p = &input      //Assigns the address of input as content to p
```

The same is diagrammatically represented as

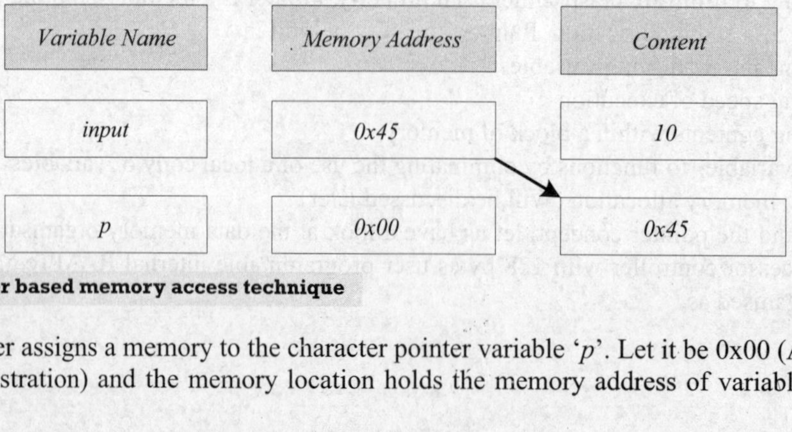

Fig. 9.7 **Pointer based memory access technique**

The compiler assigns a memory to the character pointer variable '*p*'. Let it be 0x00 (Arbitrary value chosen for illustration) and the memory location holds the memory address of variable *input* (0x45) as content. In 'C' the address assignment to pointer is done using the address of operator '&' or it can be done using explicitly by giving a specific address. The pointer feature in 'C' is same as the indirect addressing technique used in *8051* Assembly instructions. The code snippet

```
MOV R0, #45H
MOV A,@R0 ; R0 & R1 are the indirect addressing registers.
```

is an example for 8bit memory pointer usage in *8051* Assembly and the code snippet

```
MOV DPTR, #0045H
MOV A,@DPTR ; DPTR is the 16bit indirect addressing register
```

is an example for 16bit memory pointer operation. The general form of declaring a pointer in 'C' is

```
data type *pointer; //'data type' is the standard data type like
            //int, char, float etc... supported by 'C' language.
```

The * (asterisk) symbol informs the compiler that the variable *pointer* is a pointer variable. Like any other variables, pointers can also be initialised in its declaration itself.

```
E.g.    char x, y;
        char *ptr = &x;
```

The contents pointed by a pointer is modified/retrieved by using * as prefix to the pointer.

```
E.g.    char x=5, y=56;
        char *ptr=&x;           //ptr holds address of x
        *ptr = y;               //x = y
```

Pointer Arithmetic and Relational Operations 'C' language supports the following Arithmetic and relational operations on pointers.

1. Addition of integer with pointer. e.g. ptr+2 (It should be noted that the pointer is advanced forward by the storage length supported by the compiler for the data type of the pointer multiplied by the integer. For example for integer pointer where storage size of int = 4, the above addition advances the pointer by $4 \times 2 = 8$)
2. Subtraction of integer from pointer, e.g. ptr–2 (Above rule is applicable)
3. Incremental operation of pointer, e.g. ++ptr and ptr++ (Depending on the type of pointer, the ++ increment context varies). For a character pointer ++ operator increments the pointer by 1 and for an integer pointer the pointer is incremented by the storage size of the integer supported by the compiler (e.g. pointer ++ results in pointer + 4 if the size for integer supported by compiler is 4)
4. Decrement operation of pointer, e.g. – –ptr and ptr– – (Context rule for decrement operation is same as that of incremental operation)
5. Subtraction of pointers, e.g. ptr1– ptr2
6. Comparison of two pointers using relational operators, e.g. ptr1 > ptr2, ptr1 < ptr2, ptr1 = = ptr2, ptr1! = ptr2 etc (Comparison of pointers of same type only will give meaningful results)

Note:

1. Addition of two pointers, say *ptr1 + ptr2* is illegal
2. Multiplication and division operations involving pointer as numerator or denominator are also not allowed

A few important points on Pointers

1. The instruction *ptr++ increments only the pointer not the content pointed by the pointer '*ptr*' and *ptr– – decrements the pointer not the contents pointed by the pointer '*ptr*'
2. The instruction (*ptr) ++ increments the content pointed by the pointer '*ptr*' and not the pointer '*ptr*'. (*ptr)-- decrements the content pointed by the pointer '*ptr*' and not the pointer '*ptr*'
3. A type-casted pointer cannot be used in an assignment expression and cannot be incremented or decremented, e.g. ((int *ptr))++; will not work in the expected way
4. '***Null Pointer***' is a pointer holding a special value called '*NULL*' which is not the address of any variable or function or the start address of the allocated memory block in dynamic memory allocations
5. Pointers of each type can have a related null pointer viz. there can be character type null pointer, integer type null pointer, etc.
6. '*NULL*' is a preprocessor macro which is literally defined as zero or ((void *) 0). #define NULL 0 or #define NULL ((void *) 0)
7. '*NULL*' is a constant zero and both can be used interchangeably as Null pointer constants
8. A '*NULL*' pointer can be checked by the operator if ( ). See the following example

```
if (ptr)   //ptr is a pointer declared
printf ("ptr is not a NULL pointer");
else
printf ("ptr is a NULL pointer");
```

   The statement if (ptr) is converted to if (ptr! =0) by the (cross) compiler. Alternatively you can directly use the statement if (ptr! =0) in your program to check the 'NULL' pointer.

9. Null pointer is a 'C' language concept and whose internal value does not matter to us. '*NULL*' always guarantee a '0' to you but Null pointer need not be.

Pointers and Arrays—Are they related? Arrays are not equivalent to pointers and vice versa. But the expression array 'name [ ]' is equivalent to a pointer, of type specified by the array, to the first element of an array, e.g. for the character array '*char arr[5]*', '*arr[ ]*' is equivalent to a character pointer pointing to the first element of array '*arr*' (This feature is referred to as '*equivalence of pointers and arrays*'). You can achieve the array features like accessing and modifying members of an array using a pointer and pointer increment/decrement operators. Arrays and pointer declarations are interchangeable when they are used as parameters to functions. Point 2 discussed under the section '**A few important points on Arrays**' for *sizeof()* operator usage explains this feature also.

9.3.3.10 Characters and Strings Character is a one byte data type and it can hold values ranging from 0 to 255 (unsigned character) or -128 to +127 (signed character). The term character literally refers to the alpha numeric characters (English alphabet A to Z (both small letters and capital letters) and number representation from '0' to '9') and special characters like *, ?, !, etc. An integer value ranging from 0 to 255 stored in a memory location can be viewed in different ways. For example, the hexadecimal number 0x30 when represented as a character will give the character '0' and if it is viewed as a decimal number it will give 48. String is an array of characters. A group of characters defined within a double quote represents a constant string.

'*H*' is an example for a character, whereas "*Hello*" is an example for a string. String always terminates with a '\0' character. The '\0' character indicates the string termination. Whenever you declare a string using a character array, allocate space for the null terminator '\0' in the array length.

```
E.g.    char name [ ] = "SHIBU"   ;
or      char name [6] = {'S', 'H', 'I', 'B', 'U', '\0'};
```

String operations are very important in embedded product applications. Many of the embedded products contain visual indicators in the form of alpha numeric displays and are used for displaying text. Though the conventional alpha numeric displays are giving way to graphic displays, they are deployed widely in low cost embedded products. The various operations performed on character strings are explained below.

Input & Output operations Conventional 'C' programs running on Desktop machines make use of the standard string inputting (*scanf()*) and string outputting (*printf()*) functions from the platform specific I/O library. Standard keyboard and monitor are used as the input and output media for desktop application. This is not the case for embedded systems. Embedded systems are compact and they need not contain a standard keyboard or monitor screen for I/O functions. Instead they incorporate application specific keyboard and display units (Alpha numeric/graphic) as user interfaces. The standard string input instruction supported by 'C' language is *scanf( )* and a code snippet illustrating its usage is given below.

```
char name [6];
scanf ("%s", name);
```

A standard ANSI C compiler converts this code according to the platform supported I/O library files and waits for inputting a string from the keyboard. The scanf function terminates when a white space (blank, tab, carriage return, etc) is encountered in the input string. Implementation of the *scanf()* function is (cross) compiler dependent. For example, for 8051 microcontroller all I/O operations are supposed to be executed by the serial interface and the C51 cross compiler implements the *scanf()* function in such a way to expect and receive a character/string (according to the scanf usage context (character if first parameter to *scanf()* is "%c" and string if first parameter is "%s")) from the serial port.

printf() is the standard string output instruction supported by 'C' language. A code snippet illustrating the usage of *printf( )* is given below.

```
char name [ ] = "SHIBU";
printf ("%s", name);
```

Similar to *scanf()* function, the standard ANSI C compiler converts this code according to the platform supported I/O library files and displays the string in a console window displayed on the monitor. Implementation of *printf()* function is also (cross) compiler specific. For 8051 microcontroller the C51 cross compiler implements the *printf()* function in such a way to send a character/string (according to the printf usage context (character if first parameter to *printf()* is "%c" and string if first parameter is "%s")) to the serial port.

String Concatenation Concatenation literally means '*joining together*'. String concatenation refers to the joining of two or more strings together to form a single string. 'C' supports built in functions for string operations. To make use of the built in string operation functions, include the header file '*string.h*' to your '*.c*' file. '*strcat()*' is the function used for concatenating two strings. The syntax of '*strcat()*' is illustrated below.

```
strcat (str1, str2); //'str1' and 'str2' are the strings to
                     //be concatenated.
```

On executing the above instruction the null character ('\0') from the end of '*str1*' is removed and '*str2*' is appended to '*str1*'. The string '*str2*' remains unchanged. As a precautionary measure, ensure that str1 (first parameter of '*strcat( )*' function) is declared with enough size to hold the concatenated string. '*strcat()*' can also be used for appending a constant string to a string variable.

```
E.g.    strcat(str1, "Hello!");
```

> ***Note:***
> 1. Addition of two strings, say *str1+str2* is not allowed
> 2. Addition of a string variable, say str1, with a constant string, say "*Hello*" is not allowed

String Comparison Comparison of strings can be performed by using the '*strcmp()*' function supported by the string operation library file. Syntax of *strcmp()*' is illustrated below.

```
strcmp (str1, str2); //str1 and str2 are two character strings
```

If the two strings which are passed as arguments to '*strcmp()*' function are equal, the return value of '*strcmp()*' will be zero. If the two strings are not equal and if the ASCII value of the first non-matching character in the string *str1* is greater than that of the corresponding character for the second string *str2*, the return value will be greater than zero. If the ASCII value of first non-matching character in the string *str1* is less than that of the corresponding character for the second string *str2*, the return value will be less than zero. '*strcmp()*' function is used for comparing two string variables, string variable and constant string or two constant strings.

```
E.g.    char str1 [ ] = "Hello world";
        char str2 [ ] = "Hello World!"  ;
        int n;
        n= strcmp(str1, str2);
```

Executing this code snippet assigns a value which is greater than zero to *n*. (since ASCII value of '*w*' is greater than that of '*W*'). *n= strcmp(str2, str1);* will assign a value which is less than zero to *n*. (since ASCII value of '*W*' is less than that of '*w*').

The function *stricmp()* is another version of *strcmp()*. The difference between the two is, *stricmp()* is not case sensitive. There won't be any differentiation between upper and lowercase letters when *stricmp()* is used for comparison. If *stricmp()* is used for comparing the two strings str1 and str2 in the above example, the return value of the function *stricmp* (str1, str2) will be zero.

> ***Note:***
> 1. Comparison of two string variables using '= =' operator is invalid, e.g. if (*str1* == *str2*) is invalid
> 2. Comparison of a string variable and a string constant using '= =' operator is also invalid, e.g. if (*str1* == *"Hello"*) is invalid

Finding String length String length refers to the number of characters except the null terminator character '\0' present in a string. String length can be obtained by using a counter combined with a search operation for the '\0' character. 'C' supplies a ready to use string function ***strlen()*** for determining the length of a string. Its syntax is explained below.

```
        strlen (str1);          //where str1 is a character string
```

```
e.g.   char str1 [ ] = "Hello World!"  ;
       int n;
       n = strlen (str1);
```

Executing this code snippet assigns the numeric value 12 to integer variable '*n*'.

Copying Strings *strcpy()* function is the 'C' supported string operation function for copying a string to another string. Syntax of *strcpy( )* function is

```
       strcpy (str1, str2);    //str1, str2 are character strings.
```

This function assigns the contents of *str2* to *str1*. The original content of str1 is overwritten by the contents of *str2*. *str2* remains unchanged. The size of the character array which is passed as the first argument the *strcpy( )* function should be large enough to hold the copied string. *strcpy()* function can also be used to assign constant string to string variables.

```
e.g.   strcpy(str1, "Hello!")
```

> ***Note:***
> A string variable cannot be copied to another string variable using the '=' operator e.g. *str1 = str2* is illegal

A few important points on Characters and Strings

1. The function *strcat()* is used for concatenating two string variables or string variable and string constants. Characters cannot be appended to a string variable using *strcat()* function. For example *strcat (str1, 'A')* may not give the expected result. The same can be achieved by *strcat (str1, "A")*
2. Strings are character arrays and they cannot be assigned directly to a character array (except the initialisation of arrays using string constants at the time of declaring character arrays)

```
//###########################################################
E.g.   unsigned char str1 [] = 'Hello"; // is valid;
       unsigned char str1 [6];
       str1= "Hello"; //is invalid.
```

3. Whenever a character array is declared to hold a string, allocate size for the null terminator character '\0' also in the character array

9.3.3.11 Functions Functions are the basic building blocks of modular programs. A function is a self-contained and re-usable code snippet intended to perform a particular task. 'Embedded C' supports two different types of functions namely, *library functions* and *user defined functions*.

Library functions are the built in functions which is either part of the standard 'Embedded C' library or user created library files. 'C' provides extensive built in library file support and the library files are categorised into various types like I/O library functions, string operation library functions, memory allocation library functions etc. *printf()*, *scanf ()*, etc. are examples of I/O library functions. *strcpy()*, *strcmp()*, etc. are examples for string operations library functions. *malloc()*, *calloc()* etc are examples of memory allocation library functions supported by 'C'. All library functions supported by a particular library is implemented and exported in the same. A corresponding header ('.*h*') file for the library file provides information about the various functions available to user in a library file. Users should include the header file corresponding to a particular library file for calling the functions from that library in the

'C' source file. For example, if a programmer wants to use the standard I/O library function *printf()* in the source file, the header file corresponding to the I/O library file ("*stdio.h*" meant for standard i/o) should be included in the 'c' source code using the #include preprocessor directive.

```
E.g.
        #include <stdio.h>
        void main ( )
        {
            printf("Hello World");
        }
```

"***string.h***" is the header file corresponding to the built in library functions for string operations and "***malloc.h***" is the header file for memory allocation library functions. Readers are requested to get info on header files for other required libraries from the standard ANSI library. As mentioned earlier, the standard 'C' library function implementation may be tailored by cross-compilers, keeping the function name and parameter list unchanged depending on Embedded 'C' application requirements. ***printf()*** function implemented by C51 cross compiler for *8051* microcontroller is a typical example. The library functions are standardised functions and they have a unique style of naming convention and arguments. Users should strictly follow it while using library functions.

User defined functions are programmer created functions for various reasons like modularity, easy understanding of code, code reusability, etc. The generic syntax for a function definition (implementation) is illustrated below.

```
Return type   function name (argument list)
        {
              //Function body (Declarations & statements)
              //Return statement
        }
```

Return type of a function tells—what is the data type of the value returning by the function on completion of its execution. The return type can be any of the data type supported by 'C' language, viz. *int*, *char*, *float*, *long*, etc. *void* is the return type for functions which do not return anything. Function name is the name by which a function is identified. For user defined functions users can give any name of their interest. For library functions the function name for doing certain operations is fixed and the user should use those standard function names. Parameters are the list of arguments to be passed to the function for processing. Parameters are the inputs to the functions. If a function accepts multiple parameters, each of them are separated using ',' in the argument list. Arguments to functions are passed by two means, namely, pass by value and pass by reference. Pass by value method passes the variables to the function using local copies whereas in pass by reference variables are passed to the function using pointers. In addition to the above-mentioned attributes, a function definition may optionally specify the function's linkage also. The linkage of the function can be either '*external*' or '*internal*'.

The task to be executed by the function is implemented within the body of the function. In certain situations, you may have a single source ('*.c*') file containing the entire variable list, user defined functions, function *main()*, etc. There are two methods for writing user defined functions if the source code is a single '*.c*' file. The first method is writing all user defined functions on top of the *main* function and other user defined functions calling the user defined function.

```
E.g.

Int xyz (int i)
{
............;
}

void abc (void)
{
............;
xyz (a)
}

void main ()
  {
      abc ();
  }
```

If you are writing the user defined functions after the entry function *main()* and calling the same inside *main*, you should specify the function prototype (function declaration) of each user defined functions before the function *main()*. Otherwise the compiler assumes that the user defined function is an extern function returning integer value and if you define the function after *main()* without using a function declaration/prototype, compiler will generate error complaining the user defined function is redefining (Compiler already assumed the function which is used inside *main()* without a function prototype as an extern function returning an integer value). The function declaration informs the compiler about the format and existence of a function prior to its use. Implicit declaration of functions is not allowed: every function must be explicitly declared before it is called. The general form of function declaration is

```
Linkage Type Return type  function name (arguments);
E.g. static int add(int a, int b);
```

The '*Linkage Type*' specifies the linkage for the function. It can be either '*external*' or '*internal*'. The '*static*' keyword for the '*Linkage Type*' specifies the linkage of the function as internal whereas the '*extern*' '*Linkage Type*' specifies 'external' linkage for the function. It is not mandatory to specify the name of the argument along with its type in the argument list of the function declaration. The declarations can simply specify the types of parameters in the argument list. This is called function *prototyping*. A function prototype consists of the function return type, the name of the function, and the parameter list. The usage is illustrated below.

```
static int add(int, int);
```

Let us have a look at the examples for the different scenarios explained above on user defined functions.

```
//######################################################################
//Example for Source code with function prototype for user defined-
//functions. Source file test.c
//######################################################################
```

```
#include <stdio.h>
//function prototype for user defined function test
void test (void);

    void main ( )
    {
    test ();        //Calling user defined function from main
    }
//Implementation of user defined function test after function main
void test (void)
{
printf ("Hello World!");
return;
}
```

```
//####################################################################
//Example for Source code without function prototype for user defined
//functions. Source file test.c
//####################################################################
#include <stdio.h>
//function prototype for user defined function test not declared
    void main ()
    {
    test ();        //Calling user defined function from main
    }

//Implementation of user defined function test after function main
    void test (void)
    {
    printf ("Hello World!");
    return;
    }
```

Compiler Output:

Compiling…
test.c
test.c(5): warning c4013: 'test' undefined; assuming extern returning int
test.c(9): error C2371: 'test': redefinition; different basic types Error executing cl.exe.
test.exe-1 error(s), 1 warning(s)

There is another convenient method for declaring variables and functions involved in a source file. This technique is a header ('*.h*') file and source ('*.c*') file based approach. In this approach, corresponding to each 'c' source file there will be a header file with same name (not necessarily) as that of the 'c' source file. All functions and global/extern variables for the source file are declared in the header file instead of declaring the same in the corresponding source file. Include the header file where the functions are declared to the source file using the "*#include*" pre-processor directive. Functions declared in a file can be either global (extern access) in scope or static in scope depending on the declaration of the function. By default all functions are global in scope (accessible from outside the file where the function is declared). If you want to limit the scope (accessibility) of the function within the file where it is declared, use the keyword '*static*' before the return type in the function declaration.

9.3.3.12 Function Pointers A function pointer is a pointer variable pointing to a function. When an application is compiled, the functions which are part of the application are also get converted into corresponding processor/compiler specific codes. When the application is loaded in primary memory for execution, the code corresponding to the function is also loaded into the memory and it resides at a memory address provided by the application loader. The function name maps to an address where the first instruction (machine code) of the function is present. A function pointer points to this address.

The general form of declaration of a function pointer is given below.

```
return_type (*pointer_name) (argument list)
```

where, '*return_type*' represents the return type of the function, '*pointer_name*' represents the name of the pointer and 'argument list' represents the data type of the arguments of the function. If the function contains multiple arguments, the data types are separated using ','. Typical declarations of function pointer are given below.

```
//Function pointer to a function returning int and takes no parameter
int (*fptr)();
//Function pointer to a function returning int and takes 1 parameter
int (*fptr)(int)
```

The parentheses () around the function pointer variable differentiates it as a function pointer variable. If no parentheses are used, the declaration will look like

```
int *fptr();
```

The cross compiler interprets it as a function declaration for function with name '*fptr*' whose argument list is void and return value is a pointer to an integer. Now we have declared a function pointer, the next step is 'How to assign a function to a function pointer?'.

Let us assume that there is a function with signature

```
int function1(void);
```

and a function pointer with declaration

```
int (*fptr)();
```

We can assign the address of the function '*function1()*' to our function pointer variable '*fptr*' with the following assignment statement:

```
fptr = &function1;
```

The '&' operator gets the address of function '*function1*' and it is assigned to the pointer variable '*fptr*' with the assignment operator '='. The address of operator '&' is optional when the name of the function is used. Hence the assignment operation can be re-written as:

```
fptr = function1;
```

Once the address of the right sort of function is assigned to the function pointer, the function can be invoked by any one of the following methods.

```
        (*fptr)();
        fptr();
```

Function pointers can also be declared using *typedef*. Declaration and usage of a function pointer with *typedef* is illustrated below.

```
//Function pointer to a function returning int and takes no parameter
        typedef int (*funcptr)();
        funcptr fptr;
```

The following sample code illustrates the declaration, definition and usage of function pointer.

```
#include <stdio.h>
void square(int x);
void main()
{
      //Declare a function pointer
      void (*fptr)(int);
      //Define the function pointer to function square
      fptr = square;
      //Style 1: Invoke the function through function pointer
      fptr(2);
      //Style 2: Invoke the function through function pointer
      (*fptr)(2);
}
//######################################################################
//Function for printing the square of a number
void square(int x)
{
      printf("Square of %d = %d\n", x, x*x);
}
```

Function pointer is a helpful feature in late binding. Based on the situational need in the application you can invoke the required function by binding the function with the right sort of function pointer (The function signature and function pointer signature should be matching). This reduces the usage of 'if' and 'switch – case' statements with function names. Function pointers are extremely useful for handling situations which demand passing of a function as argument to another function. Function pointers are often used within functions where the function should be able to work with a number of functions whose names are not known until the program is running. A typical example for this is callback functions, which requires the information about the function which needs to be called. The following sample piece of code illustrates the usage of function pointer as parameter to a function.

```
#include <stdio.h>
//######################################################################
//Function prototype declaration
void square(int x);
void cube(int x);
void power(void (*fptr)(int), int x);
```

```
void main()
{
      //Declare a function pointer
      void (*fptr)(int);
      //Define the function pointer to function square
      fptr = square;
      //Invoke the function 'square' through function pointer
      power (fptr,2);
      //Define the function pointer to function cube
      fptr = cube;
      //Invoke the function 'cube' through function pointer
      power (fptr,2);
}
//#####################################################################
//Interface function for invoking functions through function pointer

void power(void (*fptr)(int), int x)
{
      fptr(x);

}
//#####################################################################
//Function for printing the square of a number

void square(int x)
{
      printf("Square of %d = %d\n", x, x*x);

}
//#####################################################################
//Function for printing the third power (cube) of a number
void cube(int x)
{
      printf("Cube of %d = %d\n", x, x*x*x);
}
```

Arrays of Function Pointers An array of function pointers holds pointers to functions with same type of signature. This offers the flexibility to select a function using an index. Arrays of function pointers can be defined using either direct function pointers or the '*typedef*' qualifier.

```
//Declare an array of pointers to functions, which returns int and
//takes no parameters, using direct function pointer declaration
int (*fnptrarr[5])();

//Declare and initialise an array of pointers to functions, which
//return int and takes no parameters, using direct function pointer-
//declaration
int (*fnptrarr[])()= {/*initialisation*/};
```

```
//Declare and initialize to 'NULL' an array of pointers to functions,
//which return int and takes no parameters, using direct function
//pointer declaration
int (*fnptrarr[5])()= {NULL};

//Declare an array of pointers to functions, which returns int and
//takes no parameters, using typedef function pointer declaration
typedef int (*fncptr)();
fncptr fnptrarr[5])();

//Declare and initialize an array of pointers to functions, which
//return int and takes no parameters, using typedef function pointer-
//declaration
typedef int (*fncptr)();
fncptr fnptrarr[] ()= {/*initialisation*/};

//Declare and initialise to 'NULL' an array of pointers to functions,
//which return int and takes no parameters, using typedef function
//pointer declaration
typedef int (*fncptr)();
fncptr fnptrarr[5]()= {NULL};
```

The following piece of code illustrates the usage of function pointer arrays:

```
#include <stdio.h>
//######################################################################
//Function prototype definition
void square(int x);
void cube(int x);

void main()
{
      //Declare a function pointer array of size 2 and initialize
      void (*fptr[2])(int)= {NULL};
      //Define the function pointer 0 to function square
      fptr[0] = square;
      //Invoke the function square
      fptr[0](2);
      //Define the function pointer 1 to function cube
      fptr[1] = cube;
      //Invoke the function cube through function pointer
      fptr[1](2);
}
//######################################################################
//Function for printing the square of a number
void square(int x)
{
      printf("Square of %d = %d\n", x, x*x);
}
```

```
//###########################################################################
//Function for printing the third power (cube) of a number

void cube(int x)
{
      printf("Cube of %d = %d\n", x, x*x*x);
}
```

9.3.3.13 Structures and Unions *'structure'* is a variable holding a collection of data types (int, float, char, long etc). The data types can be either unique or distinct. The tag *'struct'* is used for declaring a structure. The general form of a structure declaration is given below.

```
        struct  struct_name
                {
                        //variable 1 declaration
                        //variable 2 to declaration
                        //..............
                        //variable n declaration
                };
```

struct_name is the name of the structure and the choice of the name is left to the programmer.

Let us examine the details kept in an employee record for an employee in the employee database of an organisation as example. A typical employee record contains information like *'Employee Name'*, *'Employee Code'*, and *'Date of Birth'*. This information can be represented in 'C' using a structure as given below.

```
struct  employee
        {
        char emp_name [20]; // Allowed maximum length for name = 20
        int emp_code;
        char DOB [10]; // DD-MM-YYYY Format (10 character)
        };
```

Hence in 'C', the employee record is represented by two string variables (character arrays) and an integer variable. Since these three variables are relevant to each employee, they are grouped together in the form of a structure. Literally structure can be viewed as a collection of related data. The above structure declaration does not allocate memory for the variables declared inside the structure. It's a mere representation of the data inside a structure. To allocate memory for the structure we need to create a variable of the structure. The structure variable creation is illustrated below.

```
struct employee emp1;
```

Keyword *'struct'* informs the compiler that the variable *'emp1'* is a structure of type *'employee'*. The name of the structure is referred as *'structure tag'* and the variables declared inside the structure are called *'structure elements'*. The definition of the structure variable only allocates the memory for the different elements and will not initialise the members. The members need to be initialised explicitly. Members of the structure variable can be initialised altogether at the time of declaration of the structure variable itself or can be initialised (modified) independently using the '.' operator (member operator).

```
struct employee emp1= {"SHIBU K V", 42170, "11-11-1977"};
```

This statement declares a structure variable with name 'emp1' of type employee and each elements of the structure is initialised as

```
emp_name = "SHIBU K V"
emp_code = 42170
DOB= "11-11-1977"
```

It should be noted that the variables should be initialised in the order as per their declaration in the structure variable. The selective method of initialisation/modification is used for initialising /modifying each element independently.

```
E.g.     struct employee emp1;
         emp1.emp_code = 42170;
```

All members of a structure, except character string variables can be assigned values using '.' Operator and assignment ('=') operator (character strings are character arrays and character arrays cannot be initialised altogether using the assignment operator). Character string variables can be assigned using string copy function (*strcpy*).

```
strcpy (emp1.emp_name,"SHIBU K V");
strcpy (emp1.DOB,"11-11-1977");
```

Declaration of a structure variable requires the keyword '*structure*' as the first word and it may sound awkward from a programmer point of view. This can be eliminated by using '*typedef*' in defining the structure. The above 'employee' structure example can be re-written using typedef as

```
typedef struct
      {
      char emp_name [20];// Allowed maximum length for name = 20
      int emp_code;
      char DOB [10];     // DD-MM-YYYY Format (10 character)
      } employee;
employee emp1; //No need to add struct before employee
```

This approach eliminates the need for adding the keyword '*struct*' each time a structure variable is declared.

Structure operations The following table lists the various operations supported by structures

Operator	Operation	Example

= (Assignment)	Assigns the values of one structure to another structure of same type	employee emp1,emp2;
		emp1.emp_code = 42170;
		strcpy(emp1.emp_name,"SHIBU");
		strcpy(emp1.DOB,"11/11/1977");
		emp2=emp1;

== (Checking the equality of all members of two structures)	Compare individual members of two structures of same type for equality. Return 1 if all members are identical in both structures else return 0	employee emp1,emp2;
		emp1.emp_code = 42170;
		strcpy(emp1.emp_name,"SHIBU");
		strcpy(emp1.DOB,"11/11/1977");
		if (emp2==emp1)

!= (Checking the equality of all members of two structures)	Compare individual members of two structures of same type for non equality. Return 1 if all members are not identical in both structures else return 0	employee emp1,emp2;
		emp1.emp_code = 42170;
		strcpy(emp1.emp_name,"SHIBU");
		strcpy(emp1.DOB,"11/11/1977");
		if (emp2!=emp1)

sizeof()	Returns the size of the structure (memory allocated for the structure variable in bytes)	employee emp1; sizeof (emp1);

> ***Note:***
> 1. The assignment and comparison operation is valid only if both structure variables are of the same type
> 2. Some compilers may not support the direct assignment and comparison operation. In such situation the individual members of structure should be assigned or compared separately.

Structure pointers Structure pointers are pointers to structures. It is easy to modify the memory held by structure variables if pointers are used. Functions with structure variable as parameter is a very good example for it. The structure variable can be passed to the function by two methods; either as a copy of the structure variable (pass by value) or as a pointer to a structure variable (pass by reference/address). Pass by value method is slower in operation compared to pass by pointers since the execution time for copying the structure parameter also needs to be accounted. Pass by pointers is also helpful if the structure which is given as input parameter to a function need to be modified and returned on execution of the calling function. Structure pointers can be declared by prefixing the structure variable name with '*'. The following structure pointer declaration illustrates the same.

```
struct employee *emp1;     //structure defined using the structure tag
employee *emp1;            //structure defined with typedef structure
```

For structure variables declared as pointers to a structure, the member selection of the structure is performed using the '→' operator.

```
E.g.      struct employee *emp1, emp2;
          emp1 = &emp2; //Obtain a pointer
          emp1→ emp_code = 42170;
          strcpy (emp1→DOB, "11-11-1977");
```

Structure pointers at absolute address Most of the time structures are used in Embedded C applications for representing the memory locations or registers of chip whose memory address is fixed at the time of hardware designing. Typical example is a Real Time Clock (RTC) which is memory mapped at a specific address and the memory address of the registers of the RTC is also fixed. If we use a structure to define the different registers of the RTC, the structure should be placed at an absolute address corresponding to the memory mapped address of the first register given as the member variable of the structure. Consider the structure describing RTC registers.

```
typedef struct
{
//RTC Control register (8bit) memory mapped at 0x4000
unsigned char control;
//RTC Seconds register (8bit) memory mapped at 0x4001
unsigned char seconds;
```

```
//RTC Minutes register (8bit) memory mapped at 0x4002
unsigned char minutes;
//RTC Hours register (8bit) memory mapped at 0x4003
unsigned char hours;
//RTC Day of week register (8bit) memory mapped at 0x4004
unsigned char day;
//RTC Date register (8bit) memory mapped at 0x4005
unsigned char date;
//RTC Month register (8bit) memory mapped at 0x4006
unsigned char month;
//RTC Year register (8bit) memory mapped at 0x4007
unsigned char year;
} RTC;
```

To read and write to these hardware registers using structure member variable manipulation, we need to place the RTC structure variable at the absolute address 0x4000, which is the address of the RTC hardware register, represented by the first member of structure RTC.

The implementation of structures using pointers to absolute memory location is cross-compiler dependent. Desktop applications may not give permission to explicitly place structures or pointers at an absolute address since we are not sure about the address allocated to general purpose RAM by the linker. Any attempt to explicitly allocate a structure at an absolute address may result in *access violation exception*. More over there is no need for a general purpose application to explicitly place structure or pointers at an absolute address, whereas embedded systems most often requires it if different hardware registers are memory mapped to the processor/controller memory map. The C51 cross compiler for *8051* microcontroller supports a specific Embedded C keyword '*xdata*' for external memory access and the structure absolute memory placement can be done using the following method.

```
        RTC xdata *rtc_registers = (void xdata *) 0x4000;
```

Structure Arrays In the above employee record example, three important data is associated with each employee, namely; employee name (emp_name), employee code (emp_code) and Date of Birth (DOB). This information is held together as a structure for associating the same with an employee. Suppose the organisation contains 100 employees then we need 100 such structures to hold the data related to the 100 employees. This is achieved by array of structures. For the above employee structure example a structure array with 100 structure variables can be declared as

```
struct employee emp [100]; //structure declared using struct keyword
        or
employee emp [100]; //structure declared using typedef struct
```

emp [0] holds the structure variable data for the first employee and emp [99] holds the structure variable data corresponding to the 100th employee. The variables corresponding to each structure in an array can be initialised altogether at the time of defining the structure array or can be initialised/modified using the corresponding array subscript for the structure and the '.' Operator as explained below.

```
typedef struct
        {
        char emp_name [20]; // Allowed maximum length for name = 20
        int emp_code;
```

```
      char DOB [10]; // DD-MM-YYYY Format (10 character)
      } employee;

//Initialisation at the time of defining variable
employee emp [3] = {{"JOHN", 1, "01-01-1988"}, {"ALEX", 2, "10-01-1976"},
{"SMITH", 3, "07-05-1985"}};
//Selective initialization
emp [0].emp_code = 1;
strcpy (emp [0].emp_name, "JOHN");
strcpy (emp [0].DOB, "01-01-1988");
```

Structure in Embedded 'C' programming Simple structure variables and array of structures are widely used in 'embedded 'C' based firmware development. Structures and structure arrays are used for holding various configuration data, exchanging information between Interrupt Service Routine (ISR) and application etc. A typical example for the structure usage is for holding the various register configuration data for setting up a particular baudrate for serial communication. An array of such configuration data holding structures can be used for setting different baudrates according to user needs. It is interesting to note that more than 90% of the embedded C programmers use '*typedef*' to define the structures with meaningful names.

Structure padding (Packed structure) Structure variables are always stored in the memory of the target system with structure member variables in the same order as they are declared in the structure definition. But it is not necessary that the variables should be placed in continuous physical memory locations. The choice on this is left to the compiler/cross-compiler. For multi byte processors (processors with word length greater than 1 byte (8 bits)), if the structure elements are arranged in memory in such a way that they can be accessed with lesser number of memory fetches, it definitely speeds up the operation. The process of arranging the structure elements in memory in a way facilitating increased execution speed is called *structure padding*. As an example consider the following structure:

```
      typedef struct
            {
            char x;
            int y;
            } exmpl;
```

Let us assume that the storage space for '***int***' is 4 bytes (32 bits) and for '***char***' it is 1 byte (8 bits) for the target embedded system under consideration. Suppose the target processor for embedded application, where the above structure is making use is with a 4 byte (32 bit) data bus and the memory is byte accessible. Every memory fetch operation retrieves four bytes from the memory locations $4x$, $4x + 1$, $4x + 2$ and $4x +3$, where $x = 0, 1, 2$, etc. for successive memory read operations. Hence a 4 byte (32 bit) variable can be fully retrieved in a single memory fetch if it is stored at memory locations with starting address $4x$ ($x = 0, 1, 2$, etc.). If it is stored at any other memory location, two memory fetches are required to retrieve the variable and hence the speed of operation is reduced by a factor of 2.

Let us analyse the various possibilities of storing the above structure within the memory.

Method-1 member variables of structure stored in consecutive data memory locations.

In this model the member variables are stored in consecutive data memory locations (***Note:*** the member variable storage need not start at the address mentioned here, the address given here is only

Memory Address	4x + 3	4x + 2	4x + 1	4x
Data	Byte 2 of exmpl.y	Byte 1 of exmpl.y	Byte 0 of exmpl.y	exmpl.x
Data				Byte 3 of exmpl.y
Memory Address	4(x + 1) + 3	4(x + 1) + 2	4(x + 1) + 1	4(x + 1)

Fig. 9.8 Memory representation for structure without padding

for illustration) and if we want to access the character variable exmp1.x of structure exmp1, it can be achieved with a single memory fetch. But accessing the integer member variable exmp1.y requires two memory fetches.

Method-2 member variables of structure stored in data memory with padding

In this approach, a structure variable with storage size same as that of the word length (or an integer multiple of word length) of the processor is always placed at memory locations with starting address as multiple of the word length so that the variable can be retrieved with a single data memory fetch. The memory locations coming in between the first variable and the second variable of the structure are filled with extra bytes by the compiler and these bytes are called 'padding bytes' (Fig. 9.9). The structure padding technique is solely dependent on the cross-compiler in use. You can turn ON or OFF the padding of structure by using the cross-compiler supported padding settings. Structure padding is applicable only for processors with word size more than 8bit (1 byte). It is not applicable to processors/controllers with 8bit bus architecture.

Memory Address	4x + 3	4x + 2	4x + 1	4x
Data	Padding	Padding	Padding	exmpl.x
Data	Byte 3 of exmpl.y	Byte 2 of exmpl.y	Byte 1 of exmpl.y	Byte 0 of exmpl.y
Memory Address	4(x + 1) + 3	4(x + 1) + 2	4(x + 1) + 1	4(x + 1)

Fig. 9.9 Memory representation for structure with padding

Structure and Bit fields Bit field is a useful feature supported by structures for bit manipulation operation and flag settings in embedded applications. Most of the processors/controllers used in embedded application development provides extensive Boolean (bit) operation support and a similar support in the firmware environment can directly be used to explore the Boolean processing capability of the target device.

For most of the application development scenarios we use integer and character to hold data items even though the variable is expected to vary in a range far below the upper limit of the data type used for holding the variable. A typical example is flags. Flags are used for indicating a 'TRUE' or 'FALSE' condition. Practically this can be done using a single bit and the two states of the bit (1 and 0) can be used for representing 'TRUE' or 'FALSE' condition. Unfortunately 'C' does not support a built in data type for holding a single bit and it forces us to use the minimum sized data type (quite often char (8bit data type) and short int) for representing the flag. This will definitely lead to the wastage of memory. Since memory is a big constraint in embedded applications we cannot tolerate the memory wastage. 'C' indirectly supports bit data types through '***Bit fields***' of structures. Structure bit fields can be directly accessed and manipulated. A set of bits in the structure bit field forms a '*char*' or '*int*' variable. The general format of declaration of bit fields within structure is illustrated below.

```
struct  struct_name
        {
        data type (char or int) bit_var 1_name : bit_size,
        bit_var 2_name : bit_size,
        ..........................,
        ..........................,
        bit_var n_name : bit_size;
        } ;
```

'*struct_name*' represents the name of the bit field structure. '*data type*' is the data type which will be formed by packing several bits. Only character (char) and integer (int/short int) data types are allowed in bit field structures in Embedded C applications. Some compilers may not support the 'char' data type. However our illustrative cross-compiler C51 supports 'char' data type as data type. '*bit_var 1_name*' denotes the bit variable and '*bit_size*' gives the number of bits required by the variable '*bit_var 1_name*' and so. The operator ':' associates the number of bits required with the bit variable. Bit variables that are packed to form a data type should be separated inside the structure using ',' operator. A real picture of bit fields in structures for embedded applications can be provided by the Program Status Word (PSW) register representation of *8051* controller. The PSW register of 8051 is bit addressable and its bit level representation is given below.

PSW.7	PSW.6	PSW.5	PSW.4	PSW.3	PSW.2	PSW.1	PSW.0
CY	AC	F0	RS1	RS0	OV		P

Using structure and bit fields the same can be represented as

```
struct PSW
     {
          char     P:1,      /* Bit 0 of PSW : Parity Flag */
                   :1,       /* Bit 1 of PSW : Unused */
                   OV:1,     /* Bit 2 of PSW : Overflow Flag */
                   RS0:1,    /* Bit 3 of PSW : Register Bank Select 0 bit */
                   RS1 :1,   /* Bit 4 of PSW : Register Bank Select 1 bit */
                   F0:1,     /* Bit 5 of PSW : User definable Flag */
                   AC :1,    /* Bit 6 of PSW : Auxiliary Carry Flag */
                   C:1;      /* Bit 7 of PSW : Carry Flag */
```

```
/*Note that the operator ';' is used after the last bit field to
indicate end of bit field*/

};
```

In the above structure declaration, each bit field variable is defined with a name and an associated bit size representation. If some of the bits are unused in a packed fashion, the same can be skipped by merely giving the number of bytes to be skipped without giving a name for that bit variables. In the above example Bit 1 of PSW is skipped since it is an unused bit in the PSW register.

It should be noted that the total number of bits used by the bit field variables defined for a specific data type should not exceed the maximum number of allocated bits for that specific data type. In the above example the bit field data type is '*char*' (8 bits) and 7 bit field variables each of size 1 are declared and one bit variable is declared as unused bit. Hence the total number of bits consumed by all the bit variables including the non declared bit variable sums to 8, which is same as the bit size for the data type '*char*'. The internal representation of structure bit fields depends on the size supported by the cross-compiler data type (char/int) and the ordering of bits in memory. Some processors/controllers store the bits from left to right while others store from right to left (Here comes the significance of endianness).

Unions Union is a concept derived from structure and *union* declarations follow the same syntax as that of structures (*structure* tag is replaced by *union* tag). Though *union* looks similar to structure in declaration, it differs from structure in the memory allocation technique for the member variables. Whenever a *union* variable is created, memory is allocated only to the member variable of *union* requiring the maximum storage size. But for structures, memory is allocated to each member variables. This helps in efficient data memory usage. Even if a *union* variable contains different member variables of different data types, existence is only for a single variable at a time. The size of a *union* returns the storage size of its member variable occupying the maximum storage size. The syntax for declaring *union* is given below

```
union    union_name
         {
                  //variable 1 declaration
                  //variable 2 to declaration
                  //..............
                  //variable n declaration
         };
```

or

```
typedef union
         {
         //variable 1 declaration
         //variable 2 to declaration
         //..............
         //variable n declaration
         } union_name;
```

'*union_name*' is the name of the *union* and programmers can use any name according to their programming style. As an illustrative example let's declare a *union* variable consisting of an integer member variable and a character member variable.

```
    typedef union
            {
            int y;      //Integer variable
            char z;     //Character variable
            } example;
example ex1;
```

Assuming the storage location required for '*int*' as 4 bytes and for '*char*' as 1 byte, the memory allocated to the *union* variable ex1 will be as shown below

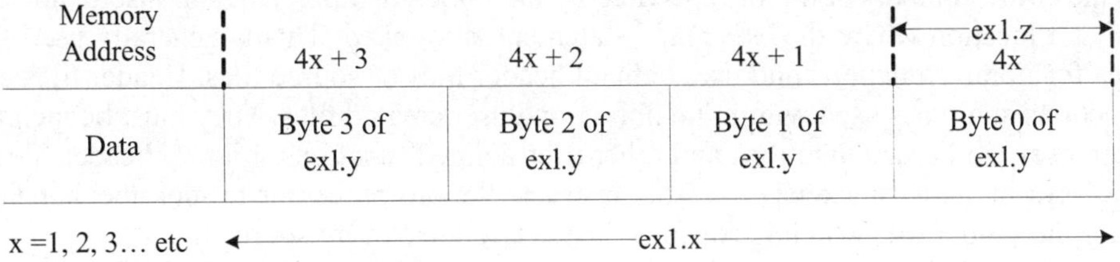

Fig. 9.10 **Memory representation for union**

Note: The start address is chosen arbitrarily for illustration, it can be any data memory. It is obvious from the figure that by using *union* the same physical address can be accessed with different data type references. Hence *union* is a convenient way of '*variant access*'.

In Embedded C applications, *union* may be used for fast accessing of individual bytes of 'long' or 'int' variables, eliminating the need for masking the other bytes of 'long' or 'int' variables which are of no interest, for checking some conditions. Typical example is extracting the individual bytes of 16 or 32 bit counters.

A few important points on Structure and Union

1. The *offsetof()* macro returns the offset of a member variable (in bytes) from the beginning of its parent structure. The usage is *offsetof (structName, memberName);* where '*structName*' is the name of the parent structure and '*memberName*' is the name of the member in the parent data structure whose offset is to be determined. For using this macro use the header file '*stddef.h*'
2. If you declare a *structure* just before the *main ()* function in your source file, ensure that the structure is terminated with the structure definition termination indicator ';'. Otherwise function *main ()* will be treated as a structure and the application may crash with exceptions.
3. A *union* variable can be initialised at the time of creation with the first member variable value only.

9.3.3.14 Pre-processors and Macros Pre-processor in 'C' is compiler/cross-compiler directives used by compiler/cross-compiler to filter the source code before compilation/cross-compilation. The pre-processor directives are mere directions to the compilers/cross compilers on how the source file should be compiled/cross compiled. No executable code is generated for pre-processor directives on compilation. They are same as pseudo ops in assembly language. Pre-processors are very useful for selecting target processor/controller dependent pieces of code for different target systems and allow a single source code to be compiled and run on several different target boards. The syntax for pre-processor directives is different from the syntax of 'C' language. Each pre-processor directive starts with the

'#' symbol and ends without a semicolon (;). Pre-processor directives are normally placed before the entry point function *main()* in a source file. Pre-processor directives are grouped into three categories; namely

1. File inclusion pre-processor directives
2. Compile control pre-processor directives
3. Macro substitution pre-processor directives

File inclusion pre processor directives The file inclusion pre processor directives include external files containing macro definitions, function declarations, constant definitions etc to the current source file. '***#include***' is the pre processor directive used for file inclusion. '*#include*' pre processor instruction reads the entire contents of the file specified by the '*#include*' directive and inserts it to the current source file at a location where the '*#include*' statement is invoked. This is generally used for reading header files for library functions and user defined header files or source files. Header files contain details of functions and types used within the library and user created files. They must be included before the program uses the library functions and other user defined functions. Library header file names are always enclosed in angle brackets, < >. This instructs the pre-processor to look the standard include directory for the header file, which needs to be inserted to the current source file.

e.g. *#include <stdio.h>* is the directive to insert the standard library file '*stdio.h*'. This file is available in the standard include directory of the development environment. (Normally inside the folder '*inc*'). If the file to be included is given in double quotes (" "), the pre-processor searches the file first in the current directory where the current source code file is present and if not found will search the standard include directory. Usually user defined files kept in the project folder are included using this technique. E.g. *#include "constants.h"* where 'constants' is a user defined header file with name *constants.h*, kept in the local project folder. An include file can include another include file in it (Nesting of include files). An include file is not allowed to include the same file itself. Source files (.c) file can also be used as include files.

Compile control pre-processor directives Compile control pre-processor directives are used for controlling the compilation process such as skipping compilation of a portion of code, adding debug features, etc. The conditional control pre-processor directives are similar to the conditional statement if else in 'C'. *#ifdef*, *#ifndef*, *#else*, *#endif*, *#undef*, etc are the compile control pre-processor directives.

#ifdef uses a name as argument and returns true if the argument (name) is already defined. *#define* is used for defining the argument (name).
#else is used for two way branching when combined with *#ifdef* (same as *if else* in 'C').
#endif is used for indicating the end of a block following *#ifdef* or *#else*

Usage of *#ifdef*, *#else* and *#endif* is given below.

```
#ifdef

#else  (optional)

#endif
```

The pre-processor directive *#ifndef* is complementary to *#ifdef*. It is used for checking whether an argument (e.g. macro) is not defined. Pre-processor directive *#undef* is used for disabling the definition of the argument or macro if it is defined. It is complementary to *#define*. Pre-processor directives are a powerful option in source code debugging. If you want to ensure the execution of a code block, for debug purpose you can define a debug variable and define it. Within the code wherever you want to ensure the execution, use the *#ifdef* and *#endif* pre-processors. The argument to *#ifdef* should be the debug variable. Insert a *printf()* function within the *#ifdef #endif* block. If no debugging is required comment or remove the definition of debug variable.

```
E.g.

#define DEBUG 1
//Inside code block
#ifdef DEBUG
printf ("Debug Enabled");
#endif
```

The #error pre-processor directive The *#error* pre-processor generates error message in case of an error and stops the compilation on accounting an error condition. The syntax of *#error* directive is given below

```
#error  error message
```

Macro substitution pre-processor directives *Macros* are a means of creating portable inline code. '*Inline*' means wherever the macro is called in a source file it is replaced directly with the code defined by the macro. In-line code improves the performance in terms of execution speed. Macros are similar to subroutines in functioning but they differ in the way in which they are coded in the source code. Functions are normally written only once with arguments. Whenever a function needs to be executed, a call to the function code is made with the required parameters at the point where it needs to be invoked. If a macro is used instead of functions, the compiler inserts the code for macro wherever it is called. From a code size viewpoint macros are non-optimised compared to functions. Macros are generally used for coding small functions requiring execution without latency. The '*#define*' pre-processor directive is used for coding macros. Macros can be either simple definitions or functions with arguments.

#define PI 3.1415 is an example for a simple macro definition.

Macro definition can contain arithmetic operations also. Proper care should be taken in giving right syntax while defining macros, keeping an eye on their usage in the source code. Consider the following example

```
#define A 12+25
#define B 45-10
```

Suppose the source contains a statement *multiplier = A*B;* the pre-processor directly replaces the macros A and B and the statement becomes

```
multiplier = 12+25*45-10;
```

Due to the operator precedence criteria, this won't give the expected result. Expected result can be obtained by a simple re-writing of the macro with necessary parentheses as illustrated below.

```
#define A (12+25)
#define B (45-10)
```

Proper care should be given to parentheses the macro arguments. As mentioned earlier macros can also be defined with arguments. Consider the following example

```
#define CIRCLE_AREA(a) (3.14 * a*a)
```

This defines a macro for calculating the area of a circle. It takes an argument and returns the area. It should be noted that there is no space between the name of the macro (macro identifier) and the left bracket parenthesis.

Suppose the source code contains a statement like *area=CIRCLE_AREA(5);* it will be replaced as

```
area = (3.14*5*5);
```

Suppose the call is like this, *area=CIRCLE_AREA(2+5);* the pre-processor will translate the same as

```
area = (3.14*2+5*2+5);
```

Will it produce the expected result? Obviously no. This shortcoming in macro definition can be eliminated by using parenthesis to each occurrence of the argument. Hence the ideal solution will be;

```
#define CIRCLE_AREA(a) (3.14 *(a)*(a))
```

9.3.3.15 Constant Declarations in Embedded 'C' In embedded applications the qualifier (keyword) '*const*' represents a 'Read only' variable. Use of the keyword '*const*' in front of a variable declares that the value of the variable cannot be altered by the program. This is a kind of defensive programming in which any attempt to modify a variable declared as '*const*' is reported as an access violation by the cross-compiler. The different types of constant variables used in embedded 'C' application are explained below.

Constant data Constant data informs that the data held by a variable is always constant and cannot be modified by the application. Constants used as scaling variables, ratio factors, various scientific computing constants (e.g. Plank's constant), etc. are represented as constant data. The general form of declaring a constant variable is given below.

```
const  data type  variable name;
```

or

```
data type  const  variable name;
```

'*const*' is the keyword informing compiler/cross compiler that the variable is constant. '*data type*' gives the data type of the variable. It can be 'int', 'char', 'float', etc. '*variable name*' is the constant variable.

```
E.g.   const float PI = 3.1417;
       float const PI = 3.1417;
```

Both of these statements declare PI as floating point constant and assign the value 3.1417 to it.
Constant variable can also be defined using the *#define* pre-processor directive as given below.

```
#define PI 3.1417
/*No assignment using = operator and no ';' at end*/
```

The difference between both approaches is that the first one defines a constant of a particular data type (int, char, float, etc.) whereas in the second method the constant is represented using a mere symbol (text) and there is no implicit declaration about the data type of the constant. Both approaches are used in declaring constants in embedded C applications. The choice is left to the programmer.

Pointer to constant data Pointer to constant data is a pointer which points to a data which is read only. The pointer pointing to the data can be changed but the data is non-modifiable. Example of pointer to constant data

```
const int* x;      //Integer pointer x to constant data
int const* x       //Same meaning as above definition
```

Constant pointer to data Constant pointer has significant importance in Embedded C applications. An embedded system under consideration may have various external chips like, data memory, Real Time Clock (RTC), etc interfaced to the target processor/controller, using memory mapped technique. The range of address assigned to each chips and their registers are dependent on the hardware design. At the time of designing the hardware itself, address ranges are allocated to the different chips and the target hardware is developed according to these address allocations. For example, assume we have an RTC chip which is memory mapped at address range 0x3000 to 0x3010 and the memory mapped address of register holding the time information is at 0x3007. This memory address is fixed and to get the time information we have to look at the register residing at location 0x3007. But the content of the register located at address 0x3007 is subject to change according to the change in time. We can access this data using a constant pointer. The declaration of a constant pointer is given below.

```
// Constant character pointer x to constant/variable data
char *const x;

/*Explicit declaration of character pointer pointing to 8bit memory location,
mapped at location 0x3007; RTC example illustrated above*/

char *const x= (char*) 0x3007;
```

Constant pointer to constant data Constant pointers pointing to constant data are widely used in embedded programming applications. Typical uses are reading configuration data held at ROM chips which are memory mapped at a specified address range, Read only status registers of different chips, memory mapped at a fixed address. Syntax of declaring a constant pointer to constant data is given below.

```
/*Constant character pointer x pointing to constant data*/
const char *const x;
char const* const x;    //Equivalent to above declaration
```

```
/*Explicit declaration of constant character pointer* pointing to constant
data/
char const* const x = (char*) 0x3007;
```

9.3.3.16 The 'Volatile' Type Qualifier in Embedded 'C' The keyword '*volatile*' prefixed with any variable as qualifier informs the cross-compiler that the value of the variable is subject to change at any point of time (subject to asynchronous modification) other than the current statement of code where the control is at present.

Examples of variables which are subject to asynchronous modifications are

1. Variables common to Interrupt Service Routines (ISR) and other functions of a file
2. Memory mapped hardware registers

3. Variables shared by different threads in a multi threaded application (Not applicable to Super loop Firmware development approach)

The '***volatile***' keyword informs the cross-compiler that the variable with '*volatile*' qualifier is subject to asynchronous change and there by the cross compiler turns off any optimisation (assumptions on the variable) for these variables. The general form of declaring a volatile variable is given below.

```
volatile data type variable name; or
data type volatile variable name;
```

'data type' refers to the data type of the variable. It can be *int*, *char*, *float*, etc. 'variable name' is the user defined name for the *volatile* variable of the specified type.

```
E.g.     volatile unsigned char x;
         unsigned char volatile x;
```

What is the catch in using 'volatile' variable? Let's examine the following code snippet.

```
//Declare a memory mapped register
char* status_reg = (char*) 0x3000;

while (*status_reg!=0x01);    //Wait till status_reg = 0x01
```

On cross-compiling the code snippet, the cross-compiler converts the code to a read operation from the memory location mapped at address 0x3000 and it will assume that there is no point where the variable is going to modify (sort of over smartness) and may keep the data in a register to speed up the execution. The actual intention of the programmer, with the above code snippet is to read a memory mapped hardware status register and halt the execution of the rest of the code till the status register shows a ready status. Unfortunately the program will not produce the expected result due to the oversmartness of the cross-compiler in optimising the code for execution speed. Re-writing the code as given below serves the intended purpose.

```
//Declares volatile variable
volatile char *status_reg = (char *) 0x3000;

while (*status_reg!=0x01);    //Wait till status_reg = 0x01
```

In embedded applications all memory mapped device registers which are subject to asynchronous modifications (e.g. status, control and general purpose registers of memory mapped external devices) should be declared with '*volatile*' keyword to inform the cross-compiler that the variables representing these registers/locations are subject to asynchronous changes and do not optimise them. Another area which needs utmost care in embedded applications is variables shared between ISR and functions (variables which can be modified by both Interrupt Sub Routines and functions). These include structure variable, union variable and other ordinary variables. To avoid unexpected behaviour of the application, always declare such variables using '*volatile*' keyword.

The 'constant volatile' Variable Some variables used in embedded applications can be both '*constant*' and '*volatile*'. A '***Read only***' status register of a memory mapped device is a typical example for this. From a user point of view the '***Read only***' status registers can only be read but cannot modify. Hence it is a constant variable. From the device point the contents can be modified at any time by the device. So it is a volatile variable. Typical declarations are given ahead.

```
volatile const int a;      // Constant volatile integer
volatile const int* a;     //Pointer to a Constant volatile integer
```

Volatile pointer Volatile pointers is subject to change at any point after they are initialised. Typical examples are pointer to arrays or buffers modifiable by Interrupt Service Routines and pointers in dynamic memory allocation. Pointers used in dynamic memory allocation can be modified by the *realloc()* function. The general form of declaration of a volatile pointer to a non-volatile variable is given below.

```
data type* volatile variable name;
e.g.   unsigned char* volatile a;
```

Volatile pointer to a volatile variable is declared with the following syntax.

```
       data type volatile* volatile variable name;
e.g.   unsigned char volatile* volatile a;
```

9.3.3.17 Delay Generation and Infinite Loops in Embedded C Almost every embedded application involves delay programming. Embedded applications employ delay programming for waiting for a fixed time interval till a device is ready, for inserting delay between displays updating to give the user sufficient time to view the contents displayed, delays involved in bit transmission and reception in asynchronous serial transmissions like I2C, 1-Wire data transfer, delay for key de-bouncing etc. Some delay requirements in embedded application may be critical, meaning delay accuracy should be within a very narrow tolerance band. Typical example is delay used in bit data transmission. If the delay employed is not accurate, the bits may lost while transmission or reception. Certain delay requirements in embedded application may not be much critical, e.g. display updating delay.

It is easy to code delays in desktop applications under DOS or Windows operating systems. The library function *delay()* in DOS and *Sleep ()* in Windows provides delays in milliseconds with reasonable accuracy. Coding delay routines in embedded applications is bit difficult. The major reason is delay is dependent on target system's clock frequency. So we need to have a trial and error approach to code delays demanding reasonably good accuracy. Refer to the code snippet given for 'Performance Analyser' in *Chapter 14* for getting a handle on how to code delay routine in embedded applications using IDEs. Delay codes are generally non-portable. Delay routine requires a complete re-work if the target clock frequency is changed. Normally *'for loops'* are used for coding delays. Infinite loops are created using various loop control instructions like while (), do while (), for and goto labels. The super loop created by while (1) instruction in a traditional super loop based embedded firmware design is a typical example for infinite loop in embedded application development.

Infinite loop using while The following code snippet illustrates '*while*' for infinite loop implementation.

```
       while (1)
       {
       }
```

Infinite loop using do while

```
       do
       {
       } while (1);
```

Infinite loop using for

```
for (; ; ;)
{
}
```

Infinite loop using goto '*goto*' when combined with a '*label*' can create infinite loops.

```
label: //Task to be repeated
       //..................
       //..................
       goto label;
```

Which technique is the best? According to all experienced Embedded 'C' programmers *while()* loop is the best choice for creating infinite loops. There is no technical reason for this. The clean syntax of while loop entitles it for the same. The syntax of *for* loop for infinite loop is little puzzling and it is not capable of conveying its intended use. '*goto*' is the favorite choice of programmers migrating from Assembly to Embedded C ☺.

break; statement is used for coming out of an infinite loop. You may think why we implement an infinite loop and then quitting it? Answer – There may be instructions checking some condition inside the infinite loop. If the condition is met the program control may have to transfer to some other location.

9.3.3.18 Bit Manipulation Operations Though Embedded 'C' does not support a built in Boolean variable (Bit variable) for holding a 'TRUE (Logic 1)' or 'FALSE (Logic 0)' condition, it provides extensive support for Bit manipulation operations. Boolean variables required in embedded application are quite often stored as variables with least storage memory requirement (obviously *char* variable). Indeed it is wastage of memory if the application contains large number of Boolean variables and each variable is stored as a *char* variable. Only one bit (Least Significant bit) in a *char* variable is used for storing Boolean information. Rest 7 bits are left unused. This will definitely lead to serious memory bottle neck. Considerable amount of memory can be saved if different Boolean variables in an application are packed into a single variable in 'C' which requires less memory storage bytes. A character variable can accommodate 8 Boolean variables. If the Boolean variables are packed for saving memory, depending upon the program requirement each variable may have to be extracted and some manipulation (setting, clearing, inverting, etc.) needs to be performed on the bits. The following Bit manipulation operations are employed for the same.

Bitwise AND Operator '&' performs Bitwise AND operations. Please note that the Bitwise AND operator '&' is entirely different from the Logical AND operator '&&'. The '&' operator acts on individual bits of the operands. Bitwise AND operations are usually performed for selective clearing of bits and testing the present state of a bit (Bitwise ANDing with '1').

Bitwise OR Operator '|' performs Bitwise OR operations. Logical OR operator '||' is in no way related to the Bitwise OR operator '|'. Bitwise OR operation is performed on individual bits of the operands. Bitwise OR operation is usually performed for selectively setting of bits and testing the current state of a bit (Bitwise ORing with '0').

Bitwise Exclusive OR- XOR Bitwise XOR operator '^' acts on individual operand bits and performs an 'Excusive OR' operation on the bits. Bitwise XOR operation is used for toggling bits in embedded applications.

Bitwise NOT Bitwise NOT operations negates (inverts) the state of a bit. The operator '~' (tilde) is used as the Bitwise NOT operator in C.

Setting and Clearing and Bits Setting the value of a bit to '1' is achieved by a Bitwise OR operation. For example consider a character variable (8bit variable) flag. The following instruction sets its 0th bit always 1.

```
flag = flag | 1;
```

Brief explanation about the above operation is given below.
Using 8 bits, 1 is represented as 00000001. Upon a Bitwise OR each bit is ORed with the corresponding bit of the operand as illustrated below.

Bit 0 of flag is ORed with 1 and Resulting o/p bit=1
Bit 1 of flag is ORed with 0 and Resulting o/p bit= Bit 1 of flag
Bit 2 of flag is ORed with 0 and Resulting o/p bit= Bit 2 of flag
Bit 3 of flag is ORed with 0 and Resulting o/p bit= Bit 3 of flag
Bit 4 of flag is ORed with 0 and Resulting o/p bit= Bit 4 of flag
Bit 5 of flag is ORed with 0 and Resulting o/p bit= Bit 5 of flag
Bit 6 of flag is ORed with 0 and Resulting o/p bit= Bit 6 of flag
Bit 7 of flag is ORed with 0 and Resulting o/p bit= Bit 7 of flag

Bitwise OR operation combined with left shift operation of '1' is used for selectively setting any bit in a variable. For example the following operation will set bit 6 of *char* variable flag.

```
//Sets 6th bit of flag. Bit numbering starts with 0.
flag = flag | (1<<6);
```

Re-writing the above code for a neat syntax will give

```
flag |= (1<<6);        //Equivalent to flag = flag | (1<<6);
```

The same can also be achieved by bitwise ORing the variable flag with a mask with 6th bit '1' and all other bits '0', i.e. mask with 01000000 in Binary representation and 0x40 in hex representation.

```
flag |= 0x40;   //Equivalent to flag = flag | (1<<6);
```

Clearing a desired bit is achieved by Bitwise ANDing the bit with '0'. Bitwise AND operation combined with left shifting of '1' can be used for clearing any desired bit in a variable.

```
Example:
        flag &= ~ (1<<6);
```

The above instruction will clear the 6th bit of the character variable *flag*. The operation is illustrated below.

Execution of (1<<6) shifts '1' to six positions left and the resulting output in binary will be 01000000. Inverting this using the Bitwise NOT operation (~ (1<<6)) inverts the bits and give 10111111 as output. When *flag* is Bitwise ANDed with 10111111, the 6th bit of *flag* is cleared (set to '0') and all other bits of *flag* remain unchanged.

From the above illustration it can be inferred that the same operation can also be achieved by a direct Bitwise ANDing of the variable *flag* and a mask with binary representation 10111111 or hex representation 0xBF.

```
flag &= 0xBF;        //Equivalent to flag = flag & ~(1<<6);
```

Shifting the mask '1' for setting or clearing a desired bit works perfectly, if the operand on which these operations are performed is 8bit wide. If the operand is greater than 8 bits in size, care should be taken to adjust the mask as wide as the operand. As an example let us assume *flag* as a 32bit operand. For clearing the 6th bit of *flag* as illustrated in the previous example, the mask 1 should be re-written as '1L' and the instruction becomes

```
flag &= ~ (1L<<6);
```

Toggling Bits

Toggling a bit is performed to negate (toggle) the current state of a bit. If current state of a specified bit is '1', after toggling it becomes '0' and vice versa. Toggling is also known as inverting bits. The Bitwise XOR operator is used for toggling the state of a desired bit in an operand.

```
flag ^= (1<<6);        //Toggle bit 6 of flag
```

The above instruction toggles bit 6 of *flag*.

Adding '1' to the desired bit position (In the above example 0x40 for 6th bit) will also toggle the current state of the desired bit. This approach has the following drawback. If the current state of the bit which is to be inverted is '1', adding a '1' to that bit position inverts the state of that bit and at the same time a carry is generated and it is propagated to the next most significant bit (MSB) and change the status of some of the other bits falling to the left of the bit which is toggled.

Extracting and Inserting Bits

Quite often it is meaningful to store related information as the bits of a single variable instead of saving them as separate variables. This saves considerable amount of memory in an embedded system where data memory is a big bottleneck. Typical scenario in embedded applications where information can be stored using the bits of single variable is, information provided by Real Time Clock (RTC). RTC chip provides various data like current date/month/year, day of the week, current time in hours/minutes/seconds, etc. If an application demands the storage of all these information in the data memory of the embedded system for some reason, it can be achieved in two ways;

1. Use separate variables for storing each data (date, month, year, etc.)
2. Club the related data and store them as the bits of a single variable

As an example assume that we need to store the date information of the RTC in the data memory in D/M/Y format. Where 'D' stands for date varying from 1 to 31, 'M' stands for month varying from 1 to 12 and 'Y' stands for year varying from 0 to 99. If we follow the first approach we need 3 character variables to store the date information separately. In the second approach, we need only 5 bits for date (With 5 bits we can represent 0 to 2^5-1 numbers (0 to 31), 4 bits for month and 7 bits for year. Hence the total number of bits required to represent the date information is 16. All these bits can be fitted into a 16 bit variable as shown in Fig. 9.11.

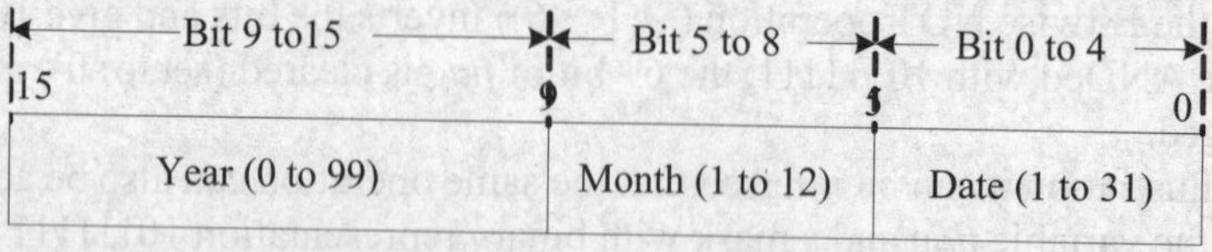

Fig. 9.11 **Packed Bits for data representation**

Suppose this is arranged in a 16bit integer variable date, for any calculation requiring 'Year', 'Month' or 'Date', each should be extracted from the single variable date. The following code snippet illustrates the extraction of 'Year'

```
char year = (date>>9) & 0x7F;
```

(*date*>>9) shifts the contents 9 bits to the left and now 'Year' is stored in the variable *date* in bits 0 to 6 (including both). The contents of other bits (7 to 15) are not relevant to us and we need only the first 7 bits (0 to 6) for getting the 'Year' value. ANDing with the mask 0x7F (01111111 in Binary) retains the contents of bits 0 to 6 and now the variable year contains the 'Year' value extracted from variable '*date*'.

Similar to the extracting of bits, we may have to insert bits to change the value of certain data. In the above example if the program is written in such a way that after each 1 minute, the RTC's year register is read and the contents of bit fields 9 to 15 in variable '*date*' needs to be updated with the new value. This can be achieved by inserting the bits corresponding to the data into the desired bit position. Following code snippet illustrates the updating of 'Year' value for the above example. To set the new 'Year' value to the variable '*date*' all the corresponding bits in the variable for 'Year' should be cleared first. It is illustrated below.

```
date = date & ~ (0x7F<<9);
```

The mask for 7 bits is 0x7F (01111111 in Binary). Shifting the mask 9 times left aligns the mask to that of the bits for storing 'Year'. The ~ operator inverts the 7 bits aligning to the bits corresponding to 'Year'. Bitwise ANDing with this negated mask clears the current bits for 'Year' in the variable '*date*'. Now shift the new value which needs to be put at the 'Year' location, 9 times for bitwise alignment for the bits corresponding to 'Year'. Bitwise OR the bit aligned new value with the '*date*' variable whose bits corresponding to 'Year' is already cleared. The following instruction performs this.

```
date |= (new_year <<9);
```

where 'new_year' is the new value for 'Year'.

In order to ensure the inserted bits are not exceeding the number of bits assigned for the particular bit variable, bitwise AND the new value with the mask corresponding to the number of bits allocated to the corresponding variable (Above example 7 bits for 'Year' and the mask is 0x7F). Hence the above instruction can be written more precisely as

```
date |= (new_year & 0x7F) <<9;
```

If all the bits corresponding to the bit field to be modified are not set to zero prior to Bitwise ORing with the new value, any existing bit with value '1' will remain as such and expected result will not be obtained.

Testing Bits So far we discussed the Bitwise operators for changing the status of a selected bit. Bitwise operators can also be used for checking the present status of a bit without modifying it for decision making operations.

```
if (flag & (1<<6))    //Checks whether 6th bit of flag is '1'
```

This instruction examines the status of the 6th bit of variable *flag*. The same can also be achieved by using a constant bit mask as

```
if (flag & 0x40)    //Checks whether 6th bit of flag is '1'
```

9.3.3.19 Coding Interrupt Service Routines (ISR) Interrupt is an event that stops the current execution of a process (task) in the CPU and transfers the program execution to an address in code memory where the service routine for the event is located. The event which stops the current execution can be an internal event or an external event or a proper combination of the external and internal event. Any trigger signal coming from an externally interfaced device demanding immediate attentions is an example for external event whereas the trigger indicating the overflow of an internal timer is an example for internal event. Reception of serial data through the serial line is a combination of internal and external events. The number of interrupts supported, their priority levels, interrupt trigger type and the structure of interrupts are processor/controller architecture dependent and it varies from processor to processor. Interrupts are generally classified into two: Maskable Interrupts and Non-maskable Interrupts (NMI). Maskable interrupt can be ignored by the CPU if the interrupt is internally not enabled or if the CPU is currently engaged in processing another interrupt which is at high priority. Non-maskable interrupts are interrupts which require urgent attention and cannot be ignored by the CPU. Reset (RST) interrupt and TRAP interrupt of *8085* processor are examples for Non-maskable interrupts.

Interrupts are considered as boon for programmers and their main motto is "*give real time behaviour to applications*". In a processor/controller based simple embedded system where the application is designed in a super loop model, each interrupt supported by the processor/controller will have a fixed memory location assigned in the code memory for writing its corresponding service routine and this address is referred as *Interrupt Vector Address*. The vector address for each interrupt will be pre-defined and the number of code memory bytes allocated for each Interrupt Service Routine, starting from the Interrupt Vector Address may also be fixed. For example the interrupt vector address for interrupt 'INT0' of *8051* microcontroller is '0003H' and the number of code memory bytes allowed for writing its Service routine is 8 bytes.

The function written for serving an Interrupt is known as Interrupt Service Routine (ISR). ISR for each interrupt may be different and they are placed at the Interrupt Vector Address of corresponding Interrupt. ISR is essentially a function that takes no parameters and returns no results. But, unlike a regular function, the ISR can be active at any time since the triggering of interrupts need not be in sync with the internal program execution (e.g. An external device connected to the external interrupt line can assert external interrupt at any time regardless at what stage the program execution is currently). Hence special care must be taken in writing these functions keeping in mind; they are not going to be executed in a pre-defined order. What all special care should be taken in writing an ISR? The following section answers this query.

Imagine a situation where the application is doing some operations and some registers are modified and an interrupt is triggered in between the operation. Indeed the program flow is diverted to the Interrupt Service Routine, if the interrupt is an enabled interrupt and the operation in progress is not a service routine of a high priority interrupt, and the ISR is executed. After completing the ISR, the program flow is re-directed to the point where it got interrupted and the interrupted operation is continued. What happens if the ISR modifies some of the registers used by the program? No doubt the application will produce unexpected results and may go for a toss. How can this situation be tackled? Such a situation can be avoided if the ISR is coded in such a way that it takes care of the following:

1. Save the current context (Important Registers which the ISR will modify)
2. Service the Interrupt
3. Retrieve the saved context (Retrieve the original contents of registers)
4. Return to the execution point where the execution is interrupted

Normal functions will not incorporate code for saving the current context before executing the function and retrieve the saved context before exiting the function. ISR should incorporate code for performing these operations. Also it is known to the programmer at what point a normal function is going to be invoked and the programmer can take necessary precautions before calling the function, it is not the case for an ISR. Interrupt Service Routines can be coded either in Assembly language or High level language in which the application is written. Assembly language is the best choice if the ISR code is very small and the program itself is written in Assembly. Assembly code generates optimised code for ISR and user will have a good control on deciding what all registers needs to be preserved from alteration. Most of the modern cross-compilers provide extensive support for efficient and optimised ISR code. The way in which a function is declared as ISR and what all context is saved within the function is cross-compiler dependent.

Keil C51 Cross-complier for 8051 microcontroller implements the Interrupt Service Routine using the keyword *interrupt* and its syntax is illustrated below.

```
void interrupt_name (void)      interrupt x using y
{
/*Process Interrupt*/
}
```

interrupt_name is the function name and programmers can choose any name according to his/her taste. The attribute '*interrupt*' instructs the cross compiler that the associated function is an interrupt service routine. The *interrupt* attribute takes an argument *x* which is an integer constant in the range 0 to 31 (supporting 32 interrupts). This number is the interrupt number and it is essential for placing the generated hex code corresponding to the ISR in the corresponding Interrupt Vector Address (e.g. For placing the ISR code at code memory location 0003H for Interrupt 0 – External Interrupt 0 for *8051* microcontroller). *using* is an optional keyword for indicating which register bank is used for the general purpose Registers R0 to R7 (For more details on register banks and general purpose registers, refer to the hardware description of *8051*). The argument *y* for *using* attribute can take values from 0 to 3 (corresponding to the register banks 0 to 3 of 8051). The *interrupt* attribute affects the object code of the function in the following way:

1. If required, the contents of registers ACC, B, DPH, DPL, and PSW are saved on the stack at function invocation time.
2. All working registers (R0 to R7) used in the interrupt function are stored on the stack if a register bank is not specified with the *using* attribute.
3. The working registers and special registers that were saved on the stack are restored before exiting the function.
4. The function is terminated by the 8051 RETI instruction.

Typical usage is illustrated below

```
void external_interrupt0 (void )    interrupt 0 using 0
{
adc_control = *adc_control_reg //Read memory mapped ADC
                                // control Register
}
```

If the cross-compiler you are using don't have a built in support for writing ISRs, What shall you do? Don't be panic you can implement the ISR feature with little tricky coding. If the cross-compiler provides support for mixing high level language-C and Assembly, write the ISR in Assembly and place the ISR code at the corresponding Interrupt Vector address using the cross compiler's support for placing the code in an absolute address location of code memory (Using keywords like *_at*. Refer to your cross compiler's documentation for getting the exact keyword). If the ISR is too complicated, you can place the body of the ISR processing in a normal C function and call it from a simple assembly language wrapper. The assembly language wrapper should be installed as the ISR function at the absolute address corresponding to the Interrupt's Vector Address. It is responsible for executing the current context saving and retrieving instructions. Current context saving instructions are written on top of the call to the 'C' function and context retrieving instructions are written just below the 'C' function call. It is little puzzling to find answers to the following questions in this approach.

1. Which registers must be saved and restored since we are not sure which registers are used by the cross compiler for implementing the 'C' function?
2. How the assembly instructions can be interfaced with high-level language like 'C'?

Answers to these questions are cross compiler dependent and you need to find the answer by referring the documentation files of the cross-compiler in use. Context saving is done by 'Pushing' the registers (using PUSH instructions) to stack and retrieving the saved context is done by 'Poping' (using POP instructions) the pushed registers. Push and Pop operations usually follow the Last In First Out (LIFO) method. While writing an ISR, always keep in mind that the primary aim of an interrupt is to provide real time behaviour to the program. Saving the current context delays the execution of the original ISR function and it creates Interrupt latency (Refer to the section on Interrupt Latency for more details) and thereby adds lack of real time behaviour to an application. As a programmer, if you are responsible for saving the current context by Pushing the registers, avoid Pushing the registers which are not used by the ISR. If you deliberately avoid the saving of registers which are going to be modified by the ISR, your application may go for a toss. Hence Context saving is an unavoidable evil in Interrupt driven programming. If you go for saving unused registers, it will increase interrupt latency as well as stack memory usage. So always take a judicious decision on the context saving operation. If the cross compiler offers the context saving operation by supporting ISR functions, always rely on it. Because most modern cross compilers are smart and capable of taking a judicious decision on context saving. In case the cross compiler is not supporting ISR function and as a programmer you are the one writing ISR functions either in Assembly or by mixing 'C' and Assembly, ensure that the size of ISR is not crossing the size of code memory bytes allowed for an Interrupt's ISR (8 bytes for *8051*). If it exceeds, it will overlap with the location for the next interrupt and may create unexpected behaviour on servicing the Interrupt whose Vector address got overlapped.

9.3.3.20 Recursive Functions A function which calls itself repeatedly is called a Recursive Function. Using recursion, a complex problem is split into its single simplest form. The recursive function only knows how to solve that simplest case. Recursive functions are useful in evaluating certain types of mathematical function, creating and accessing dynamic data structures such as linked lists or binary trees. As an example let us consider the factorial calculation of a number.

By mathematical definition

n factorial $= 1 \times 2 \times \ldots\ldots (n-2) \times (n-1) \times n$; where $n = 1, 2$, etc… and 0 factorial = 1

Using 'C' the function for finding the factorial of a number '*n*' is written as

```
int factorial (int n)
{
int count;
int factorial=1;
for (count=1; count<=n; count++)
        factorial*=count;
```

```
    return factorial;
    }
```

This code is based on iteration. The iteration of calculating the repeated products is performed until the count value exceeds the value of the number whose factorial is to be calculated. We can split up the task performed inside the function as *count * (count +1)* till count is one short of the number whose factorial is to be calculated. Using recursion we can re-write the above function as

```
int factorial (int n)
{
if (n==0)
return 1;
else
return (n*factorial (n-1));
}
```

Here the function *factorial (n)* calls itself, with a changed version of the parameter for each call, inside the same for calculating the factorial of a given number. The 'if' statement within the recursive function forces the function to stop recursion when a certain criterion is met. Without an 'if' statement a recursive function will never stop the recursion process. Recursive functions are very effective in implementing solutions expressed in terms of a successive application of the same solution to the solution subsets. Recursion is a powerful at the same time most dangerous feature which may lead to application crash. The local variables of a recursive function are stored in the stack memory and new copies of each variable are created for successive recursive calls of the function. As the recursion goes in a deep level, stack memory may overflow and the application may bounce.

Recursion vs. Iteration: A comparison Both recursion and iteration is used for implementing certain operations which are self repetitive in some form.

- Recursion involves a lot of call stack overhead and function calls. Hence it is slower in operation compared to the iterative method. Since recursion implements the functionality with repeated self function calls, more stack memory is required for storing the local variables and the function return address
- Recursion is the best method for implementing certain operations like certain mathematical operation, creating and accessing of dynamic data structures such as linked lists or binary trees
- A recursive solution implementation can always be replaced by iteration. The process of converting a recursive function to iterative method is called '*unrolling*'

Benefits of Recursion Recursion brings the following benefits in programming:

- Recursive code is very expressive compared to iterative code. It conveys the intended use.
- Recursion is the most appropriate method for certain operations like permutations, search trees, sorting, etc.

Drawbacks of Recursion Though recursion is an effective technique in implementing solutions expressed in terms of a successive application of the same solution to the solution subsets, it possesses the following drawbacks.

- Recursive operation is slow in operation due to call stack overheads. It involves lot of stack operations like local variable storage and retrieval, return address storage and retrieval, etc.
- Debugging of recursive functions are not so easy compared to iterative code debugging

9.3.3.21 Re-entrant Functions Functions which can be shared safely with several processes concurrently are called re-entrant functions. When a re-entrant function is executing, another process can interrupt the execution and can execute the same re-entrant function. The "*another process*" referred here can be a thread in a multithreaded application or can be an Interrupt Service Routine (ISR). Re-entrant function is also referred as '*pure*' function. Embedded applications extensively make use of re-entrant functions. Interrupt Service Routines (ISR) in Super loop based firmware systems and threads in RTOS based systems can change the program's control flow to alter the current context at any time. When an interrupt is asserted, the current operation is put on hold and the control is transferred to another function or task (ISR). Imagine a situation where an interrupt occurs while executing a *function x* and the ISR also contain the task of executing the *function x*. What will happen? - Obviously the ISR will modify the shared variables of *function x* and when the control is switched back to the point where the execution got interrupted, the function will resume its execution with the data which is modified by the ISR. What will be the outcome of this action? - Unpredictable result causing data corruption and potential disaster like application break-down. Why it happens so? Due to the corruption of shared data in function which is unprotected. How this situation can be avoided? By carefully controlling the sharing of data in the function.

In embedded applications, a function/subroutine is considered re-entrant if and only if it satisfies the following criteria.

1. The function should not hold static data over successive calls, or return a pointer to static data.
2. All shared variables within the function are used in an atomic way.
3. The function does not call any other non-reentrant functions within it.
4. The function does not make use of any hardware in a non-atomic way

Rule# 1 deals with variable usage and function return value for a reentrant function. In an operating system based embedded system, the embedded application is managed by the operating system services and the '*memory manager*' service of the OS kernel is responsible for allocating and de-allocating the memory required by an application for its execution. The working memory required by an application is divided into three groups namely; stack memory, heap memory and data memory (Refer to *the Dynamic Memory Allocation* section of this chapter for more details). The life time of static variables is same as that of the life time of the application to which it belongs and they are usually held in the data memory area of the memory space allocated for the application. All static variables of a function are allocated in the data memory area space of the application and each instance of the function shares this, whereas local (auto) variables of a function are stored in the stack memory and each invocation of the function creates independent copies of these variables in the stack memory. For a function to be reentrant, it should not keep any data over successive invocations (the function should not contain any static storage). If a function needs some data to be kept over successive invocations, it should be provided through the caller function instead of storing it in the function in the form of static variables. If the function returns a pointer to a static data, each invocation of the function makes use of this pointer for returning the result. This can be tackled by using caller function provided storage for passing the data back to the caller function. The 'callee' function needs to be modified accordingly to make use of the caller function provided storage for passing the data back to the caller.

Rule# 2 deals with '*atomic*' operations. So what does '*atomic*' mean in reentrancy context? Meaning the operation cannot be interrupted. If an embedded application contains variables which are shared between various threads of a multitasking system (Applicable to Operating System based embedded systems) or between the application and ISR (In Non-RTOS based embedded systems), and if the operation on the shared variable is non-atomic, there is a possibility for corruption of the variable due to concurrent access of the variable by multiple threads or thread and ISR. As an example let us assume that the variable counter is shared between multiple threads or between a thread and ISR, the instruction,

```
counter++;
```

need not operate in an '*atomic*' way on the variable *counter*. The compiler/cross-compiler in use converts this high level instruction into machine dependent code (machine language) and the objective of incrementing the variable *counter* may be implemented using a number of low level instructions by the compiler/cross compiler. This violates the 'atomic' rule of operation. Imagine a situation where an execution switch (context switch) happens when one thread is in the middle of executing the low level instructions corresponding to the high level instruction *counter++*, of the function and another thread (which is currently in execution after the context switch) or an ISR calls the same function and executes the instruction *counter++*, this will result in inconsistent result. Refer to the section '*Racing*' under the topic '*Task Synchronisation Issues*' of the chapter '*Designing with Real Time Operating Systems*' for more details on this. Eliminating shared global variables and making them as variables local to the function solves the problem of modification of shared variables by concurrent execution of the function.

Rule# 3 is selfexplanatory. If a re-entrant function calls another function which is non-reentrant, it may create potential damages due to the unexpected modification of shared variables if any. What will happen if a reentrant function calls a standard library function at run time? By default most of the run time library is reentrant. If a standard library function is not reentrant the function will no longer be reentrant.

Rule# 4 deals with the atomic way of accessing hardware devices. The term '*atomic*' in hardware access refers to the number of steps involved in accessing a specific register of a hardware device. For the hardware access to be atomic the number of steps involved in hardware access should be one. If access is achieved through multiple steps, any interruption in between the steps may lead to erroneous results. A typical example is accessing the hardware register of an I/O device mapped to the host CPU using paged addressing technique. In order to Read/Write from/to any of the hardware registers of the device a minimum of two steps is required. First write the page address, corresponding to the page in which the hardware register belongs, to the page register and then read the register by giving the address of the register within that page. Now imagine a situation where an interrupt occurs at the moment executing the page setting instruction in progress. The ISR will be executed after finishing this instruction. Suppose ISR also involves a Read/Write to another hardware register belonging to a different page. Obviously it will modify the page register of the device with the required value. What will be its impact? On finishing the ISR, the interrupted code will try to read the hardware register with the page address which is modified by the ISR. This yields an erroneous result.

How to declare a function as Reentrant The way in which a function is declared reentrant is cross-compiler dependent. For Keil C51 cross-compiler for *8051* controller, the keyword '*reentrant*' added as function attribute treats the function as reentrant. For each reentrant function, a reentrant stack area is simulated in internal or external memory depending whether the data memory is internal or external to the processor/controller. A typical reentrant function implementation for C51 cross-compiler for *8051* controller is given below.

```
int multiply (char i, int b) reentrant
{
 int x;
 x = table [i];
return (x * b);
}
```

The simulated stack used by reentrant functions has its own stack pointer which is independent of the processor stack and stack pointer. For C51 cross compiler the simulated stack and stack pointers are declared and initialised in the startup code in STARTUP.A51 which can be found in the LIB subdirectory. You must modify the startup code to specify which simulated stack(s) to initialize in order to use re-entrant functions. You can also modify the starting address for the top of the simulated stack(s) in the startup code. When calling a function with a re-entrant stack, the cross-compiler must know that the function has a re-entrant stack. The cross-compiler figures this out from the function prototype which should include the reentrant keyword (just like the function definition). The cross compiler must also know which reentrant stack to stuff the arguments for it. For passing arguments, the cross-compiler generates code that decrements the stack pointer and then "pushes" arguments onto the stack by storing the argument indirectly through R0/R1 or DPTR (*8051* specific registers). Calling reentrant function decrements the stack pointer (for local variables) and access arguments using the stack pointer plus an offset (which corresponds to the number of bytes of local variables). On returning, reentrant function adjusts the stack pointer to the value before arguments were pushed. So the caller does not need to perform any stack adjustment after calling a reentrant function.

Reentrant vs. Recursive Functions The terms Reentrant and Recursive may sound little confusing. You may find some amount of similarity among them and ultimately it can lead to the thought are Reentrant functions and Recursive functions the same? The answer is—it depends on the usage context of the function. It is not necessary that all recursive functions are reentrant. But a Reentrant function can be invoked recursively by an application.

For *8051* Microcontroller, the internal data memory is very small in size (128 bytes) and the stack as well user data memory is allocated within it. Normally all variables local to a function and function arguments are stored in fixed memory locations of the user data memory and each invocation of the function will access the fixed data memory and any recursive calls to the function use the same memory locations. And, in this case, arguments and locals would get corrupted. Hence the scope for implementing recursive functions is limited. A reentrant function can be called recursively to a recursion level dependent on the simulated stack size for the same reentrant function.

C51 Cross-compiler does not support recursive calls if the functions are non-reentrant.

9.3.3.22 Dynamic Memory Allocation Every embedded application, regardless of whether it is running on an operating system based product or a non-operating system based product (Super loop based firmware Architecture) contains different types of variables and they fall into any one of the following storage types namely; *static*, *auto*, *global* or *constant* data. Regardless of the storage type each variable requires memory locations to hold them physically. The storage type determines in which area of the memory each variable needs to be kept. For an Assembly language programmer, handling memory for different variables is quite difficult. S/he needs to assign a particular memory location for each variable and should recollect where s/he kept the variable for operations involving that variable.

Certain category of embedded applications deal with fixed number of variables with fixed length and certain other applications deal with variables with fixed memory length as well as variable with total storage size determined only at the runtime of application (e.g. character array with variable size). If the number of variables are fixed in an application and if it doesn't require a variable size at run time, the cross compiler can determine the storage memory required by the application well in advance at the run time and can assign each variable an absolute address or relative (indirect) address within the data memory. Here the memory required is fixed and allocation is done before the execution of the application. This type of memory allocation is referred as '*Static Memory Allocation*'. The term '*Static*' mentioned here refers '*fixed*' and it is no way related to the storage class static. As mentioned, some embedded applications require data memory which is a combination of fixed memory (Number of variables and variable size is known prior to cross compilation) and variable length data memory. As an example, let's take the scenario where an application deals with reading a stream of character data from an external environment and the length of the stream is variable. It can vary between any numbers (say 1 to 100 bytes). The application needs to store the data in data memory temporarily for some calculation and it can be ignored after the calculation. This scenario can be handled in two ways in the application program. In the first approach, allocate fixed memory with maximum size (say 100 bytes) for storing the incoming data bytes from the stream. In the second approach allocate memory at run time of the application and de-allocate (free) the memory once the data memory storage requirement is over. In the first approach if the memory is allocated fixedly, it is locked forever and cannot re-used by the application even if there is no requirement for the allocated number of bytes and it will definitely create memory bottleneck issues in embedded systems where memory is a big constraint. Hence it is not advised to go for fixed memory allocations for applications demanding variable memory size at run time. Allocating memory on demand and freeing the memory at run time is the most advised method for handling the storage of dynamic (changing) data and this memory allocation technique is known as '*Dynamic Memory Allocation*'.

Dynamic memory allocation technique is employed in Operating System (OS) based embedded systems. Operating system contains a '*Memory Management Unit*' and it is responsible for handling memory allocation related operations. The memory management unit allocates memory to hold the code for the application and the variables associated with the application. The conceptual view of storage of an application and the variables related to the application is represented in Fig. 9.12.

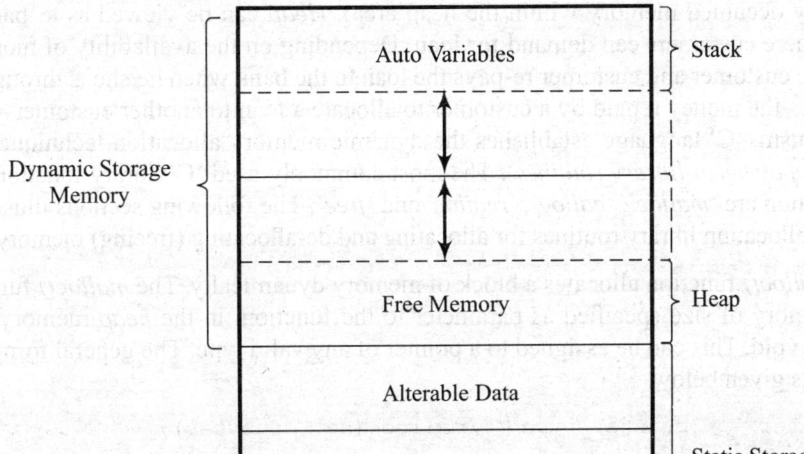

Fig. 9.12 **Static and Dynamic Memory Storage Allocation**

Memory manager allocates a memory segment to each application and the memory segment holds the source code of the application as well as data related to the application. The actual program code (executable machine code instructions) is stored at the lower address of the memory (at the beginning address of the memory segment and stores upward). Constant data related to the application (e.g. const *int x* = 10;) is stored at the memory area just above the executable code. The alterable data (global and static variables; e.g. static int *j* = 10; *int k* = 2; (global declaration), etc.) are stored at the '*Alterable Data*' memory area. The size of the executable code, the number of constant data and alterable data in an application is always fixed and hence they occupy only a fixed portion of the memory segment. Memory allocated for the executable code, constant data and alterable data together constitute the '*Static storage memory* (*Fixed storage memory*)'. The storage memory available within the memory segment excluding the fixed memory is the '*Dynamic storage memory*'. Dynamic storage memory area is divided into two separate entities namely '*stack*' and '*heap*'. '*Stack memory*' normally starts at the high memory area (At the top address) of the memory segment and grows down. Within a memory segment, fixed number of storage bytes are allocated to stack memory and the stack can grow up to this maximum allocated size. Stack memory is usually used for holding auto variables (variables local to a function), function parameters and function return values. Depending upon the function calls/return and auto variable storage, the size of the stack grows and shrinks dynamically. If at any point of execution the stack memory exceeds the allocated maximum storage size, the application may crash and this condition is called '*Stack overflow*'. The free memory region lying in between the stack and fixed memory area is called '*heap*'. Heap is the memory pool where storage for data is done dynamically as and when the application demands. Heap is located immediately above the fixed memory area and it grows upward. Any request for dynamic memory allocation by the program increases the size of *heap* (depending on the availability of free memory within heap) and the free memory request decrements the size of *heap* (size of already occupied memory within the heap area). *Heap* can be viewed as a 'bank' in real life application, where customers can demand for loan. Depending on the availability of money, bank may allot loan to the customer and customer re-pays the loan to the bank when he/she is through with his/her need. Bank uses the money repaid by a customer to allocate a loan to another customer—some kind of rolling mechanism. 'C' language establishes the dynamic memory allocation technique through a set of '*Memory management library routines*'. The most commonly used 'C' library functions for dynamic memory allocation are '*malloc*', '*calloc*', '*realloc*' and '*free*'. The following sections illustrate the use of these memory allocation library routines for allocating and de-allocating (freeing) memory dynamically.

malloc() *malloc()* function allocates a block of memory dynamically. The *malloc()* function reserves a block of memory of size specified as parameter to the function, in the *heap* memory and returns a pointer of type void. This can be assigned to a pointer of any valid type. The general form of using *malloc()* function is given below.

```
pointer =  (pointer_type *) malloc (no. of bytes);
```

where '*pointer*' is a pointer of type 'pointer_type'. 'pointer_type' can be '*int*', '*char*', '*float*' etc. *malloc()* function returns a pointer of type 'pointer_type' to a block of memory with size 'no. of bytes'. A typical example is given below.

```
ptr= (char *) malloc(50);
```

This instruction allocates 50 bytes (If there is 50 bytes of memory available in the *heap* area) and the address of the first byte of the allocated memory in the *heap* area is assigned to the pointer *ptr* of type *char*. It should be noted that the *malloc()* function allocates only the requested number of bytes and it will not allocate memory automatically for the units of the pointer in use. For example, if the programmer wants to allocate memory for 100 integers dynamically, the following code

```
x= (int *) malloc(100);
```

will not allocate memory size for 100 integers, instead it allocates memory for just 100 bytes. In order to make it reserving memory for 100 integer variables, the code should be re-written as

```
x= (int *) malloc(100 * sizeof (int));
```

malloc() function can also be used for allocating memory for complex data types such as structure pointers apart from the usual data types like 'int', 'char', 'float' etc. *malloc()* allocates the requested bytes of memory in *heap* in a continuous fashion and the allocation fails if there is no sufficient memory available in continuous fashion for the requested number of bytes by the *malloc()* functions. The return value of *malloc()* will be NULL (0) if it fails. Hence the return value of *malloc()* should be checked to ensure whether the memory allocation is successful before using the pointer returned by the *malloc()* function.

```
E.g.    int * ptr;
        if ((ptr= (int *) malloc(50 * sizeof (int)))
                  printf ("Memory allocated successfully");
        else
                   printf ("Memory allocation failed");
```

Remember malloc() only allocates required bytes of memory and will not initialise the allocated memory. The allocated memory contains random data.

calloc() The library function *calloc()* allocates multiple blocks of storage bytes and initialises each allocated byte to zero. Syntax of *calloc()* function is illustrated below.

```
pointer =  (pointer_type *) calloc (n, size of block);
```

where 'pointer' is a pointer of type 'pointer_type'. 'pointer_type' can be 'int', 'char', 'float' etc. '*n*' stands for the number of blocks to be allocated and 'size of block' tells the size of bytes required per block. The *calloc*(*n*, size of block) function allocates continuous memory for '*n*' number of blocks with 'size of block' number of bytes per block and returns a pointer of type 'pointer_type' pointing to the first byte of the allocated block of memory. A typical example is given below.

```
ptr= (char *) calloc (50,1);
```

Above instruction allocates 50 contiguous blocks of memory each of size one byte in the *heap* memory and assign the address of the first byte of the allocated memory region to the character pointer '*ptr*'. Since *malloc()* is capable of allocating only fixed number of bytes in the *heap* area regardless of the storage type, *calloc()* can be used for overcomming this limitation as discussed below.

```
ptr= (int *) calloc(50,sizeof(int));
```

This instruction allocates 50 blocks of memory, each block representing an integer variable and initialises the allocated memory to zero. Similar to the *malloc()* function, *calloc()* also returns a 'NULL' pointer if there is not enough space in the *heap* area for allocating storage for the requested number of memory by the *calloc()* function. Hence it is advised to check the pointer to which the *calloc()* assigns the address of the first byte in the allocated memory area. If *calloc()* function fails, the return value will be 'NULL' and the pointer also will be 'NULL'. Checking the pointer for 'NULL' immediately after assigning with pointer returned by *calloc()* function avoids possible errors and application crash.

Features provided by *calloc()* can be implemented using *malloc()* function as

```
pointer =  (pointer_type *) malloc (n * size of block);
memset(pointer, 0, n * size of block);
```

For example

```
ptr= (int *) malloc (10 * sizeof (int));
memset(ptr, 0, n * size of block);
```

The function *memset (ptr, 0, n * size of block)* sets the memory block of size (*n* * size of block) with starting address pointed by '*ptr*', to zero.

free() The 'C' memory management library function *free()* is used for releasing or de-allocating the memory allocated in the *heap* memory by *malloc()* or *calloc()* functions. If memory is allocated dynamically, the programmer should release it if the dynamically allocated memory is no longer required for any operation. Releasing the dynamically allocated memory makes it ready to use for other dynamic allocations. The syntax of *free()* function is given below.

```
free (ptr);
```

'*ptr*' is the valid pointer returned by the *calloc()* or *malloc()* function on dynamic memory allocation. Use of an invalid pointer with function *free()* may result in the unexpected behaviour of the application.

Note:

1. *The dynamic memory allocated using malloc () or calloc() functions should be released (deallocated) using free () function .*
2. *Any use of a pointer which refers to freed memory space results in abnormal behaviour of application.*
3. *If the parameter to free () function is not a valid pointer, the application behaviour may be unexpected.*

realloc() *realloc()* function is used for changing the size of allocated bytes in a dynamically allocated memory block. You may come across situations where the allocated memory is not sufficient to hold the required data or it is surplus in terms of allocated memory bytes. Both of these situations are handled using *realloc()* function. The *realloc()* function changes the size of the block of memory pointed to, by the *pointer* parameter to the number of bytes specified by the *modified size* parameter and it returns a new pointer to the block. The pointer specified by the *pointer* parameter must have been created with the malloc, calloc, or realloc subroutines and not been de-allocated with the free or realloc subroutines. Function *realloc()* may shift the position of the already allocated block depending on the new size, with preserving the contents of the already allocated block and returns a pointer pointing to the first byte of the re-allocated memory block. *realloc()* returns a void pointer if there is sufficient memory available for allocation, else return a 'NULL' pointer. Syntax of *realloc* is given below.

```
realloc (pointer, modified size);
```

Example illustrating the use of *realloc()* function is given below.

```
char *p;
p= (char*) malloc (10); //Allocate 10 bytes of memory
```

```
p= realloc(p,15);        //Change the allocation to 15 bytes
```

realloc(p,0) is same as free(p), provided 'p' is a valid pointer.

Summary

- ✓ Embedded firmware can be developed to run with the help of an embedded operating system or without an OS. The non-OS based embedded firmware execution runs the tasks in an infinite loop and this approach is known as 'Super loop based' execution
- ✓ Low level language (Assembly code) or High Level language (C,C++ etc.) or a mix of both are used in embedded firmware development
- ✓ In Assembly language based design, the firmware is developed using the Assembly language Instructions specific to the target processor. The Assembly code is converted to machine specific code by an assembler.
- ✓ In High Level language based design, the firmware is developed using High Level language like 'C/C++' and it is converted to machine specific code by a compiler or cross-compiler
- ✓ Mixing of Assembly and High Level language can be done in three ways namely; mixing assembly routines with a high level language like 'C', mixing high level language functions like 'C' functions with application written in assembly code and invoking assembly instructions inline from the high level code
- ✓ Embedded 'C' can be considered as a subset of conventional 'C' language. Embedded C supports almost all 'C' instructions and incorporates a few target processor specific functions/instructions. The standard ANSI 'C' library implementation is always tailored to the target processor/controller library files in Embedded C
- ✓ Compiler is a tool for native platform application development, whereas cross-compiler is a tool for cross platform application development
- ✓ Embedded 'C' supports all the keywords, identifiers and data types, storage classes, arithmetic and logical operations, array and branching instructions supported by standard 'C'
- ✓ *structure* is a collection of data types. Arrays of structures are helpful in holding configuration data in embedded applications. The *bitfield* feature of structures helps in bit declaration and bit manipulation in embedded applications
- ✓ *Pre-processor* in 'C' is compiler/cross-compiler directives used by compiler/cross-compiler to filter the source code before compilation/cross-compilation. Preprocessor directives falls into one of the categories: file inclusion, compile control and macro substitution
- ✓ 'Read only' variable in embedded applications are represented with the keyword *const*. *Pointer to constant data* is a pointer which points to a data which is read only. A *constant pointer* is a pointer to a fixed memory location. *Constant pointer to constant data* is a pointer pointing to a fixed memory location which is read only
- ✓ A variable or memory location in embedded application, which is subject to asynchronous modification should be declared with the qualifier *volatile* to prevent the compiler optimisation on the variable
- ✓ A *constant volatile pointer* represents a Read only register (memory location) of a memory mapped device in embedded application
- ✓ *while(1) { }; do { }while (1); for (;;){}* are examples for infinite loop setting instructions in embedded 'C'.
- ✓ The ISR contains the code for saving the current context, code for performing the operation corresponding to the interrupt, code for retrieving the saved context and code for informing the processor that the processing of interrupt is completed
- ✓ *Recursive function* is a function which calls it repeatedly. Functions which can be shared safely with several processes concurrently are called *re-entrant function*.
- ✓ *Dynamic memory allocation* is the technique for allocating memory on a need basis for tasks. *malloc()*, *calloc()*, *realloc()* and *free()* are the 'C' library routines for dynamic memory management

Keywords

Super Loop Model	:	An embedded firmware design model which executes tasks in an infinite loop at a predefined order
Assembly Language	:	The human readable notation of 'machine language'
Machine Language	:	Processor understandable language made up of 1s and 0s
Mnemonics	:	Symbols used in Assembly language for representing the machine language
Assembler	:	A program to translate Assembly language program to object code
Library	:	Specially formatted, ordered program collections of object modules
Linker	:	A software for linking the various object files of a project
Hex File	:	ASCII representation of the machine code corresponding to an application
Inline Assembly	:	A technique for inserting assembly instructions in a C program
Embedded C	:	'C' Language for embedded firmware development. It supports 'C' instructions and incorporates a few target processor specific functions/instructions along with tailoring of the standard library functions for the target embedded system
Compiler	:	A software tool that converts a source code written in a high level language on top of a particular operating system running on a specific target processor architecture
Cross-compiler	:	The software tools used in cross-platform development applications. It converts the application to a target processor specific code, which is different from the processor architecture on which the compiler is running
Function	:	A self-contained and re-usable code snippet intended to perform a particular task
Function Pointer	:	Pointer variable pointing to a function
structure	:	Variable holding a collection of data types (int, float, char, long, etc.) in C language
structure Padding	:	The act of arranging the structure elements in memory in a way facilitating increased execution speed
union	:	A derived form of structure, which allocates memory only to the member variable of union requiring the maximum storage size on declaring a union variable
Pre-processor	:	A compiler/cross-compiler directives used by compiler/ cross-compiler to filter the source code before compilation/cross-compilation in 'C' language
Macro	:	The 'C' pre-processor for creating portable inline code
const	:	A keyword used in 'C' language for informing the compiler/cross-compiler that the variable is constant. It represents a 'Read only' variable
Dynamic Memory Allocation	:	The technique for allocating memory on a need basis at run time
Stack	:	The memory area for storing local variables, function parameters and function return values and program counter, in the memory model for an application/task
Static Memory Area	:	The memory area holding the program code, constant variables, static and global variables, in the memory model for an application/task
Heap Memory	:	The free memory lying in between stack and static memory area, which is used for dynamic memory allocation

Objective Questions

1. Which of the following is a processor understandable language?
   (a) Assembly language (b) Machine language (c) High level language
2. Assembly language is the human readable notation of?
   (a) Machine language (b) High level language (c) None of these
3. Consider the following piece of assembly code

```
ORG 0000H
LJMP MAIN
```

   Here '*ORG*' is a
   (a) Pseudo-op (b) Label (c) Opcode (d) Operand
4. Translation of assembly code to machine code is performed by the
   (a) Assembler (b) Compiler (c) Linker (d) Locater
5. A cross-compiler converts an embedded 'C' program to
   (a) The machine code corresponding to the processor of the PC used for application development
   (b) The machine code corresponding to a processor which is different from the processor of the PC used for application development
6. '*ptr*' is an *integer* pointer holding the address of an *integer* variable say *x* which holds the value 10. Assume the address of the *integer* variable *x* as 0x12ff7c. What will be the output of the below piece of code? Assume the storage size of *integer* is 4

```
ptr+=2;
//Print the address holding by the pointer
printf("0x%x\n", ptr);
```

   (a) 0x12ff7c (b) 0x12ff7e (c) 0x12ff84 (d) None
7. '*ptr*' is a *char* pointer holding the address of a *char* variable say *x* which holds the value 10. Assume the address of the *char* variable *x* as 0x12ff7c. What will be the output of the below piece of code?

```
//Print the address holding by the pointer
printf("0x%x\n", ptr++);
```

   (a) 0x12ff7c (b) 0x12ff7d (c) 0x12ff80 (d) None
8. '*ptr*' is a *char* pointer holding the address of a *char* variable say *x* which holds the value 10. Assume the address of the *char* variable *x* as 0x12ff7c. What will be the output of the below piece of code?

```
//Print the address holding by the pointer
printf("0x%x\n", ++ptr);
```

   (a) 0x12ff7c (b) 0x12ff7d (c) 0x12ff80 (d) None
9. '*ptr1*' is a *char* pointer holding the address of the *char* variable say *x* which holds the value 10. '*ptr2*' is a *char* pointer holding the address of the *char* variable say *y* which holds the value 20. Assume the address of *char* variable *x* as 0x12ff7c and *char* variable *y* as 0x12ff78. What will be the output of the following piece of code?

```
//Print the address holding by the pointer
printf("%x\n", (ptr1+ptr2));
```

   (a) 30 (b) 4 (c) Compile error (cannot add two pointers)
   (d) 0x25fef4

10. '*ptr1*' is a *char* pointer holding the address of the *char* variable say *x* which holds the value 10. Assume the address of *char* variable *x* as 0x12ff7c. What will be the output of the following piece of code?

```
++*ptr1;
printf("%x\n", *ptr1);
```

(a) 0x0a (b) 0x0b (c) 0x12ff7c (d) 0x12ff7d

11. '*ptr1*' is a *char* pointer holding the address of the *char* variable say *x* which holds the value 10. Assume the address of *char* variable *x* as 0x12ff7c. What will be the output of the following piece of code?

```
++*ptr1;
printf("%x\n", ptr1);
```

(a) 0x0a (b) 0x0b (c) 0x12ff7c (d) 0x12ff7d

12. '*ptr1*' is a *char* pointer holding the address of the *char* variable say *x* which holds the value 10. Assume the address of *char* variable *x* as 0x12ff7c. What will be the output of the following piece of code?

```
*ptr1++;
printf("%x\n", *ptr1);
```

(a) 0x0b (b) The contents of memory location 0x12ff7d (c) 0x12ff7c (d) 0x12ff7d

13. '*ptr1*' is a *char* pointer holding the address of the *char* variable say *x* which holds the value 10. Assume the address of *char* variable *x* as 0x12ff7c. What will be the output of the following piece of code?

```
*ptr1++;
printf("%x\n", ptr1);
```

(a) 0x0b (b) The contents of memory location 0x12ff7d (c) 0x12ff7c (d) 0x12ff7d

14. Which of the following is the string termination character?

(a) '\n' (b) '\t' (c) '\0' (d) '\a'

15. What is the output of the following piece of code?

```
char name[6] = {'H','E','L','L','O','\0'};
printf("%d",strlen(name));
```

(a) 6 (b) 5 (c) 7 (d) None of the above

16. What is the output of the following piece of code?

```
char str1[] = "Hello ";
char str2[] = "World!";
str1+= str2;
printf("%s\n",str1);
```

(a) Hello (b) Hello World! (c) Compile error (d) World!

17. What is the output of the following piece of code?

```
char str1 [ ] = "Hello world!";
char str2 [ ] = "Hello World!"  ;
int n;
n= stricmp(str1, str2);
printf("%d", n);
```

(a) 1 (b) 0 (c) –1

18. What is the output of the following piece of code?

```
char str1[] = "Hello "
char str2[] = "World!";
strcpy(str1,str2);
printf("%s\n",str1);
```

(a) Hello (b) Hello World! (c) Compile error (d) World!

19. What is the output of the following piece of code?

```
char str1[] = "Hello "
char str2[] = "World!";
str1 = str2;
printf("%s\n",str1);
```

(a) Hello (b) Hello World! (c) Compile error (d) World!

20. Consider the following structure declaration

```
typedef struct
    {
        unsigned char command; // command to pass to device
        unsigned char status;   //status of command execution
        unsigned char BytesToSend;  //No. of bytes to send
       unsigned char  BytesReceived; //No. of bytes received
    }Info;
```

Assuming the size of *unsigned char* as 1 byte, what will be the memory allocated for the structure?
(a) 1 byte (b) 2 bytes (c) 4 bytes (d) 0 bytes

21. Consider the following structure declaration

```
typedef struct

    {
        unsigned char hour;      // command to pass to device
        unsigned char minute;   //status of command execution
        unsigned char seconds;   //No. of bytes to send
    }RTC_Time;
```

Assuming the size of *unsigned char* as 1 byte, what will be the output of the following piece of code when compiled for Keil C51 cross compiler

```
static volatile RTC_Time xdata *current_time = (void xdata *) 0x7000;
void main()
{
unsigned char test;
test = current_time->minute;
printf("%d", test);
}
```

(a) 0x7000 (b) 0x7001 (c) Content of memory location 0x7000
(d) Content of memory location 0x7001

22. Consider the following structure declaration

```
typedef struct
    {
      unsigned char  hour;      // Hour Reg value
      unsigned char  minute;   // Minute value
      unsigned char  seconds; // Seconds value
    }RTC_Time;
```

Assuming the size of *unsigned char* as 1 byte, what will be the output of the following piece of code when compiled for Keil C51 cross compiler

```
void main(void)
{
unsigned char test;
test = offsetof(RTC_Time, seconds);
printf("%d",test);
}
```

(a) 1 (b) 2 (c) Compile error (d) 0

23. Consider the following union definition

```
    typedef union
              {
              int intVal;
              unsigned char   charVal[3];
              }union_ichar;
```

What will be the output of the following piece of code? Assume the storage size of *int* as 2 and *unsigned char* as 1

```
union_ichar int_char;
void main(void)
{
unsigned char test;
test = sizeof (int_char);
printf("%d",test);
}
```

(a) 0 (b) 2 (c) 3 (d) 5

24. The default initialiser for a *union* with static *storage* is the default for
    (a) The first member variable
    (b) The last member variable
    (c) The member variable with the highest storage requirement
25. Which of the following is (are) True about pre-processor directives?
    (a) compiler/cross-compiler directives
    (b) executable code is generated for pre-processor directives on compilation
    (c) No executable code is generated for pre-processor directives on compilation
    (d) Start with # symbol (e) (a), (b) and (d) (f) (a), (c) and (d)
26. The 'C' pre-processor directive instruction always ends with a semicolon (;). State '*True*' or '*False*'
    (a) True (b) False
27. Which of the following is the file inclusion pre-processor directive?
    (a) #define (b) #include (c) #ifdef (d) None of these

28. Which of the following pre-processor directive is used for indicating the end of a block following *#ifdef* or *#else*?
(a) #define (b) #undef (c) #endif (d) #ifndef
29. Which of the following preprocessor directive is used for coding macros?
(a) #ifdef (b) #define (c) #undef (d) #endif
30. What will be the output of the following piece of code?

```
#define A        2+8
#define B        2+3
void main(void)
{
Unsigned char result ;
result = A/B ;
printf("%d", result) ;
}
```

(a) 0 (b) 2 (c) 9 (d) 8
31. The instruction

```
const unsigned char* x;
```

represents:
(a) Pointer to constant data (b) Constant pointer to data
(c) Constant pointer to constant data (d) None of these
32. The instruction

```
unsigned char* const x;
```

represents:
(a) Pointer to constant data (b) Constant pointer to data
(c) Constant pointer to constant data (d) None of these
33. The instruction

```
const unsigned char* const x;
```

represents:
(a) Pointer to constant data (b) Constant pointer to data
(c) Constant pointer to constant data (d) None of these
34. The instruction

```
volatile unsigned char* x;
```

represents:
(a) Volatile pointer to data (b) Pointer to volatile data
(c) Volatile pointer to constant data (d) None of these
35. The instruction

```
volatile const unsigned char* x;
```

represents:
(a) Volatile pointer to data (b) Pointer to volatile data
(c) Pointer to constant volatile data (d) None of these
36. The constant volatile variable in Embedded application represents a
(a) Write only memory location/register (b) Read only memory location/register
(c) Read/Write memory location/register

37. What will be the output of the following piece of code? Assume the data bus width of the controller on which the program is executed as 8 bits.

```
void main(void)
{
unsigned char flag = 0x00;
flag |=   (1<<7)
printf("%d", flag);
}
```

(a) 0x00 (b) 0x70 (c) 0x80 (d) 0xFF

38. The variable 'x' declared with the following code statement

```
const int x = 5;
```

will be stored in which section of the memory allocated to the program?

(a) Constant Data Memory (b) Heap Memory (c) Alterable Data Memory
(d) Stack Memory (e) Register

39. What will be the memory allocated on successful execution of the following memory allocation request? Assume the size of *int* as 2 bytes

```
x = (int *) malloc(100);
```

(a) 2 Bytes (b) 100 Bytes (c) 200 Bytes (d) 4 Bytes

40. Which of the following memory management routine is used for changing the size of allocated bytes in a dynamically allocated memory block

(a) *malloc()* (b) *realloc()* (c) *calloc()* (d) *free()*

Review Questions

1. Explain the different 'embedded firmware design' approaches in detail
2. What is the difference between 'Super loop' based and '*OS*' based embedded firmware design? Which one is the better approach?
3. What is 'Assembly Language' Programming?
4. Explain the format of assembly language instruction
5. What is 'pseudo-ops'? What is the use of it in Assembly Language Programming?
6. Explain the various steps involved in the assembling of an assembly language program
7. What is relocatable code? Explain its significance in assembly programming
8. Explain 'library file' in assembly language context. What is the benefit of 'library file'?
9. What is absolute object file?
10. Explain the advantages of 'Assembly language' based Embedded firmware development
11. Explain the limitations/drawbacks of 'Assembly language' based Embedded firmware development
12. What is the difference between compiler and cross-compiler?
13. Explain the 'High Level language' based 'Embedded firmware' development technique
14. Explain the advantages of 'High Level language' based 'Embedded firmware' development
15. Give examples for situations demanding mixing of assembly with 'C'. Explain the techniques for mixing assembly with 'C'.
16. Give examples for situations demanding mixing of 'C' with assembly. Explain the techniques for mixing 'C' with assembly.

17. What is 'inline Assembly'? How is it different from mixing assembly language with 'C'?
18. What is 'pointer' in embedded C programming? Explain its role in embedded application development.
19. Explain the different arithmetic and relational operations supported by pointers
20. What is 'NULL' Pointer? Explain its significance in embedded C programming
21. Explain the similarities and differences between strings and character arrays
22. Explain function in the Embedded C programming context. Explain the generic syntax of function declaration and implementation
23. What is static function? What is the difference between static and global functions?
24. Explain the similarities and differences between function prototype and function declaration
25. What is function pointer? How is it related to function? Explain the use of function pointers
26. Explain *structure* in the 'Embedded C' programming context. Explain the significance of *structure* over normal variables
27. Explain the declaration and initialisation of structure variables
28. Explain the different operations supported by *structures*
29. What is *structure pointer*? What is the advantage of using structure pointers?
30. Explain 'structure placement at absolute memory location' and its advantage in embedded application development. Will it be possible to place a structure at absolute memory location in desktop application development? Explain
31. What is structure padding? What are the merits and demerits of structure padding?
32. What is bit field? How bit field is useful in variant data access?
33. Explain the use of *offsetof*() macro in structure operations.
34. What is *union*? What is the difference between union and structure?
35. Explain how *union* is useful in variant data access.
36. Explain the use of *union* in 'Embedded C' applications
37. What is pre-processor directive? How is a pre-processor directive instruction differentiated from normal program code?
38. What are the different types of pre-processor directives available in 'Embedded C'? Explain them in detail
39. What is *macro* in 'Embedded C' programming?
40. What is the difference between *macros* and *functions*?
41. What are the merits and drawbacks of *macros*?
42. Write a *macro* to multiply two numbers
43. Explain the different methods of '*constant data*' declaration in 'Embedded C'. Explain the differences between the methods.
44. Explain the difference between '*pointer to constant data*' and '*constant pointer to data*' in 'Embedded C' programming. Explain the syntax for declaring both.
45. What is *constant pointer* to *constant data*? Where is it used in embedded application development?
46. Explain the significance of '*volatile*' type qualifier in Embedded C applications. Which all variables need to be declared as '*volatile*' variables in Embedded C application?
47. What is '*pointer to constant volatile data*'? What is the syntax for defining a 'pointer to constant volatile data'? What is its significance in embedded application development?
48. What is *volatile pointer*? Explain the usage of '*volatile pointer*' in 'Embedded C' application
49. Explain the different techniques for *delay* generation in 'Embedded C' programming. What are the limitations of delay programming for super loop based embedded applications?
50. Explain the different bit manipulation operations supported by 'Embedded C'
51. What is *Interrupt*? Explain its properties? What is its role in embedded application development?
52. What is *Interrupt Vector Address* and *Interrupt Service Routine* (ISR)? How are they related?
53. What is the difference between *Interrupt Service Routine* and Normal Service Routine?
54. Explain *context switching*, *context saving* and *context retrieval* in relation to Interrupts and Interrupt Service Routine (ISR)

55. What all precautionary measures need to be implemented in an Interrupt Service Routine (ISR)?
56. What is '*recursion*'? What is the difference between *recursion* and *iteration*? Which one is better?
57. What are the merits and drawbacks of '*recursion*'?
58. What is '*reentrant*' function? What is its significance in embedded applications development?
59. What is the difference between '*recursive*' and '*reentrant*' function?
60. Explain the different criteria that need to be strictly met by a function to consider it as '*reentrant*' function.
61. What is the difference between *Static* and *Dynamic memory* allocation?
62. Explain the different sections of a memory segment allocated to an application by the memory manager
63. Explain the different '*Memory management* library routines' supported by C
64. Explain the difference between the library functions *malloc*() and *calloc*() for dynamic memory allocation

Lab Assignments

1. Write a 'C' program to create a 'reentrant' function which removes the white spaces from a string which is supplied as input to the function and returns the new string without white spaces. The main 'C' function passes a string to the reentrant function and accepts the string with white spaces removed
2. Write a C program to place a character variable at memory location 0x000FF and load it with 0xFF. Compile the application using Microsoft Visual Studio compiler and run it on a desktop machine with Windows Operating System. Record the output and explain the reason behind the output behaviour
3. Write a small embedded C program to complement bit 5 (Assume bit numbering starts at 0) of the status register of a device, which is memory mapped to the CPU. The status register of the device is memory mapped at location 0x3000. The data bus of the controller and the status register of the device is 8bit wide
4. Write a small embedded C program to set bit 0 and clear bit 7 of the status register of a device, which is memory mapped to the CPU. The status register of the device is memory mapped at location 0x8000. The data bus of the controller and the status register of the device is 8bit wide. The application should illustrate the usage of bit manipulation operations.
5. Write a small embedded C program to test the status of bit 5 of the status register and reset it if it is 1, of a device, which is memory mapped to the CPU. The status register of the device is memory mapped at location 0x7000. The data bus of the controller and the status register of the device is 8bit wide. The application should illustrate the usage of bit manipulation operations.
6. Write an 'Embedded C' program for Keil C51 cross-compiler for transmitting a string data through the serial port of *8051* microcontroller as per the following requirements
   (a) Use structure to hold the communication parameters
   (b) Use a structure array for holding the configurations corresponding to various baudrates (say 2400, 4800, 9600 and 195200)
   (c) Write the code for sending a string to the serial port as function. The main routine invokes this function with the string to send. Use polling of Transmit Interrupt for ensuring the sending of a character

10 Real-Time Operating System (RTOS) based Embedded System Design

LEARNING OBJECTIVES

- ✓ *Learn the basics of an operating system and the need for an operating system*
- ✓ *Learn the internals of Real-Time Operating System and the fundamentals of RTOS based embedded firmware design*
- ✓ *Learn the basic kernel services of an operating system*
- ✓ *Learn about the classification of operating systems*
- ✓ *Learn about the different real-time kernels and the features that make a kernel Real-Time*
- ✓ *Learn about tasks, processes and threads in the operating system context*
- ✓ *Learn about the structure of a process, the different states of a process, process life cycle and process management*
- ✓ *Learn the concept of multithreading, thread standards and thread scheduling*
- ✓ *Understand the difference between multiprocessing and multitasking,*
- ✓ *Learn about the different types of multitasking (Co-operative, Preemptive and Non-preemptive)*
- ✓ *Learn about the FCFS/FIFO, LCFS/LIFO, SJF and priority based task/process scheduling*
- ✓ *Learn about the shortest remaining time (SRT), Round Robin and priority based preemptive task/process scheduling*
- ✓ *Learn about the different Inter Process Communication (IPC) mechanisms used by tasks/process to communicate and co-operate each other in a multitasking environment*
- ✓ *Learn the different types of shared memory techniques (Pipes, memory mapped object, etc.) for IPC*
- ✓ *Learn the different types of message passing techniques (Message queue, mailbox, signals, etc.) for IPC*
- ✓ *Learn the RPC based Inter Process Communication*
- ✓ *Learn the need for task synchronisation in a multitasking environment*
- ✓ *Learn the different issues related to the accessing of a shared resource by multiple processes concurrently*
- ✓ *Learn about 'Racing', 'Starvation', 'Livelock', 'Deadlock', 'Dining Philosopher's Problem', 'Producer-Consumer/Bounded Buffer Problem', 'Readers-Writers Problem' and 'Priority Inversion'*
- ✓ *Learn about the 'Priority Inheritance' and 'Priority Ceiling' based Priority avoidance mechanisms*
- ✓ *Learn the need for task synchronisation and the different mechanisms for task synchronisation in a multitasking environment*
- ✓ *Learn about mutual exclusion and the different policies for mutual exclusion implementation*
- ✓ *Learn about semaphores, different types of semaphores, mutex, critical section objects and events for task synchronisation*
- ✓ *Learn about device drivers, their role in an operating system based embedded system design, the structure of a device driver, and interrupt handling inside device drivers*
- ✓ *Understand the different functional and non-functional requirements that need to be addressed in the selection of a Real-Time Operating System*

In the previous chapter, we discussed about the *Super loop* based task execution model for firmware execution. The super loop executes the tasks sequentially in the order in which the tasks are listed within the loop. Here every task is repeated at regular intervals and the task execution is non-real time. As the number of task increases, the time intervals at which a task gets serviced also increases. If some of the tasks involve waiting for external events or I/O device usage, the task execution time also gets pushed off in accordance with the 'wait' time consumed by the task. The priority in which a task is to be executed is fixed and is determined by the task placement within the loop, in a super loop based execution. This type of firmware execution is suited for embedded devices where response time for a task is not time critical. Typical examples are electronic toys and video gaming devices. Here any response delay is acceptable and it will not create any operational issues or potential hazards. Whereas certain applications demand time critical response to tasks/events and any delay in the response may become catastrophic. Flight Control systems, Air bag control and Anti Locking Brake (ABS) systems for vehicles, Nuclear monitoring devices, etc. are typical examples of applications/devices demanding time critical task response.

How the increasing need for time critical response for tasks/events is addressed in embedded applications? Well the answer is

1. Assign priority to tasks and execute the high priority task when the task is ready to execute.
2. Dynamically change the priorities of tasks if required on a need basis.
3. Schedule the execution of tasks based on the priorities.
4. Switch the execution of task when a task is waiting for an external event or a system resource including I/O device operation.

The introduction of operating system based firmware execution in embedded devices can address these needs to a greater extent.

10.1 OPERATING SYSTEM BASICS

The operating system acts as a bridge between the user applications/tasks and the underlying system resources through a set of system functionalities and services. The OS manages the system resources and makes them available to the user applications/tasks on a need basis. A normal computing system is a collection of different I/O subsystems, working, and storage memory. The primary functions of an operating system is

- Make the system convenient to use
- Organise and manage the system resources efficiently and correctly

Figure 10.1 gives an insight into the basic components of an operating system and their interfaces with rest of the world.

10.1.1 The Kernel

The kernel is the core of the operating system and is responsible for managing the system resources and the communication among the hardware and other system services. Kernel acts as the abstraction layer between system resources and user applications. Kernel contains a set of system libraries and services. For a general purpose OS, the kernel contains different services for handling the following.

Process Management Process management deals with managing the processes/tasks. Process management includes setting up the memory space for the process, loading the process's code into the memory space, allocating system resources, scheduling and managing the execution of the process, setting

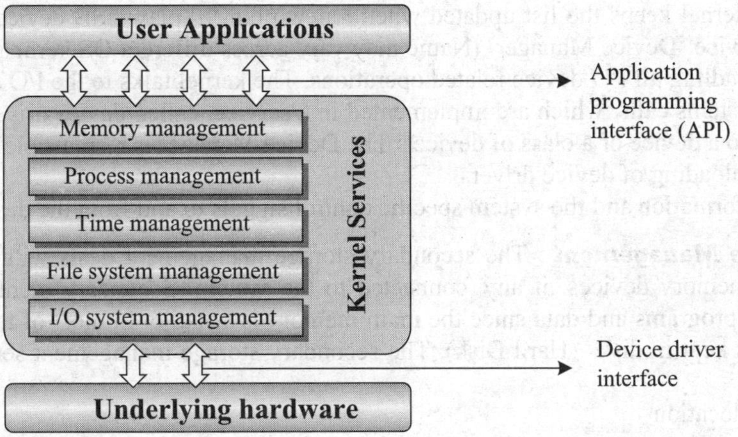

Fig. 10.1 **The Operating System Architecture**

up and managing the Process Control Block (PCB), Inter Process Communication and synchronisation, process termination/deletion, etc. We will look into the description of process and process management in a later section of this chapter.

Primary Memory Management The term primary memory refers to the volatile memory (RAM) where processes are loaded and variables and shared data associated with each process are stored. The Memory Management Unit (MMU) of the kernel is responsible for

- Keeping track of which part of the memory area is currently used by which process
- Allocating and De-allocating memory space on a need basis (Dynamic memory allocation).

File System Management File is a collection of related information. A file could be a program (source code or executable), text files, image files, word documents, audio/video files, etc. Each of these files differ in the kind of information they hold and the way in which the information is stored. The file operation is a useful service provided by the OS. The file system management service of Kernel is responsible for

- The creation, deletion and alteration of files
- Creation, deletion and alteration of directories
- Saving of files in the secondary storage memory (e.g. Hard disk storage)
- Providing automatic allocation of file space based on the amount of free space available
- Providing a flexible naming convention for the files

The various file system management operations are OS dependent. For example, the kernel of Microsoft® DOS OS supports a specific set of file system management operations and they are not the same as the file system operations supported by UNIX Kernel.

I/O System (Device) Management Kernel is responsible for routing the I/O requests coming from different user applications to the appropriate I/O devices of the system. In a well-structured OS, the direct accessing of I/O devices are not allowed and the access to them are provided through a set of Application Programming Interfaces (APIs) exposed by the kernel. The kernel maintains a list of all the I/O devices of the system. This list may be available in advance, at the time of building the kernel. Some kernels, dynamically updates the list of available devices as and when a new device is installed (e.g. Windows XP kernel keeps the list updated when a new plug '*n*' play USB device is attached to the system). The service 'Device Manager' (Name may vary across different OS kernels) of the kernel is responsible for handling all I/O device related operations. The kernel talks to the I/O device through a set of low-level systems calls, which are implemented in a service, called device drivers. The device drivers are specific to a device or a class of devices. The Device Manager is responsible for

- Loading and unloading of device drivers
- Exchanging information and the system specific control signals to and from the device

Secondary Storage Management The secondary storage management deals with managing the secondary storage memory devices, if any, connected to the system. Secondary memory is used as backup medium for programs and data since the main memory is volatile. In most of the systems, the secondary storage is kept in disks (Hard Disk). The secondary storage management service of kernel deals with

- Disk storage allocation
- Disk scheduling (Time interval at which the disk is activated to backup data)
- Free Disk space management

Protection Systems Most of the modern operating systems are designed in such a way to support multiple users with different levels of access permissions (e.g. Windows XP with user permissions like 'Administrator', 'Standard', 'Restricted', etc.). Protection deals with implementing the security policies to restrict the access to both user and system resources by different applications or processes or users. In multiuser supported operating systems, one user may not be allowed to view or modify the whole/portions of another user's data or profile details. In addition, some application may not be granted with permission to make use of some of the system resources. This kind of protection is provided by the protection services running within the kernel.

Interrupt Handler Kernel provides handler mechanism for all external/internal interrupts generated by the system.

These are some of the important services offered by the kernel of an operating system. It does not mean that a kernel contains no more than components/services explained above. Depending on the type of the operating system, a kernel may contain lesser number of components/services or more number of components/services. In addition to the components/services listed above, many operating systems offer a number of add-on system components/services to the kernel. Network communication, network management, user-interface graphics, timer services (delays, timeouts, etc.), error handler, database management, etc. are examples for such components/services. Kernel exposes the interface to the various kernel applications/services, hosted by kernel, to the user applications through a set of standard Application Programming Interfaces (APIs). User applications can avail these API calls to access the various kernel application/services.

10.1.1.1 Kernel Space and User Space As we discussed in the earlier section, the applications/services are classified into two categories, namely: user applications and kernel applications. The program code corresponding to the kernel applications/services are kept in a contiguous area (OS dependent) of primary (working) memory and is protected from the un-authorised access by user programs/applications. The memory space at which the kernel code is located is known as '*Kernel Space*'. Similarly, all user applications are loaded to a specific area of primary memory and this memory area is referred as '*User Space*'. User space is the memory area where user applications are loaded and executed. The partitioning of memory into kernel and user space is purely Operating System dependent.

Some OS implements this kind of partitioning and protection whereas some OS do not segregate the kernel and user application code storage into two separate areas. In an operating system with virtual memory support, the user applications are loaded into its corresponding virtual memory space with demand paging technique; Meaning, the entire code for the user application need not be loaded to the main (primary) memory at once; instead the user application code is split into different pages and these pages are loaded into and out of the main memory area on a need basis. The act of loading the code into and out of the main memory is termed as '*Swapping*'. Swapping happens between the main (primary) memory and secondary storage memory. Each process run in its own virtual memory space and are not allowed accessing the memory space corresponding to another processes, unless explicitly requested by the process. Each process will have certain privilege levels on accessing the memory of other processes and based on the privilege settings, processes can request kernel to map another process's memory to its own or share through some other mechanism. Most of the operating systems keep the kernel application code in main memory and it is not swapped out into the secondary memory.

10.1.1.2 Monolithic Kernel and Microkernel As we know, the kernel forms the heart of an operating system. Different approaches are adopted for building an Operating System kernel. Based on the kernel design, kernels can be classified into '*Monolithic*' and '*Micro*'.

Monolithic Kernel In monolithic kernel architecture, all kernel services run in the kernel space. Here all kernel modules run within the same memory space under a single kernel thread. The tight internal integration of kernel modules in monolithic kernel architecture allows the effective utilisation of the low-level features of the underlying system. The major drawback of monolithic kernel is that any error or failure in any one of the kernel modules leads to the crashing of the entire kernel application. LINUX, SOLARIS, MS-DOS kernels are examples of monolithic kernel. The architecture representation of a monolithic kernel is given in Fig. 10.2.

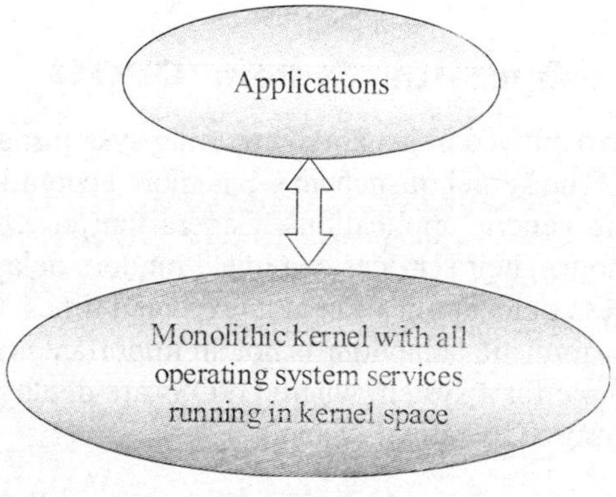

Fig. 10.2 The Monolithic Kernel Model

Microkernel The microkernel design incorporates only the essential set of Operating System services into the kernel. The rest of the Operating System services are implemented in programs known as '*Servers*' which runs in user space. This provides a highly modular design and OS-neutral abstraction to the kernel. Memory management, process management, timer systems and interrupt handlers are the essential services, which forms the part of the microkernel. Mach, QNX, Minix 3 kernels are examples for microkernel. The architecture representation of a microkernel is shown in Fig. 10.3.

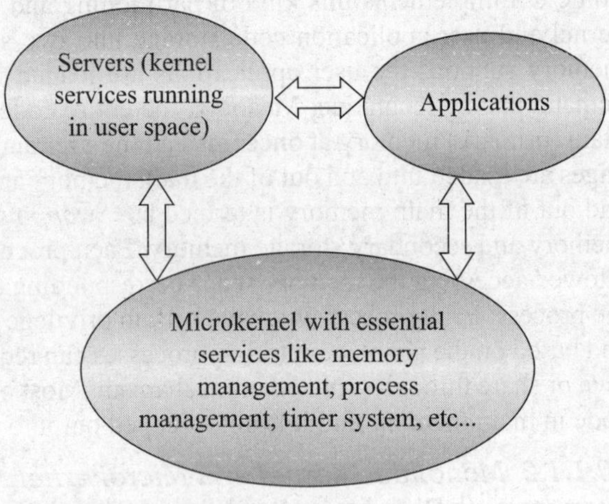

Fig. 10.3 **The Microkernel model**

Microkernel based design approach offers the following benefits

- **Robustness:** If a problem is encountered in any of the services, which runs as '*Server*' application, the same can be reconfigured and re-started without the need for re-starting the entire OS. Thus, this approach is highly useful for systems, which demands high '*availability*'. Refer Chapter 3 to get an understanding of '*availability*'. Since the services which run as '*Servers*' are running on a different memory space, the chances of corruption of kernel services are ideally zero.
- **Configurability:** Any services, which run as '*Server*' application can be changed without the need to restart the whole system. This makes the system dynamically configurable.

10.2 TYPES OF OPERATING SYSTEMS

Depending on the type of kernel and kernel services, purpose and type of computing systems where the OS is deployed and the responsiveness to applications, Operating Systems are classified into different types.

10.2.1 General Purpose Operating System (GPOS)

The operating systems, which are deployed in general computing systems, are referred as *General Purpose Operating Systems (GPOS)*. The kernel of such an OS is more generalised and it contains all kinds of services required for executing generic applications. General-purpose operating systems are often quite non-deterministic in behaviour. Their services can inject random delays into application software and may cause slow responsiveness of an application at unexpected times. GPOS are usually deployed in computing systems where deterministic behaviour is not an important criterion. Personal Computer/Desktop system is a typical example for a system where GPOSs are deployed. Windows XP/MS-DOS etc. are examples for General Purpose Operating Systems.

10.2.2 Real-Time Operating System (RTOS)

There is no universal definition available for the term '*Real-Time*' when it is used in conjunction with operating systems. What '*Real-Time*' means in Operating System context is still a debatable topic and there are many definitions available. In a broad sense, '*Real-Time*' implies deterministic timing behaviour. Deterministic timing behaviour in RTOS context means the OS services consumes only known and expected amounts of time regardless the number of services. A Real-Time Operating System or RTOS implements policies and rules concerning time-critical allocation of a system's resources. The RTOS decides which applications should run in which order and how much time needs to be allocated for each application. Predictable performance is the hallmark of a well-designed RTOS. This is best achieved by the consistent application of policies and rules. Policies guide the design of an RTOS. Rules implement those policies and resolve policy conflicts. Windows CE, QNX, VxWorks MicroC/OS-II, etc. are examples of Real-Time Operating Systems (RTOS).

10.2.2.1 The Real-Time Kernel The kernel of a Real-Time Operating System is referred as Real. Time kernel. In complement to the conventional OS kernel, the Real-Time kernel is highly specialised and it contains only the minimal set of services required for running the user applications/tasks. The basic functions of a Real-Time kernel are listed below:

- Task/Process management
- Task/Process scheduling
- Task/Process synchronisation
- Error/Exception handling
- Memory management
- Interrupt handling
- Time management

Task/Process management Deals with setting up the memory space for the tasks, loading the task's code into the memory space, allocating system resources, setting up a Task Control Block (TCB) for the task and task/process termination/deletion. A Task Control Block (TCB) is used for holding the information corresponding to a task. TCB usually contains the following set of information.

Task ID: Task Identification Number

Task State: The current state of the task (e.g. State = 'Ready' for a task which is ready to execute)

Task Type: Task type. Indicates what is the type for this task. The task can be a hard real time or soft real time or background task.

Task Priority: Task priority (e.g. Task priority = 1 for task with priority = 1)

Task Context Pointer: Context pointer. Pointer for context saving

Task Memory Pointers: Pointers to the code memory, data memory and stack memory for the task

Task System Resource Pointers: Pointers to system resources (semaphores, mutex, etc.) used by the task

Task Pointers: Pointers to other TCBs (TCBs for preceding, next and waiting tasks)

Other Parameters Other relevant task parameters

The parameters and implementation of the TCB is kernel dependent. The TCB parameters vary across different kernels, based on the task management implementation. Task management service utilises the TCB of a task in the following way

- Creates a TCB for a task on creating a task
- Delete/remove the TCB of a task when the task is terminated or deleted
- Reads the TCB to get the state of a task
- Update the TCB with updated parameters on need basis (e.g. on a context switch)
- Modify the TCB to change the priority of the task dynamically

Task/Process Scheduling Deals with sharing the CPU among various tasks/processes. A kernel application called '*Scheduler*' handles the task scheduling. Scheduler is nothing but an algorithm implementation, which performs the efficient and optimal scheduling of tasks to provide a deterministic behaviour. We will discuss the various types of scheduling in a later section of this chapter.

Task/Process Synchronisation Deals with synchronising the concurrent access of a resource, which is shared across multiple tasks and the communication between various tasks. We will discuss the various synchronisation techniques and inter task /process communication in a later section of this chapter.

Error/Exception Handling Deals with registering and handling the errors occurred/exceptions raised during the execution of tasks. Insufficient memory, timeouts, deadlocks, deadline missing, bus error, divide by zero, unknown instruction execution, etc. are examples of errors/exceptions. Errors/Exceptions can happen at the kernel level services or at task level. *Deadlock* is an example for kernel level exception, whereas *timeout* is an example for a task level exception. The OS kernel gives the information about the error in the form of a system call (API). *GetLastError()* API provided by Windows CE RTOS is an example for such a system call. Watchdog timer is a mechanism for handling the timeouts for tasks. Certain tasks may involve the waiting of external events from devices. These tasks will wait infinitely when the external device is not responding and the task will generate a hang-up behaviour. In order to avoid these types of scenarios, a proper timeout mechanism should be implemented. A watchdog is normally used in such situations. The watchdog will be loaded with the maximum expected wait time for the event and if the event is not triggered within this wait time, the same is informed to the task and the task is timed out. If the event happens before the timeout, the watchdog is resetted.

Memory Management Compared to the General Purpose Operating Systems, the memory management function of an RTOS kernel is slightly different. In general, the memory allocation time increases depending on the size of the block of memory needs to be allocated and the state of the allocated memory block (initialised memory block consumes more allocation time than un-initialised memory block). Since predictable timing and deterministic behaviour are the primary focus of an RTOS, RTOS achieves this by compromising the effectiveness of memory allocation. RTOS makes use of '*block*' based memory allocation technique, instead of the usual dynamic memory allocation techniques used by the GPOS. RTOS kernel uses blocks of fixed size of dynamic memory and the block is allocated for a task on a need basis. The blocks are stored in a '*Free Buffer Queue*'. To achieve predictable timing and avoid the timing overheads, most of the RTOS kernels allow tasks to access any of the memory blocks without any memory protection. RTOS kernels assume that the whole design is proven correct and protection is unnecessary. Some commercial RTOS kernels allow memory protection as optional and the kernel enters a *fail-safe* mode when an illegal memory access occurs.

A few RTOS kernels implement *Virtual Memory*† concept for memory allocation if the system supports secondary memory storage (like HDD and FLASH memory). In the '*block*' based memory allocation, a block of fixed memory is always allocated for tasks on need basis and it is taken as a unit. Hence, there will not be any memory fragmentation issues. The memory allocation can be implemented as constant functions and thereby it consumes fixed amount of time for memory allocation. This leaves the deterministic behaviour of the RTOS kernel untouched. The '*block*' memory concept avoids the garbage collection overhead also. (We will explore this technique under the MicroC/OS-II kernel in a

† *Virtual Memory* is an imaginary memory supported by certain operating systems. Virtual memory expands the address space available to a task beyond the actual physical memory (RAM) supported by the system. Virtual memory is implemented with the help of a Memory Management Unit (MMU) and 'memory paging'. The program memory for a task can be viewed as different pages and the page corresponding to a piece of code that needs to be executed is loaded into the main physical memory (RAM). When a memory page is no longer required, it is moved out to secondary storage memory and another page which contains the code snippet to be executed is loaded into the main memory. This memory movement technique is known as demand paging. The MMU handles the demand paging and converts the virtual address of a location in a page to corresponding physical address in the RAM.

latter chapter).The '*block*' based memory allocation achieves deterministic behaviour with the trade-of limited choice of memory chunk size and suboptimal memory usage.

Interrupt Handling Deals with the handling of various types of interrupts. Interrupts provide Real-Time behaviour to systems. Interrupts inform the processor that an external device or an associated task requires immediate attention of the CPU. Interrupts can be either *Synchronous* or *Asynchronous*. Interrupts which occurs in sync with the currently executing task is known as *Synchronous* interrupts. Usually the software interrupts fall under the Synchronous Interrupt category. Divide by zero, memory segmentation error, etc. are examples of synchronous interrupts. For synchronous interrupts, the interrupt handler runs in the same context of the interrupting task. Asynchronous interrupts are interrupts, which occurs at any point of execution of any task, and are not in sync with the currently executing task. The interrupts generated by external devices (by asserting the interrupt line of the processor/controller to which the interrupt line of the device is connected) connected to the processor/controller, timer overflow interrupts, serial data reception/ transmission interrupts, etc. are examples for asynchronous interrupts. For asynchronous interrupts, the interrupt handler is usually written as separate task (Depends on OS kernel implementation) and it runs in a different context. Hence, a context switch happens while handling the asynchronous interrupts. Priority levels can be assigned to the interrupts and each interrupts can be enabled or disabled individually. Most of the RTOS kernel implements '*Nested Interrupts*' architecture. Interrupt nesting allows the pre-emption (interruption) of an Interrupt Service Routine (ISR), servicing an interrupt, by a high priority interrupt.

Time Management Accurate time management is essential for providing precise time reference for all applications. The time reference to kernel is provided by a high-resolution Real-Time Clock (RTC) hardware chip (hardware timer). The hardware timer is programmed to interrupt the processor/controller at a fixed rate. This timer interrupt is referred as '*Timer tick*'. The '*Timer tick*' is taken as the timing reference by the kernel. The '*Timer tick*' interval may vary depending on the hardware timer. Usually the '*Timer tick*' varies in the microseconds range. The time parameters for tasks are expressed as the multiples of the '*Timer tick*'.

The System time is updated based on the '*Timer tick*'. If the System time register is 32 bits wide and the '*Timer tick*' interval is 1 microsecond, the System time register will reset in

$$2^{32} * 10^{-6} / (24 * 60 * 60) = 49700 \text{ Days} = \sim 0.0497 \text{ Days} = 1.19 \text{ Hours}$$

If the '*Timer tick*' interval is 1 millisecond, the system time register will reset in

$$2^{32} * 10^{-3} / (24 * 60 * 60) = 497 \text{ Days} = 49.7 \text{ Days} = \sim 50 \text{ Days}$$

The '*Timer tick*' interrupt is handled by the 'Timer Interrupt' handler of kernel. The '*Timer tick*' interrupt can be utilised for implementing the following actions.

- Save the current context (Context of the currently executing task).
- Increment the System time register by one. Generate timing error and reset the System time register if the timer tick count is greater than the maximum range available for System time register.
- Update the timers implemented in kernel (Increment or decrement the timer registers for each timer depending on the count direction setting for each register. Increment registers with count direction setting = '*count up*' and decrement registers with count direction setting = '*count down*').
- Activate the periodic tasks, which are in the idle state.
- Invoke the scheduler and schedule the tasks again based on the scheduling algorithm.
- Delete all the terminated tasks and their associated data structures (TCBs)
- Load the context for the first task in the ready queue. Due to the re-scheduling, the ready task might be changed to a new one from the task, which was preempted by the 'Timer Interrupt' task.

Apart from these basic functions, some RTOS provide other functionalities also (Examples are file management and network functions). Some RTOS kernel provides options for selecting the required kernel functions at the time of building a kernel. The user can pick the required functions from the set of available functions and compile the same to generate the kernel binary. Windows CE is a typical example for such an RTOS. While building the target, the user can select the required components for the kernel.

10.2.2.2 Hard Real-Time Real-Time Operating Systems that strictly adhere to the timing constraints for a task is referred as '*Hard Real-Time*' systems. A Hard Real-Time system must meet the deadlines for a task without any slippage. Missing any deadline may produce catastrophic results for Hard Real-Time Systems, including permanent data lose and irrecoverable damages to the system/users. Hard Real-Time systems emphasise the principle '*A late answer is a wrong answer*'. A system can have several such tasks and the key to their correct operation lies in scheduling them so that they meet their time constraints. Air bag control systems and Anti-lock Brake Systems (ABS) of vehicles are typical examples for Hard Real-Time Systems. The Air bag control system should be into action and deploy the air bags when the vehicle meets a severe accident. Ideally speaking, the time for triggering the air bag deployment task, when an accident is sensed by the Air bag control system, should be zero and the air bags should be deployed exactly within the time frame, which is predefined for the air bag deployment task. Any delay in the deployment of the air bags makes the life of the passengers under threat. When the air bag deployment task is triggered, the currently executing task must be pre-empted, the air bag deployment task should be brought into execution, and the necessary I/O systems should be made readily available for the air bag deployment task. To meet the strict deadline, the time between the air bag deployment event triggering and start of the air bag deployment task execution should be minimum, ideally zero. As a rule of thumb, Hard Real-Time Systems does not implement the virtual memory model for handling the memory. This eliminates the delay in swapping in and out the code corresponding to the task to and from the primary memory. In general, the presence of *Human in the loop* (*HITL*) for tasks introduces unexpected delays in the task execution. Most of the Hard Real-Time Systems are automatic and does not contain a 'human in the loop'.

10.2.2.3 Soft Real-Time Real-Time Operating System that does not guarantee meeting deadlines, but offer the best effort to meet the deadline are referred as '*Soft Real-Time*' systems. Missing deadlines for tasks are acceptable for a Soft Real-time system if the frequency of deadline missing is within the compliance limit of the Quality of Service (QoS). A Soft Real-Time system emphasises the principle '*A late answer is an acceptable answer, but it could have done bit faster*'. Soft Real-Time systems most often have a '*human in the loop (HITL)*'. Automatic Teller Machine (ATM) is a typical example for Soft-Real-Time System. If the ATM takes a few seconds more than the ideal operation time, nothing fatal happens. An audio-video playback system is another example for Soft Real-Time system. No potential damage arises if a sample comes late by fraction of a second, for playback.

10.3 TASKS, PROCESS AND THREADS

The term '*task*' refers to something that needs to be done. In our day-to-day life, we are bound to the execution of a number of tasks. The task can be the one assigned by our managers or the one assigned by our professors/teachers or the one related to our personal or family needs. In addition, we will have an order of priority and schedule/timeline for executing these tasks. In the operating system context, a task is defined as the program in execution and the related information maintained by the operating system for the program. Task is also known as '*Job*' in the operating system context. A program or part of it in execution is also called a '*Process*'. The terms '*Task*', '*Job*' and '*Process*' refer to the same entity in the operating system context and most often they are used interchangeably.

10.3.1 Process

A '*Process*' is a program, or part of it, in execution. Process is also known as an instance of a program in execution. Multiple instances of the same program can execute simultaneously. A process requires various system resources like CPU for executing the process, memory for storing the code corresponding to the process and associated variables, I/O devices for information exchange, etc. A process is sequential in execution.

10.3.1.1 The Structure of a Process The concept of '*Process*' leads to concurrent execution (pseudo parallelism) of tasks and thereby the efficient utilisation of the CPU and other system resources. Concurrent execution is achieved through the sharing of CPU among the processes. A process mimics a processor in properties and holds a set of registers, process status, a Program Counter (PC) to point to the next executable instruction of the process, a stack for holding the local variables associated with the process and the code corresponding to the process. This can be visualised as shown in Fig. 10.4.

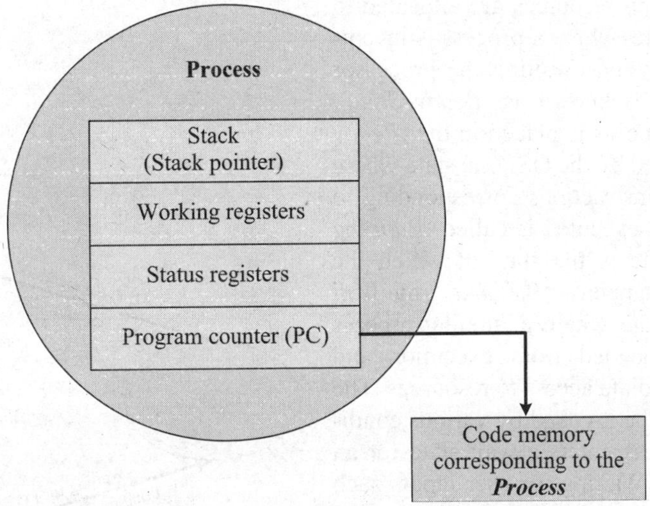

Fig. 10.4 **Structure of a *Process***

A process which inherits all the properties of the CPU can be considered as a virtual processor, awaiting its turn to have its properties switched into the physical processor. When the process gets its turn, its registers and the program counter register becomes mapped to the physical registers of the CPU. From a memory perspective, the memory occupied by the *process* is segregated into three regions, namely, Stack memory, Data memory and Code memory (Fig. 10.5).

The 'Stack' memory holds all temporary data such as variables local to the process. Data memory holds all global data for the process. The code memory contains the program code (instructions) corresponding to the process. On loading a process into the main memory, a specific area of memory is allocated for the process. The stack memory usually starts (OS Kernel implementation dependent) at the highest memory address from the memory area allocated for the process. Say for example, the memory map of the memory area allocated for the process is 2048 to 2100, the stack memory starts at address 2100 and grows downwards to accommodate the variables local to the process.

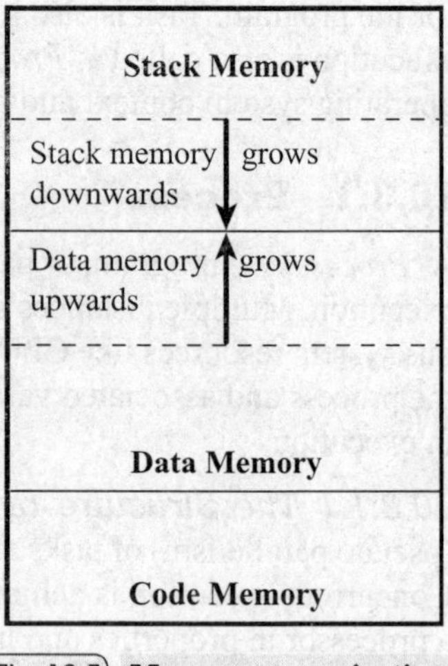

Fig. 10.5 **Memory organisation of a *Process***

10.3.1.2 Process States and State Transition The creation of a process to its termination is not a single step operation. The process traverses through a series of states during its transition from the newly created state to the terminated state. The cycle through which a process changes its state from '*newly created*' to '*execution completed*' is known as '*Process Life Cycle*'. The various states through which a process traverses through during a Process Life Cycle indicates the current status of the process with respect to time and also provides information on what it is allowed to do next. Figure 10.6 represents the various states associated with a process.

The state at which a process is being created is referred as 'Created State'. The Operating System recognises a process in the '*Created State*' but no resources are allocated to the process. The state, where a process is incepted into the memory and awaiting the processor time for execution, is known as '*Ready State*'. At this stage, the process is placed in the '*Ready list*' queue maintained by the OS. The state where in the source code instructions corresponding to the process is being executed is called '*Running State*'. Running state is the state at which the process execution happens. '*Blocked State/Wait State*' refers to a state where a running process is temporarily suspended from execution and does not have immediate access to resources. The blocked state might be invoked by various conditions like: the process enters a wait state for an event to occur (e.g. Waiting for user inputs such as keyboard input) or waiting for getting access to a shared resource (will be discussed at a later section of this chapter). A state where the process completes its execution is known as '*Completed State*'. The transition of a process from one state to another is known as '*State transition*'. When a process changes its state from Ready to running or from running to blocked or terminated or from blocked to running, the CPU allocation for the process may also change.

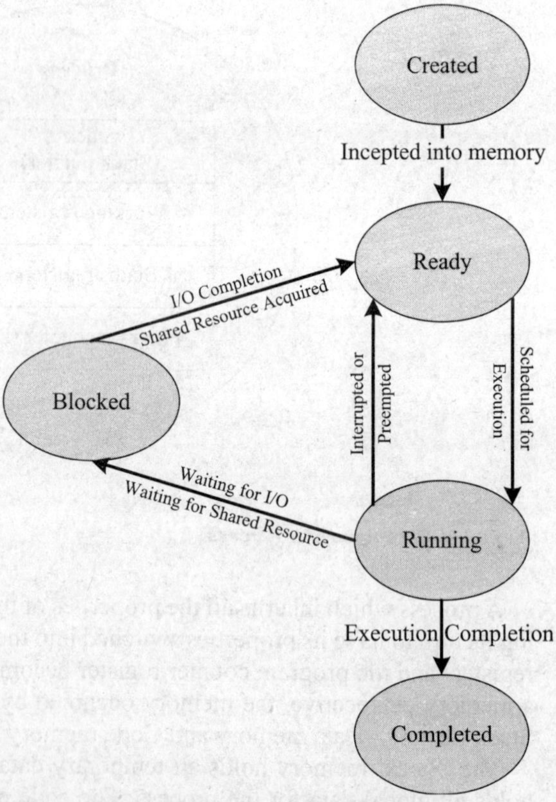

Fig. 10.6 **Process states and state transition representation**

It should be noted that the state representation for a process/task mentioned here is a generic representation. The states associated with a task may be known with a different name or there may be more or less number of states than the one explained here under different OS kernel. For example, under VxWorks' kernel, the tasks may be in either one or a specific combination of the states READY, PEND, DELAY and SUSPEND. The PEND state represents a state where the task/process is blocked on waiting for I/O or system resource. The DELAY state represents a state in which the task/process is sleeping and the SUSPEND state represents a state where a task/process is temporarily suspended from execution and not available for execution. Under MicroC/OS-II kernel, the tasks may be in one of the states, DORMANT, READY, RUNNING, WAITING or INTERRUPTED. The DORMANT state represents the 'Created' state and WAITING state represents the state in which a process waits for shared resource or I/O access. We will discuss about the states and state transition for tasks under VxWorks and uC/OS-II kernel in a later chapter.

10.3.1.3 Process Management Process management deals with the creation of a process, setting up the memory space for the process, loading the process's code into the memory space, allocating system resources, setting up a Process Control Block (PCB) for the process and process termination/deletion. For more details on Process Management, refer to the section 'Task/Process management' given under the topic 'The Real-Time Kernel' of this chapter.

10.3.2 Threads

A *thread* is the primitive that can execute code. A *thread* is a single sequential flow of control within a process. '*Thread*' is also known as lightweight process. A process can have many threads of execution. Different threads, which are part of a process, share the same address space; meaning they share the data memory, code memory and heap memory area. Threads maintain their own thread status (CPU register values), Program Counter (PC) and stack. The memory model for a process and its associated threads are given in Fig. 10.7.

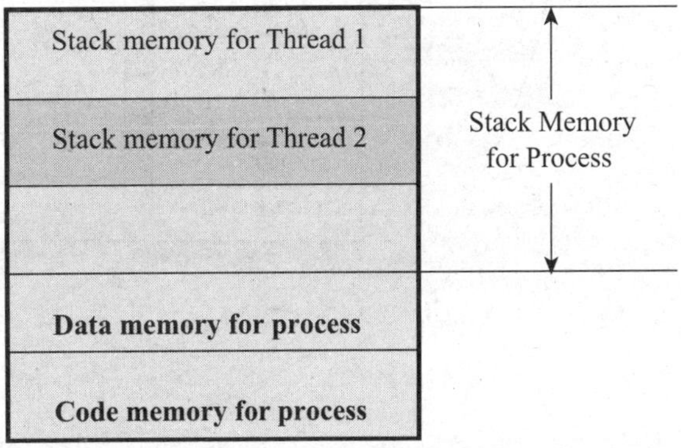

Fig. 10.7 **Memory organisation of a *Process* and its associated *Threads***

10.3.2.1 The Concept of Multithreading A process/task in embedded application may be a complex or lengthy one and it may contain various suboperations like getting input from I/O devices connected to the processor, performing some internal calculations/operations, updating some I/O devices etc. If all the subfunctions of a task are executed in sequence, the CPU utilisation may not be efficient. For example, if the process is waiting for a user input, the CPU enters the wait state for the event, and the process execution also enters a wait state. Instead of this single sequential execution of the whole process, if the task/process is split into different threads carrying out the different subfunctionalities of the process, the CPU can be effectively utilised and when the thread corresponding to the I/O operation enters the wait state, another threads which do not require the I/O event for their operation can be switched into execution. This leads to more speedy execution of the process and the efficient utilisation of the processor time and resources. The multithreaded architecture of a process can be better visualised with the thread-process diagram shown in Fig. 10.8.

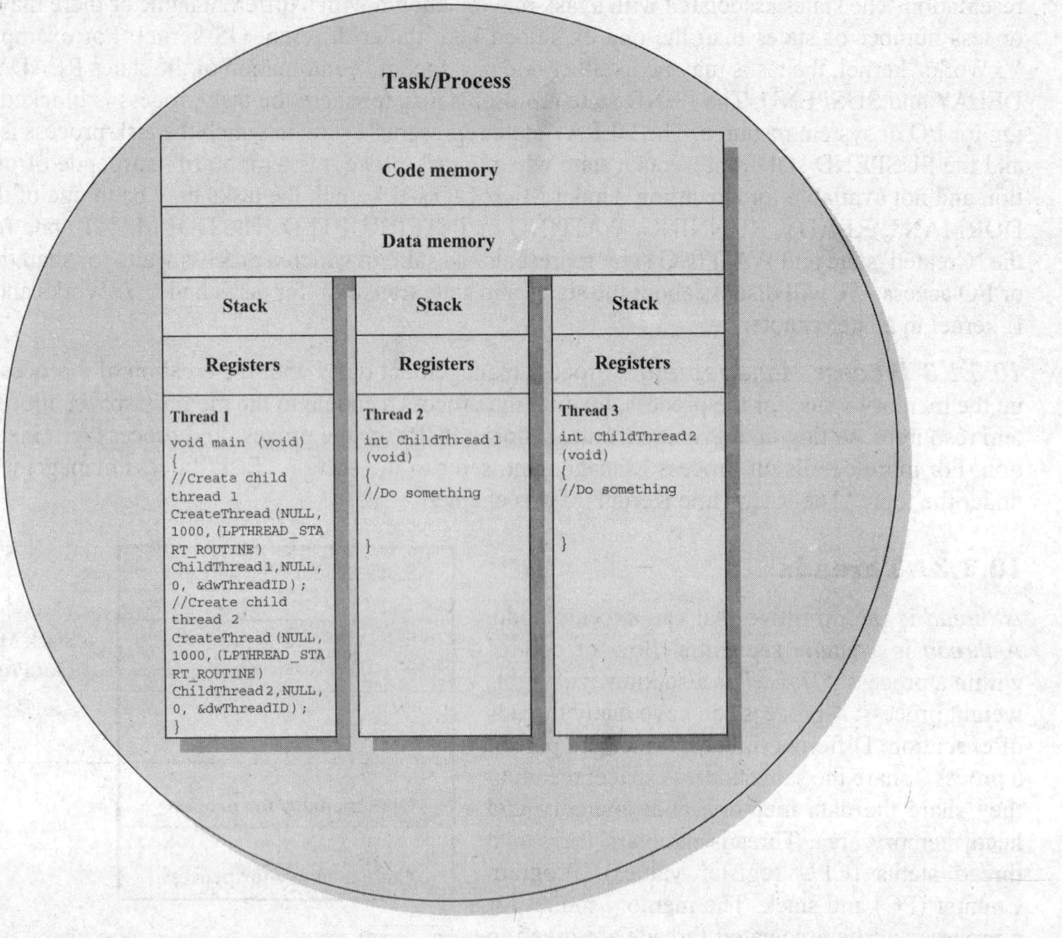

Fig. 10.8 ***Process* with multi-threads**

If the process is split into multiple threads, which executes a portion of the process, there will be a main thread and rest of the threads will be created within the main thread. Use of multiple threads to execute a process brings the following advantage.

- Better memory utilisation. Multiple threads of the same process share the address space for data memory. This also reduces the complexity of inter thread communication since variables can be shared across the threads.
- Since the process is split into different threads, when one thread enters a wait state, the CPU can be utilised by other threads of the process that do not require the event, which the other thread is waiting, for processing. This speeds up the execution of the process.
- Efficient CPU utilisation. The CPU is engaged all time.

10.3.2.2 Thread Standards Thread standards deal with the different standards available for thread creation and management. These standards are utilised by the operating systems for thread creation and thread management. It is a set of thread class libraries. The commonly available thread class libraries are explained below.

POSIX Threads: POSIX stands for Portable Operating System Interface. The *POSIX.4* standard deals with the Real-Time extensions and *POSIX.4a* standard deals with thread extensions. The POSIX standard library for thread creation and management is '*Pthreads*'. '*Pthreads*' library defines the set of POSIX thread creation and management functions in 'C' language.

The primitive

```
int pthread_create(pthread_t *new_thread_ID, const pthread_attr_t *attribute,
void * (*start_function)(void *), void *arguments);
```

creates a new thread for running the function *start_function*. Here *pthread_t* is the handle to the newly created thread and *pthread_attr_t* is the data type for holding the thread attributes. '*start_function*' is the function the thread is going to execute and *arguments* is the arguments for '*start_function*' (It is a void * in the above example). On successful creation of a *Pthread*, *pthread_create()* associates the Thread Control Block (TCB) corresponding to the newly created thread to the variable of type *pthread_t* (*new_thread_ID* in our example).

The primitive

```
int pthread_join(pthread_t new_thread,void * *thread_status);
```

blocks the current thread and waits until the completion of the thread pointed by it (In this example *new_thread*)

All the POSIX 'thread calls' returns an integer. A return value of zero indicates the success of the call. It is always good to check the return value of each call.

Example 1

Write a multithreaded application to print "Hello I'm in main thread" from the main thread and "Hello I'm in new thread" 5 times each, using the *pthread_create()* and *pthread_join()* POSIX primitives.

```
//Assumes the application is running on an OS where POSIX library is
//available
#include <pthread.h>
#include <stdlib.h>
#include <stdio.h>
//*****************************************************************
//New thread function for printing "Hello I'm in new thread"
void *new_thread( void *thread_args )
{
  int i, j;
  for( j= 0; j < 5; j++ )
   {
    printf("Hello I'm in new thread\n" );
    //Wait for some time. Do nothing
    //The following line of code can be replaced with
    //OS supported delay function like sleep(), delay () etc...
    for( i= 0; i < 10000; i++ );
   }
  return NULL;
}
```

```
//*****************************************************************
//Start of main thread
int main( void )
{
  int i, j;
  pthread_t tcb;
//Create the new thread for executing new_thread function
  if (pthread_create( &tcb, NULL, new_thread, NULL ))
    {
      //New thread creation failed
      printf("Error in creating new thread\n" );
      return -1;
    }
  for( j= 0; j < 5; j++ )
   {
    printf("Hello I'm in main thread\n" );
    //Wait for some time. Do nothing
    //The following line of code can be replaced with
    //OS supported delay function like sleep(), delay etc…
    for( i= 0; i < 10000; i++ );
   }
  if (pthread_join(tcb, NULL ))
    {
      //Thread join failed
      printf("Error in Thread join\n" );
      return -1;
    }
  return 1;
}
```

You can compile this application using the *gcc* compiler. Examine the output to figure out the thread execution switching. The lines printed will give an idea of the order in which the thread execution is switched between. The *pthread_join* call forces the main thread to wait until the completion of the thread *tcb*, if the main thread finishes the execution first.

The termination of a thread can happen in different ways. The thread can terminate either by completing its execution (natural termination) or by a forced termination. In a natural termination, the thread completes its execution and returns back to the main thread through a simple *return* or by executing the *pthread_exit()* call. Forced termination can be achieved by the call *pthread_cancel()* or through the termination of the main thread with *exit* or *exec* functions. *pthread_cancel()* call is used by a thread to terminate another thread.

pthread_exit() call is used by a thread to explicitly exit after it completes its work and is no longer required to exist. If the main thread finishes before the threads it has created, and exits with *pthread_exit()*, the other threads continue to execute. If the main thread uses *exit* call to exit the thread, all threads created by the main thread is terminated forcefully. Exiting a thread with the call *pthread_exit()* will not perform a cleanup. It will not close any files opened by the thread and files will remain in the open status even after the thread terminates. Calling *pthread_join* at the end of the main thread is the best way to achieve synchronisation and proper cleanup. The main thread, after finishing its task waits for the completion of other threads, which were joined to it using the *pthread_join* call. With a *pthread_join* call, the main thread waits other threads, which were joined to it, and finally merges to the single main thread. If a new thread spawned by the main thread is still not joined to the main thread, it will be counted against the system's maximum thread limit. Improper cleanup will lead to the failure of new thread creation.

Win32 Threads Win32 threads are the threads supported by various flavours of Windows Operating Systems. The Win32 Application Programming Interface (Win32 API) libraries provide the standard set of Win32 thread creation and management functions. Win32 threads are created with the API

```
HANDLE  CreateThread(LPSECURITY_ATTRIBUTES  lpThreadAttributes,DWORD  dwStack-
Size, LPTHREAD_START_ROUTINE lpStartAddress, LPVOID lpParameter, DWORD dwCre-
ationFlags, LPDWORD lpThreadId );
```

The parameter *lpThreadAttributes* defines the security attributes for the thread and *dwStackSize* defines the stack size for the thread. These two parameters are not supported by the Windows CE Real-Time Operating Systems and it should be kept as NULL and 0 respectively in a *CreateThread* API Call. The other parameters are

lpStartAddress: Pointer to the function which is to be executed by the thread.

lpParameter: Parameter specifying an application-defined value that is passed to the thread routine.

dwCreationFlags: Defines the state of the thread when it is created. Usually it is kept as 0 or CREATE_SUSPENDED implying the thread is created and kept at the suspended state.

lpThreadId: Pointer to a DWORD that receives the identifier for the thread.

On successful creation of the thread, *CreateThread* returns the handle to the thread and the thread identifier.

The API *GetCurrentThread(void)* returns the handle of the current thread and *GetCurrentThreadId(void)* returns its ID. *GetThreadPriority (HANDLE hThread)* API returns an integer value representing the current priority of the thread whose handle is passed as *hThread*. Threads are always created with normal priority (THREAD_PRIORITY_NORMAL. Refer MSDN documentation for the different thread priorities and their meaning). *SetThreadPriority (HANDLE hThread, int nPriority)* API is used for setting the priority of a thread. The first parameter to this function represents the thread handle and the second one the thread priority.

For Win32 threads, the normal thread termination happens when an exception occurs in the thread, or when the thread's execution is completed or when the primary thread or the process to which the thread is associated is terminated. A thread can exit itself by calling the *ExitThread (DWORD dwExitCode)* API. The parameter *dwExitCode* sets the exit code for thread termination. Calling *ExitThread* API frees all the resources utilised by the thread. The exit code of a thread can be checked by other threads by calling the *GetExitCodeThread (HANDLE hThread, LPDWORD lpExitCode)*. *TerminateThread (HANDLE hThread, DWORD dwExitCode)* API is used for terminating a thread from another thread. The handle *hThread* indicates which thread is to be terminated and *dwExitCode* sets the exit code for the thread. This API will not execute the thread termination and clean up code and may not free the resources occupied by the thread. *TerminateThread* is a potentially dangerous call and it should not be used in normal conditions as a mechanism for terminating a thread. Use this call only as a final choice. *SuspendThread(HANDLE hThread)* API can be used for suspending a thread from execution provided the *handle hThread* possesses *THREAD_SUSPEND_RESUME* access right. If the *SuspendThread* API call succeeds, the thread stops executing and increments its internal suspend count. The thread becomes suspended if its suspend count is greater than zero. The *SuspendThread* function is primarily designed for use by debuggers. One must be cautious in using this API for the reason it may cause *deadlock* condition if the thread is suspended at a stage where it acquired a mutex or shared resource and another thread tries to access the same. The *ResumeThread(HANDLE hThread)* API is used for resuming a suspended thread. The *ResumeThread* API checks the suspend count of the specified thread. A suspend count of zero indicates that the specified thread is not currently in the suspended mode. If the count is not zero, the count is decremented by one and if the resulting count value is zero, the thread is resumed. The API *Sleep (DWORD dwMilliseconds)* can be used for suspending a thread for the duration specified in milliseconds by the *Sleep* function. The *Sleep* call is initiated by the thread.

Example 2

Write a multithreaded application using Win32 APIs to set up a counter in the main thread and secondary thread to count from 0 to 10 and print the counts from both the threads. Put a delay of 500 ms in between the successive printing in both the threads.

```
#include "windows.h"
#include "stdio.h"
//*******************************************************************
//Child thread
//*******************************************************************
void ChildThread(void)
    {
    char i;
    for(i=0;i<=10;++i)
        {
        printf("Executing Child Thread:Counter = %d\n",i);
        Sleep(500);
        }
    }
//*******************************************************************
//Primary thread
//*******************************************************************
int main(int argc, char* argv[])
{
       HANDLE hThread;
       DWORD dwThreadID;
       char i;
       hThread=CreateThread(NULL,1000,(LPTHREAD_START_ROUTINE)
       ChildThread, NULL, 0, &dwThreadID);
    if(hThread==NULL)
       {
       printf("Thread Creation Failed\nError No:
       %d\n",GetLastError());
       return 1;
       }
        for(i=0;i<=10;++i)
        {
        printf("Executing Main Thread: Counter = %d\n",i);
        Sleep(500);
        }
    return 0;
}
```

To execute this program, create a new Win32 Console Application using Microsoft Visual C++ and add the above piece of code to it and compile. The output obtained on running this application on a machine with Windows XP operating system is given in Fig. 10.9.

If you examine the output, you can see the switching between main and child threads. The output need not be the same always. The output is purely dependent on the scheduling policies implemented by the windows operating system for thread scheduling. You may get the same output or a different output each time you run the application.

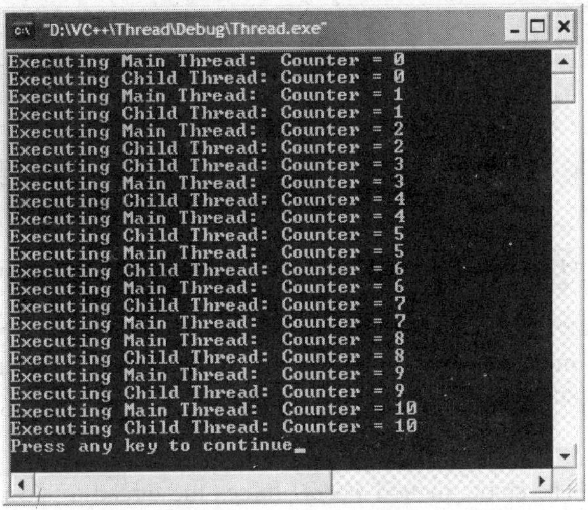

Fig. 10.9 **Output of the Win32 Multithreaded application**

Java Threads Java threads are the threads supported by Java programming Language. The java thread class '*Thread*' is defined in the package '*java.lang*'. This package needs to be imported for using the thread creation functions supported by the Java thread class. There are two ways of creating threads in Java: Either by extending the base '*Thread*' class or by implementing an interface. Extending the thread class allows inheriting the methods and variables of the parent class (Thread class) only whereas interface allows a way to achieve the requirements for a set of classes. The following piece of code illustrates the implementation of Java threads with extending the thread base class '*Thread*'.

```
import java.lang.*;
public class MyThread extends Thread
{
      public void run()
      {
            System.out.println("Hello from MyThread!");
      }
      public static void main(String args[])
      {
            (new MyThread()).start();
      }
}
```

The above piece of code creates a new class *MyThread* by extending the base class *Thread*. It also overrides the *run()* method inherited from the base class with its own *run()* method. The *run()* method of *MyThread* implements all the task for the *MyThread* thread. The method *start()* moves the thread to a pool of threads waiting for their turn to be picked up for execution by the scheduler. The thread is said to be in the 'Ready' state at this stage. The scheduler picks the threads for execution from the pool based on the thread priorities.

```
E.g.  MyThread.start();
```

The output of the above piece of code when executed on Windows XP platform is given in Fig. 10.10.

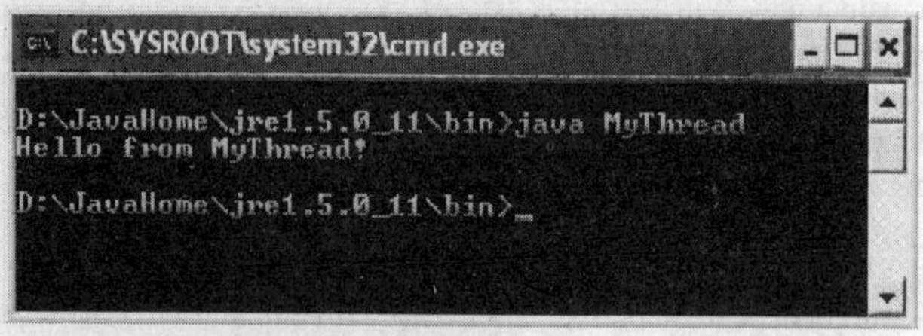

Fig. 10.10 **Output of the Java Multithreaded application**

Invoking the static method *yield()* voluntarily give up the execution of the thread and the thread is moved to the pool of threads waiting to get their turn for execution, i.e. the thread enters the 'Ready' state.

```
E.g.  MyThread.yield();
```

The static method *sleep()* forces the thread to sleep for the duration mentioned by the sleep call, i.e. the thread enters the 'Suspend' mode. Once the sleep period is expired, the thread is moved to the pool of threads waiting to get their turn for execution, i.e. the thread enters the 'Ready' state. The method *sleep()* only guarantees that the thread will sleep for the minimum period mentioned by the argument to the call. It will not guarantee anything on the resume of the thread after the sleep period. It is dependent on the scheduler.

```
E.g.  MyThread.sleep(100); Sleep for 100 milliseconds.
```

Calling a thread Object's *wait()* method causes the thread object to wait. The thread will remain in the 'Wait' state until another thread invokes the *notify()* or *notifyAll()* method of the thread object which is waiting. The thread enters the 'Blocked' state when waiting for input from I/O devices or waiting for object lock in case of accessing shared resources. The thread is moved to the 'Ready' state on receiving the I/O input or on acquiring the object lock. The thread enters the 'Finished/Dead' state on completion of the task assigned to it or when the *stop()* method is explicitly invoked. The thread may also enter this state if it is terminated by an unrecoverable error condition.

For more information on Java threads, visit Sun Micro System's tutorial on Threads, available at http://java.sun.com/tutorial/applet/overview/threads.html

Summary So far we discussed about the various thread classes available for creation and management of threads in a multithreaded system in a General Purpose Operating System's perspective. From an RTOS perspective, POSIX threads and Win32 threads are the most commonly used thread class libraries for thread creation and management. Many non-standard, proprietary thread classes are also used by some proprietary RTOS. Portable threads (*Pth*), a very portable POSIX/ANSI-C based library from GNU, may be the "next generation" threads library. *Pth* provides non-preemptive priority based scheduling for multiple threads inside event driven applications. Visit http://www.gnu.org/software/pth/ for more details on GNU Portable threads.

10.3.2.3 Thread Pre-emption Thread pre-emption is the act of pre-empting the currently running thread (stopping the currently running thread temporarily). Thread pre-emption ability is solely dependent on the Operating System. Thread pre-emption is performed for sharing the CPU time among all the threads. The execution switching among threads are known as '*Thread context switching*'. Thread context switching is dependent on the Operating system's scheduler and the type of the thread. When we say 'Thread', it falls into any one of the following types.

User Level Thread User level threads do not have kernel/Operating System support and they exist solely in the running process. Even if a process contains multiple user level threads, the OS treats it as single thread and will not switch the execution among the different threads of it. It is the responsibility of the process to schedule each thread as and when required. In summary, user level threads of a process are non-preemptive at thread level from OS perspective.

Kernel/System Level Thread Kernel level threads are individual units of execution, which the OS treats as separate threads. The OS interrupts the execution of the currently running kernel thread and switches the execution to another kernel thread based on the scheduling policies implemented by the OS. In summary kernel level threads are pre-emptive.

For user level threads, the execution switching (thread context switching) happens only when the currently executing user level thread is voluntarily blocked. Hence, no OS intervention and system calls are involved in the context switching of user level threads. This makes context switching of user level threads very fast. On the other hand, kernel level threads involve lots of kernel overhead and involve system calls for context switching. However, kernel threads maintain a clear layer of abstraction and allow threads to use system calls independently. There are many ways for binding user level threads with system/kernel level threads. The following section gives an overview of various thread binding models.

Many-to-One Model Here many user level threads are mapped to a single kernel thread. In this model, the kernel treats all user level threads as single thread and the execution switching among the user level threads happens when a currently executing user level thread voluntarily blocks itself or relinquishes the CPU. Solaris Green threads and GNU Portable Threads are examples for this. The '*PThread*' example given under the POSIX thread library section is an illustrative example for application with Many-to-One thread model.

One-to-One Model In One-to-One model, each user level thread is bonded to a kernel/system level thread. Windows XP/NT/2000 and Linux threads are examples for One-to-One thread models. The modified '*PThread*' example given under the '*Thread Pre-emption*' section is an illustrative example for application with One-to-One thread model.

Many-to-Many Model In this model many user level threads are allowed to be mapped to many kernel threads. Windows NT/2000 with *ThreadFibre* package is an example for this.

10.3.2.4 Thread v/s Process I hope, by now you got a reasonably good knowledge of *process* and *threads*. Now let us summarise the properties of *process* and *threads*.

Thread	Process
Thread is a single unit of execution and is part of process.	Process is a program in execution and contains one or more threads.
A thread does not have its own data memory and heap memory. It shares the data memory and heap memory with other threads of the same process.	Process has its own code memory, data memory and stack memory.
A thread cannot live independently; it lives within the process.	A process contains at least one thread.
There can be multiple threads in a process. The first thread (main thread) calls the main function and occupies the start of the stack memory of the process.	Threads within a process share the code, data and heap memory. Each thread holds separate memory area for stack (shares the total stack memory of the process).

Threads are very inexpensive to create	Processes are very expensive to create. Involves many OS overhead.
Context switching is inexpensive and fast	Context switching is complex and involves lot of OS overhead and is comparatively slower.
If a thread expires, its stack is reclaimed by the process.	If a process dies, the resources allocated to it are reclaimed by the OS and all the associated threads of the process also dies.

10.4 MULTIPROCESSING AND MULTITASKING

The terms *multiprocessing* and *multitasking* are a little confusing and sounds alike. In the operating system context *multiprocessing* describes the ability to execute multiple processes simultaneously. Systems which are capable of performing multiprocessing, are known as *multiprocessor* systems. *Multiprocessor* systems possess multiple CPUs and can execute multiple processes simultaneously.

The ability of the operating system to have multiple programs in memory, which are ready for execution, is referred as *multiprogramming*. In a uniprocessor system, it is not possible to execute multiple processes simultaneously. However, it is possible for a uniprocessor system to achieve some degree of pseudo parallelism in the execution of multiple processes by switching the execution among different processes. The ability of an operating system to hold multiple processes in memory and switch the processor (CPU) from executing one process to another process is known as *multitasking*. Multitasking creates the illusion of multiple tasks executing in parallel. Multitasking involves the switching of CPU from executing one task to another. In an earlier section '*The Structure of a Process*' of this chapter, we learned that a Process is identical to the physical processor in the sense it has own register set which mirrors the CPU registers, stack and Program Counter (PC). Hence, a '*process*' is considered as a '*Virtual processor*', awaiting its turn to have its properties switched into the physical processor. In a multitasking environment, when task/process switching happens, the virtual processor (task/process) gets its properties converted into that of the physical processor. The switching of the virtual processor to physical processor is controlled by the scheduler of the OS kernel. Whenever a CPU switching happens, the current context of execution should be saved to retrieve it at a later point of time when the CPU executes the process, which is interrupted currently due to execution switching. The context saving and retrieval is essential for resuming a process exactly from the point where it was interrupted due to CPU switching. The act of switching CPU among the processes or changing the current execution context is known as '*Context switching*'. The act of saving the current context which contains the context details (Register details, memory details, system resource usage details, execution details, etc.) for the currently running process at the time of CPU switching is known as '*Context saving*'. The process of retrieving the saved context details for a process, which is going to be executed due to CPU switching, is known as '*Context retrieval*'. Multitasking involves '*Context switching*' (Fig. 10.11), '*Context saving*' and '*Context retrieval*'.

Toss juggling – The skilful object manipulation game is a classic real world example for the multitasking illusion. The juggler uses a number of objects (balls, rings, etc.) and throws them up and catches them. At any point of time, he throws only one ball and catches only one per hand. However, the speed at which he is switching the balls for throwing and catching creates the illusion, he is throwing and catching multiple balls or using more than two hands ☺ simultaneously, to the spectators.

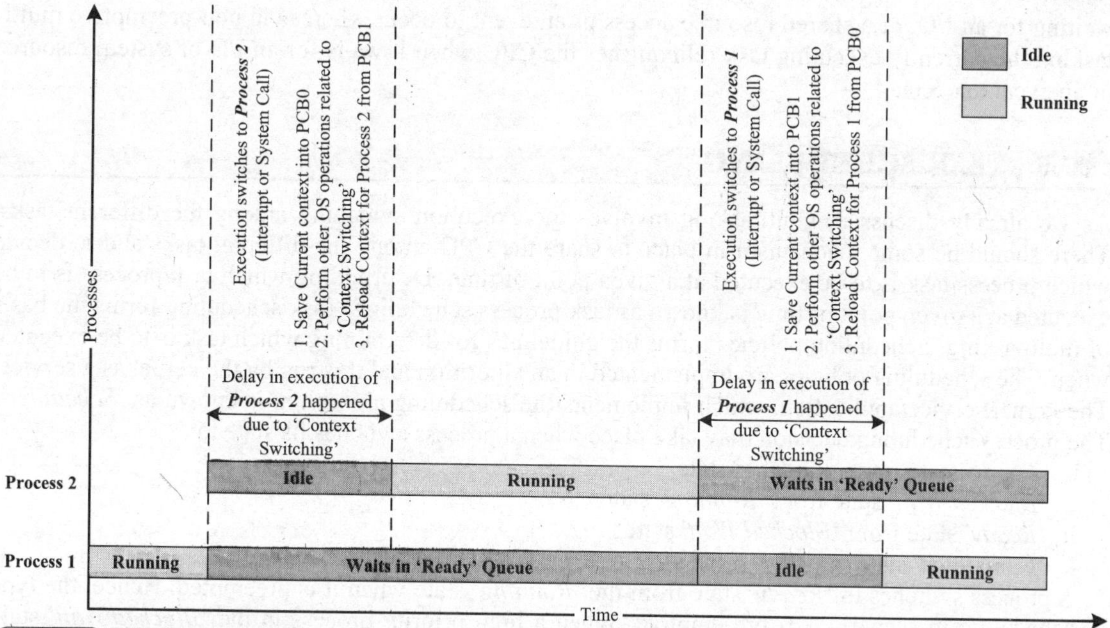

Fig. 10.11 **Context switching**

10.4.1 Types of Multitasking

As we discussed earlier, multitasking involves the switching of execution among multiple tasks. Depending on how the switching act is implemented, multitasking can be classified into different types. The following section describes the various types of multitasking existing in the Operating System's context.

10.4.1.1 Co-operative Multitasking Co-operative multitasking is the most primitive form of multitasking in which a task/process gets a chance to execute only when the currently executing task/process voluntarily relinquishes the CPU. In this method, any task/process can hold the CPU as much time as it wants. Since this type of implementation involves the mercy of the tasks each other for getting the CPU time for execution, it is known as co-operative multitasking. If the currently executing task is non-cooperative, the other tasks may have to wait for a long time to get the CPU.

10.4.1.2 Preemptive Multitasking Preemptive multitasking ensures that every task/process gets a chance to execute. When and how much time a process gets is dependent on the implementation of the preemptive scheduling. As the name indicates, in preemptive multitasking, the currently running task/process is preempted to give a chance to other tasks/process to execute. The preemption of task may be based on time slots or task/process priority.

10.4.1.3 Non-preemptive Multitasking In non-preemptive multitasking, the process/task, which is currently given the CPU time, is allowed to execute until it terminates (enters the '*Completed*' state) or enters the '*Blocked/Wait*' state, waiting for an I/O or system resource. The co-operative and non-preemptive multitasking differs in their behaviour when they are in the '*Blocked/Wait*' state. In co-operative multitasking, the currently executing process/task need not relinquish the CPU when it enters the '*Blocked/Wait*' state, waiting for an I/O, or a shared resource access or an event to occur whereas in non-preemptive multitasking the currently executing task relinquishes the CPU when it waits for an I/O or system resource or an event to occur.

10.5 TASK SCHEDULING

As we already discussed, multitasking involves the execution switching among the different tasks. There should be some mechanism in place to share the CPU among the different tasks and to decide which process/task is to be executed at a given point of time. Determining which task/process is to be executed at a given point of time is known as task/process scheduling. Task scheduling forms the basis of multitasking. Scheduling policies forms the guidelines for determining which task is to be executed when. The scheduling policies are implemented in an algorithm and it is run by the kernel as a service. The kernel service/application, which implements the scheduling algorithm, is known as '*Scheduler*'. The process scheduling decision may take place when a process switches its state to

1. '*Ready*' state from '*Running*' state
2. '*Blocked/Wait*' state from '*Running*' state
3. '*Ready*' state from '*Blocked/Wait*' state
4. '*Completed*' state

A process switches to '*Ready*' state from the '*Running*' state when it is preempted. Hence, the type of scheduling in scenario 1 is pre-emptive. When a high priority process in the '*Blocked/Wait*' state completes its I/O and switches to the '*Ready*' state, the scheduler picks it for execution if the scheduling policy used is priority based preemptive. This is indicated by scenario 3. In preemptive/non-preemptive multitasking, the process relinquishes the CPU when it enters the '*Blocked/Wait*' state or the '*Completed*' state and switching of the CPU happens at this stage. Scheduling under scenario 2 can be either preemptive or non-preemptive. Scheduling under scenario 4 can be preemptive, non-preemptive or co-operative.

The selection of a scheduling criterion/algorithm should consider the following factors:

CPU Utilisation: The scheduling algorithm should always make the CPU utilisation high. CPU utilisation is a direct measure of how much percentage of the CPU is being utilised.

Throughput: This gives an indication of the number of processes executed per unit of time. The throughput for a good scheduler should always be higher.

Turnaround Time: It is the amount of time taken by a process for completing its execution. It includes the time spent by the process for waiting for the main memory, time spent in the ready queue, time spent on completing the I/O operations, and the time spent in execution. The turnaround time should be a minimal for a good scheduling algorithm.

Waiting Time: It is the amount of time spent by a process in the '*Ready*' queue waiting to get the CPU time for execution. The waiting time should be minimal for a good scheduling algorithm.

Response Time: It is the time elapsed between the submission of a process and the first response. For a good scheduling algorithm, the response time should be as least as possible.

> To summarise, a good scheduling algorithm has high CPU utilisation, minimum Turn Around Time (TAT), maximum throughput and least response time.

The Operating System maintains various queues† in connection with the CPU scheduling, and a process passes through these queues during the course of its admittance to execution completion.

† Queue is a special kind of arrangement of a collection of objects. In the operating system context queue is considered as a buffer.

The various queues maintained by OS in association with CPU scheduling are:

Job Queue: Job queue contains all the processes in the system

Ready Queue: Contains all the processes, which are ready for execution and waiting for CPU to get their turn for execution. The Ready queue is empty when there is no process ready for running.

Device Queue: Contains the set of processes, which are waiting for an I/O device.

A process migrates through all these queues during its journey from '*Admitted*' to '*Completed*' stage. The following diagrammatic representation (Fig. 10.12) illustrates the transition of a process through the various queues.

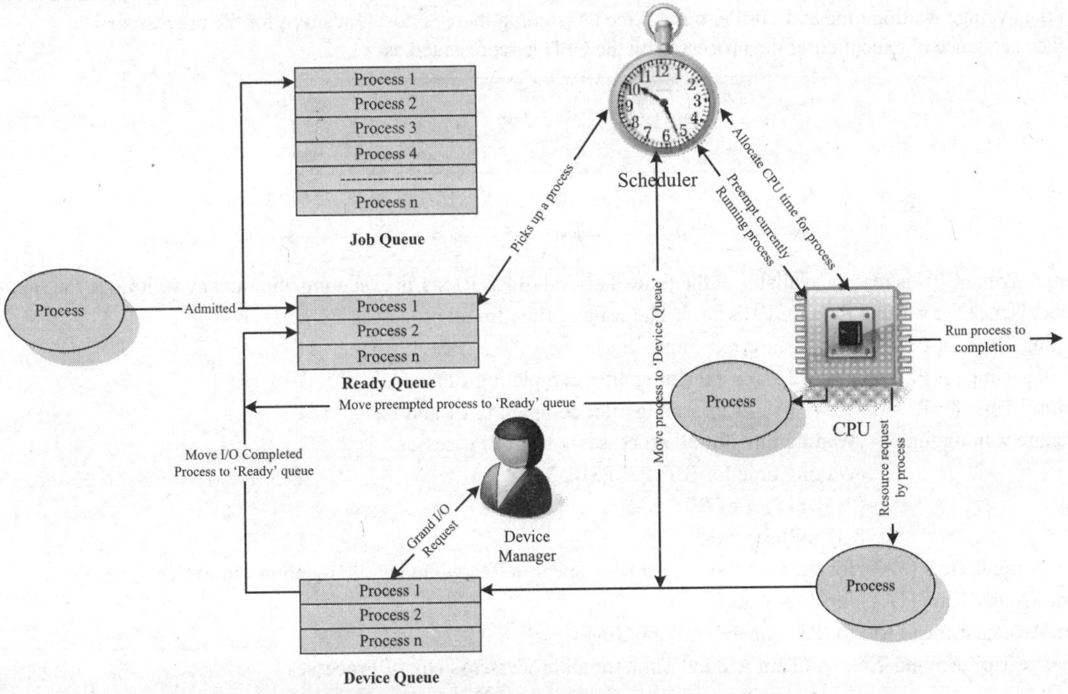

Fig. 10.12 **Illustration of process transition through various queues**

Based on the scheduling algorithm used, the scheduling can be classified into the following categories.

10.5.1 Non-preemptive Scheduling

Non-preemptive scheduling is employed in systems, which implement non-preemptive multitasking model. In this scheduling type, the currently executing task/process is allowed to run until it terminates or enters the '*Wait*' state waiting for an I/O or system resource. The various types of non-preemptive scheduling adopted in task/process scheduling are listed below.

10.5.1.1 First-Come-First-Served (FCFS)/ FIFO Scheduling As the name indicates, the First-Come-First-Served (FCFS) scheduling algorithm allocates CPU time to the processes based on the order in which they enter the '*Ready*' queue. The first entered process is serviced first. It is same as any real world application where queue systems are used; e.g. Ticketing reservation system where people need to stand in a queue and the first person standing in the queue is serviced first. FCFS scheduling is also known as First In First Out (FIFO) where the process which is put first into the '*Ready*' queue is serviced first.

Example 1

Three processes with process IDs P1, P2, P3 with estimated completion time 10, 5, 7 milliseconds respectively enters the ready queue together in the order P1, P2, P3. Calculate the waiting time and Turn Around Time (TAT) for each process and the average waiting time and Turn Around Time (Assuming there is no I/O waiting for the processes).

The sequence of execution of the processes by the CPU is represented as

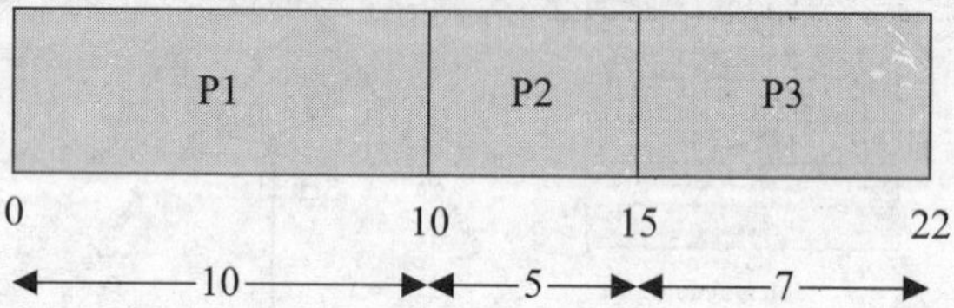

Assuming the CPU is readily available at the time of arrival of P1, P1 starts executing without any waiting in the '*Ready*' queue. Hence the waiting time for P1 is zero. The waiting time for all processes are given as

Waiting Time for P1 = 0 ms (P1 starts executing first)

Waiting Time for P2 = 10 ms (P2 starts executing after completing P1)

Waiting Time for P3 = 15 ms (P3 starts executing after completing P1 and P2)

Average waiting time = (Waiting time for all processes) / No. of Processes
= (Waiting time for (P1+P2+P3)) / 3
= (0+10+15)/3 = 25/3
= 8.33 milliseconds

Turn Around Time (TAT) for P1 = 10 ms (Time spent in Ready Queue + Execution Time)

Turn Around Time (TAT) for P2 = 15 ms (-Do-)

Turn Around Time (TAT) for P3 = 22 ms (-Do-)

Average Turn Around Time = (Turn Around Time for all processes) / No. of Processes
= (Turn Around Time for (P1+P2+P3)) / 3
= (10+15+22)/3 = 47/3
= 15.66 milliseconds

Average Turn Around Time (TAT) is the sum of average waiting time and average execution time.

Average Execution Time = (Execution time for all processes)/No. of processes
= (Execution time for (P1+P2+P3))/3
= (10+5+7)/3 = 22/3
= 7.33

Average Turn Around Time = Average waiting time + Average execution time
= 8.33 + 7.33
= 15.66 milliseconds

Example 2

Calculate the waiting time and Turn Around Time (TAT) for each process and the Average waiting time and Turn Around Time (Assuming there is no I/O waiting for the processes) for the above example if the process enters the 'Ready' queue together in the order P2, P1, P3.

The sequence of execution of the processes by the CPU is represented as

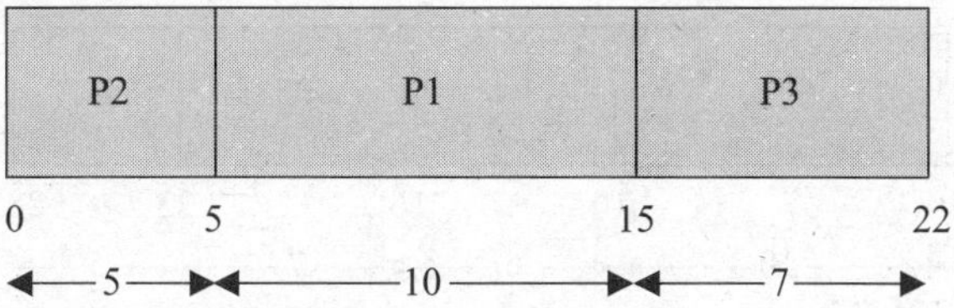

Assuming the CPU is readily available at the time of arrival of P2, P2 starts executing without any waiting in the '*Ready*' queue. Hence the waiting time for P2 is zero. The waiting time for all processes is given as

Waiting Time for P2 = 0 ms (P2 starts executing first)
Waiting Time for P1 = 5 ms (P1 starts executing after completing P2)
Waiting Time for P3 = 15 ms (P3 starts executing after completing P2 and P1)
Average waiting time = (Waiting time for all processes) / No. of Processes
= (Waiting time for (P2+P1+P3)) / 3
= (0+5+15)/3 = 20/3
= 6.66 milliseconds

Turn Around Time (TAT) for P2 = 5 ms (Time spent in Ready Queue + Execution Time)
Turn Around Time (TAT) for P1 = 15 ms (-Do-)
Turn Around Time (TAT) for P3 = 22 ms (-Do-)
Average Turn Around Time = (Turn Around Time for all processes) / No. of Processes
= (Turn Around Time for (P2+P1+P3)) / 3
= (5+15+22)/3 = 42/3
= 14 milliseconds

The Average waiting time and Turn Around Time (TAT) depends on the order in which the processes enter the '*Ready*' queue, regardless there estimated completion time.

From the above two examples it is clear that the Average waiting time and Turn Around Time improve if the process with shortest execution completion time is scheduled first.

The major drawback of FCFS algorithm is that it favours monopoly of process. A process, which does not contain any I/O operation, continues its execution until it finishes its task. If the process contains any I/O operation, the CPU is relinquished by the process. In general, FCFS favours CPU bound processes and I/O bound processes may have to wait until the completion of CPU bound process, if the currently executing process is a CPU bound process. This leads to poor device utilisation. The average waiting time is not minimal for FCFS scheduling algorithm.

10.5.1.2 Last-Come-First Served (LCFS)/LIFO Scheduling The Last-Come-First Served (LCFS) scheduling algorithm also allocates CPU time to the processes based on the order in which they are entered in the '*Ready*' queue. The last entered process is serviced first. LCFS scheduling is also known as Last In First Out (LIFO) where the process, which is put last into the '*Ready*' queue, is serviced first.

Example 1

Three processes with process IDs P1, P2, P3 with estimated completion time 10, 5, 7 milliseconds respectively enters the ready queue together in the order P1, P2, P3 (Assume only P1 is present in the '*Ready*' queue when the scheduler picks it up and P2, P3 entered '*Ready*' queue after that). Now a new process P4 with estimated completion time 6 ms enters the 'Ready' queue after 5 ms of scheduling P1. Calculate the waiting time and Turn Around Time (TAT) for each process and the Average waiting time and Turn Around Time (Assuming there is no I/O waiting for the processes).Assume all the processes contain only CPU operation and no I/O operations are involved.

Initially there is only P1 available in the Ready queue and the scheduling sequence will be P1, P3, P2. P4 enters the queue during the execution of P1 and becomes the last process entered the '*Ready*' queue. Now the order of execution changes to P1, P4, P3, and P2 as given below.

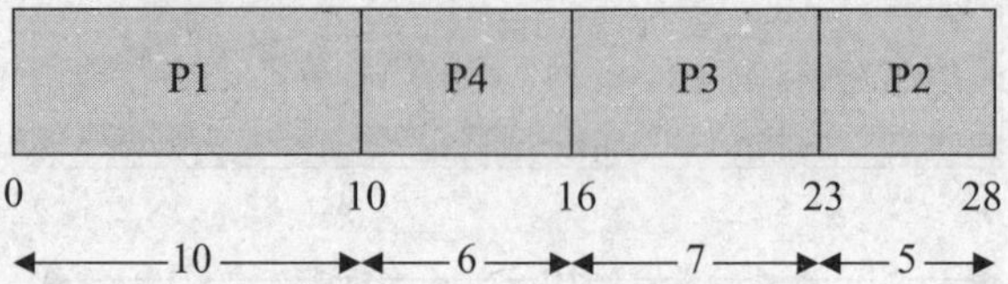

The waiting time for all the processes is given as
Waiting Time for P1 = 0 ms (P1 starts executing first)
Waiting Time for P4 = 5 ms (P4 starts executing after completing P1. But P4 arrived after 5 ms of execution of P1. Hence its waiting time = Execution start time – Arrival Time = 10 – 5 = 5)
Waiting Time for P3 = 16 ms (P3 starts executing after completing P1 and P4)
Waiting Time for P2 = 23 ms (P2 starts executing after completing P1, P4 and P3)
Average waiting time = (Waiting time for all processes) / No. of Processes
= (Waiting time for (P1+P4+P3+P2)) / 4
= (0 + 5 + 16 + 23)/4 = 44/4
= 11 milliseconds
Turn Around Time (TAT) for P1 = 10 ms (Time spent in Ready Queue + Execution Time)
Turn Around Time (TAT) for P4 = 11 ms (Time spent in Ready Queue + Execution Time = (Execution Start Time – Arrival Time) + Estimated Execution Time = (10 – 5) + 6 = 5 + 6)
Turn Around Time (TAT) for P3 = 23 ms (Time spent in Ready Queue + Execution Time)
Turn Around Time (TAT) for P2 = 28 ms (Time spent in Ready Queue + Execution Time)
Average Turn Around Time = (Turn Around Time for all processes) / No. of Processes
= (Turn Around Time for (P1+P4+P3+P2)) / 4
= (10+11+23+28)/4 = 72/4
= 18 milliseconds

LCFS scheduling is not optimal and it also possesses the same drawback as that of FCFS algorithm.

10.5.1.3 Shortest Job First (SJF) Scheduling Shortest Job First (SJF) scheduling algorithm 'sorts the '*Ready*' queue' each time a process relinquishes the CPU (either the process terminates or enters the '*Wait*' state waiting for I/O or system resource) to pick the process with shortest (least) estimated completion/run time. In SJF, the process with the shortest estimated run time is scheduled first, followed by the next shortest process, and so on.

Example 1

Three processes with process IDs P1, P2, P3 with estimated completion time 10, 5, 7 milliseconds respectively enters the ready queue together. Calculate the waiting time and Turn Around Time (TAT) for each process and the Average waiting time and Turn Around Time (Assuming there is no I/O waiting for the processes) in SJF algorithm.

The scheduler sorts the '*Ready*' queue based on the shortest estimated completion time and schedules the process with the least estimated completion time first and the next least one as second, and so on. The order in which the processes are scheduled for execution is represented as

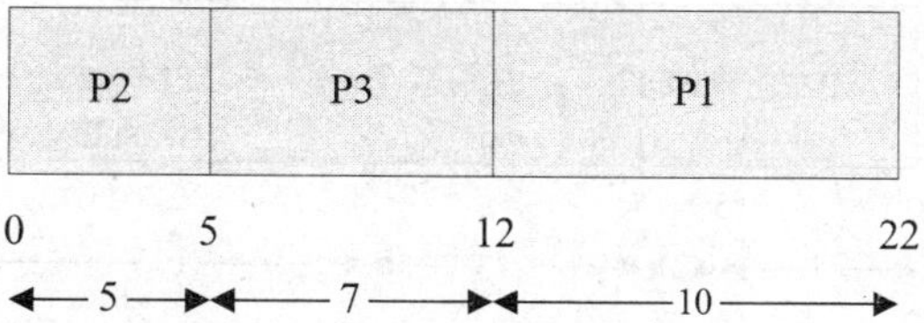

The estimated execution time of P2 is the least (5 ms) followed by P3 (7 ms) and P1 (10 ms).
The waiting time for all processes are given as
Waiting Time for P2 = 0 ms (P2 starts executing first)
Waiting Time for P3 = 5 ms (P3 starts executing after completing P2)
Waiting Time for P1 = 12 ms (P1 starts executing after completing P2 and P3)
Average waiting time = (Waiting time for all processes) / No. of Processes
= (Waiting time for (P2+P3+P1)) / 3
= (0+5+12)/3 = 17/3
= 5.66 milliseconds

Turn Around Time (TAT) for P2 = 5 ms (Time spent in Ready Queue + Execution Time)
Turn Around Time (TAT) for P3 = 12 ms (-Do-)
Turn Around Time (TAT) for P1 = 22 ms (-Do-)
Average Turn Around Time = (Turn Around Time for all processes) / No. of Processes
= (Turn Around Time for (P2+P3+P1)) / 3
= (5+12+22)/3 = 39/3
= 13 milliseconds

Average Turn Around Time (TAT) is the sum of average waiting time and average execution time.
The average Execution time = (Execution time for all processes)/No. of processes
= (Execution time for (P1+P2+P3))/3
= (10+5+7)/3 = 22/3 = 7.33
Average Turn Around Time = Average Waiting time + Average Execution time
= 5.66 + 7.33
= 13 milliseconds

From this example, it is clear that the average waiting time and turn around time is much improved with the SJF scheduling for the same processes when compared to the FCFS algorithm.

Example 2

Calculate the waiting time and Turn Around Time (TAT) for each process and the Average waiting time and Turn Around Time for the above example if a new process P4 with estimated completion time 2 ms enters the 'Ready' queue after 2 ms of execution of P2. Assume all the processes contain only CPU operation and no I/O operations are involved.

At the beginning, there are only three processes (P1, P2 and P3) available in the '*Ready*' queue and the SJF scheduler picks up the process with the least execution completion time (In this example P2 with execution completion time 5 ms) for scheduling. The execution sequence diagram for this is same as that of Example 1.

Now process P4 with estimated execution completion time 2 ms enters the '*Ready*' queue after 2 ms of start of execution of P2. Since the SJF algorithm is non-preemptive and process P2 does not contain any I/O operations, P2 continues its execution. After 5 ms of scheduling, P2 terminates and now the scheduler again sorts the '*Ready*' queue for process with least execution completion time. Since the execution completion time for P4 (2 ms) is less than that of P3 (7 ms), which was supposed to be run after the completion of P2 as per the '*Ready*' queue available at the beginning of execution scheduling, P4 is picked up for executing. Due to the arrival of the process P4 with execution time 2 ms, the '*Ready*' queue is re-sorted in the order P2, P4, P3, P1. At the beginning it was P2, P3, P1. The execution sequence now changes as per the following diagram

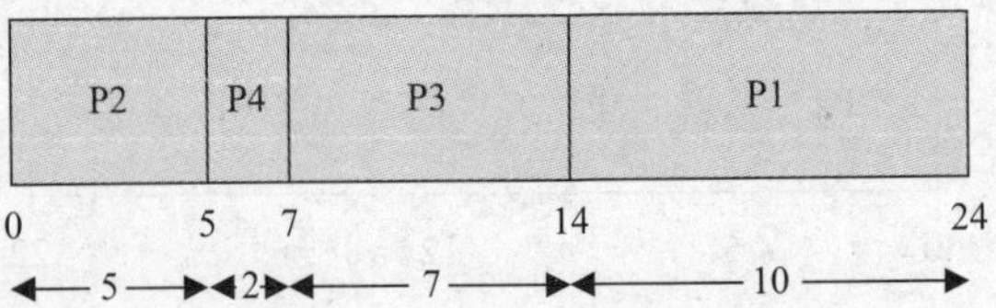

The waiting time for all the processes are given as

Waiting time for P2 = 0 ms (P2 starts executing first)

Waiting time for P4 = 3 ms (P4 starts executing after completing P2. But P4 arrived after 2 ms of execution of P2. Hence its waiting time = Execution start time – Arrival Time = 5 – 2 = 3)

Waiting time for P3 = 7 ms (P3 starts executing after completing P2 and P4)

Waiting time for P1 = 14 ms (P1 starts executing after completing P2, P4 and P3)

Average waiting time = (Waiting time for all processes) / No. of Processes
= (Waiting time for (P2+P4+P3+P1)) / 4
= (0 + 3 + 7 + 14)/4 = 24/4
= 6 milliseconds

Turn Around Time (TAT) for P2 = 5 ms (Time spent in Ready Queue + Execution Time)

Turn Around Time (TAT) for P4 = 5 ms (Time spent in Ready Queue + Execution Time = (Execution Start Time – Arrival Time) + Estimated Execution Time = (5 – 2) + 2 = 3 + 2)

Turn Around Time (TAT) for P3 = 14 ms (Time spent in Ready Queue + Execution Time)

Turn Around Time (TAT) for P1 = 24 ms (Time spent in Ready Queue + Execution Time)

Average Turn Around Time = (Turn Around Time for all Processes) / No. of Processes
= (Turn Around Time for (P2+P4+P3+P1)) / 4
= (5+5+14+24)/4 = 48/4
= 12 milliseconds

The average waiting time for a given set of process is minimal in SJF scheduling and so it is optimal compared to other non-preemptive scheduling like FCFS. The major drawback of SJF algorithm is that a process whose estimated execution completion time is high may not get a chance to execute if more and more processes with least estimated execution time enters the '*Ready*' queue before the process with longest estimated execution time started its execution (In non-preemptive SJF). This condition is known as '*Starvation*'. Another drawback of SJF is that it is difficult to know in advance the next shortest process in the '*Ready*' queue for scheduling since new processes with different estimated execution time keep entering the '*Ready*' queue at any point of time.

10.5.1.4 Priority Based Scheduling The Turn Around Time (TAT) and waiting time for processes in non-preemptive scheduling varies with the type of scheduling algorithm. Priority based non-preemptive scheduling algorithm ensures that a process with high priority is serviced at the earliest compared to other low priority processes in the 'Ready' queue. The priority of a task/process can be indicated through various mechanisms. The Shortest Job First (SJF) algorithm can be viewed as a priority based scheduling where each task is prioritised in the order of the time required to complete the task. The lower the time required for completing a process the higher is its priority in SJF algorithm. Another way of priority assigning is associating a priority to the task/process at the time of creation of the task/process. The priority is a number ranging from 0 to the maximum priority supported by the OS. The maximum level of priority is OS dependent. For Example, Windows CE supports 256 levels of priority (0 to 255 priority numbers). While creating the process/task, the priority can be assigned to it. The priority number associated with a task/process is the direct indication of its priority. The priority variation from high to low is represented by numbers from 0 to the maximum priority or by numbers from maximum priority to 0. For Windows CE operating system a priority number 0 indicates the highest priority and 255 indicates the lowest priority. This convention need not be universal and it depends on the kernel level implementation of the priority structure. The non-preemptive priority based scheduler sorts the 'Ready' queue based on priority and picks the process with the highest level of priority for execution.

Example 1

Three processes with process IDs P1, P2, P3 with estimated completion time 10, 5, 7 milliseconds and priorities 0, 3, 2 (0—highest priority, 3—lowest priority) respectively enters the ready queue together. Calculate the waiting time and Turn Around Time (TAT) for each process and the Average waiting time and Turn Around Time (Assuming there is no I/O waiting for the processes) in priority based scheduling algorithm.

The scheduler sorts the '*Ready*' queue based on the priority and schedules the process with the highest priority (P1 with priority number 0) first and the next high priority process (P3 with priority number 2) as second, and so on. The order in which the processes are scheduled for execution is represented as

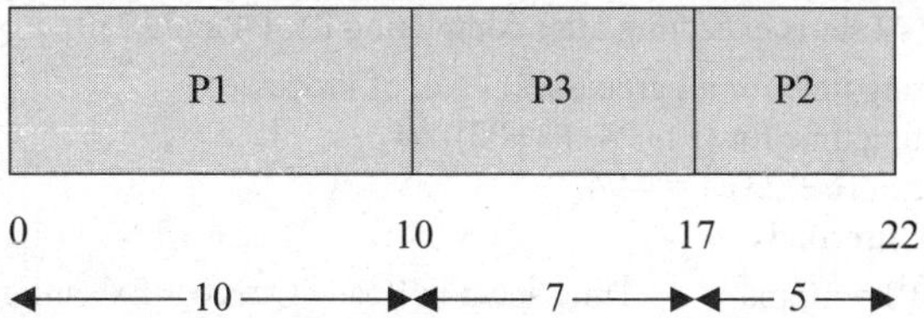

The waiting time for all the processes are given as

Waiting time for P1 = 0 ms (P1 starts executing first)

Waiting time for P3 = 10 ms (P3 starts executing after completing P1)

Waiting time for P2 = 17 ms (P2 starts executing after completing P1 and P3)

Average waiting time = (Waiting time for all processes) / No. of Processes
= (Waiting time for (P1+P3+P2)) / 3
= (0+10+17)/3 = 27/3
= 9 milliseconds

Turn Around Time (TAT) for P1 = 10 ms (Time spent in Ready Queue + Execution Time)

Turn Around Time (TAT) for P3 = 17 ms (-Do-)

Turn Around Time (TAT) for P2 = 22 ms (-Do-)

Average Turn Around Time = (Turn Around Time for all processes) / No. of Processes
= (Turn Around Time for (P1+P3+P2)) / 3
= (10+17+22)/3 = 49/3
= 16.33 milliseconds

Example 2

Calculate the waiting time and Turn Around Time (TAT) for each process and the Average waiting time and Turn Around Time for the above example if a new process P4 with estimated completion time 6 ms and priority 1 enters the 'Ready' queue after 5 ms of execution of P1. Assume all the processes contain only CPU operation and no I/O operations are involved.

At the beginning, there are only three processes (P1, P2 and P3) available in the '*Ready*' queue and the scheduler picks up the process with the highest priority (In this example P1 with priority 0) for scheduling. The execution sequence diagram for this is same as that of Example 1. Now process P4 with estimated execution completion time 6 ms and priority 1 enters the '*Ready*' queue after 5 ms of execution of P1. Since the scheduling algorithm is non-preemptive and process P1 does not contain any I/O operations, P1 continues its execution. After 10 ms of scheduling, P1 terminates and now the scheduler again sorts the '*Ready*' queue for process with highest priority. Since the priority for P4 (priority 1) is higher than that of P3 (priority 2), which was supposed to be run after the completion of P1 as per the '*Ready*' queue available at the beginning of execution scheduling, P4 is picked up for executing. Due to the arrival of the process P4 with priority 1, the '*Ready*' queue is resorted in the order P1, P4, P3, P2. At the beginning it was P1, P3, P2. The execution sequence now changes as per the following diagram

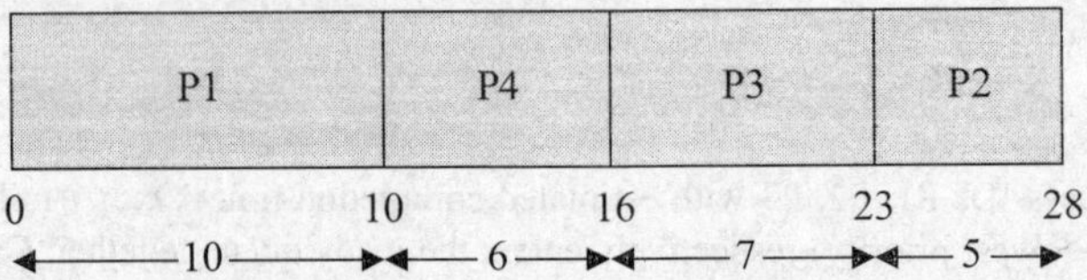

The waiting time for all the processes are given as

Waiting time for P1 = 0 ms (P1 starts executing first)

Waiting time for P4 = 5 ms (P4 starts executing after completing P1. But P4 arrived after 5 ms of execution of P1. Hence its waiting time = Execution start time – Arrival Time = 10 – 5 = 5)

Waiting time for P3 = 16 ms (P3 starts executing after completing P1 and P4)

Waiting time for P2 = 23 ms (P2 starts executing after completing P1, P4 and P3)

Average waiting time = (Waiting time for all processes) / No. of Processes
= (Waiting time for (P1+P4+P3+P2)) / 4
= (0 + 5 + 16 + 23)/4 = 44/4
= 11 milliseconds

Turn Around Time (TAT) for P1 = 10 ms (Time spent in Ready Queue + Execution Time)

Turn Around Time (TAT) for P4 = 11 ms (Time spent in Ready Queue + Execution Time = (Execution Start Time – Arrival Time) + Estimated Execution Time = (10 – 5) + 6 = 5 + 6)

Turn Around Time (TAT) for P3 = 23 ms (Time spent in Ready Queue + Execution Time)

Turn Around Time (TAT) for P2 = 28 ms (Time spent in Ready Queue + Execution Time)

Average Turn Around Time = (Turn Around Time for all processes) / No. of Processes
= (Turn Around Time for (P2 + P4 + P3 + P1)) / 4
= (10 + 11 + 23 + 28)/4 = 72/4
= 18 milliseconds

Similar to SJF scheduling algorithm, non-preemptive priority based algorithm also possess the drawback of '*Starvation*' where a process whose priority is low may not get a chance to execute if more and more processes with higher priorities enter the '*Ready*' queue before the process with lower priority started its execution. '*Starvation*' can be effectively tackled in priority based non-preemptive scheduling by dynamically raising the priority of the low priority task/process which is under starvation (waiting in the ready queue for a longer time for getting the CPU time). The technique of gradually raising the priority of processes which are waiting in the 'Ready' queue as time progresses, for preventing '*Starvation*', is known as '*Aging*'.

10.5.2 Preemptive Scheduling

Preemptive scheduling is employed in systems, which implements preemptive multitasking model. In preemptive scheduling, every task in the '*Ready*' queue gets a chance to execute. When and how often each process gets a chance to execute (gets the CPU time) is dependent on the type of preemptive scheduling algorithm used for scheduling the processes. In this kind of scheduling, the scheduler can preempt (stop temporarily) the currently executing task/process and select another task from the '*Ready*' queue for execution. When to pre-empt a task and which task is to be picked up from the '*Ready*' queue for execution after preempting the current task is purely dependent on the scheduling algorithm. A task which is preempted by the scheduler is moved to the '*Ready*' queue. The act of moving a '*Running*' process/task into the '*Ready*' queue by the scheduler, without the processes requesting for it is known as

'*Preemption*'. Preemptive scheduling can be implemented in different approaches. The two important approaches adopted in preemptive scheduling are time-based preemption and priority-based preemption. The various types of preemptive scheduling adopted in task/process scheduling are explained below.

10.5.2.1 Preemptive SJF Scheduling/Shortest Remaining Time (SRT) The non-preemptive SJF scheduling algorithm sorts the 'Ready' queue only after completing the execution of the current process or when the process enters 'Wait' state, whereas the preemptive SJF scheduling algorithm sorts the 'Ready' queue when a new process enters the 'Ready' queue and checks whether the execution time of the new process is shorter than the remaining of the total estimated time for the currently executing process. If the execution time of the new process is less, the currently executing process is preempted and the new process is scheduled for execution. Thus preemptive SJF scheduling always compares the execution completion time (It is same as the remaining time for the new process) of a new process entered the 'Ready' queue with the remaining time for completion of the currently executing process and schedules the process with shortest remaining time for execution. Preemptive SJF scheduling is also known as Shortest Remaining Time (SRT) scheduling.

Now let us solve Example 2 given under the Non-preemptive SJF scheduling for preemptive SJF scheduling. The problem statement and solution is explained in the following example.

Example 1

Three processes with process IDs P1, P2, P3 with estimated completion time 10, 5, 7 milliseconds respectively enters the ready queue together. A new process P4 with estimated completion time 2 ms enters the 'Ready' queue after 2 ms. Assume all the processes contain only CPU operation and no I/O operations are involved.

At the beginning, there are only three processes (P1, P2 and P3) available in the '*Ready*' queue and the SRT scheduler picks up the process with the shortest remaining time for execution completion (In this example, P2 with remaining time 5 ms) for scheduling. The execution sequence diagram for this is same as that of example 1 under non-preemptive SJF scheduling.

Now process P4 with estimated execution completion time 2 ms enters the '*Ready*' queue after 2 ms of start of execution of P2. Since the SRT algorithm is preemptive, the remaining time for completion of process P2 is checked with the remaining time for completion of process P4. The remaining time for completion of P2 is 3 ms which is greater than that of the remaining time for completion of the newly entered process P4 (2 ms). Hence P2 is preempted and P4 is scheduled for execution. P4 continues its execution to finish since there is no new process entered in the 'Ready' queue during its execution. After 2 ms of scheduling P4 terminates and now the scheduler again sorts the '*Ready*' queue based on the remaining time for completion of the processes present in the 'Ready' queue. Since the remaining time for P2 (3 ms), which is preempted by P4 is less than that of the remaining time for other processes in the 'Ready' queue, P2 is scheduled for execution. Due to the arrival of the process P4 with execution time 2 ms, the '*Ready*' queue is re-sorted in the order P2, P4, P2, P3, P1. At the beginning it was P2, P3, P1. The execution sequence now changes as per the following diagram

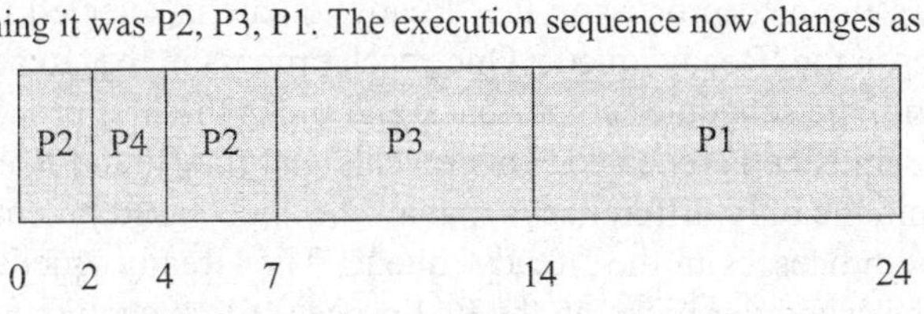

The waiting time for all the processes are given as

Waiting time for P2 = 0 ms + (4 – 2) ms = 2 ms (P2 starts executing first and is interrupted by P4 and has to wait till the completion of P4 to get the next CPU slot)

Waiting time for P4 = 0 ms (P4 starts executing by preempting P2 since the execution time for completion of P4 (2 ms) is less than that of the Remaining time for execution completion of P2 (Here it is 3 ms))
Waiting time for P3 = 7 ms (P3 starts executing after completing P4 and P2)
Waiting time for P1 = 14 ms (P1 starts executing after completing P4, P2 and P3)
Average waiting time = (Waiting time for all the processes) / No. of Processes
= (Waiting time for (P4+P2+P3+P1)) / 4
= (0 + 2 + 7 + 14)/4 = 23/4
= 5.75 milliseconds

Turn Around Time (TAT) for P2 = 7 ms (Time spent in Ready Queue + Execution Time)
Turn Around Time (TAT) for P4 = 2 ms (Time spent in Ready Queue + Execution Time = (Execution Start Time – Arrival Time) + Estimated Execution Time = (2 – 2) + 2)
Turn Around Time (TAT) for P3 = 14 ms (Time spent in Ready Queue + Execution Time)
Turn Around Time (TAT) for P1 = 24 ms (Time spent in Ready Queue + Execution Time)
Average Turn Around Time = (Turn Around Time for all the processes) / No. of Processes
= (Turn Around Time for (P2+P4+P3+P1)) / 4
= (7+2+14+24)/4 = 47/4
= 11.75 milliseconds

Now let's compare the Average Waiting time and Average Turn Around Time with that of the Average waiting time and Average Turn Around Time for non-preemptive SJF scheduling (Refer to Example 2 given under the section Non-preemptive SJF scheduling)

Average Waiting Time in non-preemptive SJF scheduling = 6 ms
Average Waiting Time in preemptive SJF scheduling = 5.75 ms

Average Turn Around Time in non-preemptive SJF scheduling = 12 ms
Average Turn Around Time in preemptive SJF scheduling = 11.75 ms

This reveals that the Average waiting Time and Turn Around Time (TAT) improves significantly with preemptive SJF scheduling.

10.5.2.2 Round Robin (RR) Scheduling The term *Round Robin* is very popular among the sports and games activities. You might have heard about 'Round Robin' league or 'Knock out' league associated with any football or cricket tournament. In the 'Round Robin' league each team in a group gets an equal chance to play against the rest of the teams in the same group whereas in the 'Knock out' league the losing team in a match moves out of the tournament ☺.

In the process scheduling context also, '*Round Robin*' brings the same message "Equal chance to all". In Round Robin scheduling, each process in the 'Ready' queue is executed for a pre-defined time slot. The execution starts with picking up the first process in the 'Ready' queue (see Fig. 10.13). It is executed for a pre-defined time and when the pre-defined time elapses or the process completes (before the pre-defined time slice), the next process in the 'Ready' queue is selected for execution. This is repeated for all the processes in the 'Ready' queue. Once each process in the 'Ready' queue is executed for the pre-defined time period, the scheduler comes back and picks the first process in the 'Ready' queue again for execution. The sequence is repeated. This reveals that the Round Robin scheduling is similar to the FCFS scheduling and the only difference is that a time slice based preemption is added to switch the execution between the processes in the 'Ready' queue. The 'Ready' queue can be considered as a circular queue in which the scheduler picks up the first process for execution and moves to the next till the end of the queue and then comes back to the beginning of the queue to pick up the first process.

The time slice is provided by the *timer tick* feature of the time management unit of the OS kernel (Refer the Time management section under the subtopic '*The Real-Time kernel*' for more details on Timer tick). Time slice is kernel dependent and it varies in the order of a few microseconds to milliseconds. Certain OS kernels may allow the time slice as user configurable. Round Robin scheduling ensures that

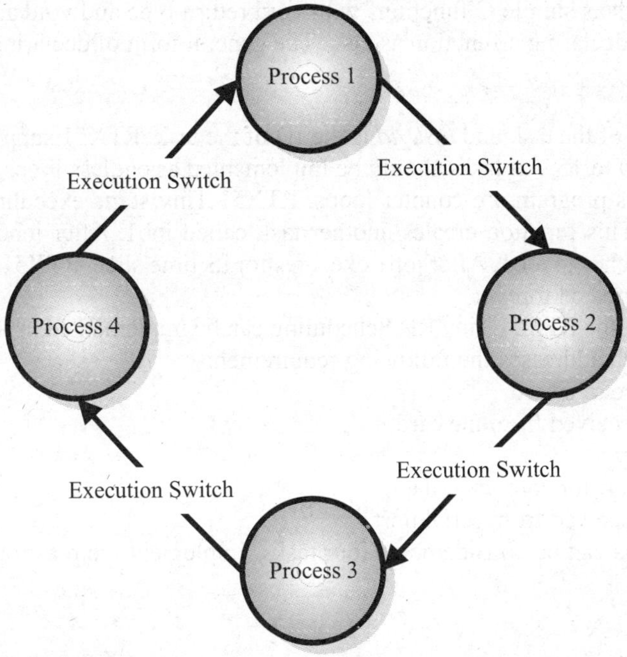

Fig. 10.13 **Round Robin Scheduling**

every process gets a fixed amount of CPU time for execution. When the process gets its fixed time for execution is determined by the FCFS policy (That is, a process entering the Ready queue first gets its fixed execution time first and so on…). If a process terminates before the elapse of the time slice, the process releases the CPU voluntarily and the next process in the queue is scheduled for execution by the scheduler. The implementation of RR scheduling is kernel dependent. The following code snippet illustrates the RR scheduling implementation for RTX51 Tiny OS, an 8bit OS for *8051* microcontroller from Keil Software (www.keil.com), an ARM® Company.

```
#include <rtx51tny.h>      /* Definitions for RTX51 Tiny */
int counter0;
int counter1;

job0 () _task_ 0 {
  os_create_task (1);      /* Mark task 1 as "ready"       */

  while (1)  {             /* Endless loop                 */
    counter0++;            /* Increment counter 0          */
  }
}
job1 () _task_ 1 {
  while (1)  {             /* Endless loop                 */
    counter1++;            /* Increment counter 1          */
  }
}
```

RTX51 defines the tasks as simple C functions with void return type and void argument list. The attribute *_task_* is used for declaring a function as task. The general form of declaring a task is

```
void func (void) _task_ task_id
```

where *func* is the name of the task and *task_id* is the ID of the task. RTX51 supports up to 16 tasks and so *task_id* varies from 0 to 15. All tasks should be implemented as endless loops.

The two tasks in this program are counter loops. RTX51 Tiny starts executing task 0 which is the function named job0. This function creates another task called job1. After job0 executes for its time slice, RTX51 Tiny switches to job1. After job1 executes for its time slice, RTX51 Tiny switches back to job0. This process is repeated forever.

Now let's check how the RTX51 Tiny RR Scheduling can be implemented in an embedded device (A smart card reader) which addresses the following requirements.

- Check the presence of a card
- Process the data received from the card
- Update the Display
- Check the serial port for command/data
- Process the data received from serial port

These four requirements can be considered as four tasks. Implement them as four RTX51 tasks as explained below.

```
void check_card_task (void) _task_ 1
{
/* This task checks for the presence of a card */
/* Implement the necessary functionality here */
}
void process_card_task (void) _task_ 2
{
/* This task processes the data received from the card */
/* Implement the necessary functionality here */
}
void check_serial_io_task (void) _task_ 3
{
/* This task checks for serial I/O */
/* Implement the necessary functionality here */
}
void process_serial_data_task (void) _task_ 4
{
/* This task processes the data received from the serial port */
/* Implement the necessary functionality here */
}
```

Now the tasks are created. Next step is scheduling the tasks. The following code snippet illustrates the scheduling of tasks.

```
void startup_task (void) _task_ 0
{
os_create_task (1);    /* Create check_card_task Task */
os_create_task (2);    /* Create process_card_task Task */
os_create_task (3);    /* Create serial_io_task Task */
```

```
os_create_task (4);     /* Create serial_data_task Task */
os_delete_task (0);     /* Delete the Startup Task */
}
```

The *os_create_task* (task_ID) RTX51 Tiny kernel call puts the task with task ID *task_ID* in the 'Ready' state. All the ready tasks begin their execution at the next available opportunity. RTX51 Tiny does not have a *main ()* function to begin the code execution; instead it starts with executing task 0. Task 0 is used for creating other tasks. Once all the tasks are created, task 0 is stopped and removed from the task list with the *os_delete_task* kernel call. The RR scheduler selects each task based on the time slice and continues the execution. If we observe the tasks we can see that there is no point in executing the task *process_card_task* (Task 2) without detecting a card and executing the task *process_serial_data_task* (Task 4) without receiving some data in the serial port. In summary task 2 needs to be executed only when task 1 reports the presence of a card and task 4 needs to be executed only when task 3 reports the arrival of data at serial port. So these tasks (tasks 2 and 4) need to be put in the 'Ready' state only on satisfying these conditions. Till then these tasks can be put in the 'Wait' state so that the RR scheduler will not pick them for scheduling and the RR scheduling is effectively utilised among the other tasks. This can be achieved by implementing the wait and notify mechanism in the related tasks. Task 2 can be coded in a way that it waits for the card present event and task 1 signals the event 'card detected'. In a similar fashion Task 4 can be coded in such a way that it waits for the serial data received event and task 3 signals the reception of serial data on receiving serial data from serial port. The following code snippet explains the same.

```
void check_card_task (void) _task_ 1
{
/* This task checks for the presence of a card */
/* Implement the necessary functionality here */
while (1)
{
//Function for checking the presence of card and card reading
//..............................
if (card is present)
//Signal card detected to task 2
os_send_signal (2)
}
}

void process_card_task (void) _task_ 2
{
/* This task processes the data received from the card */
/* Implement the necessary functionality here */
while (1)
{
//Function for checking the signaling of card present event
os_wait1(K_SIG);
//Process card data
}
}
```

```
void check_serial_io_task (void) _task_ 3
{
/* This task checks for serial I/O */
/* Implement the necessary functionality here */
while (1)
{
//Function for checking the reception of serial data
//..............................
if (data is received)
//Signal serial data reception to task 4
os_send_signal (4)
}
}

void process_serial_data_task (void) _task_ 4
{
/* This task processes the data received from the serial port */
/* Implement the necessary functionality here */
while (1)
{
//Function for checking the signaling of serial data received event
os_wait1(K_SIG);
//Process card data
}
}
```

The *os_send_signal* (*Task ID*) kernel call sends a signal to task *Task ID*. If the specified task is already waiting for a signal, this function call readies the task for execution but does not start it. The *os_wait1* (*event*) kernel call halts the current task and waits for an event to occur. The *event* argument specifies the event to wait for and may have only the value K_SIG which waits for a signal. RTX51 uses the Timer 0 of *8051* for time slice generation. The time slice can be configured by the user by changing the time slice related parameters in the RTX51 Tiny OS configuration file **CONF_TNY.A51** file which is located in the **\KEIL\C51\RTXTINY2** folder. Configuration options in **CONF_TNY.A51** allow users to:

- Specify the Timer Tick Interrupt Register Bank.
- Specify the Timer Tick Interval (in *8051* machine cycles).
- Specify user code to execute in the Timer Tick Interrupt.
- Specify the Round-Robin Timeout.
- Enable or disable Round-Robin Task Switching.
- Specify that your application includes long duration interrupts.
- Specify whether or not code banking is used.
- Define the top of the RTX51 Tiny stack.
- Specify the minimum stack space required.
- Specify code to execute in the event of a stack error.
- Define idle task operations.

The RTX51 kernel provides a set of task management functions for managing the tasks. At any point of time each RTX51 task is exactly in any one of the following state.

Task State	State Description
RUNNING	The task that is currently running is in the RUNNING State. Only one task at a time may be in this state. The *os_running_task_id* kernel call returns the task number (ID) of the currently executing task.
READY	Tasks which are ready to run are in the READY State. Once the Running task has completed processing, RTX51 Tiny selects and starts the next Ready task. A task may be made ready immediately (even if the task is waiting for a timeout or signal) by setting its ready flag using the *os_set_ready or isr_set_ready* kernel functions.
WAITING	Tasks which are waiting for an event are in the WAITING State. Once the event occurs, the task is switched to the READY State. The *os_wait function* is used for placing a task in the WAITING State.
DELETED	Tasks which have not been started or tasks which have been deleted are in the DELETED State. The *os_delete_task* routine places a task that has been started (with *os_create_task*) into the DELETED State.
TIME - OUT	Tasks which were interrupted by a Round-Robin Time-Out are in the TIME-OUT State. This state is equivalent to the READY State for Round-Robin programs.

Refer the documentation available with RTX51 Tiny OS for more information on the various RTX51 task management kernel functions and their usage.

RR scheduling with interrupts is a good choice for the design of comparatively less complex *Real-Time Embedded Systems*. In this approach, the tasks which require less *Real-Time* attention can be scheduled with Round Robin scheduling and the tasks which require *Real-Time* attention can be scheduled through Interrupt Service Routines. RTX51 Tiny supports Interrupts with RR scheduling. For RTX51 the time slice for RR scheduling is provided by the Timer interrupt and if the interrupt is of high priority than that of the timer interrupt and if its service time (ISR) is longer than the timer tick interval, the RTX51 timer interrupt may be interrupted by the ISR and it may be reentered by a subsequent RX51 Tiny timer interrupt. Hence proper care must be taken to limit the ISR time within the timer tick interval or to protect the timer tick interrupt code from reentrancy. Otherwise unexpected results may occur. The limitations of RR with interrupt generic approach are the limited number of interrupts supported by embedded processors and the interrupt latency happening due to the context switching overhead.

RR can also be used as technique for resolving the priority in scheduling among the tasks with same level of priority. We will discuss about how RR scheduling can be used for resolving the priority among equal tasks under the VxWorks kernel in a later chapter.

Example 1

Three processes with process IDs P1, P2, P3 with estimated completion time 6, 4, 2 milliseconds respectively, enters the ready queue together in the order P1, P2, P3. Calculate the waiting time and Turn Around Time (TAT) for each process and the Average waiting time and Turn Around Time (Assuming there is no I/O waiting for the processes) in RR algorithm with Time slice = 2 ms.

The scheduler sorts the '*Ready*' queue based on the FCFS policy and picks up the first process P1 from the 'Ready' queue and executes it for the time slice 2 ms. When the time slice is expired, P1 is preempted and P2 is scheduled for execution. The Time slice expires after 2ms of execution of P2. Now P2 is preempted and P3 is picked up for execution. P3 completes its execution within the time slice and the scheduler picks P1 again for execution for the next time slice. This procedure is repeated till all the processes are serviced. The order in which the processes are scheduled for execution is represented as

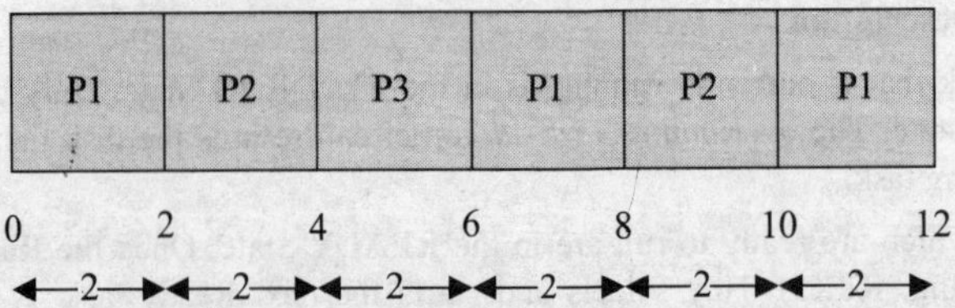

The waiting time for all the processes are given as

Waiting time for P1 = 0 + (6 – 2) + (10 – 8) = 0 + 4 + 2 = 6 ms

(P1 starts executing first and waits for two time slices to get execution back and again 1 time slice for getting CPU time)

Waiting time for P2 = (2 – 0) + (8 – 4) = 2 + 4 = 6 ms

(P2 starts executing after P1 executes for 1 time slice and waits for two time slices to get the CPU time)

Waiting time for P3 = (4 – 0) = 4 ms

(P3 starts executing after completing the first time slices for P1 and P2 and completes its execution in a single time slice)

Average waiting time = (Waiting time for all the processes) / No. of Processes

= (Waiting time for (P1 + P2 + P3)) / 3

= (6 + 6 + 4)/3 = 16/3

= 5.33 milliseconds

Turn Around Time (TAT) for P1 = 12 ms (Time spent in Ready Queue + Execution Time)

Turn Around Time (TAT) for P2 = 10 ms (-Do-)

Turn Around Time (TAT) for P3 = 6 ms (-Do-)

Average Turn Around Time = (Turn Around Time for all the processes) / No. of Processes

= (Turn Around Time for (P1 + P2 + P3))/3

= (12 + 10 + 6)/3 = 28/3

= 9.33 milliseconds

Average Turn Around Time (TAT) is the sum of average waiting time and average execution time.

Average Execution time = (Execution time for all the process)/No. of processes

= (Execution time for (P1 + P2 + P3))/3

= (6 + 4 + 2)/3 = 12/3

= 4

Average Turn Around Time = Average Waiting time + Average Execution time

= 5.33 + 4

= 9.33 milliseconds

RR scheduling involves lot of overhead in maintaining the time slice information for every process which is currently being executed.

10.5.2.3 Priority Based Scheduling Priority based preemptive scheduling algorithm is same as that of the non-preemptive priority based scheduling except for the switching of execution between tasks. In preemptive scheduling, any high priority process entering the 'Ready' queue is immediately scheduled for execution whereas in the non-preemptive scheduling any high priority process entering the 'Ready' queue is scheduled only after the currently executing process completes its execution or only when it voluntarily relinquishes the CPU. The priority of a task/process in preemptive scheduling is indicated in the same way as that of the mechanism adopted for non-preemptive multitasking. Refer the non-preemptive priority based scheduling discussed in an earlier section of this chapter for more details.

Example 1

Three processes with process IDs P1, P2, P3 with estimated completion time 10, 5, 7 milliseconds and priorities 1, 3, 2 (0—highest priority, 3—lowest priority) respectively enters the ready queue together. A new process P4 with estimated completion time 6 ms and priority 0 enters the 'Ready' queue after 5 ms of start of execution of P1. Assume all the processes contain only CPU operation and no I/O operations are involved.

At the beginning, there are only three processes (P1, P2 and P3) available in the '*Ready*' queue and the scheduler picks up the process with the highest priority (In this example P1 with priority 1) for scheduling.

Now process P4 with estimated execution completion time 6 ms and priority 0 enters the '*Ready*' queue after 5 ms of start of execution of P1. Since the scheduling algorithm is preemptive, P1 is preempted by P4 and P4 runs to completion. After 6 ms of scheduling, P4 terminates and now the scheduler again sorts the '*Ready*' queue for process with highest priority. Since the priority for P1 (priority 1), which is preempted by P4 is higher than that of P3 (priority 2) and P2 ((priority 3), P1 is again picked up for execution by the scheduler. Due to the arrival of the process P4 with priority 0, the '*Ready*' queue is resorted in the order P1, P4, P1, P3, P2. At the beginning it was P1, P3, P2. The execution sequence now changes as per the following diagram

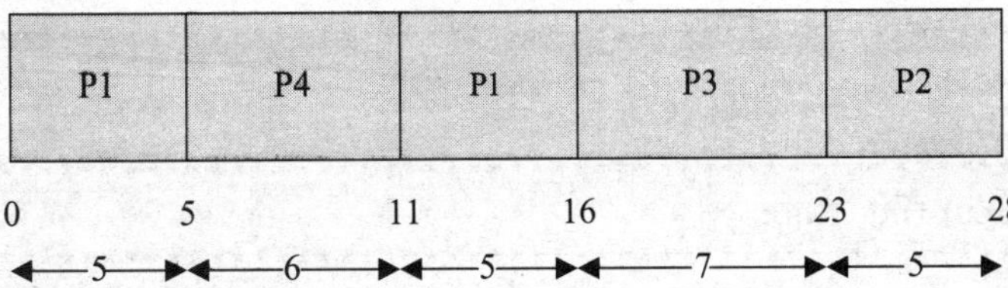

The waiting time for all the processes are given as

Waiting time for P1 = 0 + (11 – 5) = 0 + 6 = 6 ms

(P1 starts executing first and gets preempted by P4 after 5 ms and again gets the CPU time after completion of P4)

Waiting time for P4 = 0 ms

(P4 starts executing immediately on entering the 'Ready' queue, by preempting P1)

Waiting time for P3 = 16 ms (P3 starts executing after completing P1 and P4)

Waiting time for P2 = 23 ms (P2 starts executing after completing P1, P4 and P3)

Average waiting time = (Waiting time for all the processes) / No. of Processes

= (Waiting time for (P1+P4+P3+P2)) / 4

= (6 + 0 + 16 + 23)/4 = 45/4

= 11.25 milliseconds

Turn Around Time (TAT) for P1 = 16 ms (Time spent in Ready Queue + Execution Time)

Turn Around Time (TAT) for P4 = 6 ms

(Time spent in Ready Queue + Execution Time = (Execution Start Time – Arrival Time) + Estimated Execution Time = (5 – 5) + 6 = 0 + 6)

Turn Around Time (TAT) for P3 = 23 ms (Time spent in Ready Queue + Execution Time)

Turn Around Time (TAT) for P2 = 28 ms (Time spent in Ready Queue + Execution Time)

Average Turn Around Time = (Turn Around Time for all the processes) / No. of Processes

= (Turn Around Time for (P2 + P4 + P3 + P1)) / 4

= (16 + 6 + 23 + 28)/4 = 73/4

= 18.25 milliseconds

Priority based preemptive scheduling gives Real-Time attention to high priority tasks. Thus priority based preemptive scheduling is adopted in systems which demands 'Real-Time' behaviour. Most of the RTOSs make use of the preemptive priority based scheduling algorithm for process scheduling. Preemptive priority based scheduling also possesses the same drawback of non-preemptive priority based scheduling–'*Starvation*'. This can be eliminated by the '*Aging*' technique. Refer the section Non-preemptive priority based scheduling for more details on '*Starvation*' and '*Aging*'.

10.6 THREADS, PROCESSES AND SCHEDULING: PUTTING THEM ALTOGETHER

So far we discussed about threads, processes and process/thread scheduling. Now let us have a look at how these entities are addressed in a real world implementation. Let's examine the following pieces of code.

```
//*****************************************************************
//Process 1
//*****************************************************************
#include <windows.h>
#include <stdio.h>
//*****************************************************************
//Thread for executing Task
//*****************************************************************
void Task(void) {

while (1)
{
//Perform some task
//Task execution time is 7.5 units of execution
//Sleep for 17.5 units of execution
Sleep(17.5); //Parameter given is not in milliseconds
//Repeat task
}
}
//*****************************************************************
//Main Thread.
//*****************************************************************
void main(void) {
      DWORD id;
      HANDLE hThread;
//Create thread with normal priority
//*****************************************************************
      hThread = CreateThread(NULL,0,
                (LPTHREAD_START_ROUTINE)Task,
                (LPVOID) 0, 0, &id);
      if (NULL==hThread)
      {//Thread Creation failed. Exit process
      printf("Creating thread failed: Error Code =
      %d",GetLastError());
```

```
        return;
        }
        WaitForSingleObject(hThread, INFINITE);
        return;
}
//**************************************************************
//Process 2
//**************************************************************
#include <windows.h>
#include <stdio.h>
//**************************************************************
//Thread for executing Task
//**************************************************************
void Task(void) {
while (1)
{
//Perform some task
///Task execution time is 10 units of execution
//Sleep for 5 units of execution
Sleep(5); //Parameter given is not in milliseconds
//Repeat task
}
}
//**************************************************************
//Main Thread.
//**************************************************************
void main(void) {
        DWORD id;
        HANDLE hThread;
//Create thread with above normal priority
//**************************************************************
        hThread = CreateThread(NULL,0,
                        (LPTHREAD_START_ROUTINE)Task,
                        (LPVOID) 0, CREATE_SUSPENDED, &id);
        if (NULL==hThread)
        {//Thread Creation failed. Exit process
        printf("Creating thread failed: Error Code =
        %d",GetLastError());
        return;
        }
        SetThreadPriority(hThread,THREAD_PRIORITY_ABOVE_NORMAL);
        ResumeThread(hThread);
        WaitForSingleObject(hThread, INFINITE);
        return;
}
```

The first piece of code represents a process (Process 1) with priority normal and it performs a task which requires 7.5 units of execution time. After performing this task, the process sleeps for 17.5 units of execution time and this is repeated forever. The second piece of code represents a process (Process

2) with priority above normal and it performs a task which requires 10 units of execution time. After performing this task, the process sleeps for 5 units of execution time and this is repeated forever. Process 2 is of higher priority compared to process 1, since its priority is above 'Normal'.

Now let us examine what happens if these processes are executed on a Real-Time kernel with pre-emptive priority based scheduling policy. Imagine Process 1 and Process 2 are ready for execution. Both of them enters the 'Ready' queue and the scheduler picks up Process 2 for execution since it is of higher priority (Assuming there is no other process running/ready for execution, when both the processes are 'Ready' for execution) compared to Process 1. Process 2 starts executing and runs until it executes the Sleep instruction (i.e. after10 units of execution time). When the Sleep instruction is executed, Process 2 enters the wait state. Since Process 1 is waiting for its turn in the 'Ready' queue, the scheduler picks up it for execution, resulting in a context switch. The Process Control Block (PCB) of Process 2 is updated with the values of the Program Counter (PC), stack pointer, etc. at the time of context switch. The estimated task execution time for Process 1 is 7.5 units of execution time and the sleeping time for Process 2 is 5 units of execution. After 5 units of execution time, Process 2 enters the 'Ready' state and moves to the 'Ready' queue. Since it is of higher priority compared to the running process, the running process (Process 1) is pre-empted and Process 2 is scheduled for execution. Process 1 is moved to the 'Ready' queue, resulting in context switching. The Process Control Block of Process 1 is updated with the current values of the Program Counter (PC), Stack pointer, etc. when the context switch is happened. The Program Counter (PC), Stack pointer, etc. for Process 2 is loaded with the values stored in the Process Control Block (PCB) of Process 2 and Process 2 continues its execution form where it was stopped earlier. Process 2 executes the Sleep instruction after 10 units of execution time and enters the wait state. At this point Process 1 is waiting in the 'Ready' queue and it requires 2.5 units of execution time for completing the task associated with it (The total time for completing the task is 7.5 units of time, out of this it has already completed 5 units of execution when Process 2 was in the wait state). The scheduler schedules Process 1 for execution. The Program Counter (PC), Stack pointer, etc. for Process 1 is loaded with the values stored in the Process Control Block (PCB) of Process 1 and Process 1 continues its execution form where it was stopped earlier. After 2.5 units of execution time, Process 1 executes the Sleep instruction and enters the wait state. Process 2 is already in the wait state and the scheduler finds no other process for scheduling. In order to keep the CPU always busy, the scheduler runs a dummy process (task) called '*IDLE PROCESS (TASK)*'. The '*IDLE PROCESS (TASK)*' executes some dummy task and keeps the CPU engaged. The execution diagram depicted in Fig. 10.24 explains the sequence of operations.

The implementation of the '*IDLE PROCESS (TASK)*' is dependent on the kernel and a typical implementation for a desktop OS may look like. It is simply an endless loop.

```
void Idle_Process (void)
{
//Simply wait.
//Do nothing...
While (1);
}
```

The Real-Time kernels deployed in embedded systems, where operating power is a big constraint (like systems which are battery powered); the '*IDLE TASK*' is used for putting the CPU into *IDLE* mode for saving the power. A typical example is the RTX51 Tiny Real-Time kernel, where the '*IDLE TASK*' sets the 8051 CPU to *IDLE* mode, a power saving mode. In the '*IDLE*' mode, the program execution is

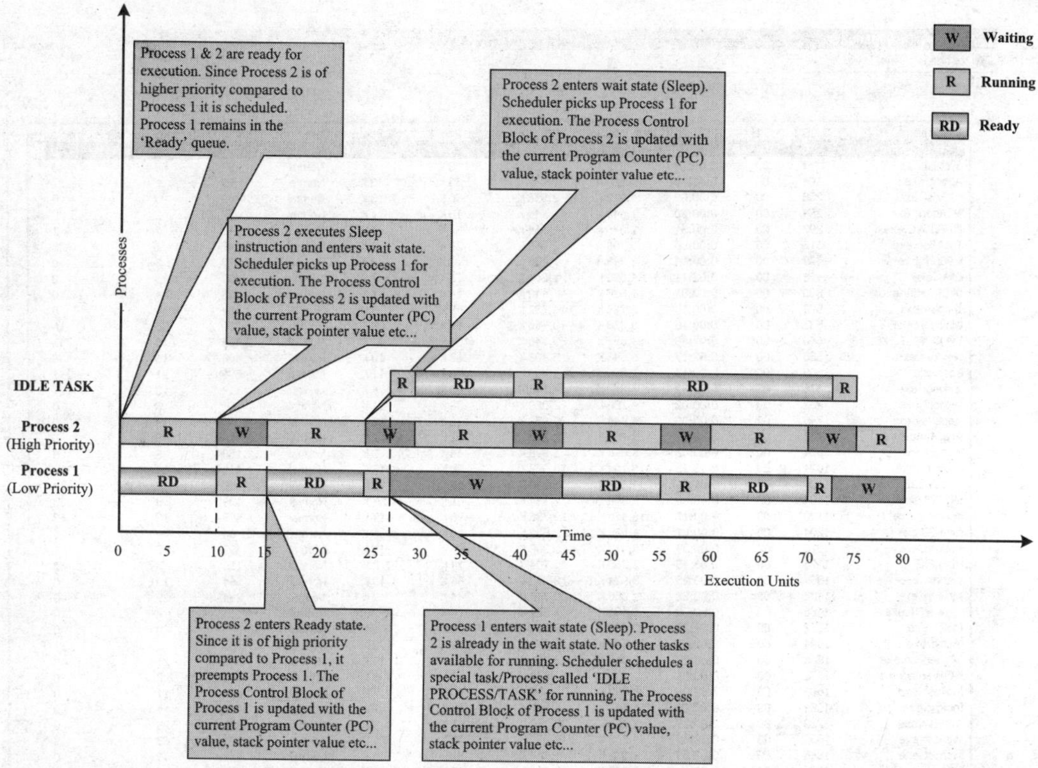

Fig. 10.14 **Process scheduling and context switch**

halted and all peripherals and the interrupt system continues its operation. Once the CPU is put into the '*IDLE*' mode, it comes out of this mode when an Interrupt occurs or when the RTX51 Tiny Timer Tick Interrupt (The timer interrupt used for task scheduling in Round robin scheduling) occurs. It should be noted that the '*IDLE PROCESS (TASK)*' execution is not pre-emptive priority scheduling specific, it is applicable to all types of scheduling policies which demand 100% CPU utilisation/CPU power saving.

Back to the desktop OS environment, let's analyse the process, threads and scheduling in the Windows desktop environment. Windows provide a utility called *task manager* for monitoring the different process running on the system and the resources used by each process. A snapshot of the process details returned by the task manager for Windows XP kernel is shown in Fig. 10.15. It should be noted that this snapshot is purely machine dependent and it varies with the number of processes running on the machine.

'*Image Name*' represents the name of the process. '*PID*' represents the Process Identification Number (Process ID). As mentioned in the 'Threads and Process' section, when a process is created an ID is associated to it. CPU usage gives the % of CPU utilised by the process during an interval. '*CPU Time*' gives the total CPU time used by a process after its commencement. '*Mem Usage*' represents the total main memory, in kilobytes, used by the process. '*VM Size*' represents the total virtual memory (paged memory), in kilobytes, used by a process. '*Paged Pool*' represents the paged memory, in kilobytes, currently used by the system. '*NP Pool*' is the non-paged pool or system memory used by a process. The non-paged memory is not swapped to the secondary storage disk. '*Base Pri*' represents the priority of

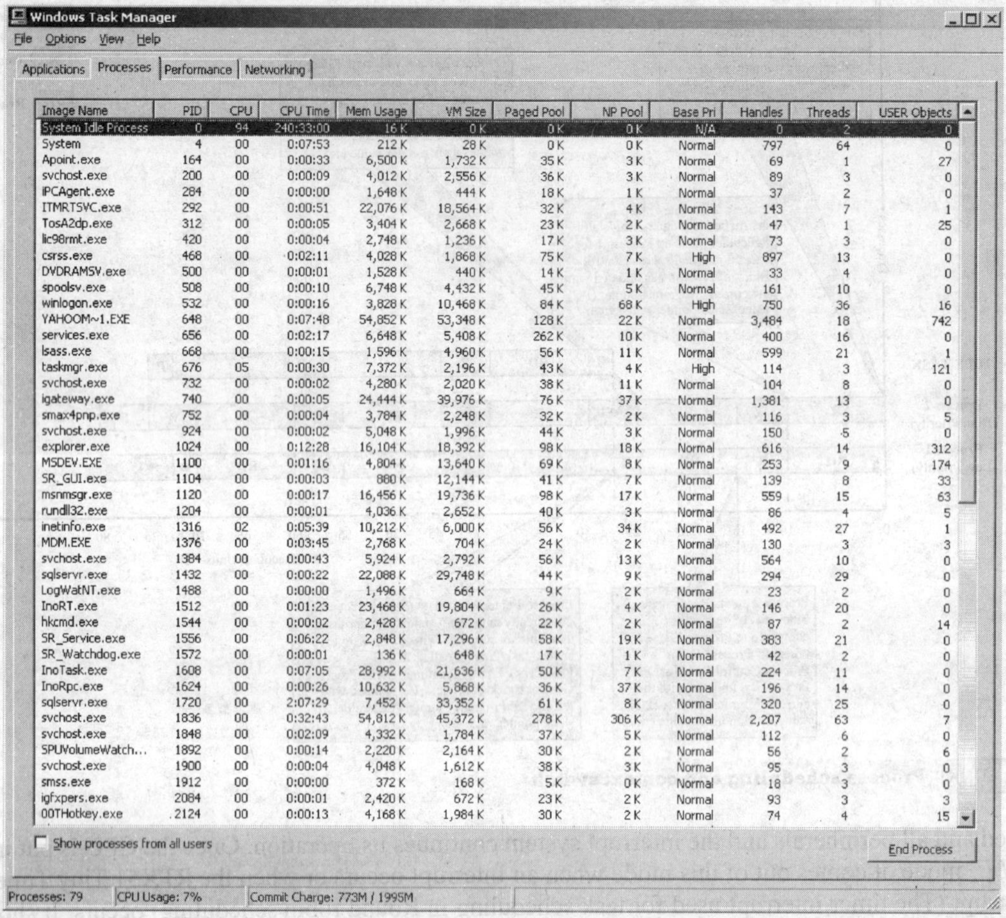

Image Name	PID	CPU	CPU Time	Mem Usage	VM Size	Paged Pool	NP Pool	Base Pri	Handles	Threads	USER Objects
System Idle Process	0	94	240:33:00	16 K	0 K	0 K	0 K	N/A	0	2	0
System	4	00	0:07:53	212 K	28 K	0 K	0 K	Normal	797	64	0
Apoint.exe	164	00	0:00:33	6,500 K	1,732 K	35 K	3 K	Normal	69	1	27
svchost.exe	200	00	0:00:09	4,012 K	2,556 K	36 K	3 K	Normal	89	3	0
iPCAgent.exe	284	00	0:00:00	1,648 K	444 K	18 K	1 K	Normal	37	2	0
ITMRTSVC.exe	292	00	0:00:51	22,076 K	18,564 K	32 K	4 K	Normal	143	7	1
TosA2dp.exe	312	00	0:00:05	3,404 K	2,668 K	23 K	2 K	Normal	47	1	25
lic98rmt.exe	420	00	0:00:04	2,748 K	1,236 K	17 K	3 K	Normal	73	3	0
csrss.exe	468	00	0:02:11	4,028 K	1,868 K	75 K	7 K	High	897	13	0
DVDRAMSV.exe	500	00	0:00:01	1,528 K	440 K	14 K	1 K	Normal	33	4	0
spoolsv.exe	508	00	0:00:10	6,748 K	4,432 K	45 K	5 K	Normal	161	10	0
winlogon.exe	532	00	0:00:16	3,828 K	10,468 K	84 K	68 K	High	750	36	16
YAHOOM~1.EXE	648	00	0:07:48	54,852 K	53,348 K	128 K	22 K	Normal	3,484	18	742
services.exe	656	00	0:02:17	6,648 K	5,408 K	262 K	10 K	Normal	400	16	0
lsass.exe	668	00	0:00:15	1,596 K	4,960 K	56 K	11 K	Normal	599	21	1
taskmgr.exe	676	05	0:00:30	7,372 K	2,196 K	43 K	4 K	High	114	3	121
svchost.exe	732	00	0:00:02	4,280 K	2,020 K	38 K	11 K	Normal	104	8	0
igateway.exe	740	00	0:00:05	24,444 K	39,976 K	76 K	37 K	Normal	1,381	13	0
smax4pnp.exe	752	00	0:00:04	3,784 K	2,248 K	32 K	2 K	Normal	116	3	5
svchost.exe	924	00	0:00:02	5,048 K	1,996 K	44 K	3 K	Normal	150	5	0
explorer.exe	1024	00	0:12:28	16,104 K	18,392 K	98 K	18 K	Normal	616	14	312
MSDEV.EXE	1100	00	0:01:16	4,804 K	13,640 K	69 K	8 K	Normal	253	9	174
SR_GUI.exe	1104	00	0:00:03	880 K	12,144 K	41 K	7 K	Normal	139	8	33
msnmsgr.exe	1120	00	0:00:17	16,456 K	19,736 K	98 K	17 K	Normal	559	15	63
rundll32.exe	1204	00	0:00:01	4,036 K	2,652 K	40 K	3 K	Normal	86	4	5
inetinfo.exe	1316	02	0:05:39	10,212 K	6,000 K	56 K	34 K	Normal	492	27	1
MDM.EXE	1376	00	0:03:45	2,768 K	704 K	24 K	2 K	Normal	130	3	3
svchost.exe	1384	00	0:00:43	5,924 K	2,792 K	56 K	13 K	Normal	564	10	0
sqlservr.exe	1432	00	0:00:22	22,088 K	29,748 K	44 K	9 K	Normal	294	29	0
LogWatNT.exe	1488	00	0:00:00	1,496 K	664 K	9 K	2 K	Normal	23	2	0
InoRT.exe	1512	00	0:01:23	23,468 K	19,804 K	26 K	4 K	Normal	146	20	0
hkcmd.exe	1544	00	0:00:02	2,428 K	672 K	22 K	2 K	Normal	87	2	14
SR_Service.exe	1556	00	0:06:22	2,848 K	17,296 K	58 K	19 K	Normal	383	21	0
SR_Watchdog.exe	1572	00	0:00:01	136 K	648 K	17 K	1 K	Normal	42	2	0
InoTask.exe	1608	00	0:07:05	28,992 K	21,636 K	50 K	7 K	Normal	224	11	0
InoRpc.exe	1624	00	0:00:26	10,632 K	5,868 K	36 K	37 K	Normal	196	14	0
sqlservr.exe	1720	00	2:07:29	7,452 K	33,352 K	61 K	8 K	Normal	320	25	0
svchost.exe	1836	00	0:32:43	54,812 K	45,372 K	278 K	306 K	Normal	2,207	63	7
svchost.exe	1848	00	0:02:09	4,332 K	1,784 K	37 K	5 K	Normal	112	6	0
SPUVolumeWatch...	1892	00	0:00:14	2,220 K	2,164 K	30 K	2 K	Normal	56	2	6
svchost.exe	1900	00	0:00:04	4,048 K	1,612 K	38 K	3 K	Normal	95	3	0
smss.exe	1912	00	0:00:00	372 K	168 K	5 K	0 K	Normal	18	3	0
igfxpers.exe	2084	00	0:00:01	2,420 K	672 K	23 K	2 K	Normal	93	3	3
00THotkey.exe	2124	00	0:00:13	4,168 K	1,984 K	30 K	2 K	Normal	74	4	15

Fig. 10.15 **Windows XP task manager for monitoring process and resource usage**

the process. As mentioned in an earlier section, a process may contain multiple threads. The '*Threads*' section gives the number of threads present in a process. '*Handles*' reflects the number of object handles owned by the process. This value is the reflection of the object handles present in the process's object table. '*User Objects*' reflects the number of objects active in the user mode for a process. Use '*Ctrl*' + '*Alt*' + '*Del*' key for accessing the task manager and select the '*View*' → '*Select Columns*' option to select the different monitoring parameters for a process.

10.7 TASK COMMUNICATION

In a multitasking system, multiple tasks/processes run concurrently (in pseudo parallelism) and each process may or may not interact between. Based on the degree of interaction, the processes running on an OS are classified as

Co-operating Processes: In the co-operating interaction model one process requires the inputs from other processes to complete its execution.

Competing Processes: The competing processes do not share anything among themselves but they share the system resources. The competing processes compete for the system resources such as file, display device, etc.

Co-operating processes exchanges information and communicate through the following methods.

Co-operation through Sharing: The co-operating process exchange data through some shared resources.

Co-operation through Communication: No data is shared between the processes. But they communicate for synchronisation.

The mechanism through which processes/tasks communicate each other is known as Inter Process/Task Communication (IPC). Inter Process Communication is essential for process co-ordination. The various types of Inter Process Communication (IPC) mechanisms adopted by process are kernel (Operating System) dependent. Some of the important IPC mechanisms adopted by various kernels are explained below.

10.7.1 Shared Memory

Processes share some area of the memory to communicate among them (Fig. 10.16). Information to be communicated by the process is written to the shared memory area. Other processes which require this information can read the same from the shared memory area. It is same as the real world example where 'Notice Board' is used by corporate to publish the public information among the employees (The only exception is; only corporate have the right to modify the information published on the Notice board and employees are given 'Read' only access, meaning it is only a one way channel).

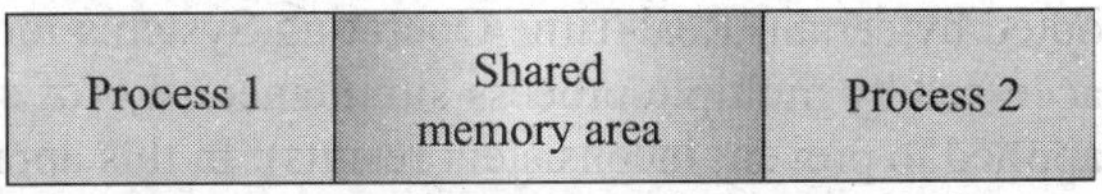

Fig. 10.16 **Concept of Shared Memory**

The implementation of shared memory concept is kernel dependent. Different mechanisms are adopted by different kernels for implementing this. A few among them are:

10.7.1.1 Pipes 'Pipe' is a section of the shared memory used by processes for communicating. Pipes follow the client-server† architecture. A process which creates a pipe is known as a pipe server and a process which connects to a pipe is known as pipe client. A pipe can be considered as a conduit for information flow and has two conceptual ends. It can be unidirectional, allowing information flow in one direction or bidirectional allowing bi-directional information flow. A unidirectional pipe allows the process connecting at one end of the pipe to write to the pipe and the process connected at the other end of the pipe to read the data, whereas a bi-directional pipe allows both reading and writing at one end. The unidirectional pipe can be visualised as

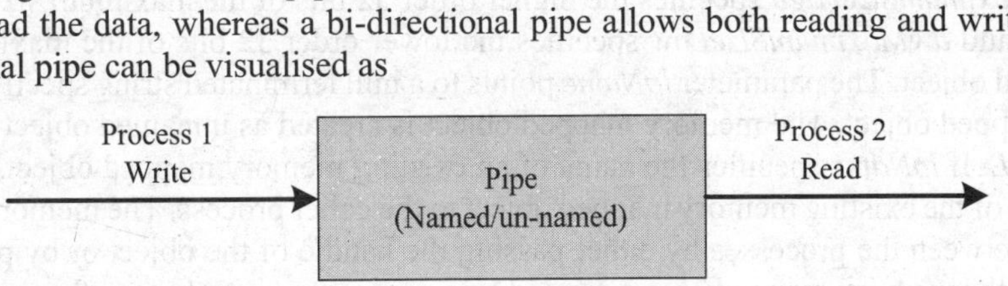

Fig. 10.17 **Concept of Pipe for IPC**

†Client Server is a software architecture containing a client application and a server application. The application which sends request is known as client and the application which receives the request process it and sends a response back to the client is known as server. A server is capable of receiving request from multiple clients.

The implementation of 'Pipes' is also OS dependent. Microsoft® Windows Desktop Operating Systems support two types of 'Pipes' for Inter Process Communication. They are:

Anonymous Pipes: The anonymous pipes are unnamed, unidirectional pipes used for data transfer between two processes.

Named Pipes: Named pipe is a named, unidirectional or bi-directional pipe for data exchange between processes. Like anonymous pipes, the process which creates the named pipe is known as pipe server. A process which connects to the named pipe is known as pipe client. With named pipes, any process can act as both client and server allowing point-to-point communication. Named pipes can be used for communicating between processes running on the same machine or between processes running on different machines connected to a network.

Please refer to the Online Learning Centre for details on the Pipe implementation under Windows Operating Systems.

Under VxWorks kernel, *pipe* is a special implementation of message queues. We will discuss the same in a latter chapter.

10.7.1.2 Memory Mapped Objects Memory mapped object is a shared memory technique adopted by certain Real-Time Operating Systems for allocating a shared block of memory which can be accessed by multiple process simultaneously (of course certain synchronisation techniques should be applied to prevent inconsistent results). In this approach a mapping object is created and physical storage for it is reserved and committed. A process can map the entire committed physical area or a block of it to its virtual address space. All read and write operation to this virtual address space by a process is directed to its committed physical area. Any process which wants to share data with other processes can map the physical memory area of the mapped object to its virtual memory space and use it for sharing the data.

Windows CE 5.0 RTOS uses the memory mapped object based shared memory technique for Inter Process Communication (Fig. 10.18). The *CreateFileMapping (HANDLE hFile, LPSECURITY_ATTRIBUTES lpFileMappingAttributes, DWORD flProtect, DWORD dwMaximumSizeHigh, DWORD dwMaximumSizeLow, LPCTSTR lpName)* system call is used for sharing the memory. This API call is used for creating a mapping from a file. In order to create the mapping from the system paging memory, the handle parameter should be passed as *INVALID_HANDLE_VALUE (–1)*. The *lpFileMappingAttributes* parameter represents the security attributes and it must be *NULL*. The *flProtect* parameter represents the read write access for the shared memory area. A value of *PAGE_READONLY* makes the shared memory read only whereas the value *PAGE_READWRITE* gives read-write access to the shared memory. The parameter *dwMaximumSizeHigh* specifies the higher order 32 bits of the maximum size of the memory mapped object and *dwMaximumSizeLow* specifies the lower order 32 bits of the maximum size of the memory mapped object. The parameter *lpName* points to a null terminated string specifying the name of the memory mapped object. The memory mapped object is created as unnamed object if the parameter *lpName* is *NULL*. If *lpName* specifies the name of an existing memory mapped object, the function returns the handle of the existing memory mapped object to the caller process. The memory mapped object can be shared between the processes by either passing the handle of the object or by passing its name. If the handle of the memory mapped object created by a process is passed to another process for shared access, there is a possibility of closing the handle by the process which created the handle while it is in use by another process. This will throw OS level exceptions. If the name of the memory object is passed for shared access among processes, processes can use this name for creating a shared memory object which will open the shared memory object already existing with the given name. The OS will maintain a

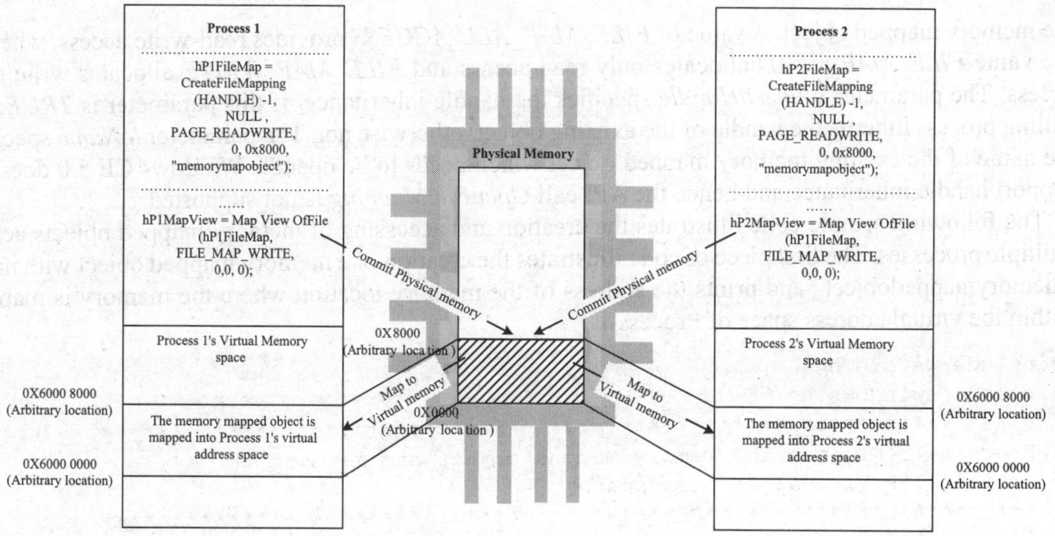

Fig. 10.18 **Concept of memory mapped object**

usage count for the named object and it is incremented each time when a process creates/opens a memory mapped object with existing name. This will prevent the destruction of a shared memory object by one process while it is being accessed by another process. Hence passing the name of the memory mapped object is strongly recommended for memory mapped object based inter process communication. The *MapViewOfFile (HANDLE hFileMappingObject DWORD dwDesiredAccess, DWORD dwFileOffsetHigh, DWORD dwFileOffsetLow, DWORD dwNumberOfBytesToMap)* system call maps a view of the memory mapped object to the address space of the calling process. The parameter *hFileMappingObject* specifies the handle to an existing memory mapped object. The *dwDesiredAccess* parameter represents the read write access for the mapped view area. A value of *FILE_MAP_WRITE* makes the view access read-write, provided the memory mapped object *hFileMappingObject* is created with read-write access, whereas the value *FILE_MAP_READ* gives read only access to the shared memory, provided the memory mapped object *hFileMappingObject* is created with read-write/read only access. The parameter *dwFileOffsetHigh* specifies the higher order 32 bits and *dwFileOffsetLow* specifies the lower order 32 bits of the memory offset where mapping is to begin from the memory mapped object. A value of '0' for both of these maps the view from the beginning memory area of the memory object. *dwNumberOfBytesToMap* specifies the number of bytes of the memory object to map. If *dwNumberOfBytesToMap* is zero, the entire memory area owned by the memory mapped object is mapped. On successful execution, *MapViewOfFile* call returns the starting address of the mapped view. If the function fails it returns *NULL*. A mapped view of the memory mapped object is unmapped by the API call *UnmapViewOfFile (LPCVOID lpBaseAddress)*. The *lpBaseAddress* parameter specifies a pointer to the base address of the mapped view of a memory object that is to be unmapped. This value must be identical to the value returned by a previous call to the *MapViewOfFile* function. Calling *UnmapViewOfFile* cleans up the committed physical storage in a process's virtual address space. In other words, it frees the virtual address space of the mapping object. Under Windows NT/XP OS, a process can open an existing memory mapped object by calling the API *OpenFileMapping(DWORD dwDesiredAccess, BOOL bInheritHandle, LPCTSTR lpName)*. The parameter *dwDesiredAccess* specifies the read write access permissions for the memory mapped object. A value of *FILE_MAP_ALL_ACCESS* provides read-write access, whereas the value *FILE_MAP_READ* allocates only read access and *FILE_MAP_WRITE* allocates write only access. The parameter *bInheritHandle* specifies the handle inheritance. If this parameter is *TRUE*, the calling process inherits the handle of the existing object, otherwise not. The parameter *lpName* specifies the name of the existing memory mapped object which needs to be opened. Windows CE 5.0 does not support handle inheritance and hence the API call *OpenFileMapping* is not supported.

The following sample code illustrates the creation and accessing of memory mapped objects across multiple processes. The first piece of code illustrates the creation of a memory mapped object with name "memorymappedobject" and prints the address of the memory location where the memory is mapped within the virtual address space of Process 1.

```
#include <stdio.h>
#include <windows.h>
//*****************************************************************
//Process 1: Creates the memory mapped object and maps it to
//Process 1's Virtual Address space
//*****************************************************************
void main() {
      //Define the handle to Memory mapped Object
      HANDLE hFileMap;
      //Define the handle to the view of Memory mapped Object
      LPTSTR hMapView;
      printf("//*******************************************\n");
      printf("                    Process 1\n");
      printf("//*******************************************\n");
      //Create an 8 KB memory mapped object
      hFileMap = CreateFileMapping( (HANDLE) -1,
       NULL,          // default security attributes
       PAGE_READWRITE, // Read-Write Access
      0, //Higher order 32 bits of the memory mapping object
      0x2000, //Lower order 32 bits of the memory mapping object
       TEXT("memorymappedobject")); // Memory mapped object name
if (NULL == hFileMap)
{
printf ("Memory mapped Object Creation Failed: Error Code: %d\n", GetLastError
());
//Memory mapped Object Creation failed. Return
return;
}

//Map the memory mapped object to Process 1's address space
hMapView= (LPTSTR) MapViewOfFile(hFileMap,
            FILE_MAP_WRITE,
            0,      //Map the entire view
            0,
            0);
if (NULL == hMapView)
```

```
{
      printf ("Mapping of Memory mapped view Failed: Error Code:
      %d\n", GetLastError ());
      //Memory mapped view Creation failed. Return
      return;
}
else
{
      //Successfully created the memory mapped view.
      //Print the start address of the mapped view
      printf ("The memory is mapped to the virtual address starting
      at 0x%08x\n", hMapView);
}
//Wait for user input to exit. Run Process 2 before providing
//user input
printf ("Press any key to terminate Process 1");
getchar();
//Unmap the view
UnmapViewOfFile(hMapView);
//Close memory mapped object handle
CloseHandle(hFileMap);
return;
}
```

The piece of code given below corresponds to Process 2. It illustrates the accessing of an existing memory mapped object (memory mapped object with name "memorymappedobject" created by Process 1) and prints the address of the memory location where the memory is mapped within the virtual address space of Process 2. To demonstrate the application, the program corresponding to Process 1 should be executed first and the program corresponding to Process 2 should be executed following Process 1.

```
#include <stdio.h>
#include <windows.h>
//*******************************************************************
//Process 2: Opens the memory mapped object created by Process 1
//Maps the object to Process 2's virtual address space.
//*******************************************************************
void main() {
      //Define the handle for the Memory mapped Object
      HANDLE hChildFileMap;
      //Define the handle for the view of Memory mapped Object
      LPTSTR hChildMapView;
      printf("//*******************************************\n");
      printf("            Process 2\n");
      printf("//*******************************************\n");
      //Create an 8 KB memory mapped object
      hChildFileMap = CreateFileMapping( INVALID_HANDLE_VALUE,
      NULL,           // default security attributes
      PAGE_READWRITE, // Read-Write Access
      0, //Higher order 32 bits of the memory mapping object
```

```
      0x2000, //Lower order 32 bits of the memory mapping object
      TEXT("memorymappedobject"));    // Memory mapped object name
if (NULL == hChildFileMap || INVALID_HANDLE_VALUE == hChildFileMap)
{
printf ("Memory mapped Object Creation Failed: Error Code: %d\n",
GetLastError ());
//Memory mapped Object Creation failed. Return
return;
}
else

      if (ERROR_ALREADY_EXISTS == GetLastError ())
      {
      //A memory mapped object with given name exists already.
       printf ("The named memory mapped object is already
      existing\n");
      }
//Map the memory mapped object to Process 2's address space

hChildMapView=(LPTSTR)MapViewOfFile(hChildFileMap,
                    FILE_MAP_WRITE, //Read-Write access
                    0,    //Map the entire view
                    0,
                    0);
if (NULL == hChildMapView)
{
printf ("Mapping of Memory mapped view Failed: Error Code: %d\n", GetLastError
());
//Memory mapped view Creation failed. Return
return;
}

else
{
//Successfully created the memory mapped view.
//Print the start address of the mapped view
printf ("The memory mapped view starts at memory location 0x%08x\n", hChild-
MapView);
}

//Unmap the view
UnmapViewOfFile(hChildMapView);
//Close memory mapped object handle
CloseHandle(hChildFileMap);
return;
}
```

The output of the above programs when run in the sequence, Process 1 is executed first and Process 2 is executed while Process 1 waits for the user input from the keyboard, is given in Fig. 10.19.

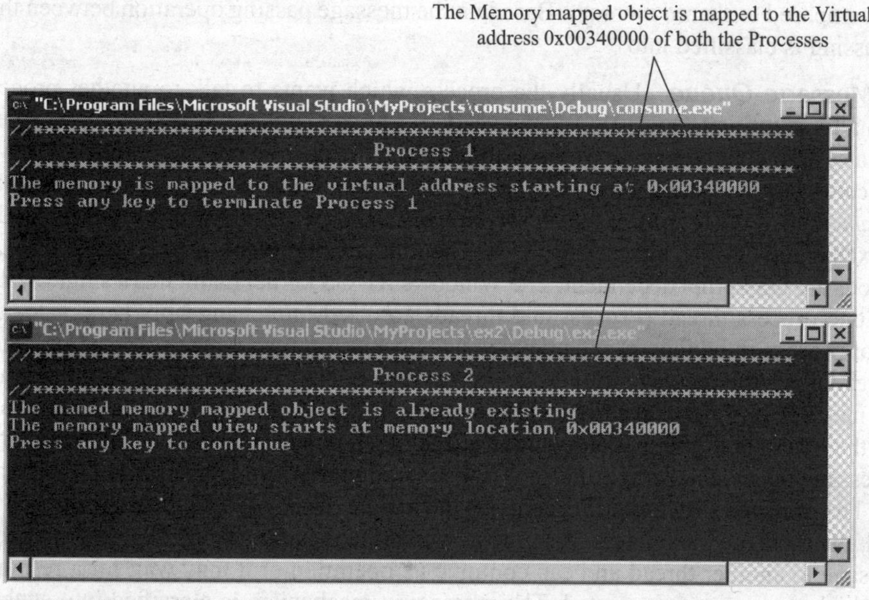

Fig. 10.19 **Output of Win32 memory mapped object illustration program**

This reveals that using memory mapped objects with same name across multiple processes running on the same system maps the object to the same virtual address space of the processes.

Reading and writing to a memory mapped area is same as any read write operation using pointers. The pointer returned by the API call *MapViewOfFile* can be used for this. The exercise of Read and Write operation is left to the readers. Proper care should be taken to avoid any conflicts that may arise due to the simultaneous read/write access of the shared memory area by multiple processes. This can be handled by applying various synchronisation techniques like events, mutex, semaphore, etc.

For using a memory mapped object across multiple threads of a process, it is not required for all the threads of the process to create/open the memory mapped object and map it to the thread's virtual address space. Since the thread's address space is part of the process's virtual address space, which contains the thread, only one thread, preferably the parent thread (main thread) is required to create the memory mapped object and map it to the process's virtual address space. The thread which creates the memory mapped object can share the pointer to the mapped memory area as global pointer and other threads of the process can use this pointer for reading and writing to the mapped memory area. If one thread of a process tries to create a memory mapped object with the same name as that of an existing mapping object, which is created by another thread of the same process, a new view of the mapping object is created at a different virtual address of the process. This is same as one process trying to create two views of the same memory mapped object☺.

10.7.2 Message Passing

Message passing is an (a)synchronous information exchange mechanism used for Inter Process/Thread

Communication. The major difference between shared memory and message passing technique is that, through shared memory lots of data can be shared whereas only limited amount of info/data is passed through message passing. Also message passing is relatively fast and free from the synchronisation overheads compared to shared memory. Based on the message passing operation between the processes, message passing is classified into

10.7.2.1 Message Queue Usually the process which wants to talk to another process posts the message to a First-In-First-Out (FIFO) queue called 'Message queue', which stores the messages temporarily in a system defined memory object, to pass it to the desired process (Fig. 10.20). Messages are sent and received through *send* (*Name of the process to which the message is to be sent, message*) and *receive* (*Name of the process from which the message is to be received, message*) methods. The messages are exchanged through a message queue. The implementation of the message queue, *send* and *receive* methods are OS kernel dependent. The Windows XP OS kernel maintains a single system message queue and one process/thread (Process and threads are used interchangeably here, since thread is the basic unit of process in windows) specific message queue. A thread which wants to communicate with another thread posts the message to the system message queue. The kernel picks up the message from the system message queue one at a time and examines the message for finding the destination thread and then posts the message to the message queue of the corresponding thread. For posting a message to a thread's message queue, the kernel fills a message structure *MSG* and copies it to the message queue of the thread. The message structure *MSG* contains the handle of the process/thread for which the message is intended, the message parameters, the time at which the message is posted, etc. A thread can simply post a message to another thread and can continue its operation or it may wait for a response from the thread to which the message is posted. The messaging mechanism is classified into synchronous and asynchronous based on the behaviour of the message posting thread. In asynchronous messaging, the message posting thread just posts the message to the queue and it will not wait for an acceptance (return) from the thread to which the message is posted, whereas in synchronous messaging, the thread which posts a message enters waiting state and waits for the message result from the thread to which the message is posted. The thread which invoked the send message becomes blocked and the scheduler will not pick it up for scheduling. The *PostMessage (HWND hWnd, UINT Msg, WPARAM wParam, LPARAM*

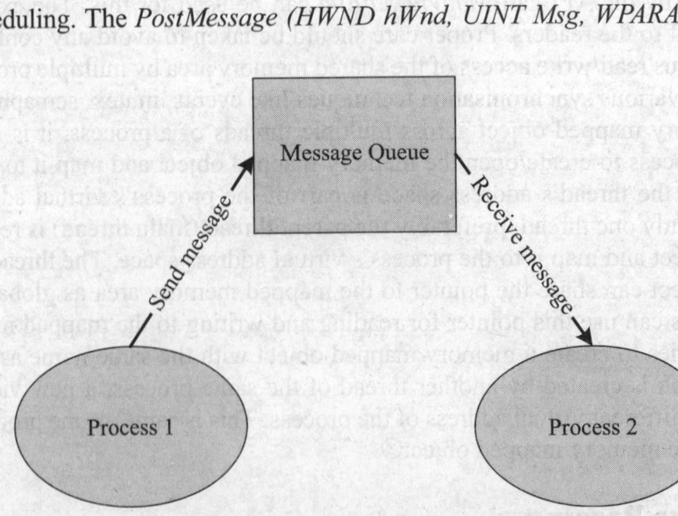

Fig. 10.20 Concept of message queue based indirect messaging for IPC

lParam) or *PostThreadMessage (DWORD idThread, UINT Msg, WPARAM wParam, LPARAM lParam)* API is used by a thread in Windows for posting a message to its own message queue or to the message queue of another thread. The *PostMessage* API does not always guarantee the posting of messages to message queue. The *PostMessage* API will not post a message to the message queue when the message queue is full. Hence it is recommended to check the return value of *PostMessage* API to confirm the posting of message. The *SendMessage (HWND hWnd, UINT Msg, WPARAM wParam, LPARAM lParam)* API call sends a message to the thread specified by the handle *hWnd* and waits for the callee thread to process the message. The thread which calls the *SendMessage* API enters waiting state and waits for the message result from the thread to which the message is posted. The thread which invoked the *SendMessage* API call becomes blocked and the scheduler will not pick it up for scheduling.

The Windows CE operating system supports a special Point-to-Point Message queue implementation. The OS maintains a First In First Out (FIFO) buffer for storing the messages and each process can access this buffer for reading and writing messages. The OS also maintains a special queue, with single message storing capacity, for storing high priority messages (Alert messages). The creation and usage of message queues under Windows CE OS is explained below.

The *CreateMsgQueue(LPCWSTR lpszName, LPMSGQUEUEOPTIONS lpOptions)* API call creates a message queue or opens a named message queue and returns a read only or write only handle to the message queue. A process can use this handle for reading or writing a message from/to of the message queue pointed by the handle. The parameter *lpszName* specifies the name of the message queue. If this parameter is *NULL*, an unnamed message queue is created. Processes can use the handle returned by the API call if the message queue is created without any name. If the message queue is created as named message queue, other processes can use the name of the message queue for opening the named message queue created by a process. Calling the *CreateMsgQueue* API with an existing named message queue as parameter returns a handle to the existing message queue. Under the Desktop Windows Operating Systems (Windows 9x/XP/NT/2K), each object type (viz. mutex, semaphores, events, memory maps, watchdog timers and message queues) share the same namespace and the same name is not allowed for creating any of this. Windows CE kernel maintains separate namespace for each and supports the same name across different objects. The *lpOptions* parameter points to a *MSGQUEUEOPTIONS* structure that sets the properties of the message queue. The member details of the *MSGQUEUEOPTIONS* structure is explained below.

```
typedef MSGQUEUEOPTIONS_OS{
  DWORD dwSize;
  DWORD dwFlags;
  DWORD dwMaxMessages;
  DWORD cbMaxMessage;
  BOOL bReadAccess;
} MSGQUEUEOPTIONS, FAR* LPMSGQUEUEOPTIONS, *PMSGQUEUEOPTIONS;
```

The members of the structure are listed below.

Member	Description
dwSize	Specifies the size of the structure in bytes
dwFlags	Describes the behaviour of the message queue. Set to MSGQUEUE_NOPRECOMMIT to allocate message buffers on demand and to free the message buffers after they are read, or set to MSGQUEUE_ALLOW_BROKEN to enable a read or write operation to complete even if there is no corresponding writer or reader present.

dwMaxMessages	Specifies the maximum number of messages to queue at any point of time. Set this value to zero to specify no limit on the number of messages to queue at any point of time.
cbMaxMessage	Specifies the maximum number of bytes in each message. This value must be greater than zero.
bReadAccess	Specifies the Read Write access to the message queue. Set to TRUE to request read access to the queue. Set to FALSE to request write access to the queue.

On successful execution, the *CreateMsgQueue* API call returns a 'Read Only' or 'Write Only' handle to the specified queue based on the *bReadAccess* member of the *MSGQUEUEOPTIONS* structure *lpOptions*. If the queue with specified name already exists, a new handle, which points to the existing queue, is created and a following call to *GetLastError* returns *ERROR_ALREADY_EXISTS*. If the function fails it returns *NULL*. A single call to the *CreateMsgQueue* creates the queue for either 'read' or 'write' access. The *CreateMsgQueue* API should be called twice with the *bReadAccess* member of the *MSGQUEUEOPTIONS* structure *lpOptions* set to TRUE and FALSE respectively in successive calls for obtaining 'Read only' and 'Write only' handles to the specified message queue. The handle returning by *CreateMsgQueue* API call is an *event* handle and, if it is a 'Read Only' access handle, it is signalled by the message queue if a new message is placed in the queue. The signal is reset on reading the message by *ReadMsgQueue* API call. A 'Write Only' access handle to the message queue is signalled when the queue is no longer full, i.e. when there is room for accommodating new messages. Processes can monitor the handles with the help of the wait functions, viz. *WaitForSingleObject* or *WaitForMultipleObjects*, supported by Windows CE. The *OpenMsgQueue(HANDLE hSrcProc, HANDLE hMsgQ, LPMSGQUEUEOPTIONS lpOptions)* API call opens an existing named or unnamed message queue. The parameter *hSrcProc* specifies the process handle of the process that owns the message queue and *hMsgQ* specifies the handle of the existing message queue (Handle to the message queue returned by the CreateMsgQueue function). As in the case of *CreateMsgQueue*, the *lpOptions* parameter points to a *MSGQUEUEOPTIONS* structure that sets the properties of the message queue. On successful execution the *OpenMsgQueue* API call returns a handle to the message queue and *NULL* if it fails. Normally the *OpenMsgQueue* API is used for opening an unnamed message queue. The *WriteMsgQueue(HANDLE hMsgQ, LPVOID lpBuffer, DWORD cbDataSize, DWORD dwTimeout, DWORD dwFlags)* API call is used for writing a single message to the message queue pointed by the handle *hMsgQ*. *lpBuffer* points to a buffer that contains the message to be written to the message queue. The parameter *cbDataSize* specifies the number of bytes stored in the buffer pointed by *lpBuffer*, which forms a message. The parameter *dwTimeout* specifies the timeout interval in milliseconds for the message writing operation. A value of zero specifies the write operation to return immediately without blocking if the write operation cannot succeed. If the parameter is set to *INFINITE*, the write operation will block until it succeeds or the message queue signals the 'write only' handle indicating the availability of space for posting a message. The *dwFlags* parameter sets the priority of the message. If it is set to *MSGQUEUE_MSGALERT*, the message is posted to the queue as high priority or alert message. The Alert message is always placed in the front of the message queue. This function returns *TRUE* if it succeeds and *FALSE* otherwise.

The *ReadMsgQueue(HANDLE hMsgQ, LPVOID lpBuffer, DWORD cbBufferSize, LPDWORD lpNumberOfBytesRead, DWORD dwTimeout, DWORD* pdwFlags)* API reads a single message from the message queue. The parameter *hMsgQ* specifies a handle to the message queue from which the message needs to be read. *lpBuffer* points to a buffer for storing the message read from the queue. The parameter *cbBufferSize* specifies the size of the buffer pointed by *lpBuffer*, in bytes. *lpNumberOfBytesRead* specifies the number of bytes stored in the buffer. This is same as the number of bytes present in the message which is read from the message queue. *dwTimeout* specifies the timeout interval in milliseconds for the message reading operation. The timeout values and their meaning are same as that of the write message timeout parameter. The *dwFlags* parameter indicates the priority of the message. If the message read from the message queue is a high priority message (alert message), *dwFlags* is set to *MSGQUEUE_MSGALERT*. The function returns *TRUE* if it succeeds and *FALSE* otherwise. The *GetMsgQueueInfo (HANDLE hMsgQ, LPMSGQUEUEINFO lpInfo)* API call returns the information about a message queue specified by the handle *hMsgQ*. The message information is returned in a *MSGQUEUEINFO* structure pointed by *lpInfo*. The details of the *MSGQUEUEINFO* structure is explained below.

```
typedef MSGQUEUEINFO{
  DWORD dwSize;
  DWORD dwFlags;
  DWORD dwMaxMessages;
  DWORD cbMaxMessage;
  DWORD dwCurrentMessages;
  DWORD dwMaxQueueMessages;
  WORD wNumReaders;
  WORD wNumWriters;
} MSGQUEUEINFO, *PMSGQUEUEINFO, FAR* LPMSGQUEUEINFO;
```

The member variable details are listed below.

Member	Description
DwSize	Specifies the size of the buffer passed in.
dwFlags	Describes the behaviour of the message queue. It retrieves the *MSGQUEUEOPTIONS. dwFlags* passed when the message queue is created with *CreateMsgQueue* API call.
dwMaxMessages	Specifies the maximum number of messages to queue at any point of time. This reflects the *MSGQUEUEOPTIONS. dwMaxMessages* value passed when the message queue is created with *CreateMsgQueue* API call.
cbMaxMessage	Specifies the maximum number of bytes in each message. This reflects the *MSGQUEUEOPTIONS.cbMaxMessage* value passed when the message queue is created with *CreateMsgQueue* API call.
dwCurrentMessages	Specifies the number of messages currently existing in the specified message queue.
dwMaxQueueMessages	Specifies maximum number of messages that have ever been in the queue at one time.
wNumReaders	Specifies the number of readers (processes which opened the message queue for reading) subscribed to the message queue for reading.
wNumWriters	Specifies the number of writers (processes which opened the message queue for writing) subscribed to the message queue for writing.

The *GetMsgQueueInfo* API call returns *TRUE* if it succeeds and *FALSE* otherwise. The *CloseMsgQueue(HANDLE hMsgQ)* API call closes a message queue specified by the handle *hMsgQ*. If a process holds a 'read only' and 'write only' handle to the message queue, both should be closed for closing the message queue.

'Message queue' is the primary inter-task communication mechanism under VxWorks kernel. Message queues support two-way communication of messages of variable length. The two-way messaging between tasks can be implemented using one message queue for incoming messages and another one for outgoing messages. Messaging mechanism can be used for task-to task and task to Interrupt Service Routine (ISR) communication. We will discuss about the VxWorks' message queue implementation in a separate chapter.

10.7.2.2 Mailbox Mailbox is an alternate form of 'Message queues' and it is used in certain Real-Time Operating Systems for IPC. Mailbox technique for IPC in RTOS is usually used for one way messaging. The task/thread which wants to send a message to other tasks/threads creates a mailbox for posting the messages. The threads which are interested in receiving the messages posted to the mailbox by the mailbox creator thread can subscribe to the mailbox. The thread which creates the mailbox is known as 'mailbox server' and the threads which subscribe to the mailbox are known as 'mailbox clients'. The mailbox server posts messages to the mailbox and notifies it to the clients which are subscribed to the mailbox. The clients read the message from the mailbox on receiving the notification. The mailbox creation, subscription, message reading and writing are achieved through OS kernel provided API calls. Mailbox and message queues are same in functionality. The only difference is in the number of messages supported by them. Both of them are used for passing data in the form of message(s) from a task to another task(s). Mailbox is used for exchanging a single message between two tasks or between an Interrupt Service Routine (ISR) and a task. Mailbox associates a pointer pointing to the mailbox and a wait list to hold the tasks waiting for a message to appear in the mailbox. The implementation of mailbox is OS kernel dependent. The MicroC/OS-II implements mailbox as a mechanism for inter-task communication. We will discuss about the mailbox based IPC implementation under MicroC/OS-II in a latter chapter. Figure 10.21 given below illustrates the mailbox based IPC technique.

10.7.2.3 Signalling Signalling is a primitive way of communication between processes/threads. *Signals* are used for asynchronous notifications where one process/thread fires a signal, indicating the occurrence of a scenario which the other process(es)/thread(s) is waiting. Signals are not queued and they do not carry any data. The communication mechanisms used in RTX51 Tiny OS is an example for Signalling. The *os_send_signal* kernel call under RTX 51 sends a signal from one task to a specified task. Similarly the *os_wait* kernel call waits for a specified signal. Refer to the topic 'Round Robin Scheduling' under the section 'Priority based scheduling' for more details on Signalling in RTX51 Tiny OS. The VxWorks RTOS kernel also implements 'signals' for inter process

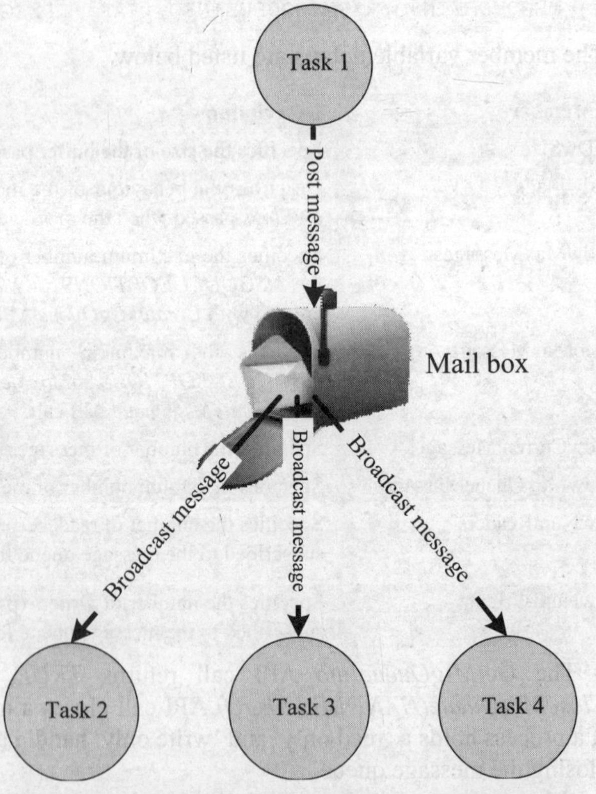

Fig. 10.21 Concept of Mailbox based indirect messaging for IPC

communication. Whenever a specified signal occurs it is handled in a signal handler associated with the signal. We will discuss about the signal based IPC mechanism for VxWorks' kernel in a later chapter.

10.7.3 Remote Procedure Call (RPC) and Sockets

Remote Procedure Call or RPC (Fig. 10.22) is the Inter Process Communication (IPC) mechanism used by a process to call a procedure of another process running on the same CPU or on a different CPU which is interconnected in a network. In the object oriented language terminology RPC is also known as *Remote Invocation* or *Remote Method Invocation (RMI)*. RPC is mainly used for distributed applications like client-server applications. With RPC it is possible to communicate over a heterogeneous network (i.e. Network where Client and server applications are running on different Operating systems). The CPU/process containing the procedure which needs to be invoked remotely is known as server. The CPU/process which initiates an RPC request is known as client.

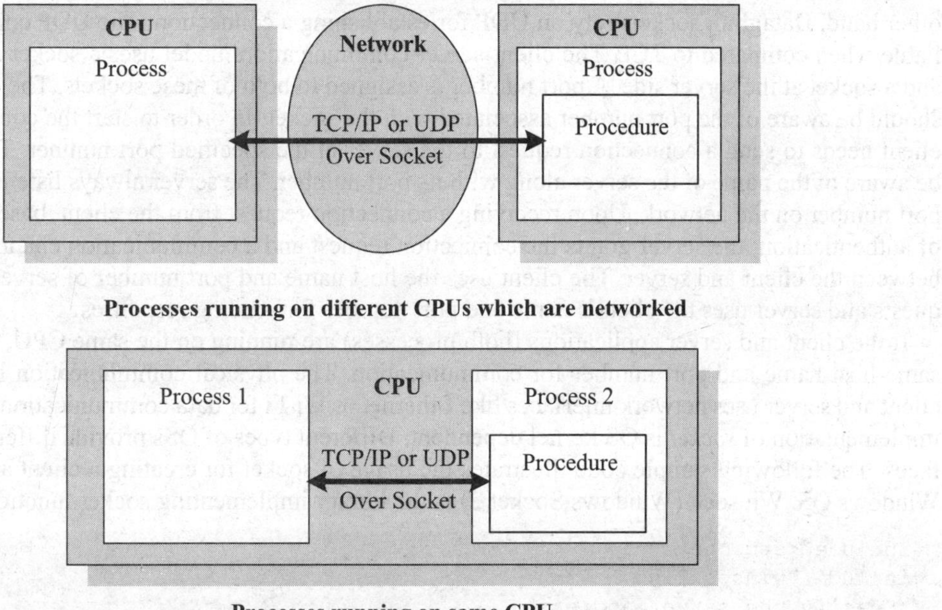

Fig. 10.22 **Concept of Remote Procedure Call (RPC) for IPC**

It is possible to implement RPC communication with different invocation interfaces. In order to make the RPC communication compatible across all platforms it should stick on to certain standard formats. Interface Definition Language (IDL) defines the interfaces for RPC. Microsoft Interface Definition Language (MIDL) is the IDL implementation from Microsoft for all Microsoft platforms. The RPC communication can be either Synchronous (Blocking) or Asynchronous (Non-blocking). In the Synchronous communication, the process which calls the remote procedure is blocked until it receives a response back from the other process. In asynchronous RPC calls, the calling process continues its execution while the remote process performs the execution of the procedure. The result from the remote procedure is returned back to the caller through mechanisms like callback functions.

On security front, RPC employs authentication mechanisms to protect the systems against vulnerabilities. The client applications (processes) should authenticate themselves with the server for getting access. Authentication mechanisms like IDs, public key cryptography (like DES, 3DES), etc. are used by the client for authentication. Without authentication, any client can access the remote procedure. This may lead to potential security risks.

Sockets are used for RPC communication. *Socket is a logical endpoint in a two-way communication link between two applications running on a network. A port number is associated with a socket so that the network layer of the communication channel can deliver the data to the designated application.* Sockets are of different types, namely, Internet sockets (INET), UNIX sockets, etc. The INET socket works on internet communication protocol. TCP/IP, UDP, etc. are the communication protocols used by INET sockets. INET sockets are classified into:

1. Stream sockets
2. Datagram sockets

Stream sockets are connection oriented and they use TCP to establish a reliable connection. On the other hand, Datagram sockets rely on UDP for establishing a connection. The UDP connection is unreliable when compared to TCP. The client-server communication model uses a socket at the client side and a socket at the server side. A port number is assigned to both of these sockets. The client and server should be aware of the port number associated with the socket. In order to start the communication, the client needs to send a connection request to the server at the specified port number. The client should be aware of the name of the server along with its port number. The server always listens to the specified port number on the network. Upon receiving a connection request from the client, based on the success of authentication, the server grants the connection request and a communication channel is established between the client and server. The client uses the host name and port number of server for sending requests and server uses the client's name and port number for sending responses.

If the client and server applications (both processes) are running on the same CPU, both can use the same host name and port number for communication. The physical communication link between the client and server uses network interfaces like Ethernet or Wi-Fi for data communication. The underlying implementation of *socket* is OS kernel dependent. Different types of OSs provide different socket interfaces. The following sample code illustrates the usage of socket for creating a client application under Windows OS. Winsock (Windows Socket 2) is the library implementing socket functions for Win32.

```
#include <stdio.h>
#include "winsock2.h"
//Specify the server address
#define SERVER          "172.168.0.1"
//Specify the server port
#define PORT 5000
int buflength = 100;
char *sendbuf = "Hi from Client";
char buffer[buflength];
void main() {
  //*****************************************************
  // Initialize Winsock
  WSADATA wsaData;
  if (WSAStartup(MAKEWORD(2,2), &wsaData) == NO_ERROR)
      printf("Winsock Initialisation succeeded…\n");
```

```
else
{
  printf("Winsock Initialisation failed…\n");
  return;
}
//*********************************************************
// Create a SOCKET for connecting to server
SOCKET MySocket;
MySocket = socket(AF_INET, SOCK_STREAM, IPPROTO_TCP);
if (MySocket == INVALID_SOCKET)
{
  printf("Socket Creation failed…\n");
  WSACleanup();
  return;
}
else
 {
  printf("Successfully created the socket…\n");
//*********************************************************
// Set the Socket type, IP address and port of the server
sockaddr_in ServerParams;
ServerParams.sin_family = AF_INET;
ServerParams.sin_addr.s_addr = inet_addr( SERVER );
ServerParams.sin_port = htons( PORT );
//*********************************************************
// Connect to server.
if ( connect( MySocket, (SOCKADDR*) & ServerParams, sizeof(ServerParams) )
  == SOCKET_ERROR) {
  printf( "Connecting to Server failed…\n" );
  WSACleanup();
  return;
}
else
{
printf("Successfully Connected to the server…\n");
//*********************************************************
// Send command to server
if (send(MySocket, sendbuf, (int)strlen(sendbuf), 0)
     == SOCKET_ERROR) {
  printf("Sending data to server failed…\n");
  closesocket(MySocket);
  WSACleanup();
  return;
}
else
{
printf("Successfully sent command to server…\n");
```

```
//************************************************************
// Receive a data packet
  if (recv(MySocket, recvbuf, recvbuflen, 0) > 0 )
      printf("Successfully Received a byte…\n
    The received byte is %s\n", recvbuf);
  else
    printf("No response from server…\n");
//************************************************************
//Close Socket
  closesocket(MySocket);
  WSACleanup();
  return;
}
}
}
}
}
```

The above application tries to connect to a server machine with IP address 172.168.0.1 and port number 5000. Change the values of *SERVER* and *PORT* to connect to a machine with different IP address and port number. If the connection is success, it sends the data "Hi from Client" to the server and waits for a response from the server and finally terminates the connection.

Under Windows, the socket function library *Winsock* should be initiated before using the socket related functions. The function *WSAStartup* performs this initiation. The *socket()* function call creates a socket. The socket type, connection type and protocols for communication are the parameters for socket creation. Here the socket type is *INET* (*AF_INET*) and connection type is stream socket (*SOCK_STREAM*). The protocol selected for communication is *TCP/IP* (*IPPROTO_TCP*). After creating the socket it is connected to a server. For connecting to server, the server address and port number should be indicated in the connection request. The *sockaddr_in* structure specifies the socket type, IP address and port of the server to be connected to. The *connect ()* function connects the socket with a specified server. If the server grants the connection request, the *connect ()* function returns success. The *send()* function is used for sending data to a server. It takes the socket name and data to be sent as parameters. Data from server is received using the function call *recv()*. It takes the socket name and details of buffer to hold the received data as parameters. The TCP/IP network stack expects network byte order (Big Endian: Higher order byte of the data is stored in lower memory address location) for data. The function *htons()* converts the byte order of an unsigned short integer to the network order. The *closesockct()* function closes the socket connection. On the server side, the server creates a socket using the function *socket()* and binds the socket with a port using the *bind()* function. It listens to the port bonded to the socket for any incoming connection request. The function *listen()* performs this. Upon receiving a connection request, the server accepts it. The function *accept()* performs the accepting operation. Now the connectivity is established. Server can receive and transmit data using the function calls *recv()* and *send()* respectively. The implementation of the server application is left to the readers as an exercise.

10.8 TASK SYNCHRONISATION

In a multitasking environment, multiple processes run concurrently (in pseudo parallelism) and share the system resources. Apart from this, each process has its own boundary wall and they communicate with each other with different IPC mechanisms including shared memory and variables. Imagine a situation where two processes try to access display hardware connected to the system or two processes try to access a shared memory area where one process tries to write to a memory location when the other process is trying to read from this. What could be the result in these scenarios? Obviously unexpected results. How these issues can be addressed? The solution is, make each process aware of the access of a shared resource either directly or indirectly. The act of making processes aware of the access of shared resources by each process to avoid conflicts is known as '*Task/Process Synchronisation*'. Various synchronisation issues may arise in a multitasking environment if processes are not synchronised properly. The following sections describe the major task communication synchronisation issues observed in multitasking and the commonly adopted synchronisation techniques to overcome these issues.

10.8.1 Task Communication/Synchronisation Issues

10.8.1.1 Racing Let us have a look at the following piece of code:

```
#include <windows.h>
#include <stdio.h>
//****************************************************************
//counter is an integer variable and Buffer is a byte array shared
//between two processes Process A and Process B
char Buffer[10] = {1,2,3,4,5,6,7,8,9,10};
short int counter = 0;
//****************************************************************
// Process A
void Process_A (void) {
int i;
  for (i =0; i<5; i++)
{
    if (Buffer[i] > 0)
       counter++;
}
}
//****************************************************************
// Process B
void Process_B(void) {
int j;
  for (j =5; j<10; j++)
{
    if (Buffer[j] > 0)
       counter++;
}
}
//****************************************************************
//Main Thread.
int main() {
       DWORD id;
```

```
    CreateThread(NULL,0,
                    (LPTHREAD_START_ROUTINE)Process_A,
                    (LPVOID)0,0,&id);
    CreateThread(NULL,0,
                    (LPTHREAD_START_ROUTINE)Process_B,
                    (LPVOID)0,0,&id);
    Sleep(100000);
    return 0;
}
```

From a programmer perspective the value of *counter* will be 10 at the end of execution of processes A & B. But 'it need not be always' in a real world execution of this piece of code under a multitasking kernel. The results depend on the process scheduling policies adopted by the OS kernel. Now let's dig into the piece of code illustrated above. The program statement *counter++;* looks like a single statement from a high level programming language ('C' language) perspective. The low level implementation of this statement is dependent on the underlying processor instruction set and the (cross) compiler in use. The low level implementation of the high level program statement *counter++;* under Windows XP operating system running on an *Intel Centrino Duo* processor is given below. The code snippet is compiled with Microsoft Visual Studio 6.0 compiler.

```
mov eax,dword ptr [ebp-4];Load counter in Accumulator
add eax,1 ; Increment Accumulator by 1
mov dword ptr [ebp-4],eax ;Store counter with Accumulator
```

At the processor instruction level, the value of the variable *counter* is loaded to the Accumulator register (***EAX*** register). The memory variable *counter* is represented using a pointer. The base pointer register (***EBP*** register) is used for pointing to the memory variable *counter*. After loading the contents of the variable *counter* to the Accumulator, the Accumulator content is incremented by one using the add instruction. Finally the content of Accumulator is loaded to the memory location which represents the variable counter. Both the processes Process A and Process B contain the program statement *counter++;* Translating this into the machine instruction.

Process A	Process B
mov eax,dword ptr [ebp-4]	mov eax,dword ptr [ebp-4]
add eax,1	add eax,1
mov dword ptr [ebp-4],eax	mov dword ptr [ebp-4],eax

Imagine a situation where a process switching (context switching) happens from Process A to Process B when Process A is executing the *counter++;* statement. Process A accomplishes the *counter++;* statement through three different low level instructions. Now imagine that the process switching happened at the point where Process A executed the low level instruction, 'mov eax,dword ptr [ebp-4]' and is about to execute the next instruction 'add eax,1'. The scenario is illustrated in Fig. 10.23.

Process B increments the shared variable 'counter' in the middle of the operation where Process A tries to increment it. When Process A gets the CPU time for execution, it starts from the point where it got interrupted (If Process B is also using the same registers *eax* and *ebp* for executing *counter++;*

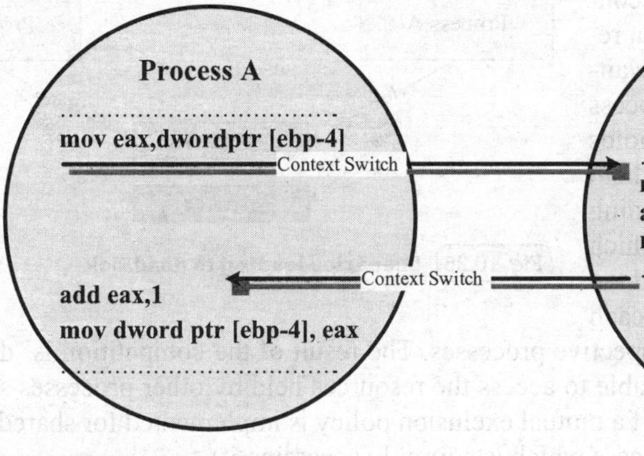

Fig. 10.23 **Race condition**

instruction, the original content of these registers will be saved as part of the context saving and it will be retrieved back as part of context retrieval, when process A gets the CPU for execution. Hence the content of *eax* and *ebp* remains intact irrespective of context switching). Though the variable *counter* is incremented by Process B, Process A is unaware of it and it increments the variable with the old value. This leads to the loss of one increment for the variable *counter*. This problem occurs due to non-atomic† operation on variables. This issue wouldn't have been occurred if the underlying actions corresponding to the program statement *counter++;* is finished in a single CPU execution cycle. The best way to avoid this situation is make the access and modification of shared variables mutually exclusive; meaning when one process accesses a shared variable, prevent the other processes from accessing it. We will discuss this technique in more detail under the topic '*Task Synchronisation techniques*' in a later section of this chapter.

To summarise, *Racing* or *Race condition* is the situation in which multiple processes compete (race) each other to access and manipulate shared data concurrently. In a Race condition the final value of the shared data depends on the process which acted on the data finally.

10.8.1.2 Deadlock A race condition produces incorrect results whereas a deadlock condition creates a situation where none of the processes are able to make any progress in their execution, resulting in a set of deadlocked processes. A situation very similar to our traffic jam issues in a junction as illustrated in Fig. 10.24.

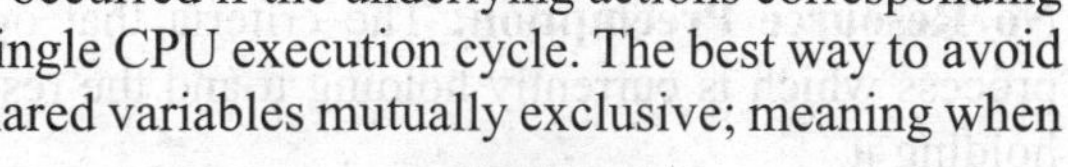
Fig. 10.24 **Deadlock visualisation**

† Atomic Operation: Operations which are non-interruptible.

In its simplest form 'deadlock' is the condition in which a process is waiting for a resource held by another process which is waiting for a resource held by the first process (Fig. 10.25). To elaborate: Process A holds a resource x and it wants a resource y held by Process B. Process B is currently holding resource y and it wants the resource x which is currently held by Process A. Both hold the respective resources and they compete each other to get the resource held by the respective processes. The result of the competition is 'deadlock'. None of the competing process will be able to access the resources held by other processes since they are locked by the respective processes (If a mutual exclusion policy is implemented for shared resource access, the resource is locked by the process which is currently accessing it).

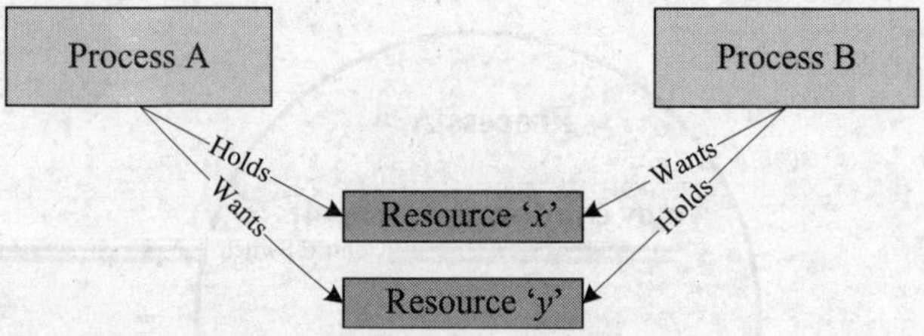

Fig. 10.25 **Scenarios leading to deadlock**

The different conditions favouring a deadlock situation are listed below.

Mutual Exclusion: The criteria that only one process can hold a resource at a time. Meaning processes should access shared resources with mutual exclusion. Typical example is the accessing of display hardware in an embedded device.

Hold and Wait: The condition in which a process holds a shared resource by acquiring the lock controlling the shared access and waiting for additional resources held by other processes.

No Resource Preemption: The criteria that operating system cannot take back a resource from a process which is currently holding it and the resource can only be released voluntarily by the process holding it.

Circular Wait: A process is waiting for a resource which is currently held by another process which in turn is waiting for a resource held by the first process. In general, there exists a set of waiting process P0, P1 … Pn with P0 is waiting for a resource held by P1 and P1 is waiting for a resource held by P0, …, Pn is waiting for a resource held by P0 and P0 is waiting for a resource held by Pn and so on… This forms a circular wait queue.

'Deadlock' is a result of the combined occurrence of these four conditions listed above. These conditions are first described by E. G. Coffman in 1971 and it is popularly known as *Coffman conditions*.

Deadlock Handling A smart OS may foresee the deadlock condition and will act proactively to avoid such a situation. Now if a deadlock occurred, how the OS responds to it? The reaction to deadlock condition by OS is nonuniform. The OS may adopt any of the following techniques to detect and prevent deadlock conditions.

Ignore Deadlocks: Always assume that the system design is deadlock free. This is acceptable for the reason the cost of removing a deadlock is large compared to the chance of happening a deadlock. UNIX is an example for an OS following this principle. A life critical system cannot pretend that it is deadlock free for any reason.

Detect and Recover: This approach suggests the detection of a deadlock situation and recovery from it. This is similar to the deadlock condition that may arise at a traffic junction. When the vehicles from different directions compete to cross the junction, deadlock (traffic jam) condition is resulted. Once a deadlock (traffic jam) is happened at the junction, the only solution is to back up the vehicles from one direction and allow the vehicles from opposite direction to cross the junction. If the traffic is too high, lots of vehicles may have to be backed up to resolve the traffic jam. This technique is also known as 'back up cars' technique (Fig. 10.26).

Fig. 10.26 ***'Back up cars'* technique for deadlock recovery**

Operating systems keep a resource graph in their memory. The resource graph is updated on each resource request and release. A deadlock condition can be detected by analysing the resource graph by graph analyser algorithms. Once a deadlock condition is detected, the system can terminate a process or preempt the resource to break the deadlocking cycle.

Avoid Deadlocks: Deadlock is avoided by the careful resource allocation techniques by the Operating System. It is similar to the traffic light mechanism at junctions to avoid the traffic jams.

Prevent Deadlocks: Prevent the deadlock condition by negating one of the four conditions favouring the deadlock situation.

- Ensure that a process does not hold any other resources when it requests a resource. This can be achieved by implementing the following set of rules/guidelines in allocating resources to processes.
    1. A process must request all its required resource and the resources should be allocated before the process begins its execution.
    2. Grant resource allocation requests from processes only if the process does not hold a resource currently.

- Ensure that resource preemption (resource releasing) is possible at operating system level. This can be achieved by implementing the following set of rules/guidelines in resources allocation and releasing.
    1. Release all the resources currently held by a process if a request made by the process for a new resource is not able to fulfil immediately.
    2. Add the resources which are preempted (released) to a resource list describing the resources which the process requires to complete its execution.
    3. Reschedule the process for execution only when the process gets its old resources and the new resource which is requested by the process.

Imposing these criterions may introduce negative impacts like low resource utilisation and starvation of processes.

Livelock The *Livelock* condition is similar to the deadlock condition except that a process in livelock condition changes its state with time. While in deadlock a process enters in wait state for a resource and continues in that state forever without making any progress in the execution, in a livelock condition a process always does something but is unable to make any progress in the execution completion. The livelock condition is better explained with the real world example, two people attempting to cross each other in a narrow corridor. Both the persons move towards each side of the corridor to allow the opposite person to cross. Since the corridor is narrow, none of them are able to cross each other. Here both of the persons perform some action but still they are unable to achieve their target, cross each other. We will make the livelock, the scenario more clear in a later section–*The Dining Philosophers' Problem*, of this chapter.

Starvation In the multitasking context, *starvation* is the condition in which a process does not get the resources required to continue its execution for a long time. As time progresses the process starves on resource. Starvation may arise due to various conditions like byproduct of preventive measures of deadlock, scheduling policies favouring high priority tasks and tasks with shortest execution time, etc.

10.8.1.3 The Dining Philosophers' Problem The '*Dining philosophers' problem*' is an interesting example for synchronisation issues in resource utilisation. The terms 'dining', 'philosophers', etc. may sound awkward in the operating system context, but it is the best way to explain technical things abstractly using non-technical terms. Now coming to the problem definition:

Five philosophers (It can be '*n*'. The number 5 is taken for illustration) are sitting around a round table, involved in eating and brainstorming (Fig. 10.37). At any point of time each philosopher will be in any one of the three states: eating, hungry or brainstorming. (While eating the philosopher is not involved in brainstorming and while brainstorming the philosopher is not involved in eating). For eating, each philosopher requires 2 forks. There are only 5 forks available on the dining table ('*n*' for '*n*' number of philosophers) and they are arranged in a fashion one fork in between two philosophers. The philosopher can only use the forks on his/her immediate left and right that too in the order pickup the left fork first and then the right fork. Analyse the situation and explain the possible outcomes of this scenario.

Let's analyse the various scenarios that may occur in this situation.

Scenario 1: All the philosophers involve in brainstorming together and try to eat together. Each philosopher picks up the left fork and is unable to proceed since two forks are required for eating the spaghetti present in the plate. Philosopher 1 thinks that Philosopher 2 sitting to the right of him/her will put the fork down and waits for it. Philosopher 2 thinks that Philosopher 3 sitting to the right of him/her will

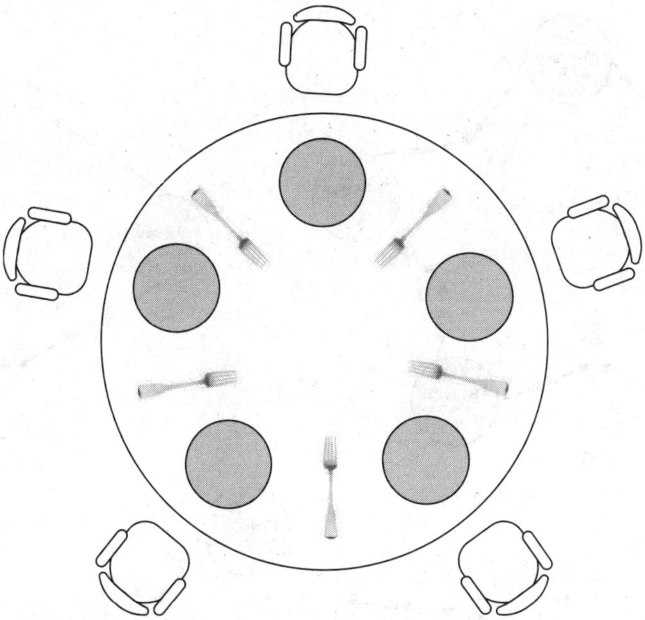

Fig. 10.27 **Visualisation of the '*Dining Philosophers problem*'**

put the fork down and waits for it, and so on. This forms a circular chain of un-granted requests. If the philosophers continue in this state waiting for the fork from the philosopher sitting to the right of each, they will not make any progress in eating and this will result in *starvation* of the philosophers and *deadlock*.

Scenario 2: All the philosophers start brainstorming together. One of the philosophers is hungry and he/she picks up the left fork. When the philosopher is about to pick up the right fork, the philosopher sitting to his right also become hungry and tries to grab the left fork which is the right fork of his neighbouring philosopher who is trying to lift it, resulting in a '*Race condition*'.

Scenario 3: All the philosophers involve in brainstorming together and try to eat together. Each philosopher picks up the left fork and is unable to proceed, since two forks are required for eating the spaghetti present in the plate. Each of them anticipates that the adjacently sitting philosopher will put his/her fork down and waits for a fixed duration and after this puts the fork down. Each of them again tries to lift the fork after a fixed duration of time. Since all philosophers are trying to lift the fork at the same time, none of them will be able to grab two forks. This condition leads to *livelock* and *starvation* of philosophers, where each philosopher tries to do something, but they are unable to make any progress in achieving the target.

Figure 10.28 illustrates these scenarios.

Solution: We need to find out alternative solutions to avoid the *deadlock*, *livelock*, *racing* and *starvation* condition that may arise due to the concurrent access of forks by philosophers. This situation can be handled in many ways by allocating the forks in different allocation techniques including Round Robin allocation, FIFO allocation, etc. But the requirement is that the solution should be optimal, avoiding

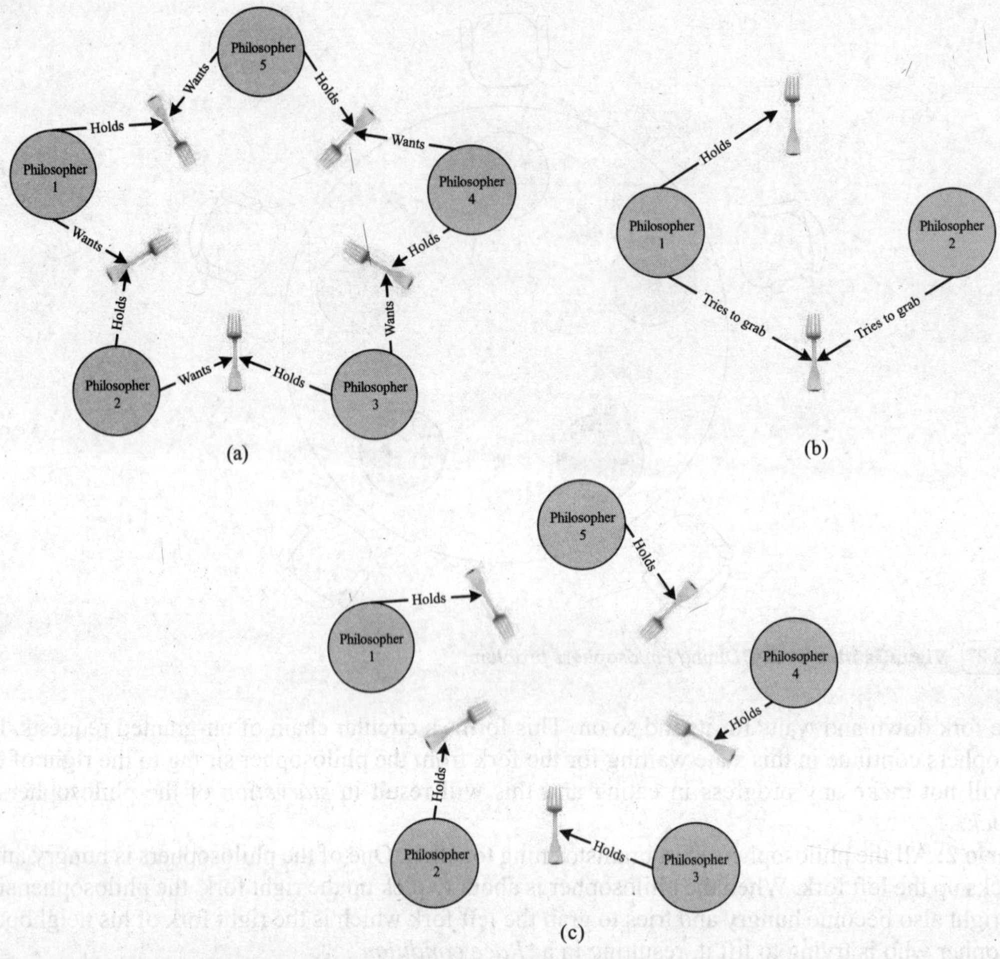

Fig. 10.28 **The 'Real Problems' in the '*Dining Philosophers problem*' (a) Starvation and Deadlock (b) Racing (c) Livelock and Starvation**

deadlock and starvation of the philosophers and allowing maximum number of philosophers to eat at a time. One solution that we could think of is:

- Imposing rules in accessing the forks by philosophers, like: The philosophers should put down the fork he/she already have in hand (left fork) after waiting for a fixed duration for the second fork (right fork) and should wait for a fixed time before making the next attempt.

This solution works fine to some extent, but, if all the philosophers try to lift the forks at the same time, a *livelock* situation is resulted.

Another solution which gives maximum concurrency that can be thought of is each philosopher acquires a semaphore (mutex) before picking up any fork. When a philosopher feels hungry he/she checks whether the philosopher sitting to the left and right of him is already using the fork, by checking the state of the associated semaphore. If the forks are in use by the neighbouring philosophers, the philosopher waits till the forks are available. A philosopher when finished eating puts the forks down and informs the philosophers sitting to his/her left and right, who are hungry (waiting for the forks), by signalling the semaphores associated with the forks. We will discuss about semaphores and mutexes at a latter section of this chapter. In the operating system context, the dining philosophers represent the processes and forks represent the resources. The dining philosophers' problem is an analogy of processes competing for shared resources and the different problems like racing, deadlock, starvation and livelock arising from the competition.

10.8.1.4 Producer-Consumer/Bounded Buffer Problem Producer-Consumer problem is a common data sharing problem where two processes concurrently access a shared buffer with fixed size. A thread/process which produces data is called '*Producer thread/process*' and a thread/process which consumes the data produced by a producer thread/process is known as '*Consumer thread/process*'. Imagine a situation where the producer thread keeps on producing data and puts it into the buffer and the consumer thread keeps on consuming the data from the buffer and there is no synchronisation between the two. There may be chances where in which the producer produces data at a faster rate than the rate at which it is consumed by the consumer. This will lead to '*buffer overrun*' where the producer tries to put data to a full buffer. If the consumer consumes data at a faster rate than the rate at which it is produced by the producer, it will lead to the situation '*buffer under-run*' in which the consumer tries to read from an empty buffer. Both of these conditions will lead to inaccurate data and data loss. The following code snippet illustrates the producer-consumer problem

```
#include <windows.h>
#include <stdio.h>
#define N 20 //Define buffer size as 20
int buffer[N];//Shared buffer for producer & consumer
//*********************************************************************
//Producer thread
void producer_thread(void) {
        int x;
        while(true) {
                for(x=0;x<N;x++)
                {
                //Fill buffer with random data
                buffer[x]= rand()%1000;
                printf("Produced : Buffer [%d] = %4d\n", x,
                buffer[x]);
                Sleep(25);
                }
        }
}
//*********************************************************************
//Consumer thread
void consumer_thread(void) {
        int y=0,value;
        while(true) {
                for(y=0;y<N;y++)
```

```
            {
            value=buffer[y];
            printf("Consumed : Buffer [%d] = %4d\n", y, value);
            Sleep(20);
            }
    }
}
//*************************************************************************
//Main Thread
int main()
{
    DWORD thread_id;
    //Create Producer thread
    CreateThread(NULL,0,
                (LPTHREAD_START_ROUTINE)producer_thread,
                NULL,0,&thread_id);
    //Create Consumer thread
    CreateThread(NULL,0,
                (LPTHREAD_START_ROUTINE)consumer_thread,
                NULL,0,&thread_id);
    //Wait for some time and exit
    Sleep(500);
    return 0;
}
```

Here the 'producer thread' produces random numbers and puts it in a buffer of size 20. If the 'producer thread' fills the buffer fully it re-starts the filling of the buffer from the bottom. The 'consumer thread' consumes the data produced by the 'producer thread'. For consuming the data, the 'consumer thread' reads the buffer which is shared with the 'producer thread'. Once the 'consumer thread' consumes all the data, it starts consuming the data from the bottom of the buffer. These two threads run independently and are scheduled for execution based on the scheduling policies adopted by the OS. The different situations that may arise based on the scheduling of the 'producer thread' and 'consumer thread' is listed below.

1. 'Producer thread' is scheduled more frequently than the 'consumer thread': There are chances for overwriting the data in the buffer by the 'producer thread'. This leads to inaccurate data.
2. Consumer thread' is scheduled more frequently than the 'producer thread': There are chances for reading the old data in the buffer again by the 'consumer thread'. This will also lead to inaccurate data.

The output of the above program when executed on a Windows XP machine is shown in Fig. 10.29.

The output shows that the consumer thread runs faster than the producer thread and most often leads to buffer under-run and thereby inaccurate data.

> **Note**
> It should be noted that the scheduling of the threads '*producer_thread*' and '*consumer_thread*' is OS kernel scheduling policy dependent and you may not get the same output all the time when you run this piece of code in Windows XP.

The producer-consumer problem can be rectified in various methods. One simple solution is the '*sleep and wake-up*'. The '*sleep and wake-up*' can be implemented in various process synchronisation techniques like semaphores, mutex, monitors, etc. We will discuss it in a latter section of this chapter.

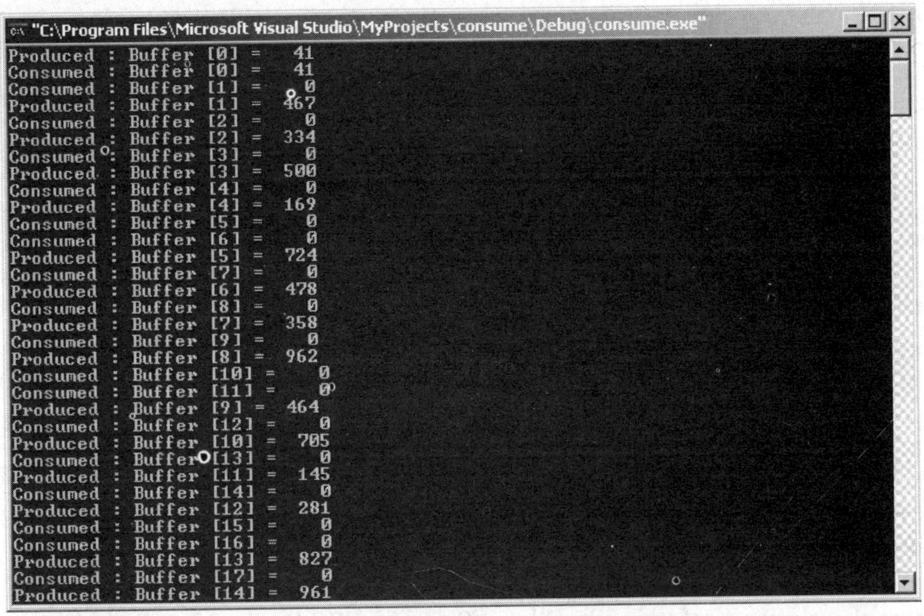

Fig. 10.29 **Output of Win32 program illustrating producer consumer problem**

10.8.1.5 Readers-Writers Problem The Readers-Writers problem is a common issue observed in processes competing for limited shared resources. The Readers-Writers problem is characterised by multiple processes trying to read and write shared data concurrently. A typical real-world example for the Readers-Writers problem is the banking system where one process tries to read the account information like available balance and the other process tries to update the available balance for that account. This may result in inconsistent results. If multiple processes try to read a shared data concurrently it may not create any impacts, whereas when multiple processes try to write and read concurrently it will definitely create inconsistent results. Proper synchronisation techniques should be applied to avoid the readers-writers problem. We will discuss about the various synchronisation techniques in a later section of this chapter.

10.8.1.6 Priority Inversion Priority inversion is the byproduct of the combination of blocking based (lock based) process synchronisation and pre-emptive priority scheduling. '*Priority inversion*' is the condition in which a high priority task needs to wait for a low priority task to release a resource which is shared between the high priority task and the low priority task, and a medium priority task which doesn't require the shared resource continue its execution by preempting the low priority task (Fig. 10.30). Priority based preemptive scheduling technique ensures that a high priority task is always executed first, whereas the lock based process synchronisation mechanism (like mutex, semaphore, etc.) ensures that a process will not access a shared resource, which is currently in use by another process. The synchronisation technique is only interested in avoiding conflicts that may arise due to the concurrent access of the shared resources and not at all bothered about the priority of the process which tries to access the shared resource. In fact, the priority based preemption and lock based synchronisation are the two contradicting OS primitives. Priority inversion is better explained with the following scenario:

Let Process A, Process B and Process C be three processes with priorities High, Medium and Low respectively. Process A and Process C share a variable 'X' and the access to this variable is synchronised

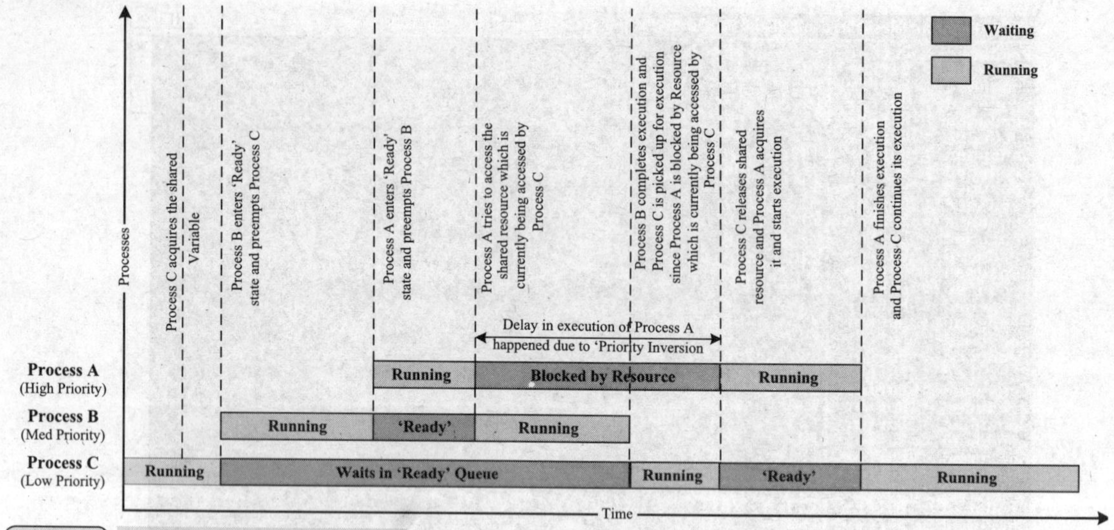

Fig. 10.30 Priority Inversion Problem

through a mutual exclusion mechanism like *Binary Semaphore S*. Imagine a situation where Process C is ready and is picked up for execution by the scheduler and 'Process C' tries to access the shared variable 'X'. 'Process C' acquires the 'Semaphore S' to indicate the other processes that it is accessing the shared variable 'X'. Immediately after 'Process C' acquires the 'Semaphore S', 'Process B' enters the 'Ready' state. Since 'Process B' is of higher priority compared to 'Process C', 'Process C' is preempted and 'Process B' starts executing. Now imagine 'Process A' enters the 'Ready' state at this stage. Since 'Process A' is of higher priority than 'Process B', 'Process B' is preempted and 'Process A' is scheduled for execution. 'Process A' involves accessing of shared variable 'X' which is currently being accessed by 'Process C'. Since 'Process C' acquired the semaphore for signalling the access of the shared variable 'X', 'Process A' will not be able to access it. Thus 'Process A' is put into blocked state (This condition is called Pending on resource). Now 'Process B' gets the CPU and it continues its execution until it relinquishes the CPU voluntarily or enters a wait state or preempted by another high priority task. The highest priority process 'Process A' has to wait till 'Process C' gets a chance to execute and release the semaphore. This produces unwanted delay in the execution of the high priority task which is supposed to be executed immediately when it was 'Ready'.

Priority inversion may be sporadic in nature but can lead to potential damages as a result of missing critical deadlines. Literally speaking, priority inversion 'inverts' the priority of a high priority task with that of a low priority task. Proper workaround mechanism should be adopted for handling the priority inversion problem. The commonly adopted priority inversion workarounds are:

Priority Inheritance: A low-priority task that is currently accessing (by holding the lock) a shared resource requested by a high-priority task temporarily '*inherits*' the priority of that high-priority task, from the moment the high-priority task raises the request. Boosting the priority of the low priority task to that of the priority of the task which requested the shared resource holding by the low priority task eliminates the preemption of the low priority task by other tasks whose priority are below that of the task requested the shared resource and thereby reduces the delay in waiting to get the resource requested by the high priority task. The priority of the low priority task which is temporarily boosted to high is brought to the original value when it releases the shared resource. Implementation of Priority inheritance workaround in the priority inversion problem discussed for Process A, Process B and Process C example will change the execution sequence as shown in Fig. 10.31.

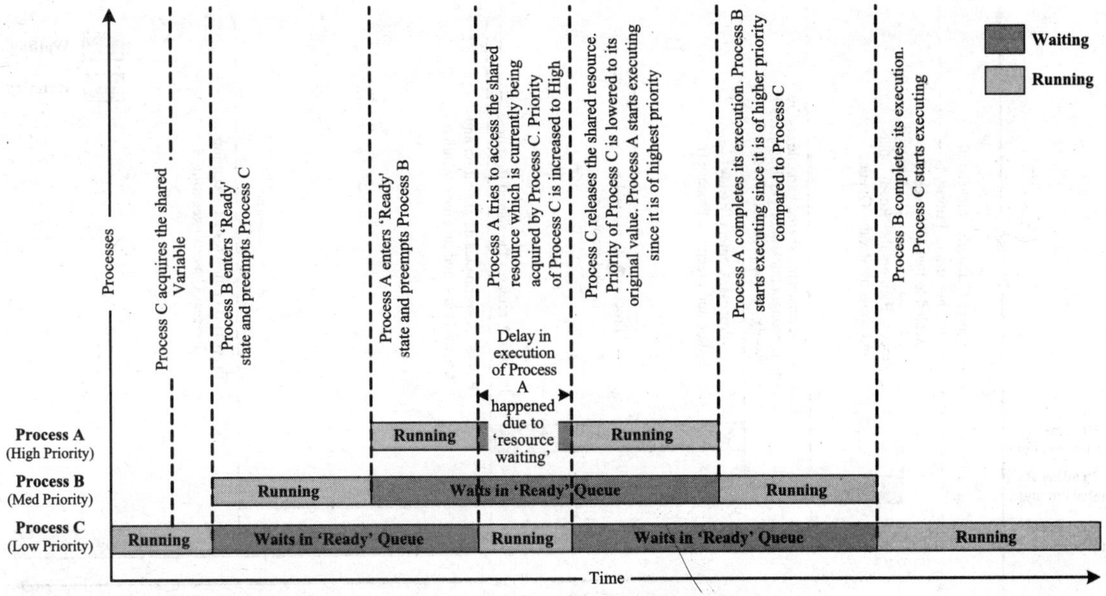

Fig. 10.31 **Handling Priority Inversion Problem with Priority Inheritance**

Priority inheritance is only a work around and it will not eliminate the delay in waiting the high priority task to get the resource from the low priority task. The only thing is that it helps the low priority task to continue its execution and release the shared resource as soon as possible. The moment, at which the low priority task releases the shared resource, the high priority task kicks the low priority task out and grabs the CPU – A true form of selfishness☺. Priority inheritance handles priority inversion at the cost of run-time overhead at scheduler. It imposes the overhead of checking the priorities of all tasks which tries to access shared resources and adjust the priorities dynamically.

Priority Ceiling: In '*Priority Ceiling*', a priority is associated with each shared resource. The priority associated to each resource is the priority of the highest priority task which uses this shared resource. This priority level is called 'ceiling priority'. Whenever a task accesses a shared resource, the scheduler elevates the priority of the task to that of the ceiling priority of the resource. If the task which accesses the shared resource is a low priority task, its priority is temporarily boosted to the priority of the highest priority task to which the resource is also shared. This eliminates the pre-emption of the task by other medium priority tasks leading to priority inversion. The priority of the task is brought back to the original level once the task completes the accessing of the shared resource. 'Priority Ceiling' brings the added advantage of sharing resources without the need for synchronisation techniques like locks. Since the priority of the task accessing a shared resource is boosted to the highest priority of the task among which the resource is shared, the concurrent access of shared resource is automatically handled. Another advantage of 'Priority Ceiling' technique is that all the overheads are at compile time instead of run-time. Implementation of 'priority ceiling' workaround in the priority inversion problem discussed for Process A, Process B and Process C example will change the execution sequence as shown in Fig. 10.32.

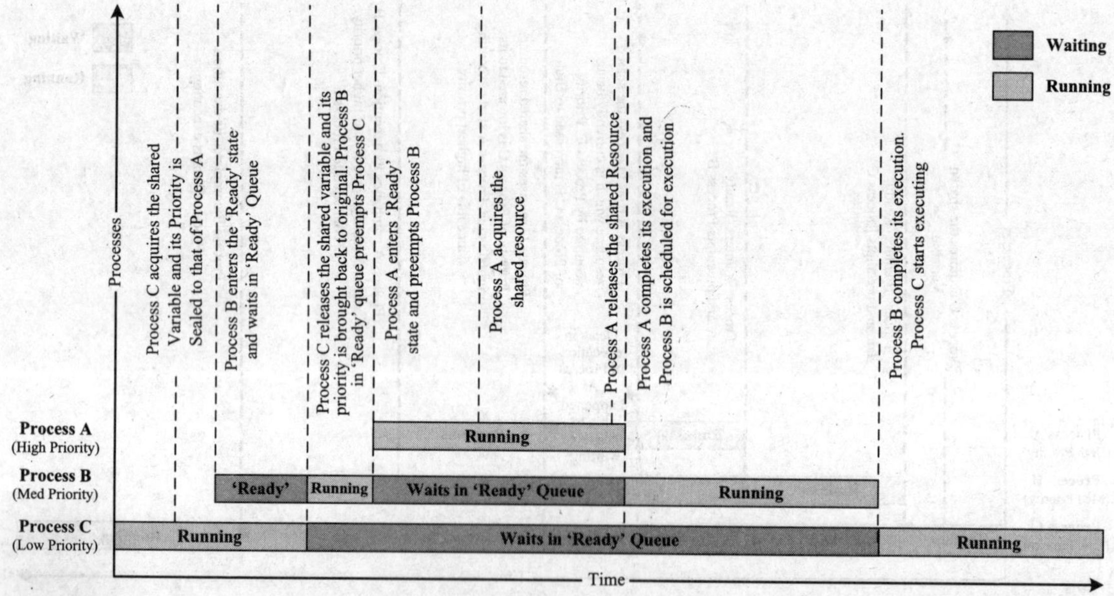

Fig. 10.32 **Handling Priority Inversion Problem with Priority Ceiling**

The biggest drawback of 'Priority Ceiling' is that it may produce *hidden priority inversion*. With 'Priority Ceiling' technique, the priority of a task is always elevated no matter another task wants the shared resources. This unnecessary priority elevation always boosts the priority of a low priority task to that of the highest priority tasks among which the resource is shared and other tasks with priorities higher than that of the low priority task is not allowed to preempt the low priority task when it is accessing a shared resource. This always gives the low priority task the luxury of running at high priority when accessing shared resources☺.

10.8.2 Task Synchronisation Techniques

So far we discussed about the various task/process synchronisation issues encountered in multitasking systems due to concurrent resource access. Now let's have a discussion on the various techniques used for synchronisation in concurrent access in multitasking. Process/Task synchronisation is essential for

1. Avoiding conflicts in resource access (racing, deadlock, starvation, livelock, etc.) in a multitasking environment.
2. Ensuring proper sequence of operation across processes. The producer consumer problem is a typical example for processes requiring proper sequence of operation. In producer consumer problem, accessing the shared buffer by different processes is not the issue, the issue is the writing process should write to the shared buffer only if the buffer is not full and the consumer thread

should not read from the buffer if it is empty. Hence proper synchronisation should be provided to implement this sequence of operations.

3. Communicating between processes.

The code memory area which holds the program instructions (piece of code) for accessing a shared resource (like shared memory, shared variables, etc.) is known as '*critical section*'. In order to synchronise the access to shared resources, the access to the critical section should be exclusive. The exclusive access to critical section of code is provided through mutual exclusion mechanism. Let us have a look at how mutual exclusion is important in concurrent access. Consider two processes *Process* A and *Process B* running on a multitasking system. *Process A* is currently running and it enters its critical section. Before *Process A* completes its operation in the critical section, the scheduler preempts *Process A* and schedules *Process B* for execution (*Process B* is of higher priority compared to *Process A*). *Process B* also contains the access to the critical section which is already in use by *Process A*. If *Process B* continues its execution and enters the critical section which is already in use by *Process A*, a racing condition will be resulted. A mutual exclusion policy enforces mutually exclusive access of critical sections.

Mutual exclusions can be enforced in different ways. Mutual exclusion blocks a process. Based on the behaviour of the blocked process, mutual exclusion methods can be classified into two categories. In the following section we will discuss them in detail.

10.8.2.1 Mutual Exclusion through Busy Waiting/Spin Lock '*Busy waiting*' is the simplest method for enforcing mutual exclusion. The following code snippet illustrates how 'Busy waiting' enforces mutual exclusion.

```
//Inside parent thread/main thread corresponding to a process
bool bFlag; //Global declaration of lock Variable.
bFlag= FALSE; //Initialise the lock to indicate it is available.
//...............................................................................................................................
//Inside the child threads/threads of a process
while(bFlag == TRUE); //Check the lock for availability
bFlag=TRUE; //Lock is available. Acquire the lock
//Rest of the source code dealing with shared resource access
```

The 'Busy waiting' technique uses a lock variable for implementing mutual exclusion. Each process/thread checks this lock variable before entering the critical section. The lock is set to '*1*' by a process/thread if the process/thread is already in its critical section; otherwise the lock is set to '*0*'. The major challenge in implementing the lock variable based synchronisation is the non-availability of a single atomic instruction† which combines the reading, comparing and setting of the lock variable. Most often the three different operations related to the locks, viz. the operation of Reading the lock variable, checking its present value and setting it are achieved with multiple low level instructions. The low level implementation of these operations are dependent on the underlying processor instruction set and the (cross) compiler in use. The low level implementation of the 'Busy waiting' code snippet, which we discussed earlier, under Windows XP operating system running on an *Intel Centrino Duo* processor is given below. The code snippet is compiled with Microsoft Visual Studio 6.0 compiler.

```
--- D:\Examples\counter.cpp -----------------------------------
      #include <stdio.h>
      #include <windows.h>
```

† Atomic Instruction: Instruction whose execution is uninterruptible.

```
3:
4:     int main()
5:     {
//Code memory          Opcode       Operand
00401010               push         ebp
00401011               mov          ebp,esp
00401013               sub          esp,44h
00401016               push         ebx
00401017               push         esi
00401018               push         edi
00401019               lea          edi,[ebp-44h]
0040101C               mov          ecx,11h
00401021               mov          eax,0CCCCCCCCh
00401026               rep stos     dword ptr [edi]
6:     //Inside parent thread/ main thread corresponding to a process
7:     bool bFlag; //Global declaration of lock Variable.
8:     bFlag= FALSE; //Initialise the lock to indicate it is //available.
00401028    mov          byte ptr [ebp-4],0
9:     //..............................................................
10:    //Inside the child threads/ threads of a process
11:    while(bFlag == TRUE); //Check the lock for availability
0040102C    mov          eax,dword ptr [ebp-4]
0040102F    and          eax,0FFh
00401034    cmp          eax,1
00401037    jne          main+2Bh (0040103b)
00401039    jmp          main+1Ch (0040102c)
12:    bFlag=TRUE; //Lock is available. Acquire the lock
0040103B    mov          byte ptr [ebp-4],1
```

The assembly language instructions reveals that the two high level instructions (*while(bFlag==false);* and *bFlag=true;*), corresponding to the operation of reading the lock variable, checking its present value and setting it is implemented in the processor level using six low level instructions. Imagine a situation where 'Process 1' read the lock variable and tested it and found that the lock is available and it is about to set the lock for acquiring the critical section (Fig. 10.33). But just before 'Process 1' sets the lock variable, 'Process 2' preempts 'Process 1' and starts executing. 'Process 2' contains a critical section code and it tests the lock variable for its availability. Since 'Process 1' was unable to set the lock variable, its state is still '**0**' and 'Process 2' sets it and acquires the critical section. Now the scheduler preempts 'Process 2' and schedules 'Process 1' before 'Process 2' leaves the critical section. Remember, 'Process 1' was preempted at a point just before setting the lock variable ('Process 1' has already tested the lock variable just before it is preempted and found that the lock is available). Now 'Process 1' sets the lock variable and enters the critical section☺. It violates the mutual exclusion policy and may produce unpredicted results.

The above issue can be effectively tackled by combining the actions of reading the lock variable, testing its state and setting the lock into a single step. This can be achieved with the combined hardware and software support. Most of the processors support a single instruction '*Test and Set Lock (TSL)*' for testing and setting the lock variable. The '*Test and Set Lock (TSL)*' instruction call copies the value of the lock variable and sets it to a nonzero value. It should be noted that the implementation and usage of

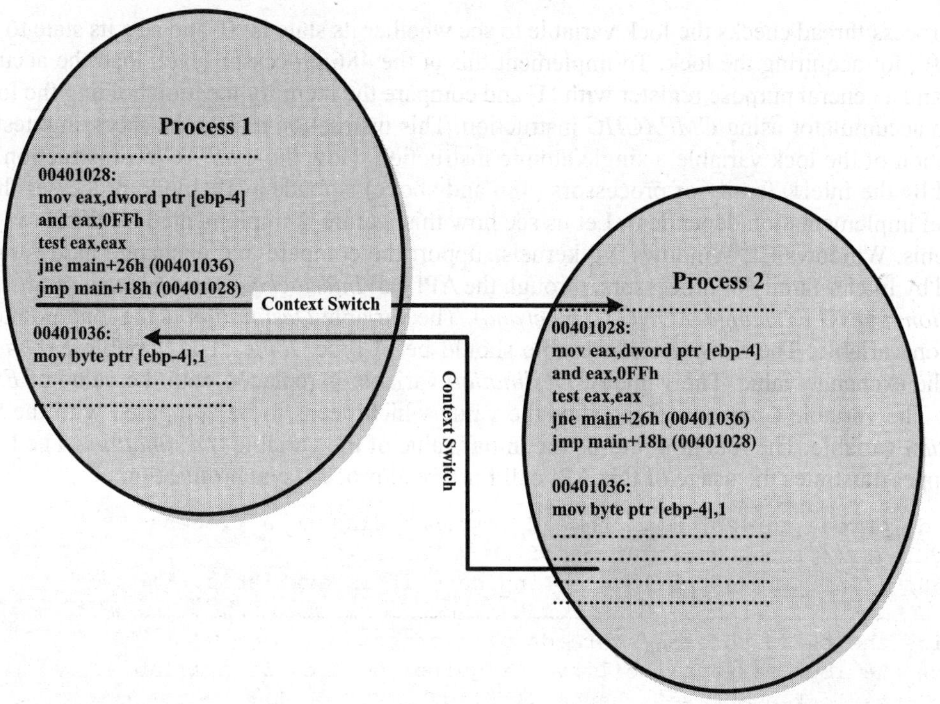

Fig. 10.33 **Issue with locks**

'*Test and Set Lock (TSL)*' instruction is processor architecture dependent. The *Intel 486* and the above family of processors support the '*Test and Set Lock (TSL)*' instruction with a special instruction *CMPXCHG*—Compare and Exchange. The usage of *CMPXCHG* instruction is given below.

```
CMPXCHG dest,src
```

This instruction compares the Accumulator (*EAX* register) with 'dest'. If the Accumulator and 'dest' contents are equal, 'dest' is loaded with 'src'. If not, the Accumulator is loaded with 'dest'. Executing this instruction changes the six status bits of the Program Control and Status register *EFLAGS*. The destination ('dest') can be a register or a memory location. The source ('src') is always a register. From a programmer's perspective the operation of *CMPXCHG* instruction can be viewed as:

```
if (accumulator == destination)
        {
        ZF =1; //Set the Zero Flag of EFLAGS Register
        destination =source;
        }
else
        {
        ZF = 0; //Reset the Zero Flag of EFLAGS Register
        accumulator = destination;
        }
```

The process/thread checks the lock variable to see whether its state is '0' and sets its state to '1' if its state is '0', for acquiring the lock. To implement this at the 486 processor level, load the accumulator with '0' and a general purpose register with '1' and compare the memory location holding the lock variable with accumulator using *CMPXCHG* instruction. This instruction makes the accessing, testing and modification of the lock variable a single atomic instruction. How the *CMPXCHG* instruction support provided by the Intel® family of processors (486 and above) is made available to processes/threads is OS kernel implementation dependent. Let us see how this feature is implemented by Windows Operating systems. Windows CE/Windows XP kernels support the compare and exchange hardware feature provided by Intel® family of processors, through the API call *InterlockedCompareExchange (LPLONG Destination, LONG Exchange, LONG Comperand)*. The variable *Destination* is the long pointer to the destination variable. The *Destination* variable should be of type '*long*'. The variable *Exchange* represents the exchange value. The value of *Destination* variable is replaced with the value of *Exchange* variable. The variable *Comperand* specifies the value which needs to be compared with the value of *Destination* variable. The function returns the initial value of the variable '*Destination*'. The following code snippet illustrates the usage of this API call for thread/process synchronisation.

```
//Inside parent thread/ main thread corresponding to a process
long bFlag; //Global declaration of lock Variable.
bFlag=0; //Initialise the lock to indicate it is available.
//..........................................................................
//Inside the child threads/ threads of a process
//Check the lock for availability & acquire the lock if available.
while (InterlockedCompareExchange (&bFlag, 1, 0) == 1);

//Rest of the source code dealing with shared resource access
```

The *InterlockedCompareExchange* function is implemented as '*Compiler intrinsic function*'. The 'code for *Compiler intrinsic functions*' are inserted inline while compiling the code. This avoids the function call overhead and makes use of the built-in knowledge of the optimisation technique for intrinsic functions. The compiler can be instructed to use the intrinsic implementation for a function using the compiler directive *#pragma intrinsic (intrinsic-function-name)*. A sample implementation of the *InterlockedCompareExchange* interlocked intrinsic function for Windows XP OS is given below.

```
#include "stdafx.h"
#include <intrin.h>
#include <windows.h>
long bFlag; //Global declaration of lock Variable.
//Declare InterlockedCompareExchange as intrinsic function
#pragma intrinsic(_InterlockedCompareExchange)
void child_thread(void)
{
//Inside the child thread of a process
//Check the lock for availability & acquire the lock if available.
//The lock can be set by any other threads
while (_InterlockedCompareExchange (&bFlag, 1, 0) == 1);
//Rest of the source code dealing with shared resource access
//...........................................................
return;
}
```

```
//.........................................................................
int _tmain(int argc, _TCHAR* argv[])
{
//Inside parent thread/ main thread corresponding to a process
DWORD thread_id;
//Define handle to the child thread
HANDLE tThread;
//Initialize the lock to indicate it is available.
bFlag =0;
//Create child thread
tThread = CreateThread    (NULL,0,
                          (LPTHREAD_START_ROUTINE) child_thread,
                          NULL, 0, &thread_id);
if(NULL== tThread)
{
//Child thread creation failed.
printf ("Creation of Child thread failed. Error Code =
%d",GetLastError());
return -1;
}
//Wait for the completion of the child thread.
WaitForSingleObject(tThread,INFINITE);
return 0;
}
```

Note: Visual Studio 2005 or a later version of the compiler, which supports interlocked intrinsic functions, is required for compiling this application. The assembly code generated for the intrinsic interlocked function *while (_InterlockedCompareExchange (&bFlag, 1, 0) == 1);* when compiled using Visual Studio 2005 compiler, on Windows XP platform with Service Pack 2 running on an Intel® Centrino® Duo processor is given below. It clearly depicts the usage of the *cmpxchg* instruction

```
//Inside the child threads/ threads of a process
//Check the lock for availability & acquire the lock if available.
//The lock can be set by any other threads
while (_InterlockedCompareExchange (&bFlag, 1, 0) == 1);
004113DE        mov   ecx,1
004113E3        mov   edx,offset bFlag (417178h)
004113E8        xor         eax,eax
004113EA        lock        cmpxchg dword ptr [edx],ecx
004113EE        cmp         eax,1
004113F1        jne         child_thread+35h (4113F5h)
004113F3        jmp         child_thread+1Eh (4113DEh)
//Rest of the source code dealing with shared resource access
//.......................................................................
```

The Intel 486 and above family of processors provide hardware level support for atomic execution of increment and decrement operations also. The *XADD* low level instruction implements atomic execution of increment and decrement operations. Windows CE/XP kernel makes these features available to the users through a set of *Interlocked* function API calls. The API call *InterlockedIncrement (LPLONG lpAddend)* increments the value of the variable pointed by *lpAddend* and the API *InterlockedDecrement (LPLONG lpAddend)* decrements the value of the variable pointed by *lpAddend*.

The lock based mutual exclusion implementation always checks the state of a lock and waits till the lock is available. This keeps the processes/threads always busy and forces the processes/threads to wait for the availability of the lock for proceeding further. Hence this synchronisation mechanism is popularly known as '*Busy waiting*'. The '*Busy waiting*' technique can also be visualised as a lock around which the process/thread spins, checking for its availability. Spin locks are useful in handling scenarios where the processes/threads are likely to be blocked for a shorter period of time on waiting the lock, as they avoid OS overheads on context saving and process re-scheduling. Another drawback of Spin lock based synchronisation is that if the lock is being held for a long time by a process and if it is preempted by the OS, the other threads waiting for this lock may have to spin a longer time for getting it. The '*Busy waiting*' mechanism keeps the process/threads always active, performing a task which is not useful and leads to the wastage of processor time and high power consumption.

The interlocked operations are the most efficient synchronisation primitives when compared to the classic lock based synchronisation mechanism. Interlocked function based synchronisation technique brings the following value adds.

- The interlocked operation is free from waiting. Unlike the mutex, semaphore and critical section synchronisation objects which may require waiting on the object, if they are not available at the time of request, the interlocked function simply performs the operation and returns immediately. This avoids the blocking of the thread which calls the interlocked function.
- The interlocked function call is directly converted to a processor specific instruction and there is no user mode to kernel mode transition as in the case of mutex, semaphore and critical section objects. This avoids the user mode to kernel mode transition delay and thereby increases the overall performance.

The types of interlocked operations supported by an OS are underlying processor hardware dependent and so they are limited in functionality. Normally the bit manipulation (Boolean) operations are not supported by interlocked functions. Also the interlocked operations are limited to integer or pointer variables only. This limits the possibility of extending the interlocked functions to variables of other types. Under windows operating systems, each process has its own virtual address space and so the interlocked functions can only be used for synchronising the access to a variable that is shared by multiple threads of a process (Multiple threads of a process share the same address space) (Intra Process Synchronisation). The interlocked functions can be extended for synchronising the access of the variables shared across multiple processes if the variable is kept in shared memory.

10.8.2.2 Mutual Exclusion through Sleep & Wakeup The '*Busy waiting*' mutual exclusion enforcement mechanism used by processes makes the CPU always busy by checking the lock to see whether they can proceed. This results in the wastage of CPU time and leads to high power consumption. This is not affordable in embedded systems powered on battery, since it affects the battery backup time of the device. An alternative to '*busy waiting*' is the '*Sleep & Wakeup*' mechanism. When a process is not allowed to access the critical section, which is currently being locked by another process, the process undergoes '*Sleep*' and enters the '*blocked*' state. The process which is blocked on waiting for access to the critical section is awakened by the process which currently owns the critical section. The process which owns the critical section sends a wakeup message to the process, which is sleeping as a result of waiting for the access to the critical section, when the process leaves the critical section. The '*Sleep & Wakeup*' policy for mutual exclusion can be implemented in different ways. Implementation of this policy is OS kernel dependent. The following section describes the important techniques for '*Sleep & Wakeup*' policy implementation for mutual exclusion by Windows XP/CE OS kernels.

Semaphore Semaphore is a sleep and wakeup based mutual exclusion implementation for shared resource access. Semaphore is a system resource and the process which wants to access the shared resource can first acquire this system object to indicate the other processes which wants the shared resource that the shared resource is currently acquired by it. The resources which are shared among a process can be either for exclusive use by a process or for using by a number of processes at a time. The display device of an embedded system is a typical example for the shared resource which needs exclusive access by a process. The Hard disk (secondary storage) of a system is a typical example for sharing the resource among a limited number of multiple processes. Various processes can access the different sectors of the hard-disk concurrently. Based on the implementation of the sharing limitation of the shared resource, semaphores are classified into two; namely '*Binary Semaphore*' and '*Counting Semaphore*'. The binary semaphore provides exclusive access to shared resource by allocating the resource to a single process at a time and not allowing the other processes to access it when it is being owned by a process. The implementation of binary semaphore is OS kernel dependent. Under certain OS kernel it is referred as *mutex*. Unlike a binary semaphore, the '*Counting Semaphore*' limits the access of resources by a fixed number of processes/threads. '*Counting Semaphore*' maintains a count between zero and a

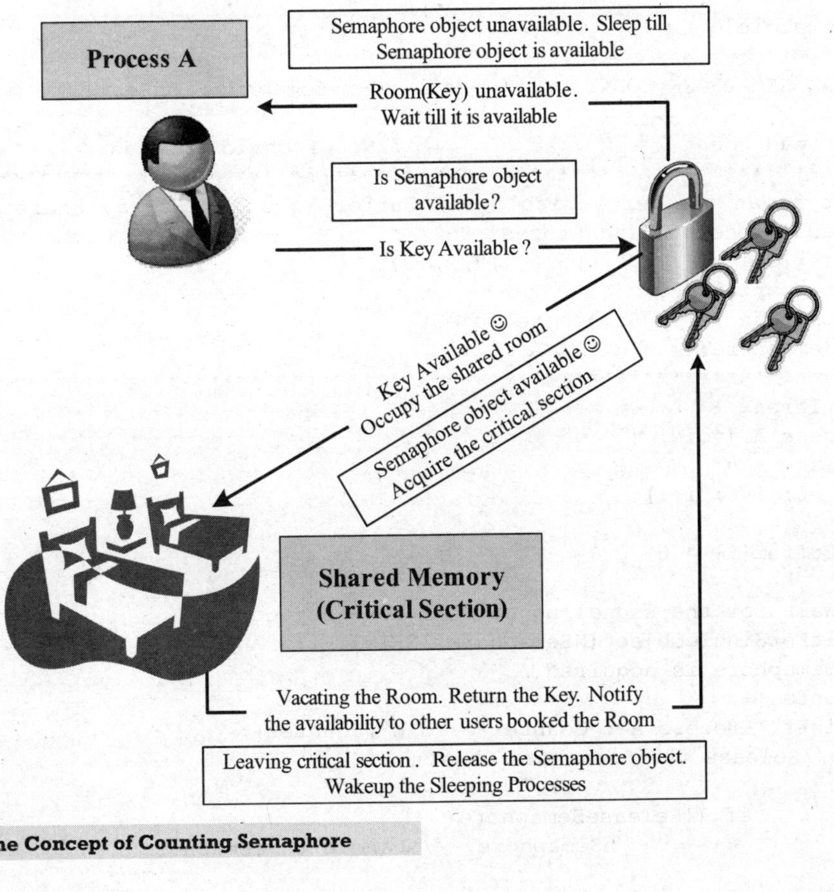

Fig. 10.34 **The Concept of Counting Semaphore**

value. It limits the usage of the resource to the maximum value of the count supported by it. The state of the counting semaphore object is set to 'signalled' when the count of the object is greater than zero. The count associated with a '*Semaphore object*' is decremented by one when a process/thread acquires it and the count is incremented by one when a process/thread releases the '*Semaphore object*'. The state of the '*Semaphore object*' is set to non-signalled when the semaphore is acquired by the maximum number of processes/threads that the semaphore can support (i.e. when the count associated with the '*Semaphore object*' becomes zero). A real world example for the counting semaphore concept is the dormitory system for accommodation (Fig. 10.34). A dormitory contains a fixed number of beds (say 5) and at any point of time it can be shared by the maximum number of users supported by the dormitory. If a person wants to avail the dormitory facility, he/she can contact the dormitory caretaker for checking the availability. If beds are available in the dorm the caretaker will hand over the keys to the user. If beds are not available currently, the user can register his/her name to get notifications when a slot is available. Those who are availing the dormitory shares the dorm facilities like TV, telephone, toilet, etc. When a dorm user vacates, he/she gives the keys back to the caretaker. The caretaker informs the users, who booked in advance, about the dorm availability.

The creation and usage of '*counting semaphore object*' is OS kernel dependent. Let us have a look at how we can implement semaphore based synchronisation for the '*Racing*' problem we discussed in the beginning, under the Windows kernel. The following code snippet explains the same.

```
#include <stdio.h>
#include <windows.h>
#define MAX_SEMAPHORE_COUNT 1    //Make the semaphore object for //exclusive
use
#define thread_count 2                    //No.of Child Threads
//*****************************************************************
//counter is an integer variable and Buffer is a byte array shared //between
two threads Process_A and Process_B
char Buffer[10] = {1,2,3,4,5,6,7,8,9,10};
short int counter = 0;
//Define the handle to Semaphore object
HANDLE hSemaphore;
//*****************************************************************
// Child Thread 1
void Process_A (void) {
int i;
  for (i =0; i<5; i++)
{
    if (Buffer[i] > 0)
       {
       //Wait for the signaling of Semaphore object
       WaitForSingleObject(hSemaphore,INFINITE);
       //Semaphore is acquired
       counter++;
       printf("Process A : Counter = %d\n",counter);
          //Release the Semaphore Object

             if (!ReleaseSemaphore(
                      hSemaphore, // handle to semaphore
```

```
                    1,          // increase count by one
                    NULL))     // not interested in previous count
            {
            //Semaphore Release failed. Print Error code &
            return.
            printf("Release Semaphore Failed with Error Code:
            %d\n", GetLastError());
            return;
            }
       }
}
  return;
}
//*******************************************************************
// Child Thread 2
void Process_B(void) {
int j;
  for (j =5; j<10; j++)
{
    if (Buffer[j] > 0)
       {
      //Wait for the signalling of Semaphore object
      WaitForSingleObject(hSemaphore,INFINITE);
      //Semaphore is acquired
      counter++;
      printf("Process B : Counter = %d\n",counter);
         //Release Semaphore
         if (!ReleaseSemaphore(
                    hSemaphore, // handle to semaphore
                    1,          // increase count by one
                    NULL) )    // not interested in previous count
                 {
            //Semaphore Release failed. Print Error code &
            //return.
            printf("Release Semaphore Failed Error Code: %d\n",
            GetLastError());
            return;
            }
       }
}
  return;
}
//*******************************************************************
// Main Thread
void main() {

      //Define HANDLE for child threads
      HANDLE child_threads[thread_count];
```

```
        DWORD thread_id;
        int i;

        //Create Semaphore object
        hSemaphore = CreateSemaphore(
         NULL,            // default security attributes
         MAX_SEMAPHORE_COUNT,  // initial count. Create as signaled
         MAX_SEMAPHORE_COUNT,  // maximum count
         "Semaphore");    // Semaphore object with name "Semaphore"

    if (NULL == hSemaphore)
        {
        printf ("Semaphore Object Creation Failed: Error Code: %d",
        GetLastError ());
        //Semaphore Object Creation failed. Return
        return;
        }
//Create Child thread 1
child_threads[0]=        CreateThread(NULL,0,
                         (LPTHREAD_START_ROUTINE)Process_A,
                         (LPVOID)0,0,&thread_id);
//Create Child thread 2
child_threads[1]=        CreateThread(NULL,0,
                         (LPTHREAD_START_ROUTINE)Process_B,
                         (LPVOID)0,0,&thread_id);
//Check the success of creation of child threads
for (i=0;i<thread_count; i++)
{
        if(NULL==child_threads[i])
        {
        //Child thread creation failed.
        printf ("Child thread Creation failed with Error Code: %d",
        GetLastError ());
        return;
        }
}
// Wait for the termination of child threads
WaitForMultipleObjects(thread_count, child_threads, TRUE,
INFINITE);
//Close handles of child threads
    for( i=0; i < thread_count; i++ )
        CloseHandle(child_threads[i]);
//Close Semaphore object handle
        CloseHandle(hSemaphore);
        return;
}
```

Please refer to the Online Learning Centre for details on the various Win32 APIs used in the program for counting semaphore creation, acquiring, signalling, and releasing. The VxWorks and MicroC/OS-II

Real-Time kernels also implements the Counting semaphore based task synchronisation/shared resource access. We will discuss them in detail in a later chapter.

Counting Semaphores are similar to *Binary Semaphores* in operation. The only difference between *Counting Semaphore* and *Binary Semaphore* is that *Binary Semaphore* can only be used for exclusive access, whereas *Counting Semaphores* can be used for both exclusive access (by restricting the maximum count value associated with the semaphore object to one (1) at the time of creation of the semaphore object) and limited access (by restricting the maximum count value associated with the semaphore object to the limited number at the time of creation of the semaphore object).

Binary Semaphore (Mutex) Binary Semaphore (Mutex) is a synchronisation object provided by OS for process/thread synchronisation. Any process/thread can create a '*mutex object*' and other processes/threads of the system can use this '*mutex object*' for synchronising the access to critical sections. Only one process/thread can own the '*mutex object*' at a time. The state of a mutex object is set to signalled when it is not owned by any process/thread, and set to non-signalled when it is owned by any process/thread. A real world example for the mutex concept is the hotel accommodation system (lodging system) Fig. 10.35. The rooms in a hotel are shared for the public. Any user who pays and follows the norms of the hotel can avail the rooms for accommodation. A person wants to avail the hotel room facility can contact the hotel reception for checking the room availability (see Fig. 10.35). If room is available the receptionist will handover the room key to the user. If room is not available currently, the user can book

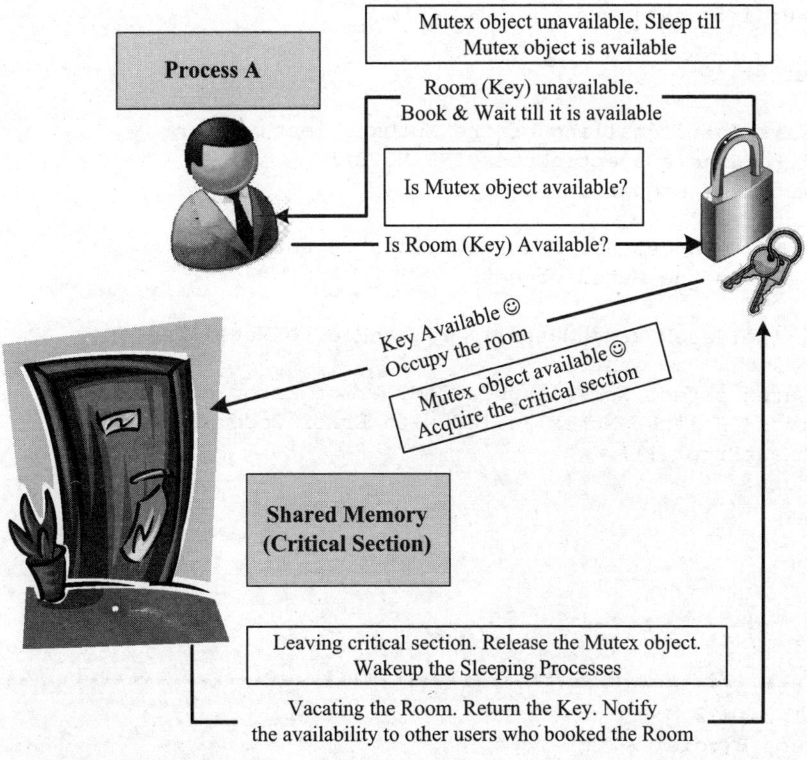

Fig. 10.35 **The Concept of Binary Semaphore (Mutex)**

the room to get notifications when a room is available. When a person gets a room he/she is granted the exclusive access to the room facilities like TV, telephone, toilet, etc. When a user vacates the room, he/she gives the keys back to the receptionist. The receptionist informs the users, who booked in advance, about the room's availability.

Let's see how we can implement mutual exclusion with mutex object in the '*Racing*' problem example given under the section '*Racing*', under Windows kernel.

```
#include <stdio.h>
#include <windows.h>
#define thread_count 2                    //No.of Child Threads
//*******************************************************************
//counter is an integer variable and Buffer is a byte array shared
//between two
//threads Process_A and Process_B
char Buffer[10] = {1,2,3,4,5,6,7,8,9,10};
short int counter = 0;
//Define the handle to Mutex Object
HANDLE hMutex;
//*******************************************************************
// Child Thread 1
void Process_A (void) {
int i;
  for (i =0; i<5; i++)
{
    if (Buffer[i] > 0)
      {
      //Wait for signalling of the Mutex object
      WaitForSingleObject(hMutex,INFINITE);
      //Mutex is acquired
      counter++;
      printf("Process A : Counter = %d\n",counter);
      //Release the Mutex Object

      if (!ReleaseMutex(hMutex))  // handle to Mutex Object
      {
      //Mutex object Releasing failed. Print Error code & return.
      printf("Release Mutex Failed with Error Code: %d\n",
      GetLastError());
      return;
      }

      }
}
  return;
}
//*******************************************************************
// Child Thread 2
void Process_B(void) {
int j;
```

```
  for (j =5; j<10; j++)
{
   if (Buffer[j] > 0)
      {
      //Wait for signalling of the Mutex object
      WaitForSingleObject(hMutex,INFINITE);
      //Mutex object is acquired
      counter++;
      printf("Process B : Counter = %d\n",counter);
      //Release Mutex object
      if (!ReleaseMutex(hMutex))  // handle to Mutex Object
        {
         //Mutex object Release failed. Print Error code & return.
         printf("Release Mutex Failed with Error Code: %d\n",
         GetLastError());
         return;
        }
      }
}
  return;
}
//*************************************************************
// Main Thread
void main() {

      //Define HANDLE for child threads
      HANDLE child_threads[thread_count];
      DWORD thread_id;
      int i;

      //Create Mutex object
      hMutex = CreateMutex(
       NULL,        // default security attributes
       FALSE, // Not initial ownership
       "Mutex");  // Mutex object with name "Mutex"
    if (NULL == hMutex)
      {
       printf ("Mutex Object Creation Failed: Error Code: %d",
      GetLastError ());
       //Mutex Object Creation failed. Return
       return;
      }
//Create Child thread 1
child_threads[0]=    CreateThread(NULL,0,
                     (LPTHREAD_START_ROUTINE)Process_A,
                     (LPVOID)0,0,&thread_id);
```

```
//Create Child thread 2
child_threads[1]=        CreateThread(NULL,0,
                         (LPTHREAD_START_ROUTINE)Process_B,
                         (LPVOID)0,0,&thread_id);
//Check the success of creation of child threads
for (i=0;i<thread_count; i++)
{
       if(NULL==child_threads[i])
       {
       //Child thread creation failed.
       printf ("Child thread Creation failed with Error Code: %d",
       GetLastError ());
       return;
       }
}
// Wait for the termination of child threads

WaitForMultipleObjects(thread_count, child_threads, TRUE,
INFINITE);
    //Close child thread handles
       for( i=0; i < thread_count; i++ )
        CloseHandle(child_threads[i]);
       //Close Mutex object handle
       CloseHandle(hMutex);
       return;
}
```

Please refer to the Online Learning Centre for details on the various Win32 APIs used in the program for mutex creation, acquiring, signalling, and releasing.

The mutual exclusion semaphore is a special implementation of the binary semaphore by certain real-time operating systems like VxWorks and MicroC/OS-II to prevent priority inversion problems in shared resource access. The mutual exclusion semaphore has an option to set the priority of a task owning it to the highest priority of the task which is being pended while attempting to acquire the semaphore which is already in use by a low priority task. This ensures that the low priority task which is currently holding the semaphore, when a high priority task is waiting for it, is not pre-empted by a medium priority task. This is the mechanism supported by the mutual exclusion semaphore to prevent priority inversion.

VxWorks kernel also supports binary semaphores for synchronising shared resource access. We will discuss about it in detail in a later chapter.

Critical Section Objects In Windows CE, the '*Critical Section object*' is same as the '*mutex object*' except that '*Critical Section object*' can only be used by the threads of a single process (Intra process). The piece of code which needs to be made as '*Critical Section*' is placed at the '*Critical Section*' area by the process. The memory area which is to be used as the '*Critical Section*' is allocated by the process. The process creates a '*Critical Section*' area by creating a variable of type *CRITICAL_SECTION*. The *Critical Section*' must be initialised before the threads of a process can use it for getting exclusive access. The *InitializeCriticalSection(LPCRITICAL_SECTION lpCriticalSection)* API initialises the critical section pointed by the pointer *lpCriticalSection* to the critical section. Once the critical section is initialized, all threads in the process can use it. Threads can use the API call *EnterCriticalSection (LPCRITICAL_SECTION lpCriticalSection)* for getting the exclusive ownership of the critical section pointed by the pointer *lpCriticalSection*. Calling the *EnterCriticalSection()* API blocks the execution of the caller thread if the critical section is already in use by other threads and the thread waits for the critical section object. Threads which are blocked by the *EnterCriticalSection()* call, waiting on a critical section are added to a wait queue and are woken when the critical section is available to the requested thread. The API call *TryEnterCriticalSection(LPCRITICAL_SECTION lpCriticalSection)* attempts to enter the critical section pointed by the pointer *lpCriticalSection* without blocking the caller thread. If the critical section is not in use by any other thread, the calling thread gets the ownership of the critical section. If the critical section is already in use by another thread, the *TryEnterCriticalSection()* call indicates it to the caller thread by a specific return value and the thread resumes its execution. A thread can release the exclusive ownership of a critical section by calling the API *LeaveCriticalSection(LPCRITICAL_SECTION lpCriticalSection)*. The threads of a process can use the API *DeleteCriticalSection (LPCRITICAL_SECTION lpCriticalSection)* to release all resources used by a critical section object which was created by the process with the *CRITICAL_SECTION* variable.

Now let's have a look at the '*Racing*' problem we discussed under the section '*Racing*'. The racing condition can be eliminated by using a critical section object for synchronisation. The following code snippet illustrates the same.

```
#include <stdio.h>
#include <windows.h>
//******************************************************************
//counter is an integer variable and Buffer is a byte array shared
//between two threads
char Buffer[10] = {1,2,3,4,5,6,7,8,9,10};
short int counter = 0;
//Define the critical section
CRITICAL_SECTION CS;
//******************************************************************
// Child Thread 1
void Process_A (void) {
int i;
  for (i =0; i<5; i++)
{
   if (Buffer[i] > 0)
     {
     //Use critical section object for synchronisation
     EnterCriticalSection(&CS);
     counter++;
     LeaveCriticalSection(&CS);
     }
    printf("Process A : Counter = %d\n",counter);
}
}
//******************************************************************
// Child Thread 2
void Process_B(void) {
```

```
int j;
 for (j =5; j<10; j++)
{
   if (Buffer[j] > 0)
      {
      //Use critical section object for synchronisation
      EnterCriticalSection(&CS);
      counter++;
      LeaveCriticalSection(&CS);
      }
     printf("Process B : Counter = %d\n",counter);
}
}
//*************************************************************
// Main Thread

int main() {

      DWORD id;

      //Initialize critical section object
      InitializeCriticalSection(&CS);
      CreateThread(NULL,0,
                          (LPTHREAD_START_ROUTINE) Process_A,
                          (LPVOID)0,0,&id);
      CreateThread(NULL,0,
                          (LPTHREAD_START_ROUTINE) Process_B,
                          (LPVOID)0,0,&id);
      Sleep(100000);
      return 0;
}
```

Here the shared resource is the shared variable '*counter*'. The concurrent access to this variable by the threads '*Process_A*' and '*Process_B*' may create race condition and may produce incorrect results. The critical section object '*CS*' holds the piece of code corresponding to the access of the shared variable '*counter*' by each threads. This ensures that the memory area containing the low level instructions corresponding to the high level instruction '*counter++*' is accessed exclusively by threads '*Process_A*' and '*Process_B*' and avoids a race condition. The output of the above piece of code when executed on Windows XP machine is given in Fig. 10.36.

The final value of '*counter*' is obtained as 10, which is the expected result for this piece of code. If you observe this output window you can see that the text is not outputted to the o/p window in the expected manner. The *printf ()* library routine used in this sample code is re-entrant and it can be preempted while in execution. That is why the outputting of text happened in a non expected way.

> ***Note***
> It should be noted that the scheduling of the threads '*Process_A*' and '*Process_B*' is OS kernel scheduling policy dependent and you may not get the same output all the time when you run this piece of code under Windows XP.

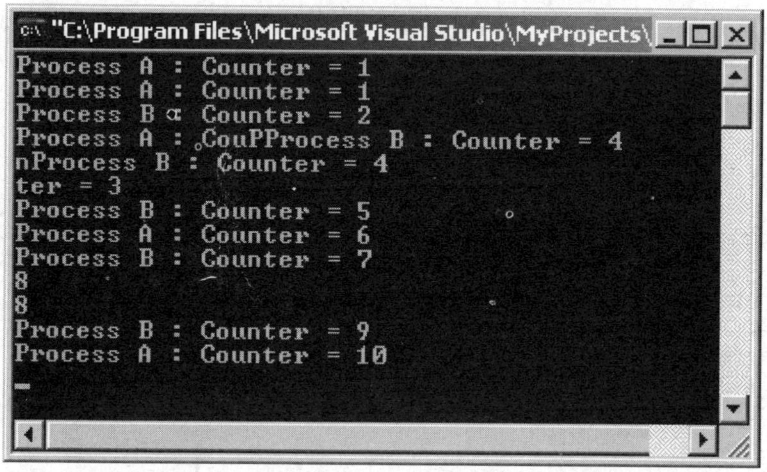

Fig. 10.36 **Output of the Win32 application resolving racing condition through critical section object**

The critical section object makes the piece of code residing inside it non-reentrant. Now let's try the above piece of code by putting the *printf ()* library routine in the critical section object.

```
#include <stdio.h>
#include <windows.h>
//*******************************************************************
//counter is an integer variable and Buffer is a byte array shared
//between two threads Process A and Process B
char Buffer[10] = {1,2,3,4,5,6,7,8,9,10};
short int counter = 0;
//Define the critical section
CRITICAL_SECTION CS;
//*******************************************************************
// Child Thread 1
void Process_A (void) {

int i;
  for (i =0; i<5; i++)
{
    if (Buffer[i] > 0)
       {
       //Use critical section object for synchronisation
       EnterCriticalSection(&CS);
       counter++;
       printf("Process A : Counter = %d\n",counter);
       LeaveCriticalSection(&CS);
       }
}
}
```

```
//*******************************************************************
// Child Thread 2
void Process_B(void) {

int j;
  for (j = 5; j<10; j++)
{
    if (Buffer[j] > 0)
        {
        //Use critical section object for synchronisation
        EnterCriticalSection(&CS);
        counter++;
        printf("Process B : Counter = %d\n",counter);
        LeaveCriticalSection(&CS);
        }
}
}
//*******************************************************************
// Main Thread

int main() {

        DWORD id;

        //Initialize critical section object
        InitializeCriticalSection(&CS);
        CreateThread(NULL,0,
                    (LPTHREAD_START_ROUTINE)Process_A,
                    (LPVOID)0,0,&id);
        CreateThread(NULL,0,
                    (LPTHREAD_START_ROUTINE)Process_B,
                    (LPVOID)0,0,&id);
        Sleep(100000);
        return 0;
}
```

The output of the above piece of code when executed on a Windows XP machine is given below.

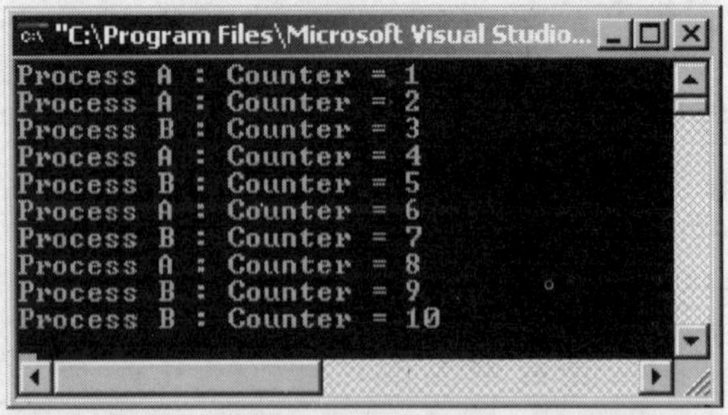

Fig. 10.37 **Output of the Win32 application resolving racing condition through critical section object**

> **Note**
> It should be noted that the scheduling of the threads '*Process_A*' and '*Process_B*' is OS kernel scheduling policy dependent and you may not get the same output all the time when you run this piece of code in Windows XP. The output of the above program when executed at three different instances of time is given shown in Fig. 10.38.

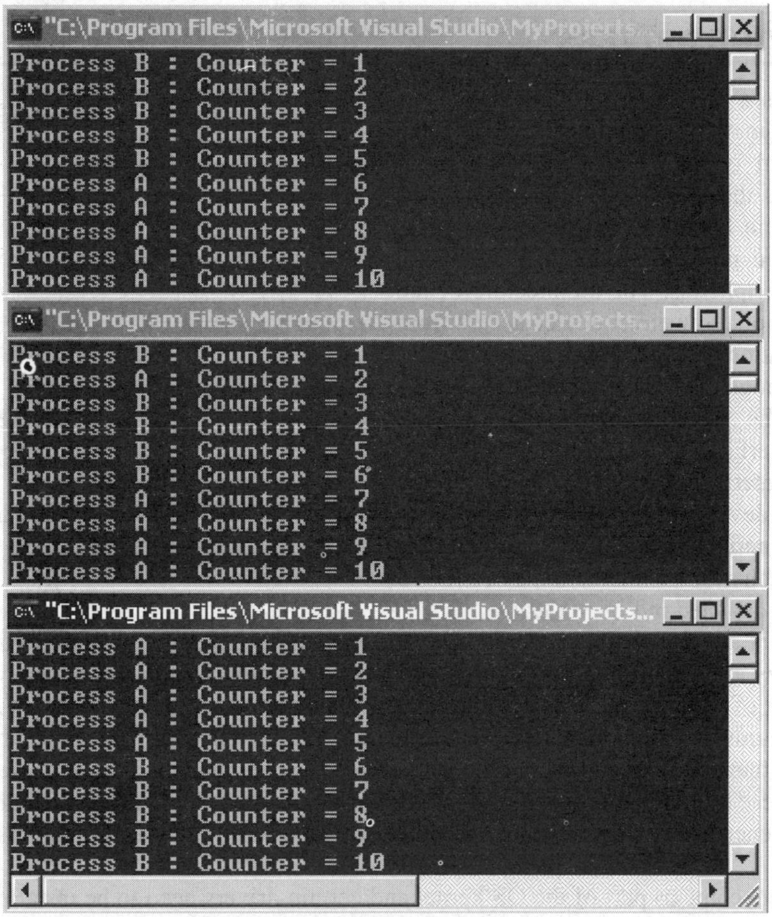

Fig. 10.38 **Illustration of scheduler behaviour under Windows XP kernel**

Events Event object is a synchronisation technique which uses the notification mechanism for synchronisation. In concurrent execution we may come across situations which demand the processes to wait for a particular sequence for its operations. A typical example of this is the producer consumer threads, where the consumer thread should wait for the consumer thread to produce the data and producer thread should wait for the consumer thread to consume the data before producing fresh data. If this sequence is not followed it will end up in producer-consumer problem. Notification mechanism is used for handling this scenario. Event objects are used for implementing notification mechanisms.

A thread/process can wait for an event and another thread/process can set this event for processing by the waiting thread/process. The creation and handling of event objects for notification is OS kernel dependent. Please refer to the Online Learning Centre for information on the usage of 'Events' under Windows Kernel for process/thread synchronisation.

The MicroC/OS-II kernel also uses 'events' for task synchronisation. We will discuss it in a later chapter.

10.9 DEVICE DRIVERS

Device driver is a piece of software that acts as a bridge between the operating system and the hardware. In an operating system based product architecture, the user applications talk to the Operating System kernel for all necessary information exchange including communication with the hardware peripherals. The architecture of the OS kernel will not allow direct device access from the user application. All the device related access should flow through the OS kernel and the OS kernel routes it to the concerned hardware peripheral. OS provides interfaces in the form of Application Programming Interfaces (APIs) for accessing the hardware. The device driver abstracts the hardware from user applications. The topology of user applications and hardware interaction in an RTOS based system is depicted in Fig. 10.39.

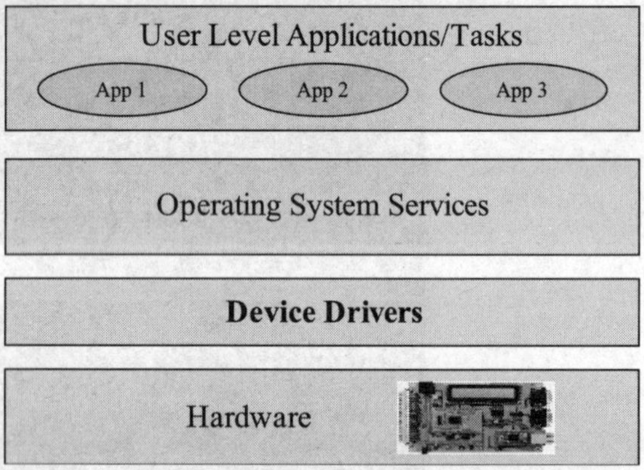

Fig. 10.39 **Role of Device driver in Embedded OS based products**

Device drivers are responsible for initiating and managing the communication with the hardware peripherals. They are responsible for establishing the connectivity, initialising the hardware (setting up various registers of the hardware device) and transferring data. An embedded product may contain different types of hardware components like Wi-Fi module, File systems, Storage device interface, etc. The initialisation of these devices and the protocols required for communicating with these devices may be different. All these requirements are implemented in drivers and a single driver will not be able to satisfy all these. Hence each hardware (more specifically each class of hardware) requires a unique driver component.

Certain drivers come as part of the OS kernel and certain drivers need to be installed on the fly. For example, the program storage memory for an embedded product, say NAND Flash memory requires a NAND Flash driver to read and write data from/to it. This driver should come as part of the OS kernel image. Certainly the OS will not contain the drivers for all devices and peripherals under the Sun. It contains only the necessary drivers to communicate with the onboard devices (Hardware devices which are part of the platform) and for certain set of devices supporting standard protocols and device class (Say USB Mass storage device or HID devices like Mouse/keyboard). If an external device, whose driver software is not available with OS kernel image, is connected to the embedded device (Say a medical device with custom USB class implementation is connected to the USB port of the embedded product), the OS prompts the user to instal its driver manually. Device drivers which are part of the OS image are known as 'Built-in drivers' or 'On-board drivers'. These drivers are loaded by the OS at the time of booting the device and are always kept in the RAM. Drivers which need to be installed for accessing a device are known as 'Installable drivers'. These drivers are loaded by the OS on a need basis. Whenever the device is connected, the OS loads the corresponding driver to memory. When the device is removed, the driver is unloaded from memory. The Operating system maintains a record of the drivers corresponding to each hardware.

The implementation of driver is OS dependent. There is no universal implementation for a driver. How the driver communicates with the kernel is dependent on the OS structure and implementation. Different Operating Systems follow different implementations.

It is very essential to know the hardware interfacing details like the memory address assigned to the device, the Interrupt used, etc. of on-board peripherals for writing a driver for that peripheral. It varies on the hardware design of the product. Some Real-Time operating systems like 'Windows CE' support a layered architecture for the driver which separates out the low level implementation from the OS specific interface. The low level implementation part is generally known as Platform Dependent Device (PDD) layer. The OS specific interface part is known as Model Device Driver (MDD) or Logical Device Driver (LDD). For a standard driver, for a specific operating system, the MDD/LDD always remains the same and only the PDD part needs to be modified according to the target hardware for a particular class of devices.

Most of the time, the hardware developer provides the implementation for all on board devices for a specific OS along with the platform. The drivers are normally shipped in the form of *Board Support Package*. The *Board Support Package* contains low level driver implementations for the onboard peripherals and OEM Adaptation Layer (OAL) for accessing the various chip level functionalities and a bootloader for loading the operating system. The OAL facilitates communication between the Operating System (OS) and the target device and includes code to handle interrupts, timers, power management, bus abstraction, generic I/O control codes (IOCTLs), etc. The driver files are usually in the form of a dll file. Drivers can run on either user space or kernel space. Drivers which run in user space are known as *user mode drivers* and the drivers which run in kernel space are known as *kernel mode drivers*. User mode drivers are safer than kernel mode drivers. If an error or exception occurs in a user mode driver, it won't affect the services of the kernel. On the other hand, if an exception occurs in the kernel mode driver, it may lead to the kernel crash. The way how a device driver is written and how the interrupts are handled in it are operating system and target hardware specific. However regardless of the OS types, a device driver implements the following:

1. Device (Hardware) Initialisation and Interrupt configuration
2. Interrupt handling and processing
3. Client interfacing (Interfacing with user applications)

The Device (Hardware) initialisation part of the driver deals with configuring the different registers of the device (target hardware). For example configuring the I/O port line of the processor as Input or output line and setting its associated registers for building a General Purpose IO (GPIO) driver. The interrupt configuration part deals with configuring the interrupts that needs to be associated with the hardware. In the case of the GPIO driver, if the intention is to generate an interrupt when the Input line is asserted, we need to configure the interrupt associated with the I/O port by modifying its associated registers. The basic Interrupt configuration involves the following.

1. Set the interrupt type (Edge Triggered (Rising/Falling) or Level Triggered (Low or High)), enable the interrupts and set the interrupt priorities.
2. Bind the Interrupt with an Interrupt Request (IRQ). The processor identifies an interrupt through IRQ. These IRQs are generated by the Interrupt Controller. In order to identify an interrupt the interrupt needs to be bonded to an IRQ.

3. Register an Interrupt Service Routine (ISR) with an Interrupt Request (IRQ). ISR is the handler for an Interrupt. In order to service an interrupt, an ISR should be associated with an IRQ. Registering an ISR with an IRQ takes care of it.

With these the interrupt configuration is complete. If an interrupt occurs, depending on its priority, it is serviced and the corresponding ISR is invoked. The processing part of an interrupt is handled in an ISR. The whole interrupt processing can be done by the ISR itself or by invoking an Interrupt Service Thread (IST). The IST performs interrupt processing on behalf of the ISR. To make the ISR compact and short, it is always advised to use an IST for interrupt processing. The intention of an interrupt is to send or receive command or data to and from the hardware device and make the received data available to user programs for application specific processing. Since interrupt processing happens at kernel level, user applications may not have direct access to the drivers to pass and receive data. Hence it is the responsibility of the Interrupt processing routine or thread to inform the user applications that an interrupt is occurred and data is available for further processing. The client interfacing part of the device driver takes care of this. The client interfacing implementation makes use of the Inter Process communication mechanisms supported by the embedded OS for communicating and synchronising with user applications and drivers. For example, to inform a user application that an interrupt is occurred and the data received from the device is placed in a shared buffer, the client interfacing code can signal (or set) an event. The user application creates the event, registers it and waits for the driver to signal it. The driver can share the received data through shared memory techniques. IOCTLs, shared buffers, etc. can be used for data sharing. The story line is incomplete without performing an interrupt done (Interrupt processing completed) functionality in the driver. Whenever an interrupt is asserted, while vectoring to its corresponding ISR, all interrupts of equal and low priorities are disabled. They are re-enable only on executing the interrupt done function (Same as the Return from Interrupt RETI instruction execution for *8051*) by the driver. The interrupt done function can be invoked at the end of corresponding ISR or IST.

We will discuss more about device driver development in a dedicated book coming under this book series.

10.10 HOW TO CHOOSE AN RTOS

The decision of choosing an RTOS for an embedded design is very crucial. A lot of factors needs to be analysed carefully before making a decision on the selection of an RTOS. These factors can be either functional or non-functional. The following section gives a brief introduction to the important functional and non-functional requirements that needs to be analysed in the selection of an RTOS for an embedded design.

10.10.1 Functional Requirements

Processor Support It is not necessary that all RTOS's support all kinds of processor architecture. It is essential to ensure the processor support by the RTOS.

Memory Requirements The OS requires ROM memory for holding the OS files and it is normally stored in a non-volatile memory like FLASH. OS also requires working memory RAM for loading the OS services. Since embedded systems are memory constrained, it is essential to evaluate the minimal ROM and RAM requirements for the OS under consideration.

Real-time Capabilities It is not mandatory that the operating system for all embedded systems need to be Real-time and all embedded Operating systems are 'Real-time' in behaviour. The task/process scheduling policies plays an important role in the 'Real-time' behaviour of an OS. Analyse the real-time capabilities of the OS under consideration and the standards met by the operating system for real-time capabilities.

Kernel and Interrupt Latency The kernel of the OS may disable interrupts while executing certain services and it may lead to interrupt latency. For an embedded system whose response requirements are high, this latency should be minimal.

Inter Process Communication and Task Synchronisation The implementation of Inter Process Communication and Synchronisation is OS kernel dependent. Certain kernels may provide a bunch of options whereas others provide very limited options. Certain kernels implement policies for avoiding priority inversion issues in resource sharing.

Modularisation Support Most of the operating systems provide a bunch of features. At times it may not be necessary for an embedded product for its functioning. It is very useful if the OS supports modularisation where in which the developer can choose the essential modules and re-compile the OS image for functioning. Windows CE is an example for a highly modular operating system.

Support for Networking and Communication The OS kernel may provide stack implementation and driver support for a bunch of communication interfaces and networking. Ensure that the OS under consideration provides support for all the interfaces required by the embedded product.

Development Language Support Certain operating systems include the run time libraries required for running applications written in languages like Java and C#. A Java Virtual Machine (JVM) customised for the Operating System is essential for running java applications. Similarly the .NET Compact Framework (.NETCF) is required for running Microsoft® .NET applications on top of the Operating System. The OS may include these components as built-in component, if not, check the availability of the same from a third party vendor for the OS under consideration.

10.10.2 Non-functional Requirements

Custom Developed or Off the Shelf Depending on the OS requirement, it is possible to go for the complete development of an operating system suiting the embedded system needs or use an off the shelf, readily available operating system, which is either a commercial product or an Open Source product, which is in close match with the system requirements. Sometimes it may be possible to build the required features by customising an Open source OS. The decision on which to select is purely dependent on the development cost, licensing fees for the OS, development time and availability of skilled resources.

Cost The total cost for developing or buying the OS and maintaining it in terms of commercial product and custom build needs to be evaluated before taking a decision on the selection of OS.

Development and Debugging Tools Availability The availability of development and debugging tools is a critical decision making factor in the selection of an OS for embedded design. Certain Operating Systems may be superior in performance, but the availability of tools for supporting the development may be limited. Explore the different tools available for the OS under consideration.

Ease of Use How easy it is to use a commercial RTOS is another important feature that needs to be considered in the RTOS selection.

After Sales For a commercial embedded RTOS, after sales in the form of e-mail, on-call services, etc. for bug fixes, critical patch updates and support for production issues, etc. should be analysed thoroughly.

Summary

- ✓ The *Operating System* is responsible for making the system convenient to use, organise and manage system resources efficiently and properly.
- ✓ Process/Task management, Primary memory management, File system management, I/O system (Device) management, Secondary Storage Management, protection implementation, Time management, Interrupt handling, etc. are the important services handled by the OS kernel.
- ✓ The core of the operating system is known as *kernel*. Depending on the implementation of the different kernel services, the kernel is classified as *Monolithic* and *Micro*. *User Space* is the memory area in which user applications are confined to run, whereas *kernel space* is the memory area reserved for kernel applications.
- ✓ Operating systems with a generalised kernel are known as *General Purpose Operating Systems* (*GPOS*), whereas operating systems with a specialised kernel with deterministic timing behaviour are known as *Real-Time Operating Systems* (*RTOS*).
- ✓ In the operating system context a task/process is a program, or part of it, in execution. The process holds a set of registers, process status, a Program Counter (PC) to point to the next executable instruction of the process, a stack for holding the local variables associated with the process and the code corresponding to the process.
- ✓ The different states through which a process traverses through during its journey from the newly created state to finished state is known as *Process Life Cycle*
- ✓ Process management deals with the creation of a process, setting up the memory space for the process, loading the process's code into the memory space, allocating system resources, setting up a Process Control Block (PCB) for the process and process termination/deletion.
- ✓ A thread is the primitive that can execute code. It is a single sequential flow of control within a process. A process may contain multiple threads. The act of concurrent execution of multiple threads under an operating system is known as *multithreading.*
- ✓ Thread standards are the different standards available for thread creation and management. POSIX, Win32, Java, etc. are the commonly used thread creation and management libraries.
- ✓ The ability of a system to execute multiple processes simultaneously is known as *multiprocessing*, whereas the ability of an operating system to hold multiple processes in memory and switch the processor (CPU) from executing one process to another process is known as *multitasking*. Multitasking involves *Context Switching*, *Context Saving* and *Context Retrieval.*
- ✓ *Co-operative* multitasking, *Preemptive* multitasking and *Non-preemptive* multitasking are the three important types of multitasking which exist in the Operating system context.
- ✓ CPU utilisation, Throughput, Turn Around Time (TAT), Waiting Time and Response Time are the important criterions that need to be considered for the selection of a scheduling algorithm for task scheduling.
- ✓ Job queue, Ready queue and Device queue are the important queues maintained by an operating system in association with CPU scheduling.
- ✓ First Come First Served (FCFS)/First in First Out (FIFO), Last Come First Served (LCFS)/Last in First Out (LIFO), Shortest Job First (SJF), priority based scheduling, etc. are examples for Non-preemptive scheduling, whereas Preemptive SJF Scheduling/Shortest Remaining Time (SRT), Round Robin (RR) scheduling and priority based scheduling are examples for preemptive scheduling.
- ✓ Processes in a multitasking system falls into either *Co-operating* or *Competing*. The co-operating processes share data for communicating among the processes through *Inter Process Communication* (IPC), whereas competing

processes do not share anything among themselves but they share the system resources like display devices, keyboard, etc.

- ✓ *Shared memory*, *message passing* and *Remote Procedure Calls* (RPC) are the important IPC mechanisms through which the co-operating processes communicate in an operating system environment. The implementation of the IPC mechanism is OS kernel dependent.
- ✓ Racing, deadlock, livelock, starvation, producer-consumer problem, Readers-Writers problem and priority inversion are some of the problems involved in shared resource access in task communication through sharing.
- ✓ The 'Dining Philosophers' 'Problem' is a real-life representation of the deadlock, starvation, livelock and 'Racing' issues in shared resource access in operating system context.
- ✓ *Priority inversion* is the condition in which a medium priority task gets the CPU for execution, when a high priority task needs to wait for a low priority task to release a resource which is shared between the high priority task and the low priority task.
- ✓ *Priority inheritance* and *Priority ceiling* are the two mechanisms for avoiding *Priority Inversion* in a multitasking environment.
- ✓ The act of preventing the access of a shared resource by a task/process when it is currently being held by another task/process is known as *mutual exclusion*. Mutual exclusion can be implemented through either *busy waiting* (*spin lock*) or *sleep and wakeup* technique.
- ✓ *Test and Set*, *Flags*, etc. are examples of *Busy waiting* based *mutual exclusion* implementation, whereas *Semaphores*, *mutex*, *Critical Section Objects* and *events* are examples for *Sleep and Wakeup* based mutual exclusion.
- ✓ *Binary semaphore* implements exclusive shared resource access, whereas *counting semaphore* limits the concurrent access to a shared resource, and *mutual exclusion semaphore* prevents priority inversion in shared resource access.
- ✓ *Device driver* is a piece of software that acts as a bridge between the operating system and the hardware. Device drivers are responsible for initiating and managing the communication with the hardware peripherals.
- ✓ Various functional and non-functional requirements need to be evaluated before the selection of an RTOS for an embedded design.

Keywords

Operating System : A piece of software designed to manage and allocate system resources and execute other pieces of the software

Kernel : The core of the operating system which is responsible for managing the system resources and the communication among the hardware and other system services

Kernel space : The primary memory area where the kernel applications are confined to run

User space : The primary memory area where the user applications are confined to run

Monolithic kernel : A kernel with all kernel services run in the kernel space under a single kernel thread

Microkernel : A kernel which incorporates only the essential services within the kernel space and the rest is installed as loadable modules called *servers*

Real-Time Operating System (RTOS) : Operating system with a specialised kernel with a deterministic timing behaviour

Scheduler : OS kernel service which deals with the scheduling of processes/tasks

Hard Real-Time : Real-time operating systems that strictly adhere to the timing constraints for a task

Soft Real-Time : Real-time operating systems that does not guarantee meeting deadlines, but, offer the best effort to meet the deadline

Task/Job/Process : In the operating system context a task/process is a program, or part of it, in execution

Process Life Cycle	:	The different *states* through which a process traverses through during its journey from the newly created state to completed state
Thread	:	The primitive that can execute code. It is a single sequential flow of control within a process
Multiprocessing systems	:	Systems which contain multiple CPUs and are capable of executing multiple processes simultaneously
Multitasking	:	The ability of an operating system to hold multiple processes in memory and switch the processor (CPU) from executing one process to another process
Context switching	:	The act of switching CPU among the processes and changing the current execution context
Co-operative multitasking	:	Multitasking model in which a task/process gets a chance when the currently executing task relinquishes the CPU voluntarily
Preemptive multitasking	:	Multitasking model in which a currently running task/process is preempted to execute another task/process
Non-preemptive multitasking	:	Multitasking model in which a task gets a chance to execute when the currently executing task relinquishes the CPU or when it enters a wait state
First Come First Served (FCFS)/First in First Out (FIFO)	:	Scheduling policy which sorts the *Ready Queue* with FCFS model and schedules the first arrived process from the *Ready queue* for execution
Last Come First Served (LCFS)/Last in First Out (LIFO)	:	Scheduling policy which sorts the *Ready Queue* with LCFS model and schedules the last arrived process from the *Ready queue* for execution
Shortest Job First (SJF)	:	Scheduling policy which sorts the *Ready queue* with the order of the shortest execution time for process and schedules the process with least estimated execution completion time from the *Ready queue* for execution
Priority based Scheduling	:	Scheduling policy which sorts the *Ready queue* based on priority and schedules the process with highest priority from the *Ready queue* for execution
Shortest Remaining Time (SRT)	:	Preemptive scheduling policy which sorts the *Ready queue* with the order of the shortest remaining time for execution completion for process and schedules the process with the least remaining time for estimated execution completion from the *Ready queue* for execution
Round Robin	:	Preemptive scheduling policy in which the currently running process is preempted based on time slice
Co-operating processes	:	Processes which share data for communicating among them
Inter Process/Task Communication (IPC)	:	Mechanism for communicating between co-operating processes of a system
Shared memory	:	A memory sharing mechanism used for inter process communication
Message passing	:	IPC mechanism based on exchanging of messages between processes through a message queue or mailbox
Message queue	:	A queue for holding messages for exchanging between processes of a multitasking system
Mailbox	:	A special implementation of message queue under certain OS kernel, which supports only a single message
Signal	:	A form of asynchronous message notification
Remote Procedure Call or RPC	:	The IPC mechanism used by a process to invoke a procedure of another process running on the same CPU or on a different CPU which is interconnected in a network
Racing	:	The situation in which multiple processes compete (race) each other to access and manipulate shared data concurrently

Deadlock : A situation where none of the processes are able to make any progress in their execution. Deadlock is the condition in which a process is waiting for a resource held by another process which is waiting for a resource held by the first process

Livelock : A condition where a process always does something but is unable to make any progress in the execution completion

Starvation : The condition in which a process does not get the CPU or system resources required to continue its execution for a long time

Dining Philosophers' Problem : A real-life representation of the *deadlock*, *starvation*, *livelock* and *racing* issues in shared resource access in operating system context

Producer-Consumer problem : A common data sharing problem where two processes concurrently access a shared buffer with fixed size

Readers-Writers problem : A data sharing problem characterised by multiple processes trying to read and write shared data concurrently

Priority inversion : The condition in which a medium priority task gets the CPU for execution, when a high priority task needs to wait for a low priority task to release a resource which is shared between the high priority task and the low priority task

Priority inheritance : A mechanism by which the priority of a low-priority task which is currently holding a resource requested by a high priority task, is raised to that of the high priority task to avoid priority inversion

Priority Ceiling : The mechanism in which a priority is associated with a shared resource (The priority of the highest priority task which uses the shared resource) and the priority of the task is temporarily boosted to the priority of the shared resource when the resource is being held by the task, for avoiding priority inversion

Task/Process synchronisation : The act of synchronising the access of shared resources by multiple processes and enforcing proper sequence of operation among multiple processes of a multitasking system

Mutual Exclusion : The act of preventing the access of a shared resource by a task/process when it is being held by another task/process

Semaphore : A system resource for implementing mutual exclusion in shared resource access or for restricting the access to the shared resource

Mutex : The *binary semaphore* implementation for exclusive resource access under certain OS kernel

Device driver : A piece of software that acts as a bridge between the operating system and the hardware

Objective Questions

Operating System Basics

1. Which of the following is true about a kernel?
   (a) The kernel is the core of the operating system
   (b) It is responsible for managing the system resources and the communication among the hardware and other system services
   (c) It acts as the abstraction layer between system resources and user applications.
   (d) It contains a set of system libraries and services
   (e) All of these
2. The user application and kernel interface is provided through
   (a) System calls (b) Shared memory (d) None of these

3. The process management service of the kernel is responsible for
   (a) Setting up the memory space for the process
   (b) Allocating system resources
   (c) Scheduling and managing the execution of the process
   (d) Setting up and managing the Process Control Block (PCB), inter-process communication and synchronisation
   (e) All of these
4. The Memory Management Unit (MMU) of the kernel is responsible for
   (a) Keeping track of which part of the memory area is currently used by which process
   (b) Allocating and de-allocating memory space on a need basis (Dynamic memory allocation)
   (c) Handling all virtual memory operations in a kernel with virtual memory support
   (d) All of these
5. The memory area which holds the program code corresponding to the core OS applications/services is known as
   (a) User space (b) Kernel space (c) Shared memory (d) All of these
6. Which of the following is true about *Privilege separation*?
   (a) The user applications/processes runs at user space and kernel applications run at kernel space
   (b) Each user application/process runs on its own virtual memory space
   (c) A process is not allowed to access the memory space of another process directly
   (d) All of these
7. Which of the following is true about monolithic kernel?
   (a) All kernel services run in the kernel space under a single kernel thread.
   (b) The tight internal integration of kernel modules in monolithic kernel architecture allows the effective utilisation of the low-level features of the underlying system
   (c) Error prone. Any error or failure in any one of the kernel modules may lead to the crashing of the entire kernel
   (d) All of these
8. Which of the following is true about microkernel?
   (a) The microkernel design incorporates only the essential set of operating system services into the kernel. The rest of the operating system services are implemented in programs known as '*servers*' which runs in user space.
   (b) Highly modular and OS neutral
   (c) Less Error prone. Any 'Server' where error occurs can be restarted without restarting the entire kernel
   (d) All of these

Real-Time Operating System (RTOS)

1. Which of the following is true for Real-Time Operating Systems (RTOSes)?
   (a) Possess specialised kernel (b) Deterministic in behaviour
   (c) Predictable performance (d) All of these
2. Which of the following is (are) example(s) for RTOS?
   (a) Windows CE (b) Windows XP (c) Windows 2000 (d) QNX
   (e) (a) and (d)
3. Interrupts which occur in sync with the currently executing task are known as
   (a) Asynchronous interrupts (b) Synchronous interrupts
   (c) External interrupts (d) None of these
4. Which of the following is an example of a synchronous interrupt?
   (a) TRAP (b) External interrupt (c) Divide by zero (d) Timer interrupt
5. Which of the following is true about 'Timer tick' for RTOS?
   (a) The high resolution hardware timer interrupt is referred as 'Timer tick'
   (b) The 'Timer tick' is taken as the timing reference by the kernel
   (c) The time parameters for tasks are expressed as the multiples of the 'Timer tick'
   (d) All of these

6. Which of the following is true about hard real-time systems?
   (a) Strictly adhere to the timing constraints for a task
   (b) Missing any deadline may produce catastrophic results
   (c) Most of the hard real-time systems are automatic and may not contain a human in the loop
   (d) May not implement virtual memory based memory management
   (e) All of these.
7. Which of the following is true about soft real-time systems?
   (a) Does not guarantee meeting deadlines, but offer the best effort to meet the deadline are referred
   (b) Missing deadlines for tasks are acceptable
   (c) Most of the soft real-time systems contain a human in the loop
   (d) All of these

Tasks, Process and Threads

1. Which of the following is true about *Process* in the operating system context?
   (a) A '*Process*' is a program, or part of it, in execution
   (b) It can be an instance of a program in execution
   (c) A process requires various system resources like CPU for executing the process, memory for storing the code corresponding to the process and associated variables, I/O devices for information exchange, etc.
   (d) A process is sequential in execution
   (e) All of these
2. A process has
   (a) Stack memory (b) Program memory (c) Working Registers (d) Data memory
   (e) All of these
3. The 'Stack' memory of a process holds all temporary data such as variables local to the process. State 'True' or 'False'
   (a) True (b) False
4. The data memory of a process holds
   (a) Local variables (b) Global variables (c) Program instructions (d) None of these
5. A process has its own memory space, when residing at the main memory. State 'True' or 'False'
   (a) True (b) False
6. A process when loaded to the memory is allocated a virtual memory space in the range 0x08000 to 0x08FF8. What is the content of the Stack pointer of the process when it is created?
   (a) 0x07FFF (b) 0x08000 (c) 0x08FF7 (d) 0x08FF8
7. What is the content of the program counter for the above example when the process is loaded for the first time?
   (a) 0x07FFF (b) 0x08000 (c) 0x08FF7 (d) 0x08FF8
8. The state where a process is incepted into the memory and awaiting the processor time for execution, is known as
   (a) Created state (b) Blocked state (c) Ready state (d) Waiting state
   (e) Completed state
9. The CPU allocation for a process may change when it changes its state from ________?
   (a) 'Running' to 'Ready' (b) 'Ready' to 'Running'
   (c) 'Running' to 'Blocked' (d) 'Running' to 'Completed'
   (e) All of these
10. Which of the following is true about threads?
    (a) A thread is the primitive that can execute code
    (b) A thread is a single sequential flow of control within a process
    (c) '*Thread*' is also known as lightweight process
    (d) All of these (e) None of these
11. A process can have many threads of execution. State 'True' or 'False'
    (a) True (b) False

12. Different threads, which are part of a process, share the same address space. State 'True' or 'False'
    (a) True (b) False
13. Multiple threads of the same process share ________?
    (a) Data memory (b) Code memory
    (c) Stack memory (d) All of these
    (e) only (a) and (b)
14. Which of the following is true about multithreading?
    (a) Better memory utilisation
    (b) Better CPU utilisation
    (c) Reduced complexity in inter-thread communication
    (d) Faster process execution (e) All of these
15. Which of the following is a thread creation and management library?
    (a) POSIX (b) Win32
    (c) Java Thread Library (d) All of these
16. Which of the following is the POSIX standard library for thread creation and management
    (a) Pthreads (b) Threads (c) Jthreads (d) None of these
17. What happens when a thread object's *wait()* method is invoked in Java?
    (a) Causes the thread object to wait
    (b) The thread will remain in the 'Wait' state until another thread invokes the *notify()* or *notifyAll()* method of the thread object which is waiting
    (c) Both of these
    (d) None of these
18. Which of the following is true about user level threads?
    (a) Even if a process contains multiple user level threads, the OS treats it as a single thread
    (b) The user level threads are executed non-preemptively in relation to each other
    (c) User level threads follow co-operative execution model
    (d) All of these
19. Which of the following are the valid thread binding models for user level to kernel level thread binding?
    (a) One to Many (b) Many to One (c) One to One (d) Many to Many
    (e) All of these (f) only (b), (c) and (d)
20. If a thread expires, the stack memory allocated to it is reclaimed by the process to which the thread belongs. State 'True' or 'False'
    (a) True (b) False

Multiprocessing and Multitasking

1. Multitasking and multiprocessing refers to the same entity in the operating system context. State 'True' or 'False'
   (a) True (b) False
2. Multiprocessor systems contain
   (a) Single CPU (b) Multiple CPUs (c) No CPU
3. The ability of the operating system to have multiple programs in memory, which are ready for execution, is referred as
   (a) Multitasking (b) Multiprocessing (c) Multiprogramming
4. In a multiprocessing system
   (a) Only a single process can run at a time (b) Multiple processes can run simultaneously
   (c) Multiple processes run in pseudo parallelism
5. In a multitasking system
   (a) Only a single process can run at a time (b) Multiple processes can run simultaneously
   (c) Multiple processes run in pseudo parallelism (d) Only (a) and (c)
6. Multitasking involves
   (a) CPU execution switching of processes (b) CPU halting (c) No CPU operation

7. Multitasking involves
   (a) Context switching (b) Context saving (c) Context retrieval (d) All of these
   (e) None of these
8. What are the different types of multitasking present in operating systems?
   (a) Co-operative (b) Preemptive (c) Non-preemptive (d) All of these
9. In Co-operative multitasking, a process/task gets the CPU time when
   (a) The currently executing task terminates its execution
   (b) The currently executing task enters 'Wait' state
   (c) The currently executing task relinquishes the CPU before terminating
   (d) Never get a chance to execute (e) Either (a) or (c)
10. In Preemptive multitasking
    (a) Each process gets an equal chance for execution
    (b) The execution of a process is preempted based on the scheduling policy
    (c) Both of these (d) None of these
11. In Non-preemptive multitasking, a process/task gets the CPU time when
    (a) The currently executing task terminates its execution
    (b) The currently executing task enters 'Wait' state
    (c) The currently executing task relinquishes the CPU before terminating
    (d) All of these
    (e) None of these
12. MSDOS Operating System supports
    (a) Single user process with single thread
    (b) Single user process with multiple threads
    (c) Multiple user process with single thread per process
    (d) Multiple user process with multiple threads per process

Task Scheduling

1. Who determines which task/process is to be executed at a given point of time?
   (a) Process manager (b) Context manager (c) Scheduler (d) None of these
2. Task scheduling is an essential part of multitasking.
   (a) True (b) False
3. The process scheduling decision may take place when a process switches its state from
   (a) 'Running' to 'Ready' (b) 'Running' to 'Blocked'
   (c) 'Blocked' to 'Ready' (d) 'Running' to 'Completed'
   (e) All of these
   (f) Any one among (a) to (d) depending on the type of multitasking supported by OS
4. A process switched its state from 'Running' to 'Ready' due to scheduling act. What is the type of multitasking supported by the OS?
   (a) Co-operative (b) Preemptive (c) Non-preemptive (d) None of these
5. A process switched its state from 'Running' to 'Wait' due to scheduling act. What is the type of multitasking supported by the OS?
   (a) Co-operative (b) Preemptive (c) Non-preemptive (d) (b) or (c)
6. Which one of the following criteria plays an important role in the selection of a scheduling algorithm?
   (a) CPU utilisation (b) Throughput (c) Turnaround time (d) Waiting time
   (e) Response time (f) All of these
7. For a good scheduling algorithm, the CPU utilisation is
   (a) High (b) Medium (c) Non-defined

8. Under the process scheduling context, 'Throughput' is
   (a) The number of processes executed per unit of time
   (b) The time taken by a process to complete its execution
   (c) None of these
9. Under the process scheduling context, 'Turnaround Time' for a process is
   (a) The time taken to complete its execution
   (b) The time spent in the 'Ready' queue
   (c) The time spent on waiting on I/O
   (d) None of these
10. Turnaround Time (TAT) for a process includes
   (a) The time spent for waiting for the main memory
   (b) The time spent in the ready queue
   (c) The time spent on completing the I/O operations
   (d) The time spent in execution
   (e) All of these
11. For a good scheduling algorithm, the Turn Around Time (TAT) for a process should be
   (a) Minimum (b) Maximum (c) Average (d) Varying
12. Under the process scheduling context, 'Waiting time' for a process is
   (a) The time spent in the 'Ready queue'
   (b) The time spent on I/O operation (time spent in wait state)
   (c) Sum of (a) and (b)
   (d) None of these
13. For a good scheduling algorithm, the waiting time for a process should be
   (a) Minimum (b) Maximum (c) Average (d) Varying
14. Under the process scheduling context, 'Response time' for a process is
   (a) The time spent in 'Ready queue'
   (b) The time between the submission of a process and the first response
   (c) The time spent on I/O operation (time spent in wait state)
   (d) None of these
15. For a good scheduling algorithm, the response time for a process should be
   (a) Maximum (b) Average (c) Least (d) Varying
16. What are the different queues associated with process scheduling?
   (a) Ready Queue (b) Process Queue (c) Job Queue (d) Device Queue
   (e) All of the Above (f) (a), (c) and (d)
17. The 'Ready Queue' contains
   (a) All the processes present in the system
   (b) All the processes which are 'Ready' for execution
   (c) The currently running processes
   (d) Processes which are waiting for I/O
18. Which among the following scheduling is (are) Non-preemptive scheduling
   (a) First In First Out (FIFO/FCFS)
   (b) Last In First Out (LIFO/LCFS)
   (c) Shortest Job First (SJF)
   (d) All of these
   (e) None of these
19. Which of the following is true about FCFS scheduling
   (a) Favours CPU bound processes
   (b) The device utilisation is poor
   (c) Both of these
   (d) None of these
20. The average waiting time for a given set of process is ______ in SJF scheduling compared to FIFO scheduling
   (a) Minimal (b) Maximum (c) Average
21. Which among the following scheduling is (are) preemptive scheduling
   (a) Shortest Remaining Time First (SRT)
   (b) Preemptive Priority based
   (c) Round Robin (RR)
   (d) All of these
   (e) None of these
22. The Shortest Job First (SJF) algorithm is a priority based scheduling. State 'True' or 'False'
   (a) True (b) False

23. Which among the following is true about preemptive scheduling
    (a) A process is moved to the 'Ready' state from 'Running' state (preempted) without getting an explicit request from the process
    (b) A process is moved to the 'Ready' state from 'Running' state (preempted) on receiving an explicit request from the process
    (c) A process is moved to the 'Wait' state from the 'Running' state without getting an explicit request from the process
    (d) None of these
24. Which of the following scheduling technique(s) possess the drawback of 'Starvation'
    (a) Round Robin (b) Priority based preemptive
    (c) Shortest Job First (SJF) (d) (b) and (c)
    (e) None of these
25. Starvation describes the condition in which
    (a) A process is ready to execute and is waiting in the 'Ready' queue for a long time and is unable to get the CPU time due to various reasons
    (b) A process is waiting for a shared resource for a long time, and is unable to get it for various reasons.
    (c) Both of the above
    (d) None of these
26. Which of the scheduling policy offers equal opportunity for execution for all processes?
    (a) Priority based scheduling (b) Round Robin (RR) scheduling
    (c) Shortest Job First (SJF) (d) All of these
    (e) None of these
27. Round Robin (RR) scheduling commonly uses which one of the following policies for sorting the 'Ready' queue?
    (a) Priority (b) FCFS (FIFO) (c) LIFO (d) SRT
    (e) SJF
28. Which among the following is used for avoiding 'Starvation' of processes in priority based scheduling?
    (a) Priority Inversion (b) Aging (c) Priority Ceiling (d) All of these
29. Which of the following is true about 'Aging'
    (a) Changes the priority of a process at run time
    (b) Raises the priority of a process temporarily
    (c) It is a technique used for avoiding 'Starvation' of processes
    (d) All of these
    (e) None of these
30. Which is the most commonly used scheduling policy in Real-Time Operating Systems?
    (a) Round Robin (RR) (b) Priority based preemptive
    (c) Priority based non-preemptive
    (d) Shortest Job First (SJF)
31. In the process scheduling context, the IDLE TASK is executed for
    (a) To handle system interrupts
    (b) To keep the CPU always engaged or to keep the CPU in idle mode depending on the system design
    (c) To keep track of the resource usage by a process
    (d) All of these

Task Communication and Synchronisation

1. Processes use IPC mechanisms for
   (a) Communicating between process (b) Synchronising the access of shared resource
   (c) Both of these (d) None of these
2. Which of the following techniques is used by operating systems for inter process communication?
   (a) Shared memory (b) Messaging (c) Signalling (d) All of these

3. Under Windows Operating system, the input and output buffer memory for a named pipe is allocated in
   (a) Non-paged system memory (b) Paged system memory
   (c) Virtual memory (d) None of the above
4. Which among the following techniques is used for sharing data between processes?
   (a) Semaphores (b) Shared memory (c) Messages d) (b) and (c)
5. Which among the following is a shared memory technique for IPC?
   (a) Pipes (b) Memory mapped Object
   (c) Message blocks (d) Events (e) (a) and (b)
6. Which of the following is best advised for sharing a memory mapped object between processes under windows kernel?
   (a) Passing the handle of the shared memory object (b) Passing the name of the memory mapped object
   (c) None of these
7. Why is message passing relatively fast compared to shared memory based IPC?
   (a) Message passing is relatively free from synchronisation overheads
   (b) Message passing does not involve any OS intervention
   (c) All of these
   (d) None of these
8. In asynchronous messaging, the message posting thread just posts the message to the queue and will not wait for an acceptance (return) from the thread to which the message is posted. State 'True' or 'False'
   (a) True (b) False
9. Which of the following is a blocking message passing call in Windows?
   (a) PostMessage (b) PostThreadMessage (c) SendMessage (d) All of these
   (e) None of these
10. Under Windows operating system, the message is passed through ______ for Inter Process Communication (IPC) between processes?
    (a) Message structure (b) Memory mapped object
    (c) Semaphore (d) All of these
11. Which of the following is true about 'Signals' for Inter Process Communication?
    (a) Signals are used for asynchronous notifications (b) Signals are not queued
    (c) Signals do not carry any data (d) All of these
12. Which of the following is true about *Racing* **or** *Race condition*?
    (a) It is the condition in which multiple processes compete (race) each other to access and manipulate shared data concurrently
    (b) In a race condition the final value of the shared data depends on the process which acted on the data finally
    (c) Racing will not occur if the shared data access is atomic
    (d) All of these
13. Which of the following is true about *deadlock*?
    (a) Deadlock is the condition in which a process is waiting for a resource held by another process which is waiting for a resource held by the first process
    (b) Is the situation in which none of the competing process will be able to access the resources held by other processes since they are locked by the respective processes
    (c) Is a result of chain of circular wait
    (d) All of these
14. What are the conditions favouring deadlock in multitasking?
    (a) Mutual Exclusion (b) Hold and Wait (c) No kernel resource preemption at kernel level
    (d) Chain of circular waits (e) All of these
15. Livelock describes the situation where
    (a) A process waits on a resource is not blocked on it and it makes frequent attempts to acquire the resource. But unable to acquire it since it is held by other process

(b) A process waiting in the 'Ready' queue is unable to get the CPU time for execution
(c) Both of these
(d) None of these

16. *Priority inversion* is
(a) The condition in which a high priority task needs to wait for a low priority task to release a resource which is shared between the high priority task and the low priority task
(b) The act of increasing the priority of a process dynamically
(c) The act of decreasing the priority of a process dynamically
(d) All of these

17. Which of the following is true about Priority inheritance?
(a) A low priority task which currently holds a shared resource requested by a high priority task temporarily inherits the priority of the high priority task
(b) The priority of the low priority task which is temporarily boosted to high is brought to the original value when it releases the shared resource
(c) All of these
(d) None of these

18. Which of the following is true about Priority Ceiling based Priority inversion handling?
(a) A priority is associated with each shared resource
(b) The priority associated to each resource is the priority of the highest priority task which uses this shared resource
(c) Whenever a task accesses a shared resource, the scheduler elevates the priority of the task to that of the ceiling priority of the resource
(d) The priority of the task is brought back to the original level once the task completes the accessing of the shared resource
(e) All of these

19. Process/Task synchronisation is essential for?
(a) Avoiding conflicts in resource access in multitasking environment
(b) Ensuring proper sequence of operation across processes.
(c) Communicating between processes
(d) All of these
(e) None of these

20. Which of the following is true about *Critical Section*?
(a) It is the code memory area which holds the program instructions (piece of code) for accessing a shared resource
(b) The access to the critical section should be exclusive
(c) All of these
(d) None of these

21. Which of the following is true about mutual exclusion?
(a) Mutual exclusion enforces mutually exclusive access of resources by processes
(b) Mutual exclusion may lead to deadlock
(c) Both of these
(d) None of these

22. Which of the following is an example of mutual exclusion enforcing policy?
(a) Busy Waiting (Spin lock) (b) Sleep & Wake up
(c) Both of these (d) None of these

23. Which of the following is true about lock based synchronisation mechanism?
(a) It is CPU intensive
(b) Locks are useful in handling situations where the processes is likely to be blocked for a shorter period of time on waiting the lock

(c) If the lock is being held for a long time by a process and if it is preempted by the OS, the other threads waiting for this lock may have to spin a longer time for getting
(d) All of these
(e) None of these

24. Which of the following synchronisation techniques follow the '*Sleep & Wakeup*' mechanism for mutual exclusion?
(a) Mutex (b) Semaphore (c) Critical Section (d) Spin lock
(e) (a), (b) and (c)

25. Which of the following is true about *mutex objects* for IPC synchronisation under Windows OS?
(a) Only one process/thread can own the '*mutex object*' at a time
(b) The state of a mutex object is set to non-signalled when it is not owned by any process/thread, and set to signalled when it is owned by any process/thread
(c) The state of a mutex object is set to signalled when it is not owned by any process/thread, and set to non-signalled when it is owned by any process/thread
(d) Both (a) & (b) (e) Both (a) & (c)

26. Which of the following is (are) the *wait functions* provided by windows for synchronisation purpose?
(a) WaitForSingleObject (b) WaitForMultipleObjects
(c) Sleep (d) Both (a) and (b)

27. Which of the following is true about *Critical Section object*?
(a) It can only be used by the threads of a single process (Intra process)
(b) The 'Critical Section' must be initialised before the threads of a process can use it
(c) Accessing Critical Section blocks the execution of the caller thread if the critical section is already in use by other threads
(d) Threads which are blocked by the Critical Section access call, waiting on a critical section, are added to a wait queue and are woken when the Critical Section is available to the requested thread
(e) All of these

28. Which of the following is a non-blocking Critical Section accessing call under windows?
(a) *EnterCriticalSection* (b) *TryEnterCriticalSection*
(c) Both of these (d) None of these

29. The Critical Section object makes the piece of code residing inside it ____?
(a) Non-reentrant (b) Re-entrant (c) Thread safe (d) Both (a) and (c)

30. Which of the following synchronisation techniques is exclusively used for synchronising the access of shared resources by the threads of a process (Intra Process Synchronisation) under Windows kernel?
(a) Mutex object (b) Critical Section object (c) Interlocked functions
(d) Both (c) and (d)

Review Questions

Operating System Basics

1. What is an Operating System? Where is it used and what are its primary functions?
2. What is kernel? What are the different functions handled by a general purpose kernel?
3. What is kernel space and user space? How is kernel space and user space interfaced?
4. What is monolithic and microkernel? Which one is widely used in real-time operating systems?
5. What is the difference between a General Purpose kernel and a Real-Time kernel? Give an example for both.

Real-Time Operating System (RTOS)

1. Explain the basic functions of a real-time kernel?
2. What is task control block (TCB)? Explain the structure of TCB

3. Explain the difference between the memory management of general purpose kernel and real-time kernel.
4. What is virtual memory? What are the advantages and disadvantages of virtual memory?
5. Explain how 'accurate time management' is achieved in real-time kernel
6. What is the difference between 'Hard' and 'Soft' real-time systems? Give an example for 'Hard' and 'Soft' Real-Time kernels

Tasks, Process and Threads

1. Explain *Task* in the operating system context
2. What is *Process* in the operating system context?
3. Explain the memory architecture of a process
4. What is *Process Life Cycle*?
5. Explain the various activities involved in the creation of process and threads
6. What is *Process Control Block* (*PCB*)? Explain the structure of *PCB*
7. Explain *Process Management* in the Operating System Context
8. What is *Thread* in the operating system context?
9. Explain how *Threads* and *Processes* are related? What are common to *Process* and *Threads*?
10. Explain the memory model of a 'thread'.
11. Explain the concept of 'multithreading'. What are the advantages of multithreading?
12. Explain how multithreading can improve the performance of an application with an illustrative example
13. Why is thread creation faster than process creation?
14. Explain the commonly used thread standards for thread creation and management by different operating systems
15. Explain *Thread context switch* and the various activities performed in thread context switching for user level and kernel level threads
16. What all information is held by the thread control data structure of a user/kernel thread?
17. What are the differences between user level and kernel level threads?
18. What are the advantages and disadvantages of using user level threads?
19. Explain the different thread binding models for user and kernel level threads
20. Compare threads and processes in detail

Multiprocessing and Multitasking

1. Explain multiprocessing, multitasking and multiprogramming
2. Explain context switching, context saving and context retrieval
3. What all activities are involved in context switching?
4. Explain the different multitasking models in the operating system context

Task Scheduling

1. What is *task scheduling* in the operating system context?
2. Explain the various factors to be considered for the selection of a scheduling criteria
3. Explain the different *queues* associated with process scheduling
4. Explain the different types of *non-preemptive* scheduling algorithms. State the merits and de-merits of each
5. Explain the different types of *preemptive* scheduling algorithms. State the merits and de-merits of each
6. Explain *Round Robin (RR)* process scheduling with interrupts
7. Explain *starvation* in the process scheduling context. Explain how starvation can be effectively tackled?
8. What is *IDLEPROCESS*? What is the significance of IDLEPROCESS in the process scheduling context?
9. Three processes with process IDs P1, P2, P3 with estimated completion time 5, 10, 7 milliseconds respectively enters the ready queue together in the order P1, P2, P3. Process P4 with estimated execution completion time 2 milliseconds enters the ready queue after 5 milliseconds. Calculate the waiting time and Turn Around Time (TAT) for each process and the Average waiting time and Turn Around Time (Assuming there is no I/O waiting for the processes) in the FIFO scheduling
10. Three processes with process IDs P1, P2, P3 with estimated completion time 12, 10, 2 milliseconds respectively enters the ready queue together in the order P2, P3, P1. Process P4 with estimated execution completion time

4 milliseconds enters the Ready queue after 8 milliseconds. Calculate the waiting time and Turn Around Time (TAT) for each process and the average waiting time and Turn Around Time (Assuming there is no I/O waiting for the processes) in the FIFO scheduling

11. Three processes with process IDs P1, P2, P3 with estimated completion time 8, 4, 7 milliseconds respectively enters the ready queue together in the order P3, P1, P2. P1 contains an I/O waiting time of 2 milliseconds when it completes 4 milliseconds of its execution. P2 and P3 do not contain any I/O waiting. Calculate the waiting time and Turn Around Time (TAT) for each process and the average waiting time and Turn Around Time in the LIFO scheduling. All the estimated execution completion time is excluding I/O wait time
12. Three processes with process IDs P1, P2, P3 with estimated completion time 12, 10, 2 milliseconds respectively enters the ready queue together in the order P2, P3, P1. Process P4 with estimated execution completion time 4 milliseconds enters the Ready queue after 8 milliseconds. Calculate the waiting time and Turn Around Time (TAT) for each process and the Average waiting time and Turn Around Time (Assuming there is no I/O waiting for the processes) in the LIFO scheduling
13. Three processes with process IDs P1, P2, P3 with estimated completion time 6, 8, 2 milliseconds respectively enters the ready queue together. Process P4 with estimated execution completion time 4 milliseconds enters the Ready queue after 1 millisecond. Calculate the waiting time and Turn Around Time (TAT) for each process and the Average waiting time and Turn Around Time (Assuming there is no I/O waiting for the processes) in the non-preemptive SJF scheduling
14. Three processes with process IDs P1, P2, P3 with estimated completion time 4, 6, 5 milliseconds and priorities 1, 0, 3 (0—highest priority, 3 lowest priority) respectively enters the ready queue together. Calculate the waiting time and Turn Around Time (TAT) for each process and the average waiting time and Turn Around Time (Assuming there is no I/O waiting for the processes) in non-preemptive priority based scheduling algorithm
15. Three processes with process IDs P1, P2, P3 with estimated completion time 4, 6, 5 milliseconds and priorities 1, 0, 3 (0—highest priority, 3 lowest priority) respectively enters the ready queue together. Process P4 with estimated execution completion time 6 milliseconds and priority 2 enters the 'Ready' queue after 5 milliseconds. Calculate the waiting time and Turn Around Time (TAT) for each process and the average waiting time and Turn Around Time (Assuming there is no I/O waiting for the processes) in non-preemptive priority based scheduling algorithm
16. Three processes with process IDs P1, P2, P3 with estimated completion time 8, 4, 7 milliseconds respectively enters the ready queue together. P1 contains an I/O waiting time of 2 milliseconds when it completes 4 milliseconds of its execution. P2 and P3 do not contain any I/O waiting. Calculate the waiting time and Turn Around Time (TAT) for each process and the average waiting time and Turn Around Time in the SRT scheduling. All the estimated execution completion time is excluding I/O waiting time
17. Three processes with process IDs P1, P2, P3 with estimated completion time 12, 10, 6 milliseconds respectively enters the ready queue together. Process P4 with estimated execution completion time 2 milliseconds enters the Ready queue after 3 milliseconds. Calculate the waiting time and Turn Around Time (TAT) for each process and the Average waiting time and Turn Around Time (Assuming there is no I/O waiting for the processes) in the SRT scheduling
18. Three processes with process IDs P1, P2, P3 with estimated completion time 10, 14, 20 milliseconds respectively, enters the ready queue together in the order P3, P2, P1. Calculate the waiting time and Turn Around Time (TAT) for each process and the Average waiting time and Turn Around Time (Assuming there is no I/O waiting for the processes) in RR algorithm with Time slice = 2 ms
19. Three processes with process IDs P1, P2, P3 with estimated completion time 12, 10, 12 milliseconds respectively enters the ready queue together in the order P2, P3, P1. Process P4 with estimated execution completion time 4 milliseconds enters the Ready queue after 8 milliseconds. Calculate the waiting time and Turn Around Time (TAT) for each process and the Average waiting time and Turn Around Time (Assuming there is no I/O waiting for the processes) in RR algorithm with Time slice = 4 ms
20. Three processes with process IDs P1, P2, P3 with estimated completion time 4, 6, 5 milliseconds and priorities 1, 0, 3 (0—highest priority, 3 lowest priority) respectively enters the ready queue together. Calculate the waiting time

and Turn Around Time (TAT) for each process and the average waiting time and Turn Around Time (Assuming there is no I/O waiting for the processes) in preemptive priority based scheduling algorithm
21. Three processes with process IDs P1, P2, P3 with estimated completion time 6, 2, 4 milliseconds respectively, enters the ready queue together in the order P1, P3, P2. Process P4 with estimated execution time 4 milliseconds entered the 'Ready' queue 3 milliseconds later the start of execution of P1. Calculate the waiting time and Turn Around Time (TAT) for each process and the Average waiting time and Turn Around Time (Assuming there is no I/O waiting for the processes) in RR algorithm with Time slice = 2 ms

Task Communication and Synchronisation

1. Explain the various process interaction models in detail.
2. What is Inter Process Communication (IPC)? Give an overview of different IPC mechanisms adopted by various operating systems.
3. Explain how multiple processes in a system co-operate.
4. Explain how multiple threads of a process co-operate.
5. Explain the shared memory based IPC.
6. Explain the concept of memory mapped objects for IPC.
7. Explain the handle sharing and name sharing based memory mapped object technique for IPC under Windows Operating System.
8. Explain the message passing technique for IPC. What are the merits and de-merits of message based IPC?
9. Explain the synchronous and asynchronous messaging mechanisms for IPC under Windows kernel.
10. Explain *Race condition* in detail, in relation to the shared resource access.
11. What is *deadlock*? What are the different conditions favouring deadlock?
12. Explain by *Coffman conditions*?
13. Explain the different methods of handling deadlocks.
14. Explain *livelock* in the resource sharing context.
15. Explain *starvation* in the resource sharing context.
16. Explain the *Dining Philosophers* problem in the process synchronisation context.
17. Explain the *Produces-consumer* problem in the inter process communication context.
18. Explain *bounded-buffer* problem in the interprocess communication context.
19. Explain *buffer overrun* and *buffer under-run*.
20. What is *priority inversion*? What are the different techniques adopted for handling priority inversion?
21. What are the merits and de-merits of *priority ceiling*?
22. Explain the different task communication synchronisation issues encountered in Interprocess Communication
23. What is *task (process) synchronisation*? What is the role of process synchronisation in IPC?
24. What is *mutual exclusion* in the process synchronisation context? Explain the different mechanisms for mutual exclusion
25. What are the merits and de-merits of *busy-waiting* (*spinlock*) based mutual exclusion?
26. Explain the *Test and Set Lock (TSL)* based mutual exclusion technique. Explain how *TSL* is implemented in Intel family of processors
27. Explain the *interlocked functions* for lock based mutual exclusion under Windows OS
28. Explain the advantages and limitations of *interlocked function* based synchronisation under Windows
29. Explain the *sleep & wakeup* mechanism for mutual exclusion
30. What are the merits and de-merits of *sleep & wakeup* mechanism based mutual exclusion?
31. What is *mutex*?
32. Explain the *mutex* based process synchronisation under Windows OS
33. What is *semaphore*? Explain the different types of semaphores. Where is it used?
34. What is binary *semaphore*? Where is it used?
35. What is the difference between *mutex* and *semaphore*?
36. What is the difference between *semaphore* and *binary semaphore*?
37. What is the difference between *mutex* and *binary semaphore*?

38. Explain the *semaphore* based process synchronisation under Windows OS
39. Explain the *critical section problem*?
40. What is *critical section*? What are the different techniques for controlling access to *critical section*?
41. Explain the *critical section object* for process synchronisation. Why is critical section object based synchronisation fast?
42. Explain the *critical section object* based process synchronisation under Windows OS.
43. Explain the *Event* based synchronisation mechanism for IPC.
44. Explain the *Event object* based synchronisation mechanism for IPC under Windows OS.
45. What is a *device driver*? Explain its role in the OS context.
46. Explain the architecture of device drivers.
47. Explain the different functional and non-functional requirements that needs to be evaluated in the selection of an RTOS.

Lab Assignments

1. Write a multithreaded Win32 console application satisfying:
   (a) The main thread of the application creates a child thread with name "child_thread" and passes the pointer of a buffer holding the data "Data passed from Main thread".
   (b) The main thread sleeps for 10 seconds after creating the child thread and then quits.
   (c) The child thread retrieves the message from the memory location pointed by the buffer pointer and prints the retrieved data to the console and sleeps for 100 milliseconds and then quits.
   (d) Use appropriate error handling mechanisms wherever possible.
2. Write a multithreaded Win32 console application for creating '*n*' number of child threads (*n* is configurable). Each thread prints the message "I'm in thread thread no" ('thread no' is the number passed to the thread when it is created. It varies from 0 to $n - 1$) and sleeps for 50 milliseconds and then quits. The main thread, after creating the child threads, wait for the completion of the execution of child threads and quits when all the child threads are completed their execution.
3. Write a multithreaded application using 'PThreads' for creating '*n*' number of child threads (*n* is configurable). The application should receive '*n*' as command line parameter. Each thread prints the message "I'm in thread thread no" ('thread no' is the number passed to the thread when it is created. It varies from 0 to $n - 1$) and sleeps for 1 second and then quits. The main thread, after creating the child threads, wait for the completion of the execution of child threads and quits when all the child threads are completed their execution. Compile and execute the application in Linux.
4. Write a multithreaded application in Win32 satisfying the following:
   (a) Two child threads are created with normal priority
   (b) Thread 1 retrieves and prints its priority and sleeps for 500 milliseconds and then quits
   (c) Thread 2 prints the priority of thread 1 and raises its priority to above normal and retrieves the new priority of thread 1, prints it and then quits
   (d) The main thread waits for the completion of both the child threads and then terminates.
5. Write a Win32 console application illustrating the usage of anonymous pipes for data sharing between a parent and child thread of a process. The application should satisfy the following conditions:
   (a) The main thread of the process creates an anonymous pipe with size 512KB and assigns the handle of the pipe to a global handle
   (b) The main thread creates an event object "synchronise" with state non-signalled and a child thread with name 'child_thread'.
   (c) The main thread waits for the signalling of the event object "synchronise" and reads data from the anonymous pipe when the event is signalled and prints the data read from the pipe on the console window.

(d) The main thread waits for the execution completion of the child thread and quits when the child thread completes its execution.
(e) The child thread writes the data "Hi from child thread" to the anonymous pipe and sets the event object "synchronise" and sleeps for 500 milliseconds and then quits.

Compile and execute the application using Visual Studio under Windows XP/NT OS.

6. Write a Win32 console application (Process 1) illustrating the creation of a memory mapped object of size 512KB with name "mysharedobject". Create an event object with name "synchronise" with state non-signalled. Read the memory mapped object when the event is signalled and display the contents on the console window. Create a second console application (Process 2) for opening the memory mapped object with name "mysharedobject" and event object with name "synchronise". Write the message "Message from Process 2" to the memory mapped object and set the event object "synchronise". Use appropriate error handling mechanisms wherever possible. Compile both the applications using Visual Studio and execute them in the order Process 1 followed by Process 2 under Windows XP/NT OS.
7. Write a multithreaded Win32 console application where:
   (a) The main thread creates a child thread with default stack size and name 'Child_Thread'.
   (b) The main thread sends user defined messages and the message 'WM_QUIT' randomly to the child thread.
   (c) The child thread processes the message posted by the main thread and quits when it receives the 'WM_QUIT' message.
   (d) The main thread checks the termination of the child thread and quits when the child thread completes its execution.
   (e) The main thread continues sending random messages to the child thread till the WM_QUIT message is sent to child thread.
   (f) The messaging mechanism between the main thread and child thread is synchronous.

   Compile the application using Visual Studio and execute it under Windows XP/NT OS.
8. Write a Win32 console application illustrating the usage of anonymous pipes for data sharing between a parent and child processes using handle inheritance mechanism. Compile and execute the application using Visual Studio under Windows XP/NT OS.
9. Write a Win32 console application for creating an anonymous pipe with 512 bytes of size and pass the 'Read handle' of the pipe to a second process (another Win32 console application) using a memory mapped object. The first process writes a message "Hi from Pipe Server". The second process reads the data written by the pipe server to the pipe and displays it on the console window. Use event object for indicating the availability of data on the pipe and mutex objects for synchronising the access to the pipe.
10. Write a multithreaded Win32 Process addressing:
    (a) The main thread of the process creates an unnamed memory mapped object with size 1K and shares the handle of the memory mapped object with other threads of the process
    (b) The main thread writes the message "Hi from main thread" and informs the availability of data to the child thread by signalling an event object
    (c) The main thread waits for the execution completion of the child thread after writing the message to the memory mapped area and quits when the child thread completes its execution
    (d) The child thread reads the data from the memory mapped area and prints it on the console window when the event object is signalled by the main thread
    (e) The read write access to the memory mapped area is synchronised using a mutex object
11. Write a multithreaded application using Java thread library satisfying:
    (a) The first thread prints "Hello I'm going to the wait queue" and enters wait state by invoking the wait method.
    (b) The second thread sleeps for 500 milliseconds and then prints "Hello I'm going to invoke first thread" and invokes the first thread.
    (c) The first thread prints "Hello I'm invoked by the second thread" when invoked by the second thread.

11 An Introduction to Embedded System Design with VxWorks and MicroC/OS-II RTOS

LEARNING OBJECTIVES

- ✓ *Learn about the VxWorks RTOS from Wind River Systems*
- ✓ *Learn about the task states, task creation and management under VxWorks kernel*
- ✓ *Learn about the task scheduling policies supported by VxWorks kernel*
- ✓ *Learn about the important kernel services of VxWorks*
- ✓ *Learn about the different Inter-Task Communications supported by the VxWorks kernel*
- ✓ *Learn about the task synchronisation and mutual exclusion policies supported by VxWorks for shared resource access*
- ✓ *Learn about the interrupt handling mechanism and implementation of Interrupt Service Routines under VxWorks kernel*
- ✓ *Learn about watchdog timer implementation of VxWorks for task execution monitoring*
- ✓ *Learn about timing and reference implementation by VxWorks for delay generation and timing operations*
- ✓ *Learn about the Integrated Development Environment for OS customisation and application development for VxWorks*
- ✓ *Learn about MicroC/OS-II Real-time kernel from Micrium Inc.*
- ✓ *Learn about task states, task creation and management under MicroC/OS-II kernel*
- ✓ *Learn about MicroC/OS-II kernel services and initialisation*
- ✓ *Learn about task scheduling under MicroC/OS-II kernel*
- ✓ *Learn about inter-task communication mechanisms supported by MicroC/OS-II kernel*
- ✓ *Learn about the task communication and synchronisation under MicroC/OS-II kernel*
- ✓ *Learn about timing and reference implementation by MicroC/OS-II kernel for delay generation and timing operations*
- ✓ *Learn the dynamic memory management under MicroC/OS-II kernel*
- ✓ *Learn about the interrupt handling mechanism and implementation of Interrupt Service Routines under MicroC/OS-II kernel*
- ✓ *Learn about the Integrated Development Environment for OS customisation and application development for MicroC/OS-II*

In Chapter 10 we discussed about the fundamentals of RTOS, the different kernel services of an RTOS, the different techniques used for implementing multitasking, the different mechanisms used for communicating between multiple concurrently running tasks and the mechanisms to synchronise the execution of tasks and accessing of shared resources. The implementation of the multitasking strategy, inter-task communication and synchronisation is OS kernel dependent. It varies across kernels. Let's have a look at these implementations for the VxWorks and MicroC/OS-II Real Time Operating Systems.

11.1 VxWORKS

VxWorks is a popular hard real-time, multitasking operating system from Wind River Systems (http://www.windriver.com/). It is fully compatible with the POSIX Standard (1003.1b) for real-time extension. It supports a variety of target processors/controllers including Intel x-86, ARM, MIPS, Power PC (PPC) and 68K. Please refer to the Wind Driver System's VxWorks documentation for the complete list of processors supported.

The kernel of VxWorks is popularly known as *wind*. The latest release of VxWorks introduces the concept of Symmetric multiprocessing (SMP) and thereby facilitates multicore processor based Real Time System design. The presence of VxWorks RTOS platform spans across aerospace and defence applications to robotics and industrial applications, networking and consumer electronics, and car navigation and telematics systems.

VxWorks follows the task based execution model. Under VxWorks kernel, it is possible to run even a 'subroutine' as separate task with own context and stack. The '*wind*' kernel uses the priority based scheduling policy for tasks. The inter-task communication among the tasks is implemented using message queues, sockets, pipes and signals, and task synchronisation is achieved through semaphores.

11.1.1 Task Creation and Management

Under VxWorks kernel, the tasks may be in one of the following primary states or a specific combination of it at any given point of time.

READY: The task is 'Ready' for execution and is waiting for its turn to get the CPU

PEND: The task is in the blocked (pended) state waiting for some resources

DELAY: The task is sleeping

SUSPEND: The task is unavailable for execution. This state is primarily used for halting a task for debugging. Suspending a task prevents it only from the execution and will not block it from state transition. It is possible for a suspended task to change the task state (For example, if a task is suspended when the task is in the state 'DELAY', sleeping for a specified duration, its state will change to 'READY' 'SUSPEND' when the sleeping delay is over.

A task may run to completion from its inception ('READY') state or it may get pended or delayed or suspended during its execution. If a task is picked up for execution by the scheduler, and suppose another task of higher priority becomes 'READY' for execution, and if the scheduling policy is pre-emptive priority based, the currently executing task is pre-empted and the high priority task is executed. The pre-empted task enters the 'READY' state. If a currently executing task requires a shared resource, which is currently held by another task, the currently executing task is preempted and it enters the 'PEND' state until the resource is released by the task holding it. If a task contains sleeping requirement like polling an external device at a periodic interval or sampling data from the external world at a periodic time, the task sleeps during the periodic interval. The task is said to be in the 'DELAY' state during this time. If a debug request for debugging a task in execution or if an exception happens during the execution of a task, it is moved to the state 'SUSPEND'.

When a task is created with the task creation kernel system call *taskInit()*, the task is created with the state 'SUSPEND'. In order to run the newly created task, it should be brought to the 'READY' state. It is achieved by activating the task with the system call *taskActivate()*. The system call *taskSpawn()* can be used for creating a task with 'READY' state. The *taskSpawn()* call follows the syntax

```
taskSpawn (task_name, task_priority, task_options, task_stack size, routine_
name, arg1, arg2, arg3, arg4, arg5, arg6, arg7, arg8, arg9, arg10 );
```

where *task_name* is the name of the task and it is unique. The parameter *task_priority* defines the priority for the task. It can vary from 0 (Highest priority) to 255. The *task_options* parameter specifies the options for the task. For example, if the task requires any floating point operation, it should be set as VX_FP_TASK. Set the option as VX_UNBREAKABLE for disabling breakpoints in the task. Refer to VxWorks' documentation for more details on the task options. The parameter *routine_name* specifies the entry point for the task. It can be function main or a subroutine. 'arg1' to 'arg10' specifies the arguments required for executing the task. It is possible to have multiple tasks with the same *routine_name* and different argument list. Each task will have its own stack and context. On creating the task, *taskSpawn* returns a task ID which is a 4 byte handle to the task's data structure. The following table gives a snapshot of various task creation and management routines supported by VxWorks.

Function Call†	Description
taskInit()	Create a task
taskActivate()	Initialise a task
taskSpawn()	Create and initialise a task
taskName( )	Return the task name associated with a task ID
taskNameToId( )	Return the task ID associated with a task name
taskIdSelf( )	Return the task ID of the calling task
taskIdVerify( )	Check whether the task with given ID exists.
taskOptionsGet( )	Retrieve the options associated with a task
taskOptionsSet( )	Set the options for a task
taskIsReady( )	Check whether a task is 'Ready' to execute
taskIsSuspended( )	Check whether a task is in the 'Suspend' sate
taskPriorityGet( )	Get the task's priority
taskRegsGet( )	Get the register details of a task
taskRegsSet( )	Set the registers for a task
taskInfoGet( )	Retrieve information about the task
taskTcb( )	Retrieve a pointer to the task's Task Control Block
taskIdListGet( )	Retrieve the list of all 'Active' tasks.
taskSuspend( )	Suspend a task (Change state to 'SUSPEND')
taskResume( )	Resume a task (Change state to 'READY')

† Please refer to the VxWorks library reference manual for the parameter details of each function call.

taskRestart( )	Restart a task. It recreates a task with original task creation parameters
taskDelay( )	Sleep the task (Sleep period is given in timer tick units). The state of the task changes to 'DELAY'. The task is moved to the end of the ready queue for tasks of the same priority.
nanosleep( )	Sleep the task (Sleep period is given in nanoseconds). The state of the task changes to 'DELAY'
exit()	Terminate the calling task and free the memory occupied its stack and TCB.
taskDelete( )	Terminate the task specified and free the memory occupied by its stack and TCB.
taskSafe( )	Protects a task from deletion by other tasks. It is essential for ensuring that the task is not deleted by other tasks, when it is holding a shared resource and executing in the critical section.
taskUnsafe( )	Used by a task to inform other tasks that it is available for deletion. A task uses this if it is already declared as an undeletable task by the function call *taskSafe( )*

The task creation and management system routines are part of the library *taskLib*. The following piece of code illustrates the creation of task.

```
//Header for VxWorks kernel specific implementations
#include "vxWorks.h"
#include "taskLib.h"
#include "stdio.h"

//Function Prototype
void print_task(void);

//*****************************************************************
//Main task

void main_task(void)
{
int tasked;

//Spawn Task A
if((taskId = taskSpawn("task1",90,VX_NO_STACK_FILL,2000,
        (FUNCPTR) print_task,0,0,0,0,0,0,0,0,0,0)) == ERROR)
        printf("Creation of print_task failed\n");
exit();
}

//*****************************************************************
//Task print_task

void print_task (void)
{
int ID;
//Get the task ID
ID = taskIdSelf( );
//Print the task ID
```

```
printf(" The ID of the task is: %d\n", ID);
//Delete the task
taskDelete(ID)
}
```

The main task *main_task* creates a new task with name *task1*, priority 90, stack size 2000 and option NO_STACK_FILL and terminates. The new task *task1* retrieves its task ID, prints it and finally deletes the task.

11.1.2 Task Scheduling

On the scheduling front, VxWorks supports two types of scheduling interfaces, namely 'POSIX scheduling' and 'wind' scheduling interfaces. The 'POSIX scheduling' interface is based on the concept of 'process' and it defines a portable interface, whereas the 'wind scheduling' is based on the concept of 'tasks'. The POSIX standard for task scheduling allows setting the scheduling policies independently for process (i.e. It is possible to set the scheduling policy of a process as 'Round Robin', whereas for another process it can be 'Priority-based' scheduling, provided the scheduler have the implementation for both). But the VxWorks' implementation of POSIX scheduling interface does not allow the setting of different scheduling policies for different tasks. It allows only a single system wide scheduling policy for the different tasks running on it. The table given below gives a snapshot of various POSIX scheduling calls supported by VxWorks.

Function Call†	Description
sched_setparam( )	Sets the priority for the task
sched_getparam( )	Retrieves the priority of the given task
sched_setscheduler( )	Set the scheduling policy and priority for the task
sched_yield( )	Stop task execution and relinquish the CPU to other tasks
sched_getscheduler( )	Retrieve the current scheduling policy. VxWorks supports two types of scheduling, namely; priority based pre-emptive (SCHED_FIFO) and priority based Round Robin (SCHED_RR)
sched_get_priority_max( )	Retrieve the maximum possible POSIX priority value
sched_get_priority_min( )	Retrieve the minimum possible POSIX priority value
sched_rr_get_interval( )	Retrieve the Time slice interval for Round Robin scheduling policy

VxWorks supports two different types of scheduling policies namely; Round Robin (Time slice based) and Priority based pre-emptive. The Round Robin scheduling policy is adopted for priority resolution among equal priority tasks. Imagine a situation where more than one tasks with equal priority are in the 'READY' state and the currently executing task is also with the same priority, if the scheduling policy adopted is pre-emptive, these tasks may not be able to pre-empt the currently running tasks since they are of equal priority. The other tasks will get a chance to execute only when the running task voluntarily relinquishes the CPU or it is pended on a resource request. This issue can be addressed if Round Robin policy is adopted for resolving the priority among equal priority tasks. Round Robin scheduling can be enabled with the function call *kernelTimeSlice()*. This function takes the time slice in the form of

† Please refer to the VxWorks library reference manual for the parameter details of each function call.

timer tick. Each task is executed for the amount of time specified, if there are multiple tasks with equal priority exist. The task relinquishes the CPU to the other task with equal priority when this time interval is completed. Setting a time interval value of 0 for the time slice interval disables Round Robin scheduling for equal priority tasks.

VxWorks kernel has a well-defined exception handling module which takes care of the handling of exceptions that arises during the execution of a task. In case of an exception, the task caused the exception is suspended and the state of the task at the point of exception is saved. All other tasks and kernel continue their operation without any interruption.

11.1.3 Kernel Services

The kernel functionalities of VxWorks is also implemented as tasks and they are known as system tasks. The system tasks exist concurrently with user defined tasks. The root task *tUsrRoot* is the first task executed by the scheduler. The function *usrRoot()* is the entry point to this task and it performs the following:

- Spawns the logging task *tLogTask*, the exception task *tExcTask*, the network task *tNetTask*, the target agent task *tWdbTask* and tasks for optional components (like shell service *tShell*, Remote login *tRlogind*, etc.) selected by the user while building the kernel.

The Root task is user customisable and user can add necessary additional initialisation code to this task during the kernel build time. The root task's responsibility gets over with the starting of all necessary initialisations and it is terminated and deleted after the initialisation process is completed. The kernel modules use the logging task for logging system messages without current task context IO. The exception handling task is responsible for handling the exceptions/errors encountered during the execution of a task. It has the highest priority. The priority of it should not be altered in any form by suspending or deleting the task or by assigning a lower priority. The *tRlogind* daemon is responsible for managing remote login request from another VxWorks target or a host machine. For this functionality to work the VxWorks' target shell *tShell* and the remote login service components *rlogin* should be included in the kernel build configuration.

11.1.4 Inter-Task Communication

The inter-task communication is facilitated through shared memory, message queues, pipes, sockets, Remote Procedure Call (RPC) and signals. Mutual exclusion and synchronisation in shared resource access is implemented through semaphores.

VxWorks kernel follows a single linear address space for tasks. The data can be shared in the form of global variable, linear buffer, linked list and ring buffer.

'Message queue' is the primary inter-task communication mechanism under VxWorks. Message queues support two-way communication of messages of variable length. The two-way messaging between tasks can be implemented using one message queue for incoming messages and another one for outgoing messages. Messaging mechanism can be used for task-to task and task to Interrupt Service Routine (ISR) communication. Two different versions of message queues are supported by VxWorks. They are; POSIX based message queues and Wind driver kernel (wind) specific message queues. The table given below gives a snapshot of various Wind message queue based function calls for messaging.

Function Call†	Description
msgQCreate( )	Create and initialise a message queue. The parameters are maximum number of messages supported and the maximum length in bytes for a message.
msgQDelete( )	Delete a message queue and free the messages
msgQSend( )	Send a message to the message queue. Used by a task or ISR to send a message. If any task is waiting from a message from the message queue, the message is delivered to the first waiting task. If no tasks are waiting for a message, the message is added to the buffer holding the messages.
msgQReceive( )	Retrieve a message from the message queue. If the message queue already contains messages, the first message is removed from the queue and it is supplied to the calling task. If there is no messages present in the message queue at the time of calling this function, the task is blocked and it is moved to the message waiting queue. The message waiting queue can be ordered on the basis of either priority or FIFO policy. The task will be in the 'PEND' state.

It is not necessary that a message queue always have space to accommodate a message when a task tries to write a message to it. The message queue may be full and may not have room for accommodating a message. In such case the task can either wait until a space available in the queue or can return immediately. Similarly when a task tries to read a message from the message queue, there may be situations in which the message queue is empty. The task needs to wait until a message is available or it can return immediately. The choice on whether the task needs to wait or return immediately is determined by the timeout parameters used in conjunction with message sending and reception. A time out value *NO_WAIT* (0), allows the task to return immediately and the value *WAIT_FOREVER* (–1) forces the task to wait until a space is available for posting a message in the case of message sending and a message is available for reading in the case of message reception.

A message can be posted as either normal message or high priority (urgent) message. The *msgQSend()* function provides options to set a message as either normal or high priority. A normal message is placed at the bottom of the message queue and a high priority message is always placed at the top of the message queue. A value *MSG_PRI_NORMAL* for the message priority option declares it as normal message whereas the value *MSG_PRI_URGENT* sets a message as urgent.

The following piece of code illustrates the implementation of Wind message queue based communication in a multitasking application.

Example 1

Here a main task creates two tasks, namely, '*task_a*' and '*task_b*' with priority 100, stack size 10000 and option NO_STACK_FILL. It also creates a message queue with number of messages supported as 50 and the maximum length in bytes for a message as 20. The message queue is created with an option for queuing the pended tasks (tasks waiting for a message to arrive in the message queue) as FIFO. '*task_a*' sends the message "*Hi from Task A*" with message priority 'urgent' and with option for waiting if there is no space available in the message queue for posting the message. '*task_b*' receives the message from the message queue and waits for the availability of a message if the message queue is empty.

```
//Header for VxWorks kernel specific implementations
#include "vxWorks.h"
////Header for Wind task related functions
#include "taskLib.h"
```

† Please refer to the VxWorks library reference manual for the parameter details of each function call.

```
#include "stdio.h"
//Header for Wind Message queue related functions
#include "msgQLib.h"

#define MAX_MESSAGES (50)
#define MAX_MESSAGE_LENGTH (20)
#define MESSAGE "Hi From Task A"

MSG_Q_ID MsgQueueID;

//**************************************************************
//Task_A

void task_A(void)
{
//Send message to message queue
if((msgQSend(MsgQueueID, MESSAGE, MAX_MESSAGE_LENGTH, WAIT_FOREVER,
      MSG_PRI_URGENT)) == ERROR)
      printf("Message Sending failed…\n");
}

//**************************************************************
//Task_B

void task_B(void)
{
char msgBuf[MAX_MESSAGE_LENGTH];

//Receive message from message queue
if(msgQReceive(mesgQueueId,msgBuf,MAX_MESSAGE_LENGTH, WAIT_FOREVER)
      == ERROR)
      printf("Message reception failed…\n");
else
      printf("Message Received from Queue: %s\n",msgBuf);
}

//**************************************************************
//Main task for creating the message queue and creating tasks A & B

void main_task(void)
{
int taskId;

// Create message queue
if ((mesgQueueId = msgQCreate(MAX_MESSAGES,MAX_MESSAGE_LENGTH,MSG_Q_FIFO))
      == NULL)
      printf("Message Queue creation failed…\n");
```

```
//Spawn Task A
if((taskId = taskSpawn("task_a",100,VX_NO_STACK_FILL,10000,
      (FUNCPTR)task_A,0,0,0,0,0,0,0,0,0,0)) == ERROR)
      printf("Creation of Task A failed\n");

//Spawn Task B
if((taskId = taskSpawn("task_b",100,VX_NO_STACK_FILL,10000,
      (FUNCPTR)task_B,0,0,0,0,0,0,0,0,0,0)) == ERROR)
      printf("Creation of Task B failed\n");
}
```

The POSIX standard supports named message queues with options for setting message level priorities. The table given below summarises the list of POSIX Message queue function calls supported by VxWorks.

Function Call†	Description
mqPxLibInit( )	Initialises the POSIX message library. The initialisation should be done before any task can make use of the message queue
mq_open( )	Opens a message queue. The message queue must be created/opened by the task for posting and receiving messages. A message queue is created by calling this function with parameter *O_CREAT*. A task can open a message queue in read only mode, write only mode or read write mode. This option is specified by the flags *O_RDONLY*, *O_WRONLY* and *O_RDWR*.
mq_send( )	Posts a message to the queue. The option *O_NONBLOCK* specifies the task to return immediately if there is no room left for a message to place in the message queue. Otherwise the task will wait until there is space for writing the message in the message queue. Messages can be sent with different priorities. The priority ranges from 0 (lowest) to 31 (highest priority). The highest priority message is always placed in front of the message queue.
mq_receive( )	Retrieves a message from the message queue. The option *O_NONBLOCK* specifies the task to return immediately if there is no message available in the message queue. Otherwise the task will wait until there is a message to read in the message queue.
mq_close( )	Used by a task to indicate it is not using the message queue anymore.
mq_unlink( )	Used by a task to destroy a message queue. Unlinking destroys the message queue only after all tasks which are using the queue close it.
mq_notify( )	Notifies a task, when a message for the task arrives in an empty message queue. The *mq_notify()* call specifies a signal to be sent to the task when a message is placed in an empty queue. A task can cancel the notification registration at any point during the waiting by passing a NULL in place of the signal value to the *mq_notify()* function call.
mq_setattr( )	Sets the attributes for the message queue. The attributes are: 1. Blocking flag *O_NONBLOCK*. 2. Allowed maximum number of messages in the queue. 3. Allowed maximum size of a message. 4. The number of messages currently present in the queue. A task can change only the blocking flag.
mq_getattr( )	Retrieves the attributes for the message queue.

† Please refer to the VxWorks library reference manual for the parameter details of each function call

Pipes are another form of IPC mechanism supported by VxWorks. Pipes use the message queue based technique for communication. The only difference is that pipe acts as a virtual I/O device and it can be accessed with I/O access calls in the same way as accessing an I/O device. The syntax for pipe creation function is given below.

```
pipeDevCreate ("/pipe/name", max_msgs, max_length);
```

where the first parameter is the name of the pipe, the parameter *max_msgs* represents the maximum number of messages and the allowed maximum size of a message. Normal Input/ Output routines like open, read, write and I/O controls are used for accessing pipes. Interrupt Service Routines are only allowed to write to a pipe and not reading from the pipe.

Sockets are the mechanism utilised by VxWorks to communicate between processes running on different targets which are networked and for executing a procedure (function) which is part of another process running on the same CPU or on a different CPU within the network (Remote Procedure Call (RPC)). Sockets works on Internet communication protocols. VxWorks supports TCP/IP and UDP based protocols for socket communication.

'Signals' is a form of software event notification based Inter Process Communication (IPC) mechanism supported by VxWorks. The 'signal' mechanism of VxWorks supports 31 different signals. A signal is associated with an event and the occurrence of the event asserts the signal. Any task or Interrupt Service Routine (ISR) can generate a signal which is intended for a task. Upon receiving the signal notification, the task is suspended and it executes the 'signal handler' associated with the signal on its next scheduling. As a rule of thumb the signal handler should not contain any routines which contain code (e.g. Accessing a shared resource, critical section, etc.) that may cause the blocking of the task and thereby leading to a deadlock situation. 'Signal' based IPC mechanism is more appropriate for exception and error handling than general purpose communication mechanism. The definition for a typical signal handler is given below.

```
void sigHandler (int sigNum)
```

where *sigHandler* is the name of the signal handler function and *sigNum* is the signal number.

The definition for a signal handler for passing additional arguments will look like

```
void sigHandler (int sigNum, int code, struct sigcontext *pSigContext)
```

where *sigHandler* is the name of the signal handler function, *sigNum* is the signal number, code is the additional argument and *pSigContext* is the context of task before signal.

The Signal handler function should be attached to the signal using the function *sigaction( )* (For POSIX compliant signal usage) or *sigvec( )* for *Wind* signal usage.

VxWorks support two kinds of 'signal' interfaces, namely;

1. UNIX BSD Style Signals
2. POSIX Compatible Signals

The table given below summarises the list of basic 'Signal' function calls supported by VxWorks.

Function Call†	Description
sigInit( )	Signal library initialisation routine. It must be executed during the OS initialisation before enabling interrupts.
signal( )	Specifies the handle associated with a signal. Supported by both *Wind* signal interface and POSIX interface.

† Please refer to the VxWorks library reference manual for the parameter details of each function call.

kill()	Sends a signal to a specified task. Supported by both *Wind* signal interface and POSIX interface.
raise()	Sends a signal to the same task. Supported by only POSIX interface.
sigaction( ) *sigvec()*	Binds a signal handler to a particular signal. *sigaction()* is the call corresponding to POSIX interface and *sigvec()* is the call corresponding to *Wind* Signal interface.
sigsetmask()	Sets the mask of blocked signals. It selectively inhibits a signal. Supported by *Wind* signal interface.
sigblock()	Add a signal to the set of blocked signals. It selectively inhibits a signal. Supported by *Wind* signal interface.

11.1.5 Task Synchronisation and Mutual Exclusion

Data sharing is one of the inter-task communication mechanism adopted by VxWorks. VxWorks follows a single linear address space for all user tasks. Imagine a situation where a global variable is being accessed by a task and it is pre-empted by a high priority task (or by an ISR) and the high priority task (or ISR) also tries to modify the global variable. It may result in inconsistent result, if the operation on the global variable is not atomic. Hence it is advised to give exclusive access to a shared resource when it is being used by a task. In other words make the access to shared resources mutually exclusive. It is essential for task synchronisation. VxWorks implements mutual exclusion policies in three different ways. They are

1. Task Locking (Disabling task preemption)
2. Disabling interrupts
3. Locking resource with semaphores

Task locking (Disabling of task preemption) provides restrictive access to shared resources. The function call *taskLock* prevents the kernel from pre-empting the task. However it will not prevent the execution of Interrupt Service Routines (ISRs). This method is suited when there is no global data shared between tasks and ISR. Otherwise the problem will be in the half solved state. The major drawback of this approach is the deviation from real-time behaviour. With task preemption disabled, a high priority task may not be serviced until the currently running task relinquishes the CPU by enabling the pre-emption (By calling *taskUnlock)*. It is not an acceptable behaviour if the high priority task doesn't involve accessing of shared resource which is held by the currently executing task. An overview of the implementation of task locking based mutual exclusion is given below.

```
#include "vxWorks.h"
//*************************************************************
//Task_A

void task_A(void)
{
//.........
//.........
//Disable task preemption
taskLock ();
//Shared data access code
//...........
//Enable task preemption
taskUnlock();
}
```

Interrupt locking based mutual exclusion implementation disables interrupts. It is appropriate for exclusive access of resource shared between tasks and Interrupt Service Routine (ISR). The major drawback of this method is that the system will not respond to interrupts when the task is executing the critical section code (Accessing shared resource). It is not acceptable for a real time system.

An overview of the implementation of interrupt locking based mutual exclusion is given below.

```
#include "vxWorks.h"
//*************************************************************
//Task_A

void task_A(void)
{
//.........
//.........
//Disable Interrupts
int lock = intLock ();
//Shared data access code
//............
//Enable Interrupts
intUnlock(lock);
}
```

It should be noted that the implementation of the *intLock* routine is processor architecture dependent. The *intLock* routine returns an architecture-dependent lock-out key representing the interrupt level prior to the call. For example, for ARM processors, interrupts (IRQs) are disabled by setting the 'I' bit in the CPSR.

Semaphores provide both exclusive access to shared resource and synchronisation among tasks. VxWorks has the implementation for *Wind* specific and POSIX compliant versions of semaphores. The Wind specific semaphores supported by VxWorks are:

1. Binary semaphore
2. Mutual exclusion semaphore
3. Counting semaphore

The binary semaphore provides exclusive access to resource by locking it exclusively. At any given point of time the state of the binary semaphore is either 'available' or 'unavailable'. Counting semaphore is used for sharing resources among a fixed number of tasks. It associates a count with it and the count is decremented each time when a resource acquires it. When the count reaches '0' the semaphore will not be available and a task requesting the semaphore is pended. The count associated with a counting semaphore is specified at the time of creating the counting semaphore. Counting semaphores are usually used for protecting multiple copies of resources. On releasing the semaphore by a task, the count associated with it is incremented by one. The inherent problem with binary semaphore is that they are not deletion safety, meaning whenever a task holding the semaphore is deleted, the semaphore is not released. Also the 'binary' semaphore doesn't support a mechanism for priority inheritance for avoiding priority inversion. These limitations are addressed in a special implementation of 'binary' semaphore called 'mutual exclusion' semaphore.

The semaphores are distinguished with the way they created. The access and control routines for all semaphores remain the same. The following table gives a snapshot of the different semaphore related function calls.

Function Call†	Description
semBCreate( )	Create and initialise a binary semaphore. Successful creation returns a semaphore ID which can be used as the semaphore handle for all semaphore related actions. When a task tries to access a semaphore, if the semaphore is not available the task is put in a wait queue. The queue is ordered either in FIFO model or priority model. It can be specified at the time of creation of the semaphore. A value of SEM_Q_FIFO sets FIFO model whereas SEM_Q_PRIORITY sets the priority model. The semaphore creation also specifies its status at the time of creation (Available or unavailable).
semMCreate( )	Create and initialise a mutual exclusion semaphore. Successful creation returns a semaphore ID which can be used as the semaphore handle for all semaphore related actions. When a task tries to access a semaphore, if the semaphore is not available the task is put in a wait queue. The queue is ordered either in FIFO model or priority model. It can be specified at the time of creation of the semaphore. A value of SEM_Q_FIFO sets FIFO model whereas SEM_Q_PRIORITY sets the priority model. The semaphore creation also specifies its status at the time of creation (Available or unavailable).
semBCCreate( )	Create and initialise a counting semaphore. Successful creation returns a semaphore ID which can be used as the semaphore handle for all semaphore related actions. When a task tries to access a semaphore, if the semaphore is not available the task is put in a wait queue. The queue is ordered either in FIFO model or priority model. It can be specified at the time of creation of the semaphore. A value of SEM_Q_FIFO sets FIFO model whereas SEM_Q_PRIORITY sets the priority model. The semaphore creation also specifies its status at the time of creation (Available or unavailable).
semDelete( )	Terminate and free a semaphore.
semTake( )	Acquires a semaphore.
semGive( )	Release a semaphore.
semFlush( )	Unblock all tasks which are waiting (pended) for the specified semaphore.

The mutual exclusion semaphore has an option to set its priority to the highest priority of the task which is being pended while attempting to acquire a semaphore which is already in use by a low priority task. This ensures that the low priority task which is currently holding the semaphore, when a high priority task is waiting for it, is not pre-empted by a medium priority task. This is the mechanism supported by the mutual exclusion semaphore to prevent priority inversion. To make use of this feature, the mutual exclusion semaphore should be created with the option *SEM_INVERSION_SAFE* and the queue holding the pended tasks waiting for the semaphore should be sorted on priority basis. These two options should be specified while creating the semaphore. The syntax for this is given below.

```
Id = semMCreate (SEM_Q_PRIORITY | SEM_INVERSION_SAFE);
```

where Id is the 4 byte ID returned by the system on creating the semaphore. It is used as the handle for accessing the semaphore. The option *SEM_Q_PRIORITY* sets the ordering of the queue, holding the pended tasks which are waiting for the semaphore, as priority based. The option *SEM_INVERSION_SAFE* enables priority inheritance.

The mutual exclusion semaphore protects a task from deletion when it is currently in the critical section. If the task is not protected from deletion when it is holding a semaphore and is executing in the critical section, the semaphore will not be released properly and it may not be available for access to

† Please refer to the VxWorks library reference manual for the parameter details of each function call.

other resources. This may lead to starvation and deadlock. In order to make a semaphore 'task deletion safe', it should be created with the option *SEM_DELETE_SAFE*. The queue holding the pended tasks waiting for the semaphore can be sorted on either priority basis or first come first served (FIFO) basis. The task safe option should be specified while creating the semaphore. The syntax for this is given below.

```
Id = semMCreate (SEM_Q_PRIORITY | SEM_DELETE_SAFE);
```

The *semFlush()* operation is illegal for mutual exclusion semaphores.

Whenever a task tries to acquire a semaphore and if the semaphore is not available (It is acquired and being in use by other task(s)), the task enters the pended state and it waits for the semaphore in a pended queue. The *wind* semaphores support a timeout mechanism to specify how long the task needs to wait. It is useful for tasks which are not interested in wasting the time on waiting for the semaphore. The timeout option can be set in the *semTake()* call used for accessing/acquiring the semaphore. Wind supports three different timeout options. They are explained below.

Return immediately: If the semaphore is not available when the task tries to acquire it, the task returns immediately and it will not enter the pended state. The return value in case of nonavailability of semaphore is *S_objLib_OBJ_UNAVAILABLE*. The timeout option *NO_WAIT* is used for specifying this.

Wait for a predefined time: If the semaphore is not available when the task tries to acquire it, the task is pended and it waits in the pended queue for semaphores for the specified timeout duration. The timeout is usually specified in terms of the 'kernel tick'. If the semaphore is not available even after the specified timeout duration, the task times out and it returns the value *S_objLib_OBJ_TIMEOUT*.

Wait Forever: If the semaphore is not available when the task tries to acquire it, the task is pended and it waits in the pended queue for semaphores until it is available. The timeout option *WAIT_FOREVER* is used for specifying this.

As mentioned earlier the pended queue holding the pended tasks waiting for the semaphore can be ordered based on either priority or FIFO. It is specified by the option parameters *SEM_Q_PRIORITY* or *SEM_Q_FIFO* respectively at the time of creating the semaphore. The priority based sorting enhances the priority based execution with expense of kernel overhead. Whereas FIFO based mechanism is simple to implement and is free from overheads.

VxWorks also supports the implementation of POSIX standard semaphores. POSIX supports named and unnamed semaphores and are counting semaphores. The interface for POSIX semaphores is defined by the library *semPxLib*.

11.1.6 Interrupt Handling

VxWorks support a well-defined interrupt handling mechanism for handling hardware interrupts. Efficient and fast handling of external interrupts is a key requirement for real-time systems. The salient features of VxWorks' interrupt handling mechanism are summarised below.

1. The Interrupt Service Routine (ISR) runs in a special context outside any task's context. This eliminates the delay in context saving and context retrieval (Context switch delay) in contrast to task execution. This greatly reduces interrupt latency.
2. A separate stack is maintained for use by all ISRs. It is allocated and initialised by the kernel at the time of system startup. For processor architectures supporting this option, the same stack is used by all ISRs. If the processor architecture doesn't support a single stack for all ISRs, the stack

of the task which is currently preempted by the ISR is used by ISR. In this case the stack size for each task should be large enough to accommodate ISR stack requirement also.

3. Supports connecting of 'C' function with system hardware interrupts which are not used by VxWorks kernel. The connecting of 'C function' with the interrupt vector is achieved through the function call *intConnect()*. It is responsible for saving the processor registers, setting up the stack entry point, pushing the argument, to be passed to the ISR function, on the stack and invoking the 'C function' as ISR. The *intConnect()* function takes the arguments; byte offset of the interrupt vector to connect to, the address of the 'C function' to be connected with the interrupt vector and an argument to the 'C' function. The 'C function' becomes the ISR for the interrupt. On completion of the ISR, the registers are restored to the original state.
4. To avoid starvation and deadlock situations, as a rule of thumb, ISRs are not allowed invoking routines (involving the access of shared resource protected through semaphores) that may block the ISR.
5. ISRs are not allowed to acquire (take) a semaphore. But are allowed to release (give) a semaphore (except mutual exclusion semaphore).
6. ISRs are not allowed to invoke memory allocation and de-allocation functions like *malloc(), calloc(), free()* etc. The memory allocation functions internally make use of semaphores for synchronisation and they may block the ISR.
7. ISRs are not allowed to call any creation or deletion routines. The creation and deletion calls may use semaphores internally and it may block the ISR.
8. ISRs must not perform I/O operations through VxWorks drivers. The restriction is put for the reason, most of the device drivers require a task context and it may block the ISR. However, ISRs are allowed write operations for pipes, which is a virtual I/O device.
9. ISR must not call routines/instructions involving floating point operations. The reason is that the floating point registers are not saved and re-stored by the ISR connecting code. It is the responsibility of the user to save and re-store floating point registers explicitly, if the ISR involves floating point calculation.
10. ISRs can make use of the logging service supplied by logger component to send text messages to the system console.
11. If an exception happens during the execution of an ISR, *wind* stores the exception details and resets the system. During the boot-up time, the boot ROM checks for captured exception messages and displays it on the display console.
12. Interrupts communicate with tasks using shared memory, message queues, pipes, semaphore (can give a semaphore but can't take one), pipes and signals.
13. The *intLock()*function performs a system wide lockout of all interrupts to the highest priority level supported by the kernel. If the intention is to lockout only interrupts up to a certain level and the system wants to preserve the occurrence of high priority interrupts, it can be achieved through the system call *intLockLevelSet()*, which sets the lock-out priority level to a desired one than locking out all interrupts including high priority. With an *intLockLevelSet()*, the *intLock()*function locks only interrupts with priority level specified by the lock level in *intLockLevelSet()*. All other enabled, high priority interrupts are acknowledged.
14. For interrupts whose priority is higher than that of the lock level set by the function *intLockLevelSet()* and Non-maskable interrupts, the system call *intVecSet()* should be used for connecting a C function as ISR for the interrupt and also the ISR should not use any kernel facilities that depend on interrupt locks for their operation.

The following table gives a snapshot of the Interrupt handling related function calls under VxWorks.

Function Call†	Description
*IntConnect (VOIDFUNCPTR * vector, VOIDFUNCPTR routine, int parameter)*	Used for connecting a 'C' routine with an interrupt vector. The 'C' routine acts as the ISR. It also contains the necessary code for saving and retrieving required registers, and setting up the stack for ISR
intContext( )	Checks whether the current execution context is at interrupt level. Returns *TRUE* if the current execution context is at interrupt level. If not *FALSE* is returned
intCount( )	Returns the current interrupt nesting level in a nested interrupt environment
intLevelSet(int level)	Sets the interrupt mask in the interrupt status register. Interrupts are locked out at or below this level
intLock( )	Disables the processor interrupts. Its operation is processor architecture dependent. Used for interrupt locking based mutual exclusion implementation
intUnlock(int lockKey)	Re-enable the interrupts. Used for interrupt locking based mutual exclusion implementation
*intVecBaseSet(FUNCPTR * baseAddr)*	Sets the CPU's vector base register to the specified value. Initially it will be 0 for almost all processors (Exceptions are their). The subsequent calls to *intVecSet( )* and *intVecGet( )* uses this base address value
intLockLevelSet (int newLevel)	Sets the current interrupt lock-out level. When the interrupt lock-out level is set only the interrupts which belong to this specified level are locked by the function call *intLock( )*
intLockLevelGet()	Returns the current interrupt lock-out level
intVecBaseGet( )	Returns the vector base address from the CPU's vector base register
*intVecSet(FUNCPTR * vector, FUNCPTR function)*	It attaches an exception/interrupt/trap handler to a specified vector. The vector is specified as an offset into the CPU's vector table. It takes an interrupt vector as parameter, which is the byte offset into the vector table and the address of the 'C function' to be connected with the interrupt vector
*intVecGet(FUNCPTR * vector)*	Returns a pointer to the exception/interrupt handler attached to a specified vector. The vector is specified as an offset into the CPU's vector table. It takes an interrupt vector as parameter, which is the byte offset into the vector table

11.1.7 Watchdog for Task Execution Monitoring

Watchdog timers are essential for bringing the system out of 'system hang-up' condition. If a task hangs at some point of execution due to some unexpected situations (like the peripheral device is not responding while accessing it in an infinite loop), it should be brought out of the situation to make the system operational. Watchdog timers are used for this. You can set a watchdog timer for the time expected for the execution completion of the task or a portion of the task which is more prone to hang-up. Start the watchdog timer when the task is started or when the task is executing in the suspected portion of the code. If the execution of the task or portion of the task is not completed within the time set in the

† Please refer to the VxWorks library reference manual for the parameter details of each function call.

watchdog timer, the watchdog expires and it raises a watchdog timeout event. The necessary actions to handle the situation can be written in the watchdog timeout handler. Under VxWorks, watchdog timeout is handled as part of the system clock ISR. User can associate a 'C' function with the Watchdog timer. The 'C' function is executed when the watchdog expires. The time is specified in terms of system timer tick. The timer is created using the function call *wdCreate()*. The timer is started with the function call *wdStart()* and it takes the number of ticks as timer value, 'C' function to be executed in case of timeout and the parameter to the 'C' function as parameters. The watchdog timer can be stopped and cancelled at any time prior to its expiration by calling the function *wdCancel()*.

The following table gives a snapshot of the watchdog timer related function calls.

Function Call†	Description
wdCreate()	Allocate and initialise a watchdog timer
wdStart()	Start the watchdog timer
wdCancel()	Cancel the currently running watchdog timer
wdDelete()	Terminate and de-allocate a watchdog timer

11.1.8 Timing and Reference

In many of the scenarios the application may require timing reference. VxWorks provides access to the system wide real-time clock for timing reference. Software timers and time reference can be generated using these interfaces. For timer operations, the task can create a timer and set it for the desired time. The timer runs with the system timer tick and it generates the 'signal', SIGALRM when it expires. The task can associate a signal handler with this signal for performing the necessary operations in the event of timer expire.

11.1.9 The VxWorks Development Environment

Tornado® II is the development environment from Wind River Systems for VxWorks 5.x development. It includes the Tornado tools and the VxWorks run-time environment. The Tornado tools include the Integrated Development Environment (IDE) for OS customisation and building. Debug interface for debugging and simulator (VxSim) for simulating the target environment. Tornado® II development environment is available for both Windows and UNIX development hosts. The Tornado (R) IDE is re-placed by the Eclipse based IDE Wind River Workbench for VxWorks 6.x.

11.2 MicroC/OS-II

MicroC/OS-II (μC/OS-II) is a simple, easy to use real-time kernel written in 'C' language for embedded application development. MicroC OS 2 is the acronym for Micro Controller Operating System Version 2. The μC/OS-II features:

- Multitasking (Supports multi-threading)
- Priority based pre-emptive task scheduling

MicroC/OS-II is a commercial real-time kernel from Micrium Inc (www.micrium.com). The MicroC/OS-II kernel is available for different family of processors/controllers and supports processors/controllers ranging from 8bit to 64bit. ARM family of processors, Intel 8085/x86/8051, Freescale

† Please refer to the VxWorks library reference manual for the parameter details of each function call.

68K series and Altera Nios II are examples for some of the processors/controllers supported by MicroC/OS-II. Please check the Micrium Inc website for complete details about the different family of processors/controllers for which the MicroC/OS-II kernel port is available. MicroC OS follows the task based execution model. Each task is implemented as infinite loop.

11.2.1 Task Creation and Management

Under MicroC OS kernel, the tasks may be in one of the following state at a given point of time.

Dormant: The dormant state corresponds to the state where a task is created but no resources are allocated to it. This means the task is still present in the program memory and is not moved to the RAM for execution.

Ready: Corresponds to a state where the task is incepted into memory and is awaiting the CPU for its turn for execution.

Running: Corresponds to a state where the task is being executed by CPU.

Waiting: Corresponds to a state where a running task is temporarily suspended from execution and does not have immediate access to resources. The waiting state might be invoked by various conditions like —the task enters a wait state for an event to occur (e.g. Waiting for user inputs such as keyboard input) or waiting for getting access to a shared resource.

Interrupted: A task enters the Interrupted (or ISR) state when an interrupt is occurred and the CPU executes the ISR.

A task is usually created as non-ending function. The creation of a task is illustrated below.

```
//*******************************************************************
//Creates a task with name MicroCTask
void MicroCTask(void *arg)
{
        while (1)
        {
        //Code corresponding to task.
        //..........................................
        }
}
```

It creates a task with name *MicroCTask*. The task doesn't return anything. The argument to the task is passed through a pointer to void. Depending on the argument required the pointer can pass structure variables, other data types or function pointers to the task. The task *MicroCTask* is in the 'Dormant' state now.

You need to pass this task to the MicroC kernel to make it ready for execution. It is essential for assigning resources to the task *MicroCTask*. The MicroC kernel call *OSTaskCreate()* or *OSTaskCreateEx()* is used for this. These function calls take the address of the task, the priority assigned to it and the stack size requirement for the task as parameters. *OSTaskCreate()* is the older version of the task allocation call and *OSTaskCreateEx()* is the enhanced version of it. Calling these functions allocate the memory for the task and put the task in the 'Ready' state. The usage of these functions is illustrated below.

```
//*****************************************************************
//Allocate resources for the task MicroCTask
//Make the task MicroCTask 'Ready' for execution
//Declare stack as type OS_STK
OS_STK TaskStk[1024];
OSTaskCreateEx(MicroCTask,(void *)0, & TaskStk[1023], 10,10, &TaskStk[0],1024,
(void*) 0, OS_TASK_OPT_STK_CHK );
```

The parameter *MicroCTask* specifies the entry point of the task *MicroCTask*. The second parameter specifies the arguments for executing the task. The parameter *TaskStk[1023]* sets the top of stack and *TaskStk[0]* sets the bottom of the stack for the task. The other parameters are the task priority (10), task ID (10), stack size (1024) and a pointer to user supplied memory location used as an extension of TCB. Here it is not used. The last parameter specifies a task specific option like whether stack checking is allowed or not, whether the stack needs to be cleared, etc. Here it is set for enabling stack check option. It should be noted that the stack should be declared with type OS_STK. The value *OS_STK_GROWTH* specifies whether stack grows downwards (*OS_STK_GROWTH=1*) or upwards (*OS_STK_GROWTH=0*). This value should be configured properly depending on the processor architecture and the stack bottom, top and size should also be configured accordingly for creating a task.

uC/OS-II supports up to 64 tasks. Out of this 8 are reserved for the uC/OS-II kernel. Each task should have a unique task priority assigned. No two tasks can have the same priority. In effect uC/OS-II supports 56 user level tasks. The priority of tasks varies from 0 to 63, with 0 being the highest priority. Considering the future expansions, uC/OS-II advices developers not to use the priority values 0, 1, 2, 3, OS_LOWEST_PRIO-3, OS_LOWEST_PRIO-2, OS_LOWEST_PRIO-1 and OS_LOWEST_PRIO. Currently, the uC/OS-II reserves only two task priorities for kernel tasks. Under the uC/OS-II kernel, the ID of the task is its priority. A Task Control Block (TCB) is assigned to a task when a task is created. TCB is a data structure for holding the state of a task. It is essential for handling the state information during a context switch. The TCB under uC/OS-II is represented by OS_TCB. The following table gives a snapshot of the important task creation and management routines supported by uC/OS-II.

Function Call†	Description
OSTaskCreate()	Create a task and makes it 'Ready' for execution.
OSTaskCreateEx()	Create a task and makes it 'Ready' for execution. This is an enhanced version of *OSTaskCreate()*.
OSTaskStkCheck()	Checks stack overflow for the creation of tasks. uC/OS-II does not automatically check for the status of stack on task creation.
OSTimeDly()	Delay the task for the specified duration. The delay is mentioned in number of clock ticks. It ranges from 0 to 65535 ticks.
OSTimeDlyHMSM()	Delay the task for the specified duration. The delay time is specified by the combination of hours (H), minutes (M), seconds (S) and milliseconds (M). Hour value can range from 0 to 255, minutes value can range from 0 to 59, second's value can range from 0 to 59 and millisecond value can range from 0 to 999. Resolution depends on clock rate.
OSTimeDlyResume()	Resumes a task which is delayed by a call to either *OSTimeDly()* or *OSTimeDlyHMSM()*.

† Please refer to the MicroC library reference manual for the parameter details of each function call.

OSTaskDel()	Deletes a specified task. The task is specified by its priority. Calling this routine places the task in 'Dormant' state. The task can be recreated later, if needed, by calling *OSTaskCreate* or *OSTaskCreateExt*. It is the responsibility of the calling function to ensure that the task doesn't hold resources like semaphores and mailboxes. A task can delete itself by passing *OS_PRIO_SELF* as the argument to this function call.
OSTaskDelReq()	Same as *OSTaskDel()* function. It sends a task delete request to the MicroC kernel. This call makes the deletion safe and protects the task from deletion when it is holding shared resources like semaphore and mail boxes.
OSTaskNameGet()	Returns the name associated with a task. The task is identified using its priority.
OSTaskNameSet()	Sets the name for a task. The task is identified using its priority.
OSTaskQuery()	Retrieves the information about a task in a Task Control block structure (OS_TCB).
OSTaskSuspend()	Suspends or blocks a task from execution. On task suspension, the kernel reschedules the next highest priority task for execution. A task can suspend itself by passing the argument *OS_PRIO_SELF* to this call.
OSTaskResume()	Resumes a suspended task.

Interrupt Service Routines (ISRs) are not allowed to create a task. The stack statistics of a task can be examined by calling the function *OSTaskStkCheck()*. In order to get the stack statistics for a task, the task should be created with the option *OS_TASK_OPT_STK_CHK*. The stack details of the stack for a task in terms of no. of bytes used and no. of bytes free in the stack are returned in a structure variable of type *OS_STK_DATA*. The execution time of this call is determined by the size of the stack and hence the call is non-deterministic. It is advised not to call this function from ISR due to its non-deterministic nature. The following code snippet illustrates the usage of this function.

```
//********************************************************************
//Define variable of type OS_STK_DATA
OS_STK_DATA stack_mem;
//Define 32 bit integer for holding stack size
INT32U stack_size;
//Define variable for holding return value
INT8U err;

//Get the stack details for task with priority 5
err = OSTaskStkChk(5, &stack_mem);
if (OS_NO_ERR == err)
stack_size = stack_mem.OSFree + stack_mem.OSUsed;
```

The function calls *OSTaskSuspend()* and *OSTaskResume()* are used in combination to suspend and resume a task. Whenever an *OSTaskSuspend()* call is made by a task, the task is put in the 'Waiting' state and the scheduler picks up the highest priority task from the 'Ready' list for execution. Suspending of *IDLE* task is not allowed. The following code snippet illustrates the usage of the task suspend function.

```
//********************************************************************
//Task implementation
void task(void *args)
{
while (1)
```

```
{
//Execute the task specific details….
//.........................................................
//.........................................................
//Suspend task with priority 5
OSTaskSuspend(5);
//Rest of the task
//.........................................................
//.........................................................
}
}
```

A task can delay itself by calling either *OSTimeDly()* or *OSTimeDlyHMSM()* function. Upon calling these functions, the task is put into the 'Waiting' state. The task becomes ready for execution when the delay time expires or when another task resumes the delayed task by calling a task resume function. Task delaying is the mechanism by which a task can voluntarily relinquish the CPU to other tasks when it is waiting for any events to occur. A task can only delay itself and cannot impose delaying of other tasks. The activation of the delayed task to 'Ready' state from 'Waiting' state, when the wait period expires is done by the function *OSTimeTick()*. The function *OSTimeTick()* is the Interrupt Service Routine (ISR) for the system timer clock and the kernel executes it. Users don't need to bother about it. A task which is currently in the waiting state introduced by the self delaying can be resumed by another task. The function call *OSTimeDlyResume()* resumes a specified task which is currently in the 'waiting' state induced by self delaying. A task which is self delayed by invoking *OSTimeDlyHMSM()* function cannot be resumed by another tasks if the combined delay set by the hour, minute, seconds and milliseconds parameter exceeds 65535 timer ticks.

The task self delaying and resuming it from another tasks technique is a good approach for building applications where one task requires waiting for I/O operations. The task involving Input operation (e.g. Waiting for a key press) can self delay it and key press event can be handled in an Interrupt Service Routine (ISR) and the ISR can resume the delayed task upon receiving the key press event. The following code snippet illustrates the usage of task delay and task resuming functions.

```
//**************************************************************
//Task implementation
void taskA(void *args)
{
while (1)
{
//Execute the task specific details
//.........................................................
//.........................................................
//Delay the task for 5 Timer ticks.
OSTimeDly(5);
//Rest of the task
//.........................................................
}
}
```

```
//**************************************************************
//Task implementation
void taskB(void *args)
{
while (1)
{
//Execute the task specific details
//.................................................
//.................................................
//Resume task 5.
OSTimeDlyResume(5);
//Rest of the task
//.................................................
}
}
```

The function pair *OSTaskSuspend()* and *OSTaskResume()* can be used for suspending a task unconditionally and resuming the suspended task. If a task which is being suspended is delayed by task delay call, the task is resumed only after the task is resumed from suspension and both the time expires.

Tasks can be deleted by calling *OSTaskDel()*. The task which is being deleted is kept in the 'Dormant' state and it can be recreated, if needed by calling task creation functions like *OSTaskCreate()* or *OSTaskCreateEx()*. Proper care should be applied in the usage of *OSTaskDel()* function. Imagine a situation where Task 1 is holding a shared resource, a semaphore and Task 2 attempts to delete Task 1 by executing *OSTaskDel()*. Task 1 will be moved to the 'Dormant' state and this will lead to the locking of the semaphore used by Task 1 and this semaphore will not be available to other tasks – leading to starvation of tasks. The function *OSTaskDelReq()* makes task deletion safe by ensuring that the task is not deleted when it is holding a shared resource.

11.2.2 Kernel Functions and Initialisation

The kernel needs to be initialised and started before executing the user tasks. MicroC/OS-II provides OS kernel initialisation and start routines. The MicroC/OS-II kernel initialisation and OS kernel start is written as part of the startup code which is executed before the execution of user tasks. The OS kernel initialisation function *OSInit()* is executed first. It performs the following operations.

1. Initialise the different OS kernel data structure
2. Creates the idle task *OSIdle()*

The idle task is the lowest priority task under the MicroC/OS-II kernel and it is executed to keep the CPU always busy when there are no user tasks to execute. User tasks are not allowed to delete or suspend the 'Idle' task. The following code snippet illustrates the implementation of 'Idle' task.

```
//**************************************************************
//Idle Task implementation
void OS_TaskIdle(void *args)
{
while (1)
{
OS_ENTER_CRITICAL();
OSIdleCtr++;
```

```
OS_EXIT_CRITICAL();
OSTaskIdleHook();
}
}
```

It simply increments a counter to keep the CPU always active. Depending on the power saving requirements, the IDLE task can be re-written to include the CPU specific power down modes.

The MicroC/OS-II kernel runs a statistical task for computing the percentage of CPU usage. The statistical task is created with priority *OS_LOWEST_PRIO – 1* and it is executed in every second. The function call *OSStatinit()* sets up the statistical task related activities. This function must be called before *OSStart()*. The *OSStart()* function starts the multitasking. It is invoked only after invoking *OSInit()*. It starts the execution of the highest priority task from the 'Ready' list. It never returns to the calling function. There should be at least one task to execute. The following code snippet illustrates the OS initialisation and start operations.

```
//***********************************************************************
#include <includes.h>     ;The include file for uC functions
//Main task
void main(void)
{
//Initialise the kernel
OSInit();
//Create the first task. The function OSStatinit() should be-
//called from this task.
//Start OS by executing the highest priority task
OSStart();
}
```

11.2.3 Task Scheduling

The MicroC/OS-II support preemptive priority based scheduling. Each task should be assigned a unique priority ranging from 0 to 63 with 0 being the highest priority level. The four highest priorities (0 to 3) and the four lowest priorities (63 to *OS_LOWEST_PRIO – 3*) are reserved for the kernel. When the kernel starts, it executes the first available highest priority task. A task rescheduling happens if any one of the following situation occurs.

1. Whenever high priority task becomes 'Ready' to run or when a task enters the 'Waiting' state due to the invocation of system calls like *OSTaskSuspend()*,*OSTaskResume()*,*OSTaskDel()*,*OSTimeDly()*, *OSTimeDlyHMSM()*, *OSTimeDlyResume()*, etc.
2. Whenever an Interrupt occurs, the tasks are rescheduled upon return from the Interrupt Service Routine (ISR).

In general, the task scheduling happens at the task level and ISR level. The task level scheduling is executed by the kernel service *OS_Sched()* when a system call occurs. The ISR level task scheduling is done by the function call *OSIntExit()*. When an *OSIntExit()* call is executed, the kernel is notified that the ISR is complete and the kernel checks whether there is any high priority task is 'Ready' for scheduling. If a high priority task is ready for scheduling, the ISR returns to the high priority task instead of returning to the interrupted task.

For task level scheduling, the software interrupt *OS_TASK_SW()* is triggered and the context switch handler *OSCtxSw()* is executed as ISR for this interrupt. The service *OSCtxSw()* is part of the MicroC/

OS-II kernel service and is responsible for handling the context switch operation. It saves the CPU registers and Program Status Word (PSW) to the stack of the preempted task (context saving) and loads the CPU registers and PSW from the stack of the highest priority task (context retrieval) which is going to execute.

The task rescheduling will not take place if the scheduler is in the locked state. The scheduler can be locked by invoking the system call *OSSchedLock()*. Proper care should be applied in the usage of *OSSchedLock()*. Once the scheduler is locked with this call, the application should not call any other function calls, which suspends the execution of the current task, like *OSTaskSuspend(),OSTaskResume ()*, *OSTaskDel()*, *OSTimeDly()*, *OSTimeDlyHMSM()*. Since the scheduler is in the locked state it will not be able to schedule another task for execution and the current task is already in the suspended stage, the system hangs-up.

The scheduling can be resumed by calling *OSSchedUnlock()*. The MicroC/OS-II kernel supports nested locking of scheduling up to 255 levels deep. Scheduling is enabled only when the same number of scheduler unlocking calls as that of scheduler locking calls is executed. Interrupts are serviced even when the scheduler is in the locked state. The scheduler locking and unlocking mechanism is used as a technique for exclusive access to shared resources (An implementation of mutual exclusion). The following piece of code illustrates the usage of scheduler locking and unlocking functions.

```
//***************************************************************
//Task implementation
void taskA(void *args)
{
while (1)
{
//Execute the task specific details
//.......................................................
//.......................................................
//Lock the scheduler.
OSSchedLock();
//Perform shared resource access
//.......................................................
//Unlock the scheduler.
OSSchedUnlock();
//Rest of the task
//.......................................................
//.......................................................
}
}
```

The priorities associated with a task can be changed dynamically. The function call *OSTaskChange-Prio()* changes the priority associated with a task. The function takes current priority and new priority as arguments.

11.2.4 Inter-Task Communication

The MicroC/OS-II kernel supports the following inter-process communication techniques for data sharing and co-operation among tasks

1. Mailbox
2. Message queue

Mailbox and message queues are same in functionality. The only difference is in the number of messages supported by them. Both of them are used for passing data in the form of message(s) from a task to another task(s) or from an ISR to task(s).

Mailbox is used for exchanging a single message between two tasks or between an Interrupt Service Routine (ISR) and a task. Mailbox associates a pointer pointing to the mailbox and a wait list to hold the tasks waiting for a message to appear in the mailbox. The following table gives a snapshot of the important mailbox related routines supported by MicroC/OS-II.

Function Call†	Description
OSMboxCreate()	Creates and initialises a mailbox.
OSMboxPost()	Posts a message to the mailbox. The parameters are pointer to the mailbox (which is obtained on creating a mailbox) and a pointer variable pointing to the message. If a message is already present in the mailbox, the message posting fails and the message posting task returns immediately. Upon the arrival of a message in the mailbox it is routed to the highest priority task waiting for the message.
OSMboxPostOpt()	Same as *OSMboxPost()* function call. Allows the broadcasting of message to all tasks waiting for the message. The broadcast option can be set in the options parameter.
OSMboxPend()	Used for retrieving message from a mailbox. If a message is available in the mailbox at the time of calling this function, it is retrieved through the pointer and the message is deleted from the mailbox. If message is not available in the mailbox at the time of calling this function, the calling task is blocked and it is put in the message wait list queue associated with the mailbox. A task can wait until a message is available in the mailbox or till a timeout occurs. The timeout value for waiting can be specified in the 'timeout' argument of this function call. The 'timeout' value is specified in terms of clock ticks. It can take values ranging from 0 to 65535. A value of 0 indicates wait until a message is available.
OSMboxAccept()	Used for retrieving message from a mailbox. Similar to *OSMboxPend()* in functioning but differ in the way it operates. It allows a task to check whether a message is available in the mailbox. Unlike *OSMboxPend()*, the calling task is not blocked ('Pended') if there is no message to read in the mailbox.
OSMboxQuery()	Retrieves information about the mailbox. The information is retrieved in a data structure of type *OS_MBOX_DATA*. It is used for getting information like, whether a message is available in the mailbox, is there any tasks waiting for the messages and if yes how many tasks, etc.
OSMboxDel()	Deletes a mailbox. Option for specifying whether the mailbox needs to be deleted immediately or only when the pending operations on this mailbox are completed.

A mailbox is created with the function call *OSMboxCreate(void *msg)*, where the parameter *msg* is a pointer holding the initial message. If this is a non-null value, the mailbox holds the message pointed by *msg*. If *msg* is a null pointer, the mailbox is created without any messages present initially. This function allocates an Event Control Block (ECB) to the mailbox and returns a pointer of type *OS_EVENT* to the allocated ECB. The Event Control Block (ECB) is a data structure holding information like, the event associated, list of tasks waiting for this event to occur, etc. A task can post a message to the mailbox if the task knows the ECB pointer for the mailbox. Along with the ECB pointer of the mailbox, the task passes a pointer to the message which is to be posted to the mailbox, as argument to the *OSMboxPost(OS_EVENT *pevent, void *msg)* function. If the mailbox is not empty when a task is

† Please refer to the MicroC library reference manual for the parameter details of each function call.

trying to post a message, the task returns immediately. On the arrival of a message in the mailbox, it is delivered to the highest priority task waiting for the event and the message is deleted from the mailbox. If the priority of the highest priority task waiting for the message is higher than that of the message posting task, the message posting task is preempted and the highest priority task is executed by the scheduler. A task can broadcast a message to all tasks waiting for a message by posting the message with the function call *OSMboxPostOpt(OS_EVENT *pevent, void *msg, INT8U opt)*. The '*opt*' parameter should be set as *OS_POST_OPT_BROADCAST* for broadcasting a message. If this parameter is set as *OS_POST_OPT_NONE*, this function becomes equivalent to *OSMboxPost*. The functions *OSMbox-Pend()*, and *OSMboxAccept()* can be used for retrieving a message from the mailbox. *OSMboxPend()* provides option to set the function call as either a blocking call till a message is available in the mailbox or till a wait period specified in the parameter list. *OSMboxAccept()* is a non-blocking call. This function will not block a calling task when there is no message available in the mailbox. This can be used by ISRs to check the availability of messages in a mailbox. A task can delete a mailbox by calling *OSMboxDel(OS_EVENT *pevent, INT8U opt, INT8U *err)*. The parameter '*opt*' specifies whether a mailbox needs to be deleted immediately or only when the pending operations on this mailbox are over. The value *OS_DEL_NO_PEND* for '*opt*' sets the first choice and a value *OS_DEL_ALWAYS* deletes the mailbox immediately. Proper care should be applied in the usage of this function. There are possibilities for tasks to access a deleted mailbox. This may result in unpredicted behaviour. Also tasks which are using the function *OSMboxAccept()* for checking the availability of a message may never know about the non-availability of a mailbox. Hence use this function judiciously and as a precautionary measure delete all tasks which uses the specified mailbox before it is being deleted. The following piece of code illustrates the usage of mailbox functions:

```
//********************************************************************
#include <includes.h>
//Define Task IDs for First Task, Task 1 and Task 2
#define TASK_FIRST_ID 1
#define TASK_1_ID 2
#define TASK_2_ID 3

//Define Task Priorities for First Task, Task 1 and Task 2
#define TASK_FIRST_PRIO 5
#define TASK_1_PRIO 6
#define TASK_2_PRIO 7

//Set the default stack size for all tasks
#define TASK_STK_SIZE      1024

//Define stack size for tasks
OS_STK TaskFirstStk[TASK_STK_SIZE];    // First task's stack
OS_STK Task1Stk[TASK_STK_SIZE];        // Task 1's task stack
OS_STK Task2Stk[TASK_STK_SIZE];        // Task 2's task stack

//Define ECB pointer for the mailbox
OS_EVENT *Mbox;

void main (void)
```

```
{
//Initialise MicroC OS
OSInit();

//Create the first task.
OSTaskCreateExt(TaskFirst,
                (void *)0,
                &TaskFirstStk[TASK_STK_SIZE - 1],
                TASK_FIRST_PRIO,
                TASK_FIRST_ID,
                &TaskStartStk[0],
                TASK_STK_SIZE,
                (void *) 0,
                OS_TASK_OPT_STK_CHK);
// Start multitasking
OSStart();

}

//********************************************************************
//Implementation of TaskFirst
void TaskFirst(void *args)
{
//Initialise statistics task
OSStatInit();
//Create Mailbox
Mbox = OSMboxCreate((void *)0);
//Create Task1
OSTaskCreateExt(Task1,
                (void *)0,
                &Task1Stk[TASK_STK_SIZE - 1],
                TASK_1_PRIO,
                TASK_1_ID,
                &Task1Stk[0],
                TASK_STK_SIZE,
                (void *) 0,
                OS_TASK_OPT_STK_CHK);

//Create Task2
OSTaskCreateExt(Task2,
                (void *)0,
                &Task2Stk[TASK_STK_SIZE - 1],
                TASK_2_PRIO,
                TASK_2_ID,
                &Task2Stk[0],
                TASK_STK_SIZE,
                (void *) 0,
                OS_TASK_OPT_STK_CHK);
```

```
while (1)
{
//Do Nothing. Simply sleep for one timer tick
OSTimeDly(OS_TICKS_PER_SEC);
}
}

//**********************************************************************
//Implementation of Task1
void Task1(void *args)
{
//Define pointer to message
char msg;

msg = '0';
while (1)
{
//Execute the task specific details
//.................................................
//.................................................
//Post a message to the mailbox Mbox.
OSMboxPost(Mbox, (void *)&msg);
//Rest of the task
//.................................................
//.................................................
}
}
//**********************************************************************
//Implementation of Task2
void Task2(void *args)
{
//Define pointer to message
char * msg;
//Define Return value handling variable
INT8U err;

while (1)
{
//Execute the task specific details
//.................................................
//.................................................
//Receive a message from the mailbox Mbox.
//Wait till a message is available.
msg = (char *)OSMboxPend(Mbox, 0, &err);
//Rest of the task
//.................................................
//.................................................
}
}
```

The sample application creates a main task *TaskFirst* which creates a mailbox and two tasks namely *Task1* and *Task2*. *Task1* posts the message '0' to the mailbox and *Task2* reads the mailbox to retrieve the message present in it. The startup tasks, viz. the initialisation of MicroC kernel (*OSInit()*), main task creation and starting of multitasking (*OSStart()*) is done by the *main* function.

Message queue is same as that of mailbox in operation; the only difference is—mailbox is designed for handling only a single message whereas message queue is designed for the handling of multiple messages. Message queue is used for exchanging a message data between two or more tasks or between an Interrupt Service Routine (ISR) and tasks. Message queue associates a pointer pointing to the Message queue and a wait list to hold the tasks waiting for a message to appear in the Message queue. The following table gives a snapshot of the important message queue related routines supported by MicroC/OS-II.

Function Call†	Description
OSQCreate()	Creates and initializes a message queue. An array of pointers is allocated for storing the message. The size of the message storage area (size of the pointer array) is specified as the parameter to this function.
OSQPost()	Posts a message to the message queue. The parameters are pointer to the message queue (which is obtained on creating a message queue) and a pointer variable pointing to the message. If there is no room for a new message in the message queue, the message posting fails and the message posting task returns immediately. Upon the arrival of a message in the message queue it is routed to the highest priority task waiting for the message. Message queue normally follows the FIFO structure for operation.
OSQPostFront()	Same as *OSQPost()* function call. Only difference is that it posts the message in front of the message queue.
OSQPostOpt()	Same as *OSQPost()* function call. It allows the broadcasting of message to all tasks waiting for the message, or posts the message at the front of the message queue. The broadcast or post in front of queue option is set by the options parameter.
OSQPend()	Used for retrieving messages from a message queue. If a message is available in the message queue at the time of calling this function, it is retrieved through the pointer and the message is deleted from the message queue. If message is not available in the message queue at the time of calling this function, the calling task is blocked and it is put in the message wait list queue associated with the message queue. A task can wait until a message is available in the message queue or till a timeout occurs. The timeout value for waiting can be specified in the 'timeout' argument of this function call. The 'timeout' value is specified in terms of clock ticks. It can take values ranging from 0 to 65535. A value of 0 indicates wait until a message is available.
OSQAccept()	Used for retrieving messages from a message queue. Similar to *OSQPend()* in functioning but differ in the way it operates. It allows a task to check whether a message is available in the message queue. Unlike *OSQPend()*, the calling task is not blocked ('Pended') if there is no message to read in the message queue.
OSQQuery()	Retrieves information about the message queue. The information is retrieved in a data structure of type *OS_Q_DATA*. It is used for getting information like, what is the message queue size, whether a message is available in the message queue, is there any tasks waiting for the messages and if yes how many tasks, etc.
OSQFlush()	Flushes the message queue and deletes all the messages present in it. The time required to execute this function is fixed regardless of the number of messages present, and the number of tasks waiting (in case no messages are present in the message queue).
OSQDel()	Deletes a message queue. Option for specifying whether the message queue needs to be deleted immediately or only when the pending operations on this message queue are completed.

† Please refer to the MicroC library reference manual for the parameter details of each function call.

A message queue is created with the function call *OSQCreate(void **start, INT8U size)*, where *start* is the base address of the message storing area and *size* is the size of the message storage area in bytes. This function allocates an Event Control Block (ECB) to the message queue and returns a pointer of type *OS_EVENT* to the allocated ECB. A task can post a message to the message queue if the task knows the ECB pointer for the message queue. Along with the ECB pointer of the mailbox, the task passes a pointer to the message which is to be posted to the message queue, as argument to the *OSQPost(OS_EVENT *pevent, void *msg)* function. If there is no room for a message in the message queue when a task is trying to post a message, the task returns immediately. On the arrival of a message in the message queue, it is delivered to the highest priority task waiting for the event and the message is deleted from the message queue. If the priority of the highest priority task waiting for the message is higher than that of the message posting task, the message posting task is preempted and the highest priority task is executed by the scheduler. A task can broadcast a message to all tasks waiting for a message by posting the message with the function call *OSQPostOpt(OS_EVENT *pevent, void *msg, INT8U opt)*. The '*opt*' parameter should be set as *OS_POST_OPT_BROADCAST* for broadcasting a message. If this parameter is set as *OS_POST_OPT_NONE*, this function becomes equivalent to *OSQPost*. This function can also serve the purpose of the function *OSQPostFront()*, which posts the message to the front of the message queue. For this, set the '*opt*' parameter as *OS_POST_OPT_FRONT*. The functions *OSQPend()*, and *OQSAccept()* can be used for retrieving a message from the message queue. *OSQPend()* provides option to set the function call as either a blocking call till a message is available in the message queue or till a wait period specified in the parameter list. *OSQAccept()* is a non-blocking call. This function will not block a calling task when there is no message available in the message queue. This can be used by ISRs to check the availability of messages in a message queue. A task can delete a message queque by calling *OSQDel(OS_EVENT *pevent, INT8U opt, INT8U *err)*. The parameter '*opt*' specifies whether a message queue needs to be deleted immediately or only when the pending operations on this message queue are over. The value *OS_DEL_NO_PEND* for '*opt*' sets the first choice and a value *OS_DEL_ALWAYS* deletes the message queue immediately. Proper care should be applied in the usage of this function. There are possibilities for tasks to access a deleted message queue. This may result in unpredicted behaviour. Also tasks which are using the function *OSQAccept()* for checking the availability of a message may never know about the non-availability of a message queue. Hence use this function judiciously and as a precautionary measure delete all task which uses the specified message queue before it is being deleted.

Message queue and mailbox operates on the same principle. However message queue supports multiple messages and also provides option to post a message as urgent message, by posting it in front of the message queue. Mailbox holds only one message at a time and there is no provision to post a message to the mailbox until the existing message is read by a task. Message queue supports emptying of the message queue by flushing it.

11.2.5 Mutual Exclusion and Task Synchronisation

In multitasking environment multiple tasks execute concurrently and share the system resources and data. The access to shared resources should be made mutually exclusive to prevent data corruption and 'race' conditions. Synchronisation techniques are used by tasks to synchronise their execution. For example, one task may be waiting for a resource while it is being held by another task. The task which is currently holding the resource can inform the waiting tasks when it releases the resource. MicroC/OS-II provides exclusive access to shared resources through the following techniques.

1. Disabling task scheduling

2. Disabling interrupts
3. Semaphores for mutual exclusion
4. Events (Flags) for synchronisation

In a multitasking environment, problems arise only when a task is preempted by another task, when the task was accessing a shared resource and the task which preempted it also tries to access the resource. This may lead to inconsistent results. The easiest option to solve this problem is prevent task preemption by disabling the task scheduling when a task is accessing a shared resource. The task scheduling is re-enabled only when the task completes the accessing of the shared resource. Interrupts are still identified and serviced even if the scheduler is in the locked state. This technique is suited for controlling the access to resources shared between tasks and it will not serve the purpose of exclusive access of resources shared between a task and Interrupt Service Routine (ISR). The function calls *OSSchedLock()* and *OSSchedUnlock()* are used for locking and unlocking the scheduler respectively.

We have seen that the disabling of task scheduling will not serve the purpose of exclusive access to resources shared between a task and ISR. The interrupts should be disabled to ensure error-free operation when a task is executing in the critical section of code (The piece of code which corresponds to the shared resource access). The interrupts are re-enabled when the task complete the execution of the critical section code. Disabling and enabling of interrupts can be done by the MicroC/OS-II supplied macros; *OS_ENTER_CRITICAL()* and *OS_EXIT_CRITICAL()* respectively. The implementation of these macros is processor specific. These macros need to be ported as per the target processor specific implementation of Interrupt enabling and disabling. These macros are defined in the MicroC/OS-II header file '*os_cpu.h*'. The usage of these 'macros' are illustrated below.

```
//*************************************************************************
//Implementation of Task
void Task1(void *args)
{
while (1)
{
//Execute the task specific details
//..............................................................
//..............................................................
//Disable Interrupts
OS_ENTER_CRITICAL();
//Enter Critical section.
//Access shared resource
Counter++;
//Leave Critical section.
//Enable Interrupts
OS_EXIT_CRITICAL();
//Rest of the task
//..............................................................
//..............................................................
}
}
```

Here the variable 'Counter' is shared between a task and ISR. The accessing of it is made exclusive in the task by disabling the interrupt just before accessing the variable and re-enabling the interrupts when the operation on the variable is over.

Disabling of interrupts may produce adverse effects like impact on the real time response of the system. It is advised not to disable interrupts for critical section access operations which are lengthy.

Semaphore based mutual execution is the most efficient and easy technique for implementing exclusive resource access. Semaphores control the access to shared resources as well as synchronise the execution of tasks. The MicroC/OS-II supports two different types of semaphores namely counting semaphore and mutual exclusion semaphore (mutex).

The counting semaphore is used for restricting the access to shared resources and as a signalling mechanism for task synchronisation. It associates a count for keeping track of the number of tasks using the semaphore at a given point of time. It also holds a wait list queue for holding the tasks which are waiting for the semaphore. The following table gives a snapshot of the important counting semaphore related routines supported by MicroC/OS-II.

Function Call†	**Description**
OSSemCreate()	Creates and initialises a counting semaphore. It takes a count value as parameter. The count value can range from 0 to 65535. Each time the semaphore is acquired by a task its count is decremented by 1. When the count reaches 0, the semaphore is not available and the task trying to acquire the semaphore is pended (blocked).
OSSemPost()	Signals the availability of a semaphore. A task can use this call to inform the waiting task that the semaphore is available. The count associated with the semaphore is incremented by one. Upon executing this call the highest priority task waiting (If the count associated with the semaphore is 0) for this semaphore is granted access to the semaphore. If the priority of the task waiting for the semaphore is greater than that of the priority of the task signalled the availability of the semaphore, it is preempted.
OSSemPend()	Used by a task for acquiring a semaphore. If the semaphore is available (The count associated with the semaphore is greater than 0) at the time of calling this function, access is granted to the task and the count associated with the semaphore is decremented by one. If the semaphore is not available (The count associated with the semaphore is zero) at the time of calling this function, the calling task is blocked and it is put in the semaphore wait list queue associated with the semaphore. A task can wait until the semaphore is available or till a timeout occurs. The timeout value for waiting can be specified in the 'timeout' argument of this function call. The 'timeout' value is specified in terms of clock ticks. It can take values ranging from 0 to 65535. A value of 0 indicates wait until the semaphore is available.
OSSemAccept()	Used for acquiring a semaphore. Similar to *OSSemPend()* in functioning but differ in the way it operates. It allows a task to check whether a semaphore is available. Unlike *OSSemPend()*, the calling task is not blocked ('Pended') if the semaphore is not available.
OSSemQuery()	Retrieves the information about the semaphore. The information is retrieved in a data structure of type *OS_SEM_DATA*. It is used for getting information like, the semaphore count, whether a semaphore is available, is there any tasks waiting for the semaphore and if yes how many tasks etc.
OSSemSet()	It is used for changing the current count value associated with the semaphore. The count associated with the semaphore is reset to the value specified in the 'count' parameter to this function. If the semaphore count is 0 at the time of executing this call, the count is changed only if there are no tasks waiting for this semaphore. This function call is primarily used for signalling mechanism for task synchronisation and not for protecting shared resources.

† Please refer to the MicroC library reference manual for the parameter details of each function call.

OSSemDel()	Deletes a semaphore. Option for specifying whether the semaphore needs to be deleted immediately or only when the pending operations on this semaphore are over. Proper care should be applied in the usage of this function. There are possibilities for tasks to access a deleted semaphore. This may result in unpredicted behaviour.

The mutual exclusion semaphore or mutex is a binary semaphore. It differs from the ordinary semaphore in the sense it implements provisions for handling priority inversion problems in task scheduling. The mutual exclusion semaphore (mutex) temporarily raises the priority of a low priority task holding the mutex to a priority above the highest priority of the task which tries to acquire the mutex when it is being in use by a low priority task. The mutex object associates a flag to indicate whether the mutex object is available or currently in use and a priority to assign to the task owning the mutex, when another high priority task tries to acquire it. It also holds a waitlist queue for holding the tasks waiting for the mutex.

Normally the mutex object elevates the priority of a task holding it to a priority value same as that of the priority of the highest priority task trying to acquire it. However MicroC/OS-II doesn't support the existence of two tasks of the same priority. Hence a small work around is implemented to overcome this issue. Under MicroC/OS-II, the priority of the task holding the mutex is elevated to a value which is greater than the highest priority of the task which is trying to acquire it, when it is being held by a low priority task. The priority reserved to the mutex is known as *Priority Inheritance Priority* (*PIP*). PIP should be an unused priority by tasks. The following table gives a snapshot of the important mutual exclusion semaphore (mutex) related routines supported by MicroC/OS-II.

Function Call†	**Description**
OSMutexCreate()	Creates and initialises a mutex. It takes Priority Inheritance Priority (PIP) as one parameter. The mutex is created with state available (The flag associated with it is set as 1). On successful creation of the mutex a pointer to an Event Control Block (ECB) is returned.
OSMutexPend()	Used by a task for acquiring a mutex. If the mutex is available (The mutex value is 0xFF) at the time of calling this function, access is granted to the task and the mutex value is set to 0 to indicate the non-availability of mutex. If the mutex is not available (The mutex value is zero) at the time of calling this function, the calling task is blocked and it is put in the mutex wait list queue associated with the mutex. A task can wait until the mutex is available or till a timeout occurs. The timeout value for waiting can be specified in the 'timeout' argument of this function call. The 'timeout' value is specified in terms of clock ticks. It can take values ranging from 0 to 65535. A value of 0 indicates wait until the mutex is available.
OSMutexAccept()	Used for acquiring a mutex. Similar to *OSMutexPend()* in functioning but differ in the way it operates. It allows a task to check whether a mutex is available. The function returns 1 if the mutex is available, else returns 0. Unlike *OSMutexPend()*, the calling task is not blocked ('Pended') if the mutex is not available.
OSMutexPost()	Signals the availability of a mutex. A task can use this call to inform the waiting task that the mutex is available. The following actions take place on the execution of this call. 1. The flag associated with the mutex is set as 1, i.e. (Mutex value is set as 0xFF). 2. If the priority of the task holding the mutex was raised to the PIP, it is brought back to the original priority of the task. 3. If more than one task is waiting for the mutex, the mutex is given to the highest priority task and the flag associated with the mutex is set as 0 (Mutex value is set as 0x00) indicating mutex is not available. 4. If the priority of the task which acquired the mutex is greater than that of the task which released the mutex, the task which released the mutex is pended. 5. A rescheduling of tasks is performed.

† Please refer to the MicroC library reference manual for the parameter details of each function call.

OSMutexQuery()	Retrieves the information about the mutex. The information is retrieved in a data structure of type *OS_MUTEX_DATA*. It is used for getting information like, whether a mutex is available or not, What is the PIP for the mutex, is there any tasks waiting for the mutex and if yes how many tasks, etc.
OSMutexDel()	Deletes a mutex. Option for specifying whether the mutex needs to be deleted immediately or only when the pending operations on this mutex are over. Proper care should be applied in the usage of this function. There are possibilities for tasks to access a deleted mutex. This may result in unpredicted behaviour.

The following code snippet illustrates the usage of mutex.

```
//*****************************************************************
#include <includes.h>
//Define Task IDs for First Task, Task 1 and Task 2
#define TASK_FIRST_ID 1
#define TASK_1_ID 2
#define TASK_2_ID 3

//Define Task Priorities for First Task, Task 1 and Task 2
#define TASK_FIRST_PRIO 10
#define TASK_1_PRIO 11
#define TASK_2_PRIO 12

//Set the default stack size for all tasks
#define TASK_STK_SIZE      1024

//Define stack size for tasks
OS_STK TaskFirstStk[TASK_STK_SIZE];      // First task's stack
OS_STK Task1Stk[TASK_STK_SIZE];          // Task 1's task stack
OS_STK Task2Stk[TASK_STK_SIZE];          // Task 2's task stack

//Define ECB pointer for the mutex
OS_EVENT *MyMutex;

void main (void)
{
//Initialize MicroC OS
OSInit();

//Create the first task.
OSTaskCreateExt(TaskFirst,
               (void *)0,
               &TaskFirstStk[TASK_STK_SIZE - 1],
               TASK_FIRST_PRIO,
               TASK_FIRST_ID,
               &TaskStartStk[0],
               TASK_STK_SIZE,
               (void *) 0,
               OS_TASK_OPT_STK_CHK);
```

```
// Start multitasking
OSStart();

}

//****************************************************************
//Implementation of TaskFirst
void TaskFirst(void *args)
{
//Variable for holding function return values
INT8U err;
//Initialize statistics task
OSStatInit();
//Create Mutex with PIP 9
MyMutex = OSMutexCreate(9,&err);
//Create Task1
OSTaskCreateExt(Task1,
               (void *)0,
               &Task1Stk[TASK_STK_SIZE - 1],
               TASK_1_PRIO,
               TASK_1_ID,
               &Task1Stk[0],
               TASK_STK_SIZE,
               (void *) 0,
               OS_TASK_OPT_STK_CHK);

//Create Task2
OSTaskCreateExt(Task2,
               (void *)0,
               &Task2Stk[TASK_STK_SIZE - 1],
               TASK_2_PRIO,
               TASK_2_ID,
               &Task2Stk[0],
               TASK_STK_SIZE,
               (void *) 0,
               OS_TASK_OPT_STK_CHK);
while (1)
{
//Do Nothing. Simply sleep for one timer tick
OSTimeDly(OS_TICKS_PER_SEC);
}
}
//****************************************************************
//Implementation of Task1
void Task1(void *args)
{
//Variable for holding function return values
INT8U err;
while (1)
```

```
{
//Execute the task specific details
//..............................................
//..............................................
//Acquire Mutex
OSMutexPend(MyMutex, 0, &err);
//Code for accessing Shared Resource
//..............................................
//Release Mutex
OSMutexPost(MyMutex);
//Rest of the task
//..............................................
//..............................................
}
}
//*****************************************************************
//Implementation of Task2
void Task2(void *args)
{
//Variable for holding function return values
INT8U err;
while (1)
{
//Execute the task specific details
//..............................................
//..............................................
//Acquire Mutex
OSMutexPend(MyMutex,0,&err);
//Code for accessing Shared Resource
//..............................................
//Release Mutex
OSMutexPost(MyMutex);
//Rest of the task
//..............................................
//..............................................
}
}
```

The sample application creates a main task *TaskFirst* with priority 10, which creates a mutex *MyMutex* with PIP 9 and two tasks namely *Task1* (with priority 11) and *Task2* (with priority 12). *Task1* and *Task2* contain critical section access. The mutex *MyMutex* is used for acquiring exclusive access to the critical section. Each task releases the mutex after they exit the critical section of code.

It is possible to associate a name to the Event Control Block (ECB) which is associated with a semaphore, mailbox, message queue or a mutex object. The function call *OSEventNameSet (OS_EVENT *pevent, char *pname, INT8U *err)* associates the name holding by the character string pointed by *pname* to the entity pointed by the ECB pointer *pevent*. Similarly the function *OSEventNameSGet (OS_EVENT *pevent, char *pname, INT8U *err)* retrieves the name associated with the object pointed by the ECB pointer *pevent* into a character string pointed by *pname*. These functions are mainly used for associating a name with a resource for debugging purpose.

Event flags are another mechanism supported by MicroC/OS-II for task synchronisation. You can create a group of event flags and can assign specific meaning to each bit present in the event flags group. Tasks or Tasks and ISRs can modify or access these event flag bits to synchronise their execution. The following table gives a snapshot of the important event flag related routines supported by MicroC/OS-II for task synchronisation.

Function Call†	Description
OSFlagCreate()	Creates and initialises an event flag group. It takes the initial value that needs to be set for flags as one parameter. Successful creation of the event flag group returns a pointer to the Event Flag Group (*OS_FLAG_GRP*) associated with the event flag group.
OSFlagPost()	Sets or clears the individual flag bits in the event flag group. A task can make another task ready by setting the event flag bit pattern expected by the other task. The *OSFlagPost* function call readies each task that has its desired bits satisfied by this call. The 'flags' parameter of the function call specifies which all bits to be set or reset and the parameter 'opt' specifies whether the operation is a set or reset. For setting the bits, this parameter is set as *OS_FLAG_SET* and for clearing, it is set as *OS_FLAG_CLR*. For example for setting the 0th, 3rd and 5th bit, set the 'flags' parameter as 0x29 (00101001) and 'opt' parameter as *OS_FLAG_SET*. If the priority of the task waiting for the specified bit pattern is greater than that of the priority of the task signalled the availability of the specified bit pattern, it is preempted.
OSFlagPend()	Used by a task to wait for the arrival of a specific combination of flag bits in the event flag group. The 'flags' parameter of the function call specifies which all event flag bits to be checked and the parameter 'opt' specifies the type of event bit checking. It can be any one of the following type. 1. *OS_FLAG_WAIT_CLR_ALL* : Check all specified bits in the flags is clear (0) 2. *OS_FLAG_WAIT_CLR_ANY* : Check any specified bit in the flags is clear (0) 3. *OS_FLAG_WAIT_SET_ALL* : Check all specified bits in the flags is set (1) 4. *OS_FLAG_WAIT_SET_ANY* : Check any specified bit in the flags is set (1) The flag *OS_FLAG_CONSUME* can be combined with the above flag to clear the bits of the flag group when the specified condition occurs. For example a task can use *OS_FLAG_WAIT_SET_ANY + OS_FLAG_CONSUME* to wait for the setting of any specified flag bit and the flag bits are automatically reset (cleared) when the condition occurs. If the priority of the task waiting for the specified bit pattern is greater than that of the priority of the task signalled the availability of the specified bit pattern, it is preempted. If the event flag bits satisfy the conditions specified by the task, the task is readied. If the event flag bits don't satisfy the conditions specified by the task, at the time of calling this function, the calling task is blocked and it is put in the event flag wait list queue associated with the event flags group. A task can wait until the specified flag pattern arrives or till a timeout occurs. The timeout value for waiting can be specified in the 'timeout' argument of this function call. The 'timeout' value is specified in terms of clock ticks. It can take values ranging from 0 to 65535. A value of 0 indicates wait until the specified event flag condition occurs.
OSFlagAccept()	Used for checking the occurrence of a specified flag bit pattern in the event flag group. Similar to *OSFlagPend()* in functioning but differ in the way it operates. It allows a task to check whether the specified bit pattern is available. Unlike *OSFlagPend()*, the calling task is not blocked ('Pended') if the specified flag event is not occurred.

† Please refer to the MicroC library reference manual for the parameter details of each function call.

OSFlagPendGetFlagsRdy()	Returns the flag value that made the task ready from blocked state.
OSFlagQuery()	Retrieves the current value of the event flags in the event flags group. The function returns the state of the flag bits in the event group.
OSFlagNameSet()	Associates a name with the specified event flag group. The name is passed as a character pointer. This function is mainly used for associating a name with a resource for debugging purpose.
OSFlagNameGet()	Retrieves the name associated with the specified event flag group. The name is retrieved in a character pointer, which is passed as argument to this function. This function is mainly used for associating a name with a resource for debugging purpose.
OSFlagDel()	Deletes an event flags group. Option for specifying whether the event flags group needs to be deleted immediately or only when the pending operations on this event flags group are over. Proper care should be applied in the usage of this function. There are possibilities for tasks to access a deleted event flags group. This may result in unpredicted behaviour.

The following code snippet illustrates the usage of event flags.

```
//*******************************************************************
#include <includes.h>

//Define Task IDs for First Task, Task 1 and Task 2
#define TASK_FIRST_ID 1
#define TASK_1_ID 2
#define TASK_2_ID 3

//Define Task Priorities for First Task, Task 1 and Task 2
#define TASK_FIRST_PRIO 10
#define TASK_1_PRIO 12
#define TASK_2_PRIO 11

//Set the default stack size for all tasks
#define TASK_STK_SIZE     1024

//Define stack size for tasks
OS_STK TaskFirstStk[TASK_STK_SIZE];    // First task's stack
OS_STK Task1Stk[TASK_STK_SIZE];        // Task 1's task stack
OS_STK Task2Stk[TASK_STK_SIZE];        // Task 2's task stack

//Define Even Flags Group pointer for the mutex
OS_FLAG_GRP *StatusFlags;

void main (void)
{
//Initialize MicroC OS
OSInit();

//Create the first task.
OSTaskCreateExt(TaskFirst,
```

```
              (void *)0,
              &TaskFirstStk[TASK_STK_SIZE - 1],
              TASK_FIRST_PRIO,
              TASK_FIRST_ID,
              &TaskStartStk[0],
              TASK_STK_SIZE,
              (void *) 0,
              OS_TASK_OPT_STK_CHK);
// Start multitasking
OSStart();

}

//*********************************************************************
//Implementation of TaskFirst
void TaskFirst(void *args)
{
//Variable for holding function return values
INT8U err;
//Initialize statistics task
OSStatInit();
//Create the event flag group with all flags in reset state.
StatusFlags = OSFlagCreate(0x00, &err);
//Create Task1
OSTaskCreateExt(Task1,
              (void *)0,
              &Task1Stk[TASK_STK_SIZE - 1],
              TASK_1_PRIO,
              TASK_1_ID,
              &Task1Stk[0],
              TASK_STK_SIZE,
              (void *) 0,
              OS_TASK_OPT_STK_CHK);

//Create Task2
OSTaskCreateExt(Task2,
              (void *)0,
              &Task2Stk[TASK_STK_SIZE - 1],
              TASK_2_PRIO,
              TASK_2_ID,
              &Task2Stk[0],
              TASK_STK_SIZE,
              (void *) 0,
              OS_TASK_OPT_STK_CHK);
while (1)
{
//Do Nothing. Simply sleep for one timer tick
OSTimeDly(OS_TICKS_PER_SEC);
}
}
```

```
//*****************************************************************
//Implementation of Task1
void Task1(void *args)
{
//Variable for holding function return values
INT8U err;
while (1)
{
//Execute the task specific details
//.......................................................
//.......................................................
//Set the Flag bits 0, 2
OSFlagPost(StatusFlags, 0x05, &err);
//Rest of the task
//.......................................................
//.......................................................
}
}

//*****************************************************************
//Implementation of Task2
void Task2(void *args)
{
//Variable for holding function return values
INT8U err;
while (1)
{
//Execute the task specific details
//.......................................................
//.......................................................
//Wait for the signaling of either flag bit 0 or 2
OSFlagPend(StatusFlags, OS_FLAG_WAIT_SET_ANY,0, &err);
if (OS_NO_ERR == err)
{
//Find out the flag bit value readied the task and print it
err = OSFlagPendGetFlagsRdy();
printf("The Flag state readied the task is %x", err);
}
else
{
//Rest of the task
//.......................................................
//.......................................................
}
}
}
```

The sample application creates a main task *TaskFirst* with priority 10, which creates an event flag group *StatusFlags* and two tasks namely *Task1* (with priority 12) and *Task2* (with priority 11). *Task2* requires the signalling of two flags to continue its execution. At some point of execution *Task2* waits for the occurring of any one of the specified event. *Task1* sets the flags at some point of its execution. Since the priority of *Task2* is higher than that of *Task1*, *Task2* preempts *Task1* when the signalling of event flag occurs. *Task2* also prints the event flag bits value which made *Task2* 'Ready' for execution.

The flag based task execution synchronisation is the best choice for synchronising the execution of cooperating tasks which requires the occurring of a particular sequence of operation for completion. A typical example is a 'Smart Card Reader' interfaced with a PC. The card reading operation can be controlled from an application running on the PC. Obviously there are two tasks running in the Smart Card Reader Device. Task 1, 'The Communication task', checks the serial port or USB port to receive the commands from PC. The second task 'The card Reading task' waits until a command is received from the PC, to continue its operation. The 'Communication task' can inform the 'Card reading task' that a command is received, by setting a flag in the event flags group.

11.2.6 Timing and Reference

The 'Clock Tick' acts as the time source for providing timing reference for time delays and timeouts. 'Clock Tick' generates periodic interrupts. The clock ticker interrupt should be enabled for handling the clock ticks. The clock tick ISR (*OSTickISR(void)*) calls the function *OSTimeTick()* to service the clock tick interrupt. The *OS_TICKS_PER_SEC* configuration parameter should be set properly for the proper functioning of the system timer. It defines how many clock ticks are there in one second. It depends on the clock frequency of the target board. The functions which relay upon *OSTimeTick()* are summarised in the table given below.

Function Call†	Description
OSTimeDly()	Delay the task for the specified duration. The delay is mentioned in number of clock ticks. It ranges from 0 to 65535 ticks.
OSTimeDlyHMSM()	Delay the task for the specified duration. The delay time is specified by the combination of hours (H), Minutes (M), Seconds (S) and Milliseconds (M). Hour value can range from 0 to 255, Minutes value can range from 0 to 59, second's value can range from 0 to 59 and millisecond value can range from 0 to 999. Resolution depends on clock rate.
OSTimeDlyResume()	Resumes a task which is delayed by a call to either *OSTimeDly()* or *OSTimeDlyHMSM()*.
OSTimeGet()	Returns the current value of the system clock. System clock is a 32 bit counter and it accumulates the clock tick numbers since a power on or a system reset.
OSTimeSet()	Sets the value for the system clock counter.

11.2.7 Memory Management

MicroC/OS-II supports runtime memory allocation and de-allocation on a need basis. The memory is divided into multiple sectors (partitions). Each sector is further divided into blocks. Each block holds fixed bytes of memory. Figure 11.1 illustrates the same.

Each partition contains a minimum of two memory blocks. The block size is uniform throughout a partition. Each memory partition associates a memory control block (MCB) with it. The following table gives a snapshot of various function calls supported by uC/OS-II for memory management.

† Please refer to the MicroC library reference manual for the parameter details of each function call.

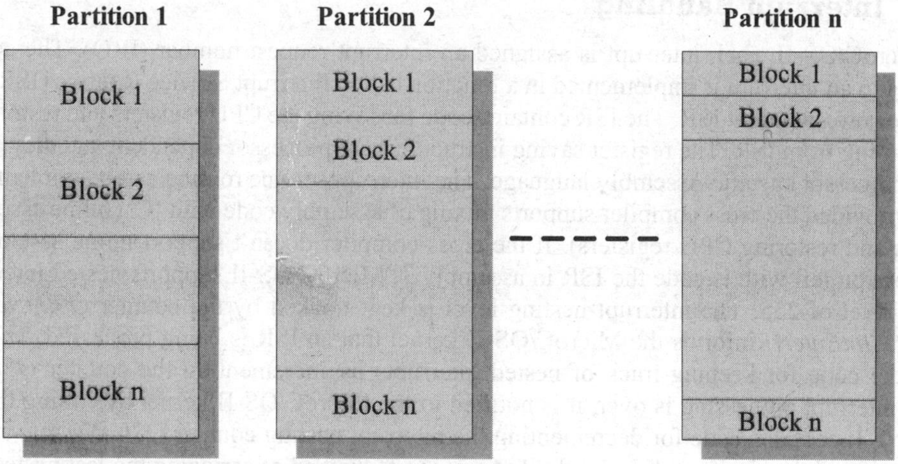

Fig. 11.1 **Memory partitioning under Micro C/OS-II**

Function Call	Description
*OSMemCreate(void *addr, INT32U nblks, INT32U blksize, INT8U *err)*	Creates and initialises a memory partition. The parameter *addr* specifies the start address of the partition, *nblks* specifies the number of blocks in the partition and *blksize* specifies the size of the block. On successful creation of memory partition, the function returns a pointer to the created memory partition control block.
*OSMemGet(OS_MEM *pmem, INT8U *err)*	Acquires a memory block from a partition. *pmem* is a pointer to the memory partition control block which is obtained while creating the memory partition. If the memory block is allocated, this function returns a pointer to the allocated memory block.
*OSMemPut(OS_MEM *pmem, void *pblk)*	Releases the specified memory block to the memory partition. *pmem* is a pointer to the memory partition control block which is obtained while creating the memory partition and *pblk* is the pointer to the memory block to be released. Returns the code *OS_NO_ERR* if the memory block de-allocation is success.
*OSMemQuery(OS_MEM *pmem, OS_MEM_DATA *pdata)*	Retrieves the information about a memory partition. The information is retrieved in a data structure of type *OS_MEM_DATA*. It is used for getting information like, the start address of memory partition, number of memory blocks in the partition, size of a memory block, number of used memory blocks, number of free memory blocks, etc.
*OSMemNameSet(OS_MEM *pmem, char *pname, INT8U *err)*	Associates a name with the specified memory partition. The name is passed as a character pointer *pname*. This function is mainly used for associating a name with a resource for debugging purpose.
*OSMemNameGSet(OS_MEM *pmem, char *pname, INT8U *err)*	Retrieves the name associated with the specified memory partition. The name is retrieved in a character pointer *pname*, which is passed as argument to this function. This function is mainly used for associating a name with a resource for debugging purpose.

11.2.8 Interrupt Handling

Under MicroC/OS-II, each interrupt is assigned an interrupt request number (IRQ). The actions corresponding to an interrupt is implemented in a function called Interrupt Service Routine (ISR).The IRQ links to the corresponding ISR. The ISR contains code for saving the CPU registers and restoring it back when returning from ISR. The register saving instructions are processor dependent and they are usually coded in processor specific Assembly language. The interrupt service routine can be implemented in C function, provided the cross compiler supports mixing of assembly code with 'C' (Inline assembly code for saving and restoring CPU registers). If the cross-compiler doesn't support inline assembly codes, the only option left with is code the ISR in assembly☹. MicroC/OS-II supports nested interrupts with a nesting level of 255. The interrupt nesting level is kept tracked by the counter *OSIntNesting*. The function *OSIntEnter()* informs the MicroC/OS-II kernel that an ISR is being processed. This function contains the code for keeping track of nested interrupts by incrementing the counter *OSIntNesting*. When an interrupt processing is over, it is notified to the MicroC/OS-II kernel by calling the function *OSIntExit()*. It contains code for decrementing the interrupt nesting counter *OSIntNesting* and task re-scheduling if a high priority task is 'ready' for running at the end of servicing the last nested interrupt. The ISR returns to the interrupted task if there is no high priority task 'ready' for running at the time of execution completion. If there is a high priority task 'ready' for running at the time of ISR completion, the execution is not returned to the low priority task which is preempted by the ISR. Instead it executes the high priority task. The implementation of an ISR is illustrated below.

```
//*******************************************************************
//Implementation of Interrupt
void interrupt xyzInterrupt(int vector)
{
_asm
//Assembly instructions to save (PUSH) CPU registers
//..............................................................
//..............................................................
_endasm
//Track Interrupt nesting
OSIntEnter();
//Execute the ISR specific code
//..............................................................
//..............................................................
//Return from ISR
OSIntExit();
_asm
//Assembly instructions to retrieve (POP) CPU registers
//..............................................................
//..............................................................
_endasm
}
}
```

The keyword *interrupt* identifies a function as Interrupt Service Routine (ISR). The parameter *vector* specifies the interrupt vector address corresponding to the ISR. It should be noted that an ISR neither takes and nor returns any variables. All CPU registers are saved (PUSHed) to the stack of the task which is interrupted by the ISR. However certain processor architecture like Motorola 68030 requires a separate stack for ISR.

11.2.9 The MicroC/OS-II Development Environment

Various processor manufacturers, who develop the MicroC/OS-II port for their product, may also supply an IDE for MicroC based development. The Nios® II IDE from Altera (www.altera.com) is an IDE supplied by Altera for their Nios® II family of processors. Some third party developers also provide IDE for MicroC/OS-II development for various processor architectures. The Micro-IDE is an example for a 3rd party development tool. It supports Micro C compilers 6808, 6809, 6811, 6812, 6816, AVR, 8051/52, 8080/85, 8086 and 8096.

Summary

- ✓ VxWorks is a POSIX compliant popular hard real time, multitasking operating system from Wind River Systems. The kernel of VxWorks is popularly known as *wind*
- ✓ Under VxWorks kernel, the tasks may be in one of the primary states 'READY', 'PEND', 'DELAY', 'SUSPEND' or a specific combination of it at any given point of time
- ✓ VxWorks supports priority levels from 0 to 255, with 0 being the highest priority, for tasks. VxWorks' scheduler implements the pre-emptive priority based scheduling of tasks with Round Robin scheduling for priority resolution among equal priority tasks
- ✓ The kernel functionalities of 'VxWorks' is also implemented as tasks and they are known as system tasks. The root task *tUsrRoot* is the first task executed by the scheduler. The function *usrRoot()* is the entry point to this task
- ✓ VxWorks implements Inter Task communication through shared memory, message queues, pipes, sockets, Remote Procedure Call (RPC) and signals
- ✓ VxWorks' kernel follows a single linear address space for tasks. The data can be shared in the form of global variable, linear buffer, linked list and ring buffer
- ✓ VxWorks implements mutual exclusion policies in three different ways namely; Task Locking (Disabling task preemption), Disabling Interrupts, Locking resource with semaphores
- ✓ VxWorks supports three types of semaphores namely; Binary semaphore, counting semaphore and mutual exclusion semaphore
- ✓ Under VxWorks kernel, Interrupt Service Routines (ISRs) run at a special context outside any task's context. A separate stack is maintained for use by all ISRs
- ✓ The watchdog timer interface provided by VxWorks kernel can be utilised for monitoring task execution. The watchdog timeout is handled as part of the system clock ISR. User can associate a 'C' function with the watchdog timeout handler
- ✓ Wind River Workbench is the development environment from Wind River Systems for VxWorks development
- ✓ MicroC/OS-II is a portable, ROMable, scalable, preemptive, real-time, multitasking kernel from Micrium Inc
- ✓ MicroC/OS-II follows the task based execution model and each task is implemented as infinite loop. Under MicroC/OS-II kernel, the tasks may be in one of the states *Ready*, *Running*, *Waiting*, *Interrupted* at a given point of time
- ✓ MicroC/OS-II supports tasks up to 64. Out of this 8 are reserved for the MicroC/OS-II kernel. Each task will have a unique task priority assigned. No two tasks can have the same priority

- ✓ The OS kernel initialisation function *OSInit()* is the first task executed by MicroC kernel. It initialises the different OS kernel data structure and creates the Idle task *OSIdle()*. The Idle task is the lowest priority task under the MicroC/OS-II kernel and it is executed to keep the CPU always busy when there are no user tasks to execute.
- ✓ MicroC/OS-II executes a statistical task with priority *OS_LOWEST_PRIO – 1* in every second to capture the percentage of CPU usage.
- ✓ The MicroC/OS-II supports preemptive priority based scheduling. Each task is assigned a unique priority ranging from 0 to 63 with 0 being the highest priority level. The four highest priorities (0 to 3) and the four lowest priorities (63 to OS_LOWEST_PRIO – 3) are reserved for the kernel
- ✓ The MicroC/OS-II kernel starts executing the first available highest priority task and a task re-scheduling happens whenever a task enters the 'Waiting' state due to the invocation of system calls, and whenever an Interrupt occurs, the tasks are rescheduled upon return from the Interrupt Service Routine
- ✓ The MicroC/OS-II kernel supports Inter Task Communication through mailbox and message queues.
- ✓ The MicroC/OS-II kernel implements mutual exclusion through disabling task scheduling, disabling interrupts, using semaphores and events
- ✓ MicroC/OS-II supports two different types of semaphores, namely, counting semaphore and mutual exclusion semaphore (mutex)
- ✓ Under MicroC/OS-II, the 'Clock Tick' acts as the time source for providing timing reference for time delays and timeouts. 'Clock Tick' generates periodic interrupts
- ✓ Under MicroC/OS-II, each interrupt is assigned an Interrupt Request number (IRQ). The actions corresponding to an interrupt is implemented in a function called Interrupt Service Routine (ISR). The IRQ links to the corresponding ISR
- ✓ The Micro-IDE is an example for 3rd party development tool for MicroC/OS-II

Keywords

VxWorks : A popular hard real-time, multitasking operating system from Wind River Systems

wind : The kernel of VxWorks

Task Scheduling : The act of allocating the CPU to different tasks

Kernel : A set of services which forms the heart of an operating system

Message Queue : An inter-task communication mechanism used in VxWorks. It comprises queue for sending and receiving messages

Pipe : A message queue based IPC mechanism under VxWorks

Socket : The mechanism utilised by VxWorks to communicate between processes running on different targets which are networked and for executing a procedure (function) which is part of another process running on the same CPU or on a different CPU within the network

Signals : A form of software event notification based Inter Process Mechanism supported by VxWorks

Mutual Exclusion Semaphore : A binary semaphore implementation under VxWorks kernel, which implements mechanisms to prevent priority inversion

Watchdog Timer : A special timer implementation for monitoring the task execution time and triggering precautionary actions in case the execution exceeds the allowed time

Tornado® II : The VxWorks development environment from Wind River Systems

MicroC/OS-II : A portable, ROMable, scalable, preemptive, real-time, multitasking kernel from Micrium Inc

Mailbox : An IPC mechanism supported by MicroC/OS-II kernel, for exchanging a single message between two tasks or between an ISR and a task

Objective Questions

1. Which of the following is true about VxWorks OS
   (a) Hard real-time (b) Soft real-time (c) Multitasking (d) (a) and (c)
   (e) (b) and (c)
2. A task is waiting for a semaphore for its operation. Under VxWorks task state terminology, the task is said to be in ________ state
   (a) READY (b) RUNNING (c) PEND (d) SUSPEND
   (e) None of these
3. Under VxWorks kernel the state of a task which is currently executing is changed to SUSPEND. Which of the following system call might have occurred?
   (a) *taskSpawn()* (b) *taskActivate()* (c) *taskSuspend()* (d) *msgQSend()*
   (e) None of these
4. Under VxWorks kernel the state of a task is SUSPEND. Which of the following statement is true?
   (a) It is a new task created with system call *taskInit()* and not yet activated
   (b) It is a new task created with system call *taskSpawn()* and not yet activated
   (c) The task is suspended by the system call *taskSuspend()*
   (d) Execution of the task created some exception
   (e) All of the above (f) Only (a), (c) and (d) (g) Only (b), (c) and (d)
5. Which of the following is not part of a task's context under standard VxWorks kernel?
   (a) Program counter (b) CPU Registers (c) Memory address space (d) Signal Handlers
   (e) None of these
6. Under VxWorks kernel, executing the system call *kernelTimeSlice (0)* produces the impact
   (a) The scheduling becomes pre-emptive priority based with Round Robin for Priority resolution
   (b) The scheduling becomes pre-emptive priority based with no priority resolution
   (c) The scheduling becomes Round Robin (d) None of these
7. What is the priority level supported by VxWorks for tasks?
   (a) 10 (b) 255 (c) 256 (d) Unlimited
8. Which of the following is(are) true about the system call *taskDelete()*
   (a) Terminates a specified task (b) Frees the task memory occupied by stack
   (c) Frees the memory occupied by the task control block
   (d) Frees the memory allocated by the task during its execution
   (e) All of these (f) Only (a), (b) and (c)
9. Which is the first task executed by VxWorks kernel on a system boot-up?
   (a) *tNetTask* (b) *tUsrRoot* (c) *tRlogind* (d) *tWdbTask*
10. Which of the following is not an IPC mechanism supported by VxWorks
    (a) Shared memory (b) Message queue (c) mailslot (d) Sockets
11. While executing a task under VxWorks kernel, an address error exception occurred. Which of the following actions are performed by the default exception handler service?
    (a) The task caused the error is suspended
    (b) The state of the task at the point of exception is saved (c) Initiates a system reset
    (d) All of these (e) Only (a) and (b)
12. Which of the following is not a mechanism supported by VxWorks for Inter Task Synchronisation?
    (a) Binary semaphore (b) Test and set (c) Counting semaphore
    (d) Mutual exclusion semaphore
13. Which of the following is true about the scheduler locking based synchronisation under VxWorks kernel?
    (a) May lead to unacceptable real-time response (b) May increase interrupt latency
    (c) Both of these (d) None of these

14. The mutual exclusion semaphore under VxWorks kernel is a type of
    (a) Counting semaphore (b) Binary semaphore
15. The mutual exclusion semaphore prevents priority inversion by
    (a) Priority ceiling (b) Priority inheritance
16. Which of the following is true about Interrupt Service Routine under VxWorks kernel
    (a) It runs in a separate context
    (b) It runs on the same context as that of the interrupted task
    (c) It depends on the processor architecture in which the VxWorks kernel is running
    (d) None of these
17. Which of the following is true about the stack implementation for ISR under VxWorks?
    (a) All ISRs share a common stack
    (b) The ISR uses the stack of the interrupted task
    (c) It depends on the processor architecture in which the kernel is running
    (d) None of these
18. What is the priority levels supported by MicroC/OS-II kernel
    (a) 64 (b) 56 (c) 256 (d) Unlimited
19. Which of the following is true about task scheduling under MicroC/OS-II kernel
    (a) Priority based pre-emptive scheduling
    (b) Priority based non-preemptive scheduling
    (c) Round Robin
    (d) Pre-emptive priority based with Round Robin for priority resolution
20. Which of the following is not true about tasks under MicroC/OS-II kernel
    (a) Supports multiple tasks with same priority (b) ISRs are allowed to create tasks
    (c) The stack can be specified as either upward growing or downward growing
    (d) All of these (e) Only (a) and (b) (f) Only (a) and (c) (g) Only (b) and (c)
21. Under MicroC/OS-II kernel changes its state from 'RUNNING' to 'WAITING', which of the following conditions might have invoked this?
    (a) The task attempted to acquire a shared resource which is currently in use by another task
    (b) The task involves some I/O operation and is waiting for I/O
    (c) The task undergoes sleeping
    (d) The task is suspended by itself or by another task
    (e) Any one of these (f) None of these
22. Which is the MicroC function responsible for initialising the different OS kernel data structure
    (a) *OSInit()* (b) *OSStart()* (c) *OSIdle()* (d) None of these
23. Which of the following is not an IPC mechanism under MicroC/OS-II kernel
    (a) Message queue (b) Mailbox (c) Pipes (d) None of these
24. Which is the function call used by an ISR to indicate the occurrence of an interrupt to the MicroC/OS-II kernel
    (a) *Interrupt* (b) *OSIntEnter* (c) *OSIntExit* (d) *OSIntNesting*
25. Under the MicroC/OS-II kernel, the ISR for normal processor architecture makes use of which stack?
    (a) Stack of the Interrupted Task (b) Separate stack
    (c) A mix of a separate stack and stack of interrupted task
    (d) ISR doesn't use any stack

Review Questions

1. Explain 'task' in 'VxWorks' context? Explain the different possible states of a task under VxWorks kernel.
2. Explain the state transition under VxWorks kernel with a state transition diagram. Give an example for the scenarios for each state transitions.

3. Explain the task creation and management under VxWorks kernel.
4. Explain the difference between *taskInit()* and *taskSpawn()* system calls for task creation under VxWorks kernel.
5. Explain the task scheduling supported by VxWorks kernel.
6. Explain the priority based pre-emptive scheduling with Round Robin scheduling for priority resolution under VxWorks, with execution diagram for the following:
   (a) There are 3 tasks T1, T2 and T3 with priority 15 READY to run and the execution time for the tasks are 20, 15 and 20 Timer Tick respectively
   (b) The Time slice for Round Robin scheduling is 5 timer ticks
   (c) The scheduler selects the tasks in the order T1,T3,T2 for Round Robin execution
   (d) After 7 timer ticks, task 4 with priority 14 and execution completion time 10 becomes 'READY'
7. Explain the exception handling mechanisms for tasks and interrupts under VxWorks kernel
8. Explain how a task can be made safe from unwanted deletion under VxWorks kernel, when it is holding a system resource
9. Explain the kernel services of VxWorks
10. Explain the different types of Inter Process Communication Mechanisms supported by VxWorks
11. Explain the implementation of a two-way message queue between two tasks under VxWorks kernel, with a block diagram
12. Explain the different mutual exclusion mechanisms supported by VxWorks. State the relative merits and limitations of each
13. What is semaphore? Explain the different types of semaphores supported by VxWorks
14. Explain how a mutual exclusion semaphore prevents priority inversion in task execution under VxWorks kernel
15. Explain the different system calls for *wind* message queue creation and management under VxWorks kernel
16. Explain the different system calls for POSIX standard message queue creation and management under VxWorks kernel
17. Explain pipe based IPC implementation under VxWorks kernel. How is it different form the message queue based IPC?
18. Explain the 'Signals' based IPC implementation under VxWorks kernel
19. Explain the interrupt handling mechanism under VxWorks kernel
20. Explain how a 'C function' can be used as the ISR for an interrupt under VxWorks
21. Under VxWorks it is required to mask interrupts with priority less than 2 while allowing the other interrupts to be serviced. Explain how it can be achieved?
22. Explain the watchdog timer operation under VxWorks kernel
23. Explain the time delay generation under VxWorks kernel
24. Explain the different possible states of a task under MicroC/OS-II kernel
25. Explain the state transition under MicroC/OS-II kernel with a state transition diagram. Give an example for the scenarios for each state transitions
26. Explain the task creation and management under MicroC/OS-II kernel
27. Explain the task scheduling supported by MicroC/OS-II kernel
28. Explain the kernel functions and initialisation under MicroC/OS-II kernel
29. Explain the role of Idle Task under MicroC/OS-II kernel
30. Explain the different types of Inter Task Communication mechanisms supported by MicroC/OS-II kernel
31. Explain the different mutual exclusion mechanisms supported by MicroC/OS-II kernel. State the relative merits and limitations of each
32. Explain the different types of semaphores supported by MicroC/OS-II kernel
33. Explain the *event* based task synchronisation under MicroC/OS-II kernel
34. Compare the *signal* based synchronisation under VxWorks and *event* based task synchronisation under MicroC/OS-II kernel
35. Compare the VxWorks and MicroC/OS-II kernel
36. Explain the time delay generation under MicroC/OS-II kernel
37. Explain the dynamic memory management under MicroC/OS-II kernel
38. Explain the Interrupt handling mechanism supported by MicroC/OS-II kernel

Lab Assignments

1. Write a VxWorks multitasking application to create two tasks as per the following requirements
   (a) The stack size for both the tasks are 2000
   (b) Priority for both the tasks are 100
   (c) Task 1 prints the message "Hello from Task 1" continuously with a delay of 500 timer ticks between successive printing
   (d) Task 2 prints the message "Hello from Task 2" continuously with a delay of 500 timer ticks between successive printing
2. Write a VxWorks multitasking application to retrieve and change the POSIX priority assigned to the tasks as per the following requirements
   (a) Create two tasks with names "Task1" and "Task2" respectively. The stack size for both the tasks are 2000
   (b) Priority for both the tasks are initially set at 100
   (c) Task1 is spawned first and then Task2
   (d) Task1 retrieves its priority and prints it on the console and then changes it to current priority-1, if the current priority is an even number, else changes to priority+1
   (e) Task2 retrieves its priority and prints it on the console and then changes it to current priority-1, if the current priority is an even number, else changes to priority+1
   (f) Use Round Robin scheduling with time slice 20 timer tick for priority resolution
3. An embedded application involves reading data from an Analog to Digital Converter. The ADC indicates the availability of data by asserting the interrupt line which is connected to the processor of the system. The interrupt vector for the external interrupt line to which the ADC is interfaced is 0x0003. The ISR for the external interrupt reads the data and stores it in a shared buffer of size 512 bytes. The received data is processed by a task. The task reads the data and prints it on the console. The communication between the ISR and task is synchronised using a binary semaphore. The task waits for the availability of the binary semaphore and the ISR signals the availability of the binary semaphore when an interrupt occurs and the data is read from the device. Write an application to implement this requirement under VxWorks kernel
4. Re-write the message queue example given under the Inter Task Communication section of VxWorks for posting the message as a high priority message
5. Create a POSIX based message queue under VxWorks for communicating between two tasks as per the requirements given below
   (a) Use a named message queue with name "MyQueue"
   (b) Create two tasks (Task1 and Task2) with stack size 4000 and priorities 99 and 100 respectively
   (c) Task1 creates the specified message queue as Read Write and reads the message present, if any, from the message queue and prints it on the console
   (d) Task2 opens the message queue and posts the message "Hi From Task2"
   (e) Handle all possible error scenarios appropriately
6. Implement the above requirements with 'notification' based POSIX message queue (**Hint:** Use signal for handling the notification)
7. Write a VxWorks application as per the requirements given below
   (a) Three tasks with names Task1, Task2 and Task3 with priorities 100, 99 and 98 respectively are created with stack size 2000
   (b) Task1 checks the availability of a binary semaphore 'binarySem' and if it is available, it prints the message "Hi from Task1" 50 times and then releases the binary semaphore and completes its execution
   (c) Task2 prints the message "Hi from Task2" 50 times and completes its execution
   (d) Task3 checks the availability of a binary semaphore 'binarySem' and if it is available, it prints the message "Hi from Task2" 50 times and then releases the binary semaphore and completes its execution

(e) The tasks are spawned in the order Task1, Task2 and Task3
(f) Handle all possible error scenarios appropriately

Observe the output and record your inference on the behaviour of the program

8. Write a complete MicroC program for implementing multitasking as per the following requirements
   (a) Create two tasks with names Task1 and Task2 with stack size 1024 and priorities 9 and 10 respectively
   (b) Task1 prints the message "Hi from Task1" (Assume that the compiler in use has a MicroC library implementation for the printf() function tailored for the target processor port) and sleeps for 20 Timer Ticks
   (c) Task2 prints the message "Hi from Task2" (Assume that the compiler in use has a MicroC library implementation for the printf() function tailored for the target processor port) and sleeps for 20 Timer Ticks
   (d) The tasks are created in the order Task2, Task1
9. Write a complete MicroC program for synchronising the access of an integer variable 'Var' shared between two tasks using 'disabling task scheduling technique' as per the following requirements
   (a) Create two tasks with names Task1 and Task2 with stack size 1024 and priorities 9 and 10 respectively
   (b) Task1 increments the shared variable and prints its value with the message "From Task1 : Var = " (Assume that the compiler in use has a MicroC library implementation for the printf() function tailored for the target processor port) and sleeps for 20 Timer Ticks
   (c) Task2 decrements the shared variable and prints its value with the message "From Task2 : Var = " (Assume that the compiler in use has a MicroC library implementation for the printf() function tailored for the target processor port) and sleeps for 20 Timer Ticks
   (d) The tasks are created in the order Task2, Task1
10. An embedded system involves the reception of serial data through a serial port and displaying the current time in HH:MM:SS format on the first line of a 2 line 16 character display and indicating serial data reception on the second line of the LCD. Design the system based on MicroC/OS-II as per the requirements given below
   (a) Task1 is created for polling the serial receive interrupt flag of the processor (Assume that MicroC implementation provides a variable called RI for indicating the status. It is set on the reception of a data byte). Task1 is created with stack size 512 bytes and priority 9
   (b) Upon receiving serial data, Task1 displays the message "Data Received = " and appends the received data byte to the display
   (c) Task2 is created for reading the time from a MicroC/OS-II time structure, which is assumed to be updated every second by the system timer interrupt, and displaying the time on the first line of the LCD in HH:MM:SS format. The Display should be centralised to the first line with packing with blank characters on both sides ("   HH:MM:SS   ")
   (d) Task2 is created with stack size 512 bytes and priority 10
   (e) It is assumed that the function for initialising the LCD, *LCDInit()* is available. You can use a dummy function call *LCDInit()* to indicate the initialisation of the LCD. Similarly a dummy function *LCDWrite(x, y, char)* is also available for displaying character on the LCD at position *x,y*. $x = 0$ for line 1 and 1 for line 2. *y* varies from 0 to 15
   (f) Task3 displays the message "HAVE A GREAT DAY" on the second line of the LCD if there is no data reception activity in progress. Task3 is created with stack size 512 bytes and priority 11
   (g) Each task should contain self-delaying for a period of 5 timer ticks to give another task a chance to execute
   (h) When the system starts up, the current time is displayed on the first line and the message "HAVE A GREAT DAY" is displayed on the second line of the LCD
   (i) The learning objective of this application is the usage of semaphore under MicroC/OS-II kernel for enforcing mutual exclusion in shared resource access

12 Integration and Testing of Embedded Hardware and Firmware

LEARNING OBJECTIVES

- ✓ *Learn about the different techniques for embedding firmware into hardware*
- ✓ *Learn about the steps involved in the Out of system Programming*
- ✓ *Learn about the In System Programming (ISP) for firmware embedding*
- ✓ *Learn about the In Application Programming (IAP) for altering an area of the program storage memory for updating configuration data, tables, etc.*
- ✓ *Learn the technique used for embedding OS image and applications into the program storage memory of an embedded device*
- ✓ *Know the various things to be taken care in the 'board bring up'*

Integration testing of the embedded hardware and firmware is the immediate step following the embedded hardware and firmware development. Embedded hardware and firmware are developed in various steps as described in the earlier chapters. The final embedded hardware constitute of a PCB with all necessary components affixed to it as per the original schematic diagram. Embedded firmware represents the control algorithm and configuration data necessary to implement the product requirements on the product. Embedded firmware will be in a target processor/controller understandable format called machine language (sequence of 1s and 0s–Binary). The target embedded hardware without embedding the firmware is a dumb device and cannot function properly. If you power up the hardware without embedding the firmware, the device may behave in an unpredicted manner. As described in the earlier chapters, both embedded hardware and firmware should be independently tested (*Unit Tested*) to ensure their proper functioning. Functioning of individual hardware sections can be done by writing small utilities which checks the operation of the specified part. As far as the embedded firmware is concerned, its targeted functionalities can easily be checked by the simulator environment provided by the embedded firmware development tool's IDE. By simulating the firmware, the memory contents, register details, status of various flags and registers can easily be monitored and it gives an approximate picture of "What happens inside the processor/controller and what are the states of various peripherals" when the firmware is running on the target hardware. The IDE gives necessary support for simulating the various inputs required from the external world, like inputting data on ports, generating an interrupt condition, etc. This really helps in debugging the functioning of the firmware without dumping the firmware in a real target board.

12.1 INTEGRATION OF HARDWARE AND FIRMWARE

Integration of hardware and firmware deals with the embedding of firmware into the target hardware board. It is the process of '***Embedding Intelligence***' to the product. The embedded processors/controllers used in the target board may or may not have built in code memory. For non-operating system based embedded products, if the processor/controller contains internal memory and the total size of the firmware is fitting into the code memory area, the code memory is downloaded into the target controller/processor. If the processor/controller does not support built in code memory or the size of the firmware is exceeding the memory size supported by the target processor/controller, an external dedicated EPROM/FLASH memory chip is used for holding the firmware. This chip is interfaced to the processor/controller. (The type of firmware storage, either processor storage or external storage is decided at the time of hardware design by taking the firmware complexity into consideration). A variety of techniques are used for embedding the firmware into the target board. The commonly used firmware embedding techniques for a non-OS based embedded system are explained below. The non-OS based embedded systems store the firmware either in the onchip processor/controller memory or offchip memory (FLASH/NVRAM, etc.).

12.1.1 Out-of-Circuit Programming

Out-of-circuit programming is performed outside the target board. The processor or memory chip into which the firmware needs to be embedded is taken out of the target board and it is programmed with the help of a programming device (Fig. 12.1). The programming device is a dedicated unit which contains the necessary hardware circuit to generate the programming signals. Most of the programmer devices available in the market are capable of programming different family of devices with different pin outs (Pin counts). The programmer contains a ZIF socket with locking pin to hold the device to be programmed. The programming device will be under the control of a utility program running on a PC. Usually the programmer is interfaced to the PC through RS-232C/USB/Parallel Port Interface. The commands to control the programmer are sent from the utility program to the programmer through the interface (Fig. 12.2).

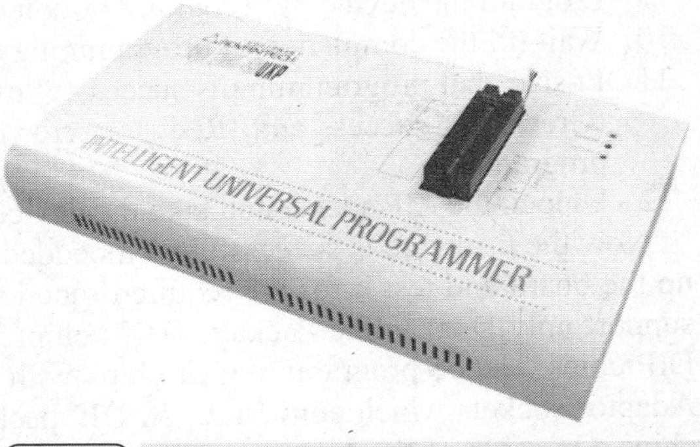

Fig. 12.1 **Firmware Embedding Tool-Device Programmer: LabTool-48UXP)**
(Courtesy of Burn Technology Limited www.burntec.com & Advantech Equipment Corp www.aec.com.tw)

The sequence of operations for embedding the firmware with a programmer is listed below.

1. Connect the programming device to the specified port of PC (USB/COM port/parallel port)
2. Power up the device (Most of the programmers incorporate LED to indicate Device power up. Ensure that the power indication LED is ON)
3. Execute the programming utility on the PC and ensure proper connectivity is established between PC and programmer. In case of error, turn off device power and try connecting it again

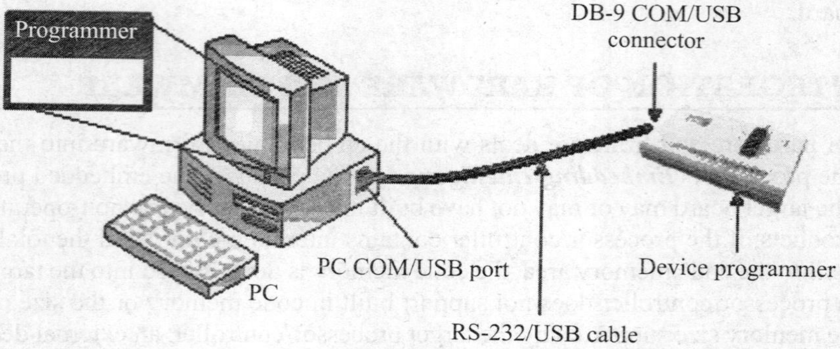

Fig. 12.2 **Interfacing of Device Programmer with PC**

4. Unlock the ZIF socket by turning the lock pin
5. Insert the device to be programmed into the open socket as per the insert diagram shown on the programmer
6. Lock the ZIF socket
7. Select the device name from the list of supported devices
8. Load the hex file which is to be embedded into the device
9. Program the device by 'Program' option of utility program
10. Wait till the completion of programming operation (Till busy LED of programmer is off)
11. Ensure that programming is successful by checking the status LED on the programmer (Usually 'Green' for success and 'Red' for error condition) or by noticing the feedback from the utility program
12. Unlock the ZIF socket and take the device out of programmer

Now the firmware is successfully embedded into the device. Insert the device into the board, power up the board and test it for the required functionalities. It is to be noted that the most of programmers support only Dual Inline Package (DIP) chips, since its ZIF socket is designed to accommodate only DIP chips. Hence programming of chips with other packages is not possible with the current setup. Adaptor sockets which convert a non-DIP package to DIP socket can be used for programming such chips. One side of the Adaptor socket contains a DIP interface and the other side acts as a holder for holding the chip with a non-DIP package (say VQFP). Option for setting firmware protection will be available on the programming utility. If you really want the firmware to be protected against unwanted external access, and if the device is supporting memory protection, enable the memory protection on the utility before programming the device. The programmer usually erases the existing content of the chip before programming the chip. Only EEPROM and FLASH memory chips are erasable by the programmer. Some old embedded systems may be built around UVEPROM chips and such chips should be erased using a separate 'UV Chip Eraser' before programming.

The major drawback of out-of-circuit programming is the high development time. Whenever the firmware is changed, the chip should be taken out of the development board for re-programming. This is tedious and prone to chip damages due to frequent insertion and removal. Better use a socket on the board side to hold the chip till the firmware modifications are over. The programmer facilitates programming of only one chip at a time and it is not suitable for batch production. Using a 'Gang Programmer' resolves this issue to certain extent. A gang programmer is similar to an ordinary programmer except that it contains multiple ZIF sockets (4 to 8) and capable of programming multiple devices at a time. But it is bit expensive compared to an ordinary programmer. Another big drawback of this programming technique is that once the product is deployed in the market in a production environment, it is very difficult to upgrade the firmware.

The out-of-system programming technique is used for firmware integration for low end embedded products which runs without an operating system. Out-of-circuit programming is commonly used for development of low volume products and Proof of Concept (PoC) product Development.

12.1.2 In System Programming (ISP)

With ISP, programming is done '*within the system*', meaning the firmware is embedded into the target device without removing it from the target board. It is the most flexible and easy way of firmware embedding. The only pre-requisite is that the target device must have an ISP support. Apart from the target board, PC, ISP cable and ISP utility, no other additional hardware is required for ISP. Chips supporting ISP generates the necessary programming signals internally, using the chip's supply voltage. The target board can be interfaced to the utility program running on PC through Serial Port/Parallel Port/USB. The communication between the target device and ISP utility will be in a serial format. The serial protocols used for ISP may be 'Joint Test Action Group (JTAG)' or 'Serial Peripheral Interface (SPI)' or any other proprietary protocol. In order to perform ISP operations the target device (in most cases the target device is a microcontroller/microprocessor) should be powered up in a special '*ISP mode*'. ISP mode allows the device to communicate with an external host through a serial interface, such as a PC or terminal. The device receives commands and data from the host, erases and reprograms code memory according to the received command. Once the ISP operations are completed, the device is re-configured so that it will operate normally by applying a reset or a re-power up.

12.1.2.1 In System Programming with SPI Protocol Devices with SPI In System Programming support contains a built-in SPI interface and the on-chip EEPROM or FLASH memory is programmed through this interface. The primary I/O lines involved in SPI – In System Programming are listed below.

MOSI – Master Out Slave In
MISO – Master In Slave Out
SCK – System Clock
RST – Reset of Target Device
GND – Ground of Target Device

PC acts as the master and target device acts as the slave in ISP. The program data is sent to the MOSI pin of target device and the device acknowledgement is originated from the MISO pin of the device. SCK pin acts as the clock for data transfer. A utility program can be developed on the PC side to generate the above signal lines. Since the target device works under a supply voltage less than 5V (TTL/CMOS), it is better to connect these lines of the target device with the parallel port of the PC. Since Parallel port operations are also at 5V logic, no need for any other intermediate hardware for signal conversion. The pins of parallel port to which the ISP pins of device needs to be connected are dependent on the program, which is used for generating these signals, or you can fix these lines first and then write the program according to the pin inter-connection assignments. Standard SPI-ISP utilities are feely available on the internet and there is no need for going for writing own program. What you need to do is just connect the pins as mentioned by the program requirement. As mentioned earlier, for ISP operations, the target device needs to be powered up in a pre-defined sequence. The power up sequence for In System Programming for Atmel's AT89S series microcontroller family is listed below.

1. Apply supply voltage between VCC and GND pins of target chip.
2. Set RST pin to "HIGH" state.
3. If a crystal is not connected across pins XTAL1 and XTAL2, apply a 3 MHz to 24 MHz clock to XTAL1 pin and wait for at least 10 milliseconds.
4. Enable serial programming by sending the Programming Enable serial instruction to pin MOSI/P1.5. The frequency of the shift clock supplied at pin SCK/P1.7 needs to be less than the CPU clock at XTAL1 divided by 40.
5. The Code or Data array is programmed one byte at a time by supplying the address and data together with the appropriate Write instruction. The selected memory location is first erased before the new data is written. The write cycle is self-timed and typically takes less than 2.5 ms at 5V.
6. Any memory location can be verified by using the Read instruction, which returns the content at the selected address at serial output MISO/P1.6.
7. After successfully programming the device, set RST pin low or turn off the chip power supply and turn it ON to commence the normal operation.

Note

This sequence is applicable only to Atmel AT89S Series microcontroller and it need not be the same for other series or family of microcontroller/ISP device. Please refer to the datasheet of the device which needs to be programmed using ISP technique for the sequence of operations.

The key player behind ISP is a factory programmed memory (ROM) called '*Boot ROM*'. The *Boot ROM* normally resides at the top end of code memory space and it varies in the order of a few Kilo Bytes (For a controller with 64K code memory space and 1K Boot ROM, the Boot ROM resides at memory location FC00H to FFFFH). It contains a set of Low-level Instruction APIs and these APIs allow the processor/controller to perform the FLASH memory programming, erasing and Reading operations. The contents of the *Boot ROM* are provided by the chip manufacturer and the same is masked into every device. The *Boot ROM* for different family or series devices is different. By default the Reset vector starts the code memory execution at location 0000H. If the ISP mode is enabled through the special ISP Power up sequence, the execution will start at the *Boot ROM* vector location. In System Programming technique is the best advised programming technique for development work since the effort required to re-program the device in case of firmware modification is very little. Firmware upgrades for products supporting ISP is quite simple.

12.1.3 In Application Programming (IAP)

In Application Programming (IAP) is a technique used by the firmware running on the target device for modifying a selected portion of the code memory. It is not a technique for first time embedding of user written firmware. It modifies the program code memory under the control of the embedded application. Updating calibration data, look-up tables, etc., which are stored in code memory, are typical examples of IAP. The *Boot ROM* resident API instructions which perform various functions such as programming, erasing, and reading the Flash memory during ISP mode, are made available to the end-user written firmware for IAP. Thus it is possible for an end-user application to perform operations on the Flash memory. A common entry point to these API routines is provided for interfacing them to the end-user's application. Functions are performed by setting up specific registers as required by a specific operation and performing a call to the common entry point. Like any other subroutine call, after completion of the function, control will return to the end-user's code. The *Boot ROM* is shadowed with the user code memory in its address range. This shadowing is controlled by a status bit. When this status bit is set, accesses to the internal code memory in this address range will be from the *Boot ROM*. When cleared, accesses will be from the user's code memory. Hence the user should set the status bit prior to calling the common entry point for IAP operations (The IAP technique described here is for PHILIPS' 89C51RX series microcontroller. Though the underlying principle in IAP is the same, the shadowing technique used for switching access between *Boot ROM* and code memory may be different for other family of devices).

12.1.4 Use of Factory Programmed Chip

It is possible to embed the firmware into the target processor/controller memory at the time of chip fabrication itself. Such chips are known as '*Factory programmed chips*'. Once the firmware design is over and the firmware achieved operational stability, the firmware files can be sent to the chip fabricator to embed it into the code memory. Factory programmed chips are convenient for mass production applications and it greatly reduces the product development time. It is not recommended to use factory programmed chips for development purpose where the firmware undergoes frequent changes. Factory programmed ICs are bit expensive.

12.1.5 Firmware Loading for Operating System Based Devices

The OS based embedded systems are programmed using the In System Programming (ISP) technique. OS based embedded systems contain a special piece of code called '*Boot loader*' program which takes control of the OS and application firmware embedding and copying of the OS image to the RAM of the system for execution. The '*Boot loader*' for such embedded systems comes as pre-loaded or it can be loaded to the memory using the various interface supported like JTAG. The bootloader contains necessary driver initialisation implementation for initialising the supported interfaces like UART, TCP/IP etc. Bootloader implements menu options for selecting the source for OS image to load (Typical menu item examples are 1. Load from FLASH ROM, Load from Network, Load through UART etc). In case of the network based loading, the bootloader broadcasts the target's presence over the network and the host machine on which the OS image resides can identify the target device by capturing this message. Once a communication link is established between the host and target machine, the OS image can be directly downloaded to the FLASH memory of the target device. We will discuss about the role of '*Boot loader*', '*Boot loader*' development and embedding, firmware and OS embedding and booting process for an OS based embedded system in detail in a dedicated book coming under this series. Please be patient till then.

12.2 BOARD POWER UP

Now the firmware is embedded into the target board using one of the programming techniques described above. 'What Next?' The answer is power up the board. You may be expecting the device functioning exactly in a way as you designed. But in real scenario it need not be and if the board functions well in the first attempt itself you are very lucky. Sometimes the first power up may end up in a messy explosion leaving the smell of burned components behind. It may happen due to various reasons, like Proper care was not taken in applying the power and power applied in reverse polarity (+ve of supply connected to

–ve of the target board and vice versa), components were not placed in the correct polarity order (E.g. a capacitor on the target board is connected to the board with +ve terminal to –ve of the board and vice versa), etc… etc… *I would like to share a very interesting incident which happened in my development career during the power up of a new board. Though the board was well checked and extreme care was taken in applying the power, when I powered the board after embedding the firmware, I heard an explosion followed by the burning of a capacitor on the target board and I really struggled hard to stop the fire from spreading by a strong puff of air—It is not a joke, It's a true incident*. The reason was very simple, the power applied to the board was 9V and the filter capacitor placed at the regulator IC input side was with a rating of 6V (220MFD/6V). Since the capacitor voltage rating was below the input supply, the dielectric of capacitor got burned. Be cautious: Before you power up the board make sure everything is intact. We will discuss about the various tools used for troubleshooting the target hardware in a later chapter.

Summary

- ✓ Integration of hardware and firmware deals with the embedding of firmware into the target hardware board.
- ✓ For non-operating system based embedded products, if the processor/controller contains internal memory and the total size of the firmware is fitting into the code memory area, the code memory is downloaded into the target controller/processor. If the processor/controller does not support built-in code memory or the size of the firmware is exceeding the memory size supported by the target processor/controller, the firmware is held in an external dedicated EPROM/FLASH memory chip
- ✓ Out-of-circuit programming and In System Programming (ISP) are the two different methods for embedding firmware into a non Operating System based product
- ✓ In the out-of-circuit programming, the device is removed from the target board and is programmed using a 'Device Programmer', whereas in the In System Programming technique, the firmware is embedded into the controller memory/program memory chip without removing the chip from the target board
- ✓ JTAG, SPI, etc. are the commonly used serial protocols for transferring the embedded firmware into the target device
- ✓ In Application Programming (IAP) is a technique used by the firmware running on the target device for modifying a selected portion of the code memory. It is not a technique for first time embedding of user written firmware. It modifies the program code memory under the control of the embedded application
- ✓ IAP is normally used for updating calibration data, look-up tables, etc. which are stored in code memory
- ✓ Factory programmed chip embeds firmware into the chip at the time of chip fabrication
- ✓ In System Programming (ISP) is used for embedding the OS image and application program into the non-volatile storage memory of the embedded product. The bootloader program running in the target device implements the necessary routine for embedding the OS image into the non-volatile memory and booting the system

Keywords

JTAG	:	An Interface for hardware troubleshooting like boundary scan testing
In System Programming (ISP)	:	Firmware embedding technique in which the firmware is embedded into the program memory without removing the chip from the target board
Serial Peripheral Interface (SPI)	:	Serial interface for connecting devices

In Application Programming (IAP)	:	A technique used by the firmware running on the target device for modifying a selected portion of the code memory
BootROM	:	A program, which contains the libraries for implementing In System Programming, which is embedded into the memory at the time of chip fabrication
Bootloader	:	Program which takes control of the OS and application firmware embedding and copying of the OS image to the RAM of the system for execution

Review Questions

1. Explain the different techniques for embedding the firmware into the target board for a non-OS based embedded system
2. Explain the major drawbacks of *out-of-circuit* programming
3. Explain the firmware embedding process for OS based embedded products
4. What is the difference between In System Programming (ISP) and In Application Programming (IAP)?

13 The Embedded System Development Environment

LEARNING OBJECTIVES

- ✓ *Learn about the different entities of the embedded system development environment*
- ✓ *Learn about the Integrated Development Environments (IDEs) for embedded firmware development and debugging*
- ✓ *Learn the usage of μVision3 IDE from Keil software (www.keil.com) for embedded firmware development, simulation and debugging for 8051 family of microcontrollers*
- ✓ *Familiarise with the different IDEs for firmware development for different family of processors/controllers and Embedded Operating Systems*
- ✓ *Learn about the different types of files (List File, Preprocessor output file, Object File, Map File, Hex File, etc.) generated during the cross compilation of a source file written in high level language like Embedded C and during the cross assembling of a source file written in Assembly Language*
- ✓ *Learn about disassembler and decompiler, and their role in embedded firmware development*
- ✓ *Learn about Simulators, In Circuit Emulators (ICE), and Debuggers and their role in embedded firmware debugging*
- ✓ *Learn about the different tools and techniques used for embedded hardware debugging*
- ✓ *Learn the use of magnifying glass, multimeter, CRO, logic analyser and function generator in embedded hardware debugging*
- ✓ *Learn about the boundary scanning technique for testing the interconnection among the various chips in a complex hardware board*

This chapter is designed to give you an insight into the embedded-system development environment. The various tools used and the various steps followed in embedded system development are explained here. It is a summary of the various design and development phases we discussed so far and an introduction to the various design/development/debug tools employed in embedded system development. A typical embedded system development environment is illustrated in Fig. 13.1.

As illustrated in the figure, the development environment consists of a Development Computer (PC) or Host, which acts as the heart of the development environment, Integrated Development Environment (IDE) Tool for embedded firmware development and debugging, Electronic Design Automation (EDA) Tool for Embedded Hardware design, An emulator hardware for debugging the target board, Signal sources (like Function generator) for simulating the inputs to the target board, Target hardware

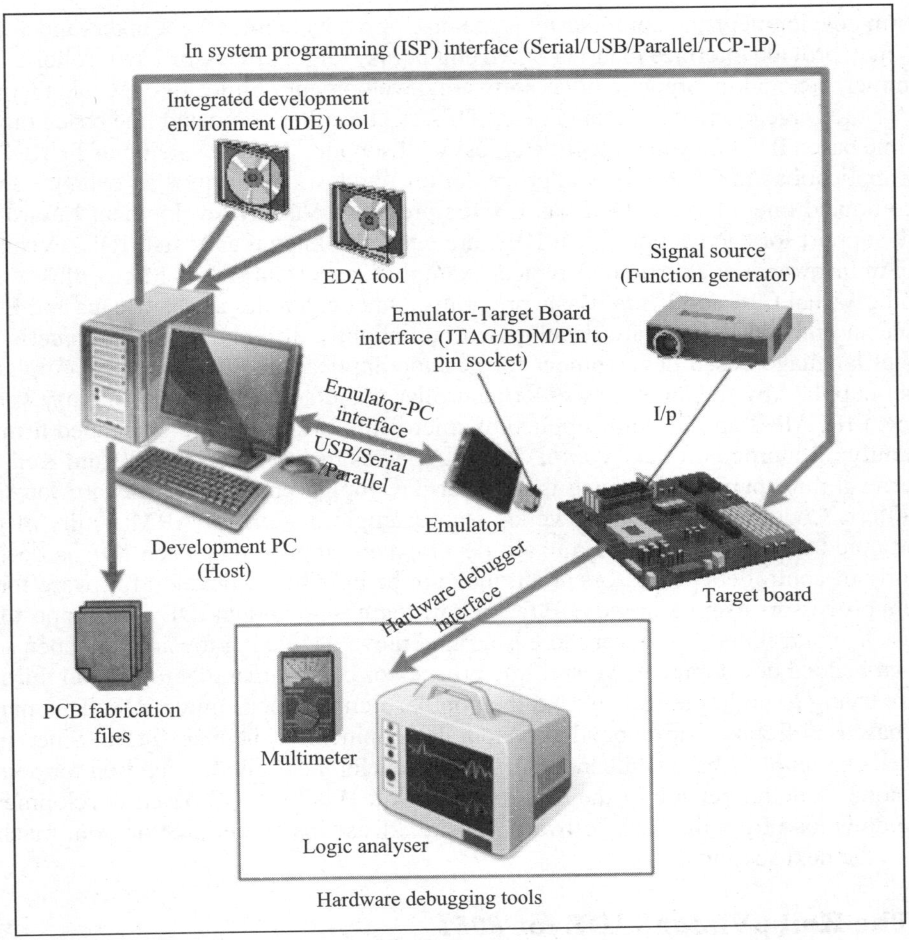

Fig. 13.1 The Embedded System Development Environment

debugging tools (Digital CRO, Multimeter, Logic Analyser, etc.) and the target hardware. The Integrated Development Environment (IDE) and Electronic Design Automation (EDA) tools are selected based on the target hardware development requirement and they are supplied as Installable files in CDs by vendors. These tools need to be installed on the host PC used for development activities. These tools can be either freeware or licensed copy or evaluation versions. Licensed versions of the tools are fully featured and fully functional whereas trial versions fall into two categories, tools with limited features, and full featured copies with limited period of usage.

13.1 THE INTEGRATED DEVELOPMENT ENVIRONMENT (IDE)

In embedded system development context, Integrated Development Environment (IDE) stands for an integrated environment for developing and debugging the target processor specific embedded firmware. IDE is a software package which bundles a 'Text Editor (Source Code Editor)', 'Cross-compiler (for cross platform development and compiler for same platform development)', 'Linker' and a 'Debugger'. Some IDEs may provide interface to target board emulators, Target processor's/controller's Flash memory programmer, etc. and incorporate other software development utilities like 'Version Control Tool', 'Help File for the Development Language', etc. IDEs can be either command line based or GUI based. Command line based IDEs may include little or less GUI support. The old version of TURBO C IDE for developing applications in C/C++ for x86 processor on Windows platform is an example for a generic IDE with command line interface. GUI based IDEs provide a Visual Development Environment with mouse click support for each action. Such IDEs are generally known as Visual IDEs. Visual IDEs are very helpful in firmware development. A typical example for a Visual IDE is Microsoft® Visual Studio for developing Visual C++ and Visual Basic programs. Other examples are NetBeans and Eclipse.

IDEs used in embedded firmware development are slightly different from the generic IDEs used for high level language based development for desktop applications. In Embedded Applications, the IDE is either supplied by the target processor/controller manufacturer or by third party vendors or as Open Source. MPLAB is an IDE tool supplied by microchip for developing embedded firmware using their PIC family of microcontrollers. Keil µVision3 (spelt as micro vision three) from Keil software is an example for a third party IDE, which is used for developing embedded firmware for *8051* family microcontrollers. CodeWarrior by Metrowerks is an example of IDE for ARM family of processors. It should be noted that in embedded firmware development applications each IDE is designed for a specific family of controllers/processors and it may not be possible to develop firmware for all family of controllers/processors using a single IDE (as of now there is no known IDE with support for all family of processors/controllers). However there is a rapid move happening towards the open source IDE, Eclipse for embedded development. Most of the proccessor/control manufacturers and third party IDE providers are trying to build the IDE around the popular Eclipse open source IDE. This may lead to a single IDE based on Eclipse for embedded system development in the near future. Since this book is primarily focusing on *8051* based embedded firmware development, the IDE chosen for demonstration is Keil µVision3. A demo version of the tool for Microsoft Windows OS based development is available for free download from the Keil Software website. Please instal the same on your machine before proceeding to the next sections.

13.1.1 The Keil µVision3 IDE for *8051*

Keil µVision3 is a licensed IDE tool from Keil Software (www.keil.com), an ARM company, for *8051* family microcontroller based embedded firmware development. To start with the IDE (after installing the demo tool) execute the program Uv3.exe (or the short cut 'Keil µVision3' from desktop or 'All Programs' tab from 'Start Menu' – For Host machine with Microsoft® Windows Operating System). The IDE view is shown in Fig. 13.2.

The IDE looks very similar to the Microsoft® Visual Studio IDE and it contains various menu options, a project window showing files, Register view, Books and Functions Tab and an output window. To start a new project, go to the '*Project*' tab on the menu, select '*New Project*' option. Give a name to your workspace in the '*File Name*' section of the '*Create New Project*' Pop-up dialog Box (Let it be 'sample'). Choose the directory to save the project from the pop-up dialog. The default extension of a project workspace file is .uv2. On clicking the '***Save***' button of the '*Create New Project*' pop-up dialog, a device selection dialog as shown in Fig. 13.3 appears on the screen.

This Dialog Box lists out all the vendors (manufacturers) for *8051* family microcontroller, supported by IDE. Choose the manufacturer of the chip for your design (Let it be 'Atmel' for our design). Atmel itself manufactures a variety of *8051* flavours. Choose the exact part number of the device used as the

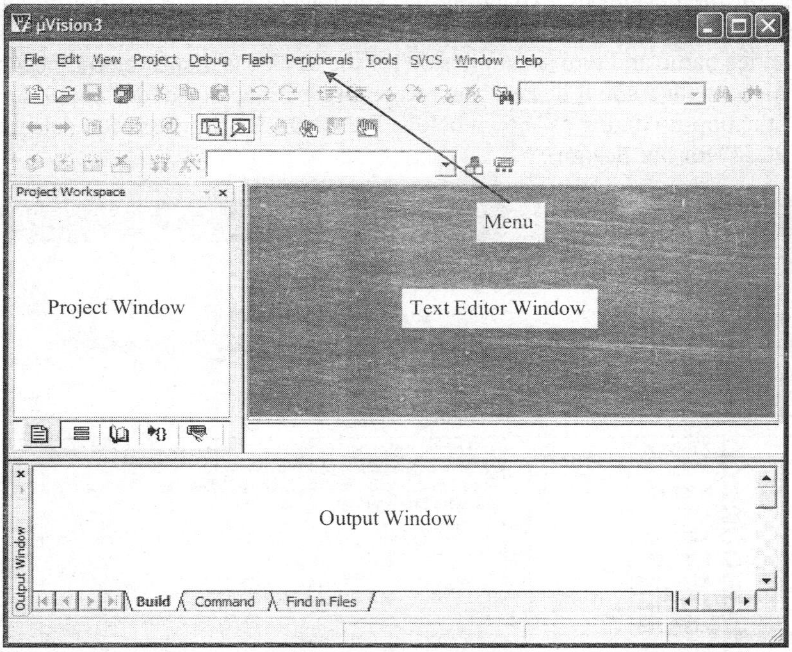

Fig. 13.2 **Keil µVision3 Integrated Development Environment (IDE)**

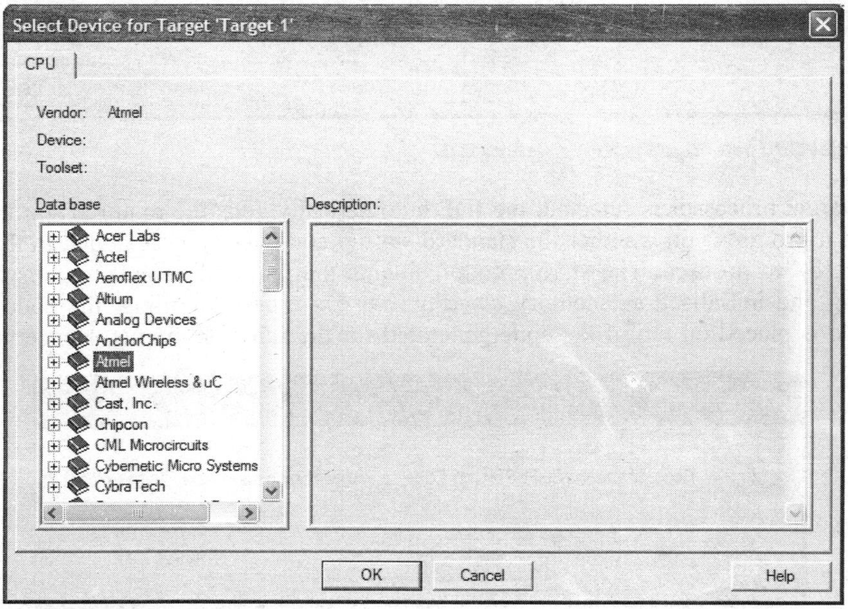

Fig. 13.3 **Target CPU Vendor selection for Keil µVision3 IDE**

target processor for the design, by expanding the vendor node. It will list out all supported CPUs by the selected vendor under the vendor node. On selecting the target processor's exact part number, the vendor name, device name and tool set supported for the device is displayed on the appropriate fields of the dialog box along with a small description of the target processor under the *Description* column on the right side of the pop-up dialog as shown below. Press 'OK' to proceed after selecting the target CPU (Let it be 'AT89C51' for our design).

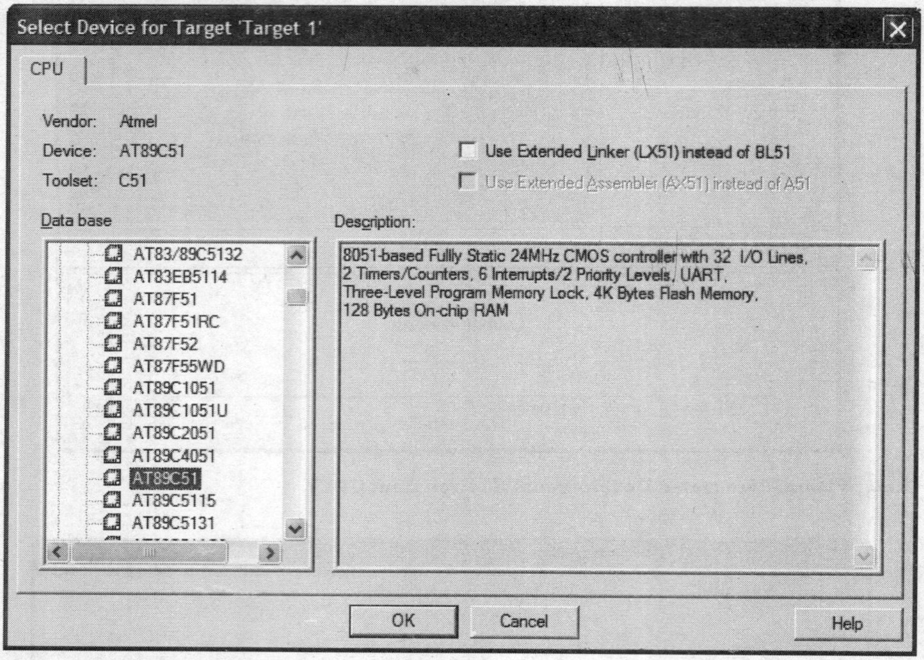

Fig. 13.4 **Target CPU selection for Keil μVision3 IDE**

Once the target processor is selected, the IDE automatically adds the required startup code for the firmware and it prompts you whether the standard startup code needs to be added to the project (Fig. 13.5). Press '***Yes***' to proceed. The startup code contains the required default initialisation like stack pointer setting and initialisation, memory clearing, etc, On cross-compiling, the code generated for the startup file is placed on top of the code generated for the function *main()*. Hence the reset vector

Fig. 13.5 **Startup file addition to the project**

(0000H) always starts with the execution of startup code before the main code. For more details on the contents and code of startup file please go through the µVision help files which is listed under the '*Books*' section of the project workspace window.

A '*Target*' group with the name '*Target1*' is automatically generated under the '*Files*' section of the project Window. '*Target1*' contains a '*Source Group*' with the name '*Source Group1*' and the startup file (STARTUP.A51) is kept under this group (Fig. 13.6). All these groups are generated automatically. If you want you can rename these groups by clicking the respective group names.

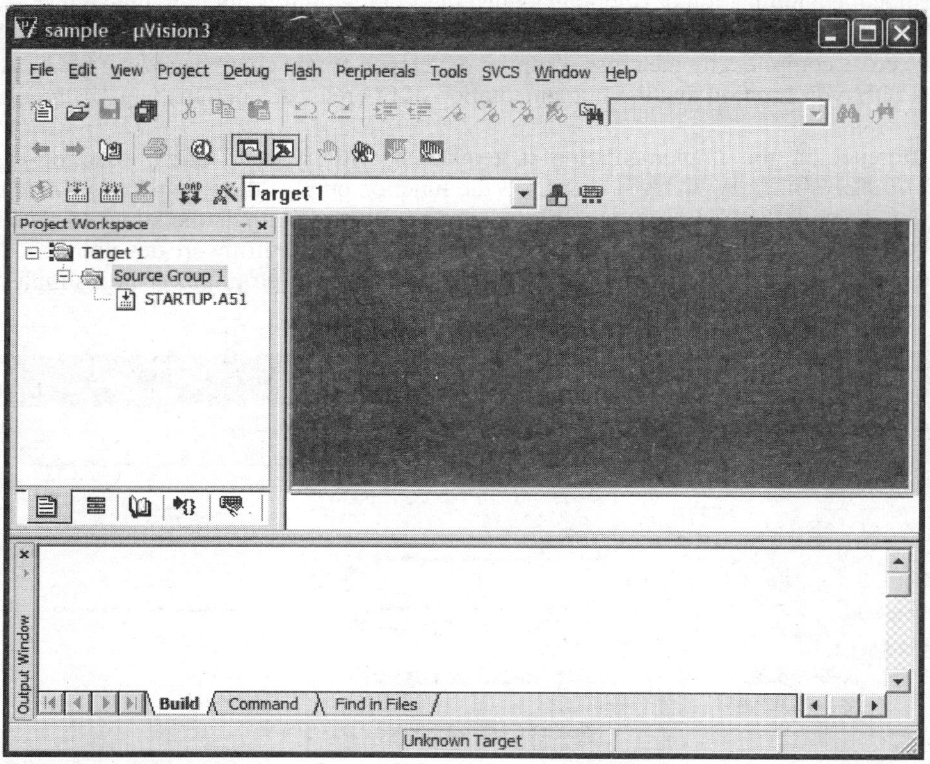

Fig. 13.6 **Startup file added to the project**

You can see that similar to the Visual Studio IDE's '*Project Window*' for VC++ development, Keil IDE's '*Project Window*' also contains multiple tabs. They are the '*Files*' tab, which gives the file details for the current project, '*Regs*' tab, giving the Register details while debugging the source code, '*Books*' tab showing all the available help and documentation files supplied by the IDE, '*Functions*' tab lists out the functions present in a '*C*' source file and finally a '*Templates*' tab which generate automatic code framework (function body) for *if*, *if else*, *switch case* etc and code documentation template (Header). These steps create a project workspace. To start with the firmware development we need to create a source file and then add that source file to the '*Source Group*' of the '*Target*'. Click on the '*File*' tab on the menu tool of the IDE and select the option '*New*'. A blank text editor will be visible on the IDE to the right of the '*Project Window*'. Start writing the code on the text editor as per your design (Refer to the Keil help file for using Keil supported specific Embedded C instructions for *8051* family). You can write the program in ANSI C and *8051* specific codes (like Port Access, bit manipulation instruction etc) using Keil specific Embedded C codes. For using the Keil specific Embedded code, you need to add the specific header file to the text editor using the *#include* compiler directive. For example, *#include <reg51.h>* is the header file including all the target processor specific declarations for *8051* family processors for Keil C51 Compiler. Standard '*C*' programs (Desktop applications) calls the library routines for accessing the I/O and they are defined in the *stdio.h* file, whereas these library files cannot be used as such for embedded application development since the I/O medium is not a graphic console as in the *C* language based development on DOS Operating system and they are re-defined for the target processor I/Os for the cross compilers by the cross compiler developer. If you open the *stdio.h* file by ANSI C and Keil for its IDE, you can find that the implementation of I/O related functions (e.g. *printf()*) are entirely different.

The difference in the implementation is explained with typical *stdio.h* function-*printf() (*e.g. *printf("Hello World\n"))*. With ANSI C & DOS the function outputs the string *Hello World* to the DOS console whereas with the C51 cross-compiler, the same function outputs the string *Hello World* to the serial port of the device with the default settings. Coming back to the firmware development, let's follow the universal unwritten law of first 'C' program- The "*Hello World*" program. Write a simple 'C' code to print the string Hello world.

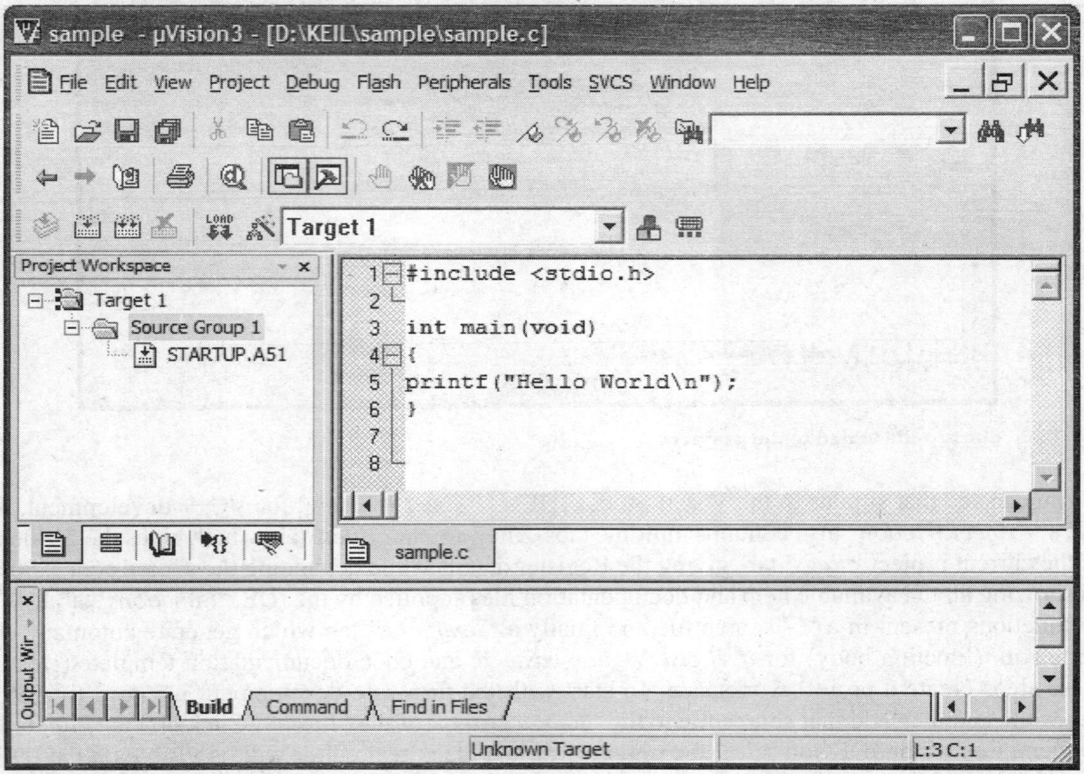

Fig. 13.7 **Writing the first Embedded C code**

The code is written in the text editor which appears within the IDE on selecting the '*New*' tab from the '*File*' Menu. Write the code in *C* language syntax (Fig. 13.7). Add the necessary header files. You can make use of the standard template files available under the '*Templates*' tab of the '*Project Window*' for adding functions, loops, conditional instructions, etc. for writing the code. Once you are done with the code, save it with extension .c in a desired folder (Preferably in the current project directory). Let the name of the file be '*sample.c*'. At the moment you save the program with extension .c, all the keywords (like #include, int, void, etc.) appear in a different colour and the title bar of the IDE displays the name of the current .c file along with its path. By now we have created a 'c' source file. Next step is adding the created source file to the project. For this, right click on the '*Source Group*' from the '*Project Window*' and select the option '*Add Files to Group 'Source Group'*'. Choose the file '*sample.c*' from the file selection Dialog Box and press '*Add*' button and exit the file selection dialog by pressing '*Close*' button. Now the file is added to the target project (Fig. 13.8). You can see the file in the '*Project Window*' under '*Files*' tab beneath the '*Source Group*'.

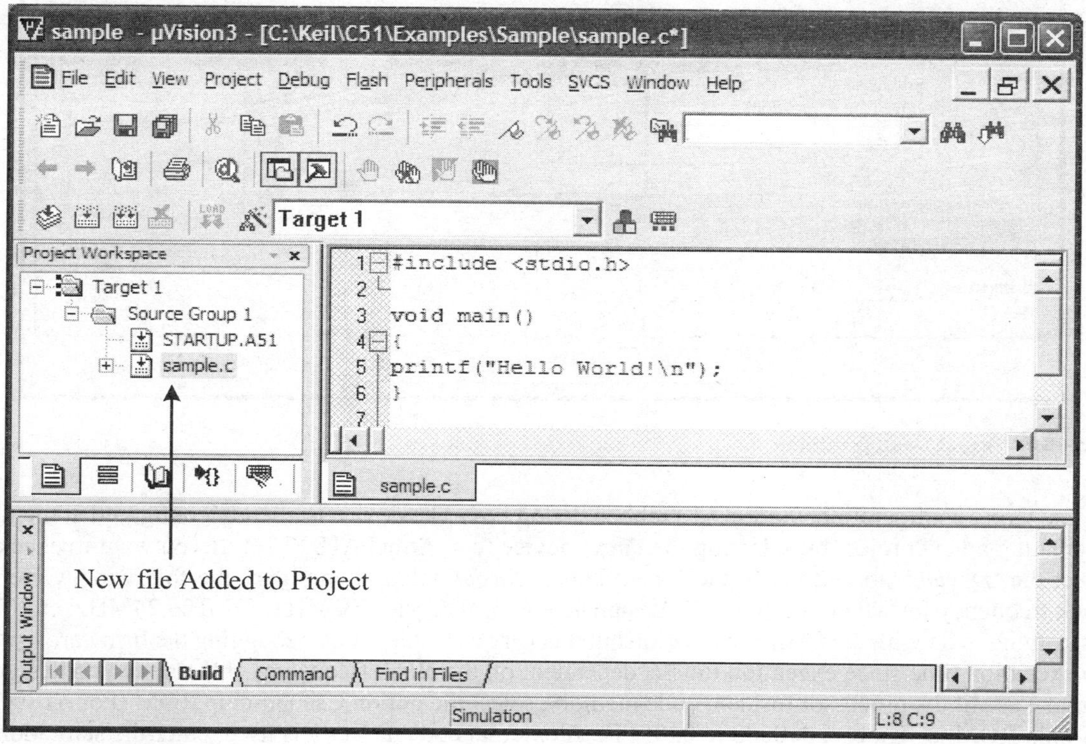

Fig. 13.8 **Adding Files to the Project**

If you are following the modular programming technique, you may have different source files for performing an intended operation. Add all those files to the project as described above. It should be noted that function *main()* is the only entry point and only one '*.c*' file among the files added to the project is allowed to contain the function *main()*. If more than one file contains a function with the name *main()*, compilation will end up in error. The next step is configuring the target. To configure the target, go to '*Project*' tab on the Menu and select '*Options for Target*'. The configuration window as shown in Fig. 13.9 is displayed.

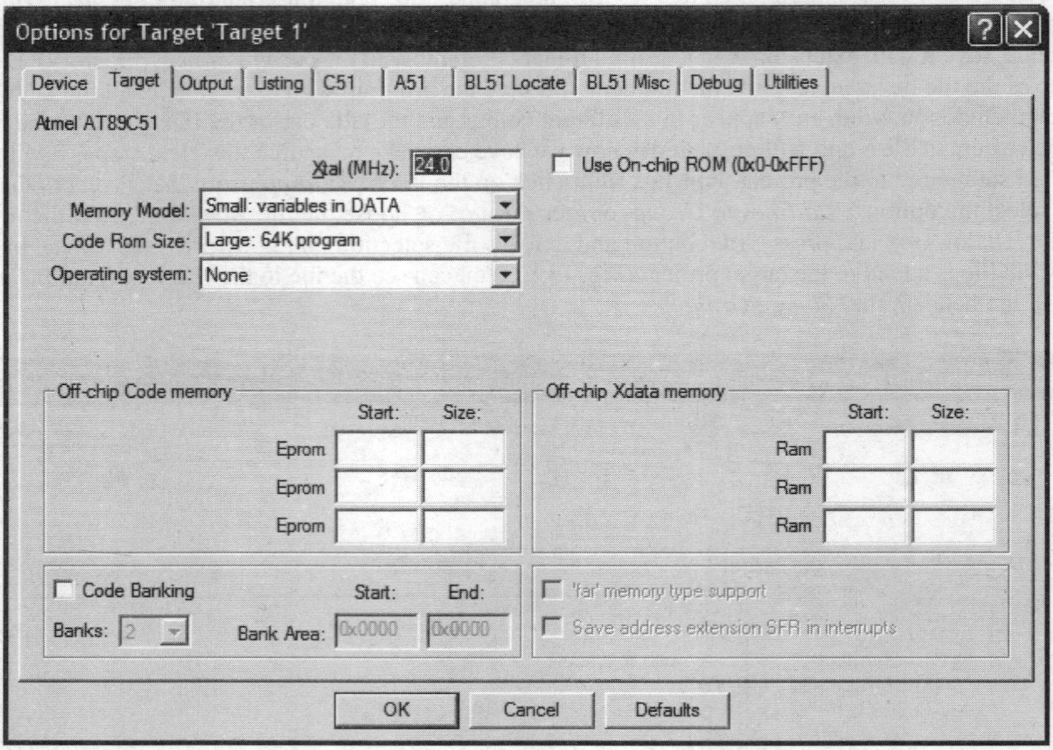

Fig. 13.9 **Target Configuration**

The target configuration window is a tabbed dialog box. The device is already configured at the time of creating a new project by selecting the target device (e.g. Atmel AT89C51). If you want to check it, select the '*Device*' tab and verify the same. Select '*Target*' tab and configure the following. Give the clock frequency for which the system is designed. e.g. 6MHz, 11.0592MHz, 12MHz, 24MHz, etc. This has nothing to do with the firmware creation but it is very essential while debugging the firmware to note the execution time since execution time is dependent on the clock frequency. If the system is designed to make use of the processor resident code memory, select the option Use On-chip ROM (For AT89C51 On-chip ROM is 4K only; 0x0000 to 0x0FFF). If external code memory is used, enter the start address and size of the code memory at the Off-chip Code memory column (e.g. Eprom Start: 0x0000 and Size 0x0FFF). The working memory (data memory or RAM) can also be either internal or external to the processor. If it is external, enter the memory map starting address of the external memory along with the size of external memory in the 'Off-chip Xdata memory section (e.g. Ram Start: 0x8000 and Size 0x 1000). Select the memory model for the target. Memory model refers to the data memory. Keil supports three types of data memory model; internal data memory (Small), external data memory in paged mode (Compact) and external data memory in non-paged mode (Large). Now select the Code memory size.

Code memory model is also classified into three; namely, Small (code less than 2K bytes), Compact (2K bytes functions and 64K bytes code memory) and Large (Plain 64K bytes memory). Choose the type depending on your target application and target hardware design. If your design is for an RTOS based system, select the supported RTOS by the IDE. Keil supports two 8 bit RTOS namely, RTX51 Tiny and RTX51 Full. Choose none for a non RTOS based design.

Move to the next Tab, '***Output***'. The output tab holds the settings for output file generation from the source code (Fig. 13.10). The source file can either be converted into an executable machine code or a library file.

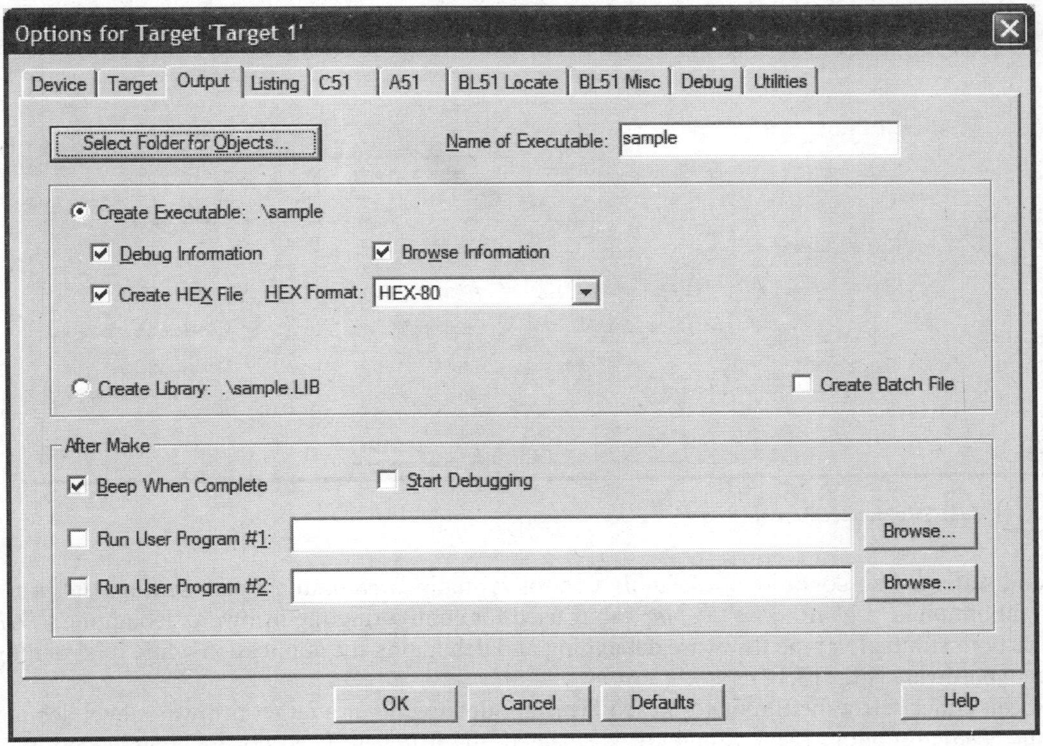

Fig. 13.10 **Output File creation settings**

You can select one of the output settings (viz. executable binary file (hex) or library file (lib)). For executable file, tick the 'Create Hex File' option and select the target processor specific hex file format. Depending on the target processor architecture the hex file format may vary, e.g. Intel Hex file and Motorola hex file. For *8051*, only one choice is available and it is Intel hex File HEX-80. The list files section coming under the tab '*Listing*' tells what all listing files should be created during cross-compilation process (Fig. 13.11).

'*C51*' tab settings are used for cross compiler directives and settings like/Pre-processor symbols, code optimisation settings, type of optimisation (viz. code optimised for execution speed and code optimised for size), *include* file's path settings, etc. The '*A51*' tab settings are used for assembler direc-

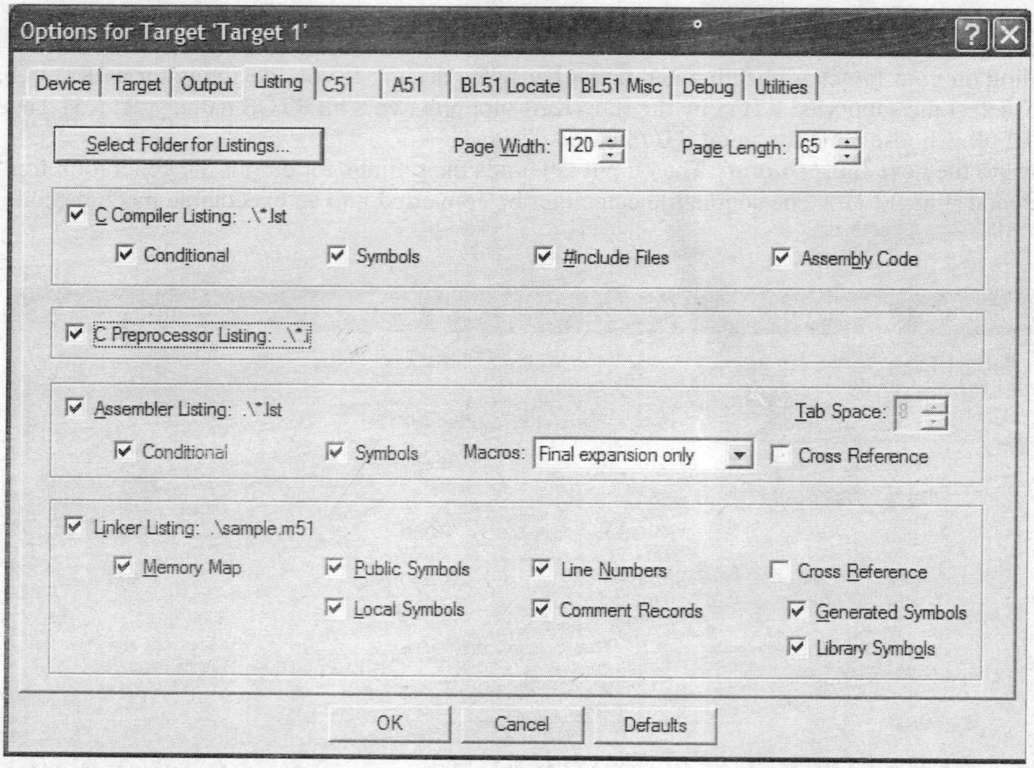

Fig. 13.11 **List File generation settings**

tives and settings like conditional assembly control symbols, *include* file's path settings etc. Another important option is '*Debug*'. The '*Debug*' tab is used for configuring the firmware debugging. '*Debug*' supports both simulation type firmware debugging and debugging the application while it is running on the target hardware (Fig. 13.12).

You can either select the Simulator based firmware debugging or a target firmware level debugging from the '*Debug*' option. If the Simulator is selected, the firmware need not be downloaded into the target machine. The IDE provides an application firmware debugging environment by simulating the target hardware in a software environment. It is most suitable for offline analysis and rapid code developments. If target level debugging is selected, the binary file created by the cross-compilation process needs to be downloaded into the target hardware and the debugging is done by single stepping the firmware. A physical link should be established between the target hardware and the PC on which the IDE is running for target level debugging. Target level hardware debugging is achieved using the Keil supported monitor programs or through an emulator interface. Select the same from the Drop-down list. Normally the link between target hardware and IDE is established through a Serial interface. Use the settings tab to configure the Serial interface. Select the '*Comm Port*' to which the target device is connected and the baudrate for communication (Fig. 13.13).

If the Debug mode is configured to use the Target level debugging using any one of the monitor program or the emulator interface supported by the Keil IDE, the created binary file is downloaded into

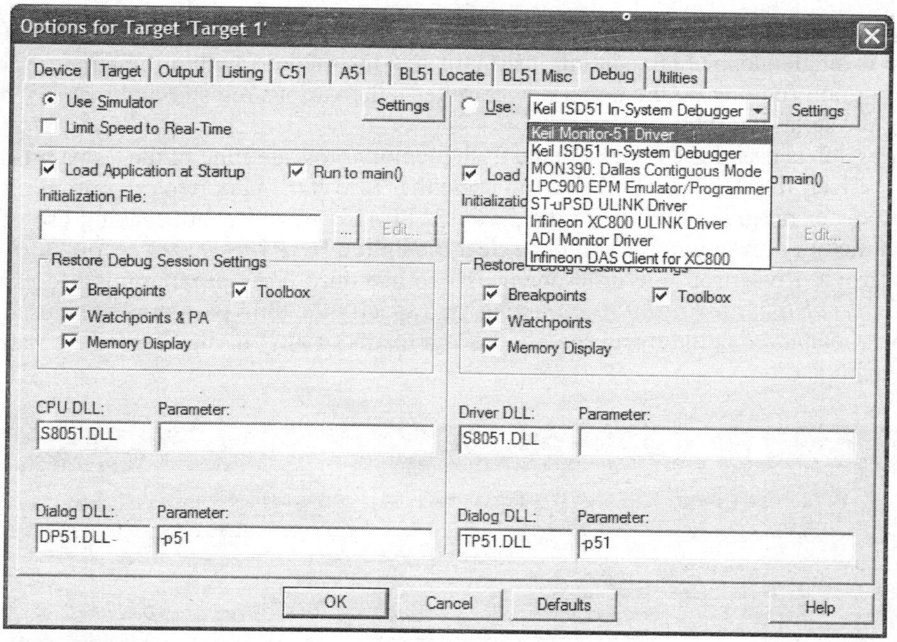

Fig. 13.12 **Firmware debugging options**

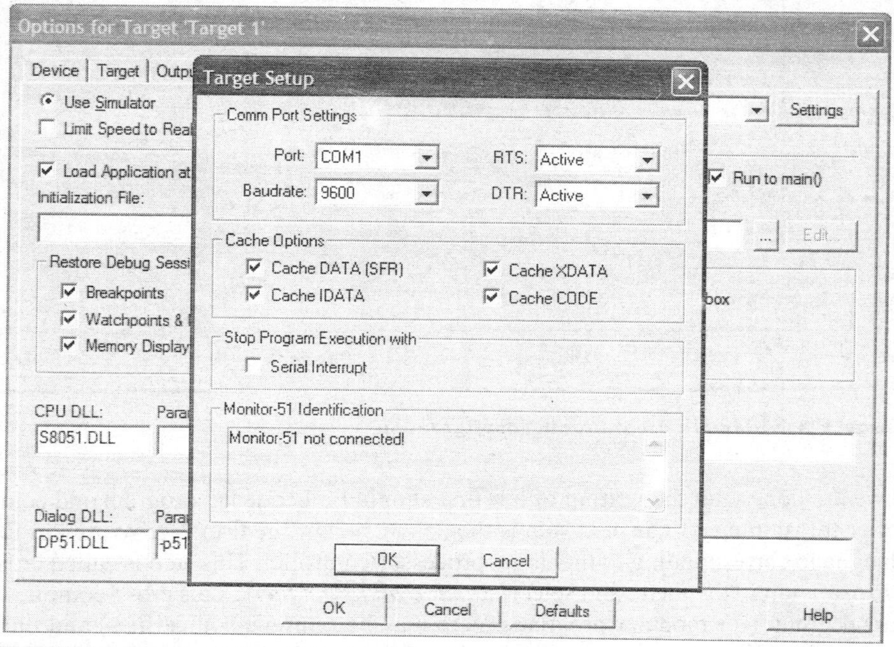

Fig. 13.13 **Target hardware debug serial link configuration**

the target board using the configured serial connection and the firmware execution occurs in real time. The firmware is single stepped (Executing instruction-by-instruction) within the target processor and the monitor program running on the target device reflects the various register and memory contents in the IDE using the serial interface.

The '*Utilities*' tab is used for configuring the flash memory programming of the target processor/controllers from the Keil IDE (Fig. 13.14). You can use either Keil IDE supported programming drivers or a third party tool for programming the target system's FLASH memory. For making use of Keil IDE provided flash memory programming drivers, select the option '*Use Target Driver for Flash Programming*' and choose a driver from the drop-down list. To use third party programming tools, select the option '*Use External Tool for Flash Programming*' and specify the third party tool to be used by giving the path in the '*Command*' column and specify the arguments (if any) in the '*Arguments*' tab to invoke the third party application.

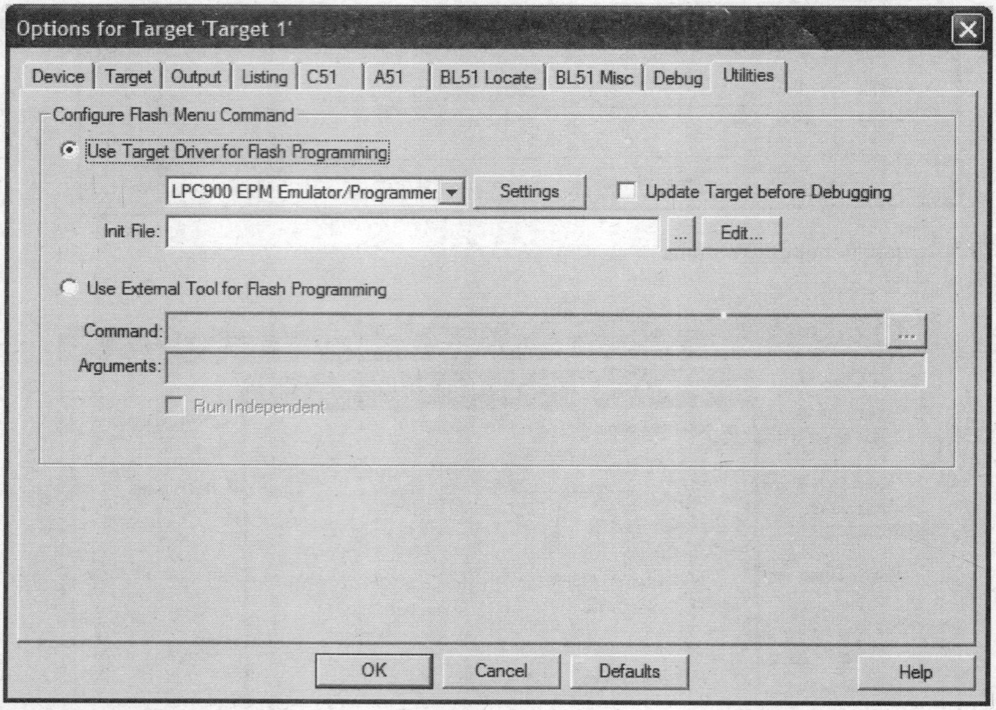

Fig. 13.14 **Target Flash Memory Programming configuration**

With this we are done with the writing of our first simple Embedded C program and configuring the target controller for running it. The next step is the conversion of the firmware written in Embedded C to machine language corresponding to the target processor/controller. This step is called cross-compilation. Go to '*Project*' tab in the menu and select '*Rebuild all target files*'. This cross-compiles all the files within the target group (for modular programs there may be multiple source files) and link the object codes created by each file to generate the final binary. The output of cross-compilation for the "*Hello World*" application is given in Fig. 13.15.

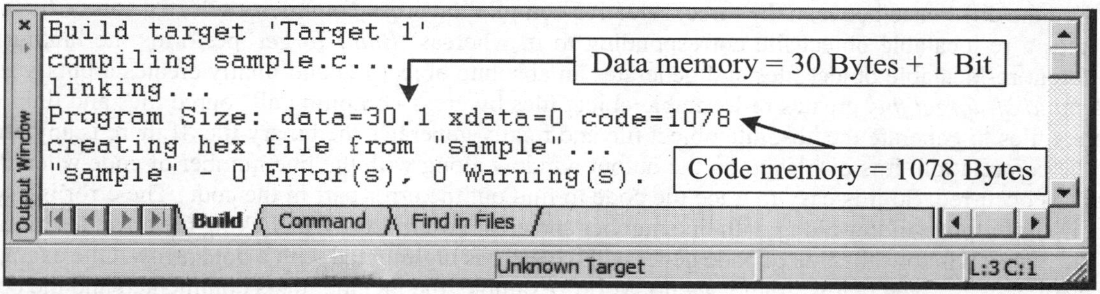

Fig. 13.15 **Conversion of the Embedded C program to *8051* Machine code**

You can see the cross-compilation step & linking in the o/p window along with cross-compilation error history. Now perform a '*Build Target*' operation. This links all the object files created (in a multi-file system where each source files are cross-compiled separately) (Fig. 13.16).

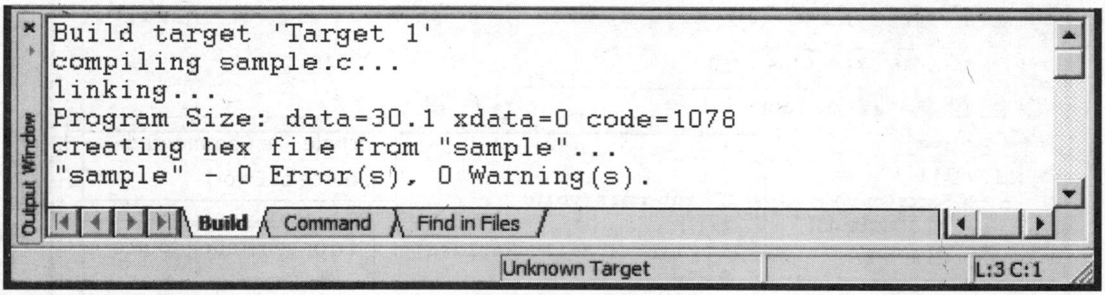

Fig. 13.16 **Linking of all object Files**

In a multi source file project (source group containing multiple .c files) each file can be separately cross-compiled by selecting the '*Translate current file*' option. This is known as Selective Compilation. Remember this generates the object file for the current file only and it needs to be combined with object files generated for other files, by using '*Build Target*' option for creating the final executable (Fig. 13.17). Selective compilation is very helpful in a multifile project where a modified file only needs to be re-compiled and it saves the time in re-compiling all the files present in the target group.

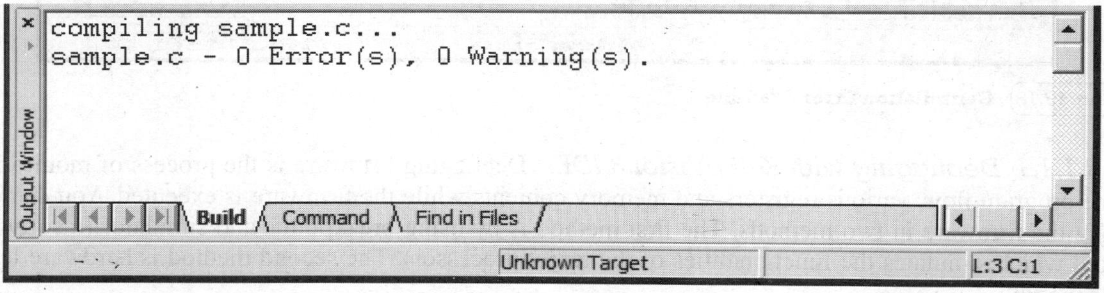

See the difference between the three; selective compilation cross-compiles a selected source file and creates a re-locatable object file corresponding to it, whereas '*Build Target*' performs the linking of different re-locatable object files and generates an absolute object file and finally creates a binary file. '*Rebuild all target file*' creates re-locatable object files by cross-compiling all source files and links all object files to generate the absolute object file and finally generates the binary file. If there is any error in the compilation, it is displayed on the output window along with the line number of code where the error is occurred. So it is easy to trace the code to find out the error part in the code. The error is listed out in the output window along with line number and error description. On clicking the error description at the output window, the line of code generated the error is highlighted with a bold arrow. One example of error code is given below. In the "Hello World" example, the include file is commented and the code while compiling will generate the error indicating *printf* function is not defined. Have a look at the same (Fig. 13.18).

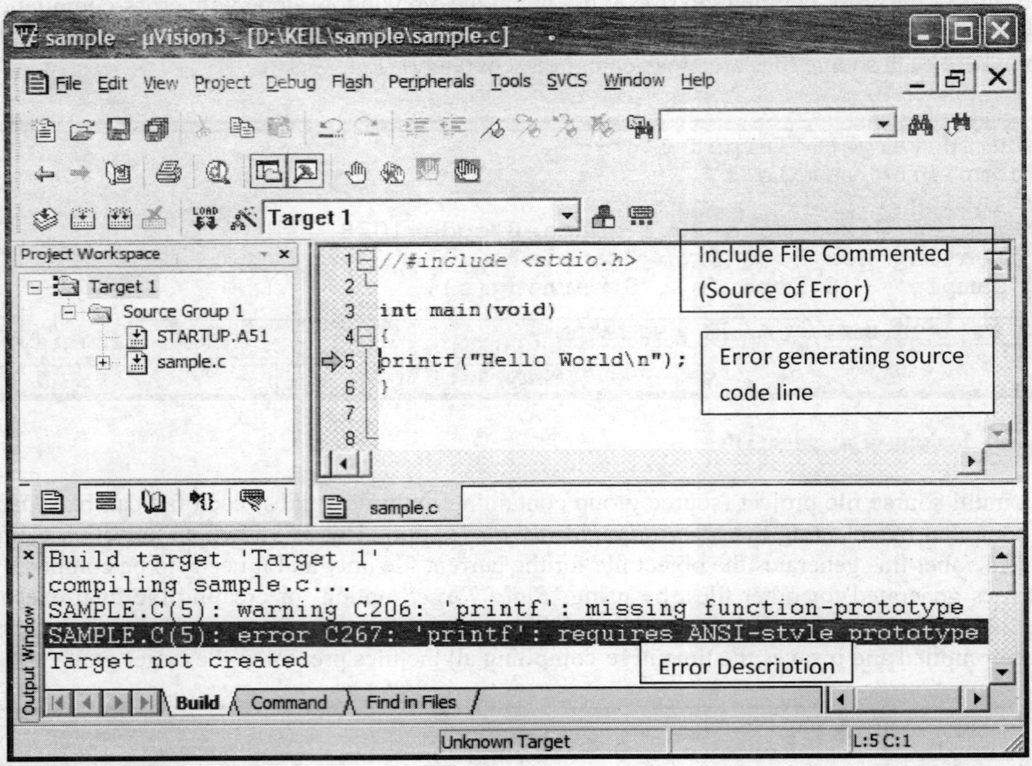

Fig. 13.18 Compilation Error Example

13.1.1.1 Debugging with Keil µVision3 IDE Debugging firmware is the process of monitoring the program flow, various registers and memory contents while the firmware is executed. You can debug the firmware in two methods. The first method is by using breakpoints and simulator (a software tool which simulates the functionalities of the target processor). The second method is hardware level debugging.

For simulator-based debugging, select the option '*Use Simulator*' from the '*Debug*' tab of the '*Options for Target*' as illustrated in a previous section on debug. Insert a '*Breakpoint*' in the code line of the source program where debugging needs to be started. Breakpoints can be inserted by right clicking on the desired source code line and by selecting the '*Insert/Remove Breakpoint*' option. It can also be inserted by using the '*Debug*' tab present in the menu of the IDE (Not the debug tab of Options for Target Pop-up dialog). It toggles the breakpoint (if the breakpoint is already inserted, it is removed and if not a breakpoint is added). The breakpoint breaks the firmware execution at the selected point and further execution requires user interaction. After a break, the code can be executed by single stepping or by a complete run again. For the above 'Hello World' example, we are going to debug the firmware at the source code line *printf* and a breakpoint is inserted as shown in Fig. 13.19.

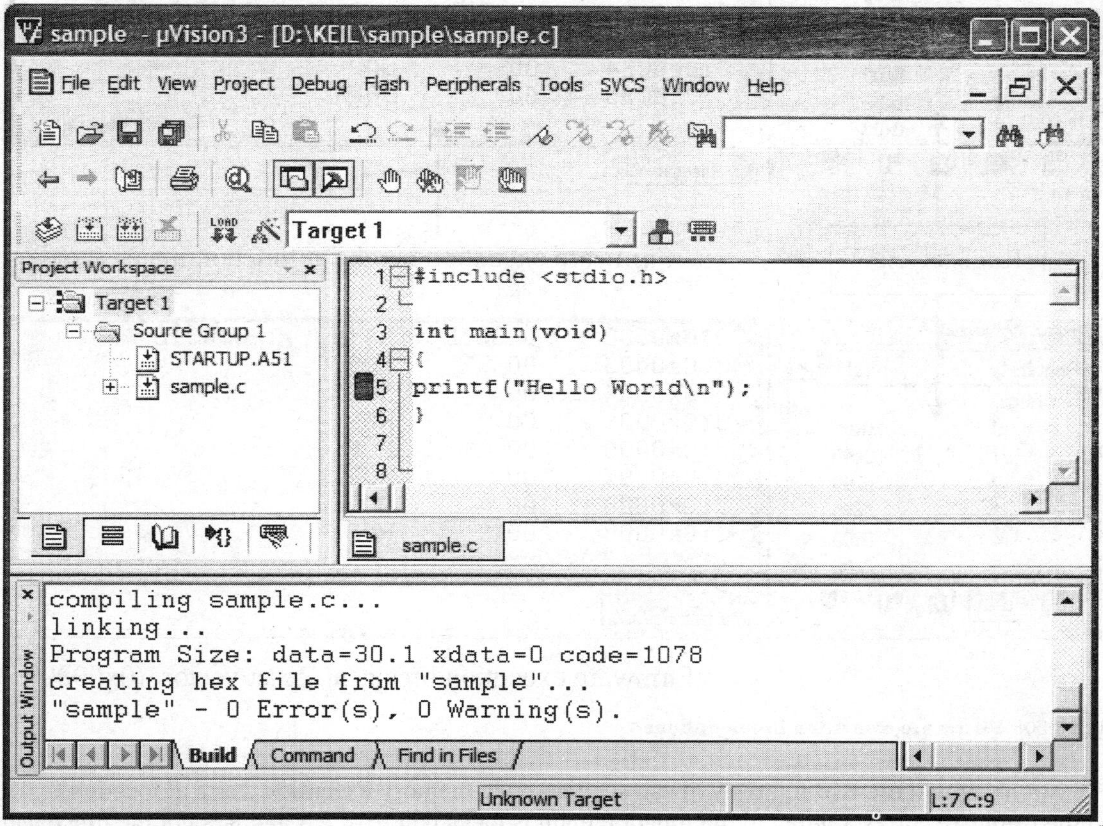

Fig. 13.19 **Breakpoint insertion and debugging**

The '*breakpoint*' is distinguishable with a special visible mark. All debug related actions are grouped within the '*Debug*' tab of the IDE menu. Each debug instruction has a hot key (e.g. Ctrl+F5 for start and stop of debugging) associated with it. Identify the hotkey and use it or use mouse to activate the debug related action each time from the debug menu. To start debugging, select the option '*Start/Stop Debug Session (Ctrl+F5)*' from the '*Debug*' menu. If you set the option '*Go till main()*' on the '*Debug*' tab of

'*Options for Target*', the application runs till the code memory where the main() function starts. If this option is not selected, the execution breaks at the Reset vector (0x0000) itself. Both of these options are shown below. Note that while debugging, the project window tab automatically selects the '*Regs*' tab and shows the various register contents in this window when the program is at the break stage. You can switch the project window in between the '*Files*' section and '*Regs*' section to find out the changes happening to various registers on executing each line of code (Fig. 13.20).

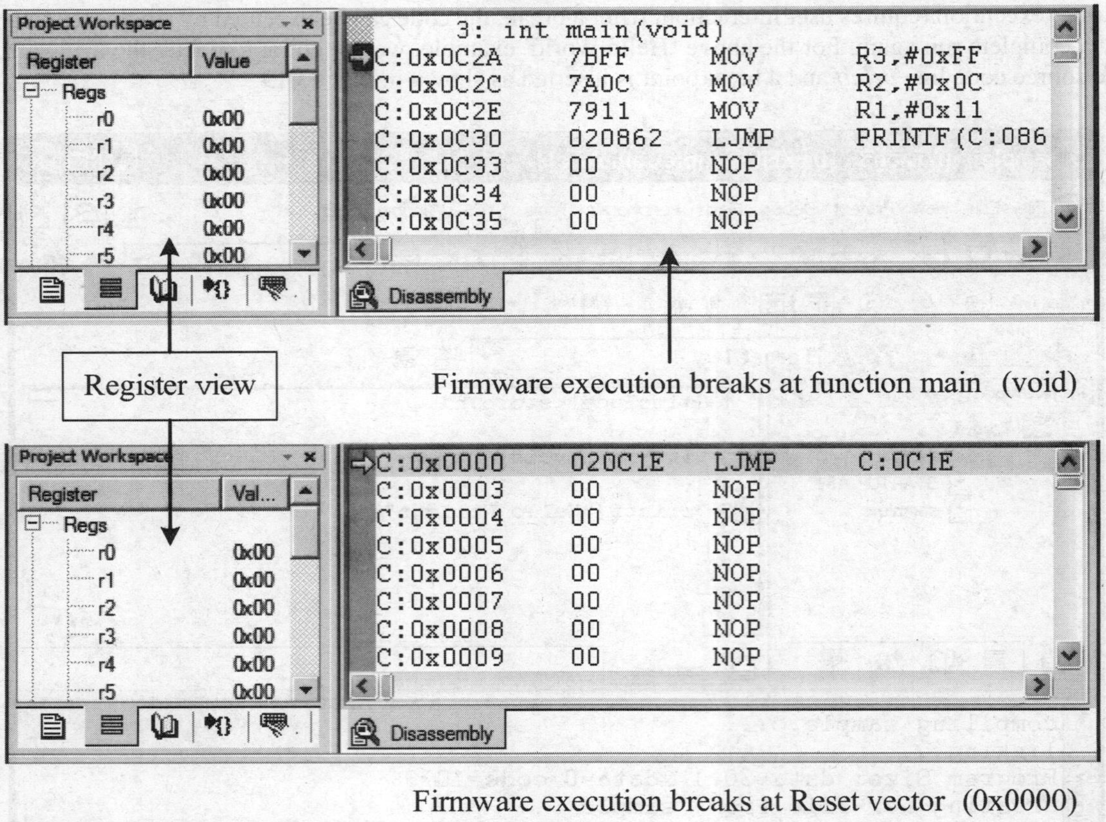

Fig. 13.20 Firmware execution Break options

If you observe these two figures you can see that code memory execution starts at location 0x0000 and the firmware corresponding to the function main is located at 0x0C2A and it is not the first executable code. Before executing *main ()* some other code placed at location 0x0C1E (jump from the reset vector to location 0x0C1E) is executed. The code at this memory location is the code memory generated for the startup file. Startup file code is always executed before entering the function *main*. It should be noted that the code memory location mentioned here for function *main* is not always fixed. It varies depending on the changes made to the startup file. From this breakpoint you can go to the breakpoint you set in the code memory either by single stepping ('*Step*' command (*F11*)) or by a run to the next breakpoint ('*Go*' command (*F5*)).

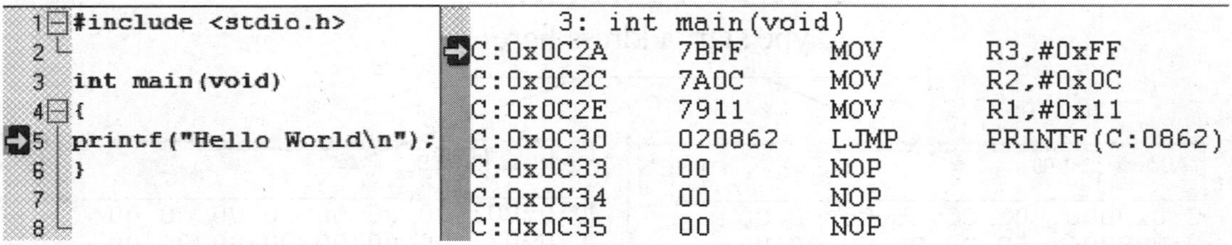

Fig. 13.21 **Source Code and corresponding Disassembly View**

By default, the text editor window in debug mode contains two tabs, namely Source code view tab and Disassembly tab. The Source code and corresponding Disassembly view is shown in Fig. 13.21. While debugging the firmware you can switch the view between Assembly code and original source code lines by selecting the corresponding tab. This switches the view between the original source code and the corresponding Assembly code for it. The Disassembly view disappears temporarily if you click the '*Disassembly Window*' option under the '*View*' tab of the IDE menu. To enable Disassembly View click again on the '*Disassembly Window*' option under the '*View*' tab of the IDE menu (Fig. 13.22).

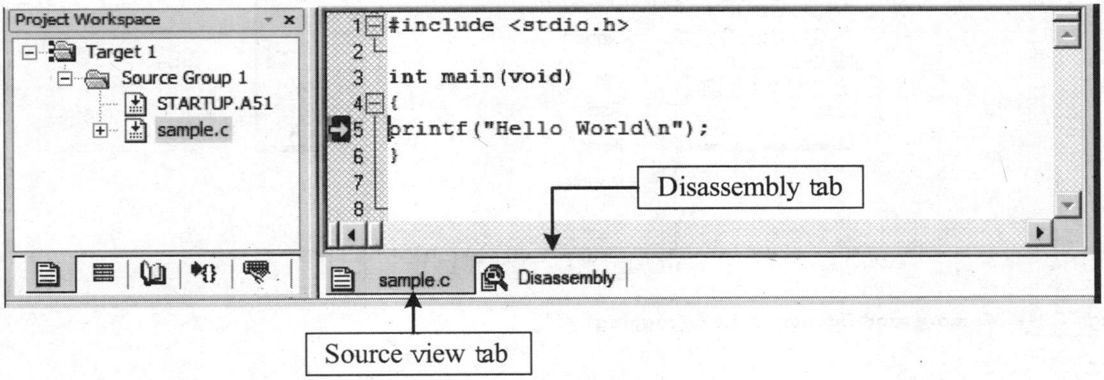

Fig. 13.22 **Workbook Mode for Source – Disassembly code View**

During debugging the content of various CPU and general purpose registers are displayed under the '*Regs*' tab of the project Window. Apart from this you can inspect the data memory and code memory by invoking the '*Memory Window*' under the '*View*' tab of the IDE menu (Fig. 13.23).

For viewing the Data memory, use the Prefix 'D:' before the address and type it at the Address edit box and press enter (For example, for viewing the data memory starting from 0x00, type D:0x00 at the Address box and press enter). You can edit the content of the desired data memory by right clicking on the current contents pointed by the address or just by a double click on the current content. Code memory can also be inspected and modified in a similar way to the Data memory. The only difference is instead of D: use 'C:' (D stands for Data and C stands for Code) (Fig. 13.24).

Similar to other Desktop application development IDEs, this also provides option for viewing local variables and call stack details. Invoke '*Watch & Call Stack Window*' from the '*View*' tab of the IDE menu (Fig. 13.25).

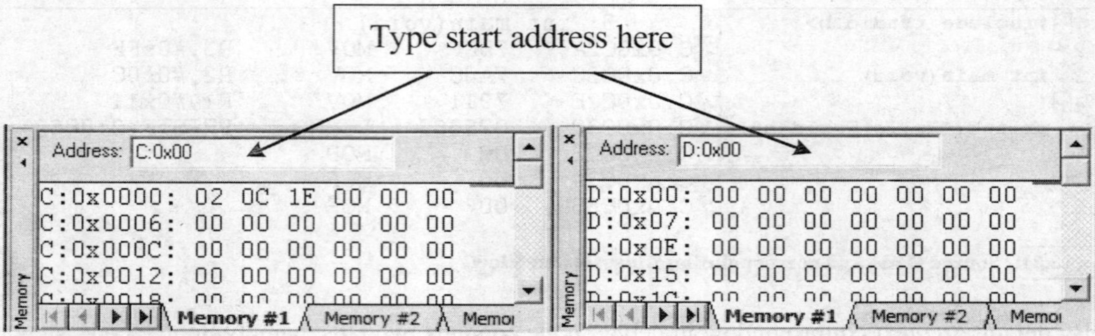

Fig. 13.23 **Memory Window for memory inspection in firmware debugging**

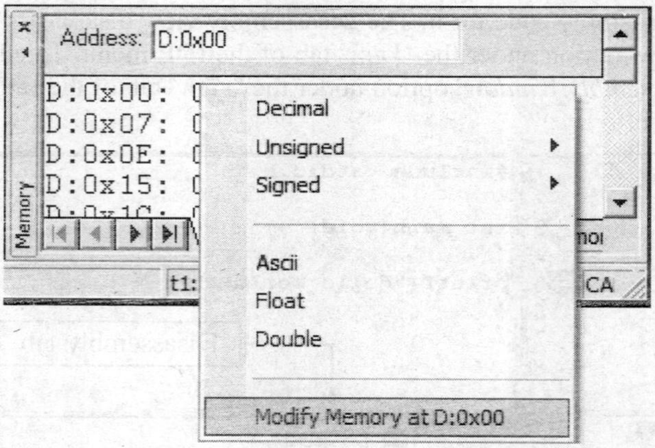

Fig. 13.24 **Memory modification while debugging**

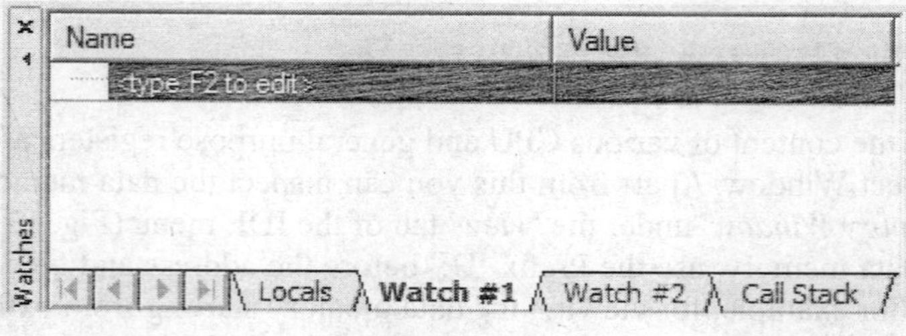

Fig. 13.25 **Watch and Call Stack Window for Debugging**

The local variables can be viewed in the '*Locals*' section of '*Watch and call Stack Window*' whereas users can add other variables to the '*Watch*' window to get their values. '*Call Stack*' gives the '*Callee-Caller*' details for subroutine calls. Invoking '*Symbol Window*' under the '*View*' tab of IDE menu while debugging, displays the list of '*Publics*', '*Locals*' and '*Lines*' used by the application, in the disassembly window (Assembly code). Selecting '*Publics*' shows the different variables and functions present in the Assembly code along with their 'Address', 'Name' and 'Type'. Address can either be Data memory address or Code memory address. 'Type' indicates whether it is a variable or a function. The different variables supported are 'unsigned char (*uchar*)', 'signed char (*char*)', *bit*, unsigned integer (*uint*), signed int (*int*), etc. Figure 13.26 shows the Symbols Window displaying the various symbols used in Assembly for our sample application.

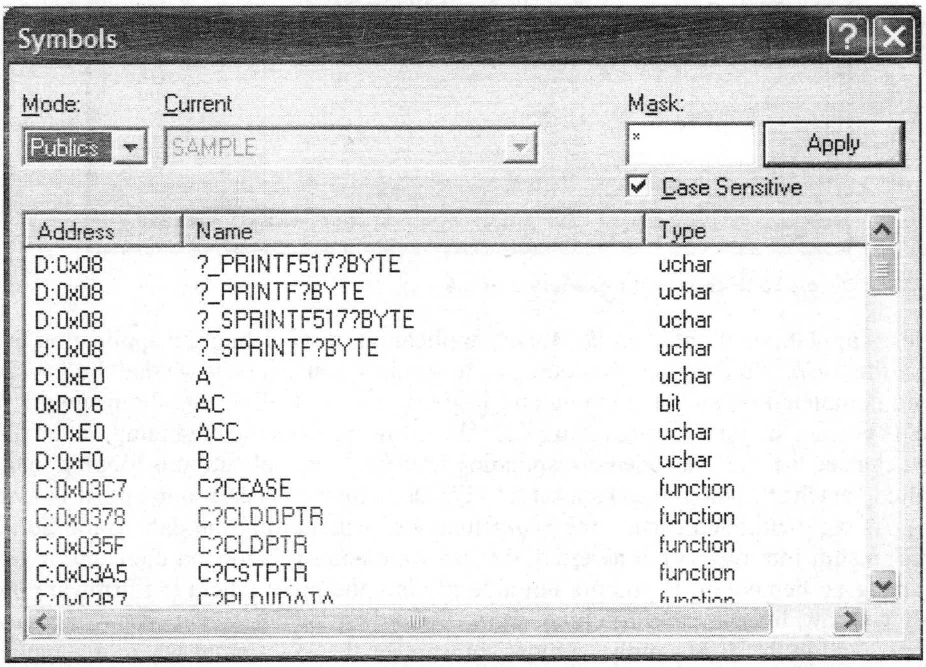

Fig. 13.26 **Symbols Window showing the various symbols used in Assembly**

Activating the '*Code Coverage*' option under the '*View*' tab of the IDE menu when the execution is at halted stage, gives the details of instructions in each function/module and how many of them are executed till execution break. Figure 13.27 illustrates the same.

13.1.1.2 Simulating Peripherals and Interrupts with Keil µVision3 IDE Embedded systems are designed to interact with real world and the actions performed by them may depend on the inputs from various sensors connected to the processor/controller of the embedded system. By a mere software simulation of the firmware, we can only inspect the memory, register contents, etc. of the processor and cannot infer anything on the real-time performance of the system since the inputs provided by the sensors are real-time and dynamic. To a certain extent, we can simulate these inputs using the simulator support provided by the IDE. Keil provides extensive support for simulating various peripherals like; ports, memory mapped I/O, etc. and Interrupts (External, Timer and Serial interrupts). The main limitation of simulation is that we can simulate it with only known values (in a real application the simulated value may not be the real input) and also it is difficult to predict the real-time behaviour of the system

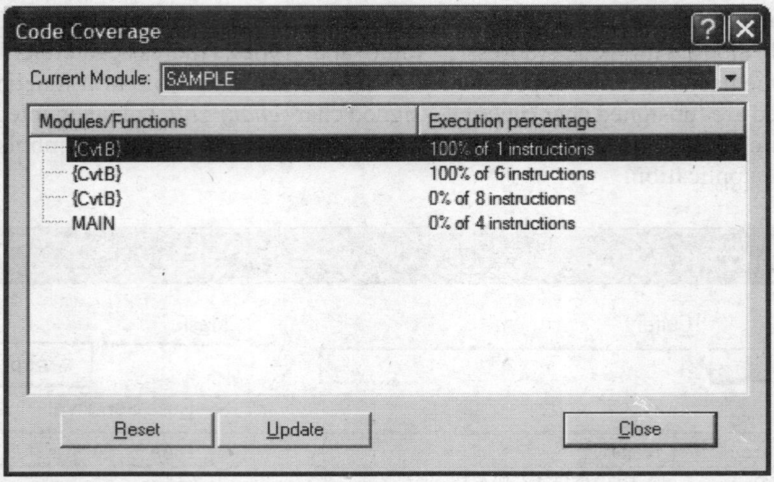

Fig. 13.27 **Code Coverage Details at the execution break**

based on these simulations. In our "*Hello World*" application, if we debug the application by placing a breakpoint at the '*printf*' function, in the source code window you can observe that the '*printf*' function is not getting completed on single stepping and it gives you the feeling that the firmware is hang up somewhere. If you are single stepping (using *F11*) the firmware from the beginning, in the disassembly window you can see that for the code corresponding to *printf*, the application is looping inside another function called 'putchar', which checks a bit TI (Transmit Interrupt) and loops till it is asserted high (Fig. 13.28). As we mentioned earlier, the *printf* function is outputting the data to the Serial port. As long as the Transmit Interrupt is not asserted, the firmware control is looped there and it generates an application hang-up behaviour. If you are not able to view the point where the firmware loops in the Disassembly window, invoke '*Stop Running*' from '*Debug*' tab of IDE menu. The firmware execution will be stopped and in the disassembly window you can see the exact point where the application was looping.

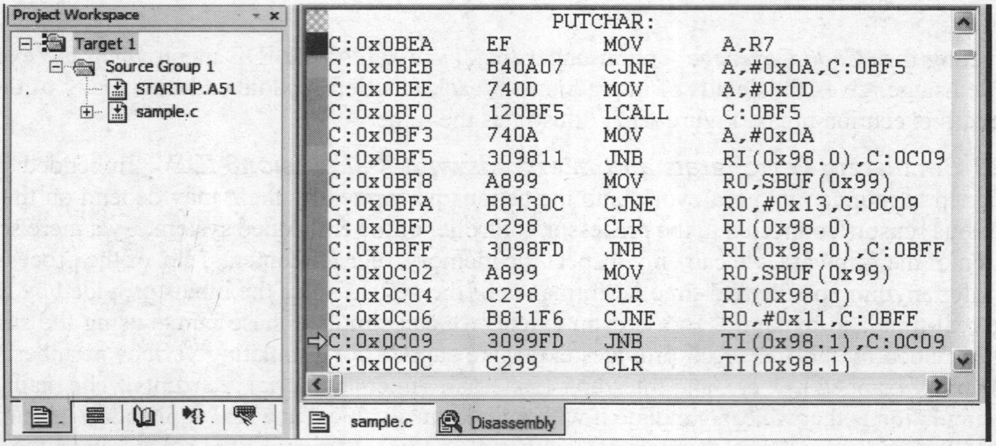

Fig. 13.28 **Firmware Execution waiting for Transmit Interrupt (TI)**

We can simulate the Transmit Interrupt '*TI*' using the simulator support provided by Keil. If you have already stopped the execution, continue the code execution by invoking '*Go*' option from '*Debug*' tab or by pressing '*F5*' key. Now select '*Interrupt*' option from the '*Peripherals*' tab of the IDE menu. The interrupt simulation window will pop-up. Select the '*Serial Xmit*' interrupt and enable the Global Interrupt Enable (*EA*) as well as Transmit Interrupt (*TI*) (Fig. 13.29).

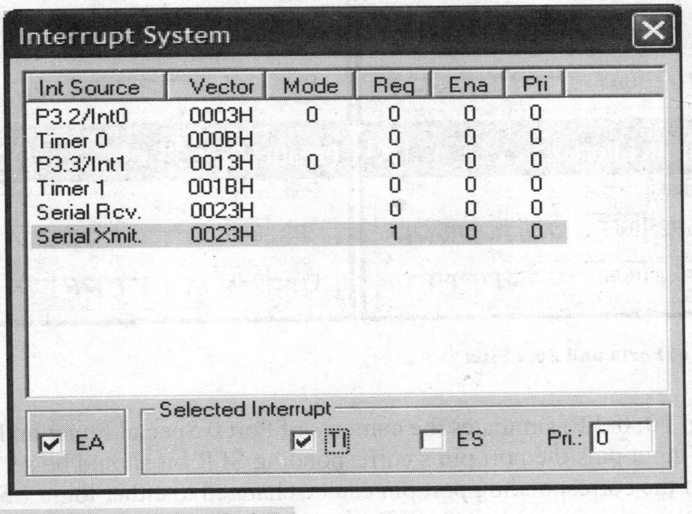

Fig. 13.29 **Serial Transmit Interrupt Simulation**

You can simulate any other interrupt listed in the interrupt system in a similar fashion. On enabling TI, firmware execution comes out of the infinite loop and dumps the string "Hello World" to the serial port. The output of 'Hello World' application is shown in Fig. 13.30. You can capture whatever data going through the serial port while simulation. For this invoke '*Serial Window #1*' from the '*View*' tab of the IDE menu.

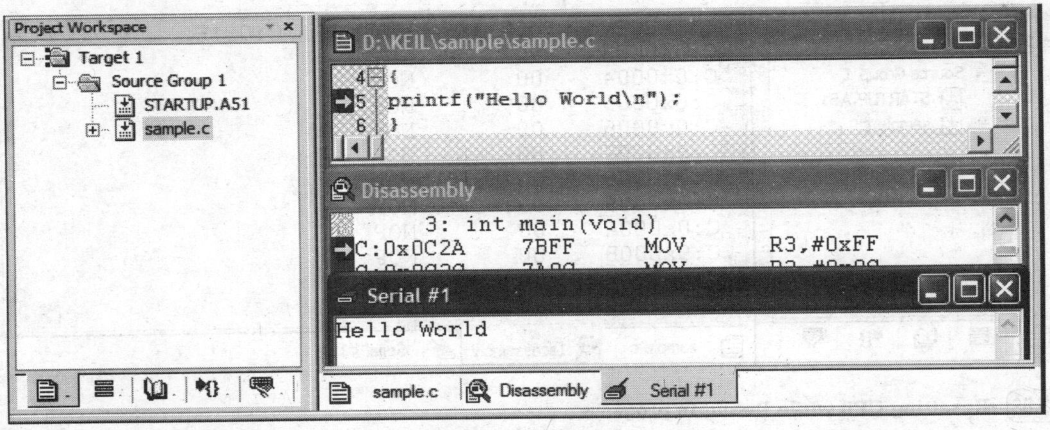

Fig. 13.30 **Output of 'Hello World' Application at Serial Port**

To simulate the Ports and their status, select '*I/O-Ports*' from the '*Peripherals*' tab of IDE menu (Fig. 13.31).

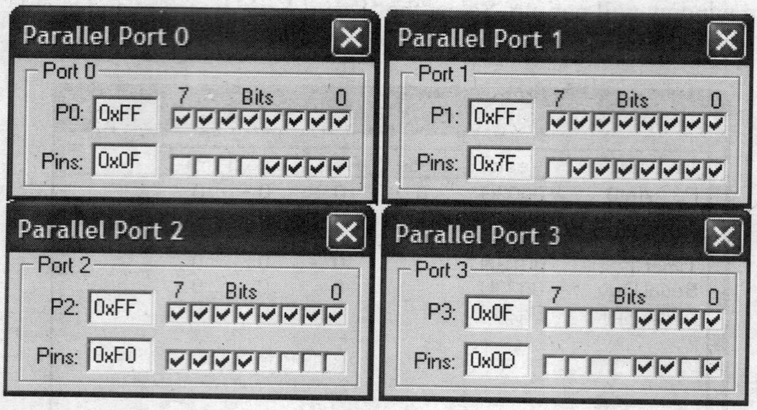

Fig. 13.31 **Simulation of Ports and Port Pins**

The first value (E.g. P0: 0xFF) simulates the contents of Port 0 Special Function Register. In order to make the port pins as input pins the port pin's corresponding SFR bit should be set as 1. With the SFR bit set to 1, the state of the corresponding port pin can be changed to either logic 1 or logic 0. To output logic 0 to a port pin, clear the corresponding SFR bit and for outputting logic 1, set the corresponding port bit in the SFR bit. In the above example, if Port 0 is viewed as an output port, the port will be outputting all 1s. If it is treated as an input port, the value inputted will be 0x0F (which is the state of the port pins). Serial Port and Timers can also be simulated by selecting the respective commands from the '*Peripherals*' tab of the IDE menu. It is left for the readers for experimenting. The '*Reset CPU*' option available under the '*Peripherals*' tab is used for resetting the firmware execution. Resetting the CPU while debugging brings the program execution to the reset vector (0x0000).

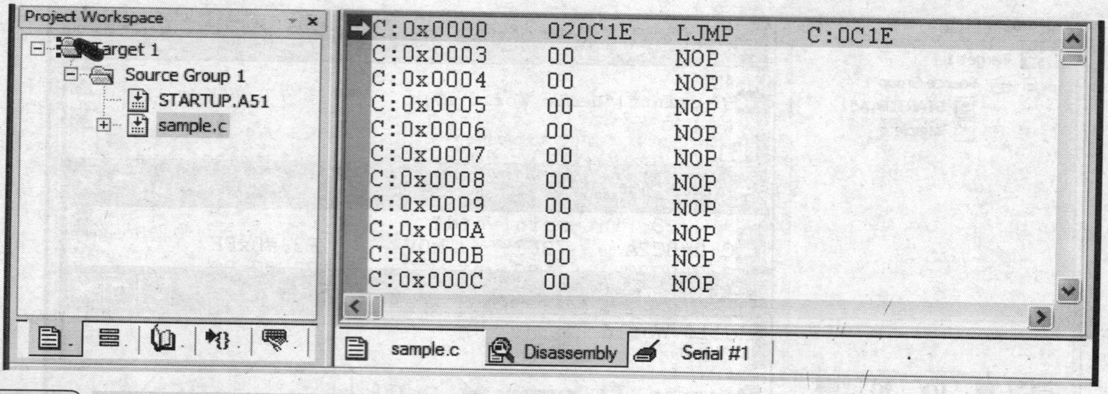

Fig. 13.32 **Resetting CPU while Debug in progress**

Generating precise delays in software for super loop based embedded applications are often quite difficult and there are no standard functions available for generating precise delays. If the '*C*' program is running on DOS platform, there is a standard function '*delay()*' available which generates delay with multiples of millisecond. There are no such standard functions available for generating delays in non-operating system based embedded programming. The only way of generating delays is writing a loop and set its parameters according to the clock frequency used. Often we need to do a trial and error method to finetune the parameters depending on the crystal used. The '*Performance analyser*' support by the Keil IDE helps in calculating the time consumed by a function. To activate this, select '*Performance Analyser...*' from the '*Debug*' tab of the IDE menu while debugging is on, before entering the function whose execution time needs to be calculated. A Performance analyser set up for selected function is shown in Fig. 13.33.

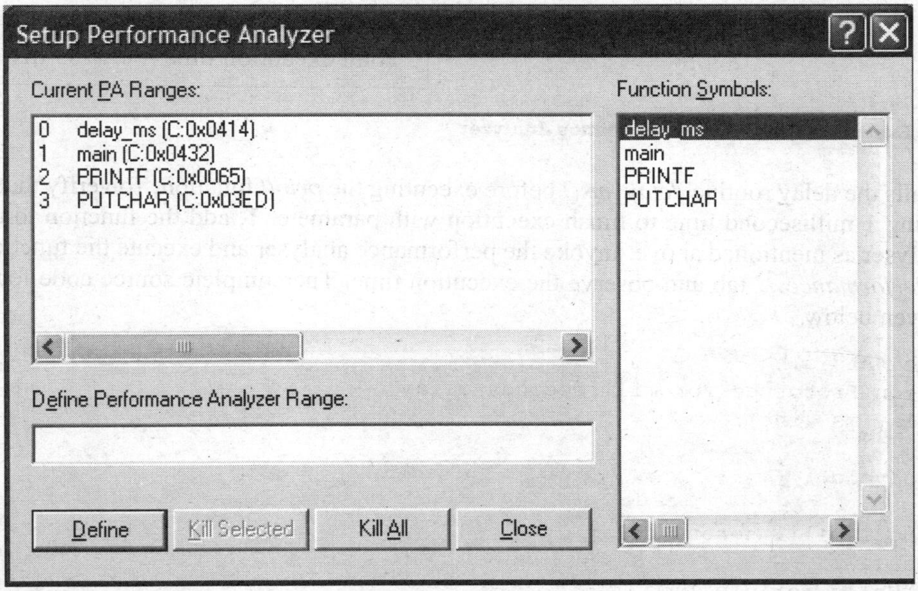

Fig. 13.33 Performance Analyser setup for selected function

The various functions available on the current module is listed on the right side of the '*Setup Performance analyser*' window under the '*Function symbols:*' section. Double clicking on the function of interest displays the same on the '*Define Performance Analyser Range:*' Click the 'Define' button to add it to the analyser. Invoke the '*Performance analyser window*' from the '*View*' tab of the IDE menu. A new tab with name '*Performance...*' will be added to the text editor window. Now execute the function whose execution time is to be analysed by single step (*F11*) or by giving a step Over (*F10*) command. Select the tab '*Performance...*' and click on the function name for which the analysis is performed. The time taken for executing the function is displayed at the '*total time*' display window. This gives a rough estimate on the execution time of the function (Fig. 13.34). Note that in addition to this time, the time taken for calling this function also needs to be taken into account. Moreover, all these calculations are based on the target clock frequency set on the target options. We will discuss the same for a new function for generating milliseconds delay added to our program 'Hello World' application. The main

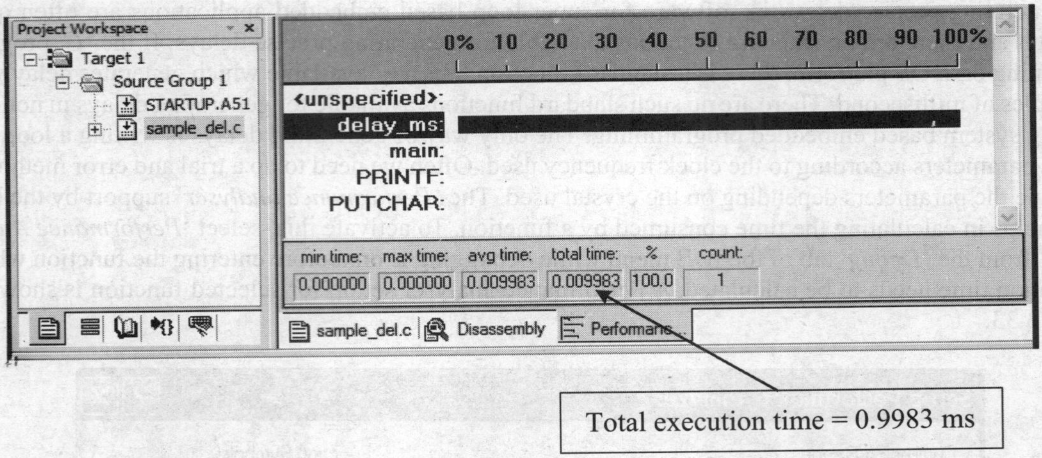

Fig. 13.34 **Execution time from Performance Analyzer**

function calls the delay routine *delay_ms()* before executing the *printf* function. To verify that this function is taking 1 millisecond time to finish execution with parameter 1, add the function to the performance analyser as mentioned above. Invoke the performance analyser and execute the function. Switch view to '*Performance...*' tab and observe the execution time. The complete source code for including delay is given below.

```
#include <stdio.h>
//Function Prototype for milliseconds delay
void delay_ms (int);

int main(void)
{
//Calling 1 milli second delay
delay_ms (1);
printf("Hello World\n");
}
//######################################################################
//Function for generating milli seconds delay
//Assumes clock frequency=24MHz

void delay_ms (int n)
{
int j, k;
for (j=0; j<n; j++)
{
for (k=0; k<247; k++);
}
}
```

It should be noted that generating highly precise delay is very difficult and there may be a tolerance of +/– fraction of milliseconds in the delay. Also the delay is purely dependent on the system clock frequency. In a real world scenario, the stability of the clock is expressed in terms of +/– some parts per million (ppm) of the fundamental frequency. Any change in the target clock frequency needs the re-tuning of the code to bring it back to the desired tolerance level. Precise time delay can be generated using the hardware timer unit of the microcontroller.

13.1.1.3 Target Level Firmware Debugging with Keil μVision3 IDE Simulation based debugging technique lacks real-time behaviour and various input conditions needs to be simulated using the IDE support for debugging the firmware. Target level hardware debugging involves debugging the firmware which is embedded in the target board. This technique is also known as In Circuit Debugging/ Emulation (ICD/E). For performing target level debugging with Keil, the target board should be connected to the development machine through a serial interface. The IDE debug settings should be modified to activate target level debugging. Select the '*Debug*' option from '*Options for Target*' and change '*Use Simulator*' to '*Use:*' selected debug support from a list of available target debug supports (Fig. 13.35).

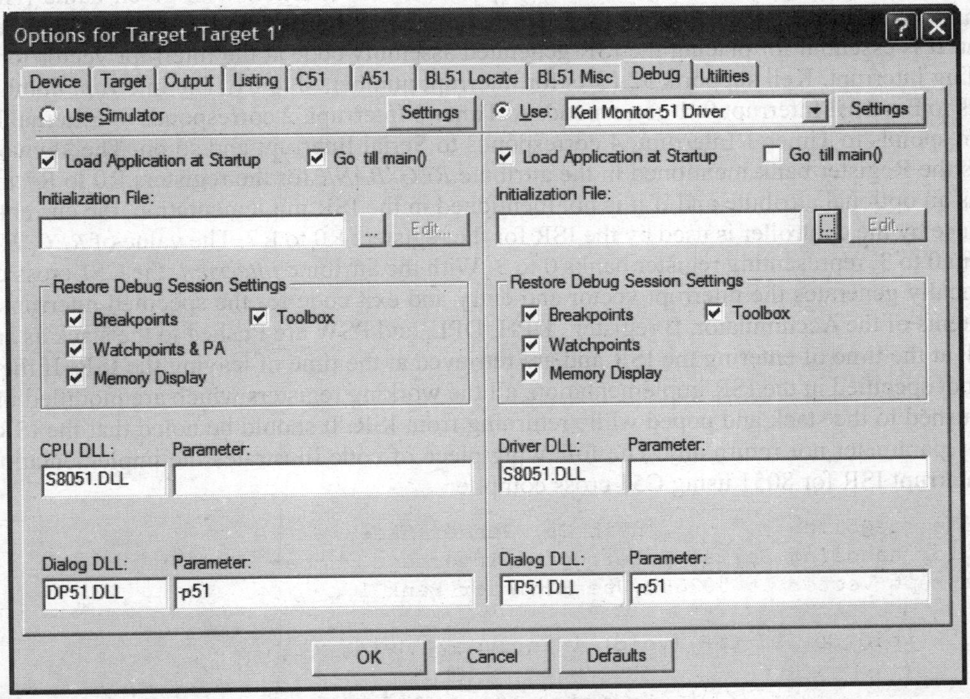

Fig. 13.35 **Configuring IDE Debug settings for target level debugging**

Select the target supported debug option from the drivers available on the drop-down list and configure the serial link properties using the 'Settings' tab. Keil supports two types of target level debugging, namely '*Monitor program based debugging*' and '*Emulator based debugging*'. For Monitor program based debugging, the target processor should have Keil IDE supported monitor program installed and the target hardware should be configured to run the monitor program. Debug instructions from the IDE communicates with the monitor program running on the target processor and it returns the debug information to the IDE using the configured serial link. For Emulator based debugging, Keil IDE acts as an interface between a Keil supported third party Emulator hardware and the target board. The Serial link should be connected to the emulator hardware and other end of the emulator hardware should be interfaced to the target hardware using any ICE supported interfaces like JTAG, BDM or pin-to-pin socket (For JTAG/BDM interface, target processor/controller should have this support at processor/controller side. If not, pin-to-pin socket is used).

13.1.1.4 Writing ISR in Embedded C using the µVision3 IDE The C51 cross-compiler from Keil supports the implementation of Interrupt Service Routines (ISRs) in Embedded C. The general form of writing an Interrupt Service Routine in C for C51 cross-compiler is illustrated below.

```
void ISR_Name (void) interrupt INTR_NO using REG_BANK
{
//Body of ISR
}
```

The attribute *interrupt* informs the cross compiler that the function with given name (Here *ISR_Name*) is an Interrupt Service Routine. The attribute *INTR_NO* indicates the interrupt number for an interrupt. It is essential for placing the ISR generated assembly code at the Interrupt Vector for the corresponding interrupt. Keil supports 32 ISRs for interrupt numbers 0 to 31. The interrupt number 0 corresponds to External Interrupt 0, 1 corresponds to Timer 0 Interrupt, 2 corresponds to External Interrupt 1, 3 corresponds to Timer 1 Interrupt, 4 corresponds to Serial Interrupt and so on. The keyword *using* specifies the Register bank mentioned in the attribute *REG_BANK* for the registers R0 to R7 inside the ISR. It is an optional attribute and if it is not mentioned in the ISR implementation, the current register bank in use by the controller is used by the ISR for the registers R0 to R7. The value of *REG_BANK* can vary from 0 to 3, representing register banks 0 to 3. With the attribute *interrupt*, the C51 cross compiler automatically generates the interrupt vector and entry and exit code for the specified interrupt routine. The contents of the Accumulator, B register , DPH, DPL, and PSW are Pushed to the stack as and when required, at the time of entering the ISR and are retrieved at the time of leaving the ISR. If the register bank is not specified in the ISR implementation, all the working registers which are modified inside the ISR is pushed to the stack and poped while returning from ISR. It should be noted that the ISR neither takes any parameter nor return any. The following piece of code illustrates the implementation of the Serial Interrupt ISR for 8051 using C51 cross compiler.

```
#include <reg51.h>            //Keil C51 Header file
//ISR for handling Serial Interrupts. Interrupt number = 4
//Interrupt Vector at 0023H. Use Register Bank 1

    void Serial_ISR (void) interrupt 4 using 1
    {
            if (TI)     //Check transmit Interrupt (TI) Flag
            {
            //Transmit Interrupt Handler
            }
            else
            {
            //Receive Interrupt Handler
            }
    }
```

13.1.1.5 Assembly Based Firmware Development with μVision3 IDE Apart from Embedded C based development, Keil IDE also supports Assembly language based firmware development. The steps involved in creating a project for writing assembly instructions are same as that of Embedded C based development. The only difference is that there is no need to include the standard startup file at the time of creating a project. Select the option '***No***' to the query '*Copy standard 8051 startup Code to Project Folder and add File to Project?*' while creating a new project (Refer to Section 13.1.1 for details on creating a new project). Since we are not using the IDE supplied startup code, the actions performed by startup code (mainly initialisation of stack pointer), should be written by the programmer before the start of the main program in the assembly file. Create a new file and start writing Assembly instructions in the file. Save the file with extension '*.src*' and add the file to the 'Source Group' of the target as illustrated in embedded C based development (Section 13.1.1). A program written in Assembly Language corresponding to the "Hello World" program written in Embedded C is illustrated below.

```
;####################################################################
;                        Start of Main Program
;####################################################################
ORG     0000H
               JMP MAIN
ORG     0003H  ; External Interrupt 0 Handler
               RETI
ORG     000BH  ; Timer0 Interrupt Handler
               RETI
ORG     0013H  ; External Interrupt 1 Handler
               RETI
ORG     001BH  ; Timer1 Interrupt Handler
               RETI
ORG     0023H  ; Serial Interrupt Handler
               RETI
ORG     0100H
MAIN:          MOV SP, #50H        ; Initialise stack pointer at 50H
;####################################################################
               ; 8051 Serial Routine Parameter settings
               MOV SCON, #50h      ; Configure Serial Communication
                                   ; Register.
               MOV TMOD, #21h      ; Baud Generation Settings
               MOV TH1, #0FDH      ; Re-Load Value for TIMER 1 in Auto
                                   ; Re-Load
               MOV TL1, #0FDH      ; 9600 baud
               MOV A, PCON
               ANL A, #7FH
               MOV PCON, A
               SETB TR1            ; Start Timer1
;####################################################################
OUT_TEXT:      CALL    TEXT_OUT
               JMP     OUT_TEXT
;####################################################################
; Text outputting Routine
; Same as printf () in Embedded C
```

```
TEXT_OUT:        MOV DPTR, #HELLO_WORLD
SERIAL_OUT:      CLR TI              ; Clear Transmit Interrupt
                 CLR A
                 MOVC A,@A+DPTR
                 CJNE A, #'\', FOLLOW
                 MOV SBUF, #0AH      ; Send new line character
                 JNB TI, $
                 RET
FOLLOW:MOV       SBUF, A
                 JNB TI, $           ; Wait till Transmit Interrupt before
                                     ; sending next byte
                 INC DPTR
                 JMP SERIAL_OUT
;#####################################################################
; Store the string "Hello World" in program memory
;#####################################################################
HELLO_WORLD:

DB        'Hello World\'
          END                        ; End of Assembly
```

Compile this source code using the same compile options illustrated for Embedded C based development. Here also you can have multiple source (*.src*) files. Add all source files to the 'Source Group' and compile the program. The Assembly program is written to store the string "Hello World" in the code memory and it is retrieved from the code memory for sending to the serial port. The string can also be stored in the data memory and retrieve it from there for sending to the serial port. In that case the storage memory for the string "*Hello World*" (12 bytes with string termination character '\') in the code memory will be released and the same will occupy in the data memory. Figure 13.36 shows the assembling of source code written in assembly language.

If you observe the output window while compiling, you can see that the source code is '*assembled*' instead of '*compiling*'. Why this strange thing happens? - The answer is conversion of program written in assembly language to object code is carried out by the utility '*Assembler*'. Assembler is same as compiler in functioning but the input is different. You can debug this application using the simulator in a similar way as that of debugging the '*C*' source code. On debugging the assembly code you can view the output on the '*Serial Window*' and it is exactly the same as the output produced by the "*Hello World*" Application written in Embedded C.

Now let's have a comparison between the application written in Embedded C and Assembly Language for outputting the string "Hello World" to the Serial port. Read carefully.

Q1. How many lines of code you wrote for the program "Hello World"?
Embedded C: Only a single line of Code excluding the framework of main
Assembly: More than 25 lines

Q2. How many registers of the target processor you are familiar with for writing the "Hello World" program?
Embedded C: None
Assembly: Almost all

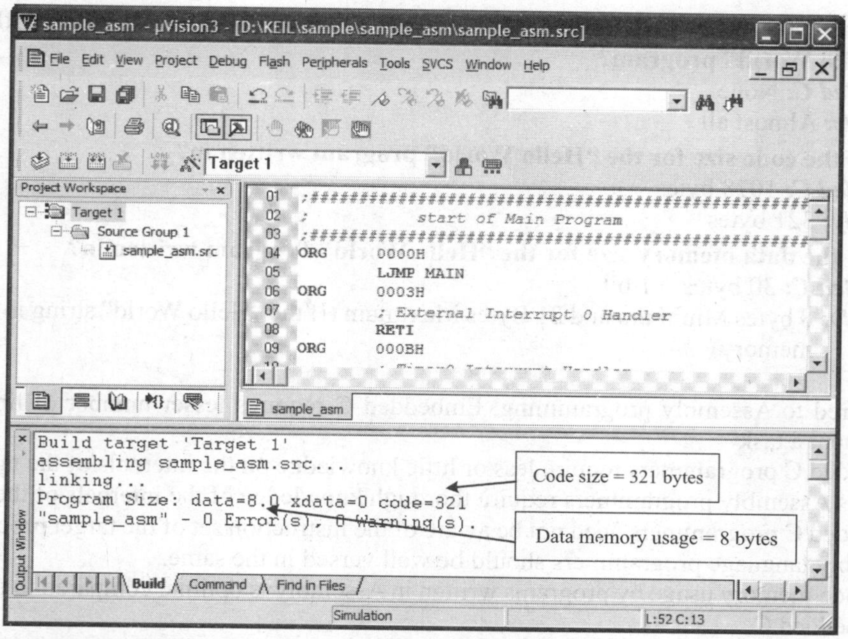

Fig. 13.36 **Assembling of source code written in Assembly Language**

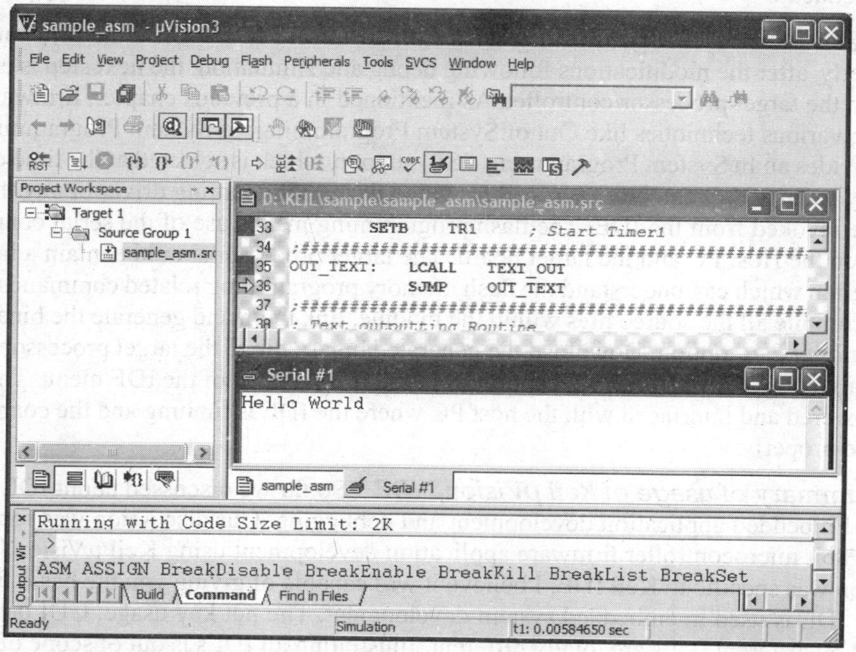

Fig. 13.37 **Debugging the Source code written in Assembly Language for outputting the text "*Hello World*" to serial port**

Q3. How many Assembly Instructions of the target processor you are familiar with for writing the "Hello World" program?
Embedded C: None
Assembly: Almost all

Q4. What is the code size for the "Hello World" program written in?
Embedded C: 1078 bytes
Assembly: 321 bytes

Q5. What is the data memory size for the "Hello World" Program written in?
Embedded C: 30 bytes + 1 bit
Assembly: 8 bytes Minimum and 21 Bytes Maximum (If the "Hello World" string is stored in Data memory)

Summary

1. Compared to Assembly programming, Embedded C requires lesser number of lines of code to implement a task
2. Embedded C programmers require less or little knowledge on the internals of the target processor whereas Assembly programmers require thorough knowledge of the internals of the processor
3. Embedded C programmers need not be aware of the instruction set of the target processor whereas Assembly language programmers should be well versed in the same.
4. The Code memory usage by programs written in Assembly is optimal compared to the one written in Embedded C
5. The Data memory usage by programs written in Assembly is optimal compared to the one written in Embedded C

13.1.1.6 Flash Memory Programming with Keil μVision3 IDE Once the firmware starts functioning properly, after the modifications following debug and simulation, the next step is embedding the firmware into the target processor/controller. As mentioned in a previous chapter, firmware can be embedded using various techniques like Out of System Programming, In System Programming (ISP), etc. Keil IDE provides an In System Programming (ISP) support which is selected at the time of configuring the '*Options for Target*'. It can be either Keil provided flash programming driver or any third party tool which can be invoked from the IDE. The flash programming makes use of the serial connection established between the Host PC and the target board. The target processor should contain a bootloader or a monitor program which can understand the flash memory programming related commands sent from the IDE. Cross-compile all the source files within the module, link them and generate the binary code using '*Rebuild all target files*' option. Download the generated binary file to the target processor's/controller's memory by invoking '*Flash Download*' option from the '*Project*' tab of the IDE menu. The target board should be powered and interfaced with the host PC where the IDE is running and the connection should be configured properly.

13.1.1.7 Summary of usage of Keil μVision3 IDE So far we discussed about IDE and how IDE is helpful in Embedded application development and debugging. Our discussion was focusing only on *8051* family 8bit microcontroller firmware application development using Keil μVision3 IDE. Though the discussion was specific to Keil IDE, I believe it was capable of giving you the basic fundas of IDEs and how the IDE is used in embedded system development. The hot key usage, GUI details and functions offered by different IDEs are totally different. Illustrating all IDEs is out of scope of this book and also there is no common IDE supporting multiple family devices that can be used for illustrating the same. Users are requested to go through the respective manuals of the IDE they are using for firmware development. Also, IDEs undergo rapid changes by adding new features, functions, etc. and whatever we discussed here need not be the same after three months or six months or one year, in terms of features, UI, hot keys, menu options, etc. When I started the work of this book, the IDE offered from Keil was Keil µVision2 and at the time of finishing this work, the latest IDE available from Keil is Keil µVision3. It incorporated lots of new features and changes compared to the old IDE. Users are requested to visit the web site www.keil.com to get the latest updates on the new versions of the IDE. You can directly download the trial version of the IDE from the above site.

13.1.2 An Overview of IDEs for Embedded System Development

The table shown below gives an overview of the Integrated Development Environments (IDEs) used for developing embedded systems for various processors/Real-time operating systems.

Processor Family/ RTOS	IDE Name	Supplier/Remarks
8051	Keil Micro Vision	Keil Software. An ARM Company. www.keil.com
8051	RIDE	Raisonance http://www.raisonance.com/products/info/RIDE.php
8051	SC51	SPJ Embedded Technologies http://www.spjsystems.com/sc51.htm
8051	IAR Embedded Workbench FOR 8051	IAR Systems http://www.iar.com/website1/1.0.1.0/244/1/index.php
PIC	MPLAB	Microchip Technology Inc http://www.microchip.com/
PIC	IAR Embedded Workbench for PIC	IAR Systems http://www.iar.com/website1/1.0.1.0/214/1/index.php
AVR	AVR Studio AVR32 Studio	Atmel Corporation http://www.atmel.com/dyn/Products/tools_card.asp?tool_id=2725
ARM	RealView MDK	Keil Software. An ARM Company http://www.keil.com/arm/
ARM	IAR Embedded Workbench for ARM	IAR Systems http://www.iar.com/website1/1.0.1.0/68/1/index.php
ARM	CodeWarrior	Freescale Semiconductor http://www.freescale.com/
ARM	Sourcery G++	CodeSourcery http://www.codesourcery.com/gnu_toolchains/sgpp It is a complete software development environment based on the GNU Tool chain. Sourcery G++ includes the GNU C and C++ compilers, the Eclipse IDE. Supports ARM®, ColdFire®, fido™, MIPS®, Power Architecture™, Stellaris®, x86
Infineon Family	DAvE	Infineon Technologies. For the 8, 16 and 32 bit Infineon processors/controllers. http://www.infineon.com/

MIPS	Eclipse Ganymede	Macraigor Systems. Eclipse based GNU tool suite. http://www.macraigor.com/Eclipse/index.htm
PowerPC	Eclipse Ganymede	Macraigor Systems. Eclipse based GNU tool suite. http://www.macraigor.com/Eclipse/index.htm
ST Family	ST Visual Develop	IDE for ST Microelectronics processor/controller products. http://www.st.com/mcu/contentid-44.html
Blackfin Family DSP	VisualDSP	Analog Devices www.analog.com
TI Family of DSP	Code Composer Studio	Texas Instruments. http://www.ti.com/
Windows CE RTOS	Platform Builder	Microsoft. www.microsoft.com Available as bundled package with Visual Studio IDE
VxWorks RTOS	Wind River Workbench	Wind River Systems. www.windriver.com
QNX RTOS	QNX Momentics	QNX Software Systems www.qnx.com
3rd Party Tools	MULTI IDE	Green Hills Software Supports a variety of family of processors. Visit www.ghs.com for more details

And…. The list continues. There are thousands of IDEs available in the market as either commercial or non-commercial and as either Open source tools or proprietary tools. Listing all of them is out of the scope of this book. The intention is to just make the readers familiar with some of the popular IDEs for some commonly used processors/controllers and RTOSs for embedded development.

13.2 TYPES OF FILES GENERATED ON CROSS-COMPILATION

Cross-compilation is the process of converting a source code written in high level language (like 'Embedded C') to a target processor/controller understandable machine code (e.g. ARM processor or *8051* microcontroller specific machine code). The conversion of the code is done by software running on a processor/controller (e.g. x86 processor based PC) which is different from the target processor. The software performing this operation is referred as the 'Cross-compiler'. In a single word cross-compilation is the process of cross platform software/firmware development. Cross assembling is similar to cross-compiling; the only difference is that the code written in a target processor/controller specific Assembly code is converted into its corresponding machine code. The application converting Assembly instruction to target processor/controller specific machine code is known as cross-assembler. Cross-compilation/cross-assembling is carried out in different steps and the process generates various types of intermediate files. Almost all compilers provide the option to select whatever intermediate files needs to be retained after cross-compilation. The various files generated during the cross-compilation/cross-assembling process are:

List File (.lst), Hex File (.hex), Pre-processor Output file, Map File (File extension linker dependent), Object File (.obj)

13.2.1 List File (*.LST File*)

Listing file is generated during the cross-compilation process and it contains an abundance of information about the cross compilation process, like cross compiler details, formatted source text **('C' code)**, assembly code generated from the source file, symbol tables, errors and warnings detected during the cross-compilation process. The type of information contained in the list file is cross-compiler specific. As an example let's consider the cross-compilation process of the file *sample.c* given as the first illustrative embedded C program under Keil µVision3 IDE discussion. The '*list file*' generated contains the following sections.

Page Header A header on each page of the listing file which indicates the compiler version number, source file name, date, time, and page number.

```
C51 COMPILER V8.02 SAMPLE                    05/23/2006 11:29:58 PAGE 1
```

Command Line Represents the entire command line that was used for invoking the compiler.

```
C51 COMPILER V8.02, COMPILATION OF MODULE SAMPLE
OBJECT MODULE PLACED IN sample.OBJ
COMPILER INVOKED BY: C:\Keil\C51\BIN\C51.EXE sample.c BROWSE DEBUG OBJECTEXTEND
CODE LISTINCLUDE SYMBOLS
```

Source Code The source code listing outputs the line number as well as the source code on that line. Special cross compiler directives can be used to include or exclude the conditional codes (code in #if blocks) in the source code listings. Apart from the source code lines, the list file will include the comments in the source file and depending on the list file generation settings the entire contents of all include files may also be included. Special cross compiler directives can be used to include the entire contents of the include file in the list file.

```
line level    source
 1          //Sample.c for printing Hello World!
 2          //Written by xyz
 3          #include <stdio.h>
 1     =1  /*-------------------------------------------------------------------
 2     =1  STDIO.H
 3     =1
 4     =1  Prototypes for standard I/O functions.
 5     =1  Copyright © 1988–2002 Keil Elektronik GmbH and Keil Software, Inc.
 6     =1  All rights reserved.
 7     =1  --------------------------------------------------------------------*/
 8     =1
 9     =1  #ifndef __STDIO_H__
10     =1  #define __STDIO_H__
11     =1
12     =1  #ifndef EOF
13     =1   #define EOF -1
14     =1  #endif
15     =1
16     =1  #ifndef NULL
```

```
17    =1   #define NULL ((void *) 0)
18    =1  #endif
19    =1
20    =1  #ifndef _SIZE_T
21    =1  #define _SIZE_T
22    =1   typedef unsigned int size_t;
23    =1  #endif
24    =1
25    =1  #pragma SAVE
26    =1  #pragma REGPARMS
27    =1  extern char _getkey (void);
28    =1  extern char getchar (void);
29    =1  extern char ungetchar (char);
30    =1  extern char putchar (char);
31    =1  extern int printf   (const char *, ...);
32    =1  extern int sprintf (char *, const char *, ...);
33    =1  extern int vprintf  (const char *, char *);
34    =1  extern int vsprintf (char *, const char *, char *);
35    =1  extern char *gets (char *, int n);
36    =1  extern int scanf (const char *, ...);
37    =1  extern int sscanf (char *, const char *, ...);
38    =1  extern int puts (const char *);
39    =1
40    =1  #pragma RESTORE
41    =1
42    =1  #endif
43    =1
4
5         void main()
6         {
7   1     printf("Hello World!\n");
8   1     }
9
```

Assembly Listing Assembly listing contains the assembly code generated by the cross compiler for the 'C' source code. Assembly code generated can be excluded from the list file by using special compiler directives.

```
ASSEMBLY LISTING OF GENERATED OBJECT CODE
          ; FUNCTION main (BEGIN)
                                  ; SOURCE LINE # 5
                                  ; SOURCE LINE # 6
                                  ; SOURCE LINE # 7
0000 7BFF                       MOV     R3, #0FFH
0002 7A00        R              MOV     R2, #HIGH ?SC_0
```

```
0004 7900      R    MOV   R1, #LOW ?SC_0
0006 020000    E    LJMP  _printf

    ; FUNCTION main (END)
```

Symbol Listing The symbol listing contains symbolic information about the various symbols present in the cross compiled source file. Symbol listing contains the sections symbol name (NAME) symbol classification (CLASS (Special Function Register (SFR), structure, typedef, static, public, auto, extern, etc.)), memory space (MSPACE (code memory or data memory)), data type (TYPE (int, char, Procedure call, etc.)), offset ((OFFSET from code memory start address)) and size in bytes (SIZE). Symbol listing in list file output can be turned on or off by cross-compiler directives.

NAME	CLASS	MSPACE	TYPE	OFFSET	SIZE
====	=====	======	====	======	====
size_t	TYPEDEF	-----	U_INT	-----	2
main	PUBLIC	CODE	PROC	0000H	-----
_printf.	EXTERN	CODE	PROC	-----	-----

Module Information The module information provides the size of initialised and un-initialised memory areas defined by the source file

```
MODULE INFORMATION:          STATIC     OVERLAYABLE
   CODE SIZE           =     9          ----
   CONSTANT SIZE       =     14         ----
   XDATA SIZE          =     ----       ----
   PDATA SIZE          =     ----       ----
   DATA SIZE           =     ----       ----
   IDATA SIZE          =     ----       ----
   BIT SIZE            =     ----       ----
END OF MODULE INFORMATION.
```

Warnings and Errors Warnings and Errors section of list file records the errors encountered or any statement that may create issues in application (warnings), during cross compilation. The warning levels can be configured before cross compilation. You can ignore certain warnings, e.g. a local variable is declared within a function and it is not used anywhere in the program. Certain warnings require prompt attention.

```
C51 COMPILATION COMPLETE.  0 WARNING(S),  0 ERROR(S)
```

List file is a very useful tool for application debugging in case of any cross compilation issues.

13.2.2 Preprocessor Output File

The preprocessor output file generated during cross-compilation contains the preprocessor output for the preprocessor instructions used in the source file. Preprocessor output file is used for verifying the operation of macros and conditional preprocessor directives. The preprocessor output file is a valid C source file. File extension of preprocessor output file is cross compiler dependent.

13.2.3 Object File (*.OBJ* File)

Cross-compiling/assembling each source module (written in C/Assembly) converts the various Embedded C/Assembly instructions and other directives present in the module to an object (*.OBJ*) file. The format (internal representation) of the *.OBJ* file is cross compiler dependent. OMF51 or OMF2 are the two objects file formats supported by C51 cross compiler. The object file is a specially formatted file with data records for symbolic information, object code, debugging information, library references, etc. The list of some of the details stored in an object file is given below.

1. Reserved memory for global variables.
2. Public symbol (variable and function) names.
3. External symbol (variable and function) references.
4. Library files with which to link.
5. Debugging information to help synchronise source lines with object code.

The object code present in the object file are not absolute, meaning, the code is not allocated fixed memory location in code memory. It is the responsibility of the linker/locater to assign an absolute memory location to the object code. During cross-compilation process, the cross compiler sets the address of references to external variables and functions as 0. The external references are resolved by the linker during the linking process. Hence it is obvious that the code generated by the cross-compiler is not executable without linking it for resolving external references.

13.2.4 Map File (*.MAP*)

As mentioned above, the cross-compiler converts each source code module into a re-locatable object (OBJ) file. Cross-compiling each source code module generates its own list file. In a project with multiple source files, the cross-compilation of each module generates a corresponding object file. The object files so created are re-locatable codes, meaning their location in the code memory is not fixed. It is the responsibility of a *linker* to link all these object files. The *locater* is responsible for locating absolute address to each module in the code memory. Linking and locating of re-locatable object files will also generate a list file called '*linker list file*' or '*map file*'. Map file contains information about the link/locate process and is composed of a number of sections. The different sections listed in a map file are cross compiler dependent. The information generally held by map files is listed below. It is not necessary that the map files generated by all *linkers/locaters* should contain all these information. Some may contain less information compared to this or others may contain more information than given in this. It all depends on the *linker/locater*.

Page Header A header on each page of the linker listing (MAP) file which indicates the linker version number, date, time, and page number.

```
e.g.   BL51 LINKER/LOCATER V3.62    02/29/2004  09:59:51  PAGE 1
```

Command Line Represents the entire command line that was used for invoking the linker.

```
e.g.  BL51 BANKED LINKER/LOCATER V6.00, INVOKED BY:
      C:\KEIL\C51\BIN\BL51.EXE STARTUP.obj, sample.obj TO sample
```

CPU Details Details about the target CPU and memory model (internal data memory, external data memory, paged data memory, etc.) come under this category.

```
e.g.    MEMORY MODEL: SMALL
```

Input Modules This section includes the names of all object modules, and library files and modules that are included in the linking process. This section can be checked for ensuring all the required modules are lined in the linking process
e.g.

```
INPUT MODULES INCLUDED:
STARTUP.obj (?C_STARTUP)
  sample.obj (SAMPLE)
  C:\KEIL\C51\LIB\C51S.LIB (PRINTF)
  C:\KEIL\C51\LIB\C51S.LIB (?C?CLDPTR)
  C:\KEIL\C51\LIB\C51S.LIB (?C?CLDOPTR)
  C:\KEIL\C51\LIB\C51S.LIB (?C?CSTPTR)
  C:\KEIL\C51\LIB\C51S.LIB (?C?PLDIIDATA)
  C:\KEIL\C51\LIB\C51S.LIB (?C?CCASE)
  C:\KEIL\C51\LIB\C51S.LIB (PUTCHAR)
```

Memory Map Memory map lists the starting address, length, relocation type and name of each segment in the program.
e.g.

```
TYPE  BASE    LENGTH   RELOCATION  SEGMENT NAME
-------------------------------------------------
************ D A T A   M E M O R Y *************
REG     0000H    0008H     ABSOLUTE    "REG BANK 0"
DATA    0008H    0014H     UNIT        _DATA_GROUP_
        001CH    0004H                 *** GAP ***
BIT     0020H.0  0001H.1   UNIT        _BIT_GROUP_
        0021H.1  0000H.7               *** GAP ***
IDATA   0022H    0001H     UNIT        ?STACK
************ C O D E   M E M O R Y *************
CODE    0000H    0003H     ABSOLUTE
        0003H    07FDH                 *** GAP ***
CODE    0800H    035CH     UNIT        ?PR?PRINTF?PRINTF
CODE    0B5CH    008EH     UNIT        ?C?LIB_CODE
CODE    0BEAH    0027H     UNIT        ?PR?PUTCHAR?PUTCHAR
CODE    0C11H    000EH     UNIT        ?CO?SAMPLE
CODE    0C1FH    000CH     UNIT        ?C_C51STARTUP
CODE    0C2BH    0009H     UNIT        ?PR?MAIN?SAMPLE
```

Symbol Table It contains the value, type and name for all symbols from the different input modules e.g.

SYMBOL TABLE OF MODULE: sample (?C_STARTUP)

VALUE	TYPE	NAME
-------	MODULE	?C_STARTUP
C:0C1FH	SEGMENT	?C_C51STARTUP
I:0022H	SEGMENT	?STACK
C:0000H	PUBLIC	?C_STARTUP
D:00E0H	SYMBOL	ACC
D:00F0H	SYMBOL	B
D:0083H	SYMBOL	DPH
D:0082H	SYMBOL	DPL

Inter Module Cross Reference The cross reference listing includes the section name, memory type and the name of the modules in which it is defined and all modules in which it is accessed.

e.g.

NAME..................USAGE	MODULE NAMES
?C?CCASE ....CODE;	?C?CCASE PRINTF
?C?CLDOPTR ....CODE;	?C?CLDOPTR PRINTF
?C?CLDPTR............CODE;	?C?CLDPTR PRINTF
?C?CSTPTR..............CODE;	?C?CSTPTR PRINTF
?C?PLDIIDATA.......CODE;	?C?PLDIIDATA PRINTF

Program Size Program size information contain the size of various memory areas as well as constant and code space for the entire application

e.g. Program Size: data=30.1 xdata=0 code=1079

Warnings and Errors Errors and warnings generated while linking a program are written to this section. It is very useful in debugging link errors.

e.g. `LINK/LOCATE RUN COMPLETE.  0 WARNING(S),  0 ERROR(S)`

NB: The file extension for MAP files generated by different *linkers/locaters* need not be the same. It varies across *linker/locater* in use. For example the map file generated for BL51 Linker/locater is with extension *.M51*

13.2.5 HEX File (*.HEX*)

Hex file is the binary executable file created from the source code. The absolute object file created by the linker/locater is converted into processor understandable binary code. The utility used for converting an object file to a hex file is known as *Object to Hex file converter*. Hex files embed the machine code in a particular format. The format of Hex file varies across the family of processors/controllers. *Intel HEX* **and** *Motorola HEX* are the two commonly used hex file formats in embedded applications. Intel HEX file is an ASCII text file in which the HEX data is represented in ASCII format in lines. The lines in an

Intel HEX file are corresponding to a HEX Record. Each record is made up of hexadecimal numbers that represent machine-language code and/or constant data. Individual records are terminated with a carriage return and a linefeed. *Intel HEX* file is used for transferring the program and data to a ROM or EPROM which is used as code memory storage.

13.2.5.1 Intel HEX File Format As mentioned, *Intel HEX* file is composed of a number of HEX records. Each record is made up of five fields arranged in the following format:

:llaaaattdd...cc

Each group of letters corresponds to a different field, and each letter represents a single hexadecimal digit. Each field is composed of at least two hexadecimal digits (which make up a byte) as described below:

Field	Description
:	The colon indicating the start of every Intel HEX record
ll: **aaaa**: **tt**:	Record length field representing the number of data bytes (**dd**) in the record Address field representing the starting address for subsequent data in the record Field indicating the HEX record type. According to its value it can be of the following types 00: Data Record 01: End of File Record 02: 8086 Segment Address Record 04: Extended Linear Address record
dd:	Data field that represents one byte of data. A record can have number of data bytes. The number of data bytes in the record must match to the number specified by the'**ll**' field
cc:	Checksum field representing the checksum of the record. Checksum is calculated by adding the values of all hexadecimal digit pairs in the record and taking modulo 256. Resultant o/p is 2's complemented to get the checksum.

An extract from the Intel hex file generated for "Hello World" application example is given below.

```
:03000000020C1FD0
:0C0C1F00787FE4F6D8FD758121020C2BD3
:0E0C110048656C6C6F20576F726C64210A008E
:090C2B007BFF7A0C7911020862CA
:10080000E517240BF8E60517227808300702780B65
:10081000E475F001120BB4020B5C2000EB7F2ED2CA
:1008200008018EF540F2490D43440D4FF30040BD0
:10083000EF24BFB41A0050032461FFE518600215CD
:1008400018051BE51B7002051A30070D7808E475C2
:100BFA00B8130CC2983098FDA899C298B811F6306B
:070C0A0099FDC299F5992242
:00000001FF
```

Let's analyse the first record

:	l	l	a	a	a	a	t	t	d	d	d	d	d	d	c	c
:	0	3	0	0	0	0	0	0	0	2	0	C	1	F	D	0

: field indicates the start of a new record. 03 (*ll*) gives the number of data bytes in the record. For this record,'*ll*' is 03 and the number of data bytes in the corresponding record is 03. The start address (*aaaa*) of data in the record is 0000H. The record type byte (*tt*) for this record is 00 and it indicates that this record is a data record. The data for the above record is 02, 0C and 1F. They are supposed to place at three consecutive memory locations in the EEPROM with starting address 0000H. The arrangement is given below.

Memory Address in Hex	Data in Hex
0000H	02
0001H	0C
0002H	1F

If you are familiar with 8051 Machine code you can easily identify that 02 is the machine code for the instruction LJMP and the next two bytes represent the 16bit address of the location to which the jump is intended. Obviously the instruction is *LJMP 0C1F*. The last two digits (*cc*) of the record holds the checksum of the values present in the record. The checksum is calculated by adding all the bytes in the record and then taking modulo 256 of the result. The resultant is 2's complemented and represented as checksum in the record field. Above example it is 0xD0. Intel hex files end with an end of file record indicating the end of records in the hex file. Let's examine the end of record structure.

:	l	l	a	a	a	a	t	t	c	c
:	0	0	0	0	0	0	0	1	F	F

End of record also starts with the start of record symbol ':'. Since End of record does not contain any data bytes, field '*ll*' will be 00. The field '*aaaa*' is not significant since the number of data bytes are zero. Field '*tt*' will hold the value 01 to indicate that this record is an End of record. Field '*cc*' holds the checksum of all the bytes present in the record and it is calculated as 2's complement of Modulo 256 of (0 + 0 + 0 + 1) = 0xFF

13.2.5.2 Motorola HEX File Format Similar to the Intel HEX file, Motorola HEX file is also an ASCII text file where the HEX data is represented in ASCII format in lines. The lines in *Motorola HEX* file represent a HEX Record. Each record is made up of hexadecimal numbers that represent machine-language code and/or constant data. The general form of Motorola Hex record is given below.

SOR	RT	Length	Start Address	Data/Code	Checksum

In other words it can be represented as **Stllaaaadddd...cc**
The fields of the record are explained below.

Field	Description
SOR	Stands for Start of record. The ASCII Character 'S' is used as the Start of Record. Every record begins with the character 'S'
RT	Stands for Record type. The character't' represents the type of record in the general format. There are different meanings for the record depending on the value of 't' 0: Header. Indicates the beginning of Hex File 1: Data Record with 16bit start address 2: Data record with 24bit start address 9: End of File Record

Length (*ll*):	Stands for the count of the character pairs in the record, excluding the type and record length (Count includes the number of data/code bytes, data bytes representing start address and character pair representing the checksum). Two ASCII characters '*ll*' represent the length field .Each '*l*' in the representation can take values 0 to 9 and A to F.
Start Address (*aaaa*):	Address field representing the starting address for subsequent data in the record.
Code/Data (dd):	Data field that represents one byte of data. A record can have number of data bytes. The number of data bytes in the record must match to the number specified by (*ll - no. of character pairs for start address–1*)
Checksum (cc):	Checksum field representing the checksum of the record. Checksum is calculated by adding the values of all hexadecimal digit pairs in the record and taking modulo 256. Resultant o/p is 1's complemented to get the checksum.

Typical example of a Motorola Hex File format is given below.

```
S011000064656D6F5F68637331322E616273E5
S11311000002000800082629001853812341001812
S9030000FC
```

You can see that each Record starts with the ASCII character 'S'. For the first record, the value for field '*t*' is 0 and it implies that this record is the first record in the hex file (Header Record). The second record is a data record. The field '*t*' for second record is 1. Number of character pairs held by second record is 0x13 (19 in decimal). Out of this two character pairs are used for holding the start address and one character pair for holding the checksum. Rest 16 bytes are the data bytes. The start address for placing the data bytes is 0x1100. The data bytes that are going to be placed in 16 consecutive memory locations starting from address 0x1100 are 0x00, 0x02, 0x00, 0x08, 0x00, 0x08, 0x26, 0x29, 0x00, 0x18, 0x53, 0x81, 0x23, 0x41, 0x00 and 0x18. The last two digits (here 0x12) represent the checksum of the record. Checksum is calculated as the least significant byte of the one's complement of the sum of the values represented by the pairs of characters making up the record length, address, and data fields. The third record represents the End of File record. The value for field '*t*' for this record is 9 and it is an indicative of End of Hex file. Number of character pairs held by this record is 03; two for address and one for the checksum. The address is insignificant here since the record does not contain any values to dump into memory. Only one End of File Record is allowed per file and it must be the last line of the file.

13.3 DISASSEMBLER/DECOMPILER

Disassembler is a utility program which converts machine codes into target processor specific Assembly codes/instructions. The process of converting machine codes into Assembly code is known as 'Disassembling'. In operation, disassembling is complementary to assembling/cross-assembling. Decompiler is the utility program for translating machine codes into corresponding high level language instructions. Decompiler performs the reverse operation of compiler/cross-compiler. The disassemblers/decompilers for different family of processors/controllers are different. Disassemblers/Decompilers are deployed in reverse engineering. Reverse engineering is the process of revealing the technology behind the working of a product. Reverse engineering in Embedded Product development is employed to find out the secret behind the working of popular proprietary products. Disassemblers/decompilers help the reverse-engineering process by translating the embedded firmware into Assembly/high level language instructions.

Disassemblers/Decompilers are powerful tools for analysing the presence of malicious codes (virus information) in an executable image. Disassemblers/Decompilers are available as either freeware tools readily available for free download from internet or as commercial tools. It is not possible for a disassembler/decompiler to generate an exact replica of the original assembly code/high level source code in terms of the symbolic constants and comments used. However disassemblers/decompilers generate a source code which is somewhat matching to the original source code from which the binary code is generated.

13.4 SIMULATORS, EMULATORS AND DEBUGGING

Simulators and emulators are two important tools used in embedded system development. Both the terms sound alike and are little confusing. Simulator is a software tool used for simulating the various conditions for checking the functionality of the application firmware. The Integrated Development Environment (IDE) itself will be providing simulator support and they help in debugging the firmware for checking its required functionality. In certain scenarios, simulator refers to a soft model (GUI model) of the embedded product. For example, if the product under development is a handheld device, to test the functionalities of the various menu and user interfaces, a soft form model of the product with all UI as given in the end product can be developed in software. Soft phone is an example for such a simulator. Emulator is hardware device which emulates the functionalities of the target device and allows real time debugging of the embedded firmware in a hardware environment.

13.4.1 Simulators

In a previous section of this chapter, describing the Integrated Development Environment, we discussed about simulators for embedded firmware debugging. Simulators simulate the target hardware and the firmware execution can be inspected using simulators. The features of simulator based debugging are listed below.

1. Purely software based
2. Doesn't require a real target system
3. Very primitive (Lack of featured I/O support. Everything is a simulated one)
4. Lack of Real-time behaviour

13.4.1.1 Advantages of Simulator Based Debugging Simulator based debugging techniques are simple and straightforward. The major advantages of simulator based firmware debugging techniques are explained below.

No Need for Original Target Board Simulator based debugging technique is purely software oriented. IDE's software support simulates the CPU of the target board. User only needs to know about the memory map of various devices within the target board and the firmware should be written on the basis of it. Since the real hardware is not required, firmware development can start well in advance immediately after the device interface and memory maps are finalised. This saves development time.

Simulate I/O Peripherals Simulator provides the option to simulate various I/O peripherals. Using simulator's I/O support you can edit the values for I/O registers and can be used as the input/output value in the firmware execution. Hence it eliminates the need for connecting I/O devices for debugging the firmware.

Simulates Abnormal Conditions With simulator's simulation support you can input any desired value for any parameter during debugging the firmware and can observe the control flow of firmware. It really helps the developer in simulating abnormal operational environment for firmware and helps the firmware developer to study the behaviour of the firmware under abnormal input conditions.

13.4.1.2 Limitations of Simulator based Debugging Though simulation based firmware debugging technique is very helpful in embedded applications, they possess certain limitations and we cannot fully rely upon the simulator-based firmware debugging. Some of the limitations of simulator-based debugging are explained below.

Deviation from Real Behaviour Simulation-based firmware debugging is always carried out in a development environment where the developer may not be able to debug the firmware under all possible combinations of input. Under certain operating conditions we may get some particular result and it need not be the same when the firmware runs in a production environment.

Lack of real timeliness The major limitation of simulator based debugging is that it is not real-time in behaviour. The debugging is developer driven and it is no way capable of creating a real time behaviour. Moreover in a real application the I/O condition may be varying or unpredictable. Simulation goes for simulating those conditions for known values.

13.4.2 Emulators and Debuggers

What is debugging and why debugging is required? Debugging in embedded application is the process of diagnosing the firmware execution, monitoring the target processor's registers and memory while the firmware is running and checking the signals from various buses of the embedded hardware. Debugging process in embedded application is broadly classified into two, namely; hardware debugging and firmware debugging. Hardware debugging deals with the monitoring of various bus signals and checking the status lines of the target hardware. The various tools used for hardware debugging will be explaining in detail in a later section of this chapter. Firmware debugging deals with examining the firmware execution, execution flow, changes to various CPU registers and status registers on execution of the firmware to ensure that the firmware is running as per the design. This section deals with the debugging of firmware.

Why is debugging required? Well the counter question why you go for diagnosis when you are ill answers this query. Firmware debugging is performed to figure out the bug or the error in the firmware which creates the unexpected behaviour. Firmware is analogous to the human body in the sense it is widespread and/or modular. Any abnormalities in any area of the body may lead to sickness. How is the region causing illness identified correctly when you are sick? If we look back to the 1900s, where no sophisticated diagnostic techniques were available, only a skilled doctor was capable of identifying the root cause of illness, that too with his solid experience. Now, with latest technologies, the scenario is totally changed. Sophisticated diagnostic techniques provide offline diagnosis like Computerized Tomography (CT), MRI and ultrasound scans and online diagnosis like micro camera based imaging techniques. With the intrusion of a micro camera into the body, the doctors can view the internals of the body in real time.

During the early days of embedded system development, there were no debug tools available and the only way was "*Burn the code in an EEPROM and pray for its proper functioning*". If the firmware does not crash, the product works fine. If the product crashes, the developer is unlucky and he needs to sit back and rework on the firmware till the product functions in the expected way. Most of the time the developer had to seek the help of an expert to figure out the exact problem creator. As technology has achieved a new dimension from the early days of embedded system development, various types of debugging techniques are available today. The following section describes the improvements over firmware debugging starting from the most primitive type of debugging to the most sophisticated On Chip Debugging (OCD).

13.4.2.1 Incremental EEPROM Burning Technique This is the most primitive type of firmware debugging technique where the code is separated into different functional code units. Instead of burning the entire code into the EEPROM chip at once, the code is burned in incremental order, where the code corresponding to all functionalities are separately coded, cross-compiled and burned into the chip one by one. The code will incorporate some indication support like lighting up an "LED (every embedded product contains at least one LED). If not, you should include provision for at least one LED in the target board at the hardware design time such that it can be used for debugging purpose)" or activate a "BUZZER (In a system with BUZZER support)" if the code is functioning in the expected way. If the first functionality is found working perfectly on the target board with the corresponding code burned into the EEPROM, go for burning the code corresponding to the next functionality and check whether it is working. Repeat this process till all functionalities are covered. Please ensure that before entering into one level up, the previous level has delivered a correct result. If the code corresponding to any functionality is found not giving the expected result, fix it by modifying the code and then only go for adding the next functionality for burning into the EEPROM. After you found all functionalities working properly, combine the entire source for all functionalities together, re-compile and burn the code for the total system functioning.

Obviously it is a time-consuming process. But remember it is a onetime process and once you test the firmware in an incremental model you can go for mass production. In incremental firmware burning technique we are not doing any debugging but observing the status of firmware execution as a debug method. The very common mistake committed by firmware developers in developing non-operating system-based embedded application is burning the entire code altogether and fed up with debugging the code. Please don't adopt this approach. Even though you need to spend some additional time on incremental burning approach, you will never lose in the process and will never mess up with debugging the code. You will be able to figure out at least 'on which point of firmware execution the issue is arising'–"A stitch in time saves nine". Incremental firmware burning technique is widely adopted in small, simple system developments and in product development where time is not a big constraint (e.g. R&D projects). It is also very useful in product development environments where no other debug tools are available.

13.4.2.2 Inline Breakpoint Based Firmware Debugging Inline breakpoint based debugging is another primitive method of firmware debugging. Within the firmware where you want to ensure that firmware execution is reaching up to a specified point, insert an inline debug code immediately after the point. The debug code is a *printf()* function which prints a string given as per the firmware. You can insert debug codes (*printf()*) commands at each point where you want to ensure the firmware execution is covering that point. Cross-compile the source code with the debug codes embedded within it. Burn the corresponding hex file into the EEPROM. You can view the *printf()* generated data on the '*HyperTerminal*—A communication facility available with the Windows OS coming under the *Communications* section of *Start Menu*' of the Development PC. Configure the serial communication settings of the '*HyperTerminal*' connection to the same as that of the serial communication settings configured in the firmware (Say Baudrate = 9600; Parity = None; Stop Bit = 1; Flow Control = None); Connect the target board's serial port (COM) to the development PC's COM Port using an RS232 Cable. Power up the target board. Depending on the execution flow of firmware and the inline debug codes inserted in the firmware, you can view the debug information on the '*HyperTerminal*'. Typical usage of inline debug codes and the debug info retrieved on the *HyperTerminal* is illustrated below.

```
//First Inline Debug Code
printf ("Starting Configuration…\n");
Configurations……
…………………
//Inline Debug code ensuring execution of Configuration section
printf ("End of Configuration…\n");
printf ("Beginning of Firmware Execution…\n");
Code segment1….
…………………
//Inline Debug code ensuring execution of Code Segment 1
printf ("End of Code segment 1…\n");
Code segment2….
…………………
//Inline Debug code ensuring execution of Code Segment 2
printf ("End of Code segment 2…\n");
```

If the firmware is error free and the execution occurs properly, you will get all the debug messages on the *HyperTerminal*. Based on this debug info you can check the firmware for errors (Fig. 13.38).

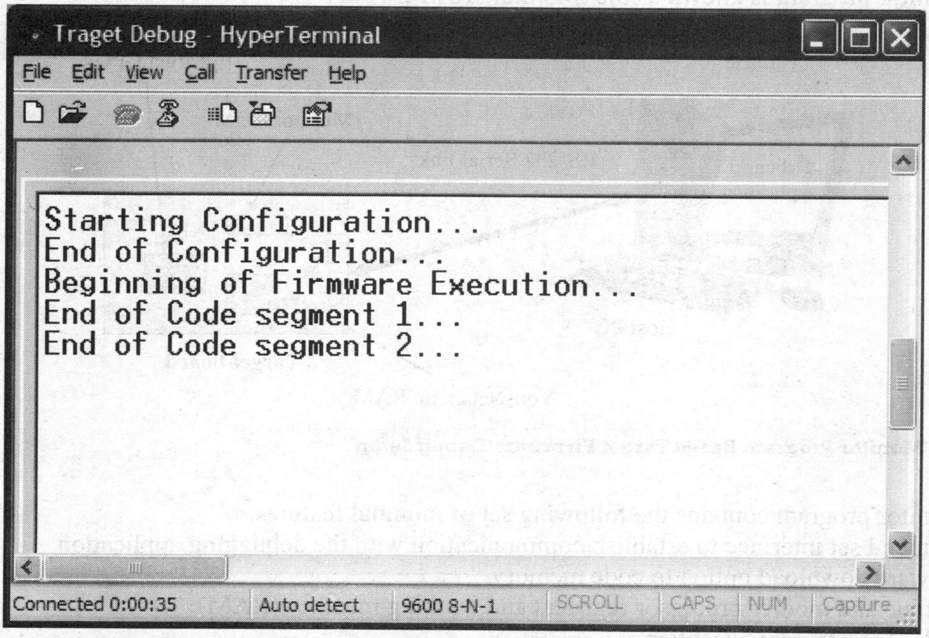

Fig. 13.38 **Inline Breakpoint Based Firmware Debugging with HyperTerminal**

13.4.2.3 Monitor Program Based Firmware Debugging Monitor program based firmware debugging is the first adopted invasive method for firmware debugging (Fig. 13.39). In this approach a monitor program which acts as a supervisor is developed. The monitor program controls the downloading of user code into the code memory, inspects and modifies register/memory locations; allows single stepping of source code, etc. The monitor program implements the debug functions as per a pre-defined command set from the debug application interface. The monitor program always listens to the serial port of the target device and according to the command received from the serial interface it performs command specific actions like firmware downloading, memory inspection/modification, firmware single stepping and sends the debug information (various register and memory contents) back to the main debug program running on the development PC, etc. The first step in any monitor program development is determining a set of commands for performing various operations like firmware downloading, memory/register inspection/modification, single stepping, etc. Once the commands for each operation is fixed, write the code for performing the actions corresponding to these commands. As mentioned earlier, the commands may be received through any of the external interface of the target processor (e.g. RS-232C serial interface/parallel interface/USB, etc.). The monitor program should query this interface to get commands or should handle the command reception if the data reception is implemented through interrupts. On receiving a command, examine it and perform the action corresponding to it. The entire code stuff handling the command reception and corresponding action implementation is known as the "*monitor program*". The most common type of interface used between target board and debug application is RS-232C Serial interface. After the successful completion of the '*monitor program*' development, it is compiled and burned into the FLASH memory or ROM of the target board. The code memory containing the monitor program is known as the '*Monitor ROM*'.

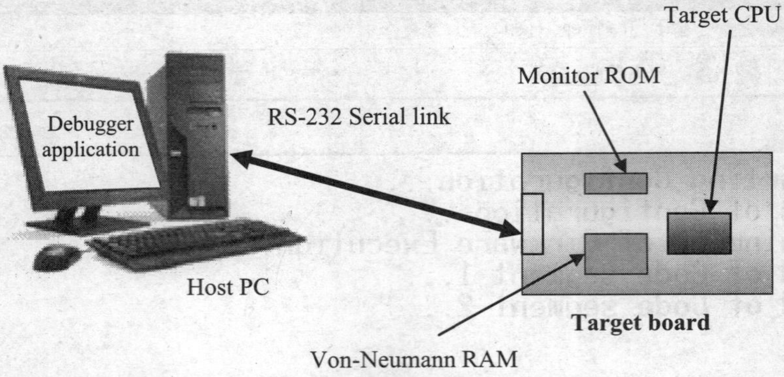

Fig. 13.39 **Monitor Program Based Target Firmware Debug Setup**

The monitor program contains the following set of minimal features.

1. Command set interface to establish communication with the debugging application
2. Firmware download option to code memory
3. Examine and modify processor registers and working memory (RAM)
4. Single step program execution
5. Set breakpoints in firmware execution
6. Send debug information to debug application running on host machine

The monitor program usually resides at the reset vector (code memory 0000H) of the target processor. The monitor program is commonly employed in development boards and the development board supplier provides the monitor program in the form of a ROM chip. The actual code memory is downloaded into a RAM chip which is interfaced to the processor in the Von-Neumann architecture model. The Von-Neumann architecture model is achieved by ANDing the PSEN\ and RD\ signals of the target processor (In case of *8051*) and connecting the output of AND Gate to the Output Enable (RD\) pin of RAM chip. WR\ signal of the target processor is interfaced to The WR\ signal of the Von Neumann RAM. Monitor ROM size varies in the range of a few kilo bytes (Usually 4K). An address decoder circuit maps the address range allocated to the monitor ROM and activates the Chip Select (CS\) of the ROM if the address is within the range specified for the Monitor ROM. A user program is normally loaded at locations 0x4000 or 0x8000. The address decoder circuit ensures the enabling of the RAM chip (CS\) when the address range is outside that allocated to the ROM monitor. Though there are two memory chips (Monitor ROM Chip and Von-Neumann RAM), the total memory map available for both of them will be 64K for a processor/controller with 16bit address space and the memory decoder units take care of avoiding conflicts in accessing both. While developing user program for monitor ROM-based systems, special care should be taken to offset the user code and handling the interrupt vectors. The target development IDE will help in resolving this. During firmware execution and single stepping, the user code may have to be altered and hence the firmware is always downloaded into a Von-Neumann RAM in monitor ROM-based debugging systems. Monitor ROM-based debugging is suitable only for development work and it is not a good choice for mass produced systems. The major drawbacks of monitor based debugging system are

1. The entire memory map is converted into a Von-Neumann model and it is shared between the monitor ROM, monitor program data memory, monitor program trace buffer, user written firmware and external user memory. For *8051*, the original Harvard architecture supports 64K code memory and 64K external data memory (Total 128K memory map). Going for a monitor based debugging shrinks the total available memory to 64K Von-Neumann memory and it needs to accommodate all kinds of memory requirement (Monitor Code, monitor data, trace buffer memory, User code and External User data memory).
2. The communication link between the debug application running on Development PC and monitor program residing in the target system is achieved through a serial link and usually the controller's On-chip UART is used for establishing this link. Hence one serial port of the target processor becomes dedicated for the monitor application and it cannot be used for any other device interfacing. Wastage of a serial port! It is a serious issue in controllers or processors with single UART.

13.4.2.4 In Circuit Emulator (ICE) Based Firmware Debugging The terms 'Simulator' and 'Emulator' are little bit confusing and sounds similar. Though their basic functionality is the same – "Debug the target firmware", the way in which they achieve this functionality is totally different. As mentioned before, 'Simulator' is a software application that precisely duplicates (mimics) the target CPU and simulates the various features and instructions supported by the target CPU, whereas an 'Emulator' is a self-contained hardware device which emulates the target CPU. The emulator hardware contains necessary emulation logic and it is hooked to the debugging application running on the development PC on one end and connects to the target board through some interface on the other end. In summary, the simulator '*simulates*' the target board CPU and the emulator '*emulates*' the target board CPU.

There is a scope change that has happened to the definition of an emulator. In olden days emulators were defined as special hardware devices used for emulating the functionality of a processor/controller and performing various debug operations like halt firmware execution, set breakpoints, get or set internal RAM/CPU register, etc. Nowadays pure software applications which perform the functioning of a hardware emulator is also called as 'Emulators' (though they are 'Simulators' in operation). The emulator application for emulating the operation of a PDA phone for application development is an example of a 'Software Emulator'. A hardware emulator is controlled by a debugger application running on the development PC. The debugger application may be part of the Integrated Development Environment (IDE) or a third party supplied tool. Most of the IDEs incorporate debugger support for some of the emulators commonly available in the market. The emulators for different families of processors/controllers are different. Figure 13.40 illustrates the different subsystems and interfaces of an 'Emulator' device.

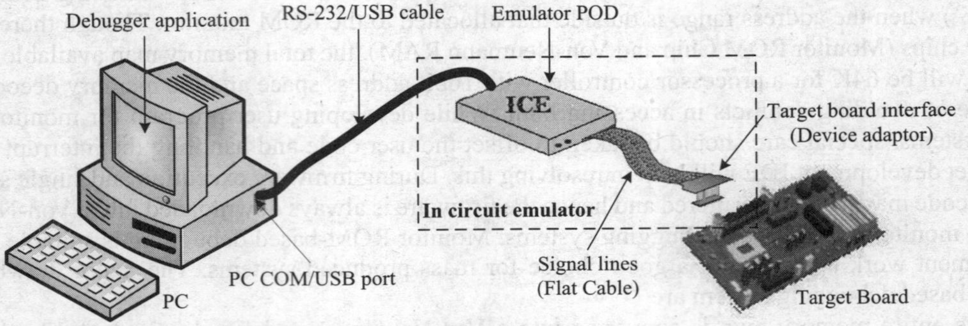

Fig. 13.40 **In Circuit Emulator (ICE) Based Target Debugging**

The Emulator POD forms the heart of any emulator system and it contains the following functional units.

Emulation Device Emulation device is a replica of the target CPU which receives various signals from the target board through a device adaptor connected to the target board and performs the execution of firmware under the control of debug commands from the debug application. The emulation device can be either a standard chip same as the target processor (e.g. AT89C51) or a Programmable Logic Device (PLD) configured to function as the target CPU. If a standard chip is used as the emulation device, the emulation will provide real-time execution behaviour. At the same time the emulator becomes dedicated to that particular device and cannot be re-used for the derivatives of the same chip. PLD-based emulators can easily be re-configured to use with derivatives of the target CPU under consideration. By simply loading the configuration file of the derivative processor/controller, the PLD gets re-configured and it functions as the derivative device. A major drawback of PLD-based emulator is the accuracy of replication of target CPU functionalities. PLD-based emulator logic is easy to implement for simple target CPUs but for complex target CPUs it is quite difficult.

Emulation Memory It is the Random Access Memory (RAM) incorporated in the Emulator device. It acts as a replacement to the target board's EEPROM where the code is supposed to be downloaded after each firmware modification. Hence the original EEPROM memory is emulated by the RAM of emulator. This is known as '*ROM Emulation*'. ROM emulation eliminates the hassles of ROM burning and it offers the benefit of infinite number of reprogrammings (Most of the EEPROM chips available in the market supports only 100 to 1000 re-program cycles). Emulation memory also acts as a trace buffer in debugging. Trace buffer is a memory pool holding the instructions executed/registers modified/related data by the processor while debugging. The trace buffer size is emulator dependent and the trace buffer holds the recent trace information when the buffer overflows. The common features of trace buffer memory and trace buffer data viewing are listed below:

- Trace buffer records each bus cycle in frames
- Trace data can be viewed in the debugger application as Assembly/Source code
- Trace buffering can be done on the basis of a Trace trigger (Event)
- Trace buffer can also record signals from target board other than CPU signals (Emulator dependent)
- Trace data is a very useful information in firmware debugging

Emulator Control Logic Emulator control logic is the logic circuits used for implementing complex hardware breakpoints, trace buffer trigger detection, trace buffer control, etc. Emulator control logic circuits are also used for implementing logic analyser functions in advanced emulator devices. The 'Emulator POD' is connected to the target board through a 'Device adaptor' and signal cable.

Device Adaptors Device adaptors act as an interface between the target board and emulator POD. Device adaptors are normally pin-to-pin compatible sockets which can be inserted/plugged into the target board for routing the various signals from the pins assigned for the target processor. The device adaptor is usually connected to the emulator POD using ribbon cables. The adaptor type varies depending on the target processor's chip package. DIP, PLCC, etc. are some commonly used adaptors.

The above-mentioned emulators are almost dedicated ones, meaning they are built for emulating a specific target processor and have little or less support for emulating the derivatives of the target processor for which the emulator is built. This type of emulators usually combines the entire emulation control logic and emulation device (if present) in a single board. They are known as '*Debug Board Modules (DBMs)*'. An alternative method of emulator design supports emulation of a variety of target processors. Here the emulator hardware is partitioned into two, namely, '*Base Terminal*' and '*Probe Card*'. The Base terminal contains all the emulator hardware and emulation control logic except the emulation chip (Target board CPU's replica). The base terminal is connected to the Development PC for establishing communication with the debug application. The emulation chip (Same chip as the target CPU) is mounted on a separate PCB and it is connected to the base terminal through a ribbon cable. The '*Probe Card*' board contains the device adaptor sockets to plug the board into the target development board. The board containing the emulation chip is known as the '*Probe Card*'. For emulating different target CPUs the '*Probe Card*' will be different and the base terminal remains the same. The manufacturer of the emulator supplies '*Probe Card*' for different CPUs. Though these emulators are capable of emulating different CPUs, the cost for '*Probe Cards*' is very high. Communication link between the emulator base unit/ Emulator POD and debug application is established through a Serial/Parallel/USB interface. Debug commands and debug information are sent to and from the emulator using this interface.

13.4.2.5 On Chip Firmware Debugging (OCD) Advances in semiconductor technology has brought out new dimensions to target firmware debugging. Today almost all processors/controllers incorporate built in debug modules called On Chip Debug (OCD) support. Though OCD adds silicon complexity and cost factor, from a developer perspective it is a very good feature supporting fast and efficient firmware debugging. The On Chip Debug facilities integrated to the processor/controller are chip vendor dependent and most of them are proprietary technologies like Background Debug Mode

(BDM), OnCE, etc. Some vendors add 'on chip software debug support' through JTAG (Joint Test Action Group) port. Processors/controllers with OCD support incorporate a dedicated debug module to the existing architecture. Usually the on-chip debugger provides the means to set simple breakpoints, query the internal state of the chip and single step through code. OCD module implements dedicated registers for controlling debugging. An On Chip Debugger can be enabled by setting the OCD enable bit (The bit name and register holding the bit varies across vendors). Debug related registers are used for debugger control (Enable/disable single stepping, Freeze execution, etc.) and breakpoint address setting. BDM and JTAG are the two commonly used interfaces to communicate between the Debug application running on Development PC and OCD module of target CPU. Some interface logic in the form of hardware will be implemented between the CPU OCD interface and the host PC to capture the debug information from the target CPU and sending it to the debugger application running on the host PC. The interface between the hardware and PC may be Serial/Parallel/USB. The following section will give you a brief introduction about Background Debug Mode (BDM) and JTAG interface used in On Chip Debugging.

Background Debug Mode (BDM) interface is a proprietary On Chip Debug solution from Motorola. BDM defines the communication interface between the chip resident debug core and host PC where the BDM compatible remote debugger is running. BDM makes use of 10 or 26 pin connector to connect to the target board. Serial data in (DSI), Serial data out (DSO) and Serial clock (DSCLK) are the three major signal lines used in BDM. DSI sends debug commands serially to the target processor from the remote debugger application and DSO sends the debug response to the debugger from the processor. Synchronisation of serial transmission is done by the serial clock DSCLK generated by the debugger application. Debugging is controlled by BDM specific debug commands. The debug commands are usually 17-bit wide. 16 bits are used for representing the command and 1 bit for status/control.

Chips with JTAG debug interface contain a built-in JTAG port for communicating with the remote debugger application. JTAG is the acronym for Joint Test Action Group. JTAG is the alternate name for IEEE 1149.1 standard. Like BDM, JTAG is also a serial interface. The signal lines of JTAG protocol are explained below.

Test Data In (TDI): It is used for sending debug commands serially from remote debugger to the target processor.

Test Data Out (TDO): Transmit debug response to the remote debugger from target CPU.

Test Clock (TCK): Synchronises the serial data transfer.

Test Mode Select (TMS): Sets the mode of testing.

Test Reset (TRST): It is an optional signal line used for resetting the target CPU.

The serial data transfer rate for JTAG debugging is chip dependent. It is usually within the range of 10 to 1000 MHz.

13.5 TARGET HARDWARE DEBUGGING

Even though the firmware is bug free and everything is intact in the board, your embedded product need not function as per the expected behaviour in the first attempt for various hardware related reasons like dry soldering of components, missing connections in the PCB due to any un-noticed errors in the PCB layout design, misplaced components, signal corruption due to noise, etc. The only way to sort out these issues and figure out the real problem creator is debugging the target board. Hardware debugging is not similar to firmware debugging. Hardware debugging involves the monitoring of various signals of the target board (address/data lines, port pins, etc.), checking the inter. connection among various components, circuit continuity checking, etc. The various hardware debugging tools used in Embedded Product Development are explained below.

13.5.1 Magnifying Glass (Lens)

You might have noticed watch repairer wearing a small magnifying glass while engaged in repairing a watch. They use the magnifying glass to view the minute components inside the watch in an enlarged manner so that they can easily work with them. Similar to a watch repairer, magnifying glass is the primary hardware debugging tool for an embedded hardware debugging professional. A magnifying glass is a powerful visual inspection tool. With a magnifying glass (lens), the surface of the target board can be examined thoroughly for dry soldering of components, missing components, improper placement of components, improper soldering, track (PCB connection) damage, short of tracks, etc. Nowadays high quality magnifying stations are available for visual inspection. The magnifying station incorporates magnifying glasses attached to a stand with CFL tubes for providing proper illumination for inspection. The station usually incorporates multiple magnifying lenses. The main lens acts as a visual inspection tool for the entire hardware board whereas the other small lens within the station is used for magnifying a relatively small area of the board which requires thorough inspection.

13.5.2 Multimeter

I believe the name of the instrument itself is sufficient to give an outline of its usage. A multimeter is used for measuring various electrical quantities like voltage (Both AC and DC), current (DC as well as AC), resistance, capacitance, continuity checking, transistor checking, cathode and anode identification of diode, etc. Any multimeter will work over a specific range for each measurement. A multimeter is the most valuable tool in the toolkit of an embedded hardware developer. It is the primary debugging tool for physical contact based hardware debugging and almost all developers start debugging the hardware with it. In embedded hardware debugging it is mainly used for checking the circuit continuity between different points on the board, measuring the supply voltage, checking the signal value, polarity, etc. Both analog and digital versions of a multimeter are available. The digital version is preferred over analog the one for various reasons like readability, accuracy, etc. Fluke, Rishab, Philips, etc. are the manufacturers of commonly available high quality digital multimeters.

13.5.3 Digital CRO

Cathode Ray Oscilloscope (CRO) is a little more sophisticated tool compared to a multimeter. You might have studied the operation and use of a CRO in your basic electronics lab. Just to refresh your brain, CRO is used for waveform capturing and analysis, measurement of signal strength, etc. By connecting the point under observation on the target board to the Channels of the Oscilloscope, the waveforms can be captured and analysed for expected behaviour. CRO is a very good tool in analysing interference noise in the power supply line and other signal lines. Monitoring the crystal oscillator signal from the target board is a typical example of the usage of CRO for waveform capturing and analysis in target board debugging. CROs are available in both analog and digital versions. Though Digital CROs are costly, featurewise they are best suited for target board debugging applications. Digital CROs are available for high frequency support and they also incorporate modern techniques for recording waveform over a period of time, capturing waves on the basis of a configurable event (trigger) from the target board (e.g. High to low transition of a port pin of the target processor). Most of the modern digital CROs contain more than one channel and it is easy to capture and analyse various signals from the target board using multiple channels simultaneously. Various measurements like phase, amplitude, etc. is also possible with CROs. Tektronix, Agilent, Philips, etc. are the manufacturers of high precision good quality digital CROs.

13.5.4 Logic Analyser

A logic analyser is the big brother of digital CRO. Logic analyser is used for capturing digital data (logic 1 and 0) from a digital circuitry whereas CRO is employed in capturing all kinds of waves including logic signals. Another major limitation of CRO is that the total number of logic signals/waveforms that can be captured with a CRO is limited to the number of channels. A logic analyser contains special connectors and clips which can be attached to the target board for capturing digital data. In target board debugging applications, a logic analyser captures the states of various port pins, address bus and data bus of the target processor/controller, etc. Logic analysers give an exact reflection of what happens when a particular line of firmware is running. This is achieved by capturing the address line logic and data line logic of target hardware. Most modern logic analysers contain provisions for storing captured data, selecting a desired region of the captured waveform, zooming selected region of the captured waveform, etc. Tektronix, Agilent, etc. are the giants in the logic analyser market.

13.5.5 Function Generator

Function generator is not a debugging tool. It is an input signal simulator tool. A function generator is capable of producing various periodic waveforms like sine wave, square wave, saw-tooth wave, etc. with different frequencies and amplitude. Sometimes the target board may require some kind of periodic waveform with a particular frequency as input to some part of the board. Thus, in a debugging environment, the function generator serves the purpose of generating and supplying required signals.

13.6 BOUNDARY SCAN

As the complexity of the hardware increase, the number of chips present in the board and the interconnection among them may also increase. The device packages used in the PCB become miniature to reduce the total board space occupied by them and multiple layers may be required to route the interconnections among the chips. With miniature device packages and multiple layers for the PCB it will be very difficult to debug the hardware using magnifying glass, multimeter, etc. to check the interconnection among the various chips. Boundary scan is a technique used for testing the interconnection among the various chips, which support JTAG interface, present in the board. Chips which support boundary scan associate a boundary scan cell with each pin of the device. A JTAG port which contains the five signal lines namely TDI, TDO, TCK, TRST and TMS form the Test Access Port (TAP) for a JTAG supported chip. Each device will have its own TAP. The PCB also contains a TAP for connecting the JTAG signal lines to the external world. A boundary scan path is formed inside the board by interconnecting the devices through JTAG signal lines. The TDI pin of the TAP of the PCB is connected to the TDI pin of the first device. The TDO pin of the first device is connected to the TDI pin of the second device. In this way all devices are interconnected and the TDO pin of the last JTAG device is connected to the TDO pin of the TAP of the PCB. The clock line TCK and the Test Mode Select (TMS) line of the devices are connected to the clock line and Test mode select line of the Test Access Port of the PCB respectively. This forms a boundary scan path. Figure 13.41 illustrates the same.

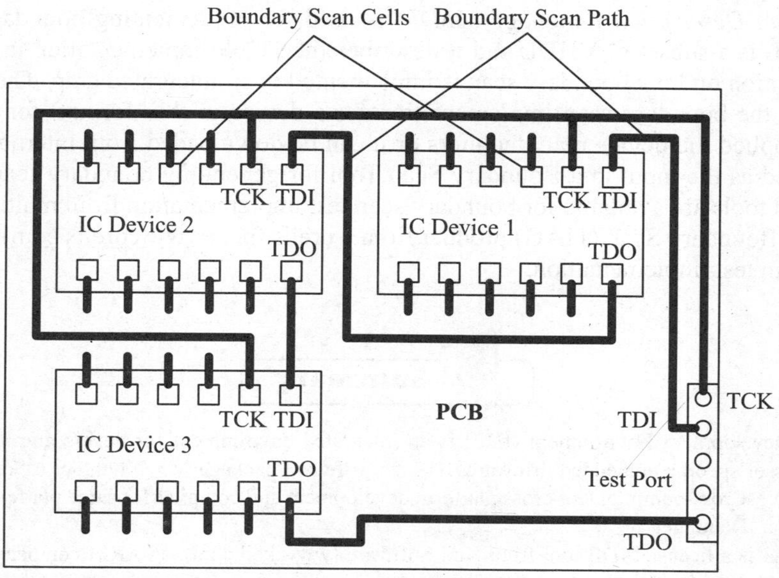

Fig. 13.41 **JTAG based boundary scanning for hardware testing**

As mentioned earlier, each pin of the device associates a boundary scan cell with it. The boundary scan cell is a multipurpose memory cell. The boundary scan cell associated with the input pins of an IC is known as 'input cells' and the boundary scan cells associated with the output pins of an IC is known as 'output cells'. The boundary scan cells can be used for capturing the input pin signal state and passing it to the internal circuitry, capturing the signals from the internal circuitry and passing it to the output pin, and shifting the data received from the Test Data In pin of the TAP. The boundary scan cells associated with the pins are interconnected and they form a chain from the TDI pin of the device to its TDO pin. The boundary scan cells can be operated in Normal, Capture, Update and Shift modes. In the Normal mode, the input of the boundary scan cell appears directly at its output. In the Capture mode, the boundary scan cell associated with each input pin of the chip captures the signal from the respective pins to the cell and the boundary scan cell associated with each output pin of the chip captures the signal from the internal circuitry. In the Update mode, the boundary scan cell associated with each input pin of the chip passes the already captured data to the internal circuitry and the boundary scan cell associated with each output pin of the chip passes the already captured data to the respective output pin. In the shift mode, data is shifted from TDI pin to TDO pin of the device through the boundary scan cells. ICs supporting boundary scan contain additional boundary scan related registers for facilitating the boundary scan operation. Instruction Register, Bypass Register, Identification Register, etc. are examples of boundary scan related registers. The Instruction Register is used for holding and processing the instruction received over the TAP. The bypass register is used for bypassing the boundary scan path of the device and directly interconnecting the TDI pin of the device to its TDO. It disconnects a device from the boundary scan path. Different instructions are used for testing the interconnections and the functioning of the chip. *Extest*, *Bypass*, *Sample* and *Preload*, *Intest,* etc. are examples for instructions for different types of boundary scan tests, whereas the instruction *Runbist* is used for performing a self test on the internal functioning of the chip. The *Runbist* instruction produces a pass/fail result.

Boundary Scan Description Language (*BSDL*) is used for implementing boundary scan tests using JTAG. BSDL is a subset of VHDL and it describes the JTAG implementation in a device. BSDL provides information on how boundary scan is implemented in an integrated chip. The BSDL file (File which describes the boundary scan implementation for a device in *.bsd* format) for a JTAG compliant device is supplied the device manufacturers or it can be downloaded from internet repository. The BSDL file is used as the input to a Boundary Scan Tool for generating boundary scan test cases for a PCB. Automated tools are available for boundary scan test implementation from multiple vendors. The ScanExpress™ Boundary Scan (JTAG) product from Corelis Inc. (www.corelis.com) is a popular tool for boundary scan test implementation.

Summary

- ✓ Integrated Development Environment (IDE) is an integrated environment for developing and debugging the target processor specific embedded firmware. IDE is a software package which bundles a 'Text Editor (Source Code Editor)', 'Cross-compiler (for cross platform development and compiler for same platform development)', 'Linker' and a 'Debugger'
- ✓ Keil µVision3 is a licensed IDE tool from Keil Software (www.keil.com), an ARM company, for *8051* family microcontroller based embedded firmware development
- ✓ *List File* (.lst), *Pre-processor Output file*, *Map File* (File extension linker dependent), *Object File* (.obj), *Hex File* (.hex). etc. are the files generated during the cross-compilation process of a source file
- ✓ Hex file is the binary executable file created from the source code. The absolute object file created by the linker/locater is converted into processor understandable binary code. Object to Hex file converter is the utility program for converting an object file to a hex file
- ✓ *Intel HEX* and *Motorola HEX* are the two commonly used Hex file formats in embedded applications
- ✓ *Disassembler* is a utility program which converts machine codes into target processor specific Assembly codes/instructions. *Disassembling* is the process of converting machine codes into Assembly code
- ✓ *Decompiler* is the utility program for translating machine codes into corresponding high level language instructions
- ✓ *Simulator* is a software application that precisely duplicates (mimics) the target CPU and simulates the various features and instructions supported by the target CPU
- ✓ *Emulator* is a self-contained hardware device which emulates the target CPU. Emulator hardware contains necessary emulation logic and it is hooked to the debugging application running on the development PC on one end and connects to the target board through some interface on the other end
- ✓ Incremental EEPROM Burning technique, Inline breakpoint based Firmware Debugging, Monitor Program based Firmware Debugging, In Circuit Emulator (ICE) based Firmware Debugging and On Chip Firmware Debugging (OCD) are the techniques used for debugging embedded firmware on the target hardware
- ✓ Background Debug Mode (BDM) Interface and JTAG are the two commonly used interfaces for On Chip Firmware Debugging (OCD)
- ✓ Magnifying glass, Multimeter, Cathode Ray Oscilloscope (CRO), Logic Analyser and Function generator are the commonly used hardware debugging tools
- ✓ Boundary scan is a technique for testing the interconnection among the various chips, which support boundary scanning, in a complex board containing too many interconnections and multiple planes for routing
- ✓ *Boundary Scan Description Language* (*BSDL*) is a language similar to VHDL, which describes the boundary

scan implementation of a device and is used for implementing boundary scan tests using JTAG. BSDL file is a file containing the boundary scan description for a device in boundary scan description language, which is supplied as input to a Boundary scan tool for generating the boundary scan test cases

Keywords

Integrated Development Environment (IDE) : A software package which bundles a 'Text Editor (Source Code Editor)', 'Cross-compiler (for cross platform development and compiler for same platform development)', 'Linker' and a 'Debugger'

Keil µVision3 : A licensed IDE tool from Keil Software (www.keil.com), an ARM company, for 8051 family microcontroller based embedded firmware development

Listing file (.LST File) : File generated during cross compilation of a source code and it contains information about the cross compilation process, like cross compiler details, formatted source text ('C' code), assembly code generated from the source file, symbol tables, errors and warnings detected during the cross-compilation process, etc.

Object File (.OBJ File) : A specially formatted file with data records for symbolic information, object code, debugging information, library references, etc. generated during the cross-compilation of a source file

Map file : File generated during cross-compilation process and it contains information about the link/locate process.

Hex file : The binary executable file created from the source code

Intel HEX : HEX file representation format

Motorola HEX : HEX file representation format

Disassembler : Utility program which converts machine codes into target processor specific Assembly codes/instructions.

Decompiler : Utility program for translating machine codes into corresponding high level language instructions

Simulator : Software application that precisely duplicates (mimics) the target CPU and simulates the various features and instructions supported by the target CPU

Monitor Program : Program which acts as a supervisor and controls the downloading of user code into the code memory, inspects and modifies register/memory locations, allows single stepping of source code, etc.

In Circuit Emulator (ICE) : A hardware device for emulating the target CPU for debug purpose

Debug Board Module (DBM) : ICE device which contains the emulation control logic and emulation chip in a single hardware unit and is designed for a particular family of device

Background Debug Mode (BDM) : A proprietary serial interface from Motorola for On Chip Debugging

JTAG : A serial interface for target board diagnostics and debugging

Boundary Scan : A target hardware debug method for checking the interconnections among the various chips of a complex board

Boundary Scan Description Language (BSDL) : A language similar to VHDL, which describes the boundary scan implementation of a JTAG supported device

Objective Questions

1 Which of the following intermediate file, generated during cross-compilation of an Embedded C file holds the assembly code generated corresponding to the c source code.
(a) List File (b) Preprocessor output file (c) Object file (d) Map file

2 Which of the following detail(s) is(are) kept in an object file generated during the process of cross-compiling an Embedded C file.
(a) Variable and function names (b) Variable and function reference
(c) Reserved memory for global variables (d) All of these
(e) None of these

3 Which of the following intermediate file, generated during the cross-compilation of an Embedded C files holds the information about the link/locate process for the multiple object modules of the project?
(a) List file (b) Preprocessor output file (c) Object file (d) Map file

4 Which of the following file generated during the cross-compilation process of an Embedded C project holds the machine code corresponding to the target processor?
(a) List file (b) Preprocessor output file (c) Object file (d) Map file

5 Examine the following Intel HEX Record
:03000000020C1FD0
This record is ?
(a) a Data Record (b) an End of File Record (c) a Segment Address Record
(d) an Extended Linear Address record

6 Examine the following Intel HEX record
:03000000020C1FD0
What is the number of data bytes in this record?
(a) 0 (b) 3 (c) 2 (d) 20

7 Examine the following Intel HEX record
:03000000020C1FD0
What is the start address of the data bytes in this record?
(a) 0x0000 (b) 0x3000 (c) 0x1FD0 (d) 0x20C1

8 Examine the following Intel HEX Record
:03000000020C1FD0
Which all are the data bytes present in this record?
(a) 03, 00, 00 (b) 02, 0C, 1F (c) 0C, 1F, D0 (d) 00, 00, 20

9 The program that converts machine codes into target processor specific Assembly code is known as
(a) Disassembler (b) Assembler (c) Cross-compiler (d) Decompiler

10 Which of the following is true about a *simulator* used in embedded software debugging?
(a) It is a software tool (b) It requires target hardware for simulation
(c) It doesn't require target hardware for simulation (d) (a) and (b) (e) (a) and (c)

11 Which of the following is an example for on chip firmware debugging?
(a) OnCE (b) BDM (c) All of these

Review Questions

1 Explain the various elements of an embedded system development environment.
2 Explain the role of *Integrated Development Environment* (IDE) for Embedded Software Development.

3 What are the different files generated during the cross-compilation of an Embedded C file? Explain them in detail.
4 Explain the various details held by a *List file* generated during the process of cross-compiling an Embedded C project.
5 Explain the various details held by a *Map file* generated during the process of cross-compiling an Embedded C project.
6 Explain the various details stored in an *Object file* generated during the cross-compilation of an Embedded C file.
7 Explain the difference between *Intel Hex* and *Motorola Hex* file format.
8 Explain the format of *Hex records* in an *Intel Hex* File.
9 Explain the format of *Hex records* in a *Motorola Hex* File.
10 What is the difference between an *assembler* and a *disassembler*? State their use in Embedded Application development.
11 What is a *decompiler*?
12 What is the difference between a *simulator* and an *emulator*?
13 Explain the advantages and limitations of *simulator* based debugging.
14 What are the different techniques available for embedded firmware debugging? Explain them in detail.
15 What is a *Monitor program*? Explain its role in embedded firmware debugging?
16 What is *ROM emulation*? Explain *In Circuit Emulator* (ICE) based debugging in detail.
17 Explain *On Chip Debugging* (OCD).
18 Explain the different tools used for hardware debugging.
19 Explain the *Boundary Scan* based hardware debugging in detail.

Lab Assignments

1 Write an Embedded C program for building a dancing LED circuit using *8051* as per the requirements given below
(a) 4 Red LEDs are connected to Port Pins P1.0, P1.2, P1.4 and P1.6 respectively
(b) 4 Green LEDs are connected to Port Pins P1.1, P1.3, P1.5 and P1.7 respectively
(c) Turn On and Off the Green and Red LEDs alternatively with a delay of 100 milliseconds
(d) Use a clock frequency of 12 MHz
(e) Use Keil μVision 3 IDE and simulate the application for checking the firmware
(f) Write the application separately for delay generation using timer and software routines
2 Implement the above requirement in Assembly Language
3 Write an Embedded C application for reading the status of 8 Dip switches connected to the Port P1 of the *8051* microcontroller using μVision 3 IDE. Debug the application using the simulator and simulate the state of DIP switches using the Port simulator for P1
4 Implement the above requirement in Assembly language
5 Write an Embedded C program to count the pulses appearing on the C/T0 input pin of *8051* microcontroller for a duration of 100 milliseconds using μVision 3 IDE
6 Implement the above requirement in Assembly language
7 Write an Embedded C program for configuring the INT0 Pin of the *8051* microcontroller as edge triggered and print the message "External 0 Interrupt in Progress" to the serial port of *8051* when the External 0 interrupt occurs. Use Keil μVision 3 IDE. Assume the crystal frequency for the controller as 11.0592 MHz. Configure the serial Port for baudrate 9600, No parity, 1 Start bit, 1 Stop bit and 8 data bits.
8 Implement the above requirement in Assembly language

9 Write an Interrupt Service Routine in Embedded C to handle the INT0 interrupt as per the requirements given below
   (a) Use Register Bank 1
   (b) Read port P1 and save it in register R7
   (c) Use Keil µVision 3 IDE and simulate the application

10 Write an embedded 'C' program using Keil µVision 3 IDE to control the stepping of a unipolar 2-phase stepper motor in full step mode with a delay of 5 second between the steps. The stepper motor coils, A is connected to P1.0, B is connected to Port pins P1.1, C is connected to P1.2 and D to P1.3 of 8051 through NPN transistor driving circuits. Assume the clock frequency of operation as 12.00MHz

11 Write an Embedded C program using Keil µVision 3 IDE to interface 8255 PPI device with *8051* microcontroller. The 8255 is memory interfaced to *8051* in the address map 8000H to FFFFH. Initialise the Port A, Port B and Port C of 8255 as Output ports in Mode0

12 Write an Embedded C program using Keil µVision 3 IDE to interface ADC *0801* with *8051* microcontroller as per the requirements given below
   (a) Data lines of ADC is interfaced to Port 1
   (b) The Chip Select of ADC is supplied through Port Pin P3.3, Read signal through P3.0 and Write signal through P3.1 of *8051* microcontroller
   (c) ADC interrupt line is interfaced to External Interrupt 0 of *8051*
   (d) The ADC Data is read when an interrupt is asserted. The data is kept in a buffer in the data memory
   (e) The buffer is located at 20H and its size is 15 bytes. When the buffer is full, the buffer address for the next sample is reset to location 20H

14 Product Enclosure Design and Development

LEARNING OBJECTIVES

- ✓ *Learn about the different techniques for product enclosure design and development*
- ✓ *Learn about the Computer Aided Design (CAD) tools for Product enclosure design*
- ✓ *Learn about handmade enclosure development and Rapid Prototyping for product enclosure development*
- ✓ *Learn about Steriolithography (SLA), Selective Laser Sintering (SLS) and Fused Deposition Modelling (FDM) based Rapid Prototyping for product enclosure development*
- ✓ *Learn about the tooling and moulding techniques for product enclosure development*
- ✓ *Learn about Room Temperature Vulcanised (RTV), Computer Numeric Control (CNC) and Injection Moulding based Tooling techniques for mould development*
- ✓ *Learn the sheet metal based product enclosure development process*
- ✓ *Know the use of commercial off-the-shelf enclosures (CoEs) in product enclosure development*

The saying "The first Impression is the last impression" is really meaningful in the commercial embedded product market. No matter whatever features a commercial product offers compared to its competitor's product, the aesthetics of the product plays an important role on its demand and popularity. A mobile handset is a typical example for this. Most of the end users prefer handy, compact, rugged handsets with user friendly keypads among a set of handsets by various manufacturers offering more or less the same features. For a successful commercial embedded product, the features offered and product aesthetics must be well balanced. Product aesthetics refers to the look 'n' feel, size, weight and shape of the product. User friendliness (Navigation key order, placement, accessibility, etc.) is another important factor that should be considered for products involving extensive user interactions. In most of the product development process, the engineering design of the product is carried out by a mechanical engineering wing. The mechanical engineering team and embedded hardware development team should work hands on hand to develop products with nice aesthetics. The mechanical design team is responsible for designing the product enclosure and this design is executed in parallel with the design of embedded hardware and firmware. However, the aesthetics of the product should be finalized before the development of the real embedded hardware (PCB). The PCB size and shape are restricted by the suggested product enclosure. The PCB should be routed in a way to incorporate the directions (like placement of keyboard if any, display unit if any, PCB mounting holes, placement of connectors, etc.) from the engineering design team. Apart from the product aesthetics, the engineering design team should be well aware of the budget limitations for the product and they should be capable of suggesting a design fitting into the allocated budget. Some technical aspects also need to be considered while selecting materials for product enclosures. For example, certain products involving RF signals cannot use metal enclosures since they absorb the RF signals and reduce the field strength, hence in such cases some cheap alternatives should be put forward. The enclosure design should also take into account various protections like mechanical shock, water resistance, etc.

14.1 PRODUCT ENCLOSURE DESIGN TOOLS

Frankly speaking, product enclosure design is an art. As a sculpture shows the artistic ability of its creator, the product's enclosure reflects the design capabilities of its designer. With the latest design technologies, the custom drawing using pen and pencil on paper for a design (front, top and end view of the design) has given way to Computer Aided Design (CAD). A variety of CAD tools are available for Product Enclosure Design. 'Solidworks', 'AutoCAD', 'ProEngineer', 'Catia Interface', etc. are examples of CAD tools. By combining the artistic ability of the designer with the design flexibility offered by the automated tools, good product enclosures maintaining very good aesthetics can be developed.

14.2 PRODUCT ENCLOSURE DEVELOPMENT TECHNIQUES

Choosing the right enclosure (housing) for a design is dependent upon a variety of product specifications like size, shielding, materials and construction, ergonomics, customisability, operating conditions and protection requirements. Various techniques and materials are used for the enclosure (housing) development of the product. The commonly used materials for enclosure (housing) development are metal and variants of plastic. The de facto standard for plastic is ABS (acrylonitrile-butadiene-styrene). ABS is used in a multitude of consumer products ranging from children's toys to mobile handsets. Metal is been pushed down in most modern products for the requirement lightweight and compactness. Plastic is the right choice for products demanding lightweight and compactness whereas metal is the right candidate for products requiring ruggedness and extensive shielding from external RF interference. Certain applications demand products with tight sealing and watertight enclosures conforming to protection standards like IP 65, NEMA 4, etc. The following sections give an overview of various techniques adopted in Product enclosure (housing) development.

14.2.1 Handmade Enclosures

This is the best choice for enclosure development for prototype products and low volume product requirements. The capital investment required is very small for handmade enclosures. Commonly used materials for handmade enclosures are plastics like Poly Vinyl Chloride (PVC) and Acrylic. The PVC/Acrylic sheet can be cut into desired shape and combined using a suitable adhesive. It is a low cost technology but limited to the fabrication of low volume products. The manpower involved is comparatively high and development time is also high.

14.2.2 Rapid Prototyping Development

Rapid prototyping is a 3-Dimensional Computer Assisted Manufacturing (3D CAM) technique used for prototype development as well as mass production. The 3D model designed using any of the 3D CAD tools is used as input for this. Rapid prototyping is also known as generative manufacturing or solid freeform fabrication or layered manufacturing. Rapid prototyping is best suggested for Proof of Concept (PoC) models. The various techniques adopted in rapid prototyping are listed below.

14.2.2.1 Stereolithography (SLA) Prototyping Stereolithography is considered as the first rapid prototyping technology and it was developed by 3D systems of Valencia, CA, USA. It is commercially introduced in the year 1988. Stereolithography is a process in which liquid plastic is solidified in precise patterns by a UV laser beam, resulting in a solid epoxy realisation of a 3D design of the enclosure. SLA prototyping machine uses a computer to direct UV laser to solidify photosensitive polymer layer upon layer to produce a physical object. On completion of each layer, the surface is re-wetted and the laser hardens the next layer. Upon completion of the entire layer, the part is cleaned and cured. This technique is also referred as 3D layering or 3D printing.

14.2.2.2 Selective Laser Sintering (SLS) Prototyping Selective Laser Sintering (SLS) is similar to SLA, except that the 3D prototypes are created from the drawing by fusing or sintering powdered thermoplastic materials layer by layer. SLS system consists of a part chamber, laser unit and a computerised controller. The part chamber contains a building platform, powder cartridge and levelling roller. The powder cartridge sinters the material over the building platform. The advantage of SLS over SLA is the range of materials available; including nylon, metals, and elastomers.

14.2.2.3 Fused Deposition Modelling (FDM) Fused Deposition Modelling (FDM) is a solid-based rapid prototyping method. It makes use of melted thermoplastic polymer in the form of paste for building the layers. The FDM system consists of a build platform, extrusion nozzle, and control system. In order to generate a two-dimensional cross section of the model under consideration, production quality thermoplastics (largely ABS) is melted and then extruded through a specially designed head onto a platform. The platform is lowered down once the newly extruded layer is solidified, for extruding the next layer. This process is repeated until the model is complete. On completion the model is taken out of the build platform chamber and cleaned properly.

14.2.3 Tooling and Moulding

The tooling and moulding techniques are mainly used for developing plastic and metal housings for high volume production. ABS, nylon, polycarbonate, acrylic and a variety of other polymers are the commonly used plastic. The initial investment for making a tool or mould is too high and hence it is profitable only for high volume productions. Once a tool or mould is developed, thousands of pieces can be developed from it and this will convert the initial investment into per piece housing price. The widely adopted tooling and moulding techniques are:

14.2.3.1 Room Temperature Vulcanised (RTV) Tooling Room Temperature Vulcanised (RTV) tooling technique is used for polyurethane housings. First an RTV rubber tools is created by pouring liquid silicone rubber around a master pattern. The resulting model is taken out of the master pattern, finished well and then used for casting polyurethane housings. These housings are painted according to the user needs. Text and graphics can be printed on top of the painted housing. The key advantage of RTV is the ability to produce high volume prototypes at a nominal cost.

14.2.3.2 Computer Numeric Control (CNC) Tooling In Computer Numeric Control (CNC) tooling, CNC machines are used for milling the block of plastic according to the input from a design file generated by the 3D modelling tool to develop desired housing.

14.2.3.3 Injection Moulding Injection moulding system consists of a moulding machine and mould plates (dummy shape of the product to be developed). Plastic/resin is fed into the injection barrel of the machine through the hopper and in the barrel it is heated to the appropriate melting temperature. Molted resin is injected to the space between the mould plates through a nozzle to create moulds. Mould is cooled constantly to a temperature that allows the resin to solidify. Mould plates are held together by hydraulic or mechanical force.

14.2.4 Sheet Metal Work

Sheet metal is the foil (thin) form of metal sheets, which can be cut or bend into different shapes. Copper, brass, mild steel, aluminum, tin, nickel, titanium, etc. are examples for metals used in sheet metal work. The thickness of metal sheets used for sheet metal work normally falls below 6 mm. Sheet metal is the best choice for product enclosures where aesthetics are not a big constraint, where a functional product is the only requirement. Sheet metal is best suited for products demanding high ruggedness. Sheet metal is not a good choice for products including any RF circuitry, since the enclosure tend to attenuate the RF field. Also fancy works like contours, curves are not possible to build on housing using sheet metal work.

14.2.5 Commercial Off-the-Shelf Enclosures (COE)

Commercial off-the-shelf enclosures are the readily available enclosures in the market. It can be either plastic or metal. They are generally available with rectangular, square and circular shapes and with various dimensions. Multimeter housings, plastic boxes, etc. are typical examples for COE. If the product is important only in terms of functionalities and not in terms of aesthetics, you can go for a commercial off-the-shelf enclosure. Before building the hardware, identify the best suiting COE and tailor the PCB to fit into the selected COE. COE is best suited for concept development projects and product development work with low budget.

14.3 SUMMARY

Competitive products where features as well as aesthetics are important should always require attractive enclosures. Mobile handsets, children toys, etc. are examples of it. The more you make the enclosure attractive, the more is the demand. Custom enclosure development is required for such products. Proof of Concept (PoC) design products and products which are not aiming a commercial market can go for either custom enclosure or Commercial off-the-shelf enclosure. Moreover the enclosure should consider any special needs by the product like protection standards, shielding requirements, etc.

Summary

- ✓ Product enclosure is essential for protecting the hardware from dust, water, corrosion, etc. to provide ruggedness and to provide a good aesthetics (look and feel) to the product
- ✓ Product enclosure design should take care of the aesthetics, protection requirements, shielding requirements, etc.
- ✓ Product enclosure design deals with the design of the enclosure for the embedded product (Hardware with firmware integrated). Various computer aided design (CAD) tools like 'Solidworks', 'AutoCAD', 'ProEngineer', 'Catia Interface', etc. can be used for product enclosure design

- ✓ Product enclosure can be developed manually or using Computer Assisted Manufacturing (CAM) tools based on the design file generated from the Computer Aided Design
- ✓ Handmade enclosure is a typical example for manually developed product enclosure. It is the best choice for prototype and low volume production. It uses plastics like ABS or PVC and sheet metal for enclosure design
- ✓ Rapid prototyping is a 3-Dimentional Computer Assisted Manufacturing (3D CAM) technique used for prototype development as well as mass production
- ✓ Stereolithography (SLA), Selective Laser Sintering (SLS), Fused Deposition Modelling (FDM), etc. are examples for various types of rapid prototyping
- ✓ Stereolithography is a process in which liquid plastic is solidified in precise patterns by a UV laser beam, resulting in a solid epoxy realisation of a 3D design of the enclosure
- ✓ Selective Laser Sintering (SLS) is similar to SLA, except that the 3D prototypes are created from the drawing by fusing or sintering powdered thermoplastic materials layer by layer
- ✓ Fused Deposition Modelling (FDM) is a solid-based rapid prototyping method, which uses melted thermoplastic polymer in the form of paste for building the layers
- ✓ The tooling and moulding techniques are mainly used for developing plastic and metal housings for high volume production. Here a tool or mould is developed first and the enclosure is developed from this mould. Room Temperature Vulcanised (RTV), Computer Numeric Control (CNC), injection moulding, etc. are examples for tooling techniques
- ✓ Room Temperature Vulcanised (RTV) tooling technique is used for polyurethane housings. First an RTV rubber tool is created by pouring liquid silicone rubber around a master pattern. The resulting model is taken out of the master pattern, finished well and then used for casting polyurethane housings
- ✓ In Computer Numeric Control (CNC) tooling, CNC machines are used for milling the block of plastic according to the input from a design file generated by the 3D modeling tool to develop desired housing
- ✓ Injection moulding system consists of a moulding machine and mould plates (dummy shape of the product to be developed). Plastic/resin is fed into the injection barrel of the machine through the hopper and in the barrel it is heated to the appropriate melting temperature. Molted resin is injected to the space between the mould plates through a nozzle to create moulds
- ✓ Sheet metal is the foil (thin) form of metal sheets, which can be cut or bent into different shapes
- ✓ Commercial off-the-shelf enclosure is the readily available enclosures in the market. It can be either plastic or metal

Keywords

Product Enclosure	:	A protective casing for the hardware product
Acrylonitrile-Butadiene-Styrene (ABS)	:	A type of plastic used in product enclosure development
Handmade Enclosure	:	Manually developed enclosure using plastic or sheet metal
Computer Assisted Design (CAD)	:	Design using software tools
Computer Aided Manufacturing	:	Manufacturing process with the aid of software tools
Rapid Prototyping	:	A 3-Dimensional Computer Assisted Manufacturing (3D CAM) technique for prototype development as well as mass production
Stereolithography (SLA)	:	A rapid prototyping technique in which liquid plastic is solidified in precise patterns by a UV laser beam, resulting in a solid epoxy realisation of a 3D design of the enclosure

Selective Laser Sintering (SLS)	:	A rapid prototyping technique in which the 3D prototype is created by fusing or sintering powdered thermoplastic materials layer by layer
Fused Deposition Modelling (FDM)	:	A solid-based rapid prototyping method, which uses melted thermoplastic polymer in the form of paste for building the layers
Room Temperature Vulcanised (RTV) Tooling	:	A tooling technique for building polyurethane enclosures, in which an RTV rubber tools is created by pouring liquid silicone rubber around a master pattern
Computer Numeric Control (CNC) Tooling	:	A tooling mechanism for generating the mould by milling the block of plastic according to the input from a design file generated by the 3D modelling tool to develop desired housing
Injection Moulding	:	A moulding technique in which molted resin is injected into the space between the mould plates through a nozzle to create moulds
Commercial Off-the-Shelf Enclosure	:	Ready to use plastic or metal enclosures available in the market

Objective Questions

1 Which of the following is not a Rapid Prototyping technology for product enclosure development?
(a) Selective Laser Sintering (SLS) (b) Fused Deposition Modelling (FDM)
(c) Room Temperature Vulcanisation (RTV) (d) Stereolithography (SLA)

2 Which of the following is not a Tooling and Moulding technology for product enclosure development?
(a) Room Temperature Vulcanisation (RTV) (b) Sheet metal
(c) Injection moulding (d) CNC tooling

Review Questions

1 Explain the various factors that need to be addressed while selecting an enclosure for an embedded product.
2 Explain the different product enclosure development techniques in detail
3 What are the merits and limitations of Handmade Enclosures?
4 What is Rapid Prototyping? What are the different techniques available for Rapid Prototyping? Explain the merits and limitations of each.
5 Explain the Tooling and Moulding techniques used for product enclosure development
6 Explain the Sheet Metal based product enclosure development

15 The Embedded Product Development Life Cycle (EDLC)

LEARNING OBJECTIVES

- ✓ *Learn about the life-cycle stages in embedded product development, the modelling of the life cycle stages and the objectives for modelling the life cycle*
- ✓ *Learn about the project management and its objectives in embedded product development*
- ✓ *Learn about the techniques for productivity improvement in embedded product development*
- ✓ *Learn the different phases (Need, Conceptualisation, Analysis, Design, Development, Testing, Deployment, Support, Upgrades and Disposal) of the product development life cycle and the activities happening in each stage of the life cycle*
- ✓ *Learn about the different modelling techniques for modelling the stages involved in the embedded product development life cycle*
- ✓ *Learn about the application, advantages and limitations of Linear/Waterfall Model in embedded product development life cycle management*
- ✓ *Learn about the application, advantages and limitations of Iterative/Incremental or Fountain Model in embedded product development life cycle management*
- ✓ *Learn about the application, advantages and limitations of prototyping/evolutionary model in embedded product development life cycle management*
- ✓ *Learn about the application, advantages and limitations of Spiral Model in embedded product development life cycle management*

Just imagine about your favourite chicken dish that your mom served during a holiday lunch. Have you ever thought of the effort behind preparing the delicious chicken dish? Frankly speaking No, Isn't it? Okay let's go back and analyse how the yummy chicken in the chicken stall became the delicious chicken dish served on the dining table. One fine morning Mom thinks "Wohh!! It's Sunday and why can't we have a special lunch with our favourite chicken dish." Mom tells this to Papa and he agrees on it and together they decide how much quantity of chicken is required for the four-member family (may be based on past experience) and lists out the various ingredients required for preparing the dish. Now the list is ready and papa checks his purse to ensure whether the item list is at the reach of the money in his purse. If not, both of them sit together and make some reductions in the list. Papa goes to the market to buy the items in the list. Finds out a chicken stall where quality chicken is selling at a nominal rate. Procures all the items and returns back home with all the items in the list and hands over the packet to Mom. Mom starts cleaning the chicken pieces and chopping the ingredient/vegetables and then puts them in a vessel and starts boiling them. Mom may go on to preparing other side dishes or rice and comes back to the chicken dish preparation at regular intervals to add the necessary ingredients (like chicken masala, chilly powder, coriander powder, tamarind, coconut oil, salt, etc.) in time and checks whether all ingredients are in correct proportion, if not adjust them to the required proportion. Papa gives an overall supervision to the preparation and informs mom if she forgot to add any ingredients and also helps her in verifying the proportion of the ingredients. Finally the fragrance of spicy boiled chicken comes out of the vessel and mom realises that chicken dish is ready. She takes it out from the stove and adds the final taste building ingredients. Mom tastes a small piece from the dish and ensures that it meets the regular quality. Now the dish is ready to serve. Mom takes the responsibility of serving the same to you and what you need to do is taste it and tell her how tasty it is. If you closely observe these steps with an embedded product developer's mind, you can find out that this simple chicken dish preparation contains various complex activities like overall management, development, testing and releasing. Papa is the person who did the entire management activity starting from item procurement to giving overall supervision. Mom is responsible for developing the dish, testing the dish to certain extent and serving the dish (release management) and finally you are the one who did the actual field test. All embedded products will have a design and development life cycle similar to our chicken dish preparation example, with management, design, development, test and release activities.

15.1 WHAT IS EDLC?

Embedded Product Development Life Cycle (Let us call it as EDLC, though it is not a standard and universal term) is an 'Analysis-Design-Implementation' based standard problem solving approach for Embedded Product Development. In any product development application, the first and foremost step is to figure out what product needs to be developed (analysis), next you need to figure out a good approach for building it (design) and last but not least you need to develop it (implementation).

15.2 WHY EDLC

EDLC is essential for understanding the scope and complexity of the work involved in any embedded product development. EDLC defines the interaction and activities among various groups of a product development sector including project management, system design and development (hardware, firmware and enclosure design and development), system testing, release management and quality assurance. The standards imposed by EDLC on a product development makes the product, developer independent in terms of standard documents and it also provides uniformity in development approaches.

15.3 OBJECTIVES OF EDLC

The ultimate aim of any embedded product in a commercial production setup is to produce marginal benefit. Marginal benefit is usually expressed in terms of Return on Investment (ROI). The investment for a product development includes initial investment, manpower investment, infrastructure investment, etc. A product is said to be profitable only if the turnover from the selling of the product is more than that of the overall investment expenditure. For this, the product should be acceptable by the end user and it should meet the requirements of end user in terms of quality, reliability and functionality. So it is very essential to ensure that the product is meeting all these criteria, throughout the design, development, implementation and support phases. Embedded Product Development Life Cycle (EDLC) helps out in ensuring all these requirements. EDLC has three primary objectives, namely

1. Ensure that high quality products are delivered to end user.
2. Risk minimisation and defect prevention in product development through project management.
3. Maximise the productivity.

15.3.1 Ensuring High Quality for Products

The primary definition of quality in any embedded product development is the Return on Investment (ROI) achieved by the product. The expenses incurred for developing the product may fall in any of the categories; initial investment, developer recruiting, training, or any other infrastructure requirement related. There will be some budgetary and cost allocation given to the development of the product and it will be allocated by some higher officials based on the assumption that the product will produce a good return or a return justifying the investment. The budget allocation might have done after studying the market trends and requirements of the product, competition, etc. EDLC must ensure that the development of the product has taken account of all the qualitative attributes of the embedded system. The qualitative attributes are discussed separately in an earlier chapter of this book. Please refer back for the same.

15.3.2 Risk Minimisation and Defect Prevention through Management

You may be thinking what is the significance of project management, or why project management is essential in product development. Nevertheless it is an additional expenditure to the project! If we look back to the chicken dish example, we can find out that the management activity from dad is essential in the beginning phase but in the preparation phase it can be handled by mom itself. There are projects in embedded product development which requires 'loose' or 'tight' project management. If the product development project is a simple one, a senior developer itself can take charge of the management activity and no need for a skilled project manager to look after this with dedicated effort throughout the development process, but there should be an overall supervision from a skilled project management team for ensuring that the development process is going in the right direction. Projects which are complex and requires timeliness should have a dedicated and skilled project management part and hence they are said to be "tightly" bounded to project management. '*Project management is essential for predictability, co-ordination and risk minimisation*'. Whenever a product development request comes, an estimate on the duration of the development and deployment activity should be given to the end user/client. The timeframe may be expressed in number of person days PDS (The effort in terms of single person working for this much days) or 'X person for X week (e.g. 2 person 2 week) etc. This is one aspect of predictability. The management team might have reached on this estimate based on past experience in handling similar project or on the analysis of work summary or data available for a similar project, which was logged in using an activity tool. Resource (Developer) allocation is another aspect of predictability in management. Resource allocations like how many resources should work for this project for how many days, how many resources are critical with respect to the work handling by them and how many backups required for the resources to overcome a critical situation where a resource is not available (Risk minimisation). Resource allocation is critical and it is having a direct impact on investment.

The communication aspect of the project management deals with co-ordination and interaction among resources and client from which the request for the product development aroused. Project management adds an extra cost on the budget but it is essential for ensuring the development process is going in the right direction and the schedules of the development activity are meeting. Without management, the development work may go beyond the stipulated time frame (schedule slipping) and may end up in a product which is not meeting the requirements from the client side, as a result re-works should be done to rectify the possible deviations occurred and it will again put extra cost on the development. Project management makes the proverb "A stitch in time saves nine" meaningful in an embedded product development. Apart from resource allocation, project management also covers activities like task allocation, scheduling, monitoring and project tracking. Computer Assisted Software Engineering (CASE) Tools and Gantt charts help the manager in achieving this. Microsoft® Project Tool is a typical example of CASE tool for project management.

15.3.3 Increased Productivity

Productivity is a measure of efficiency as well as Return on Investment (ROI). One aspect of productivity covers how many resources are utilised to build the product, how much investment required, how much time is taken for developing the product, etc. For example, the productivity of a system is said to be doubled if a product developed by a team of 'X' members in a period of 'X' days is developed by another team of 'X/2' members in a period of 'X' days or by a team of 'X' members in a period of 'X/2' days. This productivity measurement is based on total manpower efficiency. Productivity in terms of Returns is said to be increased, if the product is capable of yielding maximum returns with reduced investment. Saving manpower effort will definitely result in increased productivity. Usage of automated tools, wherever possible, is recommended for this. The initial investment on tools may be an additional burden in terms of money, but it will definitely save efforts in the next project also. It is a one-time investment. "Pay once use many time". Another important factor which can help in increased productivity is "re-usable effort". Some of the works required for the current product development may have some common features which you built for some of the other product development in the projects you executed before. Identify those efforts and design the new product in such a way that it can directly be plugged into the new product without any additional effort. (For example, the current product you are developing requires an RS-232C serial interface and one of the product you already developed have the same feature. Adapt this part directly from the existing product in terms of the hardware and firmware required for the same.) This will definitely increase the productivity by reducing the development effort. Another advised method for increasing the productivity is by using resources with specific skill sets which matches the exact requirement of the entire or part of the product (e.g. Resource with expertise in Bluetooth technology for developing a Bluetooth interface for the product). This reduces the learning time taken by a resource, who does not have prior expertise in the particular feature or domain. This is not possible in all product development environments, since some of the resources with the desired skill sets may be engaged with some other work and releasing them from the current work is not possible. Recruiting people with desired skill sets for the current product development is another option; this is worth only if you expect to have more work on the near future on the same technology or skill sets. Use of Commercial Off-the-Shelf Components (COTS) wherever possible in a product is a very good way of reducing the development effort and thereby increasing the productivity (Refer back to the topic 'Commercial Off-the-shelf components' given in Chapter 2 for more details on COTS). COTS component is a ready to use component and you can use the same as plug-in modules in your product. For example, if the product under development requires a 10 base T Ethernet connectivity, you can either implement the same in your product by using the TCP/IP chip and related components or can use a readily available TCP/IP full functional plug-in module. The second approach will save effort and time. EDLC should take all these aspects into consideration to provide maximum productivity.

15.4 DIFFERENT PHASES OF EDLC

The life cycle of a product development is commonly referred to as models. Model defines the various phases involved in the life cycle. The number of phases involved in a model may vary according to the complexity of the product under consideration. A typical simple product contains five minimal phases namely: 'Requirement Analysis', 'Design', 'Development and Test', 'Deployment' and 'Maintenance'. The classic Embedded Product Life Cycle Model contains the phases: 'Need', 'Conceptualisation', 'Analysis', 'Design', 'Development and Testing', 'Deployment', 'Support', 'Upgrades' and 'Retirement/ Disposal' (Fig. 15.1). In a real product development environment, the phases given in this model may vary and can have submodels or the models contain only certain important phases of the classic model. As mentioned earlier, the number of phases involved in the EDLC model depends on the complexity of the product. The following section describes each phases of the classic EDLC model in detail.

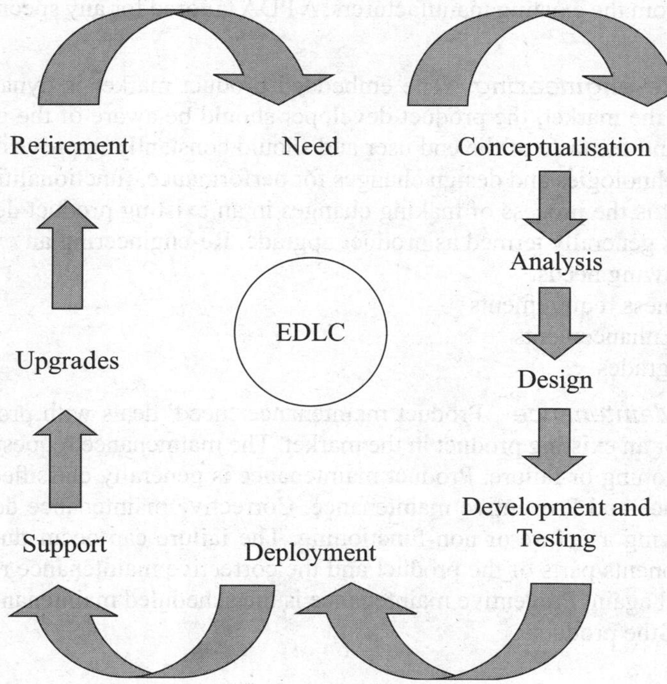

Fig. 15.1 **Classic Embedded Product Development Life Cycle Model**

15.4.1 Need

Any embedded product evolves as an output of a '*Need*'. The need may come from an individual or from the public or from a company (Generally speaking from an end user/client). 'Need' should be articulated to initiate the Product Development Life Cycle and based on the need for the product, a 'Statement of Need' or 'Concept Proposal' is prepared. The 'Concept Proposal' must be reviewed by the senior management and funding agency and should get necessary approval. Once the proposal gets approval, it goes to a product development team, which can either be an organisation from which the need arise or a third party product development/service company (If a product development company approaches a client/sponsor with the idea of a product, the business needs for the product will be prepared by the company itself). The product development need can be visualised in any one of the following three needs.

15.4.1.1 New or Custom Product Development The need for a product which does not exist in the market or a product which acts as competitor to an existing product in the current market will lead to the development of a completely new product. The product can be a commercial requirement or an individual requirement or a specific organisation's requirement. Example for an Embedded Product which acts a competitor in the current market is 'Mobile handset' which is going to be developed by a new company apart from the existing manufacturers. A PDA tailored for any specific need is an example for a custom product.

15.4.1.2 Product Re-engineering The embedded product market is dynamic and competitive. In order to sustain in the market, the product developer should be aware of the general market trends, technology changes and the taste of the end user and should constantly improve an existing product by incorporating new technologies and design changes for performance, functionalities and aesthetics. Re-engineering a product is the process of making changes in an existing product design and launching it as a new version. It is generally termed as product upgrade. Re-engineering an existing product comes as a result of the following needs.

1. Change in Business requirements
2. User Interface Enhancements
3. Technology Upgrades

15.4.1.3 Product Maintenance Product maintenance 'need' deals with providing technical support to the end user for an existing product in the market. The maintenance request may come as a result of product non-functioning or failure. Product maintenance is generally classified into two categories; Corrective maintenance and Preventive maintenance. Corrective maintenance deals with making corrective actions following a failure or non-functioning. The failure can occur due to damages or non-functioning of components/parts of the product and the corrective maintenance replaces them to make the product functional again. Preventive maintenance is the scheduled maintenance to avoid the failure or non-functioning of the product.

15.4.2 Conceptualisation

Conceptualisation is the 'Product Concept Development Phase' and it begins immediately after a Concept Proposal is formally approved. Conceptualisation phase defines the scope of the concept, performs cost benefit analysis and feasibility study and prepares project management and risk management plans. Conceptualisation can be viewed as a phase shaping the "Need" of an end-user or convincing the end user, whether it is a feasible product and how this product can be realised (Fig. 15.2).

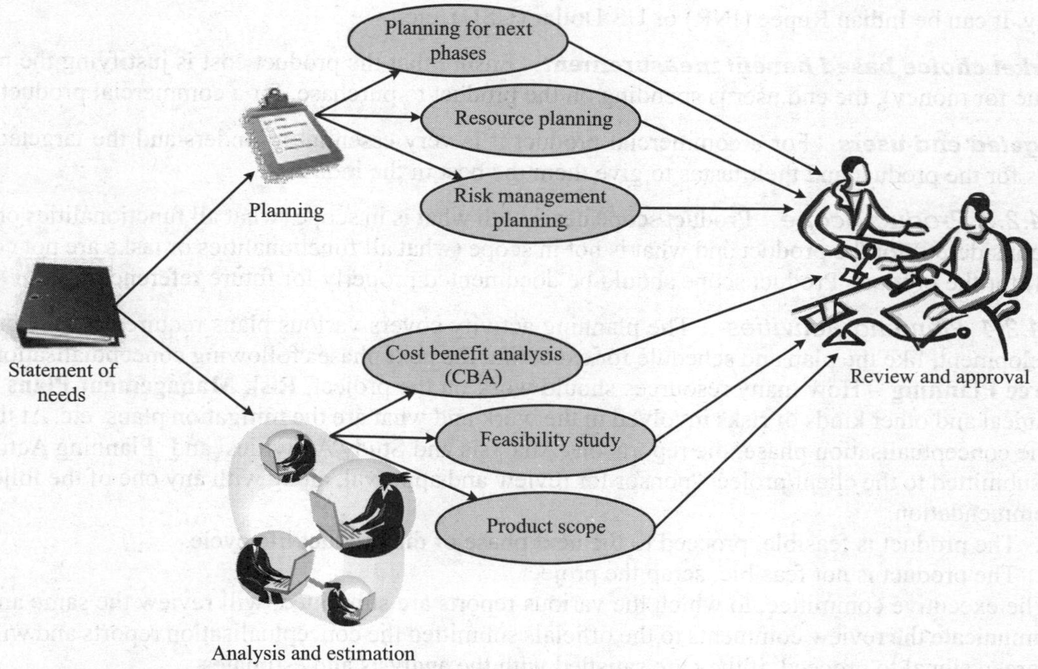

Fig. 15.2 **Various activities involved in Conceptualisation Phase**

The 'Conceptualisation' phase involves two types of activities, namely; 'Planning Activity' and 'Analysis and Study Activity'. The Analysis and Study Activities are performed to understand the opportunity of the product in the market (for a commercial product). The following are the important 'Analysis and Study activities' performed during 'Conceptualisation Phase'.

15.4.2.1 Feasibility Study Feasibility study examines the need for the product carefully and suggests one or more possible solutions to build the need as a product along with alternatives. Feasibility study analyses the Technical (Technical Challenges, limitations, etc.) as well as financial feasibility (Financial requirements, funding, etc.) of the product under consideration.

15.4.2.2 Cost Benefit Analysis (CBA) The Cost Benefit Analysis (CBA) is a means of identifying, revealing and assessing the total development cost and the profit expected from the product. It is somewhat similar to the loss-gain analysis in business term except that CBA is an assumption oriented approach based on some rule of thumb or based on the analysis of data available for similar products developed in the past. In summary, CBA estimates and totals up the equivalent money value of the benefits and costs of the product under consideration and give an idea about the worthwhile of the product. Some common underlying principles of Cost Benefit Analysis are illustrated below.

Common Unit of Measurement In order to make the analysis sensible and meaningful, all aspects of the product, either plus points or minus points should be expressed in terms of a common unit. Since the ultimate aim of a product is "Marginal Profit" and the marginal profit is expressed in terms of money in most cases, 'money' is taken as the common unit of measurement. Hence all benefits and costs of the product should be expressed in terms of money. Money in turn may be represented by a common currency. It can be Indian Rupee (INR) or US Dollar (USD), etc.

Market choice based benefit measurement Ensure that the product cost is justifying the money (value for money), the end user is spending on the product to purchase, for a commercial product.

Targeted end users For a commercial product it is very essential to understand the targeted end-users for the product and their tastes to give them the best in the industry.

15.4.2.3 Product Scope Product scope deals with what is in scope (what all functionalities or tasks are considered) for the product and what is not in scope (what all functionalities or tasks are not considered) for the product. Product scope should be documented properly for future reference.

15.4.2.4 Planning Activities The planning activity covers various plans required for the product development, like the plan and schedule for executing the next phases following conceptualisation, **Resource Planning** – How many resources should work on the project, **Risk Management Plans** – The technical and other kinds of risks involved in the work and what are the mitigation plans, etc. At the end of the conceptualisation phase, the reports on 'Analysis and Study Activities' and 'Planning Activities' are submitted to the client/project sponsor for review and approval, along with any one of the following recommendation.

1. The product is feasible; proceed to the next phase of the product life cycle.
2. The product is not feasible; scrap the project

The executive committee, to which the various reports are submitted, will review the same and will communicate the review comments to the officials submitted the conceptualisation reports and will give the green signal to proceed, if they are satisfied with the analysis and estimates.

15.4.3 Analysis

Requirements Analysis Phase starts immediately after the documents submitted during the 'Conceptualisation' phase is approved by the client/sponsor of the project. Documentation related to user requirements from the Conceptualisation phase is used as the basis for further user need analysis and the development of detailed user requirements. Requirement analysis is performed to develop a detailed functional model of the product under consideration. During the Requirements Analysis Phase, the product is defined in detail with respect to the inputs, processes, outputs, and interfaces at a functional level. Requirement Analysis phase gives emphasis on determining 'what functions must be performed by the product' rather than how to perform those functions. The various activities performed during 'Requirement Analysis' phase is illustrated in Fig. 15.3.

15.4.3.1 Analysis and Documentation The analysis and documentation activity consolidates the business needs of the product under development and analyses the purpose of the product. It addresses various functional aspects (product features and functions) and quality attributes (non-functional requirements) of the product, defines the functional and data requirements and connects the function-

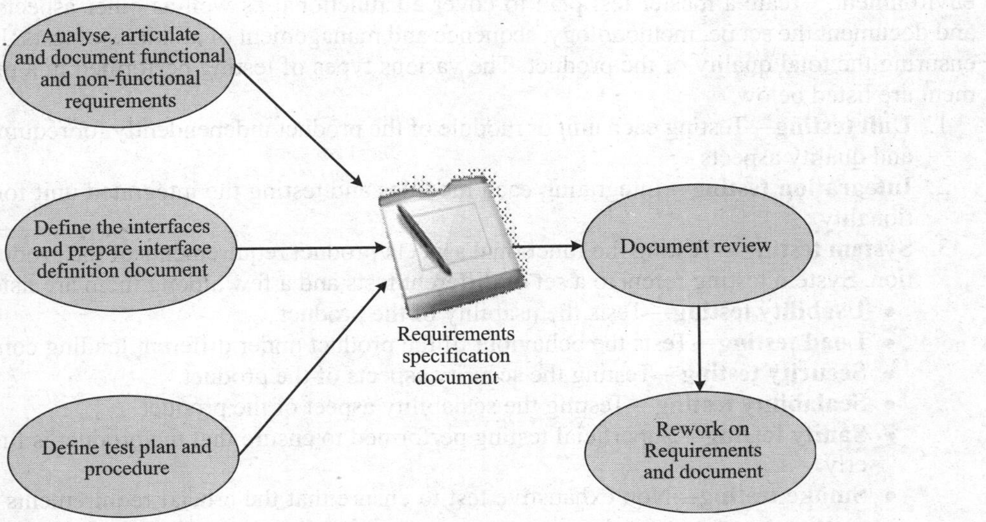

Fig. 15.3 **Various activities involved in Requirements Analysis Phase**

al requirements with the data requirements. In summary, the analysis activities address all business functionalities of the product and develop a logical model describing the fundamental processes and the data required to support the functionalities. The various requirements that need to be addressed during the requirement analysis phase for a product under consideration are listed below.

1. Functional capabilities like performance, operational characteristics (Refer to Chapter 3 for details on operational characteristics), etc.
2. Operational and non-operational quality attributes (Refer to Chapter 3 for Quality attributes of embedded products)
3. Product external interface requirements
4. Data requirements
5. User manuals
6. Operational requirements
7. Maintenance requirements
8. General assumptions

15.4.3.2 Interface Definition and Documentation The embedded product under consideration may be a standalone product or it can be a part of a large distributed system. If it is a part of another system there should be some interface between the product and the other parts of the distributed system. Even in the case of standalone products there will be some standard interfaces like serial, parallel etc as a provision to connect to some standard interfaces. The interface definition and documentation activity should clearly analyse on the physical interface (type of interface) as well as data exchange through these interfaces and should document it. It is essential for the proper information flow throughout the life cycle.

15.4.3.3 Defining Test Plan and Procedures Identifies what kind of tests are to be performed and what all should be covered in testing the product. Define the test procedures, test setup and test environment. Create a master test plan to cover all functional as well as other aspects of the product and document the scope, methodology, sequence and management of all kinds of tests. It is essential for ensuring the total quality of the product. The various types of testing performed in a product development are listed below.

1. **Unit testing**—Testing each unit or module of the product independently for required functionality and quality aspects
2. **Integration testing**—Integrating each modules and testing the integrated unit for required functionality
3. **System testing**—Testing the functional aspects/product requirements of the product after integration. System testing refers to a set of different tests and a few among them are listed below.
   - **Usability testing**—Tests the usability of the product
   - **Load testing**—Tests the behaviour of the product under different loading conditions.
   - **Security testing**—Testing the security aspects of the product
   - **Scalability testing**—Testing the scalability aspect of the product
   - **Sanity testing**—Superficial testing performed to ensure that the product is functioning properly
   - **Smoke testing**—Non exhaustive test to ensure that the crucial requirements for the product are functioning properly. This test is not giving importance to the finer details of different functionalities
   - **Performance testing**—Testing the performance aspects of the product after integration
   - **Endurance testing**—Durability test of the product
4. **User acceptance testing**—Testing the product to ensure it is meeting all requirements of the end user.

At the end, all requirements should be put in a template suggested by the standard (e.g. ISO-9001) Process Model (e.g. CMM Level 5) followed for the Quality Assurance. This document is referred as 'Requirements Specification Document'. It is sent out for review by the client and the client, after reviewing the requirements specification document, communicates back with the review comments. According to the review comments more requirement analysis may have to be performed and re-work required is performed on the initial 'Requirement Specification Document'.

15.4.4 Design

Product 'Design phase' deals with the entire design of the product taking the requirements into consideration and it focuses on 'how' the required functionalities can be delivered to the product. The design phase identifies the application environment and creates an overall architecture for the product. Product design starts with '*Preliminary Design/High Level Design*'. Preliminary design establishes the top-level architecture for the product, lists out the various functional blocks required for the product, and defines the inputs and outputs for each functional block. The functional block will look like a 'black box' at this design point, with only inputs and outputs of the block being defined. On completion, the 'Preliminary Design Document (PDD) is sent for review to the end-user/client who come up with a need for the product. If the end-user agrees on the preliminary design, the product design team can take the work to the next level – *'Detailed Design'*. Detailed design generates a detailed architecture, identifies and lists out the various components for each functional block, the inter connection among various functional blocks, the control algorithm requirements, etc. The 'Detailed Design' also needs to be reviewed and get approved by the end user/customer. If the end user wants modifications on the design, it can be informed to the design team through review comments.

An embedded product is a real mix of hardware, embedded firmware and enclosure. Hence both *Preliminary Design* and *Detailed Design* should take the design of these into consideration. For traditional embedded system design approach, the functional requirements are classified into either hardware or firmware at an early stage of the design and the hardware team works on the design of the required hardware, whereas the software team works on the design of the embedded firmware. Today the scenario is totally changed and a hardware software co-design approach is used. In this approach, the functional requirements are not broken down into hardware and software, instead they are treated as system requirements and the partitioning of system requirements into either hardware or software is performed at a later stage of the design based on hardware-software trade-offs for implementing the required functionalities. The hardware and software requirements are modelled using different modelling techniques. Please refer to Chapter 7 for more details on hardware-software co-design and program models used in hardware-software co-design. The other activities performed during the design phase are 'Design of Operations and maintenance manual' and 'Design of Training materials' (Fig. 15.4). The operations manual is necessary for educating the end user on 'how to operate the product' and the maintenance manual is essential for providing information on how to handle the product in situations like non-functioning, failure, etc.

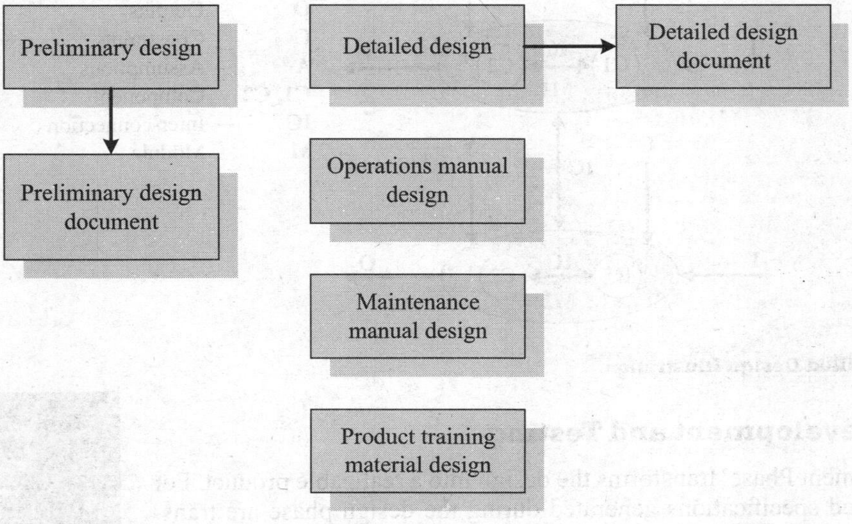

Fig. 15.4 Various Activities involved in Design Phase

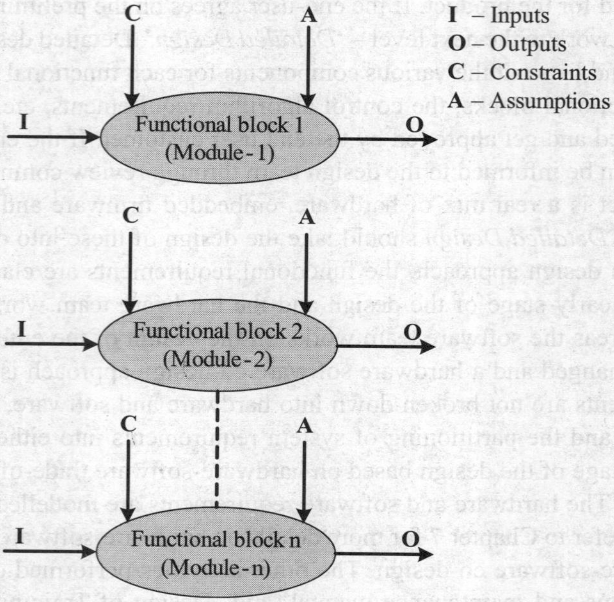

Fig. 15.5 **Preliminary Design Illustration**

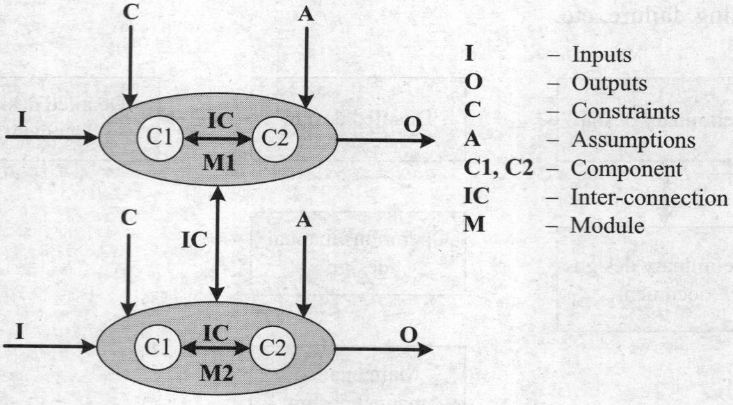

Fig. 15.6 **Detailed Design Illustration**

15.4.5 Development and Testing

The 'Development Phase' transforms the design into a realizable product. For this the detailed specifications generated during the design phase are translated into hardware and firmware. During development phase, the installation and setting up of various development tools is performed and the product hardware and firmware is developed using different tools and associated production setup. The development activities can be partitioned into embedded hardware development, embedded firmware development and product enclosure development. Embedded hardware development refers to the development of the component placement platform – PCB using CAD tools and its fabrication using CAM Tools. Embedded firmware development is performed using the embedded firmware development tools. The mechanical enclosure design is performed with CAD Tools like Solid Works, AutoCAD, etc. "Look and Feel" of a commercial product plays an important role on its market demand. So the entire product design and development should concentrate on the product aesthetics (Size, Weight, Appearance, etc.) and special requirements like protection shielding, etc.

Component procurement also carried out during this phase. As mentioned in one of the earlier chapters, some of the components may have "*lead time* – The time required for the component to deliver after placing the purchase order for the component" and the component procurement should be planned well in advance to avoid the possible delay in the product development. The other important activities carried out during this phase are preparation of test case procedures, preparation of test files and development of detailed user, deployment, operations and maintenance manual. The embedded firmware development may be divided into various modules and the firmware (code) review for each module as well as the schematic diagram and layout file review for hardware is carried out during the development phase and the changes required should be incorporated in the development from time to time.

The testing phase can be divided into independent testing of firmware and hardware (Unit Testing), testing of the product after integrating the firmware and hardware (Integration Testing), testing of the whole system on a functionality and non-functionality basis (System Testing) and testing of the product against all acceptance criteria mentioned by the client/end user for each functionality (User Acceptance Testing). The Unit testing deals with testing the embedded hardware and its associated modules, the different modules of the firmware for their functionality independently. A test plan is prepared for the unit testing (Unit Test plan) and test cases (Unit Test cases) are identified for testing the functionality of the product as per the design. Unit test is normally performed by the hardware developer or firmware developer as part of the development phase. Depending on the product complexity, rest of the tests can be considered as the activities performed in the 'Testing phase' of the product. Once the hardware and firmware are unit tested, they are integrated using various firmware integration techniques and the integrated product is tested against the required functionalities. An integration test plan is prepared for this and the test cases for integration testing (Integration test cases) is developed. The Integration testing ensures that the functionality which is tested working properly in an independent mode remains working properly in an integrated product (Hardware + Firmware). The integration test results are logged in and the firmware/hardware is reworked against any flaws detected during the Integration testing. The purpose of integration testing is to detect any inconsistencies between the firmware modules units that are integrated together or between any of the firmware modules and the embedded hardware. Integration testing of various modules, hardware and firmware is done at the end of development phase depending on the readiness of hardware and firmware.

The system testing follows the Integration testing and it is a set of various tests for functional and non-functional requirements verification. System testing is a kind of black box testing, which doesn't require any knowledge on the inner design logic or code for the product. System testing evaluates the product's compliance with the requirements. User acceptance test or simply Acceptance testing is the product evaluation performed by the customer as a condition of the product purchase. During user Acceptance testing, the product is tested against the acceptance value set by customer/end user for each requirement (e.g. The loading time for the application running on the PDA device is less than 1 millisecond ☺). The deliverables from the 'Design and Testing' phase are firmware source code, firmware binaries, finished hardware, various test plans (Hardware and Firmware Unit Test plans, Integration Test plan, System Test plan and Acceptance Test plan), test cases (Hardware and Firmware Unit Test cases,

Integration Test cases, System Test cases and Acceptance Test cases) and test reports (Hardware and Firmware Unit Test Report, Integration Test Report, System Test Report and Acceptance Test Report).

15.4.6 Deployment

Deployment is the process of launching the first fully functional model of the product in the market (for a commercial embedded product) or handing over the fully functional initial model to an end user/client. It is also known as *First Customer Shipping* (*FCS*). During this phase, the product modifications as per the various integration tests are implemented and the product is made operational in a production environment. The 'Deployment Phase' is initiated after the system is tested and accepted (User Acceptance Test) by the end user. The important tasks performed during the Deployment Phase are listed below.

15.4.6.1 Notification of Product Deployment Whenever the product is ready to launch in the market, the launching ceremony details should be communicated to the stake holders (all those who are related to the product in a direct or indirect way) and to the public if it is a commercial product. The notifications can be sent out through e-mail, media, etc. mentioning the following in a few words.

1. Deployment Schedule (Date Time and Venue)
2. Brief description about the product
3. Targeted end users
4. Extra features supported with respect to an existing product (for upgrades of existing model and new products having other competitive products in the market)
5. Product support information including the support person name, contact number, contact mail ID, etc.

15.4.6.2 Execution of Training Plan Proper training should be given to the end user to get them acquainted with the new product. Before launching the product, conduct proper training as per the training plan developed during the earlier phases. Proper training will help in reducing the possible damages to the product as well as the operating person, including personal injuries and product mal-functioning due to inappropriate usage. User manual will help in understanding the product, its usage and accessing its functionalities to certain extend.

15.4.6.3 Product Installation Instal the product as per the installation document to ensure that it is fully functional. As a typical example take the case of a newly purchased mobile handset. The user manual accompanying it will tell you clearly how to instal the battery, how to charge the battery, how many hours the battery needs to be charged, how the handset can be switched on/off, etc.

15.4.6.4 Product post-Implementation Review Once the product is launched in the market, conduct a post-implementation review to determine the success of the product. The ultimate aim behind post-implementation review is to document the problems faced during installation and the solutions adopted to overcome them which will act as a reference document for future product development. It also helps in understanding the customer needs and the expectations of the customer on the next version of the product.

15.4.7 Support

The support phase deals with the operations and maintenance of the product in a production environment. During this phase all aspects of operations and maintenance of the product are covered and the product is scrutinised to ensure that it meets the requirements put forward by the end user/client. 'Bugs (product mal-functioning or unexpected behaviour or any operational error)' in the products may be observed and reported during the operations phase. Support should be provided to the end user/client to fix the bugs in the product. The support phase ensures that the product meets the user needs and it continues functioning in the production environment. The various activities involved in the 'Support' phase are listed below.

15.4.7.1 Set up a Dedicated Support Wing The availability of certain embedded products in terms of product functioning in production environment is crucial and they may require 24x7 support in case of product failure or malfunctioning. For example the patient monitoring system used in hospitals is a very critical product in terms of functioning and any malfunctioning of the product requires immediate technical attention/support from the supplier. Set up a dedicated support wing (customer care unit) and ensure high quality service is delivered to the end user. 'After service' plays significant role in product movement in a commercial market. If the manufacturer fails to provide timely and quality service to the end user, it will naturally create the talk '*the product is good but the after service is very poor*' among the end users and people will refrain from buying such products and will opt for competitive products which provides more or less same functionalities and high quality service. The support wing should be set up in such a way that they are easily reachable through e-mail, phone, fax, etc.

15.4.7.2 Identify Bugs and Areas of Improvement None of the products are bug-free. Even if you take utmost care in design, development and implementation of the product, there can be bugs in it and the bugs reveal their real identity when the conditions are favouring them, similar to the harmless microbes living in human body getting turned into harmful microbes when the body resistance is weak. You may miss out certain operating conditions while design or development phase and if the product faces such an operating condition, the product behaviour may become unexpected and it is addressed with the familiar nick name '*Bug*' by a software/product engineer. Since the embedded product market is highly competitive, it is very essential to stay connected with the end users and know their needs for the survival of the product. Give the end user a chance to express their views on the product and suggestions, if any, in terms of modifications required or feature enhancements (areas of improvement), through user feedbacks. Conduct product specific surveys and collect as much data as possible from the end user.

15.4.8 Upgrades

The upgrade phase of product development deals with the development of upgrades (new versions) for the product which is already present in the market. Product upgrade results as an output of major bug fixes or feature enhancement requirements from the end user. During the upgrade phase the system is subject to design modification to fix the major bugs reported or to incorporate the new feature addition requirements aroused during the support phase. For embedded products, the upgrades may be for the product resident firmware or for the hardware embedding the firmware. Some bugs may be easily fixed by modifying the firmware and it is known as firmware up-gradation. Some feature enhancements can also be performed easily by mere firmware modification. The product resident firmware will have a version number which starts with version say 1.0 and after each firmware modification or bug fix, the firmware version is changed accordingly (e.g. version 1.1). Version numbering is essential for backward traceability. Releasing of upgrades is managed through release management. (Embedded Product Engineers might have used the term "Today I have a release" at least once in their life). Certain feature enhancements and bug fixes require hardware modification and they are generally termed as hardware upgrades. Firmware also needs to be modified according to the hardware enhancements. The upgraded product appears in the market with the same name as that of the initial product with a different version number or with a different name.

15.4.9 Retirement/Disposal

We are living in a dynamic world where everything is subject to rapid changes. The technology you feel as the most advanced and best today may not be the same tomorrow. Due to increased user needs and revolutionary technological changes, a product cannot sustain in the market for a long time. The disposal/retirement of a product is a gradual process. When the product manufacture realises that there is another powerful technology or component available in the market which is most suitable for the production of the current product, they will announce the current product as obsolete and the newer version/upgrade of the same is going to be released soon. The retirement/disposition phase is the final phase in a product development life cycle where the product is declared as obsolete and discontinued from the market. There is no meaning and monetary benefit in continuing the production of a device or equipment which is obsolete in terms of technology and aesthetics. The disposition of a product is essential due to the following reasons.

1. Rapid technology advancement
2. Increased user needs

Some products may get a very long 'Life Time' in the market, beginning from the launch phase to the retirement phase and during this time the product will get reasonably good amount of maturity and stability and it may be able to create sensational waves in the market (e.g. Nokia 3310 Mobile Handset; Launched in September 2000 and discontinued in early 2005, more than 4 years of continued presence in the market with 126 million pieces sold). Some products get only small 'Life Time' in the market and some of them even fails to register their appearance in the market.

By now we covered all the phases of embedded product development life cycle. We can correlate the various phases of the product development we discussed so far to the various activities involved in our day-today life. Whenever you are a child you definitely have the ambition to become an earning person like your mom/dad (There may be exceptions too ☺). The need for a job arises here. To get a good job you must have a good academic record and hence you should complete the schooling with good marks and should perform very well in interviews. Finally you are managed to get a good job and your professional career begins here. You may get promotions to next senior level depending on your performance. At last that day comes—Your retirement day from your professional life.

15.5 EDLC APPROACHES (MODELING THE EDLC)

The term 'Modelling' in Embedded Product Development Life Cycle refers to the interconnection of various phases involved in the development of an embedded product. The various approaches adopted or models used in Modelling EDLC are described below.

15.5.1 Linear or Waterfall Model

Linear or waterfall approach is the one adopted in most of the olden systems and in this approach each phase of EDLC is executed in sequence. The linear model establishes a formal analysis and design methodology with highly structured development phases. In linear model, the various phases of EDLC are executed in sequence and the flow is unidirectional with output of one phase serving as the input to the next phase. In the linear model all activities involved in each phase are well documented, giving an insight into what should be done in the next phase and how it can be done. The feedback of each phase is available locally and only after they are executed. The linear model implements extensive review mechanisms to ensure the process flow is going in the right direction and validates the effort during a phase. One significant feature of linear model is that even if you identify bugs in the current design, the corrective actions are not implemented immediately and the development process proceeds with the current design. The fixes for the bugs are postponed till the support phase, which accompanies the deployment phase. The major advantage of 'Linear Model' is that the product development is rich in terms of documentation, easy project management and good control over cost and schedule. The major drawback of this approach is that it assumes all the analysis can be done and everything will be in right place without doing any design or implementation. Also the risk analysis is performed only once throughout the development and risks involved in any changes are not accommodated in subsequent phases, the working product is available only at the end of the development phase and bug fixes and corrections are performed only at the maintenance/support phase of the life cycle. 'Linear Model' (Fig. 15.7) is best

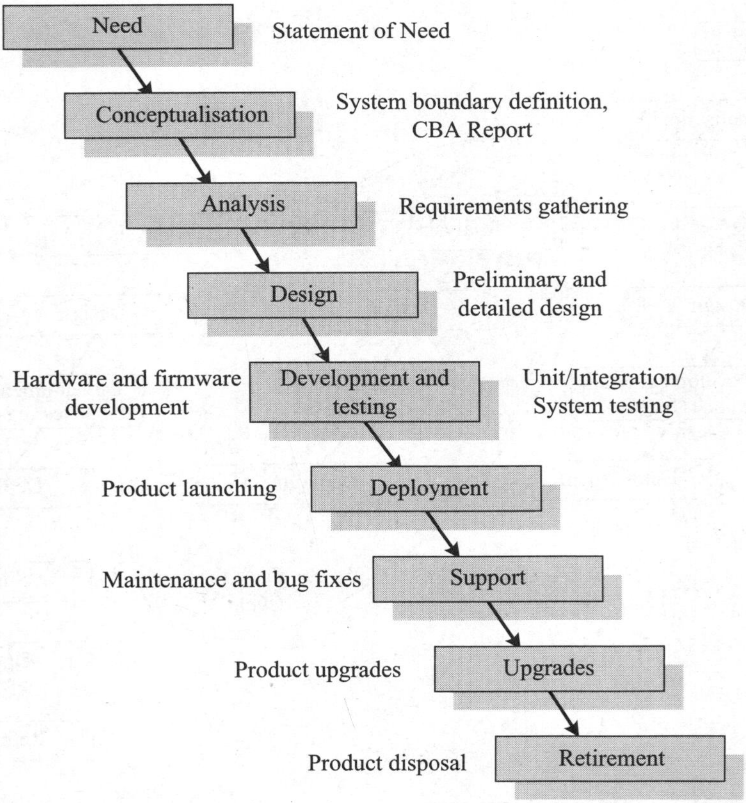

Fig. 15.7 **Linear (Waterfall) EDLC Model**

suited for product developments, where the requirements are well defined and within the scope, and no change requests are expected till the completion of the life cycle.

15.5.2 Iterative/Incremental or Fountain Model

Iterative or fountain model follows the sequence—Do some analysis, follow some design, then some implementation. Evaluate it and based on the shortcomings, cycle back through and conduct more analysis, opt for new design and implementation and repeat the cycle till the requirements are met completely. The iterative/fountain model can be viewed as a cascaded series of linear (waterfall) models. The incremental model is a superset of iterative model where the requirements are known at the beginning and they are divided into different groups. The core set of functions for each group is identified in the first cycle and is built and deployed as the first release. The second set of requirements along with the bug fixes and modification for first release is carried out in the second cycle and the process is repeated until all functionalities are implemented and they are meeting the requirements. It is obvious that in an iterative/incremental model (Fig. 15.8), each development cycle act as the maintenance phase for the previous cycle (release). Another approach for the iterative/interactive model is the 'Overlapped' model where development cycles overlap; meaning subsequent iterative/incremental cycle may begin before the completion of previous cycle.

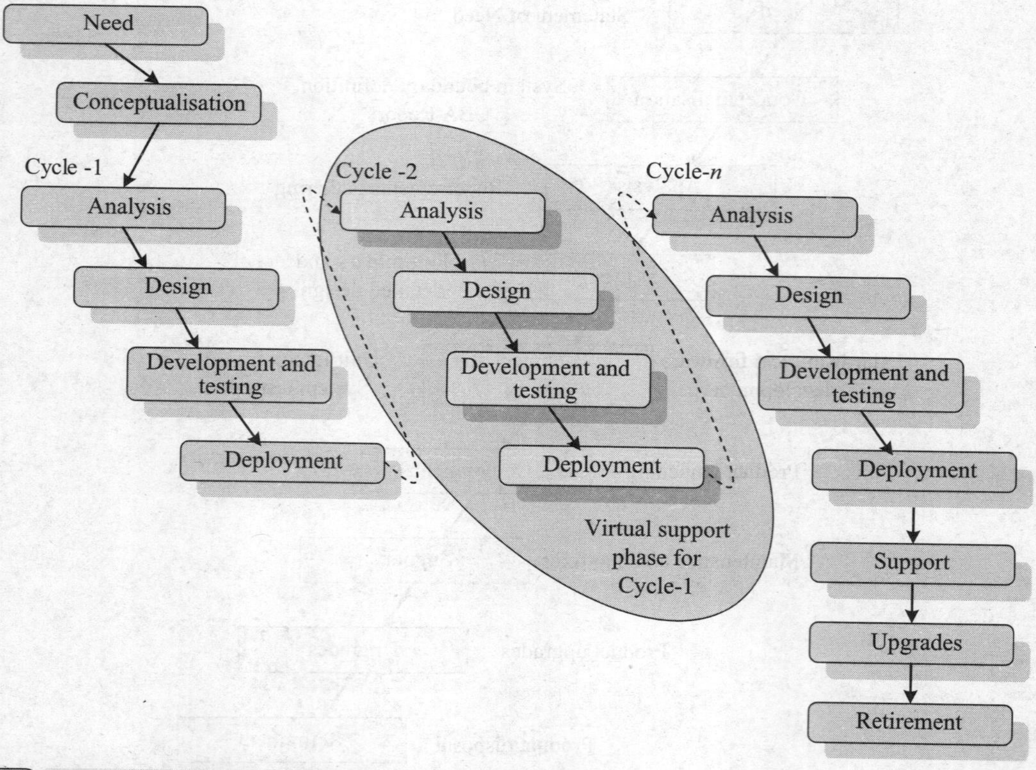

Fig. 15.8 Iterative/Incremental/Fountain EDLC Model

If you closely observe this model you can see that each cycle is interconnected in a similar fashion of a fountain, where water first moves up and then comes down, again moves up and comes down. The major advantage of iterative/fountain model is that it provides very good development cycle feedback at each function/feature implementation and hence the data can be used as a reference for similar product development in future. Since each cycle can act as a maintenance phase for previous cycle, changes in feature and functionalities can be easily incorporated during the development and hence more responsive to changing user needs. The iterative model provides a working product model with at least minimum features at the first cycle itself. Risk is spread across each individual cycle and can be minimised easily. Project management as well as testing is much simpler compared to the linear model. Another major advantage is that the product development can be stopped at any stage with a bare minimum working product. Though iterative model is a good solution for product development, it possess lots of drawbacks like extensive review requirement at each cycle, impact on operations due to new releases, training requirement for each new deployment at the end of each development cycle, structured and well documented interface definition across modules to accommodate changes. The iterative/incremental model is deployed in product developments where the risk is very high when the development is carried out by linear model. By choosing an iterative model, the risk is spread across multiple cycles. Since each cycle produces a working model, this model is best suited for product developments where the continued funding for each cycle is not assured.

15.5.3 Prototyping/Evolutionary Model

Prototyping/evolutionary model is similar to the iterative model and the product is developed in multiple cycles. The only difference is that this model produces a more refined prototype of the product at the end of each cycle instead of functionality/feature addition in each cycle as performed by the iterative model. There won't be any commercial deployment of the prototype of the product at each cycle's end. The shortcomings of the proto-model after each cycle are evaluated and it is fixed in the next cycle.

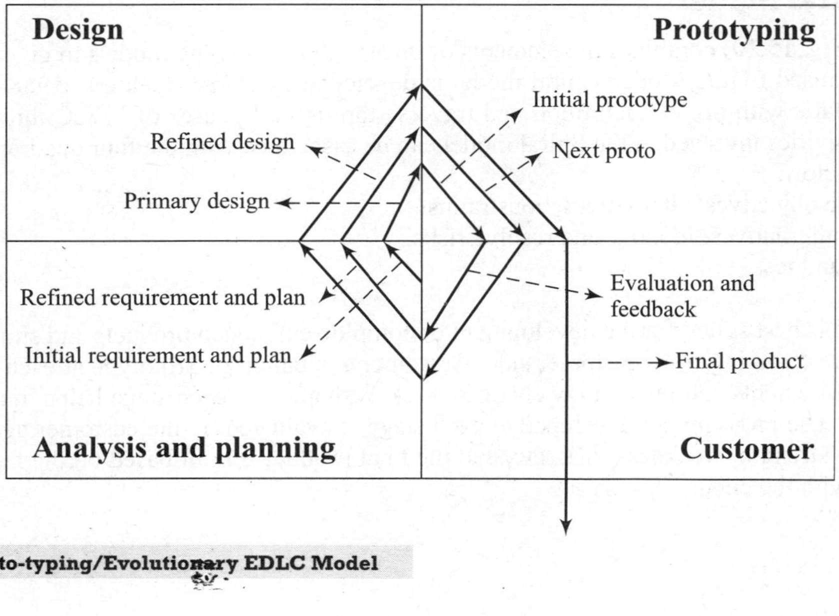

Fig. 15.9 **Proto-typing/Evolutionary EDLC Model**

After the initial requirement analysis, the design for the first prototype is made, the development process is started. On finishing the prototype, it is sent to the customer for evaluation. The customer evaluates the product for the set of requirements and gives his/her feedback to the developer in terms of shortcomings and improvements needed. The developer refines the product according to the customer's exact expectation and repeats the proto development process. After a finite number of iterations, the final product is delivered to the customer and launches in the market/operational environment. In this approach, the product undergoes significant evolution as a result of periodic shuttling of product information between the customer and developer. The prototyping model follows the approach – 'Requirements definition, proto-type development, proto-type evaluation and requirements refining'. Since the requirements undergo refinement after each proto model, it is easy to incorporate new requirements and technology changes at any stage and thereby the product development process can start with a bare minimum set of requirements. The evolutionary model relies heavily on user feedback after each implementation and hence finetuning of final requirements is possible. Another major advantage of proto-typing model is that the risk is spread across each proto development cycle and it is well under control. The major drawbacks of proto-typing model are

1. Deviations from expected cost and schedule due to requirements refinement
2. Increased project management
3. Minimal documentation on each prototype may create problems in backward prototype traceability
4. Increased Configuration Management activities

Prototyping model is the most popular product development model adopted in embedded product industry. This approach can be considered as the best approach for products, whose requirements are not fully available and are subject to change. This model is not recommended for projects involving the upgradation of an existing product. There can be slight variations in the base prototyping model depending on project management.

15.5.4 Spiral Model

Spiral model (Fig. 15.10) combines the elements of linear and prototyping models to give the best possible risk minimised EDLC Model. Spiral model is developed by Barry Boehm in 1988. The product development starts with project definition and traverse through all phases of EDLC through multiple phases. The activities involved in the Spiral model can be associated with the four quadrants of a spiral and are listed below.

1. Determine objectives, alternatives, constraints.
2. Evaluate alternatives. Identify and resolve risks.
3. Develop and test.
4. Plan.

Spiral model is best suited for the development of complex embedded products and situations where requirements are changing from customer side. Customer evaluation of prototype at each stage allows addition of requirements and technology changes. Risk evaluation in each stage helps in risk planning and mitigation. The proto model developed at each stage is evaluated by the customer against various parameters like strength, weakness, risk, etc. and the final product is built based on the final prototype on agreement with the client.

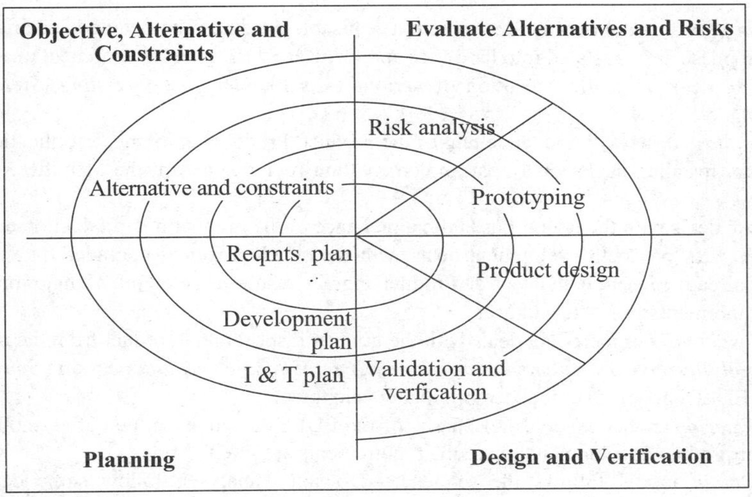

Fig. 15.10 **Spiral Model**

Summary

- ✓ Embedded Product Development Life Cycle (EDLC) is an 'Analysis-Design-Implementation' based standard problem solving approach for Embedded Product Development
- ✓ EDLC defines the interaction and activities among various groups of a product development sector including project management, system design and development (hardware, firmware and enclosure design and development), system testing, release management and quality assurance
- ✓ Project management, productivity improvement and ensuring quality of the product are the primary objectives of EDLC
- ✓ *Project Management* is essential for predictability, co-ordination and risk minimisation in product development
- ✓ The Life Cycle of a product development is commonly referred as Models and a *Model* defines the various phases involved in a product's life cycle
- ✓ The classic Embedded Product Life Cycle Model contains the phases: *Need*, *Conceptualisation*, *Analysis*, *Design*, *Development and Testing*, *Deployment*, *Support*, *Upgrades* and *Retirement/Disposal*
- ✓ The product development *need* falls into three categories namely, New or custom product development, Product Re-engineering and product maintenance
- ✓ *Conceptualisation phase* is the phase dealing with product concept development. Conceptualisation phase includes activities like product feasibility analysis, cost–benefit analysis, product scoping and planning for next phases
- ✓ The *Requirements analysis* phase defines the inputs, processes, outputs, and interfaces of the product at a functional level. Analysis and documentation, interface definition and documentation, high level test plan and procedure definition, etc. are the activities carried out during requirement analysis phase
- ✓ Product design phase deals with the implementation aspects of the required functionalities for the product.
- ✓ The *Preliminary design* establishes the top-level architecture for the product, lists out the various functional blocks required for the product, and defines the inputs and outputs for each functional block
- ✓ *Detailed Design* generates a detailed architecture, identifies and lists out the various components for each functional block, the inter-connection among various functional blocks, the control algorithm requirements, etc.

- ✓ The *Development phase* transforms the design into a realisable product. The detailed specifications generated during the design phase are translated into hardware and firmware during the development phase
- ✓ The *Testing phase* deals with the execution of various tests like *Integration testing*, *System testing*, *User acceptance testing*, etc.
- ✓ The *Deployment phase* deals with the launching of the product. Product deployment notification, Training plan execution, product installation, Product post-implementation review, etc. are the activities performed during *Deployment phase*
- ✓ The *Support phase* deals with the operations and maintenance of the product in a production environment
- ✓ The *Upgrade phase* of product development deals with the development of upgrades (new versions) for the product which is already present in the market. Product upgrade results as an output of major bug fixes or feature enhancement requirements from the end user
- ✓ *Retirement/Disposal phase* of a product deals with the gradual disposal of a product from the market
- ✓ *Linear or Waterfall*, *Iterative or incremental or fountain*, *Prototyping or evolutionary* and *Spiral models* are the commonly used EDLC models in embedded product development
- ✓ The *Linear* or *Waterfall* model executes all phases of the EDLC in sequence, one after another. It is the best suited method for product development where the requirements are fixed
- ✓ *Iterative* or *Fountain* model follows the sequence—Do some analysis, follow some design, then some implementation. Evaluate it and based on the short comings, cycle back through and conduct more analysis, opt for new design and implementation and repeat the cycle till the requirements are met completely.
- ✓ *Prototyping model* is a variation to the *Iterative model*, in which a more refined prototype is produced at the end of each iteration. It is the best suited model for developing embedded products whose requirements are not fully available at the time of starting the project, and are subject to change
- ✓ *Spiral model* is the EDLC model combining linear and prototyping model to give the best possible risk minimisation in product development

Keywords

Embedded Product Development Life Cycle (EDLC)	:	An 'Analysis-Design-Implementation' based standard problem solving approach for Embedded Product Development
Model	:	The various phases involved in a product development life cycle
Need	:	Demand for a custom product or re-engineering of an existing product or maintenance of an existing product
Conceptualisation	:	Product Life Cycle stage which deals with the concept development for a product
Requirement Analysis	:	Product Life Cycle stage which deals with the activities for developing a detailed functional model of the product under consideration
Design Phase	:	Product Life Cycle stage which deals with the implementation aspects of the required functionalities for the product
Development Phase	:	Product Life Cycle stage which transforms the design into a realisable product
Testing Phase	:	Phase which deals with the execution of various tests like Integration testing, System testing, User acceptance testing. etc,
Unit Testing	:	Tests carried out to verify the functioning of the individual modules of the firmware and hardware
Integration Testing	:	Tests carried out to verify the functioning of a product for the required functionalities after the integration of embedded firmware and hardware

System Testing	:	A set of various tests for functional and non-functional requirements verification of the product
User Acceptance Testing (UAT)	:	Tests performed by the user (customer) against the acceptance values for each requirement
Deployment Phase	:	Product Life Cycle stage which deals with the launching of the product
First Customer Shipping (FCS)	:	The process of handing over the fully functional initial model of the product to an end user/client
Support Phase	:	Product Life Cycle stage which deals with the operations and maintenance of the product in a production environment
Upgrade Phase	:	Product Life Cycle stage which deals with the development of upgrades (new versions) for the product which is already present in the market
Retirement/Disposal	:	Product Life Cycle stage which deals with the gradual disposal of a product from the market
Linear or Waterfall Model	:	EDLC Model which executes all phases of the EDLC in sequence, one after another
Iterative or Fountain Model	:	EDLC Model which follows the sequence—Do some analysis, follow some design, then some implementation.
Prototyping Model	:	EDLC Model which is the variation of the iterative model in which a more refined prototype is produced at the end of each iteration
Spiral Model	:	EDLC model combining linear and prototyping model to give the best possible risk minimisation in product development

Objective Questions

1. Which of the following is not in the scope of EDLC
   (a) Maximise Return on Investment (RoI)
   (b) Minimise the risks involved in the product development
   (c) Advertise the product
   (d) Defect prevention in Product development
2. The term 'model' in EDLC represents
   (a) The various phases in the life cycle of the product (b) The various analysis of the product
   (c) The various designs of the product (d) The various architecture of the product
3. Which of the following is(are) a driving factor(s) for 'Product Re-engineering'?
   (a) Change in business requirement (b) User interface enhancements
   (c) Technology upgrades (d) All of these
   (e) (a) and (b) (f) (a) and (c)
4. An embedded product requires interfacing with another subsystem of an enterprise for data logging and information exchange. The interface for this is defined during?
   (a) Conceptualisation phase (b) Requirement analysis phase
   (c) Design phase (d) Development phase
   (e) Deployment phase
5. An embedded product requires a TCP/IP interface and it is decided that the TCP/IP interface can be implemented using Commercial of the Shelf (COTS) component. The COTS module for the TCP/IP Module is finalised and selected during?
   (a) Conceptualisation phase (b) Requirement analysis phase
   (c) Design phase (d) Development phase
   (e) Deployment phase

6. An embedded product contains LCD interfacing and a developer is assigned to work on this module. The developer coded the module and tested its functioning using a simulator. The test performed by the developer falls under?
   (a) Integration Testing (b) Unit Testing
   (c) System Testing (d) Acceptance Testing
7. For an Embedded product, the requirements are well defined and are within the scope and no change requests are expected till the completion of the life cycle. Which is the best-suited life cycle model for developing this product?
   (a) Linear (b) Iterative (c) Prototyping (d) Spiral
8. Which of the following is(are) not a feature of prototyping model
   (a) Requirements refinement (b) Documentation intensive
   (c) Intensive Project Management (d) Controlled risk
9. An embedded product under consideration is very complex in nature and there is a possibility for change in requirements of the product. Also the risk associated with the development of this product is very high. Which is the best-suited life cycle method to handle this product development?
   (a) Linear (b) Iterative (c) Prototyping (d) Spiral

Review Questions

1. What is EDLC? Why EDLC is essential in embedded product development?
2. What are the objectives of EDLC?
3. Explain the significance of *Productivity* in embedded product development. Explain the techniques for productivity improvements
4. Explain the different phases of Embedded Product Development Life Cycle (EDLC)
5. Explain the term '*model*' in relation to EDLC
6. Explain the different types of *Product Development* needs
7. Explain the *Product Re-engineering* need in detail
8. Explain the various activities performed during the *Conceptualisation* phase of an Embedded product development.
9. Explain the various activities performed during the *Requirement Analysis* phase of an embedded product development.
10. Explain the various activities performed during the *Design* phase of an embedded product development.
11. Explain the various activities performed during the *Development* phase of an embedded product development.
12. Explain the various types of tests performed in the development of an embedded product.
13. Explain the various activities performed during the *Deployment* phase of an embedded product.
14. Explain the various activities performed during the *Support* phase of an embedded product.
15. Explain the need for *Product upgrades* in the Embedded Product development. Explain the different types of product upgrades.
16. Explain the various factors leading to the *Retirement/Disposal* of an embedded product
17. Explain the different *Life Cycle Models* adopted in embedded product development
18. Explain the merits and drawbacks of *Linear* model for embedded product development
19. Explain the similarities and differences between *Iterative* and *Incremental* life cycle model
20. Explain the merits and drawbacks of *Fountain* model for embedded product development
21. Explain the similarities and differences between *Iterative* and *Evolutionary* life cycle model
22. Explain the merits and drawbacks of *Prototyping* model for embedded product development
23. Explain the need for *Spiral* life cycle model in embedded product development

16 Trends in the Embedded Industry

EPILOGUE

The embedded industry has evolved a lot from the first mass produced embedded system, Autonetics D-17, to the recently launched Apple iPhone (Apple iPhone was the sensational gadget in the embedded device market at the time of writing this book (Year 2008-09)) in terms of miniaturisation, performance, features, development cost and time to market. Revolutions in processor technology is a prime driving factor in the embedded development arena. The embedded industry has witnessed the improvements over processor design from the 8bit processors of the 1970s to today's system on chip and multicore processors. The embedded operating system vendors, standards bodies, alliances, and open source communities are also playing a vital role in the growth of Embedded domain.

I hope this book was able to give you the fundamentals of embedded system, the steps involved in their design and development. I know this book itself is not complete in all aspects. It is quite difficult to present all the aspects of embedded design in a single book with limited page count. Moreover, the embedded industry is the one growing at a tremendous pace and whatever we feel superior in terms of performance and features may not be the same tomorrow. Wait for the rest of the books planned under this series to get an in-depth knowledge on the various aspects of embedded system design

So what next? Get your hands dirty with the design and development of Embedded Systems☺.

Wishing you good luck and best wishes in your new journey....

From the first mass produced embedded system, Autonetics D-17, to the recently launched Apple iPhone†, the embedded industry has evolved a lot, in terms of miniaturisation, performance, features, development cost and time to market. This book will not be complete without throwing some light into the current trends and bottlenecks in the embedded development.

16.1 PROCESSOR TRENDS IN EMBEDDED SYSTEM

Indeed, the advances in the processor technology are the prime driving factor in the embedded development arena. In the 1970s we started developing our embedded devices based on the 8bit microprocessors/controllers. Later we moved to the 16 and 32bit processor based designs, depending on our

†Apple iPhone was the sensational gadget in the embedded device market at the time of writing this book (Year 2008–09).

system requirement, as and when they appear in the market. Even today the 8bit processors/controllers are widely used in low-end applications. The only difference between the olden days 8bit processors/controllers and today's 8bit processors/controllers is that today's 8bit processors/controllers are more power and feature packed. In the olden days we used '*n*' number of ICs for building a device, but today, with the high degree of integration and IP Core re-use techniques, processors/controllers are integrating multiple IC functionalities into a single chip (System on Chip). In the olden days we required a processor/controller, Brown out circuit, reset circuit, watch dog timer ICs, and ADC/DAC ICs separately for building a simple Data Acquisition System, today a single microcontroller with all these components integrated is available in the market and it leads to the concept of miniaturisation and cost saving. Embedded industry has also witnessed the architectural changes for processors. In the beginning of the processor revolution, the speed at which an *8085* microprocessor executing a piece of code was awesome to us. Because it was beyond our imaginations. As we experienced the performance enhancements offered by general computing processors like x86, P-I, P-II, P-III, P-IV, Celeron, Centrino and Core 2 Duo, today we are unsatisfied with the performance offered by even the most powerful processor, because we have witnessed the rapid growth in the processor technology and our expectations are sky high today. Reduced Instruction Set Computing (RISC) and execution pipelining contributed a lot to the improvement on processor performance. From the procedural execution, the processor architecture moved to the single stage instruction pipelining and today processor families like ARM are supporting 8-stage pipelining (The latest ARM family ARM11 at the time of writing this book) with instruction and data cache.

The operating clock frequency was a bottleneck in processor designs. The earlier versions of processors/controllers were designed to operate at a few MHz. Advances in the semiconductor technology has elevated the bar on the operating frequency limitations. Nowadays processors/controllers with operating frequency in the range of Giga hertz (GHz) are available. Indeed, increase in operating frequency increases the total power consumption. Another trend in the embedded processor market is the 'Device oriented' design of processors. As mentioned earlier, in the beginning of the embedded revolution, we started building our embedded products around the available processors/controllers. As embedded industry started gaining momentum, the need for device specific processor design is flagged and processor manufactures started thinking in that direction. Today, when we think about developing a product, say Set Top Box or Handheld Device, we have a bunch of processors to select for the design. Intel is offering a variety of device specific processors. Intel PXA family of StrongARM processor (Now owned by Marvell Technology Group) is specifically designed for PDA applications and Intel has an x86 version for Set Top Box devices. The following section gives an overview of the key processor architecture/trends in embedded development.

16.1.1 System on Chip (SoC)

As the name indicates, a System on Chip (SoC) makes a system on a single chip. The System on Chip technology places multiple function 'systems' on a single chip. As mentioned earlier, in the beginning of the embedded revolution, we used separate ICs in an interconnected fashion for implementing a system. Innovations in the semiconductor area introduced the concept of integration of multiple function 'systems' on a single chip. With this it is possible to integrate almost all functional systems required to build an embedded product into a single chip. SoCs changed the concept of embedded processor from general purpose design to device specific design. Nowadays SoCs are available for diverse application needs like Set Top Boxes, Portable media players, PDAs, etc. iMX31 SoC from freescale semiconductor is a typical example for SoC targeted for multimedia applications. It integrates a powerful ARM 11 Core and other system functions like USB OTG interface, Multimedia and human interface (Graphics Accelerator, MPEG 4, Keypad Interface), Standard Interfaces (Timers, Watch Dog Timer, general purpose I/O), Image Processing Unit (Camera Interface, Display/TV control, Image Inversion and rotation, etc.) etc. on a single silicon wafer. On a first look SoC and Application Specific Integrated Circuit (ASIC) resembles the same. But they are not. SoCs are built by integrating the proven reusable IPs of different sub-systems, whereas ASICs are IPs developed for a specific application. By integrating multiple functions into a single chip, SoCs greatly save the board space in embedded hardware development and thereby leads to the concept of miniaturisation. SoCs are also cost effective.

16.1.2 Multicore Processors/Chiplevel Multi Processor (CMP)

One way of achieving increased performance is to increase the operating clock frequency. Indeed it will increase the speed of execution with the cost of high power consumption. In today's world most embedded devices are demanding battery power source for their operation. Here we don't have the luxury to offer high performance with the cost of reduced battery life. Here comes the role of Multicore processors. Multicore processors incorporate multiple processor cores on the same chip and works on the same clock frequency supplied to the chip. Based on the number of cores, the processors are known as dual core (2 cores), tri core (3 cores), quad core (4 cores), etc. Multicore processors implement multiprocessing (Simultaneous execution. Don't confuse it with multitasking). Each core of the CMP implements pipelining, multithreading and superscalar execution. Current implementations† of Intel multicore processors support cores up to 4, whereas Freescale multicore processors support cores up to 2. It is amazing to note that the multicore processor OCTEON™ CN3860, developed by Cavium Networks (http://www.caviumnetworks.com) is supporting 16 MIPS processor cores capable of operating at a clock frequency of 1GHz.

16.1.3 Reconfigurable Processors

Reconfigurable processor is a microprocessor/controller with reconfigurable hardware features. They contain an array of Programming Elements (PE) along with a microprocessor (Typically a RISC processor). The PE can be either a computational engine or a memory element. The hardware feature of the reconfigurable processor can be changed statically or dynamically. The dynamic changing of hardware configuration brings the advantage of making the chip adaptable to the firmware running on the processor. Depending on the situational need, the reconfigurable processor can entirely change their functionality to adapt to the new requirements. For example, a chip can configure itself to function as the heart of a camera system or a media player in a single device by downloading the appropriate firmware. Billions of Operations and Chameleon Systems are the key players of reconfigurable processor market. Reconfigurable SoCs (RSoCs) implement the IP for different subsystems through a reconfigurable matrix. This enables configurable hardware functionality for an SoC. The SoC needs to be configured to the required hardware functionality, through software support at the time of system initialisation (startup task). The hardware configuration can also be changed on the fly. A typical example for this is configuring the hardware codec for the required compression like MPEG1, MPEG 2, etc. by a media player application on a need basis. The Field Programmable System Level Integrated Circuit (FPSLIC)

†The statistics shown here is based on the data available till Dec 2008. Since processor technology is undergoing rapid changes, this data may not be relevant in future.

from Atmel Corporation is a typical example for RSoC. It integrates an 8bit AVR processor and a dynamically reconfigurable Field Programmable Gate Array (FPGA). The system is reconfigured from a library of pre-compiled IP cores stored in a FLASH memory on a need basis. RSoCS bring the concept of silicon sharing and thereby leads to less silicon usage and low power consumption.

16.2 EMBEDDED OS TRENDS

The Embedded OS industry is also undergoing revolutionary changes to take advantage of the potential offered by the trends in processor technologies. Today we have lot of options to select from a bunch of commercial and open source embedded OSs for building embedded devices. Most of the embedded OSs are trying to bring the virtualisation concept to the embedded device industry by adopting the microkernel architecture in place of the monolithic architecture. In microkernel architecture, the kernel contains very limited and essential features/services and rest of the features or services are installed as service and they run at the user space. Another noticeable trend adopting by OS suppliers is the 'Device oriented' design similar to the processor trends. In the olden days for building a device, we have to select an OS matching the device requirements and then customise it. Today OS suppliers are providing off-the-shelf OS customised for the device. Microsoft Embedded OS product line is a typical example of this. Microsoft has a range of OSs targeted for a group of device families like point of sale terminal, media player, set top box, etc. The Windows Mobile OS from Microsoft is specifically designed for mobile handsets. Open source embedded OS (Mostly centered around Embedded Linux) are gaining attention in the embedded market and the open source community is also offering off the shelf OS customised for specific group/family of devices. The Ubuntu MID edition which is specifically designed for Mobile Internet Device (MID) is a typical example for this. Since the processor technology is shifting the paradigm of computing from single core to multicore processors, the OS suppliers are also forced to change their strategies for supporting multicore processors. The latest version of the VxWorks (VxWorks 6.6SMP†) RTOS is designed to support the latest market-leading multicore processors.

16.3 DEVELOPMENT LANGUAGE TRENDS

When we talk about languages for embedded development, there are two aspects. One is the system side application (embedded device platform development) and the other one is the user application development. The system side application is responsible for managing the embedded device, interacting with low level hardware, scheduling and executing user applications, memory management, etc. whereas the user application runs on top of the system applications and requires the intervention of system application for performing system resource access (Like hardware access, memory access, etc.). In Embedded terminology the system side applications are referred as '*Embedded Firmware*' and the user applications are known as '*Embedded Software*'. The embedded firmware always comes as embedded into the program memory of the device and it is unalterable by the end user. Embedded software comes as either embedded with the firmware or user can install the software applications later on the device (A typical example is PDA, where the OS comes as embedded in the device and along with the OS certain application software like document viewer, mail client, etc. also comes as embedded in the device. Users can download and install rest of the applications in the device).

Whenever we think of development languages for embedded firmware, the first and foremost language that comes into our mind is 'C'. The reason being historic, the flexibility provided by 'C'

† At the time of writing this book (Year 2008–09).

language in hardware access and the bunch of cross-compilers and IDEs available for different platforms. We lived in an era where imagining a language beyond 'C' and Assembly (ALP) for embedded firmware was impossible. Now the scenario is totally changed. We have object-oriented languages like C++ for embedded firmware development. Efficient cross platform development tools and compilers from providers like Microsoft® played a significant role in this transformation. Advances in the compiler implementations and processor support brings java as one of the emerging language for system software development. Though java lacks lot of features essential for system software development, a move towards improving the missing factors is in progress. Still it is in the infancy stage. We will discuss the java based development under a separate thread. When it comes to embedded software development, a bunch of languages, including 'C', 'C++', Microsoft C#, ASP.NET, VB, Java, etc. are available. The following sections illustrate the role of Java and Microsoft .NET framework supported languages for embedded development.

16.3.1 Java for Embedded Development

Java being considered as the popular language for enterprise applications due to its platform independent implementations, but when it comes to embedded application development (firmware and software), it is not so popular due to its inherent shortcomings in real time system development support. In a basic java development, the java code is compiled by a java class compiler to platform independent code called *java bytecode*. The *java bytecode* is converted into processor specific object code by a utility called Java Virtual Machine (JVM). JVM abstracts the processor dependency from Java applications. JVM performs the operation of converting the bytecode into the processor specific machine code implementations. During run time, the bytecode is interpreted by the JVM for execution. The interpretation technique makes java applications slower than the other (cross) compiled applications. JVM can be implemented as either a piece of software code or hardware unit. Nowadays processors are providing built-in support for Java bytecode execution. The ARM processor implements hardware JVM called jazelle for supporting java. Figure 16.1 given below illustrates the implementation of Java applications in an embedded device with Operating System.

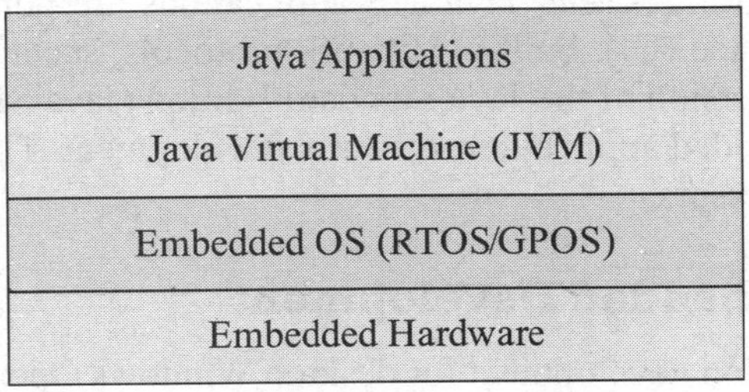

Fig. 16.1 **Java based embedded application development**

As mentioned earlier, JVM interprets the bytecode and thereby greatly affects the speed of execution. Another technique called Just In Time (JIT) compiler speeds up the Java program execution by caching all the previously interpreted bytecode. This avoids the delay in interpreting a bytecode which was already interpreted earlier.

The limitations of standard Java in embedded application development are:

1. The interpreted version of Java is quite slower and is not meeting the real-time requirement demanding by most embedded systems (For real-time applications)
2. The garbage collector of Java is non-deterministic in execution behaviour. It is not acceptable for a hard real-time system.
3. Processors which don't have a built-in JVM support or an off-the-shelf software JVM, require the JVM ported for the processor architecture.
4. The resource access (Hardware registers, memory, etc.) supported by Java is limited.
5. The runtime memory requirement for JVM and Java class libraries or JIT is a bit high and embedded systems which are constrained on memory cannot afford this.

Some movements to overcome these limitations are in the process and lot of novel ideas are emerging out to make Java suitable for embedded applications. The Ahead-of-Time (AOT) compilers for Java is intended for converting the Java bytecodes to target processor specific assembly code during compile time. It eliminates the need for a JVM/JIT for executing Java code. However there should be a piece of code for implementing the garbage collection in place of JVM/JIT. AOT compiler also brings the advantage of linking the compiled bytecode with other modules developed in languages like C/C++ and Assembly.

Java provides an interface named Java Native Interface (JNI), which can be used for invoking the functions written in other languages like C and Assembly. The JNI feature of Java can be explored for implementing system software like, user mode device drivers which has access to the JVM. Since JVM runs on top of the OS, device drivers which are statically linked with the OS kernel during OS image building or drivers which are loaded as shared object cannot be implemented using Java. In the Java based drivers, the low level hardware access is implemented in native languages like C.

The Java Community Process within the Safety Critical Java Technology expert group has come up with a real-time version for the JVM which is capable of providing comparable execution speed with C and also with predictable latency and reduced memory footprint.

Java Platform Micro Edition (Java ME), which was known as J2ME earlier, is a customised Java version specifically designed for 'Embedded application software' development for devices like mobile phones, PDAs, Set Top Boxes, printers, etc. Java ME applications are portable across devices. Java ME provides flexible User Interface (UI), built-in network protocols, security, etc. Sun Microsystems has also released an Embedded version of the Java Standard Edition (Java SE) with optimised memory footprint requirements for 'embedded application software' development. The embedded edition of the Java SE supports multicore processors.

16.3.2 .NET CF for Embedded Development

.NET is a framework for application development for desktop Windows Operating Systems (The UNIX version is also under development) from Microsoft®. It is a collection of pre-coded libraries and it acts as the run time component for .NET supported languages (C++, C#, VB, J#, etc.). It contains class libraries for User Interface, database connectivity, network connectivity, image editing, cryptography etc. The runtime environment of .NET is known as Common Language Runtime (CLR). The CLR resembles JVM in operation. It abstracts the target processor from application programmer. Like JVM, CLR also provides memory management (garbage collection), exception handling, etc. The CLR provides a language neutral platform for application development and execution. Applications written in .NET supported languages are compiled to a platform neutral intermediate language called Common Intermediate Language (CIL). For actual execution, the CIL is converted to the target processor specific machine code by the Common Language Runtime (CLR). Fig. 16.2 illustrates the concept of .NET framework based program execution.

The .NET framework is targeted for enterprise application development for desktop systems. The .NET framework consumes significant amount of memory. When it comes to embedded application development, the .NET framework is not a viable choice due to its memory requirement. For embedded and small devices running on Microsoft Embedded Operating Systems (like Windows Mobile and Windows CE), Microsoft® is providing a stripped down customised version of .NET framework called .NET Compact Framework or simply .NET CF for application development. Obviously .NET CF doesn't support all features of the .NET Framework. But it supports all necessary components required for application development for small devices. Users can develop applications in any .NET supported language including C++, C#, VB, J# etc.

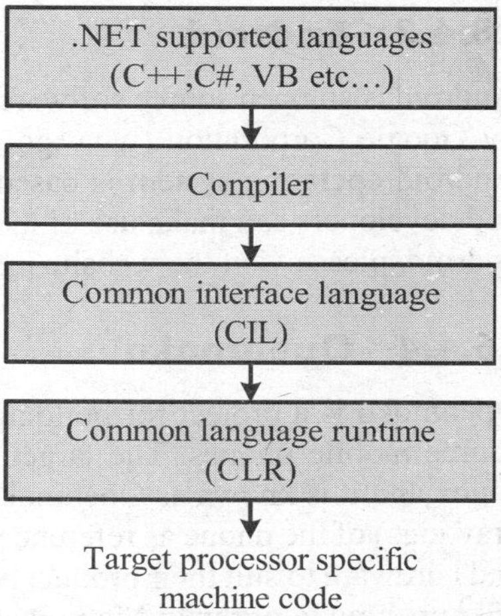

Fig. 16.2 **.NET based Embedded Application Development**

16.4 OPEN STANDARDS, FRAMEWORKS AND ALLIANCES

Certain areas of the embedded industry are highly 'hot' and competitive. It demands strategic alliances to sustain in the market and bring innovations through combined R&D. A typical example is the handset industry. The combined R&D helps hardware manufacturers to come up with new designs and software developers to support the new hardware. With diverse market players it is essential to have formal specifications to ensure interoperability in operations. The Open Alliances and standards body are aimed towards defining and formulating the standards. Time to market is a critical factor in the sensational embedded market segments. Open sources and frameworks reduce the time to market in product development. The following sections highlight the popular strategic alliances, open source standards and frameworks in the mobile handset industry.

16.4.1 Open Mobile Alliance (OMA)

The Open Mobile Alliance (OMA) is a standards body for developing open standards for *mobile phone industry*. The OMA alliance was formed in 2002 by stakeholders from the world's leading network operators, device manufacturers, Information technology companies and content providers. The mission of OMA is 'To create interoperable services across countries, operators and mobile terminals by acting as the centre of the mobile service enabler specification work'. Please visit http://www.openmobilealliance.org/ for more details on OMA.

16.4.2 Open Handset Alliance (OHA)

The Open Handset Alliance (OHA) is a business alliance formed by various handset manufacturers (HTC, Samsung, LG, Motorola etc), chip manufacturers (Intel, Nvidia, Qualcomm, etc.), platform providers (Google, Wind River Systems, etc.) and carriers (T-Mobile, China Mobile, Sprint Nextel, etc.) for developing standards for *mobile devices*. Please visit http://www.openhandsetalliance.com/ for more details on OHA.

16.4.3 Android

Android is an open source software platform and operating system for mobile devices. It was developed by Google Corporation (www.google.com) and retained by the Open Handset Alliance (OHA). The Android operating system is based on the Linux kernel. Google has developed a set of Java libraries and developers can make use of these libraries for application development in java. For more details on android, please visit the website http://www.android.com/

16.4.4 Openmoko

Openmoko is a project for building open hardware and firmware (OS) standards for a family of open source mobile phones. The target operating system under consideration by openmoko is Embedded Linux and it is known as Openmoko Linux. It also supplies the hardware details (schematics and CAD drawings) of the phone as reference design for developers. Developers can customise the software stack and hardware to suit their product needs. For more details on Openmoko, please visit the website http://wiki.openmoko.org/wiki/Main_Page

16.5 BOTTLENECKS

So far we discussed about the positives of the embedded technology. Now let's have a look at the bottlenecks faced by the embedded industry today.

16.5.1 Memory Performance

Memory performance is a real road blocker in embedded development. Though processor technologies are supporting high speed operations through increased clock, the current memory technology is not yet up to the mark to catch up the speed offered by processors. It is high time to think about alternate memory techniques that can at least offer a performance somewhat near to that of processors.

16.5.2 Lack of Standards/Conformance to Standards

Though we talk about various alliances and open standards for specific areas of embedded system, there are no specific standards in place to ensure interoperability in all areas of embedded development. Even though, standards are in place for certain areas of the embedded development like mobile handset market, only a minor proportion of the players are sticking on to these standards and majority of the players are still sticking on to their own proprietary architecture and designs. To bring innovations and cutting edge feature rich products, it is essential to have a combined effort and standardisation. It is high time to think about strategic alliances in all areas of embedded development.

16.5.3 Lack of Skilled Resources

This is the most crucial problem faced by the embedded industry today. 'Design of Embedded System is an Art' and it requires highly skilled, self motivated and talented people to meet the time criticalities of embedded product development. Though most of our engineering graduates are highly talented, they lack proper orientation towards the design and development of embedded systems. Lack of good books on the embedded fundamentals is also a major reason for it. It is high time to think about teaching embedded system as a special branch of undergraduate course in all major universities.

Appendix

I

Overview of PIC and AVR Family Microcontrollers and ARM Processors

INTRODUCTION TO PIC® FAMILY OF MICROCONTROLLERS

PIC® is a popular 8/16/32 bit RISC microcontroller family from Microchip Technology (www.microchip.com). The 8bit PIC family comprises the products PIC10F, PIC12F, PIC16F and PIC18F. They differ in the amount of program memory supported, performance, instruction length and pin count. Based on the architecture, the 8bit PIC family is grouped into three namely;

Baseline Products based on the original PIC architecture. They support 12bit instruction set with very limited features. They are available in 6 to 40 pin packages. The 6 pin 10F series, some 12F series (8 pin 12F629) and some 16F series (The 20-pin 16F690 and 40-pin 16F887) falls under this category.

Mid-Range This is an extension to the baseline architecture with added features like support for interrupts, on-chip peripherals (Like A/D converter, Serial Interfaces, LCD interface, etc.), increased memory, etc. The instruction set for this architecture is 14bit wide. They are available in 8 to 64 pin packages with operating voltage in the range 1.8V to 5.5V. Some products of the 12F (The 8 pin 12F629) and the 16F (20-pin 16F690 and 40-pin 16F887) series comes under this category.

High Performance The PIC 18F J and K series comes under this category. The memory density for these devices is very high (Up to 128KB program memory and 4KB data memory). They provide built-in support for advanced peripherals and communication interfaces like USB, CAN, etc. The instruction set for this architecture is 16bit wide. They are capable of delivering a speed of 16MIPS.

As mentioned earlier we have a bunch of devices to select for our design, from the PIC 8bit family. Some of them have limited set of I/O capabilities, on-chip Peripherals, data memory (SRAM) and program memory (FLASH) targeting low end applications. The 12F508 controller is a typical example for this. It contains 512 × 12 bits of program memory, 25 bytes of RAM, 6 I/O lines and comes in an 8-pin package. On the other hand some of the PIC family devices are feature rich with a bunch of on-chip peripherals (Like ADC, UART, I2C, SPI, etc.), higher data and program storage memory, targeting high end applications. The 16F877 controller is a typical example for this. It contains 8192 × 14 bits of FLASH program memory, 368 bytes of RAM, 256 bytes of EEPROM, 33 I/O lines, On-chip peripherals like 10-bit A/D converter, 3-Timer units, USART, Interrupt Controller, etc. It comes in a 40-pin package.

Here, the 16F877 device is selected as the candidate for illustrating the generic PIC architecture. Figure A1.1 illustrates the architectural details of PIC 16F877 device.

The 16F877 PIC family devices contain three types of memory namely; FLASH memory for storing program code, data memory for storing data and holding registers and EEPROM for holding non-volatile data. PIC follows the Harvard architecture and thereby contains two separate buses for program memory and data memory fetching. The data bus is 8bit wide and program memory bus is 14bit wide. The Program Counter is 13bit wide and is capable of addressing 8K

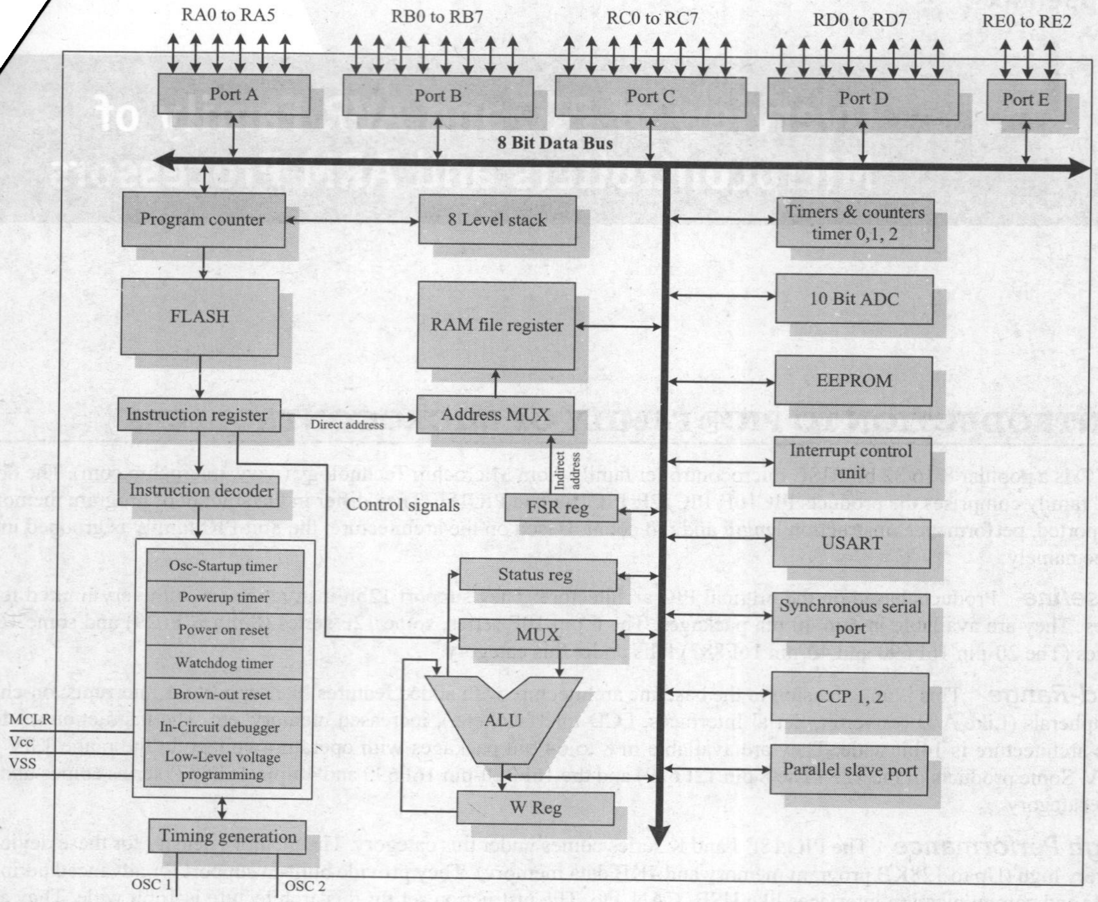

Fig. A1.1

program memory locations. The On-chip FLASH memory is partitioned into pages of size 2K bytes each. The program counter is formed by two register, an 8bit register PCL and a 5bit register PCH. PCL is a read/writable register whereas PCH is not directly accessible. PCH can be written indirectly through the register PCLATH. A write to the PCLATH register copies the least significant 5 bits to PCH. The W register holds the result of an operation performed in the ALU. The data memory contains the general purpose and special function registers and it is partitioned into multiple banks. Each bank contains 128 bytes. The special function registers are located at the lower memory address area of each bank. The working RAM is implemented as general purpose registers. The data memory bank is selected by setting the memory bank selector bits RPI and RP0 in the STATUS register. The RP0, RP1 combinations for selecting different data memory banks is given in the following table.

RP1	RP0	Memory Bank
0	0	0
0	1	1
1	0	2
1	1	3

General purpose registers are the memory locations available to users for data storage. They can be accessed directly or indirectly through the File Select Register (FSR). Special Function Registers are used by the CPU and peripherals for configuration, status indication, data association, etc. They are located in the lower memory area of a memory bank. The size of the SFR memory varies across device families and the typical size for 16F877 is 96 bytes. The status of arithmetic operations and reset along with the data memory bank selector bits RP0 and RP1 are held in the STATUS register. The bit details of the status register is explained below.

B7	B6	B5	B4	B3	B2	B1	B0
IRP	RP1	RP0	TO\	PD\	Z	DC	C

The table given below explains the meaning and use of each bit.

Bit	Name	Explanation
C	Carry/Borrow Flag	C = 1 for addition operation indicates a carry generated by the addition operation and C = 0 for subtraction operation indicates borrow generated by the subtraction operation executed by ALU.
DC	Digit Carry/Borrow Flag	C = 1 for addition operation indicates a carry generated out of the fourth bit by the addition operation and C = 0 for subtraction operation indicates borrow generated out of the fourth bit by the subtraction operation executed by ALU.
Z	Zero Flag	Z=1 when the result of an arithmetic or logic operation executed by the ALU is zero.
PD\	Power Down Flag	PD\= 1 After power up or on execution of the CLRWDT instruction. PD\= 0 On executing a SLEEP instruction.
TO\	Time out Flag	TO\= 1 After power up or on execution of the CLRWDT or SLEEP instruction. PD\= 0 On the expiration of Watchdog Timer (WDT)
RP0	Memory Bank select bit 0	Memory bank selector bit
RP1	Memory Bank select bit 1	
IRP	Register Bank Select	Memory bank selector for indirect addressing IRP = 0 : Bank 0, 1 (Indirect Address 000H to 0FFH) IRP = 1 : Bank 2, 3 (Indirect Address 100H to 1FFH)

The stack of 16F877 is an 8 level deep 13bit wide hardware stack. The stack pointer register which holds the current address of the stack is not readable and writeable. The stack space for PIC is an independent implementation and it is not part of either data memory or program memory. The program counter PC is PUSHed to the stack on execution of a CALL instruction or when an Interrupt is occurred. The Program Counter is POPed on the execution of a Return instruction (RETURN or RETLW or RETFIE). The stack operates as a circular queue. When all the 8 locations are PUSHed, a 9th PUSH operation stores the pushed data at the start of the stack.

The indirect addressing of data memory is accomplished by the registers INDF and File Select Register (FSR). INDF is a virtual register. Any instructions using the INDF register internally accesses the FSR register. In indirect addressing the memory bank is indicated by the IRP bit of the STATUS register and the 7th bit (In 0 to 7 numbering) of FSR. The memory location within the memory bank is pointed by the bits 0 to 6 of FSR register.

16F877 contains five bi-directional ports namely; PORTA, PORTB, PORTC, PORTD and PORTE. Ports B, C and D are 8bit wide, whereas Port A is 6bit wide and Port E is 3bit wide. Each Port associates a data direction register called TRISx (x= A for PORTA, B for PORTB, C for PORTC, D for PORTD and E for PORTE). It sets the Input or Output mode for the port. If the TRISx.n bit (where 'n' is the port pin number, 0 to 5 for Port A, 0 to 7 for Port B, C and D, and 0 to 2 for Port E) is set, the corresponding port pin configures as Input Port. PORTx (x = A or B or C or D or E) is the data register associated with each port. Some of the ports have alternate functions associated with them. The alternate functions are enabled by setting the corresponding bit in the register controlling the alternate functions for a Port. It should be noted that TRISx is the register deciding I/O direction even when the port is operating in the alternate function mode. The number of ports available in a device is device family specific.

The PIC 16F877 supports 14 interrupt sources. The interrupt control register INTCON holds the global and individual interrupt enable bits and bits for recording the status of all interrupts. 16F877 supports only one Interrupt vector for servicing all the interrupts. The interrupt vector is located at code memory location 0004H. The trigger type for external interrupts can be configured as either rising edge or falling edge, in the OPTION_REG by setting or clearing the INTEDG flag respectively. RETFIE is the instruction for returning from an interrupt service routine.

A watchdog timer is implemented to keep track of the proper execution of instructions. The watchdog timer is implemented as a free running RC oscillator. Watchdog timer doesn't require an external clock for its operation. During normal operation, a watchdog timeout resets the controller, whereas if the device is in the SLEEP mode, the watchdog timeout wakes up the CPU and put the controller in the normal operation mode. The watchdog timer can be enabled or disabled by setting or clearing the WDTE bit of the CONFIGURATION WORD register.

The 16F877 device undergoes reset if any one of the following conditions is met:

Power on Reset (POR) The power on reset signal is generated internally when the voltage supply to the device reaches in the range 1.2V to 1.7V when it is raised from 0V. In order to ensure a proper voltage level and stabilised clock, for proper operation of the device, some delays are introduced upon the detection of a POR. The Power up Timer (PWRT) is started on detecting a POR. PWRT runs for a period of 72 ms allowing the supply voltage to stabilise. When PWRT expires, the Oscillator Start-up Timer (OST) is started when PWRTs time delay expires. OST provides a delay of 1024 oscillator periods. This ensures that the crystal resonator for the oscillator circuit is properly stabilised before the code execution begins.

Brown-out Reset (BOR) BOR ensures that the program execution flow is not corrupted when the supply voltage falls below the threshold value for proper operation of the device. Whenever the supply voltage falls below this threshold, the BOR holds the device under reset till the voltage raises above the threshold value. The Brown-out Reset can be enabled by setting the bit BODEN. Brown-out reset follows the same sequence of operation for PWRT and OST as in the case of the Power on Reset.

Watchdog Reset Watchdog reset occurs when the watchdog timer overflows (if the watchdog timer is in the enabled state). Watchdog reset can happen either in the normal operation mode or when the controller is in the SLEEP mode. During normal operation, a watchdog timeout resets the controller, whereas if the device is in the SLEEP mode, the watchdog timeout wakes up the CPU and put the controller in the normal operation mode. The Watchdog reset in the normal operation mode follows the same sequence of operation for PWRT and OST as in the case of the Power on Reset.

External Reset The controller can be brought into the reset state at any time during program execution by applying a reset pulse at the RESET pin (MCLR\). Similar to watchdog timer reset, external reset can happen either in the normal operation mode or when the controller is in the SLEEP mode. During normal operation, the external reset assertion resets the controller, whereas if the device is in the SLEEP mode, the external reset wakes up the CPU and put the controller in the normal operation mode. The external reset in the normal operation mode follows the same sequence of operation for PWRT and OST as in the case of the Power on Reset.

PIC microcontrollers support power saving, by executing the SLEEP instruction. During SLEEP mode, the watchdog timer can be kept either in the enabled or disabled. If the watchdog timer is in the enabled state, the controller resumes its operation when the watchdog timer expires. During SLEEP mode, the I/O pins maintain their status at the time of entering the SLEEP state. The device is wakeup from the SLEEP mode by one of the following events.

1. An external reset signal at pin MCLR\
2. Watchdog timer expiration
3. Occurrence of external Interrupts, port change interrupt or peripheral interrupt

16F877 contains three timers/counters namely Timer 0, 1 and 2. Timer 0 can act as an 8bit timer/counter with internal or external clock. Timer 0 interrupt is generated when the timer count rolls over to 00H from FFH. Timer 0 mode can be selected by the T0CS bit of the OPTION_REG register. In the timer mode, Timer 0 increments on every instruction cycle (If the timer pre-scaler is not set). Timer 1 is a 16bit timer/counter (TMR1) consisting of two 8bit registers (TMR1H and TMR1L). Timer 1 can function as either a timer or counter. In counter mode, timer 1 counts the external pulses occurring at the corresponding I/O pin. Timer 2 is an 8bit timer which is specially designed for generating Pulse Width Modulation (PWM) signals. Timer 2 generates the PWM time base for Capture Compare PWM module (CCP) 1 and 2. Timer 2 associates a prescaler and a postscaler.

The Capture Compare PWM Modules (CCP) are associated with PWM signal generation and each CCP module contains a 16bit register which acts as either 16bit capture register or 16bit compare register or 16bit PWM master/slave duty cycle register.

The Parallel Slave Port (PSP) acts as a slave port which can be directly interfaced to the 8bit data bus of an external microprocessor/controller. Port D operates as the Parallel Slave Port. In PSP mode, the external microprocessor can read or write the PORTD latch.

The Universal Synchronous Asynchronous Receiver Transmitter (USART) acts as the serial communication interface (SCI) for the device. It supports full duplex asynchronous serial data transfer and half duplex synchronous serial data transfer. In synchronous half duplex communication, the USART can act as either master or slave. The baudrate for serial data communication is configurable.

Master Synchronous Serial Port (MSSP) or Synchronous Serial Port (SSP) is another serial interface supported by the 16F877 device. MSSP can operate as either Serial Peripheral Interface (SPI) or Inter Integrated Circuit (I2C) interface. The SPI mode requires minimum 3 wires and I2C requires minimum 2 wires for communication.

The 16F877 family device contains an on-chip Analog to Digital Converter ADC for analog signal conversion. The resolution of the ADC is 10bit. The ADC is controlled by the ADC register ADCON0 and the register ADCCON1 configures the port pin used for supplying Analog input signal.

PIC 24 and dsPIC series are the 16bit PIC microcontrollers and PIC32 is the 32bit PIC microcontroller from microchip. MPLAB from Microchip Technologies is the Integrated Development Environment for the PIC family of microcontrollers.

INTRODUCTION TO AVR® FAMILY OF MICROCONTROLLERS

AVR® 8bit RISC is a popular high performance low power 8bit RISC microcontroller family from Atmel (www.atmel.com). AVR microcontrollers operate at voltages ranging from 1.8V to 5.5V and execute instructions in a single clock cycle. They contain on-chip FLASH memory, EEPROM, SDRAM and built-in peripherals like ADC. The various microcontroller products coming under the AVR family of umbrella are listed below.

tinyAVR® Smallest version of 8bit AVR microcontroller. Limited pin counts. It contains up to 8K bytes of internal FLASH program memory and 512 bytes of SRAM and EEPROM. The *tinyAVR®* microcontrollers are commonly used for general purpose applications.

megaAVR® High performance AVR microcontroller with hardware multiplier. It contains up to 256K bytes of internal FLASH program memory and 8K bytes of SRAM and 4K bytes of EEPROM.

XMEGA™ High performance AVR microcontrollers with advanced peripherals like DMA and event systems.

AVR microcontrollers are also available as application oriented controllers specifically designed for certain applications like Automotive (Automotive AVR), CAN networking (CAN AVR), LCD driver (LCD AVR), Motor control, lighting applications (Lighting AVR), ZigBee, Remote Access Control, USB connectivity, etc. The AVR microcontroller may contain built-in peripherals like ADC, UART, SPI bus interface, etc. Figure A1.3 illustrates the architecture of the AVR ATmega8 Microcontroller.

The AVR 8 CPU contains an 8bit ALU, 32, 8bit general purpose registers, Stack pointer, program counter, instruction register, instruction decoder, and status and control register.

AVR follows the 'Harvard' architecture and supports separate memories and buses for program and data. AVR implements single level 'pipelining' with pre-fetching of instruction while an instruction is being executed.

All the 32 registers are directly connected to the ALU and it allows the accessing of two independent registers in one single instruction execution. The register access time is one clock cycle. Out of the 32 registers, 6 can be used as three 16bit indirect address registers. These 16bit registers are known as 'X', 'Y' and 'Z' registers. The address map of the general purpose registers are shown below in Fig. A1.2.

The higher 6 registers can be grouped into three 16bit registers as shown in the register map. Registers R26 and R27 forms the X register with lower order byte of X register in R26. Similarly registers R28 and R29 forms the Y register with lower order byte of Y register in R28. Register Z is formed by registers R30 and R31 with the lower order byte of Z register in R30. These registers are used as indirect addressing registers in data memory access and lookup table access registers for FLASH memory.

The Stack pointer register is a 16bit register holding the current address of the stack. For AVR architecture, the stack memory grows down (From a highest memory address to lower address). The stack is implemented in the SRAM memory area and the stack pointer points to the current location of the stack in the SRAM. The reset value of stack pointer is

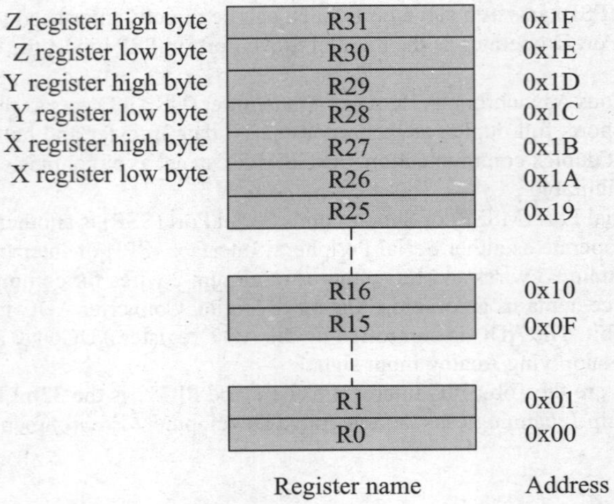

Fig. A1.2

0000H. It should be initialised to a value higher than 0060H for proper functioning. Whenever a data byte is 'PUSHed' to the stack, the stack pointer register is decremented by one. Whenever a data byte is 'POPed' from the stack, the stack pointer register is incremented by one. This is contradictory with the *8051* stack operation where the stack is located at the lowest address and it grows up. The stack pointer register is implemented as a combination of two eight bit registers namely Stack Pointer High (SPH) and Stack Pointer Low (SPL). Both the registers are required only if the size of the SRAM is greater than 256 bytes. For AVR processors with SRAM less than 256 bytes only the SPL register is physically implemented see Fig. A1.3.

The status register SREG holds the status of the most recently executed arithmetic instruction in the ALU. The bit details of the status register is explained below.

B7	B6	B5	B4	B3	B2	B1	B0
I	T	H	S	V	N	Z	C

The table given below explains the meaning and use of each bit.

Bit	Name	Explanation
C	Carry Flag	C = 1 indicates a carry generated by the arithmetic or logic operation executed by ALU.
Z	Zero Flag	Sets when the result of an arithmetic or logic operation is zero.
N	Negative Flag	Sets when the result of an arithmetic or logic operation is negative.
V	Over Flow	Two's complement overflow flag. Sets when overflow occurs in two's complement operation.
S	Sign Flag	Exclusive OR (XOR) between Negative Flag (N) and Overflow flag (V).
H	Half Carry Flag	Sets when a carry generated out of bit 3 (bit index starts from 0) in arithmetic operation. Useful in BCD arithmetic.
T	Bit Copy Storage	Acts as source and destination for the Bit Copy storage instructions, Bit Load (BLD) and Bit Store (BST) respectively. BLD loads the specified bit in the register with the value of T. BST loads T with the value of the specified bit in the specified register.
I	Global Interrupt Enable	Activates or de-activates the interrupts. If set to 1 all interrupts configured through their corresponding interrupt enabler register, are serviced. If set to 0 none of the interrupts are serviced. I bit is cleared by hardware when an interrupt is occurred and it is set automatically on executing a RETI instruction.

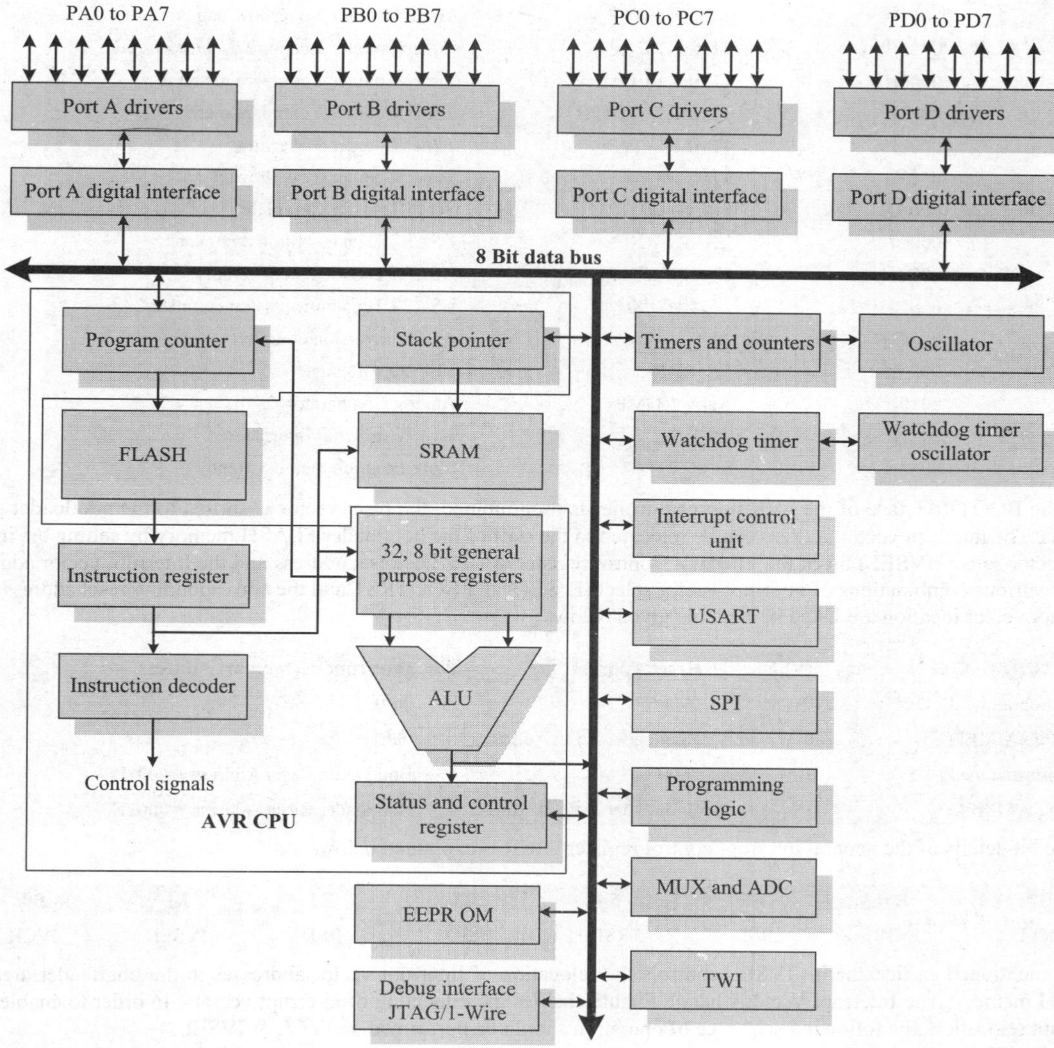

Fig. A1.3

AVR supports a number of interrupts including AVR CPU specific and additional On-chip hardware specific (These are implemented only if the microcontroller integrates the hardware in it. Examples are SPI interrupt). The table given below summarises the various interrupts supported by ATmega8 and their interrupt vectors.

Interrupt Vector No#	Interrupt Vector address	Interrupt Name	Explanation
1	0000H	RESET	Microcontroller Reset occurred
2	0001H	INT0	External Interrupt 0
3	0002H	INT1	External Interrupt 1
4	0003H	TIMER2 COMP	Timer/Counter 2 compare match

5	0004H	TIMER2 OVF	Timer/Counter 2 overflow flag
6	0005H	TIMER1 CAPT	Timer/Counter 2 capture event occurred
7	0006H	TIMER1 COMPA	Timer/Counter 1 compare match A
8	0007H	TIMER1 COMPB	Timer/Counter 1 compare match B
9	0008H	TIMER1 OVF	Timer/Counter 1 overflow
10	0009H	TIMER0 OVF	Timer/Counter 0 overflow
11	000AH	SPI, STC	Serial Transfer Complete
12	000BH	USART RXC	USART Data reception complete
13	000CH	USART UDRE	USART Data register is empty
14	000DH	USART TXC	USART Data transmission complete
15	000EH	ADC	ADC conversion complete
16	000FH	EE_RDY	EEPROM Ready
17	0010H	ANA_COMP	Analog Comparator
18	0011H	TWI	Two Wire Serial Interface
19	0012H	SPM_RDY	Store Program memory Ready

If the BOOTRST fuse of the AVR microcontroller is programmed, the reset vector is shifted to the bootloader start address. The interrupt vector address can be relocated to the start of the bootloader FLASH memory by setting the interrupt vector select (IVSEL) bit of the Interrupt Control register GICR. The reset address and the Interrupt vector address for the various combinations of interrupt vector select (IVSEL) and BOOTRST and the corresponding reset address and interrupt vector location are listed in the table given below.

BOOTRST	IVSEL	Reset Address	Interrupt vector start Address
Non-programmed	0	0000H	0001H
PROGRAMMED	0	Bootloader Reset Address	0001H
Non-programmed	1	0000H	Bootloader Reset Address + 0001H
PROGRAMMED	1	Bootloader Reset Address	Bootloader Reset Address + 0001H

The bit details of the general interrupt control register GICR is explained below.

B7	B6	B5	B4	B3	B2	B1	B0
INT1	INT0	RSD	RSD	RSD	RSD	IVSEL	IVCE

As mentioned earlier, the bit IVSEL controls the relocation of Interrupt vector addresses to the bootloader area of FLASH memory. The Interrupt Vector Change Enable enables the relocating of interrupt vectors. In order to enable the interrupt relocation, the following sequence of operation should be performed on IVCE & IVSEL.

1. Set IVCE
2. Within 4 machine cycles of setting IVCE, write the desired value to IVSEL (1 for interrupt vector relocation enabling and 0 for disabling interrupt vector relocation) along with a value of 0 for IVCE flag.

Interrupts are automatically disabled during the setting up of IVCE and for 4 machine cycles following the instruction setting up IVCE. If IVSEL is not modified within this 4 machine cycles, interrupts are automatically re-enabled. The global interrupt enabler bit in the status register SREG remains unchanged.

The reset of AVR can happen in four ways. They are:

1. *Power ON Reset:* The microcontroller is reset when the supply voltage is below the Power ON Reset threshold value
2. *External Reset:* The reset pin of the microcontroller is held low for a specified period.
3. *Watchdog Reset:* The watchdog Timer is expired. It happens due to flaws in program execution.
4. *Brown Out Reset:* The supply voltage to the microcontroller falls below a specified threshold. This is essential for preventing data corruptions and unexpected program execution.

During reset, all I/O registers are set to their initial values; all ports are reset to their initial states. When the reset sources go inactive, a delay counter is started to wait for a specified period set by the CKSEL fuses of the device. It ensures the proper stabilisation of the power source before the start of program execution. The program execution starts at either the rest vector (0000H) or the Reset address of Boot FLASH depending on the configuration of the BOOTRST fuse. The MCU Control and Status Register MCUCSR keep track of the source of reset. The bit details of this register are shown below.

B7	B6	B5	B4	B3	B2	B1	B0
RSD†	RSD	RSD	RSD	WDRF	BORF	EXTRF	PORF

WDRF is the flag corresponding to a watchdog initiated reset and BORF flag indicates a reset triggered by Brown Out detection (The operating voltage goes beyond a threshold). If the reset is initiated by the external RESET line, the EXTRF flag is set. A power On reset sets the PORF flag.

Watchdog timer is a mechanism to bring the controller out of a system hang-up condition. Unexpected program flow may result in unexpected behaviour and thereby leading to an illusion of total system hang-up. This can be prevented by using a watchdog timer to monitor the time taken to execute the code segment, which is prone to create system hang-up behaviour.

The AVR watchdog timer unit contains a built in watchdog timer oscillator which runs at a separate on-chip oscillator at a frequency of 1MHz. The watchdog reset interval can be adjusted by changing the pre-scaler values of the watchdog timer. The watchdog timeout event triggers a reset when the watchdog timer exceeds the time period set. The Watchdog Timer Control Register (WDTCR) controls the operation of the watchdog timer. The bit details of the watchdog timer register are given below.

B7	B6	B5	B4	B3	B2	B1	B0
RSD*	RSD	RSD	WDCE	WDE	WDP2	WDP1	WDP0

The bits, WDP0, WDP1 and WDP2 set the oscillator cycles in which the watchdog timer expires (sets the watchdog timer pre-scaler). It varies from 16K oscillator cycles (WDP0, WDP1, WDP2 = 000) to 2048K oscillator cycles (WDP0, WDP1, WDP2 =111). The bit WDE controls the enabling and disabling the watchdog timer. Setting it to 1 starts the watchdog timer. The bit, Watchdog Change Enable, controls the disabling of the Watchdog timer. In order to disable a watchdog timer this bit should be set before clearing the watchdog enable bit WDE. Writing a 0 to the Watchdog Enable bit takes effect only when the WDCE bit is at logic 1. Before starting the watchdog timer, it should be resetted using the instruction WDR.

Apart from the general purpose registers, AVR holds various status, control and configuration registers for configuring, controlling and providing feedback on various operations like Port setting, initialisation, read write, watch dog timer management, interrupt management, serial data communication, etc. These registers are known as special function registers. These registers fall under the I/O space and they are accessed by the I/O access instructions *IN* and *OUT*. I/O Registers within the address range 0x00–0x1F are directly bit accessible using the *SBI* and *CBI* instructions. In these registers, the value of single bits can be checked by using the *SBIS* and *SBIC* instructions. If the I/O registers are addressed as data space using the *LD* and *SD* instructions, add 0x20 to these addresses.

The external interrupts INT0 and INT1 are configurable for either level triggering or edge triggering. This can be configured by setting or clearing the Interrupt Sense Control bits of the MCU Control Register (MCUCR). The bit details of this register are shown below.

B7	B6	B5	B4	B3	B2	B1	B0
SE	SM2	SM1	SM0	ISC11	ISC10	ISC01	ISC00

Bits ISC11, ISC10 configures the external interrupt INT1 and bits ISC01, ISC00 configures the external interrupt INT0. The various settings for the bits ISC1 and ISC0 and the corresponding interrupt triggering conditions are listed below.

† RSD – Reserved for Future Use

ISCx1	ISCx0	Interrupt Trigger
0	0	Low level
0	1	Any logical change on INTx generates an interrupt request (x=0 for INT0 and 1 for INT1)
1	0	Falling Edge
1	1	Raising Edge

The AVR mega architecture supports multiple bidirectional ports (Up to 4 Ports: Port A, Port B, Port C and Port D) with configurable pull-up option. The ports can be configured as either input port or output port. Each port contains a group of port pins (up to 8 pins). Port pins are internally pulled to logic 'High' using pull-up resistors. All I/O pins have protection diodes to both +ve supply voltage and ground. Three I/O mapped registers are associated with each port. They are:

Data Direction Register (DDRx) The data direction register associated with Port x (where x can be A or B or C or D). If the bit corresponding to a port pin is set as 1, the port pin is configured as output pin. If the bit is set as 0, the corresponding pin of the port is configured as input pin.

Data Register (PORTx) The data register associated with Port x (where x can be A or B or C or D). It is used for holding the data to output to the port when it is configured as an Output port. When the Port is configured as I/p port, the Data register is used for turning ON and OFF the pull-up resistors associated with each pin of the port.

Port Input Pin (PINx) This register holds the Pin status.

Three register bits namely DD*xn* (bits in (DDRx Register), PORT*xn* and PIN*xn* (where x = A or B or C or D and n = 0 to 7) are associated with each port pin. The DDxn bit selects the direction of the port. A value of 1 sets the port pin as Output port and a value of 0 sets the port pin as input port. If PORTxn is set at logic 1 when the DDxn for the corresponding port pin is configured as input pin, the Pull-up associated with the port pin is activated. The pull up associated with the pin can be turned Off by writing a logic 0 to the corresponding PORTxn register bit or by setting the Pin as Output pin. If port pin PORT*xn* is written with logic 1 when the DDxn pin of it is configured as Output pin, the port pin is driven 'High'. The port pin is driven 'Low' in the output mode by writing a 0 to the PORTxn register bit.

Apart from bi-directional I/O operation, some of the port pins support alternate functions. The alternate functions for a port pin can be enabled by overriding the port pin I/O functionality with alternate functions. These overriding is enabled by setting the override bit corresponding to the alternate function in the corresponding special function register holding the override bit. The override value can be mentioned in the corresponding bit. Hence for each alternate function, two bits are required; 1 for enabling the override and the other one for setting the override value.

The mega8 AVR supports two 8bit Timers/Counters and a 16bit Timer/Counter. Timer/counter 0 can operate in any one of the modes; Single Channel Counter, Frequency Generator, External Event Counter and 10-bit Clock pre-scaler:

The clock to the timer unit is supplied via the internal clock or via a clock prescaler or via an external clock source on the port pin T0. The Timer/Counter is incremented at each clock tick. The counting happens in the upward direction and the Timer/Counter register overflows to 00H on next clock pulse when the count value is maximum, i.e. 0FFH. Whenever a Timer/Counter overflow occurs, it is indicated through the flag corresponding to the timer.

Each 8bit timer 'x' (x = 0 or 2) associates the following registers with it for operation

1. A Timer/Counter Control Register (TCCR*x*) for selecting the clock source
2. A Timer/Counter Register (TCNT*x*) for holding the count
3. A Timer/Counter Interrupt mask register (TIMSK). It contains the bit TOIE*x* for individually enabling or disabling the Timer/Counter *x* interrupt.
4. Timer/Counter Interrupt Flag Register (TIFR). It contains the bit TOV*x* for indicating the overflow of Timer/Counter *x*. It is cleared by hardware when the interrupt vectors to its ISR.

The 16bit timer (Timer/Counter 1) serves as Pulse Width Modulation (PWM) generator/Frequency generator and external event counter.

AVR has a built-in USART for full duplex synchronous or asynchronous serial data communication. It supports Serial Frames with 5, 6, 7, 8, or 9 data bits and 1 or 2 Stop Bits, with hardware based odd or even parity generation and parity check. Port D bit 0 and bit 1 when configured in the alternate function mode serves as the Receive Pin and Transmit Pin respectively for serial data communication. The USART Transmitter has two flags namely; USART Data Register Empty

(UDRE) and Transmit Complete (TXC) for indicating its state. The flag UDRE is set when the transmit buffer is empty. The flag TXC is set upon transmission of data. Both of these flags can be used for generating interrupts. Similarly the USART receiver has one flag named Receive Complete (RXC) for indicating the availability of data in the receive buffer.

AVR microcontroller contains a special program called bootloader located in the FLASH memory. It has the capability to load program into the FLASH memory area of the controller. It facilitates firmware upgrades. The bootloader is self modifiable, and it can also erase itself from the code if it is not required anymore. The bootloader memory size is configurable with fuses and it has two independently configurable boot lock bits for locking the bootloader for security reasons. The bootloader program can be configured to execute either on power on reset (If the BOOTRST fuse of the AVR microcontroller is programmed, the reset vector is shifted to the bootloader start address) or on receiving a specific command from a host PC through the USART or SPI interface.

The AVR architecture incorporates multiple levels of power saving. The different levels correspond to a power saving mode and the device should put in the corresponding mode to take advantage of the power savings. The power saving mode is activated by executing the SLEEP instruction. The power saving mode is set in the MCU Control Register (MCUCR) before executing the SLEEP instruction. The details of the MCUCR bits associated with power saving is illustrated below.

B7	B6	B5	B4	B3	B2	B1	B0
SE	SM2	SM1	SM0	ISC11	ISC10	ISC01	ISC00

The Sleep Enable (SE) bit enables the CPU to enter sleep state on executing a SLEEP instruction. Bits SM0, SM1 and SM2 sets the power saving mode. The different power saving modes supported by AVR are listed below.

Idle Mode This mode is set by configuring the bits SM2:SM1:SM0 as 0:0:0 with SE = 1. The clock to CPU is frozen. CPU stops execution. Other units like SPI, USART, Analog Comparator, ADC, Two-wire Serial Interface, Timer/Counters, Watchdog, and the interrupt system continue operational. The Idle mode is terminated by an externally or internally triggered interrupt like external interrupts, Timer Overflow and USART Transmit Complete interrupts and Analog Comparator interrupt, etc.

ADC Noise Reduction Mode This mode is set by configuring the bits SM2:SM1:SM0 as 0:0:1 with SE = 1. The clock to I/O system, CPU is frozen. CPU stops execution. Other units like ADC, external interrupts, two-wire Serial Interface address watch, Timer/Counter2 and the Watchdog timer (if enabled) continue operational. This mode is terminated by an ADC Conversion Complete interrupt, or an External reset, or a Watchdog Reset, or a Brown-out Reset, or a Two-wire Serial Interface address match interrupt, or a Timer/Counter2 interrupt, or an SPM/EEPROM ready interrupt, or an external interrupt (INT0 or INT1)

Power down Mode This mode is set by configuring the bits SM2:SM1:SM0 as 0:1:0 with SE = 1. The external oscillator is halted and stops all internally generated clocks. All modules using the generated clock are frozen. External interrupts, Two-wire Serial Interface address watch, and the watchdog continue operational. The power down mode is terminated by an External Reset, or a Watchdog Reset, or a Brown-out Reset, or a Two-wire Serial Interface address match interrupt, or an external level interrupt.

Power save Mode This mode is set by configuring the bits SM2:SM1:SM0 as 0:1:1 with SE = 1. This mode is same as Power down mode except that Timer/Counter 2 continue runs in this mode if it is clocked asynchronously. Along with the power down mode termination conditions, a Timer Overflow or an Output Compare event from Timer/Counter2 also triggers the termination of this mode.

Standby Mode This mode is set by configuring the bits SM2:SM1:SM0 as 1:1:0 with SE = 1 and when the external clock is used. The device wakes up from the standby mode in 6 clock cycles.

The size of on-chip FLASH memory, SRAM and EEPROM varies across different members of the AVR family. AVR 8 family supports FLASH memory up to 256KB, EEPROM from 64 bytes to 4KB and SRAM up to 8KB. Also the presence of on-chip peripherals like ADC, Two Wire Interface (TWI), SPI, etc. varies across the family members.

AVR normally does not support the execution of program from external program memory. The code is always executed form the internal FLASH memory.

AVR provides built in On-Chip debug support in the form of either JTAG interface or DebugWIRE (1-Wire) interface. All AVR mega family devices with 16KB or more FLASH memory supports built in JTAG interface for On-chip debugging and In System Programming. All new AVR mega family devices with FLASH memory less than 16KB supports the 1-Wire debug interface.

Please refer to the website http://www.atmel.com/dyn/resources/prod_documents/doc0856.pdf for details on the Instruction set for 8bit AVR.

AVR® 32 is a 32bit microcontroller family from Atmel featuring Single Instruction Multiple Data (SIMD) and DSP instructions. It also supports audio and video processing features.

INTRODUCTION TO ARM® FAMILY OF PROCESSORS

Advanced RISC Machines (or ARM) is a powerful 32bit RISC processor from ARM Holdings (www.arm.com). ARM holdings is a joint venture between Acorn Computers (http://www.acorncomputers.co.uk/), Apple Computers (www.apple.com) and VLSI Technology (www.vlsi.com www.nxp.com) and is founded in 1990. ARM Holdings is the Intellectual Property (IP) supplier of ARM processor core and it doesn't manufacture ARM processor chips. ARM designs the ARM processor core and licences its ARM IP to their networked partners. The partners can utilise the ARM IP for building System On Chip devices. Freescale semiconductors, Texas Instruments, NXP (Philips) Semiconductors, etc. are some of the channel partners of ARM, which fabricates ARM processors. Please visit the ARM website http://www.arm.com/community/all_partners.php for the complete list of ARM community partners.

The ARM architecture has evolved a lot from its first version ARM1 to the latest ARM11 Processor core. ARM1, ARM2, ARM3, ARM 4&5, ARM6, ARM7, ARM8, StrongARM, ARM9, ARM10 and ARM11 are the product families from ARM since its introduction to the market. Some ARM processor extensions like Thumb, EI Segundo, Jazelle, etc. are also introduced by ARM during its journey from ARM1 to ARM11.

ARM is a RISC processor and it supports multiple levels of pipelines for instruction execution. ARM contains thirty-seven 32bit registers. Out of the 37 registers 30 are general purpose registers and 16 general purpose registers (Registers r0 to r15) are available in the user mode of operation. Register r15 is the program counter (pc). Register r13 functions as the stack pointer register (sp). Register r14 is used as link register (lr) for the branch and link instructions. The Current Program Status Register (CPSR) holds execution status of the processor, processor operation mode, interrupt enable bit status, etc. The details of the bits associated with the CPSR register is illustrated below.

B31	B30	B29	B28	B27	B25 to B26	B 24	B8 to B23	B7	B6	B5	B0 to B4
N	Z	C	V	Q		J		I	F	T	Mode Select

The condition code flags' status reflects the following scenarios:

N = 1: The result of ALU operation is negative
Z = 1: The result of ALU operation is zero
C = 1: Carry generated as a result of the operation executed in ALU
V = 1: ALU operation resulted in Overflow

The J bit specifies whether the processor is in Jazelle state or not. The T bit indicates whether the ARM is using 32bit ARM instruction or 16bit Thumb instruction. The 'I' and 'F' flags are used for disabling Interrupts. If 'I' is set to 1, the Normal interrupts are disabled. Setting 'F' to 1 disables the Fast Interrupts. The Mode select bits, B0 to B4, select the operating mode for the processor. ARM supports the following operating modes:

User Mode It is the main execution mode for user applications. This mode is also known as 'Unprivileged Mode'. It enables the protection and isolation of operating system from user applications.

Fast Interrupt Processing (FIQ) Mode The processor enters this mode when a high priority interrupt is raised.

Normal Interrupt Processing (IRQ) Mode The processor enters this mode when a normal priority interrupt (Interrupts other than high priority) is raised.

Supervisor/Software Interrupt Mode The processor enters this mode on reset and when a software interrupt instruction is executed.

Abort Mode Enters this mode when a memory access violation occurs

Undefined Instruction Mode Enters this mode when the processor tries to execute an undefined instruction.

System Mode This mode is used for running operating system tasks. It uses the same register as the User mode.

All the above modes, except User mode, are privileged modes. The privileged mode uses several other registers than the registers available in the user mode. Figure A1.4 illustrates the register organisation for the various modes.

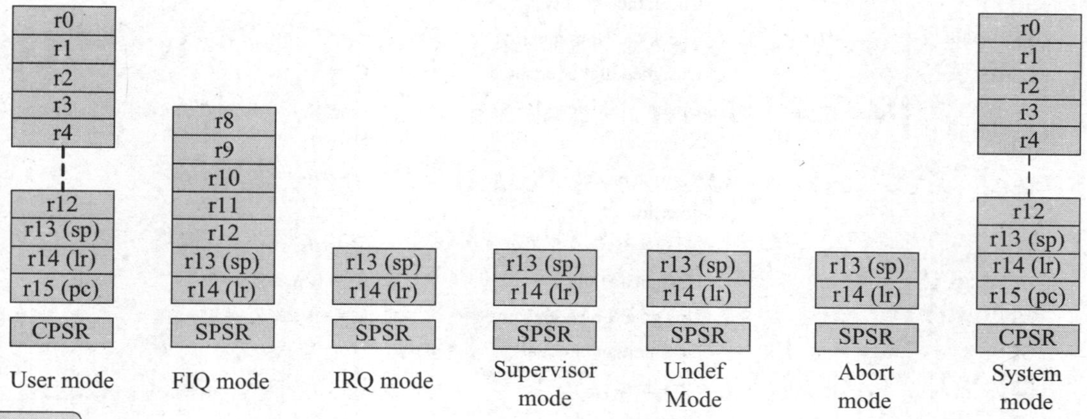

Fig. A1.4

ARM supports multiple levels of pipelining for improving the speed of operation. The first generation of ARM processors implemented 3-stage pipelining. This pipelining model was followed till ARM7TDMI core. This pipeline model was based on the classical fetch-decode-execute sequence and it executed one instruction per cycle in the absence of pipelining. The ARM9 family implements a 5-stage pipelining with separate instruction and data cache. The continuous improvements over the pipelining model brought a new pipeline architecture, which supports 6-stage pipelining for the ARM10 family of devices. In this model, both the instruction and data buses are 64bit wide and it enabled the fetching of two instructions on each cycle. The ARM11 family of devices is designed to support 8-stage pipelining. Here the shift operation is segregated to a separate pipeline and both instruction and data cache access are distributed across 2 pipeline stages.

The Instruction Set Architecture (ISA) of ARM supports three different types of Instruction sets, namely:

ARM Instruction Set The original ARM instruction set. Here all instructions are 32bit wide and are word aligned. Since all instructions are word aligned, one single fetch reads four 8bit memory locations. Hence there is no significance for the lower 2 bits (b0 and b1 which generates 4) of the program counter. Only bits 2 to 31 of PC are significant for ARM instructions.

Thumb Instruction Set Thumb is the 16bit subset for the 32bit ARM instructions. These instructions can be considered as a 16bit compressed form of the original 32bit ARM instructions. These instructions can be executed either by decompressing the instruction to the original 32bit ARM instruction or by using a dedicated 16bit Instruction decoding unit. Here all instructions are half word aligned; meaning one single fetch reads two 8bit memory locations. Hence there is no significance for the lower bit (b0 which generates 2) of the program counter. Only bits 1 to 31 of PC are significant for Thumb instructions. Thumb instructions provide higher code density than the 32bit original ARM instructions. The concept of thumb instruction was introduced in the ARM V4 (Version 4.0) architecture.

Jazelle Instruction Set Jazelle is the hardware implementation of the Java Virtual Machine (JVM) for executing java byte codes. The 140 Java instructions are implemented directly in the Jazelle hardware unit, rest 94 Java instructions are implemented by emulating them with multiple ARM instructions. All instructions related to the Jazelle are 8bit wide. Here the processor reads 4 instructions at a time by a word access.

All ARM instructions are conditional, meaning all instructions associate a conditional code with them. The condition code specifies the condition to be checked (Flags to be tested) for executing the instruction. A typical instruction looks like *Opcode <condition code> Operands*, e.g. ADDAL r0,r1,r2 always adds r1 and r2 and stores the result in register r0, whereas the instruction ADDEQ r0,r1,r2 adds r1 and r2 only if the zero flag (Z) is set. The table given below gives a snapshot of the different condition codes supported by ARM.

Condition Code	**Description**	**Flag to Test**
EQ	Check the equality	Z == 1
NE	Check the Non-equality	Z == 0
CS/HS	Unsigned higher or same	C == 1
CC/LO	Unsigned Lower	C == 0
MI	Negative	N == 1
PL	Positive or Zero	N == 0
VS	Overflow	V == 1
VC	No Overflow	V == 0
HI	Unsigned Higher	C == 1 && Z == 0
LS	Unsigned Lower or same	C == 0 && Z == 1
GE	Greater than or equal	N == V
LT	Less than	N != V
GT	Greater than	Z == 0 & N == V
LE	Less than or equal	Z == 1 & N != V
AL	Execute Always	None

Use the condition code AL for executing the instruction regardless of any conditions. The ARM instruction set can be broadly classified into:

Data Processing Instructions The data processing instructions include the arithmetical and logical operation instructions, comparison and data movement instructions. The following table summarises the data processing operations supported by ARM.

Operation Category	**Instructions**
Arithmetic	ADD, ADC, SUB, SBC, RSB, RSC
Logical	AND, ORR, EOR, BIC
Comparisons	CMP, CMN,TST, TEQ
Data Movement	MOV, MVN

These instructions work only on registers. Not on memory.

Single Register and Multiple Register Data transfer Instructions
The instructions related to register data transfer come under this category. These instructions involve either a single register data transfer or multiple register data transfer

Program Control (Branching) Instructions Diverts the program flow. It can be either a conditional execution or unconditional branching. BX, B, BL, etc. are examples for branching instructions.

Multiplication Instructions Multiply (MUL), Multiply Accumulate (MLA), Multiply Long (MLL) and Multiply Long Accumulate (MLAL) instructions are the multiply instructions supported by ARM Instruction set.

Barrel shift Operations ARM ISA doesn't implement shift instructions by default. However shift operations are implemented as part of other instructions, with the help of a barrel shifter. Bit shifting operations like Logical Left Shift (LSL), Arithmetic Right Shift (ASR), Logical Right Shift (LSR), Rotate Right (ROR), and Rotate Right Extended (RRE) are examples for this.

Branching Instructions For changing the program execution flow. It can be either conditional branching or unconditional branching.

Co-Processor Specific Instructions ARM does not execute certain instructions and lets a co-processor to execute these instructions. CDP, LDC, STC, MRC, MCR, etc. are examples for this.

Under ARM architecture, Interrupts, Reset, memory access error, etc. are considered as exceptions and ARM has a well defined exception mechanism to handle them. The different exceptions defined by ARM are listed below.

Exception	Description	Priority
Reset	Start the processor from a well defined state.	High
Data Abort	Occurs when a load store instruction violates the memory access restrictions. It is asserted by the Memory Management Unit (MMU).	↓
Fast Interrupt	This exception is raised when a high priority interrupt is asserted.	
Normal Interrupt	This exception is raised when any interrupt other than the high priority interrupt is asserted.	
Pre-fetch Abort	Occurs when an instruction fetch violates the memory access permissions. It is asserted by the Memory Management Unit (MMU).	
Software Interrupt	It is raised by a special instruction to request operating system service. It is used by operating system to implement a set of privileged operations which applications running in user mode can request.	
Undefined Instruction Execution	Asserted on the decoding of an instruction which is not supported by the ARM architecture.	Low

For all exceptions except the 'Reset', the various operations performed are listed below.

1. Copy the contents of the CPSR register to the SPSR register of the new mode.
2. Set the following states in the CPSR register
   (a) Change the state to ARM
   (b) Change the mode to exception mode, e.g. FIQ mode for Fast Interrupts.
   (c) Disable interrupts if needed
3. Save the address of the instruction following the instruction generated the exception to the register 'r14' LR (register) of the mode corresponding to the exception.
4. Set Program counter with the vector address corresponding to the exception.

Figure A1.5 given below explains the vector address for all exceptions.

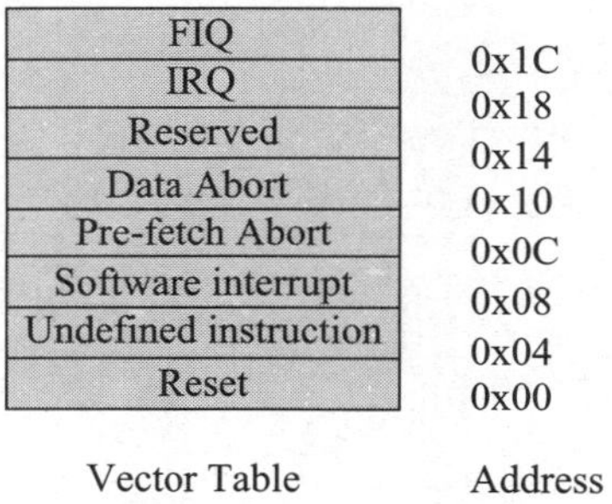

Fig. A1.5

Upon the execution completion of the exception code, the following actions are performed.

1. Restore CPSR register from the SPSR register of the current mode
2. Restore Program counter from register 'r14', (LR) of the current mode.

The processor bus architecture followed by ARM is known as Advanced Microcontroller Bus Architecture (AMBA). The AMBA architecture standardises the on-chip connection of different IP cores and enables IP reusability. The AMBA specifications define three different buses for on-chip device communication. They are:

Advanced High Performance Bus (AHB) AHB acts as the backbone for connecting high-performance, high clock frequency system modules like memory controllers, DMA bus master, etc.

Advanced System Bus (ASB) ASB is used for connecting high performance system modules. ASB is an alternative system bus for AHB, for system modules which don't require performance up to the mark offered by AHB.

Advanced Peripheral Bus (APB) APB is a simple, low performance, low power bus used for connecting low speed peripherals.

ARM supplies the high performance processor core and the specification for the different buses for connecting with the ARM core. The ARM partners can build System on Chip (SoC) devices by integrating various peripherals to the ARM core using the AMBA specified bus. A typical SoC architecture using the ARM core and AMBA bus standard is given in Fig. A1.6.

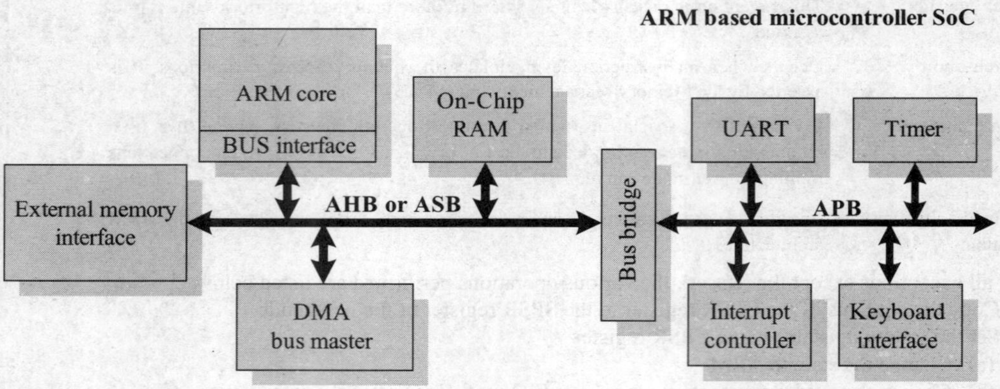

Fig. A1.6

Appendix

II Design Case Studies

1. DIGITAL CLOCK

Design and Implement a Digital Clock as per the requirements given below.

1. Use a 16 character 2-line display for displaying the current Time. Display the time in DAY HH:MM:SS format on the first line. Display the message 'Have A Nice Day!' on the second line. DAY represents the day of the Week (SUN, MON, TUE, WED, THU, FRI and SAT). HH represents the hour in 2 digit format. Depending on the format settings it may vary from 00 to 12 (12 Hour Format) or from 00 to 23 (24 Hour format). MM represents the minute in 2 digit format. It varies from 00 to 59. SS represents the seconds in 2 digit format. It varies from 00 to 59. The alignment of display character should be centre justified (Meaning if the characters to display are 12, pack it with 2 blank space each at right and left and then display).
2. Interface a Hitachi HD44780 compatible LCD with 8051 microcontroller as per the following interface details
   Data Bus: Port P2
   Register Select Control line (RS): Port Pin P1.4
   Read/Write Control Signal (RW): Port Pin P1.5
   LCD Enable (E): P1.6
3. The Backlight of the LCD should be always ON
4. Use AT89C51/52 or AT89S8252 microcontroller. Use a crystal Oscillator with frequency 12.00 MHz. This will provide accurate timing of 1 microsecond/machine cycle.
5. A 2 × 2 matrix key board (4 keys) is interfaced to Port P1 of the microcontroller. The key details are MENU key connected to Row 0, and Column 0 of the matrix; ESC key connected to Row 0, and Column 1 of the matrix; UP key connected to Row 1, and Column 0 of the matrix; DOWN key connected to Row 1, and Column 1 of the matrix. The Rows 0, 1 and columns 0, 1 of matrix keyboard are interfaced to Port pins P1.0, P1.1, P1.2 and P1.3 respectively.
6. The hour (HH) and minutes (MM) should be adjustable through a Menu Screen. The Menu screen is invoked by pressing the MENU key of the matrix key.
7. The selection of an item in the menu is achieved by pressing the MENU key (Performs the Enter Key function). Exit from the menu is achieved through pressing the ESC key. Pressing the ESC key takes the user to the previous menu.
8. The menu contains 4 submenu items, namely 'Adjust Hour', 'Adjust Minute', 'Adjust Day' and 'Adjust Format'. The 'Adjust Hour' adjusts the hour, 'Adjust Minute' adjusts the minute, 'Adjust Day' adjusts the day of the week (SUN to SAT) and 'Adjust Format' adjusts the hour display format (12 hour/24 hour format). 'Adjust Hour' is the default submenu item and on invoking the menu this prompt is displayed on the screen. The user can select other menus by pressing the UP or DOWN key. Once the submenu is selected, the User can enter that submenu by press-

ing the MENU key. The Submenu lists the current Hour or the Current Minute or the Current Day or the Current Format according to the submenu selected. User can adjust the values for each by pressing the UP or DOWN key. Once a value is selected, it can be applied by pressing the MENU key. Pressing the MENU key applies the new value and takes the user to the previous menu. Pressing ESC from any point takes the user to the previous menu. The menu arrangement is illustrated in A2.1.

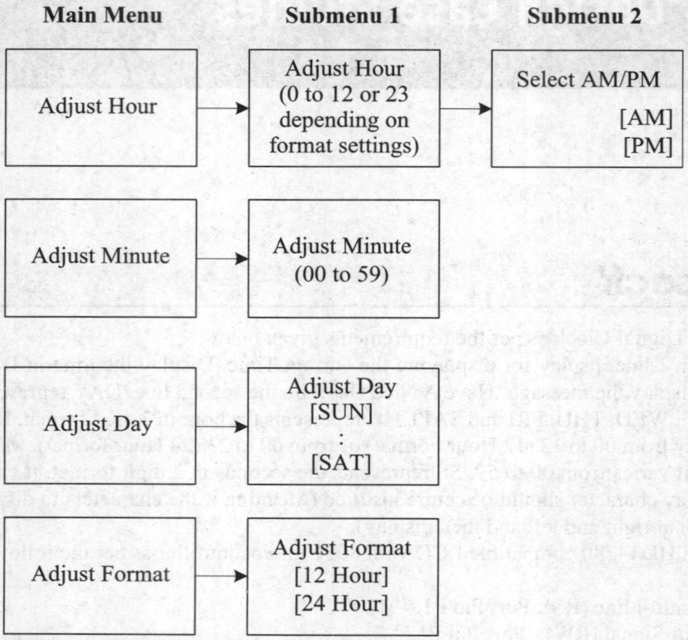

Fig. A2.1 **Menu implementation for Digital Clock**

Solution:

The HD44780 standard for LCD defines a unique set of control signals, data bus and command set for Alpha numeric Liquid Crystal Display (LCD) units. This makes the interfacing and controlling of Alpha numeric LCD unit built using the Display Controller Hitachi 44780, independent of the LCD manufacturer. As per the HD44780 standard, the LCD contains 3 controlling signal and a 4 bit/8bit data bus. The 4 bit/8 bit mode of operation is configurable. The Display modules come in different varieties like single line 8 character, single line 16 character, 2 line 8 character, 2 line 16 character, etc. The Pin details for an HD44780 compatible, 2 line 16-character LCD module (ODM16112) from ORIOLE Electronics (www.orioleindia.com) is given in Fig. A2.2.

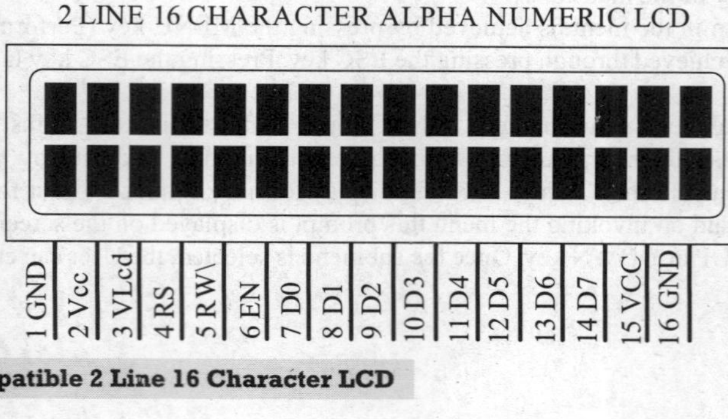

Fig. A2.2 **HD44780 Compatible 2 Line 16 Character LCD**

The LCD module contains interface pins for power supply, backlight control, LCD control and data lines. They are explained below.

Power Supply and Backlight Control Interface

The Power supply and Backlight control interface for the LCD module is tabulated below.

Pin No#	Pin Name*	Description
1	GND	Power Supply Ground Pin for LCD module
2	V_{cc}	Power Supply + ve for LCD module
3	VLcd	The Power supply for Liquid crystal units. Usually it is connected through a variable resistor and it should be adjusted for adjusting the brightness of display characters on the LCD
15*	VCC	Backlight +ve supply. Power supply for backlight LED
16*	GND	Backlight –ve supply. Power supply for backlight LED

Control and Data Interface

The LCD unit can accept either 4bit data or 8bit data. The data bit width can be set programmatically. There are three control signals associated with controlling the data/control command exchange with LCD. The control and data bus signal details are tabulated below.

Pin No#	Pin Name	Description
		Data Interface
7	D0	Data line 0
8	D1	Data line 1
9	D2	Data line 2
10	D3	Data line 3
11	D4	Data line 4
12	D5	Data line 5
13	D6	Data line 6
14	D7	Data line 7
		Control Interface
4	RS	RS = 0 Selects Command Register RS = 1 Selects Data Register
5	RW	RW = 0 Enables Data/Command Write RW = 1 Enables Data/Command Register Read
6	EN	Enable Signal. Signal for latching the data present on the data bus to the LCD unit. This signal is active falling edge triggered (1 to 0 transition is required for asserting this signal)

The HD44780 display controller contains an Instruction register and a data register for holding the commands and the data respectively to the controller. The commands and data to the controller is sent through the same data bus interface. The RS control signal interface is asserted accordingly and the RW signal is asserted low to inform the controller that the incoming data is command data or display data. For reading from the controller, the RW signal is asserted high and the RS signal is asserted low or high according to the requirement (RS = 0 for reading the command register. RS = 1 for reading from the data register).

* It may vary depending on the LCD module manufacturer.

The command register holds the different commands sent by the host controller (8051) CPU to control the various options of the LCD. We will discuss the various control commands at a later section. For displaying a character on the LCD, the ASCII value of the character (For example 30H for displaying 0) is written to the data port of LCD. The LCD module contains two types of memory; namely; Display Data RAM (DDR) and Character Generator RAM. Display Data RAM is the memory which holds the ASCII value of the characters written to the LCD. The display data RAM size for the ODM16112 module is 80 characters. Each Crystal cell in the LCD module is mapped to the DDRAM location. The first 40 DDRAM address locations (00H to 27H) are mapped for the crystal cells corresponding to the first line. The next 40 DDRAM memory locations are mapped to the crystal cells for the second line and the address range for these DDRAM is from 40H to 67H.

The Character Generator RAM (CGRAM) is used for generating and storing user generated character patterns. Readers are requested to go through the LCD module manual for generating and storing user generated character pattern.

The various parameters for configuring and controlling the LCD is sent as commands to the Instruction register of the LCD. These parameters include, the interface length setting (4 or 8 bit interface), Display Data Address Selection, LCD cursor movement, Clear the LCD, display character scrolling, etc. For more details on the supported command set for the LCD module, refer to the LCD manual. The common commands supported for executing the commands for an HD44780 standard LCD module is listed below.

D7	D6	D5	D4	D3	D2	D1	D0	Command Description
0	0	1	DL	N	F	X	X	Function Set DL = 1 8Bit Interface; 0 = 4bit N = 0 :1- Line Display; 0 = 2Line F = 1: 5*10 Dots; = 0 : 5*7 Dots
0	0	0	0	0	0	0	1	Clear Display
0	0	0	0	0	0	1	X*	Move Cursor to Home Position
0	0	0	0	1	D	C	B	Display ON/OFF and Cursor ON/OFF/Blink D = 1 Display ON; 0 – OFF C = 1 Cursor ON; 0 – OFF B =1 Cursor Blink; 0 – Non blink
0	0	0	0	0	1	ID	S	Entry Mode Set ID = 1 Increment Cursor after writing a character S = 1 Shift Display on writing a character; 0 No shift
1	A6	A5	A4	A3	A2	A1	A0	DDRAM Address select A0 to A6 Address bits
BF	X	X	X	X	X	X	X	Check Busy Flag. BF represents the busy flag bit read from LCD

For all the commands listed above, except the Busy flag check, the RS signal is 0 (RS = 0 Command Register Selection) and RW signal is 0 (RW = 0 Write to LCD).

For the Busy Flag check instruction, the RS signal is 0 and RW signal is 1 (Read Operation). The busy flag gives an indication of whether the system is busy in processing a command. The busy flag (BF) should be checked before writing a command to the LCD.

For proper operation of the LCD, it should be initialised properly as per the initialisation sequence listed in the LCD manual. The LCD undergoes an internal power on initialisation following the application of VCC to the LCD module. During this period the LCD will not accept any external commands. The Initialisation sequence for a standard HD44780 display is illustrated in Fig. A2.3.

Please refer to the datasheet of the LCD module for exact details on the initialisation routine.

Now let us have a look at the matrix keyboard. You can either buy a ready to use 2 × 2 matrix keyboard or can build own 2 × 2 matrix keyboard using 4 push button switches. The arrangement of push buttons and the interfacing of the matrix keyboard is shown in Fig. A2.4.

In a matrix keyboard, the keys are arranged in matrix fashion (i.e. they are connected in a row and column style). For detecting a keypress, the keyboard uses the scanning technique, where each row of the matrix is pulled low and the col-

* Don't Care. It can be either 0 or 1

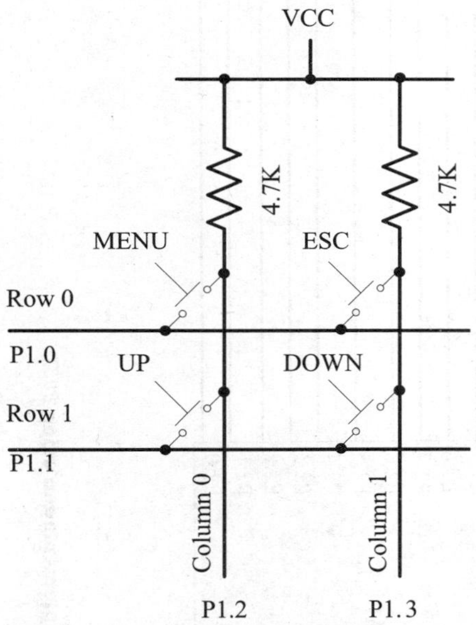

Fig. A2.4 **Interfacing of 2 × 2 matrix keyboard with *8051* Port P1**

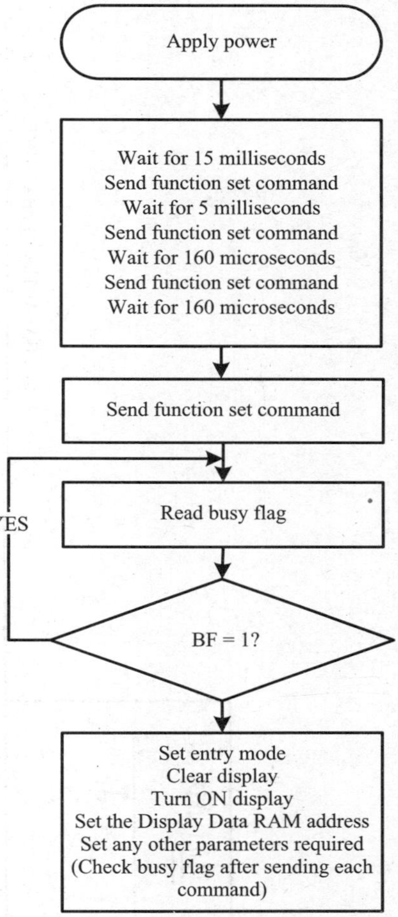

Fig. A2.3 **Flow chart illustrating initialisation of HD44780 Compatible LCD**

umns are read. After reading the status of each columns corresponding to a row, the row is pulled high and the next row is pulled low one by one and the status of the columns are read. This process is repeated until the scanning for all rows are completed. When a row is pulled low and if a key connected to the row is pressed, reading the column to which the key is connected will give logic 0. Since keys are mechanical devices, there is a possibility for debounce issues, which may give multiple key press effect for a single keypress. To prevent this, a proper key debouncing technique should be applied. Hardware keydebouncer circuits and software keydebounce techniques are the keydebouncing techniques available. The software keydebouncing technique doesn't require any additional hardware and is easy to implement. In the software debouncing technique, on detecting a keypress, the key is read again after a debounce delay. If the keypress is a genuine one, the state of the key will remain as 'pressed' on the second read also. Pull-up resistors are connected to the column lines to limit the current that flows to the row line on a keypress.

The necessary hardware interfacing and circuit diagram for implementing the digital clock is given in Fig. A2.5.

The next step is the design of the firmware for implementing the digital clock. Timer 0 is used for generating precise time generation. Timer 0 when configured in the 16bit timer mode can generate precise timing of 65536 (FFFFH +1) machine cycles. For a clock frequency of 12MHz, the time for 1 machine cycle is 1 microsecond. Timer 0 in 16bit Timer

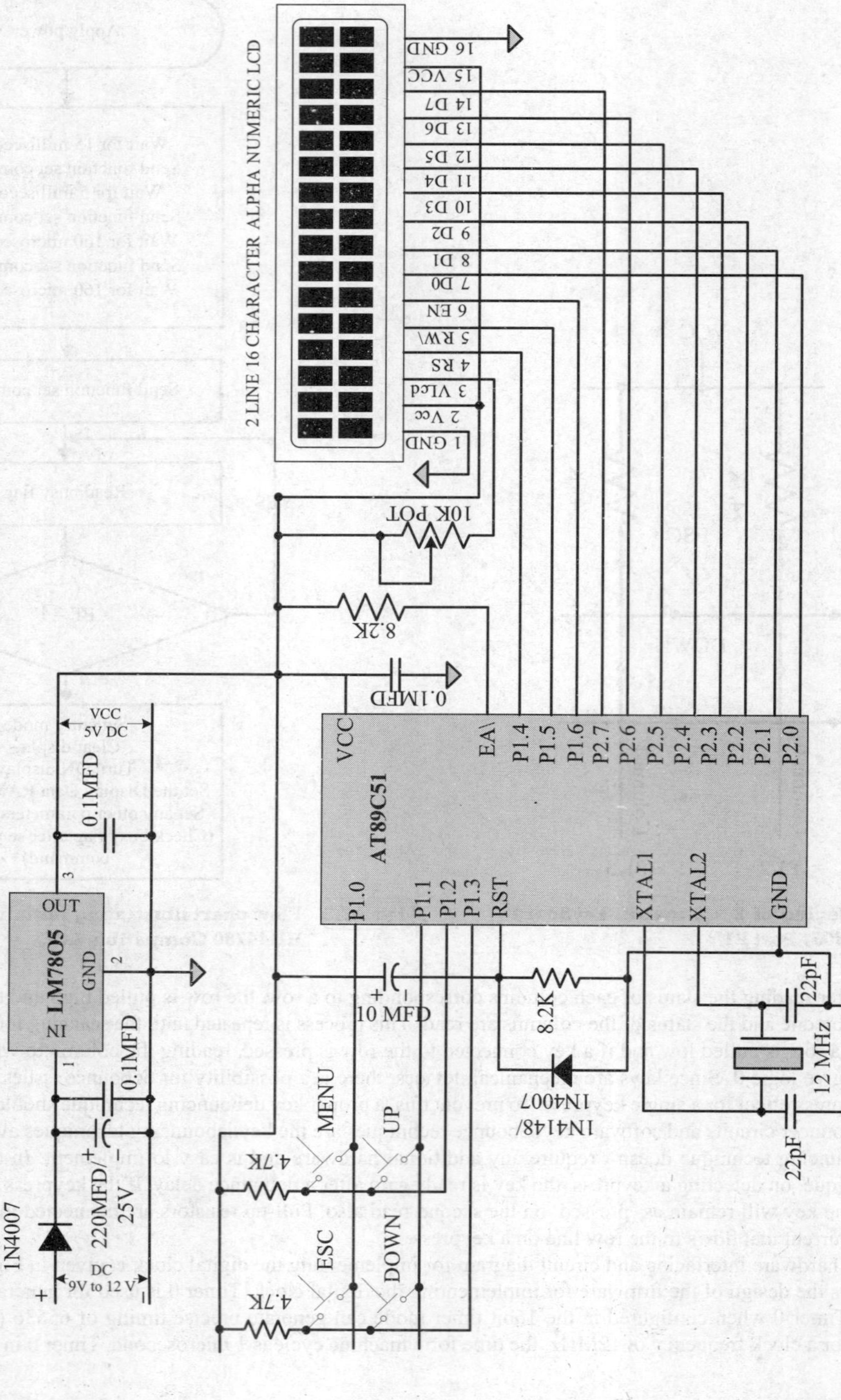

Fig. A2.5 **Circuit diagram for Digital Clock implementation using *8051***

mode, with a count loaded 00H, generates Timer Interrupt after 65536 machine cycles (i.e. after 65536 microseconds = ~ 65 milliseconds). For generating a timing of 1 second, timer 0 can be loaded with a count for generating 50 milliseconds. A Timer multiplier counter can be used to generate 1 second timing. The Timer multiplier counter is incremented by one each time the timer 0 rolls over from FFFFH to 0000H. The seconds register is incremented each time when the Timer multiplier counter becomes 20. The minutes register is incremented each time when the 'seconds' register become 60. The hour register is incremented by one each time when the minutes register become 60. The hour is adjusted according to the hour format, i.e. hour is adjusted in the range 1 to 12 for 12 Hour format and 0 to 23 for 24 Hour format. For 24 hour format, the day register is incremented by one when the hour register rolls over from 23 to 0. For 12 hour time format the day register is incremented by one when the hour register rolls over from 12 to 1 and the time format changes from PM to AM.

Two sets of registers or memory locations for hour, minute, seconds, day, time format and AM/PM selection is used. The first set of registers is the real registers for representing the time. These registers are modified inside the Timer 0 interrupt in accordance with the seconds, minute, hour, day and AM/PM change. The register details are given below.

R7: Seconds Register
R6: Minute Register
R5: Hour Register
R4: Day Register
Bit 0: Format Register (only 1 bit is required since format falls into either of (12/24)
Bit 1: AM/PM Register (only 1 bit is required since the time falls into either AM/PM
(The memory location 20H is the physical storage location for bits with address 00H and 01H)

The second set of registers is used within the menu to adjust these values as and when the user changes it through menu. Here data memory locations are used for holding the variables. The details of the memory variables are given below.

30H: Seconds Register
31H: Minute Register
32H: Hour Register
33H: Day Register
Bit 2: Format Register (only 1 bit is required since format falls into either of (12/24)
Bit 3: AM/PM Register (only 1 bit is required since the time falls into either AM/PM
(The memory location 20H is the physical storage location for bits with address 02H and 03H)

The LCD needs to be updated only when there is a change in time or when the user exits from the menu. This is indicated by setting a flag. The flag name is time_changed and it is a bit variable with bit address 04H. The flow chart given in Fig. A2.6 below models the firmware requirements for building the Digital Clock.

The detection of keypress and the triggering of corresponding action are performed by the 'Key Handler' function implementation. The key handler scans the rows and columns of the keyboard and identifies which key is pressed. On detecting a keypress the actions corresponding to that key is invoked by the 'Key Handler' function. The keybouncing is implemented using a 20 milliseconds delay. If a key is found closed during a scan, the same key is read after 20 milliseconds to confirm it is a deliberate key closure. Hence a key should be held in pressed condition for at least 20 milliseconds to identify it as valid key closure input. Otherwise the key closure is considered as an accidental one and it is ignored. The flow chart given in Fig. A2.7 illustrates the implementation of the 'Key Handler'.

The 'Menu Key Handler' function implements the handling of the '*MENU*' key in different contexts. In the normal scenario, the '*MENU*' key is used for invoking the 'Main Menu'. Within the 'Menu', the '*MENU*' key functions as an '*ENTER*' key. The flow chart given in Fig. A2.8 illustrates the implementation of '*MENU*' key handling.

The 'Up Key Handler' function implements the handling of the '*UP*' key in different contexts. Inside the '*MENU*', this key is used for navigating between the menu items and setting the values for menu items. This key doesn't have a function when the user is not inside the '*MENU*', meaning, pressing this key will not produce any impact when the user hasn't invoked the '*MENU*'. The flow chart given in Fig. A2.9 illustrates the implementation of '*UP*' key handling.

The 'Down Key Handler' function implements the handling of the '*DOWN*' key in different contexts. Inside the '*MENU*', this key is used for navigating between the menu items and setting the values for menu items. This key doesn't have a function when the user is not inside the '*MENU*', meaning, pressing this key will not produce any impact when the user hasn't invoked the '*MENU*'. The flow chart given in Fig. A2.10 illustrates the implementation of '*DOWN*' key handling.

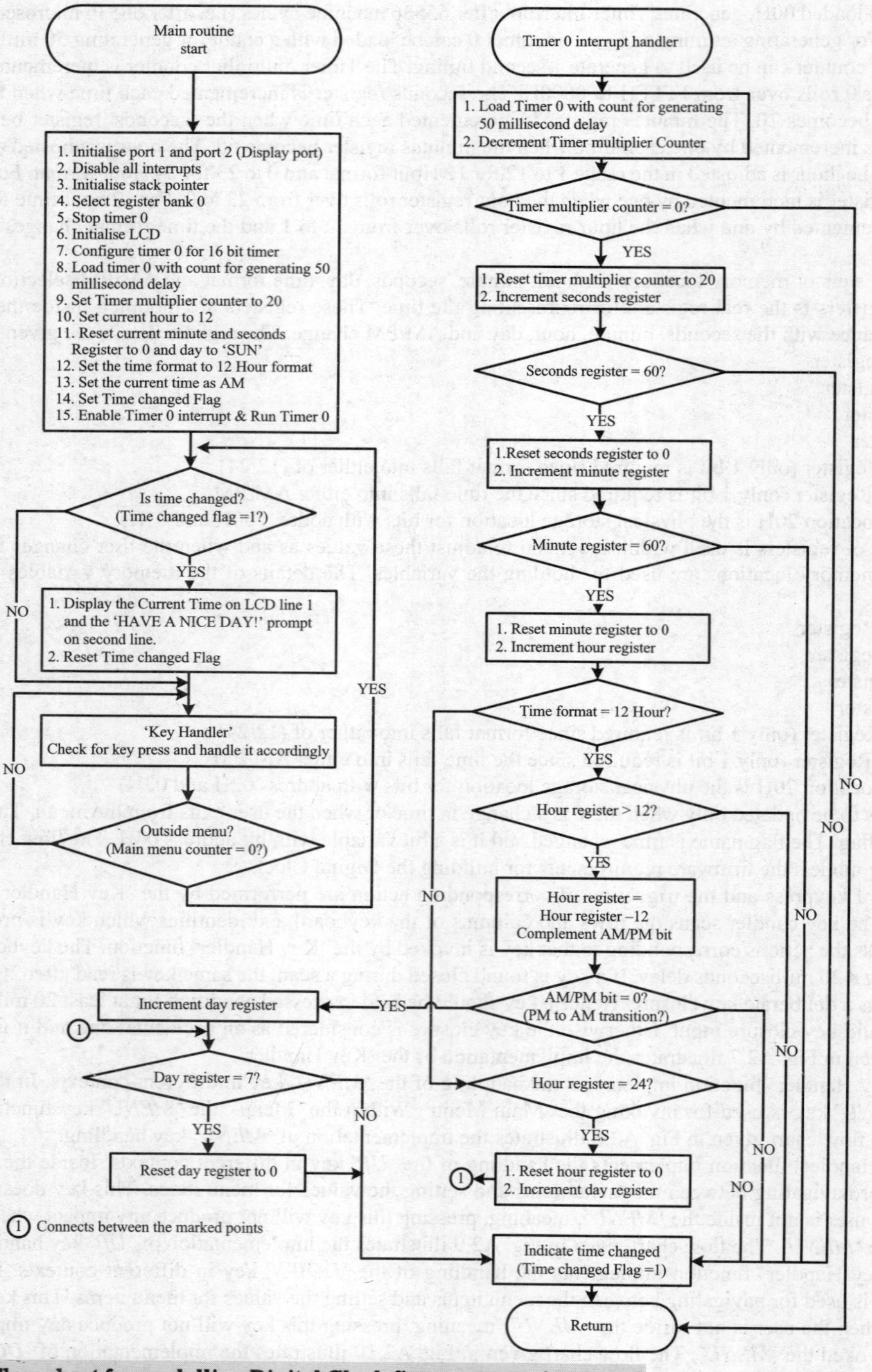

Fig. A2.6 Flow chart for modelling Digital Clock firmware requirements

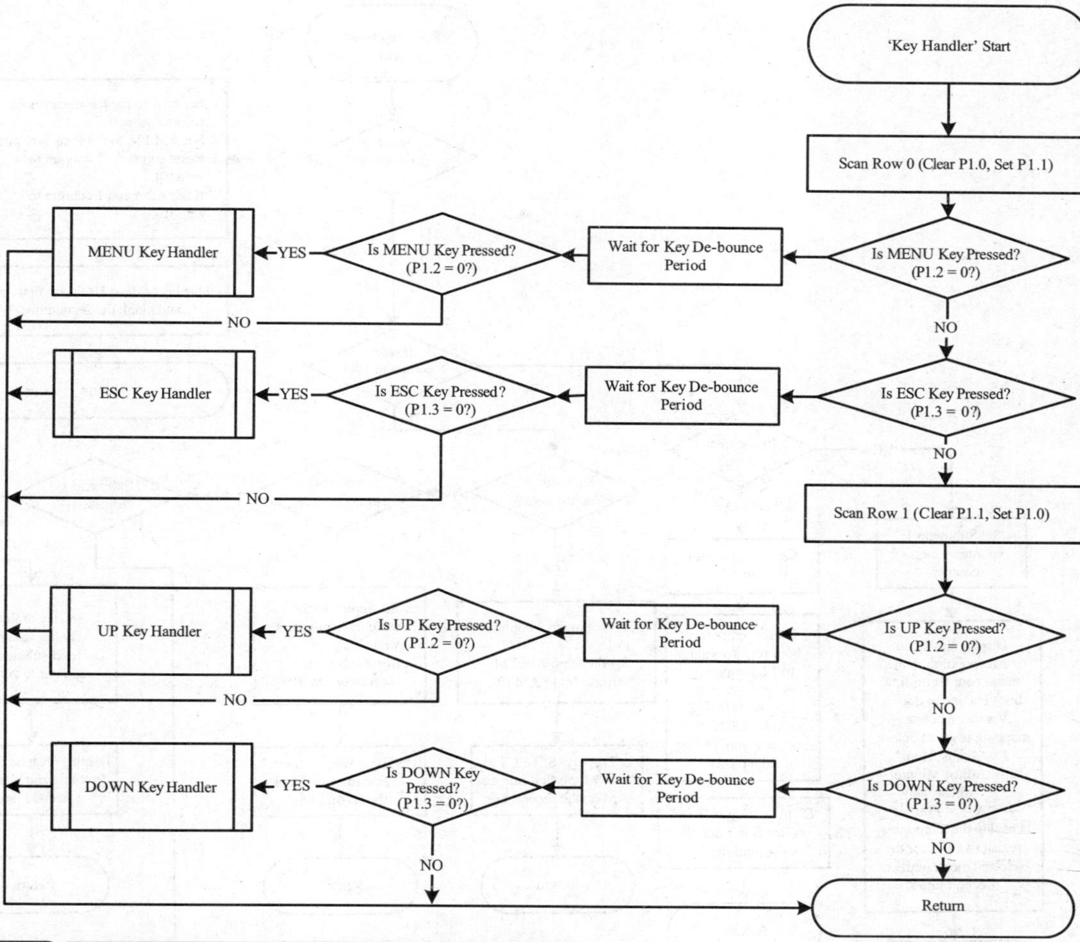

Fig. A2.7 **Flow chart for implementing Keypress handler**

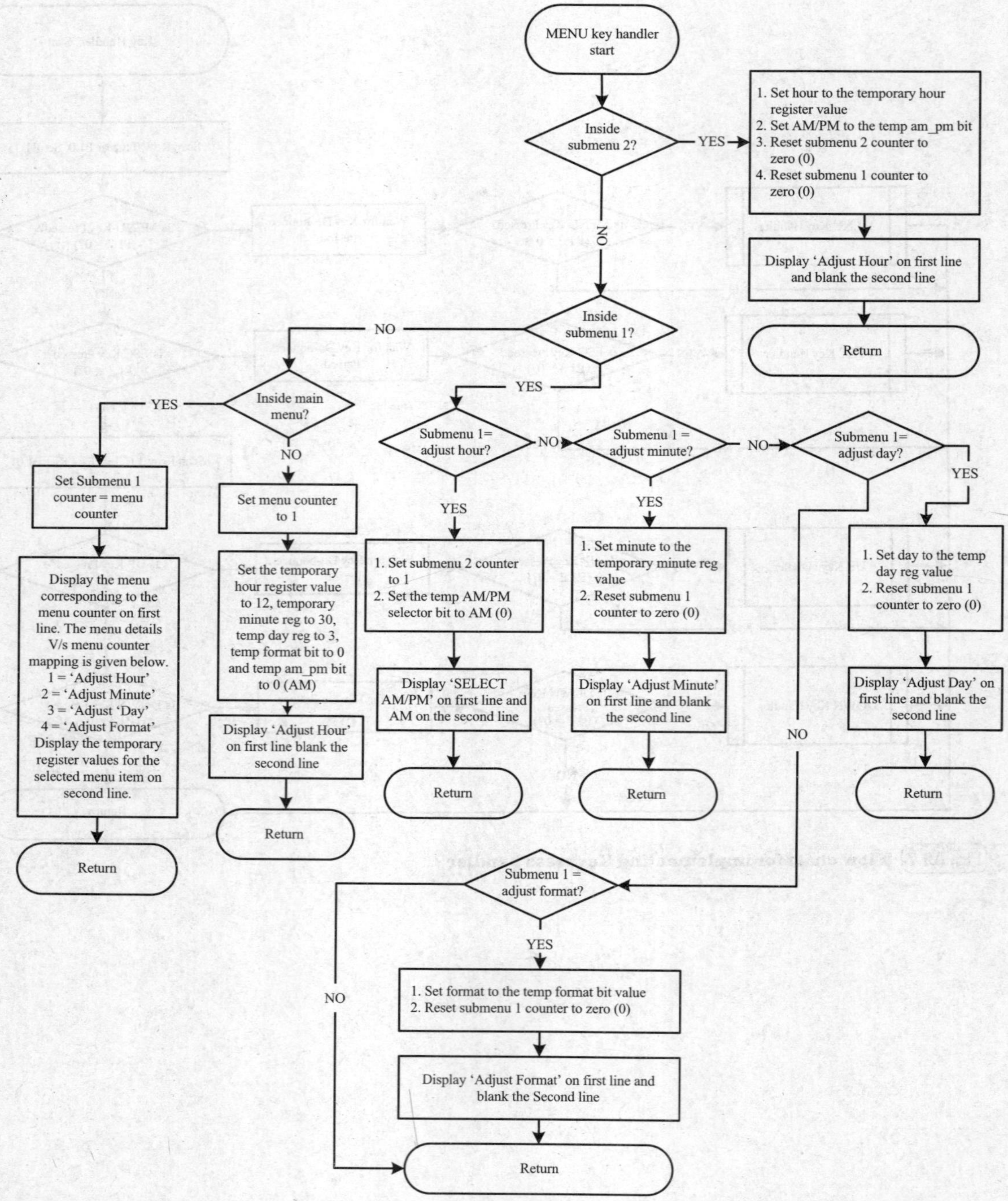

Fig. A2.8 **Flow chart for implementing 'MENU' Key handler**

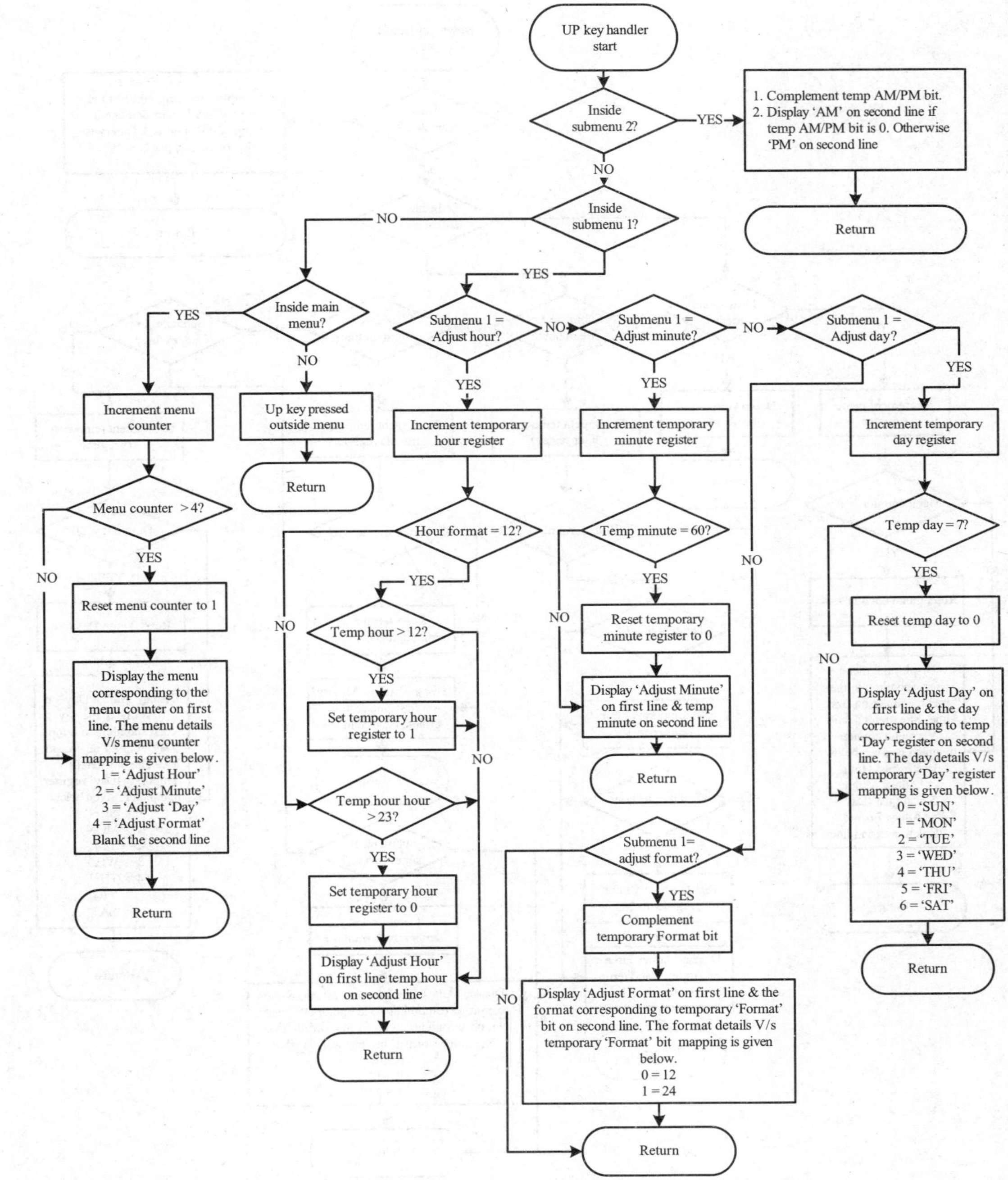

Fig. A2.9 **Flow chart for implementing 'UP' Key handler**

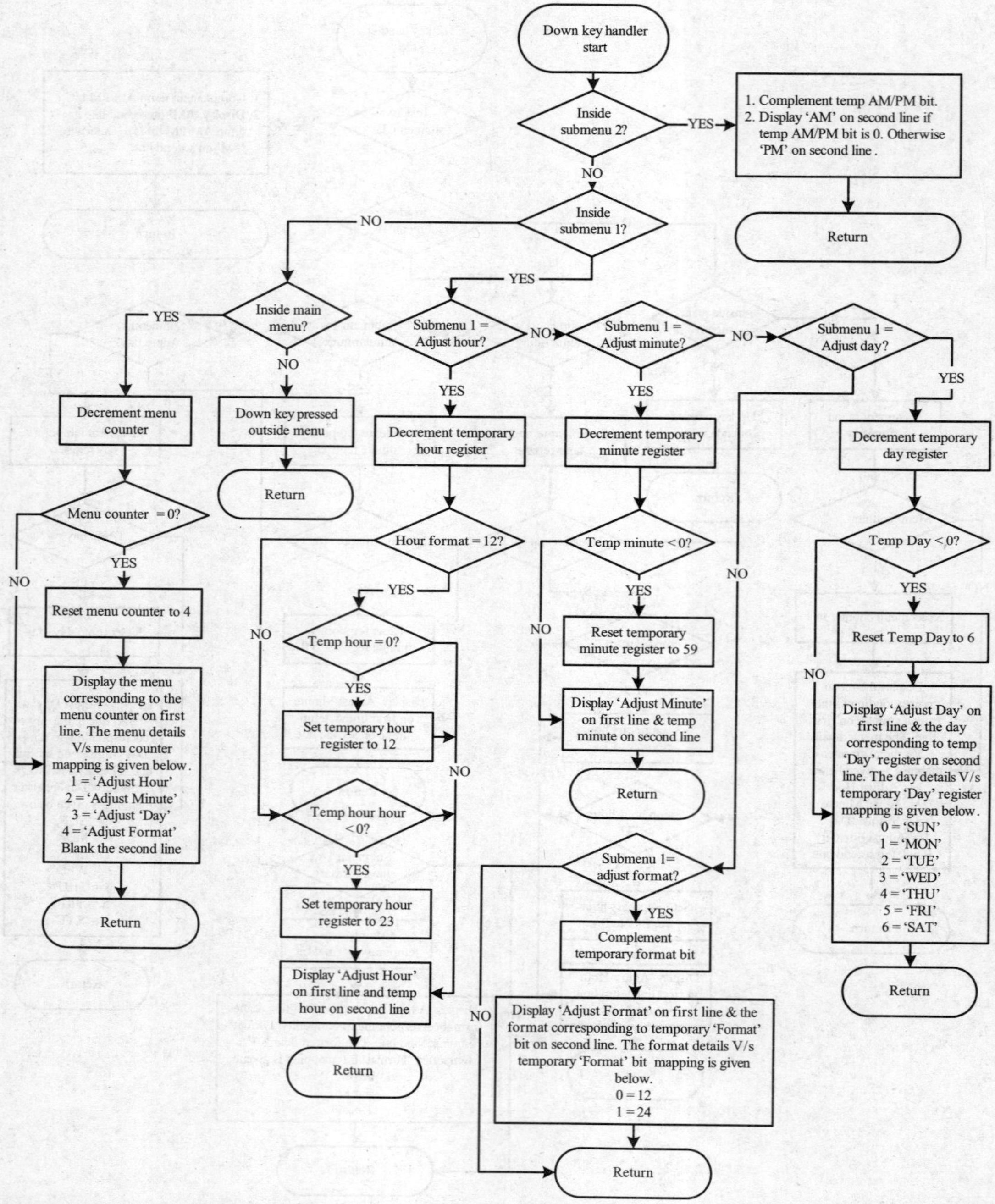

Fig. A2.10 **Flow chart for implementing 'DOWN' Key handler**

The 'ESC Key Handler' function implements the handling of the '*ESC*' key in different contexts. Inside the '*MENU*', this key is used for traversing to the previous menu and finally to come out of the '*MENU*'. This key doesn't have a function when the user is outside the '*MENU*', meaning, pressing this key will not produce any effect when the user hasn't invoked the '*MENU*'. The flow chart given in Fig. A2.11 illustrates the implementation of '*ESC*' key handling.

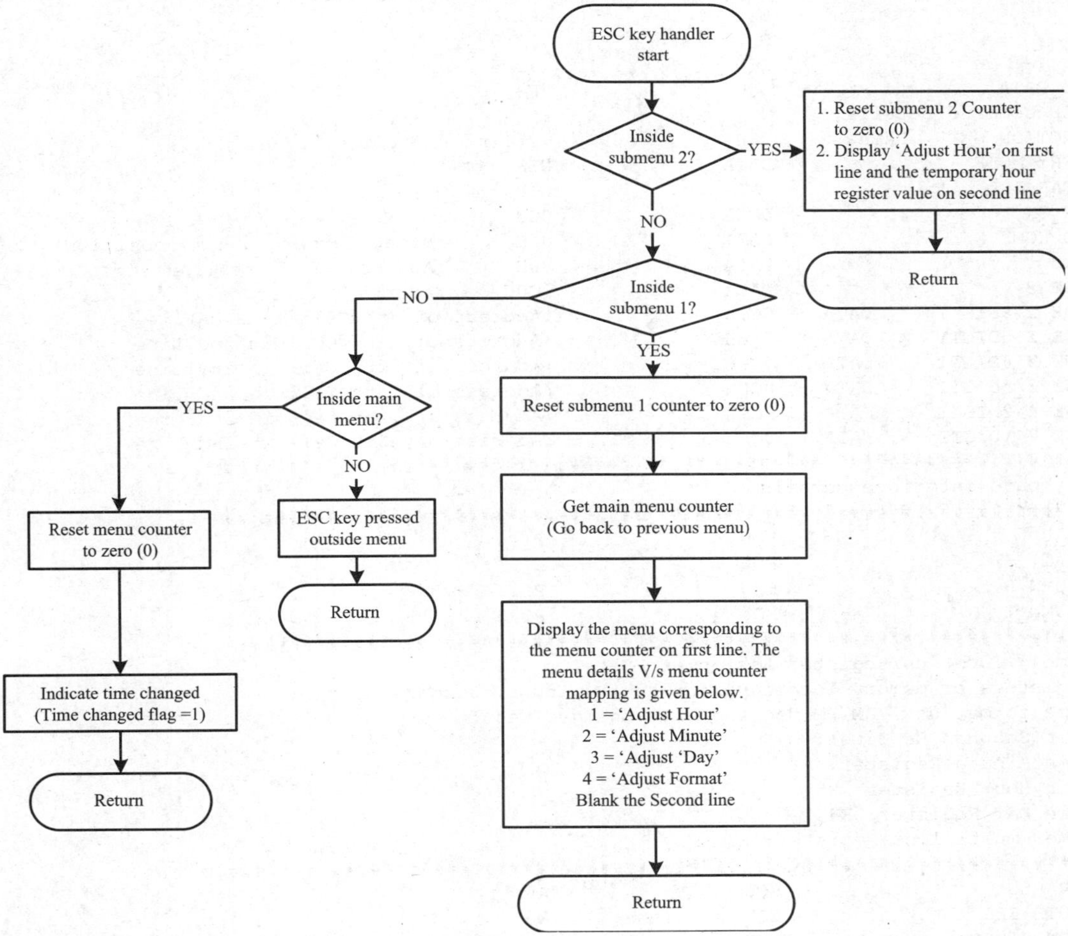

Fig. A2.11 **Flow chart for implementing 'ESC' Key handler**

Now comes the final part, implementation of the firmware requirements, which are modelled above, in Assembly Language. The firmware implementation is given below.

```
;####################################################################
;Digital_Clock.src
;Firmware for Displaying the Current Day and Time
;Written & assembled for A51 Assembler
;Written by Shibu K V. Copyright (C) 2008
;####################################################################
;LCD interface details
;Register Select RS connected to Port Pin P1.4
```

```
;Read/Write connected to Port Pin P1.5
;LCD Enable EN connected to Port Pin P1.6
;LCD Data bus connected to Port 2
;#####################################################################
RS                          EQU                 P1.4
RW                          EQU                 P1.5
EN                          EQU                 P1.6
LCD_DATA                    EQU                 P2
;LCD Command Details
FUNCTION_SET    DATA        38H                ;2 line 8 bit interface
ENTRY_MODE                  DATA               06H
CLEAR_LCD                   DATA               01H
LCD_ON                      DATA               0CH
LCD_HOME                    DATA               02H      ;Bring Cursor to home position
LINE_1                      DATA               80H      ;Address of First line start
LINE_2                      DATA               0C0H     ;Address of Second line start
LINE_2_9DIGIT       DATA    0C7H               ;Address of 7th Cell in 2nd Line
LINE_2_5DIGIT       DATA    0CBH               ;Address of 11th Cell in 2nd Line
LINE_2_4DIGIT       DATA    0CCH               ;Address of 12th Cell in 2nd Line
LINE_2_3DIGIT       DATA    0CDH               ;Address of 13th Cell in 2nd Line
LINE_2_2DIGIT       DATA    0CEH               ;Address of 14th Cell in 2nd Line
LINE_2_1DIGIT       DATA    0CFH               ;Address of 15th Cell in 2nd Line
;#####################################################################
;Keyboard interface details
;#####################################################################
ROW_0                       EQU                 P1.0
ROW_1                       EQU                 P1.1
COLUMN_0                    EQU                 P1.2
COLUMN_1                    EQU                 P1.3
;#####################################################################
;Memory location/Register Assignment Details
;Registers or memory locations for hour, minute, seconds, day,
;time format flag, AM/PM flag and Time changed flag
;Main Seconds Register: R7
;Main Minute Register: R6
;Main Hour Register: R5
;Main Day Register: R4
;Timer multiplier Register: R3
;#####################################################################
HOUR_REG                    EQU                 R5
MINUTE_REG                  EQU                 R6
SECONDS_REG                 EQU                 R7
DAY_REG                     EQU                 R4
TEMP_SECONDS                EQU                 30H
TEMP_MINUTE                 EQU                 31H
TEMP_HOUR                   EQU                 32H
TEMP_DAY                    EQU                 33H
SBIT        FORMAT                    = 00H
SBIT        AM_PM                     = 01H
SBIT        TEMP_FORMAT               = 02H
SBIT        TEMP_AM_PM                = 03H
SBIT        TIME_CHANGED              = 04H
;The memory locations for Holding the information on
;which all menus are traversed
MAIN_MENU_COUNTER                   EQU                 35H
SUBMENU1_COUNTER                    EQU                 36H
```

```
SUBMENU2_COUNTER                  EQU             37H
;##################################################################
ORG 0000H                         ;Reset vector
            JMP 0050H             ;Jump to code mem location 0100H to
                                  ;start of execution
ORG 0003H                         ; External Interrupt 0 ISR location
            RETI                  ; Simply return. Do nothing
ORG 000BH                         ; Timer 0 Interrupt ISR location
            ;The ISR will not fit in 8 bytes. Make it a
            ;subroutine and Call the routine.
            CALL TIMER0_INTERRUPT
            RETI        ; Return
ORG 0013H                         ; External Interrupt 1 ISR location
            RETI                  ; Simply return. Do nothing
ORG 001BH                         ; Timer 1 Interrupt ISR location
            RETI                  ; Simply return. Do nothing
ORG 0023H                         ; Serial Interrupt ISR location
            RETI                  ; Simply return. Do nothing
;##################################################################
; Start of main Program
ORG 0050H   MOV P1, #0FFH         ; Initialise Port 1
            MOV P2, #0FFH         ; Initialise Port 1
            CLR     EA            ; Disable All interrupts
            MOV SP, #50H          ; Set stack at memory location 50H
            CLR RS0               ; Select Register Bank 0
            CLR RS1               ; "
            CLR TR0               ; Stop Timer 0
            CALL INITIALISE_LCD
        ; Configure Timer 0 as Timer in mode 1 (16 bit Timer)
            MOV TMOD, #00000001b
            MOV TL0, #0B4H
            MOV TH0, #3CH
        ; The multiplier for the time delay generated by Timer
            MOV R3, #20
            CLR A
        ;Current Day, Time, Hour Format and AM/PM Initialisation
            MOV HOUR_REG,#12             ; Set Current Hour to 12
            MOV MINUTE_REG, A            ; Set Current Minutes to 0
            MOV SECONDS_REG, A           ; Set Current Seconds to 0
            MOV DAY_REG, A               ; Set Current Day to SUNDAY
            CLR FORMAT ; Set the time format to 12 Hour format
            CLR AM_PM      ; Set the current time as AM
            MOV IE, #10000010b; Enable only Timer 0 interrupt
            SETB TR0       ; Start Timer 0
            SETB TIME_CHANGED            ;Set Time changed Flag to-
                           ;refresh LCD
CHECK_UPDATE:JNB TIME_CHANGED,SKIP_REFRESH
            CALL DISPLAY_TIME
            CLR TIME_CHANGED
SKIP_REFRESH:CALL KEY_HANDLER
            ;Check whether inside menu. If yes loop till exit
            MOV A,MAIN_MENU_COUNTER
            CJNE A,#00H,SKIP_REFRESH
            JMP CHECK_UPDATE
;##################################################################
; SUBROUTUINE FOR DISPLAYING TIME
```

```
; Displays Time in "  DAY HH:MM:SS  " on First line and
; "HAVE A NICE DAY!" on second line
; Input: DAY_REG, HOUR_REG, MINUTE_REG, SECONDS_REG, DPTR Register
; Output: None
;####################################################################
DISPLAY_TIME:     MOV A,#LINE_1
                  CALL SEND_COMMAND
                  MOV DPTR,#TEXT_2BLANK
                  CALL DISPLAY_STRING
                  ;Pass the DAY_REG Value through Accumulator
                  ;Retrieve the String value for DAY corresponding-
                  ;to the DAY index passed
                  MOV A,DAY_REG
                  CALL GET_DAY_STRING
                  ;Adjust DAY_REG If it holds an invalid value (>6)
                  ;The GET_DAY_STRING Loads Accumulator with 0, if
                  ;DAY_REG > 6
                  MOV DAY_REG,A
                  CALL DISPLAY_STRING
                  MOV A, #' '
                  CALL DISPLAY_CHAR
                  MOV A,HOUR_REG
                  CALL DISPLAY_NUMBER
                  MOV A,#':'
                  CALL DISPLAY_CHAR
                  MOV A,MINUTE_REG
                  CALL DISPLAY_NUMBER
                  MOV A,#':'
                  CALL DISPLAY_CHAR
                  MOV A,SECONDS_REG
                  CALL DISPLAY_NUMBER
                  MOV DPTR,#TEXT_2BLANK
                  CALL DISPLAY_STRING
                  MOV A,#LINE_2
                  CALL SEND_COMMAND
                  MOV DPTR,#TEXT_NICEDAY
                  CALL DISPLAY_STRING
                  RET
;####################################################################
; Key Handler
; Handles the key press.
; Implements the Row-wise scanning of Keyboard with keydebouncing.
; Input: None
; Output: None
;####################################################################
KEY_HANDLER:   SETB COLUMN_0         ;Configure Column 0 Pin as input pin
                  SETB COLUMN_1      ;Configure Column 1 Pin as input pin
                  CLR ROW_0          ;Scan Row 0
                  SETB ROW_1
                  JB COLUMN_0, CHECK_R0C1
                  ;Menu key press detected
                  ;Wait for keydebounce time, 20 milliseconds
                  MOV R0, #20
                  CALL MILLISECOND_DELAY
                  JB COLUMN_0, INVALID_PRESS
                  ;Menu Key press is valid
```

```
                ;Call menu handler Routine
                CALL MENU_KEY_HANDLER
                RET
CHECK_R0C1: JB COLUMN_1, SCAN_ROW1
                ;ESC key press detected
                ;Wait for keydebounce time, 20 milliseconds
                MOV R0, #20
                CALL MILLISECOND_DELAY
                JB COLUMN_1, INVALID_PRESS
                ;ESC Key press is valid
                ;Call ESC Key handler Routine
                CALL ESC_KEY_HANDLER
                RET
SCAN_ROW1:  CLR ROW_1                    ;Scan Row 1
                SETB ROW_0
                JB COLUMN_0, CHECK_R1C1
                ;UP key press detected
                ;Wait for keydebounce time, 20 milliseconds
                MOV R0, #20
                CALL MILLISECOND_DELAY
                JB COLUMN_0, INVALID_PRESS
                ;UP Key press is valid
                ;Call UP Key handler Routine
                CALL UP_KEY_HANDLER
                RET
CHECK_R1C1: JB COLUMN_1, INVALID_PRESS
                ;DOWN key press detected
                ;Wait for keydebounce time, 20 milliseconds
                MOV R0, #20
                CALL MILLISECOND_DELAY
                JB COLUMN_1, INVALID_PRESS
                ;DOWN Key press is valid
                ;Call DOWN handler Routine
                CALL DOWN_KEY_HANDLER
INVALID_PRESS:  RET
;######################################################################
;MENU KEY HANDLER
;Handles the MENU Key press in Main menu, Submenu 1 and Submenu 2
;Inputs: SUBMENU2_COUNTER, SUBMENU1_COUNTER, MAIN_MENU_COUNTER
;Output: None
;######################################################################
MENU_KEY_HANDLER:MOV A,SUBMENU2_COUNTER
                  ;Check whether inside Submenu 2
                  CJNE A,#00H, INSIDE_SUBMENU2
                  JMP      CHECK_SUBMENU1
                  ;Inside Submenu 2
                  ;Set Hour to the temporary hour register value
INSIDE_SUBMENU2:MOV HOUR_REG, TEMP_HOUR
                  ;Set AM/PM to the temp am_pm bit
                  MOV C,TEMP_AM_PM
                  MOV AM_PM, C
                  ;Reset Submenu 2 Counter to zero
                  CLR A
                  MOV SUBMENU2_COUNTER, A
                  ;Reset Submenu 1 Counter to zero
                  MOV SUBMENU1_COUNTER, A
```

```
                  ;Display 'Adjust Hour' on First Line and
                  ;blank the Second line
                  CALL DISPLAY_HOUR_BL
                  RET
CHECK_SUBMENU1:   MOV A,SUBMENU1_COUNTER
                  ;Check whether inside Submenu 1
                  CJNE A,#00H, INSIDE_SUBMENU1
                  ;Not inside Submenu 1
                  ;Check whether inside Main Menu
                  JMP CHECK_MAINMENU
                  ;Inside Submenu 1
INSIDE_SUBMENU1: CJNE A,#01H, ADJUST_MINUTE
                  ;Enter from Submenu 1
                  ;Indicate inside Submenu 2
                  MOV SUBMENU2_COUNTER, A
                  MOV A,#LINE_1
                  CALL SEND_COMMAND
                  MOV DPTR,#TEXT_AMPM
                  CALL DISPLAY_STRING
                  ;Default AM/PM to AM
                  ;For AM the bit should be reset. The TEMP_AM_PM bit
                  ;is complemented inside DISPLAY_AMPM
                  SETB TEMP_AM_PM
                  ;Display the AM/PM on second Line
                  CALL DISPLAY_AMPM
                  RET
                  ;Reset Submenu 1 Counter to zero
ADJUST_MINUTE: MOV SUBMENU1_COUNTER, #00H
                  CJNE A,#02H, ADJUST_DAY
                  ;Set Minute to the temporary hour register value
                  MOV MINUTE_REG, TEMP_MINUTE
                  ;Display 'Adjust Minute' on First Line
                  ;Blank the second line of LCD
                  CALL DISPLAY_MINUTE_BL
                  RET
ADJUST_DAY:    CJNE A,#03H, ADJUST_FORMAT
                  ;Set Day to the temporary Day register value
                  MOV DAY_REG, TEMP_DAY
                  ;Display 'Adjust Day' on First Line
                  ;Blank the second line of LCD
                  CALL DISPLAY_DAY_BL
                  RET
ADJUST_FORMAT:    CJNE A,#04H, SUBMENU1_INVALID
                  ;Set FORMAT to the temp format bit
                  MOV C,TEMP_FORMAT
                  MOV FORMAT, C
                  ;Display 'Adjust Format' on First Line
                  ;Blank the second line of LCD
                  CALL DISPLAY_FORMAT_BL
SUBMENU1_INVALID:RET
CHECK_MAINMENU:   MOV A,MAIN_MENU_COUNTER
                  CJNE A,#00H, INSIDE_MAINMENU
                  ;Outside Mainmenu
                  MOV MAIN_MENU_COUNTER, #1
                  ;Set Temp Hour Reg to 12
                  MOV TEMP_HOUR, #12
```

```
                ;Set Temp Minute Reg to 30
                MOV TEMP_MINUTE, #30
                ;Set Temp Day Reg to WED (3)
                MOV TEMP_DAY, #3
                ;Set Temp AM_PM to AM
                ;The common Subroutine DISPLAY_AMPM complements-
                ;this bit. Hence take the inverse logic
                SETB TEMP_AM_PM
                ;Set Temp FORMAT to 12
                CLR TEMP_FORMAT
                ;Display 'Adjust Hour' on First Line and
                ;blank the Second line
                CALL DISPLAY_HOUR_BL
                RET
INSIDE_MAINMENU:MOV SUBMENU1_COUNTER,A
                CJNE A,#01H, INSIDE_MINUTE
                ;The Submenu 1 selected is hour
                ;Display the temp hour on second line
                MOV A,TEMP_HOUR
                CALL DISPLAY_HR_MT
                RET
INSIDE_MINUTE: CJNE A,#02H, INSIDE_DAY
                ;The Submenu 1 selected is Minute
                ;Display the temp minute on second line
                MOV A,TEMP_MINUTE
                CALL DISPLAY_HR_MT
                RET
INSIDE_DAY:    CJNE A,#03H, INSIDE_FORMAT
                ;The Submenu 1 selected is DAY
                ;Display the String for temp Day on second line
                MOV A, TEMP_DAY
                CALL GET_DAY_STRING
                ;Perform day correction if day passed is invalid
                MOV TEMP_DAY,A
                MOV A,#LINE_2_5DIGIT
                CALL SEND_COMMAND
                CALL DISPLAY_STRING
                RET
INSIDE_FORMAT: CJNE A,#04H, INVALID_MENU
                ;The Submenu 1 selected is Format
                ;Display the temp format on second line
                CALL DISPLAY_FORMAT
INVALID_MENU:  RET
;#####################################################################
;Subroutine for Displaying the hour/minute on the last 2 cells of
;the second line of LCD.
;The hour/minute value to be displayed on LCD is passed through-
;Accumulator Register A
;Input Variable: Accumulator
;Output Variable: None
;#####################################################################
DISPLAY_HR_MT: PUSH ACC
                MOV A,#LINE_2_2DIGIT
                CALL SEND_COMMAND
                POP ACC
                CALL DISPLAY_NUMBER
                RET
```

```
;##################################################################
;Subroutine for retrieving the DAY string corresponding to the day
;index passed. The Day index is passed through Accumulator
;Input Variable: Through Accumulator Register
;Output Variable: The start address of the corresponding string is-
;loaded in DPTR register.
;##################################################################
GET_DAY_STRING:     CJNE A, #0H, IS_MONDAY
                    MOV DPTR,#TEXT_SUN
                    RET
IS_MONDAY:          CJNE A, #1H, IS_TUESDAY
                    MOV DPTR,#TEXT_MON
                    RET
IS_TUESDAY:         CJNE A, #2H, IS_WEDNESDAY
                    MOV DPTR,#TEXT_TUE
                    RET
IS_WEDNESDAY:       CJNE A, #3H, IS_THURSDAY
                    MOV DPTR,#TEXT_WED
                    RET
IS_THURSDAY:        CJNE A, #4H, IS_FRIDAY
                    MOV DPTR,#TEXT_THU
                    RET
IS_FRIDAY:          CJNE A, #5H, IS_SATURDAY
                    MOV DPTR,#TEXT_FRI
                    RET
IS_SATURDAY:        CJNE A, #6H, INVALID_DAY
                    MOV DPTR,#TEXT_SAT
                    RET
INVALID_DAY:        MOV A, #00H
                    MOV DPTR,#TEXT_SUN
                    RET
;##################################################################
;Subroutine for Displaying the Time Format on the last 9 cells of
;the second line of LCD. The bit corresponding to the Format string-
;to be displayed on LCD is passed through TEMP_FORMAT bit
;Input Variable: TEMP_FORMAT bit
;Output Variable: None
;##################################################################
DISPLAY_FORMAT:     JB TEMP_FORMAT, NXT_HOUR_FORMAT
                    MOV DPTR,#TEXT_12HR
                    JMP DISP_HOUR_FORMAT
NXT_HOUR_FORMAT:    MOV DPTR,#TEXT_24HR
DISP_HOUR_FORMAT:   MOV A,#LINE_2_9DIGIT
                    CALL SEND_COMMAND
                    CALL DISPLAY_STRING
                    RET
;##################################################################
;Subroutine for Displaying AM/PM on the last 4 cells of the second-
;line of LCD. The bit corresponding to the AM/PM string to be-
;displayed on LCD is passed through TEMP_AM_PM bit. This bit is-
;complemented first. This helps in calling this subroutine for-
;handling both UP/DOWN key in Submenu 2 (for AM_PM Adjust)
;Input Variable: TEMP_AM_PM bit
;Output Variable: None
;##################################################################
```

```
DISPLAY_AMPM:  CPL TEMP_AM_PM
               JB TEMP_AM_PM, AFTERNOON_TIME
               ;The TEMP_AM_PM is in reset state
               ;The time is morning. Display AM on second line
               MOV DPTR,#TEXT_AM
               JMP DISPLAY_AM_PM
               ;The TEMP_AM_PM is in set state
               ;The time is Afternoon. Display PM on second line
AFTERNOON_TIME:     MOV DPTR,#TEXT_PM
DISPLAY_AM_PM: MOV A,#LINE_2_4DIGIT
               CALL SEND_COMMAND
               CALL DISPLAY_STRING
               RET
;####################################################################
; ESC KEY HANDLER
;Handles the ESC Key press in Main menu, Submenu 1 and Submenu 2
;Inputs: SUBMENU2_COUNTER, SUBMENU1_COUNTER, MAIN_MENU_COUNTER
;Output: None
;####################################################################
ESC_KEY_HANDLER:    MOV A,SUBMENU2_COUNTER
                    ;Check whether inside Submenu 2
                    CJNE A,#00H, ESC_IN_SUBMENU2
                    ;Not inside Submenu 2
                    ;Check whether inside Submenu 1
                    JMP ESC_CHECK_SUBMENU1
                    ;Inside Submenu 2
                    ;Go back to the previous menu
ESC_IN_SUBMENU2:    ;Reset Submenu 2 Counter to zero
                    CLR A
                    MOV SUBMENU2_COUNTER, A
                    ;Display 'Adjust Hour' on First Line
                    MOV A,#LINE_1
                    CALL SEND_COMMAND
                    MOV DPTR,#TEXT_HOUR
                    CALL DISPLAY_STRING
                    ;Blank the second line
                    MOV A,#LINE_2
                    CALL SEND_COMMAND
                    MOV DPTR,#TEXT_LCD_BLANK
                    CALL DISPLAY_STRING
                    ;Display current temporary hour on the Second line
                MOV A,TEMP_HOUR
                    CALL DISPLAY_HR_MT
                    RET
ESC_CHECK_SUBMENU1: MOV A,SUBMENU1_COUNTER
                    ;Check whether inside Submenu 1
                    CJNE A,#00H, ESC_IN_SUBMENU1
                    ;Not inside Submenu 1
                    ;Check whether inside Main Menu
                    JMP ESC_CHECK_MAINMENU
                    ;Inside Submenu 1
                    ;Reset Submenu 1 Counter to zero
ESC_IN_SUBMENU1:    MOV SUBMENU1_COUNTER, #00H
                    ;ESC pressed inside submenu 1
                    ;Call the common subroutine for handling ESC key
                    ;inside submenu 1 and UP/DOWN key in main menu
```

```
                    CALL MAIN_SM1_CMNHLR
                    RET
ESC_CHECK_MAINMENU: MOV A,MAIN_MENU_COUNTER
                    CJNE A,#00H, ESC_INSIDE_MAINMENU
                    ;ESC Press Outside Mainmenu
                    ;Do Nothing
                    RET
ESC_INSIDE_MAINMENU:;ESC from Main Menu
                    ;Reset all menu related counters
                    CLR A
                    MOV MAIN_MENU_COUNTER, A
                    MOV SUBMENU1_COUNTER, A
                    MOV SUBMENU2_COUNTER, A
                    ;Set Time changed Flag.
                    ;This is mandatory for Refreshing LCD Display
                    SETB TIME_CHANGED
                    RET
;######################################################################
;Common Handler for ESC key in Submenu 1 and UP/DOWN Key in Main Menu
;Handles ESC Key in Submenu 1 and UP/DOWN Key in Main Menu
;Before Calling this routine, Accumulator Register should be loaded-
;with the value of Submenu 1 counter or main menu counter
;Input: Accumulator Register
;Output: None
;######################################################################
MAIN_SM1_CMNHLR:CJNE A,#01H, SM1_ADJUST_MINUTE
                    ;ESC from Submenu 1
                    CALL DISPLAY_HOUR_BL
                    RET
SM1_ADJUST_MINUTE:CJNE A,#02H, SM1_ADJUST_DAY
                    CALL DISPLAY_MINUTE_BL
                    RET
SM1_ADJUST_DAY: CJNE A,#03H, SM1_ADJUST_FORMAT
                    CALL DISPLAY_DAY_BL
                    RET
SM1_ADJUST_FORMAT: CJNE A,#04H, SM1_INVALID
                    CALL DISPLAY_FORMAT_BL
SM1_INVALID:   RET
;######################################################################
;UP KEY HANDLER
;Handles the UP Key press in Main menu, Submenu 1 and Submenu 2
;Inputs: SUBMENU2_COUNTER, SUBMENU1_COUNTER, MAIN_MENU_COUNTER
;Output: None
;######################################################################
UP_KEY_HANDLER:     MOV A,SUBMENU2_COUNTER
                    ;Check whether inside Submenu 2
                    CJNE A,#00H, UP_IN_SUBMENU2
                    ;Not inside Submenu 2
                    ;Check whether inside Submenu 1
                    JMP UP_CHECK_SUBMENU1
                    ;Inside Submenu 2
                    ;Complement AM_PM
UP_IN_SUBMENU2:     ;Display the AM/PM on second Line
                    CALL DISPLAY_AMPM
                    RET
UP_CHECK_SUBMENU1:MOV A,SUBMENU1_COUNTER
```

```
                ;Check whether inside Submenu 1
                CJNE A,#00H, UP_INSIDE_SUBMENU1
                ;Not inside Submenu 1
                ;Check whether inside Main Menu
                JMP UP_CHECK_MAINMENU
UP_INSIDE_SUBMENU1:
                CJNE A,#01H, UP_ADJUST_MINUTE
                ;Inside Adjust Hour Menu
                ;Increment Temp_Hour by 1
                MOV A, TEMP_HOUR
                INC A
                ;Check the time format. For 12 hour format, reset-
                ;Temp_Hour to 1 if it exceeds 12
                JB FORMAT, UP_HR_FORMAT_24
                CJNE A,#13,UP_HOUR_SM1_RTRN
                MOV A, #1
UP_HOUR_SM1_RTRN:MOV TEMP_HOUR, A
                ;Display the temp hour on second line
                CALL DISPLAY_HR_MT
                RET
UP_HR_FORMAT_24:CJNE A,#24,UP_HOUR_SM1_RTRN
                ;For 24 hour format reset the Temp_Hour to 0-
                ;if Temp_hour > 23
                CLR A
                MOV TEMP_HOUR, A
                ;Display the temp hour on second line
                CALL DISPLAY_HR_MT
                RET
UP_ADJUST_MINUTE: CJNE A,#02H, UP_ADJUST_DAY
                ;Inside Adjust Minute Menu
                ;Increment Temp_Minute by 1
                MOV A, TEMP_MINUTE
                INC A
                CJNE A,#60,UP_MNT_SM1_RTRN
                ;Reset the Temp_Minute to 0-
                ;if Temp_Minute > 59
                CLR A
UP_MNT_SM1_RTRN:MOV TEMP_MINUTE, A
                ;Display the temp minute on second line
                CALL DISPLAY_HR_MT
                RET
UP_ADJUST_DAY:  CJNE A,#03H, UP_ADJUST_FORMAT
                ;Inside Adjust Day Menu
                ;Increment Temp_Day by 1
                MOV A, TEMP_DAY
                INC A
                CJNE A,#7,UP_DAY_SM1_RTRN
                CLR A
UP_DAY_SM1_RTRN:CALL GET_DAY_STRING
                MOV TEMP_DAY,A
                ;Display the DAY string on second line
                ;DPTR Register holds the start address of the string
                MOV A,#LINE_2_5DIGIT
                CALL SEND_COMMAND
                CALL DISPLAY_STRING
                RET
```

```
UP_ADJUST_FORMAT:CJNE A,#04H, UP_SM1_INVALID
                 ;Toggle Temporary Format bit
                 CPL TEMP_FORMAT
                 ;Display the current temp format on second line
                 CALL DISPLAY_FORMAT
UP_SM1_INVALID:  RET
                 ;Check whether inside mainmenu
UP_CHECK_MAINMENU:MOV A,MAIN_MENU_COUNTER
                 CJNE A,#00H, UP_IN_MAINMENU
                 ;UP Key pressed outside menu
                 ;Do nothing
                 RET
                 ;UP Key pressed inside main menu
                 ;Scroll down in main menu
                 ;Increment the main menu counter for this
UP_IN_MAINMENU: INC A
                 CJNE A,#5, UP_WITHIN_LIMIT
                 MOV A,#1
UP_WITHIN_LIMIT:MOV MAIN_MENU_COUNTER,A
                 ;Display the main menu item corresponding to the
                 ;new menu counter
                 CALL MAIN_SM1_CMNHLR
                 RET
;####################################################################
;DOWN KEY HANDLER
;Handles the DOWN Key press in Main menu, Submenu 1 and Submenu 2
;Inputs: SUBMENU2_COUNTER, SUBMENU1_COUNTER, MAIN_MENU_COUNTER
;Output: None
;####################################################################
DOWN_KEY_HANDLER:MOV A,SUBMENU2_COUNTER
                 ;Check whether inside Submenu 2
                 CJNE A,#00H, DN_IN_SUBMENU2
                 ;Not inside Submenu 2
                 ;Check whether inside Submenu 1
                 JMP DN_CHECK_SUBMENU1
                 ;Inside Submenu 2
                 ;Complement AM_PM
DN_IN_SUBMENU2:  ;Display the AM/PM on second Line
                 CALL DISPLAY_AMPM
                 RET
DN_CHECK_SUBMENU1:MOV A,SUBMENU1_COUNTER
                 ;Check whether inside Submenu 1
                 CJNE A,#00H, DN_INSIDE_SUBMENU1
                 ;Not inside Submenu 1
                 ;Check whether inside Main Menu
                 JMP DN_CHECK_MAINMENU
                 ;Inside Submenu 1
DN_INSIDE_SUBMENU1:
                 CJNE A,#01H, DN_ADJUST_MINUTE
                 ;Inside Adjust Hour Menu
                 ;Decrement Temp_Hour by 1
                 MOV A, TEMP_HOUR
                 DEC A
                 ;Check the time format. For 12 hour format, reset-
                 ;Temp_Hour to 12 if it goes below 1
                 JB FORMAT, DN_HR_FORMAT_24
```

```
                 CJNE A,#0,DN_HOUR_SM1_RTRN
                 MOV A, #12
DN_HOUR_SM1_RTRN:MOV TEMP_HOUR, A
                 ;Display the temp hour on second line
                 CALL DISPLAY_HR_MT
                 RET
DN_HR_FORMAT_24:CJNE A,#0FFH,DN_HOUR_SM1_RTRN
                 ;For 24 hour format reset the Temp_Hour to 23-
                 ;if Temp_hour < 0
                 MOV A, #23
                 MOV TEMP_HOUR, A
                 ;Display the temp hour on second line
                 CALL DISPLAY_HR_MT
                 RET
DN_ADJUST_MINUTE: CJNE A,#02H, DN_ADJUST_DAY
                 ;Inside Adjust Minute Menu
                 ;Decrement Temp_Minute by 1
                 MOV A, TEMP_MINUTE
                 DEC A
                 CJNE A,#0FFH,DN_MNT_SM1_RTRN
                 ;Reset the Temp_Minute to 59-
                 ;if Temp_Minute < 0
                 MOV A,#59
DN_MNT_SM1_RTRN:MOV TEMP_MINUTE, A
                 ;Display the temp minute on second line
                 CALL DISPLAY_HR_MT
                 RET
DN_ADJUST_DAY:  CJNE A,#03H, DN_ADJUST_FORMAT
                 ;Inside Adjust Day Menu
                 ;Decrement Temp_Day by 1
                 MOV A, TEMP_DAY
                 DEC A
                 CJNE A,#0FFH,DN_DAY_SM1_RTRN
                 MOV A, #6
DN_DAY_SM1_RTRN:CALL GET_DAY_STRING
                 MOV TEMP_DAY,A
                 ;Display the DAY string on second line
                 ;DPTR Register holds the start address of the string
                 MOV A,#LINE_2_5DIGIT
                 CALL SEND_COMMAND
                 CALL DISPLAY_STRING
                 RET
DN_ADJUST_FORMAT:CJNE A,#04H, DN_SM1_INVALID
                 ;Toggle Temporary Format bit
                 CPL TEMP_FORMAT
                 ;Display the current temp format on second line
                 CALL DISPLAY_FORMAT
DN_SM1_INVALID:  RET
                 ;Check whether inside mainmenu
DN_CHECK_MAINMENU:MOV A,MAIN_MENU_COUNTER
                 CJNE A,#00H, DN_IN_MAINMENU
                 ;DOWN Key pressed outside menu
                 ;Do nothing
                 RET
                 ;DOWN Key pressed inside main menu
```

```
                  ;Scroll Up in main menu
                  ;Decrement the main menu counter for this
DN_IN_MAINMENU: DEC A
                  CJNE A,#0H, DN_WITHIN_LIMIT
                  MOV A,#4
DN_WITHIN_LIMIT:MOV MAIN_MENU_COUNTER,A
                  ;Display the main menu item corresponding to the
                  ;new menu counter
                  CALL MAIN_SM1_CMNHLR
                  RET
;####################################################################
;Display 'Adjust Hour' on First Line and blank the Second line
;Input: None
;Output: None
;####################################################################
DISPLAY_HOUR_BL:MOV A,#LINE_1
                  CALL SEND_COMMAND
                  MOV DPTR,#TEXT_HOUR
                  CALL DISPLAY_STRING
                  MOV A,#LINE_2
                  CALL SEND_COMMAND
                  MOV DPTR,#TEXT_LCD_BLANK
                  CALL DISPLAY_STRING
                  RET
;####################################################################
;Display 'Adjust Minute' on First Line and blank the Second line
;Input: None
;Output: None
;####################################################################
DISPLAY_MINUTE_BL:MOV     A,#LINE_1
                  CALL SEND_COMMAND
                  MOV DPTR,#TEXT_MINUTE
                  CALL DISPLAY_STRING
                  MOV A,#LINE_2
                  CALL SEND_COMMAND
                  MOV DPTR,#TEXT_LCD_BLANK
                  CALL DISPLAY_STRING
                  RET
;####################################################################
;Display 'Adjust Day' on First Line and blank the Second line
;Input: None
;Output: None
;####################################################################
DISPLAY_DAY_BL:MOV A,#LINE_1
                  CALL SEND_COMMAND
                  MOV DPTR,#TEXT_DAY
                  CALL DISPLAY_STRING
                  MOV A,#LINE_2
                  CALL SEND_COMMAND
                  MOV DPTR,#TEXT_LCD_BLANK
                  CALL DISPLAY_STRING
                  RET
;####################################################################
;Display 'Adjust Format' on First Line and blank the Second line
;Input: None
;Output: None
```

```
;####################################################################
DISPLAY_FORMAT_BL:MOV A,#LINE_1
                  CALL SEND_COMMAND
                  MOV DPTR,#TEXT_FORMAT
                  CALL DISPLAY_STRING
                  MOV A,#LINE_2
                  CALL SEND_COMMAND
                  MOV DPTR,#TEXT_LCD_BLANK
                  CALL DISPLAY_STRING
                  RET
;####################################################################
; LCD Initialisation Routine
; Subroutine for initialising LCD.
; Written for ORIOLE ODM1611 Module.
; Refer to the LCD Datasheet for timing parameters and commands
; Fine tune this subroutine as per the LCD Module
; Input: None
; Output: None
;####################################################################
INITIALISE_LCD:   MOV A,#FUNCTION_SET
                  CALL WRITE_COMMAND

                  MOV A,#FUNCTION_SET
                  CALL WRITE_COMMAND

                  MOV A,#FUNCTION_SET
                  CALL WRITE_COMMAND

                  MOV A,#FUNCTION_SET
                  CALL SEND_COMMAND

                  MOV A,#ENTRY_MODE
                  CALL SEND_COMMAND

                  MOV A,#CLEAR_LCD
                  CALL SEND_COMMAND

                  MOV A,#LCD_ON
                  CALL SEND_COMMAND
                  RET
;####################################################################
;Subroutine for writing to the command register of LCD with 'BUSY'-
;checking. Command to be written is passed through Accumulator
;Input: Accumulator
;Output: None
;####################################################################
SEND_COMMAND:  SETB P2.7  ;Configure Pin P2.7 as input Pin
                  CLR RS             ;RS=0, Select Command Register of LCD
                  SETB RW            ;RD=1, Read Operation
READ_BUSY:     SETB EN      ;Toggle LCD Enable to generate a High to
                  CLR EN             ;Low transition. This latches the data
                  JB P2.7,READ_BUSY  ;Loop till Busy Flag is Reset
                  MOV P2, A          ;Load Display port with the command
                  CLR RS             ;RS=0, Select Command Register of LCD
                  CLR RW             ;RD=0, Write Operation
                  SETB EN            ;Toggle LCD Enable to generate a High to
```

```
                 CLR EN              ;Low transition. This latches the data
                 RET                 ;Return
;####################################################################
;Subroutine for writing to the command register of LCD without-
;'BUSY' checking. Before writing to the command register, waits for-
;100 millisecond. Command to be written is passed through Accumulator
;Input: Accumulator
;Output: None
;####################################################################
WRITE_COMMAND: MOV P2, A
                 CLR RS              ;RS=0, Select Command Register of LCD
                 CLR RW              ;RD=0, Write Operation
                 SETB EN  ;Toggle LCD Enable to generate a High to
                 CLR EN              ;Low transition. This latches the data
                 MOV R0,#100
                 CALL MILLISECOND_DELAY
                 RET
;####################################################################
;String Display Subroutine
;This Routine Displays a string on the LCD Screen
;DPTR contains the start address of the String
;The character # indicates the string termination
;Input: DPTR Register
;Output: None
;####################################################################
DISPLAY_STRING:  CLR A
                 MOVC A,@A+DPTR
                 CJNE A,#'#',CONTINUE
                 RET
CONTINUE:        CALL DISPLAY_CHAR
                 INC DPTR
                 SJMP DISPLAY_STRING
;####################################################################
;Subroutine for generating milliseconds delay
;ms Parameter passed through R0
;Input: R0
;Output: None
;####################################################################
MILLISECOND_DELAY:
                 MOV R1,#250
DELAY_LOOP1:     NOP
                 NOP
                 DJNZ R1,DELAY_LOOP1
                 DJNZ R0,MILLISECOND_DELAY
                 RET
;####################################################################
;Routine for Displaying a Character on LCD
;The ASCII Value of the character to be displayed is passed through A
;Input: Accumulator Register A
;Output: None
;####################################################################
DISPLAY_CHAR:  SETB P2.7                ;Configure Pin P2.7 as input Pin
                 CLR RS                 ;RS=0, Select Command Register of LCD
                 SETB RW                ;RD=1, Read Operation
CHECK_BUSY:    SETB EN      ;Toggle LCD Enable to generate a High to
                 CLR EN                 ;Low transition. This latches the data
```

```
            JB P2.7,CHECK_BUSY
            MOV P2, A              ;Load LCD Data bus with Data
            SETB RS                ;RS=1, Select Data Register of LCD
            CLR RW                 ;RD=0, Write Operation
            SETB EN                ;Toggle LCD Enable to generate a High to
            CLR EN                 ;Low transition. This latches the data
            RET
;#####################################################################
; Subroutine for Displaying a decimal number in the range-
;0 to 99 t0 corresponding ASCII. Displays the ASCII value of the-
;number on second line of LCD at position starting from 14
;(0 to 15 are the positions on 16 character LCD)
;The decimal number is passed through Accumulator Register
;Input: Accumulator Register A
;Output: None
;#####################################################################
DIPLAY_NUMBER: MOV R0,#2
            MOV B, #10
            DIV AB
            XCH A,B
LOOP1:      XCH A,B
            ADD A, #30H
            CALL DISPLAY_CHAR
            DJNZ R0,LOOP1
            RET
;#####################################################################
;Timer 0 Interrupt Routine
;Occurs at every 50 milliseconds. 20 consecutive interrupts generate-
;1 second delay.
;Input: R3 (Timer Multiplier)
;Output: SECONDS_REG, HOUR_REG, MINUTE_REG, DAY_REG, AM_PM
;#####################################################################
TIME0_INTERRUPT:
            ;Reload timer 0 with a count for 50 milliseconds
            MOV TL0, #0B4H
            MOV TH0, #3CH
            PUSH ACC               ; Save Accumulator
            PUSH PSW               ; Save PSW Register
            ;Check whether 1 second is elapsed. One timer
            ;interrupt corresponds to 50ms. 20 consecutive
            ;timer interrupts generate 1 second. This is
            ;implemented by loading a timer multiplier register-
            ;with 20. This is decremented on interrupt.
            ;A value of 0 for this register indicates 1 second
            ;delay happened.
            DJNZ R3, TIME_NOT_ELAPSED
            MOV R3, #20
            ;1 Second elapsed. Increment seconds Register
            INC SECONDS_REG
            CJNE SECONDS_REG, #60,DISPLAY_UPDATE
            ;60 Seconds elapsed. Reset Seconds Register and
            ;Increment Minute Register by 1
            MOV SECONDS_REG, #00H
            INC MINUTE_REG
            CJNE MINUTE_REG, #60,DISPLAY_UPDATE
            ;60 Minutes elapsed. Reset Minute Register and
```

```
                    ;Increment Hour Register
                    MOV MINUTE_REG, #00H
                    INC HOUR_REG
                    ;Check the time format. For 12 hour format change-
                    ;the day when hour goes beyond 12 and the time-
                    ;transition from PM to AM
                    JB FORMAT, HOUR_FORMAT_24
                    CJNE HOUR_REG,#13,DISPLAY_UPDATE
                    CLR C
                    MOV A,HOUR_REG
                    ;If the existing time format was 24hr and the user
                    ;changed it through menu option when the hour is
                    ;greater than 12. This may result in erroneous
                    ;result. So use the following set of instructions.
                    ;Otherwise it should have been replaced by MOV
                    ;HOUR_REG, #1
                    SUBB A,#12
                    MOV HOUR_REG, A
                    CPL AM_PM
                    JB AM_PM, DISPLAY_UPDATE
CHECK_DAY:          INC DAY_REG
                    ;Reset day to SUNDAY (0) if it overflows beyond
                    ;SATURDAY (6)
                    CJNE DAY_REG,#7, DISPLAY_UPDATE
                    MOV DAY_REG, #0
DISPLAY_UPDATE:     SETB TIME_CHANGED
TIME_NOT_ELAPSED:POP PSW  ;Retrieve PSW
                    POP ACC                  ;Retrieve Accumulator
                    RET
HOUR_FORMAT_24:     CJNE HOUR_REG,#24,DISPLAY_UPDATE
                    ;For 24 hour format reset the hour to 0and change
                    ;the day when hour goes beyond 23
                    MOV HOUR_REG, #0
                    JMP CHECK_DAY
;#####################################################################
;Define the String Constants to be displayed on LCD for different-
;Menus. The String is stored in code memory after the above-
;instruction. The start address for each string constant is-
;indicated by the text label. ;The character # is used as string-
;terminator
; Some strings are aligned for 16 characters by packing with blank
;#####################################################################
TEXT_NICEDAY:
DB          'HAVE A NICE DAY!#'
TEXT_HOUR:
DB          '  ADJUST HOUR   #'
TEXT_MINUTE:
DB          '  ADJUST MINUTE #'
TEXT_DAY:
DB          '   ADJUST DAY   #'
TEXT_FORMAT:
DB          '  ADJUST FORMAT #'
TEXT_AMPM:
DB          '  SELECT AM/PM  #'
TEXT_2BLANK:
DB          '  #'
```

```
TEXT_LCD_BLANK:
DB              '                #'
TEXT_SUN:
DB              '[SUN]#'
TEXT_MON:
DB              '[MON]#'
TEXT_TUE:
DB              '[TUE]#'
TEXT_WED:
DB              '[WED]#'
TEXT_THU:
DB              '[THU]#'
TEXT_FRI:
DB              '[FRI]#'
TEXT_SAT:
DB              '[SAT]#'
TEXT_12HR:
DB              '[12 HOUR]#'
TEXT_24HR:
DB              '[24 HOUR]#'
TEXT_AM:
DB              '[AM]#'
TEXT_PM:
DB              '[PM]#'
END             ;END of Assembly Program
```

The timer interrupt generates 'seconds' timing with a tolerance of 1 to 6 microseconds/Second. This code may not be optimised for code size or performance. Fine tuning of the code, instruction usage, redundant and dead code elimination, etc. are left to the readers as an assignment.

2. BATTERY-OPERATED SMARTCARD READER

Smartcard is a credit card sized plastic card containing a memory or a 'CPU and memory'. Smartcard contains memory in the order of a few bytes to a few kilo bytes. Smartcard follows a specific command sequence for data read/write operations. The data read write operation is controlled by a Smartcard Reader/Writer IC. Based on the interface between the Smartcard and the Reader unit, smartcards are classified as 'Contact type' and 'Contactless'. The Contact type smartcard requires physical contact between the reader and the smartcard. The contact type smartcard follows the ISO-7816 standard and its physical contact looks exactly the same as that of the contacts of a GSM cell phone's SIM card. Whereas the contactless smartcard doesn't require a physical contact between the reader and the smartcard for data communication. The data communication for a contactless smartcard happens over air interface and it uses radio frequency waves for data transmission. 13.56 MHz is the commonly used radio frequency for smartcard operation.

We are going to design a battery operated contactless smartcard reader (Handheld Reader). A rechargeable Li-Io battery (Say 7V with capacity 1000mAh) is used as the power source for the handheld. The battery parameter (capacity and voltage) monitoring and charging is controlled using a battery monitor and charge control IC (Like DS2770 from Maxim Dallas Semiconductor). The host processor can be an 8 or 16bit microcontroller (Like *8051* or PIC family of controller). The device power ON is controlled through a push button switch. A single chip contactless smartcard read/write IC is used for data read write operation with the smartcard. The smartcard reader IC is interfaced to the host processor and the data communication will be under the control of the host processor. The smartcard read/write IC contains CPU (Or control logic implementation), read/write memory, analog circuits for data modulation and demodulation, transceiver unit for RF data transmission and reception, and antenna driver circuitry. For the handheld reader to communicate with a desktop machine, a communication channel using either USB or RS-232C is implemented in the reader. The I/O unit of the system includes a matrix keyboard for user inputs and a graphical/alpha-numeric LCD for visual indications. LEDs are used for various status indications like 'Charging', 'Battery Low', 'Busy/Error', etc.

The Oscillator and Reset circuitry generates the necessary clock and reset signals for the proper operation of the host processor and smartcard read/write IC. The watchdog timer unit provides the necessary reset to the system in case of system misbehaviour. Sometimes the watchdog timer hardware comes as part of the host processor; if not a separate watchdog timer IC is used. The watchdog interrupt is connected to one of the interrupt lines of the processor. Most of the microcontrollers contain built in data memory and program memory. If the on-chip program and data memory are not sufficient for the application, external data memory and program memory chips can be used in the design. The block diagram depicted in Fig. A2.12 illustrates the various components required for building the handheld, contactless smartcard reader.

The firmware requirements for building the handheld smartcard reader can be divided into the following tasks.

1. Startup task
2. Battery monitoring and Charge controlling task
3. Card read/write operation task
4. Communication Task
5. Keyboard scanning task
6. LCD update task
7. Watchdog timer expire event

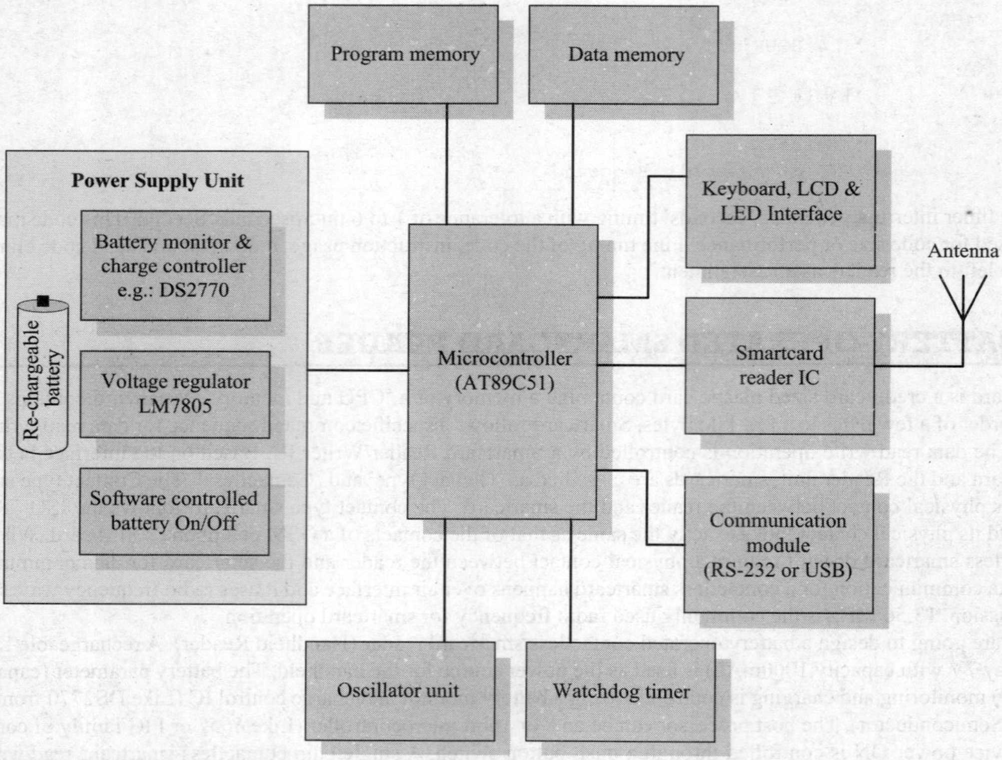

Fig. A2.12 Block Diagram of a Handheld Contactless Smart Card Reader

The communication task and keyboard scanning task can be implemented either as a polling task or an interrupt driven task. The watchdog timer expiration event is captured as an interrupt.

The startup task implements the necessary startup operations like setting up the interrupts, configuring the ports of the host processor, initialising the LCD, initialising the battery monitor and charge control IC, initialising the smart card reader IC, etc.

The battery monitoring and charge controlling task reads the various registers (Voltage, capacity registers, etc.) of the battery monitor IC, checks the presence of a charger and initiates a charge command, terminates the charging when the battery is full, produces warning signal when the battery voltage is below a threshold value and switch off the unit if the battery voltage falls below the critical threshold value. This task is assigned highest priority to avoid data corruption in case of a power down.

The card read/write operation task is responsible for implementing the communication sequence for data read/write operation with the card. The smartcard read/write operation follows a specific sequence of operation. The sequence varies with the standards (Like ISO/IEC 14443 A/B, ISO/IEC 15693, etc.) supported by the read write IC. A typical read write operation follows the sequence:

1. Reader initiates a 'Request' command for checking the presence of cards in the vicinity of the reader. If a card is present in the field it responds to the reader with *Answer To Request* (*ATR*).
2. Upon receiving the ATR, the reader sends a command to capture the serial number of all cards present in the field. Most of the reader ICs implement special algorithms to decode and capture the serial number of all cards present in the field.
3. Reader selects the serial number of a card from the list of serial numbers received and sends a command to select the specified card. The card whose serial number matches with the one sent by the reader responds to the reader and all other cards in the field enters sleep state. Now the communication channel is established exclusively between the reader and a card.
4. The Reader authenticates the card with an encrypted key. If the key matches with the key stored in the card, the authentication succeeds. Different security mechanisms are used by different family of cards and readers for implementing authentication.
5. The reader sends a read/write command to the card along with the details of the memory area which the reader wants to read/write and the data to write in case of a write operation. The memory of the card is segmented into different sectors and each sector may be further divided into blocks. Each block holds a fixed number of data bytes. Each memory segment contains a key for authentication. The memory organisation of the card is manufacturer specific.

The keyboard scanning task scans the keyboard and identifies a key press and performs the operation corresponding to the key press. This can be implemented as a task or an Interrupt Service Routine if the keyboard hardware supports interrupt generation on a key press.

The LCD update task updates the LCD with new data. This task can be invoked by other tasks like keyboard scanning task, battery monitoring task, card read/write task and communication task for displaying the various information.

The communication task handles reader communication with the host PC. The communication interface can be either USB or RS-232. This task can also be implemented as Interrupt Service Routine. Most of the processors support Serial Interrupt for handling Serial data transmission using UART and RS-232. If USB is used as the interface, the interrupt line of the USB chip can be connected to the Interrupt line of the processor and communication can be controlled in the ISR.

The watchdog timer expiration ISR handles the actions corresponding to a watchdog timer event.

The firmware for controlling the handheld reader can be implemented in either a 'Super loop' model where the tasks are executed in sequence in a super loop with interrupts running in the background or using an RTOS scheduler like uC/OS-II or RTX-51 or VxWorks for scheduling the tasks.

3. AUTOMATED METER READING SYSTEM (AMR)

An Automated Meter Reading (AMR) system automates the utility metering (like electricity, water and gas consumption). AMR technique replaces the existing manual meter reading operation. AMR systems transfer the meter reading data automatically to a central station or operator for billing and usage monitoring purposes. The meter reading data is transferred over a wireless communication channel or a wired communication medium. Radio Frequency (RF) transceivers, GPRS based communication over GSM network are examples of wireless AMR data transfer, whereas Power Line Communication (PLC) in electricity metering is an example for wired AMR data transfer. PLC uses the power carrying lines for data communication with a substation. The AMR system contains an AMR data transmission unit, which is interfaced with the utility meter and a remote AMR data receiver unit which collects the data for billing and usage monitoring purpose. The AMR data transmission interface can be built as an integral part of the utility meter or can be built as an add-on module for existing utility readers. Nowadays, Application Specific Standard Product (ASSP) ICs integrating both utility metering capability and AMR interface is available for building a utility meter with integrated AMR interface. The AMR enabled utility meter can also be built using a low-cost microcontroller with an AMR interface. Our discussion is focused only on AMR interfaces for energy metering for single phase power supply.

The implementation of a microcontroller-based AMR enabled energy metering device is shown in Fig. A2.13. It contains an energy metering unit and a wireless/wired automated meter reading interface. The energy metering unit records the electricity consumption. A single chip energy meter IC forms the heart of the energy metering unit. It contains a high performance microcontroller (typically a 16bit RISC microcontroller), integrated ADCs and LCD controller, etc. The instantaneous power consumption in an electric circuit is given as P = VI; where V is the instantaneous voltage and I is the instantaneous current. The electronic energy meter records the current consumption by integrating the instantaneous power. The instantaneous current is measured using a current sensor circuit. The current sensor circuit essentially contains a current sensing resistor and an instrumentation amplifier for signal conditioning. The signal conditioned current value is fed to the energy metering IC. The ADC present in the energy metering IC digitises the instantaneous current value. The voltage sensor circuit senses the instantaneous voltage and it is fed to the energy metering IC for digitisation. The microcontroller present in the energy metering IC computes the instantaneous power, the average power consumption and stores it in the EEPROM memory. It also displays the parameters like instantaneous current, voltage, electricity consumed in KWh units on an LCD through a built-in LCD controller interface. The MSP430 chip from Texas Instruments is a typical example of a single chip energy metering IC.

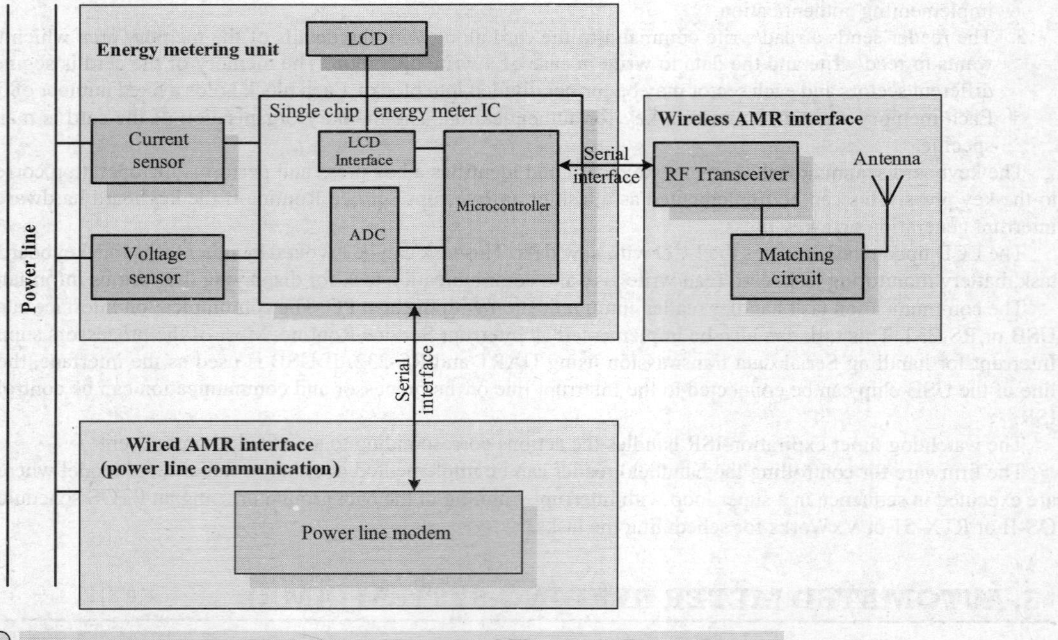

Fig. A2.13 **Block Diagram of an AMR enabled Integrated Electronic Energy Meter**

The Automated Meter Reading (AMR) interface to the energy metering unit can be provided through an RF interface or through Power Line Communication (PLC) module. The RF based wireless AMR interface is best suited for short range automated reading applications like handheld device based recording of energy consumption. The meter reading official carries a handheld for recording the energy meter reading through a Wireless AMR interface. The specific energy meter whose reading is to be recorded can be selected by sending the unique meter identification number (Meter ID) of the meter and then initiating an automated meter reading operation. The RF interface consists of an RF Transceiver (RF transmitter cum receiver), and impedance matching circuit and an antenna for RF data transfer. The impedance matching circuit consists of capacitor, resistors and inductors and it tunes the circuit for the required frequency. The RF transceiver unit is responsible for RF Data modulation and de-modulation. The antenna is a metallic coil for transmitting and receiving RF modulated data. The interface between the energy metering unit and the RF module is implemented through serial interfaces like SPI, I2C, etc. The firmware running in the microcontroller of the single chip energy meter IC controls the communication with the RF module.

The Power Line Carrier Communication (PLCC) based AMR interface makes use of a power line modem for interfacing the power lines with the energy metering unit for data communication. The PLC modem provides bi-directional half-duplex data communication over the mains. The PLC modem can be interfaced to the microcontroller of the energy metering unit through serial interfaces like UART, SPI, etc. The firmware running in the microcontroller controls the communication with the PLC modem. Texas Instruments' F28x controller platform provides a cost-effective means to implement PLC technology.

GPRS based data communication over GSM network is another option for implementing AMR interface for long range communication. A GPRS modem is required for establishing the communication with the GSM network. The GPRS modem can be interfaced to the microcontroller of the energy metering unit for data communication. ZigBee, Wi-Fi, etc. are other wireless interface options for AMR interface.

The firmware requirements for building the AMR enabled energy meter can be divided into the following tasks:

1. Startup task
2. Energy consumtion recording task
3. Automatic meter data transfer task
4. LCD update task

The 'Startup task' deals with the initialisation of various port pins, interrupt configuration, stack pointer setting, etc. for the microcontroller, initialisation of the RF interface for the communication parameter, and initialisation of the LCD. The energy consumption task records the energy consumption. The energy metering SoC may contain dedicated hardware units for calculating the energy consumption based on the instantaneous voltage and current and the meter reading will be available in some dedicated registers of the SoC. The energy consumprion recording task can read this register periodically and update the EEPROM storage memory (Which may be part the SoC or an external chip interfaced to the SoC). The automatic meter data transfer task can be implemented as a periodic task or a command driven operation in which the meter reading is sent upon receiving a command from the host system (the system which requests energy consumption for billing and usage purpose like the central electricity office or handheld terminal carried by the meter reading official). For the command driven communication model, a set of command interfaces are defined for communication between the AMR enabled meter and the host system. Each AMR enabled meter holds a unique Meter ID and the firmware can be implemented in such a way that the AMR module responds only when the Meter ID sent by the host along with the command matches the Meter ID stored in the EEPROM of the Meter. The LCD update task updates the LCD when a change in display parameter (like instantaneous current and voltage, energy consumption, etc.) occurs. These tasks can be implemented in a super loop with interrupts or under an RTOS like uC/OS-II. The firmware requirements in the super loop based implementation is modelled here with the flow chart as shown in Fig. A2.14.

4. DIGITAL CAMERA

Digital camera is a device for capturing and storing images in the form digital data (series of 1s and 0s) in place of the conventional paper/film based image storage. It is a typical example of an embedded computing system for data collection/storage application. It contains a lens and image sensors for capturing the image, LCD for displaying the captured image, user interface buttons to control the operation of the device and Communication interface to connect it with a PC to transfer captured images. Figure A2.15 given below illustrates the various subsystems of a digital camera.

In today's digital world people are accustomed to digital devices. Indeed they use digital camera for capturing their favourite moments in life. But how the camera converts their favourite moments into a digital picture is still a surprising thing to most of them. Let us have a closer look at the internals of a digital camera to explore its functioning. Figure A2.16 illustrates the various components of a digital camera.

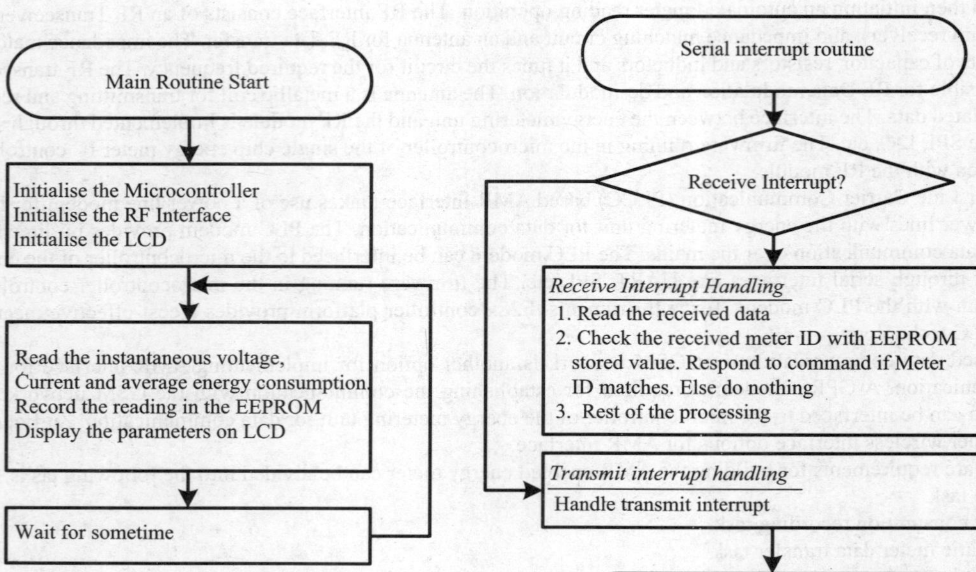

Fig. A2.14

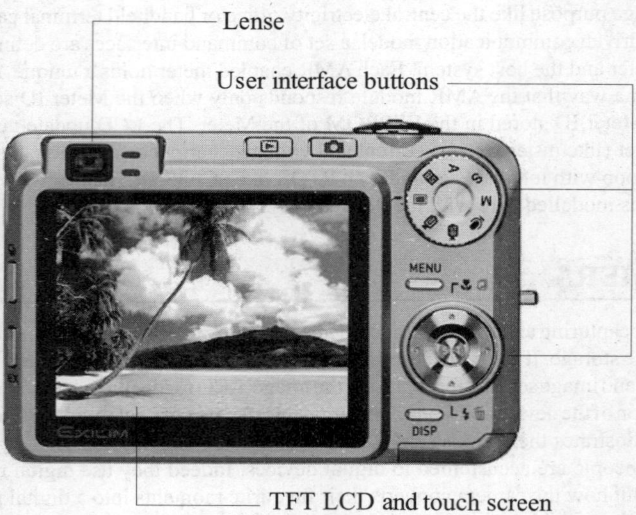

Fig. A2.15 **Subsystems of a Digital Camera**
(Photo courtesy of Casio)

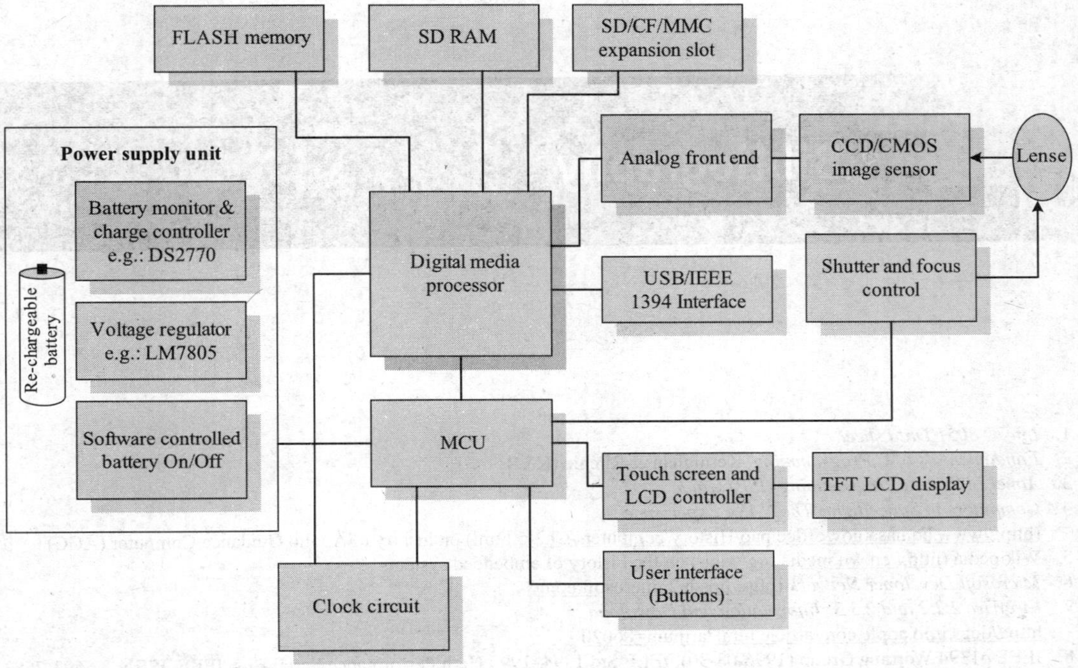

Fig. A2.16 Components of a Digital Camera

Like a normal film camera, it uses a lens to focus the scene which is going to be captured as an image. The only difference is in 'how the scene is captured'. In a normal film camera, the image is captured in a photo film and the photo film is later developed to recreate the image, whereas in a digital camera, the image is captured electronically. Charge Coupled Device (CCD) or CMOS image sensors are used for capturing the image. When exposed to light these sensors produce electrons which in turn generates analog voltage signals. These analog signals are post-processed (filtered, amplified and digitised) by an Analog Front End (AFE) system. Analog Front End ICs are available from various manufactures like Texas Instruments. The digitised data is supplied to a Digital Media processor, which implements various compression algorithms like JPEG, TIFF, etc. for compressing the raw image data. The digital media processor may contain a DMA unit to transfer the compressed, digitised image directly to the storage memory.

The various system functions like shutter control and zooming control is performed by the 'System Control' unit of the camera which is implemented using a 16/32 microprocessor/microcontroller. Stepper motors are used for shutter and zoom control. The system control unit is also responsible for handling the I/O (Buttons) and graphical user interface (LCD control).

The digital camera is powered by a re-chargeable battery and the monitoring and charging control is carried out by a battery charge control and monitoring IC, which is under the control of the 'System Control Unit'.

Provisions for interfacing various storage memory devices like SD/CF/MMC cards are implemented in the digital camera. The camera device can be connected to a host PC through the communication interface (Like USB, IEEE 1394, etc.) supported by the device, for image transfer.

Nowadays, a single-chip called System on Chip (SoC), incorporating both image processing unit and 16/32 processor in a single IC are available and they simplify the design. The resolution of a digital camera is expressed in terms of mega pixels. You may be familiar with the terms 3.2 mega pixels, 5.1 mega pixels, 7.2 mega pixels, etc. It represents the pixels per inch of the image sensing device (CCD/CMOS). As the number of pixels increase, the image quality also increases.

The various system control tasks and image capturing and processing tasks for the digital camera are implemented using an embedded operating system.

Bibliography

1. *Intel® 8051 Data sheet*
2. *Fundamentals of C Programming*, Kernighan & Ritchie (K&R)
3. *Atmel In System Programming (ISP) Guide*
4. *Computers in Spaceflight: The NASA Experience* (http://www.hq.nasa.gov/office/pao/History/computers/Ch2-5.html) on history of Apollo Guidance Computer (AGC)
5. Wikipedia (http://en.wikipedia.org/wiki/) on the history of embedded systems
6. *Microsoft Developer Network* (http://msdn2.microsoft.com/)
7. *FireWire 2.2.2 and 2.3.3: Information and Download* http://docs.info.apple.com/article.html?artnum=86020
8. IEEE p1394 Working Group (1996-08-30), IEEE Std 1394–1995 High Performance Serial Bus, IEEE. ISBN 1-5593-7583-3
9. *WiFi Wireless LAN Data Rates and Range* http://www.networkdictionary.com/Wireless/WiFi-Wireless-LAN-Data-Rates.php
10. *USB Complete: Everything You Need to Develop Custom USB Peripherals*, Jan Axelson, published by Lakeview research llc, 2005, ISBN 1931448027, 9781931448024
11. *Quick reference for RS485, RS422, RS232 and RS423* http://www.rs485.com/rs485spec.html
12. *Latest ZIGBEE SPECIFICATION including the PRO Feature Set from Zigbee Alliance* http://www.zigbee.org/en/index.asp
13. *Home Networking with Zigbee*, Mikhail Galeev http://www.embedded.com/columns/technicalinsights/18902431?_requestid=94796
14. *ZigBee Wireless Networking Overview*, Texas Instruments http://focus.ti.com/lit/ml/slyb134a/slyb134a.pdf
15. *Piezo Electric Sound Components Application Manual*, muRata http://www.murata.com/catalog/p15e6.pdf
16. *CMOS: Circuit Design, Layout, and Simulation*, revised second edition, Baker, R Jacob (2008), Wiley-IEEE, ISBN 978-0-470-22941-5. http://CMOSedu.com/
17. *The VLSI Handbook*, second edition (electrical engineering handbook), Chen, Wai-Kai (ed) (2006), Boca Raton: CRC, ISBN 0-8493-4199-X
18. *82C55A Datasheet from Intersil Corporation*. http://www.intersil.com/data/fn/fn2969.pdf
19. *MicroC/OS-II: The Real-Time Kernel*, Jean J. Labresse, CMP Book, ISBN: 1-57820-103-9
20. *AVR Instruction set summary* http://www.atmel.ru/Disks/AVR%20Technical%20Library/appnotes/pdf/AVR_Instruction_set.pdf
21. *Datasheet of PIC 16F877* http://ww1.microchip.com/downloads/en/DeviceDoc/30292c.pdf
22. *ARM Architecture Reference Manual*, David Seal, Addison-Wesley, 2nd edition, 2000.
23. *AMBA Specification* (Rev 2.0) © Copyright ARM Limited 1999
24. *74F148 8 to 3 encoder* http://www.standardics.nxp.com/products/fast/datasheet/74f148.pdf
25. *Embedded Power Line Carrier Modem* http://www.archnetco.com/english/product/ATL90.htm

26. *MCT2M, MCT2EM, MCT210M, MCT271M Phototransistor Optocouplers* http://www.fairchildsemi.com/ds/MC/MCT2-M.pdf
27. *Trends in the High-speed Embedded Market* http://www.embeddedintel.com/market_watch.php?market=643
28. *Reconfigurable Processors: Changing the Systems Design Paradigm* http://www.embedded.com/192200275?_requestid=25912
29. *Reconfigurable SoCs* http://electronicdesign.com/Articles/ArticleID/4861/4861.html
30. *Inside the JAVA Virtual Machine*, Bill Venners, McGraw-Hill, 1999, ISBN 0-07-135093-4
31. *Java ME at a Glance* http://java.sun.com/javame/index.jsp
32. *UML forum–UML tools list* http://www.uml-forum.com/tools.htm
33. *IBM Software Design Tools* http://www-01.ibm.com/software/rational/offerings/architecture/softwaredesign.html
34. *The Unified Modeling Language Reference Manual*, second edition, Grady Booch, James Rumbaugh & Ivar Jacobson, Addison-Wesley, ISBN 978-0-321-24562-5
35. *The Unified Modeling Language User Guide*, second edition, Grady Booch, James Rumbaugh & Ivar Jacobson, Addison-Wesley, ISBN 978-0-321-26797-9
36. *Hardware/Software Co-Design Comes of Age*, David Maliniak http://electronicdesign.com/Articles/Index.cfm?AD=1&ArticleID=19301
37. *Hardware/software Co-design: Principles and Practice*, Jørgen Staunstrup & Wayne Hendrix Wolf, published by Springer, 1997, ISBN 0792380134, 9780792380139
38. *8-bit Flash Microcontroller* AT89C51RD2/AT89C51ED2 http://www.atmel.com/dyn/resources/prod_documents/doc4235.pdf
39. *DS80C320/DS80C323 High Speed Low-power Microcontrollers* http://www.maxim-ic.com/quick_view2.cfm/qv_pk/2955
40. *8-Lead JEDEC SOIC Package Material Declaration Data Sheet* http://www.atmel.com/green/documents/pmdds/SOIC_JEDEC_8_Sn.pdf
41. *SOIC Package details for AT17LV65 from Atmel* http://www.atmel.com/dyn/resources/prod_documents/doc2321.pdf
42. *TSSOP Package details for AT24C1024B from Atmel* http://www.atmel.com/dyn/resources/prod_documents/doc5194.pdf
43. *AD570–Complete 8-Bit A-to-D Converter* http://www.analog.com/static/imported-files/Data_Sheets/AD570.pdf
44. *DM9370 7-Segment Decoder/Driver/Latch with Open-Collector Outputs* http://www.datasheetcatalog.org/datasheet/fairchild/DM9370.pdf
45. *Use reentrant functions for safer signal handling* http://www.ibm.com/developerworks/linux/library/l-reent.html
46. *Cx51 User's Guide Listing (LST) File* http://www.keil.com/support/man/docs/C51/c51_cm_lstfile.htm
47. *BL51 User's Guide Listing (MAP) File* http://www.keil.com/support/man/docs/bl51/bl51_ln_mapfile.htm
48. *Cx51 User's Guide Object (OBJ) File* http://www.keil.com/support/man/docs/C51/c51_cm_objfile.htm
49. *Cx51 User's Guide Preprocessor (I) File* http://www.keil.com/support/man/docs/C51/c51_cm_ifile.htm
50. *Boundary-Scan Tutorial from Corelis Inc* http://www.corelis.com/products/Boundary-Scan_Tutorial.htm
51. *Boundary-Scan Description Language (BSDL) Tutorial*, Corelis Inc http://www.corelis.com/products/BSDL_Tutorial.htm
52. *Operating System Concepts* seventh edition, Avi Silberschatz, Peter Baer Galvin & Greg Gagne, John Wiley & Sons, Inc., ISBN 0-471-69466-5
53. *VxWorks® Programmer's Guide 5.4*, Wind River Systems
54. *What is Programmable Logic?* www.xilinx.com/company/about/programmable.html
55. *Adidas Designs A Winner With "Smart" Running Shoes*, Mark David www.electronicdesign.com/Articles/Index.cfm?AD=1&ArticleID=10113

Index